AUDIO ENGINEERING HANDBOOK

Other McGraw-Hill Reference Books of Interest

Handbooks

Avalone and Baumeister • STANDARD HANDBOOK FOR MECHANICAL ENGINEERS

Beeman • INDUSTRIAL POWER SYSTEMS HANDBOOK

Benson • TELEVISION ENGINEERING HANDBOOK

Coombs • BASIC ELECTRONIC INSTRUMENT HANDBOOK

Coombs • PRINTED CIRCUITS HANDBOOK

Croft and Summers • AMERICAN ELECTRICIANS' HANDBOOK

Di Giacomo • VLSI HANDBOOK

Fink and Beaty • STANDARD HANDBOOK FOR ELECTRICAL ENGINEERS

Fink and Christiansen • ELECTRONICS ENGINEERS' HANDBOOK

Harper • HANDBOOK OF COMPONENTS FOR ELECTRONICS

Harper • HANDBOOK OF ELECTRONIC SYSTEMS DESIGN

Harper • HANDBOOK OF THICK FILM HYBRID MICROELECTRONICS

Harper • HANDBOOK OF WIRING, CABLING, AND INTERCONNECTING FOR ELECTRONICS

Hecht • THE LASER GUIDEBOOK

Hicks • STANDARD HANDBOOK OF ENGINEERING CALCULATIONS

Inglis • ELECTRONIC COMMUNICATIONS HANDBOOK

Johnson and Jasik • ANTENNA ENGINEERING HANDBOOK

Juran • QUALITY CONTROL HANDBOOK

Kaufman and Seidman • HANDBOOK OF ELECTRONICS CALCULATIONS

Kaufman and Seidman • HANDBOOK FOR ELECTRONICS ENGINEERING TECHNICIANS

Kurtz • HANDBOOK OF ENGINEERING ECONOMICS

Perry • ENGINEERING MANUAL

Stout • HANDBOOK OF MICROPROCESSOR DESIGN AND APPLICATIONS

Stout and Kaufman • HANDBOOK OF MICROCIRCUIT DESIGN AND APPLICATION

Stout and Kaufman • HANDBOOK OF OPERATIONAL AMPLIFIER DESIGN

Tuma • ENGINEERING MATHEMATICS HANDBOOK

Williams • DESIGNER'S HANDBOOK OF INTEGRATED CIRCUITS

Williams and Taylor • ELECTRONIC FILTER DESIGN HANDBOOK

Encyclopedias

CONCISE ENCYCLOPEDIA OF SCIENCE AND TECHNOLOGY

ENCYCLOPEDIA OF ELECTRONICS AND COMPUTERS

ENCYCLOPEDIA OF ENGINEERING

Dictionaries

DICTIONARY OF SCIENTIFIC AND TECHNICAL TERMS

DICTIONARY OF COMPUTERS

DICTIONARY OF ELECTRICAL AND ELECTRONIC ENGINEERING

DICTIONARY OF ENGINEERING

Markus • ELECTRONICS DICTIONARY

For more information about other McGraw-Hill materials,
call 1-800-2-MCGRAW in the United States. In other
countries, call your nearest McGraw-Hill office.

AUDIO
ENGINEERING
HANDBOOK

K. Blair Benson Editor

Consultant
Member, Audio Engineering Society
Senior and Life Member, Institute of Electrical
and Electronic Engineers
Fellow and Life Member, Society of Motion Picture
and Television Engineers

McGRAW-HILL BOOK COMPANY

New York   St. Louis   San Francisco   Auckland
Bogotá   Hamburg   London   Madrid   Mexico
Milan   Montreal   New Delhi   Panama
Paris   São Paulo   Singapore
Sydney   Tokyo   Toronto

Library of Congress Cataloging-in-Publication Data

Audio engineering handbook.

 1. Sound—Recording and reproducing—Handbooks,
manuals, etc.   2. Sound—Digital techniques—Handbooks,
manuals, etc.   I. Benson, K. Blair
TK7881.4.A923 1988   621.389′3   87-29719
ISBN 0-07-004777-4

 234567890   DOC/DOC   954321

ISBN 0-07-004777-4

The editors for this book were Daniel A. Gonneau and Beatrice E. Eckes
and the production supervisor was Richard Ausburn. It was set in Times
Roman by University Graphics, Inc.
Printed and bound by R. R. Donnelley & Sons Company.

*For more information about other McGraw-Hill materials,
call 1-800-2-MCGRAW in the United States. In other
countries, call your nearest McGraw-Hill office.*

*To Carole, Candi, Kathi, and Kenneth
for their encouragement and patience*

CONTENTS

Chapter 3. Architectural Acoustic Principles and Design Techniques *Richard G. Cann and K. Anthony Hoover*

Chapter 4. Digital Audio *P. Jeffrey Bloom, Guy W. McNally, Leonard Sherman, and Jerry Whitaker*   **4.1**

Chapter 8. Analog Disk Recording and Reproduction   *Gregory A. Bogantz and Joseph C. Ruda*   **8.1**

Chapter 9. Digital Disk Recording and Reproduction   *Hiroshi Ogawa, Kentaro Odaka, and Masanobu Yamato; Toshi T. Doi, technical consultant*   **9.1**

Chapter 10. Analog Magnetic-Tape Recording and Reproduction   *E. Stanley Busby, Jr.*   **10.1**

Chapter 13. Studio Production Systems   *Ernst-Joachim Voelker*   **13.1**

CONTRIBUTORS

Dr. P. Jeffrey Bloom, *Digital Audio Research Limited, Chessington, Surrey, England* (CHAPTER 4)

Gregory A. Bogantz, *Manager, Quality Assurance, RCA Records, BMG Music, Indianapolis, Indiana* (CHAPTER 8)

E. Stanley Busby, Jr., *Senior Staff Engineer, Ampex Corporation, Redwood City, California* (CHAPTER 10)

Dr. Richard C. Cabot, *P.E., Principal Engineer, Audio Precision, Inc., Beaverton, Oregon* (CHAPTER 16)

Richard C. Cann, *President, Grozier Technical Systems, Inc., Brookline, Massachusetts* (CHAPTER 3)

James R. Carpenter, *Manager, Audio Engineering, Broadcast Electronics Inc., Quincy, Illinois* (CHAPTER 5)

H. G. de Haan, *Philips Consumer Electronics, Eindhoven, Netherlands* (CHAPTER 11)

Dr. Toshi T. Doi, *Deputy General Manager, MC/OA Division, Sony Corporation, Tokyo, Japan* (*Technical Consultant,* CHAPTER 9)

Ray Dolby, *Chairman, Dolby Laboratories Inc., San Francisco, California* (CHAPTER 15)

Wesley L. Dooley, *Chief Engineer, Audio Engineering Associates, Pasadena, California* (CHAPTER 6)

Tomlinson Holman, *Assistant Professor, School of Cinema-Television, University of Southern California; Corporate Technical Director, Lucasfilm Ltd., San Rafael, California* (CHAPTER 14)

K. Anthony Hoover, *Staff Consultant, Cavanaugh Tocci Associates, Inc., Sudbury, Massachusetts* (CHAPTER 3)

Guy W. McNally, *Digital Audio Research Limited, Chessington, Surrey, England* (CHAPTER 4)

Donald L. Markley, *P.E., D. L. Markley & Associates, Inc., Peoria, Illinois* (CHAPTER 5)

T. J. G. A. Martens, *Philips Consumer Electronics, Eindhoven, Netherlands* (CHAPTER 11)

Kentaro Odaka, *Audio Technology Center, Sony Corporation, Tokyo, Japan* (CHAPTER 9)

Hiroshi Ogawa, *Optical Disk Drive Division, Sony Corporation, Tokyo, Japan* (CHAPTER 9)

Dr. Douglas Preis, *Professor of Electrical Engineering, Tufts University, Medford, Massachusetts* (CHAPTER 2)

Daniel Queen, *Daniel Queen Associates, New York* (CHAPTER 17)

David P. Robinson, *Vice President, Engineering, Dolby Laboratories Inc., San Francisco, California* (CHAPTER 15)

Joseph C. Ruda, *Manager, Equipment and Process Development, RCA Records, BMG Music, Indianapolis, Indiana* (CHAPTER 8)

Jon R. Sank, *Cross County Consultants, Haddonfield, New Jersey* (CHAPTER 6)

Katsuaki Satoh, *Chief Engineer, Acoustic Research Laboratory, Matsushita Electric Industrial Co., Ltd., Osaka, Japan* (CHAPTER 7)

Leonard Sherman, *Maxim Integrated Products, Sunnyvale, California* (CHAPTER 4)

Ronald D. Streicher, *President, Pacific Audio-Visual Enterprises, Monrovia, California* (CHAPTER 6)

Dr. Floyd E. Toole, *Division of Physics, National Research Council, Ottawa, Canada* (CHAPTER 1)

Leslie B. Tyler, *Vice President, Engineering, dbx Inc., Newton, Massachusetts* (CHAPTER 15)

Ronald E. Uhlig, *Senior Photographic Engineer, Motion Picture and Audio Visual Product Department, Eastman Kodak Company, Rochester, New York* (CHAPTER 12)

W. J. van Gestel, *Philips Research Laboratories, Eindhoven, Netherlands* (CHAPTER 11)

Ernst-Joachim Voelker, *Institut für Akustik und Bauphysik, Oberursel, West Germany* (CHAPTER 13)

Daniel R. von Recklinghausen, *Consultant, Hudson, New Hampshire* (CHAPTER 6)

Jerry Whitaker, *Editorial Director,* Broadcast Engineering and Video Systems, *Overland Park, Kansas* (CHAPTER 4)

Masanobu Yamamoto, *Disk Development Division, Sony Corporation, Tokyo, Japan* (CHAPTER 9)

PREFACE

The term *audio* is defined as pertaining to audible sound, normally considered to extend over the range of 15 to 20,000 Hz. *Engineering* involves putting scientific knowledge to practical use; thus *audio engineering* involves the application of electrical and acoustic technology to audio equipment and systems.

Covering a span of over a century, audio engineering dates back to 1876, when Alexander Graham Bell first demonstrated the electrical transmission and reproduction of voice signals. Although sound had been converted to electrical signals 15 years earlier by Philip Reiss, the revolutionary feature of Bell's invention was the use of an electromagnetic transducer for reproducing the voice signals. Thus, audio engineering, as demonstrated by the telephone, is an old and established scientific discipline.

On the other hand, the use of audio technology for applications beyond voice communication over very limited distances was not to be realized until 50 years later with the invention of the dynamic loudspeaker, by Kellogg and Rice in 1925, and the availability of the vacuum-tube amplifier. Consequently, audio engineering can be considered a relatively new discipline, since it involves a variety of electronic devices and the wide application to many entertainment, educational, and industrial fields, most of which have been developed in the last few decades. Most recently, the use of digital processing and laser recording has required a significant broadening of the audio engineer's expertise. Another new development of great importance in both professional and consumer fields is the rapidly expanding use of noise reduction by analog as well as digital processing.

In addition to a working knowledge of current technology and hardware, engineers engaged in the design or utilization of audio equipment and systems require an understanding of the fundamental and underlying principles of sound and acoustics. The *Audio Engineering Handbook* thus encompasses all aspects of sound involving the generation, transmission, media storage, and reproduction of audio signals, including the new technologies of digital magnetic-tape recording and laser disk recording. The chapter subjects generally can be classified as follows:

Fundamental concepts of sound, hearing, and acoustics

Audio-signal spectrum and transmission

Digital and analog processing and recording

Sound pickup, amplification, and reproduction

Program production

Measurements and standards

The introductory chapter acquaints the reader with the basic principles of audio technology in order to provide a better understanding of the underlying principles governing the equipment and systems designs discussed in subsequent chapters. This is followed by a chapter on the fundamental waveform characteristics and the related spectrum of audio signals. Also included is a chapter on architectural design aspects related to acoustic characteristics.

A full chapter on digital fundamentals and the application of digital techniques to audio component and system design is followed by a review of the practical aspects of analog AM, FM, and TV broadcast transmission of audio signals.

Digital disk and magnetic-tape recording and reproduction are each the subject of two chapters, followed by a chapter on related digital and analog noise reduction technology for both professional and consumer applications.

Studio program production and editing and related film-recording techniques are the subjects of Chaps. 12 through 14.

The last two chapters cover measurement techniques and standards adopted by industry agreement both in the United States and worldwide. Included in the last chapter is a heretofore unpublished tabulation of applicable audio standards and recommended practices in the United States.

Publication of a handbook of this size and scope required the cooperation and hard work of a large number of recognized experts in many different engineering fields in order to provide an authoritative treatise. To all the contributors, I offer my sincere appreciation and thanks for their dedicated efforts.

K. Blair Benson

CHAPTER 1
PRINCIPLES OF SOUND AND HEARING*

Floyd E. Toole
Division of Physics, National Research Council, Ottawa, Canada

Sound would be of little interest if we could not hear. It is through the production and perception of sounds that it is possible to communicate and monitor events in our surroundings. Some sounds are functional, others are created for aesthetic pleasure, and still others yield only annoyance. Obviously a comprehensive examination of sound must embrace not only the physical properties of the phenomenon but also the consequences of interaction with listeners.

This chapter deals with sound in its various forms, beginning with a description of what it is and how it is generated, how it propagates in various environments, and, finally, what happens when sound impinges on the ears and is transformed into a perception. Part of this examination is a discussion of the factors that influence the opinions about sound and spatial qualities that so readily form when listening to music, whether live or reproduced.

Audio engineering, in virtually all its facets, benefits from an understanding of these basic principles. A foundation of technical knowledge is a useful instrument, and, fortunately, most of the important ideas can be understood without recourse to complex mathematics. It is the intuitive interpretation of the principles that is stressed in this chapter; more detailed information may be found in the reference material.

1.1 PHYSICAL NATURE OF SOUND

Sound is a physical disturbance in the medium through which it is propagated. Although the most common medium is air, sound can travel in any solid, liquid, or gas. In air, sound consists of localized variations in pressure above and below normal atmospheric pressure (*compressions* and *rarefactions*).

---

* The author is indebted to E. A. G. Shaw, G. A. Daigle, and M. R. Stinson for their helpful suggestions and detailed reading of the manuscript.

Air pressure rises and falls routinely, as environmental weather systems come and go, or with changes in altitude. These fluctuation cycles are very slow, and no perceptible sound results, although it is sometimes evident that the ears are responding in a different way to these *infrasonic* events. At fluctuation frequencies in the range from about 20 cycles per second up to about 20,000 cycles per second the physical phenomenon of sound can be perceived as having pitch or tonal character. This generally is regarded as the *audible* or *audio-frequency range,* and it is the frequencies in this range that are the concern of this chapter. Frequencies above 20,000 cycles per second are classified as *ultrasonic.*

1.2 SOUND WAVES

The essence of sound waves is illustrated in Fig. 1.1, which shows a tube with a piston in one end. Initially, the air within and outside the tube is all at the prevailing atmospheric pressure. When the piston moves quickly inward, it compresses the air in contact with its surface. This energetic compression is rapidly passed on to the adjoining layer of air, and so on, repeatedly. As it delivers its energy to its neighbor, each layer of air returns to its original uncompressed state. A longitudinal sound pulse is moving outward through the air in the tube, causing only a passing disturbance on the way. It is a pulse because there is only an isolated action, and it is longitudinal because the air movement occurs along the axis of sound propagation. The rate at which the pulse propagates is the speed of sound. The pressure rise in the compressed air is proportional to the velocity with which the piston moves, and the perceived loudness of the resulting sound pulse is related to the incremental amplitude of the pressure wave above the ambient atmospheric pressure.

Percussive or impulsive sounds such as these are common, but most sounds do not cease after a single impulsive event. Sound waves that are repetitive at a regular rate are called *periodic.* Many musical sounds are periodic, and they embrace a very wide range of repetitive patterns. The simplest of periodic sounds is a pure tone, similar to the sound of a tuning fork or a whistle. An example is presented when the end of the tube is driven by a loudspeaker reproducing a

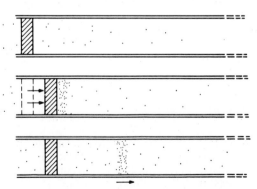

FIG. 1.1 Generation of a longitudinal sound wave by the rapid movement of a piston in the end of a tube, showing the propagation of the wave pulse at the speed of sound down the length of the tube.

recording of such a sound (Fig. 1.2). The pattern of displacement versus time for the loudspeaker diaphragm, shown in Fig. 1.2*b*, is called a *sine wave* or *sinusoid*.

If the first diaphragm movement is inward, the first event in the tube is a pressure compression, as seen previously. When the diaphragm changes direction, the adjacent layer of air undergoes a pressure rarefaction. These cyclic compressions and rarefactions are repeated, so that the sound wave propagating down the tube has a regularly repeated, periodic form. If the air pressure at all points along the tube were measured at a specific instant, the result would be the graph of air pressure versus distance shown in Fig. 1.2*c*. This reveals a smoothly sinusoidal waveform with a repetition distance along the tube symbolized by λ (lambda), the *wavelength* of the periodic sound wave.

If a pressure-measuring device were placed at some point in the tube to record the instantaneous changes in pressure at that point as a function of time, the result would be as shown in Fig. 1.2*d*. Clearly the curve has the same shape as the previous one except that the horizontal axis is time instead of distance. The periodic nature of the waveform is here defined by the time period *T*, known simply as the *period* of the sound wave. The inverse of the period, $1/T$, is the *frequency* of the sound wave, describing the number of repetition cycles per second passing a

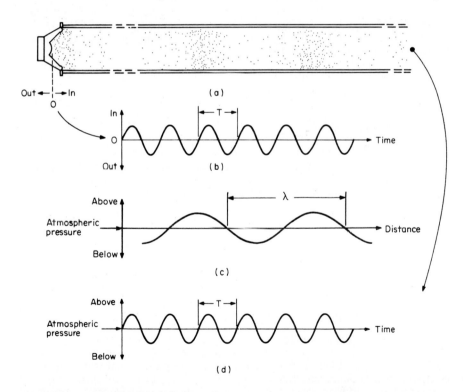

FIG. 1.2 (*a*) A periodic sound wave, a sinusoid in this example, is generated by a loudspeaker placed at the end of a tube. (*b*) Waveform shows the movement of the loudspeaker diaphragm as a function of time: displacement versus time. (*c*) Waveform shows the instantaneous distribution of pressure along a section of the tube: pressure versus distance. (*d*) Waveform shows the pressure variation as a function of time at some point along the tube: pressure versus time.

fixed point in space. An ear placed in the path of a sound wave corresponding to the musical tone middle C would be exposed to a frequency of 261.6 cycles per second or, using standard scientific terminology, a frequency of 261.6 hertz (Hz). The perceived loudness of the tone would depend on the magnitude of the pressure deviations above and below the ambient air pressure.

The parameters discussed so far are all related by the *speed of sound*. Given the speed of sound and the duration of one period, the wavelength can be calculated as follows:

$$\lambda = cT \tag{1.1}$$

where λ = wavelength
      c = speed of sound
      T = period

By knowing that the frequency $f = 1/T$, the following useful equation and its variations can be derived:

$$\lambda = \frac{c}{f} \quad f = \frac{c}{\lambda} \quad c = f\lambda \tag{1.2}$$

The speed of sound in air at a room temperature of 22°C (72°F) is 345 m/s (1131 ft/s). At any other ambient temperatures the speed of sound in air is given by the following approximate relationships:[1,2]

$$c(\text{m/s}) = 331.29 + 0.607t \ (°C) \tag{1.3}$$

$$\text{or} \quad c(\text{ft/s}) = 1051.5 + 1.106t \ (°F) \tag{1.4}$$

where t = ambient temperature.

The relationships between the frequency of a sound wave and its wavelength are essential to understanding many of the fundamental properties of sound and hearing. The graph of Fig. 1.3 is a useful quick reference illustrating the large ranges of distance and time embraced by audible sounds. For example, the tone middle C with a frequency of 261.6 Hz has a wavelength of 1.3 m (4.3 ft) in air at 20°C. In contrast, an organ pedal note at C1, 32.7 Hz, has a wavelength of 10.5 m (34.5 ft), and the third-harmonic overtone of C8, at 12,558 Hz, has a wavelength of 27.5 mm (1.1 in). The corresponding periods are, respectively, 3.8 ms, 30.6 ms, and 0.08 ms. The contrasts in these dimensions are remarkable, and they result in some interesting and troublesome effects in the realms of perception and audio engineering. For the discussions that follow it is often more helpful to think in terms of wavelengths rather than in frequencies.

1.2.1 Complex Sounds

The simple sine waves used for illustration reveal their periodicity very clearly. Normal sounds, however, are much more complex, being combinations of several such pure tones of different frequencies and perhaps additional transient sound components that punctuate the more sustained elements. For example, speech is a mixture of approximately periodic vowel sounds and staccato consonant sounds. Complex sounds can also be periodic; the repeated wave pattern is just more intricate, as is shown in Fig. 1.4a. The period identified as T_1 applies to the *fundamental frequency* of the sound wave, the component that normally is related to the characteristic pitch of the sound. Higher-frequency components of the complex wave are also periodic, but since they are typically lower in amplitude, that

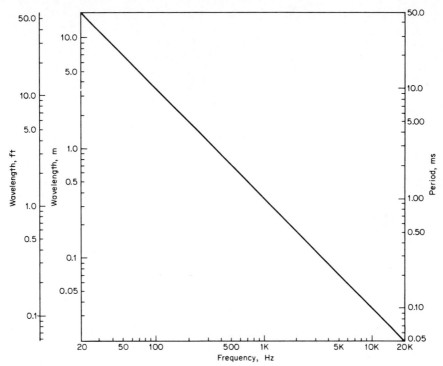

FIG. 1.3 Relationships between wavelength, period, and frequency for sound waves in air. To use the graph, select a frequency and move upward to the diagonal line. From the point of intersection move horizontally to the left to read the wavelength or to the right to read the period. For conversions between wavelength and period simply move horizontally between the scales. For accurate data use Eq. (1.1) or Eq. (1.2).

aspect tends to be disguised in the summation of several such components of different frequency. If, however, the sound wave were analyzed, or broken down into its constituent parts, a different picture emerges: Fig. 1.4*b*, *c*, and *d*. In this example the analysis shows that the components are all *harmonics,* or whole-number multiples, of the fundamental frequency; the higher-frequency components all have multiples of entire cycles within the period of the fundamental.

To generalize, it can be stated that *all complex periodic waveforms are combinations of several harmonically related sine waves.* The shape of a complex waveform depends upon the relative amplitudes of the various harmonics and the position in time of each individual component with respect to the others. If one of the harmonic components in Fig. 1.4 is shifted slightly in time, the shape of the waveform is changed, although the frequency composition remains the same (Fig. 1.5). Obviously a record of the time locations of the various harmonic components is required to completely describe the complex waveform. This information is noted as the *phase* of the individual components.

1.2.2   Phase

Phase is a notation in which the time of one period of a sine wave is divided into 360°. It is a relative quantity, and although it can be defined with respect to any reference point in a cycle, it is convenient to start (0°) with the upward, or posi-

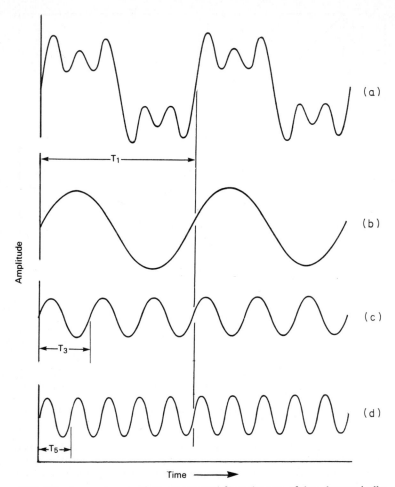

FIG. 1.4 A complex waveform constructed from the sum of three harmonically related sinusoidal components, all of which start at the origin of the time scale with a positive-going zero crossing. Extending the series of odd-harmonic components to include those above the fifth would result in the complex waveform's progressively assuming the form of a square wave, a shape that is already suggested in this example. (*a*) Complex waveform: sum of *b*, *c*, and *d*. (*b*) f_1 = fundamental = first harmonic = $1/T_1$ Hz. (*c*) f_3 = third harmonic = $3/T_1 = 3f_1 = 1/T_3$ Hz. (*d*) f_5 = fifth harmonic = $5/T_1 = 5f_1 = 1/T_5$ Hz.

tive-going, zero crossing and to end (360°) at precisely the same point at the beginning of the next cycle (Fig. 1.6). *Phase shift* expresses in degrees the fraction of a period or wavelength by which a single-frequency component is shifted in the time domain. For example, a phase shift of 90° corresponds to a shift of one-fourth period. For different frequencies this translates into different time shifts. Looking at it from the other point of view, if a complex waveform is time-delayed, the various harmonic components will experience different phase shifts, depending on their frequencies.

A special case of phase shift is a *polarity reversal,* an inversion of the wave-

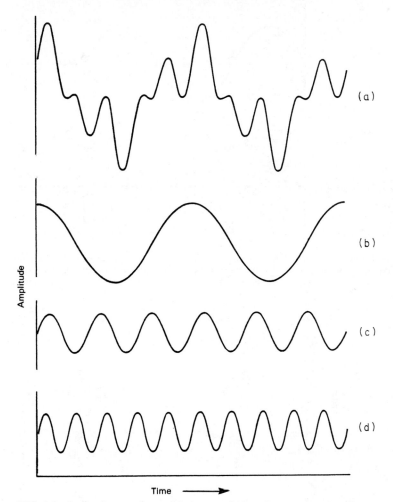

FIG. 1.5 A complex waveform with the same harmonic-component amplitudes as in Fig. 1.4 but with the starting time of the fundamental advanced by one-fourth period: a phase shift of 90°.

form, where all frequency components undergo a 180° phase shift. This occurs when, for example, the connections to a loudspeaker are reversed.

1.2.3 Spectra

Translating time-domain information into the frequency domain yields an *amplitude-frequency spectrum* or, as it is commonly called, simply a *spectrum*. Figure 1.7*a* shows the spectrum of the waveform in Figs. 1.4 and 1.5, in which the height of each line represents the amplitude of that particular component and the position of the line along the frequency axis identifies its frequency. This kind of display is a line spectrum because there are sound components at only certain spe-

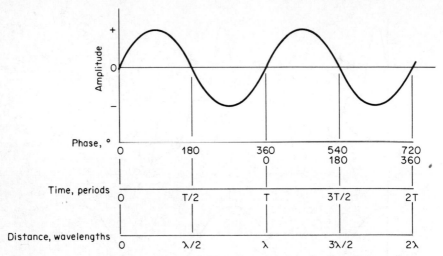

FIG. 1.6 Relationship between the period (T) and wavelength λ of a sinusoidal waveform and the phase expressed in degrees. Although it is normal to consider each repetitive cycle as an independent 360°, it is sometimes necessary to sum successive cycles starting from a reference point in one of them.

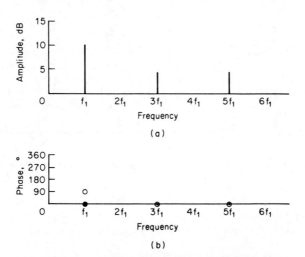

FIG. 1.7 The amplitude-frequency spectra (a) and the phase-frequency spectra (b) of the complex waveforms shown in Figs. 1.4 and 1.5. The amplitude-frequency spectra are identical for both waveforms, but the phase-frequency spectra show the 90° phase shift of the fundamental component in the waveform of Fig. 1.5. Note that frequency is expressed as a multiple of the fundamental frequency f_1. The numerals are the harmonic numbers. Only the fundamental f_1 and the third and fifth harmonics (f_3 and f_5) are present.

cific frequencies. The phase information is shown in Fig. 1.7*b*, where the difference between the two waveforms is revealed in the different *phase-frequency spectra.*

The equivalence of the information presented in the two domains—the waveform in the time domain and the amplitude- and phase-frequency spectra in the frequency domain—is a matter of considerable importance. The proofs have been throroughly worked out by a French mathematician, Fourier, and the well-known relationships bear his name. The breaking down of waveforms into their constituent sinusoidal parts is known as *Fourier analysis.* The construction of complex waveshapes from summations of sine waves is called *Fourier synthesis. Fourier transformations* permit the conversion of time-domain information into frequency-domain information, and vice versa. These interchangeable descriptions of waveforms form the basis for powerful methods of measurement and, at the present stage, provide a convenient means of understanding audio phenomena (see Chap. 2). In the examples that follow the relationships between time-domain and frequency-domain descriptions of waveforms will be noted from time to time.

Figure 1.8 illustrates the sound waveform that emerges from the larynx, the buzzing sound that is the basis for vocalized speech sounds. This sound is modified in various ways in its passage down the vocal tract before it emerges from the mouth as speech. The waveform is a series of periodic pulses, corresponding to the pulses of air that are expelled, under lung pressure, from between the vibrating vocal cords. The spectrum of this waveform consists of a harmonic series of components, with a fundamental frequency, for this male talker, of 100 Hz. The gently rounded contours of the waveform suggest the absence of strong high-frequency components, and the amplitude-frequency spectrum confirms it. The *spectrum envelope,* the overall shape delineating the amplitudes of the components of the line spectrum, shows a progressive decline in amplitude as a function of frequency. The amplitudes are described in *decibels,* abbreviated dB. This is the common unit for describing sound-level *differences,* as will be discussed in more detail in Sec. 1.3. The rate of this decline is about -12 dB per octave (an *octave* is a 2:1 ratio of frequencies).

Increasing the pitch of the voice brings the pulses closer together in time and raises the fundamental frequency. The harmonic-spectrum lines displayed in the frequency domain are then spaced farther apart but still within the overall form of the spectrum envelope, which is defined by the shape of the pulse itself. Reducing the pitch of the voice has the opposite effect, increasing the spacing between pulses and reducing the spacing between the spectral lines under the envelope. Continuing this process to the limiting condition, if it were possible to emit just a single pulse, would be equivalent to an infinitely long period, and the spacing between the spectral lines would vanish. The discontinuous, or *aperiodic,* pulse waveform therefore yields a *continuous* spectrum having the form of the spectrum envelope.

Isolated pulses of sound occur in speech as any of the variations of consonant sounds and in music as percussive sounds and as transient events punctuating more continuous melodic lines. All these aperiodic sounds exhibit continuous spectra with shapes that are dictated by the waveforms. The leisurely undulations of a bass drum waveform contain predominantly low-frequency energy, just as the more rapid pressure changes in a snare drum waveform require the presence of higher frequencies with their more rapid rates of change. A technical waveform of considerable use in measurements consists of a very brief impulse which has the important feature of containing equal amplitudes of all frequencies within the

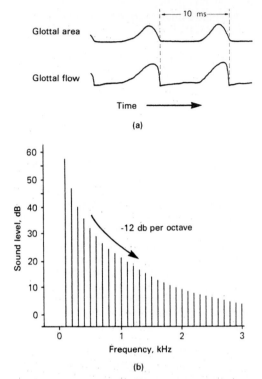

FIG. 1.8 (*a*) Waveforms showing the varying area between vibrating vocal cords (glottal area) and the corresponding airflow (glottal flow) during vocalized speech as functions of time. The measurement was made close to the larynx, before the sounds traveled out of the throat and mouth. (*b*) The amplitude-frequency spectrum of the glottal-flow waveform, showing the 100-Hz fundamental frequency for this male speaker. *(From J. M. Pickett,* The Sounds of Speech Communication, *University Park Press, Baltimore, 1980.)*

audio-frequency bandwith. This is moving toward a limiting condition in which an infinitely short event in the time domain is associated with an infinitely wide amplitude-frequency spectrum.

1.3 *DIMENSIONS OF SOUND*

The descriptions of sound in the preceding section involved only pressure variation, and while this is the dimension that is most commonly referred to, it is not the only one. Accompanying the pressure changes are temporary movements of the air "particles" as the sound wave passes (in this context a particle is a volume of air that is large enough to contain many molecules while its dimensions are small compared with the wavelength). Other measures of the magnitude of the sound event are the displacement amplitude of the air particles away from their rest positions and the velocity amplitude of the particles during the movement cycle. In the physics of sound the *particle displacement* and the *particle velocity* are useful concepts, but the difficulty of their measurement limits their practical application. They can, however, help in understanding other concepts.

In a normally propagating sound wave, energy is required to move the air particles; they must be pushed or pulled against the elasticity of the air, causing the incremental rises and falls in pressure. Doubling the displacement doubles the pressure change, and this requires double the force. Since the work done is the product of force times distance and both are doubled, the energy in a sound wave is therefore proportional to the square of the particle displacement amplitude or, in more practical terms, to the square of the sound pressure amplitude.

Sound energy spreads outward from the source in the three dimensions of space, in addition to those of amplitude and time. The energy of such a sound field is usually described in terms of the energy flow through an imaginary surface. The sound energy transmitted per unit of time is called *sound power*. The sound power passing through a unit area of a surface perpendicular to a specified direction is called the *sound intensity*. Since intensity is a measure of energy flow, it also is proportional to the square of the sound pressure amplitude.

The ear responds to a very wide range of sound pressure amplitudes. From the smallest sound that is audible to sounds large enough to cause discomfort there is a ratio of approximately 1 million in sound pressure amplitude or 1 trillion (10^{12}) in sound intensity or power. Dealing routinely with such large numbers is impractical, so a logarithmic scale is used. This is based on the *bel,* which represents a ratio of 10:1 in sound intensity or sound power (the power can be acoustical or electrical). More commonly the decibel, one-tenth of a bel, is used. A difference of 10 dB therefore corresponds to a factor-of-10 difference in sound intensity or sound power. Mathematically this can be generalized as

$$\text{Level difference} = \log \frac{P_1}{P_2} \quad \text{bels} \tag{1.5}$$

or
$$= 10 \log \frac{P_1}{P_2} \quad \text{decibels} \tag{1.6}$$

where P_1 and P_2 are two levels of power.

For ratios of sound pressures (analogous to voltage or current ratios in electrical systems) the squared relationship with power is accommodated by multiplying the logarithm of the ratio of pressures by 2, as follows:

$$\text{Level difference} = 10 \log \frac{p_1^2}{p_2^2} = 20 \log \frac{p_1}{p_2} \quad \text{dB} \tag{1.7}$$

where p_1 and p_2 are sound pressures.

The relationship between decibels and a few power and pressure ratios is shown in Table 1.1. The footnote to the table describes a simple process for interpolating between these values, an exercise that helps to develop a feel for the meaning of the quantities.

The representation of the relative magnitudes of sound pressures and powers in decibels is important, but there is no indication of the absolute magnitude of either quantity being compared. This limitation is easily overcome by the use of a universally accepted reference level with which others are compared. For con-

TABLE 1.1   Various Power and Amplitude Ratios and Their Decibel Equivalents*

Sound or electrical power ratio	Decibels	Sound pressure, voltage, or current ratio	Decibels
1	0	1	0
2	3.0	2	6.0
3	4.8	3	9.5
4	6.0	4	12.0
5	7.0	5	14.0
6	7.8	6	15.6
7	8.5	7	16.9
8	9.0	8	18.1
9	9.5	9	19.1
10	10.0	10	20.0
100	20.0	100	40.0
1,000	30.0	1,000	60.0
10,000	40.0	10,000	80.0
100,000	50.0	100,000	100.0
1,000,000	60.0	1,000,000	120.0

* Other values can be calculated precisely by using Eqs. (1.6) and (1.7) or estimated by using this table and the following rules:

Power ratios that are multiples of 10 are converted into their decibel equivalents by multiplying the appropriate exponent by 10. For example, a power ratio of 1000 is 10^3, and this translates into $3 \times 10 = 30$ dB. Since power is proportional to the square of amplitude, the exponent of 10 must be doubled to arrive at the decibel equivalent of an amplitude ratio.

Intermediate values can be estimated by combining values in this table by means of the rule that the multiplication of power or amplitude ratios is equivalent to adding level differences in decibels. For example, increasing a sound level by 27 dB requires increasing the power by a ratio of 500 (20 dB is a ratio of 100, and 7 dB is a ratio of 5; the product of the ratios is 500). The corresponding increase in sound pressure or electrical signal amplitude is a factor of just over 20 (20 dB is a ratio of 10, and 7 dB falls between 6.0 and 9.5 and is therefore a ratio of something in excess of 2); the calculated value is 22.4. Reversing the process, if the output from a power amplifier is increased from 40 to 800 W, a ratio of 20, the sound pressure level would be expected to increase by 13 dB (a power ratio of 10 is 10 dB, a ratio of 2 is 3 dB, and the sum is 13 dB). The corresponding voltage increase measured at the output of the amplifier would be a factor of between 4 and 5 (by calculation, 4.5).

venience the standard reference level is close to the smallest sound that is audible to a person with normal hearing. This defines a scale of *sound pressure level* (SPL), in which 0 dB represents a sound level close to the hearing-threshold level for middle and high frequencies (the most sensitive range). The SPL of a sound therefore describes, in decibels, the relationship between the level of that sound and the reference level. Table 1.2 gives examples of SPLs of some common sounds, with the corresponding intensities and some indications of listener reactions. From this it is clear that the musically useful range of SPLs extends from the level of background noises in quiet surroundings to levels at which listeners begin to experience auditory discomfort and nonauditory sensations of feeling or pain in the ears themselves.

While some sound sources, such as chain saws and power mowers, produce a relatively constant sound output, others, like a 75-piece orchestra, are variable. The sound from such an orchestra might have a *peak factor* of 20 to 30 dB; the momentary, or peak, levels can be this amount higher than the long-term average SPL indicatd here.[3]

The sound power produced by sources gives another perspective on the quantities being described. In spite of some impressively large sounds, a full symphony orchestra produces only about 1 acoustic watt when working through a typical musical passage. On crescendos with percussion, though, the levels can be of the order of 100 W. A bass drum alone can produce about 25 W of acoustic power of peaks. All these levels are dependent on the instruments and how they are played. Maximum sound output from cymbals might be 10 W; from a trombone, 6 W; and from a piano, 0.4 W.[4] By comparison, average speech generates about 25 μW, and a present-day jet liner at takeoff between 50 and 100 kW. Small gasoline engines produce from 0.001 to 1.0 acoustic watt, and electric home appliances less than 0.01 W.[5]

1.4 SOUND PROPAGATION

Sound propagating away from a source diminishes in strength at a rate depending on a variety of circumstances. It also encounters situations that can cause changes in amplitude and direction. Simple reflection is the most obvious process for directional change, but with sound there are also some less obvious mechanisms.

1.4.1 Inverse-Square and Other Laws

At increasing distances from a source of sound the level is expected to decrease. The rate at which it decreases is dictated by the directional properties of the

TABLE 1.2 Typical Sound Pressure Levels and Intensities for Various Sound Sources.*

Sound source	Sound pressure level, dB	Intensity, W/m²	Listener reaction
	160		Immediate damage
Jet engine at 10 m	150	10^3	
	140		Painful feeling
	130		
SST takeoff at 500 m	120	1	Discomfort
Amplified rock music	110		
Chain saw at 1 m	100		fff
Power mower at 1.5 m	90	10^{-3}	
75-piece orchestra at 7 m	80		f
City traffic at 15 m	70		
Normal speech at 1 m	60	10^{-6}	p
Suburban residence	50		
Library	40		ppp
Empty auditorium	30	10^{-9}	
Recording studio	20		
Breathing	10		
0†		10^{-12}	Inaudible

*The relationships illustrated in this table are necessarily approximate because the conditions of measurement are not defined. Typical levels should, however, be within about 10 dB of the stated values.

† O-dB sound pressure level (SPL) represents a reference sound pressure of 0.0002 μbar, or 0.00002 N/m².

source and the environment into which it radiates. In the case of a source of sound that is small compared with the wavelength of the sound being radiated, a condition that includes many common situations, the sound spreads outward as a sphere of ever-increasing radius. The sound energy from the source is distributed uniformly over the surface of the sphere, meaning that the intensity (see Sec. 1.3) is the sound power output divided by the surface area at any radial distance from the source. Since the area of a sphere is $4\pi r^2$, the relationship between the sound intensities at two different distances is

$$\frac{I_1}{I_2} = \frac{r_2^2}{r_1^2} \qquad (1.8)$$

where I_1 = intensity at radius r_1
$\quad\ \ I_2$ = intensity at radius r_2

and $\qquad\qquad$ Level difference $= 10 \log \dfrac{r_2^2}{r_1^2} = 20 \log \dfrac{r_2}{r_1} \quad$ dB $\qquad$ (1.9)

This translates into a change in sound level of 6 dB for each doubling or halving of distance, a convenient mnemonic.

In practice, however, this relationship must be used with caution because of the constraints of real environments. For example, over long distances outdoors the absorption of sound by the ground and the air can modify the predictions of simple theory.[6] Indoors, reflected sounds can sustain sound levels to greater distances than predicted, although the estimate is correct over moderate distances for the *direct sound* (the part of the sound that travels directly from source to receiver without reflection). Large sound sources present special problems because the sound waves need a certain distance to form into an orderly wavefront combining the inputs from various parts of the source. In this case measurements in what is called the *near field* may not be representative of the integrated output from the source, and extrapolations to greater distances will contain errors. In fact the *far field* of a source is sometimes defined as being distances at which the inverse-square law holds true. In general, the far field is where the distance from the source is at least 2 to 3 times the distance between the most widely separated parts of the sound source that are radiating energy at the same frequency.

If the sound source is not small compared with the wavelength of the radiated sound, the sound will not expand outward with a spherical wavefront and the rate at which the sound level reduces with distance will not obey the inverse-square law. For example, a sound source in the form of a line, such as a long column of loudspeakers or a long line of traffic on a highway, generates sound waves that expand outward with a cylindrical wavefront. In the idealized case, such sounds attenuate at the rate of 3 dB for each doubling of distance.

1.4.2 Sound Reflection and Absorption

A sound source suspended in midair radiates into a *free field* because there is no impediment to the progress of the sound waves as they radiate in any direction. The closest indoor equivalent of this is an *anechoic room,* in which all the room boundaries are acoustically treated to be very highly absorbing, thus preventing sounds from being reflected back into the room. It is common to speak of such situations as sound propagation in *full space,* or *4π steradians* (sr; the units by which solid angles are measured).

In normal environments sound waves run into obstacles, such as walls, and the direction of their propagation is changed. Figure 1.9 shows the *reflection* of sound from various surfaces. In this diagram the pressure crests of the sound waves are represented by the curved lines, spaced one wavelength apart. The radial lines show the direction of sound propagation and are known as *sound rays.* For reflecting surfaces that are large compared with the sound wavelength, the normal *law of reflection* applies: the angle that the incident sound ray makes with the reflecting surface equals the angle made by the reflected sound ray.

This law also holds if the reflecting surface has irregularities that are small compared with the wavelength, as shown in Fig. 1.9c, where it is seen that the irregularities have negligible effect. If, however, the surface features have dimensions similar to the wavelength of the incident sound, the reflections are *scattered* in all directions. At wavelengths that are small compared with the dimensions of the surface irregularities, the sound is also sent off in many directions but, in this case, as determined by the rule of reflections applied to the geometry of the irregularities themselves.

If there is perfect reflection of the sound, the reflected sound can be visualized as having originated at an image of the real source located behind the reflector and emitting the same sound power. In practice, however, some of the incident sound energy is *absorbed* by the reflecting surface; this fraction is called the *sound absorption coefficient* of the surface material. A coefficient of 0.0 indicates a perfect reflector, and a coefficient of 1.0 a perfect absorber; intermediate values indicate the portion of the incident sound energy that is dissipated in the surface and is not reflected. In general, the sound absorption coefficient for a material is dependent on the frequency and the angle of incidence of the sound. For simplicity published values are normally given for octave bands of frequencies and for random angles of incidence.

1.4.3   Interference: The Sum of Multiple Sound Sources

The principle of *superposition* states that multiple sound waves (or electrical signals) appearing at the same point will add linearly. Consider two sound waves of identical frequency and amplitude arriving at a point in space from different directions. If the waveforms are exactly in step with each other, i.e., there is no phase difference (see Sec. 1.2.2), they will add perfectly and the result will be an identical waveform with double the amplitude of each incoming sound (6-dB-higher SPL). Such *in-phase* signals produce *constructive interference.* If the waveforms are shifted by one-half wavelength (180° phase difference) with respect to each other, they are *out of phase;* the pressure fluctuations are precisely equal and opposite, *destructive interference* occurs, and perfect cancellation results.

In practice interference occurs routinely as a consequence of direct and reflected sounds adding at a microphone or a listener's ear. The amplitude of the reflected sound is reduced because of energy lost to absorption at the reflecting surface and because of inverse-square-law reduction related to the additional distance traveled. This means that constructive interference yields sound levels that are increased by less than 6 dB and that destructive interference results in imperfect cancellations that leave a residual sound level. Whether the interference is constructive or destructive depends on the relationship between the extra distance traveled by the reflection and the wavelength of the sound.

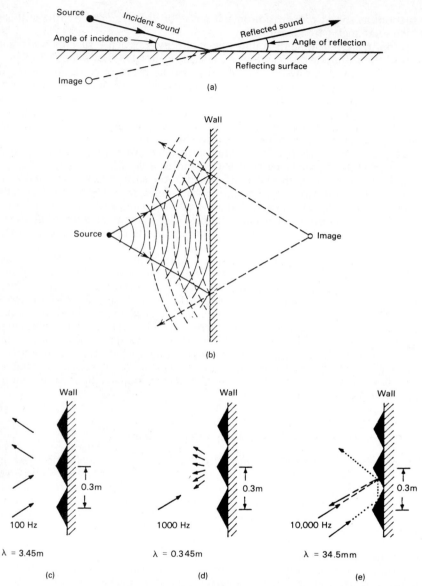

FIG. 1.9 (*a*) The relationship between the incident sound, the reflected sound, and a flat reflecting surface, illustrating the law of reflection: the angle of incidence is equal to the angle of reflection. The image and the real sources are equidistant from the reflecting surface. (*b*) A more elaborate version of *a*, showing the progression of wavefronts (the curved lines) in addition to the sound rays (arrowed lines). Note that the reflecting surface is very large compared with the wavelength of the sound (the wavelength λ is the distance between successive wavefronts). (*c*) The reflection of sound having a frequency of 100 Hz (wavelength, 3.45 m) from a surface with irregularities (splays or diffusers) that are small compared with the wavelength. In this case the irregularities are ignored, and the sound is reflected as if the surface were flat. (*d*) When the wavelength of the sound is similar to the dimensions of the irregularities, the sound is scattered in all directions. (*e*) When the wavelength of the sound is small compared with the dimensions of the irregularities, the law of reflection applies to the detailed interactions with the surface features.

Figure 1.10 shows the direct and reflected sound paths for an omnidirectional source and receivers interacting with a reflecting plane. Note that there is an acoustically mirrored source, just as there would be a visually mirrored one if the plane were optically reflecting. If the distance traveled by the direct sound and that traveled by the reflected sound are different by an amount that is small and is also small compared with a wavelength of the sound under consideration (receiver R_1), the interference at the receiver will be constructive. If the plane is perfectly reflecting, the sound at the receiver will be the sum of two essentially identical sounds and the SPL will be about 6 dB higher than the direct sound alone. Constructive interference will also occur when the difference between the distances is an even multiple of half wavelengths. Destructive interference will occur for odd multiples of half wavelengths.

As the path length difference increases, or if there is absorption at the reflective surface, the difference in the sound levels of the direct and reflected sounds increases. For receivers R_2 and R_3 in Fig. 1.10 the situation will differ from that just described only in that, because of the additional attenuation of the reflected signal, the constructive peaks will be significantly less than 6 dB and the destructive dips will be less than perfect cancellations.

For a fixed geometrical arrangement of source, reflector, and receiver, this means that at sufficiently low frequencies the direct and reflected sounds add. As the wavelength is reduced (frequency rising), the sound level at the receiver will decline from the maximum level in the approach to the first destructive interference at $\lambda/2 = r_2 - r_1$, where the level drops to a null. Continuing upward in frequency, the sound level at the receiver rises to the original level when $\lambda = r_2 - r_1$, falls to another null at $3\lambda/2 = r_2 - r_1$, rises again at $2\lambda = r_2 - r_1$, and so on, alternating between maxima and minima at regular intervals in the frequency domain. The plot of the frequency response of such a transmission path is called an *interference pattern*. It has the visual appearance of a comb, and the phenomenon has also come to be called *comb filtering* (see Fig. 1.10b).

Taking a more general view and considering the effects *averaged over a range of frequencies,* it is possible to generalize as follows for the influence of a single reflecting surface on the sound level due to the direct sound alone.[7]

1. When $r_2 - r_1$ is much less than a wavelength, the sound level at the receiver will be elevated by 6 dB or less, depending on the surface absorption and distances involved.

2. When $r_2 - r_1$ is approximately equal to a wavelength, the sound level at the receiver will be elevated between 3 and 6 dB, depending on the specific circumstances.

3. When $r_2 - r_1$ is much greater than a wavelength, the sound level at the receiver will be elevated by between 0 and 3 dB, depending on the surface absorption and distances involved.

A special case of Par. 1 occurs when the sound source, such as a loudspeaker, is mounted in the reflecting plane itself. There is no path length difference, and the source radiates into a hemisphere of free space, more commonly called *a half space,* or 2π sr. The sound level at the receiver is then elevated by 6 dB at frequencies where the sound source is truly omnidirectional, which, in practice, is only at low frequencies.

Other reflecting surfaces contribute additively to the elevation of the sound level at the receiver in amounts that can be arrived at by independent analysis of each one. Consider the situation in which a simple point monopole (omnidirectional) source of sound is progressively constrained by reflecting planes intersect-

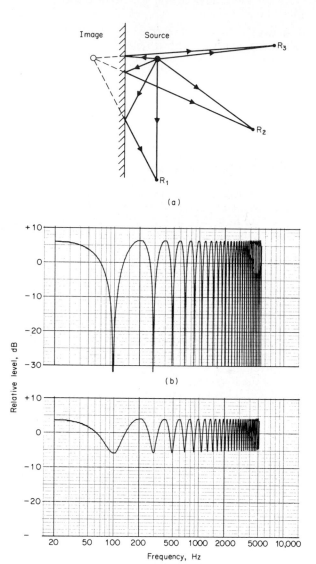

(a)

(b)

(c)

FIG. 1.10 (*a*) Differing direct and reflected path lengths as a function of receiver location. The quantity $r_2 - r_1$ increases as the receiver is moved from R_1 to R_2 and on to R_3. (r_1 = distance traveled by direct sound = distance from source to receiver R; r_2 = distance traveled by reflected sound = distance from image to receiver R.) (*b*) The interference pattern resulting when two sounds, each at the same sound level (0 dB), are summed with a time delay of just over 5 ms (a path length difference of about 1.7 m). No allowance was made for the additional attenuation of the reflected sound due to the extra distance traveled or for sound absorption at the reflecting surface. Note that the sound level at the receiver is +6 dB at the frequencies of constructive interference and that there are perfect nulls at the frequencies of destructive interference. (*c*) The reflected signal has been attenuated by 6 dB (it is now at a relative level of −6 dB, while the direct sound remains at 0 dB); the maximum sound level is reduced, and perfect nulls are no longer possible. The familiar comb-filtering pattern remains.

ing at right angles. In practice this could be the boundaries of a room that are immediately adjacent to a loudspeaker which, at very low frequencies, is effectively an omnidirectional source of sound. Figure 1.11 summarizes the relationships between four common circumstances, where the sound output from the source radiates into solid angles that reduce in stages by a factor of 2. These correspond to a loudspeaker radiating into free space (4π sr), placed against a large reflecting surface (2π sr), placed at the intersection of two reflecting surfaces (π sr), and placed at the intersection of three reflecting surfaces ($\pi/2$ sr). In all cases the dimensions of the source and its distance from any of the reflecting surfaces are assumed to be a small fraction of a wavelength. The source is also assumed to produce a constant volume velocity of sound output; i.e., the volumetric rate of air movement is constant throughout.

By using the principles outlined above and combining the outputs from the appropriate number of image sources that are acoustically mirrored in the reflective surfaces, it is found that the sound pressure at a given radius increases in inverse proportion to the reduction in solid angle; sound pressure increases by a factor of 2, or 6 dB, for each halving of the solid angle.

The corresponding sound intensity (the sound power passing through a unit surface area of a sphere of the given radius) is proportional to pressure squared (see Sec. 1.3). Sound intensity therefore increases by a factor of 4 for each halving of the solid angle. This also is 6 dB for each reduction in angle because the quantity is power rather than pressure.

Finally, multiplying the sound intensity by the surface area at the given radius yields the total sound power radiated into the solid angle. Since the surface area at each transition is reduced by a factor of 2, the total sound power radiated into the solid angle increases by a factor of 2, or 3 dB, for each halving of the solid angle.

By applying the reverse logic, reducing the solid angle by half increases the rate of energy flow into the solid angle by a factor of 2. At a given radius, this energy flows through half of the surface area that it previously did, so that the sound intensity is increased by a factor of 4; i.e., pressure squared is increased by a factor of 4. This means that sound pressure at that same radius is increased by a factor of 2.

The simplicity of this argument applies when the surfaces shown in Fig. 1.11 are the only ones present; this can only happen outdoors. In rooms there are the other boundaries to consider, and the predictions discussed here will be modified by the reflections, absorption, and standing-wave patterns therein (see Sec. 1.5.2).

1.4.4 Diffraction

The leakage of sound energy around the edges of an opening or around the corners of an obstacle results in a bending of the sound rays and a distortion of the wavefront. The effect is called *diffraction*. Because of diffraction it is possible to hear sounds around corners and behind walls—anywhere there might have been an "acoustical shadow." In fact, acoustical shadows exist, but to an extent that is dependent on the relationship between the wavelength and the dimensions of the objects in the path of the sound waves.

When the openings or obstructions are small compared with the wavelength of the sound, the waves tend to spread in all directions and the shadowing effect is small. At higher frequencies, when the openings or obstructions are large compared with the wavelengths, the sound waves tend to continue in their original

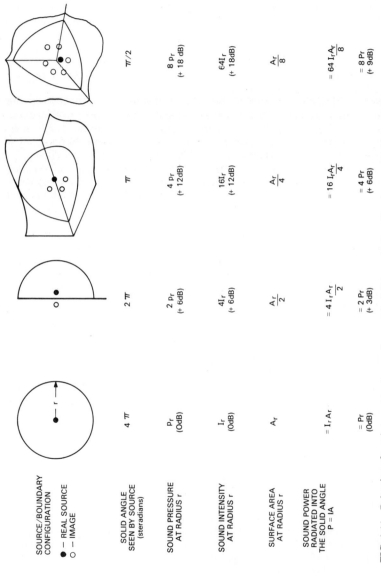

SOURCE/BOUNDARY CONFIGURATION ● – REAL SOURCE ○ – IMAGE			
SOLID ANGLE SEEN BY SOURCE (steradians)	4π	2π	π	$\pi/2$
SOUND PRESSURE AT RADIUS r	p_r (0dB)	$2p_r$ (+6dB)	$4p_r$ (+12dB)	$8p_r$ (+18 dB)
SOUND INTENSITY AT RADIUS r	I_r (0dB)	$4I_r$ (+6dB)	$16I_r$ (+12dB)	$64I_r$ (+18dB)
SURFACE AREA AT RADIUS r	A_r	$\dfrac{A_r}{2}$	$\dfrac{A_r}{4}$	$\dfrac{A_r}{8}$
SOUND POWER RADIATED INTO THE SOLID ANGLE P = IA	$= I_r A_r$	$= 4 I_r \dfrac{A_r}{2}$	$= 16 I_r \dfrac{A_r}{4}$	$= 64 I_r \dfrac{A_r}{8}$
	$= P_r$ (0dB)	$= 2 P_r$ (+3dB)	$= 4 P_r$ (+6dB)	$= 8 P_r$ (+9dB)

FIG. 1.11 Behavior of a point monopole sound source in full space (4π) and in close proximity to reflecting surfaces that constrain the sound radiation to progressively smaller solid angles. The relationships between sound pressure and intensity at a given radius and total sound power into the solid angle are shown by using the full-space (4π) situation as a reference. *(Adapted from Harry F. Olson, Acoustical Engineering, Van Nostrand, New York, 1957.)*

direction of travel and there is significant shadowing. Figure 1.12 illustrates the effect.

The principle is maintained if the openings are considered to be the diaphragms of loudspeakers. If one wishes to maintain wide dispersion at all frequencies, the radiating areas of the driver units must progressively reduce at higher frequencies. Conversely, large radiating areas can be used to restrict the dispersion, though the dimensions required may become impractically large at low frequencies. As a consequence, most loudspeakers are approximately omnidirectional at low frequencies.

Sounds radiated by musical instruments obey the same laws. Low-frequency sounds from most instruments and the human voice radiate in all directions. Higher-frequency components can exhibit quite strong directional biases that are dependent on the size and orientation of the major sound-radiating elements. Figure 1.13a shows the frequency-dependent directivities of a trumpet, a relatively simple source. Compare this with the complexity of the directional characteristics of a cello (Fig. 1.13b). It is clear that no single direction is representative of the total sound output from complex sound sources—a particular difficulty when it comes to choosing microphone locations for sound recordings. Listeners at a live performance hear a combination of all the directional components as spatially integrated by the stage enclosure and the hall itself.

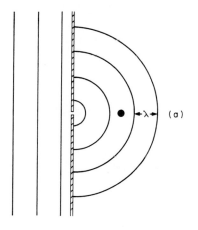

1.4.5 Refraction

Sound travels faster in warm air than in cold and faster downwind than upwind. These factors can cause sound rays to be bent, or *refracted*, when propagating over long distances in vertical gradients of wind or temperature.

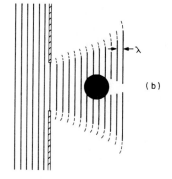

FIG. 1.12 Stylized illustration of the diffraction of sound waves passing through openings and around obstacles. The sound waves are depicted by their wavefronts. The distance between successive wavefronts is the wavelength λ. The sound waves approaching the barriers are shown as plane waves, as is approximately the case when the source of sound is far away. (*a*) The wavelength is large compared with the size of the opening and the obstacle. The sound radiates from the small opening as a spherical wave, dispersing equally in all directions and displaying no shadowing behind the small obstacle. (*b*) The wavelength is small compared with the size of the opening and the obstacle. The plane wave continues through the opening with only slight spreading, and there is a substantial shadow zone behind the obstacle. Although it is not shown, some of the sound would also be reflected back toward the source.

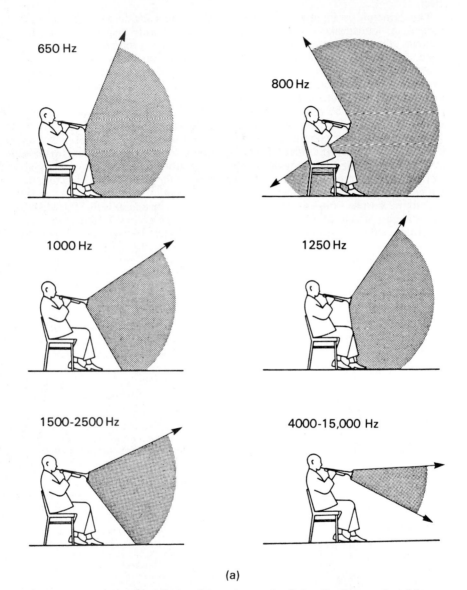

650 Hz

800 Hz

1000 Hz

1250 Hz

1500-2500 Hz

4000-15,000 Hz

(a)

FIG. 1.13 A much simplified display of the main sound radiation directions at selected frequencies for (*a*) a trumpet and (*b*) a cello. *(From J. Meyer,* Acoustics and the Performance of Music, *Verlag das Musikinstrument, Frankfurt am Main, 1978.)*

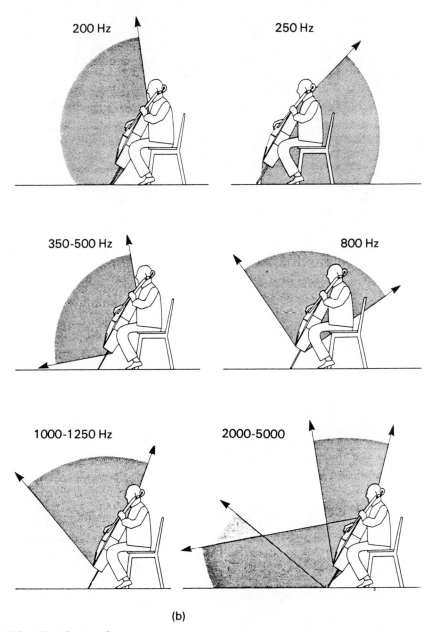

(b)

FIG. 1.13 (*Continued*)

Figure 1.14 shows the downward refraction of sound when the propagation is downwind or in a *temperature inversion,* as occurs at night when the temperature near the ground is cooler than the air higher up. Upward refraction occurs when the propagation is upwind or in a *temperature lapse,* a typical daytime condition when the air temperature falls with increasing altitude. Thus the ability to hear sounds over long distances is a function of local climatic conditions; the success of outdoor sound events can be significantly affected by the time of day and the direction of prevailing winds.

1.5 RESONANCE

A vibrating system of any kind that is driven by and is completely under the control of an external source of energy is in a state of *forced vibration.* The activity within such a system after the external force has been removed is known as *free vibration.* In this condition most systems exhibit a tendency to move at a *natural,* or *resonance,* frequency, declining with time at a rate determined by the amount

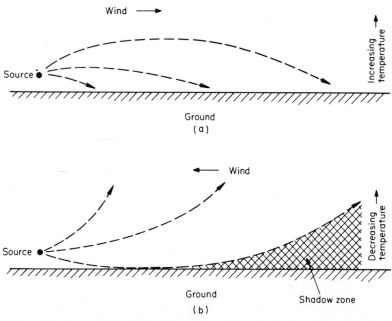

FIG. 1.14 The refraction of sound by wind and by temperature gradients. The conditions in *a,* downwind or in a temperature inversion, are favorable for the propagation of sound over long distances, while those in *b,* upwind or in a temperature lapse, are not. In the latter case the excess attenuation of the sound in the shadow zone can be as much as 20 dB. [*J. E. Piercy and T. F. W. Embleton, "Sound Propagation in the Open Air,"* in C. M. Harris (ed.), Handbook of Noise Control, 2d ed., McGraw-Hill, New York, 1978, *chap. 2.*]

of energy dissipation, or *damping,* in the system. The resonances in some musical instruments have little damping, as the devices are intended to resonate and produce sound at specific frequencies in response to inputs, such as impacts or turbulent airflow, that do not have any specific frequency characteristics. Most instruments provide the musician with some control over the damping so that the duration of the notes can be varied.

If the frequency of the driving force is matched to the natural frequency of the resonant system, the magnitude of the vibration and the efficiency of the energy transfer are maximized.

These and other points are illustrated in Fig. 1.15, which shows three versions of a resonant system having different amounts of damping. The term commonly used to describe this characteristic of resonant systems is the *quality factor, Q,* a measure of the lightness of damping in a system. The system in Fig. 1.15a has a Q of 1; it is well damped. The system in b is less well damped and has a Q of 10, while that in c has little damping and is described as having a Q of 50. As a practical example, the resonance of a loudspeaker in an enclosure would typically have a Q of 1 or less. Panel resonances in enclosures might have Q's in the region of 10 or so. Resonances with a Q of 50 or more would be rare in sound reproducers but common in musical instruments.

On the left in Fig. 1.15 can be seen the behavior of these systems when they are forced into oscillation by a pure tone tuned to the resonance frequency of the systems, 1000 Hz. When the tone is turned on and off, the systems respond with a speed that is in inverse proportion to the Q. The low-Q resonance (a) responds quickly to the onset of the tone and terminates its activity with equal brevity. The medium-Q system (b) responds at a more leisurely rate and lets the activity decay at a similar rate after the cessation of the driving signal. The high-Q system (c) is slow to respond to the driving signal and sustains the activity for some time after the interval of forced oscillation.

In the preceding example the forcing signal was optimized in frequency, in that it matched the resonance frequency of the system, and it was sustained long enough for the system to reach its level of maximum response. On the right of Fig. 1.15 are shown the responses of these systems to an impulse signal brief in the time domain but having energy over a wide range of frequencies including that of the resonant system. In a the low-Q system is shown responding energetically to this signal but demonstrating little sustained activity. In b and c the higher-Q systems respond with progressively reduced amplitude but with progressively sustained ringing after the pulse has ended. Note that the ringing is recognizably at the resonance frequency, 1 cycle/ms.

In the center of Fig. 1.15 are shown the *amplitude-frequency responses* or, more commonly, the *frequency responses* of the systems. These curves show the amplitude of system response when the frequency of a constant driving signal is varied from well below the resonance frequency to well above it. The low-Q system (a) is seen to respond to signals over a wide frequency range, but the higher-Q systems become progressively more frequency-selective.

In this illustration the maximum amplitudes of the system responses at resonance were adjusted to be approximately equal. Such is often the case in electronic resonators used in filters, frequency equalizers, synthesizers, etc. In simple resonant systems in which everything else is held equal and only the damping is varied, the maximum amplitude response would be highest in the system with the least dissipation: the high-Q system (c). Adding damping to the system would reduce the maximum amplitude, so that the system with the lowest Q, having the

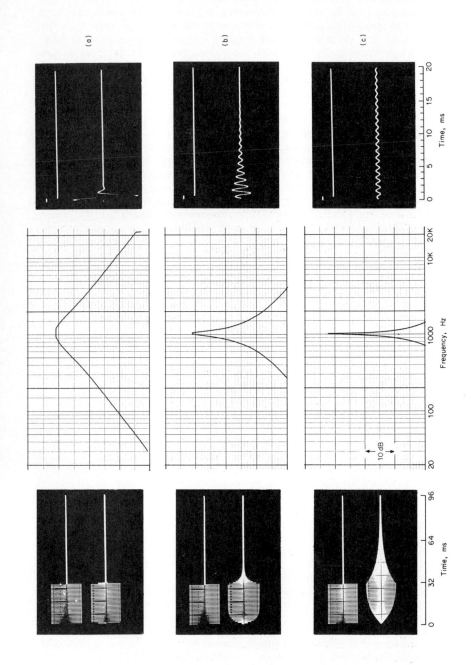

highest damping or losses, would respond to the widest range of frequencies, but with reduced amplitude.[8]

Figure 1.16 shows the frequency responses of two systems with multiple resonances. In *a* the resonances are such that they respond independently to driving forces at single frequencies. In *b* an input at any single frequency would cause some activity in all the resonators but at different amplitudes in each one. The series of high-*Q* resonators in *a* is characteristic of musical instruments, where the purpose is the efficient production of sound at highly specific frequencies. The overlapping set of low-*Q* resonators in *b* are the filters of a parametric equalizer in which the frequency, *Q*, and amplitude of the filters are individually adjustable to provide a variable overall frequency response for a sound-recording or -reproducing system.

A special case of Fig. 1.16*b* would be a multiway loudspeaker system intended for the reproduction of sounds of all kinds. In this case the selection of loudspeaker units and their associated filters (crossovers) would be such that, in combination, they resulted in an overall amplitude response that is flat (the same at all frequencies) over the required frequency range. Such a system would be capable of accurately re-creating any signal spectrum. As noted in Secs. 1.2.1 and 1.2.2, the shape of a waveform is dependent also on the phase relationships between its various components. For the loudspeaker or any system of multiple filters or resonant elements to accurately pass or reproduce a complex waveform, there must be no phase shift at the important frequencies. In technical terms this would be assessed by the *phase-frequency response,* or *phase response,* of the system showing the amount of phase shift at frequencies within the system bandwidth. The audible significance of accurate waveform reproduction is a matter for separate discussion (see Sec. 1.8.5).

Resonant systems can take any of several forms of electrical, mechanical, or acoustical elements or combinations thereof. In electronics, resonators are the basis for frequency-selective or tuned circuits of all kinds, from radios to equalizers and music synthesizers. Mechanical resonances are the essential pitch determinants of tuning forks, bells, xylophones, and glockenspiels. Acoustical resonances are the essential tuning devices of organs and other wind instruments. Stringed instruments involve combinations of mechanical and acoustical resonances in the generation and processing of their sounds, as do reed instruments and the human voice.

The voice is a good example of a complex resonant system. The sound originates as a train of pulses emanating from the voice box, as shown in Fig. 1.8. This excites a set of resonances in the vocal tract, so that the sound output from the mouth is emphasized at certain frequencies. In spectral terms, the envelope of the line spectrum shown in Fig. 1.8 is modified by the frequency response of the

← ────────────────────────────────────

FIG. 1.15 The frequency responses of three resonant systems and their behavior in conditions of forced and free vibration. The system shown in *a* has the highest amount of internal damping ($Q = 1$), system *b* has moderate damping ($Q = 10$), and system *c* has the least damping ($Q = 50$). The oscilloscope traces on the left show the system responses to a driving signal that consists of 32 cycles of a sinusoid at the system resonance frequency, 1000 Hz. The top trace of each pair shows the driving signal, a tone burst, and the lower trace shows the system response. On the right are shown the system responses to a brief impulse, a signal containing uniform energy over a very wide frequency range. The top trace in each pair is the 0.5-ms pulse, and the lower trace is the system response. To bring out clearly the differences in shape, the three frequency-response curves are presented with the same maximum amplitude; in reality the response at resonance is almost proportional to the *Q*.

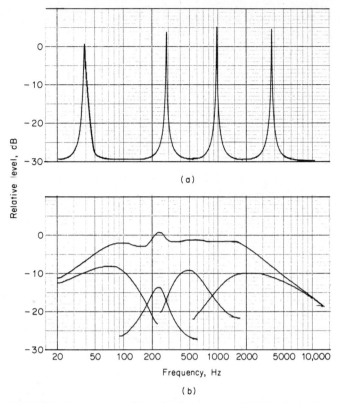

FIG. 1.16 Two systems with multiple resonances. (*a*) Here are well-separated high-*Q* (poorly damped) resonances that can respond nearly independently of each other, as in the notes of a musical instrument. (*b*) Here the four filters of a parametric equalizer produce overlapping low-*Q* (well-damped) resonance curves (bottom curves) which are combined to produce a total response (top curve) that may bear little resemblance to the individual contributions.

resonators in the vocal tract. These resonances are called *formants,* and their frequencies contribute to the individual character of voices. The relative amplitudes of the resonances are altered by changing the physical form of the vocal tract to create different vowel sounds, as illustrated in Fig. 1.17.[9,10,11]

1.5.1   Resonance in Pipes

When the diameter of a pipe is small compared with the wavelength, sound will travel as plane waves perpendicular to the length of the pipe, as shown in Fig. 1.2. At a closed end the sound is reflected back down the pipe in the reverse direction. At an open end, some of the sound radiates outward and the remainder is reflected backward, but with a pressure reversal (180° phase shift). The pressure distribution along the pipe is therefore the sum of several sound waves traveling

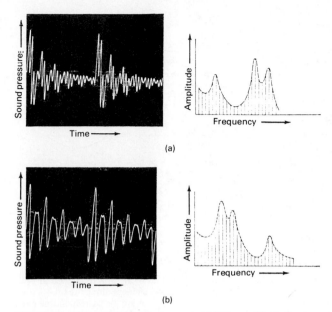

FIG. 1.17 The waveforms and corresponding amplitude-frequency spectra of the vowel sounds uh (*a*) and ah (*b*). *(From Peter B. Denes and E. N. Pinson, The Speech Chain, Waverly, Bell Telephone Laboratories, 1963.)*

backward and forward. At most frequencies the summation of these several waves results in varying degrees of destructive interference, but at some specific frequencies the interference is only constructive and a pattern stabilizes in the form of *standing waves*. At these frequencies the wavelengths of the sounds are such that specific end conditions of the tube are simultaneously met by the waves traveling in both directions, the sounds reinforce each other, and a resonant condition exists.

Figures 1.18 and 1.19 show the first three *resonant modes* for pipes open at both ends and for those with one end closed. The open ends prevent the pressures from building up, but the particle displacements are unimpeded; the end condition for resonance is therefore a displacement maximum *(antinode)* and a pressure minimum *(node)* in the standing-wave pattern. A closed end does the reverse, forcing displacements to zero but permitting pressure to build up; the end condition for resonance is therefore a displacement node and a pressure antinode.

For a pipe open at both ends the fundamental frequency has a wavelength that is double the length of the pipe; conversely, the pipe is one-half wavelength long. The fundamental frequency is therefore $f_1 = c/2L_o$, where L_o is the length of the pipe in meters, and c is the speed of sound: 345 m/s. Other resonances occur at all harmonically related frequencies: $2f_1$, $3f_1$, and so on.

A pipe closed at one end is one-quarter wavelength long at the fundamental resonance frequency; thus $f_1 = c/4L_c$. In this case, however, the other resonances occur at odd harmonics only: $3f_1$, $5f_1$, etc. A very simplistic view of the vocal tract considers it as a pipe, closed at the vocal cords, open at the mouth, and 175 mm long.[11] This yields a fundamental frequency of about 500 Hz and harmonics at

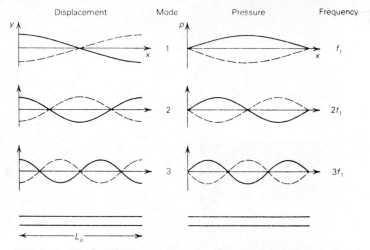

FIG. 1.18 The first three resonant modes of air in a tube open at both ends. On the left are the patterns of particle displacement along the tube, showing the antinodes at the ends of the tube. At the right are the corresponding patterns of pressure, with the required nodes at the ends. The fundamental frequency is $c/2L_o$. *(From Donald E. Hall,* Musical Acoustics: An Introduction, *Wadsworth, Belmont, Calif., 1980.)*

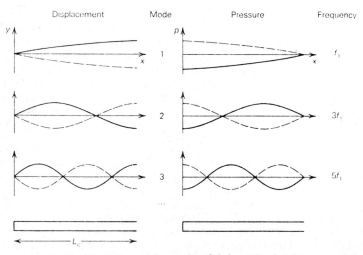

FIG. 1.19 The first three resonant modes of air in a tube closed at one end. On the left are the patterns of particle displacement along the tube, and on the right are the pressure distributions. The fundamental frequency is $c/4L_c$. *(From Donald E. Hall,* Musical Acoustics: An Introduction, *Wadsworth, Belmont, Calif., 1980.)*

1500, 2500, and 3500 Hz. These are close to the formant frequencies appearing as resonance humps in the spectra of Fig. 1.17.

Organ pipes are of both forms, although the pipes open at both ends produce the musically richer sound. To save space pipes closed at one end are sometimes used for the lowest notes; these need be only one-fourth wavelength long, but they produce only odd harmonics.

In practice this simple theory must be modified slightly to account for what is called the *end correction*. This can be interpreted as the distance beyond the open end of the pipe over which the plane waves traveling down the pipe make the transition to spherical wavefronts as they diverge after passing beyond the constraints of the pipe walls. The pipe behaves as if it is longer than its physical length by an amount equal to 0.62 times its radius. If the pipe has a flange or opens onto a flat surface, the end correction is 0.82 times the radius.

1.5.2 Resonance in Rooms and Large Enclosures

Sounds propagating in rectangular rooms and large enclosures are subject to standing waves between the reflecting boundaries. In taking a one-dimensional view for illustration, sounds reflecting back and forth between two parallel surfaces form standing waves at frequencies satisfying the boundary conditions requiring pressure antinodes and particle displacement nodes at the reflecting surfaces. The fundamental resonance frequency is that at which the separation is one-half wavelength. Other resonances occur at harmonics of this frequency. This same phenomenon exists between all opposing pairs of parallel surfaces, establishing three sets of resonances, dependent on the length, width, and height, known as the *axial modes* of the enclosure. Other resonances are associated with sounds reflected from four surfaces and propagating in a plane parallel to the remaining two. For example, sound can be reflected from the four walls and travel parallel to the floor and ceiling. The three sets of these resonances are called *tangential modes*. Finally, there are resonances involving sounds reflected from all surfaces in the enclosure, called *oblique modes.* All these resonant modes, or *eigentones,* can be calculated from the following equation:

$$f_n = \frac{c}{2} \sqrt{\left(\frac{n_x}{\ell_x}\right)^2 + \left(\frac{n_y}{\ell_y}\right)^2 + \left(\frac{n_z}{\ell_z}\right)^2} \tag{1.8}$$

where f_n = frequency of the nth mode
n_x, n_y, n_z = integers with independently chosen values between 0 and ∞
ℓ_x, ℓ_y, ℓ_z = dimensions of enclosure, m (ft)
c = speed of sound, m/s (ft/s)

It is usual to identify the individual modes by a combination of n_x, n_y, and n_z, as in (2, 0, 0), which identifies the mode as being the second-harmonic resonance along the x dimension of the enclosure. All axial modes are described by a single integer and two zeros. Tangential modes are identified by two integers and one zero, and oblique modes by three integers. The calculation of all modes for an enclosure would require the calculation of Eq. (1.8) for all possible combinations of integers for n_x, n_y, and n_z.

The sound field inside an enclosure is therefore a complex combination of many modes, and after the sound input has been terminated, they can decay at quite different rates depending on the amount and distribution of acoustical absorption on the room boundaries. Since some energy is lost at every reflection, the modes that interact most frequently with the room boundaries will decay first. The oblique modes have the shortest average distance between reflections and are the first to decay, followed by the tangential modes and later by the axial modes. This means that the sound field in a room is very complex immediately following the cessation of sound production, and it rapidly deteriorates to a few energetic tangential and axial modes.[12,13]

The ratio of length to width to height of an enclosure determines the distribution of the resonant modes in the frequency domain. The dimensions themselves determine the frequencies of the modes. The efficiency with which the sound source and receiver couple to the various modes determines the relative influence of the modes in the transmission of sound from the source to the receiver. These factors are important in the design of enclosures for specific purposes. In a listening or control room, for example, the locations of the loudspeakers and listeners are largely determined by the geometrical requirements for good stereo listening and by restrictions imposed by the loudspeaker design. Accurate communication from the source to the receiver over a range of frequencies requires that the influential room modes be uniformly distributed in frequency. Clusters or gaps in the distribution of modes can cause sounds at some frequencies to be accentuated and others to be attenuated, altering the frequency response of the sound propagation path through the room. This causes the timbre of sounds propagated through the room to be changed, a principle illustrated in Fig. 1.17 for vocal sounds.

Certain dimensional ratios have been promoted as having especially desirable mode distributions. Indeed, there are shapes like cubes and corridors that clearly present problems, but the selection of an ideal rectangular enclosure must accommodate the particular requirements of the application. Generalizations based on the simple application of Eq. (1.8) assume that the boundaries of the enclosure are perfectly reflecting and flat, that all modes are equally energetic, and that the source and receiver are equally well coupled to them all. In practice it is highly improbable that these conditions will be met.

1.5.3 Resonance in Small Enclosures: Helmholtz Resonators

At frequencies where the wavelength is large compared with the interior dimensions of an enclosure, there is negligible wave motion because the sound pressure is nearly uniform throughout the volume. In these circumstances the *lumped-element* properties of the enclosed air dominate, and another form of resonance assumes control. Such *Helmholtz resonators* form an important class of acoustic resonators.

Figure 1.20 shows a simple cavity with a short ducted opening, like a bottle with a neck. Here the volume of air within the cavity acts as a spring for the mass of air in the neck, and the system behaves as the acoustical version of a mechanical spring-mass resonant system. It is also analogous to the electrical resonant circuit with elements as shown in the figure.

Acoustical compliance increases with the volume, meaning that the resonance frequency falls with increasing cavity volume. The acoustic mass (inertance) in the duct increases with the length of the duct and decreases with increasing duct area, leading to a resonance frequency that is proportional to the square root of the duct area and inversely proportional to the square root of the duct length.

Helmholtz resonators are the simplest form of resonating systems. They are

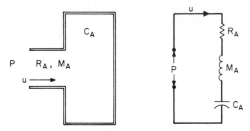

FIG. 1.20 Physical representation of a Helmholtz resonator (left) and the corresponding symbolic representation as a series resonant acoustical circuit (right). P = sound pressure at mouth; u = volume velocity in the port = particle velocity $\times$ port area; R_A = acoustical resistance; M_A = acoustical mass (inertance) of the port; C_A = acoustical compliance of the volume.

found as the air resonance in the body of guitars, violins, and similar instruments, and they are the principal frequency-determining mechanism in whistles and ocarinas. They also describe the performance of loudspeaker-enclosure systems at low frequencies. The acoustical-mechanical-electrical analogs introduced here are the basis for the design of closed-box and reflex loudspeaker systems, resulting in closely predictable performance at low frequencies. At higher frequencies, standing waves form inside the box, and the tidy lumped-element concepts no longer apply.

1.6 HORNS

If the open end of a tube has a diameter which is small compared with the wavelength of sound being propagated within it, most of the sound is reflected back into the tube, and if the wavelength is appropriate, standing waves result. At resonance, the acoustical activity is at its maximum, but the small tube opening is nevertheless a rather inefficient radiator of sound. If strong resonances are important and adequate input power is available, as in organ pipes, this is a desirable situation. Other devices, however, require the maintenance of strong standing waves, but with an improved radiation efficiency. With care this is achieved through the use of a flared development, or *horn,* at the end of the pipe. The shape and size of the horn determine, for every frequency, how much of the sound is reflected back into the tube and how much radiates outward.

The musical instruments of the brass family are all combinations of resonant pipes with a flaring bell at the output end. The shape of a trumpet bell, for example, is such that it has radiation efficiency that is low below about 1500 Hz and high above. By establishing strong resonances at the fundamental playing frequencies, the bell makes the instrument playable while imparting a bright sound character by efficiently radiating the higher harmonics of the basic pitch.[14,15]

On the other hand, a loudspeaker horn must have high radiation efficiency at all frequencies within its operating range; otherwise there will be resonances in a system that is intended to be free of such sources of tone color. The key to nonresonant behavior lies in the choice of flare shape and mouth size. The sound waves propagating outward must be allowed to expand at just the proper rate, maintaining close control over the directions of the particle velocities, so that the waves can emerge from the enlarged mouth with little energy reflected back to the loudspeaker.[12]

1.7 HEARING

The process of hearing begins with acoustical modifications to the sound waves as they interact with the head and the external ear, the visible portion of the system. These acoustical changes are followed by others in the ear canal and by a conversion of the sound pressure fluctuations into mechanical displacements by the eardrum. Transmitted through the mechanical coupling system of the middle ear to the inner ear, the displacement patterns are partially analyzed and then encoded in the form of neural signals. The signals from the two ears are cross-compared at several stages on the way to the auditory centers of the brain, where finally there is a transformation of the streams of data into perceptions of sound and acoustical space.

By these elaborate means we are able to render intelligible acoustical signals that, in technical terms, can be almost beyond description. In addition to the basic information, the hearing process keeps us constantly aware of spatial dimensions, where sounds are coming from, and the general size, shape, and decor of the space around us—a remarkable process indeed.

1.7.1 Anatomy of the Ear

Figure 1.21a shows a cross section of the ear in a very simplified form in which the outer, middle, and inner ear are clearly identified. The head and the outer ear interact with the sound waves, providing acoustical amplification that is dependent on both direction and frequency, in much the same way as an antenna. At frequencies above about 2 kHz there are reflections and resonances in the complex folds of the pinna.[16] Consequently, sounds of some frequencies reach the tympanic membrane (eardrum) with greater amplitude than sounds of other frequencies. The amount of the sound pressure gain or loss depends on both the frequency and the angle of incidence of the incoming sound. Thus the external ear is an important first step in the perceptual process, encoding sounds arriving from different directions with distinctive spectral characters. For example, the primary resonance of the external ear, at about 2.6 kHz, is most sensitive to sounds arriving from near 45° azimuth. This can be demonstrated by listening to a source of broadband sound while looking directly at it and then slowly rotating the head until one ear is pointing toward it. As the head is rotated through 45°, the sound should take on a "brighter" character as sounds in the upper midrange are accentuated. People with hearing problems use this feature of the ear to improve the intelligibility of speech when they unconsciously tilt the head, directing the ear toward the speaker. Continuing the rotation reveals a rapid dulling of the sound as the source moves behind the head. This is caused by acoustical shadowing due to diffraction by the pinna, a feature that helps to distinguish between front and back in sound localization.

At the *eardrum* the sound pressure fluctuations are transformed into move-

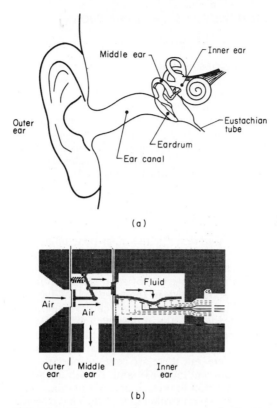

(a)

(b)

FIG. 1.21 The human ear: (*a*) a cross-sectional view showing the major anatomical elements and (*b*) a simplified functional representation. The pressure fluctuations in the air drive the eardrum, which is coupled to the inner ear by means of the middle-ear lever system. The movement of the fluid in the inner ear causes displacement of the cochlear partition, which, in turn, stimulates nerve endings to generate the neural signals that convey the essential information about the sound to the auditory centers of the brain. (b *from C. T. Morgan, J. S. Cook, A. Chapanis, and M. W. Lund,* Human Engineering Guide to Equipment Design, *McGraw-Hill, New York, 1963.*)

ment that is coupled by means of the *middle-ear* bones (the *ossicular chain*) to the *oval window,* the input to the *inner ear (cochlea).* The middle ear increases the efficiency of sound energy transfer by providing a partial impedance match between sound in air, on the one hand, and wave motion in the liquid-filled inner ear, on the other. The inner ear performs the elaborate function of analyzing the sound into its constituent frequencies and converting the result into neural signals that pass up the auditory (eighth) nerve to the auditory cortex of the brain. From there sound is transformed into the many and varied perceptions that we take for granted. In the following discussions we shall be dealing with some of these functions in more detail.

1.8 PSYCHOACOUSTICS AND THE DIMENSIONS OF HEARING

The physical dimensions of sound, discussed in previous sections, have parallels in the perceptual processes. The relationships are usually nonlinear, more complex than at first appearance, and somewhat variable among individuals as well as with time and experience. Nevertheless, they are the very essence of hearing.

The study of these relationships falls under the general umbrella of *psychoacoustics*. A more specialized study, known as *psychophysics* or *psychometrics,* is concerned with quantification of the magnitudes of the sensation in relation to the magnitude of the corresponding physical stimulus. In the following sections an overview of these relationships will be presented.

1.8.1 Loudness

Loudness is the term used to describe the magnitude of an auditory sensation. It is primarily dependent upon the physical magnitude (sound pressure) of the sound producing the sensation, but many other factors are influential.

Sounds come in an infinite variety of frequencies, timbres, intensities, temporal patterns, and durations; each of these, as well as the characteristics of the individual listener and the context within which the sound is heard, has an influence on loudness. Consequently, it is impossible for a single graph or equation to accurately express the relationship between the physical quality and quantity of sound and the subjective impression of loudness. Our present knowledge of the phenomenon is incomplete, but there are some important experimentally determined relationships between loudness and certain measurable quantities of sound. Although it is common to present and discuss these relationships as matters of fact, it must always be remembered that they have been arrived at through the process of averaging the results of many experiments with many listeners. These are not precise engineering data; they are merely indicators of trends.

Loudness as a Function of Frequency and Amplitude. The relationship between loudness and the frequency and SPL of the simplest of sounds, the pure tone, was first established by Fletcher and Munson, in 1933.[17] There have been several subsequent redeterminations of loudness relationships by experimenters incorporating various refinements in their techniques. The data of Robinson and Dadson,[18] for example, provide the basis for the International Organization for Standardization (ISO) recommendation R226.[19] The presentation of loudness data is usually in the form of *equal-loudness contours,* as shown in Fig. 1.22. Each curve shows the SPLs at which tones of various frequencies are judged to sound equal in loudness to a 1-kHz reference tone; the SPL of the reference tone identifies the curve in units called *phons.* According to this method, the *loudness level* of a sound, in phons, is the SPL level of a 1-kHz pure tone that is judged to be equally loud.

The equal-loudness contours of Fig. 1.22 show that the ears are less sensitive to low frequencies than to middle and high frequencies and that this effect increases as sound level is reduced. In other words, as the overall sound level of a broadband signal such as music is reduced, the bass frequencies will fade faster than middle or high frequencies. In the curves, this appears as a crowding together of the contours at low frequencies, indicating that, at the lower sound levels, a small change in SPL of low-frequency sounds produces the same change in loud-

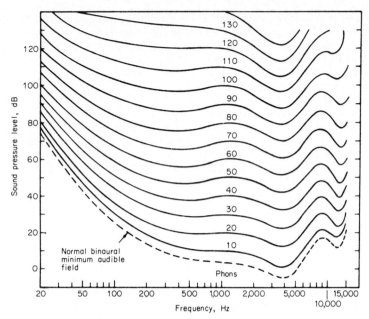

FIG. 1.22 Contours of equal loudness showing the sound pressure level required for pure tones at different frequencies to sound as loud as a reference tone of 1000 Hz. *(From International Organization for Standardization, Recommendation R226.)*

ness as a larger change in SPL at middle and high frequencies. This may be recognized as the basis for the loudness compensation controls built into many domestic hi-fi amplifiers, the purpose of which is to boost progressively the bass frequencies as the overall sound level is reduced. The design and use of such compensation have often been erroneous because of a confusion between the shape of the loudness contours themselves and the *differences* between curves at various phon levels.[20] Sounds reproduced at close to realistic levels should need no compensation, since the ears will respond to the sound just as they would to the "live" version of the program. By the same token, control-room monitoring at *very* high sound levels can result in program equalization that is not appropriate to reproduction at normal domestic sound levels (combined with this are the effects of temporary and permanent changes in hearing performance caused by exposure to loud sounds (see Sec. 1.10).

It is difficult to take the interpretations of equal-loudness contours much beyond generalizations since, as mentioned earlier, they are composites of data from many individuals. There is also the fact that they deal with pure tones and the measurements were done either through headphones (Fletcher and Munson[17]) or in an anechoic chamber (Robinson and Dadson[18]). The relationship between these laboratory tests and the common application for these data, the audition of music in normal rooms, is one that is only poorly established.

The lowest equal-loudness contour defines the lower limit of perception: the *hearing-threshold level.* It is significant that the ears have their maximum sensitivity at frequencies that are important to the intelligibility of speech. This optimization of the hearing process can be seen in various other aspects of auditory performance as well.

The rate of growth of loudness as a function of the SPL is a matter of separate interest. Units of *sones* are used to describe the magnitude of the subjective sensation. One sone is defined as the loudnesss of a tone at the 40-phon loudness level. A sound of loudness 2 sones would be twice as loud, and a sound of 0.5 sone would be half as loud. The *loudness function* relating the subjective sensation to the physical magnitude has been studied extensively,[21] and while there are consistencies in general behavior, there remain very large differences in the performance of individuals and in the effect of the temporal and spectral structure of the sound. A common approximation relates a change of 10 dB in SPL to a doubling or halving of loudness. Individual variations on this may be a factor of 2 or more, indicating that one is not dealing with precise data. For example, the growth of loudness at low frequencies, as shown in the curves of Fig. 1.22, indicates a clear departure from the general rule. Nevertheless, it is worth noting that significant changes in loudness require large differences in SPL and sound power [a doubling of loudness that requires a 10-dB increase in sound level translates into a factor of 3.16 in sound pressure (or voltage) and a factor of 10 in power].

Loudness as a Function of Bandwidth. The studies of loudness that used pure tones leave doubts about how they relate to normal sounds that are complexes of several frequencies or continuous bands of sound extending over a range of frequencies. If the bandwidth of a sound is increased progressively while maintaining a constant overall measured sound level, it is found that loudness remains constant from narrow bandwidths up to a value called the *critical bandwidth*. At larger bandwidths the loudness increases as a function of bandwidth because of a process known as *loudness summation*. For example, the broadband sound of an orchestra playing a chord will be louder than the simple sound of a flute playing a single note even when the sounds have been adjusted to the same SPL.

The critical bandwidth varies with the center frequency of the complex sound being judged. At frequencies below about 200 Hz it is fairly constant at about 90 Hz; at higher frequencies the critical bandwidth increases progressively to close to 4000 Hz at 15 kHz. The sound of the orchestra therefore occupies many critical bandwidths while the sound of the flute is predominantly within one band.

Loudness as a Function of Duration. Brief sounds can appear to be less loud than sounds with the same maximum sound level but longer duration. Experiments show that there is a progressive growth of loudness as signal duration is increased up to about 200 ms; above that, the relationship levels out. The implication is that the hearing system integrates sound energy over a time interval of about 200 ms. In reality, the integration is likely to be of neural energy rather than acoustical energy, which makes the process rather complicated, since it must embrace all the nonlinearities of the perceptual mechanism.

The practical consequence of this is that numerous temporal factors, such as duration, intermittency, repetition rate, and so on, all influence the loudness of sounds that are separate from SPL.

Measuring the Loudness of Complex Sounds. Given the numerous variables and uncertainties in ascertaining the loudness of simple sounds, it should come as no surprise that measuring the loudness of the wideband, complex, and ever-changing sounds of real life is a problem that has resisted simple interpretation. Motivated by the need to evaluate the annoyance value of sounds as well as the more neutral quantity of loudness, various methods have been developed for arriving at single-number ratings of complex sounds. Some methods make use of spectral analysis of the sound, adjusted by correction factors and weighting, to compute a single-number loudness rating. These tend to require expensive apparatus and are, at best, cumbersome to use; they also are most accurate for steady-state sounds.

Simplifying the loudness compensation permits the process to be accomplished with relatively straightforward electronics providing a direct-reading output in real time, a feature that makes the device practical for recording and broadcasting applications. Such devices are reported to give rather better indications of the loudness of typical music and speech program material than the very common and even simpler *volume-unit (VU) meters* or *sound-level meters.*[22]

The VU meter responds to the full audio-frequency range, with a flat frequency response but with some control of its dynamic (time) response. A properly constructed VU meter should exhibit a response time of close to 300 ms, with an overswing of not more than 1.5 percent, and a return time similar to the response time. The dial calibrations and reference levels are also standardized. Such devices are therefore useful for measuring the magnitudes of steady-state signals and for giving a rough indication of the loudness of complex and time-varying signals, but they fail completely to take into account the frequency dependence of loudness.

The sound-level meters used for acoustical measurements are adjustable in both amplitude and time response. Various *frequency-weighting* curves, *A-weighting* being the most popular, acknowledge the frequency-dependent aspects of loudness, and "fast" and "slow" time responses deal differently with temporal considerations. Although these instruments are carefully standardized and find extensive use in acoustics, noise control, and hearing conservation, they are of limited use as program-level indicators. Figure 1.23 shows the common frequency-weighting options found in sound-level meters: A weighting has become the almost universal choice for measurements associated with loudness, annoyance, and the assessment of hearing-damage risk (see Sec. 1.10).

Peak program meters (PPM) are also standardized,[23] and they find extensive use in the recording and broadcast industries. However, they are used mainly as a means of avoiding overloading recorders and signal-processing equipment. Consequently, the PPM has a very rapid response (an integration time of about 10 ms in the normal mode), so that brief signal peaks are registered, and a slow

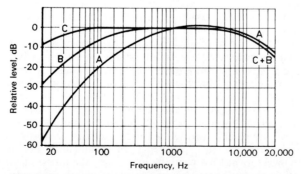

FIG. 1.23 The standard frequency-weighting networks used in sound-level meters.

return (around 3 s), so that the peak levels can be easily seen. These devices therefore are not useful indicators of loudness of fluctuating signals.

1.8.2 Masking

Listening to a sound in the presence of another sound, which for the sake of simplicity we shall call noise, results in the desired sound being, to some extent, less audible. This effect is called *masking*. If the noise is sufficiently loud, the signal can be completely masked, rendering it inaudible; at lower noise levels the signal will be partially masked, and only its apparent loudness may be reduced. If the desired sound is complex, it is possible for masking to affect only portions of the total sound. All this is dependent on the specific nature of both the signal and the masking sound.

In audio it is possible for the low-level sounds of music, for example, to be masked by background noise in a sound system. That same noise can mask distortion products, so the effects need not be entirely undesirable. In addition to the unwanted noises that have been implied so far, there can be masking of musical sounds by other musical sounds. Thus we encounter the interesting situation of the perceived sound of a single musical instrument modified by the sounds of other instruments when it is joined in an ensemble.

In addition to the partial and complete masking that occurs when two sounds occur simultaneously, there are instances of temporal masking, when the audibility of a sound is modified by a sound that precedes it in time *(forward masking)* or, strange as it may seem, by a sound that follows it *(backward masking)*.

Simultaneous Masking.   At the lowest level of audibility, the threshold, the presence of noise can cause a *threshold shift,* wherein the amplitude of the signal must be increased to restore audibility. At higher sound levels the masked sound may remain audible but, owing to partial masking, its loudness can be reduced.

In *simultaneous masking* the signal and the masking sound coexist in the time domain. It is often assumed that they must also share the same frequency band. While this seems to be most effective, it is not absolutely necessary. The effect of a masking sound can extend to frequencies that are both higher and lower than those in the masker itself. At low sound levels a masking sound tends to influence signals with frequencies close to its own, but at higher sound levels the masking effect spreads to include frequencies well outside the spectrum of the masker. The dominant effect is an *upward spread* of masking which can extend several octaves above the frequency of the masking sound. There is also a *downward spread* of masking, but the effect is considerably less. In other words, a low-frequency masking sound can reduce the audibility of higher-frequency signals, but a high-frequency masking sound has relatively little effect on signals of lower frequency. Figure 1.24 shows that a simple masking sound elevates the hearing threshold over a wide frequency range but that the elevation is greater for frequencies above the masking sound.

In the context of audio, this means that we have built-in noise and distortion suppression. Background noises of all kinds are less audible while the music is playing but stand out clearly during the quiet intervals. Distortions generated in the recording and reproduction processes are present only during the musical sound and are therefore at least partially masked by the music itself. This is especially true for harmonic distortions, in which the objectionable distortion products are at frequencies higher than the masking sound—the sound that causes

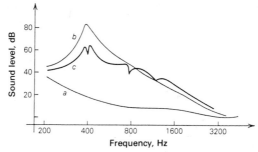

FIG. 1.24 Detection threshold for pure tones of various frequencies (*a*) in isolation, (*b*) in the presence of a narrowband (365 to 455 Hz) of masking noise centered on 400 Hz at a sound level of 80 dB, and (*c*) in the presence of a masking tone of 400 Hz at 80 dB. The asymmetrical shapes of the elevated curves indicate that tones with frequencies above the masking sound are more strongly masked than tones with lower frequencies. The notches in curve *c* indicate reduction in the masking effect because of audible beats between the test tone and the masker and its harmonics. *(From Donald E. Hall,* Musical Acoustics: An Introduction, *Wadsworth, Belmont, Calif., 1980.)*

them to exist. Intermodulation-distortion products, on the other hand, are at frequencies both above and below the frequencies of the signals that produce the distortion. In this case, the upper distortion products will be subject to greater masking by the signal than the lower distortion products.

Studies of distortion have consistently noted that all forms of distortion are less audible with music than with simple signals such as single tones or combinations of tones; the more effective masking of the spectrally complex music signal is clearly a factor in this. Also noted is that intermodulation distortion is more objectionable than its harmonic equivalent. A simple explanation for this may be that not only are the difference-frequency components of intermodulation distortion unmusical, but they are not well masked by the signals that produce them.

Temporal Masking. The masking that occurs between signals not occurring simultaneously is known as *temporal masking.* It can operate both ways, from an earlier to a later sound (forward masking) or from a later to an earlier sound (backward masking). The apparent impossibility of backward masking (going backward in time) has a physiological explanation. It takes time for sounds to be processed in the peripheral auditory system and for the neural information to travel to the brain. If the later sound is substantially more intense than the earlier sound, information about it can take precedence over information about the earlier sound. The effect can extend up to 100 to 200 ms, but because such occurrences are rare in normal hearing, the most noteworthy auditory experiences are related to forward masking.

Forward masking results from effects of a sound that remain after the physical stimulus has been removed. The masking increases with the sound level of the masker and diminishes rapidly with time, although effects can sometimes be seen for up to 500 ms.[24] Threshold shifts of 10 to 20 dB appear to be typical for moderate sound levels, but at high levels these may reach 40 to 50 dB. Combined with these substantial effects is a broadening of the frequency range of the masking; at masker sound levels above about 80 dB maximum masking no longer occurs at the frequency of the masking sound but at higher frequencies.

There are complex interactions among the numerous variables in the masking process, and it is difficult to translate the experimental findings into factors specifically related to audio engineering. The effects are not subtle, however, and it is clear that in many ways they influence what we hear.

1.8.3 Acoustic Reflex

One of the less-known features of hearing is the *acoustic reflex,* an involuntary activation of the middle-ear muscles in response to sound and some bodily functions. These tiny muscles alter the transmission of sound energy through the middle ear, changing the quantity and quality of the sound that reaches the inner ear. As the muscles tighten, there may be a slight reduction in the overall sound level reaching the inner ear, but mainly there is a change in spectral balance as the low frequencies are rolled off. Below approximately 1 kHz the attenuation is typically 5 to 10 dB, but it can be as much as 30 dB.

The reflex is activated by sounds above 80- to 85-dB SPL, which led to the early notion that it was a protective mechanism; however, the most hazardous sounds are at frequencies that are little affected by the reflex, and, furthermore, the reflex is too slow to block the passage of loud transients. The reflex activates rather slowly, in 10 to 20 ms for loud sounds and up to 150 ms for sounds near the activation threshold; then, after an interval, it slowly relaxes. Obviously there have to be other reasons for its existence. Although there is still some speculation as to its purpose, the fact that it is automatically activated when we talk and when we chew suggests that part of the reason is simply to reduce the auditory effects of our own voice and eating sounds.

Some people can activate the reflex voluntarily, and they report a reduction in the loudness of low frequencies during the period of activation. The behavior of the reflex also appears to depend on the state of the listener's attention to the sound itself. This built-in tone control clearly is a complication in sound quality assessments since the spectral balance appears to be a function of sound level, the pattern of sound-level fluctuations in time, and the listener's attitude or attention to the sound.

1.8.4 Pitch

Pitch is the subjective attribute of frequency, and while the basic correspondence between the two domains is obvious—low pitch to low frequencies and high pitch to high frequencies—the detailed relationships are anything but simple.

Fortunately waveforms that are periodic, however complex they may be (see Sec. 1.2.1), tend to be judged as having the same pitch as sine waves of the same repetition frequency. In other words, when a satisfactory pitch match has been made, the fundamental frequency of a complex periodic sound and a comparison sinusoid will normally be found to have the same frequency.

The exceptions to this simple rule derive from those situations where there is no physical energy at the frequency corresponding to the perceived pitch. Examples of pitch being associated with a *missing fundamental* are easily demonstrated by using groups of equally spaced tones, such as 100, 150, and 200 Hz, and observing that the perceived pitch corresponds to the difference frequency, 50 Hz. Common experience with sound reproducers, such as small radios, that have limited low-frequency bandwidth, illustrates the strength of the phenomenon, as do experiences with musical instruments, such as some low-frequency organ sounds, that may have little energy at the perceived fundamental frequency.

Scientifically, pitch has been studied on a continuous scale, in units of *mels*. It has been found that there is a highly nonlinear relationship between subjectively judged ratios of pitch and the corresponding ratios of frequency, with the subjective pitch interval increasing in size with increasing frequency. All this, though, is of little interest to traditional musicians, who have organized the frequency domain into intervals having special tonal relationships. The octave is particularly notable because of the subjective similarity of sounds spaced an octave apart and the fact that these sounds commonly differ in frequency by factors of 2. The musical fifth is a similarly well-defined relationship, being a ratio of 3:2 in repetition frequencies. These and the other intervals used in musical terminology gain meaning as one moves away from sine waves, with their one-frequency purity, into the sounds of musical instruments with their rich collection of overtones, many of which are harmonically related. With either pure tones[25] or some instrumental sounds in which not all the overtones are exactly harmonically related, the subjective octave may differ slightly from the physical octave; in the piano this leads to what is called *stretched tuning.*[26]

The incompatibility of the mel scale of pitch and the hierarchy of musical intervals remains a matter for discussion. These appear to be quite different views of the same phenomenon, with some of the difference being associated with the musical expertise of listeners. It has been suggested, for example, that the mel scale might be better interpreted as a scale of *brightness* rather than one of pitch.[27] With periodic sounds brightness and pitch are closely related, but there are sounds, such as bells, hisses, and clicks, that do not have all the properties of periodic sounds and yet convey enough of a sense of pitch to enable tunes to be played with them, even though they cannot be heard as combining into chords or harmony. In these cases, the impressions of brightness and pitch seem to be associated with a prominence of sound energy in a band of frequencies rather than with any of the spectral components (partials, overtones, or harmonics) that may be present in the sound. A separate confirmation of this concept of brightness is found in subjective assessments of reproduced sound quality, where there appears to be a perceptual dimension along a continuum of "darkness" to "brightness" in which brightness is associated with a frequency response that rises toward the high frequencies or in which there are peaks in the treble.[28] At this, we reach a point in the discussion where it is more relevant to move into a different but related domain.

1.8.5 Timbre, Sound Quality, and Perceptual Dimensions

Sounds may be judged to have the same subjective dimensions of loudness and pitch and yet sound very different from one another. This difference in *sound quality,* known as *timbre* in musical terminology, can relate to the tonal quality of sounds from specific musical instruments as they are played in live performance, to the character of tone imparted to all sounds processed through a system of recording and reproduction, and to the tonal modifications added by the architectural space within which the original performance or a reproduction takes place. Timbre is, therefore, a matter of fundamental importance in audio, since it can be affected by almost anything that occurs in the production, processing, storage, and reproduction of sounds.

Timbre has many dimensions, not all of which have been confidently identified and few of which have been related with any certainty to the corresponding physical attributes of sound. There is, for example, no doubt that the shape and composition of the frequency spectrum of the sound are major factors, as are the temporal behaviors of individual elements comprising the spectrum, but progress has been slow in identifying those measurable aspects of the signal that correlate with specific perceived dimensions, mainly because there are so many interactions between the dimensions themselves and between the physical and psychological factors underlying them.

The field of electronic sound synthesis has contributed much to the understanding of why certain musical instruments sound the way they do, and from this understanding have followed devices that permit continuous variations of many of the sound parameters. The result has been progressively better imitations of acoustical instruments in electronic simulations, as well as an infinite array of new "instruments" exhibiting tonal colors, dynamics, and emotional connotations that are beyond the capability of traditional instruments. At the same time as this expansion of timbral variety is occurring on one front of technical progress, there is an effort on another front to faithfully preserve the timbre of real and synthesized instruments through the complex process of recording and reproduction. The original intentions of *high-fidelity reproduction* exist today in spite of the manifest abuses of the term in the consumer marketplace.

A fundamental problem in coming to grips with the relationship between the technical descriptions of sounds and the perception of timbre is in establishing some order in the choice and quantitative evaluation of words and phrases used by listeners to describe aspects of sound quality. Some of the descriptors are fairly general in their application and seem to fall naturally to quantification on a continuous scale from say, "dull" to "bright" or from "full" to "thin." Others, though, are specific to particular instruments or lapse into poetic portrayals of the evoked emotions.

From carefully conducted assessments of reproduced sound quality involving forms of multivariate statistical analysis, it has become clear that the extensive list can be reduced to a few relatively independent dimensions. As might be expected, many of the descriptors are simply different ways of saying the same thing, or they are responses to different perceptual manifestations of the same physical phenomenon.

From such analyses can come useful clarifications of apparently anomalous results since these responses need not be unidirectional. For example, a relatively innocent rise in the high-frequency response of a sound reproducer might be perceived as causing violins to sound unpleasantly strident but cymbals to sound unusually clear and articulate. A nice sense of air and space might be somewhat offset by an accentuation of background hiss and vocal sibilants, and so on.

Inexperienced listeners tend to concentrate unduly on a few of the many descriptors that come to mind while listening, while slightly more sophisticated subjects may become confused by the numerous contradictory indications. Both groups, for different reasons, may fail to note that there is but a single underlying technical flaw. The task of critical listening is one that requires a broad perspective and an understanding of the meaning and relative importance of the many timbral clues that a varied musical program can reveal. Trained and experienced listeners tend to combine timbral clues in a quest for logical technical explanations for the perceived effects. However, with proper experimental controls and the necessary prompting through carefully prepared instructions and a questionnaire, listeners with little prior experience can arrive at similar evaluations of accuracy without understanding the technical explanations.[29] The procedure for controlled listening tests is outlined in Sec. 1.9.2.

The following list of perceptual dimensions is derived from the work of Gabrielsson and various colleagues[28,30] and is the basis for listening questionnaires used extensively by those workers and the author.[29] The descriptions are slightly modified from the original.[28]

1. *Clarity, or definition:* This dimension is characterized by adjectives such as clear, well defined, distinct, clean or pure, and rich in details or detailed, as opposed to adjectives such as diffuse, muddy or confused, unclear, blurred, noisy, rough, harsh, or sometimes rumbling, dull, and faint. High ratings in this dimension seem to require that the reproduction system perform well in several respects, exhibiting a wide frequency range, flat frequency response, and low nonlinear distortion. Systems with limited bandwidth, spectral irregularities due to resonances, or audible distortion receive lower ratings. Low-frequency spectral emphasis seems also to be detrimental to performance in this dimension, resulting in descriptions of rumbling, for the obvious reason, and dullness, probably due to the upward masking effects (see Sec. 1.8.2) of the strong low frequencies. Increased sound levels result in increased clarity and definition.

2. *Sharpness, or hardness, versus softness:* Adjectives such as sharp, hard, shrill, screaming, pointed, and clashing are associated with this dimension, contrasted with the opposite qualities of soft, mild, calm or quiet, dull, and subdued. A rising high-frequency response or prominent resonances in the high-frequency region can elicit high ratings in this dimension, as can certain forms of distortion. A higher or lower sound level also contributes to movement within this dimension, with reduced levels enhancing the aspect of softness.

3. *Brightness versus darkness:* This dimension is characterized by the adjective bright, as opposed to dark, rumbling, dull, and emphasized bass. There appears to be a similar relationship between this dimension and the physical attributes of the sound system as exists with the preceding dimension, sharpness, or hardness, versus softness. In experiments the two dimensions sometimes appear together and sometimes separately. The sense of pitch associated with brightness, mentioned in Sec. 1.8.4, might be a factor in distinguishing between these two dimensions, but the matter awaits clarification.

4. *Fullness versus thinness:* This dimension also can appear in combination with brightness versus darkness, and there are again certain similarities in the relationship to measured spectrum balance and smoothness. There appears to be an association with the bandwidth of the system, especially at the low frequencies, and with sound level. It seems possible that this dimension is a representation of one encountered elsewhere as volume, which has been found to increase with increasing sound level but to decrease with increasing frequency.

5. *Spaciousness:* Almost self-explanatory, this dimension elicits expressions of spacious, airy, wide, and open, as opposed to closed or shut up, narrow, and dry. The phenomenon appears to be related to poorly correlated sounds at the two ears of the listener (sec Secs. 1.8.6 and 1.8.7). Other aspects of spaciousness are related to the spectrum of the reproduced sound. Gabrielsson points out that increased treble response enhances spaciousness, while reducing the bandwidth encourages a closed or shut-up impression. It is well known that the directional

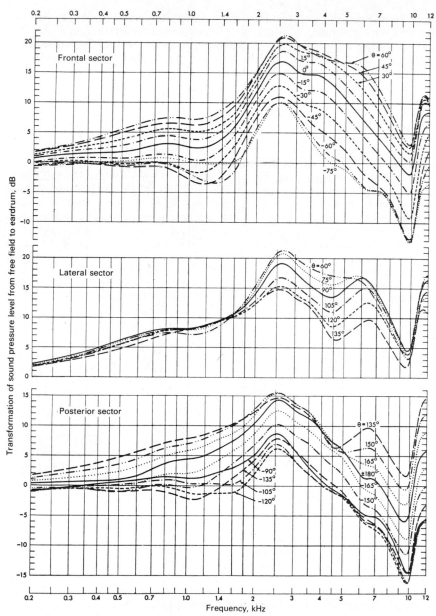

FIG. 1.25 Family of curves showing the transformation of sound pressure level from the free field to the eardrum in the horizontal plane as a function of frequency, averaged over many listeners in several independent studies. The horizontal angles are referred to zero (the forward direction) and increase postively toward the ear in which the measurement is made and negatively away from it; 90° would be facing the measurement ear, and −90° would be facing the opposite ear. [*From E. A. G. Shaw, "Transformation of Sound Pressure Level from the Free Field to the Eardrum in the Horizontal Plane," J. Acoust. Soc. Am., **56**, 1848–1861 (1974). These data also appear in numerical form in Ref. 48.*]

properties of the external ear (see Fig. 1.25 and Sec. 1.8.6) encode incoming sounds with spectral cues that can be significant influences in sound localization.[31] One such cue is a moving spectral notch and an increase in the sound level reaching the eardrum over the band from 5 to 10 kHz for progressively elevated sources (Fig. 1.26). The appropriate manipulation of the sound spectrum in this frequency region can alone create impressions of height[32,33] and, in this sense, alter the impression of spaciousness. It is worthy of note that the dimension of spaciousness is clearly observed in monophonic as well as stereophonic reproductions, indicating that it is a rather fundamental aspect of sound quality.[28,34]

6. *Nearness:* Differences in the apparent proximity of sound sources are regularly observed in listening tests. It is clear that sound level affects perception of distance, especially for sounds such as the human voice that are familiar to listeners. Evidence from other studies indicates that impressions of distance are also influenced by the relationship betweeen the direct, early-reflected, and reverberant sounds and the degree of coherence that exists in these sounds as they appear appear at the listener's ears.[32]

7. *Absence of extraneous sounds:* This dimension refers to nonmusical sounds that either exist in the original program material and are accentuated by aspects of the reproducer (such as tape hiss being aggravated by a treble boost) or are generated within the device itself (such as electronic amplifier clipping or mechanical noises from a loudspeaker).

8. *Loudness:* This self-explanatory dimension is a useful check on the accuracy with which the sound levels of comparison sounds have been matched. It should, however, be noted that some listeners seem to regard the adjective loud as a synonym for sharp, hard, or painful.

The relative importance of these dimensions in describing overall sound quality changes slightly according to the specific nature of the devices under test, the form of the listener questionnaire, the program material, and, to some extent, the listeners themselves. In general, Gabrielsson and colleagues[28,30] have found that

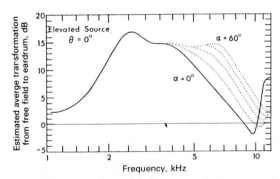

FIG. 1.26 The estimated average transformation of sound pressure level from the free field to the eardrum as a function of frequency, showing the variations as a function of the angle of elevation for sounds arriving from the forward direction. *(From E. A. G. Shaw, "The Acoustics of the External Ear," in W. D. Keidel and W. D. Neff (eds.),* Handbook of Sensory Physiology, *vol. V/1: Auditory System, Springer-Verlag, Berlin, 1974.)*

clarity, or definition, brightness versus darkness, and sharpness, or hardness, versus softness are major contributors to the overall impression of sound quality.

In an elaborate independent study von Bismarck[35,36] concluded that the dominant factor was sharpness, along with the associated descriptors hard, loud, angular, tense, obtrusive, unpleasant, bright, and high. Bearing in mind that clarity, or definition, was not in the list of 30 dimensions that his listeners rated, the results appear to be very much in agreement with those described above. Von Bismarck went on to investigate sharpness as an isolated perceptual variable, finding that sounds could be rated on a scale of sharpness with about the same ease as the scaling of loudness. It was found that sharpness increased with both the upper and lower limiting (cutoff) frequencies as well as with the slope of the spectral envelope. Sharpness appeared not to be seriously influenced by the fine structure of the spectra, being similar for both harmonic complex tones and noise. In general, the sharpness of sounds appeared to be related to the position of spectral energy concentration in the frequency domain.

Further investigations of this kind may reveal other perceptual dimensions, some of them specific to particular devices or forms of signal processing and their individualistic technical signal modifications.

It will have been noted by now that several of the perceptual dimensions are influenced by sound level. There is clearly a connection between this and the earlier discussions of loudness (Sec. 1.8.1), showing the dependence of this dimension on frequency and sound level. Since sound level alone can affect so many different aspects of the perception of sound quality or timbre, it is essential to ensure that sounds being compared are adjusted to equal sound levels. By the same token, one should be skeptical of any opinions of tonal quality formed in circumstances where this factor has not been carefully controlled.

Audibility of Variations in Amplitude and Phase.   Other things being equal, very small differences in sound level can be heard: down to a fraction of a decibel in direct A/B comparisons. Level differences that exist over only a small part of the spectrum tend to be less audible than differences that occupy a greater bandwidth. In other words, a small difference that extends over several octaves may be as significant as a much larger difference that is localized in a narrow band of frequencies. Spectral tilts of as little as 0.1 dB per octave are audible. For simple sounds the only audible difference may be loudness, but for complex sounds differences in timbre may be more easily detectable.

The audibility of phase shift is a very different matter. This hotly debated issue assumes major proportions because of the implication that if phase shifts are not audible, then the waveform of a complex sound, per se, is not important (see Sec. 1.2). Several independent investigations over many years have led to the conclusion that while there are some special signals and listening situations where phase effects can be heard, their importance when listening to music in conventional environments is small (see discussion in Ref. 34). Psychophysical studies indicate that, in general, sensitivity to phase is small compared with sensitivity to the amplitude spectrum and that sensitivity to phase decreases as the fundamental frequency of the signal increases. At the same time, it appears to be phase shifts in the upper harmonics of a complex signal that contribute most to changes in timbre.[37]

The notion that phase, and therefore waveform, information is relatively unimportant is consistent with some observations of normal hearing. Sounds from real sources (voices and musical instruments) generally arrive at our ears after traveling over many different paths, some of which may involve several reflections. The waveform at the ear therefore depends on various factors other than the source itself. Even the argument that the direct sound is especially selected for audition and that later arrivals are perceptually suppressed does not substantially change the situation because sources themselves do not radiate waveforms that are invariably distinctive. With musical instruments radiating quite different components of their sound in different directions (consider the complexity of a grand piano or the cello in Fig. 1.13, for example), the sum of these components, the waveform at issue, will itself be different at every different angle and distance; a recording microphone is in just such a situation.

The fact that the ear seems to be relatively insensitive to phase shifts would therefore appear to be simply a condition born of necessity. It would be incorrect to assume, however, that the phase performance of devices is *totally* unimportant. Spectrally localized phase anomalies are useful indicators of the presence of resonances in systems, and very large accumulations of phase shift over a range of frequencies can become audible as group delays.

While the presence of resonances can be inferred from phase fluctuations, their audibility may be better predicted from evidence in the amplitude domain.[34] It should be added that resonances of low Q in sound reproduction systems are more easily heard than those of higher Q.[38,39,40] This has the additional interesting ramification that evidence of sustained ringing in the time domain may be less significant than ringing that is rapidly damped (Fig. 1.15); waveform features and other measured evidence that attract visual attention do not always correspond directly with the sound colorations that are audible in typical listening situations.

1.8.6 Perception of Direction and Space

Sounds are commonly perceived as arriving from specific directions, usually coinciding with the physical location of the sound source. This perception may also carry with it a strong impression of the acoustical setting of the sound event, which normally is related to the dimensions, locations, and sound-reflecting properties of the structures surrounding the listener and the sound source as well as objects in the intervening path.

Blauert, in his thorough review of the state of knowledge in this field,[32] defines *spatial hearing* as embracing "the relationships between the locations of auditory events and other parameters—particularly those of sound events, but also others such as those that are related to the physiology of the brain." This statement introduces terms and concepts that may require some explanation. The adjective *sound,* as in *sound event,* refers to a physical source of sound, while the adjective *auditory* identifies a perception. Thus the perceived location of an auditory event usually coincides with the physical location of the source of sound. Under certain circumstances, however, the two locations may differ slightly or even substantially. The difference is then attributed to other parameters having nothing whatever to do with the physical direction of the sound waves impinging on the ears of the listener, such as subtle aspects of a complex sound event or the processing of the sound signals within the brain.

Thus have developed the parallel studies of *monaural,* or one-eared, hearing and *binaural,* or two-eared, hearing. Commercial sound reproduction has stimulated a corresponding interest in the auditory events associated with sounds emanating from a single source *(monophonic)* and from multiple sources that may be caused to differ in various ways *(stereophonic).* In common usage it is assumed that stereophonic reproduction involves only two loudspeakers, but there are many other possible configurations, the best known of which is probably four-channel stereophony, or *quadraphonics*. In stereophonic reproduction the objective is to create many more auditory events than the number of real sound sources would seem to permit. This is accomplished by presenting to the listener combinations of sounds that take advantage of certain inbuilt perceptual processes in the brain to create auditory events in locations other than those of the sound events and in auditory spaces that may differ from the space within which the reproduction occurs.

Understanding the processes that create auditory events would ideally permit the construction of predictable auditory spatial illusions in domestic stereophonic reproduction, in cinemas, in concert halls, and in auditoria. Although this ideal is far from being completely realized, there are some important patterns of auditory behavior that can be used as guides for the processing of sound signals reproduced through loudspeakers as well as for certain aspects of listening room, concert hall, and auditorium design. It is in this context that the following survey of spatial hearing is undertaken. Readers who wish to study this aspect of hearing in greater detail are referred to the books by Blauert[32] and Ando[41] and chapters by Durlach and Colburn[42] and Rasch and Plomp.[43]

Monaural Transfer Functions of the Ear. Sounds arriving at the ears of the listener are subject to modification by sound reflection, diffraction, and resonances in the structures of the external ear, head, shoulders, and torso. The amount and form of the modification are dependent on the frequency of the sound and the direction and distance of the source from which the sound emanates. In addition to the effect that this has on the sensitivity of the hearing process, which affects signal detection, there are modifications that amount to a kind of directional encoding, wherein sounds arriving from specific directions are subject to changes characteristic of those directions.

Each ear is partially sheltered from sounds arriving from the other side of the head. The effect of diffraction (see Sec. 1.4.4) is such that low-frequency sounds, with wavelengths that are large compared with the dimensions of the head, pass around the head with little or no attenuation, while higher frequencies are progressively more greatly affected by the directional effects of diffraction. There is, in addition, the acoustical interference that occurs among the components of sound that have traveled over paths of slightly different length around the front and back and over the top of the head.

Superimposed on these effects are those of the pinna, or external ear. The intriguingly complex shape of this structure has prompted a number of theories of its behavior, but only relatively recently have some of its important functions been properly put into perspective. According to one view, the folds of the pinna form reflecting surfaces, the effect of which is to create, at the entrance to the ear canal, a system of interferences between the direct and these locally reflected sounds that depends on the direction and distance of the incoming sound.[44] The small size of the structures involved compared with the wavelengths of audible sounds indicates that dispersive scattering, rather than simple reflection, is likely to be the dominant effect. Nevertheless, measurements have identified some acoustical interferences resembling those that such a view would predict, and these have been found to correlate with some aspects of localization.[33,45]

In the end, however, the utility of the theory must be judged on the basis of how effectively it explains the physical functions of the device and how well it predicts the perceptual consequences of the process. From this point of view, time-domain descriptions would appear to be at a disadvantage since the hearing process is demonstrably insensitive to the fine structure of signals at frequencies above about 1.5 kHz.[32] Partly for this reason most workers have favored descriptions in terms of spectral cues.

It is therefore convenient that the most nearly complete picture of external-ear function has resulted from examinations of the behavior of the external ear in the frequency domain. By carefully measuring the pressure distributions in the standing-wave patterns, the dominant resonances in the external ear have been identified.[46] These have been related to the physical structures and to the measured acoustical performance of the external ear.[16]

A particularly informative view of the factors involved in the above discussion comes from an examination of curves showing the transformation of SPL from the free field to the eardrum.[47] These curves reveal, as a function of frequency, the amplitude modifications imposed on incident sounds by the external hearing apparatus. Figure 1.25 shows the family of curves representing this transformation for sounds arriving from different directions in the horizontal plane. Figure 1.26 shows the estimated transformations for sound sources at different elevations.

An interesting perspective on these data is shown in Fig. 1.27, where it is possible to see the contributions of the various acoustical elements to the total acoustical gain of the ear. It should be emphasized that there is substantial acoustical interaction among these components, so that the sum of any combination of them is not a simple arithmetic addition. Nevertheless, this presentation is a useful means of acquiring a feel for the importance of the various components.

It is clear from these curves that there are substantial direction-dependent spectral changes, some rather narrowband in influence and others amounting to significant broadband tilts. Several studies in localization have found that, especially with pure tones and narrowband signals, listeners could attribute direction to auditory events resulting from sounds presented through only one ear (monaural localization) or presented identically in two ears, resulting in localization in the *median plane* (the plane bisecting the head vertically into symmetrical left-

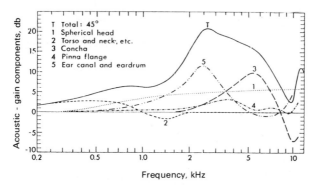

FIG. 1.27 Contributions of various body parts to the total acoustic gain of the external hearing system for a sound source at a horizontal angle of 45°. Note that the interactions between these components prevent simple arithmetic addition of their individual contributions. [*From E. A. G. Shaw, "The Acoustics of the External Ear," in W. D. Keidel and W. D. Neff (eds.),* Handbook of Sensory Physiology, *vol. V/1:* Auditory System, *Springer-Verlag, Berlin, 1974.*]

right halves). So strong are some of these effects that they can cause auditory events to appear in places different from the sound event, depending only on the spectral content of the sound. Fortunately such confusing effects are not common in the panorama of sounds we normally encounter, partly because of familiarity with the sounds themselves, but the process is almost certainly a part of the mechanism by which we are able to distinguish between front and back and between up an down, directions that otherwise would be ambiguous because of the symmetrical locations of the two ears.

Interaural Differences.   As useful as the monaural cues are, it is sound localization in the horizontal plane that is dominant, and for this the major cues come from the comparison of the sounds at the two ears and the analysis of the differences between them. From the data shown in Fig. 1.25 it is evident that there is a substantial frequency-dependent *interaural amplitude difference* (IAD) that characterizes sounds arriving from different horizontal angles. Because of the path length differences there will also be an associated *interaural time difference* (ITD) that is similarly dependent on horizontal angle.

Figure 1.28 shows IADs as a function of frequency for three angles of incidence in the horizontal plane. These have been derived from the numerical data in Ref. 48, from which many other such curves can be calculated.

The variations in IAD as a function of both frequency and horizontal angle are natural consequences of the complex acoustical processes in the external hearing apparatus. Less obvious is the fact that there is frequency dependency in the ITDs. Figure 1.29 shows the relationship between ITD and horizontal angle for various pure tones and for broadband clicks. Also shown are the predictive curves for low-frequency sounds, based on diffraction theory, and for high-frequency sounds, based on the assumption that the sound reaches the more remote ear by traveling as a creeping wave that follows the contour of the head. At intermediate frequencies (0.5 to 2 kHz) the system is dispersive, and the temporal differences become very much dependent on the specific nature of the signal.[49,50]

It is evident from these data that at different frequencies, especially the higher frequencies, there are different combinations of ITD and IAD associated with each horizontal angle of incidence. Attempts at artificially manipulating the localization of auditory events by means of frequency-independent variations of these parameters are therefore unlikely to achieve the image size and positional precision associated with natural sound events.

Localization Blur.   In normal hearing the precision with which we are able to identify the direction of sounds depends on a number of factors. The measure of this precision is called *localization blur,* the smallest displacement of the sound event that produces a just-noticeable difference in the corresponding auditory event. The concept of localization blur characterizes the fact that auditory space (the perception) is less precisely resolved than physical space and the measures we have of it.

The most precise localization is in the horizontal forward direction with broadband sounds preferably having some impulsive content. The lower limit of localization blur appears to be about 1°, with typical values ranging from 1 to 3°, though for some types of sound values of 10° or more are possible. Moving away from the forward axis, localization blur increases, with typical values for sources on either side of the head and to the rear being around 10 to 20°. Vertically, localization blur is generally rather large, ranging from about 5 to 20° in the forward direction to 30 to 40° behind and overhead.[32]

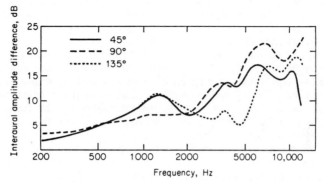

FIG. 1.28 The interaural amplitude difference as a function of frequency for three angles of incidence. [*Derived from E. A. G. Shaw and M. M. Vaillancourt, "Transformation of Sound-Pressure Level from the Free Field to the Eardrum Presented in Numerical Form,"* J. Acoust. Soc. Am.,**78,** *1120–1123 (1985).*]

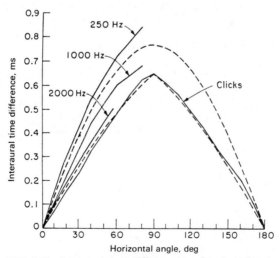

FIG. 1.29 Interaural time difference as a function of horizontal angle. The curves show measured data for clicks and pure tones (solid lines) and predictive curves for low frequencies (top dashed curve), based on diffraction theory, and for high frequencies (bottom dashed curve), based on creeping-wave concepts (see text). [*From N. I. Durlach and H. S. Colburn, "Binaural Phenomena," in E. C. Carterette and M. P. Friedman (eds.),* Handbook of Perception, *vol. 4, Academic, New York, 1978, chap. 10.*]

Lateralization versus Localization.   In exploring the various ways listeners react to interaural signal differences, it is natural that headphones be used, since the sounds presented to the two ears can then be independently controlled. The auditory events that result from this process are distinctive, however, in that the perceived images occur inside or very close to the head and image movement is predominantly lateral. Hence, this phenomenon has come to be known as *lateralization,* as opposed to *localization,* which refers to auditory events perceived to be external and at a distance. Overcoming the in-head localization characteristic of headphone listening has been a major difficulty, inhibiting the widespread use of these devices for critical listening.

In headphone listening it is possible to move the auditory event by independently varying the interaural time or amplitude difference. Manipulating interaural time alone yields auditory image trajectories of the kind shown in Fig. 1.30, indicating that the ITD required to displace the auditory image from center completely to one side is about 0.6 ms, a value that coincides with the maximum ITD occurring in natural hearing (Fig. 1.29). Although most listeners would normally be aware of a single dominant auditory image even when the ITD exceeds this normal maximum value, it is possible for there to be multiple auditory images of lesser magnitude, each with a distinctive tonal character and each occupying a different position in perceptual space. With complex periodic signals, experienced listeners indicate that some of these images follow trajectories appropriate to the individual harmonics for frequencies that are below about 1 kHz.[51] This spatial complexity would not be expected in normal listening to a simple sound source, except when there are delayed versions of the direct sounds caused by strong reflections or introduced electronically. The result, if there are several such delayed-sound components, is a confused and spatially dispersed array of images, coming and going with the changing spectral and temporal structure of the sound. It seems probable that this is the origin of the often highly desirable sense of spaciousness in live and reproduced musical performances (see Subsec. "Spatial Impression").

The sensitivity of the auditory system to changes in ITD in the lateralization

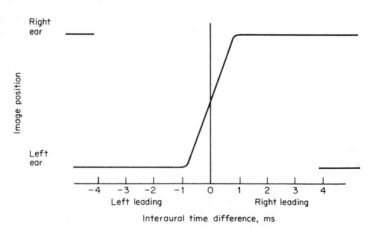

FIG. 1.30 Perceived positions of the dominant auditory images resulting from impulsive signals (clicks) presented through headphones when the interaural time difference is varied.

of auditory images, or *lateralization blur,* is dependent on both the frequency and the amplitude of the signal. According to various experimenters, lateralization blur varies from around 2 μs to about 60 μs, increasing as a function of signal frequency and sound level, and is at a minimum around ITD = 0.

Introducing an IAD displaces the auditory event toward the ear receiving the louder sound. An IAD of between 10 and 20 dB seems to be sufficient to cause the image to be moved completely to one side. The precise figure is difficult to ascertain because of the rapid increase in lateralization blur as a function of IAD; the auditory event becomes wider as it approaches the side of the head. Close to center, however, the lateralization blur is consistently in the vicinity of 1 to 2 dB.

Spatial Impression. Accompanying the auditory impression of images in any normal environment is a clear impression of the type and size of the listening environment itself. Two aspects appear to be distinguishable: *reverberance,* associated with the temporal stretching and blurring of auditory events caused by reverberation and late reflections; and *spaciousness,* often described as a spreading of auditory events so that they occupy more space than the physical ensemble of sound sources. Other descriptors such as ambience, width, or envelopment also apply. Spaciousness is a major determinant of listener preference in concert halls and as such has been the subject of much recent study.

In general, the impression of spaciousness is closely related to a lack of correlation between the input signals to the two ears. This appears to be most effectively generated by strong early lateral reflections (those arriving within about the first 80 ms after the direct sound). While all spectral components appear to add positively to the effect and to listener preference, they can contribute differently. Frequencies below about 3 kHz seem to contribute mainly to a sense of depth and envelopment, while high frequencies contribute to a broadening of the auditory event.[52]

The acoustical interaction of several time-delayed and directionally displaced sounds at the ears results in a reduced interaural cross correlation; the sense of spaciousness is inversely proportional to this correlation. In other terms, there is a spectral and temporal incoherence in the sounds at the ears, leading to the fragmentation of auditory events as a function of both frequency and time. The fragments are dispersed throughout the perceptual space, contributing to the impression of a spatially extended auditory event.

Distance Hearing. To identify the distance of a sound source listeners appear to rely on a variety of cues, depending on the nature of the sound and the environment. In the absence of strong reflections, as a sound source is moved farther from a listener, the sound level diminishes. It is possible to make judgments of distance on this factor alone, but only for sounds that are familiar, where there is a memory of absolute sound levels to use as a reference. With any sound, however, this cue provides a good sense of relative distance.

In an enclosed space the listener has more information to work with, because as a sound source is moved away, there will be a change in the relationship between the direct sound and the reflected and reverberant sounds in the room. The hearing mechanism appears to take note of the relative strengths of the direct and indirect sounds in establishing the distance of the auditory event. When the sound source is close, the direct sound is dominant and the auditory image is very compact; at greater distances, the indirect sounds grow proportionately stronger until eventually they dominate. The size of the auditory event increases with distance, as does the localization blur.

1.8.7   Stereophonic Imaging

Consider the conventional stereophonic arrangement shown in Fig. 1.31. If the two loudspeakers are radiating coherent sounds with identical levels and timing, the listener should perceive a single auditory event midway between the loudspeakers. This phantom, or virtual, sound source is the result of *summing localization,* the basis for the present system of two-channel stereophonic recording and reproduction.

Progressively increasing the time difference between the signals in the channels displaces the auditory event, or image, toward the side radiating the earlier sound until, at about 1 ms, the auditory image is coincident with the source of the earlier sound. At time differences greater than about 1 ms the perception may become spatially more dispersed, but the principal auditory event is generally perceived to remain at the position of the earlier sound event until, above some rather larger time difference, there will be two auditory events occurring separately in both time and space, the later of which is called an *echo.*

The region of time difference between that within which simple summing localization occurs and that above which echoes are perceived is one of considerable interest and complexity. In this region the position of the dominant auditory event is usually determined by the sound source that radiates the first sound to arrive at the listener's location. However, depending on the nature of the signal, simple summing localization can break down and there can be subsidiary auditory images at other locations as well. The later sound arrivals also influence loudness, timbre, and intelligibility in ways that are not always obvious.

The cause of this complexity can be seen in Fig. 1.32, showing the sounds arriving at the two ears when the sound is symbolically represented by a brief impulse. It is immediately clear that the fundamental difference between the situation of summing localization and that of natural localization is the presence of four sound components at the ears instead of just two.

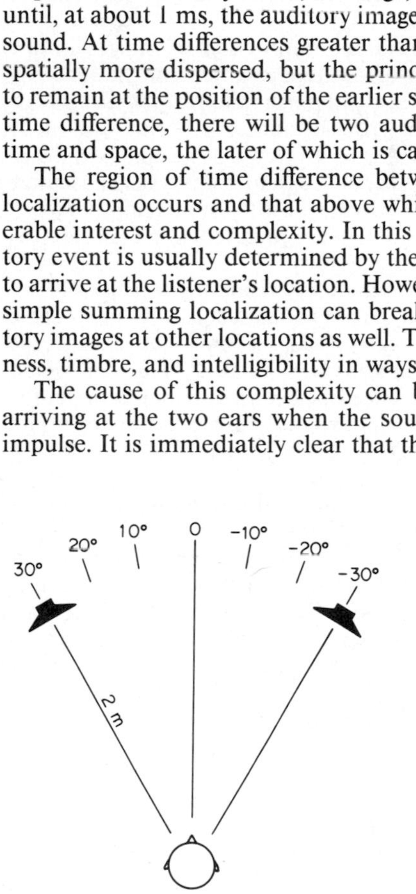

In all cases the listener responds to identical ear input signals by indicating a single auditory event in the forward direction. Note, however, that in both stereo situations the signals at the two ears are not the same as the signals in normal localization. Thus even though the spatial aspects have been simulated in stereo, the sounds at the two ears are modified by the *acoustical crosstalk* from each speaker to the opposite ear, meaning that perfectly accurate timbral reproduction for these sounds is not possible. This aspect of stereo persists

FIG. 1.31 Standard stereophonic listening configuration.

FIG. 1.32 Comparison between sound localization in natural listening and localization in stereophonic listening within the range of simple summing. For the purposes of this simplified illustration the sound waveform is an impulse. To the right of the pictorial drawings showing a listener receiving sound from either a single source (natural localization) or a stereo pair of loudspeakers (summing localization) are shown the sounds received by the left and right ears of the listener. In the stereo illustrations sounds from the left loudspeaker are indicated by dark bars and sounds from the right loudspeaker by light bars.

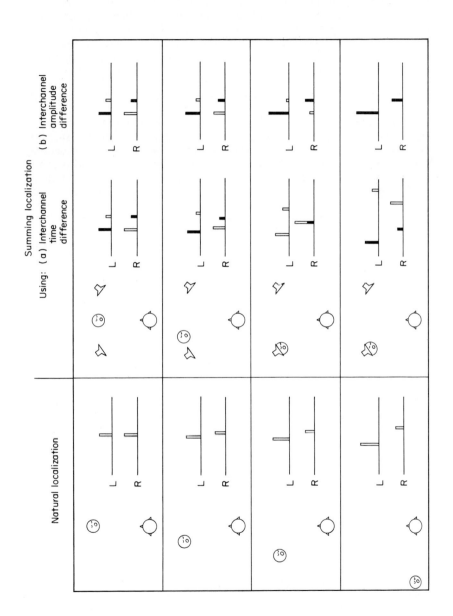

through all conditions for time-difference manipulation of the auditory image, but with amplitude-difference manipulation the effect diminishes with increasing amplitude difference until, in the extreme, the listener hears only sound from a single speaker, a monophonic presentation. In summary, then, accurate waveform reproduction is possible only in amplitude-difference stereo, and then only for auditory images that have been displaced completely to one side or the other.

Although impressions of image movement between the loudspeakers can be convincingly demonstrated by using either interchannel time or amplitude differences, there is an inherent limitation in the amount of movement: in both cases the lateral displacement of the principal auditory event is bounded by the loudspeakers themselves.

With time differences temporal masking (see Sec. 1.8.2) inhibits the contributions of the later arrivals, and the localization is dominated by the first sound to arrive at each ear. With small time differences the image can be moved between the loudspeakers, the first arrivals are from different loudspeakers, and it can be seen that an interchannel time difference is perceived as an ITD. At larger values of interchannel time difference the first arrivals are from the same loudspeaker, and the dominant auditory image remains at that location. This is because of the *law of the first wavefront,* also known as the precedence effect, according to which the dominant auditory event is perceived to be coincident with the loudspeaker radiating the earlier sound (see also Sec. 1.8.8). The other sound components are still there nonetheless, and they can contribute to complexity in the spatial illusion as well as to changes in timbre.

With amplitude differences (also known as *intensity stereo*), the temporal pattern of events in the two ears is unchanged until the difference approaches infinity. At this point the ears receive signals appropriate to a simple sound source with the attendant sound and localization accuracy. It is a real (monophonic) sound source generating a correspondingly real auditory event.

Summing Localization with Interchannel Time and Amplitude Differences. Figure 1.33 shows the position of the auditory image as a function of interchannel time difference for the conventional stereophonic listening situation shown in Fig. 1.31. The curves shown are but a few of the many that are possible since, as is apparent, the trajectory of the auditory image is strongly influenced by signal type and spectral composition.

In contrast, the curves in Fig. 1.34, showing the position of the auditory image as a function of interchannel amplitude difference, are somewhat more orderly. Even so there are significant differences in the slopes of the curves for different signals.

With a signal like music that is complex in all respects it is to be expected that, at a fixed time or amplitude difference, the auditory event will not always be spatially well defined or positionally stable. There are situations where experienced listeners can sometimes identify and independently localize several coexisting auditory images. Generally, however, listeners are inclined to respond with a single compromise localization, representing either the "center of gravity" of a spatially complex image display or the dominant component of the array. If the spatial display is ambiguous, there can be a strong flywheel effect in which occasional clear spatial indications from specific components of the sound engender the perception that all of that sound is continuously originating from a specific region of space. This is especially noticeable with the onset of transient or any small mechanical sounds that are easily localized compared with the sustained portion of the sounds.

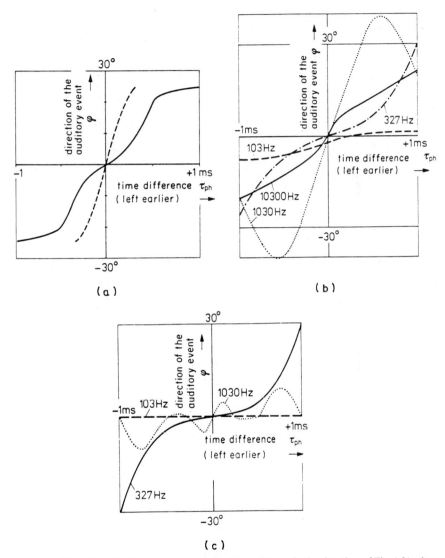

FIG. 1.33 Direction of auditory images perceived by a listener in the situation of Fig. 1.31 when the interchannel time difference is varied from 0 to $+1$ ms (left channel earlier) and -1 ms (right channel earlier). The curves show the results of using different sounds. (*a*) – – – = speech; ——— = impulses. (*b*) Tone bursts. (*c*) Continuous tones. *(From J. Blauert, Spatial Hearing, M.I.T., Cambridge, Mass., 1983, using speech data from a thesis by K. de Boer, Institute of Technology, Delft, 1940, and other data from a thesis by K. Wendt, Technische Hochschule, Aachen, 1963.)*

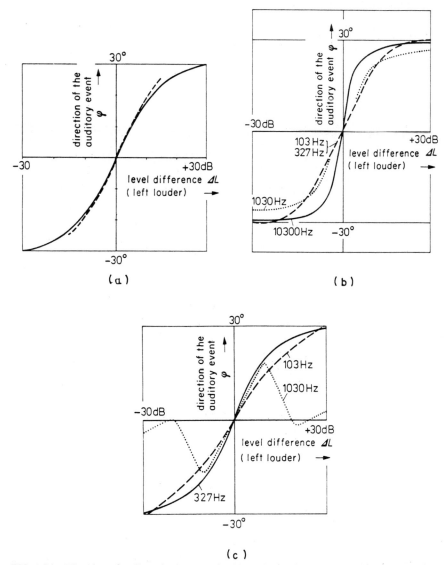

FIG. 1.34 Direction of auditory images perceived by a listener in the situation of Fig. 1.31 when the interchannel amplitude difference is varied from 0 to +30 dB (left louder) and −30 dB (right louder). The curves show the results with different sounds. (a) - - - - = speech; ———— = impulses. (b) Tone bursts. (c) Continuous tones. *(From J. Blauert, Spatial Hearing, M.I.T., Cambridge, Mass., 1983, using speech data from a thesis by K. de Boer, Institute of Technology, Delft, 1940, and other data from a thesis by K. Wendt, Technische Hochschule, Aachen, 1963.)*

The blur in stereo localization, as in natural localizaton, is least for an image localized in the forward direction, where, depending on the type of sound, the *stereo localization blur* is typically about 3 to 7°. With the image fully displaced by amplitude difference (IAD = 30 dB), the blur increases to typical values of 5 to 11°. With the image fully displaced by means of time difference (ITD = 1 ms), the blur increases to typical values of 10 to 16°.[32]

Effect of Listener Position.   Sitting away from the line of symmetry between the speakers causes the central auditory images to be displaced toward the nearer loudspeaker. Interaural time differences between the sound arrivals at the ears are introduced as the path lengths from the two speakers change. Within the first several inches of movement away from the axis of symmetry the sound components from the left and right loudspeakers remain the first arrivals at the respective ears. In this narrow region it is possible to compensate for the effect of the ITD by adding the appropriate opposite bias of interchannel amplitude difference (see Fig. 1.35). This process is known as *time-intensity trading,* and it is the justification for the balance control on home stereo systems, supposedly allowing the listener to sit off the axis of symmetry and to compensate for it by introducing an interchannel amplitude bias. There are some problems, however, the first one being that the trading ratio is different for different sounds, so that the centering compensations do not work equally for all components of a complex signal; the image becomes blurred. The second problem arises when the listener moves beyond the limited range discussed above, the simple form of summing localization breaks down, and the more complicated precedence effect (see Sec. 1.8.8) comes into effect. In this region, it is to be expected that the auditory image will become rather muddled, increasing in size and spaciousness. Localization will tend to be related to the center of gravity of a spatially diffuse auditory event rather than of a specific compact event. Nevertheless, in recordings of ensembles with natural ambience the trading may be judged to be satisfactory, since the initial effect is, by design, rather diffuse. As the listener moves about, there will also be progressive changes to the timbre due to the directional properties of the loudspeakers and wave interference between essentially similar sounds arriving at the ears with various time delays.

Stereo Image Quality and Spaciousness.   The position of auditory events is but a part of the total spatial impression. In stereo reproduction as in live performances, listeners appreciate the aspect of spaciousness as long as it creates a realistic impression (see Sec. 1.8.6: "Spatial Impression"). The process by which an impression of spaciousness is generated in stereo is much the same as in normal hearing—a reduction in interaural cross correlation. The tradeoff is also similar, in that as the feeling of space increases, the width of the auditory images also increases.[53] The extent to which the interchannel cross-correlation coefficient is altered to manipulate these effects is, therefore, a matter of artistic judgment depending on the type of music involved.

Special Role of the Loudspeakers.   In the production of stereophonic recordings the impressions of image position, size, and spaciousness are controlled by manipulating the two-channel signals. However, the impressions received by the listener are also affected by the loudspeakers used for reproduction and their interaction with the listening room.

The directionality of the loudspeakers and the location of reflecting room boundaries together determine the relative strengths of the direct, early-reflected,

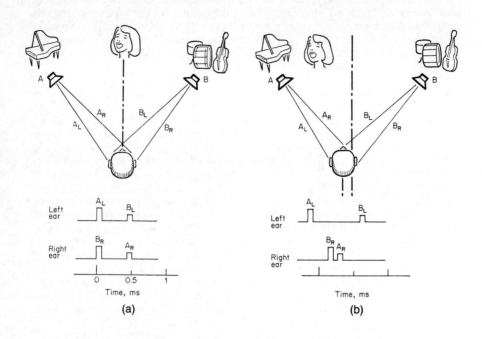

(a)

(b)

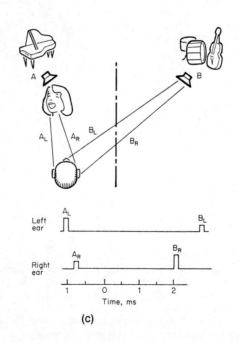

(c)

1.62

and reverberant sounds that impinge on the listener. To the extent that the reflected sounds can reduce the correlation between the sounds at the two ears, it is clear that loudspeakers with substantial off-axis sound radiation can enhance the sense of spaciousness. For this to be effective, however, the listening room boundaries must be sound-reflecting at least at the points of the first reflections, especially the wall (lateral) reflections.

There is evidence that listeners in domestic situations prefer a certain amount of locally generated spaciousness.[34,54,55] In part this may be due to the more natural spatial distribution of the reflected sounds in the listening room as opposed to the recorded ambient sounds which are reproduced only as direct sounds from the loudspeakers. Loudspeakers placed in a room where the early reflections have been absorbed or directional loudspeakers placed in any type of room would be expected to yield a reproduction lacking spaciousness. This, it seems, is preferred by some listeners at home and many audio professionals in the control room,[55,56] especially with popular music. The fact that opinions are influenced by the type of music, individual preferences, and whether the listening is done for record production or for pleasure makes this a matter for careful consideration. Once selected, the loudspeaker and the room tend to remain as fixed elements in a listening situation.

1.8.8 Sound in Rooms: The General Case

Taking the broadest view of complex sound sources, one can consider the combination of real sources and their reflected images as multiple sources. In this way, it is possible to deal with situations other than the special case of stereophonic reproduction.

Precedence Effect and the Law of the First Wavefront. For well over 100 years it has been known that the first sound arrival dominates sound localizaton. The phenomenon is known as the law of the first wavefront or the precedence effect. With time delays between the first and second arrivals of less than about 1 ms we are in the realm of simple summing localization, as discussed in Sec. 1.8.7. At longer delays the location of the auditory event is dictated by the location of the source of the first sound, but the presence of the later arrival is indicated by a distinctive timbre and a change in the spatial extent of the auditory event; it may be smeared toward the source of the second sound. At still longer time delays the second event is perceived as a discrete echo.

These interactions are physically complex, with many parametric variations possible. The perceived effects are correspondingly complex, and, as a consequence, the literature on the subject is extensive and not entirely unambiguous.

←————————————————————————————————

FIG. 1.35 Sequence of events as a listener moves progressively away from the axis of symmetry in stereophonic listening. In (*a*) the listener hears a left-channel piano, a right-channel percussion and bass, and a centrally localized vocalist. The vocal signals at the listener's ears are indicated beneath the pictorial diagram, with impulses representing the real vocal sounds. In (*b*), when the listener moves just slightly away from the axis of symmetry, the auditory image of the vocalist moves in the same direction. The waveforms at the ears are similar to those in ITD stereophony (see Fig. 1.32). In (*c*) the listener has moved well away from the axis of symmetry, and the auditory image of the vocalist has moved into the position of the nearer loudspeaker. The waveforms at the ears are like those in ITD stereophony with large time differences (see Fig. 1.32). Throughout these maneuvers the simple monophonic images remain at their respective loudspeakers.

One of the best-known studies of the interaction of two sound events is that by Haas,[57] who was concerned with the perception and intelligibility of speech in rooms, especially where there is sound reinforcement. He formed a number of conclusions, the most prominent of which is that for delays in the range of 1 to 30 ms, the delayed sound can be up to 10 dB higher in level than the direct sound before it is perceived as an echo. Within this range, there is an increase in loudness of the speech accompanied by "a pleasant modification of the quality of the sound [and] an apparent enlargement of the sound source." Over a wide range of delays the second sound was judged not to disturb the perception of speech, but this was found to depend on the syllabic rate. This has come to be known as the *Haas effect,* although the term has been extensively misused because of improper interpretation.

Examining the phenomenon more closely reveals a number of effects related to sound quality and to the localization dominance of the first-arrived sound. In general, the precedence effect is dependent on the presence of transient information in the sounds, but even this cannot prevent some interference from reflections in rooms. Several workers have noted that high frequencies in delayed sounds were more disturbing than low frequencies, not only because of their relative audibility but because they were inclined to displace the localization. In fact, the situation in rooms is so complicated that it is to be expected that interaural difference cues will frequently be contradictory, depending on the frequency and temporal envelope of the sound. There are suggestions that the hearing process deals with the problem by means of a running plausibility analysis that pieces together evidence from the eyes and ears.[58] That this is true for normal listening where the sound sources are visible underlines the need in stereo reproduction to provide unambiguous directional cues for those auditory events that are intended to occupy specific locations.

Binaural Discrimination. The *cocktail-party effect,* in which it is demonstrably easier to carry on a conversation in a crowded noisy room when listening with two ears than with one, is an example of *binaural discrimination.* The spatial concentration that is possible with two ears has several other ramifications in audio. Reverberation is much less obtrusive in two-eared listening, as are certain effects of isolated reflections that arrive from directions away from that of the direct sound. For example, the timbral modifications that normally accompany the addition of a signal to a time-delayed duplicate (comb filtering) are substantially reduced when the delayed component arrives at the listener from a different direction.[59] This helps to explain the finding that listeners frequently enjoy the spaciousness from lateral reflections without complaining about the coloration. In this connection it has been observed that the disturbing effects of delayed sounds are reduced in the presence of room reverberation[57] and that reverberation tends to reduce the ability of listeners to discriminate differences in the timbre of sustained sounds like organ stops and vowels.[37]

1.9 LISTENING AND THE PERCEPTION OF SOUND QUALITY

Listening is a fundamental activity in audio. It affects everything from the production of live music, through the production of recordings, to the reproduction of sound in the home. The opinions of listeners influence the designers of the equipment used at each of these stages as well as the selection of specific makes and models by individuals.

1.9.1 Controlling the Variables

Many factors contribute to the formation of opinions during listening, and several of them may have little to do with the equipment or sound under examination. Because of these numerous and often-uncontrolled variables, opinions may vary not only among individuals but from occasion to occasion, though the object of the examination may be constant. Most of the sources of variability can be controlled, at least to some extent, and where opinions are considered important, efforts should be made to do so. With enough care it is possible, in fact, to elevate opinion to the status of fact.[29,60]

In the following discussion the major nuisance variables are identified. Readers wishing more detailed information should see Refs. 29, 60, and 61.

Physical Variables. Because the *listening room* is the final coupling device between the loudspeaker and the listener, it should be selected or designed for its appropriateness to the listening task. Within the room, the *loudspeaker position* affects the sound radiated by the source, and the *listener position* influences the portion of the total sound that is heard. Together these three factors determine the appropriateness of the manner in which the loudspeakers and all prior elements in the chain, including the recording, are represented and the potential for agreement among several listeners sharing the experience.

The *relative loudness* of sounds being compared can affect many aspects of timbre; if other factors are equal, even a difference in level of a small fraction of a decibel can cause a preference bias. The *absolute loudness* of all sounds should be appropriate to the wishes of the listeners and to the demands of the program. Once decided, it should be constant throughout any repetitions.

Program material, often a subject of scrutiny itself, is almost always the test signal through which other devices or systems are examined. It is patently not a constant factor and thus requires careful choice if biases are to be avoided. In examining the performance of equipment intended for a wide market, it is important to use program material from a wide variety of sources, thus statistically reducing the effect of bias in any one of them.

Technical imperfections in the apparatus surrounding the object of the test must be minimized for obvious reasons. The item of greatest challenge in this respect is the loudspeaker, since changing this is likely to alter the overall sound quality more than changing any other single component.

Physiological and Psychological Variables. So that prior experience or expectations do not bias the opinions, the tests should be designed so that listeners cannot have *knowledge of the devices under examination.* Anonymity can be ensured in several ways, but the basis is usually simply to hide them from view. If several devices are being compared, the *order of presentation* should be randomized and the sounds repeated so that perceptions affected by the sequence of sounds are properly balanced. In *single-blind* tests only the person running the test knows the identities of the test objects and the sequence of presentation. In *double-blind* tests even the experimenter is unaware of these details until after the test has been completed.

Few people have had experience in organized blind tests, so that *familiarity* with the task can be a problem. Likewise, the equipment, the room, and the program material often are not familiar to the listener. Practice is the only solution. In this context also must be included the total accumulation of *prior experience* of the listeners, which will have an effect on the context in which new auditory experiences are judged and, to some extent, the ability with which the judgments are made. There is no doubt that listeners who have had extensive experience in critical listening to sound quality are best equipped to make reliable judgments of this kind. Musical training or regular concert attendance is not enough.

As might be expected, *hearing sensitivity* is a factor. Listeners with the nearest to normal hearing thresholds exhibit the least variability in their opinions in repeated trials and, as a group, show the closest agreement. With diminished hearing sensitivity and with age, listeners tend to be less consistent in their opinions and to show evidence of bias, in that their opinions deviate from those of listeners with hearing thresholds closer to normal. This would not be surprising if it were not for the fact that these trends are well developed within the range of hearing sensitivity that is regarded as normal in conventional audiometry. The difference seems to be that the requirements for the comprehension of speech are less demanding than those for the auditioning of high-quality sound.[29]

In any collection of listeners there are inevitably sounds and gestures that can communicate impressions or attitudes. Since it is a collection of opinions that is desired, not a group reaction, such *group interactions* must be suppressed. Although they can be tedious, tests with single listeners are best.

To ensure consistency among the ratings it is advisable to *standardize the terminology* by requiring listeners to respond on the scales of the perceptual dimensions discussed in Sec. 1.8.5. Even if the final result is a single-number rating on a scale of fidelity of pleasantness, for example, the exercise of criticizing the sound from several points of view appears to be an important factor in achieving balanced appraisals. Individual comments should not be discouraged; from these come some of the most colorful and penetrating analyses. A *standard questionnaire* is a convenient way to lead listeners into these modes of listening. Examples of these may be found in Refs. 28 and 29. Thorough and standardized *instructions to the listeners* reduce the possibility of simple misunderstandings.

Finally, there is the issue of whether to listen in *stereo* or in *mono*. If the stereophonic spatial effects are important to the evaluation, the answer is clear. However, there are instances when the test involves the audibility of a phenomenon such as a distortion or coloration. In these cases, monophonic listening may prove to be more revealing, as it has in the evaluation of loudspeaker sound quality.[29]

1.9.2   Listening Tests

Combining the preceding controls into a properly ritualized structure is the basis for listening tests. Such tests go far beyond the usual experiences with sounds. They can, in the extreme, be treated as *subjective measurements,* with the standards and tolerances expected of any measurement; the indicator, however, is a human listener. Everyday experiences result in opinions and differences in opinions, but it is rare that the differences can be explained in terms other than preferences, differing aptitudes, or knowledge—all personal attributes. The results of controlled listening tests indicate that many of the suspected personal differences may merely be evidence of other influences. The essential attribute of controlled listening tests may be simply that there is a greater confidence that listener opinions relate to the matter at issue rather than to untold numbers of other influences.

Simple tests attempt merely to ascertain whether or not a difference can be heard. Some of the "great debate" issues (for example, the audibility of differences between wires, amplifiers, and digital encoders) are of this kind, and, judging from the longevity of the debates, it appears that even simple tests may not be straightforward.[62,63,64] Given a situation in which differences undoubtedly can be heard, it is possible to construct elaborate tests that can reveal not only the direction of listener preference but the degree of that preference, the reliability of the results, the extent to which the opinions apply to a wider population, and, sometimes, the reasons for the preference.[29,30,34]

In an attempt to introduce some controls into an area of audio that has been noted for its idiosyncrasies, the International Electrotechnical Commission has published a document defining procedures for loudspeaker listening tests.[65] Although the statistical procedures may be difficult for some users, the basic recommendations appear to be sound. They are also adaptable to other experimental methods, such as those employed by the author.[29]

The choice of procedure determines certain aspects of the findings of a test. For example, the popular and highly useful A/B or A/B/X comparison[62,63] is probably the best way to determine whether differences exist between two sounds. However, unless there are repeated *paired comparisons* with a variety of quite different sounds (more than just two devices, for example), there is the risk that a problem that the A and B sounds have in common will not be noticed. Similarly, the quality of the devices being compared determines the subjective scaling of the differences and absolute qualities that are being assessed. For example, listening intently to the subtle differences between two recording devices might lead to a result that, on a scale of 10, the qualities range from 5 to 8. Combining this test with comparisons of loudspeakers, even very good ones, would reduce the rating differences between the recorders because of the relatively large differences between the loudspeakers, which themselves might rate between 5 and 8. It is by this process that many arguments arise about the relative merits of devices; the difficulty is the subjective scaling of the *absolute* magnitude of the differences.

A convenient means of easing the problem of scaling the qualities of sounds in a comparison test is to compare several at a time. *Multiple-comparison tests,* using four sounds in each listening session, have proved to be highly reliable,[29] especially when "anchor" sounds are built into the test. These sounds are introduced to ensure that listeners are exposed to a fairly consistent *range* of sound qualities in the course of a test, thus helping to stabilize the subjective scales used in quantifying the results. For example, listeners need not try to imagine what truly good or poor loudspeakers sound like if such devices are auditioned as part of the test population.

The *single-stimulus test,* wherein sounds are evaluated one at a time, is another common procedure, but the results may be rather strongly dependent on the choice of interval between listening sessions. It has been found that, other things being equal, variability in listener ratings can increase with the time intervals between comparisons. If the test is run as an uninterrupted series of presentations, with only brief intervals, the procedure can be viewed as an extreme form of the multiple-comparison technique. At the other extreme, this method amounts to living with a sound for some time, perhaps days or weeks, before responding. In the latter case experimental controls are difficult if not impossible to manage, and a new variable, adaptation, is introduced.

1.10 HEARING CONSERVATION

The contents of this book would be of no real interest if one could not hear and of little interest if one could not hear well. Yet, it is highly probable that many of the readers of this book, all serious about audio in some way or other, have less than good hearing.

According to some findings, listeners with even modest elevations in hearing thresholds exhibit increased variability in their opinions about sound quality.[29] Furthermore, because they can contain strongly individual biases, the opinions expressed by such people cannot be assumed to be representative of a larger population. For those individuals this is a personal inconvenience, since satisfaction may be difficult to achieve; for product reviewers, manufacturers, and recording engineers and producers it is a professional handicap, since their crucial judgments may not apply to the audience they wish to attract in one way or other.

Hearing loss is most often a result of aging, disease, or exposure to excessively loud sounds. The former causes are unfortunate and beyond our control, but the latter is one over which one has some individual influence. *Noise-induced* hearing loss is a matter of fact, but the extent to which any one person is likely to be affected by exposure to high sound levels is a complex issue.

In the short term, exposure to loud sounds can cause *temporary* hearing loss, which will disappear gradually over a period of hours or days of relative quiet. These temporary losses also affect listener performances in critical situations. Tests with recording engineers showed that 25-min exposures to 100-dB (A-weighted) popular music produced measurable temporary threshold shifts, which in turn were related to differences in the spectral balance in recordings made before and after the exposures.[66]

If the exposure is repeated, the probability increases that some of the temporary loss will remain as *permanent* hearing loss. The amount of this loss depends on the level, spectrum, and duration of the sound and the recovery intervals between repeated exposures.

Statistics accumulated over many years permit fairly good predictions of the risk of hearing damage for people who are exposed to loud sounds as a matter of their workday routine. These data have been compiled into rules that are used as the basis for occupational hearing conservation programs.

Many such programs set the limit for 8 h of occupational exposure to steady noise at 90 dBA. For shorter exposure times the sound level is allowed to rise. Current United States regulations,[67] based on the Occupational Safety and Health Act, permit a 5-dB increase in sound level for every halving of the daily exposure time (95 dBA for 4 h, 100 dBA for 2 h, and so on, to 115 dBA for 15 min). In Europe and elsewhere, a trading ratio permitting a 3-dB increase for every halving of the daily exposure time is generally used. There appears to be some agreement on an absolute maximum of 140 dBA for exposures to impulse or impact sounds.

It is sobering to bear in mind that these safe exposures are based on the premise of preserving the ability to understand normal conversational speech. Even by abiding by these restrictions there will be some noise-induced hearing loss, but not enough to result in a serious handicap for people whose highest auditory priority is to be able to carry on a conversation. For listeners who wish to preserve their hi-fi ears into old age, a stricter regimen is recommended.

Musicians, recording engineers, and other audio professionals can be exposed to comparably high sound levels but not necessarily on the same routine schedule; therefore, accurate predictions are difficult. Nevertheless, there appear to be enough accounts of audio professionals with hearing problems to conclude that there is a significant risk. A recent study revealed that some members of professional concert bands reached their permissible daily noise dose in about 2 h of practice time (equivalent to 90 dBA for 8 h).[68] Compounding the situation is the fact that many nonprofessional activities, like sport shooting, motorcycling, mowing the lawn, or using power tools, add to the total noise exposure that ears must endure. There are many occasions where hearing protection in the form of sound-attenuating earplugs or earmuffs can be worn without interfering with the activity. It comes down to a task of preserving the ears for the sounds that matter most by protecting them from some of the sounds that matter less.

REFERENCES

1. Leo L. Beranek, *Acoustics,* McGraw-Hill, New York, 1954.
2. G. S. K. Wong, "Speed of Sound in Standard Air," *J. Acoust. Soc. Am.,* **79,** 1359–1366 (1986).
3. Shiro Ehara, "Instantaneous Pressure Distributions of Orchestra Sounds," *J. Acoust. Soc. Japan,* **22,** 276–289 (1966).
4. R. W. B. Stephens and A. E. Bate, *Acoustics and Vibrational Physics,* 2d ed., E. Arnold, London, 1966.
5. E. A. G. Shaw, "Noise Pollution—What Can be Done?" *Phys. Today,* **28**(1), 46–58 (1975).
6. J. E. Piercy and T. F. W. Embleton, "Sound Propagation in the Open Air," in C. M. Harris (ed.), *Handbook of Noise Control,* 2d ed., McGraw-Hill, New York, 1979, chap. 2.
7. R. V. Waterhouse and C. M. Harris, "Sound in Enclosed Spaces," in C. M. Harris (ed.), *Handbook of Noise Control,* 2d ed., McGraw-Hill, New York, 1979, chap. 4.
8. Iain G. Main, *Vibrations and Waves in Physics,* Cambridge, London, 1978.
9. J. M. Pickett, *The Sounds of Speech Communication,* University Park Press, Baltimore, 1980.
10. Peter B. Denes and E. N. Pinson, *The Speech Chain,* Bell Telephone Laboratories, Waverly, 1963.
11. Johan Sundberg, "The Acoustics of the Singing Voice," in *The Physics of Music,* introduction by C. M. Hutchins, Scientific American/Freeman, San Francisco, 1978.
12. Philip M. Morse, *Vibrations and Sound,* 1964, reprinted by the Acoustical Society of America, New York, 1976.
13. V. S. Mankovsky, *Acoustics of Studios and Auditoria,* Focal Press, London, 1971.
14. Donald E. Hall, *Musical Acoustics: An Introduction,* Wadsworth, Belmont, Calif., 1980.
15. A. H. Benade, *Fundamentals of Musical Acoustics,* Oxford University Press, New York, 1976.
16. E. A. G. Shaw, "The Acoustics of the External Ear," in W. D. Keidel and W. D. Neff (eds.), *Handbook of Sensory Physiology,* vol. V/1: *Auditory System,* Springer-Verlag, Berlin, 1974.
17. H. Fletcher and W. A. Munson, "Loudness, Its Definition, Measurement and Calculation," *J. Acoust. Soc. Am.,* **5,** 82–108 (1933).
18. D. W. Robinson and R. S. Dadson, "A Re-determination of the Equal-Loudness Relations for Pure Tones," *Br. J. Appl. Physics,* **7,** 166–181 (1956).
19. International Organization for Standardization, *Normal Equal-Loudness Contours for Pure Tones and Normal Threshold for Hearing under Free Field Listening Conditions,*

Recommendation R226, December 1961, copyrighted by the American National Standards Institute, New York.

20. F. E. Toole, "Loudness—Applications and Implications to Audio," *dB—The Sound Engineering Magazine,* part 1, **7**(5), 27–30; part 2, **7**(6), 25–28, (1973).

21. B. Scharf, "Loudness," in E. C. Carterette and M. P. Friedman (eds.), *Handbook of Perception,* vol. 4: *Hearing,* Academic, New York, 1978, chap. 6.

22. B. L. Jones and E. L. Torick, "A New Loudness Indicator for Use in Broadcasting," *J. Soc. Motion Pict. Telev. Eng.,* **90,** 772–777 (1981).

23. International Electrotechnical Commission, *Sound Sytem Equipment,* part 10: *Programme Level Meters,* Publication 268-10A, 1978.

24. J. J. Zwislocki, "Masking: Experimental and Theoretical Aspects of Simultaneous, Forward, Backward and Central Masking," in E. C. Carterette and M. P. Friedman (eds.), *Handbook of Perception,* vol. 4: *Hearing,* Academic, New York, 1978, chap. 8.

25. W. D. Ward, "Subjective Musical Pitch," *J. Acoust. Soc. Am.,* **26,** 369–380 (1954).

26. John Backus, *The Acoustical Fundations of Music,* Norton, New York, 1969.

27. John R. Pierce, *The Science of Musical Sound,* Scientific American Library, New York, 1983.

28. A. Gabrielsson and H. Sjogren, "Perceived Sound Quality of Sound-Reproducing Systems," *J. Acoust. Soc. Am.,* **65,** 1019–1033 (1979).

29. F. E. Toole, "Subjective Measurements of Loudspeaker Sound Quality and Listener Performance," *J. Audio Eng. Soc.,* **33,** 2–32 (1985).

30. A. Gabrielsson and B. Lindstrom, "Perceived Sound Quality of High-Fidelity Loudspeakers," *J. Audio Eng. Soc.,* **33,** 33–53, (1985).

31. E. A. G. Shaw, "External Ear Response and Sound Localization," in R. W. Gatehouse (ed.), *Localization of Sound: Theory and Applications,* Amphora Press, Groton, Conn., 1982, chap. 2.

32. J. Blauert, *Spatial Hearing,* translation by J. S. Allen, M. I. T., Cambridge, Mass., 1983.

33. P. J. Bloom, "Creating Source Elevation Illusions by Spectral Manipulations," *J. Audio Eng. Soc.,* **25,** 560–565 (1977).

34. F. E. Toole, "Loudspeaker Measurements and Their Relationship to Listener Preferences," *J. Audio Eng. Soc.,* **34,** part 1, 227–235; part 2, 323–348 (1986).

35. G. von Bismarck, "Timbre of Steady Sounds: A Factorial Investigation of Its Verbal Attributes," *Acustica,* **30,** 146–159 (1974).

36. G. von Bismarck, "Sharpness as an Attribute of the Timbre of Steady Sounds," *Acustica,* **30,** 159–172 (1974).

37. R. Plomp, *Aspects of Tone Sensation—A Psychophysical Study,* Academic, New York, 1976.

38. R. Buchlein, "The Audibility of Frequency Response Irregularities" (1962), reprinted in English translation in *J. Audio Eng. Soc.,* **29,** 126–131 (1981).

39. W. R. Stevens, "Loudspeakers—Cabinet Effects," *Hi-Fi News Record Rev.,* **21,** 87–93 (1976).

40. P. Fryer, "Loudspeaker Distortions—Can We Hear Them?" *Hi-Fi News Record Rev.,* **22,** 51–56 (1977).

41. Y. Ando, *Concert Hall Acoustics,* Springer-Verlag, Berlin, 1985.

42. N. I. Durlach and H. S. Colburn, "Binaural Phenomena," in E. C. Carterette and M. P. Friedman (eds.), *Handbook of Perception,* vol. 4, Academic, New York, 1978, chap. 10.

43. R. A. Rasch and R. Plomp, "The Listener and the Acoustic Environment," in D. Deutsch (ed.), *The Psychology of Music,* Academic, New York, 1982, chap. 5.

44. D. W. Batteau, "The Role of the Pinna in Human Localization," *Proc. R. Soc. London,* **B168,** 158–180 (1967).

45. A. J. Watkins, "Psychoacoustical Aspects of Synthesized Vertical Locale Cues," *J. Acoust. Soc. Am.,* **63,** 1152–1165 (1978).

46. E. A. G. Shaw and R. Teranishi, "Sound Pressure Generated in an External-Ear Replica and Real Human Ears by a Nearby Sound Source," *J. Acoust. Soc. Am.,* **44,** 240–249 (1968).

47. E. A. G. Shaw, "Transformation of Sound Pressure Level from the Free Field to the Eardrum in the Horizontal Plane," *J. Acoust. Soc. Am.,* **56,** 1848–1861 (1974).

48. E. A. G. Shaw, and M. M. Vaillancourt, "Transformation of Sound-Pressure Level from the Free Field to the Eardrum Presented in Numerical Form," *J. Acoust. Soc. Am.,* **78,** 1120–1123 (1985).

49. G. F. Kuhn, "Model for the Interaural Time Differences in the Azimuthal Plane," *J. Acoust. Soc. Am.,* **62,** 157–167 (1977).

50. E. A. G. Shaw, "Aural Reception," in A. Lara Saenz and R. W. B. Stevens (eds.), *Noise Pollution,* Wiley, New York, 1986, chap. 5.

51. F. E. Toole and B. McA. Sayers, "Lateralization Judgments and the Nature of Binaural Acoustic Images," *J. Acoust. Soc. Am.,* **37,** 319–324 (1965).

52. J. Blauert and W. Lindemann, "Auditory Spaciousness: Some Further Psychoacoustic Studies," *J. Acoust. Soc. Am.,* **80,** 533–542 (1986).

53. K. Kurozumi and K. Ohgushi, "The Relationship between the Cross-Correlation Coefficient of Two-Channel Acoustic Signals and Sound Image Quality," *J. Acoust. Soc. Am.,* **74,** 1726–1733 (1983).

54. A. G. Bose, "On the Design, Measurement and Evaluation of Loudspeakers," presented at the 35th convention of the Audio Engineering Society (1962), preprint 622.

55. W. Kuhl and R. Plantz, "The Significance of the Diffuse Sound Radiated from Loudspeakers for the Subjective Hearing Event," *Acustica,* **40,** 182–190 (1978).

56. E.-J. Voelker, "Control Rooms for Music Monitoring," *J. Audio Eng. Soc.,* **33,** 452–462 (1985).

57. H. Haas, "The Influence of a Single Echo on the Audibility of Speech", *Acustica,* **1,** 49–58 (1951); English translation reprinted in *J. Audio Eng. Soc.,* **20,** 146–159 (1972).

58. B. Rakerd and W. M. Hartmann, "Localization of Sound in Rooms, II: The Effects of a Single Reflecting Surface," *J. Acoust. Soc. Am.,* **78,** 524–533 (1985).

59. P. M. Zurek, "Measurements of Binaural Echo Suppression," *J. Acoust. Soc. Am.,* **66,** 1750–1757 (1979).

60. F. E. Toole, "Listening Tests—Turning Opinion into Fact," *J. Audio Eng. Soc.,* **30,** 431–443 (1982).

61. F. E. Toole, "Subjective Evaluation," in J. N. Borwick (ed.), *Loudspeaker and Headphone Handbook,* Butterworth, London, in press, chap. 11.

62. S. P. Lipshitz and J. Vanderkooy, "The Great Debate: Subjective Evaluation," *J. Audio Eng. Soc.,* **29,** 482–491 (1981).

63. D. Clark, "High-Resolution Subjective Testing Using a Double-Blind Comparator," *J. Audio Eng. Soc.,* **30,** 330–338 (1982).

64. L. Leventhal, "Type 1 and Type 2 Errors in the Statistical Analysis of Listening Tests," *J. Audio Eng. Soc.,* **34,** 437–453 (1986).

65. International Electrotechnical Commission, *Sound System Equipment, Part 13: Listening Tests on Loudspeakers,* Publication 268-13, 1985.

66. D. H. Woolford, "An Aspect of Aural Perception Related to Loudspeaker Monitoring," *14th Nat. Conv. Dig. Inst. Radio Electron. Eng. (Australia),* 226–227 (1973).

67. 29 CFR §1910.95(b).

68. R. B. Crabtree, "Rehearsal Studio Acoustics and the Sound Exposure Experienced by Military Bandsmen," *Proc. 12th Int. Cong. Acoustics,* Toronto, **1,** paper C7-5 (1986).

CHAPTER 2
AUDIO SPECTRUM AND SIGNAL CHARACTERISTICS

Douglas Preis

Tufts University, Department of Electrical Engineering, Medford, Massachusetts

2.1 INTRODUCTION AND OVERVIEW

Intensity, duration, and repetition in time are perceptually important character-istics of audio signals. Consider, for example, speech, music, and natural and elec-tronically generated sounds when heard by a listener. Most audio signals do have rather complicated waveforms in time, however, and these are difficult to analyze visually. The *spectrum* of the signal offers an alternative representation which dis-plays the strengths of the signal's oscillating parts arranged in order of increasing oscillation. The spectrum also contains information about relative displacements or time shifts of these oscillating parts. In simple terms, the spectrum is a decom-position of the signal into several different oscillating components which later can be reassembled to re-create the original signal. All the information in the signal is contained in its spectrum, but the spectrum is a different way of representing the signal.

Frequency—the number of oscillations per second, or hertz—is the significant new concept associated with the spectrum. Time is no longer explicitly used but is implicitly contained in the notion of frequency. A time interval, called a *period* and equal to the time taken for one full oscillation, is associated with every fre-quency, however. The period is simply the reciprocal of frequency (number of oscillations per second). A signal's overall repetitive nature as well as any hidden periodicities are revealed in its spectrum. The relative importance of the individ-ual frequency components is also clear even though this may not be obvious from inspection of the signal itself. In the spectrum, frequency is the independent var-iable, or *domain,* rather than time.

These two different ways of viewing the signal, in time or in frequency, are called the *time domain* and the *frequency domain,* respectively. The two domains are interrelated by a mathematical operation known as a *transformation* which either resolves the frequency components from a time-domain signal or reconstructs the signal from its frequency components. Insight into audio signal properties is gained by careful study of the signal in each domain. Furthermore, if the signal is passed through a system, the effects of that system on the signal also will be observed in both domains. The spectrum of the output signal can reveal important signal modifications such as, for example, which frequency components are reinforced or reduced in strength, which are delayed, or what is added, missing, or redistributed. Comparison of spectra can be used to identify and measure signal corruption or signal distortion. Thus, the spectrum plays a significant role in both signal analysis and signal processing.

With more advanced mathematical techniques it is possible to combine the two domains and form a *joint-domain* representation of the signal. This representation forms the basis for what is called *time-frequency analysis.* Its justification is that tones or pitch (which are frequencylike) can exist and be perceived over a short time interval, after which they may change as indicated by notes in a musical score, for example. The *spectrogram* used in speech research is an early example of this approach. The objective of time-frequency analysis is to locate the signal energy in various frequency ranges during different time intervals.

Digital computers with special algorithms (software) are now available to perform rapid transformations between time and frequency domains or to generate joint-domain representations of signals. Many computationally difficult or burdensome operations are carried out quickly and accurately. With the aid of a computer, virtually all the interesting audio spectrum and signal characteristics can be computed, displayed, and studied.

In computer-aided analysis of audio signals, *discrete-time* signals are used. These are formed by sampling the actual continuum of signal values at equally spaced instants in time. In principle, no information is lost through the sampling process if it is performed properly. More advanced digital signal analysis techniques promise to play an increasing important role both in objective technical assessment of audio equipment and in human auditory perception of sound quality.

In summary, analysis of signal and spectrum characteristics or, simply, *spectral analysis* is a quantitative means to assess audio signals and audio signal-processing systems as well as general audio quality. Additionally, certain features contained in or derived from the spectrum do correlate well with human perception of sound. Although the basis of spectral analysis is mathematical, considerable insight and understanding can be gained from a study of the several examples of time-domain and frequency-domain interrelationships provided in this chapter. The bibliography at the end of the chapter lists several interesting books that extend the depth and breadth of the technical material presented here.

The technical material in this chapter is divided into two major sections. First, properties of different signals and various spectra are explained, beginning with first principles. Sinusoids, phasors, line spectra, Fourier series, discrete Fourier series, the fast Fourier transform, and Fourier transformation are discussed. Second, measures of linear distortion (loss of waveform fidelity) of linearly processed signals are defined and exemplified.

The bibliography includes additional references which serve to extend this introductory material. They cover response of linear systems to signals, relations between frequency and transient responses, spectral modification by audio devices (including perceptual studies and equalization), and more advanced spectral analysis methods such as coherence analysis and time-frequency analysis.

2.2 SIGNALS AND SPECTRA

Signals serve several purposes in audio engineering. Primarily, they carry information, for example, electrical analogs of music or speech or numerical data representing such information. Discrete-time signals, formed from sampled values of continuous signals, are now used extensively in digital recording, processing, storage, and reproduction of audio signals. Signals devised and used solely to elicit a response from an audio system are called test signals. Control signals modify the internal operation of signal-processing devices. Certain signals, such as electronic thermal noise, magnetic-tape hiss, or quantization noise in digital systems, may be present but unwanted.

Essential to a deeper understanding of all kinds of signals is the spectrum. The spectrum is defined in slightly different ways for different classes of signals, however. For example, deterministic signals have a mathematical functional relationship to time that can be described by an equation, whereas nondeterministic signals, such as noise generated by a random process, are not predictable but are described only by their statistical properties. Their spectra are defined in different ways. There are also two types of deterministic signals, classified by total energy content or average energy content; and, again, their spectra are defined differently. All spectral representations provide information about the underlying oscillatory content of the signal. This content can be concentrated at specific frequencies or distributed over a continuum of frequencies, or both.

2.2.1 Signal Energy and Power

A deterministic, real-valued signal $f(t)$ is called a *finite-energy* or *transient* signal if

$$0 < \int_{-\infty}^{\infty} f^2(t) \, dt < \infty \tag{2.1}$$

where t is time. The integrand $f^2(t)$ can be interpreted as the instantaneous power (energy/time) if $f(t)$ is assumed to be a time-varying voltage across a 1-Ω resistor. The numerical value of the integral in Eq. (2.1) is the signal's total energy. A *finite-power* deterministic signal satisfies

$$0 < \lim_{T \to \infty} \frac{1}{T} \int_{-T/2}^{T/2} f^2(t) \, dt < \infty \tag{2.2}$$

That is, the average energy per time or average power is finite. For example, $f(t)$ could be a constant dc voltage existing for all time across a 1-Ω resistor.

Fundamental to understanding spectral analysis is an elementary periodic signal, that is, one that oscillates with constant frequency and does not decay as time progresses. This simplest oscillating signal is called a *sinusoid*. It predicts, for example, the motion of a swinging pendulum (without friction) or the exchange of energy between inductor and capacitor in a lossless resonant circuit. The sinusoid is the solution to a differential equation that describes a wide variety of physical oscillatory and vibrational phenomena.

2.2.2 Sinusoids and Phasor Representation

The sinusoidal signal illustrated in Fig. 2.1a and described mathematically by

$$f(t) = A \cos(\omega t + \theta) \tag{2.3}$$

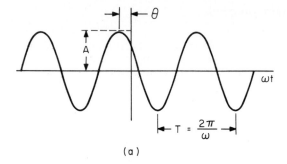

(a)

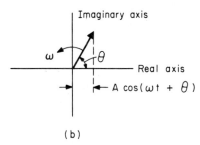

(b)

FIG. 2.1   (a) Sinusoid $A \cos (\omega t + \theta)$. (b) Phasor diagram representation of sinusoid.

is a finite-power signal characterized by its real amplitude A, radian frequency ω rad/s, and θ, which is a constant phase angle (in radians). The quantity $\omega/(2\pi)$ is the cyclic frequency or number of oscillations per second, called hertz, and equals the reciprocal of the sinusoid's period T, the time taken for one full oscillation. These relationships are illustrated in Fig. 2.1a.

The peak, or maximum, value of the signal is A. Its root-mean-square (rms) value, found from taking the square root of the expression in Eq. (2.2), is $A/\sqrt{2} = 0.7071A$, and the average value of $|f(t)|$ over one period is $2A/\pi = 0.6366A$. The average power, from Eq. (2.2), equals $A^2/2$, or simply the rms value squared. By appropriately changing the phase angle θ, a pure cosine wave or sine wave is realized. For example, $\theta = 0, \pi/2, \pi, 3\pi/2, 2\pi$ corresponds to $A \cos (\omega t)$, $-A \sin (\omega t)$, $-A \cos (\omega t)$, $A \sin (\omega t)$, $A \cos (\omega t)$, respectively. If the phase of a sine wave is increased by $\pi/2$ (that is, $90°$ positive phase shift, or phase lead), it becomes a cosine wave. A phase shift of π rad, or $180°$, inverts the polarity of a sinusoid.

By using the Euler identity,

$$e^{jx} = \cos (x) + j \sin (x) \qquad (2.4)$$

where $j = \sqrt{-1}$, $f(t)$ in Eq. (2.3), can also be written as the real part of a time-varying complex number *(phasor)*, namely,

$$f(t) = \text{real } [Ae^{j(\omega t + \theta)}] \qquad (2.5a)$$

A conceptual picture of Eq. (2.5a), called a phasor diagram, is given in Fig. 2.1b. The tip of the arrow describes the locus of points in the complex plane of the expression in brackets in Eq. (2.5a) as the arrow itself rotates counterclockwise with angular velocity ω rad/s. As time progresses, the projection (or shadow) of the arrow's length A onto the horizontal (real) axis has the values $A \cos (\omega t + \theta)$. By convention, the phasor diagram is drawn when $t = 0$ or, equivalently, showing the phase θ of the sinusoid relative to a cosine reference phasor, $\cos (\omega t)$, which would lie on the positive real axis. Note that multiplication of this phasor by $e^{j\psi}$ advances its phase by ψ rad, as can be shown by using Eq. (2.5a). For example, multiplication of the phasor by $j = e^{j\pi/2}$ advances its phase by $\pi/2$, or 90°.

The phasor concept can be extended on the basis of the following two identities derived from Eq. (2.4):

$$\cos (\omega t) = \tfrac{1}{2} (e^{j\omega t} + e^{-j\omega t}) \tag{2.5b}$$

and
$$\sin (\omega t) = \tfrac{1}{2j} (e^{j\omega t} - e^{-j\omega t}) \tag{2.5c}$$

where the negative signs in the exponents are associated with ω, implying negative angular velocity $-\omega$. Thus, $\cos (\omega t)$ and $\sin (\omega t)$ in Eq. (2.4) each can be interpreted simply as a sum of two counterrotating phasors, as shown in Fig. 2.2. On the left side of this figure, the imaginary parts of the two phasors always cancel because they are equal and opposite, and the real parts add to form $\cos (\omega t)$. On the right side, imaginary parts cancel at all times, and the real parts add to yield $\sin (\omega t)$.

There are two ways to represent a sinusoid $A \cos (\omega t + \theta)$ in terms of counterrotating phasors. The simpler method is to scale the lengths of the phasors for $\cos (\omega t)$ in Fig. 2.2 by the amplitude A and then to change the phase of each phasor by rotating it in its direction of rotation θ rad. This operation corresponds to advancing or leading the phase of the $+\omega$ phasor and advancing or leading the phase of the $-\omega$ phasor by θ rad. The other way makes use of the trigonometric identity

$$A \cos (\omega t + \theta) = A \cos \theta \cos (\omega t) - A \sin \theta \sin (\omega t) \tag{2.6}$$

which states that a sinusoid with an arbitrary phase angle can always be represented as a sum of a cosine wave and a sine wave whose coefficients are $A \cos \theta$ and $-A \sin \theta$, respectively. Depending on the phase angle θ, these coefficients can be positive, negative, or zero. When either is negative, the polarity of the associ-

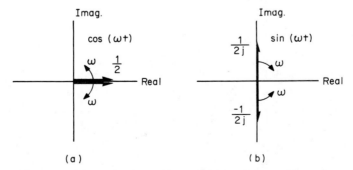

FIG. 2.2   Cosine wave (left) and sine wave (right) represented by counterrotating phasors.

ated sine wave or cosine wave is just inverted; i.e., its phase is changed by π rad, or 180°, so that the negative sign is absorbed and the coefficients represent nonnegative amplitudes. So, the phasors for cos (ωt) and sin (ωt) in Fig. 2.2 with their lengths multiplied by the coefficients in Eq. (2.6) also represent A cos $(\omega t + \theta)$.

2.2.3 Line Spectrum

An alternative to counterrotating phasors is the *line spectrum* (discrete spectrum). Because each phasor shown in Fig. 2.2 contains only three pieces of information, its length (amplitude), its angular velocity $+\omega$ or $-\omega$, and its phase (measured relative to the positive horizontal axis shown in Fig. 2.2), the same information can be presented differently as shown in Fig. 2.3. At points $-\omega$ and $+\omega$ on the horizontal frequency axis, a vertical line is drawn whose length equals that of its corresponding phasor to give the amplitude. The phase of each phasor is plotted above or below its frequency on a separate graph called the *phase spectrum*. The range of the phase spectrum is from $-\pi$, or $-180°$, to $+\pi$, or 180°. Consider, for example, sin (ωt) as represented on the right side of Fig. 2.2 and Fig. 2.3. The phase of the counterclockwise phasor is $-\pi/2$, or $-90°$, and that of clockwise phasor is $+\pi/2$, or $+90°$.

The real advantage of the line-spectrum representation is evident when the signal is composed of several different frequency components $\pm\omega_1,\ \pm\omega_2,\ \pm\omega_3,$ ..., because a separate phasor diagram would be needed for each frequency pair $\pm\omega_n$, whereas all frequencies can be displayed in one line-spectrum plot. A slight and apparent disadvantage is that the concept of negative frequencies is used and signal amplitude is split evenly between the positive and negative frequencies. This representation is a matter of convention, however. If only the total amplitude at each specific frequency is of interest, then phases can be ignored and line spectra drawn at dc (zero frequency) and only at positive values of frequency. The

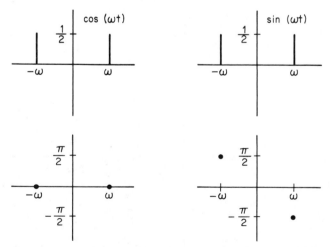

FIG. 2.3   Line-spectrum representation of cos (ωt) at left and sin (ωt) at right.

amplitudes are simply doubled at positive frequencies from their values in the "two-sided" line-spectra representation. It is also possible, by a different convention, to define the spectrum by using only positive frequencies and simply giving the amplitude A and phase θ for each sinusoid in the form of Eq. (2.3). In some applications, it is more useful to give the power $A^2/2$, rather than the amplitude A, associated with each spectral line.

The complex exponentials not only have an interesting interpretation as counterrotating phasors but also have the advantage of representing arbitrary sinusoids without explicitly using the sine and cosine functions themselves or having to take the real part of a complex number as in Eq. (2.5a). Because complex exponentials form the basis for all mathematical transformations between time domain and frequency domain, their use has become the method of choice.

While a sinusoid mathematically represents a *pure tone* at a specific frequency $\omega_0/2\pi = 1/T$ Hz, most periodic musical sounds or periodic signal waveforms have *harmonic structure,* meaning that they also contain frequencies that are integer multiples of the lowest or *fundamental* frequency ω_0 which determines the period T. These higher frequencies do, in general, have different amplitudes and phases. Within the period T each higher frequency or higher harmonic will have an integer number, e.g., 2 or 3 or 4, etc., of full oscillations. The line spectrum is a meaningful way to represent such a signal in the frequency domain. Before the line spectrum can be drawn, the amplitudes and phases of the frequency components in the time waveform are required. These can be found from a specific mathematical analysis of the waveform called Fourier analysis. An understanding of Fourier analysis is essential to the general concept of the spectrum, frequency-domain representation of signals, transformations, and linear signal processing.

2.2.4 Fourier-Series Analysis

To determine whether a periodic $f(t)$ has a sinusoidal component, say, cos (ωt), at frequency ω, the product $f(t)$ cos (ωt) is integrated over one full period $T = 2\pi/\omega$. If, for example, $f(t) = A$ cos (ωt), then

$$\int_{-T/2}^{T/2} f(t) \cos(\omega t)\, dt = A \int_{T/2}^{T/2} \cos^2(\omega t)\, dt = \frac{AT}{2} \qquad (2.7)$$

because $\cos^2(\omega t) = \frac{1}{2} + \frac{1}{2} \cos(2\omega t)$ and the second term integrates to zero. Thus, the amplitude A of cos (ωt) in $f(t)$ is simply $2/T$ times the integral (2.7). The left integral in Eq. (2.7) would equal zero if $f(t) = A$ cos $(n\omega t)$, $n \neq 1$, but $n = 0, 2, 3, \ldots$. The same method applies by using sin (ωt) if $f(t)$ contains the sinusoidal component A sin (ωt). This forms the basis for *Fourier analysis,* that is, a systematic way to determine the harmonic content, in terms of sin $(n\omega_0 t)$ and cos $(n\omega_0 t)$, for $n = 0, 1, 2, \ldots$, of a periodic $f(t)$ whose period $T = 2\pi/\omega_0$.

A *Fourier series* is a mathematical way to represent a real, periodic, finite power signal in terms of a sum of harmonically related sinusoids. If $f(t)$ is periodic with period T, it repeats itself every T so that

$$f(t + T) = f(t) \qquad (2.8)$$

and its Fourier series is given by

$$f(t) = \frac{a_0}{2} + \sum_{n=1}^{\infty} a_n \cos(n\omega_0 t) + \sum_{n=1}^{\infty} b_n \sin(n\omega_0 t) \qquad (2.9)$$

where $\omega_0 = 2\pi/T$ and the *Fourier coefficients* are real numbers given by

$$a_n = \frac{2}{T} \int_{-T/2}^{T/2} f(t) \cos(n\omega_0 t)\, dt \qquad (2.10)$$

and

$$b_n = \frac{2}{T} \int_{-T/2}^{T/2} f(t) \sin(n\omega_0 t)\, dt \qquad (2.11)$$

The frequency ω_0 is called the *fundamental frequency* (or first harmonic) and, for $n = 2, 3, 4, \ldots, n_0$ are the second, third, fourth, etc., *harmonics,* respectively. The $a_0/2$ term is the average value or dc (zero-frequency) content of $f(t)$. The Fourier coefficients in Eqs. (2.10) and (2.11) can be interpreted as the *average content* of $\cos(n\omega_0 t)$ and $\sin(n\omega_0 t)$, respectively, in $f(t)$.

By using the Euler identity, Eqs. (2.4), (2.10), and (2.11) can be combined to yield

$$c_n = \frac{a_n - jb_n}{2} = \frac{1}{T} \int_{-T/2}^{T/2} f(t) e^{-jn\omega_0 t}\, dt \qquad (2.12)$$

where each c_n is a *complex* Fourier coefficient whose magnitude and (phase) angle ϕ are, respectively,

$$|c_n| = \sqrt{(a_n^2 + b_n^2)/2} \qquad (2.13a)$$

$$\phi_n = \arctan(-b_n/a_n) \qquad (2.13b)$$

By defining $c_0 = a_0/2$ and, for $n \neq 0$,

$$c_{-n} = c_n^* = \frac{a_n + jb_n}{2} \qquad (2.14)$$

the Fourier series (2.9) can be written as

$$f(t) = c_0 + \sum_{n=1}^{\infty} c_n e^{jn\omega_0 t} + \sum_{n=-1}^{-\infty} c_n e^{jn\omega_0 t} \qquad (2.15a)$$

$$= \sum_{n=-\infty}^{\infty} c_n e^{jn\omega_0 t} \qquad (2.15b)$$

which can be derived from Eq. (2.9) by using Eqs. (2.12), (2.14), and (2.4). Equation (2.15b) is the *complex form* of the Fourier series and can be interpreted by using Eq. (2.15a), which shows the sum of the dc term, positive-frequency terms, and negative-frequency terms (n has only negative values in the second sum), respectively.

When a periodic signal is represented in the form (2.15b), its corresponding line spectrum can be viewed, first, as pairs of pure sine waves and cosine waves with different real coefficients a_n and b_n, as prescribed by Eqs. (2.10) and (2.11) at positive frequencies $n\omega_0$ which sum to form sinusoids like Eq. (2.6). Using identities (2.5), however, these sine waves and cosine waves also can be written as sums of complex exponentials $e^{+jn\omega_0 t}$ and $e^{-jn\omega_0 t}$ with amplitudes and phases given by the complex coefficients c_n. Alternatively, the line spectrum can be viewed as sinusoids at positive frequencies $n\omega_0$ in the form (2.6) and each represented as the sum of a pair of phasors counterrotating with angular velocities $+n\omega_0$ and $-n\omega_0$ whose lengths equal $|c_n|$ and whose initial phase angle is specified by the angle of c_n. In both interpretations negative frequencies are used, but this results in the very compact complex exponential notation in Eq. (2.15b), where sine and cosine functions are no longer needed.

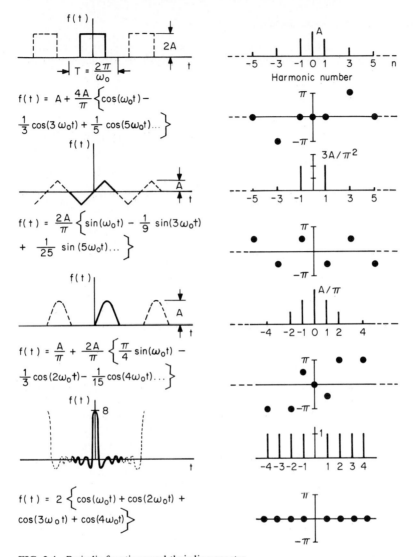

FIG. 2.4   Periodic functions and their line spectra.

sum of a pair of phasors counterrotating with angular velocities $+n\omega_0$ and $-n\omega_0$ whose lengths equal $|c_n|$ and whose initial phase angle is specified by the angle of c_n. In both interpretations negative frequencies are used, but this results in the very compact complex exponential notation in Eq. (2.15b), where sine and cosine functions are no longer needed.

Figure 2.4 shows different periodic functions of time and their corresponding line spectra determined from the magnitude and phase (or angle) of the complex Fourier coefficients c_n.

2.2.5 Discrete Fourier Series

If a Fourier series has only a finite number of terms (i.e., its frequency band is limited) and the highest frequency equals $K\omega_0$ rad/s (the Kth harmonic), then Eq. (2.15b) simplifies to the finite sum

$$f(t) = \sum_{n=-K}^{K} c_n e^{jn\omega_0 t} \tag{2.16}$$

In certain applications the values of $f(t)$ are needed only at N instants in time (within the period T) that are spaced T/N apart. The values $f(t)$ at these N points in time, from Eq. (2.16), are given by

$$f(mT/N) = \sum_{n=-K}^{K} c_n e^{jn\omega_0 mT/N} \tag{2.17}$$

where m is an integer. Choosing the number of points $N = 2K$, that is, the time interval between points equal to half of the period of the highest frequency ($T/N = T/2K$) and substituting $2\pi/T$ for ω_0 in Eq. (2.17) gives

$$f(mT/N) = \sum_{n=-N/2}^{N/2} c_n w_N^{nm} \tag{2.18}$$

where
$$w_N = e^{j2\pi/N} \tag{2.19}$$

which is called the Nth root of unity. The quantity w_n^m, for N values of m, mathematically represents specific points on the unit circle in the complex plane spaced $2\pi/N$, or $360°/N$, apart (beginning from $e^{j0} = 1$). Each of these points is physically interpreted as the location of the tip of a phasor of unit length, which rotates through 2π rad, or $360°$, during the period T at the instants in time mT/N. Because the phasor for the nth harmonic has an angular velocity n times faster than that of the fundamental ($n = 1$), the term w_N^{nm} appears in Eq. (2.18). One way to interpret the term $2\pi/N$ in Eq. (2.19) is that, for any one of the $N/2$ harmonics, only N discrete values of phase are possible after sampling regardless of frequency. The coefficients c_n in Eq. (2.18) are complex numbers of the form $|c_n|\ e^{j\psi_n}$ that scale the unit amplitudes and shift the phases of the sampled harmonics represented by w_N^{nm}.

The Fourier coefficients are related to the sampled values of $f(t)$ by the similar equation

$$c_n = \frac{1}{N} \sum_{m=-M/2}^{M/2} f(mT/N) w_N^{-nm} \tag{2.20}$$

where the integer M is even and numerically equal to N. Equation (2.20) can be substituted into Eq. (2.18), or vice versa, to yield an identity. These two equations define an N-point *discrete Fourier-series pair* which is often called a *discrete Fourier transform (DFT) pair*. They relate the N equally spaced sampled values of $f(t)$ in Eq. (2.18) to its line spectrum, which contains $N/2$ negative-frequency components, a dc term, and $N/2$ positive-frequency components as well as their phases as prescribed by Eq. (2.20). For an example, see the last line spectrum in Fig. 2.4

Equation (2.20) is a discrete-time version of Eq. (2.12) and is valid only if the periodic function $f(t)$ is sampled throughout its period T at a rate that is twice the highest frequency it contains. If $f(t)$ contains harmonics higher than $N/2$, then the c_n coefficients in Eq. (2.20) are not identical to those in Eq. (2.12); they will become corrupted or *aliased* because higher frequencies (with a harmonic number greater than $N/2$) in $f(t)$ influence the value of c_n as computed from Eq. (2.20), but these frequencies cannot be reconstructed by using the harmonics up to harmonic number $N/2$ as in Eq. (2.18). Furthermore, the resulting line spectrum itself will be incorrect.

The DFT can be computed very efficiently from sampled values of $f(t)$, as contained in Eq. (2.20), or $f(t)$ can be reconstructed at the sample points, as in Eq. (2.18), using a numerical algorithm called the *fast Fourier transform* (FFT). The algorithm exploits, in computation, the fact that w_N^{mn} represents only N distinct values of phase.

2.2.6 Spectral Density and Fourier Transformation

Line spectra, where each line $|c_n|$ represents a sinusoid whose average power is $|c_n|^2/2$, cannot be used to represent the spectrum of a finite-energy signal $f(t)$ because the average power of $f(t)$, as given in Eq. (2.2), is zero by definition. Furthermore, while a finite-energy signal can exist for all time, subject to the constraint given in Eq. (2.1), it has no finite period T associated with itself. For finite-energy signals, an *amplitude-density spectrum* is defined in the following way:

$$F(\omega) = \int_{-\infty}^{\infty} f(t)e^{-j\omega t}\, dt \qquad (2.21)$$

The dimensions of $F(\omega)$ are amplitude $\times$ time or amplitude/(1/time) and are interpreted as amplitude/frequency. The quantity $F(\omega)$ is called amplitude spectral density or, simply, *spectral density* of $f(t)$. By comparing Eq. (2.21) with Eq. (2.12), $F(\omega)$ is seen to be defined for all rather than discrete frequencies, and the limits of integration include all time rather than one period. Similar to Fourier analysis in concept, the integral (2.21) extracts from $f(t)$ its average spectral density $F(\omega)$ and associated phase at each frequency ω throughout a continuum of frequencies. The original signal $f(t)$, again analogously to Fourier analysis, can be reconstructed from its spectral density by using the relation

$$f(t) = \frac{1}{2\pi} \int_{-\infty}^{\infty} F(\omega)e^{j\omega t}\, d\omega \qquad (2.22)$$

where all frequencies, instead of discrete frequencies, are used. Equations (2.21) and (2.22) form a *Fourier-transform pair*. By comparing these two equations it is seen that the value of $f(t)$ at, say, $t = t_1$ depends on contributions from $F(\omega)$ at all frequencies and, conversely, that the value of the spectral density $F(\omega)$ at $\omega = \omega_1$ depends on contributions from $f(t)$ at all times. In both cases integrals with infinite limits are evaluated. In Fig. 2.5 several Fourier-transform pairs are illustrated.

The relations (2.21) and (2.22) can be derived from the Fourier-analysis Eqs. (2.12) and (2.15b) by using a limiting process where the period T becomes infinite and the frequency interval between harmonics approaches zero.

The continuous Fourier transform (Eq. 2.21) is often approximated or estimated by using the discrete Fourier transform (2.18) by assuming that $f(t)$ is peri-

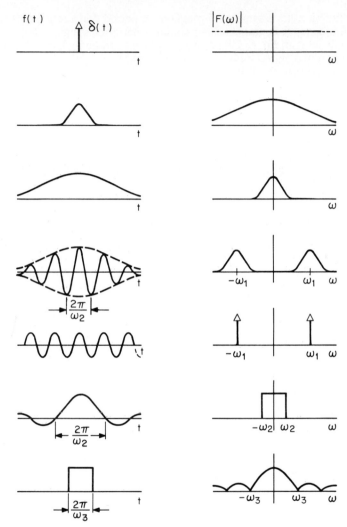

FIG. 2.5 Amplitude spectral density $|F(\omega)|$ corresponding to time-domain signals $f(t)$.

odic, with period T, and that its high-frequency content is zero beyond harmonic number $N/2$, where N equals the number of equally spaced sampled values of $f(t)$ within the assumed period.

The *Laplace transformation* $F(s)$ uses the complex variable $s = \sigma + j\omega$ in place of $j\omega$ in Eq. (2.21) with the lower limit of integration set equal to zero. The quantity $\sigma > 0$ is a convergence factor that exponentially damps out $f(t)$ as $t \to +\infty$. This transform is used in applications where finite-power signals (like sinusoids) that are zero for negative values of time are needed. While the inversion of the Laplace transform is more complicated than Eq. (2.22), tables of transform pairs are available for commonly used signals.

2.2.7 Impulse Signal

A very important finite-energy signal is the unit impulse which is denoted by $\delta(t)$ and defined by the constant spectral density $F(\omega) = 1$ and zero phase for all frequencies. Substituting $F(\omega) = 1$ in Eq. (2.22) gives

$$\delta(t) = \frac{1}{2\pi} \int_{-\infty}^{\infty} e^{j\omega t} \, d\omega \tag{2.23}$$

Because $e^{j\omega t} = \cos(\omega t) + j\sin(\omega t)$ and the odd function $\sin(\omega t)$ integrates to zero, Eq. (2.23) can be interpreted as summing (integrating) unit-amplitude cosine waves of every frequency. When $t = 0$, $\cos(\omega t) = 1$ regardless of the frequency ω, so that all the cosine waves reinforce one another, giving $\delta(t)$ infinite value. At times other than $t = 0$, the cosine waves destructively interfere and cancel, so that $\delta(t) = 0$ for $t \neq 0$. Consider, for example, the last example given in Fig. 2.4 as the number of harmonics and length of the period are increased without limit. By using Eq. (2.21) with $f(t) = \delta(t)$ and the fact that $F(\omega) = 1$,

$$1 = \int_{-\infty}^{\infty} \delta(t) e^{-j\omega t} \, dt \tag{2.24}$$

which implies that the value of the integral is simply the value of the integrand, in this case $e^{-j\omega t}$, evaluated or sampled at $t = 0$. If the numerical value 1 is substituted for $e^{-j\omega t}$ in Eq. (2.24), then the integral of $\delta(t)$ itself results, which also equals 1. By interpreting this latter integral as the area underneath $\delta(t)$, the entire contribution to the value of the integral must come when $t = 0$ because $\delta(t)$ is zero at other times. The unit impulse $\delta(t)$, also called a *delta function,* belongs to a class of *singularity functions.* It has many different interpretations in terms of limits of sequences of functions, one of which is the limit of a rectangularly shaped pulse whose width shrinks to zero and whose height increases to maintain constant area under the pulse so that the integrated value always is unity. The dimensions of $\delta(t)$ are 1/time or frequency.

The delta function provides an interesting link between line spectra and spectral density because finite-power signals can be interpreted as delta functions (in frequency) in the spectral density. For example, the finite-power signal $A \cos(\omega_1 t)$ has spectral density

$$F(\omega) = 2\pi \left[\frac{A}{2} \delta(\omega - \omega_1) + \frac{A}{2} \delta(\omega + \omega_1) \right] \tag{2.25}$$

This can be verified by inserting Eq. (2.25) into Eq. (2.22) and evaluating the integral by using the sampling property of the delta function. The result is

$$f(t) = \frac{A}{2} (e^{j\omega_1 t} + e^{-j\omega_1 t}) = A \cos(\omega_1 t) \tag{2.26}$$

From this example, it is clear that spectral density is a more general concept than line spectra.

2.2.8 Power Spectrum

In Fourier analysis, the product $f(t) e^{-j\omega t}$ is integrated with respect to time to resolve or extract the frequency components, either discrete as in Eq. (2.12) or continuous as in Eq. (2.21), from $f(t)$. These frequency components also manifest themselves as a function of τ in the product $f(t)f(t + \tau)$, where τ is a time-shift parameter. For example, if $f(t) = A \cos(\omega_1 t)$, this latter product is

$$A^2 \cos(\omega_1 t) \cos(\omega_1 t + \omega_1 \tau) = \frac{A^2}{2} \cos(2\omega_1 t + \omega_1 \tau) + \frac{A^2}{2} \cos(\omega_1 \tau) \quad (2.27)$$

For a fixed value of the parameter τ, the first term on the right of Eq. (2.27) oscillates in time t at $2\omega_1$ and has constant phase angle $\omega_1 \tau$—it is a sinusoid, while the second term does not depend on time t—it is a constant. By defining $r(\tau)$ as the time average of the product,

$$r(\tau) = \lim_{T \to \infty} \frac{1}{T} \int_{-T/2}^{T/2} f(t)f(t + \tau) \, dt \quad (2.28)$$

and inserting Eq. (2.27) into Eq. (2.28), the sinusoid at $2\omega_1$ with fixed phase integrates to zero for every choice of τ, and the second term contributes to yield

$$r(\tau) = \frac{A^2}{2} \cos(\omega_1 \tau) \quad (2.29)$$

The coefficient $A^2/2$ equals the power of $f(t) = A \cos(\omega_1 t)$, and the function $r(\tau)$ oscillates at the same frequency ω_1 but as a function of τ rather than t. Because $f(t)$ generally would contain a multitude of different frequencies, it is worthwhile to examine the spectral properties of $r(\tau)$. The Fourier transform of $r(\tau)$ in Eq. (2.28), using the variable τ instead of t in Eq. (2.21), is

$$P(\omega) = \int_{-\infty}^{\infty} r(\tau)e^{-j\omega\tau} \, d\tau \quad (2.30)$$

and defined as the *power spectrum* or *power spectral density* of the finite-power signal $f(t)$. In Eq. (2.28), $r(\tau)$ is called the *autocorrelation function* of $f(t)$, and its value for $\tau = 0$ is the average power of $f(t)$ as defined in Eq. (2.2). The autocorrelation function also equals the inverse Fourier transform of the power spectral density, which, from Eq. (2.22), is

$$r(\tau) = \frac{1}{2\pi} \int_{-\infty}^{\infty} P(\omega)e^{j\omega\tau} \, d\omega \quad (2.31)$$

Similarly to Eqs. (2.25) and (2.26) for spectral density, the power spectral density associated with Eq. (2.29) would consist of delta functions of strength $2\pi(A^2/4)$ at frequencies $\pm\omega_1$.

Equations (2.28) and (2.30) are very useful when spectral properties of a nondeterministic, finite-power signal $f(t) = n(t)$, arising, say, from a noise process, are studied. By definition, no functional relationship exists between $n(t)$ and t. The signal has finite average power but does not, in general, consist of pure sinusoids at fixed frequencies with constant phase that are representable by line spectra. Therefore, Fourier-analysis methods are not directly applicable. Normally, the autocorrelation function $r(\tau)$ in Eq. (2.28) is a finite-energy signal which first can be estimated from a sufficient number of samples of $f(t)$, then Fourier-transformed as in Eq. (2.30). The result is a power spectral density as a function of continuous frequency. The autocorrelation function contains oscillations at all the frequencies contained in $f(t)$ with amplitudes equal to their respective powers, as illustrated by Eq. (2.29) for a single frequency ω_1, and the power spectral density integral defined in Eq. (2.30) extracts, via Fourier transformation, the distribution of power in frequency $P(\omega)$ of the underlying noise process. The power spectra density has zero phase because $r(\tau)$ is always an even function of τ.

White noise is a term used to characterize a noise process whose *power* spectral density is constant or flat as a function of frequency. In contrast to an impulse, whose *amplitude* spectral density is flat and is interpreted as a sum of cosine waves of all frequencies each with identically zero phase, the phases of the similar cosine waves in white noise would vary randomly in time. The former is a finite-energy signal existing for one instant in time and the latter a finite-power signal existing for all time; both have continuous, flat spectra.

2.2.9 Analytic Signal

The actual waveshapes of certain signals, viewed in the time domain, appear to have identifiable amplitude-modulation (AM) and frequency-modulation (FM) effects that may vary as time progresses. This is not easily recognized in the signal's spectrum unless the modulation and signal to be modulated are simple, such as that generated by AM or FM between two sinusoids. The *analytic signal* is one procedure used to define AM or FM effects and extract quantitative information about them from the spectrum of $f(t)$. The analytic signal $f_A(t)$ is a linear transformation of the signal $f(t)$ which also has an interesting spectral interpretation.

Consider the signal

$$f(t) = \cos (\omega t) \tag{2.32}$$
$$= \tfrac{1}{2}(e^{j\omega t} + e^{-j\omega t})$$

and from it form a second signal $\hat{f}(t)$ by leading the phase of $e^{j\omega t}$ by 90° and leading the phase of $e^{-j\omega t}$ by 90°, which corresponds to multiplication by j and $-j$, respectively. The second signal is, by using Eq. (2.5c),

$$\hat{f}(t) = \tfrac{1}{2}(je^{j\omega t} - je^{-j\omega t}) \tag{2.33}$$
$$= - \sin (\omega t)$$

The analytic signal associated with $f(t)$ is defined as [see Eq. (2.4)],

$$f_A(t) = f(t) - j\hat{f}(t) \tag{2.34}$$
$$= e^{j\omega t}$$

The analytic signal is a complex function of time, and its (line) spectrum contains no negative-frequency components. Figure 2.6 illustrates, with phasors, the successive operations in forming the analytic signal for $\cos (\omega t)$.

The amplitude or *envelope* $E(t)$ and phase $\theta(t)$ of the analytic signal are defined by

$$E(t)e^{j\theta(t)} = f(t) - j\hat{f}(t) \tag{2.35}$$

so that, in terms of $f(t)$ and $\hat{f}^2(t)$, *they are*

$$E(t) = \sqrt{f^2(t) + \hat{f}^2(t)} \tag{2.36a}$$

$$\theta(t) = \arctan\,[-\hat{f}(t)/f(t)] \tag{2.36b}$$

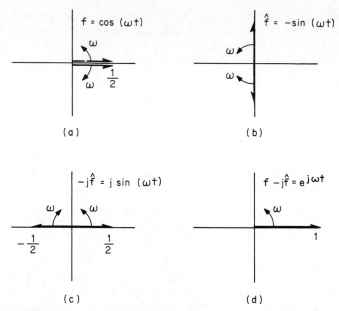

FIG. 2.6 Formation of analytic signal $e^{j\omega t}$ of cos (ωt). (a) Counterrotating phasors representing $f = $ cos (ωt). (b) $\hat{f}$, the Hilbert transform of f. (c) $-j$ times each phasor in b. (d) Analytic signal given by sum of phasors in a and c.

and, from Eq. (2.36b), the *instantaneous frequency* is defined as

$$\omega_i(t) = \frac{d\theta(t)}{dt} \tag{2.37}$$

In the example $f(t) = $ cos (ωt), the amplitude and instantaneous frequency of the associated analytic signal are 1 and ω, respectively.

While the analytic signal is a linear transformation of the signal that, in effect, converts negative-frequency components in the spectrum of $f(t)$ to positive-frequency components, the envelope $E(t)$ and instantaneous frequency $\omega_i(t)$ are nonlinear functions of $f(t)$ and $\hat{f}(t)$. For more complicated signals, $\omega_i(t)$ is, in general, not the same as ω in the spectrum.

The spectral operation of advancing the phases of all positive-frequency components by 90° and advancing the phases of all negative-frequency components by 90° is called *Hilbert transformation;* that is, $\hat{f}(t)$ is the Hilbert transform of $f(t)$.

2.3 SPECTRAL CHANGES AND LINEAR DISTORTION

2.3.1 Signal Distortion

When a reproduced signal is not a replica of the original signal, it is *distorted*. Distortionless transmission of a time-varying signal through a system requires that the signal's shape be preserved. The two general mechanisms of signal distortion are *nonlinear* and *linear*.

In a broad context, *nonlinear distortion* includes all forms of output-signal corruption that are not linearly related to (i.e., statistically linearly dependent on or correlated with) the input signal. *Modulation* (amplitude or frequency) of the signal (or even its time derivatives) by an imperfect system produces a certain amount of up conversion and down conversion of the signal's frequency components. For example, squaring or cubing of the signal resulting from a nonlinear transfer characteristic is a form of (self) amplitude modulation, whereas time-base errors, like speed variations, are equivalent to frequency modulation of the signal. These converted frequencies, like noise, are not linearly related to the input. The coherence function $\gamma^2(\omega)$ is a quantitative measure of the cumulative effect, at each frequency, of these various forms of signal corruption (see Bibliography).

Linear distortion implies that even though the output signal is linearly related to the input, the shape of the output signal is different from that of the input signal. The system itself is linear and does process signals linearly (i.e., scale factors are preserved, and superposition is valid), but linear mathematical operations on the input signal such as differentiation or integration are permissible. Linear distortion changes the *relative* relationships among the existing constituents of the signal by altering either intensity or timing, or both, of its different frequency components. As a consequence, the output signal has a different shape. The system function (or complex frequency response) only predicts the spectral changes that the spectrum of the input signal will undergo and not the change of signal shape in time. The actual time-domain signal must be computed from direct convolution or inverse Fourier transformation.

When a single sinusoid is used as an input to a linear system, the corresponding steady-state output is also a sinusoid of the same frequency but, generally, with different amplitude and phase as prescribed by the complex frequency response. This single sinusoid is never linearly distorted because it always is a replica of the input. In contrast, if the frequency content of the input signal is discrete (e.g., a square wave) or continuous (e.g., a single rectangular pulse), then linear distortion is observable as waveshape change. The extent to which an input signal will be linearly distorted depends on both its spectrum and the system function or complex frequency response of the linear system that processes it. Linear distortion encompasses what is sometimes called *transient distortion,* meaning the waveshape change of a finite-energy (transient) input signal (e.g., a short tone burst or pulse) under linear operating conditions. Finite-power input signals such as square waves, random noise, music, or speech also can be linearly distorted, however. Nonlinear effects such as clipping or slew-rate limiting of transient signals are a form of nonlinear distortion, which implies that transient distortion can be ambiguous terminology.

In summary, linear distortion changes the magnitude and/or phase of the input signal's spectrum. As a consequence, signal waveform fidelity is impaired.

The range of linear operation of a system is usually established with sine-wave signals. The most frequently used procedure is to verify, using a single sine-wave input, whether the magnitude-scale factor is preserved as input amplitude is changed and/or to verify, using two sinusoids of different frequency simultaneously as an input, whether superposition is valid. Both procedures examine the linearity hypothesis under sinusoidal, steady-state operating conditions. Because the input spectrum is as narrow as possible (a line spectrum consisting of one or two discrete frequencies), the spectrum of the output can easily reveal the existence of other, or "new," frequencies which would constitute nonlinear distortion corresponding to the chosen input signal. The ratio of total power contained in these other frequencies to the output power at the input frequency (or frequencies), expressed in percentage or decibels, is often used as both a measure and a specification of nonlinear distortion (e.g., harmonic distortion, intermodulation distortion, or so-called dynamic intermodulation distortion, depending on the specific choice of input frequencies). This method of testing linearity is relatively simple and can be very sensitive. With modern, wide-dynamic-range, high-resolution spectrum analyzers and high-purity sine-wave generators, the effects of very small amounts of nonlinearity can be measured for sinusoidal steady-state operation. Some aspects of this kind of spectral analysis are questionable, however. Incoherent (uncorrelated) power can exist at the test frequency itself (e.g., due to cubic nonlinearity, time-base errors, noise), and, even more important, the system is never excited throughout its full operating bandwidth by the test signal. Because nonlinear effects do not superpose, the percentage of sine-wave nonlinear distortion measured, say, as a function of test-signal frequency for fixed-output-power level, is not the same as the percentage of uncorrelated output power as a function of frequency for broadband operation with nonsinusoidal input signals. The latter can be expressed by using the coherence function to define a frequency-dependent signal-to-noise ratio as the ratio of coherent power to incoherent power, expressed in percentage or decibels (see Bibliography).

Comparison of input and output spectra of a system is worthwhile. Spectral changes can indicate, in the frequency domain, the existence of linear distortion as well as nonlinear distortion. For linear operation, the spectral changes that any input signal undergoes are predicted by the system function or complex frequency response. For nonlinear operation, the portion of the output signal's spectrum not linearly related to the input signal depends, in detail, on each specific input signal and how it is nonlinearly processed by the system.

2.3.2   Sinusoidal Steady-State Measurements

The complex frequency response or system function

$$H(\omega) = |H(\omega)| e^{j\phi(\omega)} \tag{2.38}$$

of a linear system predicts the *magnitude* (or amplitude) $|H(\omega)|$ and *phase* $\phi(\omega)$ of an output sinusoid relative to an input sinusoid for steady-state operation at the frequency ω. These two frequency-domain quantities are fundamental and form the basis for the dicussion of linear distortion of signals by a linear system.

The meaning of the magnitude response of a system is well understood and often displayed alone as *the* frequency response even though it is only the magnitude of $H(\omega)$. The phase-shift-$\phi(\omega)$-versus-frequency characteristic is not commonly shown but is equally important. Some conventions, definitions, and properties of phase shift and the phase-shift characteristic merit discussion.

Figure 2.7 illustrates the convention for phase lead or lag between sinusoids of the same frequency relative to a reference. The reference sinusoid (solid line) has an upward-sloping zero crossing at zero time, and that leading (short dashes) has its corresponding zero crossing at an earlier time or is advanced in time, whereas that lagging (long dashes) has its corresponding zero crossing at a later time or is delayed in time.

Aside from this convention, Fig. 2.7 has two ambiguities and raises a fundamental question about the nature of phase shift itself. First, a phase lead of π is indistinguishable from a phase lag of π; also shifting any of these sinusoids by a multiple of $\pm 2\pi$ would not change the relative phase shifts, and consequently Fig. 2.7 would not change. Thus more information than Fig. 2.7 shows is required to

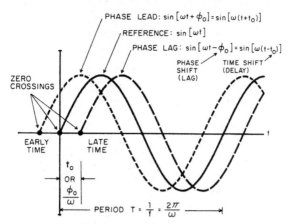

FIG. 2.7 Standard conventions for sinusoids having steady-state phase shifts relative to a reference sinusoid (solid curve). The leading sinusoid (short dashes) has its first zero crossing at an earlier time than the reference, whereas the lagging sinusoid (long dashes) has its first zero crossing at a later time. Note that the time shift $t_0 = \phi_0/\omega$ (the time shift depends upon both phase shift and frequency); therefore, if ϕ_0 is proportional to ω (varies linearly with ω), the time shift would be the same for sinusoids of any frequency.

avoid ambiguity. Second, it appears that a phase shift and a time shift are equivalent, but they are not. This is so because $\phi_0 = \omega t_0$ and for a specific phase shift ϕ_0 the corresponding amount of time shift depends upon the sinusoid's frequency ω. To illustrate this point consider Fig. 2.8a, wherein an approximate square wave is constructed from the first three nonzero harmonics of its Fourier series. Figures 2.8b and c show the difference between a constant phase shift for each harmonic and a constant time delay for each harmonic, respectively. The waveform of Fig. 2.8b is severely linearly distorted, whereas that in Fig. 2.8c is not. It is interesting to note that the amount of phase lag necessary to keep the waveform "together" is directly proportional to frequency (that is, the first, third, and fifth harmonics were lagged by $\pi/2$, $3\pi/2$, and $5\pi/2$, respectively). Therefore, in Fig. 2.8c the amount of phase lag varies linearly with frequency, and this corresponds to a uniform time delay.

The fundamental question raised by Fig. 2.7 is related to causality (i.e., cause and effect). How is it possible for a signal to be "ahead" of the reference signal in time, especially if the reference signal is the input or stimulus to a system and the phase shift of the output signal relative to the input is measured? Equivalently stated, how can the output-signal phase lead or be ahead of the input signal in time? Does this suggest that causality would permit only phase lags to occur in such a situation? It is indeed an interesting question in view of the fact that phase-shift measurements themselves can be somewhat ambiguous. The answer has to do with the fact that these are steady-state measurements, or more precisely, with how the steady state itself is achieved. Both phase lead or phase lag of a system output relative to its input are physically realizable without ambiguity or violation of causality. An example of each case is shown in Fig. 2.9. Here the actual response of two different circuits to a tone-burst input was photographed. In each

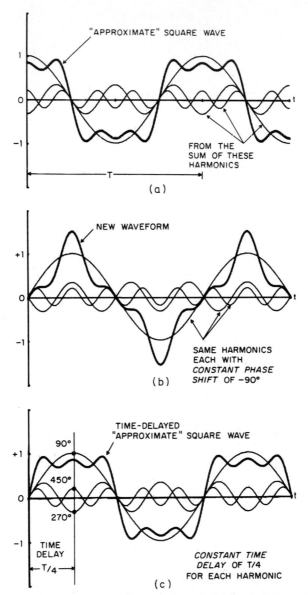

FIG. 2.8 (*a*) An approximate square wave constructed from the first three (nonzero) Fourier harmonics. (*b*) Constant phase shift for each harmonic yields a new waveform which is linearly distorted. (*c*) Constant time delay for each harmonic uniformly delays the square wave while preserving its shape. The first, third, and fifth harmonics are phase-lagged by $\pi/2$, $3\pi/2$, and $5\pi/2$ rad, respectively (i.e., the phase lag varies linearly with frequency as shown).

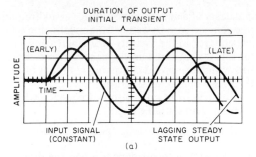

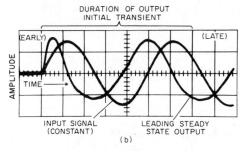

FIG. 2.9 Steady-state phase lag or lead is established only after an initial transient period. (*a*) A phase lag of about 90° occurs, and the output signal is approximately the *integral* with respect to time of the input. (*b*) A phase lead of 90° occurs, and the output is nearly the time *derivative* of the input. The input sinusoid is the same in each case. The transient buildup of phase lag or lead illustrates that the phase shift of a system is remarkably a property of the steady state.

case the input signal is also shown in time synchronization for reference purposes. It is during the initial transient state that either a phase lag or a phase lead is established. Note that in each case the output zero crossings are initially unequally spaced and that net phase lag or lead is gradually accumulated. Closer inspection of Fig. 2.9 reveals that, from a mathematical viewpoint, the output in Fig. 2.9*a* is approximately the integral with respect to time of the input, whereas in Fig. 2.9*b* the output is nearly the derivative with respect to time of the input. In the steady state the corresponding phase shifts are seen to be about $-\pi/2$ and $+\pi/2$, respectively. Circuits which have these properties are referred to as phase lag (integrators) or phase lead (differentiators). Another way of interpreting the results of Fig. 2.9 then (referring also to Fig. 2.7) is to note that the integral with respect to time of $\sin(\omega t)$ is $-1/\omega \cos(\omega t)$ or $1/\omega \sin(\omega t - \pi/2)$, whereas the time derivative of $\sin(\omega t)$ is $\omega \cos(\omega t)$ or $\omega \sin(\omega t + \pi/2)$, so that here the steady-state phase lag or lead of $\pi/2$ in the frequency domain corresponds to integration or differentiation, respectively, in the time domain. Some circuits possessing properties quite similar to these and encountered in practice are called *tone controls*.

An important conclusion to be drawn from Fig. 2.9 is that the phase shift of a system is remarkably a property of the steady state.

Two significant aspects of a general phase-shift-versus-frequency characteristic $\phi(\omega)$ at a specific frequency ω_0 are its actual numerical value $\phi(\omega_0)$ (positive, zero, or negative) and its behavior in the vicinity of ω_0 (increasing, constant, or decreasing). The reason for this is that most useful signals passed through a system have finite spectral widths which are broad compared with that of any single frequency used to measure the phase characteristic itself.

The value of the phase shift at an arbitrary frequency which is close to a specific frequency ω_0 can be represented by

$$\phi(\omega) \cong \phi(\omega_0) + \text{correction terms} \tag{2.39}$$

and in Eq. (2.39) the correction terms depend upon the difference $\Delta\omega = \omega - \omega_0$. To a first approximation and with reference to Fig. 2.10,

$$\phi(\omega) \cong \phi(\omega_0) + \Delta\phi \tag{2.40a}$$

$$\cong \phi(\omega_0) + \frac{\Delta\phi}{\Delta\omega} \Delta\omega \tag{2.40b}$$

$$\cong \phi(\omega_0) + \left(\frac{d\phi}{d\omega}\right)_{\omega_0} [\omega - \omega_0] \tag{2.40c}$$

where $(d\phi/d\omega)_{\omega_0}$ is the derivative of the phase shift at ω_0 or, equivalently, its slope there. If $\omega = \omega_0$, Eq. (2.40) is exact, and when ω is near ω_0, it is, in general, approximate. In this approximation it is the slope or first derivative of the phase characteristic at ω_0 that describes the behavior of $\phi(\omega)$ near ω_0. Thus for signals whose spectra lie in the neighborhood of ω_0 both $\phi(\omega_0)$ and $(d\phi/d\omega)_{\omega_0}$ are important because $\phi(\omega_0)$ gives the steady-state absolute phase shift of the output relative to

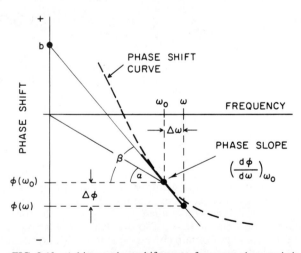

FIG. 2.10 Arbitrary phase-shift-versus-frequency characteristic (long dashes). For frequencies ω near ω_0 the slope of the phase-shift curve is nearly constant and can be approximated by the derivative $d\phi/d\omega$ evaluated at ω_0. The numerical value of the phase slope (or derivative) indicates how the phase shift varies near ω_0.

the input at ω_0, whereas $(d\phi/d\omega)_{\omega_0}[\omega - \omega_0]$ expresses the phase shift at ω relative to that at ω_0.

Because no restrictions have been placed upon the behavior of $\phi(\omega)$ or its derivative, each may assume positive, zero, or negative values throughout the frequency range of interest. There are, therefore, several different possible combination pairs of phase shift and phase slope. Each of these presumably would affect the response to a transient signal differently. A preliminary discussion of the influence of these aspects of phase response on transient signals is given in the next section together with supporting experimental measurements.

2.3.3 Some Effects of Frequency Response on Transient Signals

An important class of linear systems used in audio applications, called *minimum-phase* systems, has mathematically interrelated magnitude and phase responses. The exact mathematical relationship is given later in Eq. (2.48). These responses are not independent of one another. Specifying one determines the other.

Figure 2.11 summarizes the possible relationships between magnitude response, phase shift, and phase slope versus linear frequency for a general minimum-phase system. For example, a narrow bandpass system could have a magnitude response characteristic like that from 5–6–4–3–1, and the associated phase-shift and phase-slope characteristics would be the corresponding portions

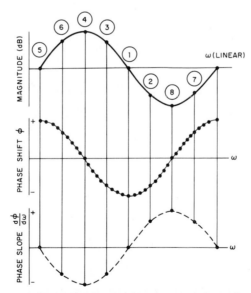

FIG. 2.11 Possible relationships among magnitude, phase, and phase slope versus linear frequency for a general minimum-phase system. The numbered vertical-line segments each connect a different combination of these three quantities (based on algebraic signs) and indicate important test frequency ranges where transient response may differ.

of those curves below. In a very wideband system the distance between points 5 and 1 on the frequency axis would be considerably greater and the curve 6–4–3 much flatter; also the corresponding sections of the phase and phase-slope curves would require appropriate modification. In a similar way, 1–2–8–7 could represent the magnitude response for a narrowband-reject filter which would have the appropriately corresponding phase and phase-slope curves as shown.

The steady-state characteristics of the minimum-phase system shown in Fig. 2.11 are also interconnected by eight numbered vertical lines. These numbers indicate important test points (or frequency ranges) where phase shift and phase slope are, in various combinations, positive, zero, and negative. Experimentally measured effects of each of these eight different combinations of $\phi(\omega)$ and $d\phi/d\omega$ on three different transient signals, illustrated along with their spectra in Fig. 2.12, are shown in Fig. 2.13. The three test signals were a 1-ms-wide rectangular pulse, a single cycle of a 1-kHz sine wave, and a 7-ms tone burst at 1 kHz.

The eight different combinations of phase shift and phase slope in Fig. 2.11 were simulated, in each case, near 1 kHz by using a five-band graphic equalizer as the minimum-phase system. In each of these eight cases, the linear distortion of transient signals is quite different. Here, the influence of complex frequency response on the system response to transient signals can be explained, qualitatively, in terms of the algebraic signs of phase shift and phase slope. Table 2.1 categorizes the eight test cases on this basis. Tables 2.2 and 2.3 summarize some

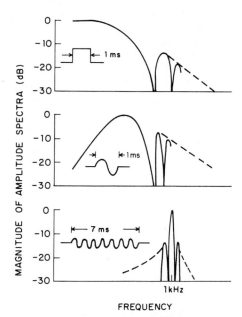

FIG. 2.12 Magnitude of the spectral density in decibels versus frequency for test signals used to evaluate the response of a general minimum-phase system to transient signals. The dashed lines indicate the upper bound for the continuing spectral peaks.

general effects which the algebraic sign of the phase shift and the phase slope (at 1 kHz) has on response to transient signals.

For the tone bursts it appears that the actual numerical value of ϕ influences the "inner" structure of the waveform, whereas $d\phi/d\omega$ mostly affects the envelope,

TABLE 2.1

		$\dfrac{d\phi}{d\omega}$ at 1 kHz	
	$+$	0	$-$
$+$	7	5	6
ϕ at 1 kHz $\quad 0$	8	*	4
$-$	2	1	3

or "outer" structure. This is consistent with the approximation in Eq. (2.40c): $\phi(\omega) = \phi(\omega_0) + (d\phi/d\omega)_{\omega_0}[\omega - \omega_0]$ with $\omega_0/2\pi = 1$ kHz.

Positive values for both ϕ and $d\phi/d\omega$ imply that ϕ is positive and increasing near ω_0, and this results in sharp and abrupt transient behavior. If ϕ and $d\phi/d\omega$

TABLE 2.2

ϕ (phase shift)	Effect
$+$	Totally or partially differentiates waveform Phase lead within first few cycles Cusplike transients
0	No phase shift at 1 kHz Tone-burst envelope shape subject to change
$-$	Totally or partially integrates waveform Phase lag within first few cycles Smooth transients

TABLE 2.3

$\dfrac{d\phi}{d\omega}$ (phase slope)	Effect
$+$	Very rapid tone-burst buildup Overshoot Some long decays
0	Little or no effect Mostly differentiation or integration due to $\phi \lessgtr 0$
$-$	Slower tone-burst buildup Slight elongation of tone burst Smooth decays

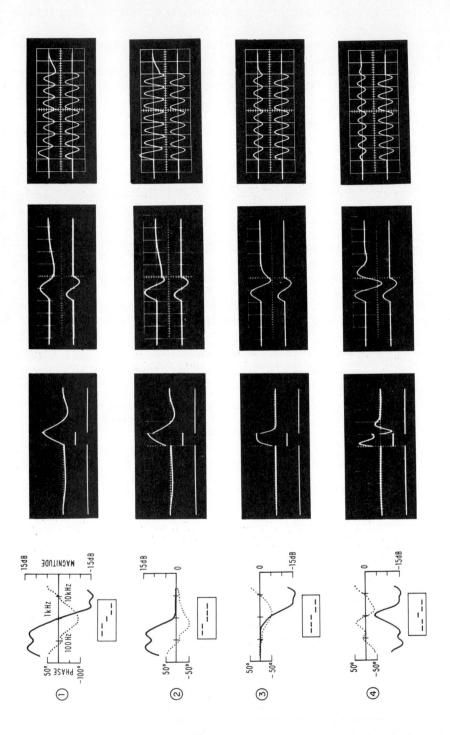

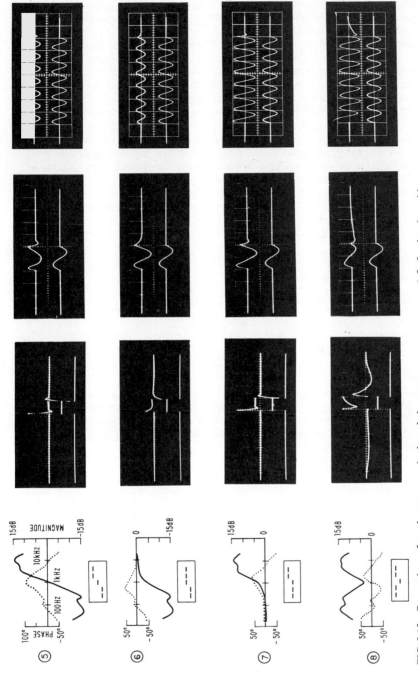

FIG. 2.13 Comparison of steady-state magnitude and phase response measurements (of a five-band graphic equalizer) with responses to the transient signals whose spectra are given in Fig. 2.12. These eight cases correspond to the eight test points for the minimum-phase system in Fig. 2.11 normalized to a frequency range near and about 1 kHz. (System output and input signals are shown in the upper and lower traces, respectively.)

are both negative, then ϕ is becoming more negative, and this yields smoother, slower transients. When the phase shift and phase slope have opposite signs, these opposing effects are seen to combine.

Perhaps the most interesting case occurs when $\phi(\omega_0) = 0$ but $[d\phi/d\omega]_{\omega_0} \neq 0$ (see Fig. 2.13, cases 4 and 8). For the very-narrow-spectrum tone burst there is no steady-state phase shift as expected; however, the response to the wide-spectrum rectangular pulse in these two cases is remarkable. These results may be interpreted in the following way. Because the rectangular pulse has a considerably wider spectrum than the tone burst, it has many spectral components both above and below $\omega_0/2\pi = 1$ kHz. In case 8 $[d\phi/d\omega]_{\omega_0} > 0$ and from the approximation (2.40c), $\phi(\omega) = [d\phi/d\omega]_{\omega_0}(\omega - \omega_0)$, so that for $\omega > \omega_0$, $\phi(\omega)$ is positive, whereas for $\omega < \omega_0$, $\phi(\omega)$ is negative. Therefore, and in simple terms, higher frequencies tend to be differentiated in time, whereas lower ones are integrated. This is seen to occur. Just the opposite occurs in case 4 because $[d\phi/d\omega]_{\omega_0} < 0$.

From the foregoing examples it is clear that the response of a system to transient signals depends on its frequency response. For minimum-phase systems, the phase and derivative of phase with respect to frequency can be used to interpret, qualitatively, important aspects of linear distortion of signals in the time domain.

2.3.4 Phase Delay and Group Delay

Phase delay and group delay are useful quantities related to the phase shift $\phi(\omega)$ and defined as

$$\tau_p(\omega) = -\phi(\omega)/\omega, \tag{2.41}$$

and

$$\tau_g(\omega) = -\frac{d\phi(\omega)}{d\omega} \tag{2.42}$$

respectively. The negative signs are required because, according to the conventions for sinusoids in Fig. 2.7, negative values of phase shift correspond to positive time delays. At a specific frequency ω_0, these two quantities are constants in the two-term Taylor-series expansion of $\phi(\omega)$ Eq. (2.40c), valid near and at ω_0, which can be rewritten as

$$\phi(\omega) \cong -\omega_0\tau_p(\omega_0) - \tau_g(\omega_0)[\omega - \omega_0] \tag{2.43}$$

Equation (2.43) restates the fact that the phase shift at ω is equal to the phase shift at ω_0 plus the phase shift at ω relative to ω_0. The steady-state phase shift for the components of a narrowband signal near ω_0 is given by Eq. (2.43), and the effect of the two terms in this equation can be interpreted in the following way. First, each component in the band undergoes a fixed phase shift $-\omega_0\tau_p(\omega_0) = \phi(\omega_0)$, then those components at frequencies different from ω_0 are subjected to additional phase shift $-\tau_g(\omega_0)[\omega - \omega_0]$. This additional phase shift is one which varies linearly with frequency, so it does not alter the waveshape (see Fig. 2.8).

An amplitude-modulated (AM) sinusoid is a narrowband signal, and the effects of phase delay and group delay on such a signal are illustrated in Fig. 2.14. Phase delay phase-lags (delays) the high-frequency carrier (inner structure), while the envelope (outer structure) is delayed by an amount equal to the group delay.

Geometrically, Fig. 2.10 shows that $\tau_g(\omega_0) = \tan \beta$ and $\tau_p(\omega_0) = \tan \alpha$. Note that $\tau_g = \tau_p$ only when $\alpha = \beta$ and the intercept $b = 0$. In this special case $\phi(0) = 0$ and $\phi(\omega)$ varies linearly as a function of ω (that is, the entire phase-shift characteristic is a straight line which passes through the origin having slope $-\tau_g$).

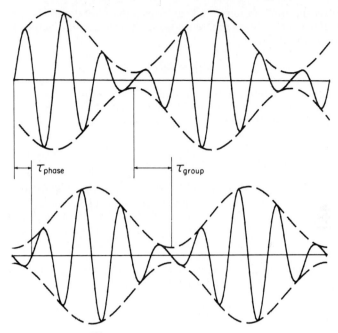

FIG. 2.14 The difference between phase delay τ_{phase} and group delay τ_{group} is illustrated by comparing these two amplitude-modulated waveforms. The lower waveform has positive phase delay and positive group delay relative to the upper waveform. Because the envelope of the high-frequency oscillations is delayed by an amount of time τ_{group} group delay is sometimes referred to as envelope delay.

Generally both τ_p and τ_g can assume positive, zero, or negative values depending upon the detailed behavior of the phase-shift characteristic. Referring to the special minimum-phase system in Fig. 2.11 and in view of definition (2.42), the group-delay characteristic is the negative of the phase slope, and therefore its shape is the same as the magnitude characteristic for this special case. It is also interesting to note from the same figure that for the bandpass system 5–6–4–3–1, $\tau_p(\omega) = -\phi(\omega)/\omega$ can be positive, negative, or zero, but $\tau_g(\omega) = -d\phi/d\omega \geq 0$. For the system 1–2–8–7, $\tau_g(\omega) \leq 0$.

The approximate nature of Eq. (2.43) deserves particular emphasis because either is valid only over a narrow range of frequencies $\Delta\omega$, and outside this range the correction terms mentioned in Eq. (2.39) contain higher-order derivatives in the Taylor series that generally cannot be neglected.

2.3.5 Distortionless Processing of Signals

In the time domain the requirement for *distortionless* linear signal processing (i.e., no waveshape change) is that the system's impulse response $h(t)$ have the form

$$h(t) = K\delta(t - T), \tag{2.44a}$$

where $\delta(t)$ is the unit impulse, and the constants $K > 0$ and $T \geq 0$. Equation (2.44a) and the convolution theorem together imply that the output signal $g(t)$ is related to the input $f(t)$ by

$$g(t) = Kf(t - T) \qquad (2.44b)$$

The distortionless system scales any input signal by a constant factor K and delays the signal as a whole by T seconds. The output is a delayed replica of the input. Substituting Eq. (2.44b) into Eq. (2.21) gives the corresponding restrictions on the frequency response, namely,

$$H(\omega) = Ke^{-j\omega T} \qquad (2.45)$$

Comparison of Eq. (2.45) with Eq. (2.38) indicates that the frequency-domain requirements are twofold: constant magnitude response $|H(\omega)| = K$ and phase response proportional to frequency $\phi(\omega) = -\omega T$. Waveform distortion or *linear distortion* is caused by deviations of $|H(\omega)|$ from a constant value K as well as departures of $\phi(\omega)$ from the linearly decreasing characteristic $-\omega T$. The former is called *amplitude distortion* and the latter *phase distortion*. From Eq. (2.45) absence of phase distortion requires that the phase and group delays in Eqs. (2.41) and (2.42) each equal the overall time delay $T \geq 0$,

$$\tau_p(\omega) = \tau_g(\omega) = T \qquad (2.46)$$

Some experimentally measured effects of the deviations of $|H(\omega)|$ and $\tau_g(\omega)$ from a constant value are illustrated in Fig. 2.15. In the experiment four bandpass filters were connected in cascade to give the attenuation magnitude (reciprocal of gain magnitude) and group-delay characteristics shown in Fig. 2.15a. The group delay is reasonably flat at midband, having a minimum value there of $\tau_g = 10.9$ ms. Near and at the passband edges τ_g deviates considerably from its minimum value. The effects in the time domain are shown in Fig. 2.15b. Here tone bursts at frequencies of 260, 300, 480, and 680 Hz were applied to the filter, and both input and output oscillographs were obtained. In each of these cases the oscillations start to build up after a time equal to the minimum value of τ_g. There is significant linear distortion for the tone bursts whose spectra lie at the passband edges. Some of this distortion can be ascribed to nonconstant attenuation, but the waveform elongation is primarily due to the group delay $\tau_g(\omega)$ deviating from its minimum value.

These experimental results indicate that, for distortionless processing of signals, the band of frequencies throughout which both magnitude response and group delay of the system are constant or flat is important *relative* to the spectral bandwidth of signals to be processed by the system.

2.3.6 Linear Phase and Minimum Phase

The impulse response of a (distortionless) unity-gain, *linear-phase,* band-limited (low-pass) system is symmetrical in time about its central peak value and described mathematically by

$$h(t) = \frac{\sin(\omega_c t)}{\pi t} \qquad (2.47)$$

where $\omega_c/2\pi = f_c$ is the cutoff frequency in hertz. The magnitude response is $|H(\omega)| = 1$, and the phase response $\phi(\omega) = 0$ (a special case of linear phase). This result, derived from Eq. (2.22) by using finite integration limits $\pm \omega_c$ can be interpreted, like the unit impulse $\delta(t)$ in Eq. (2.23), as a cophase superposition of cosine waves but up to the frequency ω_c only. In general, the group delay for such a linear-phase system is constant but otherwise arbitrary; that is, $\tau_g(\omega) = T$ s because the phase shift $\phi(\omega) = -\omega T$ is linear but can have arbitrary slope. Figure 2.16*b* illustrates $h(t)$ in Eq. (2.47) delayed, shifted to the right in time, so that its peak value occurs at, say, a positive time $t = T$ rather than $t = 0$. Regardless of the value of T, the impulse response is not causal; that is, it will have finite values for negative time. So if an impulse excitation $\delta(t)$ were applied to the system when $t = 0$, the response to that impulse would exist for negative time. Such *anticipatory transients* violate cause (stimulus) and effect (response). In practice, a causal approximation to the ideal $h(t)$ in Eq. (2.47) is realized by introducing sufficient delay T and truncating or "windowing" the response so that it is zero for negative time. This latter process would produce ripples in the magnitude response, however. Also shown in Fig. 2.16 are the corresponding magnitude response (*a*) and step response (*c*), which is the integral with respect to time of $h(t)$. In principle, this ideal system would not linearly distort signals whose spectra are zero for $\omega > \omega_c$. In practice, only approximations to this ideal response are realizable.

A minimum-phase system is causal and has the least amount of phase shift possible corresponding to its specific magnitude response $|H(\omega)|$. The phase is given by the (Hilbert-transform) relationship

$$\phi_m(\omega) = \frac{1}{\pi} \int_{-\infty}^{\infty} \frac{\ln |H(\omega')|}{\omega' - \omega} \, d\omega' \qquad (2.48)$$

and the minimum-phase group delay associated with Eq. (2.48) is

$$\tau_{gm}(\omega) = -\frac{d\phi_m(\omega)}{d\omega} \qquad (2.49)$$

While minimum-phase systems have impulse responses that are zero for negative time (causal), they are not distortionless. Because magnitude and phase responses are interrelated, the linear distortion they introduce can often be interpreted by using group delay [Eq. (2.49)].

In contrast to the preceding example, consider approximations to band limiting using realizable minimum-phase, maximally flat, low-pass systems of successively higher order. The frequency-domain and time-domain responses for three-, six-, and nine-pole systems are plotted in normalized form in Fig. 2.17. Here the impulse responses are causal but not symmetrical. The loss of symmetry is due to group-delay distortion. The group delay changes as frequency increases, and this implies that phase shift is not proportional to frequency, especially near the cutoff frequency f_c. In this example, deviations of τ_g from its low-frequency value are a measure of group-delay distortion. Note that the maximum deviation of τ_g, indicated by the length of the solid vertical bars in Fig. 2.17*b*, is quantitatively related to the broadening of the impulse response, while the low-frequency value of τ_g predicts the arrival time of the main portion of the impulse response, as indicated by the position and length of the corresponding solid horizontal bars in Fig. 2.17*c*. Actually, the low-frequency value of τ_g equals the time delay of the center of gravity of the impulse response. By increasing the rate of attenuation above f_c, the overall delay of the impulse response increases, initial buildup is

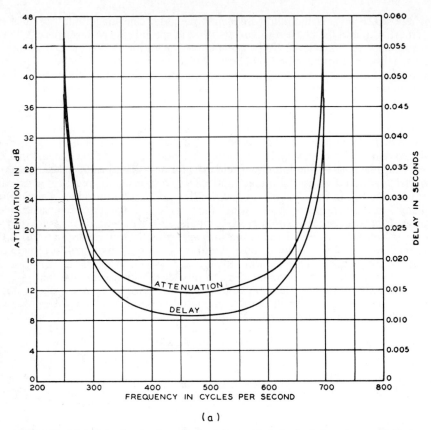

(a)

FIG. 2.15　(a) Attenuation (reciprocal of gain) magnitude in decibels and group delay in seconds versus frequency characteristics of four cascaded bandpass filters. (b) Experimentally measured responses to transient input signal (tone burst) of filtering network whose steady-state characteristics are shown in a. For this bandpass system each output signal is delayed by the minimum value of the group delay. When the tone-burst spectrum lies near either passband edge, significant amounts of linear distortion occur in the form of waveform elongation. This is due, for the most part, to the departure of the group-delay characteristic from its flat value in the midband and is called group-delay distortion.

slower, ringing is more pronounced, and the response becomes more dispersed and less symmetrical in time.

The minimum-phase group delay $\tau_{gm}(\omega)$ can be evaluated, in theory, for an arbitrary magnitude response $|H(\omega)|$ by using Eqs. (2.48) and (2.49). Consider, for example, an interesting limiting case of the previous maximally flat low-pass system where an ideal "brick wall" magnitude response is assumed, as shown in Fig. 2.18. Here the system has unity gain below the cutoff ω_c, and A dB of attenuation above ω_c. The normalized frequency $\Omega = \omega/\omega_c$. Although this magnitude response cannot be realized exactly, it could be approximated closely with an elliptic filter. The group delay is

$$\tau_g(\Omega) = \frac{T_0}{1 - \Omega^2} \qquad (2.50)$$

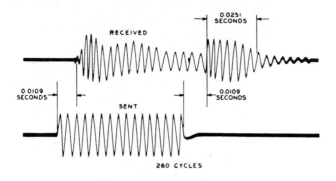

260 CYCLES

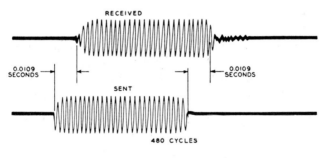

300 CYCLES

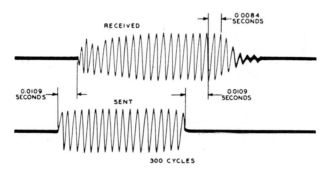

480 CYCLES

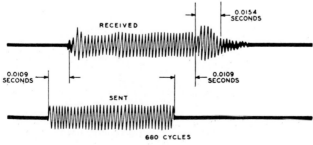

680 CYCLES

(b)

FIG. 2.15 (*Continued*)

2.33

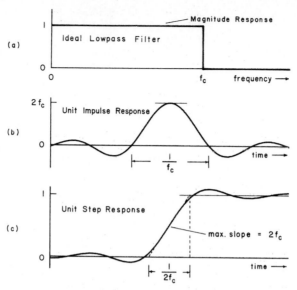

FIG. 2.16 (*a*) Magnitude response. (*b*) Impulse response. (*c*) Step response of an ideal linear-phase, band-limited (low-pass) system with cutoff frequency f_c Hz.

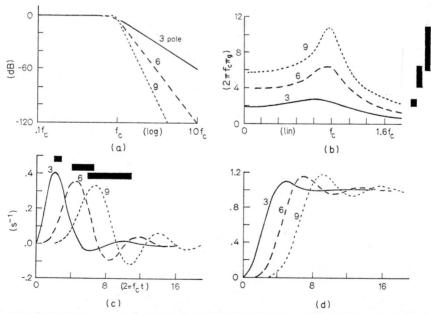

FIG. 2.17 Responses of maximally flat, minimum-phase, low-pass sytems. (*a*) Magnitude. (*b*) Group delay. (*c*) Impulse. (*d*) Step.

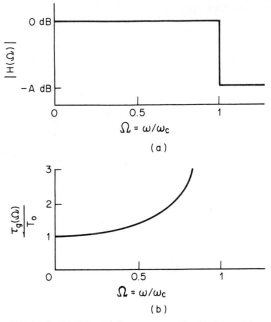

FIG. 2.18 (a) Magnitude response of a minimum-phase low-pass filter with stop-band attenuation of $-A$ dB versus normalized frequency $\Omega = \omega/\omega_c$. (b) Normalized group delay of minimum-phase filter in a.

where the constant

$$T_0 = \frac{A \ln 10}{10\pi\omega_c} \tag{2.51}$$

As predicted by Eq. (2.50) and seen in Fig. 2.18, the group delay becomes infinitely large at the band edge where $\omega = \omega_c$. This is a consequence of the assumed rectangular magnitude response. As a specific numerical example, let $A = 80$ dB and $\omega_c/2\pi = 14$ kHz. Then $T_0 = 62$ μs and $\tau_g(\omega) = 0.5$ ms when $\omega/2\pi \cong 14$ kHz. It is interesting to note that demanding greater (stop-band) attenuation for $\omega > \omega_c$ requires a larger value for the attenuation parameter A, and $\tau_g(0)$ increases, as does the deviation of the group delay within the passband.

A minimum-phase system is also a minimum-delay system since it has the least amount of phase change for a given magnitude response. (The group delay equals the negative rate of change of phase with respect to frequency.) Thus signal energy is released as fast as is physically possible without violating causality. However, in doing so, certain frequency components are released sooner than others, and this constitutes a form of phase distortion, sometimes called *dispersion*. Its presence is indicated by deviations of the group delay from a constant value. A linear-phase system necessarily introduces greater delay than a minimum-phase system with the same magnitude response. However, it has the advantage that there is no dispersion. This is accomplished by delaying all frequency components by the same amount of time.

2.3.7 Bandwidth and Rise Time

An important parameter associated with a band-limited low-pass system is the rise time. As illustrated in Figs. 2.16 and 2.17, eliminating high frequencies broadens signals in time and reduces transition times. The step response (response of the system to an input that changes from 0 to 1 when $t = 0$) shows, in the case of perfect band limiting illustrated in Fig. 2.16, that the transition from 0 to 1 requires $\pi/\omega_c = 1/(2f_c)$ s. Defining this as the rise time gives the useful result that the product of bandwidth in hertz and rise time in seconds is $f_c \times 1/(2f_c) = 0.5$. For example, with $f_c = 20$ kHz the rise time is 25 μs. The rise time equals half of the period of the cutoff frequency (for this perfectly band-limited system).

Practical low-pass systems, such as the minimum-phase systems shown in Fig. 2.17, do not have a sharp cutoff frequency, nor do they have perfectly flat group delay like the ideal low-pass model in Fig. 2.16. The product of the -3-dB bandwidth and the rise time for real systems usually lies within the range of 0.3 to 0.45. The reason that the rise time is somewhat shorter (faster) is twofold. Because the cutoff is more gradual, some frequencies beyond the -3-dB point contribute to the total output response. Also, the rise time to a unit step is conventionally defined as the time for the output to change from 10 to 90 percent of its final value.

Figure 2.19 displays this important relationship between rise time and bandwidth. Given the -3-dB bandwidth of a system, the corresponding range of typically expected rise times can be read. Conversely, knowing the rise time directly indicates nominal bandwidth requirements. Within the tolerance strip shown in Fig. 2.19, fixing the bandwidth always determines the rise time, and conversely. Figure 2.19 is a useful guide that relates a frequency-domain measurement (bandwidth) to a time-domain measurement (rise time). This fundamental relationship

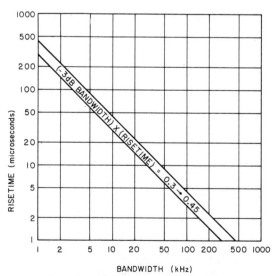

FIG. 2.19 Relationship between rise time and bandwidth of practical linear systems. For a given bandwidth the rise time will lie within the tolerance strip shown; conversely, the bandwidth requirements for a specific rise time also can be found.

suggests that testing a practical band-limited linear system with signals having rise times significantly shorter than the rise time of the linear system itself cannot yield new information about its transient response. In fact, the system may not be able to process such signals linearly.

The *slew rate* of a system is the maximum time rate of change (output units/time) for large-signal nonlinear operation when the output is required to change between extreme minimum and maximum values. It is not the same as rise time, which is a parameter defined for linear operation.

2.3.8 Echo Distortion

Ripples in the magnitude and/or phase of the system function $H(\omega)$ produce an interesting form of linear distortion of pulse signals called *echo distortion*. Assuming that these ripples are small and sinusoidal, a model for the system function $H(\omega) = |H(\omega)| e^{j\phi(\omega)}$ is

$$|H(\omega)| = 1 - m \cos(\omega c) \qquad (2.52a)$$

$$\phi(\omega) = -p \sin(\omega c) - \omega a \qquad (2.52b)$$

where c is the number of ripples per unit bandwidth, in hertz, and m and p are the maximum values of the magnitude and phase ripples, respectively. If $m = p = 0$, then there is no linear distortion of signals, just unity gain, and uniform time delay of $T = \tau_g(\omega) = a$ due to the linear-phase term $-\omega a$. By using Fourier-transform methods, it can be shown that the output $g(t)$ corresponding to an arbitrary input $f(t)$ has the form

$$g(t) = f(t - a) + \frac{m - p}{2} f(t - a - c) + \frac{m + p}{2} f(t - a + c) \quad (2.53)$$

Equation (2.53) states that the main portion of the output signal is delayed by a seconds and is undistorted, but there are, in addition, small preechoes and postechoes (replicas) which flank it being advanced and delayed in time (relative to $t = a$) by c seconds. This is shown in Fig. 2.20. Amplitude echoes are sym-

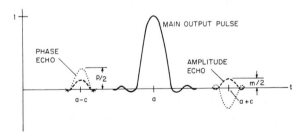

FIG. 2.20 Small preechoes and postechoes are produced at the output of a linear system having linear distortion in response to a pulselike input. The main output pulse is delayed by a seconds (minimum value of τ_g) and undistorted. Nonflat magnitude response produces symmetrical (dashed curves) "amplitude" echoes, whereas group-delay distortion produces unsymmetrical (dotted curves) "phase" echoes. These echoes *are* the linear distortion. In minimum-phase systems the non-causal echoes at $t = a - c$ are equal and opposite and cancel one another. In practical systems the echoes may overlap and change the shape of (linearly distort) the main output pulse.

metrical ($++$ or $--$), but phase echoes are asymmetrical ($+-$ or $-+$). These echoes *are* the linearly distorted portion of the output and are called echo distortion. The detection of linear distortion by observing paired echoes is possible when the echoes do not overlap and combine with the undistorted part of the signal to form a new (and linearly distorted) waveshape which may be asymmetrical and have a shifted peak time.

In connection with minimum-phase systems, if the magnitude response varies in frequency as a cosine function, then the phase response varies as a negative sine function (see Fig. 2.11 beginning at point 4) as the Hilbert-transform relationship [Eq. (2.48)] would predict. (Also, the group delay varies, like the magnitude response, as a cosine function.) This result implies that m and p in Eq. (2.52) would be equal and opposite; that is, $m = -p$. In this case the preecho vanishes because the last term in Eq. (2.53) is zero, but the postechoes reinforce. The impulse responses of many minimum-phase systems can be interpreted on this basis.

2.3.9 Classifications of Phase Distortion

When a system is causal, the minimum amount of phase shift $\phi_m(\omega)$ that it can have is prescribed by the Hilbert-transform relation [Eq. (2.48)]. There can be additional or *excess* phase shift $\phi_x(\omega)$ as well, so that in general the total phase shift is the sum

$$\phi(\omega) = \phi_m(\omega) + \phi_x(\omega) \tag{2.54}$$

A practical definition for the excess phase is

$$\phi_x(\omega) = \theta_a(\omega) - \omega T + \theta_0 \tag{2.55}$$

where θ_0 is a constant and $\theta_a(0) = 0$. In Eq. (2.55) $-\omega T$ represents pure time delay as in Eq. (2.14), $\theta_a(\omega)$ is the frequency-dependent phase shift of an all-pass filter, and θ_0 represents a frequency-independent phase shift caused by, for example, polarity reversal between input and output or a Hilbert transformer which introduces a constant phase shift for all frequencies. The group delay, defined in Eq. (2.42), is found by substituting Eq. (2.55) into Eq. (2.54) and differentiating. The result is

$$\tau_g(\omega) = T - \frac{d\phi_m(\omega)}{d\omega} - \frac{d\theta_a(\omega)}{d\omega} \tag{2.56a}$$

$$= T + \tau_{gm}(\omega) + \tau_{ga}(\omega) \tag{2.56b}$$

Because deviations of group delay from the constant value T indicate the presence of phase distortion, *group-delay distortion* is defined as

$$\Delta\tau_g(\omega) = \tau_{gm}(\omega) + \tau_{ga}(\omega) \tag{2.57}$$

This definition implies that $\Delta\tau_g(\omega) = 0$ is a *necessary* condition for no phase distortion and, further, that the peak-to-peak excursions of $\Delta\tau_g(\omega)$ are both a useful indication and a quantitative measure of phase distortion. Although the all-pass group delay $\tau_{ga}(\omega) \geq 0$, the minimum-phase group delay $\tau_{mp}(\omega)$ can be negative, zero, or positive (as can be inferred from the phase responses in Fig. 2.13 by examining their negative derivatives).

Note that when $\tau_g(\omega)$ is calculated from $\phi(\omega)$ by using Eq. (2.42), only phase-slope information is preserved. The phase intercept $\phi(0) = \phi_m(0) + \theta_0$ is lost

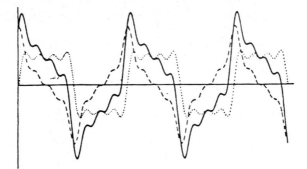

FIG. 2.21 Band-limited square wave (dotted curve), its Hilbert transform (dashed curve), and the sum of dotted and dashed curves (solid curve).

through differentiation. This result implies that when $\Delta\tau_g(\omega) = 0$ in Eq. (2.57), some phase distortion is possible if, for example, $\phi(\omega) = \phi_m(\omega) = -\pi/2$ [$H(\omega)$ is an ideal integrator] or $\phi(0) = \theta_0 = \pi/2$ [$H(\omega)$ contains a Hilbert transformer]. Thus $\Delta\tau_g(\omega) = 0$ and $\phi(0) \neq 0$ (or a multiple of π) implies no group-delay distortion but a form of phase distortion known as *phase-intercept distortion*. With reference to Fig. 2.10, the phase intercept b is zero when the phase delay and group delay are equal, as stated in Eq. (2.46), which is the *sufficient* condition for no phase distortion. Generally the total phase distortion produced by a linear system consists of both group-delay and phase-intercept distortion.

Figure 2.21 illustrates phase distortion caused by a frequency-independent phase shift or phase-intercept distortion. The dotted curve represents a band-limited square wave (sum of the first four nonzero harmonics), and the dashed curve is the Hilbert transform of the square wave obtained by shifting the phase of each harmonic $\pi/2$ rad, or 90°. This constant phase shift of each harmonic yields a linearly distorted waveshape having a significantly greater peak factor, as shown. The solid curve is the sum of the square wave and its Hilbert transform. Because corresponding harmonics in this sum are of equal amplitude and in phase quadrature, the solid curve could have been obtained by scaling the magnitude of the amplitude spectrum of the original square wave by $\sqrt{2}$ and rotating its phase spectrum by 45°. For this example, $\phi_x(\omega) = \theta_0 = \pi/4$ rad in Eq. (2.55).

In summary, there are two classifications of phase distortion: (1) group-delay distortion, which is due to the minimum-phase response and/or the frequency-dependent all-pass portion of the excess phase response; and (2) phase-intercept distortion, which is caused by a fixed or constant (frequency-independent) phase shift for all frequencies.

BIBLIOGRAPHY

Signals and Spectra

Bracewell, R.: *The Fourier Integral and Its Applications,* McGraw-Hill, New York, 1965.
Childers, D. G.: *Modern Spectral Analysis,* IEEE, New York, 1978.
Connor, F. R.: *Signals,* Arnold, London, 1972.
Jenkins, G. M., and D. G. Watts: *Spectral Analysis and Its Applications,* Holden-Day, San Francisco, 1968.

Kharkevich, A. A.: *Spectra and Analysis,* English translation, Consultants Bureau, New York, 1960.

Lynn, P. A.: *An Introduction to the Analysis and Processing of Signals,* 2d ed., Macmillan, London, 1982.

Panter, P. F.: *Modulation, Noise and Spectral Analysis,* McGraw-Hill, New York, 1965.

Papoulis, A.: *The Fourier Integral and Its Applications,* McGraw-Hill, New York, 1962.

Rabiner, L. R., and C. M. Rader (eds.): *Digital Signal Processing,* IEEE, New York, 1972.

Schwartz, M.: *Information Transmission, Modulation and Noise,* McGraw-Hill, New York, 1970.

Westman, H. P. (ed.): *ITT Reference Data for Radio Engineers,* H. W. Sams, New York, 1973.

Spectral Changes and Linear Distortion

Blinchikoff, H. J., and A. I. Zverev: *Filtering in the Time and Frequency Domains,* Wiley, New York, 1976.

Lane, C. E.: "Phase Distortion in Telephone Apparatus," *Bell Syst. Tech. J.,* **9,** 493–521 (July 1930).

Preis, D.: "Linear Distortion," *J. Audio Eng. Soc.,* **24**(5), 346–367 (June 1976).

———: "Impulse Testing and Peak Clipping," *J. Audio Eng. Soc.,* **25**(1), 2–14 (Janaury 1977).

———: "Phase Distortion and Phase Equalization in Audio Signal Processing—A Tutorial Review," *J. Audio Eng. Soc.,* **30**(11), 774–794 (November 1982).

Wheeler, H. A.: "The Interpretation of Amplitude and Phase Distortion in Terms of Paired Echoes," *Proc. IRE,* **27,** 359–385 (June 1939).

System Response to Signals

Bendat, J. S., and A. G. Piersol: *Random Data: Analysis and Measurement Procedures,* Wiley-Interscience, New York, 1971.

Cheng, D. K.: *Analysis of Linear Systems,* Addison-Wesley, Reading, Mass., 1961.

Lathi, B. P.: *Signals, Systems and Communications,* Wiley, New York, 1965.

Members of the Technical Staff of Bell Telephone Laboratories: *Transmission Systems for Communications,* 4th ed., Western Electric Company, Technical Publications, Winston-Salem, N.C., 1971.

Oppenheim, A. V., and R. W. Schafer: *Digital Signal Processing,* Prentice-Hall, Englewood Cliffs, N.J., 1975.

Papoulis, A.: *Signal Analysis,* McGraw-Hill; New York, 1977.

Catalog of Frequency and Transient Response

Application Note 63, Section II, Appendix A, Table of Important Transforms, Hewlett-Packard, Palo Alto, Calif., 1954, pp. 37, 38.

Di Toro, M. J.: "Phase and Amplitude Distortion in Linear Networks," *Proc. IRE,* **36,** 24–36 (January 1948).

Guillemin, E. A.: *Communication Networks,* vol. II, Wiley, New York, 1935.

Küpfmüller, K.: *Die Systemtheorie der elektrischen Nachrichtenübertragung,* S. Hirzel Verlag, Stuttgart, 1968.

Preis, D.: "A Catalog of Frequency and Transient Responses," *J. Audio Eng. Soc.,* **25**(12), 990–1007 (December 1977).

Spectral Modification by Audio Devices

Bloom, P. J., and D. Preis: "Perceptual Identification and Discrimination of Phase Distortions," *IEEE ICASSP Proc.*, 1396–1399 (April 1983).

Bode, H. W.: *Network Analysis and Feedback Amplifier Design,* Van Nostrand, New York, 1945.

Deer, J. A., P. J. Bloom, and D. Preis: "Perception of Phase Distortion in All-Pass Filters," *J. Audio Eng. Soc.,* **33**(10), 782–786 (October 1985).

Henderson, K. W., and W. H. Kautz: "Transient Response of Conventional Filters," *IRE Trans. Circuit Theory,* **CT-5**, 333–347 (December 1958).

Mallinson, J. C.: "Tutorial Review of Magnetic Recording," *Proc. IEEE,* **62**, 196–208 (February 1976).

Peus, S.: "Microphones and Transients," *db Mag.,* translated from *Radio Mentor* by S. Temmer, **11**, 35–38 (May 1977).

Preis, D.: "Linear Distortion," *J. Audio Eng. Soc.,* **24**, 346–367 (June 1976).

———: "Phase Equalization of Analogue Magnetic Recorders by Transversal Filtering," *Electron. Lett.,* **13**, 127–128 (March 1977).

———: "Least-Squares Time-Domain Deconvolution for Transversal-Filter Equalizers," *Electron. Lett.,* **13**(12), 356–357 (June 1977).

———: "Hilbert-Transformer Side-Chain Phase Equalizer for Analogue Magnetic Recording," *Electron. Lett.,* **13**, 616–617 (September 1977).

———: "Audio Signal Processing with Transversal Filters," *IEEE Conf. Proc.,* 1979 ICASSP, 310–313 (April 1979).

———: "Measures and Perception of Phase Distortion in Electroacoustical Systems," *IEEE Conf. Proc.,* 1980 ICASSP, 490–493 (1980).

———: "Phase Equalization for Magnetic Recording," *IEEE Conf. Proc.,* 1981 ICASSP, 790–795 (March 1981).

——— and P. J. Bloom: "Perception of Phase Distortion in Anti-Alias Filters," *J. Audio Eng. Soc.,* **32**(11), 842–848 (November 1984).

——— and C. Bunks: "Three Algorithms for the Design of Transversal-Filter Equalizers," *Proc. 1981 IEEE Int. Symp. Circuits Sys.,* 536–539.

Small, R. H.: "Closed-Box Loudspeaker Systems, part I: Analysis," *J. Audio Eng. Soc.,* **20**, 798–808 (December 1972).

Williams, A. B.: *Active Filter Design,* Artech House, Dedham, Mass., 1975.

Zverev, A. I.: *Handbook of Filter Synthesis,* Wiley, New York, 1967.

Advanced Spectral Analysis Methods

Bendat, J. S., and A. G. Riersol: "Engineering Applications of Correlation and Spectral Analysis," Wiley, New York, 1980.

Totzek, U., and D. Preis: "How to Measure and Interpret Coherence Loss in Magnetic Recording," *J. Audio Eng. Soc.* (December 1987).

Totzek, U., D. Preis, and J. F. Boehme: "A Spectral Model for Time-Base Distortions and Magnetic Recording," *Archiv. für Elektronik und Übertragungstechnik,* **41**(4), 223–231 (July–August 1987).

Preis, D., F. Hlawatsch, P. J. Bloom, and J. A. Deer: "Wigner Distribution Analysis of Filters with Perceptible Phase Distortion," *J. Audio Eng. Soc.* (December 1987).

CHAPTER 3
ARCHITECTURAL ACOUSTIC PRINCIPLES AND DESIGN TECHNIQUES

Richard G. Cann
President, Grozier Technical Systems, Inc., Brookline, Massachusetts

K. Anthony Hoover
Senior Consultant, Cavanaugh Tocci Associates, Inc., Sudbury, Massachusetts

3.1 INTRODUCTION

Each person relates to sound in a unique way that depends not only on the individual's perception but also on the context of the sound. Audiences seek the best sound quality available. Those outside the audience often find that other people's sound is noise. Thus there is a need for quality sound as well as for isolation from another sound. A general introduction to the concepts is given in this chapter.

As with other engineering applications, the objective is to assess the potential acoustical problems in advance and engineer accordingly. Acoustical solutions that are applied after the fact are compromises at best, limited mostly by cost. Doing the job right the first time is less expensive and totally avoids loss of revenue during retrofit. For example, selecting the correct floor construction for preventing sound from traveling to an adjacent floor will avoid the difficult application of sound-barrier construction to the floor or ceiling soon after the building has been commissioned.

This chapter will be a useful introduction to architectural acoustics, encouraging further reading. For those who do not seek extensive knowledge in this field, this chapter will help communication with architects, engineers, and acoustical consultants.

If assistance is needed in acoustical design, various resources are available. Sales representatives for building materials may be able to help, but one should be prepared for narrow and occasionally inappropriate advice on single-product application. More extensive help may be obtained from active members of related professional societies, such as the Audio Engineering Society or the Acoustical

Society of America. Eight years of experience specifically with noise control and a rigorous examination are requisites for membership in the Institute of Noise Control Engineering. There is also a professional group, the National Council of Acoustical Consultants, that can provide a directory of members.

3.1.1 Basic Considerations

This chapter encompasses the following basic aspects of sound propagation: the propagation of sound through air, the reflection of sound from a wall, and the transmission of sound through a wall. Also considered are the absorption of sound by materials, the criteria for desirable and/or undesirable sound, and methods for both improving the quality of desirable sound and reducing the impact of undesirable sound.

The Hearing Process.   Though each listener is unique, there are bounds within which most listeners fall. Thus over the years standards have been developed for both measurement instrumentation and measurement procedures. The Acoustical Society of America publishes, on behalf of the American National Standards Institute (ANSI), a catalog that summarizes each standard. There is also an index that lists international standards, shown in Ref. 1. In addition, there are many United States trade and professional societies that publish standards that relate to noise and their specific activities. A list is given in Ref. 9.

The manner in which the ear perceives sound is exceedingly complex. In some ways the ear is more sensitive to sound than acoustical instrumentation, being able to detect sound qualities that are extremely difficult to quantify. However, the hearing process may also interpret tonal sounds that in fact do not physically exist. The perception of sound is treated in detail in Chap. 1, Sec. 1.7.

Computer Design of Acoustic Systems.   Only recently a variety of computer programs have become available to assist the designer concerned with architectural acoustics. Some programs are supplied either gratis or for a small fee by the manufacturers of building components. For example, a program available from Monsanto, Inc., assesses the intrusion of noise through composite walls. Other manufacturers, such as Trane, Inc., have bulletins for the application of air-handling units. In addition, some programs may be purchased for generic applications. However, caution should be exercised when using these programs, for calculations performed by the computer often are not documented thoroughly and may not suit a particular application or on-the-job condition. Thus, it is possible to apply the programs improperly, resulting in substantial error.

3.2 SOUND CHARACTERISTICS

3.2.1 Simple Sound Source

The simplest source of sound expands and contracts equally in all directions as if a perfectly round balloon were rapidly inflated and deflated. The expansion and contraction of the source results in three-dimensional sound ripples which spread out unimpeded in all directions as ever-expanding spheres of compression and rarefaction at the velocity of sound. The rate at which the point source expands and contracts is the frequency in cycles per second, usually expressed numerically in hertz (Hz). The distance between consecutive spheres of either expansion or compression is identified as the wavelength, as shown in Fig. 3.1. These three parameters are related by

$$c = f\lambda \tag{3.1}$$

where c = velocity of sound, ft/s (m/s)
$\quad f$ = frequency, Hz
$\quad \lambda$ = wavelength, ft/Hz (m/Hz)

The speed of sound in air is approximately 1130 ft/s at normal room temperatures. For quick estimates, this may be rounded off to 1000 ft/s. For design surveys, it may be more convenient to use a simplification that sound travels about 1 ft/0.001 s.

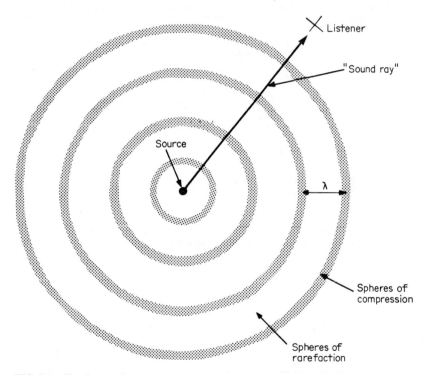

FIG. 3.1 Simple sound source.

Sound waves of all frequencies, whether from a low-frequency *woofer* or a high-frequency *tweeter,* travel at the same speed. An international standard (International Organization for Standardization, Recommendation R226, 1961) sets middle A (so-called tuning A) at 440 Hz. From Eq. (3.1) this tone has a wavelength of 2.59 ft.

Sound Spectrum.   The audible spectrum of sound ranges from 20 Hz to 20 kHz. The fundamental tone or pitch of musical instruments ranges from piano at the lowest end of human hearing to about 4 kHz. However, every instrument also develops harmonics that are frequencies many times higher than the fundamental pitch. These harmonics are important in our ability to identify types of musical instruments.

For noise control applications the frequency spectrum is conveniently divided into preferred octave bands, the frequencies of which are shown in Table 3.1. Each octave band encompasses the musical scale from F sharp to F. All noise control data are classified into these octave bands. One-third-octave bands may be used for more detailed work.

TABLE 3.1 Limits of Frequency Passbands

Band number	Nominal center frequency	One-third-octave passband	Octave passband
14	25	22.4–28.2	
15	31.5	28.2–35.5	22.4–44.7
16	40	35.5–44.7	
17	50	44.7–56.2	
18	63	56.2–70.8	44.7–89.1
19	80	70.8–89.1	
20	100	89.1–112	
21	125	112–141	89.1–178
22	160	141–178	
23	200	178–224	
24	250	224–282	178–355
25	315	282–355	
26	400	355–447	
27	500	447–562	355–708
28	630	562–708	
29	800	708–891	
30	1,000	891–1,120	708–1410
31	1,250	1,120–1,410	
32	1,600	1,410–1,780	
33	2,000	1,780–2,240	1,410–2,820
34	2,500	2,240–2,820	
35	3,150	2,820–3,550	
36	4,000	3,550–4,470	2,820–5,620
37	5,000	4,470–5,620	
38	6,300	5,620–7,080	
39	8,000	7,080–8,910	5,620–11,200
40	10,000	8,910–11,200	

3.2.2 Propagation

Expanding sound waves are sometimes depicted in acoustical diagrams by using sound rays such as those shown in Fig. 3.1. These rays are lines which are used to represent the radius of the spherical wave and are arrowed in a direction away from the source. They must not be interpreted as meaning "beams" of sound that travel only in the arrowed direction. Neither do they describe in any way the amplitude of the wave at any point. Their utility is limited to showing primary sound propagation paths in environments which are dimensionally larger than the wavelength of the sound. This limitation is explained in more detail later in this section.

Sound waves travel away from a simple source in spheres of ever-increasing diameter. The sound pressure is reduced in amplitude by a factor of 4 each time that the radius is doubled, since the sound energy is distributed over the sphere's surface, which has become 4 times larger. In decibel terms, the new sound level is decreased by 20 log (ratio of distances).

Thus, when the radius or the distance that a sound wave travels has doubled, the sound level is reduced by 20 log (2), or 6 dB. Conversely, each time that a listener's distance from the source is halved, the sound level increases by 6 dB. This is not true once a listener is close to the source.

Most speaker cabinets have dimensions of less than 1 m; this is typically the minimum distance at which the rule of 6 dB per distance doubling can be applied. At a distance of less than 1 m the sound level increases asymptotically to a maximum value at the vibrating surface.

Sound Power. Since sound pressure and sound power levels are usually expressed in decibels, a logarithmic ratio, it is important to distinguish clearly between the two. Sound power level applies only to the source, whereas sound pressure level is also dependent on the environment and the distance from the source.

As an analogy, a common light bulb is rated in lumens to indicate how much light the bulb produces regardless of the kind of room it is in. But the amount of light perceived by an observer depends on such environmental factors as the distance from the bulb to the eye and the color of the wallpaper. Sound power level cannot be measured directly but is calculated from measurement of sound pressure level made with a sound-level meter (see Chap. 1, Sec. 1.3).

Sound power is calculated from

$$L_w = L_p - 10 \log (Q/4\pi r^2) - 10.2 \qquad (3.2a)$$

where r = radius, ft
$\qquad Q$ = directivity factor

$$L_w = L_p - 10 \log (Q/4\pi r^2) \qquad (3.2b)$$

where r = radius, m.

3.2.3 Directivity

Most sound sources are not omnidirectional like the one described above. Instead, they emit sound more strongly in one direction than in another. The directivity characteristic can be specified by means of a directivity factor. If an omnidirectional source is placed against a large reflecting surface such as a floor, the sound will radiate only into a hemisphere, or half of the previous solid angle. The directivity factor Q of this source increases from 1 to 2. If the solid angle is again halved by another large plane, such as by placing the source on a floor next to a wall, the directivity factor now increases to 4. When a source is placed in the corner of a rectangular room, the sound can radiate only into one-eighth of a sphere; so the directivity factor is now 8.

Loudspeakers and microphones also show directional characteristics. Their characteristics are usually given by the manufacturer in the form of graphical polar plots which compare the sound pressure level in all directions with that of the on-axis sound. Further details may be found in Chap. 7, Sec. 7.6.5.

3.3 SOUND BUILDUP WITHIN A SPACE

3.3.1 Sound Absorption

When the spherical wavefront meets a large flat surface, some sound is reflected as a mirror image of the spherical wave with the angle of incidence of the wave equal to the angle of reflection. For most surfaces, sound is not totally reflected; some is absorbed. Regardless of the mechanism of absorption, the effectiveness of a surface material in reducing sound is given by its absorption coefficient. This is the fraction of the incident sound energy that is absorbed, with a value between 0 and 1. For example, if 25 percent of the sound is absorbed, then the coefficient is 0.25. The larger the coefficient, the more effective the absorber. Sound absorbers usually have different absorption coefficients at different frequencies. Examples of the performance of different materials are shown in Table 3.2.

It is to be noted that the coefficient of a highly effective absorber may be given as fractionally greater than 1. This is not an error but the result of the method used in testing the material.

In Eq. (3.3) the sound absorption A of a surface is measured in sabins, a parameter of which the primary dimensional system is the British imperial foot. It is calculated by multiplying its area S by its sound absorption coefficient α. The total absorption in sabins for several absorptive areas is calculated from

$$A = (S_1\alpha_1 + S_2\alpha_2 \cdots S_n\alpha_n) \tag{3.3}$$

where S = area, ft^2 (m^2), and A = total absorption, sabins (metric sabins).

For example, a 10- by 10-ft panel with an absorption coefficient of 0.68 in the 500-Hz band together with a 5- by 40-ft panel with an absorption coefficient of 0.79 in the 500-Hz band has 68 + 158 sabins of absorption.

The values of absorption coefficient in the 250-, 500-, 1000-, and 2,000-Hz octave bands are often averaged to form a composite absorption coefficient called the *noise reduction coefficient* (NRC). Typical values are shown in the last column in Table 3.2. NRC numbers are primarily used in noise reduction computations applied to speech.

Absorption must not be confused with transmission loss, which is discussed in Sec. 3.4, or mechanical damping, discussed in Sec. 3.8. The words *damping* and *deadening* are often inappropriately applied to mean the adding of sound-absorptive materials.

3.3.2 Frictional Absorbers

Most of the commonly available materials intended for the absorption of sound, such as acoustic ceiling tile and acoustic foam, are frictional absorbers. They are porous materials which allow for the passage of air and, as a result, the passage of sound waves through them. The sound waves cause molecular motion within the narrow restrictions in the material which results in friction, converting a fraction of the sound energy to heat.

As an acoustical panel is increased in thickness or moved away from a solid

TABLE 3.2 Typical Absorption Coefficients

Material	Sound absorption coefficient						NRC number
	125 Hz	250 Hz	500 Hz	1000 Hz	2000 Hz	4000 Hz	
Concrete masonry units, painted	0.08	0.05	0.05	0.07	0.08	0.08	0.06
Gypsum wallboard, ½ in thick, studs spaced 24 in on center	0.27	0.10	0.05	0.04	0.07	0.08	0.07
Typical window glass	0.30	0.22	0.17	0.13	0.07	0.03	0.15
Plaster on lath	0.15	0.10	0.06	0.05	0.05	0.03	0.07
Light fabric, flat against concrete wall	0.08	0.06	0.10	0.16	0.25	0.32	0.14
Thick drapery, draped to half area	0.15	0.36	0.55	0.70	0.73	0.75	0.59
Linoleum on concrete	0.02	0.03	0.03	0.03	0.03	0.03	0.03
Typical wood floor	0.15	0.12	0.10	0.06	0.06	0.06	0.09
Thin carpet on concrete	0.03	0.06	0.10	0.20	0.43	0.63	0.20
Thick carpet with underpadding	0.08	0.28	0.38	0.40	0.48	0.70	0.39
Typical ½-in-thick mineral-fiber acoustic ceiling tile	0.45	0.50	0.53	0.69	0.85	0.93	0.64
Typical ¾-in-thick glass-fiber acoustic ceiling tile	0.44	0.65	0.90	0.92	0.94	0.97	0.85

backing surface, its absorption at low frequency improves. The application of a facing reduces the effect of high-frequency absorption; common facings are plastic membranes, wood slats, and woven fabric. Material manufacturers provide the absorption coefficient for various frequencies and for different styles of mounting.

Frictional absorbers by themselves are not very useful for reducing sound as it is transmitted from one side of the material to the other. Materials with a good transmission loss are used for this purpose.

3.3.3 Resonant Panels

Sound energy may also be reduced when reflected from impervious resonant panels, such as those made from gypsum board or plywood. Incident sound on the panel causes it to vibrate, the air and the material behind the panel dampen the movement, some of the sound is converted to heat, and the remainder is reradiated. For these panels to be effective, they must be large compared with the wavelength of the sound, be fully baffled at the sides and rear, and be tuned to the desired resonant frequency. The maximum absorption coefficient of such a panel is typically 0.5 over a frequency range of an octave. They are most usefully applied at resonant frequencies below 300 Hz. They are usually custom-designed for specific applications.

A typical absorber may be a 4- by 8-ft sheet of plywood ½ in thick held a distance d away from a solid wall by means of studs around its periphery. It is sealed to the wall and studs, and the cavity is lightly filled with sound-absorptive material. The resonance frequency f_r is given by

$$f_r = K/\sqrt{md} \qquad (3.4)$$

where $K = 174$ ($K = 60$)
  m = surface weight, lb/ft (kg/m)
  d = panel spacing from wall, in (m)

For this example, the plywood weighs 2 lb/ft and $d = 1.5$ in; then

$$f_r = 174/\sqrt{2 \times 1.5} = 100 \text{ Hz}$$

The maximum number of sabins that this typical panel can provide at this frequency can be calculated by multiplying its area by the absorption coefficient:

$$A = 4 \times 8 \times 0.5 = 16$$

In this calculation, Eq. (3.4) is a simplified version of a much more complex equation, and its application is limited to large flexible panels that have a low resonant frequency.

In some situations, construction using such materials as gypsum wallboard for a partition that is intended to be reflective may inadvertently be absorptive in one or two octave bands because of panel resonance. Two walls, perhaps on opposite sides of a studio, may appear identical, but if one is a freestanding partition and the other is mounted to a masonry wall, their absorption coefficients may be significantly different.

3.3.4 Cavity Resonators

The most popular form of cavity resonator is a cinder block manufactured with a slot formed through to its internal cavity. This is also most effective at lower frequencies, but it has an absorption coefficient close to 1 at the resonant frequency. The volume of the cavity and the dimensions of the slot determine this frequency. When the cavity of the block is stuffed with fiberglass, the range of frequencies over which the block is effective is increased from one or two octaves to two or three. When these blocks are assembled into large walls, the total number of sabins is obtained by multiplying the manufacturer's absorption coefficient by the wall area [see Eq. (3.3)].

3.3.5 Reverberation

After the generation of sound within an enclosed space has ceased, the sound wave continues to travel, striking surfaces until it is entirely absorbed. The time taken for the sound pressure level to decay by 60 dB from its original level is called the *reverberation time*. There are two basic controlling factors: room volume and total sound absorption. The reverberation time T_{60} in seconds is given by

$$T_{60} = 0.05 V/A \qquad (3.5a)$$

where V = volume of room, ft^3
A = total area of absorption, sabins

or in metric sabins,

$$T_{60} = 0.161 V/A \qquad (3.5b)$$

where V = volume of room, m^3.

Equation (3.5) assumes that the sound pressure level is equally diffused throughout the room. In many actual situations, full diffusion does not exist because of large single areas of absorption. For example, the audience may provide most of the absorption in an auditorium, or a studio may be designed with a *dead end*. In some cases, two reverberation times may be exhibited simultaneously. The decay of sound may have an envelope of two line segments, one for each reverberation time, with the second segment being apparent only after the decay of the first. Thus caution should be exercised when using a digital reverberation-time meter, for it may obscure valuable information or give erroneous data. In most cases it is preferred that sound decay be plotted either by means of a strip-chart recorder or on a storage oscilloscope so that its slope can be viewed for anomalies.

Equation (3.5) can be expressed in an alternative way to show the result of adding to a room volume or adding acoustically absorptive material to the material already in place. From Eq. (3.5)

Change in T_{60} (percent) = (change in percent of volume)

− (change in percent of total absorption)   (3.6)

Thus, if the reverberation time of a space needs to be decreased, the percentage addition of absorptive material has to be significant. This can be understood intuitively from experience in which opening a door in a typical room that may have 200 sabins, and thus creating a totally absorptive area of an additional 20 ft^2, does not noticeably change the reverberation time. From Eq. (3.6) the change in T_{60} is only 10 percent.

3.3.6   Combination of Direct and Reverberant Sound

The sound level within a space consists of two parts: (1) the sound that comes directly from the source and (2) the reverberant sound. Very close to the source the direct sound predominates. Further away, the direct sound decreases by 6 dB at each doubling of the distance while the reverberant-sound level stays almost constant. At a distant point, the direct sound contributes insignificantly to the total sound level, and no matter how much more distance from the source is increased, the sound level remains constant at the reverberant level.

At an intermediate point, at a distance from the source known as the *critical distance,* the direct sound is equal to the reverberant sound. This distance depends on the total absorption [see Eq. (3.3) for total number of sabins] within the space and the directivity of the source.

If it is proposed to reduce sound within a space by means of absorption, applying an infinite amount will remove only the reverberant-sound contribution, not the direct sound. Of course, because of space constraints only limited amounts of absorption can be applied, with the result that not all the reverberant sound can be removed.

The critical distance is the closest distance at which any discernible sound-level reduction (3 dB) can be obtained by the application of absorptive materials. In addition, when taking into account the fact that a 3-dB reduction is just discernible but may not be significant, the cost of absorptive materials for noise reduction at the critical distance may not be justified. Noise control by means of absorption is usually practical only beyond 2 to 3 times the critical distance.

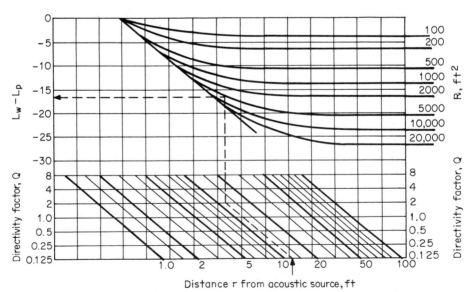

FIG. 3.2 Relationship between distance from source, directivity factor, room constant, and $L_w - L_p$.

To calculate the critical distance, first calculate the room constant R:

$$R = A[\Sigma S/(\Sigma S - A)] \qquad (3.7a)$$

The critical distance d is

$$d = \sqrt{RQ/16\pi} \qquad (3.7b)$$

The result of this calculation gives an immediate perspective on whether to control the sound through absorption within the space or to apply alternative means.

The parameters here are interrelated, as shown in Fig. 3.2. The upper half of the figure shows a diagonal line indicating the direct sound falling at 6 dB of each doubling of distance. The asymptotic lines show the contribution of reverberant sound. The lower half of the figure applies to source directivity. For example, at a distance r, 12 ft from a source with a directivity factor Q of 2, in a room with a room constant R of 5000 ft^2, the sound pressure level will be 17 dB less than the sound power level. Note that r also is approximately the critical distance where the sound level is 3 dB above the direct level.

special handling lucy 3-17-88

Though the sound level within a space can be controlled to a limited degree through the application of absorptive materials, building a partition can be much more effective in separating a noise source from a listener, although it can never totally prevent all the sound from passing through.

Actually, sound does not pass "through" a typical wall. The sound pressure on one side of the wall results in a force that shakes the wall. The shaking wall in turn disturbs the air on the other side, causing sound pressure waves to spread again and thus to establish a new sound level in the receiving space.

The difference between the levels on either side of the wall is called the *noise reduction* of the wall. The noise reduction (NR) depends not only on the characteristics of the wall but on the total absorption in the receiving space. For example, a wall enclosing a highly reverberant room is significantly less effective than the same wall protecting a well-upholstered lounge. Thus, to help in defining the acoustical performance of the wall alone, a measure that is independent of the acoustical characteristics of the receiving space is required. This is termed *transmission loss* (TL).

In one typical situation, in which the sound travels from one reverberant space to another, the transmission loss of the wall is related to noise reduction by

$$TL = NR + 10 \log (S/A) \qquad (3.9)$$

where S = surface area of the common wall, ft (m)
   A = total absorption of the receiving room, sabins (metric sabins)

In the other typical situation, in which the sound travels from a nonreverberant area to a reverberant space, for example, between a noisy highway and a studio, the noise reduction is 5 dB less:

$$TL = NR + 10 \log (S/A) + 5 \qquad (3.10)$$

The term $10 \log (S/A)$ is often called *room effect*.

In general terms, the transmission loss of a single wall is governed by its mass:

$$TL = 20 \log (f) + 20 \log (M) - K \qquad (3.11)$$

where f = frequency, Hz
$\quad M$ = mass, lb/ft (kg/m)
$\quad K$ = 34 (48 for metric units)

This shows that every time that the mass of the wall is doubled, the transmission loss increases by 6 dB. However, in practical terms the mass of a wall cannot be doubled more than a few times before running into structural and space limitations. Also, Eq. (3.11) shows that the transmission loss increases by 6 dB each time that the frequency is doubled. Thus, at high frequencies much more transmission loss is demonstrated than at bass frequencies.

Mass law essentially gives the maximum TL that can be expected from a homogenous wall. In fact, lower values are to be expected primarily as a result of *coincidence dip*. The frequency at which this dip occurs depends on the speed of

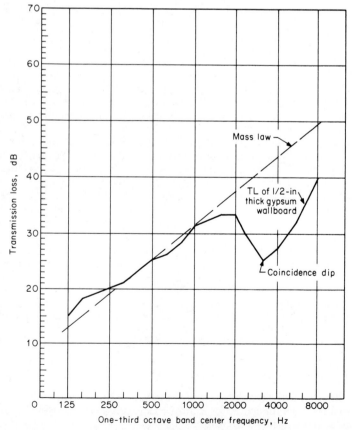

FIG. 3.3 Example of coincidence dip reducing transmission loss.

sound within the wall material. Consequently, for each material the coincidence frequency occurs at a different frequency. For example, it occurs in the 2000-Hz band for gypsum wallboard. The dip may reduce the transmission loss by up to 15 dB. Figure 3.3 shows an example. Details of how and why coincidence dip occurs can be found in Ref. 2.

Since the transmission loss can be changed or improved by more complex methods of construction, perhaps incorporating double independent walls, it is good design practice to use certified transmission-loss test data to calculate noise reduction of specific design proposals (see Ref. 3).

Reputable salespersons of acoustical products should be able to provide certified sound-transmission-loss data for their products used in specific applications, but care should be exercised when using more than one of these products back to back because acoustic coupling and resonances between the products make resulting performance difficult to predict. Since the development of complex partitions is beyond the scope of this chapter, advice of an expert in acoustics should be sought in these situations.

3.4.2   Composite Transmission Loss

Often a wall is made up of several elements such as a wall, windows, doors, or even openings. The transmission loss of each of these elements can be combined into one composite transmission loss (TL_c). The procedure is best understood by defining a transmission-loss coefficient τ, which is the fraction of the sound power passing through a unit area of the wall:

$$TL = -10 \log (\tau) \qquad \text{or} \qquad \tau = 10_{-TL/10} \tag{3.12}$$

The fraction of sound passing through the composite wall τ_c, made up of elements $1, 2 \cdots n$, is then

$$\tau_c = \tau_1 W_1/W + \tau_2 W_2/W + \tau_n W_n/W \tag{3.13}$$

where W is the wall area, ft^2 (m^2). Then the composite transmission loss is

$$TL_c = -10 \log (\tau_c) \tag{3.14}$$

The formula is also very instructive in showing how apertures in a wall influence its performance. For example, if a wall with an area of 100 ft^2 with a TL of 40 dB has a 3-ft^2 hole, then

$$\tau_c = 0.0001 \, (97/100) + 1(3/100) \qquad \text{or} \qquad = 3.0097/100$$

and $\qquad\qquad\qquad TL_c = 10 \log (100/3.0097) = 15 \text{ dB}$

Thus, a 40-dB wall has had its transmission loss reduced from 40 to 15 dB by cutting the hole. Small holes, such as cracks and slits, let much more sound through than the equations presented above would predict. The value of τ for a crack may be up to 10 times greater than would be predicted by applying its area to these equations.

3.4.3   Sound Transmission Class (STC)

To simplify handling transmission-loss data in multiple-frequency bands, a single-number descriptor, called the sound transmission class (STC), is often used to rate a wall. STC and transmission-loss data of common materials are shown in Table 3.3.

TABLE 3.3 Typical STC and Transmission-Loss Data

Material	Transmission loss, dB							STC rating
	125 Hz	250 Hz	500 Hz	1000 Hz	2000 Hz	4000 Hz		
Gypsum wallboard, ½ in thick	14	20	24	30	30	27		27
Two layers in gypsum wallboard, both ½ in thick	19	26	30	30	29	36		31
Flat concrete panel, medium weight, 6 in thick	37	43	51	59	67	73		55
One layer of ½-in-thick gypsum wallboard on each side of 2- by 4-in wood studs (16 in off center) with 2-in-thick glass-fiber batt in the cavity	20	28	33	43	43	40		38
Same as above, but with two layers of ½-in-thick gypsum wallboard on each side	24	37	44	49	50	50		46
Same as above, but with staggered studs	34	43	49	54	54	52		51
Same as above, but with double row of 2- by 4-in studs spaced 1 in apart on separate plates, using type X (fire-rated) gypsum wallboard, and two layers of 3-in glass-fiber batt in the cavity	45	54	63	66	66	64		63
Same as above, but with bracing across cavity at third points of studs	40	45	56	62	57	60		57
4-in face brick, mortared together	31	33	39	47	55	61		45
Two layers of mortared 4-in face brick separated by 2-in air space, with metal ties	36	36	46	54	61	66		50
Same as above, but air space filled with concrete grout	41	47	56	62	66	70		59
6-in-thick three-cell dense concrete masonry units, mortared together	36	38	42	49	53	60		48
2-in-thick hollow-core door, ungasketed	13	19	23	18	17	21		19
2-in-thick solid wood door with airtight gasketing and drop seal	29	31	31	31	39	43		35
Typical window glass, ⅛ in thick, single plate	15	23	26	30	32	30		29
Typical thermal glazing window (³⁄₁₆-in glass, ⅝-in air space, ³⁄₁₆-in glass)	22	21	29	34	30	32		30
½-in-thick laminated glass	34	35	36	37	40	51		39
Composite window (½-in laminated glass, 5-in air space, ¼-in glass)	33	54	60	57	55	63		55
Typical ½-in-thick mineral-fiber acoustic ceiling tile	6	10	12	16	21	21		17

However, in the process of condensing these multifrequency TL data, it is assumed that the general shape of the noise spectrum is similar to that of speech. Nevertheless, in spite of this process, STC ratings are often applied indiscriminately to the isolation of other types of sounds such as machinery or music.

The STC of a transmission-loss spectrum is determined by adjusting a fixed-shape contour over the plotted data according to the following predetermined criteria:

1. Only one-third-octave bands from 125 to 4000 Hz are considered.
2. The sum of the deficiencies (the deviations below the contour) cannot exceed 32 dB.
3. Values above the contour are ignored.
4. The deficiency in any one band cannot exceed 8 dB.

The STC rating is the ordinate of the contour at 500 Hz. Figure 3.4 shows the STC curves, and Fig. 3.5 shows an example.

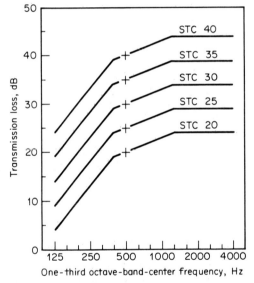

FIG. **3.4** Example of sound-transmission-class (STC) curves. *(From ASTM specification E 1413-73.)*

Transmission-loss curves are typically jagged and are not smooth and rising like the standardized STC curve. At the frequency where the STC curve may exceed the TL curve by up to 8 dB, insufficient noise reduction may be obtained. In addition, since the STC rating incorporates little transmission loss at low frequencies, it is most inappropriate to use STC ratings for the isolation of bass sounds.

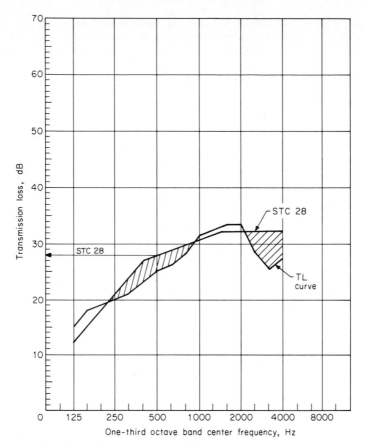

FIG. 3.5 Sound transmission class (STC) for ½-in-thick gypsum wallboard. When a TL data point falls below the STC curve, the difference is termed a *deficiency*. The sum of all deficiencies must not be greater than 32 dB. No single deficiency shall be greater than 8 dB.

3.4.4 Diffraction

In addition to being reflected or transmitted, sound waves can be diffracted. Figure 3.6 shows a barrier parallel to waves. At the free end of the barrier the waves spread around to the acoustical shadow area behind. The more the waves turn around the end of the barrier, the more the amplitude of the wave is decreased.

For example, for acoustically simple applications such as for a barrier built around rooftop equipment, the amount of noise reduction from a barrier depends on the increased distance that the sound has to travel over the top of the barrier to the listener caused by the insertion of the barrier. For the distance d, which is the additional distance which the sound must travel around the obstruction to the receiver, the Fresnel number N is defined as

$$N = 2d/\lambda \tag{3.15}$$

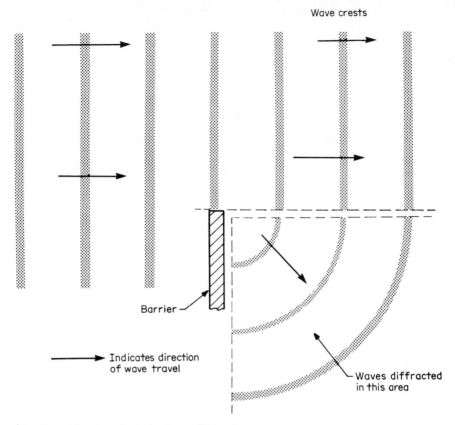

FIG. 3.6 Diffraction of sound w by a solid barrier.

where λ = wavelength of sound, ft (m)
d = total path length from the source over the barrier to the receiver less direct distance separating source and receiver, ft (m)

Thus, there is a different Fresnel number for each frequency.

From Fig. 3.7, the noise reduction can be found for each frequency band of interest. It can be seen that low-frequency sound (with lower N) is attenuated less by diffraction than high-frequency sound.

3.5 CRITERIA FOR ACCEPTABILITY OF ACOUSTICAL PERFORMANCE

3.5.1 Purpose of Criteria Specification

Before beginning the acoustical design of any space, one of the first tasks is to establish criteria for its performance. Sometimes it might appear that this is super-

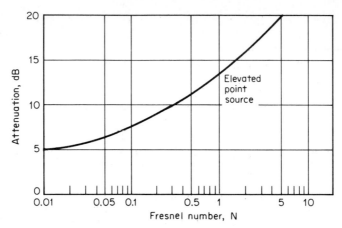

FIG. 3.7 Noise reduction of a barrier for different Fresnel numbers.

fluous, that the owner, architect, and engineer have an unwritten understanding of acoustical requirements, and that the design process can begin immediately. However, this is often not the case, and absence of thoughtfully written criteria may lead to fundamental design errors. The development of criteria is very important in defining just how spaces will be used and will ultimately determine just how well the spaces will function acoustically.

3.5.2 Reverberation Time

For example, if an auditorium will be used for both speech and music, basic design decisions will have to be made at the outset. Figure 3.8 shows a typical plot of reverberation time at 500 Hz versus room volume for auditoria used for different activities. The preferred reverberation time for music is approximately twice as long as it is for speech. Either the acoustical quality of some activities will have to be compromised by selecting a specific reverberation time, or provision will have to be made for adjusting the reverberation time for each activity.

Though there are generally accepted criteria for the reverberation time of a small auditorium, they are not nearly so clear-cut for recording studios. Some performers insist on live reverberant feedback from the space itself and directly from adjacent performers. Other artists, who work entirely through headphones, are much less concerned about the reverberant quality of a studio. The former scenario requires an architectural solution, while the latter requires none.

The design criteria for a control room often simply invoke, without acoustical reason, the currently fashionable proprietary design concept. It seems that no matter which concept is selected, there are always sound engineers who hate it or love it. There are no generally accepted design criteria even among those who record the same artist. Remembering that almost all the buying public never hear a recording with the fidelity available to sound engineers, what the engineers really want is sound quality that will allow them to project what they hear into the finished disk. And, of course, that varies from one engineer to the next, according to their past experience. Therefore, it is wise to build flexibility into

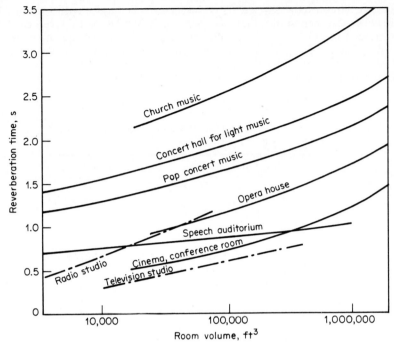

FIG. 3.8 Typical reverberation times for different sizes of rooms and auditoria according to usage.

control-room design, allowing engineers to produce their own semicustom setup. No one way is best.

3.5.3 Background Noise

The background sound level should not interfere with the perception of the desired sound, especially during quiet periods, for music is a rhythm not only of sound but also of silence. It is important not to intrude upon the latter with a rumbling fan or traffic noise. The most frequently used criteria for background noise are the noise-criterion (NC) curves which are classified according to space usage in Table 3.4. The interior octave-band sound levels are plotted on a standard graph as shown in Fig. 3.9. Each NC curve is named according to its value at 500 Hz. The NC value of a plotted spectrum is usually defined by the highest NC value that is attained in any octave band. For example, the NC value of the spectrum in Fig. 3.9 is defined by the sound pressure level at 250 Hz, which gives an NC value of 45.

However, NC curves are applicable only to essentially informationless sound, sound which is continuous and time-invariant. Where the intruding noise carries meaningful information such as intelligible speech or countermusical rhythms, more stringent criteria must be applied.

In some circumstances quieter is not necessarily better, for reducing noise levels may reveal other sounds that were previously hidden. Noise levels can often be increased to the NC value specified in Table 3.4 without causing noticeable intrusion. This masking of an intruding sound may be less expensive than controlling the sound itself. Further details are found in Sec. 3.9.4.

It may be necessary to set special criteria for a particular activity. For example,

TABLE 3.4   Design Goals for Mechanical-System Noise Levels

Type of area	NC range
Residences	
Single-family homes	20–30
Apartments and	
condominiums	25–35
Hotels and motels	
Guest rooms	30–40
Meeting or banquet rooms	30–35
Corridors and lobbies	35–45
Offices	
Boardrooms	20–30
Executive offices	30–40
Open-plan areas	35–40
Public circulation	35–45
Hospitals	
Private rooms	25–35
Operating rooms	30–40
Wards	30–40
Laboratories	30–40
Public circulation	35–45
Churches	
Sanctuaries	20–30
Public circulation	30–40
Schools and universities	
Libraries	30–40
Lecture rooms and classrooms	20–35
Laboratories	35–45
Cafeterias and recreation halls	35–45
Public buildings	
Libraries and museums	30–40
Courtrooms	25–35
Post offices and banks	30–40
Auditoria, theaters, and studios	
Concert halls	15–25
Recording studios	15–25
Multipurpose halls	20–30
TV studios	20–30
Movie theaters	30–35

for a recording studio, noise criteria may be set equal to the noise floor of the recording instrumentation. This level may be above the aural threshold of the performers, with the result that it is possible to identify clearly a source of intruding noise before a recording session begins and yet not have the offending noise be audible on tape.

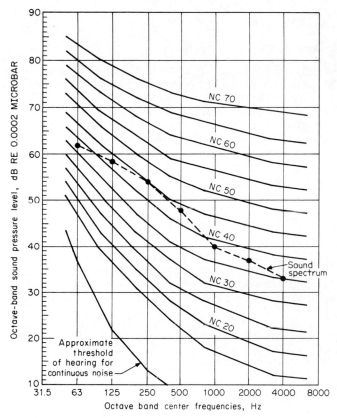

FIG. 3.9 Noise-criterion (NC) curves. *(From L. L. Beranek,* Noise and Vibration Control, *McGraw-Hill, New York, 1971.)*

3.5.4 Maximum Levels

The maximum noise expected in a space has to be determined. For example, if a space is used primarily for dining at low sound levels but if it is anticipated that the space will also be used occasionally as a nightclub when a group will bring in large loudspeaker stacks, an estimate of these higher sound levels must be made so that intrusion into adjacent spaces can be calculated. The activities in an adjacent rehearsal room may be curtailed if the dining-room sound levels are 40 dB higher.

3.5.5 Interference of Speech Communication

Mechanical equipment, air-distribution louvers, and other sources of sound may generate noise that causes speech to be unintelligible. Thus person-to-person conversations and telephone conversations rapidly become exhausting, and the efficient functioning of an administrative office can be thoroughly impaired. Criteria for adequate speech intelligibility can be developed according to Refs. 4 and 5.

3.5.6 Exterior Noise

Concern need be given not only to sound levels within the space but also to those outside in the neighborhood. The community may have a specific bylaw limiting noise levels. If not, the criteria for maximum noise levels should be based upon available annoyance data that are briefly outlined in Sec. 3.10. It is appropriate to establish these criteria up front in a permit application rather than hope that abutters will not stir up community objections at a later time.

3.6 MECHANICAL SYSTEMS

3.6.1 Introduction

Mechanical systems are the source of ventilation for recording studios, control rooms, and associated spaces. The acoustical concerns generally are mechanical systems as a source of noise produced by such items as fans and airflow and as a path for sound transmission between spaces as through ductwork. A more complete treatment of the mechanical system as a source of noise may be found in Ref. 6.

3.6.2 Sound Generation by Fans

Fans which are required to move air through a ventilation system inherently generate noise. Many factors determine the amount of noise generated, including the type of fan used, the volume of air to be delivered, the static pressure against which the fan is forcing the air, the blade passage, and the efficiency of the fan system.

The most common type of fan used for ventilation systems is the centrifugal airfoil fan, although other types of system are not unusual. Each system tends to produce its own characteristic spectrum of frequency, but in general fans used for ventilation systems tend to produce more low-frequency noise energy than high-frequency noise energy. In most cases, these fans are contained within a prefabricated housing which in turn is connected to the supply-air ductwork system and to the return-air ductwork system. It is imperative to note that the sound generated by a fan propagates as easily through the return-air system as through the supply-air system because the speed of sound is so much faster than the speed of the air within the ductwork.

The sound power level generated by a fan may be calculated by the following equation:

$$L_w = K_w + 10 \log (q) + 20 \log (p) + K \qquad (3.16)$$

where L_w = sound power level of fan, dB
  K_w = specific sound-power-level factor for type of fan, dB
  q = volume flow rate, ft³/min (m³/s)
  p = static pressure, in of water (kPa)
  $K = 0$ (metric $K = 45$)

K_w for centrifugal airflow types of fans tends to arrange itself in a smooth spectrum with values of approximately 35 to 40 dB in the 63-Hz octave band and transitioning down to 10 to 15 dB in the 8000-Hz band. It should be noted from Eq. (3.16) that a doubling of the volume flow will add 3 dB of sound power level, whereas a doubling of pressure will add 6 dB to the sound power level. Therefore, it is important to design a ventilation system with adequately sized ductwork and with smooth transitions and bends to keep the static pressure as low as possible.

An additional pure-tone component to the noise, *blade-frequency increment* (BFI), is generated by each fan blade passing by an edge or obstruction, such as the discharge opening of the fan unit. The octave band in which it falls has to be determined by calculating the blade-passage frequency and referring to Table 3.1.

Blade-passage frequency = r/min × number of fan blades/60   (3.17)

Most fan systems are of a design that gives a BFI of 3 to 10 dB in the 125- or 250-Hz band. The result is that unless this BFI is adequately attenuated, the audible pure tone will be in the same range of frequency as the fundamentals of speech and many musical instruments.

Fans should be selected for a maximum efficiency rating. A decrease in efficiency results in an increase in the sound power level generated. Most systems operate at a reduced efficiency which adds approximately 5 dB to the fan power level, and poorly selected or improperly maintained fans have been known to add as much as 20 to 25 dB to the fan power level.

Noise generated by the fan not only travels down the supply and return ductwork systems but also is radiated off the fan housing. In general, the fan housing is a very poor isolator of sound and for most practical purposes, especially in lower frequencies, can be considered to provide no isolation whatsoever. Therefore, it is good practice to locate the fan assembly well removed from the recording studio and control room.

Most reputable fan-system manufacturers provide octave-band sound-power-level data for their systems. These numbers are obviously preferable to the generic methods of calculations described here. In addition, other devices within the mechanical system may incorporate smaller fans, such as fan-powered terminal boxes. These smaller devices are generally located in the ductwork closer to the specific rooms to be ventilated, providing an extra boost to the airflow as required by the system. The accuracy of these generic methods of calculation tends to decrease as the size of the fan decreases, but the octave-band sound power level of these smaller devices is also generally available through the manufacturer.

3.6.3   Turbulent Noise in Ducts

Airflow noise is generated by turbulence within the ductwork and at diffusers and dampers. Air turbulence and, therefore, airflow noise generally increase as the speed of airflow increases. Therefore, it is good practice to keep the speed of airflow low. Several rules for controlling airflow noise are:

1. Size ductwork so that the flow of air stays below 2000 ft/min and preferably below 1500 ft/min. (The velocity of air in a duct may be calculated by dividing total cubic feet per minute in that duct by the cross-sectional area in square feet of the duct itself.)

2. Airflow velocities through diffusers should be kept below a maximum of 500 ft/min through all diffusers. For critical applications, lower speeds such as 200 to 300 ft/min are advisable.

3. Air valves and dampers should be located so that the airflow noise that they generate does not contribute to the noise ducted from upstream sources.

4. Splits and bends in the ductwork should be smooth. Abrupt corners and bends should be avoided, especially near the fan, near high-airflow-velocity locations, and near diffusers and grilles.

Airflow noise is typically a major component of mid- and high-frequency background noise in recording studios. However, when there are abrupt bends and turns in ductwork systems, especially with high airflow velocity, an enormous amount of low-frequency energy may be generated. This may be extremely difficult to control.

3.6.4 Attenuation of Noise by Ducts

Various elements within the ducted ventilation system inherently provide some attenuation of the noise as it travels through the ductwork, both down the supply-air system and up through the return-air system. Certain elements, such as internal duct lining and prefabricated silencers, can be added to the system as necessary to increase noise attenuation.

Bare ducts, that is, sheet-metal ducts which lack any added sound-absorptive lining, provide a minimal but measurable amount of attenuation to the noise. The amount of attenuation depends on such factors as width and height dimensions and the length of that section of ductwork under consideration. For ductwork, this duct attenuation is approximately 0.1 dB/ft of duct length for frequencies of 250 Hz and above regardless of width and height dimensions. For example, the 1000-Hz-band noise level inside the end of a 10-ft length of bare rectangular duct should be approximately 1 dB less than inside the beginning. For lower frequencies, this duct attenuation is approximately 0.2 dB/ft of duct length or even up to 0.3 dB/ft for ductwork as small as 5 to 15 in in either width or height. Typical data are shown in Table 3.5. It is important to note that duct attenuation increases in the lower frequencies because the thin sheet metal of which the ductwork is constructed is a poor barrier for low-frequency sound transmission, and as a result these low frequencies "break out" of the ductwork and into the surrounding space. Thus, it is advisable to reroute ductwork which is known to contain high levels of sound energy, especially low-frequency sound energy, from spaces which require low background noise.

Sheet-metal duct may be lined with sound-absorptive material. This material is generally of about 1½ lb/ft density and of either 1- or 2-in thickness (the 2-in thickness generally provides improved duct attenuation, which can be an important consideration, especially for low-frequency noise control), and it often has a mastic facing to reduce shredding and deterioration from high airflow velocities. For lined ductwork, duct attenuation is very much dependent on the width and height dimensions and on the octave frequency band of interest. Sources such as Ref. 6 or specific manufacturers' data should be consulted for a detailed analysis of lined-ductwork attenuation. It should be noted that noise breakout, especially for low frequencies, is not significantly affected by lining.

Splits, divisions, and takeoffs in the ductwork represent further attenuation to the ducted noise. It is assumed that the amount of noise energy delivered is proportional to the amount of air delivered. For example, if a fan which provides a total of 10,000 ft³/min of air delivers only 1000 ft³/min of air to a particular room (the other 9000 ft³/min of air is delivered to other rooms by means of splits and divisions), the amount of air delivered to that room is reduced to 10 percent of the total, whereas the noise or power level is reduced by 10 log (0.1) of the total. In other words, the splits and divisions have reduced the amount of noise delivered to that room by 10 dB. Similarly, a split which sends half of the air down one duct and the other half down another duct has reduced the amount of noise entering each of these two ducts by 3 dB, which is derived from 10 log (0.5) = 3 dB.

Bends and elbows in ductwork are not very effective in attenuating low-frequency noise but can provide significant attenuation of higher-frequency noise. Lined elbows and bends provide better high-frequency attenuation than bare elbows and bends. Bare elbows may provide up to 3 dB of attenuation at 2000 Hz and above, and lined elbows can provide between 5 and 10 dB of attenuation in the higher frequencies, depending on the elbow radius and duct diameter. Typical data are shown in Table 3.6.

3.6.5 Duct Silencers

Prefabricated duct silencers generally incorporate a system of parallel sound-absorptive baffles between which the air must flow (see Fig. 3.10). Silencers are available in a wide range of sizes and duct attenuations which tend to vary with frequency. Manufacturers should be able to provide detailed data on the performance of their silencers. These data should include the octave-band *dynamic insertion loss* (DIL), the pressure drop across the silencer, and the self-generated noise of the silencer. The effective attenuation of a silencer in any given octave band can change with the airflow velocity through the silencer. This is measured in terms of the DIL, which is duct attenuation in octave bands at different airflow velocities, both positive and negative. Positive DILs rate the effectiveness of a silencer when the noise and the air both flow in the same direction, as in the case of a supply-air system, and negative DILs apply where noise flows in the opposite direction of the airflow as in a return-air system. Since the baffles in a silencer restrict the flow of air to a certain degree, the silencer can add to the static pressure against which the fan must work, so that the pressure-drop ratings of silencers can become an important consideration. Since the baffles generate a certain amount of turbulence in the airflow, silencers can generate a certain amount of noise. Silencers should be positioned so that the amount of attenuated noise leaving them is still higher than the generated noise of the silencers, which implies that the silencers should be placed relatively close to fans. On the other hand, it is good

TABLE 3.5 Approximate Duct Attenuation

Duct type	Duct diameter, in	Approximate duct attenuation, dB/ft							
		63 Hz	125 Hz	250 Hz	500 Hz	1 kHz	2 kHz	4 kHz	8 kHz
Bare, rectangular or square	5–15	0.3	0.3	0.2	0.1	0.1	0.1	0.1	0.1
	16–45	0.3	0.2	0.1	0.1	0.1	0.1	0.1	0.1
	46–90	0.2	0.1	0.1	0.1	0.1	0.1	0.1	0.1
Bare, oval or round	5–15	0.15	0.15	0.1	0.05	0.05	0.05	0.05	0.05
	16–45	0.15	0.1	0.05	0.05	0.05	0.05	0.05	0.05
	46–90	0.1	0.05	0.05	0.05	0.05	0.05	0.05	0.05
1-in-thick lining, all duct shapes	5–15	0.4	0.5	1.2	2.5	5.0	4.5	3.0	1.5
	16–30	0.4	0.3	0.7	1.3	2.5	2.0	1.5	0.7
	31–45	0.4	0.3	0.3	0.8	1.4	1.2	0.9	0.5
	46–60	0.3	0.3	0.2	0.6	1.0	0.8	0.7	0.4
	61–75	0.3	0.3	0.2	0.4	0.8	0.6	0.5	0.3
	76–90	0.3	0.3	0.2	0.4	0.7	0.5	0.4	0.2
2-in-thick lining, all duct shapes	5–15	0.6	1.0	2.3	4.0	5.0	4.5	3.0	1.5
	16–30	0.4	0.4	1.0	2.0	2.5	2.1	1.5	0.7
	31–45	0.4	0.4	0.7	1.4	1.4	1.2	0.9	0.5
	46–60	0.3	0.3	0.5	0.9	1.0	0.8	0.7	0.4
	61–75	0.3	0.3	0.4	0.8	0.8	0.6	0.5	0.3
	76–90	0.3	0.3	0.3	0.7	0.7	0.5	0.4	0.2

TABLE 3.6 Approximate Elbow Attenuation

90° elbows and turns	Duct diameter, in	Approximate elbow attenuation, dB/elbow							
		63 Hz	125 Hz	250 Hz	500 Hz	1 kHz	2 kHz	4 kHz	8 kHz
Unlined round elbow or square turn	5–30	0	0	0	0	1	2	3	3
	31–45	0	0	0	1	2	3	3	3
	46–90	0	0	1	2	3	3	3	3
Lined round elbow or square turn with turning vanes	5–30	0	0	0	1	2	3	4	5
	31–45	0	1	1	2	3	4	5	5
	46–90	0	1	2	3	4	5	5	6
Lined square turn without turning vanes	5–30	0	0	1	2	3	5	7	9
	31–45	0	1	2	3	5	7	9	11
	46–90	1	2	3	5	7	9	11	11

practice to locate silencers at least five duct diameters downstream of a fan in the supply-air system; otherwise noise generated by turbulent air, especially low-frequency noise, can greatly exceed the rated self-noise of the silencers. Placement of silencers in return-air systems is less critical, but a spacing of at least three duct diameters between fan and silencer is still advisable.

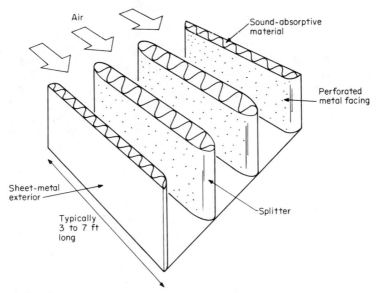

FIG. 3.10   Cutaway view of a typical duct silencer.

3.6.6   Calculating Resultant Sound Levels

A convenient method for determining the sound power levels which enter a room is to list the noise-generating and noise-attenuating devices in the ductwork system sequentially, beginning with the fan. This should be done for both supply-air systems and return-air systems. The following analysis should be performed octave band by octave band.

For each device, calculate either the sound power levels generated or the amount of attenuation provided by each element. Then sequentially subtract the attenuation provided by each element until a noise-generating device is encountered. At this point, the resultant sound power level which has made its way through the ductwork should be added to the sound power level generated by the appropriate device. Continue with this method until the octave-band sound power levels at the end of the run of ductwork (at the point at which the sound begins to enter the room) have been calculated. Then convert the sound power levels to sound pressure levels at various points of concern within the room according to Eq. (3.2).

The resultant octave-band sound pressure levels then may be plotted against NC curves, such as in Fig. 3.9, in order to determine whether the ventilation-system noise satisfies the criterion decided upon for the appropriate space. If the levels are too high, noise attenuation devices may be incorporated in the ventilation system. The calculation procedure may then be repeated to take into account the effect of the attenuation devices. If an attenuation device is inserted into the system, it is important to delete the effect of the part of the system which has been omitted. For example, if a 5-ft-long attenuator is inserted in a length of lined duct, then the effect of 5 ft of lined duct should be eliminated from subsequent calculations. Otherwise the calculations may result in inappropriately low sound pressure levels.

3.7 SOUND ISOLATION

Sound may travel to an adjacent space by a multitude of paths. Obviously it can travel through apertures. But if all these holes are sealed, the sound is ultimately received after vibrations have been transmitted through the building structure. Since they travel readily in solid materials, the vibrations may take long, devious paths before arrival. If high noise isolation is required, all paths that the vibration may take need to be interrupted; there is little value in blocking one path when a significant amount of the sound travels through a flanking path.

3.7.1 Walls

In most building applications involving audio systems a very sizable transmission loss is often required. The performance of the single homogenous wall is inadequate. As shown in Eq. (3.11), it can be seen that doubling the mass of the wall gains only 6 dB. Often space or floor-loading restrictions also limit this option. Alternatively, increased performance can be obtained from a two-wall system such as is shown in Fig. 3.11, in which one wall is completely separated from the other, over its entire area, by an air gap. Reverberant sound within the interior

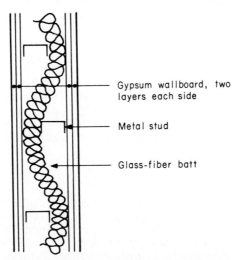

Gypsum wallboard, two layers each side

Metal stud

Glass-fiber batt

FIG. 3.11 Section of a lightweight double wall.

cavity is absorbed by fiberglass. The coincidence dip is reduced by ensuring that the frequency at which it occurs is different for each wall.

Care must be taken not to inadvertently reduce the design TL by tying the two walls together with a mechanical connection, such as a wall bolt or perhaps a pipe. Also, care must be taken with air leaks. Electrical outlet boxes on opposite sides of the wall must be staggered by at least 3 ft. Conduit and pipes should pass through the wall at its perimeter. The joints between the wall ceiling and floor must be grouted or caulked with an elastomeric compound. Never use foam caulk for acoustical isolation. If an air duct must pass through the wall, special arrangements must be made to ensure that sound does not travel into the duct wall, through the wall, and back out through the duct wall into the adjoining space. (For further details refer to Sec. 3.7.7.)

3.7.2 Partial Walls and Barriers

The effectiveness of sound barriers depends partly on the amount to which sound traveling over the top or around the sides is diffracted (see Sec. 3.5.4). In practice, the effectiveness is limited, even under the most favorable geometric layout, to about 25 dB. The material of construction does not influence a barrier's performance provided that its transmission loss is sufficient to block significant sound from passing through. For many applications, ¾-in plywood has sufficient mass and may be used effectively, but other materials are often preferred because they meet other criteria such as weatherability or structural strength.

Where barriers are also used in interior spaces such as partitions or gobos, their performance is degraded by the reflection and reverberation of sound from the adjacent walls and ceiling. Equation (3.15) and Fig. 3.7 predict the level of the diffracted sound, but to it must be added the reverberant-sound level. In many situations reverberant sound greatly exceeds the diffracted-sound level. For example, an omnidirectional sound source 4 ft above the floor has an octave-band level of 90 dB at 10 ft and a frequency of 500 Hz. The objective is to reduce sound levels by installing a 6-ft-high barrier midway between the source and the receiver. To calculate the barrier attenuation, find the Fresnel number from Eq. (3.15); $d = 2 \sqrt{5^2 - 2^2} - 10 = 0.77$, and $\lambda = 1140/500 = 2.28$, giving a Fresnel number of 2 (0.77/2.28) = 0.68. From Fig. 3.7 the noise reduction is 12 dB. However, if the source is in a room with a room constant of 1000 ft² at that same frequency, then Eq. (3.7b) shows that the receiver is beyond the critical distance (4.5 ft) and the reverberant sound level dominates. Since installing the barrier cannot reduce the reverberant field, the partition is totally ineffective at reducing sound levels.

Where barriers fully or partially enclose a source, some additional performance can be gained by reducing the local reverberant field by applying absorptive materials to the inside surface of the partition and other adjacent surfaces.

3.7.3 Doors

The door is potentially the limiting element in noise isolation for an interior wall. Not only may the frame reduce the transmission loss of the mounting wall, but improper sealing of gaskets further reduces performance. Furthermore, a good noise control design does not assume that gaskets will remain good after abuse by substantial traffic. Alternatively, a design with two well-fitting ungasketed doors should be considered. A significant increase in performance can be obtained by placing the doors a minimum of 4 in apart. Further improvements can be made by increasing the separation between the two to form an *air lock* in which acoustically absorptive materials are applied. The close-separation arrangement is awkward to use since the two doors must open in opposite directions. The air-lock design may be more convenient, though it does occupy more space.

3.7.4   Ceilings and Floors

Much of that which applies to walls also applies to ceiling and floor elements, but there are additional precautions to be taken. The addition of carpet to a floor does not decrease the airborne sound transmitted to the space below. However, carpet does reduce the generation of impact noise. Impacts on a hard floor from shoe heels and rumblings from steel-tired hand trucks are readily discernible.

In renovations where it is often the preference to refinish old wooden floors, noise isolation is difficult. The floorboards often have major cracks, and if, in addition, no solid ceiling is permitted below, the sound transmission loss is unacceptable.

If the transmission loss of the floor structure is found to be inadequate, it can be increased by applying a ceiling mounted to resilient channels, which in turn are fastened to the joists. Better still, a complete lower ceiling may be supported by resilient hangers which penetrate the upper ceiling to attach to the joists. It may be possible to use the cavity for air ducts as long as duct *breakout* is not a problem (see Sec. 3.7.7). Otherwise additional noise isolation for the duct must be provided.

3.7.5   Floating Rooms

Where maximum noise isolation is required and cost is of little concern, a room may be floated within a building space on vibration isolation pads. All building services are supplied through flexible connections. All doors are double, with the inner door and frame attached only to the floating room. The cavity around the room and under the floor is filled with sound-absorptive material. This type of construction is little used in commercial applications.

3.7.6   Windows

Most window manufacturers can supply TL data on their products. These show that single-glazed windows typically have much less transmission loss than walls, and if they represent more than a small fraction of the wall area they are usually the controlling element when the composite transmission loss of wall and window is calculated by applying Eq. (3.14). Also data show that the coincidence dip occurs in the midfrequency range, which could be of concern when controlling the compressor whine of a jet engine. However, for glass in which a plastic damping layer is sandwiched between two glass layers, the depth of the coincidence dip is reduced.

Thermal glazing, two glazings with an air space, is also commonly used. However, because the panes are close together, cavity resonance restricts any improved performance. But when the panes are separated by several inches and sound-absorptive material is applied around the cavity perimeter, there is a marked improvement in performance.

The local building code may require that a window with a specified STC be installed, but for noise control applications STC values are insufficient. The full spectral data should be used in any computations.

3.7.7 Duct Break-In Break-Out

Mechanical-system ductwork has the potential for reducing the overall transmission-loss integrity of a partition as a result of sound in one space *breaking in* through the sides of the ductwork, traveling through the duct, and *breaking out* of the ductwork into another room. Detailed calculations of this effect can be quite complicated, but the effect should be accounted for. The calculation procedure for duct break-in and break-out may be found in Ref. 6.

It is good practice to avoid running a duct through a partition which is common to two spaces that require a high degree of sound isolation between them. It is generally advisable to run the main branch of ductwork outside either room under consideration and branch ductwork from the main duct into the appropriate rooms; then, to determine the resultant sound isolation, the maximum sound pressure level expected in one room should be converted to sound power level at the point at which the ductwork serving that room begins. Then the attenuation provided by the ductwork elements between the rooms may be calculated as described above, and the sound power level may be converted to sound pressure level in the other room in question. If it is determined that the resultant sound pressure level will be too high, attenuation devices may be provided in the ductwork. For example, a silencer should be inserted into the ductwork in the manner shown in Fig. 3.12. Sometimes it is also advisable to box in the ductwork with a construction which consists of several layers of gypsum wallboard to reduce the amount of sound which breaks into a piece of ductwork. It is almost never sufficient to wrap the ductwork with fiberglass materials, and it is rarely sufficient to wrap the ductwork with lead sheet or vinyl sheet.

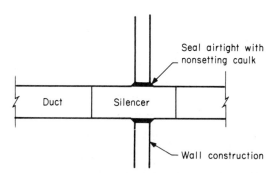

FIG. 3.12 Installation of a silencer between two rooms.

3.7.8 Site Selection

When building a new facility, it is worthwhile to evaluate in detail the suitability of the site itself for ambient and interfering noise as well as for production and aesthetic requirements. The cost of construction to meet the specified criteria may be much greater at one location than another. For example, the interior noise might be dominated by ground vibration from an adjacent railroad yard. Breaking this vibration path can be very expensive.

An industrial site might appear to be an excellent location to avoid the complaints of neighbors late at night, but the facility may not be usable if punch presses are installed next door. If jet aircraft fly close by, special construction may be required to protect the facility from low-frequency noise. Consequently, it is imperative to check with the local airport authority about flight patterns that are likely with different prevailing winds.

3.8   VIBRATION

Excessive vibration can cause several problems for audio engineers, including reradiation of vibration-induced noise from walls and direct vibration of microphone elements through mike stands. There exist quite a variety of vibration sources, such as mechanical equipment, automobile and truck traffic, and even pedestrian traffic within a building. Once vibration has entered the building structure, it may be very difficult to control, and this problem may be exaggerated by resonances found in all buildings, which commonly occur in the range of 5 to 25 Hz. Thus it is important to try to determine which sources of vibration may be problematical and to isolate them before vibration enters the building structure.

3.8.1   Driving Frequency

The driving frequency of the vibration source is the most important consideration in trying to develop a vibration isolation system. It is not unusual for a source to have several driving frequencies, but it is the lowest driving frequency that is of primary concern. The lowest driving frequency of most electrical and mechanical equipment can be determined from the lowest rotational or vibrational motion. For example, a fan that operates at 1200 r/min has a lowest driving frequency of 20 Hz (this same fan may have a harmonic at 200 Hz if the fan has 10 blades).

To isolate mechanical equipment, some sort of vibration isolation device is placed between all the supports of the piece of equipment and the building structure, such as underneath each of four legs. The vibration isolation elements generally consist of steel springs, some sort of resilient material such as neoprene rubber, or a combination of the two. As the machine is installed, it compresses the mounts by an amount known as the *static deflection*. When installation is complete, it can also be seen to have its own natural frequency. The natural frequency can be thought of as the frequency in hertz at which the machine would oscillate after it was deflected from rest. For example, an automobile with poor shock absorbers (shock absorbers add damping to the vibration isolation system) would continue to bounce up and down at a couple of hertz after it had been driven through a pothole.

The frequency ratio f_r is defined by

$$f_r = f_d/f_n \tag{3.18}$$

where f_d is the driving frequency, Hz, and f_n the natural frequency, Hz.

The static deflection d and the frequency ratio (f_r) are related in the simplest case by

$$d = 9.8(f_r/f_d)^2 \tag{3.19a}$$

where d is deflection, in,

or
$$d = 250(f_r/f_d)^2 \qquad\qquad (3.19b)$$

where d is deflection, mm.

3.8.2 Vibration Transmission

Transmissibility rates the effectiveness of the vibration isolation system. Figure 3.13 shows a plot of transmissibility against frequency ratio for a steel spring and a highly damped isolator. Steel springs are used where the driving frequency is below 30 Hz. Neoprene is used for higher driving frequencies.

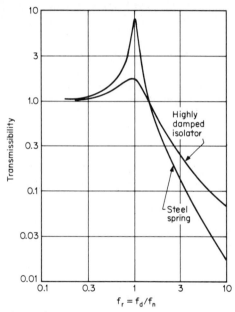

FIG. 3.13 Transmissibility of a steel spring and a highly damped isolator.

The vibration isolation system is selected according to the static deflection necessary to provide adequate transmissibility. The procedure is as follows:

1. Select the material of construction of the mounts for transmissibility according to the application. A transmissibility of 0.03 is generally acceptable. Also, if the equipment to be isolated is to be located in close proximity to a critical space, special designs should be considered.

2. Find the value of f_r, the ratio of driving frequency to the natural frequency, which intersects the transmissibility curve at the proper value of transmissibility. For example, in Fig. 3.13, which shows the transmissibility curve of a steel spring, a minimum value of 8 for f_r is necessary to achieve a transmissibility of 0.03.

3. Determine the static deflection from Eq. (3.19).

4. Select from a manufacturer's catalog mounts of the required material of a size that will deflect the calculated amount under the static load of the machine.

3.8.3 Vibration Isolation

It is important to note that several factors can significantly reduce the effectiveness of isolators. Any item that short-circuits the isolator, such as rigid conduit or solid refuse lodged under the equipment, can carry substantial vibrations to the building structure and seriously degrade the performance of an isolation system. In addition, if the isolators stand on a flexible floor span rather than a basement slab, reduced isolation must be expected. In this special situation more sophisticated methods than those outlined here must be used to ensure adequate performance. (See Ref. 6.)

3.9 INTERIOR ACOUSTICS

3.9.1 Quality of Sound

Previous sections have primarily addressed issues relating to the amplitude of sound, or sound pressure level. Here the quality of sound is considered with primary emphasis on the natural acoustics of an interior space. Those qualities that are appropriate for electronic processes are addressed elsewhere in this handbook.

Interior acoustics are graphically illustrated here with actual displays from an acoustical scale model in which wall components are progressively assembled to form a complete room. The noise source is a small electric spark that produces a short impulsive sound, and the listener is represented by a special high-frequency microphone. For each model configuration an echogram is made in which the vertical scale is in decibels and the horizontal scale is in milliseconds, with zero time being the instant when the sound is generated at its source. Though a 1:20-scale model was used, all illustrations are indicated for full scale. Similar echograms may be made in a building by using a bursting balloon as a sound source, but, of course, it is not as easy to change the room shape rapidly.

When source and microphone are located above a very reflective floor with the angles of incidence and reflection at 45°, the echogram can be seen as the spiky trace shown by the solid line in Fig. 3.14. The floor echo arrives 10 ms after the direct sound, traveling 2 times farther and also spreading 6 dB per doubling of the distance. With the two impulses arriving at less than 50 ms apart, the ear is unable to resolve the sound into two separate sounds, just hearing one. The second trace, a steplike waveform in the same figure, is calculated in the signal analyzer and is a summation of all the sound energy in arriving echoes. At any point of time it shows the total sound energy that has been received up to that moment. This display is the equivalent steady-state sound level of the impulsive sound. It can be seen from this line that the reflection adds only a step of 2 dB to the level of the direct sound. Subjectively, the echo makes the direct sound seem only just a little louder, for the ear cannot easily detect a 2-dB increase in sound level.

With the erection of a single wall, another impulse appears on the echogram,

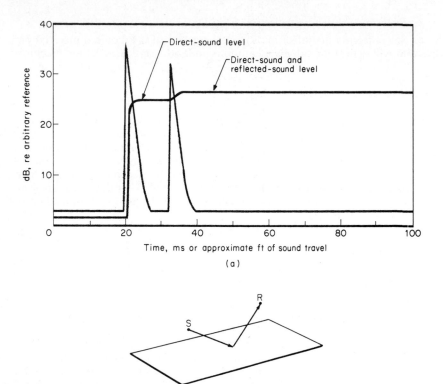

FIG. 3.14 Echogram of sound reflecting from a hard surface.

the reflection from the wall. But Fig. 3.15 shows that there is yet another echo, one that is the result of the sound traveling in sequence from floor to wall. The three echoes are not equal in strength to the direct sound. Instead, since they are attenuated by spherical spreading, they add merely 4 dB to the direct sound.

One wall may be added to the first wall at right angles as shown in Fig. 3.16. Now it becomes more complicated to calculate the number of echoes that will appear. In fact, eight spikes are now shown. They can be traced to reveal the direct sound, three single reflections, three double reflections, and one triple reflection. From the steplike trace it can be seen that they add 6 dB to the direct-sound level. An increase in level of this magnitude is readily detected by the ear.

As will be seen from the echogram in Fig. 3.16, this initial package of sound echoes typically constitutes the bulk of the sound energy that arrives at the listener in a completed room. The initial echo structure is important in the way in which the listener perceives the sound. If this package of early arrivals is no more that 50 ms wide, it will be perceived by the listener as being the direct sound. If it is stretched out, the music will lose precision and definition. In smaller, narrower halls, the sidewalls provide early reflections, but in a large fan-shaped hall lateral reflections from walls arrive too late to help. Likewise the ceiling often cannot

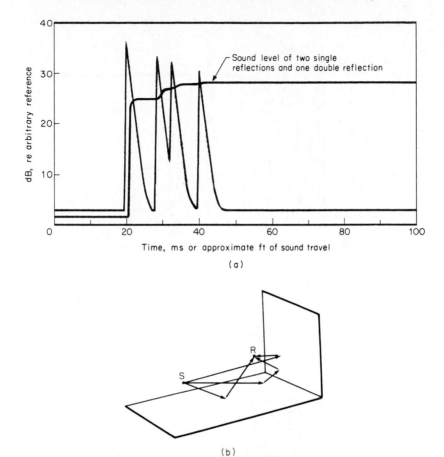

FIG. 3.15   Echogram of sound reflecting from one wall and a floor.

contribute because it is too far away. Thus to provide these early reflections, "clouds" are often hung above the stage and angled for sound dispersion.

Alternatively a parallel wall may be added as shown in Fig. 3.17. This gives an echogram reminiscent of sneaking a sideways view between parallel mirrors. The images extend with decreasing strength to infinity. They are not evenly spaced but paired because the sound travels farther in its reflection from one wall than the other. This echogram depicts the phenomenon known as *flutter,* in which sound most unpleasantly zings between parallel walls. Care must be taken in room design to prevent flutter between windows and the opposite wall or between a hard ceiling and floor. One of the pair of reflective surfaces must be made absorptive or be angled to diffuse the sound.

With the first wall replaced so that three walls are now standing, the configuration in Fig. 3.18 is similar to a complete room with an acoustically dead end, a live end, and a dead ceiling. The previous clear infinite string of images is now concealed among many other echoes, making it almost impossible to identify the

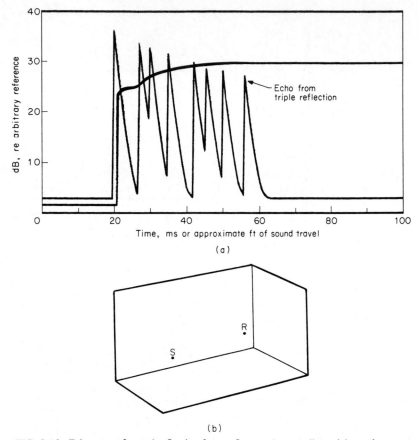

FIG. 3.16 Echogram of sound reflecting from a floor and two walls at right angles.

path of each, particularly as many echoes overlap each other. The echogram is reminiscent of a reverberation decay curve. However, its unevenness reinforces the concern given in Sec. 3.3.5 that reverberation-time measurements within such a room can lead to erroneous results.

As the remaining wall and ceiling are added, the echogram becomes more continuous until it is filled in with echoes. Figure 3.19 shows the fully reverberant echogram of the complete space. The reverberation time is 3 s. Note that the final sound level is 34 dB. This sound level is reached substantially in just 10 percent of the reverberation time.

It is important that the later-arriving echoes do not "muddy" or mask the earlier sound. Thus, to maintain good sound definition for music the sound energy arriving after the first 50 ms should increase the level by approximately 3 dB. In Fig. 3.19 note that the sound level increases by 7 dB after the early arrivals, showing too much reverberation for music. For clear speech, the increase should be approximately 1 to 2 dB above the earlier sound energy. A more in-depth treatment of preferred relationships between early- and late-arriving sound energy may be found in Refs. 7 and 8.

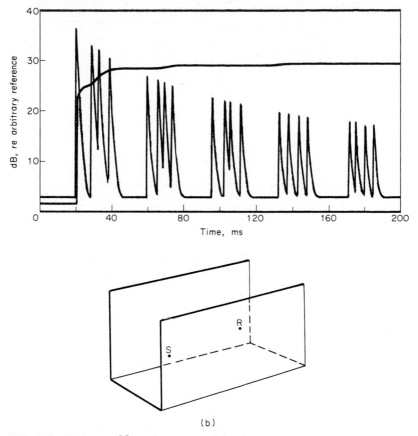

FIG. 3.17 Echogram of flutter between parallel walls.

It is most desirable to have the echoes decaying with gradually decreasing amplitude. A discrete echo can be caused by focusing, as when sound reflects from a curved wall in the rear of a fan-shaped room. For some listeners the focused sound may arrive well after the early arrivals and be clearly identifiable. For a rear wall, this effect is usually controlled by absorbing the sound at the curved wall. However, the sound may be diffused by installing angled reflecting surfaces which each have dimensions greater than the wavelength of the sound. The placement and angles will need careful determination so that other focusing is not formed.

3.9.2 Design Concerns of Spaces

It is rare that an auditorium is used for a single purpose. As outlined in Sec. 3.5 concerning acoustical criteria, it is noted that optimum acoustical requirements vary widely for each type of usage. For example, reverberation time may require changing over a range of 1 to 2 s. Some hall designs have used revealable acoustical absorption to attempt this change; solid wall panels open up so that fabric

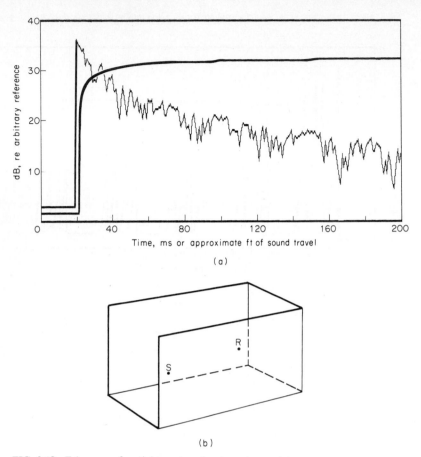

FIG. 3.18   Echogram of partial reverberation in an incomplete room.

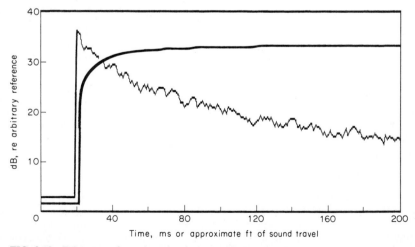

FIG. 3.19   Echogram of reverberation in a complete room.

panels can be extended. A quick reference to Eq. (3.6) shows that these panels need to reveal enough fabric to double the total acoustical absorption in the space. This may be an unwieldy solution, for not only does it require large dedicated wall spaces, but it may also kill desirable lateral reflections that enhance the early-arriving sound.

Alternatively, significant gains can be made through the application of directional loudspeakers for those activities that require a shorter reverberation time, such as speech. By aiming the majority of the sound energy at the audience, the proportion of the energy in the early-arriving sound is substantially increased compared with the sound energy entering the reverberant field, thus increasing intelligibility. Be warned that directional speakers cannot be used to full effectiveness in spaces where the basic sound absorption has not been applied.

Another choice is to build a short reverberation time into the basic acoustics of the space; then as each application warrants, the reverberant field is reinforced with a sound system that amplifies the reverberant-sound field. One advantage of these electronic methods is that sound can be readily equalized for each application over the full frequency range; in contrast, this is almost impossible with mechanical devices. These electronic techniques may be applied strategically only to selected areas of a hall, such as areas deep under balcony seating, where local reverberation is restricted.

3.9.3 Small Rooms

When the dimensions of a space become comparable with the wavelength of the sound, simple acoustic methods are inappropriate because it no longer is possible to access the properties of the whole space by using the available properties of component parts. More confidence can be placed in the design of acoustic properties of an interior space when the space has dimensions much larger than the wavelength of the sound, where, for example, flat surfaces reflect sound with the angle of incidence equal to the angle of reflection. Sound energy pumped into a small space may influence the production of the immediately following sound. Thus, as the room becomes smaller, it becomes less possible to predict the outcome accurately. Surfaces are smaller, and the popular sound-ray diagram is entirely inappropriate, especially for low frequencies. Also, the smaller-angled surfaces can become stiffer and the construction becomes less uniform, making any mathematical description of the environment very difficult.

For these reasons, no specific recommendations can be made, for each component is an integral part of a close-coupled system in which each component reacts with all others. However, two useful observations may be made:

1. If an acoustically symmetrical room is required at low frequencies, it should have symmetrical construction well beyond the interior walls. A room with a gypsum wall tied to a cinder-block wall on one side is not the same as a freestanding wall on the other. They may appear to be the same, but they are not the same acoustically.

2. A variety of construction techniques, each of a different surface weight and stiffness, can improve the uniformity of the response of the room throughout its frequency range.

When the acoustics of a space needs correction, many complex techniques are available to track down the problem. Besides microphone systems, accelerometers can be used to analyze wall vibration levels in conjunction with the sound pressure level. These analysis techniques are too specialized to be considered in this handbook.[2]

3.9.4 Masking

Masking is used in spaces in which sound sources need concealing. For example, in an open administrative office where the conversations of others are readily overheard, the noise criterion may be less than 35. But rather than applying noise-controlling devices and destroying the functionality of the space, the interior noise level may be raised to mask the conversations. This is achieved by installing an array of small loudspeakers inside the drop ceiling that uniformly distribute broadband noise throughout the plenum to the space below. Provision is made within the master broadband noise generator for adjustment of the spectral shape so that maximum speech masking can be obtained with a minimum amount of obvious sound intrusion. Even so, it is preferable to introduce such systems to the office environment slowly by increasing the sound level gradually over a period of weeks until the goal is reached. These units may also be installed above corridors to prohibit eavesdropping on conversations in adjacent rooms. In sleeping areas masking will blot out intrusive sounds.

There is a limit to the application of masking systems. The masking noise levels cannot exceed NC 40 without being regarded as a noise intrusion.

3.10 ANNOYANCE

Annoyance is very difficult to quantify. But often when sound becomes noise, pleasure becomes annoyance. Each person has his or her own way of reacting to the wide variety of sounds. Here are some factors that influence the degree to which people are annoyed.

1. *Source of sound:*   An individual will react differently to the same noise coming from different sources. The noise of a neighbor cutting a lawn is annoying. On the other hand, the noise from cutting one's own lawn is acceptable, while the noise of a neighbor cutting your lawn is music.

2. *Benefit of sound:*   If the sound is the result of an activity that brings economic benefit to the listener, tolerance increases. A town official supports renting the local stadium to a rock group because it will provide significant income, but residents fear outsiders' causing damage and congestion.

3. *Adaptation:*   People become used to certain noises. A freight train passes each night 50 ft from a sleeping family. It passes undetected. For the same family, a night in the country is disturbingly quiet.

4. *Impulsive noise:*   Impulsive noise is more annoying than steady noise, particularly if it occurs at unpredictable intervals. The slamming of automobile doors as people arrive and depart often causes complaints.

5. *Tonal noise:*   If the sound contains a tonal component such as a whine, buzz, or hum, it is more annoying than broadband noise of the same loudness. Many state and local governments recognize this by lowering the permissible noise limits for such sounds. A rooftop transformer and an exhaust air blower are typical offenders.

6. *Variability:* Sounds which vary more in amplitude with time are more annoying than steady sounds. The greater the statistical standard deviation of the sound, the more annoying it is.

7. *Speech interference:* Typical speech has a level of 60 dBA at the listener's ear. Other sounds may mask speech so that it becomes unintelligible. For example, the noise of a nearby heat pump may make speech unintelligible on the neighbors' patio. Special procedures to determine the intelligibility of speech may be found in Ref. 5.

In some instances, however, evaluation of a noise complaint in terms of the listed items may show minimal impact. But careful investigation may further show that other important issues hide behind protests. For example, residents who live near an outdoor amphitheater may be more concerned about property damage, trespassing, and parking-lot activities than about noise. It is important to consider all aspects of the operation of a facility.

REFERENCES

1. *ASA Standards Index 2,* Acoustical Society of America, New York, 1980.
2. L. L. Beranek, *Noise and Vibration Control,* McGraw-Hill, New York, 1971.
3. *Catalogue of STC and IIC Ratings for Wall and Floor/Ceiling Assemblies,* Office of Noise Control, Berkeley, Calif.
4. *Method for the Measurement of Monosyllabic Word Intelligibility,* ANSI S3.2-1960, rev. 1977, American National Standards Institute, New York, 1976.
5. *American National Standard for Rating Noise with Respect to Speech Interference,* ANSI S3.14-1977, American National Standards Institute, New York, 1977.
6. *ASHRAE Handbook—1984 Systems,* American Society of Heating, Refrigerating and Air-Conditioning Engineers, Atlanta, 1984.
7. Harold Marshall and M. Barron, "Spatial Impression Due to Early Lateral Reflections in Concert Halls: The Derivation of the Physical Measure," *JSV,* 77(2), 211–232 (1981).
8. Gary W. Siebein, *Project Design Phase Analysis Techniques for Predicting the Acoustical Qualities of Buildings,* research report to the National Science Foundation, grant CEE-8307948, Florida Architecture and Building Research Center, Gainesville, Fla., 1986.
9. Cyril M. Marris, *Handbook of Noise Control,* 2d ed., McGraw-Hill, New York, 1979.

BIBLIOGRAPHY

Beranek, L. L.: *Acoustics,* McGraw-Hill, New York, 1954.

Egan, M. D.: *Concepts in Architectural Acoustics,* McGraw-Hill, New York, 1972.

Huntington, W. C., R. A. Mickadeit, and W. Cavanaugh: *Building Construction Materials,* 5th ed., Wiley, New York, 1981.

Jones, Robert S.: *Noise and Vibration Control in Buildings,* McGraw-Hill, New York, 1980.

Kryter, K. D.: *The Effects of Noise on Man,* Academic, New York, 1985.

Lyon R. H., and R. G. Cann: *Acoustical Scale Modeling,* Grozier Technical Systems, Inc., Brookline, Mass.

Morse, P. M.: *Vibration and Sound*, American Institute of Physics, New York, 1981.

Talaske, Richard H., Ewart A. Wetherill, and William J. Cavanaugh (eds.): *Halls for Music Performance: Two Decades of Experience, 1962–1982*, American Institute of Physics for the Acoustical Society of America, New York, 1982.

CHAPTER 4
DIGITAL AUDIO

In spite of the fact that professional audio has been handled predominantly in analog form for more than a century, it would appear that a total transition to digital audio technology is under way after less than 20 years of experience. Why? The general answer is that, as the analog elements in the *audio chain* (i.e., recording, processing, transmission-distribution, and reproduction) are replaced with digital elements, a number of advantages appear. These advantages relate to audio quality, operational efficiency, new processing possibilities, or economy.

Although the introduction of digital audio is perceived by many to be revolutionary, it has been steadily introduced by broadcasters—such as the BBC in the United Kingdom and NHK in Japan—from as early as 1967. However, it is the more recent advances in high-density data recording and signal processing that have extended the technology to the recording studio, the dubbing theater, and the domestic living room.

This chapter examines the entire *digital audio chain,* that is, the signal path from origination through the processes of recording, postproduction, and transmission to the home listener, and discusses some of the remarkable technological achievements that have been made in this maturing field. Topics covered include a discussion of the advantages of digital audio over analog audio, a brief look at the history of digital audio, and an introduction to digital signal fundamentals with emphasis on the components of conversion systems and the problems of evaluating such high-quality systems. Also described are professional applications of digital audio technology in the music-recording, broadcasting, film, and video industries. Lastly, some of the consumer products available and the components utilized in digital audio conversion systems are examined.

DIGITAL TECHNIQUES*

P. Jeffrey Bloom

Digital Audio Research Limited, Chessington, Surrey, England

Guy W. McNally

Digital Audio Research Limited, Chessington, Surrey, England

4.1 OVERVIEW

4.1.1 Technical Considerations

Certainly, the advantage most apparent to a critical listener is that the fidelity of sound recorded and reproduced using current digital audio technology has reached a level of quality beyond that normally attained by the most advanced analog means. More important, this quality is now beginning to satisfy the most demanding listeners' criteria in terms of dynamic range and signal-to-noise. Furthermore, high quality can be preserved (one expects) for an indefinite period of time in a variety of media from which the reproduction should sound identical. Thus, the major appeal of digital audio to the listener is its lasting and media-independent high fidelity.

In addition, professional audio engineers, whose job it is to capture, manipulate, or sometimes generate acoustic events, are discovering advantages in the operational features and processing capabilities of digital audio processing systems. Such systems can implement precise and repeatable operations on audio signals and thereby provide signal manipulation and the generation of effects that would be largely impossible, uneconomical, or of lower quality outside the digital domain.

A further advantage of digital audio is the ability to time-multiplex a large number of signals in the transmission processes or in digital mixing consoles without significant crosstalk. This allows very efficient use of data pathways and greatly simplifies cabling and connection requirements.

4.1.2 Economic Factors

The introduction of any new technology usually is fraught with difficulties. In the case of digital audio some equipment currently tends to be more expensive than its analog counterpart, standards are difficult to establish, and testing or repair work may require a specialist's attention. Moreover, the current complexity and relatively high cost of very simple amplitude manipulation and editing in the digital domain has considerably retarded the penetration of digital audio into areas of the entertainment industry (namely, motion pictures, video, television, and radio), where in many cases the cost of audio equipment is more critical than achieving the highest possible sound quality. Fortunately, however, with every

* Reprinted with permission from Institute of Electrical and Electronics Engineers, *IEEE ASSP Magazine*, October 1985, article entitled "High-Quality Audio in the Entertainment Industry."

new generation of more highly integrated and, consequently, lower-cost digital components, the resistance to digital audio based on economic arguments is decreasing.

A more serious issue has arisen, however, whose long-term impact could be devastating. Because digital copies of audio material can be identical to the original commercial piracy (i.e., unlawful copying and selling) or even unauthorized home copying could become so widespread that the artists, producers, and recording companies using digital audio for product distribution might find this medium economically unviable. This problem is examined in detail in Sec. 4.4.2.

4.1.3 Historical Background

A few of the significant events in the history of audio and digital audio are given in Table 4.1. One can surmise that before 1960, even though the principles for binary-coded pulse-code modulation (PCM) were established around 1937,[1] digital conversion and storage technology were not sufficiently advanced to challenge analog techniques seriously. Several technical advances in the 1960s, however, began to facilitate research in the area of digital audio. The most relevant of these developments—the emergence of low-cost, high-speed digital circuits, minicomputers, and digital instrumentation technology, in addition to the rapid growth in the new field of digital signal processing—gave a few farsighted individuals, familiar with these developments, the opportunity to begin to apply them to audio products.

Yet in spite of the fact that research into digital simulation of artificial reverberation appeared as early as 1961,[2] the first demonstrations of the potential and practical impact of digital audio did not emerge until 10 years later, when stronger motivation existed for using this new technology. First, a process (i.e., variable time delay) could be implemented that previously had been impractical by analog means, and, second, some of the weakest links in the audio recording and distrib-

TABLE 4.1 Some Important Events in the History of Audio

1857	Leon Scott demonstrated the phonautograph (a talking machine).
1877	Edison filed his patent "Improvement in Phonograph or Speaking Machine."
1925	Electrical recording and reproduction introduced by Bell Laboratories.
1927	First motion picture with sound released *(The Jazz Singer).*
1937	Binary-coded PCM invented by A. H. Reeves.
1948	Columbia introduced LP (long-playing) record.
1961	Digital reverberation simulated in computers.
1967	NHK (Japan) demonstrated digital audio tape recorder.
1971	Digital delay line introduced.
1971	BBC demonstrated stereo digital audio recorder.
1972	Records digitally mastered by Nippon Columbia, Japan.
1972	PCM used in United Kingdom for high-quality sound distribution for radio and TV.
1975	Real-time digital reverberation system available.
1976	Digitally restored Caruso record released.
1976	BBC demonstrated 10-channel digital recorder.
1977	Several professional digital audio recorders released.
1980	Idea of compact-disk system announced.
1982	Compact-disk players released.
1984	First professional digital audio mixing console released.

ution chain could be replaced. Consequently, by 1971 a digital audio delay line was available commercially,[3] and the BBC was not only distributing audio digitally to some of the more remote parts of the United Kingdom, but it (and soon others) was demonstrating experimental digital audio tape recorders.[4] In the mid- and late 1970s, the potential and credibility of digital audio were advanced further by the introduction of a commercial real-time digital reverberation system,[5] the release of digitally restored Caruso recordings,[6] and the eventual introduction of several high-quality, multitrack professional digital tape recorders.[7] At last, digital audio was being used in the field (or at least being heard) by nonspecialists.

Over the next few years, a number of professional digital audio processors emerged that performed mostly single or related functions such as adding reverberation, pitch shifting, and phasing. More sophisticated audio processing still tended to be confined to general-purpose minicomputers operating in nonreal time, although some programmable digital audio processors were being built on an experimental basis.[8]

In 1982, with the release of the compact disk (CD), an unusual situation suddenly existed. For the first time, at the end of the audio chain, reproduction for the home listener could have the same quality that existed at the beginning of this chain. In fact, a CD player provides better audio quality in the home than many of the analog machines still being used in many studios to record first-generation program material.

Nevertheless, although recordings may now be made and reproduced digitally, there still may be stages of processing (such as analog mixing) which require the audio to reenter the analog domain before it is redigitized for encoding on a CD master. Such transformations, unfortunately, can each raise the background noise level by as much as 3 dB. But because digital processing and mixing are only now emerging as a commercial reality, digital "islands" exist in an ocean of analog technology (Ref. 9, p. 221). This situation is changing, however, beginning with the introduction of the first large-scale professional digital audio mixing consoles[23] in 1985. This at last demonstrated that all-digital studios are technically feasible and that the source signal, once digitized, can remain digital throughout the many stages of processing and storage until the end user converts the digital signal to analog for amplification and audition.

4.1.4   Analog Signal Shortcomings

Analog signals are so named for the reason that the physical characteristics describing a waveform originally in one medium are transformed to physical characteristics describing a waveform in another medium. Information carried thereby in the new waveform varies in a way analogous to variations in the original signal. Generally, an analog signal is a continuous-time, continuous-amplitude representation of another continuous-time, continuous-amplitude signal, and, ideally, the two signals should be linearly related.

In audio, one is primarily concerned with representing acoustic phenomena by analogs created in transducers, electrical networks, and recording media (Fig. 4.1). In the case of most transducers (such as microphones) and electrical networks, only one analog is created, and that is between the input and output signals' amplitudes. No analog is needed for the characteristic of time. Consequently, most problems encountered with analog transducers and networks result from minor nonlinearities, phase distortion, and component noise.

In conventional analog *recording* processes, however, two continuous analogies must be created by using physical characteristics of the storage medium: one for the signal amplitude and the other for time (Fig. 4.1*d*). For example, time is represented by increasing linear distance along magnetic tape in analog tape recording and, in conventional disk recordings, by decreasing nonlinear distance along the groove. In both cases, *distance,* being a continuous quantity, provides a convenient and continuous analog to time. The amplitude of the original signal is encoded into a second, continuously variable property of the physical media. If the coding of these two analogs were done ideally, an analog recording could provide a perfect representation of the original signal.

Unfortunately, in practice all analog recording techniques are susceptible of two general classes of problems: those which affect the recording medium's analog to time and those which affect the analog to amplitude. The classical terms which

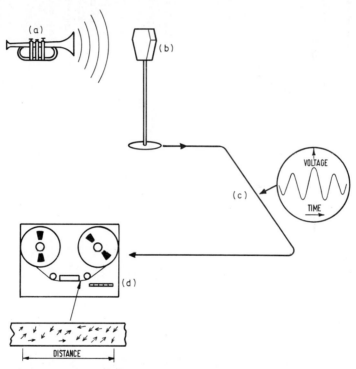

FIG. 4.1 Analog signals in the recording process. (*a*) Pressure waveform (continuous-time, continuous-amplitude). (*b*) Transducer (pressure-to-electrical). (*c*) Electrical analog waveform (amplitude: voltage is analog to pressure; time: no analog). (*d*) Analog recording (amplitude: flux produced by magnetic-particle orientation is analog to pressure; time: distance-velocity of tape past head = time).

Sources of signal degradation in analog recording:
  Time analog distortion:
    *Fluctuations in tape speed past head
    *Stretched tape
  Amplitude analog distortion:
    *Nonlinear head-to-tape transfer characteristic
    *Print-through
    *Dropouts
    *Noise floor determined by random orientation of magnetic particles
    *Limited frequency response

TABLE 4.2 Comparison of Analog and Digital Audio System Specifications

Specification or feature	LP record	Analog multitrack tape recorder (at 15 in/s)	Compact-disk system	Digital multitrack tape recorder
Frequency response	30 Hz–20 kHz ±3 dB	20 Hz–20 kHz ±3 dB	20 Hz–20 kHz +0.5/−1 dB	20 Hz–20 kHz +0.5/−1 dB
Dynamic range	70 dB (at 1 kHz)	70 dB (unweighted)	>90 dB	>90 dB
Signal-to-noise ratio	60 dB	64–68 dBA (unweighted or weighted)	>90 dB (unweighted)	>90 dB (unweighted)
Harmonic distortion	1–2%	<0.52%	0.004%	<0.05%
Separation between channels	25–30 dB	40–60 dB	>90 dB	>80 dB
Wow and flutter	0.03%	0.03%	None detectable	None detectable
Durability	High-frequency response degrades with playing	Depends on tape quality	Semipermanent	Depends on tape quality
Stylus life	500–600 h	Not available	5000 h	Not applicable
Effect of dust, scratches, or fingerprints	Causes noise	Causes dropouts	Generally correctable or concealed but occasional dropout possible	Same as for compact disk
Residual level of signal after erasing	Not available	−70-−80 dB	Not applicable	None
Print-through		<−60 dB	Not applicable	None

describe the measured performance of the complete recording and playback process (such as complex frequency response, signal-to-noise ratio, and wow and flutter) quantify different aspects of the recording chain's failure to preserve time and amplitude analogies precisely. Currently, typical figures for the preceding characteristics indicate that analog techniques are far from ideal (see Table 4.2).

Recordings made in analog media also suffer from either localized or widespread degradation of the recording medium; obvious examples of these types of defects are dropouts (in magnetic media) or scratches (on disks). Such problems again result from the fact that time is inextricably associated with a unique distance along the recording medium; consequently, if the medium is damaged in a particular region, the signal's amplitude will be corrupted at the time period corresponding to the damaged area. Moreover, very few analog techniques exist to detect signal degradation resulting from recording-medium defects and to recover the original signal waveform.

In defense of analog technologies, first, it must be said that analog transmission techniques require a lower bandwidth than comparable simple digital ones (that do not use bandwidth compression). Second, analog transducers and electrical processing systems generally can be made acceptable on a subjective, practical, and economical basis. Nevertheless, it appears that very few analog recording or broadcasting techniques are completely satisfactory in all these categories. It is mainly for this reason that digital audio attracted so much attention initially; it appeared that at least the weakest links in the audio chain could be replaced and improved through the adoption of digital technology.

4.2 DIGITAL SIGNAL FUNDAMENTALS: PERCEPTION AND CONVERSION SYSTEMS

4.2.1 Establishment of Performance Targets for High-Quality Audio Systems

General Design Criteria. In professional audio, the requirement of achieving subjectively high fidelity imposes numerous technical criteria on the performance of the optimum conversion process. However, the design specifications for the complete conversion system are governed by two general criteria.

The first criterion for an adequate system is to ensure that it can handle all possible signal-source characteristics even though they might be highly improbable. Fortunately, there is sufficient practical information about acoustical sources of interest to listeners to know that, for the most part, the dynamic range and spectral energy content of "interesting" sources are generally accommodated by the ear.

Of course, characteristics of certain signal classes, e.g., sound effects or synthesized sounds, can exceed the range humans can accommodate and, therefore, improbable but possible source characteristics must be handled satisfactorily without undue cost or complexity. In practical terms this requirement has profound engineering implications as well as economic and aesthetic ones.[11] Nevertheless, this consideration might be regarded as a demand for the initial conversion process at least to match the ear's range of audibility.

The second criterion for an adequate system is to be able to reproduce signals that are perceptually indistinguishable from the original. Note that the concept of *perceptually indistinguishable* allows the signal to be limited by the conversion system (i.e., in frequency or dynamic range) or even degraded electrically as long as the alteration is inaudible to the most sensitive listener.

Characteristics of the Human "Receiver." Because of the extreme importance of matching the conversion system's performance to the most sensitive human listener, the most relevant information related to the hearing process will be reviewed briefly. First, the limits of audibility will be considered.

1. *Limits of audibility:* For the normal listener, the ear is most sensitive to frequencies between 2000 and 5000 Hz at the threshold of hearing. This sensitivity drops for frequencies above and below this region such that by 200 Hz and 15 kHz it is approximately 20 dB lower.[12] In addition, detection of a 20-kHz pure tone is possible for some people at high levels [>80 dB sound pressure level (SPL)[15] or >100 dB SPL[14]]. Despite this possibility, some experiments reveal that even highly trained listeners cannot discriminate between conditions of 16- and 20-kHz low-pass cutoff on program material containing considerable energy at and above 20 kHz.[13,15] This result supports studies done as early as 1931, which established that a band from 40 Hz to 15 kHz is sufficient to reproduce music without an audible change in the reproduction. Nevertheless, recent work examining the low-frequency limits for reproduction suggests that the presence of frequencies below the cutoff of the audible range (20 Hz) can contribute to a more lifelike sound quality.[16] Thus, for an ideal audio system, a generous choice of bandwidth might be 0 Hz to 20 kHz, and an acceptable bandspread would be 20 Hz to 15 kHz.

2. *Dynamic-range requirements for audio reproduction:* To establish the dynamic range required for signal *playback* in the ideal system, a number of facts must be considered. The ear's effective dynamic range is 100 dB or more.[12] However, for subjectively noise-free reproduction of music in a quiet environment it has been suggested that approximately 118 dB of dynamic range is required to provide a listener with the maximum peak SPL and an undetectable noise spectrum.[17] This criterion was based partly on measurements of peak instantaneous sound levels of acoustical musical instruments (e.g., orchestral peaks registered 113-dB SPL, normal-miked percussion 122-dB SPL, and close-miked percussion 120- to 139-dB SPL), as well as electronic instruments (which could deliver 128-dB SPL and higher). At the low end, an average threshold for white-noise detection in a home and studio environment was 4-dB SPL measured over a 20-kHz bandwidth even in rooms with broadband noise levels of 50-dB SPL. This numerically unlikely feat was explained by two facts. First, a narrowband of frequencies around 4.5 kHz was probably responsible for the detection of this signal because that band was not masked by high-level, low-frequency sounds. Second, sound localization of the test noise at the loudspeaker aids the detection process.[17]

On the basis of these limited studies, an ideal system must provide for playback somewhere from 100 dB to nearly 120 dB of dynamic range to fulfill the dual requirements of capturing the range of program-material dynamics and matching the ear's range. This issue will be taken up again in a later section.

3. *Auditory masking and the perception of signal degradation:* Next, the general topic of signal degradation in the conversion process is discussed briefly because the requirement that a system be perceived as *transparent* allows signal distortion to exist as long as it is kept inaudible. The two general types of distortion for any system, analog or digital, are (*a*) the lack of waveform fidelity arising from a nonlinear response of the system and (*b*) the generation of components which are not in the original signal.

The question of sensitivity to linear distortion is examined when the conversion system is discussed in the next two main sections. Determining whether or not a particular system will produce the second type of distortion (i.e., unwanted spectral energy) at sufficiently high levels to be audible is a formidable problem. This is true because no simple models exist for describing the range of signal sources, the behavior of individual and combined elements of the conversion chain, the interaction of these two previous factors, or the hearing process. Until recently, the tendency has been to make traditional tests of a conversion system with simple signals (e.g., pure tones) to evaluate performance in easy-to-understand electrical terms. Such tests are not necessarily sufficiently sensitive to reveal some of the more subtle system defects.

Fortunately, there is a considerable body of relevant psychoacoustic data which at least provides a guide to understanding the auditory system's response to various signal and noise distributions. These data describe the phenomena associated with *auditory masking,* which may be defined as "decreased audibility of one sound due to the presence of another" (Ref. 12, p. 283).

It is known that under certain conditions one sound (a test stimulus) which is normally audible by itself may be rendered inaudible by another (masking) sound. This phenomenon occurs not only when test stimulus and masker are presented simultaneously but also when no overlapping occurs in time. Because there is such a vast number of experimental conditions,[12,18] it is difficult to summarize the results in a concise form useful to designers of professional audio systems. Such a task is especially complicated because a large proportion of the available experimental data is based on signals (such as tones and broadband or narrowband random noise) which bear little resemblance to sources of interest to listeners. Designers must be aware, however, that the fundamental aspect of masking is the auditory *critical band.*

Numerous experiments on masking and related effects[12,18] indicate that the ear displays frequency-analysis properties resembling those of highly asymmetric tuned filters. One typical and relevant masking experiment is shown in Fig. 4.2. If a narrowband of noise centered at 410 Hz is presented at 80 dB as a masking

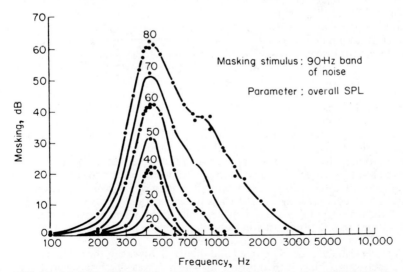

FIG. 4.2   Masked audiograms for a narrowband of noise centered at 410 Hz in which each curve shows the elevation in pure-tone threshold as a function of frequency for a particular level of the masking noise.[41]   *(From B. C. J. Moore,* An Introduction to the Psychology of Hearing, *2d ed., Academic, London, 1982.)*

stimulus, the detection thresholds of pure tones around 410 Hz are raised from their absolute threshold by approximately 60 dB. Similarly, the 410-Hz masker elevates the thresholds for tones at 200 and 2000 Hz by similar amounts (approximately 10 dB). Such results demonstrate both the asymmetry of the auditory filters and how masking spreads to frequencies above the masker more effectively than to those below.

The effective bandwidth of the auditory filter is generally described in terms of critical bands, which are roughly equal (<100 Hz wide) below around 500 Hz and above 900 Hz vary proportionally with center frequency (one-third to one-sixth octave wide). Other results reveal that signals with most of their energy concentrated in the region from 1 to 3 kHz tend to produce the most effective masking.[19]

Because masking relationships are complex and are not completely understood, one must be cautious when trying to extrapolate from one masking situation to another. As an example, "masking produced by narrow-band noise is not directly predictable from masking experiments with wide-band noise, and vice-versa" (Ref. 18, p. 295). Nevertheless, in subsequent sections regarding audible distortion, it is important not to forget the effects of the ear's limited resolving power.

4.2.2   Analog-to-Digital Conversion

Basic Principles and Advantages of Sampling and Quantizing Signals.   The generation of a digital signal from an analog signal is a simple process conceptually. In operation, the analog waveform is sampled periodically, and the samples are digitized sequentially (i.e., converted to a corresponding sequence of binary numbers). To re-create the analog signal from the digital sequence, these steps are reversed. That is, the sequence of binary numbers is consecutively converted back into a sequence of electrical samples which ideally should represent the original waveform samples. Of course, making these conversions into and out of the digital domain transparently (i.e., free from degradation) is an elusive and challenging goal for reasons that will be discussed in the following sections.

It is important to emphasize how the very different idealized processes of sampling and quantization theoretically affect the information in the input signal (Fig. 4.3). The process of sampling a band-limited signal (using a sampling frequency that is more than twice the highest frequency component in the signal) does not eliminate any of the signal's information, nor does it generate noise components or degrade the signal quality. On the other hand, even ideal quantization of a signal implies that there is a lower limit to the signal amplitude differences that can be resolved, and finer differences (i.e., signal information) will be lost. Moreover, because quantization is inherently a nonlinear process, distortion products will be created. Nevertheless, the rules for quantization may be specified so that these distortion components can be kept inaudible. There are, of course, practical limitations arising from cost and technology which currently make it very difficult to produce a perceptually adequate system.

Once a signal has been sampled and digitized, however, the explicit association that each sample has with the time at which it was taken is severed. This fact provides the basis for most of the advantages of digital audio: the samples of the signal can be processed, stored, duplicated, or fed to a digital-to-analog converter completely independently of each other. Moreover, once a signal has been digitized, it can be protected from degradation. This is true because the analog for the dimension of time is no longer a simple feature of the recording or transmitting media; it is a parameter of the signal which can be exploited in a variety of useful ways.

One example of the beneficial use of the time between samples is to employ error correction techniques, and this, coupled with the high quality of conversion

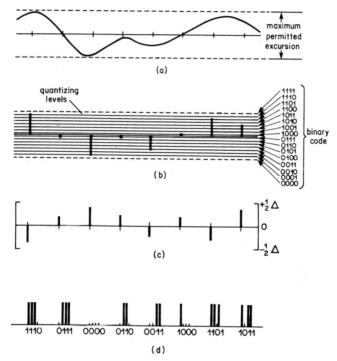

FIG. 4.3 Binary pulse-code modulation in a 4-bit system. (a) Band-limited analog input signal. (b) Sampled signal derived from a shown against quantizing levels △ apart. (c) Quantizing error (magnified) derived from b. (d) Binary pulse-code-modulated signal derived from b. (After D. E. L. Shorter, J. R. Chew, D. Howorth, and J. R. Sanders, Pulse-Code Modulation for High-Quality Sound-Signal Distribution, BBC Engineering Division Monograph 75, December 1968.)

systems in current digital audio recording and transmission systems, provides audio performance specifications (Table 4.2) measurably superior to the best analog systems.

The details of the conversion process are presented next to show how digital techniques provide such high-quality audio and why there is a limit to how high this quality can (or should) be.

System Overview. The system used to "generate" a digital signal from an existing electrical waveform involves a number of devices, the most essential set of which is shown in Fig. 4.4. The parameters of this initial conversion establish the maximum signal quality provided by the total system; moreover, any degradation introduced at this stage will remain with the digitized signal.

Of course, there are a number of different design strategies for implementing these devices as well as those discussed in Sec. 4.2.3, and each strategy will have certain advantages and limitations that must be considered in terms of interaction

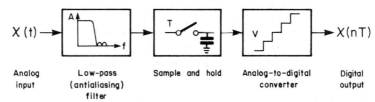

| Analog | Low-pass | Sample and hold | Analog-to-digital | Digital |
| input | (antialiasing) filter | | converter | output |

FIG. 4.4   Main components in an analog-to-digital conversion system; sampling frequency is $1/T$.

with other system components, the complexity and cost of system production, and, most important, the perceptual goals discussed previously. In addition, there is the need to handle extreme and, to some extent, unspecified signal characteristics which may be modified in certain components. Figure 4.5 presents an overview of the numerous factors that influence the design of conversion-system components.

In the following, the components of the analog-to-digital (AD) conversion system will be studied first and discussed in terms of their functions, variations in implementations, and potential sources of signal degradation. Additional discussions of certain types of degradation will be presented in Sec. 4.23.

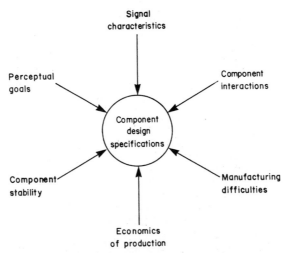

FIG. 4.5   Factors influencing the design of analog-to-digital and digital-to-analog conversion-system components.

Low-Pass Antialiasing Filter. The first device usually required in the AD conversion system is an analog low-pass filter (Fig. 4.4), whose sole function is to band-limit the input signal energy without introducing excessive linear or nonlinear distortion and without generating excessive noise. This is a critical operation because, in the following stage, when the filter's output signal is sampled at the sampling frequency (f_S), any frequencies in the signal or filter-generated noise or distortion above one-half of the sampling frequency $f_N = f_S/2$ (which is known as the Nyquist frequency) will be folded or aliased and appear as signal contributions below f_N. For a frequency f between f_N and f_S, the frequency of an alias is $f_S - f_N$. Moreover, because components generated by aliasing can relate inharmonically to the input signal's high-frequency energy variations, they are not likely to be masked completely by the true baseband spectral energy distribution. This type of distortion is not correctable in later stages and, therefore, may be audible.

Filter design specifications to ensure that aliasing distortion is not audible can be made exact only after fixing f_N and determining the following:

1. Maximum expected input spectral energy distribution above f_N and its level and slope relative to the maximum expected peak energy below f_N

2. Sensitivity of the ear around f_N

3. Permissible level of linear waveform distortion

4. Dynamic range of the following conversion system

5. Attenuation-versus-frequency characteristic of the anti-image filter in the output

At present only reasonable estimates exist for the first three items in the preceding list, thus rendering design of these filters somewhat arbitrary.

In addition, given the rather stringent filter characteristics required to reduce aliasing distortion to acceptable measurable levels, one is faced with the practical problem of designing an analog filter that meets these specifications without introducing any serious degradation of its own. In practice, a computer-aided filter design program is often used to produce between a seventh- and eleventh-order design incorporating active filter elements; and good analog engineering is required to design networks that keep the amount of distortion from high signal levels, noise, and harmonic distortion to acceptable levels.

Further signal waveform degradation arises from excessive passband ripple, which can cause not only spectral modification but dispersion (i.e., *time-smearing*) effects[20] or *echo distortion*[21] of the signal waveform, although the perceptibility of these is not well studied. Additional waveform distortion results from very steep transition bands and nonlinear phase response. It is interesting to note that whereas considerable concern is expressed for what is frequently very "visible" time-domain distortion of the high-frequency content of input waveforms (generally appearing around 15 kHz or above), it has not been shown to be audible in typical high-quality systems.

In fact, there is experimental evidence that suggests such distortion is not detectable at high cutoff frequencies except in extreme (and highly contrived) circumstances.[20,22,23] This is not necessarily true for phase distortion at lower frequencies (i.e., below 10 kHz).[20,23,24] However, it is generally accepted that a relatively linear phase response should be maintained throughout the filter's passband. What are not well specified, unfortunately, are the limits of perceptibility for music signal-phase distortion. Consequently, the filter design complexity is often increased to provide an extra stage of phase compensation.

TABLE 4.3 Typical Laboratory Specifications for Low-Pass Antialias or Anti-image Filters*

Passband	dc to 20 kHz (or 15 kHz for 32-kHz sampling frequency)
Input-output peak voltage level	± 10 V
Passband ripple	$< \pm 0.2$ to ± 0.02 dB
Transition ratio, f_{stop}/f_{edge}	1.2 (e.g., 24 kHz/20 kHz)
Stop-band attenuation	>60 dB (this may be excessive)
Signal-to-noise ratio	≥ 100 dB
Distortion	-110 dB at 15 Hz; -100 dB at 20 KHz
Phase shift	$\pm 1°$ to $2°$ from linear response up to 15 kHz

* R. Lagadec, D. Weiss, and R. Greutmann, "High Quality Analog Filters for Digital Audio," presented at the 67th Convention of the Audio Engineering Society, New York (October 1980), preprint 1707 (B-4); B. A. Blesser, "Advanced Analog-to-Digital Conversion and Filtering: Data Conversion," in B. A. Blesser, B. Locanthi, and T. G. Stockham, Jr. (eds.), *Digital Audio,* Audio Engineering Society. New York. 1983.

In designing these filters, the main degrees of freedom lie in selecting the amount of passband ripple, the stop-band attentuation, the passband edge, the transition bandwidth, and the amount of acceptable phase distortion. Obviously a "good" antialiasing filter design will keep distortion and aliased energy at levels slightly below that arising from the noise or distortion components in subsequent system components. However, it is worth noting that as yet there has not been any definitive study which measures perceptual sensitivity to passband ripple or aliasing distortion. Studies of the discrimination between passband ripple conditions of 0.1 dB versus a reference of 0.0001 dB and of aliasing distortion using a 10-kHz low-pass cutoff with 60- versus 140-dB stop-band attenuation have been initiated in the audio engineering community,[14] but the results from these studies are not published at present.

Nevertheless, high-performance antialiasing filters can be produced in the laboratory with typical specifications as shown in Table 4.3.[25,26]

Sample and Hold. The sample and hold (Fig. 4.4) is an analog device required to create alternatively a very short aperture of time during which the input-voltage level is tracked and then sampled and a much longer window during which the sampled voltage is held at the sample-and-hold output. The ADC turns the held voltage into a quantized number. The main sources of degradation which must be controlled are the following: errors in the periodicity of the sampling mechanism (timing jitter), nonlinear changes in the sampling aperture duration, and changes in the held voltage during digitization *(droop).*

Timing jitter during sampling generates a signal-dependent, broadband, additive modulation noise. Maintaining clock accuracy to between 5 and 30 ns should render this type of distortion inaudible on all but extreme test signals. For example, an 80-ps accuracy is required to hold the error signal to -100 dB for a 20-kHz full-scale sine wave sampled at 50 kHz. Similarly, sampling aperture timing errors (which are mainly significant for high-level very-high-frequency signals) will not produce audible degradation if the aperture accuracy is held to within 200 ps.[27]

To understand the errors resulting from droop in the hold phase, one must actually understand the quantization process which follows. Generally, the held voltage should not change by more than a fraction of the smallest quantizing step during the conversion interval. Although this is not too severe a requirement, if it is not met, two voltages which lie one quantizing interval apart in critical ranges at the device input can droop in the device so that the conversion process generates output voltages which are in error by several quantizing intervals. This situation leads to nonlinear distortion effects and degrades quality severely. A discussion of this distortion mechanism and the electrical properties of this device can be found in Ref. 27.

Analog-to-Digital Converter.   The analog-to-digital converter (ADC) (Fig. 4.4) is the device in which both quantization and binary coding of the sampled signal take place. Because the upper limit of the quality of a digital signal depends primarily upon the accuracy of this process and the maximum information encoded in the new signal, the ADC must be designed and constructed very carefully, bearing in mind the necessity of matching system performance to the dynamics of potential sources and the hearing process.

The coding of each signal sample is into B-bit binary words. The information capacity (I_s), in bits per second, of the digital signal can be expressed as $I = B \times f_s$, where fs is the sampling frequency. (Note that $f_s = 1/T$ where T is defined in Fig. 4.4.) It is the sampling frequency that determines the maximum system bandwidth, and this variable will be examined prior to a discussion of signal amplitude coding schemes.

Choice of Sampling Frequency.   The need to standardize sampling frequencies for professional audio applications generated a considerable amount of controversy. This controversy was not based wholly on aesthetic arguments, but primarily on the problems of integrating the digital audio data rate into the various image-carrying systems that broadcast and distribute audio and images to the public around the world. The details of these problems have been resolved, leaving a set of sampling frequencies now being recommended as standards. These are 48 kHz, the primary sampling frequency ("for origination, processing, and interchange of program material"); 44.1 kHz ("for certain consumer applications"); and 32 kHz ("for transmission-related applications"; see Ref. 28, p. 782), all of which satisfy the previously stated requirement of providing at least a 15-kHz bandwidth.

Of course, there are obvious penalties for utilizing the highest versus the lowest bandwidth. The main disadvantages of the higher sampling rate are having 33 percent less storage capacity and the same relative reduction in time between samples for signal processing. The main advantage of providing the higher bandwidth is that it preserves high frequencies which, for example, lie well above the third harmonic of the top note of a piccolo and can be heard by only a small fraction of the population. Therefore, some consideration must be given to which of these aspects is more important for specific applications.

Overview of Coding Schemes for High-Quality Digital Audio.   Because f_s is fixed at a minimum rate which still maintains the desired signal bandwidth, then it is important that B, the number of bits per sample, is used as effectively as possible to ensure that the maximum quality is achieved for a given rate. Using B bits, the maximum number of possible quantization levels is fixed at 2^B, which may be allocated in an infinite number of ways. For this reason, a large number of very different quantization schemes have been explored, each having a particular set of advantages and disadvantages. Many of these schemes exploit knowledge of the signal's amplitude characteristics or knowledge of the ear's limitations, or both.

There are two general classes of quantization schemes: uniform (or linear) quantization, in which the signal is quantized into steps of uniform size; and nonuniform (or nonlinear) quantization, in which the steps used are of nonuniform size. The choice of one over the other is dependent on a number of factors, which include a knowledge of the signal amplitude distribution, the importance of reducing the bit rate for more economic storage and transmission, the desired complexity and speed of subsequent processing, computational accuracy, complexity and speed of format changing, and the desire to spread quantization error in frequency. In this brief discussion, only those schemes most likely to be found in high-quality audio systems now and in the near future will be focused upon.

Uniform Quantization.   At present, it appears that a uniform scheme (using 16 bits) has become the temporary standard for high-quality audio ADCs for three main reasons: First, uniform codes are optimum for signals which are expected to be distributed evenly through the given system's amplitude and frequency ranges; second, these systems are the easiest to analyze and use in signal-processing hardware; and, third, high-speed 16-bit uniform converters (which represent the current limits of mass-produced technology) are available commercially.

It is also worth reminding users of audio conversion systems that two facts— that the 16-bit uniform code is nearly adequate for digital audio and that 16-bit words have very convenient lengths for digital computer hardware and storage technology—are simply lucky coincidences. Therefore, there is an obvious practical reason not to increase converter accuracy by only 1 or 2 bits. It would be very difficult for some hardware manufacturers to justify the additonal complexity required to handle word lengths of 17 or 18 bits should converters with this accuracy become available. As the next two sections will indicate, however, it may not be necessary or even desirable on a perceptual basis to settle for uniform conversion systems and the question of adequate word lengths will be examined further.

The operation of a uniform 4-bit ADC and its coding of the quantized signal into what is commonly referred to as a pulse-code-modulation (PCM) signal are shown in Fig. 4.3a, b, and d. Given a fixed quantizing step Δ, the maximum amplitude (of a zero-mean signal) which can be converted by such systems is $\Delta \times 2^{(B-1)}$.

The error signal between the analog signal and the quantized signal is represented in Fig. 4.3c, and it is this signal which generates quantization noise. Assuming that a signal does not overload the converter, a number of important features of such a system should be noted:[27,29]

1. The error ranges over $\pm \Delta/2$; therefore, if Δ is made smaller by using more bits, the error will decrease.

2. The error waveform can be viewed as a real signal which is not band-limited, that is, added to the input of an infinitely precise quantizer along with the signal.

3. Upon conversion from digital to analog (see Sec. 4.2.3), this error signal can be audible for simple signals because inharmonic aliases are created which appear in the baseband. Similarly, for more complex signals the noise spectrum will fluctuate and a type of modulation noise can be perceived.

4. A complex input signal of adequately high level will produce an error signal with statistically independent samples distributed evenly over the range from $-\Delta/2$ to $+\Delta/2$. In general, the spectrum of this signal will be approximately flat, falling by a few decibels by f_N. Consequently, this signal will sound like *white noise*.

5. The signal-to-noise power ratio for such a system usually is given in terms of the ratio of the power of the largest rms sinusoidal signal to the rms noise power computed for a complex signal as in item 4 and Refs. 27 and 29:

$$6.02B + 1.76 \text{ dB}$$

Thus, each bit contributes 6 dB to the dynamic range.

Unfortunately, the above analysis is not valid for very-low-level program signals in systems with uniform quantization because the quantizer will behave like a clipping or limiting mechanism. This mechanism generates distortion which generally produces inharmonic aliases, and the resulting reconverted signal is often perceived as having an unpleasant "gritty" quality modulated by the lower-frequency components of the signal. One solution to this problem is to increase the number of bits used in the ADC (without changing the sampling frequency), but this solution is not yet feasible technically or economically in high-quality systems which already have 16-bit converters.

Another approach that has produced an effective 18-bit performance in laboratory conditions is to use an *oversampling* converter system. Previously, such systems have been developed and effectively utilized in lower-quality telephone applications. They operate as follows. By initially sampling the audio signal at a rate many times higher than the desired sampling rate, the errors between the analog input and the digital output will also be generated at this higher rate and consequently spread the resulting noise spectrum well beyond the audible baseband. This noise spectrum can be shaped to reduce the baseband noise power much further by using carefully chosen circuit topologies for the converter. High-speed digital low-pass filters operating at the high sampling rate remove the unwanted high frequencies and allow the oversampled signal to be resampled at the desired (lower) rate. The filtering operation averages the samples to increase the effective resolution. A dynamic range of 105 dB (maximum rms signal to 20-kHz bandwidth rms noise) and a total harmonic distortion level of <0.003 percent (at full signal level) have been measured on such a system.[30]

Another practical alternative is to use nonuniform schemes, which will be discussed briefly in Sec. 4.2.2 under "Floating-Point Quantizing Schemes."

Dither. A more immediate solution to the problem of noise accompanying low-level signals in uniform converters is to add *dither* (a low-level noise signal typically having an rms value of approximately $\Delta/3$) to the input signal at the quantizer. The typical effect of adding dither to a 1-kHz sine wave with an amplitude of $\Delta/2$ is shown in Fig. 4.6a and b. There, the total power, in what would be very audible harmonic distortion (Fig. 4.6a), is converted to wideband noise (Fig. 4.6b), which will be perceived as benign white noise.[29]

Thus, the degradation obtained by adding dither appears as a "slight increase in the noise" (Ref. 29, p. 112) which will be acceptably small (typically 2 to 4 dB) in systems with a large number of bits. In addition, a ditherlike signal may be inherent in the analog electronics of the system's input or, perhaps, part of the signal itself.

An interesting alternative to simple addition of dither is to generate the dither signal digitally (from a pseudo-random sequence generator), convert it to an analog signal with an amplitude of less than 1 least significant bit (LSB), and then sum it with the held voltage at the input to the ADC. After a signal sample has been digitized, the analog noise sample value which was added may be subtracted digitally from the converted signal. This leaves a digital word which both is quantized effectively with more bits than the ADC uses and has the benefits of using dither as described previously but contains no degradation generated from the dither.[29]

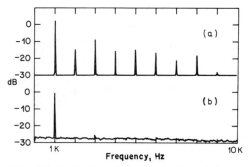

FIG. 4.6 Reduction of harmonic distortion in a DAC by use of dither. (*a*) Spectrum of digitized 1-kHz sine wave with amplitude of about 1 least significant bit (LSB) ($= \triangle$). (*b*) Spectrum of resulting signal if dither with amplitude of about ⅙ LSB rms is added to signal in *a* before digitizing. [*After J. Vanderkooy and P. Lipshitz, "Resolution below the Least Significant Bit in Digital Systems with Dither,"* J. Audio Eng. Soc., *32(3), 106–113 (March 1984).*]

Dynamic-Range Requirements.   As mentioned previously, the dynamic-range requirement for playback of musical signals to critical listeners in a quiet environment is in excess of 100 dB (see prior subsection on the dynamic-range requirements for audio reproduction). Also, the dynamics of musical-instrument peaks at the input of an ADC system could range from 120- to 140-dB SPL. The implications of these facts in the context of a uniform conversion system will be examined first.

If an untreated signal (i.e., one not undergoing any adjustment of level by human or electronic compression or limiting devices) were fed from a microphone or studio mixing console directly to a uniform PCM system, approximately 24 bits per sample would be necessary to provide the required headroom and dynamic range (i.e., approximately 24 × 6.02, or 144 dB). Of course, currently, this is not technically feasible. On the other hand, if a preset control were used to adjust the nominal maximum level reaching the ADC input, 20 bits per sample would be sufficient. Finally, if human or electronic level controls were incorporated in the audio chain before the ADC, 16 to 20 bits per sample should suffice.[31] Although 18-bit ADCs and DACs are operating in laboratories,[30,32,33] uniform audio ADCs with greater than 16-bit accuracy are not yet available commercially. Consequently, alternative coding schemes must be employed to capture the possible range of source dynamics of untreated signals. At present, the most suitable approach to achieve this end, while maintaining a sufficiently high signal-to-noise ratio, is found in *floating-point* schemes.

Floating-Point Quantizing Schemes.   Floating-point converters fall into the category of adaptive, nonuniform converters, although those considered here will have many attributes of uniform quantizers. Implementations of floating-point coding and decoding systems are shown in block form in Fig. 4.7a and b, respectively. The basic idea is that the gain of the input amplifier is adjusted to be one

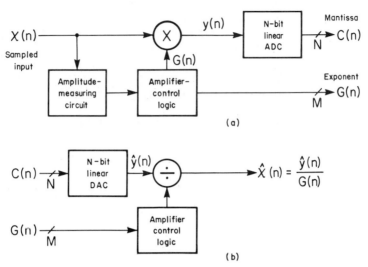

FIG. 4.7   Floating-point conversion system using a linear (i.e., uniform) ADC and DAC. (a) Encoding system whose input is a sampled waveform and whose output is an M-bit exponent and an N-bit mantissa. (b) Decoding system whose input is from the system in a and whose output is a sampled waveform value.

of several fixed levels represented by $G(n)$, such that the level of the amplified (or attenuated) sample $y(n)$ does not exceed the range of the N-bit uniform ADC which quantizes and codes $y(n)$ into the N-bit word $C(n)$. The ratios between the levels of G are arbitrary but for practical reasons are usually fixed at 6-dB intervals. These levels can then be represented in an M-bit code, forming the *exponent* of the floating-point number, whereas $C(n)$ forms the N-bit *mantissa*.

   As an example, given $M = 3$ and $N = 16$ [which will be referred to herein as a (3, 16) system], G could be adjusted over a 42-dB range (in 6-dB steps). Thus, the total range for this system would be approximately 140 dB (i.e., 42 dB + 96.3 dB + 1.76 dB). Therefore, such a system would be completely adequate for handling all but the most extreme signal conditions. Note also that this range is coded into a 19-bit word (versus a 23-bit uniform code for the same range), indicating that such systems provide considerable economy in bit rate.

   There are three other important questions to consider in assessing floating-point conversion systems, two of which largely relate to perceptual issues mentioned previously: (1) What is the signal-to-quantizing noise ratio, and is it sufficiently high? (2) How is the gain adjustment implemented to achieve optimum quality? (3) How is the floating-point data stream to be processed?

   In contrast to uniform systems, in which the dynamic range is approximately equal to the *signal-to-quantizing noise ratio with a signal present* (defined as SNR_{ws}),[27] the maximum SNR_{ws} in a floating-point converter will be determined by N (i.e., by the resolution of the uniform ADC) and will be independent of the much greater dynamic range. Changes in G will effectively alter the relative size of the quantization error, as shown in Fig. 4.8 for an ideal (3, 12) system.[27,34] It should be apparent that, by incorporating a converter with N = 14 to 16 bits (with 16 bits being suggested as the minimum-size mantissa[32]), any complex input signal will, in general, mask most quantizing components, which would be roughly on the order of at least −80 dB below the peak-signal components. With pure tones and other "simple" spectra, masking of noise cannot be guaranteed (especially for low-frequency signals), and it is recommended[27] that a dither signal be added to either $x(n)$ or $y(n)$ to remove the risk of generating audible *granular noise*.

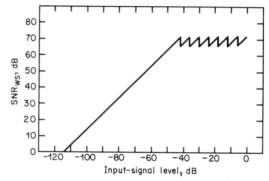

FIG. 4.8 Peak-signal-to-rms-quantizing noise ratio with signal present (SNR_{ws}) as a function of input-signal level re maximum coding range for an ideal (3, 12) floating-point conversion system.

Further use of masking principles is achieved by judiciously choosing how $G(n)$ is varied. Done on a sample-by-sample basis (known as *instantaneous algorithms*), it has been found that this approach is technically difficult to implement because of the high accuracy and stability necessary in the (wide-bandwidth) gain amplifier to avoid mismatches and offsets between gain states.[19,34] If these errors occur—and they are likely to—then waveform discontinuities will appear and generate distortion products. These may be particularly audible when gain changes occur within cycles of periodic signals.

A more acceptable class of floating-point algorithms consists of those which take advantage of masking principles to ease the technical demands on the gain-changing system. These algorithms follow general trends in signal amplitude properties according to two main operational principles. First, the gain must be allowed to increase *instantly* to the value of G which will prevent overload of the ADC. Thereby, when a waveform peak causes gain changes to occur, small discontinuities will generally be masked by the transient change in level.[34] The second principle is that the adaptation to a decreasing input level must be delayed by a time constant. In so-called syllabic algorithms this time constant is in the range of 100 to 300 ms,[27,34,35,36] i.e., commensurate with the rate at which syllables vary in speech. In *near-instantaneous* algorithms this constant is typically in the range of 0.5 to 50 ms.[19] Using either of these two *noninstantaneous* algorithms, one finds that, compared with instantaneous systems, the number and frequency of potentially audible gain and offset errors are reduced because gain changes occur much less frequently. Other benefits are that noninstantaneous algorithms reduce modulation noise which could otherwise result from low-frequency signals and also avoid the generation of quantization noise that could follow a nearly inaudible signal. One disadvantage of the syllabic and near-instantaneous systems, however, is that because noise levels can remain high longer during signal decay, the resolution required of the uniform converter is up to 2 bits greater than that in an instantaneous system[19] whose operating range is carefully set.

There are a number of other advantages of floating-point schemes. Relative to uniform ADCs, floating-point converters are less expensive to build; however, considerable engineering expertise is required to achieve low noise, wide bandwidth, and high accuracy in the gain-switching circuits.[27,34] The other advantage of floating-point converters, in which G is coded in 6-dB steps, is that the coded signal is easily converted to a uniform code for subsequent processing without hardware multiplication or division. Such conversion simply requires a shifting operation on the mantissa (possibly with sign extension) according to the value of the exponent.[37] Such a system with a (3, 16) format is in current use to provide a 24-bit range in a digital audio mixing console.[9]

One important variation on the above technique, known as block floating point, takes further advantage of the slower rate of gain changes relative to the sampling rate to reduce the aggregate data rate required to transmit high-accuracy digital audio. In this technique, a high-quality uniform or floating-point converter feeds its output words to a shift-register memory. Digital logic is used to determine the largest possible scale factor which, for a fixed number (or block) of words, maintains the block peak below full scale. All the words in this block are then scaled by this factor and read out with lower bits truncated if necessary. Because the scale factor need only be sent once per block, a considerable data reduction can be realized. Moreover, there are no scaling-related errors because the gain is digitally selected.[27]

Other Quantizing Schemes. Numerous other approaches for quantizing signals exist. Examples include *instantaneous companding,* a nonuniform system that spreads quantizing levels roughly logarithmically to make the amount of quantization error a constant percentage of the input amplitude; and *differential schemes,* which limit the total number of bits required by coding differences between successive measurements, thereby taking advantage of the signal's inherent redundancy. In addition, some of the more sophisticated examples of coders for bit rate reduction utilize properties of perception to control the quantization noise shape as a function of frequency.[35,36,38] As such, they employ principles that might be exploited in systems aiming for higher quality.

However, because most of these other quantization schemes are not currently in widespread use in high-quality audio systems and because they are discussed in considerable detail elsewhere [e.g., Refs. 26, 27, 35 (chap 5), 36, 38, 39, and 40], they will not be discussed further here.

Preemphasis. One aspect of the auditory system that is not exploited by any of the above techniques is that the ear's sensitivity decreases with decreasing frequency below around 500 Hz and with increasing frequency above approximately 5 kHz. However, this is only an approximation because threshold curves and equal-loudness contours are not monotonic above 9 kHz and the rate of growth of loudness with intensity varies considerably with frequency.[41] Nevertheless, a postemphasis characteristic which is in part complementary to the hearing-sensitivity curve can be used to shape the system-generated background-noise spectrum so that a somewhat higher level of noise power can be tolerated in spectral regions where the ear is less sensitive and provide attenuation in regions of higher sensitivity.

The benefit from using emphasis comes largely from the need to impose a complementary preemphasis frequency characteristic on the input signal in order to achieve a flat system response. Two such suggested preemphasis curves, derived from considerations of auditory characteristics and other practical considerations are shown in curves *a* and *b* of Fig. 4.9.[19] Input signals passing through a system

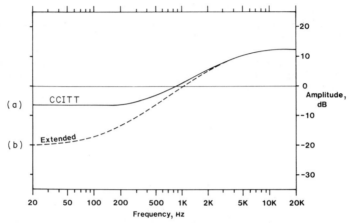

FIG. 4.9   Two proposed preemphasis curves. (*a*) A characteristic based on CCITT J.17 (which specifies a 6-dB-per-octave boost between 477 and 4134 Hz and can be implemented with a first-order filter) that has a 0.0-dB insertion gain at 1 kHz. (*b*) Version of *a* in which the low-frequency boost is "extended" to start at 100 Hz.   [*From L. D. Fielder, "The Audibility of Modulation Noise in Floating-Point Conversion Systems," J. Audio Eng. Soc., 33(10), 770–781 (October 1985).*]

with either of these characteristics will have frequencies above 1 kHz amplified and those below approximately 1 kHz attenuated. This implies that, relative to a system with no emphasis, peak levels of the low frequencies can be input by up to 8 to 20 dB higher for curves *a* and *b* respectively. Of course, if high levels of high frequencies are present, the signal may require additional attenuation. Therefore, depending on the level and the frequencies at which energy peaks occur in material being recorded, preemphasis can lead to an effective increase in dynamic range or in some (and less frequent) cases impose a decrease.

In relation to digital audio systems, it was found in one study that the use of preemphasis and postemphasis effectively reduced the dynamic-range requirements in 16-bit PCM systems by 7 to 9 dB in recording applications where the sound field in the audience position was recorded. However, in studio applications the observed reduction was only 2 to 4 dB because of the presence of substantially more high-frequency energy.[10]

In tests simulating ideal floating-point conversion systems (i.e., generating no errors other than simulated modulation noise), it was found that emphasis characteristics which improved the system's dynamic range also reduced the resolution requirements. Again, it was observed that the resolution requirements and the relative success of applying emphasis depended heavily on the distribution of spectral energy in the source material but, in general, musical passages appeared to benefit from the use of emphasis.[19]

The recommendations of this study were that a floating-point system that was adequate for capturing the full range of music signals would employ preemphasis and postemphasis, have a dynamic range of 115 dB, and provide sufficient resolution to prevent audible modulation noise. Two suggested systems that could achieve these targets were (1) a 16-bit core converter with one 18-dB step and a decay time of 0.5 ms and (2) a 13-bit core converter with 6-dB steps, a decay time of less than 0.5 ms, and extended emphasis.[19]

It should also be noted that the BBC uses CCITT preemphasis and postemphasis in its NICAM-3 companding system (in which 14 linear bits are companded to 10 bits per sample for transmission) to ensure that program-modulated noise is unobtrusive.[34] In an investigation of simulated instantaneous companding laws, it was found that the audibility of program modulated noise was reduced sufficiently through the use of emphasis such that, on average, 1 less bit was required for coding relative to the case with no emphasis.[39]

4.2.3 Digital-to-Analog Conversion

Digital-to-Analog Converter.   The conversion from a digital signal to analog typically is implemented with the three components shown in Fig. 4.10 that make up a digital-to-analog conversion system. The digital-to-analog converter (DAC) generates an analog voltage at its output which is determined by the binary word at its input. Imperfections in the DAC are, as one might expect, very similar to those in ADCs, especially since a DAC is generally employed within an ADC. The most common sources of degradation found in either of these devices are:[26,27,31]

1. Gain errors, which restrict the full voltage range from being employed and thereby increase the relative size of the quantizing error, Fig. 4.11a.

2. Static (dc offset) errors which (as in item 1) prevent the full system coding range from being activated and increase the effective level of quantizing error, Fig. 4.11b.

3. Errors in absolute linearity—the measure of the amount by which the successive output levels deviate from a straight line. These errors cause harmonic distortion.

4. Errors in relative (or differential) nonuniformity, which occur when the differences between successive quantizing steps are not of uniform size, Fig. 4.11c. The presence of relative nonuniformity introduces noise in the conversion pro-

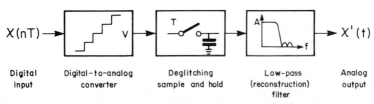

$X(nT) \rightarrow$ [Digital-to-analog converter] $V \rightarrow$ [Deglitching sample and hold] $T \rightarrow$ [Low-pass (reconstruction) filter] $A, f \rightarrow X'(t)$

| Digital input | Digital-to-analog converter | Deglitching sample and hold | Low-pass (reconstruction) filter | Analog output |

FIG. 4.10   Main components in a digital-to-analog conversion system.

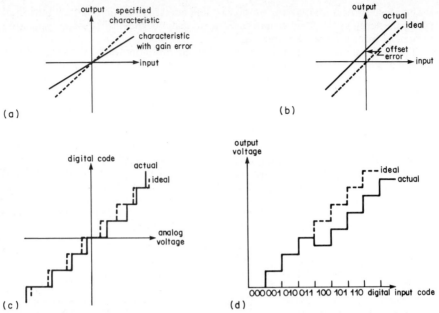

FIG. 4.11 Some examples of conversion-system errors. Items *a* to *c* can arise in both DAC and ADC systems. (*a*) Gain error. (*b*) Offset error. (*c*) Differential nonuniformity. (*d*) Nonmonotonicity in DACs. [*After N. H. C. Gilchrist, "Digital Audio Impairments and Measurements," in B. A. Blesser, B. Locanthi, and T. G. Stockham, Jr. (eds.),* Digital Audio, *Audio Engineering Society, New York, 1983, pp. 67–75.*]

cess and even a small amount (measured by conventional analog methods) can provide severe and audible waveform distortion on low-level signals if it occurs near the center of the transfer characteristic. A more severe case can produce a nonmonotonic characteristic, Fig. 4.11*d*.

Typical performance specifications of a 16-bit uniform PCM converter (ADC or DAC) should be accurate to 0.0015 percent of full range and generate no more than approximately 0.003 percent harmonic distortion. (This latter figure may be compared with 0.5 percent on a high-quality analog tape recorder.[11,26,31])

Deglitching Sample and Hold. The next component in typical DAC systems is a special sample-and-hold amplifier (Fig. 4.10) which prevents the internal switching glitches of a DAC from appearing in the analog output signal. It does this by holding the previous DAC voltage at its output for a time t' while the new DAC voltage settles at its input. This holding action introduces a $(\sin X)/X$ transfer characteristic into the system response (where $X = 2\pi f t'$) and generates so-called aperture distortion (see Fig. 4.12*a*). Thus, if $t' = 1/f_s$, attenuation will be approximately 4 dB at $f_s/2$. This is a form of linear distortion, however, which can be equalized easily in the next stage.

A more difficult problem arises if slew-rate limiting occurs on successive voltage transitions. This limiting is a nonlinear mechanism that creates inharmonic-distortion products higher than f_N; these alias and generate audible distortion. The most common solution to this problem is to provide an integrate-and-hold or exponential slewing characteristic that makes the error signal linearly related to the input signal. In the frequency domain, this is equivalent to a small amount of low-pass filtering,[27] which also may be equalized in the next stage of low-pass filtering.

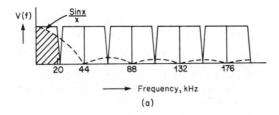

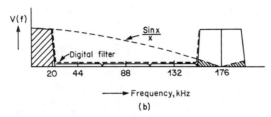

FIG. 4.12 Transfer characteristics of digital-to-analog converters (solid line). The upper broken lines indicate the attentuation from aperture distortion when $t' = 1/f_s$, and the hatched area shows the composite baseband characteristic before the analog anti-image low-pass filter. (*a*) For a standard DAC system (as in Fig. 4.10) with a sampling frequency of 44 kHz. (*b*) For a DAC system using an oversampling technique (as in Fig. 4.13) with an output sampling frequency of 176 kHz. [*After R. J. van de Plassche and E. C. Dijkmans," A Monolithic 16-Bit D/A Conversion System for Digital Audio," in B. A. Blesser, B. Locanthi, and T. G. Stockham, Jr. (eds.),* Digital Audio, *Audio Engineering Society, Anaheim, Calif. (May 1983), pp. 54–60.*]

Anti-Image Low-Pass Filter. The motivation for including this output filter in high-quality systems is vastly different from that for the input filter. The role of the anti-image filter is to remove the energy in the spectral images of the baseband which, owing to the sampling process, exist at multiples of f_s (Fig. 4.12*a*). This energy must be reduced, *not* because it is audible but because it might generate distortion in the analog system at the output of the DAC system.

The amount of reduction actually needed is impossible to specify precisely because it will depend on the effect this energy will have in the next stage of analog electronics. Naturally, overspecification of this filter's attenuation characteristics is costly and increases device complexity. More problematic is the fact that relatively more analog elements will be required to implement it, which increases the likelihood of noise and distortion arising in the filter itself. The aspect of safety in designing for worst-case situations means, however, that most anti-image filter designs have stop-band attenuation of anywhere between 50 and 75 dB. It should be emphasized that some relaxation of the specifications for this filter is possible by noting that the final attenuation of the spectral images must include both the effects of the transfer characteristics of the deglitch amplifier and the input low-pass filter.

Oversampling Digital-to-Analog Conversion Systems. It is worth restating that the uniform PCM approach, which for technical reasons is currently limited to 16 bits, is not necessarily optimally suited to coding signals for the ear. Some alternative systems have been devised which attempt to "shape" the noise spectrum generated during the coding or decoding process. The motivation for this shaping process is that although the overall quantizing noise power is not decreased for a given bit rate, it is moved to a part of the spectrum (either beyond the audible range of where it will be masked completely by higher-level signal components) such that its subjective loudness will be decreased.

One such DAC system currently used in several manufacturers' compact-disk players is shown in Fig. 4.13. It incorporates an oversampling technique to avoid

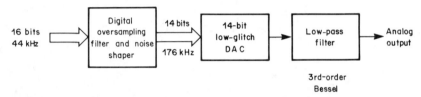

FIG. 4.13   New type of DAC conversion system using digital oversampling and simplified analog reconstruction filter requirements. The oversampling and noise-shaping operations can provide a better in-band signal-to-noise ratio than 16-bit uniform DAC systems.

using high-performance reconstruction filters and to reduce the apparent quantization noise levels.[42] Recall that in traditional DAC systems (typified by Fig. 4.10 and discussed in the preceding subsection), removing images of the baseband spectra requires an extremely sharp cutoff anti-image filter. In contrast, this new system operates as follows.

A 16-bit digital audio signal at f_s ($= 44$ kHz) is the input to a 96-tap transversal digital oversampling (or interpolating) filter, whose coefficients are 12 bits in length and whose 28-bit output is generated at a frequency of $4 \times f_s$ ($= 176$ kHz). Calculations are simplified by inserting zeros into the input signal every three out of four samples at the higher rate. The oversampling filter (designed to have a linear phase response), band-limits the quantizing noise spectra as well as the baseband spectrum, Fig. 4.12b. However, the resulting quantizing noise density at the higher sampling frequency of $4 \times f_s$ is 4 times smaller than that generated with the same number of bits at a sampling frequency of f_s. The low-passed portion of this reduced noise spectrum is shown in Fig. 4.14a. Further operations can shape this noise spectrum so that it lies predominantly outside the baseband, thereby increasing the baseband signal-to-quantizing noise ratio.

The noise-shaping operation is performed by feeding the 28-bit results, b_i, to a special rounding device which attempts to create a 14-bit output word b_o as close to b_i as possible. Because this process operates at 176 kHz, subsequent smoothing in the analog output low-pass filter (Fig. 4.13) effectively produces 16-bit performance (in terms of signal-to-quantization noise ratio) in an average sense. The resulting noise spectrum has a shape as shown by the solid line in Fig. 4.14b, whereas without noise shaping, the relative level of quantization noise from the corresponding uniform coder is shown in Fig. 4.14*a*.[42]

The total effect of these operations is the reduction of distortion products and the required rate of attenuation of the anti-image filter, illustrated in Fig. 4.12. The low-pass filter needed to remove components above $f_s/2$ ($=88$ kHz) in Fig. 4.12*b* can be satisfactorily implemented with a simple third-order Bessel filter (having extremely low phase distortion in the passband).

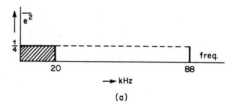

(a)

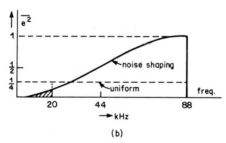

(b)

FIG. 4.14 Quantization noise density e^2 as a function of frequency for an *N*-bit DAC system using oversampling by a factor of 4. A noise density of one unit would result from an *N*-bit system without oversampling. The hatched area indicates the baseband density. (*a*) An oversampling system. (*b*) An oversampling system with noise shaping. [*After R. J. van de Plassche and E. C. Dijkmans, "A Monolithic 16-Bit D/A Conversion System for Digital Audio," in B. A. Blasser, B. Locanthi, and T. G. Stockham, Jr. (eds.), Digital Audio, Audio Engineering Society, Anaheim, Calif.* (May 1983), pp. 54–60.]

4.3 PROBLEMS IN EVALUATING HIGH-QUALITY DIGITAL AUDIO SYSTEMS

Now that the quality of digital audio conversion and storage systems can be made so high, a rather unusual set of new challenges has arisen. The first is how to devise *objective* tests that detect and measure very low levels of signal degradation in conversion-system components when these components are technically the best that currently can be built. A similar challenge is to devise reliable *subjective* tests that reveal whether detectable signal degradation is taking place in a system.

The third challenge is to find a means of avoiding these subjective evaluations (which are time-consuming and difficult) by devising objective quality measurements that correlate well with human perception. Each of these areas will be explored briefly in this section.

4.3.1 Objective Testing

One simple test for an analog-to-digital-to-analog conversion system has been suggested whereby a high-level, low-frequency sinusoid of between 5 and 30 Hz is input to the system and drives the converters through most of their quantizing steps.[26,31] The system output can then be high-pass-filtered at approximately 300 to 400 Hz to remove the test signal and any harmonic distortion, leaving only system-generated distortion and quantizing errors for analysis. In addition, examination of the noise contribution from the ADC may be performed *numerically* if the digitized signal can be digitally high-pass-filtered and the result then digitally measured, or *externally* by digitally amplifying the (digitally) high-passed signal (for example by 40 dB) and outputting it through the DAC for analog measurement (thereby reducing the DAC's relative contribution by a prescribed amount).

Such system tests do not necessarily localize the particular source of degradation, however, because a number of the defects discussed previously (e.g., clock jitter, settling times, converter nonlinearity, slew-rate defects, and analog filter limitations) can all produce similar distortions. Some suggestions for diagnosing specific types of component defects are given in Refs. 26 and 43, but the results are not always unambiguous.

In 1983 committees of professional audio engineers were organized to examine how measurements of a system component's electrical behavior could be improved and standardized. Particular areas of interest were (1) large-amplitude signals, (2) small-amplitude signals, (3) signals producing intermodulation effects, and (4) system phase response.[44] Unfortunately, this work is not completed, and professional machines are continuing to be built and sold without the benefit of such tests.

However, it should be apparent that even if good tests are derived for assessing a system's electrical performance, there are difficulties in relating such results directly to perceptible degradation. Thus, carefully controlled subjective tests are still required to provide the ultimate measuring stick of quality. Unfortunately, with very-high-quality systems, a great deal of ingenuity is required to devise such tests, and considerable care is needed to implement them, as the following example should indicate.

4.3.2 Subjective Testing

Consider a system test in which a musical instrument is played in one room and the sound is picked up by a microphone. This electrical signal is then either amplified and directly fed to a loudspeaker in a second room, or it passes through an analog-to-digital-to-analog (ADA) system before being amplified and fed to the loudspeaker. For a listener in the room with the loudspeaker to compare the "direct" sound with the signal through the ADA system, it would be necessary that the instrument ideally played the same musical passage through the two paths.

However, the slightest variation in the repetition of a performance, such as a slightly breathier sequence, will affect an evaluation and potentially invalidate the results. Obviously, a recording of the musical passage would provide a repeatable test signal; but then the problem is: How can a test signal be recorded so that the quality of the recording and reproduction process is sufficiently higher than the high-quality system being assessed to ensure that defects in the system under test are not masked?

Thus, providing a suitable source of program material is one of the most challenging aspects of subjective testing. Early experiments at the BBC, even with moderately high-quality systems, found that a number of factors governed this choice of material: (1) the need for repeatibility, (2) the desire to have several examples of critical material to cover different subjective effects, and (3) the need to devise a realistic test signal that balances the factor of the likelihood of needing to reproduce such a (possibly artificial) signal with the factor of the signal's effectiveness in revealing serious system defects. An interesting example of applying these rules emerged during an early BBC study of the effectiveness of a simple error concealment technique. The authors dryly noted:

> A previous preliminary investigation had indicated that a solo glockenspiel excerpt provided a very critical programme and it was therefore used for this series of tests. A solo glockenspiel would however represent a rather rare or unusual programme and therefore, additional excerpts were chosen (a string quarter, female reader, programme pause etc.) to be more representative of typical broadcast programmes. (Ref. 45, p. 28.)

In more recent studies of 16-bit floating-point conversion systems, the glockenspiel test was still being used at the BBC, along with an electronically genreated test signal which has the melody of "Frère Jacques,"[34] but it is no longer clear if such signals are adequate for discriminating differences between very-high-quality systems.

For example, in high-bit-rate systems the audible effect of quantizing noise or granular noise might be audible only on material like very-low-level piano notes. "Depending on the noise spectrum, the defects can sound more like a defective musical instrument or even a poor performance than an identifiable technical fault" (Ref. 4, p. 219).

For the present, however, while digital audio systems are subject to critical evaluation as replacements for analog systems, there is still a tendency to make subjective comparisons of digital audio with the best analog systems rather than with a *perfect system*. Such tests, while understandable from a purchaser's point of view, may suffer technically for a number of reasons. One example of this problem is the fact that analog recorders "crush" high-level, high-frequency components and, in doing so, subtly modify the signal, rendering it "mellower." Digital systems are often accused of being "harder" or more metallic, but it has been suggested that this may result from a *lack* of high-frequency crushing.[4]

In another recent test, which compared different analog tape recorders with digital ones, it was found that there were very few significant discernible differences in quality measures of first-generation recordings of the same musical material, except in the case of one digital machine which had an easily measured technical fault. The authors concluded that the tests being used, which were adequate for discriminating differences between high-quality loudspeakers, in fact, were not sufficiently sensitive to reveal statistically significant differences between the machines.[46] Such results again emphasize that more rigorous sets of test procedures are needed to compare machines with even more similar technical performances.

4.3.3 Objective Quality Measures Based on Models of Perception

While the preceding challenges still exist, it is also important to devise a set of quantitative measures of quality modeled on perception. However, in this area there has mainly been considerable effort in developing such measures for speech-coding systems. There, the problem is simplified somewhat by the fact that the signals of concern are of lower bandwidth, and medium- to low-quality coding schemes are the most commonly used. In these cases degradation is frequently more readily discerned both objectively and subjectively. Nevertheless, the basic principles required for high-quality objective measures are likely to be similar. For example, it has been proposed that the subjective *loudness* of noise, as determined in a mathematical formulation of the physiological process of hearing, could serve as one objective measure of (speech) quality. The main stages of this model are as follows:[47]

1. The signal passes through a transformation which accounts for the eardrum to middle-ear transfer function. For completeness, a model for high-quality audio should also account for the direction-dependent coupling of the sound field to the middle ear through the pinna, which could alter spectral components above 6 kHz by as much as 30 dB.[48]

2. A running short-term spectral analysis is performed to simulate that taking place in the inner ear. The frequency variable is converted to a spatial coordinate representing the physiologically based place of analysis along the basilar membrane, giving a critical-band scale.

3. A basilar-membrane excitation function is derived from critical-band densities by convolution with a basilar-membrane spreading function.

4. Loudness functions are obtained for both the signal and the noise spectrum. Then the loudness of the noise in the presence of the signal (masker) is computed. A sensitivity function then can be applied to remove the contribution of components that would be inaudible.

5. The (reduced) loudness of the noise then can be related to that of the signal to obtain an objective measure of perceived degradation.

Although such a model may seem unduly complex, it has been observed (in experiments with the perceptibility of quantizing error in floating-point coding schemes) that the accuracy of predictions of audibility (in contrast to simpler predictions of loudness) is very sensitive to accuracy in the implementation of auditory characteristics.[37] Thus, oversimplified models of hearing or simple electrical measures generally cannot be expected to provide reliable measures of perceptible degradation.

4.4   OTHER PROBLEMS ARISING WITH HIGH-QUALITY DIGITAL AUDIO SYSTEMS

Given that digital audio systems have clearly demonstrated that the initial promises of higher fidelity and durable media are now realities, it is important to examine potential drawbacks arising from such spectacular improvements.

4.4.1 Potential Drawbacks of Improving Audio Quality

First, the increase in dynamic range and low-frequency response will raise some interesting problems in studio design and recording techniques. As an example, for 50 years radio listeners in Scotland had British Post Office links from London, providing at best an 8-kHz bandwidth with audible telephone noise and speech crosstalk 50 dB below signal peaks. When they suddenly began to receive 15-kHz bandwidth and nearly 70-dB signal-to-noise ratio over the BBC's new PCM system, the BBC was deluged with "complaints about tape hiss, ventilation rumble, and the announcer's clock ticking" (Ref. 4, p. 220). If another 20-dB (or more) dynamic range is to become a world standard, then many of the noises present in the recording studio that were once masked by analog tape hiss or lost because of low-frequency rolloff will have to be controlled much more carefully. This is likely to imply that new architectural standards, especially for background noise levels and low frequencies, are required for recording studio environments.

Second, recording studio engineers producing analog recordings monitored a signal which never could be heard again because, once it was recorded, it would be subjected to numerous processes (each of which could degrade the signal quality) before reaching the consumer. When the entire audio chain becomes digital, because it will be easier to predict and control the signal treatment, the consumer could be provided with virtually the same signal heard over the studio monitors during recording sessions. This means that studio engineers must learn to be increasingly aware that any defects occurring during recording must be evaluated much more critically in terms of their potential annoyance for listeners.

Third, at the listening end, another problem arises from having *too much* dynamic range in a recording that is being reproduced in a moderately noisy environment such as a car or a public area. For example, if the full dynamic range of an orchestra were to be reproduced, when the loudest passages are generated at a comfortable level, many of the quieter passages will be masked by the environmental noise. Alternatively, if the quietest passages are kept audible, the loudest passages will be reproduced at levels reaching or exceeding the threshold of pain. This problem raises the issue of whether some form of dyanmic-range compression option should exist in the reproduction equipment. If the answer is yes, this raises another question: Should data for accurately controlling a digital compression circuit in the reproduction system be coded along with the audio data at a low (e.g., syllabic) data rate? Such gain-control data could be generated by sophisticated techniques[49] under the manufacturers' supervision during the mastering process, thereby removing the need to put complicated processors in the reproduction equipment. Using such a scheme, it might be feasible for a listener to select the degree of compression appropriate to his or her listening environment.

4.4.2 Piracy of Digital Audio Software

The last major problem to be discussed is much more serious than any of the above: the piracy of digital recordings. Because a digital recording is an exact replica of the master recording, "the only way to prevent piracy is to produce a recording that is not playable" (Ref. 44, p. 542). Thus, there seems to be no obvious engineering solution to piracy.

The greatest economic threat to the digital recording industry, however, does not come from illegal commercial enterprises such as in Europe—where the transferring of compact disks to high-quality cassettes for sale to consumers has started—but from home copying. At present, the best solutions to this are economic ones, one of which is to make the cost of software (i.e., digital recordings) so low that copying is not worthwhile. Another possibility is for a tax to be levied on blank tapes to cover performers' royalties. A number of experiences indicate, however, how a cost-conscious consumer population will react.

In Germany, a tax on blank tapes was about to be levied and the government was changed; the tax never materialized. In Sweden, a similar tax was imposed, but before it came into effect, tape sales skyrocketed and dropped nearly to zero afterward. Some signs of progress are emerging, however: Austria does have a tax on blank tapes, and France has managed to levy a large tax on video recorders. But, in the United States, probably one of the largest markets, there is no specific tax on blank tapes.[50]

Of course, some of the responsibility for preventing copying lies with the manufacturers of digital audio equipment. In 1982 a "gentleman's agreement" existed among manufacturers not to provide digital outputs on CD players,[50] but by 1985 a few brands of players available in Japan provided digital audio signals in the Audio Engineering Society–European Broadcasting Union (AES–EBU) format.[32] This raised the issue of whether digital copies could be easily made.

Some consideration was given to the consumer side of this question, since it was likely that by mid-1987 consumer 16-bit stereo digital cassette recorder-players would be available which would permit home copying of audio at a 48-kHz (or, optionally, 32-kHz) sampling frequency. Manufacturers of these devices agreed that all prerecorded material would be recorded and played back at a sampling frequency of 44.1 kHz.[51] Thus, both prerecorded cassettes and CDs could not be simply digitally copied on these machines. However, this would not prevent very-high-quality digital tape copies of prerecorded tapes and CDs from being made by using the analog outputs of the playback system and analog inputs to the recording system. Consequently, high-quality commercial and domestic piracy of prerecorded material might still become commonplace.

CD manufacturers have shown some foresight by including in the CD's subcode data a "digital copy prohibited" flag which, if set, would be sensed by a digital recording device and cause the recorder to refuse to copy the audio data. It appears, however, that many CD manufacturers are not even bothering to set this bit,[52] nor can one guarantee that a scheme cannot be found to disable the effect of such blocking systems.[50] Thus, it remains that one of the biggest and more serious challenges to engineers and manufacturers is to propose and implement a practicable and economical solution to this potentially disastrous situation.

4.5 PROFESSIONAL APPLICATION OF DIGITAL AUDIO TECHNOLOGY

4.5.1 Digital Audio Tape Recording

In 1983 over a dozen manufacturers provided products for professional digital audio recording,[53] in addition to large recording companies that had developed their own equipment for in-house use. One of these, Decca Recording Co., in 1984 had done all its recordings digitally for 2½ years on its 33 "homemade" stereo and four-track digital audio tape recorders. It had five digital editing rooms and its own digital audio mixer.[54] Denon (Nippon Columbia Co.) in Japan has also been making recordings digitally since the early 1970s, and in 1983 its PCM and digital recorder system recorded over 100 albums and compact disks in its first 8 months of use beginning in July 1981.[55]

In addition, most major record labels have been releasing "digital" records that are actually analog pressings of either digitally recorded material or, sometimes, of old analog recordings which have been remastered in a digital medium. The number of such digital records being released each year is increasing steadily, but it is not clear that consumers are aware that they are not getting the full benefit of digital recording and reproduction from a digital medium such as compact disks. Nevertheless, it appears that "digitally" mastered records are generally accepted as providing better quality than their analog counterparts.

Digital audio tape recorders (DATRs) have been developed with special consideration for the operational requirements of studios. These include:

1. High quality, i.e., using professional standards of 48-kHz sampling rate and 16-bit uniform quantization
2. Playing time of at least 1 h stereo on a single reel of tape (equivalent to 5.5 Gbit on 2400 ft of ¼-in magnetic tape or 0.75 Mbit/in²)
3. Resistance to tape imperfections, dropouts, dust, and fingerprints
4. Reliable overwriting of data without bulk erasure
5. Support for editing procedures such as splicing and punch-in–punch-out

Therefore, there are significant differences between a DATR and conventional magnetic-tape and disk computer peripherals. In the latter, low recording densities are used so that the size of a recorded bit cell is larger than a typical dropout and simple error correction schemes can provide residual random error rates of 1 in 10^{12}. The high densities used in digital audio demand that error correction schemes protect against burst errors of up to several thousand bits. When the performance of a recording system is evaluated, it is no longer meaningful to refer to its resistance to random errors, and one proposal[56] considers two parameters: the block error rate (BER) and block error correlation. The latter is a useful indicator of the relative contributions of burst and random errors to the total error rate. In most recording schemes, blocks of data are constructed from audio samples, parity words for correction and detection of errors, and other data for synchronization. Therefore, a block error may be induced by a single random error or short-burst error. In Fig. 4.15 a clean tape is shown to have a BER before correction of about 1 in 10^5, but in the harsh world of the sound studio dust and fingerprints may drastically impair even this figure. Both the BER and block error correlation are worsened. For acceptable performance, a BER of 1 in 10^8 must be achieved after correction and the residual errors treated by concealment methods.

To meet the operational requirements mentioned above, very high areal recording densities must be achieved. It is well known that for optimum use of magnetic media, the writing speed should be high and the tracks narrow. For the consumer digital audio cassette recorder, a decision has yet to be made to support stationary heads (S-DAT)[57] or rotating heads (R-DAT),[58] although in 1985 R-DAT machines appeared to be easier to manufacture and S-DAT required more development.[59] At short recorded wavelengths, head-tape separation losses become significant and, for a fingerprint (thickness 2.5 μm) and a recorded wavelength of 1.25 μm (40 kbit/in at 15 in/s), this loss amounts to 100 dB. Even without contamination, it is difficult to maintain good head-tape contact without higher-than-usual tape-to-head pressure which makes further demands, particularly on the heads. With rotary-head machines, the head actually deforms the tape, so high is the tape-to-head pressure needed to overcome this problem.

The alternative is to use shorter recorded wavelengths and multiple tracks per audio channel.[60] This has the additional benefit that the burst nature of errors in the longitudinal direction may be traded against random errors in the transverse direction when a limited number of discrete tracks are used (see Fig. 4.16). The

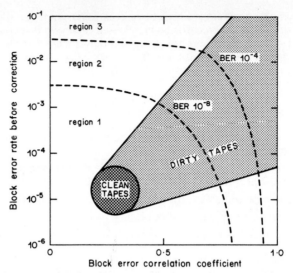

FIG. 4.15 Evaluation of an error-correcting system. Region 1: good block error rate after correction $<10^{-8}$. Region 2: warning: uncorrected errors require concealment. Region 3: prohibited, satisfactory operation not possible, and audible clicks likely.

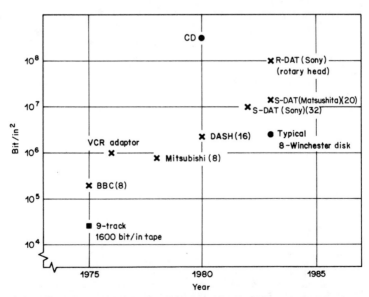

FIG. 4.16 Improvements in areal storage densities. Improvements have been made possible by developments in narrow-gap ferrite and thin-film heads, high-coercivity tapes, and precision transports with stable tape tension and minimum weaving. Figures in parentheses indicate the number of data tracks used to achieve the given density.

technique of distributing data over the tape to break up burst-error patterns is known as *interleave*. The way in which interleave is combined with error correction techniques is crucial to the ruggedness of the DATR.

In a recorder designed to accommodate cut editing and punch-in–punch-out (Fig. 4.17),interleave must be used carefully. If the interleave distance along the

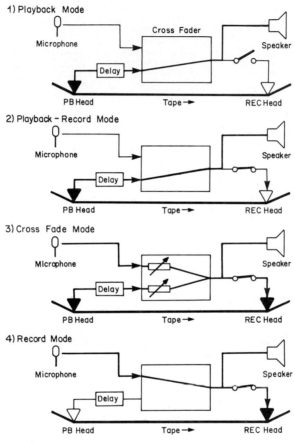

5) Cross Fade Mode

6) Playback – Record Mode

7) Playback Mode

FIG. 4.17 Punch-in–punch-out. Example of a procedure highly specific to digital audio recording. A critical application might be the replacement of a short passage of voice or soloist in an otherwise acceptable recording. In current analog recording, the playback (PB) head must be used also as the record (REC) head at the punch-in point, and quality suffers. In the digital recorder, a short delay matches the time taken for the tape to traverse from the PB head to the REC head, permitting a controlled cross-fade at the punch-in and punch-out points. A third head is usually placed after the REC head to monitor the result (not shown).

TABLE 4.4 Comparison of Two Currently Available Two-Channel Tape Formats

	DASH	Mitsubishi
Tape speed	7½ in/s	15 in/s
Data tracks	8 identically formatted	6 + 2 parity tracks
Linear density	38,400 bits/in	19,200 bits/in
Play time	120 min on 10-in reel	60 min on 10-in reel
Channel code or transition density	HDM-1/25,600 FCPI (high-density modulation)	MFM/19,200 FCPI (modified FM)
Error correction technique	Cross-interleave code plus CRC code	Reed Solomon code plus CRC code
Maximum error correction length		
l_1	5.7 mm	2.67 mm
l_2	No ability	1.25 mm
Maximum error concealment length before muting		
l_1	28.6 mm	5.33 mm
l_2	1.24 mm	1.25 mm
Block length	288 bits $\equiv$ 1 ms $\equiv$ 0.19 mm	252 bits $\equiv$ 0.875 ms $\equiv$ 0.33 mm
Interleave distance	119 and 204 blocks $\equiv$ 22.7 and 38.8 mm	Staggered from track to track and 8 blocks minimum
Maximum recommended BER before correction	1 in 10^5	1 in 10^5
Editing features	Cut-tape, punch-in–punch-out	Cut-tape
Minimum interval between edits	300 ms	25 ms

NOTES:

1. An application of the DASH format at 15 in/s is under discussion. Since it is based on a much higher redundancy, it can provide an increased resistance to errors and track loss with improved cut-tape editing.

2. An application of the Mitsubishi format at 7½ in/s is planned in the near future.

Error specification:

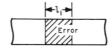 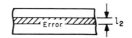

tape is large, it may be necessary to use error concealment for long periods at cut-edits or start-up. Interleaving across the tape has the disadvantage that modification to a single audio channel may require rewriting many data tracks.

Clearly, in the design of a tape format there are many compromises to be made, and in the major tape formats published[61,62,63] there are significant differences in approach. For example, Table 4.4 highlights the features of the digital audio stationary head (DASH) format for stereo machines supported by Sony, Studer, and Matsushita with the format supported by Mitsubishi.

The requirements for multichannel recorders are very different, and emphasis is on providing as many channels as possible. For example, the DASH format specifies 24 audio channels on ½-in-wide tape at 30 in/s. With expected improvements in head technology, a double-density version with 48 channels on ½-in tape is planned. All the information for each audio channel is contained in a single track on the tape. In contrast, the Mitsubishi format has 32 audio channels on 40 tracks on 1-in tape at 30 in/s. Groups of eight channels have two additional parity tracks, giving a lateral interleave. Both formats provide for smooth punch-in-punch-out and crude cut-edits, but the task of assessing the strengths and weaknesses of tape formats is a complex issue, and in the meantime the recording industry is working toward a standard.

In both tape formats, additional tracks are available for other purposes. These include Society of Motion Picture and Television Engineers (SMPTE) time code, a worldwide standard that permits synchronization of machines to about 20-ms tolerance. Some implementations of the DASH format use an additional track for control information. A pair of analog tracks is maintained with a copy or mix of the digital tracks to assist in cuing and location; in some cases, these are used as backup in case of failure of the digital tracks. Finally, and possibly most important, a track is available for auxiliary data supplied by the user and other status information, a contribution to the concept of the "smart" audio signal, described in Sec. 4.7.3.

4.5.2 All-Digital Audio Studio

An *all-digital* studio is a desirable objective because it eliminates the cost and impairments of repeated analog-to-digital and digital-to-analog conversion. Figure 4.18 illustrates the way in which digital audio studios are developing. Free-

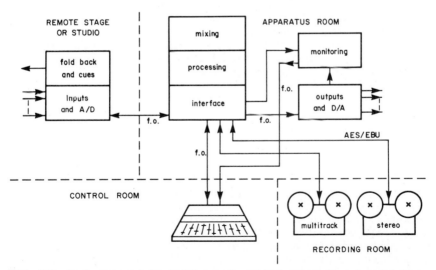

FIG. 4.18 Configuration of the all-digital studio. Multiplexing of data on optical fibers reduces the complexity of studio wiring and encourages the development of separate specialized areas. For example, the control room can be free from the noise of recorders or computer equipment so that better acoustics can be achieved. A separate apparatus room will permit maintenance while the studio is still in operation and may eventually lead to greater sharing of resources in large studio complexes.

from noise pickup and earthing problems means that equipment can be sited for operational convenience and be interconnected by high-data-rate optical fibers. For example, ADCs are sited as close to the microphone as possible, perhaps even on the sound stage; the mixing console contains a minimum of electronics, is small, and consumes little power; and digital signal-processing equipment may be housed in separate apparatus areas for easy servicing. Remote control, assignable control,[64] and system automation are inherent to the digital approach.

A multitrack recording studio is characterized by a number of independently controlled audio processing channels: as few as two for direct stereo recording and up to 128 or more in certain film-sound dubbing suites. A typical *channel strip* provides control of gain, equalization, and dynamic range. It has a multitude of *insert points* at which additional special-effects devices can be introduced. It may simultaneously generate independent multitrack outputs, stereo mixes, and *fold-back* outputs to artists in the studios or a commentator. The operator-machine interface is conventionally "one knob per function," resulting in 5000 or more controls on a large desk which may require up to four people to operate.

All this represents a significant signal-processing workload. In a digital implementation, real-time input-output (I/O) must be sustained at 48,000 words per second per channel with processing for approximately 2 million multiplications per second per channel with integer word lengths between 16 and 32 bits. Signal routing must be sufficiently flexible to isolate each processing function so that hardware can be used effectively. This has resulted in a number of solutions, including process-specific hardware,[65,66] programmable signal processors for entirely real-time execution,[67] and programmable signal processors capable of real-time and non-real-time execution.[68] The approach selected determines the overall flexibility of the system; for example, a real-time processor must complete execution of its program in one audio sample period (20.83 μs), whereas a device that can work optionally in nonreal time in principle can implement any algorithm if the operator does not need to listen to the result immediately. Therefore, there will always be the dilemma of choosing between a machine limited only by its programming and one that potentially achieves the same power in real time by modular extension to the hardware.

Signal-Processing Requirements. A digital mixing console must provide a wide selection of amplitude-equalization characteristics. These include low- and high-pass filters (6 or 12 dB per octave), presence filters (boost- or cut-centered on a single frequency), and shelving filters (lift or attenuation to a range of frequencies) (Fig. 4.19). Up to six such filters may be cascaded, although not necessarily in the same part of the signal-processing chain. These are readily implemented in a digital signal processor (DSP) as a cascade of biquadratic sections.[69,70] The current generation of signal-processing chips cannot be exploited because the required word lengths are too great and there is insufficient time for multiple precision working. However, careful selection of the filter structure can reduce the word lengths required at critical points, e.g., multiplier inputs, while maintaining good noise performance without significantly increasing the computational load.[69] Filter coefficients can be easily stored in read-only memory (ROM); there is seldom a need for more than a few thousand different equalization characteristics. Techniques based on the design of a prototype filter from which all other variations can be computed relatively simply have been proposed,[71] giving an elegant solution for a parametric equalizer.

The very high quality achievable with digital audio leads to an increased interest in the control of dynamic range. This may be applied for artistic or technical

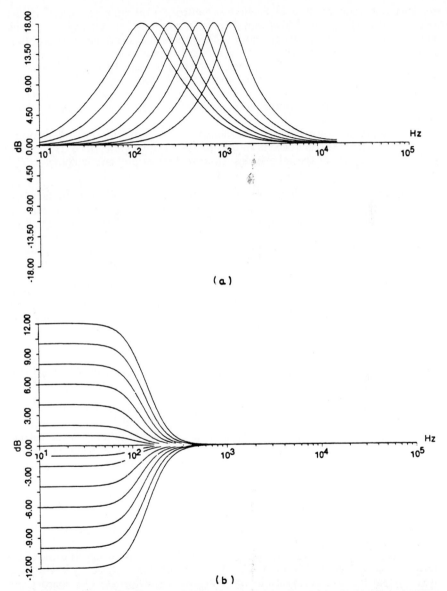

FIG. 4.19 Audio equalization with digital filters. The complete range of subjectively familiar amplitude characteristics found in analog consoles can be implemented by a cascade of biquadratic filter sections. A digital equalizer has the advantages of long-term accuracy, stability, and much greater dynamic range. The examples shown are (*a*) a family of presence filters (the *Q* of the filter is varied with the boost or cut); and (*b*) a family of shelving filters (the lift or cut is applied to a range of frequencies; a single filter section is specified by five coefficients, making the design of time-varying filters and automation features practicable).

reasons and undoubtedly will become a control on the domestic users' replay equipment in the future.[72] The input signal is monitored to determine its peak and/or root-mean-square (rms) content. Then the value is compared with a specified threshold, and gain adjustment is imposed proportional to the difference of input level and threshold.[73] The gain adjustment is related to input level by a power law and, in practice, demands that a signal processor have efficient logarithmic conversion. *Gain ducking,* caused by a compressor suddenly reducing the gain at a transient, can be minimized by a preliminary delay that gives the control side chain time to act.

The simplicity of providing digital delay leads to its use in other applications, e.g., to achieve phase coherence in multimicrophone mixes and, of course, to generate a wide variety of special effects such as reverberation[74] and flanging.

Developments in Digital Audio Studios. Although a number of manufacturers have developed simple digital mixing consoles,[70,75] only a few groups are working at the systems level on audio studios. Three such groups have been selected for comparison: Lucasfilm,[68] working on a postproduction suite for the motion-picture industry; Neve/BBC,[67,76] working on a mobile multitrack recording studio; and Denon/Nippon Columbia, builders of an editor-mixer for music recording.[77]

The Lucasfilm audio signal processor (ASP) distills a multichannel output from a very large number of independent *takes,* which might be dialogue, music, or special effects. Filtering and reverberation are needed to match the acoustics of these different takes, and extensive signal processing is needed to synthesize special effects and explore *creative* aspects. The material also must be synchronized so that a master sound track can be generated.

Most of the processing is in real time using purpose-built, microprogrammed digital signal processors. A controller supervises up to eight DSPs and interfaces to user consoles and a system master. Two features contribute significantly to the versatility of the system. First, the DSPs communicate directly with mass disk storage in real time; and, second, the DSP general-purpose architecture has, for example, the ability for multiple precision calculations and loadable microcode.

The disks can be considered *virtual* tape machines, although with current capacities and costs it is not yet practical to satisfy all audio storage needs in this way; a multichannel DATR might be used for the music tracks. However, within the disk system, resynchronization of one track relative to another is merely the adjustment to an address and does not require rerecording, as with tape.

Providing an operator-machine interface for such a complex system is clearly a difficult task. Lucasfilm has chosen to modify the UNIX kernel[78] and permit a *superprocess* to run which is locked into core for critical real-time operations, such as responding to a key press of scheduling audio I/O.

A more compact implementation of the ASP hardware, which is aimed at a mass market, is under development.[79] With an 825-Mbyte disk drive, this new ASP system [on five 16- by 16-in transistor-transistor-logic (TTL) boards] will provide an expandable eight-channel audio editing and synthesis station. The main emphasis in this system is on versatility, which results from its ability to do the following:

1. Transfer extremely high data rates to and from disk continuously (roughly 0.7 Mbyte per second per disk controller), thereby providing up to eight channels of sound at 44.1 kHz.[80]

2. Process data at very high computational rates (65 ns for pipelined multiply accumulate) and high accuracy (24- by 24-bit multiply with 48-bit results).[79]

3. Alter the processing characteristics in real time without interrupting the flow of audio data.[81]

Other aspects of this system will be mentioned in Secs. 5.5.3 and 4.5.4.

The Neve digital mixing console, developed initially in collaboration with the BBC, approaches the digital audio studio as a development from existing analog practice. The primary storage medium is tape, and facilities supplied are a superset of those currently found in well-equipped analog studios.

Signal processing is carried out on purpose-built DSPs (Fig. 4.19), each DSP normally being dedicated to two channel strips of the console. Associated with each group of 16 DSPs is a controller, two routing units for digital audio, and a mixing unit. The last-named is simple in hardware design and fulfills the need for, say, 24 independent mixes of 48 channels each. The routing unit permits efficient allocation of processing, chaining filters, compressors, special effects, etc., in any order, according to a threaded code.[82] Where the total processing load is known to be less than full facilities on every channel, fewer DSPs may be used for the same number of channels, reducing cost; and if a DSP is found to be faulty, spare processing can be patched in its place.

The DSP architecture is tailored to the processing needs of a sound studio.[83] Floating-point arithmetic is used where the dynamic range otherwise would require many bits in integer arithmetic such as high-Q filters; dedicated hardware is used for special functions such as logarithmic conversion.

The system is configured at the factory for the users' needs, and the controlling software updates the console *surface,* i.e., the fixed and assignable function knobs and displays, and interprets the data required by each of the DSPs, which run a fixed suite of microcoded programs. A real-time operating system was specially written to organize this database and share the processing among four single-board computers.

In the BBC's all-digital outside broadcast (OB) vehicle, a 48-channel mixer has been accommodated in a surface only 1.6 m wide by using assignable control systems. Rather than repeating a group of switches and displays for every channel, an equalization or dynamic-range-control (DRC) panel is *assigned* to the channel requiring adjustment. This is just one example of many ideas that now can be exploited in the person-machine interface of a digital console.

The all-digital system developed by Denon is used mainly for four-channel classical music recordings: main signals on Channels 1 and 2 and hall reverberation on Channels 3 and 4. A 32-time-slot parallel data bus provides audio data routing and connects a disk-based editing system with 1-Gbyte memory, a PCM tape recorder based on a videocassette transport, and signal-processing hardware.

Digital audio is transferred, via the bus, to disk for editing. A mix-down to two channels is implemented by special-purpose hardware, but the main emphasis is on convenient location of edit points. The disk can be played over a wide range of speeds, forward and reverse, under the control of a search dial. At any time during the recording or playback, a cue button may be used to log an approximate edit point in memory.

In contrast to the two systems described previously, the entire system is run from programs in ROM, and all hardware is dedicated to specific tasks. More than 100 classical recordings have been made on the system.

4.5.3 Editing

There are already several different strategies for editing digital audio. The use of helical-scan videocassette recorders has grown in popularity as a low-cost medium for digital audio recording, and a number of editing systems have been built around them.[84] As might be expected, the rotating heads and cassette format make dub editing a necessity, limiting the facilities that can be provided and leading to time-consuming operations. For stationary-head longitudinal recorders, some electronic editing is essential for multichannel audio.[85] Although relying on dubbing track to track or machine to machine, this allows compiling a single master track from a number of takes on other tracks, or *punching in* and *out* on preset combinations of channels. For stereo (and sometimes multichannel) work, cut-tape methods have been introduced.[86] A difficulty here is the rehearsal of an edit before cutting a valuable master tape and concealing the corrupted data at the splice. Finally, a number of off-line systems have been developed in which audio material is dubbed to the disk drive and edited via a mainframe computer.[87,88,89] Many facilities are provided, such as edit rehearsal and audition, but the systems are costly and have not yet been installed at the recording studio.

A fully engineered editor should satisfy the diverse requirements of the broadcast and recording industry. To do this, the editor must do "everything that tape does," in the sense that it must be able to insert or remove arbitrarily small sections or compile an album master from its various items in the correct sequence. However, there are more challenging applications, particularly in broadcasting, for which a digital editor must provide a solution. In interviews, it is common practice to remove stutters or add breaths to improve the flow of dialogue. Fast methods of location are needed with rehearsal and adjustment of the edit, of which there may be 100 in a half-hour program. In contrast, an opera with retakes may require few edits within several hours of material. Such edits may be necessary at nonideal times, e.g., during a sustained flute passage, and the signal level of the retake may be slightly different, requiring a gain adjustment in the vicinity of the edit. Therefore, there is a role for both direct-access and sequential-access types of editing systems.

Tape-Cut Editing.   A hierarchy of editing strategies has been identified[90] which permits a cost-performance tradeoff while preserving a degree of compatibility. At the first level there is a method similar to analog editing: the edit points on the tape are located by rocking the tape back and forth across the replay head *(rock and roll)* using an analog cue track, and the tape is then cut and spliced. Data in the immediate vicinity of the edit are unavoidably corrupted, principally by mechanical distortions at the splice, and on replay the decoding circuitry invokes an error concealment and cross-fade strategy to provide an acceptable edit. Under critical conditions, however, impairments at the edit are occasionally audible. The quality of the analog cue track is imperfect, and, of course, it is impossible to rehearse the edit.

At the second level, an improvement can be made if the notion of separate cut and edit points is introduced. The edit points are displaced to the left and right of the cut points of the lead-in and lead-out sections, respectively (Fig. 4.20). Data before and after the edit then may be decoded without recourse to error concealment, and the cross-fade made without error by "jumping" over the corrupted data at the cutting point. The displacement of the edit points and the overlap of the data lead to a gap in the audio data stream. This is smoothed by a buffer which is replenished by increasing the tape speed after the edit, a function of a servoloop already present in all digital recorders.

Additional data must be written on the tape to indicate the location of the edit points and the cross-fade parameters to be used. These data may be packaged conveniently as *labels,* a topic that recurs in many aspects of digital audio.[91] A limitation of this approach is that there must be "don't care" material recorded after the lead-in and before the lead-out, but the benefit is that perfect tape-cut edits can be achieved and a small degree of adjustment can be made even after the tape has been cut.

The third level refers to methods which are disk-assisted. The random-access nature of a hard disk can be exploited to give the user extensive rehearsal and editing facilities. Real-time and off-line signal processing can be introduced, and this opens the door to a host of production facilities that are impossible with a tape-only strategy.

In the context of tape-cut editing, the disk-assisted editor is a peripheral to the DATR. Short sections (30 s, say) of audio are dubbed to the disk where the edit is rehearsed; and the edit information including the location of the cut point is transferred back to tape. When this operation is completed, the edit on the tape is a level 2 jump edit and matches precisely that rehearsed on disk. To replay the edit, the recorder requires only the same hardware as a level 2 edit; the disk is not needed. However, this is a concept that remains to be demonstrated.

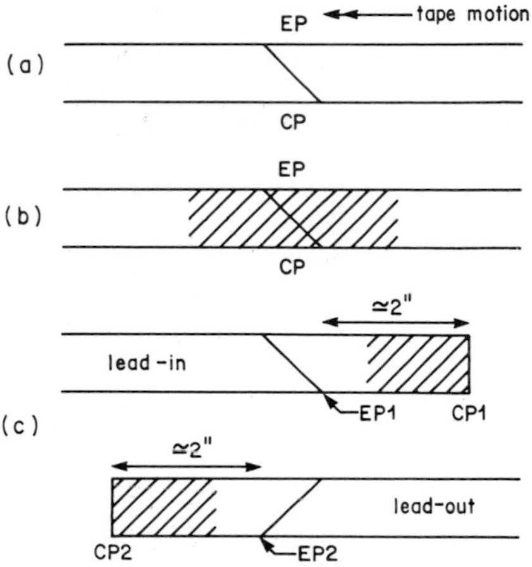

Disk-Based Editing. A number of groups are actively developing digital audio editing systems in which the need for the DATR is reduced or eliminated by the use of disks. The engineering problem, simply stated, is to provide a mechanism for the continuous real-time transfer of audio data from the disk within an acceptable user environment. The sustained high data rates, even for one audio channel, make this a nontrivial task.

Earlier work at Soundstream,[88] PCL, London,[87] and the New York

FIG. 4.20 Digital tape-cut editing. (*a*) Analog. In analog stereo editing a splice is made by making a 45° angle cut and so creating an ≈8-ms cross-fade at 15 in/s. The edit point and cutting point coincide. (*b*) Digital level 1. The equivalent cross-fade is provided electronically, and error concealment techniques are used to overcome the corrupted data at the splice (shown in the hatched area). (*c*) Digital level 2. The edit point and cutting point are separated. All data before and after the edit point can be decoded correctly without error concealment, and a repeatable result is obtained.

Institute of Technology[89] is characterized by the difficulties of producing an edited output version in real time and by limited real-time signal processing. For example, in the PCL system, the contributions to the edited output must be copied in sequence to a contiguous output file before replay. On the first Soundstream editor and at the New York Institute of Technology, cross-fades are calculated in nonreal time and stored on a scratch area of the disk. The operational delays inherent to these approaches impede the creative interaction between user and equipment.

More recently, the use of high-performance disk controllers with special-purpose I/O devices has allowed editing to be achieved by head movements, and interruptions to the data flow are accommodated by buffer memory.

Lucasfilm[92] has constructed a disk controller that permits eight channels of audio sampled at 48 kHz to be edited independently and replayed simultaneously. Particular attention has been paid to the organization of the audio data on the disk that is packeted into *allocation units* (AUs) of approximately 0.3 s. These are manipulated in a manner similar to file management under UNIX. The advantage is that there is no risk of *checkerboarding,* i.e., the creation of inaccessible areas of storage by repeated editing, deletion, etc. As the AUs are scattered over the disk, editing does not pose further demands on the scheduling algorithm except when the splices do not correspond exactly with the AUs. The user interface, by which these resources will be controlled, is still being developed and will include access to all of the signal-processing algorithms being developed for the ASP.

It is interesting to note that most of the work in digital editing is in a UNIX environment; this is not surprising when one considers the large number of utilities that can be exploited by doing so. The audio data on disk can be regarded as just another database, and the graphics support at the New York Institute of Technology for waveform display or *panoramic* viewing of down-sampled data draws on this opportunity.

However, real-time interaction is not a UNIX strong point. For example, if an instruction is given or button pressed for the system to *play,* a UNIX system may have to complete its current task before filling appropriate audio data buffers so that the audio signal can be heard.

Most sound editing can be monitored satisfactorily only by listening. An edit point is conventionally found approximately by *spooling* through the material at up to 20 times normal speed. Accurate location is then by rock and roll, i.e., manually playing the tape back and forth about the edit. In exceptional cases, a waveform display can be helpful. The demands on the operator-machine interface are enormous. In its prototype editor, Compusonics uses a UNIX-based operating system with improved real-time response called Regulus;[93] in its virtual multichannel recorder, a disk-based editor, Systex, uses the real-time operating system Versados.[94] Such operating systems can provide usable keyboard interaction but reach the limits of their performance when servicing fader movements, controlling position, organizing data transfers, and maintaining displays simultaneously.

In the BBC experimental editor,[90] data formatting and signal processing are handled by dedicated processors. Data formatting includes the organization of stereo channels and auxiliary data and blocking prior to transfer to disk. Signal processing includes cross-fading at an edit and sampling frequency conversion to give a constant output sampling rate during variable-speed operation.[95] Intimate control of these units is achieved via a separate *synchronous bus* which works outside the knowledge of the host operating system. Thus, the system is updated at a moderate rate while external hardware logs the precise address of the data samples being replayed and provides the higher updating rates required for smooth gain or speed control.

The editor is designed for two-channel working only and therefore can use contiguous data files on the disk with few penalties. The dynamic editing performance is shown in Fig 4.21, which illustrates how clusters of edits extremely close together can be managed if an adequate recovery time follows for the buffers to refill. In editing the audio, the auxiliary data are edited accordingly; this is important in new applications such as in producing compact disks where the words of a song or the score of a symphony is coded in the auxiliary data channels.[91]

4.5.4　Motion-Picture Industry

Review of Current Techniques.　Before examining the impact of digital audio technology on the motion-picture industry, it is useful to review some of the main features of the traditional treatment of motion-picture sound. There are the three main categories of sound sources for motion pictures: music, dialogue, and sound effects. Initially, music may be recorded onto a large number of tracks, which subsequently are mixed down to a small number (say, two to six) for editing purposes. In contrast, dialogue and effects mainly start out as one or two tracks of sound.

With the exception of the original recording made on a portable tape recorder (electronically synchronized with the camera) while filming takes place, music, effects, and additional dialogue are recorded independently of the picture. However, before any sound can be edited to picture, it must be transferred onto sprocketed magnetic film which has the same longitudinal running speed as the picture film. This magnetic film typically has from one to six separate tracks on it, and its sprockets ensure that it can run synchronized with picture film on manual and motor-driven systems. In contrast to a multitrack recorder, the sprocketed audio tape on one machine can be advanced or retarded in time with respect to the picture or any other audio machine, allowing the editor to adjust the synchronization.

Once the individual sounds have been selected and initially edited, they are assembled onto 10-min reels, with the desired time positioning maintained by the use of sprocketed *spacer film* containing no sound. In the final mixing process, dozens of such sound reels, each with up to six tracks, may be running with each

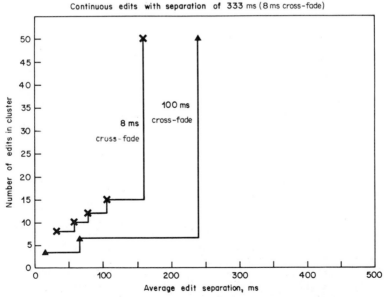

FIG. 4.21 Simulation of disk-based audio editing performance. All applications using disk media to replay audio require data buffering to eliminate gaps in data transfer caused by head movements, latency period (waiting for the required data to rotate to the head position), and system overheads such as calculating the start address of the next transfer. Audio edits achieved by direct access to appropriate locations on the disk add to this overhead. In this simulation, a buffer size of 256 kb is used with a Winchester disk storing 80 kb per cylinder and a 55-ms worst-case seek time. Two audio channels at 48-kHz sampling rate on the disk can be edited with the performance shown.

picture reel, and as many as six operators may be required to balance all the sounds (while watching the picture) by adjusting level controls, equalizers, and special processing devices.

These procedures (described in more detail in Refs. 96 and 97) have remained substantially unchanged since motion-picture sound was introduced. However, developments are beginning to introduce digital audio into key areas of motion-picture sound production.

Digital Music Recording for Motion Pictures.   The motion-picture industry has not, until recent years, been noted for providing high-fidelity audio. This is partly because prior to the early 1950s recording was done optically.[98] (Even now, most motion pictures are distributed with an optically encoded sound track with a rather limited bandwidth and signal-to-noise ratio.) Walt Disney Productions, however, has been among the first of the major film studios to make a substantial commitment to using a multitrack digital recording system in many of its productions. The main reasons given by Disney Studios for this step (besides improving audio quality considerably) were, first, to create digital sound-track masters that were ready to be released in digital form when such technology arrived and, second, to improve the archival quality of its printing masters for future use.[99]

The first use of its recording system was in January 1982 for the digital rescoring of *Fantasia* (initially recorded in 1939 on eight optical recorders). In the modern version, two 32-track DATRs were employed during the recording, dubbing, and mixing phases.[98] By late 1983 this system comprised four multitrack digital audio recorders (which provided over 90 digital sound tracks) and nine videotape players, all of which could be synchronized to support dubbing and editing of multiple-screen formats as well as conventional motion-picture and television formats. By the end of 1983 this system had produced seven multiple-screen motion pictures for the EPCOT center in Florida.[99] However, editing with this system is a complex and time-consuming operation, requiring either copying tracks from one machine to another (possibly through an analog mixing desk) or transferring the digital data to another type of editing system (made by Soundstream) at a different location and then recopying the data back to the original DATR format. The resulting digital master is then copied to analog magnetic tape for use in the tape decks at EPCOT. The entire process at Disney thus can be viewed as hybrid analog-digital operations.

Digital Sound-Effects Retrieval and Editing.   Sound effects can be derived from recordings of live or synthesized "events" such as car sounds, gunshots, wind noise, punches, etc. These are often held in sound-effects libraries (on analog disks or tapes). Alternatively, they are created specially to accompany a specific scene by recording humans making "natural" noises such as footsteps, putting a glass down, brushing against an object, etc. Such sounds are used to greatly enhance the illusion of realism for the viewer.

Traditionally, a motion-picture sound editor spends considerable time searching through an effects library or creating a new sound that is roughly what he or she wants, processing it satisfactorily, synchronizing the resulting sound with action in the picture, and documenting the points on the reel (in terms of film footage and frame or time code) at which the selected sound starts and stops. This procedure takes place for every sound effect in the film and is exceptionally time-intensive.

One of the earliest attempts to streamline this procedure by using a digital sound-retrieval and -processing system was introduced in 1977. The system, known as ACCESS,[98] uses several 200-Mbyte disk drives with removable media, each capable of holding 40 min of monaural sound. Over 250 h of sound effects are stored on disks, and any online effect can be auditioned by typing a few identifying characters. Similarly, the start and stop points can be entered by the operator, and the system memorizes the operator's *gestures* which control a sound's loudness, equalization, and pitch. When a (video) picture is run, the sound effect is played back on cue with the correct processing. In addition, this system is capable of making *loops* of sounds, producing cue sheets automatically, and updating old cues easily if a new edit is made to the picture. Completed sound effects are transferred to analog recording tape for mixing. Unfortunately, the cost of this system was so high that only a very small number were produced and installed. Nevertheless, similar machines, using new and less expensive disk technology, are beginning to appear, which also offer facilities for disk-based editing, mixing, and processing.[96,100]

Automatic Dialogue Synchronization. Usually, dialogue is recorded while filming a scene. However, this original dialogue may be unsuitable because of background noises or poor delivery. In these cases replacement dialogue must be recorded. This takes place in a special recording studio which projects the appropriate scene so that the actor can deliver lines in synchronism with the original lip movement. This procedure is known as dialogue replacement or post-synchronization.

Audiences are rarely aware that a film contains replacement dialogue, although it is common to find more than 30 percent of the original dialogue being replaced in most modern films. Unfortunately, the procedures necessary to achieve good lip sync are difficult and time-consuming. The major burden is on the actor, who must repeat a line over and over until the director and dialogue editor agree that both the sync and the performance are acceptable. The dialogue editor can do some editing of the recording afterward (mainly in silent intervals) to tighten the sync, but the speech signal generally is not cut.

To improve this situation a digital signal-processing system was introduced in London in 1984 that automatically synchronizes actors' replacement dialogue to the dialogue in the original recording. This system, known as Wordfit, is shown in block diagram form in Fig. 4.22.[101]

While the actor speaks his or her line, three main operations take place concurrently:

1. The studio dialogue is converted to digital form and stored on the disk.

2. The original recording (or *guide track*) and studio dialogue enter separate and identical digital filter banks, which analyze the respective signals' spectra every 10 ms. These time-varying spectra are input to a processor, which produces a *time-warping path*. This path is a function of the time scale of the guide track and describes the modifications to the time scale of the studio dialogue that will align best the corresponding features of the two signals. The algorithm used to compute this path is based on pattern-matching techniques used in continuous speech-recognition systems.

3. The time-warping path, along with speech and silence classifications, are input to a waveform editor, which determines if an edit is needed. If it is, the corresponding segment of the waveform is obtained from the disk and measured to find the local waveform periodicity. Then a pitch-synchronous edit is determined which will excise or repeat (as appropriate) approximately 10 ms of the

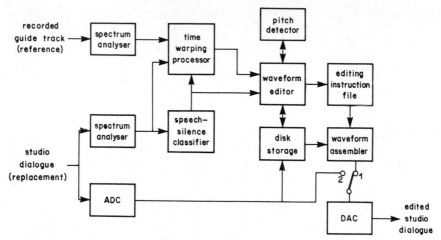

FIG. 4.22 A system for automatically synchronizing replacement dialogue to original dialogue in a motion-picture guide track. During the input and processing pass, the DAC switch is in position 2 for monitoring the digitized input waveform, which is also stored on the disk. Also during input, editing instructions are being computed and stored automatically. During output, the waveform assembler constructs the edited (and synchronized) waveform from the stored input signal according to the editing instruction file, and this signal is input to the DAC through the switch set in position 1.

signal, and a pair of pointers to the corresponding waveform segment on the disk is stored in a file from which the edited signal will be reconstructed.

The Wordfit process requires two passes of each line of dialogue. During the first pass, as described above, the actor's speech is input and processed. Then, when the actor has finished speaking, the studio equipment rewinds back to the beginning of the line, and during a second pass the fitted dialogue is reconstructed and output through the DAC both to the studio loudspeaker for evaluation and to the studio analog recorder.

Total-System Approach to Digitization of Motion-Picture Sound. Perhaps the most farsighted and ambitious approach to improving the quality and efficiency of motion-picture sound production began in 1980 at Lucasfilm Ltd. in California. The firm has now built an audio signal processor (ASP) whose software and hardware are specially tailored to maintain the vast amounts of data transfers, computations, and complex operator-machine interfacing required for sound-effects mixing and editing, music mixing, and sound synthesis for a motion picture sound-track. The prototype architecture and operational features have been described briefly in Sec. 4.5.2 and more thoroughly in Refs. 80, 81, 92, 96, 102, and 103.

Typical use of this system in sound mixing would involve an operator invoking a *cue-sheet editor,* which, via a bit-mapped graphics screen, allows sound effects and dialogue previously edited and stored on the disk to be scheduled for output at prescribed times. The editor's screen typically shows eight tracks horizontally, and sound segments are represented as labeled vertical boxes with the sound's start time (in film feet and frames) at the top and stop time at the bottom.

These segments may be shifted in time for synchronization with the picture or moved to other tracks.[102] When the sounds are played back, the ASP should also provide digital processing such as *fade-ins* and *fade-outs* (i.e., level control), filtering, and possibly artificial reverberation.

In addition, as a result of the flexibility and processing power of this system, other more complex processes such as pitch shifting, time-varying filtering, and echo deconvolution[81] should be feasible. These processes generally would be used to create the sounds used in the mixing process. Another advantage of such a system is, given that audio signals at Lucasfilm grow at 8 Gbytes per year,[104] the management of such an enormous database warrants the use of computerized hierarchical directory systems.

4.5.5   Special Digital Audio-Effects Processors

Effects Previously Implemented in Analog: Teaching Old Tricks to a New Dog.
Until the early 1970s most special audio effects were implemented predominantly by analog techniques.[105] Single "echoes" were simulated with analog tape recorders producing a time-delayed version of the original signal. By routing the delayed signal through an attenuator and mixing it with the input, multiple decaying echoes could be created. A sweeping comb-filter effect could be generated by recording a signal on two tape recorders at once and retarding one of the two supply reels while simultaneously playing and mixing their outputs. Initially realized by operators touching the tape-reel flange, this technique for creating a variable differential delay between identical signals became known as *flanging*.

More complex systems were required to create artificial reverberation, which became increasingly necessary as the popularity of close-miking and multitrack recording techniques grew. Reverberated signals were created initially acoustically in a "live" room. Later, two electromechanical devices appeared. One used springs with transducers at both ends, and the other used a metal plate with several transducers attached at various points.[106]

Because all the effects described above can be digitally implemented from the simple clements of time delay (i.e., buffered input-output), level control (i.e., multiplication), and mixing (i.e., addition), once the quality of analog-to-digital-to-analog conversion became acceptable, the first commercial digital audio devices to appear were time-delay and flanging systems. Digital reverberation units followed shortly after.

Simple Digital Time-Delay-Based Effects.   The block diagram for adding echo and flanging is shown in Fig. 4.23a. If τ is greater than approximately 40 ms, an echo will be heard. If τ is varied between 0 and 10 ms at a frequency under 1 Hz, a broadband input will be flanged by the resulting time-varying comb filter (shown for a fixed delay in Fig. 4.23b). An additional effect known as *doubling* will be produced if τ is slowly varied between 10 and 25 ms because the pitch and timing of the delayed signal changes with respect to the original. This gives the approximate impression that a second voice or instrument accompanies the first.[107] If the input is directed through four or more such doubling units with different time delays, gains, and random and independent delay variations, a convincing *chorus* effect is obtained by summing the outputs of these units.[106]

An effect commonly used known as *phasing* can be produced by replacing the delay unit in Fig. 4.23a by a digital all-pass filter or a cascade of all-pass filters.[108]

This system will have transfer-function minima at frequencies where the all-pass chain's composite phase response equals odd multiples of 180°. These notches (unlike those in the flanger) may be spaced nonuniformly in frequency and varied independently with time.

Digital Reverberation.   Although any specific reverberation process in theory could be simulated by convolving a signal with the desired measured or simulated room impulse response, it is both impractical computationally and unnecessary

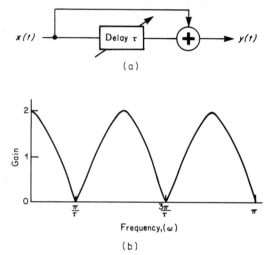

FIG. 4.23   (a) Block diagram for creating echoes (if τ is > 40 ms) or for flanging (if τ is slowly varied between approximately 0 and 10 ms). (b) The transfer function, $H(\omega) = 2|\cos(\tau\omega/2)|$, for a for a fixed value of τ. The frequency variable $\omega = 2\pi f/f_s$, and f is frequency, Hz.

perceptually to do so. Only features of room responses that are perceptually important, such as the direct path, early reflections, and the *reverberant tail* (or reverberation) need be generated to produce a perceptually satisfactory reverberation effect (Fig. 4.24). There is a general consensus in the literature indicating that the direct sound and between 4 and 20 early reflections should be generated by using a multiple-tap delay line with adjustable delays and gains on each tap (Fig. 4.25).[109,110] Optionally, the output of the delay line may be recirculated (through g_1), and the processor output may be fed through an all-pass unit such as the one shown in Fig. 4.26b.[106]

The reverberation or reverberant tail shown in Fig. 4.24 is most efficiently generated by using recursive structures such as those in Fig. 4.26a and b. These are known as *unit* reverberators, and for $g < 1$ the impulse response of the structure in Fig. 4.26a is an exponentially decreasing periodic pulse train. The corresponding frequency response is a comb filter with peaks separated by $1/\tau$. The impulse response of the filter structure in Fig. 4.26b is similar to that of the comb filter but includes a negative-going pulse at $t = 0$. With the gains shown, this gives an

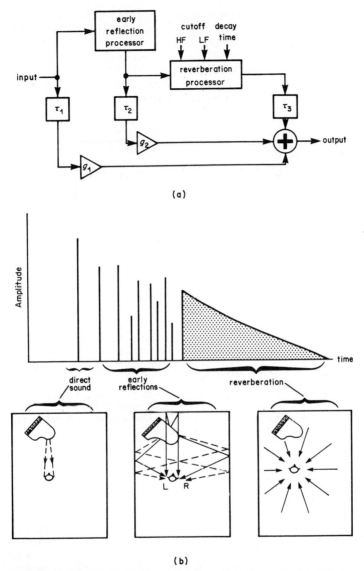

FIG. 4.24 (*a*) Typical one-channel digital reverberation system in which the direct sound, early reflections, and reverberant tail (reverberation) are created in separate processes before being summed to form the output. (*b*) The upper part of this figure indicates schematically the (somewhat artificial) separation of a room's impulse response into perceptually relevant sections. The lower part suggests paths along which sound might travel in a room from an instrument to a listener to create the corresponding sections of the impulse response.

all-pass response (i.e., flat magnitude and nonlinear phase). Used individually, these unit reverberators produce a perceptually unsatisfactory reverberant tail with noticeable spectral coloration.[106] But by feeding the input[106,109] (or alternatively the output of the early reflection process[110]) through a network typically comprising four to six parallel comb units with differing τ's and feeding their summed outputs to two all-pass units in cascade, a suitably high density of echoes and "colorless" reverberant tail can be produced.

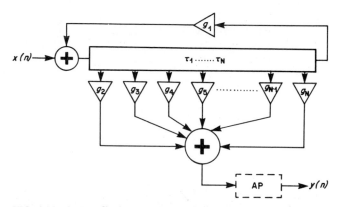

FIG. 4.25   Early reflection processor (see Fig. 4.24) using a tapped digital delay line to create the discrete repetitions of a digitized input signal $x(n)$. The time delays τ_i, typically set in the range of 40 to 100 ms   [B. A. Blesser and J. M. Kates, "Digital Processing of Audio Signals," in A. V. Oppenheim (ed.), Applications of Digital Signal Processing, Prentice-Hall, Englewood Cliffs, N.J., 1978; J. A. Moorer, "About This Reverberation Business," Comput. Music J., 3(2), 13–28 (1978)], and g_i ($g<1$) are adjustable to create perceptually different "rooms." The feedback path through g_i and the all-pass network in the output path are optional and suggested in Moorer.

The realism and flexibility of these simulations can be improved further by controlling the following:[106,109,110] (1) the time delay between the direct and reverberant components, which affects the perceived room size; (2) the time delay between the direct and first reflections, which affects the perception of presence; (3) the direct-to-reverberant energy ratio, which inversely influences the perception of distance; and (4) the high- and low-frequency rolloff, which compensates for the ear's nonuniform loudness response. In addition, the effect of air increasingly attenuating high frequencies with increasing distance can be simulated by inserting a low-pass filter in the feedback loop of the unit in Fig. 4.26a.[110]

Currently, there are about a dozen commercial manufacturers of digital two-channel reverberation units which use combinations of the structures shown in Figs. 4.24, 4.25, and 4.26,[109] plus proprietary techniques to achieve natural and easily controllable reverberation. More recent research into multichannel reverberators has indicated that spreading and increasing the echo density of the reverberation can be achieved without sacrificing system stability, by using feedback paths characterized by a feedback matrix with carefully selected elements.[111] However, more work remains to enable understanding of the relationships between the various structures and the perceived results, inasmuch as the trial-and-error method is used predominantly to find perceptually acceptable systems.

Digital Time-Scale and Pitch Modifications.   In a number of broadcasting and recording applications, the need often arises to change the pitch of a signal without altering its duration or to change the duration of a signal without altering its

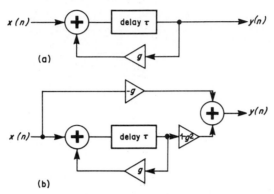

FIG. 4.26   Typical structures for unit reverberators to be used in various combinations to create the reverberant tail of a room's impulse response efficiently (Fig. 4.24). Increasing the gain g (typically set between 0.2 and 0.9) increases the decay time, and τ is usually set to values between 5 and 100 ms. (*a*) Comb-filter unit. (*b*) All-pass unit. [*B. A. Blesser and J. M. Kates, "Digital Processing of Audio Signals," in A. V. Oppenheim (ed.),* Applications of Digital Signal Processing, *Prentice-Hall, Englewood Cliffs, N.J., 1978; J. A. Moorer, "About This Reverberation Business,"* Comput. Music J.,*3(2), 13–28 (1978).*]

pitch. Several commercial real-time digital devices as well as non-real-time schemes perform these functions.

   Digital pitch changing in real time (Fig. 4.27) is generally based on the principle of loading a random-access memory (or delay line) with a signal sampled at input clock rate C_i and outputting samples at clock rate C_o. Their ratio, r = C_o/C_i, determines the relative pitch change. To maintain a continuous output signal, waveform sections in the buffer must be repeated or skipped. In practice, because the output-address pointer must repeatedly overtake the input address (for a pitch increase) or be overtaken by the recirculating input-address pointer (for a pitch decrease), the output address must occasionally *jump* to a new point in the buffer so that a relatively smooth transition is made between samples before and after the jump. To make this digital *splice* inaudible, the details of the jump must be computed, on the basis of the waveform's periodicities, and a smoothing operation is used to ramp the gain of the presplice signal to 0 and that of the postsplice signal to 1. The output is the sum of these signals.

   The performance of such systems is somewhat dependent on the complexity of the input signal and the ratio of the desired pitch change. Currently, most commercial devices tend to produce some undesirable audible effects when used on critical material.

The process of time-scale modification (or rate changing) of indeterminate-length signals is practical only when the input signal is recorded or digitally stored. For example, the input to such a system may be from a tape recorder whose play-

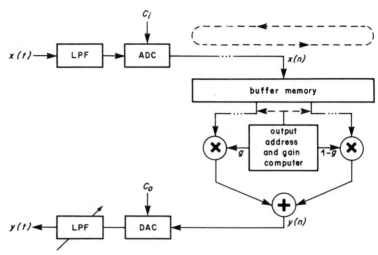

FIG. 4.27   Digital time-domain pitch-shifting device. The input signal $x(t)$ is low-pass-filtered (LPF), digitized in the ADC at clock rate C_i, and stored in a circular buffer memory. The output is constructed by taking samples from the memory at a different rate C_0. A computer is used to determine the sections in the memory to be repeated or skipped and generates the addresses and gains, $g(n)$ and $1 - g(n)$, for producing smooth transitions between noncontiguous waveform sections, thereby generating $y(n)$. The output LPF is adjusted to prevent aliases from occurring in the reconstructed output $y(t)$.

back speed is altered to a ratio r times the speed used to record (Fig. 4.28). A real-time pitch-shifting device (set to a ratio of $1/r$) is then used to restore the rate-changed output to the original pitch. Obviously, the final quality of this approach will depend primarily on that of the pitch changer.

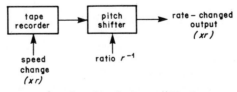

FIG. 4.28   Time-domain rate-modification system. A variable-speed tape recorder reproduces a signal at a rate r times the recording rate but with a pitch shift of r. A pitch shifter (similar to Fig. 4.27), set to shift by $1/r$, is used to restore the correct pitch to the rate-changed output signal.

Other, more complex time-domain algorithms for real-time rate modification and time-domain harmonic scaling of digitized speech have been proposed which also require periodicity estimates to achieve satisfactory quality.[112] Short-time spectral analysis, modification, and synthesis have been explored as other means for achieving similar results with speech signals (Fig. 4.29). This frequency-domain approach (often referred to as a phase vocoder) is, however, very computationally intensive and has mainly been run in non-real-time simulations.[113]

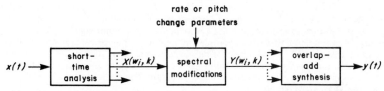

FIG. 4.29 Frequency-domain technique for producing rate or pitch changes to input signal $x(t)$. This is accomplished by interpolation or decimation (as appropriate) of the input signal's short-time spectra. $X(\omega, k)$. As shown for a frequency band centered on ω_i in analysis frame k, each complex band is individually modified before synthesis to generate output spectra $Y(\omega, k)$. The output waveform $y(t)$ is synthesized via inverse discrete Fourier transforms and overlap-add techniques. [*J. S. Lim (ed.), Speech Enhancement, Prentice-Hall, Englewood Cliffs, N.J., 1983.*]

Nevertheless, recent work indicates that such techniques may be applied to music signals with higher bandwidths and still achieve reasonably high quality.[114] Much work remains to determine how to implement any of these sophisticated approaches in real-time hardware so that they will maintain sufficiently high quality and flexibility for professional audio applications. Additional effort is required to minimize the various forms of degradation that these techniques can introduce.[114]

Other Sophisticated Processes: Restoration and Noise Reduction. Perhaps one of the most aesthetically appealing applications of digital audio technology is to improve the quality of degraded analog recordings. Already mentioned was the application of *blind deconvolution* to compensate for the recording horn resonances found in turn-of-the-century acoustic recordings.[6] It is interesting to note that a power spectrum approach is also described in the same reference that "gives more natural sounding results directly" (Ref. 6, p. 686). Both of these techniques are aimed at reshaping the spectrum of a noisy low-passed signal, and high quality is not an issue.

A more demanding task, however, is the suppression of low levels of wideband noise (such as tape hiss) on good-quality analog master recordings. The challenge in such applications is to reduce the noise without perceptibly altering signal quality.

One approach to solving this problem has been proposed,[115] in which the audio signal is passed through a linear-phase multiband filter bank (with between 64 and 512 bands) efficiently implemented by using a polyphase network and fast Fourier transforms (Fig. 4.30). The following assumptions are made: The noise is wideband, stationary, and at a very low level and may be masked by the signal. Short-term analysis of in-band noise, based on either signal-free segments, long-term averaging, or across-band or stereo pair correlation, can be used to determine at what signal level the gain of a band should be reduced. A number of enhancement

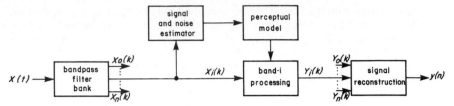

FIG. 4.30 Generalized enhancement scheme [*after R. Lagadec and D. Pelloni, "Signal Enhancement via Digital Signal Processing," presented at the 74th Convention of the Audio Engineering Society, New York (October 1984), preprint 2037 (G-6)*] which operates in the frequency domain to estimate and reduce the perceived noise components in the input signal $x(t)$. The bandpass filter bank can be implemented with a complex, nonrecursive polyphase network followed by a fast Fourier transform (FFT) and a bank of half-band filters. Estimation of the signal and noise can use information from neighboring bands, and a simple model of masking determines the attenuation applied to a particular band i. Reconstruction requires inverse FFTs and polyphase network *(Lagadec and Pelloni).*

schemes were explored by using simplified models of masking, but it was often found that in each band it was very difficult to distinguish noise from the signals and that certain settings of parameters which worked well with some signals were not optimum across a variety of musical examples.[115] Furthermore, later studies found that this implementation could introduce perceptible time-delay dispersion.[20]

A related study[116] investigated several alternative techniques for implementing digital linear-phase bandpass filter banks for multiband noise-gate applications as well as for graphic equalization. In these implementations, the input signal is analyzed into a number of bands, and the gain of band m, $g(m)$, is individually adjusted, either by the operator for equalization or automatically for noise reduction according to the suggested expansion function:

$$g(m) = (1 - \alpha) \left[\frac{s(m)}{s(m) + \lambda} \right]^{2r} + \alpha$$

which attenuates the signal at low levels and passes a high-level signal unchanged. Here, α determines the sharpness of the gain-change function, λ sets the threshold where the gain will start to reduce, and $s(m)$ is the rms signal in band m. Values of these parameters found to give good results were $\alpha = -12$ dB, $r = 1$, and $\lambda = 2.5\sigma_m$, where σ_m is an estimate of the rms value of the noise in band m, obtained from noise-only segments of the material to be processed.

The number of bands giving the best results was 256, which for efficiency could be implemented by using a fast Fourier transform. Some low-level noisy artifacts that required additional masking still remained with this method.

Another suggested approach, which also proved effective, employs four highly overlapping analysis channels. The realization of this noise suppression system is performed in the time domain directly via convolution of the signal with individual channel impulse responses, derived by using a novel theoretical analysis of the desired frequency-response characteristics of each channel. The channel outputs are then summed to form the output signal with the desired spectral modifications and no phase distortion other than pure time delay.

It is clear from both of the above studies that considerable work remains to be done in the area of signal enhancement, especially with regard to modeling the perceptibility of low-level noise with signals present.

4.6 TRANSMISSION SYSTEMS

The introduction of digital techniques in the studio presents a challenge to the broadcaster to pass on the added quality to the listener. There is now intensive effort to determine the best methods to provide new services such as stereo with terrestrial TV or new radio services based on direct-broadcasting satellites (DBS). There is some measure of agreement that these new services can be implemented best with a digitally modulated multiplex of the services required, and in many cases the current frequency-modulation (FM) techniques will be displaced gradually. Figure 4.31 depicts the scope of this work.

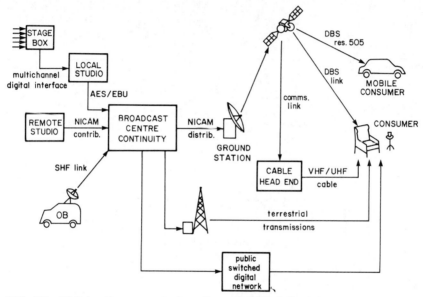

FIG. 4.31 Digital audio communications. Conveying digital signals from the sound stage to the home requires a range of communications links to be established. Digital contribution and distribution for the broadcast center have been utilized for many years. Projects currently under way and soon to be completed include multichannel links from microphone to studio (<1 km), SHF radio links from the outside broadcast (OB) vehicle to the broadcasting center, and direct-broadcasting-satellite (DBS) services to the home. Work planned included DBS services to mobile or portable users and reduced-data-rate transmission to the home via the switched-telephone network.

At the most local level, digital equipment must be interconnected, and a two-channel serial interface has been defined which operates at the agreed studio sampling rate of 48 kHz and to 24-bit resolution. In addition, it includes data for status information, users' data, sample validity, and parity in the multiplex. It is intended to operate over distances up to 300 m using RS422 differential lines and, therefore, meets most requirements for communications within a single building (Fig. 4.32).[117]

Remote contributions conventionally use the public switched-telephone service or radio links, but with the continuing move to digital telephony wider-bandwidth analog *music lines* will become rarer and eventually nonexistent. At the BBC, the *sound-in-syncs* distribution system (Fig. 4.33) was introduced in 1969. This was a method by which *all* TV sound is interleaved in digital form in the analog video signal for distribution to the various transmitters.[118] By 1972 a multiplexed scheme was in use to distribute stereo signals to the FM broadcasting

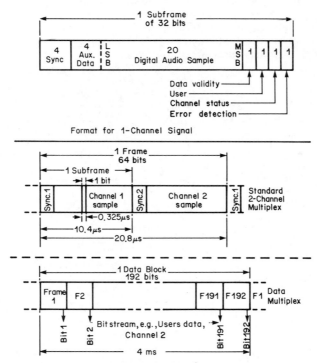

FIG. 4.32 Structure of the AES-EBU interface. A sampling frequency of 48 kHz is recommended for the origination, processing, and interchange of digital audio *(ANSI S4.28–1984)*. The interface is designed for two-channel operation and has a blocked structure which repeats after 96 sample pairs, i.e., 4 ms. A synchronizing pattern identifies the block structure so that auxiliary data for status, user data, etc., can be reformatted.

transmitters.[119] The system uses near-instantaneous companding[120] in which an initial 14-bit linear (uniform) coding is compressed to 10 bits, the degree of compression being determined by the magnitude of the largest sample in a 1-ms block. This specification has been shown to provide an acceptable idle-channel noise and program-modulated noise[121] with an efficient bit rate. A 15-kHz audio bandwidth can be maintained with a 32-kHz sampling rate and six of these high-quality channels multiplexed into the 2048-kbit/s level of the digital telephone hierarchy. The system is called *near-instantaneous companding audio multiplex* (NICAM) and is now a well-established technique in the United Kingdom for distribution which, in recent years, has been applied to contribution circuits as well.

For OBs, superhigh-frequency (SHF) links are conventionally used for the point-to-point transfer of programs either to a Postal, Telegraph, and Telephone

Administration (PTT) access point or directly to the studio. In the United Kingdom, 10 narrow 400-kHz channels are available in a 1.5-GHz subband. A digital link using a two-channel (stereo) NICAM signal of 704 kbit/s and tamed frequency modulation (TFM) went into service at the end of 1984.[122]

The consumer has yet to benefit in a dramatic way from these developments because transmission to the home is still via analog FM. However, a certain

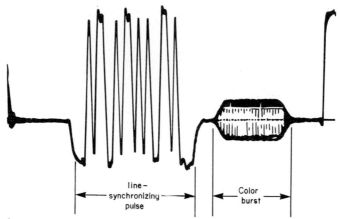

line–
◄——— synchronizing ———►   ◄——— Color ———►
pulse   burst

FIG. 4.33 Sound-in-syncs for distribution of digital audio with television signals. At a sampling frequency of 31.25 kHz (twice television-line frequency), two audio samples of 10 bits can be inserted into the unused line, synchronizing pulse interval with associated control data. This is now the most common technique for distributing audio to TV transmitter sites in Europe. A similar technique is being applied for dual-channel or stereo signals by using quaternary (four-level) data. [*J. E. Holder and N. M. Spenceley, "A Two-Channel Sound-in-Syncs Transmission System," presented at the International Broadcasting Convention, Brighton, England,* IEE Conference Publication 240, *345–348 (September 1984).*]

awareness of digital techniques was created in May 1981 when the BBC did a live concert in stereo of the BBC Symphony Orchestra from Shanghai, China, using the 2048-bit/s NICAM equipment with an analog video channel via Intelsat to return the signal to the United Kingdom. The important feature here is that no current analog transmission path of this length has a sufficiently well-controlled phase response to give a satisfactory stereo image.

Completion of the chain by broadcasting (or narrowcasting) the digital audio program to the home is being investigated extensively on several fronts as follows.

4.6.1 Stereo with Television

Many authorities are working on analog FM systems, using either an additional sound carrier (to preserve compatibility with existing receivers) or by *simulcast* using a synchronized additional broadcast on a radio network or local station. The Electronic Industries Association (EIA) announced its recommendation of the Zenith proposal for analog stereo sound on United States television.[123] Experiments in the United Kingdom[124] have shown that, for the phase-alternation-line

(PAL) system, best results are achieved when an additional subcarrier is used with a four-phase differentially-coherent-phase-shift-keying (DPSK) modulation of a digital source. By using a NICAM-encoded stereo signal and an additional carrier 0.55 MHz above the main FM sound carrier, a new service will be offered with no degradation to the existing one (Fig. 4.34).

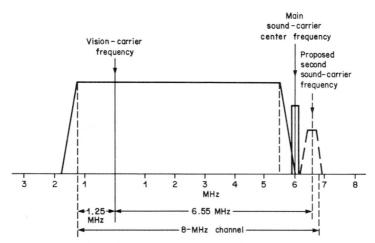

FIG. 4.34 Digital stereophony with terrestrial television. The desire for independent two-channel operation and full compatibility with existing services has led to the proposal of a digitally modulated additional carrier. This second carrier has a level 20 dB less than the peak vision carrier and uses four-phase DPSK modulation at 704 kbit/s. The low level reduces the level of any interference between the main sound carrier and the added digitally modulated carrier, which could cause picture patterning. The ruggedness of the digital signal also has the benefit that the main sound carrier can be maintained at its full level.

4.6.2   Terrestrial Digital Audio Broadcasting

Although some experiments have been conducted, terrestrial digital audio broadcasting is proving to be a less fruitful area to exploit because of the limited service area and difficulties in correcting for multipath propagation, particularly in mobile receivers.

4.6.3   Satellite Distribution

Satellite distribution is receiving much attention because it utilizes existing communications satellites. These have typical output powers of 20 W and require a large receiving dish that normally limits application to telecommunications and community-reception applications. In the United States, many organizations have considerable experience in using this kind of link to connect cable head ends, as has EUTELSAT, the operators of the European communications satellite (ECS) in Europe. When it is used for analog video distribution, only one-half of the 80-MHz channel is needed, and therefore there are clear opportunities to incorporate digital audio as well.

An excellent example of such an application was the program "Stevie Wonder Comes Home,"[125] in which a digital sound track was distributed with the video signal in June 1984. Using Scientific Atlanta 15-bit terminal equipment and the

RCA Satcom 1R communications satellite, the program was distributed to 85 earth stations in the United States for conventional simulcast transmission from local sites.

The BBC is expanding the satellite distribution of its world service to overcome the vagaries of short-wave transmission. Each audio channel has a bandwidth of approximately 6 kHz, and the digital data are conveyed in the normal bandwidth for a two-way telephone channel. The service is then relayed via the Indian Ocean region Intelsat to Cyprus, Masira, and Singapore for conventional transmission to the eastern Mediterranean, Middle East, and Far East. This service began in August 1983, and further expansion is planned.[126]

4.6.4 Direct-Broadcasting Satellites

DBS satellites are characterized by 27-MHz channels and large radio-frequency output powers in the region of 200 W which make possible individual reception using a small (1-m-diameter) dish. Such output powers have become feasible only recently (at the higher frequencies), and Table 4.5 shows a nonexhaustive list of launches.

A number of sound channels may be transmitted within any single channel of the services in Table 4.5. The International Radio Consultative Committee (CCIR) is actively considering two modulation methods: FM, with the same standards as terrestrial very-high-frequency (VHF) broadcasting; and digital, where a

TABLE 4.5 Current and Projected Launches for Direct-Broadcasting Satellites

Satellite	Country	Band	Launch date	Services	CCIR* region
Ekran	U.S.S.R.	620–790 MHz	1974	Experimental	1
ATS-6	United States	860 MHz; 2.5– 2.69 GHz		Experimental	2
INSAT 1B	India	2.5–2.69 GHz	1983	Two broadcast channels for community reception	3
Anik series	Canada	11.7–12.2 GHz	>1978		2
BS-2	Japan		1984	Two channels	3
TV-SAT and TDF-1	France and Germany	11.7–12.5 GHz	1985–1986	Three channels	
TELE-X	Scandinavia	11.7–12.5 GHz	1986	Same technology as TV-SAT	1
UNISAT	United Kingdom	11.7–12.5 GHz	>1986	Two channels	1
Olympus	ESA†	11.7–12.5 GHz	1986	FCC has authorized eight satellites with a total of 35 channels	2
	United States	12.2–12.7 GHz			

* International Radio Consultative Committee.
† European Space Agency.

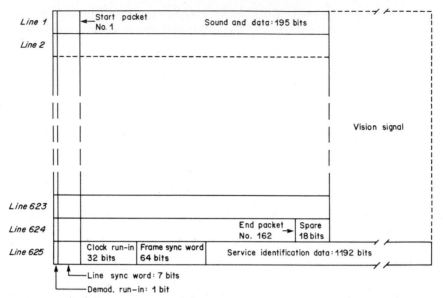

FIG. 4.35 The C-MAC-packet system for direct satellite broadcasting using 625-line television standards. One complete frame of 625 lines is shown in which 162 packets of 751 bits are conveyed. This corresponds to a rate of 4050 packets per second and may be compared with the 503 packets per second needed to transmit a single companded monophonic sound channel. The packet structure permits a variety of sound and data services to be offered, and these are rapidly identified by using the service identification data. These data may be used to automatically configure the receiver for the services selected by the user. The complete fully integrated system was first demonstrated in June 1983.

large number of sound-data services is to be offered. Presently, only two systems have been fully specified for transmission of television, digital audio, and data from satellite. These are the C-MAC(Multiplexed Analog Component)-packet system,[127,128] agreed to and adopted by the EBU; and the digital subcarrier system, for use with National Television System Committee (NTSC) picture signals.[129]

In the C-MAC-packet system, digital audio signals will be transmitted as a burst of 203 bits in each television line of which 195 data bits contribute to a transmission rate of about 3 Mbit/s. Within this burst format discrete "packets" of information may be allocated to many services, e.g., high-quality sound, data services, or conditional-access information. Particularly important is the ease with which new services can be generated (Fig 4.35).

In the digital subcarrier system a fixed-format multiplex of the contributing audio and data is used to modulate a subcarrier sited to avoid interference to the video signal.

Table 4-6 shows the relevant parameters for the audio components of the two systems; a useful comparison is detailed in Ref. 130.

As can be seen, a wide range of services can be configured. The eight-channel C-MAC-packet system could be used as four stereo sound tracks, each in a different language. If fewer languages are needed, the spare channels could be used for radio services. In addition, sound channels can be split into *commentary-grade tracks* for sporting events. In the C-MAC proposal, the multiplicity of services is recognized by providing a service identification channel that can identify the broadcast and, therefore, configure a receiver to operate correctly.

TABLE 4.6 Comparison of Audio Coding Systems in Two Direct-Broadcasting-Satellite Proposals

System	C-MAC or packet		Digital subcarrier	
Audio bandwidth, kHz	15 or 7		15	20
Sampling frequency, kHz	32 or 16		32	48
Conversion (bits/ sample)	14-14-14	14	14-10-14	16
Coding law	NICAM	Linear	NICAM	Linear
Scale factor	5 range	....	5 range	....
Preemphasis	J.17 CCITT		50/15 μs	
Instantaneous bit rate, Mbit/s	20.25		2.048	
Number of channels	8 or 6 plus auxiliary	6 or 4 plus auxiliary	4 plus 480 kb/s	2 plus 240 kb/s
Multiplexing	Packet		Continuous	
Modulation	2–4 phase-shift keying		4-phase differentially coherent phase-shift keying	

In contrast, the digital subcarrier system proposes fewer services but is capable of full studio quality. On a positive note, both systems recognize the companded 32-kHz signal.

In the United States the companded system is also being considered because it is expected that low-cost chip sets will be available for decoding.[131] Alternatively, an equivalent data rate adaptive-delta-modulation (ADM) system [132] may be preferred because of its graceful tolerance of bit errors and potential very low cost.

A different approach has been exploited in West Germany, where a project coming to fruition has been designed to broadcast 16 high-quality stereo programs in a single satellite channel [133,134] using TV-SAT. This employs a 32-kHz sampling rate and 14-bit ranging conversion to give a 16-bit effective dynamic range. Each stereo channel has a fixed allocation of 16 kbit/s for auxiliary data, a feature discussed later. Experiments are being conducted on the system's compatibility with cable systems.

The large 27-MHz bandwidth of the C-MAC-packet satellite channel can be reduced to about 14MHz if a different modulation system is used and the digital components are transmitted in binary or duobinary form. This is then compatible with VHF-UHF cable networks with minimum additional circuitry, changing only the antenna-cable feed, frequency converter, and demodulator.[127]

4.6.5 DBS to Portable and Automobile Receivers

Although there is no frequency allocation for such a service at present, it is technically feasible to provide it.[135] Both FM and digital modulation have been considered, but for mobile receivers using small antennas with limited directivity (e.g., a dipole), only the digital system can provide stereo reception in all the reception conditions anticipated by the service. It can be expected that the next World Administrative Radio Conference (WARC) will approve such a service within the 500- to 2000-MHz range.

4.6.6   Digital Audio Distribution on High-Capacity Telephone Lines

The high data rates of digital audio and the limited data-carrying capacity of conventional domestic telephone lines would appear to preclude their use as a means of distribution. However, work is in progress[136] to combine data-reduction techniques with non-real-time transmission over digital telephone links at 56 kbit/s on American Telephone & Telegraph's (AT&T's) Accunet. Presently, the lowest accepted data rate for high-quality stereo signal is 728 bit/s, achievable in NICAM-3[120] or ADPCM.[132] Therefore, it is difficult to foresee the outcome of such work.

4.7   SYSTEM ASPECTS OF PROFESSIONAL DIGITAL AUDIO

Although almost every aspect of the program chain has been implemented digitally, interconnection of digital equipment is still largely on an ad hoc basis. In comparison, the creation of an independent record-making digital studio appears almost trivial; however, there are sufficient areas of common concern that a systems approach is being sought.[137]

There are three main areas to be considered. First is synchronization, i.e., providing common timing for digital signals which may originate at a number of sources. Second is the use of auxiliary data in the so-called smart audio signal for operational reasons or for the benefit of the listener. Third is remote control, but since this has little consequence on the digital aspects of audio, it will not be considered further.

4.7.1   Synchronization

Synchronization has always been of concern even with analog signals. It is a recurring challenge in a complex production to lock sound with video (e.g., to lip-sync) or even to lock tape machines together to increase the number of recording channels. The EBU-SMPTE time code is applied almost universally to solve these problems[138] and requires the writing of hours, minutes, seconds, and frames on a spare recording track and access to the speed-control circuits of each piece of equipment used.

The block structure of the AES-EBU interface requires synchronization at the bit, sample, and block level (Fig. 4.35), whenever two or more of these digital audio signals are combined for processing. It can be expected that there will be a slowly shifting timing relationship if the clock rates are not derived from a common reference. For example, a difference in sampling frequencies of 1 ppm will cause a word loss or repetition every 20 s, causing audible clicks. Two methods have been proposed to solve this problem.

In the first, a buffer store is placed between the input and the processing equipment. Depending on the difference between the input and local sampling rates, occasionally the buffer will need to be reset to the half-full condition to avoid becoming either full or empty. The resetting involves a discarding or repetition of blocks of samples, and by arranging that this procedure occurs during quiet periods in the program the impairment caused can be minimized. The system has been tested for a wide variety of materials and gives acceptable performance for a sampling-rate difference of 1 ppm and, of course, does not contribute to an increase in the level of quantization noise.[139]

A more recent proposal again uses a buffer, but this time adjusts the *fullness* by occasionally generating a new sequence of output samples via a wideband variable-delay filter.[140] At the beginning of this transient phase, the delay through the buffer corresponds exactly to the previous steady-state delay, modified gradually by fractions of a sample until a delay of exactly one sample period has been reached. During the adjustment (which may take 32 samples), there will be a slight pitch change and quantization noise commensurate with the processing accuracy. The technique has not yet been evaluated fully but has the advantage of minimizing total delay through the synchronizer and having a more predictable behavior.

4.7.2 Sampling-Frequency Conversion

When the difference in sampling rates is greater than approximately 10 ppm, other techniques must be used. This may occur in monitoring a tape at spooling speeds or for edit-point location at low speeds by rock and roll. A sampling-frequency converter (SFC) digital filter can provide the medium quality required for these applications quite easily.[95]

However, there are a number of applications where full quality must be maintained through the converter. For example, the sampling rate for professional digital audio is 48 kHz, but it must be converted to 44.1 kHz for CD mastering. Typically, there will be an imprecise timing relationship between these rates. More challenging still is the use of variable-speed operation to make a deliberate pitch change; in this case, the effect is part of the final product, and therefore the highest quality must be maintained. In particular, the SFC must exhibit a controlled behavior as the ratio of input and output sampling rates passes through unity.

It has been shown that, in conventional approaches to sampling-frequency conversion in which the signal is first interpolated by an integer factor L and then decimated by an integer factor M, the factors L and M are of the order of 2^{15} if professional quality standards are to be maintained.[141] This corresponds to a transversal filter of length 1.8 million. One solution is to implement a multistage filter design in which a knowledge of the relative time displacements of input and output samples is used to compute selectively the contributions to a particular output-sample value.[142] Such a unit is in frequent use at CD-mastering plants.

However, an even more elegant solution can be devised by using a single-stage filter with time-varying coefficients. One proposal is to store a restricted set of coefficient values from the 1.8 million in the fully specified impulse response. Then, for each output-sample calculation, the appropriate coefficient set is calculated by interpolation from a knowledge of the relative time displacements of input and output samples.[143] Such a device remains to be demonstrated but promises to be economical and efficient for applications such as playing 44.1-kHz CDs in a studio operating at 48 kHz.

4.7.3 "Smart" Audio Signal

At almost every stage of the broadcast chain auxiliary data have been used. In the AES-EBU interface, extra bits are available for conveying machine status, time codes, routing information, etc.

The *user bits* of the interface are intended for applications where there is a benefit in the data accompanying the audio data throughout the production chain. This can be a powerful tool if formatted into an agreed structure which meets the needs of all potential users. One such format has been proposed in Ref. 91: a data packet of 48 bits termed a *label,* intended to be transmitted and recorded through the entire signal chain. Applications for labels include program identification, copyright information, song lyrics (this is very popular in Japan and is known as *karaoke*), or even gain or dynamic-range control data so that a replay device can operate at the correct volume.[133]

While labels must be transmittable and recordable, not all recorded or transmitted auxiliary data are labels. For example, routing data and other *status* information may be usefully recorded in some applications. There are many demands on auxiliary-data capacity, but the capacity available varies widely as shown in Table 4.7. However, it is generally accepted that the professional DATR must allocate a track or tracks for these purposes and that an editor must be able to edit the auxiliary data as well as the audio. How "smart" the audio signal will be when it reaches the consumer remains to be seen; current data transmissions with analog audio include *radio data* for program identification[144] and signaling at 25 bit/s on low-frequency (200-kHz) broadcasts for switching the tariffs in electricity meters.[145]

TABLE 4.7   Auxiliary-Data Capacity in a Number of Applications

Application	Auxiliary bits per audio channel	Comments	Reference
CD	22.05 kb/s	Six subcodes at 7.35 kb/s	
DASH	96.0 kb/s	One extra track serving stereo on 8 tracks	...[a]
Radio data	1200 bit/s	Conveyed with additional subcarrier with FM	...[b]
DBS	8.0 kb/s	16 kb/s for each of 16 stereo channels	...[c]
S-DAT		Two spare tracks serving stereo on 10 tracks	...[d]
NICAM-3	0.65 kb/s	Intended for operational use only	
AES-EBU interface	48.0 kb/s	User bits or formated as labels	...[e]
DTTR		Committee discussions only	
LF signaling	25.0 bit/s	Using phase modulation of carrier	...[f]

[a] *Reports on DASH (Digital Audio Stationary Head),* Sony Corp., Communication Products, International Marketing Department, March 1984.

[b] "Specifications of the Radio Data System RDS for VHF/FM Sound Broadcasting," Document 3244-D, EBU Technical Center, March, 1984.

[c] P. Tretyl (ed.), *Digital Sound Service for Direct Broadcasting Satellites,* Federal Minister of Research and Technology, Bonn, West Germany.

[d] N. Sakamoto, T. Kogure, H. Kitagawa, and T. Shimada, "Signal Processing of the Compact Cassette Digital Recorder," *J. Audio Eng. Soc.,* **32**(9), 647–658 (September 1984).

[e] R. Lagadec and G. W. McNally, "Labels and Their Formatting for Digital Trnasmission and Recording," presented at the 74th Convention of the Audio Engineering Society, New York (October 1983), preprint 2003 (A-5).

[f] S. M. Edwardson, B. E. Eyre, G. O. Hensman, and D. T. Wright, "A Radio Teleswitching System for Load Management in UK," presented at the 4th International Conference on Metering Apparatus and Tariffs for Electricity Supply, *IEE Conference Publication 217,* 40–46 (October 1982).

PROCESSING CIRCUITS AND COMPONENTS

Leonard Sherman
Maxim Integrated Products, Sunnyvale, California

Jerry Whitaker
Editorial Director, Broadcast Engineering and Video Systems, Overland Park, Kansas

4.8 EQUIPMENT EVOLUTION

The rapid growth in digitally based audio equipment is closely linked to the even faster pace set by the computer industry for data-acquisition-system development. Consequently, more uses are being found for analog-to-digital and digital-to-analog hardware as digital processing of audio signals has become commonplace in both professional and consumer equipment. For example, digital technology can be found in CD players, audio time-manipulation and -delay devices, special-effects generators, tape recorders and studio audio consoles, and transmission by fiber optics and satellites.

No longer may AD-DA processing be treated as a *black box* inserted in an analog environment. Instead, a familiarity with system disciplines and a broad knowledge of component designs are essential in the application of digital technology.

4.8.1 Analog-to-Digital Converter

The ADC is the entrance bridge to the digital domain. Converters generally fall into one of three categories that essentially define their basic modes of operation. These are successive approximation, integrating, and flash.

Successive Approximation. The most commonly encountered type of ADC is that employing a successive-approximation register (SAR). SAR designs have from 8- to 12-bit resolution and operate at a wide range of speeds from 10 to 100 μs. Conversion is accomplished by stepping through a sequence of trial-and-error comparisons between the unknown input signal and a series of binary-weighted reference levels. The result of each successive comparison serves to narrow the range of reference level used for the subsequent comparison.

A block diagram of a typical SAR ADC is shown in Fig. 4.36. The 8-bit device contains 256 series resistors and analog switches, control logic, and output latches. Conversion is performed by comparing the unknown analog voltage with the voltages at the resistor junction points by means of the analog switches. When the appropriate junction-point voltage matches the unknown voltage, conversion is complete and the digital number corresponding to the analog voltage is presented at the output.

The number of bits of resolution provided by the converter is equivalent to the number of comparisons made. The primary advantages of this technique are that (1) only one comparator is needed for the conversion and (2) higher resolution does not greatly increase the conversion time.

For example, a 10-bit ADC will only be ten-eighths slower than an 8-bit device of the same basic type because only two additional comparisons are needed to obtain 4 times the resolution. The binary nature of the SAR search also makes the converter ideal for interfacing to computers and microprocessors.

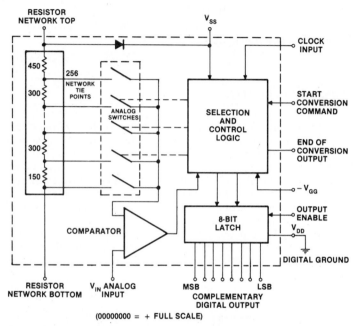

FIG. 4.36 Successive-approximation-register (SAR) analog-to-digital converter (ADC). In actual practice, the resistor network and analog switches are replaced by an 8-bit digital-to-analog converter (DAC).

Unfortunately, the SAR converter requires a large number of steps to complete an approximation routine and therefore is susceptible to error if the analog input changes in the middle of the SAR search. For this reason, the noise rejection performance usually is not high. For certain inputs, a sample-and-hold stage or filter may be needed to stabilize the input signal while AD conversion is under way.

Integrating Conversion. Integrating ADCs, including single, dual, and multi-slope designs, are most commonly found in digital meters and instrumentation systems. They are relatively slow, but this is usually not a problem because the results are used primarily for visual readout. The strong point of an integrating ADC is high resolution, offering as many as 20 bits of digital data (6 decimal digits). Even low-cost monolithic converters of this type commonly handle ±2000 counts, which is equivalent to 12 bits.

The most popular type of integrating converter is the *dual-slope design,* in which the unknown signal is used to ramp the input of an integrator up from 0 V for a time set by a fixed number of clock cycles. A reference voltage of opposite polarity is then used to discharge the integrator and return it to zero. The discharge time, which is proportional to the input voltage, is measured by counting the number of clock pulses (Fig. 4.37).

The dual-slope integrating ADC, by nature, has high noise rejection because the output represents the average value of the input signal over the integration time. This circuit is able to ignore changes in its integrator and clock because both are used to measure the reference, as well as the input, during each conversion cycle. This causes some of the drift and error terms to cancel.

A major disadvantage of the integrating ADC is the difficulty often experienced in interfacing the device with a microprocessor because of the converter's slow speed and sometimes unusual output format. Obtaining higher resolution also requires longer integration times and therefore significantly longer conversion periods. Each additional bit of resolution will typically double the AD conversion time.

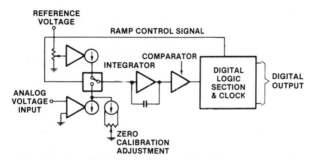

FIG. 4.37 Simplified block diagram of a dual-ramp integrating analog-to-digital converter.

Flash Conversion. Flash ADCs are the fastest devices presently available in either a discrete or a monolithic form. The operating principle of the flash converter is in some ways opposite that of the SAR. Rather than using one comparator repeatedly to make a number of comparisons, a flash converter uses a large number of comparators to make all the checks at once.

A consequence of this technique (besides high speed) is a relatively high cost per bit. The number of required comparators increases geometrically with greater resolution. For example, a 10-bit flash converter would require 1023 comparators. For this reason, flash converters are not commonly employed for applications that demand more than 8-bit resolution. They are, however, widely used in high-speed 6- and 8-bit applications such as video signal processing.

Some new ADC devices combine flash and SAR techniques to provide high speeds without using huge numbers of comparators. One example of this approach is the half-flash ADC, which performs an 8-bit conversion by combining the results of two 4-bit flashes. Figure 4.38 shows the basic concept of the half-flash converter.

Resolution and Accuracy. *Resolution* is the number of discrete segments into which a data converter divides an analog signal. It is quite different from *accuracy,* which is a converter's estimated error in deciding the absolute magnitude of an input voltage. By common definitions, data-converter accuracy and resolution have no relationship to each other, although the magnitudes of the specifications may be comparable on a given device.

Assuming that a converter's accuracy will match its resolution can be a mistake. This is especially true for higher-resolution (10- and 12-bit) devices where 0.1 percent or greater accuracies are difficult to achieve.

For example, a typical 10-bit ADC will be able to resolve a 10-V input range to within 10 mV. The output, however, will generally not be accurate to that specification without trimming the device's external circuitry.

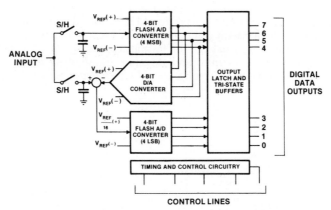

FIG. 4.38 Half-flash ADC circuit. This 8-bit converter uses 32 comparators, a most significant 4-bit flash AD and a least significant 4-bit flash AD. The input signal is sampled and then held by a pair of sample-and-hold buffer stages. This converter circuit can be cascaded for greater resolution.

4.8.2 Digital-to-Analog Converter

From an applications standpoint, discussions of process differences between semiconductor components are often academic. In the case of CMOS and bipolar DACs, however, there are significant operational differences related to fabrication which warrant attention.

Bipolar DACs are fabricated with the same process used to produce standard linear devices such as operational amplifiers and voltage regulators. The key to their performance is the ability of integrated-circuit (IC) manufacturers to build precision matched-current sources that can be switched at high speeds (Fig. 4.39).

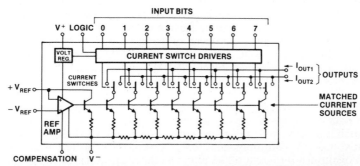

FIG. 4.39 Functional block diagram of a basic 8-bit bipolar DAC. Two outputs (I_{out} and I_{out2}) are provided to handle various external circuit requirements.

The magnitudes of these current sources are binarily weighted, and each is controlled by a digital input bit. The output current of the DAC is the sum of the current sources that have been switched on. The full-scale output of the device is set by an internal or external reference voltage.

CMOS DACs are also essentially current-output devices but differ from bipolar converters in that they are passive in the analog signal path (Fig. 4.40). The current output is controlled by using matched resistors and analog switches rather than active current sources.

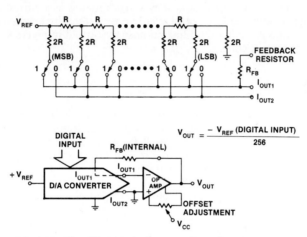

FIG. 4.40 Simplified block diagram of a typical CMOS DAC, showing the internal resistor-switching configuration (*a*) and the connection of the device to an external operational amplifier (*b*).

CMOS converter technology (basically the same process used for low-power CMOS logic devices) permits the fabrication of resistors and switches with high precision. Because a wide variety of signals can be applied to the DAC reference input and therefore be controlled by the digital input code, these devices are often called *multiplying digital-to-analog converters.*

The advantages of a CMOS DAC over a bipolar converter are lower power consumption, single-supply operation, and ability to handle a wide range of analog signals (at the reference input). CMOS devices also have excellent gain stability, which depends mainly on the tracking of the chip's monolithic resistors. On the negative side, because CMOS converters are passive, they have no output compliance as current sources. This means they cannot drive their output current linearly into any load but 0 V.

Although somewhat less versatile than CMOS, bipolar devices in general are faster and have improved settling characteristics. They can sometimes be used in multiplying applications, but only in a relatively limited fashion.

Digital-to-Analog Output Amplifier. Output amplifiers are nearly always used with CMOS DACs and are often used with bipolar devices as well. The performance limits of the output operational amplifier will have a significant impact on the output signal of the converter. The operational-amplifier output must be able to change and settle accurately to a new value within a specified time. Amplifiers with a high slew rate may respond rapidly to a change but often are of little value if they are not well behaved while settling to their new level.

The dc specifications of an output operational amplifier are important but not for the reasons usually applied in analog circuitry. Most DAC amplifiers are operated with a closed-loop gain of 1 or lower, so that device offsets appear at the circuit output unamplified. Therefore, the output shift due to operational-amplifier input offset is usually not a great concern. However, with a CMOS DAC this offset has a major effect in a completely different way by causing the converter's current output to be terminated at a nonzero level.

Because the passive CMOS output has no compliance as a current source, the interaction between this voltage and the converter's linearity becomes a complex issue. The situation is further muddied because the output impedance of the DAC changes with the input code.

4.8.3 Sample-and-Hold Circuits

The conversion of an analog audio or video signal to digital information often requires the use of a sample-and-hold (S/H) circuit to freeze the analog information so that it can be accurately measured. Trying to measure a signal while it is changing is not unlike trying to photograph an object while it is in motion. A typical S/H circuit is illustrated in Fig. 4.41.

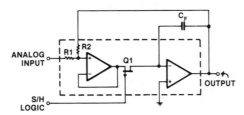

FIG. 4.41 Sample-and-hold (S/H) buffer amplifier. When the S/H logic line is low, $Q1$ conducts and the output of the device follows the analog input. When the S/H line is taken high, $Q1$ switches off and the output is held constant at the last input value by C_f.

The amount of accuracy lost during the AD conversion process when a varying signal is present depends upon the type of converter (and conversion speed) used in the application. Systems employing an SAR converter typically use an S/H circuit at the input. Flash converters, on the other hand, rarely need input-holding circuitry to maintain accuracy.

In an SAR device, the basic operating principle assumes that the input will not change by more than one-half of the magnitude of the least significant bit (LSB) during an entire conversion cycle. Because each approximation in the SAR search tells the converter what its next step will be, any change in input level during the comparison sequence can play havoc with the conversion process.

Input isolation of an analog source can be accomplished in a number of ways. The most direct is an *isolation amplifier,* usually a module or a hybrid circuit (they do not as yet exist in monolithic form) incorporating a transformer or other technique to provide an electrical barrier to interfering signals.

4.8.4 Delta Modulation

The AD conversion techniques discussed previously (SAR, integrating, and flash) make up a family of converters using the PCM method of digital encoding. There are, however, other methods of AD conversion including various types of delta modulation (DM).

The basic form of DM has been known for years to be a simple low-cost means of AD conversion. In this process, the data produced by the converter represent differences between successive sampled voltages rather than the instantaneous voltage of the input signal at each point in time (the conversion method of a conventional PCM AD system).

Delta modulation in its basic form, however, generally produces less than acceptable performance for professional applications, with a dynamic range of about 55 dB. While certain versions of DM can offer a 90-dB dynamic range, they may suffer from noise modulation problems and noise floors that exhibit a distinct tonal character.

Companded Predictive Delta Modulation. To overcome the limitations of conventional DM conversion for professional audio applications, variations on the basic concept have been developed. One is the companded-predictive-delta-modulation (CPDM) method of digital encoding. The CPDM conversion process differs from basic DM in two main respects. First, the CPDM converter uses a compander circuit in which the signal itself is varied with a voltage-controlled amplifier to avoid overloading the fixed delta modulator. Second, the DM stage uses a linear prediction filter, which relies on the history of the audio signal to predict its future. Figure 4.42 shows a block diagram of a CPDM system.

Linear Prediction. One of the problems affecting DM, adaptive DM (an improved version of delta modulation), and companded DM systems is that the noise floor can change with signal level. This occurs because the step size changes to follow the input, and it is the step size that determines the level of quantization noise.

By way of illustration, let us assume a situation where the delta modulator has a fixed step size of 10 mV. If the system's last approximation of the input signal was too high, the next will be 10 mV lower. Now, let us assume that, of the last 10 approximations to the input-signal voltages, 7 were too low and 3 were too high. We might reasonably infer that the signal level was increasing. We could then shift the step sizes from ±10 mV to +15 mV−−5 mV.

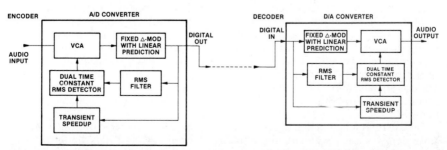

FIG. 4.42 Companded-predictive-delta-modulation AD converter (*a*) and companion DAC (*b*). (*Courtesy of dbx, Inc.*)

This is in line with our expectation (based on the recent history of the signal's behavior) that the signal is more likely to change in a positive direction than in a negative direction. Note that this process does not change or lower quantization noise: the difference is still 20 mV between $+10$ mV and -10 mV or between $+15$ mV and -5 mV. But it does increase the maximum slope (steepness, or slew rate) that the modulator can follow without slew-rate limiting. Hence, dynamic range is increased as well.

In practice, this alteration in the balance of plus and minus step sizes is achieved by a linear-prediction filter. This filter is substituted for the simpler filter (integrator) normally found in a delta modulator and is designed for maximum dynamic range.

4.8.5 Creating Special Effects

Advances in digital technology have made possible the creation of a number of new and unique special audio effects ranging from complex reverberation to comb filters.

After an audio signal has been digitized, special effects can be generated through the application of numerical calculations to the data. For example, gain control of an input signal is accomplished by multiplication of the digital word by a control constant. Audio mixing is achieved by adding together numerical samples from two or more digital signals. Limiting is performed by multiplication of the signal by a control number derived from the signal itself. Filtering and equalization are implemented in arithmetic sequences involving time-delay multiplication and addition of the resulting signals to previous samples. This arithmetic processing provides the digital equivalent of reactive circuits commonly used in analog filters.

High-speed digital filters, constructed of bit-slice processors and multipliers, can be used to create replicas of familiar audio processing circuits, such as shelving equalizers and second-order peaking filters. Because signal processing is under software control, the digital effects generator is not limited to specific characteristics. Instead, entirely new effects can be created by the user. Digital technology also allows specific effects to be stored in memory for later recall, further increasing equipment versatility.

4.8.6 Reverberation

Natural reverberation results from the combination of a source signal with a large number of time-delayed versions of the original sound. The characteristic sound produced by the original audio signal and its reflections is determined by the intensity of each reflection, its time delay, and frequency-response characteristic.

Digital reverberation is typically generated by feeding a digitized audio signal into a number of delay lines and then feeding back a controlled amount of the various signals to the different lines. This practice gives the user a wide variety of reverberation options, all under software control, at reasonable circuit complexity.

The primary factors that are used to create specific reverberation effects are the time delay of each segment, the amount of feedback used, the digital filtering applied to the feedback loops, and the mixing levels of the delay channels. The creation of reverberation special effects therefore incorporates the techniques of

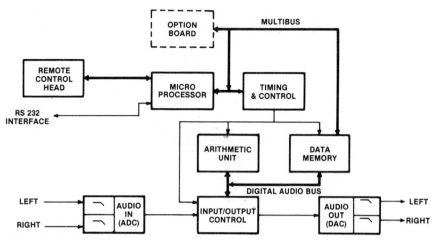

FIG. 4.43 Simplified block diagram of a programmable digital reverberation system. *(Courtesy of Lexicon, Inc.)*

gain control, mixing, limiting, and filtering previously discussed. The software program for these parameters makes up the mathematical algorithm which simulates the characteristic sounds of the desired reverberation.

Figure 4.43 shows a block diagram of a digital reverberation system. Right- and left-channel input audio is passed through a low-pass filter and digitized in an ADC. A microprocessor and an arithmetic unit processor operate on the digital data to produce the desired result. The system can store data in memory, withdraw it at specific times, perform mathematical calculations on the digitally coded audio, and then mix the various signals (at various delay points) together. The resulting sum can either be presented to the output through a DAC and low-pass filter or be placed in memory for further processing.

The complex reverberation programs required for such a system are written in advance and stored in nonvolatile memory. Users have the ability to recall a number of preset reverberation situations (such as a particular concert hall or acoustic chamber) or create their own reverberation effects. An operator can, in essence, electronically design the size and character of a room by adjusting the amplitude of each reflection, its time delay, and its frequency response.

4.9   CONCLUSION

In this chapter an attempt has been made to cover a wide range of topics in sufficient depth to indicate that considerable and rapid progress has been made in the field of digital audio since its start in the late 1960s. Furthermore, there is now sufficient momentum in the changeover from analog to digital technology, mainly because of gains in maintaining media-independent high quality, to ensure that this trend will not be reversed.

Much of the progress in digital audio has been achieved by combining the best features of the present analog practices with modern computer hardware and signal-processing techniques. In some areas, notably high-density recording and signal-processing hardware, some of the most exciting advances have been made within the digital audio community. At this stage, however, we are still connecting digital audio equipment in an ad hoc way, and it is hoped that by attempting to cover a large part of the range of activity in digital audio the reader will see more clearly how a true all-digital audio industry might mature.

REFERENCES

1. D. E. L. Shorter, J. R. Chew, D. Howorth, and J. R. Sanders, *Pulse-Code Modulation for High-Quality Sound-Signal Distribution,* BBC Engineering Division Monograph 75, December 1968.

2. M. R. Schroeder, "Improved Quasi-Stereophony and 'Colorless' Artificial Reverberation," *J. Acoust. Soc. Am.,* **33,** 1061 (1961).

3. B. A. Blesser and F. Lee, "An Audio Delay System Using Digital Technology," *J. Audio Eng. Soc.,* **19**(5), 393–397 (1971).

4. D. Stripp, "BBC Digital Audio—A Decade of On-Air Operation," in B. A. Blesser, B. Locanthi, and T. G. Stockham, Jr. (eds.), *Digital Audio,* Audio Engineering Society, New York, 1983, pp. 216–220.

5. B. A. Blesser, K. Baeder, and R. Zaorski, "A Real-Time Digital Computer for Simulating Audio Systems," *J. Audio Eng. Soc.,* **23**(9), 698–707 (November 1975).

6. T. G. Stockham, Jr., T. M. Cannon, and R. B. Ingebretsen, "Blind Deconvolution through Digital Signal Processing," *Proc. IEEE,* **63**(4), 678–692 (April 1975).

7. P. J. Bloom, "Into the Digital Studio Domain," parts I and II, *Studio Sound,* **21**(4), 56–60, and (5), 58–68 (April and May 1979).

8. G. W. McNally, *COPAS—A High Speed Real-Time Digital Audio Processor,* BBC Research Department Report 1979/26, 1979.

9. M. H. Jones, "Processing Systems for the Digital Audio Studio," in B. A. Blesser, B. Locanthi, and T. G. Stockham, Jr. (eds.), *Digital Audio,* Audio Engineering Society, New York, 1983, pp. 221–225.

10. L. D. Fielder, "Pre- and Postemphasis Techniques as Applied to Audio Recording Systems," *J. Audio Eng. Soc.,* **33**(9), 649–658 (September 1985).

11. B. A. Blesser, "Perceptual Issues in Digital Processing of Music," *IEEE Conf. Proc.,* 1981 ICASSP, Atlanta, 583–586 (March–April 1981).

12. D. M. Green, *An Introduction to Hearing,* Lawrence Erlbaum Associates, Inc., Hillsdale, N.J., 1976.

13. T. Muraoka, M. Iwahara, and Y. Yamada, "Examination of Audio-Bandwidth Requirements for Optimum Sound Signal Transmission," *J. Audio Eng. Soc.,* **29**(1/2), 2–9 (January–February 1981).

14. B. Locanthi, "Minutes of the Meeting of the Digital Audio Technical Committee," *J. Audio Eng. Soc.,* **29**(1/2), 56–78 (January–February 1981).

15. T. Muraoka, Y. Yamada, and M. Yamazaki, "Sampling-Frequency Considerations in Digital Audio," *J. Audio Eng. Soc.,* **26**(4), 252–256 (April 1978).

16. L. R. Fincham, "The Subjective Importance of Uniform Group Delay at Low Frequencies," presented at the 74th Convention of the Audio Engineering Society, New York (October 1983), preprint 2056 (H-1).

17. L. D. Fielder, "Dynamic-Range Requirement for Subjectively Noise-Free Reproduction of Music," *J. Audio Eng. Soc.,* **30**(7/8), 504–511 (July–August 1982).

18. J. J. Zwislocki, "Masking: Experimental and Theoretical Aspects of Simultaneous, Forward, Backward, and Central Masking," in *The Handbook of Perception,* vol. IV, Academic, New York, 1978.

19. L. D. Fielder, "The Audibility of Modulation Noise in Floating-Point Conversion Systems," *J. Audio Eng. Soc.,* **33**(10), 770–781 (October 1985).

20. R. Lagadec and T. G. Stockham, Jr., "Dispersive Models for A-to-D and D-to-A Conversion Systems," presented at the 75th Convention of the Audio Engineering Society, Paris (March 1984), preprint 2097 (H-8).

21. D. Preis, "Linear Distortion," *J. Audio Eng. Soc.,* **24**(5), 346–367 (June 1976).

22. P. J. Bloom and D. Preis, "Perceptual Identification and Discrimination of Phase Distortion," *IEEE Conf. Proc.,* ICASSP-83, Boston, 1396–1399 (April 1983).

23. P. S. Lidbetter, "A Technical View of a Totally Digital Audio Mixing Console," presented at the 79th Convention of the Audio Engineering Society, New York (October 1985), preprint 2277.

24. D. Preis, "Audio Spectrum and Signal Characteristics," in *Audio Engineering Handbook,* McGraw-Hill, New York, 1988, chap. 2.

25. R. Lagadec, D. Weiss, and R. Greutmann, "High Quality Analog Filters for Digital Audio," presented at the 67th Convention of the Audio Engineering Society, New York (October 1980), preprint 1707 (B-4).

26. B. A. Blesser, "Advanced Analog-to-Digital Conversion and Filtering: Data Conversion," in B. A. Blesser, B. Locanthi, and T. G. Stockham, Jr. (eds.), *Digital Audio,* Audio Engineering Society, New York, 1983.

27. B. A. Blesser, "Digitization of Audio: A Comprehensive Examination of Theory, Implementation, and Current Practice," *J. Audio Eng. Soc.,* **26**(10), 739–771 (October 1978).

28. "AES Recommended Practice for Professional Digital Audio Applications Employing Pulse-Code Modulation—Preferred Sampling Frequencies," AES5-1984 (ANSI S4.28-1984), *J. Audio Eng. Soc.,* **32**(10), 781–785 (October 1984).

29. J. Vanderkooy and P. Lipshitz, "Resolution below the Least Significant Bit in Digital Systems with Dither," *J. Audio Eng. Soc.,* **32**(3), 106–113 (March 1984).

30. R. W. Adams. "Design and Implementation of an Audio 18-Bit Analog-to-Digital Converter Using Oversampling Techniques," *J. Audio Eng. Soc.,* **34**(3), 153–166 (March 1985).

31. N. H. C. Gilchrist, "Digital Audio Impairments and Measurements," in B. A. Blesser, B. Locanthi, and T. G. Stockham, Jr. (eds.), *Digital Audio,* Audio Engineering Society, New York, 1983, pp. 67–75.

32. B. Locanthi, "Minutes of the Meeting of the Digital Audio Technical Committee, 4 March 1985," *J. Audio Eng. Soc.,* **33**(7/8), 562–565 (July–August 1985).

33. A Belcher, private communication, May 22, 1986.

34. N. H. C. Gilchrist, "Analogue-to-Digital and Digital-to-Analogue Converters for High Quality Sound," presented at the 65th Convention of the Audio Engineering Society (February 1980), preprint 1583 (C-4).

35. L. R. Rabiner and R. W. Shafer, *Digital Processing of Speech Signals,* Prentice-Hall, Englewood Cliffs, N.J., 1978.

36. N. S. Jayant and P. Noll, *Digital Coding of Waveforms,* Prentice-Hall, Englewood Cliffs, N.J., 1984.

37. J. A. Moorer, "The Digital Coding of High-Quality Musical Sound," *J. Audio Eng. Soc.,* **27**(9), 657–666 (September 1979).

38. N. S. Jayant (ed.), *Waveform Quantization and Coding,* IEEE Press, Piscataway, N.J., 1976.

39. D. Osborne, "Digital Sound Signals: Further Investigation of Instantaneous and Other Rapid Companding Systems, *BBC Eng.,* no. 96, 18–26 (November 1973).

40. R. W. Adams, "Companded Predictive Delta Modulation: A Low-Cost Conversion

Technique for Digital Recording," *J. Audio Eng. Soc.,* **32**(9), 659–672 (September 1984).

41. B. C. J. Moore, *An Introduction to the Psychology of Hearing,* 2d ed., Academic, London, 1982.

42. R. J. van de Plassche and E. C. Dijkmans, "A Monolithic 16-Bit D/A Conversion System for Digital Audio," in B. A. Blesser, B. Locanthi, and T. G. Stockham, Jr. (eds.), *Digital Audio,* Audio Engineering Society, New York, 1983, pp. 54–60.

43. R. A. Belcher, "Synthesized Test Signals for Digital Audio," presented at the 78th Convention of the Audio Engineering Society, Anaheim, Calif. (May 1985), preprint 2249.

44. B. Locanthi, "Minutes of the Meeting of the Digital Audio Technical Committee," *J. Audio Eng. Soc.,* **31**(7), 538–542 (July–August 1983).

45. G. Mitchell and M. E. B. Moffat, "Pulse Code Modulation for High-Quality Sound-Signal Distribution; Subjective Effect of Digital Error," *BBC Eng.,* no. 96, 27–33 (November 1973).

46. W. R. Woszczyk and F. E. Toole, "A Subjective Comparison of Five Analog and Digital Tape Recorders," presented at the 74th Convention of the Audio Engineering Society, New York (October 1983), preprint 2033 (H-8).

47. M. R. Schroeder, B. S. Atal, and J. L. Hall, "Optimizing Digital Speech Coders by Exploiting Masking Properties of the Human Ear," *J. Acoust. Soc. Am.,* **66**(6), 1647–1652 (June 1979).

48. J. Blauert, *Spatial Hearing: The Psychophysics of Human Sound Localization,* M.I.T., Cambridge, Mass., 1984.

49. G. W. McNally, "Dynamic Range Control of Digital Audio Signals," *J. Audio Eng. Soc.,* **32**(5), 316–327 (May 1984).

50. B. Locanthi, "Minutes of the AES Digital Audio Technical Committee Meeting, October 22, 1982," partially published in *J. Audio Eng. Soc.,* **31**(1/2), 37–40 (January–February 1983).

51. M. Kosaka, "Report of the DAT Conference," Mar. 3, 1986.

52. B. Fox, "The Little Red Book," *Which Compact Disc? + HiFi for Pleasure,* **2**(4), 67 (June 1986).

53. "Product Reference: Digital Recording Equipment," *Studio Sound,* **25**(10), 60–61 (October 1983).

54. T. Griffiths, personal communication, December 1984.

55. "Technical Information for the Denon PCM/Digital Recorder DN-035R MKII," Denon, Nippon Columbia Co., Ltd., March 1983.

56. G. Fukuda et al., "On Dropout Compensation of PCM Systems—Computer Simulation Method and a New Error Correcting Code (Crossword Code)," presented at the 60th Convention of the Audio Engineering Society (May 1978), preprint 1354 (E-7).

57. N. Sakamoto, T. Kogure, H. Kitagawa, and T. Shimada, "On the High Density Recording of the Compact Cassette Digital Recorder," *J. Audio Eng. Soc.,* **32**(9), 640–646 (September 1984).

58. H. Nakajima and K. Odaka, "A Rotary Head High Density Digital Audio Tape Recorder," *IEEE Trans. Consum. Electron.,* **CE-29**(3), 430–436 (August 1983).

59. B. Locanthi, "Minutes of the Meeting of the AES Digital Audio Technical Committee," Montreux, Switzerland (March 1986).

60. N. Wakabayashi, I. Abe, and H. Miyairi, "A Thin Film Multi-Track Recording Head," *IEEE Trans. Magn.,* **MAG-18**(6), 1140–1142 (November 1982).

61. T. Kogure, T. Doi, and R. Lagadec, "The DASH Format: An Overview," presented at the 74th Convention of the Audio Engineering Society, New York (October 1983), preprint 2038 (A-9).

62. L. Martin, K. Tanaka, and T. Yamaguchi, "Overview of RSC Tape Format for Stationary Head Type Digital Audio Recorder and Its Performance," presented at the 75th Convention of the Audio Engineering Society, Paris (March 1984), preprint 2093 (H-5).

63. F. A. Bellis and M. R. Brookhart, "An Error Correcting System for a Multichannel Digital Audio Recorder," presented at the 58th Convention of the Audio Engineering Society, New York (November 1977), preprint 1298 (M-2).

64. M. H. Jones, D. G. Longford, and D. A. Tilsley, "Digital Sound Mixing in the Analogue Studio," *Proc. Int. Broadcast. Conv.,* 371–374 (September 1984).

65. J. Richards and I. Craven, "An Experimental All-Digital Studio Mixing Desk," *J. Audio Eng. Soc.,* **30**(3), 117–126 (March 1982).

66. N. Sakamoto et al., "A Professional Digital Audio Mixer," *J. Audio Eng. Soc.,* **30**(1/2), 28–33 (January–February 1982).

67. G. W. McNally and T. A. Moore, "A Modular Signal Processor for Digital Filtering and Dynamic Range Control of High Quality Audio Signals," *IEEE Conf. Proc.,* 1981 ICASSP, Atlanta, 590–594 (March–April 1981).

68. J. A. Moorer, "The Lucasfilm Audio Signal Processor," *IEEE Conf. Proc.,* 1982 ICASSP, 85–88 (March 1982).

69. G. W. McNally, *Digital Audio: Recursive Digital Filtering for High Quality Audio Signals,* BBC Research Department Report 1981/10, 1981.

70. N. Sakamoto, S. Yamaguchi, A. Kurahashi, and T. Kogure, "Digital Equalisation and Mixing Circuit Design," presented at the 70th Convention of the Audio Engineering Society, New York (October 1981), preprint 1809 (I-6).

71. J. A. Moorer, "The Manifold Joys of Conformal Mapping: Applications to Digital Filtering in the Studio," *J. Audio Eng. Soc.,* **31**(11), 826–841 (November 1983).

72. L. D. J. Eggermont and P. J. Berkhout, "Digital Audio Circuits: Computer Simulations and Listening Tests," *Philips Tech. Rev.,* **41**(3), 99–103 (1983–1984).

73. G. W. McNally, "Dynamic Range Control of Digital Audio Signals," *J. Audio Eng. Soc.,* **32**(5), 316–327 (May 1984).

74. J. A. Moorer, "About This Reverberation Business," *Rapp. IRCAM,* Paris.

75. H. Nakagima, T. Doi, J. Fukada, and A. Ige, *Digital Audio Technology,* TAB Books, Blue Ridge Summit, Pa.

76. G. W. McNally, "Audio Processing for the BBC Digital Control Vehicle," *Int. Broadcast Eng.,* 67–76 (May 1984).

77. *Model DN-0363D PCM Editing System,* Nippon Columbia Co., Ltd., International Trade Department III, Tokyo.

78. C. Abbott, *System Level Software for the Lucasfilm ASP System,* Technical Memorandum 58, Lucasfilm Ltd., August 1982.

79. J. A. Moorer, "A Gate-Array ASP Implementation," *Proc. Int. Comput. Music Conf.,* Paris, 247–248 (October 1984).

80. C. Abbott and B. Mont-Reynaud, "Scheduling Real-Time Sound I/O on Ordinary Disks," *Proc. Int. Comput. Music Conf.,* Paris, 161–162 (October 1984).

81. J. A. Moorer, "The Audio Signal Processor: The Next Step in Digital Audio," in B. A. Blesser, B. Locanthi, and T. G. Stockham, Jr. (eds.), *Digital Audio,* Audio Engineering Society, New York, 1983, pp. 205–215.

82. P. S. Lidbetter, "Signal Processing for the Digital Audio Console," *Proc. ECCTD-83,* Stuttgart, 536–539 (September 1983).

83. G. W. McNally, *COPAS-2: A Modular Digital Audio Signal Processor for Use in a Mixing Desk,* BBC Research Department Report 1982/13, 1982.

84. T. Ohtsuki, S. Kazami, M. Watari, M. Tanaka, and T. T. Doi, "Digital Audio Editor,"

presented at the 68th Convention of the Audio Engineering Society, Hamburg (March 1981), preprint 1743 (B-5).

85. D. E. Davis and R. Youngquist, 'Electronic Editing of Digital Audio Programmes," *Proc. Int. Conf. Video Data Recording,* Southampton, England, pp. 385–393 (1979).

86. K, Tanaka, K. Onishi, and M. Kawabata, "On Tape-Cut Editing with a Fixed Head Tape PCM Tape Recorder," *IEEE Trans. ASSP,* **ASSP-27**(6), 739–745 (December 1979).

87. M. Griffiths and P. J. Bloom, "A Flexible Digital Sound Editing Program for Minicomputer Systems," *J. Audio Eng. Soc.,* **30**(3), 127–134 (March 1982).

88. R. B. Ingebretsen and T. G. Stockham, Jr., "Random Access Editing of Digital Audio," *J. Audio Eng. Soc.,* **32**(3), 114–122 (March 1984).

89. M. J. Kowalski and A. Glassner, "The N.Y.I.T. Digital Sound Editor," *Comput. Music J.,* **6**(1), 66–72 (spring 1982).

90. G. W. McNally and P. S. Gaskell, "Editing Digital Audio," *IEEE Conf. Proc.,* 1984 ICASSP, San Diego, 12B.4.1–4.4 (March 1984).

91. R. Lagadec and G. W. McNally, "Labels and Their Formatting for Digital Transmission and Recording," presented at the 74th Convention of the Audio Engineering Society, New York (October 1983), preprint 2003 (A-5).

92. C. Abbott, "Efficient Editing of Sound on Disk," *J. Audio Eng. Soc.,* **32**(6), 394–402 (June 1984).

93. D. M. Schwartz, "Specifications and Implementation of a Computer Audio Console for Digital Mixing and Recording," presented at the 76th Convention of the Audio Engineering Society, New York (October 1984), preprint 2139 (A-3).

94. *Systex 300: Audio Information Retrieval System,* Gotham Audio Corp. Engineering Bulletin, October 1983.

95. G. W. McNally, "Variable Speed Replay of Digital Audio with Constant Output Sampling Rate," presented at the 76th Convention of the Audio Engineering Society, New York (October 1984), preprint 2137 (A-9).

96. J. A. Moorer, "The Lucasfilm Audio Signal Processor," *Comput. Music J.,* **6**(3), 22–32 (Fall 1982).

97. F. Rumsey, "Sound Dubbing Techniques for Film and Video: A Comparison," *BKSTS J.,* **66**(6), 272–277 (June 1984).

98. L. Blake, "Re-recording and Post-production for Disney's Fantasia," *Recording Engineer/Producer,* **13**(5), 116–126 (1982).

99. D. W. Spencer II, *Digital Audio for Motion Picture Film Production,* WED Enterprises Notes, Nov. 5, 1983.

100. J. Stautner, D. Schwartz, and G. Schwede, "Musical Recording, Editing, and Production Using the Compusonics DSP-2000," *Proc. Int. Comput. Music Conf.,* Paris, 245 (October 1984).

101. P. J. Bloom and G. D. Marshall, "A Digital Signal Processing System for Automatic Dialogue Post-synchronization," *J. Soc. Motion Pict. Telev. Eng.,* **93**(6), 566–569 (June 1984).

102. C. Abbott, A. Marr, and J. A. Moorer, "Lucasfilm Report," *Proc. Int. Comput. Music Conf.,* Paris, 207–209 (October 1984).

103. C. Abbott, "Software for Distributed Real-Time Applications," *Proc. Int. Comput. Music Conf.,* Paris, 209–211 (October 1984).

104. J. A. Moorer, private communication, July 2, 1984.

105. H. Bode, "History of Electronic Sound Modification," *J. Audio Eng. Soc.,* **32**(10), 730–739 (October 1984).

106. B. A. Blesser and J. M. Kates, "Digital Processing of Audio Signals," in A. V. Oppen-

heim (ed.), *Applications of Digital Signal Processing,* Prentice-Hall, Englewood Cliffs, N.J., 1978.

107. C. Moore, *Studio Applications of Time Delay,* Lexicon Applications Note AN-3, Lexicon Inc., July 1976.

108. J. O. Smith, "An Allpass Approach to Digital Phasing and Flanging," *Proc. Int. Comput. Music Conf.,* Paris, 236–237 (October 1984).

109. M. R. Schroeder and B. S. Atal, "Computer Simulation of Sound Transmissions in Rooms," *IEEE Int. Conv. Rec.,* part 7, 150–155 (1963).

110. J. A. Moorer, "About This Reverberation Business," *Comput. Music J.,* **3**(2), 13–28, (1978).

111. J. Stautner and M. Puckette, "Designing Multichannel Reverberators," *Comput. Music J.,* **6**(1), 52–65 (Spring 1982).

112. R. V. Cox, R. E. Crochiere, and J. D. Johnston, "Real-Time Implementation of Time Domain Harmonic Scaling of Speech for Rate Modification and Coding," *IEEE Trans. Acoust. Speech Signal Process.,* **31**(1), 258–271 (February 1983).

113. J. S. Lim (ed.), *Speech Enhancement,* Prentice-Hall, Englewood Cliffs, N.J., 1983.

114. M. Dolson, "Refinements in Phase-Vocoder-Based Modification of Musical Sounds," *Proc. Int. Comput. Music Conf.,* Paris, 215 (October 1984).

115. R. Lagadec and D. Pelloni, "Signal Enhancement via Digital Signal Processing," presented at the 74th Convention of the Audio Engineering Society, New York (October 1984), preprint 2037 (G-6).

116. J. A. Moorer and M. Berger, "Linear-Phase Bandsplitting: Theory and Applications," *J. Audio Eng. Soc.,* **34**(3), 143–152 (March 1986).

117. R. Lagadec and T. T. Doi, "A Digital Interface for the Interconnection of Professional Audio Equipment," presented at the 71st Convention of the Audio Engineering Society, Montreux, Switzerland (March 1982), preprint 1883 (G-6).

118. A. H. Jones, *A PCM Sound-in-Syncs Distribution System: General Description,* BBC Research Department Report 1969/35, 1969.

119. D. E. L. Shorter and J. R. Chew, "Application of PCM to Sound Signal Distribution in a Broadcasting Network," *Proc. Inst. Elec. Eng.,* **119**(10), 1442–1448 (1972).

120. C. R. Caine, A. R. English, and J. W. H. O'Clarey, "NICAM-3: Near Instantaneous Companded Digital Transmission for High Quality Sound Programmes," *J. Inst. Electron. Radio Eng.,* **50**(10), 519–530 (October 1980).

121. G. W. McNally and N. H. C. Gilchrist, "The Use of a Programmed Computer to Compare the Performance of Digital Companding Systems for High Quality Audio Signals," *EBU Tech. Rev.,* no. 178, 280–290 (December 1979).

122. D. J. King and R. B. Heaton, "A Twin Channel 1.5 GHz Bearer for Digital Signals," *IEEE Colloquium on Digital Transmission for Broadcasting,* London, Digest 1984/17 (February 1984).

123. D. Looser, "Stereo TV Sound," *Television,* **34**(10), 530–534 (August 1984).

124. S. R. Ely, "Experimental Digital Stereo Sound with Terrestrial Television," presented at the International Broadcasting Convention, Brighton, England, *IEE Conference Publication 240,* 312–316 (September 1984).

125. A. Zarin, "Digital Recording and Post-production Techniques for Concert Video and Film Shoots," *Recording Engineer/Producer,* 70–81 (October 1984).

126. N. Snow, "World Service by Satellite," *Cable and Satellite Europe,* 42–43 (November 1984).

127. H. Mertens and D. Wood, "The C-MAC/Packet System for Direct Satellite Television," *EBU Tech. Rev.,* no. 200 (August 1983).

128. G. J. Phillips and P. Shelswell, "Satellite Broadcasting—Systems Concepts and the

Television Transmission Standards for Europe," *Int. J. Sat. Commun.,* **2,** 3–8 (January–March 1984).

129. T. Yoshino, N. Kawai, and K. Ohmi, *PCM Sounds on Digital Subcarrier in Television for a Satellite Broadcasting System,* NHK Laboratory Note 282, November 1982.

130. W. Zschunke, "Comparison of Direct Broadcasting Satellite TV Sound Transmission Methods," MEXICON '83, Cuernavaca (November 1983).

131. R. H. McMann, A. A. Goldberg, and J. Rossi, *A Two Channel Compatible HDTV Broadcast System,* CBS Technical Center, Stamford, Conn.

132. K. J. Gundry, D. P. Robinson, and C. C. Todd, "Recent Developments in Digital Audio Techniques," presented at the 73d Convention of the Audio Engineering Society, Eindhoven, Netherlands (March 1983), preprint 1956 (B-5).

133. P. Tretyl (ed.), *Digital Sound Service for Direct Broadcasting Satellites,* Federal Minister of Research and Technology, Bonn, West Germany.

134. H. Nakajima et al., "Satellite Broadcasting System for Digital Audio," presented at the 70th Convention of the Audio Engineering Society, New York (October 1980), preprint 1855 (L-8).

135. "Technical and Operational Information Relating to the Objectives of Resolution 505 of the WARC-79. (Satellite Sound Broadcasting System for Individual Reception by Portable and Automobile Receivers.)," CCIR Document B/143 (Rev. 1)-E.

136. H. H. Sohn, "A High Speed Telecommunications Interface or Digital Audio Transmission and Reception," presented at the 76th Convention of the Audio Engineering Society, New York (October 1984), preprint 2143 (D-2).

137. W. T. Shelton, "Signal Synchronisation in Digital Audio," presented at the 76th Convention of the Audio Engineering Society, New York (October 1984), preprint 2165 (C-1).

138. W. A. Hickman, *Time Code Handbook: Future Film Developments,* Cipher Digital Inc., Boston.

139. N. H. C. Gilchrist, "Sampling Rate Synchronisation of Digital Sound Signals by Variable Delay," *EBU Tech. Rev.,* no. 183 (October 1983).

140. R. Lagadec, "A New Approach to Sampling Rate Synchronisation," presented at the 76th Convention of the Audio Engineering Society, New York (October 1984), preprint 2166 (F-8).

141. T. A. Ramstad, "Digital Methods for the Conversion between Arbitrary Sampling Frequencies," *IEEE Trans. ASSP,* **ASSP-32**(3), 577–591 (June 1984).

142. R. Lagadec, D. P. Pelloni, and D. Weiss, "A Two Channel, 16 Bit Digital Sample Frequency Convertor for Professional Digital Audio," *IEEE Conf. Proc.,* 1982 ICASSP, Paris, 93–96, (March 1982).

143. R. Lagadec, D. P. Pelloni, and A. Koch, "Single Stage Sampling Frequency Conversion," presented at the 74th Convention of the Audio Engineering Society, New York (October 1983), preprint 2039 (G-1).

144. "Specifications of the Radio Data System RDS for VHF/FM Sound Broadcasting," Document 3244-E, EBU Technical Center, March 1984.

145. S. M. Edwardson, B. E. Eyre, G. O. Hensman, and D. T. Wright, "A Radio Teleswitching System for Load Management in UK," presented at the 4th International Conference on Metering Apparatus and Tariffs for Electricity Supply, *IEE Conference Publication 217,* 40–46 (October 1982).

CHAPTER 5

BROADCAST TRANSMISSION TECHNOLOGY

Donald L. Markley, P.E.
D. L. Markley & Associates, Inc., Peoria, Illinois

James R. Carpenter
Manager, Audio Engineering, Broadcast Electronics Inc.

5.1 OVERVIEW OF BROADCASTING TECHNOLOGY

After the recordings have been made and the audio has been processed and prepared for the end user, it is necessary to complete the task of distributing that audio to the desired audience. In the case of entertainment programs, this is done in a number of ways; compact disks, prerecorded tapes, and phonographs are three popular methods of distribution. However, the overwhelming favorite, and the manner in which the vast majority of music is distributed to the bulk of the population in the United States and around the world, is radio broadcasting. This is so primarily because of the efficiency and the low cost of distribution of information to the public by the use of modern radio transmitters. More than 10,000 AM and FM stations exist in the United States alone. Many additional thousands exist around the world in both the AM and FM bands as well as in the short-wave broadcast bands.

The one big problem which has always existed in the distribution of aural and television programming to the public has been the most efficient use of the available spectrum space while minimizing degradation of the signal being distributed. The one common feature of all types of broadcast systems is the need to modulate a higher-frequency carrier with the low-frequency program material. That is, it is necessary to place the information being transmitted on a carrier of some type. This carrier is normally higher in frequency than the information being transmitted to make use of those parts of the spectrum where the signal can be transmitted efficiently over great distances. If left at baseband, the requirements for distribution of telephone signals alone would simply overload all available wiring in the United States. By modulating carriers and using modern digital techniques, thousands of telephone conversations can be carried simultaneously on one microwave channel. Tens of thousands of these telephone conversations can be carried on one fiber-optic channel. However, it was necessary to develop modulation techniques to a fine art to permit that type of operation to occur.

The initial radio broadcasters primarily made use of switched-CW or continuous-wave (CW) signals utilizing some type of code. While those codes permitted communications to take place between fixed stations, it was necessary to have a trained operator at each end. This did not permit any type of program material other than simple message communications to be transmitted.

The first modulation system which permitted voice communications to take place was amplitude modulation (AM). In this scheme, the magnitude of the carrier wave is varied in accordance with the amplitude and frequency of an audio signal. The magnitude of the incoming audio determines the magnitude of the carrier wave, while the frequency of the modulating signal determines the rate at which the carrier wave is varied. This is the simplest type of modulation and the system which was predominant through the 1920s and 1930s. In fact, it appears that no rigorous mathematical treatment of angle or phase modulation existed until the mid-1920s. Those methods of modulation were developed subsequent to that time and now are used heavily.

The following sections of this chapter will discuss the basic modulation schemes being used at the present time. In addition, some discussions will be included of the actual circuits and hardware being utilized in modern broadcast systems to perform these various types of modulation and to permit the broadcasting of stereo program material in AM, FM, and television systems.

5.2   AMPLITUDE-MODULATION (AM) THEORY AND SYSTEMS

5.2.1   Modulation of Carrier Signal

In the simplest form of amplitude modulation an analog carrier signal is controlled by an analog modulating signal. This would be the case where a 1.0-MHz radio-frequency (RF) signal was modulated by a 1.0-kHz audio signal. The desired characteristic is to have the amplitude of the RF signal varied by the magnitude of the audio signal and at a rate equal to the frequency of the audio signal. The basic equation for amplitude modulation is shown as Eq. (5.1):

$$e(t) = kE_c \cos(\omega_c t) \qquad (5.1)$$

where k = modulation constant
E_c = peak value of carrier signal
$\omega_c = 2\pi f_c$ = carrier frequency, rad/s
$e(t)$ = instantaneous carrier signal

Here the instantaneous value of the signal is a function of a constant multiplied by the peak value of the carrier signal, which is a sinusoid varying at a radian frequency of ω_c rad/s. To carry program materials such as tone, the modulation constant must also be a function of time as shown in Eq. (5.2):

$$k(t) = 1 + E_m \cos (\omega_m t) \tag{5.2}$$

where E_m = peak value of modulating signal
ω_m = frequency of modulating signal

The 1 in this particular signal simply represents the dc value of the modulating signal. When the time-varying modulating signal is incorporated into the basic equation for the amplitude-modulated wave (5.1), the result is the signal shown in Eq. (5.3):

$$e(t) = E_c \cos (\omega_c t) + \tfrac{1}{2} m \cos(\omega_c + \omega_m)t + \tfrac{1}{2} m \cos(\omega_c - \omega_m)t \tag{5.3}$$

where $m = E_m/E_c$
$\omega_c + \omega_m$ = upper-sideband frequency
$\omega_c - \omega_m$ = lower-sideband frequency

This represents a carrier wave plus two additional signals that result from the overall modulation process. These are normally identified as the upper-sideband and lower-sideband signals. This magnitude of the upper sideband and lower sideband will not normally exceed 50 percent of the carrier amplitude. This results in an upper-sideband power of one-fourth of the carrier power. The same power exists in the lower sideband. As a result, one-half of the actual carrier power appears additionally in the sum of the sidebands of the modulated signal. A representation of these sidebands is shown in Fig. 5.1.

In this particular representation, the actual occupied bandwidth, assuming pure sinusoidal modulation signals and no distortion during the modulation process, would be equal to 2 times the frequency of the modulating signal. Again, the maximum value of the modulation index m is considered to be 1. This represents 100 percent modulation wherein the peak value of the modulated signal envelope will be equal to 2 times the value of the carrier and the minimum value of the envelope will be 0. This is shown in a phasor representation in Fig. 5.2.

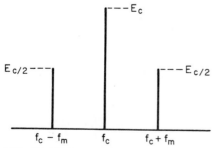

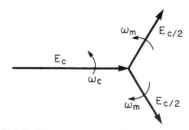

FIG. 5.1 Frequency-domain representation of an amplitude-modulated signal with $m = 1.0$ (100 percent modulation).

FIG. 5.2 Phasor representation of an amplitude-modulated signal with $m = 1.0$ (100 percent modulation).

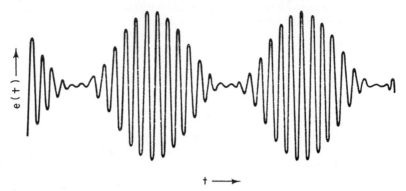

FIG. 5.3 Time-domain representation of an amplitude-modulation signal.

The overall envelope of the modulated signal in the time domain is shown in Fig. 5.3.

5.2.2 High-Level Modulation

The most widely used system of AM modulation in vacuum-tube transmitters has been what is identified as *high-level* anode modulation. In this system the modulating signal is amplified and combined with the dc supply source to the anode of the final RF amplifier stage. The RF amplifier was normally operated in Class C, and the final amplifier for the audio or modulating signal was usually a pair of tubes operating in Class B. A basic modulator of this type is shown in Fig. 5.4.

RF Signal Generation.   In a system of this type, the RF signal was normally generated in a low-level oscillator. It was then amplified by one or more stages to provide final RF drive on the appropriate frequency to the grid of the final Class C amplifier. The audio signal, upon arriving at the transmitter, was normally applied immediately to two Class A amplifier stages operating 180° out of phase with each other. These signals would then be used to drive the necessary number of intermediate power amplifiers which normally operated in Class B as push-pull amplifier stages. The final pair of amplifiers would also operate as Class B in push-pull and would provide the necessary modulating power. For 100 percent modulation, this modulating power could be 50 percent of the actual carrier power. The modulation transformer itself usually did not carry the dc supply current which was used for the final RF amplifier. The use of the capacitor and modulation reactor is shown to provide a path whereby the audio signal voltage was developed across the modulation reactor and combined with the dc supply to the final RF amplifier without the necessity of having the dc current flow through the secondary of the modulation transformer with the accompanying magnetic losses and saturation effects. In later years, the modulation reactor was sometimes eliminated from the overall scheme. This was made possible by developments in magnetic materials and transformer technology.

RF Amplifier Operation.   The RF amplifier itself normally operated as a Class C amplifier in a mode such that grid current would be drawn during the positive peaks of the cycle. By operating as a Class C amplifier, efficiencies in the upper

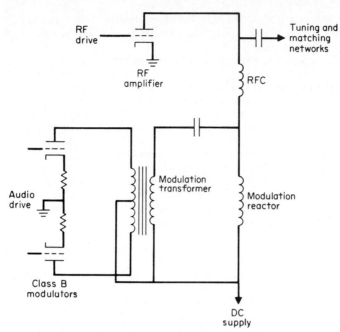

FIG. 5.4 Conventional high-level amplitude-modulated amplifier.

70 percent and lower 80 percent areas were readily achievable. This type of system was the most popular in standard broadcast use for many years, primarily because of simplicity of operation. Its primary negative aspect was the low overall system efficiency. The Class B amplifiers could not operate with greater than 50 percent efficiency for providing the audio power needed for the modulation process. Still, with inexpensive electricity this was not considered to be a significant problem.

As energy costs increased, it became more and more desirable to seek methods of modulation and signal generation that would provide the maximum amount of RF per dollar input. The increase in system efficiency normally came about only at the cost of added technical complexity. Numerous devices were developed which would provide greater system efficiency and maintain good-quality program transmission. Among these were the Doherty high-efficiency linear amplifier and various *out-phasing* modulation schemes. One of the most popular of the high-efficiency modulation systems was a screen-grid modulation technique which was first introduced by Terman and Woodward in a paper presented before the Institute of Radio Engineers (IRE)* in 1938. Systems of that type were used by various manufacturers over the years with varying degrees of success. The screen-grid modulation technique was perhaps the most successful of all these high-efficiency techniques prior to the development of pulse-modulation systems.

5.2.3 Pulse-Width Modulation

One of the most popular systems of modulation developed for modern transmitters has been the use of pulse-width modulation or pulse-duration modulation.

---

* Now the Institute of Electrical and Electronic Engineers (IEEE).

Figure 5.5 shows a scheme for pulse-width modulation identified as PDM as patented by the Harris Corporation. The PDM system works by utilizing the waveforms shown in Fig. 5.6.

Those waveforms are generated by the basic system shown in the block diagram form of Fig. 5.7. Initially, a 75-kHz waveform is generated as a simple sinusoid. The sinusoid is used to drive a square-wave generator, resulting in a simple 75-kHz square wave. That square wave is then integrated, which results in a triangular waveform as shown in Figs. 5.6 and 5.7. The triangular waveform is one input to a summing circuit where it is added to the incoming audio. For ease of demonstration, let the incoming audio be a simple sinusoid. The output of the summing circuit is now a triangular waveform which appears to be riding on the incoming audio sinusoid. These signals are then applied to a threshold amplifier. This actually is a switch which is turned on whenever the value of the input signal exceeds a certain limit or threshold value. The result is a string of pulses where the width of the pulses would be a function of the magnitude of the triangular waveform or where the width is proportional to the period of time when the triangular waveform exceeds the threshold value. This is simply applied to a pulse amplifier to obtain the necessary magnitude of pulses and to clean off whatever transients exist after this process is complete.

The output is a pulse-width-modulated signal. This is, in effect, a digital system with the audio information being sampled at a 75-kHz rate. The width of the pulses themselves contains all the audio information. The pulse-width-modulated signal is then amplified and applied to a switch or modulator tube. The tube is simply turned on, to a fully saturated state, or off in accordance with the instantaneous value of the pulse. When the pulse goes positive, the modulator tube is turned on and the voltage across the tube drops to a minimum. When the pulse returns to its minimum value, the modulator tube turns off. It effectively acts as a simple switch.

This overall signal becomes the supply to the final amplifier tube. When the modulator is switched on, the final amplifier will have current flow and RF will

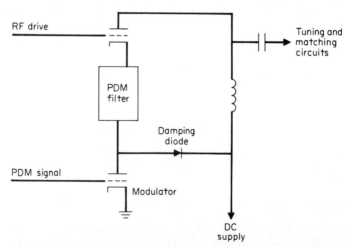

FIG. 5.5 Harris system of pulse-width modulation patented as PDM.

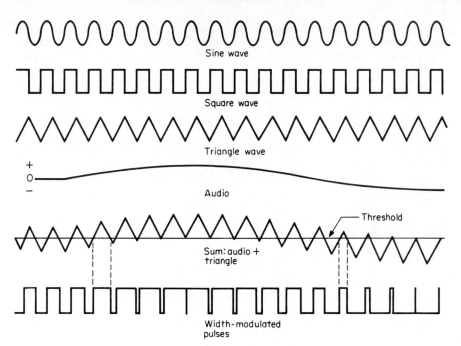

FIG. 5.6 PDM-system waveforms.

be generated. When the switch or modulator tube goes to the off mode, the final amplifier current will stop. This in effect causes the final amplifier to operate in a Class D switching mode which is an extremely high-efficiency amplifier configuration.

Low-Pass Filtering. The problem is that the 75-kHz information still exists in the sampling pulses themselves. This information is removed by use of a low-pass filter. The PDM filter removes all low-frequency components. A Fourier series of the resultant waveform would show the carrier frequency with sidebands as originally determined to be necessary for amplitude-modulated signals. A high degree of third-harmonic component will exist because of the switching-mode operation of the final amplifier. That is normally eliminated by a third-harmonic trap. The result is a very stable amplifier system normally operating in excess of 90 percent

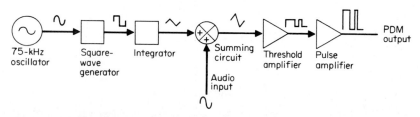

FIG. 5.7 PDM generator.

efficiency for the final amplifier itself. While some power is dissipated by the modulator or switching tube, the power consumed by the modulator and its driver stage is small in comparison with a full Class B amplifier stage.

Frequency Response.   As no tranformers are used in the modulator system, the frequency response of transmitters of this type is very good and the overall distortion is quite acceptable for standard broadcast stations. One additional component is necessary, and that is shown as the damping diode in Fig. 5.5. A problem occurs when the switching tube turns off the supply current during a period when the final amplifier is conducting. The high value of current through the large inductors contained in the PDM filters stage would cause a very large transient voltage to be created. The energy in the PDM filter at this time must be returned to the power supply by some method. If no alternative route is established, the energy will return by arcing through the modulator tube itself. Therefore, the damper diode is used to dissipate the energy stored in the PDM filter by returning it to the power supply and eliminate any problems with arcing in the switching tube.

It should be noted that variations of this amplifier and modulation scheme have been used by other manufacturers. This basic scheme has been utilized in transmitters in the standard broadcast band in the United States as well as in short-wave transmitters used in the international broadcast service.

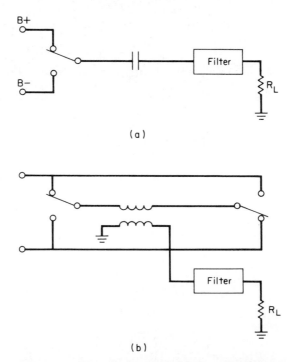

(a)

(b)

FIG. 5.8 Simple Class D radio-frequency amplifiers. (*a*) Single-ended. (*b*) Push-pull.

5.2.4 Solid-State-Transmitter Design

Solid-state transmitters make use of various schemes employing pulse-width-modulation systems and others. One solid-state system is shown in its simplest form in Fig. 5.8a. Basically, this method of generating a modulated RF signal simply uses a switch to transfer back and forth between two voltage levels at the carrier frequency. The result is a square-wave signal which is then filtered to eliminate all components except the fundamental frequency itself. A more complex version of this is shown in Fig. 5.8b.

Push-Pull Signal Generator. Figure 5.8b is a push-pull configuration which generates a larger square wave than that shown in Fig. 5.8a. This particular circuit would be suitable if all that is desired is to generate a simple sinusoid at the carrier frequency. However, this does not permit modulation. Figure 5.9 demonstrates a Class D switching system utilizing bipolar transistors. Modern solid-state transmitters use field-effect-transistor (FET) power devices as RF amplifiers. The basic operation, however, still utilizes the PDM approach as explained in the preceding section. Basically, the dc supply to the RF amplifier stages is switched on and off by an electronic switch in series with a filter. Operating in the Class D mode with the series switching of the supply function results in a composite set of signals similar to those generated by the vacuum-tube Class D amplifiers operating at much higher power. The solid-state transmitter, after the PDM filtering has been

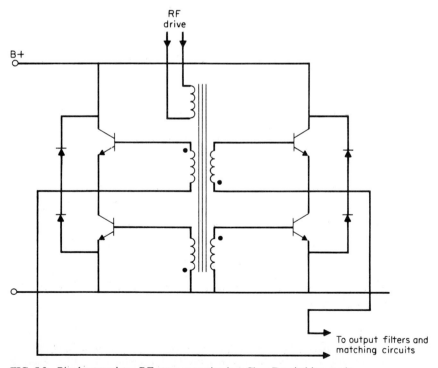

FIG. 5.9 Bipolar-transistor RF stage operating in a Class D switching mode.

completed, then combines the outputs of individual low-power amplifiers through toroidal filters. The result is a group of low-powered amplifiers operating in parallel and combined to generate the power required from the transmitting equipment itself. Transmitters up to the 50-kW power level have been constructed by using this design philosophy and have been found to exhibit very good overall performance characteristics. That is, the frequency response and distortion are well in accordance with those standards which might be expected for standard broadcast transmitters. This would normally be a frequency response flat ±1 dB from 50 Hz to 10 kHz and a distortion of not more than 1 percent at 95 percent modulation.

5.3 FREQUENCY MODULATION (FM) THEORY AND SYSTEMS

Another method of modulation, comparable in popularity to amplitude modulation, is angle or phase modulation. This is normally referred to *frequency modulation*. In this modulation scheme, the total phase angle or phase shift of the carrier is varied by the modulating signal. There are two basic mathematical derivations of frequency modulation which refer to either angle- or phase-modulated carriers. The resultant change, in the final evaluation of the mathematical characteristics, is in time.

5.3.1 Mathematical Analysis

To demonstrate one of these methods, let it be assumed that angle modulation is being performed:

$$\omega_T = \omega_c + \omega_m(t) \tag{5.4}$$

Equation (5.4) is the term showing both carrier signal and a modulating signal to be used in the frequency-modulation scheme. The angle-modulated carrier can then be mathematically expressed as Eq. (5.5):

$$e_c(t) = E_c \cos \theta(t) \tag{5.5}$$

where the total phase angle is a function of time and is constantly changing. This results in a phase angle of

$$\theta(t) = \int [\omega_c + \omega_m(t)] \, dt \tag{5.6}$$

resulting in

$$e(t) = E_c \cos \left[\omega_c t + \theta_0 + \int \omega_m(t) \, dt \right] \tag{5.7}$$

which is the resulting carrier with angle modulation. This is one of the mathematical models which may be used as representing a frequency-modulated carrier.

To analyze the frequency-modulated carrier more fully, it is necessary to do a frequency analysis to determine the bandwidth and the frequency spectrum which is necessary for this type of signal. With a single frequency-modulating signal,

$$e_m(t) = E_m \cos (\omega_m t) \qquad (5.8)$$

If this is used to angle-modulate the carrier as in the previous equations, the instantaneous angular frequency becomes

$$\omega_i = \omega_c + kE_m \cos (\omega_m t) \qquad (5.9)$$

Performing the necessary integration steps, it can be shown that the modulated carrier is

$$e(t) = E_c \cos \left[\omega_c t + \frac{\Delta\omega}{\omega_m} \sin (\omega_m t) \right] \qquad (5.10)$$

where $\Delta\omega = kE_m$. This equation definitely demonstrates that the magnitude of the frequency change of the carrier is a direct function of the magnitude of the modulating signal. The rate at which the frequency of the carrier is changed is equal to the frequency of the modulating signal. A new term is then defined: the *modulation index* (m_f), which is a function of the frequency deviation and the modulating-signal frequency:

$$m_f = \Delta\omega/\omega_m \qquad (5.11)$$

The single frequency-modulated carrier can be expanded to yield

$$e(t) = E_c \cos (\omega_c t + m_f \cos \omega_m t) \qquad (5.12)$$

This equation, while representing the actual frequency-modulated carrier, still leaves a significant degree of difficulty in establishing the actual frequency spectrum which is involved. To determine the frequency spectrum, it is necessary to determine a Fourier series or Fourier expansion to show the actual signal components involved. That action is not convenient for a waveform of this type, as the integrals which must be performed in the Fourier expansion or Fourier series are not easily solved. The actual result is that the integral produces a particular class of solution which is identified as the Bessel function. A graph of Bessel functions of the first kind, such as are involved in determining the Fourier series for the frequency-modulated signal, is shown in Fig. 5.10.

The equation which utilizes the Bessel functions to identify the frequency components of the FM modulated signal is

$$e(t) = J_0 (m_f) E_c \cos \omega_c t - J_1 (m_f) E_c \sin (\omega_c + \omega_m)t - J_1(m_f) E_c \sin$$

$$(\omega_c - \omega_m)t - J_2(m_f) E_c \cos (\omega_c + 2\omega_m)t - J_2(m_f) E_c \cos (\omega_c - 2\omega_m)t$$

$$+ J_3(m_f) E_c \sin (\omega_c + 3\omega_m)t + J_3(m_f) E_c \sin (\omega_c - 3\omega_m)t + \cdots \qquad (5.13)$$

The result is that a frequency-modulated signal using the modulation indices that would occur in a broadcast system will have a multitude of sidebands. FM broadcast stations are limited to a frequency deviation of ± 75 kHz. For a 1.0-kHz modulating frequency, this would result in a modulation index of 75, or for a 10-kHz modulating frequency the modulation index would reduce to a value of 7.5. In any case, multiple sidebands will exist.

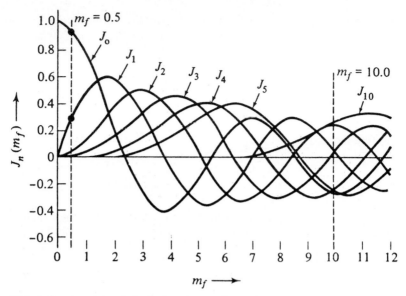

FIG. 5.10   Plot of simple Bessel functions of the first kind.

Preemphasis and Deemphasis.   Because of the reduction in the number of side-bands or the reduction in the modulation index at higher frequencies, it was found necessary to increase the amplitudes of the higher-frequency signal components in normal program material to produce more harmonics. Without this increase in the high-frequency signal magnitude, the signal-to-noise ratio at the higher frequencies would not be satisfactory for good-quality reproduction. This increase of high-frequency components is identified as preemphasis. All FM receivers utilize deemphasis to return the frequency response to normal. Standard broadcast systems use a preemphasis of 75 μs, meaning that the time constant of the resistance-inductance (RL) or resistance-capacitance (RC) circuit which is used to provide this boost of the high frequencies is 75 μs. Other values of preemphasis have been proposed and have been utilized to limited amounts in other FM broadcast systems.

Another interesting feature of FM broadcast systems is that the power is constant throughout the modulation process. That is, the total amount of energy is produced by the transmitter at all times. While the output power was increased in amplitude-modulation systems by the modulation process, FM systems simply distribute the power throughout the various frequency components which are produced by modulation. While being modulated, a wideband FM system does not have a high amount of energy present in the carrier, and most energy will be found in the sum of the sidebands themselves.

5.3.2   Modulation Systems

Reactance Modulators.   Early FM modulation systems used *reactance modulators* which operated at a low frequency. The output of the modulator was then multiplied to reach the desired output frequency of the transmitter. This was

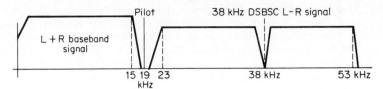

FIG. 5.11 Composite stereo signal.

acceptable in monaural FM transmitters but was not workable in modern stereo systems or other transmitting facilities which utilize subcarriers on the initial FM carriers.

Direct Modulation. Modern FM systems all utilize what is referred to as *direct modulation.* That is, the modulation occurs in a modulated oscillator which is operating on a center frequency equal to the value which is the desired output frequency of the transmitting equipment. In stereo broadcast systems, a composite FM signal is applied to the FM modulator. This composite signal is shown in Fig. 5.11.

Various techniques have been developed for this particular modulation scheme. One of the most popular and/or simple techniques uses a variable-capacity diode as the reactive element in the oscillator. The modulating signal is applied to the diode, which causes the diode capacitance to vary as a function of the magnitude of the modulating signal. As this capacitance varies, it causes the frequency of the oscillator to vary. Again, the magnitude of the frequency shift is proportional to the magnitude of the modulating signal, and the rate of the frequency shift is equal to the frequency of the incoming signal.

A block diagram of a complete FM exciter is shown in Fig. 5.12.

It should be noted that the oscillator is not normally coupled directly to a crystal but is a free-running oscillator adjusted as near as is convenient to the carrier frequency of the transmitting equipment. This frequency is then carefully maintained by shifts in a reference voltage from the automatic frequency-control circuit. That automatic frequency-control circuit itself is referenced either to a synthesized source or to a simple crystal reference.

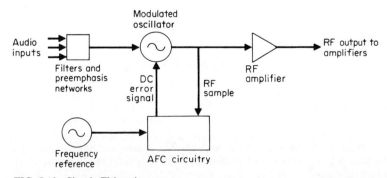

FIG. 5.12 Simple FM exciter.

Class C Mode of Operation. FM transmitters normally operate in a conventional Class C mode. As opposed to amplitude-modulation systems, frequency-modulation transmitter amplifiers can operate in Class C, as no information is lost from the frequency-modulated signal by amplitude changes. All information is contained in the magnitude of frequency change and rate of frequency change of the carrier. Therefore, the distortion introduced into the signal by utilizing a Class C amplifier does not cause the loss of any signal information.

5.3.3 Low-Noise Reception

The characteristic of Class C operation greatly assists in the low-noise advantage of FM reception. Upon being received and amplified, the FM signal normally is clipped to eliminate all amplitude variations beyond a certain level. This removes all noise which is present in the receiver as a result of human or atmospheric signals. It is not possible for these exterior signals to change the frequency of the desired signal; they can only affect its amplitude. It is this characteristic which permits the audience to listen to FM broadcast stations during periods of severe electrical storms. Even the most severe of lightning strikes in the vicinity of the receiver will be heard only as a sharp instantaneous click in the receiver as opposed to prolonged periods of static, as are observed on amplitude-modulated stations.

5.3.4 Auxiliary Services

The modern FM broadcast facility would be expected to be operating in stereo and would also probably carry one or more subsidiary channels. These channels, known as Subsidiary Communications Authorization (SCA) channels, are used for the transmission of market data, background music, control signals, and various functions for other services which are not normally part of the main programming on the FM transmitter. While significantly reduced in bandwidth from the main FM channel, they do represent valuable sources of income for the FM broadcasters and provide an efficient use of the available spectrum. The most common subcarrier frequency is 67 kHz, although higher subcarrier frequencies have been utilized. The Federal Communications Commission (FCC) permits a slightly wider frequency deviation than 75 kHz to provide spectrum for additional subcarriers. The subcarriers utilize low modulation levels, and the energy for the subcarriers themselves is maintained essentially within the 200-kHz bandwidth limitation on FM channel radiation.

5.4 TELEVISION STEREOPHONIC BROADCASTING

The adoption of the Zenith-dbx system for multichannel television sound (MTS) in December 1983 paved the way for the commercial transmission of stereo audio and second-language programming in the United States. The MTS nomenclature is a mixture of borrowed FM and some new MTS-specific terminology. This section discusses the broadcast-equipment specifications that have the most significant impact on MTS-system performance and gives brief explanations of the new MTS terminology.

A typical origination-to-end-user block diagram is shown in Fig. 5.13. Alter-

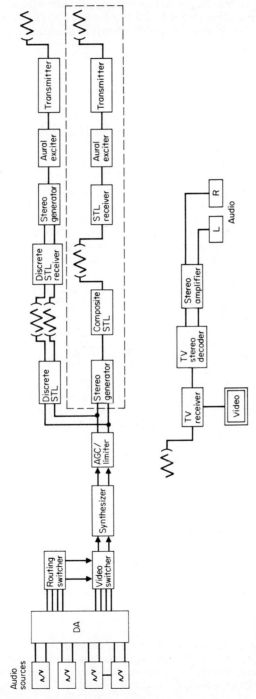

FIG. 5.13 Typical TV MTS block diagram.

nate paths are shown in the transmitter section, one for discrete encoding and the other for composite encoding in the studio-transmitter link (STL). The transmission components may be grouped into the following categories:

Audio chain

Stereo generators

Composite STL

Aural exciter

This section covers the subject under these classifications.

5.4.1   Audio Chain

The audio chain includes distribution amplifiers, mixers, switchers, processors, studio-transmitter link (STL), wiring, and connections between the audio source and the TV MTS generator. The most important performance specifications for equipment in the audio chain are frequency response, signal-to-noise ratio (SNR), distortion, separation, headroom, and channel-to-channel tracking.

Frequency Response (Refs. 1-3).   Frequency response is actually the deviation from a constant amplitude across a particular span of frequencies. Researchers have found that under some conditions variations as small as ±0.2 dB can be discerned, especially in the ear's critical 100- to 10,000-Hz range. Since the ear is less sensitive to response errors at the extremes, an audio-system specification of ±0.5 dB from 50 to 15,000 Hz and of ±0.25 dB from 100 to 10,000 Hz is adequate to deliver excellent audio.

A total-system specification of ±1 dB from 50 Hz to 15,000 Hz, including the stereo encoder and RF chain, is a realizable system performance target. Fortunately, most solid-state mixers and distribution amplifiers have frequency-response specifications much better than those given above. Unfortunately, much of the source material, such as videotape and network programming, will not be quite that good unless noise reduction or digital encoding is employed.

Signal-to-Noise Ratio (SNR).   Signal-to-noise ratio is the amplitude difference, usually expressed in decibels, between a *standard-level* audio signal and the system's residual noise and hum. The SNR of any equipment in the audio chain should be greater than 65 dB (unweighted). This will ensure that the source SNR or the transmitter FM SNR will be the limiting factor in the system noise contribution. The performance target for the entire system should be greater than 58 dB.

Total Harmonic Distortion (THD).   Total harmonic distortion is the creation by a nonlinear device of spurious signals harmonically related to the audio waveform. Research has shown that although THD levels greater than 1 percent are easily detectable during sine-wave testing, people will tolerate somewhat higher levels of THD on musical material. There is at least one audio *enhancer* that adds even-harmonic distortion to programming to give a richer sound. THD in any part of the audio chain should be less than 0.25 percent from 50 to 15,000 Hz, and the whole audio chain should be less than 0.5 percent THD from 50 to 15,000

Hz. A performance target for the entire system (RF included) should be 1 percent from 50 to 15,000 Hz.

Although harmonics of frequencies greater than 7500 Hz will be attenuated by the 15,000-Hz low-pass filters in the TV MTS generator, presence of these harmonics in the audio stages before the generator may raise the level of intermodulation-distortion products in the audio signal.

The THD test is sensitive to the SNR of the device under test. If the device has an SNR of 60 dB, the distortion analyzer's best distortion reading will be greater than 0.1 percent (60 dB = 0.001 = 0.1 percent). An audio spectrum analyzer will allow true THD readings because it will disregard the broadband noise floor of the tested device.

Intermodulation Distortion (IMD).   Intermodulation distortion is the creation by a nonlinear device of spurious signals not harmonically related to the audio waveform. These distortion components are sum-and-difference (beat notes) mixing products that research has shown are more objectionable to listeners than even harmonic-distortion products. The IMD (60 Hz/7000 Hz mixed 4:1 amplitude ratio), measured in accordance with Society of Motion Picture and Television Engineers (SMPTE), should be less than 0.25 percent for each part of the audio chain and less than 0.5 percent recommended practices (RPs) for the whole audio chain. The IMD measurement is not greatly affected by the noise floor of the tested device. A performance target for the entire system (including RF) should be 1 percent IMD.

Separation.   Separation is a specialized definition for signal crosstalk between the left and right channels of a stereo system. The minimum amount of stereo separation needed to define a stable stereo image has been found to be greater than 17 dB at the listener's position. Stereo separation is very likely to be badly degraded at every link in the transmission chain, requiring much better than the nominal 17 dB to be necessary for the audio chain. A separation requirement of greater than 50 dB from 50 to 15,000 Hz should be the minimum for each piece of equipment in the audio chain. The whole audio system should have separation greater than 40 dB from 400 to 15,000 Hz and 35 dB from 50 to 400 Hz. A performance target for the entire system (including RF) should be 30 dB from 100 to 12,000 Hz and 20 dB from 50 to 15,000 Hz.

Headroom.   Headroom is the difference (in decibels) between the normal operating level and the maximum output level of the device being tested. In equipment monitored by volume-unit (VU) types of meters the equipment should have 15 dB of headroom above 0 VU, or normal operating level, to allow for musical peaks that averaging-meter ballistics ignore. When the audio system operates without enough headroom, the time average of the program distortion becomes high enough to be audible.

Channel-to-Channel Amplitude and Phase Tracking.   Channel-to-channel amplitude and phase tracking is the match between the amplitude-versus-frequency and phase-versus-frequency responses of the stereo channels (L, R). Poor channel-to-channel tracking will result in a wandering or off-center stereo image and monaural summing errors that can be very obvious and distracting to viewers. The most obvious error is a completely out-of-phase condition ($L = -R$) which gives no mono signal ($L + R = 0$). The amplitude and phase match of the L and R channels should be good enough that with both channels driven with the same amplitude signal, but with one channel inverted ($L = -R$) and summed electrically, the residual should be 40 dB below the equivalent $L + R$ level from 50 to 15,000 Hz. The chart in Fig. 5.14 gives the amplitude and phase requirements to achieve various crosstalk performances.

5.4.2 Stereo Generators (Refs. 4–6)

To understand TV stereo-generator specifications, it is necessary to review briefly the Broadcast Television Systems Committee (BTSC) standards. The TV stereo system is a modification of the standard FM stereo system. The main differences are:

1. 25-kHz deviation for main channel ($L + R$).
2. 50-kHz deviation for subchannel ($L - R$). This is 2 times, or 6 dB, greater than for the main channel.
3. Noise reduction in the subchannel ($L - R$).
4. Pilot frequency equal to f_H (15,734 Hz).

Compatibility with existing monophonic receivers was the reason behind point 1 above. The reason for points 2 and 3 is that without noise reduction the received TV stereo SNR would be less than 50 dB in outlying areas. With the noise reduction compandor in the stereo subchannel and the 6-dB increase in level, the L and R SNR should be dependent only on the main-channel SNR, which has been better than 63 dB in system tests. The use of f_H as the pilot should result in less buzz-beat interference.

Figure 5.15 shows the FM-versus-TV stereo baseband spectrum. Table 5.1

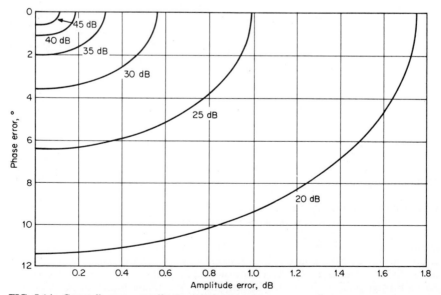

FIG. 5.14 Crosstalk versus amplitude and phase errors.

TABLE 5.1 Modulation Standards for TV MTS System

Service or signal	Modulating signal	Modulating frequency range, kHz	Audio processing or preemphasis	Subcarrier frequency*	Subcarrier modulation type	Subcarrier deviation, kHz	Aural carrier peak deviation, kHz
Monophonic	L + R	0.05–15	75 μs				25†
Pilot				f_H			5
Stereophonic	L − R	0.05–15	BTSC compression	$2f_H$	AM-DSB SC		50†
Second program		0.05–10	BTSC compression	$5f_H$	FM	10	15
Professional channel	Voice or data	0.3–3.4	150 μs	$6\frac{1}{2}f_H$	FM	3	3
		0–1.5	0		FSK		

* f_H = 15.734 kHz.
† Sum does not exceed 50 kHz.

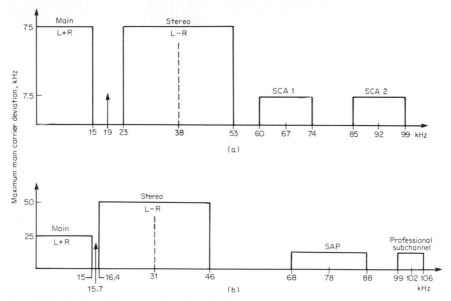

FIG. 5.15 Baseband frequency allocations. (*a*) Stereophonic FM. (*b*) BTSC TV stereophonic system; f_H (15,734.25 Hz).

shows the aural carrier-modulation standards for the TV stereo system. Figure 5.16 is a block diagram of a typical TV stereo generator.

Some of the specifications for TV stereo generators are not different from those for other audio equipment except that they cannot be verified without use of a decoder and that the decoder contribution to performance must be recognized.[7]

There are at least two operation modes for TV stereo generators: the normal (noise reduction) operational mode and a test mode called 75-μs equivalent mode. In the 75-μs equivalent mode, the noise reduction system in $L - R$ is replaced with a 75-μs preemphasis network identical to that in $L + R$. This step was taken to allow noise, distortion, and separation measurements to be made without the level-dependent degradation caused by the noise reduction. There is a disagreement about inclusion of the difficult subchannel filters in the 75-μs equivalent mode. Performance tests made without the subchannel filters in the 75-μs equivalent mode provide better frequency-response and separation measurements than those with filters in the system.

Specifications reviewed for TV stereo generators include audio filtering, frequency response, separation, crosstalk, spurious suppression, and deviation calibration.

Subchannel Filters. Subchannel filters serve to limit the noise-reduction-control-line bandwidth and to control the out-of-band energy created by the noise reduction card. When there is no audio input to the noise reduction circuitry, the spectral compressor grain is at maximum, creating a high-level parabolic noise spectrum which needs to be bandwidth-limited to audio frequencies to prevent spectrum spillover. Since the pilot is separated from the subchannel by only 734 Hz, the filter slope needs to be very sharp to provide pilot protection with flat response to 15,000 Hz.

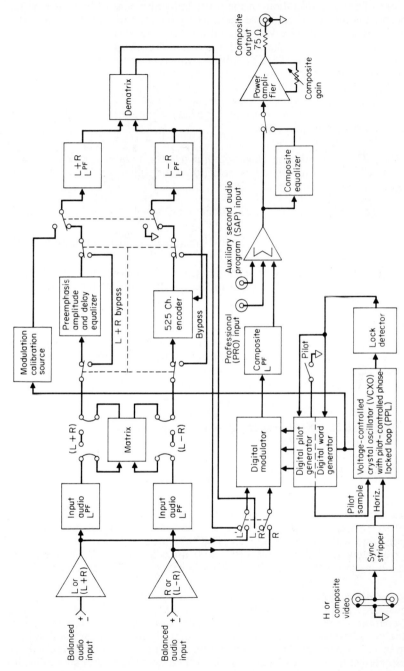

FIG. 5.16 Stereo-generator block diagram.

Any out-of-band information on the noise-reduction-control line (such as f_H) after the subchannel filter will cause the noise reduction circuitry to misencode, causing degradation of received separation and frequency response when decoded. To ensure stereo separation greater than 40 dB, the subchannel filters need to be matched within 0.08-dB amplitude difference and 1° phase difference. For good overall frequency response, the filter's response should be better than ±02 dB from 50 to 15,000 Hz.

The stereo-generator frequency response should be better than ±1 dB from 50 to 15,000 Hz (with noise reduction) and ±0.5 dB without noise reduction to help meet the total-system response goals.

Separation.   The separation specification of a stereo generator can be measured in three ways. The generator should be better than the Office of Science and Technology Bulletin 60 numbers given below.

1. Baseband (FM) generator (no audio filters included): 50-dB minimum from 50 to 15,000 Hz

2. Noise reduction bypassed (all audio filters included): 40-dB minimum from 50 to 14,000 Hz

3. Full-system BTSC mode (all filters and noise reduction included): 30-dB minimum from 100 to 8000 Hz, decreasing to 20 dB at 14,000 Hz, 26-dB minimum at 50 Hz

Linear Crosstalk.   Linear crosstalk is leakage from $L + R$ to $L - R$ or $L - R$ to $L + R$ caused by amplitude and phase matching of L and R channels which will result in a wandering or off-center stereo image and monaural summing errors that can be very obvious and distracting to viewers. The stereo-generator linear crosstalk should be better than 40 dB below 100 percent with all filters in circuit.

Nonlinear Crosstalk.   Nonlinear crosstalk is leakage from $L + R$ to $L - R$ or from $L - R$ to $L + R$ caused by distortion products in $L + R$ or $L - R$. The distortion products generated in the $L - R$ channel cause interference in the SAO (Second Audio Program) or PRO (professional) spectrum. The generator specification should be better than 70 dB below 100 percent.

Spurious Suppression.   Spurs are caused by nonlinearities in the AM-DSB (double-sideband) modulation of $L - R$. These unwanted distortion products can cause noise and whistles in the SAP and PRO channels, especially since the SAP is 10.5 dB below $L - R$ and the PRO is 20 dB below $L - R$. The generator spurious suppression should be greater than 75 dB below 100 percent $L - R$.

Deviation Calibration.   Unlike noncompanded FM stereo, the BTSC system requires precise adjustment of aural-deviation calibration for optimum received stereo separation and frequency response. Like some tape noise reduction systems, the encoder-to-decoder levels must be carefully matched for good system performance. For example, an aural-deviation error of 1 dB will degrade separation from perfect to less than 20 dB (Fig. 5.17). The stereo generator should incorporate a deviation calibration system that allows the aural deviation to be quickly and easily set and checked with an accuracy of better than 1 percent.

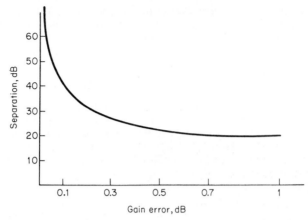

FIG. 5.17 Stereo separation versus composite gain error.

5.4.3 Composite STL

Frequency Response. To maintain a system separation greater than 40 dB, the composite amplitude response must be within ±0.08 dB, and the composite phase response must be less than ±1° from linear phase over the band from 50 to 47,000 Hz.

If a SAP or PRO is to be added, the composite amplitude and phase response must be flat (±1 dB, ±10°) to 120,000 Hz to prevent crosstalk.

Signal-to-Noise Ratio. The FM signal-to-noise ratio of the STL should be better than 65 dB (unweighted) with 75-μs deemphasis.

Distortion. The aural composite STL should have distortion better than 0.1 percent. Any distortion of the baseband signal caused by the STL will have secondary effects of the stereo, SAP, and PRO crosstalk, which is quite noticeable at the receiver with rather small amounts of distortion added to the baseband. For example, an increase of baseband harmonic distortion from 0.05 to 1.0 percent will increase crosstalk into the SAP by as much as 26 dB.

Amplitude Stability. The encoded TV stereo composite signal is highly sensitive to gain variations in the composite path. As shown in Fig. 5.17, a gain error of less than 10 percent (1 dB) will reduce the system separation to less than 20 dB. This assumes that the separation was perfect before the gain error was introduced. For good separation the composite path should have a maximum gain drift of ±0.2 dB over time and temperature. The best composite link is properly terminated coaxial cable.

5.4.4 Aural Exciter

Frequency Response. To maintain a system separation greater than 40 dB, the composite amplitude response must be within ±0.08 dB, and the composite phase response must be less than ±1° from linear phase over the band from 50 to 47,000 Hz and over an aural carrier deviation of 50,000 Hz. If a SAP or PRO is to be added, the composite amplitude and phase response must be flat (± 1 dB, $\pm 10°$) to 120,000 Hz to prevent crosstalk.

Signal-to-Noise Ratio. The FM signal-to-noise ratio of the aural exciter should be better than 65 dB (unweighted) with 75-μs deemphasis.

Amplitude Stability. The encoded TV stereo composite signal is highly sensitive to gain variations in the composite path. As shown in Fig. 5.17, a gain error of less than 10 percent (1 dB) will reduce the system separation to less than 20 dB. This assumes that the separation was perfect before the gain error was introduced. For good separation the aural exciter should have a maximum gain drift of ± 0.2 dB over time and temperature.

REFERENCES

1. R. Buecklein, "The Audibility of Frequency Response Irregularities," *J. Audio Eng. Soc.,* **29**(3), 126–131 (March 1981).

2. G. H. Plenge, H. Jakubowski, and P. Schoene, "Which Bandwidth Is Necessary for Optimal Sound Transmission?" presented at the 62d Convention of the Audio Engineering Society, Brussels (Mar. 13–16, 1979).

3. W. B. Snow, "Audible Frequency Ranges of Music, Speech and Noise," *J. Acoust. Soc. Am.,* **3**, 155–166 (1931).

4. C. Eilers, "The Zenith Multichannel TV Sound System," *Proc. 38th NAB Eng. Conf.* (1984).

5. Federal Communications Commission, *Multichannel Television Sound Transmisssion and Audio Processing Requirements for the BTSC System,* OST Bulletin 60.

6. Electronic Industries Association, *Multichannel Television Sound—BTSC System Recommended Practices,* ETA Television Systems Bulletin 5, July 1985.

7. G. Mendenhall, "Testing Television Transmission Systems for Multichannel Sound Compatibility," *Proc. 39th NAB Eng. Conf.* (1985).

CHAPTER 6
MICROPHONES AND AMPLIFIERS

Audio is defined as signal frequencies corresponding to normally audible sound waves. The initial and fundamental components involved in the engineering of audio systems are (1) the transducer to convert sound waves to electrical signals and (2) the amplification of signals for the wide variety of audio processing, recording, and reproduction devices. The design of a transducer is closely related to that of the subsequent amplifier, and in fact the latter frequently may be a part of the microphone. This close system relationship between microphones and amplifiers has been recognized by the inclusion of both subjects in Chap. 6.

The subject of microphones is introduced in Secs. 6.1 and 6.2 with a discussion of pressure-sensing means for the conversion of sound waves in air to electrical signals. In one, the pressure level is detected; in the other, the variations in the pressure, or velocity, are measured. Virtually all basic designs and their characteristics are described in detail. The design of various combinations of the two techniques is covered in Sec. 6.3.

Sections 6.4 and 6.5 describe a wide range of specialized microphone types, including stereophonic and quadraphonic. Stereophonic microphone equipment and techniques are covered in depth in Sec. 6.6.

The equipment for amplification and processing of the electrical output of microphones as well as other signal sources is covered in Sec. 6.7. From the basic single-stage amplifier, the section progresses through a detailed description of multistage amplifiers, power amplifiers, and versatile operational amplifiers. Included are feedback and feed-forward techniques and special considerations in the design of power amplifiers. Lastly, the very important, and frequently misinterpreted, terms for specification of amplifier and system characteristics in terms of gain and circuit impedances are reviewed and clarified.

MICROPHONES*

Jon R. Sank
Cross County Consultants, Haddonfield, New Jersey

STEREOPHONIC TECHNIQUES
Ronald D. Streicher
President, Pacific Audio-Visual Enterprises, Monrovia, California

Wesley L. Dooley
Chief Engineer, Audio Engineering Associates, Pasadena, California

A microphone is an electroacoustic device containing a transducer which is actuated by sound waves and delivers essentially equivalent electric waves.[1] An example of a transducer actuated by sound waves which fails to conform to this definition is the Rayleigh disk, which converts the energy of sound waves into mechanical torque.[2]

The classes of microphones are pressure, pressure-gradient (velocity), combination pressure and pressure-gradient, and wave-interference. The electrical response of a pressure microphone results from pressure variations in the air. The directional (polar) pickup pattern is omnidirectional (nondirectional) because sound pressure is a scalar quantity which possesses magnitude but no direction. The electrical response of a velocity microphone results from variations in the particle velocity of the air. The polar pattern is bidirectional (cosine or figure-of-eight) because particle velocity is a vector quantity which possesses magnitude and direction. The electrical response of the combination pressure and pressure-gradient microphone is also proportional to the particle velocity. The polar pattern may be cardioid, hypercardioid, or of a similar cosine-function limaçon shape and may be fixed or adjustable.

A particular class of microphones may include one of the following types of transducers: carbon, ceramic, condenser, moving-coil, inductor, ribbon, magnetic, electronic, or semiconductor.

The functioning of various types of microphones is described in this chapter by reference to the equivalent circuits of the acoustical and mechanical systems. The mechanical equivalent circuit is considered, for simplicity, when the discussion involves mathematical equations. In other instances, the discussion omits mathematics, and the acoustical network affords the clearest illustration of oper-

* Sections 6.1 through 6.5 presented by Jon R. Sank at the 2d AES International Conference. Anaheim, Calif., May 11–14, 1984. Reprinted with permission from the *Journal of the Audio Engineering Society,* 33(7/8) (July–August 1985).

Contributors: Patricia Macdonald of the Audio Engineering Society; Eugene Pitts III of *Audio* magazine; James Kogen, Robert Schulein, and Lee Habich of Shure Brothers; Ed Joscelyn, formerly of Telephonics; Jerry Bruck of Posthorn Recordings/Schoeps; Geoffrey Langdon of Sennheiser; Dr. J. L. Flanagan and Dr. James Snyder of Bell Laboratories; Rebecca Mercuri of RCA David Sarnoff Research Center; Geoffrey Levy of Beyer Dynamic; Nigel Branwell of Audio + Design Calrec, Inc.; Ted Telesky of Fostex; W. B. Gore of Telex; Derek Pilkington of AKG Acoustics; and Ron Streicher of Audio Engineering Associates.

ating principles. Table 4.3 in Olson (Ref. 3, pp. 86–87) lists analogous electrical, mechanical, and acoustical quantities with the pertinent units.

6.1 PRESSURE MICROPHONES

6.1.1 Carbon Microphone

A carbon microphone depends for its operation on the variation of resistance of carbon contacts. The high sensitivity of this microphone is due to the relay action of the carbon contacts. It is almost universally used in telephone communications. This is true because the high sensitivity eliminates the need for audio amplification in a telephone set. Restricted frequency range, distortion, and carbon noise limit the application of the carbon microphone in other than voice-communications applications.

A typical single-button carbon microphone and electric circuit are shown in Fig. 6.1. The carbon transducer consists of a contact cup filled with carbon granules, which are usually made from anthracite coal.[1] The granules make contact with the electrically conductive diaphragm via the contact button on the diaphragm. The diaphragm is frequently made from a thin sheet of aluminum alloy. The periodic displacement of the diaphragm causes a variation in mechanical pressure applied to the carbon granules. This results in a periodic variation in electric resistance from the diaphragm to the contact cup. For small displacements, the variation in resistance is proportional to the displacement.

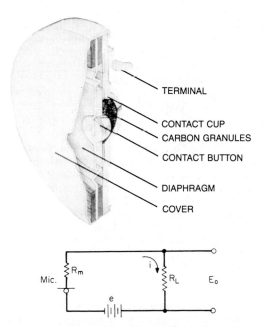

TERMINAL

CONTACT CUP
CARBON GRANULES

CONTACT BUTTON

DIAPHRAGM

COVER

FIG. 6.1 Carbon microphone and electric circuit. *(Photograph courtesy of Shure Brothers, Inc.)*

The output voltage is given by

$$E_0 = \frac{eR_L}{(R_m + R_L) + (hx \sin \omega t)} \qquad (6.1)$$

where e = dc voltage of bias source
    h = constant of carbon element, Ω/cm
    x = amplitude of diaphragm, cm
    $\omega = 2\pi f$
    f = frequency, Hz

The useful audio output is, of course, the ac component of E_0. Equation (6.1) may be expanded (Ref. 3, p. 248) to show that the ac component consists of harmonics at f, $2f$, ..., which means that the carbon transducer has intrinsic distortion. For a limited frequency range of reproduction, the distortion is not objectionable.

The large second-harmonic distortion component may be eliminated by use of two carbon buttons in push-pull. The double-button microphone is described in Ref. 3, pp. 251–253. It was used in the 1920s for broadcasting but was replaced by condenser, ribbon, and dynamic microphones. Although the double-button microphone has a wide-range frequency response and low distortion, it and the single-button types suffer from carbon compaction and carbon noise. These effects mean that the signal-to-noise ratio or dynamic range of the microphone is variable. Repeatability of frequency response, sensitivity, and noise measurements of carbon microphones is very poor.

For improved performance in telephone and speech communications, carbon microphones are being replaced by dynamic, magnetic, and electret condenser microphones, which have built-in amplifiers. These amplifiers are powered by the direct current normally provided by the communications equipment for carbon microphones. These *carbon replacements* may offer noise-canceling features as well as improved frequency response and low distortion and noise. They are offered as replacement cartridges for telephone handsets, in replacement handsets, in hand-held microphones, and in headsets.

6.1.2 Piezoelectric Microphone

The piezoelectric microphone contains a transducer element which generates a voltage when mechanically deformed. The voltage is proportional to the displacement in the frequency range below the resonance of the element. Rochelle salt crystals were used prior to 1960 but were sensitive to humidity and heat. Newer ceramic materials such as barium titanate and lead zirconate titanate are more resistant to environmental extremes and have replaced the Rochelle salt crystals. There are two general classifications of ceramic microphones: direct-actuated and diaphragm-actuated. Directly actuated transducers consist of stacked arrays of bimorph crystals or *sound cells*. These, which are now obsolete, are described in Ref. 3, pp. 248–260, where it is also reported that a directly actuated microphone was constructed with a barium titanate element but the sensitivity was low.

Figure 6.2 shows the most common construction in use today for a ceramic microphone. The element is mounted as a cantilever and actuated by the diaphragm via the drive pin. The diaphragm is frequently made from thin aluminum sheet, although paper or polyester film may also be used. The impedance of the ceramic microphone is capacitative on the order of 500 to 1000 PF. This permits use of a short length of cable with only a small loss in output level. The advantage of the ceramic microphone is that the output voltage is sufficient to drive a high-impedance input of an amplifier directly. The frequency response (with a very high input resistance) is uniform from a very low frequency up to the transducer resonance, which may be situated at 10,000 Hz or higher. The sensitivity and the frequency response are stable with time and over a wide range of temperature and humidity. The cost is relatively low. Therefore, the ceramic microphone was widely

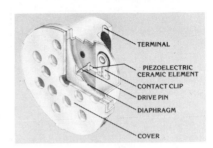

FIG. 6.2 Ceramic microphone. *(Courtesy of Shure Brothers, Inc.)*

used with tube-type home tape recorders and low-cost communications equipment. With the advent of solid-state equipment low-impedance microphones are needed, and the ceramic microphone has been replaced by inexpensive moving-coil (dynamic) microphones or electret condenser microphones. They have integral field-effect transistor (FET) preamplifiers which convert their output to low impedance.

A wide-frequency-range subminiature ceramic microphone has been developed for hearing aids.[4] The novel construction includes a thick-film preamplifier which lowers the impedance of the microphone so that noise pickup in the cable is reduced and the microphone impedance is suitable for driving a solid-state amplifier. More recently this microphone has been superseded by an electret unit with integral preamplifier with the same very small size.[5]

A recent development is the piezoelectric diaphragm transducer. A thick or thin film of the polymer polyvinylidene fluoride (PVF_2) may be processed to form a piezoelectric element. As with the ceramic element, it must be provided with plated-on output terminals. There is much in the current literature about the application of PVF_2 in underwater sound. Joscelyn and associates[6] describe a small noise-canceling (pressure-gradient) microphone employing a PVF_2 diaphragm which is partially plated with nickel chromium. The diaphragm is tensioned accurately by a device which is the subject of the patent. This is necessary to raise the diaphragm resonance to a high frequency, as with a ceramic element.

6.1.3 Electrostatic (Condenser) Microphones

Operating Principles. A condenser microphone depends for its operation on variations in its internal capacitance. Figure 6.3 shows the capsule of an omnidirectional pressure-sensing condenser microphone.[7] Condenser microphones are divided into two classes: externally polarized (air condenser) and prepolarized (electret condenser). The function of the polarizing voltage or its equivalent is to translate the diaphragm motion into a linearly related audio output voltage, which is amplified by a very-high-impedance FET or tube preamplifier, which must be located close to the capsule. Alternately, the capacitance variation may

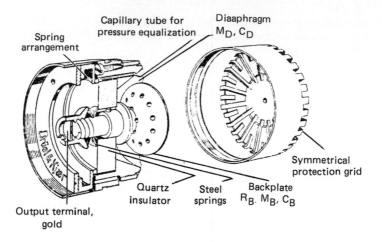

FIG. 6.3 Condenser pressure microphone and mechanical network. [*From G. Rasmussen, "A New Condenser Microphone," Tech. Rev., Brüel & Kjaer, Copenhagen, no. 1 (1959).*]

be used to frequency-modulate a radio-frequency (RF) oscillator, but this scheme will not be discussed.

The diaphragm of this microphone is a thin membrane of nickel which is spaced about 0.001 in (25 μm) from the backplate. Since the electroacoustical sensitivity is inversely proportional [Eq. (6.4)] to the spacing d, special measures must be taken to prevent this distance from changing because of temperature. The laboratory-grade microphone of Fig. 6.3 is made almost entirely of nickel and nickel alloys and has nearly constant sensitivity from 20 to 150° C.

The performance may be determined by consideration of the mechanical network (Fig. 6.3). The resonance is placed at the high end of the usable frequency range. The backplate air load includes mass M_B, compliance C_B, and resistance R_B. M_B and C_B plus the diaphragm mass M_D and compliance D_D determine the resonance frequency. R_B provides damping of the resonance. Below resonance frequency, the microphone is stiffness-controlled (reciprocal of compliance) and only C_D and C_B appear in the circuit.

The open-circuit output voltage E is given by Refs. 3, pp. 253–257, and 8:

$$E = \frac{E_0}{d} x \qquad x = \frac{\dot{x}}{j\omega} \tag{6.2}$$

where E_0 = polarizing voltage (or equivalent voltage for electrets)
d = spacing from diaphragm to backplate, m

x = diaphragm displacement, m
$\dot{x}$ = diaphragm velocity, m/s
$\omega = 2\pi f$
f = frequency, Hz

The velocity is given by

$$\dot{x} = \frac{F}{Z} = \frac{PA}{(1/j\omega)(1/C_D + 1/C_M)} \tag{6.3}$$

where F = force on diaphragm, N
P = sound pressure on diaphragm, N/m^2
A = area of diaphragm, m^2
Z = mechanical impedance system, mechanical ohms

The output voltage is obtained by combining Eqs. (6.2 and (6.3).

$$E = \frac{E_0 PA}{d(1/C_D + 1/C_B)} \tag{6.4}$$

This means that below resonance the response is independent of frequency.

The polarization field strength for most condenser microphones, independent of the polarization principle, is on the order of 100,000 V/cm[9] so that the slightest bit of contamination between diaphragm and backplate will cause impulsive noise due to arcing. Microphones used in corrosive environments may develop pinholes in the diaphragm, and the resulting corrosion behind the diaphragm eventually may short-circuit the transducer. Normally, impulsive noise is caused by humidity, which can be eliminated by desiccation. Fredericksen and associates[9] recommended the use of foam windscreens for protection in damp or corrosive environments.

Electret Microphone. The simplest type of electret microphone is the charged diaphragm type. This is illustrated in Fig. 6.4. The spacing between diaphragm and backplate is exaggerated for clarity. Figure 6.5 shows a schematic of the foil electret with the electric charge distribution illustrated. The electret foil is selected as a compromise between good electret properties and good mechanical properties as a diaphragm. Polymer materials such as polyacrylonitrile, polycarbonate,

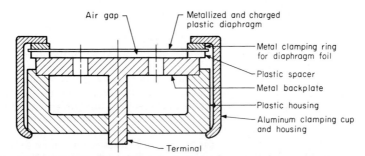

FIG. 6.4 Typical design of electret capsule with charged foil diaphragm. [*From E. Fredericksen, N. Eirby, and H. Mathiasen, "Prepolarized Condenser Microphones for Measurement Purposes," Tech. Rev., Brüel & Kjaer, Copenhagen, no. 4 (1979).*]

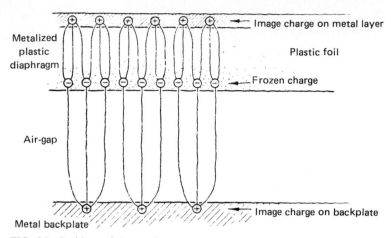

FIG. 6.5 Positions of charges for space-charge electret when electret is an integral part of the diaphragm. Frozen charge and charge on backplate produce the field in the air gap that is necessary for microphone operation. [*From E. Fredericksen, N. Eirby, and H. Mathiasen, "Prepolarized Condenser Microphones for Measurement Purposes," Tech. Rev., Brüel & Kjaer, Copenhagen, no. 4 (1979).*]

and some fluoric resins are examples of suitable plastic films used as electret diaphragms.

There are several methods of making an electret, and exact details are kept as trade secrets by the manufacturers. Typically, one side of the plastic film is coated by vacuum sputtering a conductive metal such as aluminum, gold, or nickel. The thickness of the coating is about 500 Å (50 nm). The film is then heated and charged with a high dc potential, with the electret-forming electrode facing the nonconductive side of the film.[10] A well-designed electret capsule will retain its charge and exhibit nearly constant sensitivity for 10 years, and it is predicted that it will take 30 to 100 years before the sensitivity is reduced by 3 dB.

These plastic-foil electrets generally will not stand the tension required to obtain the high resonant frequencies commonly employed in externally polarized microphones. One solution is to reduce tension and support the diaphragm at many points by means of a grooved backplate (Fig. 6.6). This and other schemes used to increase stiffness lead to short-term instability.[9]

Therefore, the charged-diaphragm electret generally does not possess the extended high-frequency response and stability of the air-condenser microphone. Its great advantage is that it can be made very cheaply by automated manufacturing methods.

An improved form of electret transducer is the *back electret,* or charged backplate design.[9-11] Figure 6-7 shows a simplified cross section of a typical design. (Dimensions are exaggerated for clarity. This is a pressure-gradient microphone, to be discussed later.) The diaphragm is a polyester film such as Mylar,* approximately 0.0002 in (5 μm) thick. This is an ideal material and thickness for a diaphragm. The diaphragm is coated on one or both sides with a thick film of gold or other metal. The electret is made of a fluoric film such as Teflon,* which must

---

* Teflon and Mylar are trademarks of E. I. du Pont de Nemours and Co., Inc.

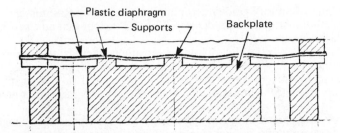

FIG. 6.6 Principle used by some manufacturers to obtain sufficiently high resonance frequency of plastic diaphragms having low creep stability. [*From E. Fredericksen, N. Eirby, and H. Mathiasen, "Prepolarized Condenser Microphones for Measurement Purposes,"* Tech. Rev., *Brüel & Kjaer, Copenhagen, no. 4 (1979).*]

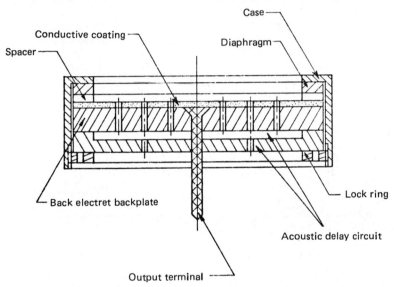

FIG. 6.7 Back-electret capsule. [*From H. Kubota, "Back Electret Microphones," presented at the 55th Convention of the Audio Engineering Society,* J. Audio Eng. Soc. (Abstracts), **24,** 862 (December 1976), preprint 1157.]

be at least 0.001 in (25 μm) thick to form a stable electret. This electret is placed on the backplate, which must have a conducting surface to form the "high" output terminal. The electret element is charged similarly to the charged-diaphragm electret. Since the electret does not function as a diaphragm, the material and thickness are chosen as optimal for high sensitivity and stability. The diaphragm-to-backplate (electret) spacing is the same as for the air condenser, approximately 0.001 in (25 μm). The equivalent polarization potential is 100 to 200 V, which is the same as that used in high-quality air-condenser microphones.

A measuring microphone must possess exceptional stability and resistance to corrosive environments. The back-electret concept permits a metal diaphragm to be used. The laboratory-grade microphone developed by Rasmussen is identical to the metal-diaphragm air condenser of Fig. 6.3, except that an electret is placed on the backplate.

Thus the back-electret microphone is essentially identical to the air condenser save for the electret element on the backplate. This means that the capsule is actually more costly to make than an air condenser. This cost is offset by the savings involved in the omission of a high-voltage power supply for polarization.

Condenser-Microphone Frequency Response.   This discussion, although about a condenser microphone, applies in principle to all pressure microphones.

Figure 6.8 shows the frequency-response curves of the Western Electric 640-AA condenser microphone. This is an ANSI type L laboratory microphone having a nominal 1-in (25-mm) diameter. It is similar to the Bruel & Kjaer microphone of Fig. 6.3, except that the latter is a newer design which eliminates the cavity in front of the diaphragm. The 640-AA is illustrated in Beranek.[13] It was the preferred calibration standard at the National Bureau of Standards (NBS) for many years.

The *pressure* response is the frequency response to a constant sound pressure on the diaphragm. This response can be very precisely measured by NBS by the closed-coupler reciprocity method.[2] This curve shows that the diaphragm resonance is approximately critically damped. The difference between the pressure response and the perpendicular incidence response (called the *free-field correction*) depends only on the geometry of the microphone and is carefully measured on a typical microphone. The perpendicular incidence response for a particular microphone is computed by adding the free-field correction to the pressure response. The parallel incidence response is similarly computed. Not shown is the random incidence response, which is the response to randomly directed sound, such as that in a reverberation chamber. The random incidence response follows the general trend of the pressure response. The 640-AA microphone has essentially flat pressure or random incidence response (to 10,000 Hz), which is called

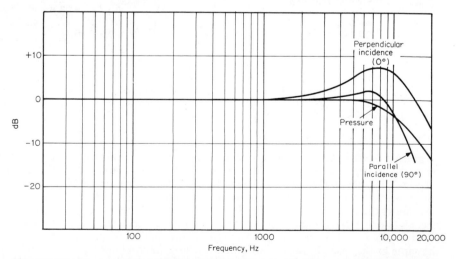

FIG. 6.8   Frequency responses of Western Electric 640-AA microphone. *(After* National Bureau of Standards Reports of Calibration, *TN-181701, July 8, 1964, and TN-199270, Aug. 4, 1969.)*

for in American National Standards Institute (ANSI) standards for laboratory microphones and sound-level meters. By contrast, International Electrotechnical Commission (IEC) standards require these microphones to have a flat response to sounds of perpendicular incidence ("flat for free field"). The response can be varied by changing the damping adjustment or the configuration of the protective grid. Therefore, most manufacturers today offer both versions to satisfy both standards. For the calibration of sound sources used in testing microphones, the IEC type is universally used. The free-field correction, being a function of diameter, vanishes (below 20,000 Hz) as the microphone diameter becomes smaller than 0.50 in (12.5 mm).

Pressure microphones used for sound and communications systems are generally larger than 1 in (25 mm) in diameter but need only have speech-range response (200 to 6300 Hz). These may have moving-coil, magnetic, or ceramic transducers. They are generally designed to have a rising axial response characteristic, which means that the off-axis and pressure responses tend to be flat. If the axial response is flattened, the off-axis response is rolled off, speech sounds muffled, and the system intelligibility is reduced. In contrast, microphones smaller than 1 in (25 mm) in diameter do not suffer when designed for flat axial response.

Boundary Microphone. Long and Wickersham have patented[14] what they call the *pressure-recording process* and a device that positions a conventional microphone very close to a plane surface such as a floor. This has given rise to a number of products which basically function as shown in Fig. 6.9. A miniature electret microphone is spaced about 0.04 in (1 mm) from a large reflecting plane. A conventional microphone, which is situated above the floor, receives the direct sound wave plus a reflected wave from the floor. It suffers from dips in frequency response, at the frequency where the spacing is one-quarter wavelength, and its harmonics, as the reflected sound wave interferes with the direct sound wave. When the spacing is reduced to about 0.04 in (1 mm), the null frequency moves far above the audible range. Therefore, in actual use the boundary microphone does not suffer from the *comb-filter series* of dips in frequency response. The sys-

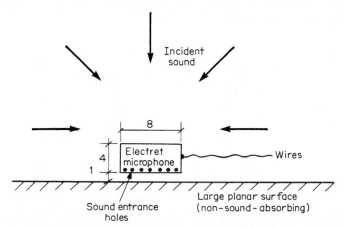

FIG. 6.9 Boundary-microphone principle. Dimensions are in millimeters.

tem has, in essence, a directional gain of 6 dB due to pressure doubling at the reflecting plane; for example, the reflected wave is in phase and adds to the amplitude of the direct wave. This results in a hemispheric pickup pattern where the 90° response (direction parallel to the plane) is 6 dB down with respect to the 0° or perpendicular incidence response. Complete test data are reported in Sank.[15]

A suitable transducer for the boundary microphone of Fig. 6.9 is the subminiature electret microphone developed by Killion and Carlson.[5] It incorporates an integral solid-state preamplifier. It is ideal for a floor-mounted microphone because it has extremely low vibration sensitivity. This type of microphone element is molded into a plastic housing which is fastened to a small metal plate in the commercial product described in Ref. 15. To obtain the measured acoustical performance, the small plate must, of course, be placed on a much larger plane surface.

In many applications it is desirable for a boundary microphone to be more directional. For instance, the rear portion of the hemispherical pattern may pick up audience noise when the microphone is mounted on a stage floor. Bullock and Woodard[16] have described a directional boundary microphone in which an electret element with a cardioid directivity is mounted close to a surface, with the principal pickup axis parallel to the surface.

Probe Microphone.   For sound pressure measurements in very small spaces, a condenser microphone may be fitted with a small-diameter probe tube, as shown in Olson.[3] This introduces a high-frequency response rolloff plus dips and peaks. The latter may be reduced by acoustic damping in the tube. The damping may be porous polyurethane foam or similar material, or the tube may be packed with pieces of music wire. Alternately, a very small capillary tube may be used as a probe which has very high acoustic resistance because of the small diameter. The need for a probe microphone in measurements is less today because condenser microphones as small as 0.125 in (3 mm) are available.

Commercial magnetic microphones have been fitted with small probe tubes for convenient use on lightweight telephone and radio communications headsets that are mounted on the ear or on eyeglass frames. Ceramic or dynamic microphones may be fitted with plastic probe tubes for diagnostic testing of machinery.

The term *probe microphone* has also been applied to pressure microphones which are small in diameter but relatively long.

6.1.4   Electrodynamic Microphones

Moving-Coil (Dynamic) Microphone.   A cross section of a moving-coil-microphone cartridge is shown in Fig. 6.10, and the complete microphone assembly in Fig. 6.11.[17] The diaphragm, which is made of Mylar polyester film 0.00035 in (9 μm) thick, is glued to a voice coil which moves in the magnetic air gap. The flux density is 10,000 G (1 Wb/m^2). The self-supporting coil is wound with four layers of no. 50 AWG coppper wire, which results in a dc resistance of 220 Ω. The ac impedance of 200 to 250 Ω is suitable for standard low-impedance microphone inputs of 150 to 600 Ω. Older microphone coils were on the order of 5- to 20-Ω resistance and required a step-up matching transformer in the microphone case. Thus the modern moving-coil microphone will drive standard bipolar integrated circuits directly. The coupler (Fig. 6.10) fits closely to the diaphragm to provide mechanical protection without frequency discrimination. The cartridge is shock-

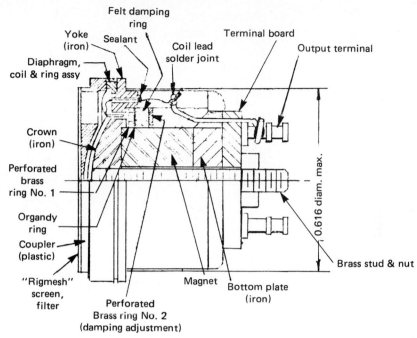

FIG. 6.10 Dynamic moving-coil-pressure-microphone cartridge (RCA type BK-16A).

mounted in the case of Fig. 6.11, which includes a foam filter screen for dirt and breath "pop" protection. (The author developed this microphone; the parameter values are from memory.)

The voltage induced in the voice coil is given by

$$E = Bl\dot{x} \qquad (6.5)$$

where E = open-circuit voltage, V
     B = air-gap flux density, Wb/m^2
     l = length of conductor in air gap, m
     $\dot{x}$ = velocity of coil, m/s

This shows that the microphone will have uniform E with respect to frequency if the coil velocity is uniform with frequency. The mechanical resonance of the coil and diaphragm (measured in a vacuum) is about 800 Hz. If the resonance is not well damped, the coil velocity will peak at 800 Hz. This resonance is heavily damped by the acoustic resistance of the felt damping ring so that the resulting response is uniform from 40 to 20,000 Hz. The coil motion is then said to be resistance-controlled. The case volume is sufficient to support this extended low-frequency response. In older microphones, it was necessary to add a vent tube inside the case, possibly as long as 4 in (10 cm). This provided a sort of bass-reflex action in which the mass of the air in the tube resonated with the compliance of the air in the case. This resulted in extended low-frequency response and was known as a Thuras tube, being incorporated in the famous Western Electric *eight-ball microphone,* which was developed in the 1930s by Wente and Thuras.[2]

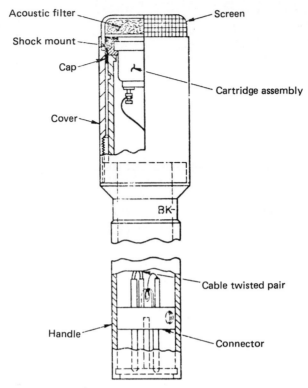

FIG. 6.11 Dynamic moving-coil microphone (RCA type BK-16A).

Inductor Microphone. Olson (Ref. 3, p. 263) shows the RCA design, now obsolete, in which a straight metal conductor is molded into a plastic diaphragm which positions the conductor in a magnetic air gap. These microphones were used in broadcasting and sound systems for many years, primarily for speech reproduction. They operated according to the acoustical principles of the moving-coil dynamic microphone described in the preceding section.

A new printed-ribbon microphone has been developed.[18] The moving system consists of a flat polyester film diaphragm with a printed-on spiral aluminum ribbon. It is different from the linear inductor microphone described above because the capsule operates according to the principle of the ribbon velocity microphone. The manufacturers state that the back of the capsule may be enclosed by a damped cavity to form an omnidirectional microphone. However, they do not presently offer a pressure-microphone version, and Ref. 18 does not mention it. Therefore, we choose to classify the printed-ribbon microphone as a pressure-gradient type (see Sec. 6.2).

Ribbon Pressure Microphone. The ribbon transducer is discussed in Sec. 6.2 because it is a pressure-gradient (particle-velocity-sensing) device. It is included in this section because an omnidirectional (pressure-sensing) ribbon microphone was developed by Olson in the 1950s (Ref. 3, p. 268) and is shown in Fig. 6.12.

The back of the ribbon transducer, which would be open to the atmosphere in a velocity (bidirectional) microphone, is terminated in an acoustic labyrinth. To save space, the labyrinth consists of a cylinder which has many holes drilled or cast in the axial direction. Slots are cut or cast between holes, thus forming a folded pipe which is much longer than the microphone itself. This damped pipe must present a constant acoustical resistance over the useful frequency range of the ribbon, so it is lightly packed with tufts of felt or ozite. The front side of the ribbon is terminated in a small pipe to form an unobtrusive interview-type microphone. The end of the pipe is flared to a horn shape which accentuates the response above 5000 Hz. This microphone was used for many years in television broadcasting but was replaced by dynamic moving-coil microphones.

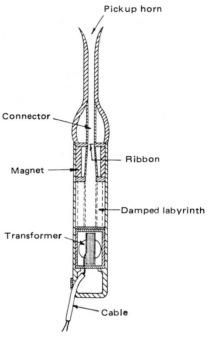

FIG. 6.12 Cross section of ribbon-type pressure microphone. *(From H. F. Olson,* Acoustical Engineering, *Van Nostrand, Princeton, N.J., 1957, pp. 271–275.)*

6.1.5 Magnetic Microphone

A magnetic microphone, shown in Fig. 6.13, consists of a diaphragm, drive pin, and magnetic assembly. The magnetic assembly includes a magnet, pole pieces, coil, and moving armature. The motion of the armature results in a corresponding variation in magnetic flux through the coil. This flux variation induces a voltage in the coil in accordance with Faraday's law:

$$E = -N \frac{d\phi}{dt} \qquad (6.6)$$

where E = open-circuit voltage, V
N = number of turns in coil
ϕ = flux in coil, Wb

Olson (Ref. 3, pp. 271–275) shows that $d\phi/dt$ is proportionate to $\dot{x}$, the velocity of the armature. As with the moving coil, flat-frequency response requires that the velocity be resistance-controlled. Therefore, the back of the cartridge of Fig. 6.13 must be enclosed and the cavity damped with acoustical resistance material.

6.1.6 Vacuum-Tube and Solid-State Electronic Microphones

Vacuum-Tube Microphone. The vacuum-tube microphone is an amplitude-sensing transducer which consists of a diaphragm and drive pin enclosed in a housing. It is a special vacuum tube, called the mechanoelectric transducer. The tube has a movable anode which modulates the flow of electrons. Olson (Ref. 3, pp. 271–275) shows the equations for the amplitude with respect to frequency. Owing

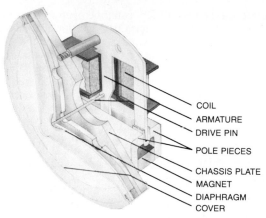

FIG. 6.13 Magnetic microphone. *(Courtesy of Shure Brothers, Inc.)*

COIL
ARMATURE
DRIVE PIN
POLE PIECES
CHASSIS PLATE
MAGNET
DIAPHRAGM
COVER

to the complicated mechanical network, uniform amplitude of diaphragm motion and flat-frequency response seem to have been difficult to obtain. This microphone was never developed as a commercial product.

Transistor and Semiconductor Microphones.   An experimental transistor microphone is described by Sikorski.[19] A sapphire indenter is fastened to the diaphragm and applies stress to the emitter region of the transistor. The output is taken from the collector, with suitable dc biasing of the transistor. The reason for the stress sensitivity of transistors is not easily explained. The frequency response of the microphone was very nonuniform. The output was adequate to drive an amplifier, but the signal-to-noise ratio was only about 40 dB. This microphone was not commercialized.

A semiconductor microphone was developed by Grover and Wood[20] and produced by Euphonics Corporation as a hand-held, close-talking communications microphone. The frequency response was smooth from 100 to 1000 Hz, then peaked at 2500 Hz. This microphone appears to have been intended as a carbon-microphone replacement. The semiconductor element was a twister silicon transducer element which was supplied by Endevco Corp. DC bias was applied to the element, which modulated the current flow. This was said to be a piezoresistive microphone.

A tunnel-diode microphone was developed by Rogers and associates.[21] This microphone functioned in two ways. First, it functioned as a piezoresistive element where the applied stress modulated the applied direct bias current. Second, by adding some inductors and capacitors, the diode was made to oscillate at about 30 MHz with FM audio modulation. However, the carrier frequency was subject to much drift.

The frequency responses of this microphone were wide-ranging, but there were many ragged peaks in the 1000- to 5000-Hz region. The signal-to-noise ratio was about 40 dB. This microphone has not been commercialized.

Integrated-Circuit Microphone.   In the piezoresistive microphone developed by Sank,[22] the transducer is a directly actuated strain-gauge deposited on a silicon chip. The chip was originally intended as a pressure transducer. This microphone is different from other solid-state microphones in that no diaphragm is used. As a result of this simple construction, it was possible to obtain a flat-frequency response from 20 to 20,000 Hz, comparable to that of a laboratory condenser microphone of a similar size (0.3 in, or 7.6 mm). The signal-to-noise ratio was not sufficient for even a close-talking microphone but was satisfactory for the intended application, which was headphone measurements. Presumably the maximum input sound-pressure-level capability was very high, but experiments along this line were not conducted. Development work was discontinued when the headphone measurements were completed. Presumably the chip could have been optimized for acoustic sensitivity. However, National Semiconductor, the manufacturer of the transducer, sold the product line, and this was another factor which slowed development work.

An interesting facet is that the military showed interest in the transducer because it has a symmetrical, low-impedance, balanced electrical output. This is important in military aircraft, which have much electromagnetic and RF interference. The military was opposed to electrets because of the high-impedance unbalanced circuitry involved, plus potential humidity and temperature problems. The silicon pressure transducers are designed to resist liquids and have a wide temperature range.

6.2 PRESSURE-GRADIENT (VELOCITY) MICROPHONES

6.2.1 Bidirectional Ribbon Microphone

A sectional view of a ribbon velocity microphone (RCA type BK-11A) developed by Sank and described by Olson[23] is shown in Fig. 6.14. This microphone has an air gap 0.125 in (3.2 mm) wide with a flux density of 6500 G (0.65 Wb/m²). The ribbon is made of pure aluminum foil weighing 0.56 mg/cm². This corresponds to a thickness of 0.000082 in (2 μm). The ribbon is 1.4 in (36 mm) long and corrugated transversely, as shown. Magnetic fine-mesh steel screens are on both sides of the ribbon to provide resistance damping of the ribbon and dirt protection. The ribbon resonance is approximately 30 Hz. The ribbon is soldered to the clamp after assembly and tuning. Soldering has no effect on tuning when done properly. Without soldering, in several years microphone impedance may rise and eventually result in an open circuit at the ribbon. The 0.2-Ω ribbon impedance is stepped up to 30/150/250 Ω by the transformer. The reactor and switch provide low-frequency rolloff for the proximity effect. The frequency response is $\pm$ 2 dB, 30 to 15,000 Hz. Olson shows an L-R equalizer which provides about 3 dB boost at 10,000 Hz with corresponding reduction in sensitivity.

The elements of the complete equivalent mechanical circuit (Fig. 6-14) are R_L and M_L, the mechanical resistance and mass of the air load on the ribbon, imposed by the damping screens; M_R and C_R, the mass and compliance of the ribbon; and M_S and R_S, the mass and mechanical resistance of the slits formed by the ribbon to pole-piece clearance, which is nominally 0.005 in (125 μm). Above resonance, the circuit is simplified as shown, and the ribbon velocity is given by

$$\dot{x} = \frac{(P_1 - P_2)A_R}{j\omega\,(M_R + M_L)} \tag{6.7}$$

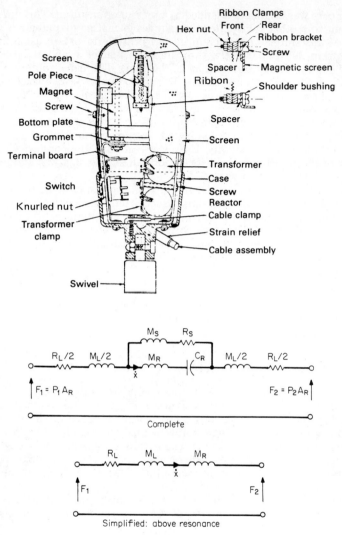

FIG. 6.14   Ribbon velocity microphone (RCA type BK-11A) and mechanical networks.

where $\dot{x}$ = ribbon velocity, m/s

$(P_1 - P_2)$ = difference in sound pressure (pressure gradient) between two sides of ribbon, N/m²

A_R = area of ribbon, m²

M_R = mass of ribbon, kg

M_L = mass of air load acting on ribbon, kg

$\omega = 2\pi f$

f = frequency, Hz

The driving sound pressure gradient $(P_1 - P_2)$ at a given frequency is proportional to the size of the baffle formed by the magnet structure. The ribbon-to-pole-piece clearance forms a *leak* which, if excessive, will reduce sensitivity. To maintain a constant ribbon velocity with mass control per Eq. (6.7), the pressure gradient must increase linearly with frequency. The open-circuit ribbon voltage is given by

$$E = Bl\dot{x} \tag{6.8}$$

where E = open-circuit voltage, V
  B = air-gap flux density, Wb/m^2
  l = length of ribbon, m
  $\dot{x}$ = ribbon velocity, m/s

At zero frequency the pressure gradient is zero. At the frequency where the path length around the baffle, from the front to back of the ribbon, corresponds to one-half of the sound wavelength, the pressure gradient departs from a linear characteristic to 65 percent of the value needed for a constant ribbon velocity. At the frequency where the path length equals one wavelength, the pressure gradient is zero. Figure 6.15 shows the resulting E versus frequency for an ideal microphone, applicable to the region well above ribbon resonance. A practical microphone may have small ripples in response in the region just above resonance frequency, plus dips or peaks at high frequencies due to pole-piece shape or transverse resonances of the ribbon.

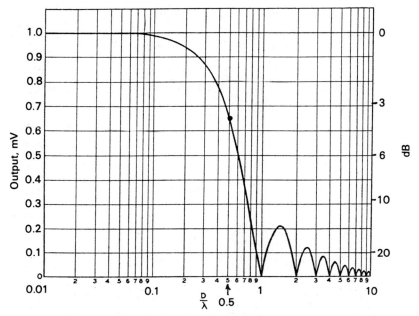

FIG. 6.15 Computed open-circuit voltage response frequency characteristic of a pressure-gradient mass-controlled electrodynamic microphone. [*From H. F. Olson, "Ribbon Velocity Microphones,"* J. Audio Eng. Soc., *18, 263–268 (June 1970).*]

Figure 6.16 shows how the figure-of-eight polar pattern becomes severely distorted above the half-wavelength frequency (D equals the path length). Below this frequency, the patterns are essentially perfect cosines. Olson describes a microphone built for measuring loudspeakers that has essentially uniform response and directivity from 20 to 20,000 Hz. He notes that the pattern in the vertical plane at high frequencies shows some sharpening, but this is not a serious problem for pickup of sound sources in the horizontal plane. A pressure condenser microphone of analogous quality must be less than 0.5 in (12.5 mm) in diameter. Unfortunately, for sound reproduction purposes the sensitivity of both of these is too low.

A compromise solution is found in the contemporary ribbon velocity microphone (Beyer M130). The head diameter is only 1.5 in (38 mm). The magnetic assembly is extremely small but efficient. The two ribbons are electrically in parallel and make use of most of the space and magnetic flux available in the air gap. They are corrugated longitudinally for most of their length, but a few conventional transverse corrugations are formed near the ends to provide compliance. This type of ribbon, while very difficult to make, can potentially solve several problems as compared with the conventional ribbons with transverse corrugations: (1) The rigid central portion resists twisting, sagging, and scraping along the pole pieces. (2) With the more rigid ribbon, the pole-piece-to-ribbon clearance may be reduced, thus increasing sensitivity. (3) The short length of transverse corrugations may reduce the need for laborious manual stretching and tuning and may greatly reduce the downward drift of tuning with time. (4) The longitudinal corrugations may reduce or eliminate transverse resonances, which produce small dips and peaks in frequency response above 8000 Hz. (5) The short length of the ribbon makes the polar pattern in the vertical plane more uniform with frequency.

How much sensitivity is adequate for an electrodynamic microphone? This is easy to calculate by first assuming that the microphone impedance is 250 Ω, resis-

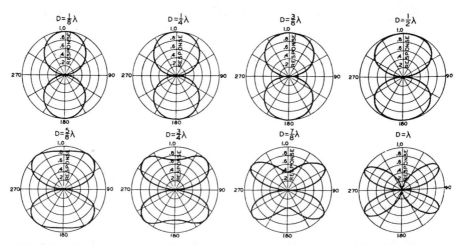

FIG. 6.16   Directional characteristics of a pressure-gradient microphone as a function of dimensions and wavelength. The polar graph depicts output, in volts, as a function of angle, in degrees. The maximum response is arbitrarily chosen as unity. [*From H. F. Olson, "Ribbon Velocity Microphones,"* J. Audio Eng. Soc., *18, 263–268 (June 1970).*]

tive. The value of 250 Ω is handy because the dBm sensitivity rating is equal *numerically* to the dBV rating. The dBm rating is the power output level in decibels with respect to 1 mW that would theoretically be obtained if the microphone were operated into a matched load with a sound pressure input of 1 Pa (94-dB sound pressure level, or SPL) (1 N/m^2). Similarly, the dBV rating is the open-circuit voltage of the microphone in decibels with respect to 1 V with a sound pressure input of 1 Pa. The latter rating corresponds to the real world, where microphones are operated into a relatively high impedance. Sank[24] discusses microphone ratings and measurements.

The thermal noise of a 250-Ω resistor in a 15,000-Hz bandwidth is calculated by Sank[25] to be −132 dBV. A typial noise figure for a modern solid-state mixer is 4 dB, which means an equivalent input noise voltage of −128 dBV. Therefore for a 250-Ω electrodynamic microphone, the mixer noise exceeds the microphone noise. A good condenser microphone (Shure SM-81) has an *unweighted* equivalent noise level of 26 dB SPL, with the A-weighted value of 16 dB. If we demand similar performance from an electrodynamic microphone, let −128 dBV equal the microphone output for a 26-dB SPL input. The output (sensitivity rating) at 1 Pa (94 dB) will therefore be −60 dBV.

Olson's ideal microphone had a sensitivity of −74 dBV/Pa, which is obviously much too low. The RCA BK-11A microphone has a sensitivity of −56 dBPa, which is more than adequate. The Beyer M130 sensitivity of −59 dB/Pa is minimal but adequate.

Most ribbon microphones have low magnetic-hum sensitivity because the ribbon circuit is easily designed to be *hum-bucking*. Ribbon microphones have the lowest vibration sensitivity because the moving mass is very low. (The printed ribbon of the following section may have high vibration sensitivity because of the relatively massive diaphragm.) Wind sensitivity of all microphones, as Olson stated on many occasions, is "proportional to electroacoustical sensitivity," so ribbon microphones, contrary to popular belief, are not inherently wind-sensitive. To the contrary, microphones such as the RCA BK-5B and Beyer M500 incorporate efficient blast filters. The latter microphone, with its accessory foam screen, resists popping by very close and loud vocalists. Most of the catastrophic ribbon failures observed by the author seem to have been caused by the checking of microphones or lines with ohmmeters or continuity checkers. Connecting a ribbon microphone to a condenser-microphone line with A-B powering can also produce the same effect: the ribbon is blasted out of the gap.

6.2.2 Printed-Ribbon Microphone

A new type of inductor microphone has been developed which is called a *printed-ribbon* type[18] The diaphragm is made of 0.0002-in (4-μm) polyester film upon which is printed a spiral ribbon of aluminum 0.0008 in (20 μm) thick. The unconventional magnetic structure includes two ring magnets in front of the diaphragm and two in the back. Like poles face each other, so the magnetic lines of force lie parallel to the diaphragm. Thus axial motion of the diaphragm causes the ribbon to cut lines of force, which induces a voltage in the ribbon, according to Eq. (6.6). The magnetic structure is symmetrical on both sides of the diaphragm, so that the transducer capsule operates according to the principle of the velocity microphone (Sec. 6.2.1). This requires a mass-controlled transducer with the resonance at the lower end of the useful frequency range. The printed-ribbon diaphragm resonance is in the region of 50 to 100 Hz. The resonance cannot be as low as for a ribbon because of the relatively high stiffness of the diaphragm. Therefore, the response of the printed-ribbon microphone is somewhat limited at low frequencies. Bidirectional and unidirectional types are available, and the frequency responses are generally uniform from 70 to 15,000 Hz. Sensitivity of the bidirectional model is quite high, -52 dBV/Pa, but this value is somewhat inflated owing to the 600-Ω impedance. These microphones are recommended for voice and pickup of individual musical instruments.

6.3 COMBINATION PRESSURE AND PRESSURE-GRADIENT MICROPHONES

6.3.1 Unidirectional-Microphone Operating Principles

Combining the Polar Patterns.   Figure 6.17 illustrates graphically how the outputs of a bidirectional and a nondirectional microphone transducer may be mixed to obtain three unidirectional polar patterns. Actually, there are an infinite number of unidirectional patterns which may be obtained. The three patterns shown are hypercardioid, cardioid, and limaçon, from left to right. The energy responses to random sounds (such as room noise and reverberant sound) are also shown relative to the nondirectional, which is assigned a value of unity. Note that the bidirectional and the cardioid have exactly the same response, but the hypercardioid is superior to both of them in discrimination against random sound. Quite a few unidirectional microphones produced today are hypercardioids, but the cardioid remains the most popular. The limaçon is not as popular, and so to obtain this pattern a microphone with variable directivity is needed. An alternate way to obtain a unidirectional pattern is by using a single transducer with an appropriate

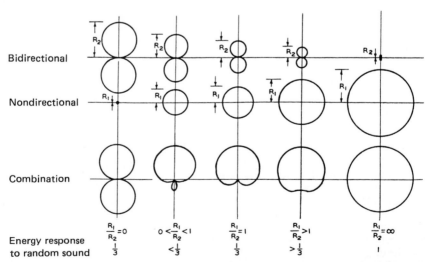

FIG. 6.17   Directional diagrams of various combinations of bidirectional and nondirectional microphones and energy response to random sounds.   *(From H. F. Olson,* Acoustical Engineering, *Van Nostrand, Princeton, N.J., 1957, pp. 293–297.)*

acoustical phase-shifting system. Some single-transducer microphones have a mechanically variable delay system so that the pattern can be varied from bidirectional to cardioid to nondirectional.

Frequency Response as a Function of Distance. The low-frequency response of the velocity microphone is accentuated when the distance between source and microphone is less than a wavelength. This happens to a lesser degree with the unidirectional microphone. Olson (Ref. 3, pp. 293–297) shows the equations. Figure 6.18 shows Olson's curves for velocity and unidirectional microphones. If the curves for 0° are plotted to a decibel scale, it turns out that the slopes follow linear 6-dB-per-octave characteristics. The unidirectional curves exhibit a corner (+3-dB) frequency which is one octave higher than those of the velocity microphone.

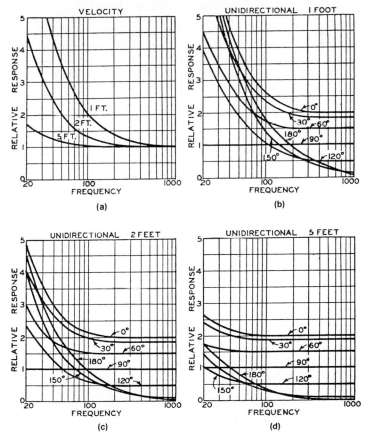

FIG. 6.18 (*a*) Relative voltage output of a velocity (or pressure-gradient) microphone as compared with a nondirectional pressure microphone for distances of 1, 2, and 5 ft (0.3, 0.6, and 1.5 m). (*b*)–(*d*) Relative voltage output of a unidirectional microphone as compared with a nondirectional pressure microphone for distances of 1, 2, and 5 ft (0.3, 0.6, and 1.5 m) and for various angles of incident sound. *(From H. F. Olson,* Acoustical Engineering, *Van Nostrand, Princeton, N.J., 1957, pp. 293–297.)*

The +3-dB frequencies rise one octave when the distance is halved. Therefore, for each distance a simple resistance-capacitance rolloff equalizer can be designed to provide flat response. This so-called proximity effect pertains to all pressure-gradient (velocity) and combination pressure and pressure-gradient (unidirectional cardioid) microphones to the same degree. These characteristics are essentially invariant between models of microphones. The exception to these rules is the variable-distance unidirectional microphone, which has a reduced proximity effect.

6.3.2 Dual-Element Unidirectional Microphones

Dual-Ribbon Unidirectional Microphone. The dual-ribbon unidirectional microphone (RCA type 77-B) was developed by Olson (Ref. 3, p. 291) and is shown in Fig. 6.19. A common magnet structure is employed for both velocity and pressure sections. The ribbons for both sections are formed from one continuous ribbon. Therefore the air-gap and ribbon dimensions and the flux density are identical for both sections. A very long folded pipe provides nearly constant acoustical resistance versus frequency to the pressure ribbon. This microphone

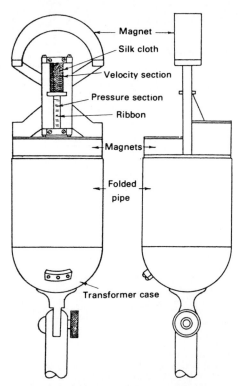

FIG.   6.19 Unidirectional microphone with screen removed; ribbon-type pressure and velocity elements.

had a fixed cardioid pattern. It was superseded by the polydirectional type 77-D, and the later model 77-DX is still in use today.

Ribbon and Moving-Coil Polydirectional Microphone. Figure 6.20 shows the Western Electric 639B microphone. The switch provides six mixing ratios of the outputs of the transducer units and six polar patterns: bidirectional, nondirectional, two cardioid patterns, and two hypercardioid patterns.[26] According to Olson, electric equalizers are incorporated to correct the amplitude and phase of the dynamic element to equal that of the velocity element.

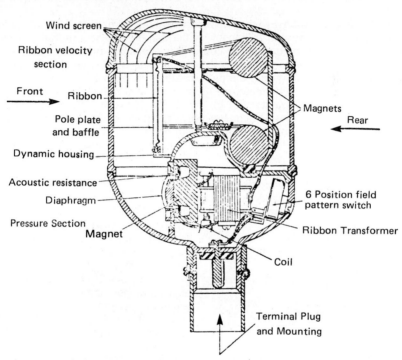

FIG. 6.20 Ribbon and moving-coil unidirectional microphone (Western Electric 639B). *(From H. Tremaine,* Audio Cyclopedia, *Howard W. Sams, Indianapolis, 1969, pp. 223–224.)*

Dual-Diaphragm Condenser Polydirectional Microphone. Eargle[27] gives a complete explanation of the workings of the dual-diaphragm polydirectional microphone transducer. This basic scheme is used in nearly all dual-diaphragm microphones. The vibrating system consists of two diaphragms, each spaced a small distance from the backplate, as in the pressure microphones of Sec. 6.1.3. The space behind each diaphragm provides acoustical resistance damping as well as acoustical capacitance (stiffness). The cavities behind the diaphragms are interconnected by small holes in the backplate. The phase shift in this system plus the variable electrical polarizing system make possible a variety of directional patterns.

With switch position 1, the diaphragms are oppositely polarized, and the transducer has a bidirectional pattern. This may be deduced by observing that sound incident at 90° or 270° will produce equal but oppositely phased outputs from each diaphragm, and thus the net voltage output is a null.

With the switch at position 5, the diaphragms are similarly polarized and the outputs are in phase at all angles of incidence, resulting in an omnidirectional pattern. At intermediate switch settings, a variety of unidirectional patterns are obtained. Note that at switch setting 3 a cardioid pattern is obtained with maximum polarizing voltage E_0 on the front diaphragm and 0 V on the back diaphragm. The unenergized diaphragm and the acoustical capacitance and resistance of the backplate form a phase-shift network similar to the rear sound aperture of a single-element unidirectional microphone, to be discussed in Sec. 6.3.3.

The frequency response of the polydirectional microphone will be flat, and the polar pattern uniform with frequency, if the diaphragms are carefully matched and the resistance elements are the controlling acoustical impedances. As in the case of the velocity microphone, acoustical characteristics deteriorate as the frequency approaches that where the path length from front to back approaches a wavelength of sound. A diameter of 0.5 in (12.5 mm) maximum is required for uniform directional characteristics to 15,000 Hz. However, the axial frequency response of a 1-in- (25-mm-) diameter polydirectional microphone can be made uniform to 20,000 Hz, so some uniformity of polar pattern is often traded for the higher sensitivity and lower noise level obtained with the larger-diaphragm transducers.

Twin-Cardioid-Element Polydirectional Condenser Microphone. The dual-diaphragm polydirectional condenser microphone may be thought of as a superposition of two single-diaphragm cardioid microphones (Sec. 6.33) back to back. Figure 6.21 shows how two cardioid capsules placed back to back will function as a polydirectional microphone. As in the case of the dual-diaphragm transducer, the front transducer has maximum polarizing voltage E_0 at all times and maintains cardioid response with maximum sensitivity. The voltage on the rear transducer is varied down to zero and up to $+E_0$, the same as in the dual-diaphragm transducer. The same polar patterns are obtained. Likewise, the same effect can be obtained by mixing the individual audio outputs in the various amplitude ratios and polarities.

This polydirectional microphone obviously has the most uniform acoustical properties in the cardioid mode because only one transducer is involved. In the other modes, the spacing between capsules, which may be 0.4 to 1.2 in (10 to 30 mm), comes into play, and the polar characteristics at high frequencies become nonuniform.

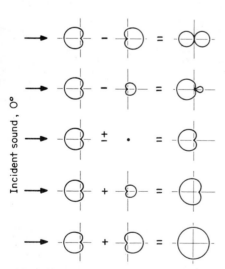

Incident sound, 0°

FIG. 6.21 Condenser polydirectional microphone using two cardioid transducers back to back. *(Adapted from J. Eargle,* The Microphone Handbook, *Elar Publishing, Plainview, N.Y., 1981.)*

6.3.3   Single-Element Unidirectional Microphones

Ribbon Polydirectional Microphone.   A single-element ribbon polydirectional microphone (RCA type 77-DX) is shown in Fig. 6.22. The ribbon is located between the pole pieces of a relatively large horseshoe magnet. The flux density is 13,000 G (13 Wb/m^2), which results in high sensitivity in all modes of operation. The vertical tube behind the magnet leads to a damped pipe (acoustic line) in the central body of the microphone. The acoustic line has a developed length of about 3 ft (1 m) and is lightly packed with ozite so as to provide a constant acoustical resistance to the ribbon over a wide frequency range. The vertical connector tube is D-shaped in cross section and has a long, narrow slot which opens to the rear. This slot is covered with an organdy screen, which is inside the tube. The rotary shutter varies the effective size of the slot or rear sound opening. This provides six polar patterns by means of a detent, but the actual number of available patterns is infinite. The shutter is shown at the bidirectional setting with the slot fully uncovered. When the shutter is rotated 60° counterclockwise, the slot is fully covered and a nondirectional pattern is obtained. An additional 60° rotation results in the slot's being about 10 percent uncovered, which yields a cardioid pattern.

The simplified acoustical equivalent circuit of the microphone (Fig. 6.22) consists of the following elements:

M_R = inertance (acoustical mass) of ribbon plus air load on ribbon

R_L = acoustical resistance of air load on ribbon

M_s = inertance of air in slot, including screens

R_s = acoustical resistance of air in slot, including screens

R_p = acoustical resistance of acoustic line

p_1 = front sound pressure

p_2 = rear sound pressure

The circuit applies to the frequency range above ribbon resonance, where the acoustical capacitative reactance of the ribbon is negligible. When the shutter fully uncovers the slot, the impedance of $(M_s + R_s)$ becomes very small and short-circuits R_p. Then the circuit becomes that of a pressure-gradient (velocity) microphone. The quantity $(p_1 - p_2)$ is the input pressure gradient. The acoustical circuit impedance is that of the ribbon plus air load and is inductive or mass-controlled. This results in a constant volume current U in $(M_R + R_L)$, constant ribbon velocity versus frequency, and uniform ribbon output voltage (Sec. 6.2.1). The polar pattern is bidirectional or figure-of-eight.

With the shutter fully closed, the impedance of $(M_s + R_s)$ becomes very large; so p_2 no longer drives the ribbon circuit. The acoustic line resistance R_p is large compared with the impedance of $(M_R + R_L)$; so the volume current U is given by

$$U = \frac{p_1}{R_p} \tag{6.9}$$

This means that the microphone is pressure-responsive and has a nondirectional polar pattern.

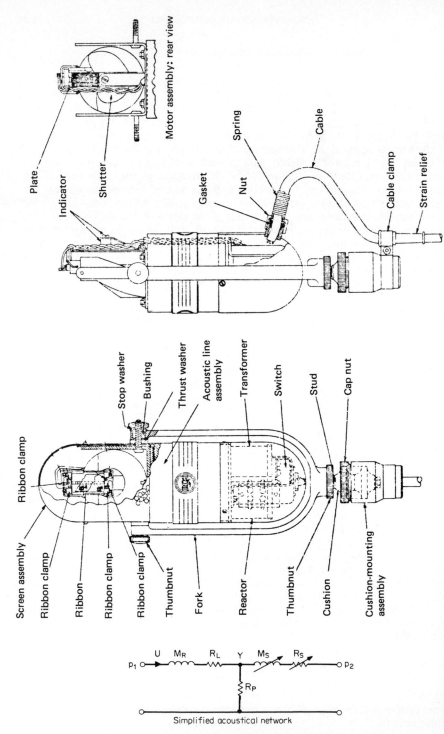

Motor assembly: rear view

Plate

Indicator

Shutter

Spring

Cable

Gasket

Nut

Cable clamp

Strain relief

Stop washer

Bushing

Thrust washer

Acoustic line assembly

Transformer

Switch

Stud

Cap nut

Ribbon clamp

Screen assembly

Ribbon clamp

Ribbon

Ribbon clamp

Ribbon clamp

Thumbnut

Fork

Reactor

Thumbnut

Cushion

Cushion-mounting assembly

$$p_1 \quad \xrightarrow{U} \quad M_R \quad R_L \quad Y \quad M_S \quad R_S \quad p_2$$

$$R_P$$

Simplified acoustical network

FIG. 6.22 Ribbon polydirectional microphone and acoustical network (RCA type 77-DX).

With the shutter set for a cardioid pattern, part of the ribbon volume current U flows through R_p and part through $(M_s + R_s)$. Thus the ribbon is partly controlled by P_1 and the line resistance R_p and is pressure-responsive. The balance of the ribbon volume current U flows through $(M_s + R_s)$; so the transducer is partly velocity-responsive. The shutter setting for a cardioid pattern is at a critical point where the phase shift through $(M_s + R_s)$ is such that sound incident from 180° arrives at point Y somewhat delayed in time so as to match the phase of sound at p_1. Thus $U = 0$, a null in response occurs at 180°, and a cardioid pattern is obtained. This is the principle by which all single-element unidirectional electrodynamic microphones operate.

Three additional directional patterns are detent-selectable. The axial frequency response at the cardioid setting is reasonably flat from 30 to 15,000 Hz. The response at the bidirectional setting slopes downward with frequency, whereas the response at the nondirectional setting slopes upward. This is a limitation of the ribbon polydirectional microphone.

Unidirectional Ribbon Microphone.   The *uniaxial* microphone (RCA type BK-5B) developed by Olson (Reg. 3, pp. 303–305) is shown in Fig. 6.23. The operation is similar to that of the polydirectional ribbon microphone with unidirectional setting. The ribbon (M_R, C_{AR}) is positioned between the pole pieces of a magnet structure which develops about 11,000 G (11 Wb/m^2) in the air gap. The lobes and screens $(M_{B1}, r_{AB1}, M_{B1}, r_{AB1})$ form a blast filter. The damped holes $(M_2, r_{A2}, M_{2s}, r_{A2s})$ provide the principal phase-shift elements for sound pressure p_2. Sound pressure p_1 is the frontal incident sound pressure; p_3 and associated elements form a third phase-shift network which sharpens the polar pattern so that the 90° response is -8 dB instead of -6 dB as in a cardioid. Therefore, the BK-5B has lower response to random sounds than a cardioid or a hypercardioid.

The simplified acoustical network of Fig. 6.23 illustrates the principle of operation in the frequency range above ribbon resonance. M_R and r_{AR} are the ribbon inertance and air-load resistance, r_{AP} is the acoustical resistance of the damped pipe, and R_s and M_s are the acoustical resistance and inertance of the damped holes. Therefore, the simplified circuit is exactly the same as Fig. 6.23, and so the basic operating principle of the unidirectional ribbon microphone is the same as that of the polydirectional microphone in the unidirectional mode.

Unidirectional Condenser Microphone.   The unidirectional condenser microphone is a relatively recent invention. An early patent is Olson's directional electrostatic microphone.[8] A modern high-quality microphone is described by Schulein and Seeler[11]. This is pictured in Fig. 6.24a. It is a prepolarized capsule where the electret is on the backplate. The construction of the diaphragm and backplate was described previously (Sec. 6.1.3). The unidirectional capsule backplate has holes which communicate through an acoustic resistance screen into the case volume (normally having a closed bottom end) and to the atmosphere through resistance screens and rear entry ports.

The operation of the microphone of Fig. 6.24b may be determined from a consideration of the simplified mechanical network. M_D and C_D are the mass and compliance of the diaphragm. R_1 is the resistance of the air film between diaphragm and backplate, R_3 is the resistance of the screen which connects to the case volume C_3, R_2 and M_2 represent the holes and screens at the rear sound entry. (This simplified network is from Ref. 8, whereas the microphone of Ref. 11 has a more complex network.)

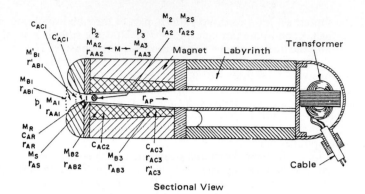

Sectional View

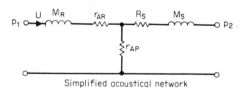

Acoustical network

Simplified acoustical network

FIG. 6.23 Unidirectional ribbon microphone. *(Adapted from H. F. Olson,* Acoustical Engineering, *Van Nostrand, Princeton, N.J., 1957, pp. 303–305.)*

The velocity $\dot{x}$ of the diaphragm is given by

$$\dot{x} = \frac{F_D}{Z_M} = \frac{j\omega \, KPA}{Z_M} \qquad (6.10)$$

where Z_M = mechanical impedance of vibrating system, mechanical ohms
F_D = force on diaphragm, N
K = transducer
P = sound pressure, N/m^2
A = area of diaphragm, m^2
$\omega = 2\pi f$
f = frequency, Hz

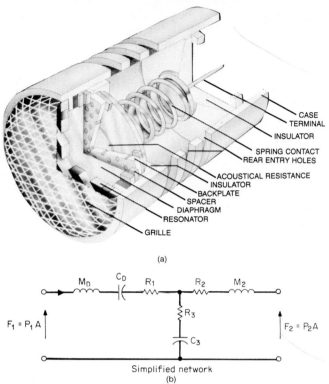

(a)

$$F_1 = P_1 A \qquad\qquad F_2 = P_2 A$$

Simplified network
(b)

FIG. 6.24 (a) Unidirectional condenser microphone. *(Courtesy of Shure Brothers, Inc.)* (b) Simplified mechanical network. *(From H. F. Olson, "Directional Electrostatic Microphone," U.S. Patent 3,007,012, Oct. 31, 1961.)*

and the displacement is given by

$$x = \frac{\dot{x}}{j\omega} = \frac{KPA}{Z_M} \tag{6.11}$$

The output voltage is given by Eq. (6.2).

Thus for the displacement (and output voltage) to be uniform with frequency, Z_M must be resistive. The resistance elements R_1, R_2, and R_3 are the controlling elements.

The phase-shift network R_2, M_2, R_3, and C_3 may take a variety of configurations similar to the various networks in ribbon and dynamic microphones. The operation of the phase-shift network in a unidirectional cardioid was described in Sec. 6.3.3.

Condenser Polydirectional Microphone. Figure 6.25 shows the microphone developed by Schoeps. It is physically symmetrical left to right. The diaphragm is centrally located between two backplates, which are perforated with holes. The mechanical assembly on the right slides left and right to provide three polar pat-

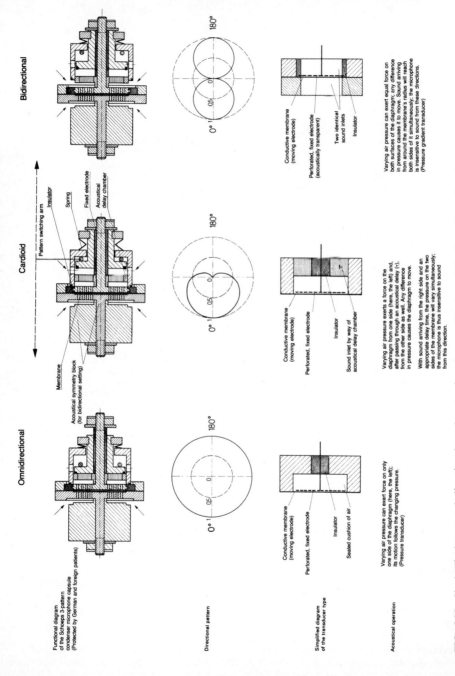

FIG. 6.25 Single-diaphragm polydirectional condenser microphone. *(Courtesy of Posthorn Recordings/ Schoeps.)*

terns. Note how the symmetry of the capsule favors a symmetrical figure-of-eight polar pattern.

When the actuating finger moves to the left, the cavity behind the diaphragm is sealed and becomes very small. The result is an omnidirectional pressure microphone where the moving system is stiffness-controlled (Sec. 6.1.3).

When the actuator moves to the right, the back of the diaphragm is open to the atmosphere and a figure-of-eight pattern results. For uniform amplitude of motion of the diaphragm, as in Sec. 6.3.3, the moving system is resistance-controlled by the perforated backplates.

When the actuator is centrally located, a phase-shift network is formed and rear entry ports provide the input to the phase-shift network. A cardioid pattern results, and the moving system is resistance-controlled.

Moving-Coil Unidirectional Microphone. Figure 6.26 shows the mechanical cross section and the acoustical network of the UNIDYNE unidirectional microphone developed by Bauer in 1941. All unidirectional moving-coil microphones which have one rear sound entry location follow these operating principles. The resonance of M_1 and C_{A1}, the diaphragm-and-coil-assembly inertance and acoustical capacitance, is at the low end of the usable audio-frequency range. Depending on the application of the microphone, this may be anywhere from approximately 70 to 140 Hz. As with the printed-ribbon transducer, the lowest attainable resonance is limited by the stiffness of the plastic-film diaphragm material.

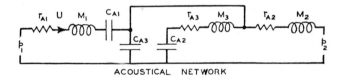

ACOUSTICAL NETWORK

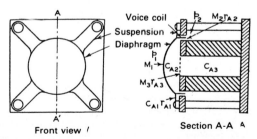

Front view

Section A-A

FIG. 6.26 Front view, sectional view, and acoustical network of UNIDYNE unidirectional microphone. In the acoustic circuit, M_1, r_{A1}, and C_{A1} = inertance, acoustical resistance, and acoustical capacitance of the diaphragm and suspension system; M_2 and r_{A2} = inertance and acoustical resistance of the slit between voice coil and pole; C_{A2} = acoustical capacitance of the air space between diaphragm and pole; M_3 and r_{A3} = inertance and acoustical resistance of the silk cloth; C_{A3} = acoustical capacitance of the air space in the magnet; p_1 = pressure at diaphragm: and p_2 = pressure at voice coil. *(From H. F. Olson,* Acoustical Engineering, *Van Nostrand, Princeton, N.J., 1957, pp. 305–307.)*

The moving-coil system is mass-controlled above resonance as in the ribbon transducer. Therefore, the difference in sound pressure between the two sides of the diaphragm must be proportional to frequency so as to maintain a constant volume current and a constant diaphragm and coil velocity throughout the useful audio-frequency range. This is done by selection of the parameter values of the phase-shift network. Also, the network values must provide for the correct delay time versus frequency such that a null is maintained at 180° for a cardioid pattern. Alternately, the network values may be adjusted for a hypercardioid pattern.

Variable-Distance Unidirectional Microphone. Figure 6.27 shows a sectional view and the acoustical network of the variable-distance unidirectional microphone. The distance from front to rear sound entry varies approximately inversely with frequency (Ref. 3, pp. 305–307). Sound pressure P_1 acts on the front of the diaphragm. Pressures P_2, P_3, and P_4 act on the back of the diaphragm through suitable acoustic impedance. P_2 acts in the high-frequency region, P_3 at middle frequencies, and P_4 at low frequencies. The advantage of this design is that

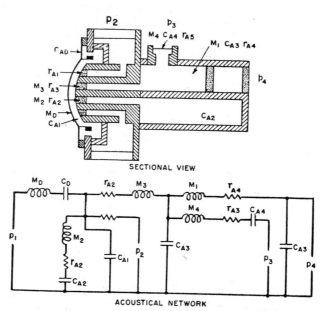

SECTIONAL VIEW

ACOUSTICAL NETWORK

FIG. 6.27 Sectional view and acoustical network of variable-distance microphone. p_1 = sound pressure on front of microphone; p_2, p_3, and p_4 = sound pressures acting at different parts on back of microphone; M_D = inertance due to mass of diaphragm: C_{AD} = acoustical capacitance of the diaphragm suspension system; C_{A1} = acoustical capacitance of volume back of the diaphragm; r_{A1} = acoustical resistance of the shortest path; M_4, C_{A4}, and r_{A5} = inertance, acoustical capacitance, and acoustical resistance of the diaphragm in the circuit of the medium path; M_1, M_3, C_{A3}, r_{A3}, and r_{A4} = inertances, acoustical capacitance, and acoustical resistances involved in the largest path; and M_2, r_{A2}, and C_{A2} = inertance, acoustical resistance, and acoustical capacitance in a side branch.

(From H. F. Olson, Acoustical Engineering, *Van Nostrand, Princeton, N.J., 1957, pp. 305–307.)*

accentuation of low frequencies due to the proximity effect is reduced. As with the UNIDYNE, the moving-system resonance is in the region of 100 Hz and is mass-controlled at higher frequencies.

6.4 ULTRADIRECTIONAL MICROPHONES

For the purpose of this discussion, an *ultradirectional microphone* is defined as one that has an energy response to random sound of less than 0.25, relative to an omnidirectional microphone, over a major portion of its useful audio-frequency range. According to Ref. 28, 0.25 is the random energy efficiency of a hypercardioid, which represents the highest directivity obtainable with a first-order gradient microphone. This category includes higher-order pressure-gradient microphones and wave-interference types of microphones. The applications of ultradirectional microphones include long-distance pickup of sound in the presence of random noise and/or reverberant sound or close talking in very-high-noise environments.

It should be noted that, of the many types of ultradirectional microphones developed since 1938, only the line-type microphone remains in common use today. It employs high-sensitivity condenser or moving-coil electrodynamic transducers.

6.4.1 Higher-Order Gradient Bidirectional Microphones

First-order pressure-gradient bidirectional microphones were described in Sec. 6.2.1. The polar pattern of the first-order gradient microphone has a cosine-squared pattern. The power of the cosine is the order of the gradient. Figure 6.28 shows a second-order bidirectional gradient microphone made up from two first-order bidirectional gradient units connected in phase opposition. The cosine-squared pattern of this microphone is shaded in Fig. 6.28. A family of cosine patterns is shown, beginning with order zero, which is the omnidirectional pattern.

The frequency response of a first-order gradient microphone with a mass-controlled moving system is uniform above the resonance frequency. The response of a similarly constructed second-order gradient microphone is proportional to frequency; that is, the response rises at 6 dB per octave. The response of a third-order gradient microphone rises at 12 dB per octave, and so forth. The useful frequency-response range of a second-order microphone extends to the frequency where the spacing d equals one wavelength, as is discussed in the next section.

The applications for higher-order bidirectional gradient microphones have been primarily limited to close-talking noise-canceling microphones. The random energy response of a gradient bidirectional microphone of order n is given by Ref. 3, pp. 312–328:

$$\text{Directional efficiency} = \frac{1}{2n + 1} \tag{6.12}$$

This equation applies when the source of sound is greater than n times a wavelength of sound from the microphone. An additional increase in discrimination against unwanted noise from distant sources occurs when the sound source is very close to the microphone. This is true because the low-frequency accentuation due to the proximity effect increases with the order number. Figure 6.28 shows an

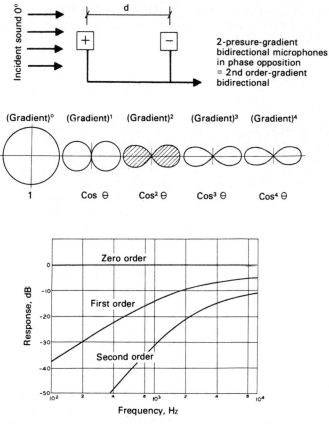

FIG. 6.28 Characteristics of higher-order gradient microphones. *(From H. F. Olson, Acoustical Engineering, Van Nostrand, Princeton, N.J., 1957, pp. 312–328.)*

example where the frequency responses of zero-, first-, and second-order microphones are compensated to be flat at a source distance of 0.75 in (19 mm). The graph shows the responses of these microphones to random sounds at a distance from the microphone. Thus the noise discrimination of a second-order microphone, relative to a pressure microphone, exceeds 30 dB at 100 Hz. This permits speech communications in very-high-noise environments. In most noisy environments, however, the first-order gradient microphone is satisfactory. Therefore, higher-order bidirectional gradient microphones are not in common use today. A novel second-order noise-canceling microphone employing a single diaphragm is found in Ref. 29.

6.4.2 Higher-Order Gradient Unidirectional Microphone

The higher-order bidirectional microphones described in the preceding section are undesirable for many applications where a unidirectional microphone is more suitable. Figure 6.29 shows that a second-order gradient unidirectional micro-

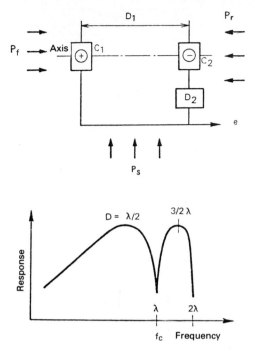

FIG. 6.29 Operating principles of a second-order gradient unidirectional microphone. *(From* Instruction Manual for SONY C-77 Telemicrophone.)

phone can be made from two cardioid elements connected in phase opposition, plus a delay network. The frequency response is proportional to frequency as shown, and the upper limit of the useful frequency range is the frequency where D equals one wavelength of sound. Figure 6.30 shows the experimental model of the second-order gradient uniaxial microphone commercialized briefly by RCA. This microphone was made from two uniaxial ribbon microphones (Fig. 6.23). It required carefully matched elements and was costly to make. The audio output was rather low when it was used at a distance from the source, and the transition to a cardioid polar pattern above 2000 Hz turned out to be a significant disadvantage compared with less costly line microphones with high-output dynamic or condenser transducers.

Beavers and Brown[30] developed a third-order gradient unidirectional microphone employing four condenser elements. The stated application was speech pickup. Woszczyk[28] reported experiments with spaced cardioid microphones where second-order unidirectionality was obtained to 200 Hz. The application was music recording.

6.4.3 Line Microphone

A simple line microphone is shown in Fig. 6.31. An acoustic line (pipe) with equally spaced sound openings along its entire length is connected to a pressure-microphone element. The transducer element may be of the electrostatic or elec-

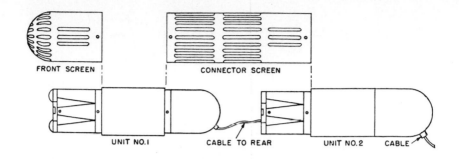

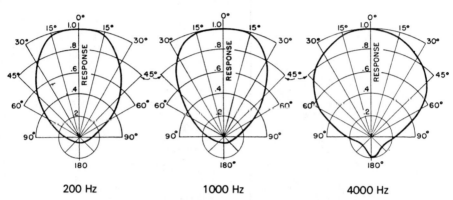

FIG. 6.30 Second-order gradient unidirectional microphone (RCA type BK-10A). *(From H. F. Olson,* Acoustical Engineering, *Van Nostrand, Princeton, N.J., 1957, pp. 312–328.)*

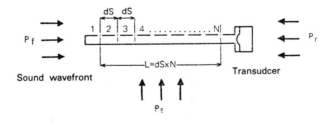

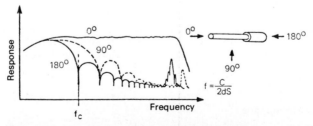

FIG. 6.31 Operating principles of the line microphone. *(From Instruction Manual for SONY C-77 Telemicrophone.)*

6.38

trodynamic varieties described previously. A high order of directivity is indicated by the frequency-response curves in the mid- and high-frequency region where the 90° and 180° responses are far below the 0° curve. The low-frequency limit of the useful range of ultradirectional characteristics is given by Ref. 31:

$$f_c = \frac{c}{2L} \tag{6.13}$$

where f_c = frequency, Hz
  c = velocity of sound = 331 m/s
  L = total length of line

The high-frequency limit of the ultradirectional region is determined by the hole spacing dS:

$$f_n = \frac{c}{2dS} \tag{6.14}$$

where dS is the hole spacing, m.

If f_c is chosen to be 100 Hz, then L must equal 65 in (1.66 m), which is too long for most practical applications. However, this requirement may be eased by substituting a pressure-gradient cardioid element. This provides good 180° rejection below f_c, and with careful optimization of parameters a microphone of practical length can have good rejection at 90°, well below f_c. It is relatively easy to achieve f_n = 10,000 Hz or higher with practical hole spacings.

Alternately, the line may consist of a bundle of small tubes of lengths which vary from dS to L in even steps of dS. Similarly, a single pipe with a series of slots may be used. With modern small-diaphragm condenser transducers, the single pipe is appropriate because the diameters of the tubes in a bundle would be so small that the acoustic resistance (viscosity) loss would reduce sensitivity and roll off the high-frequency response.

Olson[32,33] developed many types of line microphones in the late 1930s. These were generally complex, involving a lot of metal tubing. He obtained a variety of polar patterns, using pressure or pressure-gradient ribbon elements. His patents were voluminous. All modern line microphones utilize the technology developed by Olson prior to 1940, although they are much different in form and suited to today's applications. At the time RCA introduced television at the 1939 New York World's Fair, it was thought that a wide-frequency-range line microphone would be needed for long-distance pickup of voice or music. Olson developed a microphone which was 10 ft (3.05 m) long and employed five lines and five ribbon transducers covering contiguous frequency bands. It had sharp directivity down to 85 Hz.

The modern era in line microphones began in 1961, when Olson[8] patented the single-diaphragm condenser unidirectional microphone. M. Rettinger of RCA in Burbank, California, did the product design of the M1-10006A varidirectional microphone (Fig. 6.32a), which consisted of a bundle of plastic tubes attached to a cardioid condenser element based on Olson's patent. The novelty of the design was that the microphone could be changed to a cardioid by removing the pipes. This microphone was used for a time in motion-picture sound recording but reportedly suffered from electric impulse noise.

Concurrently, Electro-Voice introduced the model 642 and model 643 line microphones. Each used dynamic moving-coil cardioid transducers, which had large, heavy magnets and high sensitivity. The 642 employed a short line, only 12

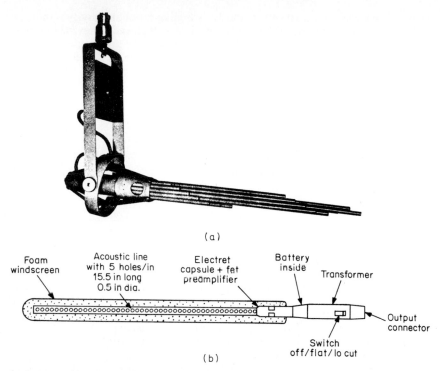

FIG. 6.32 Line microphones. (*a*) Bundled pipes (RCA type M1-10006A), varidirectional, air condenser. (*b*) Single pipe with holes (Nakamichi type CM700/CP703), electret condenser.

in (0.3 m) long, whereas the 643 was 6 ft (1.8 m) long. The 642 proved to be very popular for television and film recording and is still used today. The 643 was used for specialized applications such as presidential news conferences but is little seen today. The f_c of the 12-in (0.3-m) line is 552 Hz, but with the cardioid element plus low-frequency cutoff filters the 642 was satisfactory for voice pickup.

Figure 6.32*b* shows a modern electret condenser line microphone with a very-small-diameter line and a transducer capsule only 0.6 in (16 mm) in diameter. The capsule and line are made as an assembly which is interchangeable with standard cardioid and pressure elements. Although f_c is 420 Hz, 15-dB rejection is maintained at 90° down to 100 Hz, according to measurements by Sank.[34] The author has often used this microphone as a *direction finder* in outdoor studies where multiple sources are involved. The close spacing dS of holes in the line results in $f_n = 32,600$ Hz.

6.4.4 Combination Line and Gradient Microphone

Olson (Ref. 3, p. 319), in reference to his second-order gradient uniaxial microphone, stated: "Since operation shifts from the two microphones to the single microphone in the front in the high-frequency region, it would be a comparatively simple task to develop a microphone with a sharper directivity pattern in the high-frequency region for use as the front microphone if this appeared to be desirable."

Fourteen years later, Kishi and colleagues patented a microphone[31] which had three elements, instead of two as Olson suggested, but otherwise conformed to the idea of a second-order gradient microphone with improved high-frequency directivity. Figure 6.33 shows the principle of operation: a line microphone with a cardioid condenser capsule (Sec. 6.4.3) is combined with a second-order gradient unidirectional microphone having two cardioid condenser capsules. The line microphone operates above 1000 Hz, and the gradient microphone below 1000 Hz. The sensitivities of the transducers are balanced by adjustments in the FET preamplifiers in the microphone. Therefore, a high order of directivity is maintained over the entire audio-frequency range. This microphone was briefly commercialized by Sony as model C-77 telemicrophone.

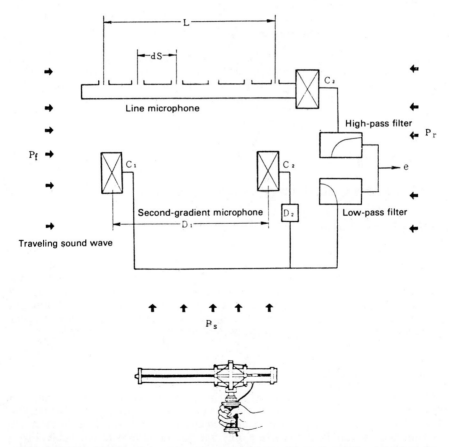

FIG. 6.33 Combination line and gradient microphone. (*From* Instructional Manual for SONY C-77 Telemicrophone.)

6.4.5 Parabolic Reflector Microphone

A parabolic reflector may be used to concentrate distant parallel rays of sound at a microphone placed at the focus (Fig. 6.34a). As in all wave-type microphones, the reflector must be large compared with a wavelength of sound to obtain a high order of directivity. Olson (Ref. 3, pp. 312–328) shows the polar patterns of a dish 3 ft (0.91 m) in diameter fitted with a pressure microphone.

6.4.6 Lens Microphone

An acoustic lens is a lenslike device made of sheet metal which can focus sound rays onto a microphone as the parabolic reflector does (Fig. 6.34b). The directivity follows the laws of wave-type microphones in much the same way as the parabola (Ref. 3, pp. 312–328).

6.4.7 Large-Surface Microphone

A large-surface microphone consisting of a large number of pressure-microphone elements arranged on a spherical surface is shown in Fig. 6.34c. Olson (Ref. 3, pp. 312–328) indicates that the polar pattern is similar to that of a curved-surface sound source, which emits uniformly over a solid angle subtended by the surface at the center of curvature. The microphone in Fig. 6.34c is 4 ft (1.22 m) in diameter and has an angular spread of 50°. The pattern is reasonably uniform above 300 Hz.

6.5 MISCELLANEOUS TYPES OF MICROPHONES

6.5.1 Stereophonic Condenser Microphone

A two-channel microphone such as the one shown in Fig. 6.35 is a convenient tool for sound pickup in the x–y or M–S stereophonic modes where coincident microphone transducers are required. The AKG C-422 utilizes two dual-diaphragm condenser transducers, which were described in Sec. 6.3.2. These are mounted on top of each other and in adjacent capsules sharing a common axis, and the capsules may be rotated with respect to each other. A remote-control unit permits any one of nine polar patterns to be selected for each channel.

6.5.2 Dual Microphone

This is a two-channel microphone similar to that in Sec. 6.5.1 except that both elements are oriented with coincident axes of maximum sensitivity. The purpose is to provide fully redundant microphones and two isolated output lines in television and film applications where only one microphone is to be visible. Figure 6.35b shows a dual microphone containing two ⅞-in- (2.2-cm-) diameter omnidirectional dynamic moving-coil transducer elements. In front of these elements is a cavity which is damped by a fine-mesh stainless-steel acoustic resistance

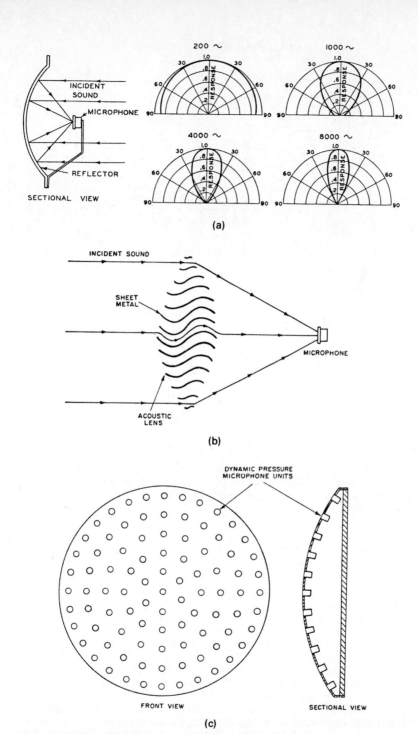

FIG. 6.34 Wave microphones. (*a*) Parabolic reflector. (*b*) Lens. (*c*) Large-surface. *(From H. F. Olson,* Acoustical Engineering, *Van Nostrand, Princeton, 1957, pp. 312–328.)*

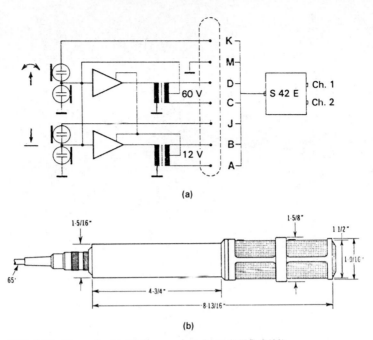

(a)

(b)

FIG. 6.35 Stereophonic condenser microphone (AKG-C422).

screen. The frequency response is designed to accentuate the region from 2000 to 6000 Hz for high-intelligibility voice reproduction. This microphone was designed by the author for the White House and was first used in the 1964 campaign of President Johnson. In that application, two microphones were used. One output of each was used for local sound reinforcement, and the other for television, film, and radio feeds.

Dual microphones are currently used on television news programs. These consist of two lavaliere microphones (see Sec. 6.5.5) mounted in one tie-clip holder. They provide functioning similar to the above but without a common housing and cable.

6.5.3 Sound-Field Microphone

The original sound-field microphone was developed for the *ambisonic* surround system patented by the United Kingdom National Research Corporation and was produced by Calrec Audio Limited. This system was a form of quadraphonic sound. As interest in quadraphonic sound waned, Calrec introduced a new version of the sound-field microphone which is essentially an electronically steerable stereophonic microphone. Four single-diaphragm cardioid condenser capsules are mounted in a tetrahedral array and connected to an electronic control unit. This unit permits selection of cardioid, figure-of-eight, and omnidirectional patterns for each stereo output. In addition, the sound pickup axes may be electronically steered in azimuth and elevation. By processing the pressure and pressure-gradient components of the audio signal, the microphone may apparently be moved fore and aft as the ratio of direct to reverberant sound is varied. The electronic steering may be done before or after the audio is recorded, allowing flexibility in the postproduction phase of sound recording.

6.5.4 Quadraphonic Microphone

Figure 6.36 shows two quadraphonic microphones developed by Yamamoto.[35] The ribbon version consists of four ribbons mounted at right angles to each other. These are apparently backed up by a common air volume and a common acoustic labyrinth which provides the resistive termination required for unidirectional polar pattrerns. Apparently this microphone was never constructed. The condenser version was constructed experimentally and consists of four cardioid condenser capsules, with pipes providing back-to-back acoustical communication between capsules.

Both the ribbon and the condenser versions include common air chambers behind the transducer elements, which essentially provide crosstalk between channels. The need for this feature is obscured by complex mathematics. The frequency response measured by Yamamoto on the condenser version extends to only 8000 Hz. This performance, plus the waning interest in quadriphony, may account for these microphones' not being commercialized.

6.5.5 Two-Way Dynamic Unidirectional Microphone

A two-way dynamic unidirectional microphone (AKG model D-202) was developed by Weingartner. His paper[36] describes a comprehensive study of acoustical networks of unidirectional dynamic microphones. He concluded that it would be difficult to manufacture a microphone with one transducer that would maintain uniform frequency response and polar pattern over the entire audio-frequency range. His solution was to divide the range at 500 Hz and use separate dynamic transducers for high and low frequencies. This resulting microphone has uniform frequency response and cardioid pattern from 30 to 15,000 Hz. According to the author, performance is comparable to that of a condenser microphone. The D-202 microphone is still in use today.

6.5.6 Lavaliere Microphone

This term refers to a small microphone which is fastened to the clothing or suspended by a lanyard around the neck. Olson, Preston, and Bleazey[37] described the application of personal microphones. They showed that a microphone mounted on the chest should have a rising high-frequency response to compensate for the loss in response due to its location off the axis of the mouth. Early models of lavaliere microphones were omnidirectional dynamic microphones which were suspended by a lanyard. Newer models include omnidirectional dynamic and electret microphones which are small and light in weight and are clipped to clothing. Very small electret condenser models available today utilize a subminiature element similar to that developed by Killion and Carlson.[5] They are light enough so that they may be fastened to the clothing by means of a small clip attached to the cable below the microphone. The flat-frequency response of

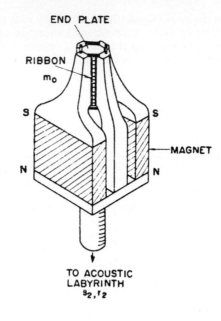

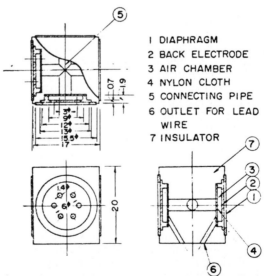

FIG. 6.36 Quadraphonic microphones. [*From T. Yamamoto, "Quadraphonic One Point Microphone," J. Audio Eng. Soc., **21**, 256–261 (May 1973).*]

these microphones requires high-frequency equalization when they are used on the chest.

The RCA BK-12A dynamic moving-coil lavaliere microphone was developed by the author. It has a 250-Ω coil, requires no output transformer, and is 0.75 in

(19 mm) in diameter by 1.5 in (38 mm) long. It clips onto the clothing, and the frequency response is acoustically equalized for use on the chest. The transducer cartridge is similar to that shown in Fig. 6.10. The microphone is designed to withstand a 6-ft (1.8-m) drop to a concrete floor and is virtually dirtproof and waterproof.

6.5.7 Wireless Microphone

VEGA model T87/R-42 uses a hand-held microphone with a built-in transmitter. This unit transmits on a very-high-frequency band to the receiver illustrated. The receiver audio is fed to the sound reinforcement, broadcast, or recording mixing console. Alternately, a *body-pack transmitter* may be used with an electret lavaliere microphone. These systems are widely used in television broadcasting and in professional entertainment. They are not as frequently used in schools and churches because of their high cost.

6.5.8 Automixer Microphone

This is a special microphone to be used with automatic mixing systems. Julstrom and Tichy[38] describe an automatic mixing system involving multiple microphones in which a particular microphone is gated on only when a talker is positioned in front of the microphone within ±60° of the microphone axis. Such microphones contain two cardioid electret condenser elements positioned back to back. The gating of the system is accomplished by measuring the ratio of the outputs of front and rear elements.

One model of the microphone (Shure AMS-22) contains two electret condenser elements placed very close to the table upon which the microphone is placed. This follows the principle of the boundary microphone described in Sec. 6.1.3. There is a more conventional style (Shure AMS-26) in which the two elements are contained in the elongated screen section.

6.5.9 Zoom Microphone

Ishigaki and associates[39] describe a microphone intended for use with video cameras which has variable directivity. The system has three unidirectional electret microphone units, and the polar pattern can be continuously varied from omnidirectional through cardioid to second-order gradient unidirectional. The directivity control is linked with the zoom lens control on the camera. The authors do not show a photograph or sketch of the experimental microphone.

6.5.10 Noise-Canceling Microphone

The Knowles BW-1789 subminiature electret noise-canceling microphone element is similar in construction to the pressure-sensing microphone developed by Killion and Carlson,[5] except that both sides of the diaphragm are open to the atmosphere as in a pressure-gradient velocity microphone. The cartridge in this microphone must be mounted in housing for use on a headset.

The far-field response to a distant sound source rises at 6 dB per octave because the displacement-sensing element is actuated by the pressure difference between the front and back sound openings, which rises with frequency. The near-field response, with a person speaking very close to the microphone, is uniform with frequency owing to the proximity effect of a velocity microphone being additive to the far-field response curve.

If the far-field sound sources are ambient noise, the noise-canceling effect is the difference between the near- and far-field curves. Therefore, the noise-canceling microphone is most effective in canceling low-frequency noise and is used in voice communications in commercial and military aircraft, spacecraft, and land mobile and marine applications. Dynamic moving-coil and magnetic transducers are used in these microphones, but the electret condenser is rapidly replacing many of these transducers. Carbon transducers were formerly used in noise-canceling microphones but are little used today. Styles of noise-canceling microphones include hand-held and stand-mounted types in addition to the boom-mounted headset models.

6.5.11   Conference Microphone

Figure 6.37 shows a teleconferencing microphone which was described by Snyder.[40] This microphone is currently being provided by Bell Telephone as part of its teleconferencing system. The microphone is placed at the center of a conference table and is claimed to provide uniform pickup of speech from all participants while rejecting reverberant sound and noise. The microphone consists of a vertical array of omnidirectional electret condenser elements which provide a 360° toroidal-shaped pickup pattern with maximum sensitivity in the plane of the talkers' mouths. The uneven spacing of the elements provides better rejection of sounds at 90° to the plane of maximum sensitivity.

Olson[32] describes a line microphone with a ribbon pressure element which has maximum sensitivity at right angles to the line axis and a toroidal pattern as shown in Fig. 6.37*a* and *b*. This line microphone is equivalent to a vertical array of pressure microphones, and so the theory developed by Olson applies to the teleconferencing microphone.

6.5.12   Hot-Wire Microphone

The hot-wire microphone consists of a fine wire which is heated by direct current and cooled by the alternating airflow of a sound wave. This causes a change in the electric resistance of the wire. The output waveform is twice the frequency of the sound wave because the wire is cooled by positive and negative particle velocities. Therefore, according to Olson (Ref. 3, pp. 329–331) it cannot be used for the reproduction of sound.

6.5.13   Throat Microphone

The throat microphone is described by Olson.[3] The carbon transducer is directly driven by contact with the throat. The acoustical impedance of the vibrating system is higher than for a microphone that is used in air because of the high acoustical impedance of the flesh of the throat. The high-frequency response of the microphone must be boosted to compensate for loss of high-frequency consonant

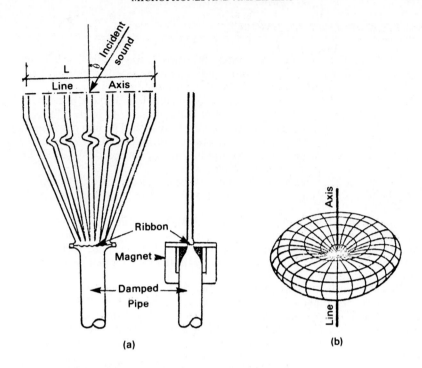

FIG. 6.37 Conference microphone. (*a*) Ribbon-line type. [*From H. F. Olson, "Line Microphones," Proc. IRE, 27 (July 1939).*] (*b*) Three-dimensional polar pattern of *a* at $L = 2\lambda$.

in passing through the throat. Other kinds of transducers may be used. The throat microphone was used in military aircraft in World War II but is now obsolete.

6.5.14 Ear Microphone

The ear microphone was introduced by Lear-Siegler for radio communications applications where the hands remain free. It is simply a magnetic earphone transducer used in reverse. The voice sound present in the ear canal misses much of the high-frequency consonant sounds, so a high-frequency boost in the amplifying system is required. The author heard a demonstration of a system, and speech was quite intelligible. An additional novelty of the system is that the transducer is used as an earphone as well, thus providing two-way communications.

6.5.15 Tooth Microphone

This was developed by Brouns[41] for providing improved intelligibility of speech from deep-sea divers who are breathing helium. It consists of a piezoelectric accelerometer fastened to a tooth. The author indicates that the microphone produces intelligible speech but reports considerable difficulty in having a wire protrude from the mouth. He recommends some form of telemetry to eliminate the hard wiring.

6.6 STEREOPHONIC TECHNIQUES*

Early acoustical recordings were made by using a single-point pickup system. Later, electrical recording made multiple-microphone pickup techniques possible and eventually encouraged the development of multichannel sound.

During the 1930s, researchers such as Alan Blumlein in the United Kingdom and Arthur Keller and Harvey Fletcher of Bell Laboratories in the United States independently experimented with stereo disk recording. The first commercial use of multichannel sound was the Disney Studios' production of *Fantasia* in 1940. Unfortunately for theaters that invested in this interlocked dual-system format, *Fantasia* was the only product released.

Various multichannel sound formats reappeared in the 1950s. Motion pictures were the first, followed soon by home consumer formats in tape, disk, and radio broadcast.

Initially, the 45-45 stereo disk was perceived as such a wonderful advance— and the corresponding product was in such short supply—that *anything* would sell. As more product became available and as listeners and their equipment became more sophisticated, the quality of these recordings came to be a factor influencing long-term sales.

Classical music is most often identified as being a long-term money-maker. However, a wide range of music from acoustical folk to Pink Floyd also fits that category. Sheffield Records' reintroduction of the direct-to-disk recording technique and Mobile Fidelity's Original Master series have shown that there is an enduring market for quality product. The discreet use of simple microphone techniques is often found among these long-term best-selling recordings.

Accurate stereo imaging is the foundation for the art of stereo recording. Experience with the basic techniques and knowledge of their attributes are essential for anyone working in stereo formats.

The *art* of recording lies in manipulating illusions. The *science* of recording involves the tools and techniques used to create these illusions.

This section is a review of the "how" of creating illusions in stereo. It describes the common stereo configurations which utilize two, three, and four microphones. It presents the placement and type of microphones used for each configuration and discusses their basic characteristics, advantages, and disadvantages. All the techniques discussed here have produced satisfying results. The use of a particular technique will depend on circumstances: the sound source, the recording environment, the desired effect, and the release format.

Some formats, for example, stereo cinema and broadcast, impose constraints, such as the need for a predictable mono-stereo relationship. Other formats have their own particular demands. The important thing is that the perspective be appropriate to the format, whether it be track building on a record album or the transience of a live broadcast. Creative use of the appropriate technique is the hallmark of the master of a craft.

6.6.1 Two-Microphone Coincident Techniques

Coincident or *intensity stereo* techniques are achieved with a pair of directional microphones, most often vertically aligned on a common axis and set at an angle

---

* Presented at the 2d AES International Conference, Anaheim, Calif., May 11–14, 1984.

to each other in the horizontal plane (Fig. 6.38). Thus there is minimum time (phase) difference between the two capsules for sound sources on the horizontal plane. Properly done, this style relies solely on intensity differences between the two signals for directional cues. The choice of the microphone pair's polar pattern can vary from subcardioid to bidirectional, depending on the specific technique being implemented. The angles formed by the microphone pair are typically symmetrical about the centerline of the sound source, and the included angles discussed in this section are the total angles between the axes of the microphones.

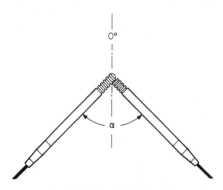

FIG. 6.38   Coincident *XY* microphone pair.

An advantage of intensity stereo is that the angular accuracy of the stereo imaging is unaffected by the distance of the microphone pair from the sound source. A disadvantage is that without the interchannel time delay common to some other miking techniques the stereo image sometimes seems to lack a *sense of space*.

XY Cardioids and Hypercardioids.   The microphone pair is typically set at an included angle of between 60 and 120°. The specific angle chosen determines the *apparent width* of the stereo image, and the choice of this angle is subjective, with consideration given to the distance of the microphone pair from the sound source, the actual width of that source, and the polar pattern of the microphones. A critical factor to consider when using these techniques is this polar response. As the individual microphones are oriented at an angle to most of the sound source, considerable off-axis coloration is possible. As with any stereo technique, the microphones comprising the pair should have as good a polar response as possible. Further, they should be closely matched with regard to polar and frequency response, since any differences will cause the image to wander with changes in pitch.

   1. *Cardioid microphone:*   Use of cardioid microphones is common in coincident techniques, typically with an included angle of 90 to 120° and placed fairly close to the sound source (Fig. 6.39). Often the axes of the microphones are aimed at a point near the extremes of the sound source. As the direct-to-reverberant-sound ratio of this approach is high, this can offer some rejection of unwanted sound from the rear of the pair. Sometimes a distant pickup with a large reverberation component is desired. In such circumstances, included angles as large as 180° may be employed.

   2. *Hypercardioid microphone:*   Using a hypercardioid pair is similar to using cardioids except that the included angle is typically narrower to preserve a solid center image (Fig. 6.40). The increased reach of the hypercardioid allows a more distant placement for a given direct-to-reverberant-sound ratio. With their small reverse-polarity lobes, using hypercardioids is a good compromise between implementing *XY* with cardioids and the Blumlein technique.

Blumlein.   The *crossed pair of figure of eights* is the earliest of the *XY* techniques and is configured with two bidirectional microphones oriented at an included

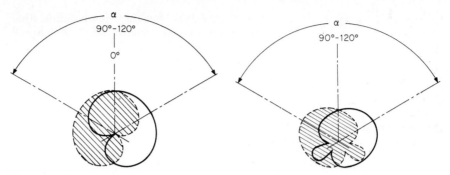

FIG. 6.39   *XY* cardioid pair.   FIG. 6.40   *XY* hypercardioid pair.

angle of 90° (Fig. 6.41). It was developed in the early 1930s by British scientist Alan Blumlein and was presented in his seminal patent.[42]

One attribute of this technique is that the rear lobes of these microphones record the rear 90° quadrant in phase but out of polarity and place this into the stereo image (cross-channeled) together with the front quadrant. Signals from the two side quadrants are picked up out of phase. Placement is therefore critical in order to maintain a proper direct-to-reverberant-sound ratio and to avoid strong out-of-phase components. Typically, this technique works very well in a wide room or one with minimal sidewall reflections, where strong signals are not presented to the side quadrants of the stereo pair. It is often commented that this configuration produces a very natural sound.

MS Stereo.   This form of intensity stereo—one variation of which is detailed by Blumlein in his patent[42]—uses one microphone (the M or midcomponent) aimed directly at the centerline of the sound source and another, a bidirectional microphone (the S or side component), oriented laterally (Fig. 6.42). Their outputs are

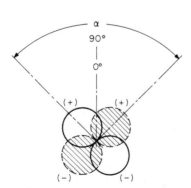

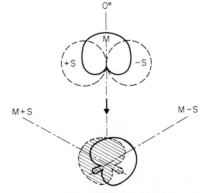

FIG. 6.41   *XY* crossed figure-of-eights. [*A. Blumlein, British Patent 394,325, Dec. 14, 1931; reprinted in J. Audio Eng. Soc.,* **6**, *91ff. (April 1958).*]

FIG. 6.42   MS conversion to *XY*.

processed by a sum-and-difference matrix network, which resolves them into conventional XY stereo signals, (M + S) and (M − S). The left-right orientation is determined by the direction of the positive lobe of the S microphone.

An advantage of this system is that it provides absolute monaural predictability: when the left and right signals are combined, the sum is solely the output of the M component: (M + S) + (M − S) = 2M. By judicious choice of polar pattern and placement of the M microphone, the monaural signal can be optimized. Conveniently this pickup is by definition on axis to the midline of the sound source and suffers minimally from off-axis coloration. The S component (the bidirectional microphone), with its null plane bisecting the sound source, provides more reverberant information than the M component. As it is generally desirable that there be less reverberation in a monaural signal than in stereo, there is a built-in advantage to MS in that it automatically has a less reverberant character when summed to mono than in its stereo image.

Finally the MS technique offers the mixing engineer greater control of the stereo image from the mixing desk than is available with any other technique. By changing the pattern of the M pickup (using a remote-pattern microphone), the apparent distance from the sound source and the amount of ambience inherent in the M signal can be adjusted. Further, by varying the M/S ratio in the sum-and-difference matrix, the apparent width of the stereo stage can also be adjusted (Fig. 6.43). This adjustment can be made either during the original recording session or later, during a postproduction session.[43]

Coincident Omnidirectional Microphones. This technique was developed by Ron Streicher for use as a soloist pickup. Since most omnidirectional microphones exhibit directionality at higher frequencies, configuring a pair of omnidirectionals at an included angle of 60 to 90° provides a stable, coherent center image combined with a sense of stereo space. Further, there will be little sense of image shift as the soloist moves, as is the case with directional microphones. The use of pressure capsules also eliminates the proximity effect and breath-blasting problems associated with gradient microphones.

6.6.2   Two-Microphone Near-Coincident Techniques

This term is used by Wes Dooley to describe that class of techniques in which a microphone pair is placed close enough together to be substantially coincident for low frequencies yet is far enough apart to have an appreciable time delay between channels for sound sources located to the far right and left. These techniques otherwise differ little from coincident microphone configurations, except that the stereo imaging results from differences in both intensity and time (phase).

The value of these techniques is that they exhibit good localization combined with a sense of depth. Close miking is not recommended in using these techniques, since small movements of the sound source can produce large image shifts. Sounds arriving from the far left or far right can also create problems for disk cutting or monaural summation owing to interchannel time delay.

ORTF. Named for the French National Broadcasting Organization (Office de Radiodiffusion-Télévision Française), this configuration consists of two cardioid microphones oriented outward from the centerline of the sound source with an included angle of 110° and with a capsule spacing of 17 cm (Fig. 6.44).

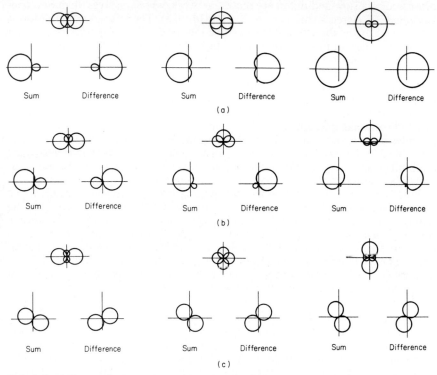

FIG. 6.43 MS to equivalent XY transformations for M/S ratios of 30:70, 50:50, and 70:30. (*a*) Omnidirectional M component. (*b*) Cardioid M. component. (*c*) Bidirectional M component.
[*From W. L. Dooley and R. D. Streicher, "M-S Stereo: A Powerful Technique for Working in Stereo," J. Audio Eng. Soc., 30, 707–718 (October 1982).*]

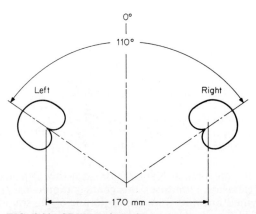

FIG. 6.44 ORTF configuration.

NOS. Adopted by the Dutch Broadcasting Organization (Nederlandsche Omroep Stichting), this standard consists of two cardioid microphones oriented outward from the centerline with an included angle of 90° and a capsule spacing of 30 cm (Fig. 6.45).

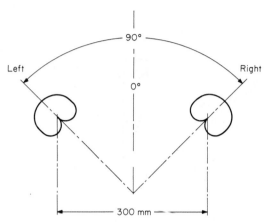

FIG. 6.45 NOS configuration.

(Note that a variety of people and organizations have their own proprietary variations on these techniques. Choices of pickup pattern, spacing, or included angle have all been altered. Be willing to experiment with variations, as did Tony Faulkner.)

Faulkner. Developed by British recording engineer Tony Faulkner,[44] this configuration uses two bidirectional microphones facing directly forward toward the sound source, spaced 20 cm apart (Fig. 6.46). This technique combines much of the coherence of the Blumlein technique with the openness afforded by the time (phase) differences resulting from the spacing between the microphones. In addition, Faulkner's recommendation that the microphone pair be placed farther back from the sound source than is common with other coincident techniques provides a more natural balance between near and more distant elements within that sound source.

Binaural. This technique is intended specifically for playback via headphones. It is often configured with two omnidirectional microphones placed into the ears of a dummy head to simulate the sound received at the ears of a listener. This technique can be quite realistic, providing a good illusion in both the horizontal and the vertical planes. (Unfortunately these illusions do not translate as well to loudspeaker playback.)

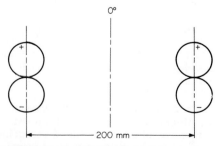

FIG. 6.46 Faulkner configuration.

Similar techniques have been configured with two omnidirectional (or even bidirectional) microphones placed approximately 3 to 4 in (75 to 100 mm) on either side of a sound-absorptive baffle (Fig. 6.47). This results in a pickup similar to the binaural method, and it provides sufficient cross-channeling information to allow for reproduction over loudspeakers as well.

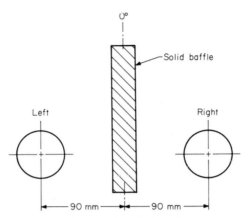

FIG. 6.47 Quasi-binaural configuration.

6.6.3 Two-Microphone Spaced Techniques

Spaced microphones were the first configuration known to relate a stereo image.[45] Generally these techniques employ two or more microphones set symmetrically along a line that is perpendicular to and bisected by the midline of the sound source. The polar pattern of the stereo pair, their spacing, and their distance from the sound source are all variables within this style. Stereo information in these configurations is created by the differences in both amplitude and time of arrival of the sound wave. A characteristic of this approach is that positional information will radically change as the distance to the sound source varies. Extremely distant sounds can present negligible directional cues to the listener.

When using spaced microphone configurations, special attention must be given to the following potential problems: (1) low-frequency comb-filter effects on sound sources to the extreme left or right of the sound stage, (2) vague center imaging, and (3) erratic monaural compatibility.

With these techniques placement and aiming are the essential elements of the art; and, as with all stereo recording, a stereo phase-monitor oscilloscope is a very useful setup and monitoring tool. Formulas for spaced microphone layouts have been widely published, and variations on these recommendations are often employed, necessitated by the physical or aesthetic needs of the recording environment.[46]

Spaced Omnidirectional Microphones. Typically this style is realized with two (or three) microphones. Common spacings are from 2 to 10 ft (0.6 to 1 m) on either side of the centerline. The spacing is determined by the width of the sound source and the distance of the microphone pair from it. A general rule is that the

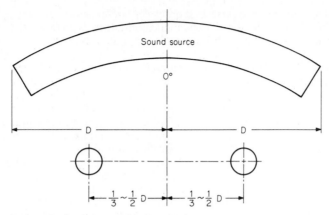

FIG. 6.48 Spaced omnidirectional pair.

microphones should be placed one-third to one-half of the distance from the centerline to the outer edge of the sound stage (Fig. 6.48).

When omnidirectional microphones are used, there is a good general sense of the acoustic space, coupled with the pressure pickup's outstanding, if sometimes overpowering, low-frequency response. Wind-noise problems are generally eliminated, although very-low-frequency sounds, such as air conditioning or traffic noise, are well recorded.

Omnidirectional microphones are designed to be either flat to an on-axis sound source (free-field) or flat to a reverberant sound field (random-incidence). In the latter case, the on-axis frequency response will be tipped up at the high end. Experimentation with the microphones' axial orientation to the sound field can therefore be productive. Omnidirectional microphones require the closest placement to the sound source for a given direct-to-reverberant-sound ratio of any polar pattern and have the maximum potential for pickup of undesirable sounds from the environment. Under the best circumstances, their sound can indeed be very open and sensual.

Pressure Boundary Microphones. Ed Long's experiments with boundary-surface-mounted transducers and the subsequent commercial success of this work have given rise to several "new" microphones, the most widely used of these being the Pressure Zone Microphone* (PZM).[47]

Use of these microphones for stereo recording is similar to using spaced omnidirectional microphones in that their polar pattern is hemispherical about the boundary surface. When baffles are employed to shape this pattern, they may then be treated similarly to spaced cardioid microphones.

Experiments have been done in simulating some of the conventional coincident and near-coincident techniques utilizing such microphones.[48]

Spaced Cardioid Microphones. This style is similar to spaced omnidirectional microphones as described above. Since these microphones are directional, they will tend to favor that segment of the sound source which is more on axis. For

---

* Registered trademark of Crown International, Inc.

reverberation, audience response, and other very off-axis sources, they will exhibit the effects of off-axis coloration. Thus their orientation and placement can sometimes be more critical than with omnidirectional microphones.

Spaced Bidirectional Microphones.   Bidirectional microphones have more reach to the front than do cardioids, but they also have an equal, though reverse-polarity, pickup lobe to the rear. Thus they must be placed farther back from the sound source than either omnidirectionals or cardioid microphones in order to achieve the same coverage. The rear lobe provides that the reverberation components and audience response will have the same sonic characteristics as the front lobe (that is, there will be little off-axis coloration of these sounds).

One advantage of this technique is provided by the null plane of these microphones. Proper orientation of this plane can reduce the pickup of unwanted sounds quite effectively. However, care must be taken that the most desired sound not be placed in the out-of-polarity rear lobes, since it is becoming increasingly evident that absolute polarity is a perceivable element in a good recording chain.

Spaced Hypercardioid Microphones.   This polar pattern is midway between cardioid and bidirectional types. The front lobe has more reach (that is, narrower) than that of a cardioid, while the small rear lobe has the reverse-polarity aspect of the bidirectional microphone. The null area is generally a cone, somewhere between the 90° null plane of the bidirectional and the 180° null point of the cardioid. The exact null cone angle, the amount of rear-lobe pickup, and the coloration of sound arriving from off axis will depend on the particular design of the microphone being used. Considerations involved in using such a spaced pair would be an amalgam of those for spaced cardioid and spaced bidirectional microphones.

6.6.4   Three- or Four-Microphone Techniques

These techniques are generally an extension of the two-microphone configurations discussed. Most of the same qualities, advantages, and disadvantages therefore apply.[49]

Three Spaced Microphones.   This technique was developed by researchers at Bell Laboratories during their experiments into stereo in the 1930s.[50] It employs a center microphone added to the two-microphone array discussed earlier. This will fill the "hole in the middle," which results from the wide spacing of the two outer microphones, and can also be used to tighten the center imaging of the configuration.

One problem arising from this additional microphone is that it compounds the effects of the phase anomalies between the microphones in the array, thus increasing the comb filtering and raising the frequencies affected into the more noticeable middle and upper ranges of the spectrum.

Two-Microphone Techniques with Accent Microphone.   Commonly an accent microphone is added to the basic two- or three-microphone technique to give special emphasis to a soloist within the overall sound stage. When more than one accent microphone is used, this leads into the realm of multimicrophone techniques and is outside the subject of this section.

When an accent microphone is used, care must be given to the placement and type employed (as well as to the amount of its signal introduced into the mix) so that it contributes only a proper representation of that soloist and does not color or change the balance of the surrounding elements of the sound stage.

With intensity stereo techniques this accent microphone can often sound out of context with the overall sound, since it is being introduced into the mix ahead in time of the basic pickup. One means of compensating for this is to delay the signal from that microphone (via a digital delay device) so that it arrives into the mix at the same time as or slightly later (10 to 15 ms) than the signal from the basic pickup. This temporal manipulation may be obviated by careful addition of this signal into the mix so that it only adds presence to the sound of the soloist but is not perceived as a separate pickup in and of itself.

Likewise, the proper panning of this pickup into the overall stereo sound stage is critical to eliminate a wandering image with changes in the intensity of the soloist.

The Sound-Field Microphone. Following theoretical development by Michael Gerzon under the auspices of the National Research Development Council in England, this special microphone system was commercially produced by Calrec Audio Ltd. It employs four transducer elements in a single housing, and via electronic manipulation the signals from these are converted into *ambisonic* surround-sound signals as well as conventional left and right stereo signals.

In their original form, the four signals are derived from four transducers arrayed in a near-coincident tetrahedron. Their outputs (the A-format signals) are electronically matrixed to produce (1) an omnidirectional component, relating the pressure of the sound wave at the microphone; (2) a pressure-gradient component, relating the vertical (up-down) information of the sound wave; (3) a pressure-gradient component relating the lateral (left-right) information; and (4) a pressure-gradient component, relating the spatial (fore-aft) information. These signals are virtually coincident, owing to the electronic manipulation, and are known as the B format, containing the overall horizontal, vertical, and pressure information.

These B-format signals can be stored on four-channel tape for postproduction, or they may be immediately processed again to resolve into quadraphonic, ambisonic, or conventional stereo signals, but with an important difference. The electronic controls of the microphone system further allow the mixing engineer the facility to steer, pan, tilt, vary the included angle, alter the directional pattern, and otherwise change the overall stereo perspective and imaging to suit his or her taste—all electronically and without ever touching the microphone itself.

6.6.5 Overview

Numerous factors must be carefully considered when planning a stereo recording. The sonic and technical characteristics of the microphones are important, and so are the visual aesthetics of their placement. During a recording session without an audience, there are few concerns other than the obvious rules of safety for both the microphones and the performers. When an audience will view the performance, the mixing engineer must also consider appearance. Live, telecast, or filmed performances all demand compromises between conflicting requirements of sight lines and microphone placement. This is particularly true with staged performances such as opera, musicals, or dramatic theater.

The discrete use of single-point coincident stereo microphones flown from above can often prove beneficial. In addition, the use of boundary-surface techniques will provide a good, clear pickup of stage activity and still be quite invisible to the audience.

The use of a single-point remote-control stereo microphone (such as the AKG C-422 or the Neumann SM-69) can also offer the engineer the added flexibility of making alterations in the stereo perspective if or when the performance or sound source dictates without the need for changing the physical position of the microphone. The ultimate example of this is the Calrec sound-field microphone previously discussed.

The final consideration in any miking situation is, of course, the sound: does it adequately represent the original sound source (if, indeed, it is supposed to)? Such aspects as localization, depth, presence, clarity of individual components, and lack of unnatural coloration are primary things to consider. Equally important: does the pickup adequately avoid the unwanted sounds in the environment?

There is no magic answer, no one right way to accomplish the task. What works well today may not suffice tomorrow. Thus it is imperative that mixing engineers learn as many approaches as they can, so that when that "impossible situation" does present itself, the relevant knowledge and the tools will be at hand to meet the situation.

REFERENCES

1. H. F. Olson (ed.)., *McGraw-Hill Encyclopedia of Science and Technology,* 5th ed., vol. 18, McGraw-Hill, New York, 1982, p.506.

2. L. L. Beranek, *Acoustic Measurements,* Wiley, New York, 1949, pp. 148–158.

3. H. F. Olson, *Acoustical Engineering,* Van Nostrand, Princeton, N.J., 1957.

4. M. C. Killion and E. V. Carlson, "A Wideband Miniature Microphone," *J. Audio Eng. Soc.,* **18,** 631–635 (December 1970).

5. M. C. Killion and E. V. Carlson, "A Subminiature Electret-Condenser Microphone of New Design," *J. Audio Eng. Soc.,* **22,** 237–243 (May 1974).

6. E. Joscelyn, M. Ferrante, and R. Saiya, "Accurately Tensioned Piezoelectric Diaphragm Microphone." U.S. Patent 4,379,211, Apr. 5, 1983.

7. G. Rasmussen, "A New Condenser Microphone," *Tech. Rev.,* Brüel & Kjaer, Copenhagen, no. 1 (1959).

8. H. F. Olson, "Directional Electrostatic Microphone," U.S. Patent 3,007,012, Oct. 31, 1961.

9. E. Fredericksen, N. Eirby, and H. Mathiasen, "Prepolarized Condenser Microphones for Measurement Purposes," *Tech. Rev.,* Brüel & Kjaer, Copenhagen, no. 4 (1979).

10. H. Kubota, "Back Electret Microphones," presented at the 55th Convention of the Audio Engineering Society, *J. Audio Eng. Soc. (Abstracts),* **24,** 862 (December 1976), preprint 1157.

11. W. R. Bevan, R. B. Schulein, and C. E. Seeler, "Design of a Studio-Quality Condenser Microphone Using Electret Technology," *J. Audio Eng. Soc. (Engineering Reports),* **26,** 947–957 (December 1978).

12. *National Bureau of Standards Reports of Calibration,* TN-181701, July 8, 1964, and TN-199270, Aug. 4, 1969.

13. L. L. Beranek, *Acoustics,* McGraw-Hill, New York, 1954, p. 158.

14. E. M. Long and R. J. Wickersham, "Pressure Recording Process and Device," U.S. Patent 4,361,736, Nov. 30, 1982.

15. J. R. Sank, "Equipment Profile: Crown PZM-30 GP Pressure Zone Microphone," *Audio,* 48–52 (March 1983).

16. J. D. Bullock and A. P. Woodard, "Performance Characteristics of Unidirectional Transducers near Reflective Surfaces," presented at the 76th Convention of the Audio Engineering Society, *J. Audio Eng. Soc. (Abstracts),* **32,** 1008 (December 1984), preprint 2122.

17. *Instruction Book for RCA BK-16A Dynamic Microphone,* IB-24898, Radio Corporation of America, Camden, N.J.

18. S. Tabuchi and S. Kawamura, "The Development and Design of a Flat Diaphragm, Printed-Ribbon Microphone Capsule," presented at the 72d Convention of the Audio Engineering Society, *J. Audio Eng. Soc. (Abstracts),* **30,** 950 (December 1982), preprint 1934.

19. M. E. Sikorski, "Transistor Microphones," *J. Audio Eng. Soc.,* **13,** 207 (July 1965).

20. H. Tremaine, *Audio Cyclopedia,* Howard W. Sams, Indianapolis, 1969, pp. 223–224.

21. E. Rogers et al., "Tunnel Diode Microphones," unpublished report, RCA Laboratories, 1961.

22. J. R. Sank, "Miniature Microphone Using an Integrated Piezoresistive Pressure Transducer," *J. Audio Eng. Soc. (Engineering Reports),* **28,** 443–436 (June 1980).

23. H. F. Olson, "Ribbon Velocity Microphones," *J. Audio Eng. Soc.,* **18,** 263–268 (June 1970).

24. J. R. Sank, "The Compleat Microphone Evaluation," *Audio* (April 1977).

25. J. R. Sank, "The Compleat Microphone Evaluation—An Update," *Audio* (September 1978).

26. *Audio Facilities Catalog,* Western Electric Co., 1947.

27. J. Eargle, *The Microphone Handbook,* Elar Publishing, Plainview, N.Y., 1981.

28. W. R. Woszczyk, "A Microphone Technique Employing the Principle of Second-Order Gradient Unidirectionality," presented at the 69th Convention of the Audio Engineering Society, *J. Audio Eng. Soc. (Abstracts),* **29,** 550 (July–August 1981), preprint 1800.

29. W. A. Beaverson and A. M. Wiggins, "Second-Order Gradient Noise Cancelling Microphone Using a Single Diaphragm," *J. Acoust. Soc. Am.,* **22,** 592 (1950).

30. B. R. Beavers and R. Brown, "Third-Order Gradient Microphone for Speech Reception," *J. Audio Eng. Soc.,* **18,** 636–640 (December 1970).

31. K. Kishi, N. Tsuchiya, and K. Shimura, "Unidirectional Microphone," U.S. Patent 3,581,012, May 25, 1971.

32. H. F. Olson, "Line Microphones," *Proc. IRE,* **27** (July 1939).

33. H. F. Olson, "Line Microphones," *J. Soc. Motion Pict. Eng.,* **36** (March 1941).

34. J. R. Sank, "Equipment Profile—Nakamichi CM-700 Electret Condenser Microphone System," *Audio* (September 1978).

35. T. Yamamoto, "Quadraphonic One Point Pickup Microphone," *J. Audio Eng. Soc.,* **21,** 256–261 (May 1973).

36. B. Weingartner, "Two-Way Cardioid Microphone," *J. Audio Eng. Soc.,* **14,** 244 (July 1966).

37. H. F. Olson, J. Preston, and J. C. Bleazey, "Personal Microphones," *J. Audio Eng. Soc.,* **9,** 278 (October 1961).

38. S. Julstrom and T. Tichy, "Direction Sensitive Gating: A New Approach to Automatic Mixing," presented at the 73d Convention of the Audio Engineering Society, *J. Audio Eng. Soc. (Abstracts),* **31,** 368 (May 1983), preprint 1976.

39. Y. Ishigaki, M. Yamamoto, K. Totsuka, and N. Miyaji, "Zoom Microphone," presented at the 67th Convention of the Audio Engineering Society, *J. Audio Eng. Soc. (Abstracts),* **28,** 923 (December 1980), preprint 1713.

40. J. H. Snyder, "The Quorum Teleconferencing Microphone," paper C3, ASA meeting, San Diego (Nov. 7–11, 1983).

41. A. J. Brouns, "Experimental Wide-Bandwidth Tooth-Contact Microphone," *J. Audio Eng. Soc.,* **19,** 41–45 (January 1971).

42. A. Blumlein, British Patent 394,325, Dec. 14, 1931; reprinted in *J. Audio Eng. Soc.,* **6,** 91ff. (April 1958).

43. W. L. Dooley and R. D. Streicher, "M-S Stereo: A Powerful Technique for Working in Stereo," *J. Audio Eng. Soc.,* **30,** 707–718 (October 1982).

44. "A Phased Array," *Hi Fi News Record Rev.,* 44ff. (July 1981).

45. "The Telephone at the Paris Opera," *Sci Amer.* (Dec. 14, 1881).

46. J. Gordon, "Recording in 2 and 4 Channels," *Audio,* 36–38 (December 1973).

47. "The PZMemo" (application notes), Crown International, Inc.

48. J. C. Lehmann and M. E. Lamm, "The Use of Boundary-Layer-Effect Microphones in Traditional Stereo Miking Techniques," presented at the 74th Convention of the Audio Engineering Society, *J. Audio Eng. Soc. (Abstracts),* **31,** 961 (December 1983), preprint 2025.

49. "Miking with the 3-Point System," *Audio,* 28–36 (December 1975).

50. A. C. Keller, "Early Hi-Fi and Stereo Recording at Bell Laboratories (1931–1932)," *J. Audio Eng. Soc.,* **29,** 274–280 (April 1981).

BIBLIOGRAPHY

Eargle, J.: *Sound Recording,* Van Nostrand Reinhold, New York, 1976.

————: *The Microphone Handbook,* Elar Publishing, Plainview, N.Y., 1982.

Lipshitz, S. P.: "Stereo Microphone Techniques: Are the Purists Wrong?" presented at the 78th Convention of the Audio Engineering Society, *J. Audio Eng. Soc. (Abstracts),* **33,** 594 (July–August 1985), preprint 2261.

Microphones—An Anthology, Audio Engineering Society, New York, 1979.

Nisbett, A.: *The Technique of the Sound Studio,* Hastings House, New York, 1974.

Olson, H.: *Music, Physics, and Engineering,* 2d ed., Dover, New York, 1967.

AMPLIFIERS

Daniel R. von Recklinghausen
Consultant, Hudson, New Hampshire

Daniel R. von Recklinghausen
Consultant, Hudson, New Hampshire

6.7 AMPLIFIERS

Amplifiers are the functional building blocks of audio systems, and each of these building blocks contains several amplifier stages coupled together. An amplifier may contain its own power supply, while an amplifier stage needs one or more external sources of power. The active component of each amplifier stage is usually a transistor or a field-effect transistor (FET). Other amplifying components, such as vacuum tubes, can also be used in amplifier circuits if the general principles of small- and large-signal voltages and current flows are followed.[1-4]

6.7.1 Single-Stage Transistor or FET Amplifier

The single-stage amplifier can best be described as using a single transistor or FET connected as a common emitter or common-source amplifier, using an NPN transistor (Fig. 6.49a) or an N-channel FET (Fig. 6.49b) and treating PNP transistors or P-channel FET circuits by simply reversing the current flow and the polarity of the voltages.

DC Conditions.   At zero frequency or dc and also at low frequencies, the transistor or FET amplifier stage requires an input voltage E_1 equal to the sum of the input voltage of the device (the transistor V_{be} or FET V_{gs}) and the voltage across the resistance R_e or R_s between the common node (ground) and the emitter or source terminal. The input current I_1 to the amplifier stage is equal to the sum of the current through the external resistor connected between ground and the base or gate and the base current I_b or gate current I_g drawn by the device. In most FET circuits the gate current may be so small that it can be neglected, while in transistor circuits the base current I_b is equal to the collector current I_c divided by the current gain beta of the transistor. The input resistance R_1 to the amplifier stage is equal to the ratio of input voltage E_1 to input current I_1.

The input voltage and the input resistance of an amplifier stage increase as the value of the emitter or source resistor becomes larger.

The output voltage E_2 of the amplifier stage, operating without any external load, is equal to the difference of supply voltage V+ and the product of collector or drain load resistor R_1 and collector current I_c or drain current I_d. An external load will cause the device to draw an additional current I_2, which increases the device output current.

As long as the collector-to-emitter voltage is larger than the saturation voltage of the transistor, collector current will be nearly independent of supply voltage. Similarly, the drain current of an FET will be nearly independent of drain-to-source voltage as long as this voltage is greater than an equivalent saturation voltage. This saturation voltage is approximately equal to the difference between gate-to-source voltage and pinch-off voltage, the latter voltage being the bias voltage which causes nearly zero drain current. In some data sheets for FETs the pinch-off voltage is given under a different name as *threshold voltage*. At lower supply

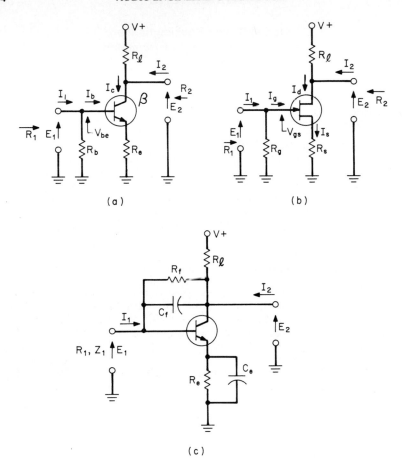

FIG. 6.49 Single-stage amplifier circuits. (*a*) Common-emitter NPN. (*b*) Common-source N-channel FET. (*c*) Single stage with current and voltage feedback.

voltages the collector or drain current will become less until it reaches zero when the drain-to-source voltage is zero or the collector-to-emitter voltage has a very small reverse value.

The output resistance R_2 of a transistor or FET amplifier stage is in effect the parallel combination of the collector or drain load resistance and the series connection of two resistors, consisting of R_e or R_s and the ratio of collector-to-emitter voltage and collector current or the equivalent drain-to-source voltage and drain current. In actual devices an additional resistor, the relatively large output resistance of the device, is connected in parallel with the output resistance of the amplifier stage.

The collector current of a single-stage transistor amplifier is equal to the base current multiplied by the current gain of the transistor. Since the current gain of a transistor may be specified as tightly as a 2:1 range at one value of collector current or may have just a minimum value, knowledge of the input current is usually not quite sufficient to specify the output current of a transistor.

Input and Output Impedance, Voltage, and Current Gain. As derived above for a common-emitter or common-source single amplifier stage, input impedance is the ratio of input voltage to input current and output impedance is the ratio of output voltage to output current. As the input current increases, the output current into the external output load resistor will increase by the current-amplification factor of the stage. The output voltage will decrease because the increased current flows from the collector or drain voltage supply source into the collector or drain of the device. Therefore, the voltage amplification is a negative number having the magnitude of the ratio of output-voltage change to input-voltage change.

The magnitude of voltage amplification is often calculated as the product of transconductance G_m of the device and load resistance value. This can be done as long as the emitter or source resistor is zero or the resistor is bypassed with a capacitor which effectively acts as a short circuit for all signal changes of interest but allows the desired bias currents to flow through the resistor. In a bipolar transistor the transconductance is approximately equal to the emitter current multiplied by 39, which is the charge of a single electron divided by the product of Boltzmann's constant and absolute temperature in kelvins. In an FET this value will be less and usually is proportional to input bias voltage with reference to the pinch-off voltage.

The power gain of the device is the ratio of output power to input power, often expressed in decibels. Voltage gain or current gain may be stated in decibels but must be so marked.

AC Gain. The resistor in series with the emitter or source causes negative feedback of most of the output current, which reduces the voltage gain of the single amplifier stage and raises its input impedance (Fig. 6.49a and b). When this resistor R_e is bypassed with a capacitor C_e (Fig. 6.49c), the amplification factor will be high at high frequencies and will be reduced by approximately 3 dB at the frequency where the impedance of capacitor C_e is equal to the emitter or source input impedance of the device, which in turn is approximately equal to the inverse of the transconductance G_m of the device (Fig. 6.50a). The gain of the stage will be approximately 3 dB higher than the dc gain at the frequency where the impedance of the capacitor is equal to the emitter or source resistor. The above simplifications hold in cases where the product of transconductance and resistance value is much larger than 1.

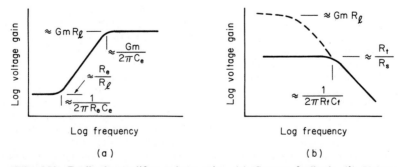

FIG. 6.50 Feedback amplifier voltage gains. (*a*) Current feedback. (*b*) Voltage feedback.

A portion of the output voltage may also be fed back to the input, which is the base or gate terminal. This resistor R_f will lower the input impedance of the single amplifier stage, reduce current amplification, reduce output impedance of the stage, and act as a supply voltage source for the base or gate. This method is used when the source of input signals and internal resistance R_s is coupled with a capacitor to the base or gate and a group of devices with a spread of current gains, transconductances, or pinch-off voltages must operate with similar amplification in the same circuit. If the feedback element is also a capacitor C_f, high-frequency current amplification of the stage will be reduced by approximately 3 dB when the impedance of the capacitor is equal to the feedback resistor R_f and voltage gain of the stage is high (Fig. 6.50b). At still higher frequencies amplification will decrease at the rate of 6 dB per octave of frequency. It should be noted at this point that the base-collector or gate-drain capacitance of the device has the same effect of limiting high-frequency amplification of the stage, but this capacitor becomes larger as collector-base or drain-gate voltage decreases.

Feedback of the output voltage through an impedance lowers the input impedance of an amplifier stage. Voltage amplification of the stage will be affected only as this lowered input impedance loads the source of input voltage. If the source of input voltage has a finite source impedance and the amplifier stage has very high voltage amplification and reversed phase, the effective amplification for this stage will approach the ratio of feedback impedance to source impedance and also have reversed phase.

Common-Base or Common-Gate Connection.   Here (Fig. 6.51a) voltage amplification is the same as in the common-emitter or common-source connection, but input impedance is approximately the inverse of the transconductance of the device. As a benefit, high-frequency amplification will be less affected because of the relatively lower emitter-collector or source-drain capacitance and the relatively low input impedance. This is the reason why the cascade connection (Fig. 6.51b) of a common-emitter amplifier stage driving a common-base amplifier stage exhibits nearly the dc amplification of a common-emitter stage with the wide bandwidth of a common-base stage. The other advantage of a common-base or common-gate amplifier stage is stable amplification at very high frequencies (VHF) and ease of matching to transmission-line impedances, usually 50 to 75 Ω.

Common-Collector or Common-Drain Connection of a Transistor or FET.   Voltage gain is slightly below 1.000, but the input impedance of a transistor so connected will be equal to the value of the load impedance multiplied by the current gain of the device plus the inverse of the transconductance of the device (Fig. 6.51c). Similarly, the output impedance of the stage will be the impedance of the source of signals divided by the current gain of the transistor plus the inverse of the transconductance of the device.

When identical resistors are connected between the collector or drain and the supply voltage and the emitter or source and ground, an increase in base or gate voltage will result in an increase of emitter or source voltage which is nearly equal to the decrease in collector or drain voltage. This type of connection is known as the *split-load phase inverter,* useful for driving push-pull amplifiers, although the output impedances at the two output terminals are unequal (Fig. 6.51d).

The current gain of a transistor decreases at high frequencies as the emitter-base capacitance shunts a portion of the transconductance, thereby reducing current gain until it reaches a value of 1 at the transition frequency of the transistor

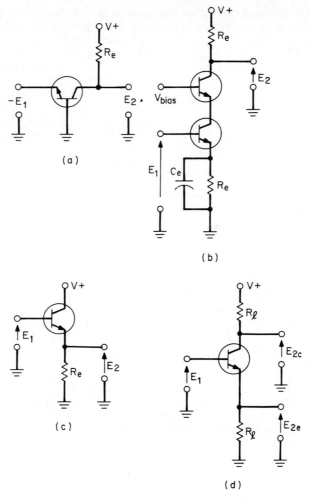

FIG. 6.51 Transistor amplifier circuits. (*a*) Common-base NPN.
(*b*) Cascade NPN. (*c*) Common-collector NPN emitter follower.
(*d*) Split-load phase inverter.

(Fig. 6.52). From this it can be seen that the output impedance of an emitter-follower or common-collector stage will increase with frequency, having the effect of an inductive source impedance when the input source to the stage is resistive. If the source impedance is inductive, as it might be with cascaded emitter followers, the output impedance of such a combination can be a negative value at certain high frequencies and be a possible cause of amplifier oscillation. Similar considerations also apply to common-drain FET stages.

Bias and Large Signals.   When large signals have to be handled by a single-stage amplifier, distortion of the signals introduced by the amplifier must be considered. Although feedback can reduce distortion, it is necessary to ensure that each stage of amplification operates in a region where normal signals will not cause the

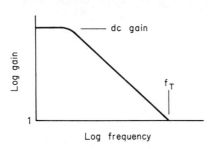

FIG. 6.52 Amplitude-frequency response of a common-emitter or common-source amplifier.

amplifier stage to operate with nearly zero voltage drop across the device or to operate the device with nearly zero current during a portion of the cycle of the signal. Although the amplifier is described primarily with respect to a single-device amplifier stage, the same holds true for any amplifier stage with multiple devices, except that here at least one device must be able to control current flow in the load without being saturated (nearly zero voltage drop) or cut off (nearly zero current).

If the single-device amplifier load consists of the collector or drain load resistor only, the best operating point should be chosen so that in the absence of a signal one-half of the supply voltage appears as a quiescent voltage across the load resistor R_1. If an additional resistive load R_1 is connected to the output through a coupling capacitor C_c (Fig. 6.53a), the maximum peak load current I_1 in one direction is equal to the difference between quiescent current I_q of the stage and the current which would flow if the collector resistor and the external load resistor were connected in series across the supply voltage. In the other direction maximum load current is limited by the quiescent voltage across the device divided by the load resistance. The quiescent current flows in the absence of an alternating signal and is caused by bias voltage or current only. Since most audio-frequency signals have positive and negative peak excursions of equal probability, it is advisable to have the two peak currents equal. This can be accomplished by increasing the quiescent current as the external load resistance decreases.

When several devices contribute current into an external load resistor (Fig. 6.53b), one useful strategy is to set bias currents so that the sum of all transconductances remains as constant as practical, which means a design for minimum distortion. This operating point for one device is near one-fourth of the peak device current for push-pull FET stages and at a lesser value for bipolar push-pull amplifiers.

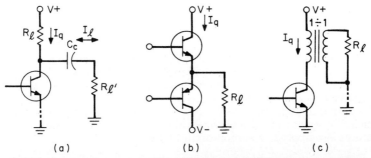

FIG. 6.53 Output load-coupling circuits. (a) AC-coupled. (b) Series-dc-parallel–ac-push-pull half-bridge. (c) Single-ended, transformer-coupled.

When the load resistance is coupled to the single-device amplifier stage with a transformer (Fig. 6.53c), the optimum bias current should be nearly equal to the peak current which would flow through the load impedance at the primary of the transformer with a voltage drop equal to the supply voltage.

6.7.2 Multistage Amplifiers

All practical audio amplifiers are multistage amplifiers in which cascaded single-stage amplifiers are connected together. Overall feedback then is used to stabilize amplification and quiescent operating points.[5]

DC-Coupled Multistage Amplifiers. Commonly, amplifier stages enclosed in an overall feedback loop are direct-coupled so that the quiescent operating point is determined primarily by the bias of the first stage.

Two cascaded common-emitter amplifier stages can form a gain block useful as a low-cost preamplifier (Fig. 6.54a). Here the collector of the first stage is connected to the base of the second stage and to a resistor which supplies collector current to the first stage and base current to the second stage from the supply voltage. Both stages have an emitter resistor connected to the common ground, with the second resistor bypassed with a large capacitor. Base current to the first

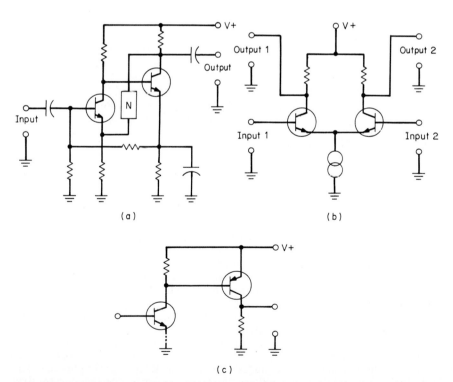

FIG. 6.54 Multistage DC-coupled circuits. (*a*) Cascaded two-transistor amplifier. (*b*) Emitter-coupled, or long-tailed-pair, phase inverter. (*c*) Cascade NPN and PNP transistors.

stage is supplied from the emitter of the second stage through a pair of voltage-divider resistors connected to ground, with audio input signals fed to the base of the first stage through a coupling capacitor. The audio-signal output is taken from the collector of the second stage through a coupling capacitor. The second collector receives its operating current through a resistor and supplies feedback current through a resistor-capacitor network to the emitter of the first stage. When using two NPN transistors and a single positive supply voltage, a low-cost preamplifier suitable for tape or disk playback with the appropriate feedback network is constructed. The maximum no-feedback voltage amplification is approximately equal to the transconductance of the first stage multiplied by the current gain of the second stage and the load resistor value of the second stage.

The cascade-amplifier stage (Fig. 6.51b) is described above.

When two transistors or FETs have their emitters or sources connected together and that junction is supplied with a constant current and output voltages are obtained from identical-value resistors connected between the supply voltage and the two collectors or drains, the long-tailed-pair or emitter-coupled or source-coupled phase-inverter stage is described (Fig. 6.54b). Here the emitter or source of one device acts as the emitter or source resistor for the other device, and an alternating signal impressed on one input will be amplified with a phase reversal in the same stage while this reversal is not experienced at the other output. This stage, then, is capable of taking one single-ended signal and transforming it into a push-pull signal. The signal applied to the other input now will arrive at the first output without a phase reversal. Thus, the emitter- or source-coupled amplifier is able to amplify the difference between two signals, where one may be an input signal and the other a feedback signal. Its voltage amplification is the same as the normal grounded emitter or grounded source stage, except that the output voltage should now be measured between the two outputs, with the voltage from either output to ground being one-half of that value. This type of input stage is the almost universal input stage of operational amplifiers.

Almost the same performance can be expected when the commonly connected emitters or sources are supplied by a resistor instead of a current source or the two input circuits have differing impedances. The long-tailed pair performs best when the two devices are matched and operate at the same temperature. For this reason, matched monolithic transistors and FET provide the best performance, with the additional benefit that, with equally shared current, even-harmonic distortion is substantially reduced when compared with single-ended amplifiers.

Two-device amplifier stages are not restricted to a construction using two devices of the same type (bipolar versus FET) or the same polarity (NPN versus PNP). Using stages of opposite polarity often results in a higher available amplification factor and output voltage when limitations of supply voltage are considered (Fig. 6.54c). In hearing-aid amplifiers it is necessary to operate silicon transistors, which have a normal base-emitter voltage of 0.7 V, from a single-cell battery voltage, which may become less than 1 V near the end of the battery's life. Here one solution is to use alternating NPN and PNP transistors as cascaded amplifiers and to use transistors operating with a collector voltage less than the base-emitter voltage, particularly when push-pull signals have to be generated to drive the transducer in the ear canal.

Another use of transistors or FETs of differing polarity is in series-connected push-pull amplifiers (Fig. 6.55), where one stage supplies current of one polarity from one supply voltage to a grounded load and the other stage supplies opposite-polarity current from a supply voltage of opposite polarity. The bias current flows from one supply to the other through the two devices without passing through the

load. Here, the two stages may have a relatively low bias current which is often stabilized by a diode per device connected in shunt with the base circuit and kept at the same temperature as the ampli-
fying transistors. As the transistors' temperature increases with heat, the base-emitter voltage decreases and the diode forward voltage decreases also, thereby keeping the quiescent current in the transistors within much smaller limits than without diode compensation.

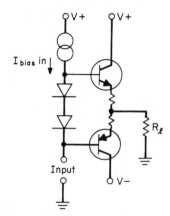

FIG. 6.55 Input signal and bias circuit in a single-ended push-pull amplifier.

CascadedTransistors.   Transistorscon-
nected in cascade with overall voltage feedback are building blocks of ampli-
fiers. When the collectors of two NPN transistors are connected together with the base signal of the second transistor derived entirely from the emitter of the first, an NPN Darlington transistor (Fig. 6.56a) is described which has only three terminals: the emitter of the sec-
ond, the base of the first, and the common collector of both. Additional internal base-emitter resistors ensure that leakage currents cannot cause conduction in the last transistor. Such a cascaded transistor may have a current gain nearly equal to the product of the two current gain factors, requires an input voltage which is two base-emitter voltages higher than the emitter voltage, and can reach in normal operation a minimum voltage drop between the external collector-emitter terminals equal to one base-emitter voltage. Two PNP transistors can be similarly interconnected.

The collector of a first PNP transistor can be connected to supply the entire base current of a second NPN transistor, with the emitter of the first transistor connected to the collector of the second transistor (Fig. 6.56b). The entire assembly now functions as a compound PNP transistor having as its base terminal the base of the first PNP transistor, as its collector the emitter of the second NPN

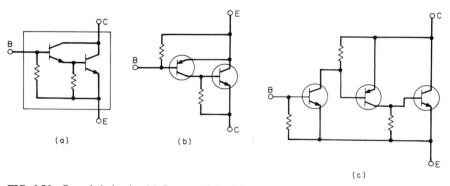

FIG. 6.56 Cascaded circuits. (*a*) Compound Darlington or coupled emitter follower. (*b*) Compound PNP-NPN transistors. (*c*) Triple compound NPN-PNP-NPN transistors.

transistor, and as its emitter the emitter of the first PNP and the collector of the second NPN transistor. The input voltage now must be one base-emitter voltage lower than the emitter voltage because of the reversed current flow in PNP transistors, and the minimum voltage drop between the collector-emitter terminals is now one base-emitter voltage. The two compound transistors described above are the compound output devices in quasi-complementary push-pull amplifiers.

Three or more transistors of like or mixed polarity may be cascaded, such as PNP-NPN-NPN or NPN-PNP-NPN (Fig. 6.56c), to form compound PNP or NPN transistors respectively. Here the polarity of the input transistor defines the polarity of the compound transistor. The minimum voltage drop and the required input voltage may be different in each connection, becoming highest when only devices of the same polarity are used.

Parallel-Connected Devices for High Currents.   When high currents have to be delivered to a load, several transistors or FETS are often connected in parallel, with each device sharing a portion of the output current (Fig. 6.57a). Nearly equal current sharing can be achieved when all devices are matched to each other as much as possible. Current sharing can be improved when each of the devices has local current feedback with equal separate emitter or source resistors connected to the common emitter or source connection and all devices share a common heat sink. The emitter resistor for bipolar transistors is typically a fraction of 1 Ω, which allows current sharing to currents as low as a fraction of 1 A.

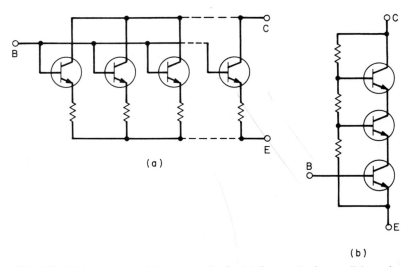

FIG. 6.57   High-voltage and high-current circuits. (*a*) Current-sharing parallel transistors. (*b*) Totem-pole series-connected transistors.

The circuit layout for a parallel connection must be done carefully to avoid constructing an oscillator circuit at very high frequencies. When using power FETs, it is necessary to connect series resistors of a few ohms in series with each gate lead and, perhaps, to have a ferrite bead in each gate lead to avoid oscillation.

Series-Connected Devices for High Voltage.   When high voltages have to be delivered to a load and single devices are incapable of operating at the maximum peak voltage, several devices may be connected in series to share the voltage while conducting nearly the same current. The resulting *totem-pole connection* for transistors involves connecting the transistors so that the emitter of the second transistor is tied to the collector of the first and the emitter of the third transistor is tied to the collector of the second, and so on (Fig. 6.57b). A series string of as many equal resistors as there are transistors has its ends connected to the collector of the last transistor and the emitter of the first transistor, and each junction is connected in the same sequence to the base of the same transistor in the sequence, except to the first transistor, whose base receives the input signal. The object of this circuit is to have the first transistor operate as a grounded-emitter device, driving all the others as grounded-base devices. This goal is not perfectly achieved, particularly at high frequencies and at high-output currents where voltage division in the resistor string under load departs from uniformity.

AC-Coupled Multistage Amplifiers.   Audio-signal amplification usually does not include amplification of the dc component of the source of signals. One or more coupling capacitors between stages of amplification reduce the low-frequency response of the system and prevent the dc offset voltages from being propagated to the output (Fig. 6.58a). When using transistor amplifiers in this fashion, the input impedance of a single-ended input stage after each capacitor may act as a partial rectifier diode for the pulsating audio signal and produce a low-frequency transient for each audio-frequency pulse. The solution to this problem may be, in part, the use of FET circuits, the use of push-pull circuits, and the selection of low-frequency time constants in the amplifier and power supply filtering circuits.

Amplifier stages may be coupled with transformers to the signal source and load and to each other (Fig. 6.58b). Transformers are excellent devices which can reject common-mode interfering signals which may appear on a program line, and they can also match the source and load impedances to the amplifier circuit. Such an impedance match is needed, for example, in amplifiers operating from a power supply directly connected to the power line where connection of external loudspeakers or headphones would present a shock hazard. Transformers are the only practical devices which can match the devices in broadband radio-frequency power amplifiers to source and load.

6.7.3   Power Output Stages

Power output stages of audio amplifiers usually are called upon to drive loudspeaker loads, which may or may not be connected when the signal or the power

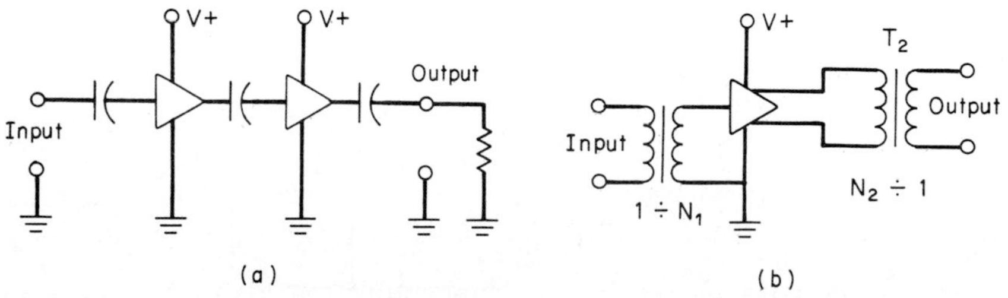

FIG. 6.58   AC amplifier circuits. (*a*) Cascaded, capacitor-coupled. (*b*) Transformer-coupled.

supply is turned on. Consequently, not only must power amplifiers be stable with any load, but they must be tolerant of excessive signals or loads unless such conditions are prevented from occurring.

The U.S. Federal Trade Commission has mandated that audio power amplifiers in excess of a 2-W rating be rated with each amplifier channel capable of delivering at least rated power simultaneously into its rated load resistance over a band of frequencies limited by a high and a low frequency. When power line variations are taken into consideration, any single channel will be capable of a higher output power and each device must be able to tolerate a much higher peak power dissipation with the reactive load that a loudspeaker may present to the amplifier and at times when excessive input signals are encountered.[6]

Single-Ended Amplifiers.   A single-ended amplifier has only one single or compound transistor or FET acting as a variable controlled resistor between power supply and load. The load may be coupled to the output stage through a capacitor or a transformer, which must also return the average direct current to the power supply (Fig. 6.53*a* and *c*). Single-ended amplifiers intended for audio-frequency amplification are usually of low power output capability and generally operate from a single power supply voltage. In a single-ended amplifier, transformer- or choke-coupled to the load, the bias current through the device must be at least equal to the peak current through the load and the peak voltage across the load must be less than the supply voltage when the turns ratio of the transformer is 1:1 between the primary and secondary windings.

Push-Pull Amplifiers.   A push-pull amplifier has at least one pair of single or compound output devices which act as variable resistors between supply and load, with the first device *pushing* load current in one direction while the other *pulls* load current in the opposite direction under control of the input signal. When the two devices have the same characteristics and the driving signal is equally balanced, the direct current and all even-harmonic distortion in the load current are canceled.[7]

Parallel-DC, Series-AC Amplifiers.   The usual transformer-coupled amplifier (Fig. 6.59) has two like devices connected between ground and the end of the primary winding of the transformer, with the supply voltage fed to the center tap of the same winding. Signal voltage is fed to the two devices with opposed phase so that one device increases conduction of current while the other decreases conduction.

The load may be connected to a secondary winding or between the ends of the primary winding. When it is connected in the latter way, maximum conduction

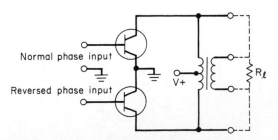

FIG. 6.59   Series-ac, parallel-dc push-pull amplifier.

of one device, resulting in nearly 0 V at that point, will raise the voltage at the opposite device to almost twice the power supply voltage, which then becomes the peak voltage across the load.

The peak-to-peak voltage across the load then becomes nearly 4 times the power supply voltage, and the peak load current becomes nearly 2 times the power supply voltage divided by the load resistance. The average power supply current is equal to the sum of the average current drawn by each device. Thus, the dc supply load is in parallel, while the ac load signal is in series between the two devices.

The parallel-dc, series-ac push-pull amplifier provides a very high relative power output when supply voltage is low, as in the 12-V automotive electrical system. The transformer- or choke-coupled amplifier makes use of two like devices and is therefore the preferred connection in radio-frequency power amplifiers.

Series-DC, Parallel-AC Amplifiers. With the availability of complementary transistors as amplifiers, the single-ended or half-bridge amplifier became practical as a transformerless power amplifier in the early 1960s. Prior to that time such amplifiers were constructed by using driver transformers or floating phase-inverter amplifiers.

A half-bridge amplifier that is fully balanced has one device connected between the load and one power supply and a second complementary device connected between the load and a second power supply of opposite polarity but the same voltage (Fig. 6.53b). The load and the two power supplies are connected to a common ground. Driving voltage is fed to both devices without phase inversion, decreasing conduction in one device while increasing conduction of an opposite current in the other direction.

The maximum peak voltage across the load will be slightly less than one supply voltage. The maximum peak-to-peak voltage thus cannot exceed the total of the two supply voltages which are series-connected. The two devices operate in parallel for ac signals, where one device increases a current of one polarity while the other decreases a current of opposite polarity.

Full-Bridge Amplifiers. Full-bridge amplifiers are constructed by using two half-bridge amplifiers with the load connected between the two output terminals and the two input terminals driven by signals of opposite polarity from a phase-inverter circuit (Fig. 6.60). Peak voltage across the load then becomes nearly equal to the total supply voltage, and peak-to-peak load voltage becomes nearly twice the total supply voltage. This type of amplifier connection is preferred over the totem-pole-transistor connection when high-voltage limitations of power devices restrict total available output power into a fixed load resistance without using a transformer.

Classes of Amplifiers. Amplifiers are described as classes depending on the angle of conduction of signal current and voltage-current relationships in the load.

Class A amplifiers (Fig. 6.61a) conduct signal current throughout the cycle of the signal waveform. They have the lowest distortion before feedback and may be single-ended or push-pull. An ideal Class A amplifier can have a sine-wave output efficiency not exceeding 50 percent at full output.

Class B amplifiers (Fig. 6.61b) conduct signal current exactly for one-half of the cycle of the input-signal waveform. In a push-pull Class B amplifier one device conducts for one half-cycle, and the other device conducts for the remaining half-cycle. Linear Class B radio-frequency amplifiers may have only one device, since

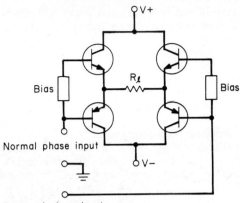

FIG. 6.60 Full-bridge amplifier coupled to a load.

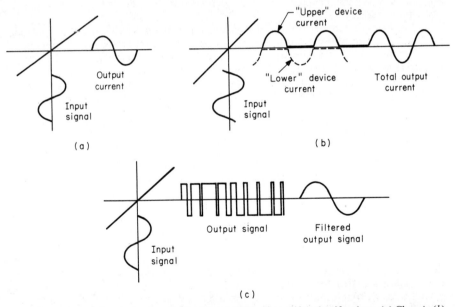

FIG. 6.61 Input-signal–output-current characteristics of amplifier classifications. (*a*) Class A. (*b*) Class B. (*c*) Class D.

the second-harmonic components are filtered out in the narrowband matching network. An ideal Class B amplifier can have a maximum sine-wave efficiency not exceeding 78 percent at full power output.

Class AB amplifiers have a conduction angle between full conduction and half-cycle conduction and efficiencies between Classes A and B. Most audio-frequency amplifiers are adjusted in this way. As lower power outputs are needed with variations in signal amplitude, efficiency of Class A, AB, and B amplifiers will decrease proportionally to output voltage, decreasing toward zero at very low output. When the load of such an amplifier is a reactive impedance, such as a loudspeaker, efficiency will decrease still further, since any voltampere energy sent to a reactance in one part of a cycle will be returned to the source and the resistance in the circuit in the other part of the cycle.

Class C amplifiers conduct for less than one-half of a complete signal cycle. These amplifiers are used primarily as radio-frequency amplifiers with the load tuned to the signal frequency.

Class D amplifiers (Fig. 6.61c) are switching amplifiers using a high-frequency carrier signal where the positive pulse on time is proportional to the audio-signal amplitude. The negative pulse on time completes the rest of the cycle as with Class A amplifiers. In other designs, separate circuits control positive and negative pulses as with Class B amplifiers. The audio-frequency load is isolated from the amplifier output stage with a low-pass filter that does not consume the high-frequency pulse energy. Class D amplifiers have a theoretical efficiency of 100 percent at all signal levels but are difficult to design for wideband low-distortion operation because of the short switching transition times required of the final high-power output stages and the difficulty of design of feedback loops.

Class E amplifiers have as input signals rectangular pulses. The output load is tuned, but the output voltage resembes a damped single pulse.

There is no agreement on naming amplifiers of classes above E. Several types of audio-frequency amplifiers have been described with differing letters. These include amplifiers in which several amplifier stages are connected in series, drawing power from several power supplies through isolation diodes to provide output signal to a load. For small signals only the stages connected to the low-voltage supplies conduct current. As these stages saturate, the next stages now conduct current from the next higher power supplies through the saturated stages into the load, and so on.

In a different version, a normal Class B amplifier obtains supply voltage from a high-efficiency switching power supply, the output voltage of which is raised as output voltage demands are increased. In all these amplifier designs attempts are made to improve efficiency with varying signal levels and with program-signal waveforms, which are nonsinusoidal.

6.7.4   Gain Block and the Operational Amplifier

A large number of audio-frequency circuits are constructed by using operational amplifiers because they permit these circuits to be designed with minimum complexity of components. In most applications, the open-circuit voltage gain of an operational amplifier will be much larger than the gain of the amplifier.

An amplifier gain block is matched to the output of the previous gain block or other circuit when it is able to extract maximum power from the previous circuit. When the amplifier gain block should draw little current from the preceding circuit, the gain block is bridged across that circuit and must have a relatively high input impedance.

An operational amplifier connected as a noninverting amplifier can have a high input impedance at its positive input while receiving feedback voltage from a voltage divider connected between output and ground, with the voltage-divider junction connected to the negative input (Fig. 6.62a). The voltage gain is the voltage ratio of the divider.

An inverting operational amplifier can be used as a gain block, with the input resistor connected between the source and the negative input and matching the

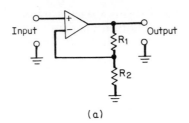

(a)

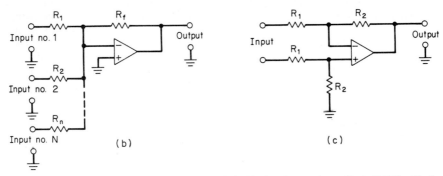

(b)   (c)

FIG. 6.62   Operational amplifier circuits. (a) Gain-block voltage gain $= (1 + R_1/R_2)$ with the same polarity of input and output signals. (b) Gain-block voltage gain $= (R_f/R_1)$, $1(R_f/R_2)$ or $-(R_f/R_n)$ with opposite polarity of input and output signals. (c) Gain-block differential voltage gain $= (R_2/R_1)$ and low common-mode gain, limited by resistor matching and loop gain.

desired load of the previous stage. A feedback resistor connected between the output and the same negative input then sets voltage gain equal to the ratio between the two resistors; the positive input is grounded (Fig. 6.62b). Since there exists only a very low voltage at the negative input, several input resistors can be connected between various input sources and the negative input. In this fashion, these input signals can be mixed together with little danger of feedthrough between signals at each source.

If resistance-capacitance networks are used in place of resistors, equalizer or tone-control blocks can be designed. With more complex networks, high-pass, low-pass, bandpass, and phase-shifting all-pass blocks result.

The above circuits make use of the common-ground mode and thus are unbalanced circuits. An operational amplifier can also amplify the voltage difference between the two wires of a balanced program line while having only little sensitivity to common-mode signals arriving in phase, thereby reducing ground-loop voltages.

The simplest connection involves the use of two identical voltage-divider resistor pairs having their junctions connected to the positive and negative inputs (Fig. 6.62c). The input terminals of the two networks are then connected to the two wires of the program line. The return terminal of the network connected to the positive input is grounded, and the other return terminal is connected to the output of the operational amplifier. The differential voltage gain of such a circuit is equal to the ratio of the resistance values, while the common-mode gain is limited by resistor accuracy and the residual errors of the operational amplifier and particularly its common-mode rejection. The input impedances of the positive and negative inputs to the circuit are not equal.

This problem is overcome in the *instrumentation amplifier* described in more detail in the section on "Differential Amplifier" below.

A number of gain blocks can then be interconnected to become a more complex amplifier or mixing console.[8]

6.7.5 Feedback and Feed Forward

Feedback is the return of a fraction of the output signal to the input (Fig. 6.63). The returned fraction is added to the input signal at the feedback node in the feedback loop of the system. The input signal to the system with feedback for the same output as before feedback is now the vector sum of the original input signal and the feedback signal. Feedback is negative when the new required input signal is larger than the signal without feedback and positive when it is smaller.

Feedback may be acoustic, mechanical, or electronic, depending upon the type of signal amplified. In amplifiers for audio-frequency signals the feedback signal is usually a portion of the output voltage or output current. When the returned fraction is negative and is obtained through a linear network, the reduction ratio of amplifier errors, such as distortion or phase shift, is proportional to the reduction in amplifier gain due to feedback. In the limit, with very high amplifier gain before feedback, the response of the amplifier with respect to frequency will nearly equal the reciprocal of the loss of the feedback network as measured from output to input.[9]

Linear Feedback.   Linear feedback exists when the feedback signal is only a level-independent portion of the output signal. Negative feedback cannot be applied in ever-increasing amounts because all amplifiers have increasing amounts of phase shift as the limits of the frequency range are approached, particularly at high frequencies (Fig. 6.64). Whenever phase shift of the feedback signal is between 90

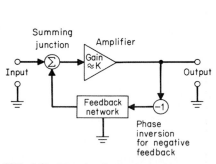

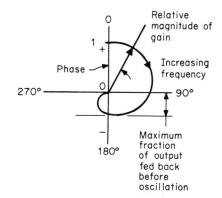

FIG. 6.63 Negative-feedback amplifier. Voltage gain = $K/[1 + (K \times b)]$, where K = amplifier voltage gain without feedback and b = gain of feedback network, usually 1 or less.

FIG. 6.64 Polar plot of amplifier gain and phase from dc relative to frequency. At higher frequencies a negative component of the gain characteristic limits the maximum usable feedback before oscillation occurs.

and 270° of phase with respect to the input signal at the feedback node, amplification with feedback will be greater with feedback than without. In the limit, no more positive feedback signal than the original input signal can be returned to the amplifier input before oscillation starts at the frequency where the returned feedback signal is equal to the original input signal in both amplitude and phase. This condition is desirable only in oscillators, not in amplifiers.

Another reason for using little negative feedback is that some intermediate stage of the amplifier may current-limit feeding a capacitor before the output stage is overloaded by input signals. This distortion is known as *slew-rate limiting* and is a cause of transient intermodulation distortion.

Feed Forward.   Feedback is a method of correcting amplifier errors after they have occurred and have been compared with the input signal (Fig. 6.65). One feed-forward method is to measure the errors that an amplifier will introduce into the output signal and then to feed these errors, inverted in phase, directly to the output summing junction through a separate path, which may also include an amplifier of lesser output range, since only the error signal will have to be supplied. A portion of the resulting output signal may also be fed back for further error correction.

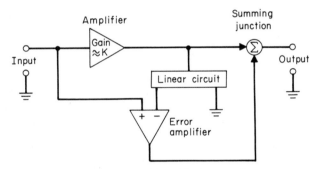

FIG. 6.65   Feed-forward amplifier with phase or gain error correction by negative feedback.

In feed-forward circuits, the error signal is handled by an amplifier, separate from the amplifier whose errors need correcting. In feedback circuits, the error signal is handled by the amplifier causing the errors.

Nonlinear Feedback.   Precision rectifier circuits make use of nonlinear feedback. Here, one or more diodes in the feedback loop of an operational amplifier result in an output signal which is the half-wave or full-wave rectified signal originally present at the input of the circuit (Fig. 6.66). Rectification of signals is a function needed in signal-processing circuits, such as compressors, expanders, meters, and noise reduction circuits for pulse or random noise.

Voltage Feedback.   The output voltage of an amplifier, attenuated in a voltage-divider network, is subtracted from the input voltage, resulting in the amplifier input voltage with feedback (Fig. 6.63). The gain reduction ratio is equal to the reduction ratio of the output impedance of the amplifier, equal to the distortion reduction ratio for signals of the same output voltage, and inversely proportional

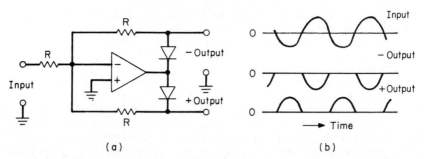

FIG. 6.66 Nonlinear precision-rectifier feedback. (*a*) Operational amplifier circuit. (*b*) Sine-wave input-output waveforms.

to the input impedance increase ratio of the amplifier. When the loop gain of the amplifier is very high, as is normal in operational amplifiers, the voltage gain of the amplifier with feedback is nearly equal to the inverse of the loss of the feedback attenuator and the output impedance of the amplifier becomes very low. Therefore, any variation in amplifier load will have little effect on output voltage until the maximum output-current capability of the amplifier is reached.

In an alternate circuit, the amplifier need not add signal and feedback voltages because only one input terminal is needed. Here, the output voltage is converted to a current using an impedance and fed to the input terminal, which also receives input current from the signal source, perhaps through a second impedance (Fig. 6.62*b*). The amplifier now amplifies the difference between the two currents. Output impedance and distortion are affected as above.

Voltage feedback causes the amplifier to become a nearly constant voltage source with a fixed input signal.[10]

Current Feedback. The output current of an amplifier may conveniently be converted to a voltage by passing this current through an impedance connected in series with the load impedance. The resulting voltage is then applied as a feedback voltage to the amplifier. With such a circuit, the internal output impedance ratio of the amplifier will be equal to the inverse of the current gain reduction ratio achieved, and the distortion reduction ratio will be the same as the output-current reduction ratio for the same input signal. Again, the feedback signal may be a feedback voltage, with the amplifier utilizing the difference in feedback and signal voltages, or a feedback current, with the amplifier supplying current gain.

Current feedback causes the amplifier to become a nearly constant current source with a fixed input signal.

Output and Input Impedance. The output impedance of an amplifier usually varies with frequency and is mostly resistive for an amplifier which has a constant fraction of the output fed back to the input or an intermediate stage. The output impedance is sometimes expressed as the *damping factor* of the amplifier, defined as the ratio of nominal load resistance to amplifier internal output impedance. The value of output impedance also includes any impedances connected between the output wiring terminals and the actual output and ground nodes of the circuit.

Another measure of output impedance of an amplifier is regulation, usually measured in percentages and defined as the change in output voltage as nominal load is changed from open-circuit to rated load. Damping factor and regulation are normally rated at midfrequencies. At the extremes of the frequency range the output impedance of an amplifier will be different from its midfrequency value since the loop gain of an amplifier decreases, particularly at high frequencies. The output impedance of an amplifier can then be described as a two-terminal network of resistors and reactive elements.

Input impedance of an amplifier may often be set by a physical resistor connected across the input terminals which shunts the input impedance of the circuit. The additional component of the input impedance sometimes rated is the *input capacitance,* partially composed of the wiring capacitance and any capacitors which are part of the radio-frequency filters of the input circuit or are capacitors designed to give the desired termination to playback heads of magnetic-tape equipment or disk playback cartridges. In low-noise amplifiers, the input resistance component will be largely determined by feedback to the input circuit.

When a number of amplifiers and other circuits are connected in series so that each amplifier amplifies the output signal from the previous circuit, the connections are often made on a voltage basis, in which each amplifier has a relatively high input impedance and a relatively low output impedance. Here, the amplifier takes very little of the load current which could be provided by the circuit at its input, and its own output voltage changes very little, whether supplying full-load current or not. This type of design is used most often in self-contained equipment or in pieces of equipment operated in close proximity to each other. Many sound reinforcement systems operate as constant-voltage systems, and the power amplifiers provide sine-wave output voltages of 25 to 75 V at full output power to the loudspeaker circuits.

Audio equipment used as part of large distributed systems or with program transmission lines is often designed to present a constant output impedance and input impedance to match the nominal impedance of transmission lines. Audio line impedances of 150 or 600 Ω are common values. At video and radio frequencies, transmission-line impedances of 50, 75, and 300 Ω are preferred.

Equipment designed to operate in constant-impedance circuits is often rated in decibels with respect to 1 mW (dBm) of output power into a matched load. Gain or loss are given in decibels, and systems are designed on a power gain or loss basis. The advantage of operating circuits at matched transmission-line impedances is that reflections or echoes of signals will not be generated at the receiving end of a traveling signal. This is of importance when the highest frequency will result in more than 30° or so of delay in the longest circuit, corresponding to one-twelfth of one wavelength transmission-line length or about ½ mi of shielded cable at 20 kHz.

Feed Forward and Correction of Estimated Errors.   Feed-forward error correction is described earlier in Section 6.7.5. Some error correction can be accomplished by making a good estimate of the error and then predistorting the signal with opposing distortion. An example is the error introduced by the nonlinear transfer curve of an analog magnetic-tape recorder, which can be established only by measurement of the playback signal, which occurs only after a time-varying delay after recording. Here a model of the tape-recorder distortion must first be devised and compared with the actual machine to be corrected. This model may contain amplitude or phase nonlinearities, or both. Then, the output signal from the amplifier may be passed through the network, and the difference between network input and network output is the error signal to be added to the amplifier output signal as an input to the tape recorder. Such a correction is very complex and needs much time to find the acceptable and achievable result, notably in the modeling of distortion.

Differential Amplifier. Amplifiers which allow the measurement or use of signals generated remote from the point of equipment location are call *instrumentation amplifiers.* These amplifiers have controlled amplification for the difference in voltage between two signals and very low amplification for the sum of the two signals, the measurement of the voltages made with the local ground reference. In audio terms, these amplifiers have a controlled differential- or transverse-mode gain and a low common- or longitudinal-mode gain. The common instrumentation amplifier connection uses three operational amplifiers, with the first two amplifiers amplifying the two signals equally and sharing a common feedback resistor R_1 between the two negative inputs. The output signals then pass through two identical resistor attenuators R_3, R_4, with the resistor junctions connected to the positive and negative inputs of the third amplifier and resistor R_4 completing the connection between positive input and ground and negative input and output.

A simplified-version instrumentation amplifier omits the two input stages and connects signal wires directly to the two resistor networks, which now present unequal loads to the two signal wires (Fig. 6.62c).

The performance of a differential or instrumentation amplifier is measured by its common-mode rejection, which is the ratio of differential- to common-mode gain. This value is largely determined by the accuracy of resistor matching and the ratio of amplifier loop gain to circuit gain. Common signals must not exceed the maximum allowable common-mode input signal for the amplifier.

Differential amplifiers are used in audio equipment when signal sources are widely separated or when ground-loop signals may exist. The two input-signal leads of a differential amplifier are brought directly to the source of signals, often as a pair of twisted wires within a common shield.

The use of a well-shielded audio-frequency input transformer ahead of a normal amplifier (Fig. 6.58b) allows this amplifier to have normal differential-mode gain and very low common-mode gain, limited primarily by the lack of balance of transformer construction and by interwinding shielding.

6.7.6 Linear Feedback Amplifiers

Specification and Tolerances. Any specifications resulting from following the methods described in the standard used have at least two values, the nominal value and the tolerance or deviation from the nominal value. When describing a group of devices, all made to the same design, the specification and tolerance may be defined as a typical value, describing the typical device, or may be a worst-case set of numbers that describes all products made. The system results then can be expressed similarly.

The allowance for overall tolerance then may be a worst-case treatment, with all tolerances of the components trending always in the same direction. This assumption may be correct for distortion or gain compression in systems. Another method involves the root-sum-square addition of errors to arrive at a tolerance to be expected. This latter method is applicable when the sources of error are not correlated, such as the generation of residual random noise or the gain adjustment of individual amplifiers.

Gain. Gain of an amplifier is given in decibels of insertion gain in a terminated system. An alternate method is to give the voltage-amplification factor. A further method is to give the amount of input voltage required to produce rated output voltage or output power into a rated load. Gain may also be given as a curve of output signal with respect to input signal.

Distortion and Noise.   Distortion of an amplifier is not a single number since it depends on signal level, frequency, load, and type of distortion measured. The standards used for defining the method of measurement often show methods of rating. The Federal Trade Commission uses a worst-case definition, which may provide a single useful number. Distortion may be given as a percentage or in decibels below sine-wave output. Multitone distortion may be given with respect to a single sine wave of the same peak-to-peak value as the peak-to-peak envelope signal.

Noise may be given similarly, or it may be described more fully as to level with respect to frequency. Noise may be rated as wideband noise, or it may be weighted according to standard methods which reflect the ability of the ear to perceive sounds more acutely at middle audio frequencies.

Input and Output Impedance.   Input and output impedances of an amplifier may be given as resistance values only or as a circuit containing resistors, capacitors, and inductors as needed. Output impedance may also be given as a damping factor which is the ratio of nominal load impedance to output impedance.

Frequency Response.   The amplitude-frequency response defines the ability of an amplifier to amplify signals over a range of frequencies. The methods of measurement define the level of operation, the source, and the load for such a test. The tolerance of response is usually given as a separate set of plus and minus decibel numbers with respect to a flat respone or a standard curve, such as the playback equalization for disk recordings.

Secondary response specifications include phase-frequency response and amplitude-time response or recovery time to a voltage tolerance after a defined voltage step.

Feedback Amplifiers for Filters and Equalizers.   Feedback amplifiers for filters and equalizers may be operational amplifiers using feedback through passive resistor-capacitor networks to achieve the desired amplitude-frequency response. Such amplifiers must not only be capable of providing an output signal but also be able to provide signal to the passive network.

Depending upon the type of network used, the response of the amplifier will affect the overall response to a greater or lesser degree. For example, second-order low-pass filters of the Sallen-Key type need only one operational amplifier but are sensitive to amplifier characteristics, while the state-variable method of filter design needs a number of operational amplifiers, most of them as integrating amplifiers and less sensitive to amplifier bandwidth.[11]

Amplifiers with Nonlinear Feedback.   The most common amplifier with nonlinear feedback is the precision rectifier, used for measuring signal level. The usual connection involves the use of two diodes connected directly to the output of an operational amplifier, one of them conducting the positive signal and the other for the negative signal. The other ends of the diodes send feedback current to the negative input of the operational amplifier, which receives signal current through a third resistor. The waveforms at the diode-resistor junctions are the half-wave rectified signal waves, with the polarities given by diode direction. The direct output of the operational amplifier is distorted by the extra voltage drop of the diodes and is not used.

The half-wave signals can be combined into a full-wave rectified signal by feeding each to the two inputs of a differential amplifier. The other method uses only one of the half-wave signals, which is fed through a fourth resistor to the negative input of a second operational amplifier, which also receives input current from the circuit input through a fifth resistor, made twice as large as the fourth, when the first three resistors are equal. A feedback resistor for the second amplifier completes the circuit, along with a capacitor to set the integrating time constant (Fig. 6.67 provides average dc output equal to peak sine-wave input).

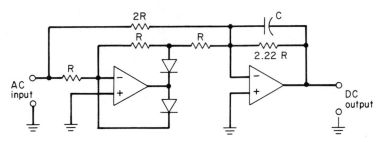

FIG. 6.67 Cascaded precision-rectifier circuit and integrating amplifier convert rms sine-wave voltage to equivalent dc value.

Variable-Gain Amplifiers. Control of signal amplitude by a voltage or a current requires a circuit portion which can vary signal current without introducing current transients.

If switching signal amplitude is sufficient, a multiplying digital-to-analog converter may be inserted in the signal path. Such a device has very low distortion, but the sudden change in amplitude will cause audible modulation sidebands.

An FET at a low source-drain voltage is a resistance which can be controlled by the gate-source voltage. When the maximum signal voltage is restricted to less than tens of millivolts, signal current can be controlled from zero to a maximum given by the on resistance of the FET (Fig. 6.68a). Distortion can be reduced by adding approximately one-half of the signal voltage across the FET channel to the gate voltage. Multiple FET channels can be controlled by a single voltage when matching monolithic FETs are used.

Photosensitive resistors made of cadmium sulfide or cadmium selenide are used in exposure meters for cameras and have also been used in light-controlled attenuators. They have a relatively low time constant of resistance change with increasing illumination but a long time constant for return to high resistance when light is extinguished. No measurable distortion is added.

Motor-driven controls have the low distortion of manual controls but suffer from mechanical problems when abused with spilled liquids.

When four matched transistors are connected as two emitter-coupled pairs and each pair receives the same-value emitter bias current, the collector currents are matched (Fig. 6.68b). If now the differential control voltage is varied and the collectors are interconnected, the sum of the collector currents in each output pair will remain constant. If a signal current is superimposed on one emitter bias current, the signal output current can be steered from one output section, through sharing in both sections, to the other section. The total signal current can be kept constant by feedback. The result is a voltage-controlled amplifier, with distortion limited principally by the accuracy of current sharing.

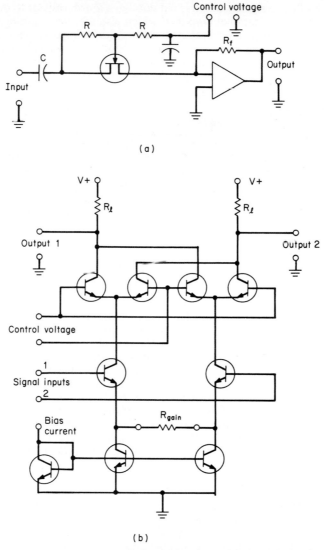

FIG. 6.68   Voltage-controlled variable-gain amplifiers. (*a*) Channel-resistance control of an FET feedback amplifier. (*b*) Monolithic circuit with coupled differential pairs.

The use of multiplier circuits creating the logarithm of the input current, then adding a voltage and passing the total to an antilogarithm element is another method of voltage-controlled amplification if four-quadrant multiplier circuits are used. Here careful device matching is needed, and close thermal coupling is required to minimize distortion to a small fraction of 1 percent and to keep gain-control transients from appearing in the signal path.

Voltage-controlled amplifiers are the active elements in compressors, expanders, noise-reducing systems, and console automation systems. They also find extensive use in music and speech synthesis equipment.

6.7.7 Special Power Amplifier Considerations

Audio power amplifiers present design problems which go beyond general amplifier design limitations. Except for power amplifiers of low power output rating, power amplifiers are not single integrated circuits but are an assembly involving multiple discrete bipolar or field-effect transistors spread over a substantial printed-circuit-board area. Power amplifiers are subject to varying input signals, including those which will cause overload. They generally drive reactive loads, need heat removal, and most often are supplied by unregulated power supplies, which also supply the other channels for stereophonic sound reproduction. Power amplifiers must be low-noise amplifiers because they are connected as the last stage of amplification after all gain and equalization controls and after all noise reduction circuitry.

Dissipation and Efficiency. In the absence of an input signal, power amplifiers dissipate as heat the products of current and voltage from each power supply voltage source. The currents may be the currents drawn by the low-level stages of the amplifier as well as the bias current of the output stage.

When supplied with an input signal, the power amplifier circuit may be considered to be one or more voltage-controlled resistors connected between the load and the supply voltage source. These resistors consume dc power and convert it to heat, which must be dissipated. If, in addition, the load has a reactive component, any energy transmitted to the load reactance must be dissipated in the load resistance and the amplifier output stage when signal polarity changes.

It is customary to rate the power output of an amplifier as the maximum sine-wave signal which can be delivered to the rated resistive load with no more than rated distortion in the rated frequency range. It is also customary to speak of ideal amplifiers which consume no idling power, except that given by their class of operation, and which can deliver an output-voltage waveform as large as the voltage supply. In such a case, the voltage-controlled resistances can vary between zero and infinite resistance.

Under these circumstances, the efficiency of an ideal Class A amplifier will be 50 percent and the efficiency of an ideal Class B amplifier will be 78.5 percent when both are delivering maximum sine-wave power output. This efficiency will decrease proportionally to output-voltage amplitude, becoming zero as zero power output is approached. The ideal Class D switching amplifier would have 100 percent efficiency at all output levels.

Any practical amplifiers will have lesser efficiency. The amplification of any real program material will show that the peak-to-average ratio of the signal is higher than that of a sine wave, further reducing attainable efficiency. Amplifier efficiency is further reduced by the energy delivered to the reactive portion of the load but dissipated in the amplifier.

When designing the heat-removing structure of an amplifier, it is fair to assume that most or nearly all the power consumed by the amplifier may be dissipated within the amplifier and its power supply. The major remaining question is to predict the probable worst-case signal to be handled by the amplifier. Here, Underwriters Laboratories, a safety agency, requires amplifier testing at 10 percent sine-wave output power for equipment used in the home and at 30 percent for commercial equipment, while the Federal Trade Commission insists on a 100 percent power test. All these tests use rated resistive load, require simultaneous operation of all amplifier channels, and specify the ventilation and temperature of the test.

Resistive and Reactive Loads.   The stresses on the output devices may be visualized by constructing the load line superimposed on the current-voltage diagram of each individual output and driver device (Fig. 6.69*a* and *b*). The load line for a resistive load is a straight line regardless of the waveform of the output voltage. The maximum instantaneous dissipation for a device occurs when the product of voltage across the device and current through the device is a maximum. This occurs at one-half of the supply voltage to the device when the current through the device is one-half of the peak current.

With reactive loads the load line becomes an ellipse when the output waveform is a sine wave. Since no reverse currents are allowed in a device, the ellipse continues as a straight line at zero current until current at some different voltage begins to rise again. As long as no overload exists, this straight line will not exist in Class A amplifiers. In Class AB amplifiers, the straight line will not exist when the combination of output voltage and phase angle is less than a critical maximum. The direction of travel along the load line depends only on the direction of the phase of the load.

When the output waveform through the device is nonsinusoidal and the load impedance is highly reactive, the load line will exist anywhere in the area limited by the maximum device current and zero and the total of positive and negative supply voltage and zero. Maximum instantaneous device dissipation can now become the product of maximum device current and total supply voltage, or 8 times higher than with resistive load.

Instantaneous device dissipation is of importance since the first thermal time constant of a transistor is the product of the thermal mass of the junction and the thermal resistance of silicon from the junction to the heat spreader within the transistor case. In FETs, the thermal mass of the channel is of importance. This time constant may be only a few microseconds, or less than a small fraction of a cycle of any audio waveform.

Allowable dissipation for a power device is usually published as a series of curves for various pulse lengths. Since heat sinks have a time constant much

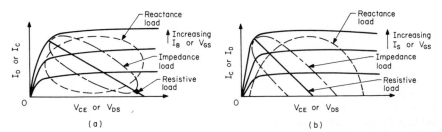

FIG. 6.69   Resistive and reactive load characteristics. (*a*) Class A amplifier with sine-wave input. (*b*) One side of a Class B amplifier, indicating the increase in instantaneous dissipation as the load phase angle increases although the sine-wave peak output currents and voltage remain constant.

longer than the syllabic rate of speech or the length of sustained musical notes, the average time-integrated dissipation of an amplifier should be used for heat-sink design, employing the highest power line voltage and the lowest impedance load.

The lowest frequency handled in an amplifier will lie below the lowest musical note and may well be a transient in power turn-on or equipment connection, with power turned on, or some other accidental event. The lowest frequency will now be determined by the low-frequency response of the amplifier following the over-loaded stage. This time of maximum dissipation may last about 1 s. This is the time when only a fraction of the heat generated within the output device has reached the heat sink through all other time constants. For such a condition, the 1-s pulse contour of a device will define the safe operating area. The shape of the voltage and current waveforms must be determined experimentally with a worst-case load.

Signal Overload and Recovery from Overload. It is not unusual for an amplifier to be subjected to input signals larger than required to produce full output. Then the amplifier will be driven into clipping. Clipping is the condition that occurs when a signal output of any stage has a flat or clipped top or bottom, or both. The avoidance of clipping would require that the supply voltage be increased in pro-portion to signal demand. This process is not practical in most amplifier designs, and all designs have a maximum safe supply voltage which must not be exceeded.

A measure of amplifier quality is the time required to recover from overload. This time may be as short as a fraction of 1 μms for comparators or amplifiers used in analog-to-digital converters. If, however, the amplifier contains coupling capacitors, recovery from overload will be longer if any capacitor is allowed to charge because of rectification of the overload signal within the amplifier.

The amplifier will recover by discharge of the capacitors charged by the exces-sive signal. This time depends on the discharge time constant of the circuit con-taining the capacitor and the amount of charge delivered to the capacitor during overload.

Amplifier overload problems can be minimized by designing the amplifier for quick recovery and by the use of direct coupling and push-pull amplifier circuits.

Output-Circuit Overload and Overload Protection. Power amplifiers are used to deliver signal power to loudspeakers, disk-recorder cutting heads, motors, and many other loads. At times the load may become misconnected, or an excessive load may be connected. One of the most severe types of loads may be a short circuit in the connecting cable to the load. With only moderate input signals to the amplifier, excessive output currents may be demanded from the output circuit because of substantial voltage feedback. If the short circuit should be in the loud-speaker wiring, human tendency is to turn up the volume because the sound is not loud enough. This condition ensures that the output devices and the power supply will be subjected to maximum stress.

As shown above, transistors and FETs must not be subjected to current pulses at voltages outside the safe-area contour for the device. Many circuits have been devised to cope with the overload problem. One method, usually employed in small amplifiers, consists of using sufficiently rugged output devices and a power supply of high impedance capable of dissipating excessive demand in resistors.

A different method senses overload and then disconnects the load terminals from the amplifier. The power supply may also become disconnected from the power line and may also be discharged, using a silicon-controlled rectifier (SCR). All devices in such a design must be sufficiently rugged to withstand overload until the protective circuit has operated. The circuit must then be restored to operation by turning the power switch on.

Some designs sense the temperature of the device or the heat sink. Excessive temperature will then cause circuit shutdown or turn on a fan to cool the heat sink.

A popular method is to sense the output current and to limit the drive signal to the output stage when excessive currents are detected (Fig. 6.70a). Current sensing may also be coupled with sensing the voltage across the output devices (Fig. 6.70b). Each output stage of a push-pull amplifier may be sensed separately, and the drive signal for each will then be controlled separately as fast as the circuit can control the signal. Time constants are sometimes included in the control circuit to simulate the safe-area contours of the affected devices.

The method of sensing device voltage and current will cause the stage to have a negative internal resistance during the limiting of the drive signal. If current and voltage levels are chosen so that reactive loads of proper nominal impedance, say, 3.2 Ω in a 4-Ω output load, will cause the protection circuit to act with a large input signal, then it may be possible that very annoying switching noises will be created as the combined circuit tries to "protect."

One effect of overload of an amplifier with a reactive load impedance is the return of energy stored in the reactance. When current is interrupted in a capacitor, the charge remains in the capacitor until the current flows again in the opposite direction after overload.

Loudspeakers and other reactive devices can act as a resonant circuit which has an inductive reactance at frequencies below resonance. Any interruption of current will now create a high voltage, limited only by any resistance or capacitance in parallel with the inductance. This voltage is in opposition to the voltage in the load just prior to overload, and current will try to flow in the amplifier stage not providing the previous output voltage, thereby stressing the stage.

More serious is the fact that the stage previously supplying current will become reversed in collector-emitter or drain-source voltage, causing excessive momentary dissipation and possible destruction of the device. The cure for this problem is to shunt each output stage with a rectifier diode which is reverse-biased for normal operation (Fig. 6.70b). This diode acts as a low resistance during overload and returns stored energy to the supply circuit.

As long as there is a reasonably constant current flowing from the supply, this returned energy can be safey dissipated. If, however, little current flows, then the supply voltage will be raised since no current can flow back to the power line through the rectifier circuit. Very efficient amplifier circuits must guard against overvoltage from this source by using a discharge circuit.

Heat Removal. Nearly all the power consumed by an amplifier in normal use will be converted to heat. The thermal resistances along the way from the device junctions or the "hot" resistances dissipating the power will cause everything to heat as the thermal power flows outward. The temperature of each critical part can then be calculated, using the thermal resistances in degrees celsius per watt, and the power in watts dissipated. These thermal resistances are published for semiconductors and heat sinks. Sometimes the amplifier chassis becomes the heat sink. Here, a heat flow of ⅛ W/in² will cause a heat rise of about 40° C with natural convection.

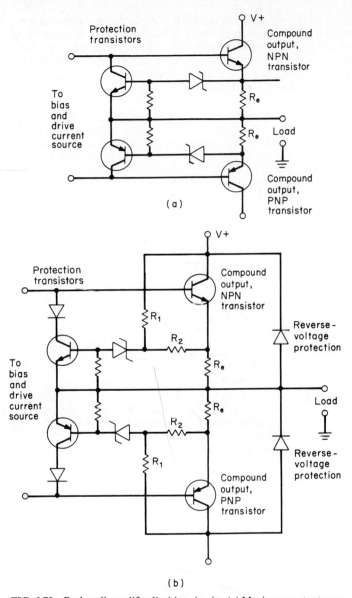

FIG. 6.70 Push-pull amplifier limiting circuits. (*a*) Maximum output-current limiting occurs when voltage drop across either emitter resistor exceeds the sum of the zener-diode and base-emitter voltage of the protection transistors, which then shunt any excess drive current directly into load. (*b*) Limiting when current and voltage on the output stage are higher than the limit set by the conduction of drive current by the protection transistors.

To estimate the actual temperature, it is necessary to know the temperature of the surroundings into which the heat must flow. Normal room temperature is often defined as being between $+10$ and $+40°$ C, while temperature in an automobile may range between -40 and $+90°$ C in the passenger compartment, with higher temperatures under the hood. If equipment installation is near heaters or has restricted airflow, temperatures higher than room temperatures will be found.

Voltage or Power Gain, dBV or dBm. The voltage gain of an amplifier can be expressed as a number which is the ratio of output voltage to input voltage. When amplifiers are cascaded, these numbers must be multiplied by each other to arrive at the overall voltage gain. The product of input voltage and gain is the output voltage. Voltage gain of an amplifier depends on the ratio of load impedance to output impedance of the amplifier. If this number is large, voltage gain will show only a small change from the open-circuit voltage gain. Passive circuits usually have a voltage loss, which may be defined as a voltage gain smaller than 1.

Voltages may be stated in decibels with reference to a known voltage. When this voltage is 1, voltages can be expressed in decibels above 1 V (dbV), where 0 dBV equals 1 V, -60 dBV equals 1 mV, and -120 dBV equals 1 mV. The voltage gain of a system may also be expressed in decibels as long as it is unmistakably stated as voltage gain because of confusion with power gain in a matched system. Voltage gain is generally used in systems where the load impedance is not a defined system impedance used for input and output.

Many sysems are designed as matched systems in which circuit impedance is equal to the output and input impedance of the amplifier. In audio systems 600 Ω is preferred. Some systems operate at 150 Ω. The preferred impedance of video systems is 75 Ω, and radio-frequency systems have a preferred impedance of 50 Ω.

When a system is matched, voltage gain and power gain are equal and *gain* alone is used to define the system components. Levels of operation are typically given in decibels above 1 mW (dBm), which is defined as the power delivered to a matched load measured in decibels with respect to 1 mW. Only rarely is dBW, the power level with respect to 1 W, used.

Power gain of an amplifier in decibels automatically assumes that the amplifier has an input impedance and an output impedance equal to the rated system impedance and that gain is measured when the amplifier is loaded with the rated system impedance load. More precisely, the gain of the amplifier is the insertion gain, with the amplifier inserted between signal source and load which were thought to be connected directly before amplifier insertion. Passive circuits have a loss, which is equal to a negative-decibel gain.

Bridging amplifiers have an input impedance which is high compared with the system impedance, and a group of them can be connected with their inputs in parallel across a channel which has a separate load equal to the circuit impedance. In this fashion, one channel can be split into several channels. The bridging gain, then, is the ratio of the power levels in the output circuit of the amplifier to the level in the input circuit.

Systems which are designed to be connected to transmission circuits, such as telephone lines, have their output and input signals measured in dBm and are rated in decibel gain. Systems which are self-contained, such as amplifiers for home use, have their output and input levels rated in volts for signal levels needed to achieve a maximum output power in watts into a nominal load.

In many systems gain may not be specified, and only an electrical output level or input level and a reference level in a different dimension are given. Examples of these differing dimensions are the sound pressure levels for microphones or loudspeakers, the magnetization of tape, or the groove velocity of disk records.

Audio-Cirucit Impedances. The many uses of audio-frequency signals have brought about various standards. The standard impedance in audio circuits in recording studios and broadcast systems is 600 Ω; circuits are usually balanced. In some systems, microphone circuit impedance may be 150 Ω.

Public address and sound reinforcement systems operate at the same impedance for low-level and line-level circuits; however, loudspeaker circuits operate from a constant-voltage circuit, with full amplifier sine-wave power equal to 70 V in many systems and 25-V circuits used less often.

Digital audio circuits now operate in a balanced 110-Ω circuit for equipment interconnection.

Most loudspeaker circuits are designed to be driven from a constant voltage into the nominal loudspeaker impedance of 4 or 8 Ω, with lesser usage of 2 or 16 Ω. The circuit usually has one wire grounded; however, bridge-mode amplifiers have a balanced output.

Pickups for analog disk recordings are most often designed to be terminated by a preamplifier input impedance of 47 kΩ, with one wire of each channel grounded to the preamplifier ground.

Almost all equipment for recording and reproduction of sound in the home operates in a constant-voltage mode, using coaxial cables to interconnect the unbalanced circuits.

REFERENCES

1. W. Shockley, "The Theory of P-N Junctions in Semiconductors and P-N Junction Transistors," *Proc. IRE,* **41** (June 1953).

2. W. Shockley, "A Unipolar Field-Effect Transistor," *Proc. IRE,* **40** (November 1952).

3. R. J. Kirchner, "Properties of Junction Transistors," *Trans. IRE PGA,* **AU-3**(4) (July–August 1955).

4. R. L. Trent, "Design Principles for Transistor Audio Amplifiers," *Trans. IRE PGA,* **AU-3**(5) (September–October 1955).

5. L. H. Garner, "High-Power Solid State Amplifiers," *Trans. IRE PGA,* **15**(4) (December 1967).

6. D. R. Fewer, "Design Principles for Junction Transistor Audio Power Amplifiers," *Trans. IRE PGA,* **AU-3**(6) (November–December 1955).

7. A. Petersen and D. B. Sinclair, "A Singled-Ended Push-Pull Audio Amplifier," *Proc. IRE,* **40**, (January 1952).

8. R. J. Widlar, "A Unique Current Design for a High Performance Operational Amplifier Especially Suited to Monolithic Construction," *Proc. NEC* (1965).

9. H. S. Black, U.S. Patent 2,102,671.

10. P. J. Walker, "A Current Dumping Audio Power Amplifier," *Wireless World* (December 1975).

11. P. J. Baxandall, "Negative Feedback Tone Control—Independent Variation of Bass and Treble without Switches," *Wireless World,* **58** (October 1952).

BIBLIOGRAPHY

Harper, C. A. (ed.): *Handbook of Components for Electronics,* McGraw-Hill, New York, 1977.

Lynn, D. K., C. S. Meyer, and D. C. Hamilton (eds.): *Analysis and Design of Integrated Circuits,* McGraw-Hill, New York, 1967.

Weinberg, L.: *Network Analysis and Synthesis,* McGraw-Hill, New York, 1967.

CHAPTER 7
SOUND REPRODUCTION DEVICES AND SYSTEMS

Katsuaki Satoh
Chief Engineer, Acoustic Research Laboratory, Matsushita Electric Industrial Co., Ltd., Osaka, Japan

7.1 OPERATIONAL ANALYSIS OF ELECTROACOUSTIC TRANSDUCERS

Conversion from electrical signals to acoustic signals ordinarily does not involve direct electroacoustic transformation; the electrical signal is transformed into mechanical vibration, which then is transformed into an acoustic signal.

The following transducers are used in the audio field generally as electromechanical transducers: electrodynamic transducers, electromagnetic transducers, electrostatic transducers, and piezoelectric transducers.

7.1.1 Basic Equations and Features of Dynamic Transducers

Among the various forms of transducers listed above, the electrodynamic type is the basis for the design of the majority of loudspeakers in use today. Invented by C. W. Rice and E. W. Kellogg in 1925, when combined with the vacuum-tube amplifier, it provided the means for the use of audio technology in applications far greater than the telephone, introduced 50 years earlier by Alexander Graham Bell. Figure 7.1 shows the principle of operation. A permanent magnet and magnetic-pole pieces form a uniform magnetic field in the gap. The coil vibrating direction is at right angles to the magnetic field so that the force acts on the coil in accordance with the Fleming rule. This relationship is expressed by the following equation:

$$F_d = B\ell I \qquad (7.1)$$

where F_d = driving force, N
B = flux density, Wb/m^2
ℓ = total length of coil, m
I = current flowing into coil, A

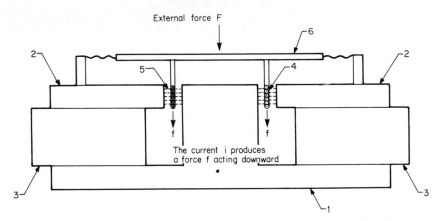

FIG. 7.1 Simplified form of a moving-coil transducer consisting of a voice coil cutting a magnetic field of a flux density B. 1, 2 = pole pieces; 3 = permanent magnet; 4 = voice coil; 5 = magnetic flux; 6 = diaphragm.

Assuming the velocity at which a coil moves by means of driving force F_d to be v, the electromotive force E_d arising from this movement is in the opposite direction to the direction of current I. Therefore, E_d is determined by

$$E_d = -Blv \qquad (7.2)$$

where E_d = counterelectromotive force, V
      v = moving-coil velocity, m/s

BI in Eqs. (7.1) and (7.2) is called the *power coefficient A*, which shows the conversion efficiency of a dynamic transducer. Assuming the mechanical impedance of the vibrating system as viewed from the coil side to be Z_m, the force acting on the coil corresponds to a summation of external forces F and driving forces F_d, which is balanced with drag $Z_m v$.

$$F + F_d = Z_m v \qquad (7.3)$$

where F = external force, N
      F_d = driving force, N
      Z_m = mechanical impedance of the vibrating system, mechanical ohms

By substituting Eq. (7.1), F is found as follows:

$$F = Z_m v - AI \qquad (7.4)$$

In the electrical system, assuming the electrical impedance of the driving coil to be Z_e, the total voltage at the coil terminals corresponds to a summation of E and E_d, whereby the following equation is obtained:

$$E + E_d = Z_e I \qquad (7.5)$$

where E = voltage applied across coil terminals, V
      Z_e = electrical impedance of coil, Ω

When Eq. (7.2) is substituted, E is determined by

$$E = Z_e I + Av \qquad (7.6)$$

Thus, Eqs. (7.4) and (7.6) are basic equations of the dynamic mechanical-electrical systems.

7.1.2 Basic Equations and Features of Electromagnetic Transducers

An electromagnetic transducer is employed most frequently as a telephone receiver. A magnetic diaphragm placed in a static magnetic field, in which a permanent magnet supplies the steady magnetic flux, is vibrated in an ac magnetic field formed by signal current flowing into a coil, thus generating a sound. This principle is shown in Fig. 7.2. In this figure, assume that the diaphragm is subjected to attraction force F_m by the static magnetic field and the external force F. At this time, the diaphragm vibrates from a summation of static displacement ξ_s by the attraction force in the static magnetic field and by the dynamic displacement generated by an ac magnetic field and external force F. Assuming this to be ξ, ξ is expressed by

$$\xi = \xi_s + \xi_d \tag{7.7}$$

where ξ = total displacement, m
   ξ_s = static displacement, m
   ξ_d = dynamic displacement, m

Assuming the equivalent circuit of the mechanical system of the diaphragm to be a single-resonance circuit with the number of degrees of freedom equal to 1, it may be regarded as being composed of the lumped constant of equivalent mass, the mechanical resistance, and the stiffness s. Therefore, from force-balanced conditions, the following is established:

$$F + F_m = m\frac{\partial^2\xi}{\partial t^2} + r\frac{\partial\xi}{\partial t} + s\xi \tag{7.8}$$

where F = external force, N
   F_m = attraction force by static magnetic field, N
   m = equivalent mass, kg
   r = mechanical resistance, N/m
   s = stiffness, Ns/m

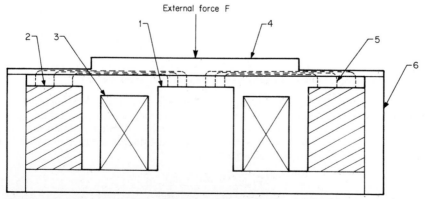

FIG. 7.2 Simplified form of an electromagnetic transducer. 1 = pole piece; 2 = permanent magnet; 3 = drive coil; 4 = diaphragm; 5 = magnet flux; 6 = frame.

If the resistance is ignored, since it is quite negligible compared with magnetic resistance in the air space, the following relation is obtained:

$$Z_m = r + j\omega m - j(s - s_n)/\omega \qquad (7.9)$$

$$A = \mu_0 s_n U_0/g_0^2 \qquad (7.10)$$

$$s_n = \mu_0 S U_0^2/g_0^2 \qquad (7.11)$$

$$Z_e = Z_c + j\omega L_m \qquad (7.12)$$

$$L_m = \mu_0 n^2 S/g_0 \qquad (7.13)$$

$$F = Z_m v - AI \qquad (7.14)$$

$$E = Z_e I + Av \qquad (7.15)$$

where Z_m = mechanical impedance of the vibrating system, mechanical ohms
  ω = angular frequency, rad/s
  A = force factor, N/A
  s_n = negative stiffness, Ns/m
  L_m = inductance, H
  Φ = total magnetic flux in space, Wb
  B = flux density, Wb/m^2
  μ_0 = magnetic permeability in space, H/m
  U_m = magnetic motive force of magnet, A/m
  S = magnetic-pole area, m^2
  g_0 = quiescent space length in magnetic-force-free conditions, m
  n = number of coil windings, turns
  I = current flowing into coil, A
  Z_c = coil electrical impedance, Ω

The difference between this transducer and the magnetic or dynamic transducer, in addition to the gap, is that negative stiffness in Eq. (7.11) is generated. This stable condition is as follows:

$$s > U_0/2\mu_0 S_0 g_0 R_{air}^2 \qquad (7.16)$$

where R_{air}^2 = magnetic resistance out of the air space, A/m. This relationship is shown in Fig. 7.3. Other differences are that since the coil is fixed, reliability is high and construction is simple, and that if the frequency is high, the force factor becomes small because of the coil inductance, thereby reducing efficiency.

7.1.3 Basic Equations and Features of Electrostatic Transducers

In the static transducer, when voltage is applied to two opposite conductive electrodes, an electrostatic attraction force is generated between them, and the action of this force causes a conductive diaphragm to be vibrated, thereby emitting sound. Figure 7.4 shows the construction. Electrostatic attraction force F_s, when signal voltage E is applied to polarized E_0, is

$$F = \frac{\varepsilon_0 S(E_0 + E)^2}{2(g_0 - \xi_0 - \xi_d)^2} \qquad (7.17)$$

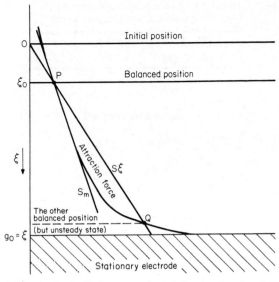

FIG. 7.3 Static displacement shows balancing the attraction and the recover force.

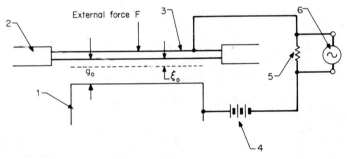

FIG. 7.4 Cross-sectional view of an electrostatic transducer. 1 = back electrode; 2 = clamping ring; 3 = diaphragm with electrode; 4 = polarizing power supply; 5 = polarizing electrical resistance; 6 = signal source.

where F = static attraction force, N
  ε_0 = dielectric constant, F/m
  S = electrode area, m^2
  E_0 = polarized voltage, V
  E = signal voltage, V
  g_0 = interelectrode distance, m
  ξ_s = static displacement, m
  ξ_d = signal displacement, m

Considering the correspondence between electromagnetic and electrostatic types, Eq. (7.17) is as shown in Table 7.1.

TABLE 7.1 Correspondence between Electromagnetic and Electrostatic Types

Electromagnetic type	nI	U_0	μ_0	F_m	ϕ
Electrostatic type	E	E_0	ε_0	F_s	q

The basic equations of the electrostatic type are

$$s_n = \varepsilon_0 S E_0^2 / g_0^3 \qquad (7.18)$$

$$A = \varepsilon_0 S E_0 / g_0^2 \qquad (7.19)$$

$$Z_m = r + j\omega m - j(s - s_n)/\omega \qquad (7.20)$$

$$Y_s = j\omega(\varepsilon_0 S / g_0) \qquad (7.21)$$

$$F = Z_m v - AE \qquad (7.22)$$

$$I = Y_s F + A v \qquad (7.23)$$

where Z_m = mechanical impedance of the vibrating system, mechanical ohms
Y_s = electrical admittance of electrostatic capacity before displacement
F = external force, N
I = current, A
s_n = negative stiffness, N/m
A = force factor, N/V
r = mechanical resistance, Ns/m
m = mass, kg
s = diaphragm stiffness, N/m
ω = angular frequency, rad/s

Equations 7.22 and 7.23 are basic equations of the electrostatic transducer. Sensitivity of this transducer can be obtained by increasing the polarized voltage and reducing the distance between electrodes. Since the electrostatic type, unlike the electromagnetic type, has nothing to restrict attraction force, the force of the diaphragm to stick to the electrode is infinite. Therefore, the diaphragm requires a very large stiffness. Electrical impedance decreases inversely proportionally to the frequency since it is quantitative. This type is simply constructed, and since it has relatively good characteristics, it is used for microphones not requiring a large-amplitude output, high-range speakers, and headphones.

7.1.4 Basic Equations and Features of Piezoelectric Transducers

If a crystal section is distorted with a force applied in one direction, positive and negative charges appear on the opposite surfaces of the crystal. This is called the *piezoelectric direct effect*. When a field is applied to the crystal section from the outside, a mechanically distorted force is generated. This is a *piezoelectric countereffect*. Ferrodielectric substances, which exhibit such a phenomenon, are polarized. These include crystal, piezoelectric crystals such as Rochelle salts, titanium oxide, and lead zirconate titanate (PZT). In general, PZT, having high reliability and a reasonable price, is used as the piezoelectric element for the speaker. By

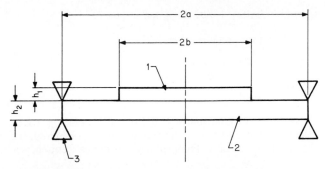

FIG. 7.5 Simplified form of a monomorphic piezoelectric transducer.
1 = piezoelectric element (E_1, ρ_1, μ_1); 2 = metal plate (E_2, ρ_2, μ_2); 3 = supporting ring.

using a configuration such as shown in Fig. 7.5, the output sound level and resonance frequency are determined as follows. Power sensitivity q, when radian frequency $\omega \rightarrow 0$, is calculated by

$$q_0 = 20 \log \left| \frac{K_1 U_0 Z_e}{E_0} \right| \tag{7.24}$$

where q_0 = power sensitivity
U_0 = volume velocity, m³/s
Z_e = electrical impedance of piezoelectric element, Ω
E_0 = input voltage, V
K_1 = constant

Assuming displacement at the piezoelectric element and laminated metal sheet to be ξ' and displacement at the peripheral metal part to be ξ, U_0 is found as follows:

$$U_0 = \int_0^b 2\pi r \xi' \, dr + \int_b^a 2\pi r \xi \, dr \tag{7.25}$$

Z, which is mainly a qualitative component, is determined by

$$Z = \frac{K_2}{\pi \omega \varepsilon_{33} T} \times \frac{h_1}{a^2 \eta^2} \tag{7.26}$$

where ε = dielectric constant of piezoelectric element
$\eta = b/a$
K_2 = constant

To find the optimum condition of η, if $\mu_1 = \mu_2 = \mu$ with radius a, material thickness $h = h_1 + h_2$, and the piezoelectric constant d_{31}, ε_{33}^T constant, the following is obtained:

$$\frac{U_0 \sqrt{Z}}{E} \propto \frac{\alpha(1 + \beta)\sqrt{\beta}}{1 + \alpha\beta}$$

$$\times \frac{\mu[3 + \mu - \eta(1 + \mu)]}{(1 + \mu)C + \eta^2[(1 - \mu)C + 2(1 - \mu^2)(1 - \frac{3}{2}\zeta + \frac{3}{4}\zeta^2)]} \tag{7.27}$$

$$C = (1 - \mu_2)(\beta_2 + \tfrac{5}{8}\beta\zeta + \tfrac{3}{4}\zeta^2)\alpha\beta \tag{7.28}$$

$$+ 2\mu(1 - \mu)(1 - \tfrac{5}{8}\zeta + \tfrac{3}{4}\zeta^2) \tag{7.29}$$

$$\zeta = (1 - \alpha\beta^2)(1 + \alpha\beta)$$

where $\alpha = Q_1/Q_2$
$\quad \mu$ = Poisson ratio*

From the above, it is found that $\eta = 0.5$ to 0.8 is better. β is dependent on α, but when the relative sensitivity of various metals is compared, $0.2 < \beta < 1.0$; therefore, aluminum is the best. The primary resonance frequency of the vibrator is

$$f_1 = \frac{2.22^2 h_1}{2\pi a^2 \beta} \sqrt{\frac{Q^2}{3\rho_2(1 - \mu_2)}\left(1 - \frac{3}{2}\zeta + \frac{3}{4}\zeta\right)} \tag{7.30}$$

where f_1 = primary resonance frequency, Hz
$\quad Q_2$ = Young's modulus, N/m^2
$\quad \rho_2$ = density, kg/m^3

Assuming radius a, thickness h, and Poisson's ratio to be constant, C is determined by

$$f_1 \propto C \sqrt{1 - \tfrac{5}{8}\zeta + \tfrac{3}{4}\zeta^2/\beta}$$
$$C = \sqrt{Q_2/\rho_2} \tag{7.31}$$

where C = sound velocity, m/s. Further, the resonance frequency of the vibrator is expressed as follows:

$$f_1 = \frac{1}{2\pi} \sqrt{\frac{s_0}{m_0}} \tag{7.32}$$

---

* Poisson's ratio is defined as the charge density at any point divided by the absolute capacitivity of the medium.

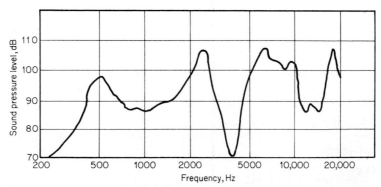

FIG. 7.6 Frequency characteristics of a typical monomorphic piezoelectric transducer.

where m_0 = vibrator mass, kg
s_0 = vibrator stiffness, N/m

However, to reduce mechanical Q, a small $s_0 \times m_0$ is preferable, and therefore aluminum is the best material. Figure 7.6 shows the sound-pressure-frequency characteristics of a speaker with this construction.

7.2 CONTROL SYSTEM AND ITS ACOUSTIC CHARACTERISTICS

For acoustic equipment, in the process of converting electrical energy to acoustic energy conversion from the electrical system to the mechanical system and from the mechanical system to the acoustic system is performed. The conversion process is expressed approximately by the equation $P/E = F/E \times V/F \times P/V$. The left-hand term shows the ratio of electrical input to sound pressure, which should be kept constant regardless of frequency. However, the first term, the ratio of electrical input to driving force, and the third term, the ratio of diaphragm velocity V to sound pressure P on the right, are fixed by the conversion and radiation systems in the relationship with frequency. For example, the sound pressure of a direct-radiation type of speaker increases in proportion to frequency if the velocity V is constant. Consequently, if V/F decreases with frequency, the ratio is not related to frequency as a whole even when F/E is constant. This corresponds to a mass when the vibrating system is regarded as a single resonance system, which is called *mass control*. Likewise, when V/F becomes unrelated to frequency, both the resistance control and the frequency increase; this is called *stiffness control*. Table 7.2 summarizes these characteristics.

TABLE 7.2 Three Control Systems

	Resistance control	Mass control	Stiffness control
Z_m approximation	r	ωm	s/ω
$vv/F\|$	$1/r$	$1/\omega m$	ω/s
Characteristics			
Applications	Horn speaker	Direct radiant-type speaker	Headphone

7.3 DIRECT-RADIATOR-LOUDSPEAKER FUNDAMENTALS

7.3.1 Piston Source in Infinite-Plane Baffle

The diameter of a speaker diaphragm normally ranges between a few centimeters and dozens of centimeters when high-amplitude sound must be produced.

An actual diaphragm has many different oscillation modes, and its motion is complicated. On the assumption, for easier analysis, that the diaphragm is rigid, radiation impedance and directivity are considered for typical circular and rectangular shapes. As shown in Fig. 7.7, part of a circular rigid wall is oscillating at

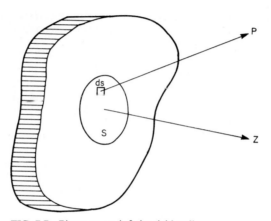

FIG. 7.7 Piston on an infinite rigid wall.

a given velocity $v \exp(j\omega t)$. The upper part of this circular piston is subdivided into the micro area d_s, and when a micro part is oscillated by the piston, the total reaction force subjected from the medium side is calculated. Thus, the radiation impedance Z_R of the diaphragm is found from the ratio of this reaction force to the diaphragm's oscillating speed. This shows how effectively sound energy from the diaphragm is used. Radiation impedance in the circular diaphragm is shown in Eq. (7.33) and the results in Fig. 7.8.

$$Z_R = (\pi a^2 \rho C)\left[\left(1 - \frac{J_1(2ka)}{ka}\right) + j\frac{S_1(2ka)}{ka}\right] \tag{7.33}$$

where J_1 = Bessel function of the first order
S_1 = Struve function

Directional characteristics of the circular diaphragm are shown in Eq. (7.34) and the results in Fig. 7.9.

$$D(\theta) = \left|\frac{2J_1(ka \sin \theta)}{ka \sin \theta}\right| \tag{7.34}$$

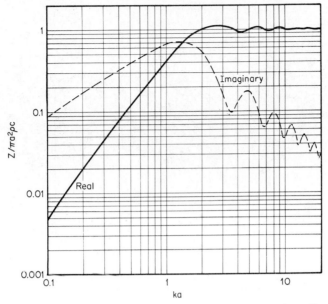

FIG. 7.8 Radiation impedance for a rigid circular diaphragm in an infinite baffle as a function of $k\,a = 2\pi\,a/\lambda$.

where $D(\theta)$ = ratio between sound pressures whose angles θ are in 0 and θ directions

θ = perpendicular on the surface center

k = number of waves

a = radius, m

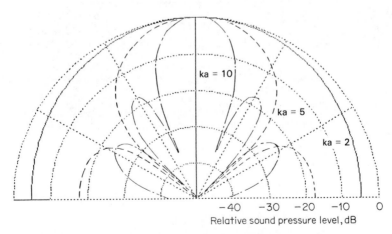

FIG. 7.9 Directional characteristics of a circular diaphragm.

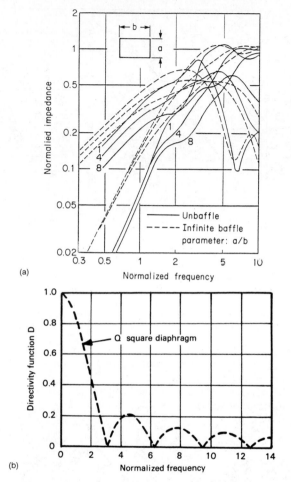

(a)

(b)

FIG. 7.10 (*a*) Radiation impedance for a rigid rectangular diaphragm. Solid lines, which have been calculated by using the finite element method (FEM), are instructive for practical designs. (*b*) Directivity function for a rigid square diaphragm.

Rectangular impedance is shown in Eq. (7.35), directional characteristics in Eq. (7.36), and the respective calculation results in Fig. 7.10*a* and *b*.

$$R(\nu, \sigma) = 1 - (2/\pi\nu^2)[1 + \cos(\nu q) + \nu q \sin(\nu q) - \cos(\nu p) - \cos(\nu/p)]$$
$$+ (2/\pi)[pI_1(\nu, \sigma) + I_1(\nu, 1/\sigma)/p]$$

$$X(\nu, \sigma) = (2/\pi\nu^2)[\sin(\nu q) - \nu q \cos(\nu q) + \nu(p + 1/p) - \sin(\nu p) - \sin(\nu/p)]$$
$$- (2/\pi)[pI_2(\nu, \sigma) + I_2(\nu, 1/\nu)/p]$$

$$\nu = k\sqrt{S}$$
$$q = (\sigma + 1/\sigma)$$

$$(7.35)$$

where ν = nondimensional frequency
$$p = \sqrt{\sigma}$$

$$I_{1,2} = \int_{\xi-1/2}^{(\xi+1/\xi)1/2} (1 - 1/\xi t^2)^{1/2} \frac{\cos}{\sin} (\nu t)\, dt$$

$$\xi = \sigma \text{ or } r - \sigma$$

1,2, subscripts of I, = cos for 1 and sin for 2 $\qquad$ (7.36)

$$D(\theta_1, \theta_2) = \frac{\sin \phi_1}{\phi_1} \cdot \frac{\sin \phi_2}{\phi_2}$$

$$\phi_{1,2} = \frac{\pi d_{1,2}}{\lambda} \sin \theta_{1,2}$$

where $D(\theta_1, \theta_2)$ = ratio between sound pressures in 0 and θ_1/θ_2 directions ($\theta_1 = \theta_2$
$\qquad$ = 0 is a perpendicular of the center on the rectangular surface)
$\quad \lambda$ = wavelength, m
$\quad d_{1,2}$ = length of each side of rectangle, m

Radiation impedance shows how effectively sound energy is radiated, while directional gain is used to show how expanding sound energy is radiated in space. The ratio of total acoustic energy W is found by integrating the sound strength from that on a spherical surface a distance r from the sound source with the sound strength that exists on the same point from the nondirectional sound source that emits the same energy. This is expressed in decibels as shown in Eq. (7.37).

$$W = \frac{r^2}{\rho C} \int_0^{2\pi} \int_0^{\pi} |\dot{P}(r, \theta, \phi)|^2 \sin^2 \theta\, d\theta d\phi \qquad (7.37)$$

$$\text{DI} = 10 \log \left(\frac{4\pi r^2}{W} \cdot \frac{|\dot{P}_{max}|^2}{\rho C} \right) \qquad (7.38)$$

where W = total acoustic energy, W
$\quad r$ = distance in the maximum sound pressure direction for standardization, m
$\quad \dot{P}_{max}$ = sound pressure at distance r, N/m^2
$\quad \text{DI}$ = directivity index (directional gain), dB

7.3.2 Baffle Shape and Acoustic Characteristics

In the preceding section an infinite baffle was discussed, but such a baffle cannot be put to practical use. Consequently, it is necessary to precheck the types of characteristics that can be obtained when a definite baffle is installed in a speaker. Since the sounds radiated to the front baffle and reflected to the rear are opposite in phase, the difference in distance between the passes of sound through the rear and front baffles from a speaker is canceled by the front and rear sounds of one-half even multiples and added to each other by the sounds of odd multiples.

Therefore, high and low sound pressures occur. To avoid this, the speaker is installed off center, resulting in a baffle with a complicated shape. One side should be a few times longer than the wavelength. However, this shape does not produce

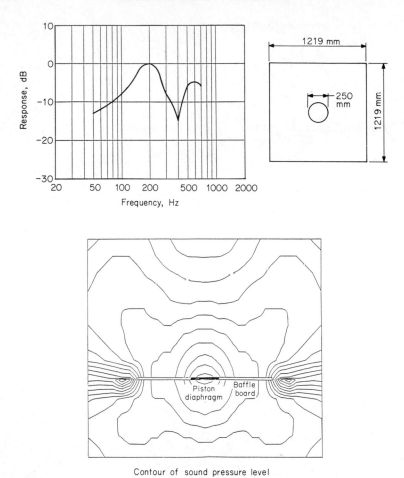

Contour of sound pressure level

FIG. 7.11 Pressure-response-frequency characteristics for a direct radiator installed in the center of a finite baffle, estimated by FEM.

favorable characteristics, and this type of baffle is not often used in practical applications. A more desirable method is discussed in Sec. 7.5. Typical baffle characteristics are shown in Figs. 7.11 and 7.12.

7.3.3 Acoustic Characteristics of Rigid Disk with Constant-Force Drive

This section comments on the types of sound-pressure-frequency characteristics produced at a remote distance on the center axis of a diaphragm and the acoustic output obtained therefrom when a circular piston diaphragm is placed in an infinite rigid wall and driven at a given force. When a circular diaphragm with radius a is subjected to a constant force F' moving in the axial direction, sound pressure $\dot{P}$ is determined by

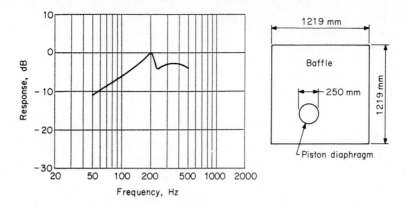

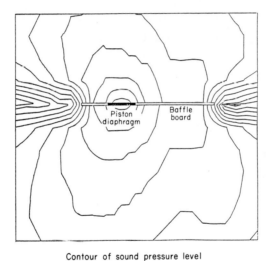

Contour of sound pressure level

FIG. 7.12 Pressure-response-frequency characteristics of a direct radiator installed off center, estimated by FEM.

$$\dot{P} = \rho_\theta \frac{\partial \phi}{\partial t} = j \frac{\omega \rho_\theta a_2}{2r} \exp(-jkr) \cdot \dot{v}$$
$$= j \frac{\omega \rho_\theta a^2}{2r} \exp(-jkr) \cdot \frac{\dot{F}}{\dot{Z}} \tag{7.39}$$

The absolute value $|\dot{P}|$ of sound pressure is shown in the following equation:

$$|\dot{P}| = \frac{\omega \rho_\theta a^2}{2r} \left| \frac{\dot{F}}{\dot{Z}} \right| \tag{7.40}$$

where $\dot{P}$ = sound pressure on the axis, N/m^2
ρ_θ = gas density, kg/m^3
ϕ = velocity potential
a = diaphragm radius, m
r = distance from diaphragm on the axis, m
$\dot{F}$ = driving force, N
ω = angular frequency, rad/s

When the oscillation system is regarded as a single resonance system, $\dot{Z}$ is obtained as follows:

$$\dot{Z} = r_m + j\omega m + \frac{1}{j\omega C_m} \tag{7.41}$$

where $\dot{Z}$ = mechanical impedance of oscillation system, mechanical ohms
r_m = mechanical resistance of oscillation system, N/m
C_m = oscillation-system compliance, m/N
m = mass of oscillation system, kg

Therefore, sound pressure $|\dot{P}|$ is determined by

$$|\dot{P}| \fallingdotseq \frac{\omega^2 \rho_\theta a^2 C_m}{2r} |\dot{F}| \qquad \omega < \omega_\theta \tag{7.42}$$

$$|\dot{P}| \fallingdotseq \frac{\rho_\theta a^2}{2rm} |\dot{F}| \qquad \omega > \omega_\theta \tag{7.43}$$

This is shown in Fig. 7.13.

$$W_a \fallingdotseq \frac{\pi \rho_\theta a^4 \omega^4 C_m}{2c_2} |\dot{F}|^2 \qquad ka < 1 \qquad \omega < \omega_\theta \tag{7.44}$$

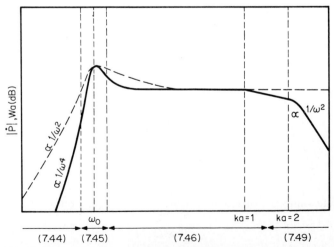

FIG. 7.13 Acoustic power and pressure-response-frequency characteristics of a piston source in an infinite-plane baffle.

$$W_a \fallingdotseq \frac{\pi \rho a^4 \omega^2}{2cr^2} |\dot{F}|^2 \qquad ka < 1 \qquad \omega = \omega_\theta \qquad (7.45)$$

$$W_a \fallingdotseq \frac{\pi \rho a^4}{2cm^2} |\dot{F}|^2 \qquad ka < 1 \qquad \omega > \omega_\theta \qquad (7.46)$$

$$W_a \fallingdotseq \pi \rho a^2 c \omega^2 C_m^2 |\dot{F}|^2 \qquad ka > 1 \qquad \omega > \omega_\theta \qquad (7.47)$$

$$W_a \fallingdotseq \frac{\pi \rho a^2}{r^2} |\dot{F}|^2 \qquad ka > 1 \qquad \omega = \omega_\theta \qquad (7.48)$$

$$W_a \fallingdotseq \frac{\pi \rho a^2 c}{\omega^2 m} |\dot{F}|^2 \qquad ka > 1 \qquad \omega > \omega_\theta \qquad (7.49)$$

where C = sound velocity, m/s
k = number of waves
ω = resonance angular frequency, rad/s

7.4 DYNAMIC-TYPE DIRECT-RADIATION SPEAKER

7.4.1 Typical Design

A typical configuration of a dynamic-type direct-radiation speaker is shown in Fig. 7.14. The speaker is divided broadly into the following components:

1. Magnetic circuit
2. Drive coil
3. Diaphragm
4. Support system
5. Frame

Most magnetic circuits are of the external type, using a ferrite magnet designed to generate a magnetic-flux density of a few thousand to a few ten thousand G in

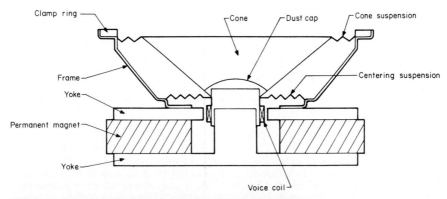

FIG. 7.14 Structure of the dynamic direct-radiator loudspeaker.

an approximately 1- to 2-mm air gap formed by the north and south poles. To control distortion the drive coil provided in the air gap is designed so that it does not move out of the uniform magnetic field formed by the magnetic pole because of vibration. Thus, the drive coil used has approximately 0.1-mm-diameter windings of several turns. The impedance normally is a multiple of 4 Ω. The diaphragm is available in a variety of shapes and materials, as described later. The dust cap is used to prevent dust from intruding into the magnetic air gap; when the cap must function as a damper, a permeable material is used. Thus, the centering suspension and cone suspension function (1) to support these vibration systems, (2) to hold the drive coil in the magnetic air gap, and (3) to generate deemphasis in the axial direction.

7.4.2 Equivalent Circuit and Frequency Response

Figure 7.15 shows the equivalent circuit of a dynamic type of speaker. The sound-pressure-frequency characteristics of the equivalent circuit in Fig. 7.15 are shown in Fig. 7.16. An examination of these characteristics divided by frequency bands follows. In low ranges the diaphragm and support system are free from split vibration, but they are considered to be a single resonance system. Thus, an equivalent circuit as shown in Fig. 7.17a is produced. The velocity, amplitude characteristics, and sound pressure characteristics on the axis are as shown in Fig. 7.17b. As can be seen from this figure, Q_0 determines sound pressure characteristics near resonance frequency. If all element constants are found, Q_0 can be obtained by calculation, but these constants must often actually be found by measurement. Voice-coil impedance near the resonance frequency is expressed as a sum of electrical impedance and motion impedance. That is,

$$Z_e = Z_c + \frac{A^2}{Z_M} \qquad (7.50)$$

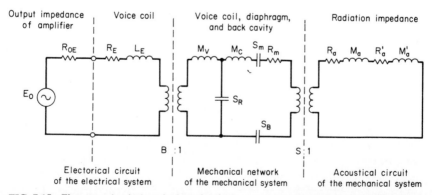

FIG. 7.15 Electromechanical equivalent circuit. R_{OE} = output impedance of amplifier, Ω; R_E = resistance of voice coil, Ω; L_E = inductance of voice cell, H; M_V = mass of voice coil, kg; S_R = stiffness between cone and voice coil, N/m; M_C = mass of cone, kg; S_m = stiffness of diaphragm, N/m; R_m = resistance of diaphragm, mechanical ohms; S_B = stiffness of back cavity, N/m; R_a, R'_a = radiation resistance of diaphragm, mechanical ohms; M_a, M'_a = radiation mass of diaphragm, kg; $B\ell$ = force factor; S = area of diaphragm, m².

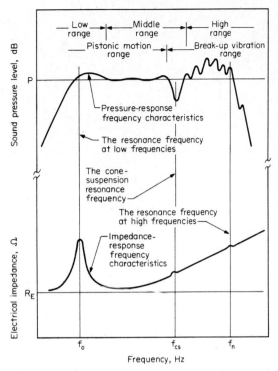

FIG. 7.16 Frequency characteristics of the dynamic direct-radiator loudspeaker.

When $R_c \gg \omega L$,

$$Z_e = R_c + \frac{A^2}{Z_M} = Re + \cfrac{1}{\cfrac{1}{\cfrac{A^2}{r_m}} + \cfrac{1}{\cfrac{A^2}{j\omega m}} + \cfrac{1}{\cfrac{A^2}{\cfrac{1}{j\omega C_m}}}} \tag{7.51}$$

The vector impedance locus is shown in Fig. 7.18. From these results, Fig. 7.19 is obtained, and Q_0 can be found directly from electrical impedance. In midrange, cone suspension less rigid than the diaphragm produces a split vibration. This phenomenon appears typically near 1000 Hz with a speaker using a paper-cone diaphragm. The analytical results of this condition, using the finite-element method (FEM), are shown in Fig. 7.20a. To eliminate this, damping material is coated and the shape is redesigned, thus controlling the resonance. For the diaphragm, specific resonance starts to appear, a peak and a dip in sound pressure response occur, and a strain may result. Regarding this shortcoming, the results of analysis by FEM are shown in Fig. 7.20b. To control this specific resonance, materials with a larger internal loss are used, the shape of the diaphragm is changed from a simple cone to a paracurve, and corrugation is provided. Furthermore, when the frequency rises, elastic deformation concentrates at the junction between the drive coil and the diaphragm, and stiffness S_R appears there

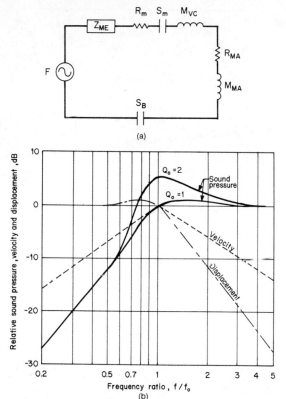

FIG. 7.17 (*a*) Mechanical equivalent circuit at a low-frequency range. Z_{ME} = motional impedance, mechanical ohms; R_m = resistance of vibrating system, mechanical ohms; S_m = stiffness of vibrating system, N/m; M_{VC} = mass of vibrating system, kg; R_{MA} = resistance of radiating system, mechanical ohms; M_{MA} = mass of radiating system, kg; S_B = stiffness of back cavity, N/m. (*b*) Frequency characteristics of sound pressure, velocity, and displacement.

equivalently. Figure 7.15 shows the equivalent circuit. Therefore, sound pressure is suddenly lowered at a higher level than the resonance frequency by S_R and the diaphragm mass, which actually presents the playback limit.

7.4.3 Efficiency

Speaker efficiency is expressed in terms of the ratio of electrical input to acoustic output. The electrical input with due regard to only the real-number part in the equivalent circuit in Fig. 7.15 is expressed by

$$W_e = R_c I^2 \qquad (7.52)$$

where W_e = electrical input, W
  R_c = coil resistance, Ω
  I = current flowing into the coil, A

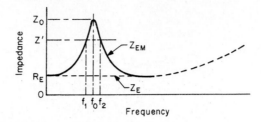

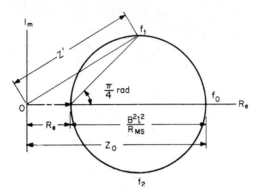

FIG. 7.18 Voice-coil impedance and impedance locus. R_E = resistance of voice coil, Ω; Z' = $Z_0/\sqrt{2}$, Ω; B = magnetic-flux density in the gap, Wb/m²; ℓ = length of wire on voice-coil winding, m; R_{MS} = resistance of vibrating system, mechanical ohms; f_o = resonance at low-frequency range, Hz; f = frequency at -3 dB, Hz.

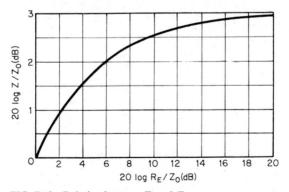

FIG. 7.19 Relation between Z' and Z.

Acoustic output W_a is determined by

$$W_a = r_R \left| \frac{F}{Z_m} \right| \tag{7.53}$$

where W_a = acoustic output, W
r_R = acoustic radiation resistance, N/m

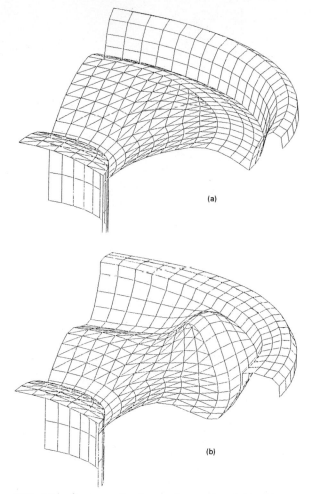

FIG. 7.20 Breakup vibrating modes, estimated by FEM. (*a*) Fundamental mode of the suspension. (*b*) Axial mode of the cone.

F = driving force, N
Z_m = vibration-system mechanical impedance, mechanical ohms

Consequently, efficiency η is found as follows:

$$\eta = \frac{W_a}{W_e + W_a}$$

$$= \frac{1}{1 + W_e/W_a}$$

(7.54)

With the diaphragm considered as a stiff disk, if it is an infinite baffle board, W_a can employ the approach shown in Sec. 7.4.3. If the acoustic output found by Eq. (7.46) is constant, η is determined by

$$\eta = \frac{1}{1 + \frac{2cm^2 R_c}{\pi \rho a^4 B^2 \ell^2}} \times 100 \qquad (7.55)$$

where η = conversion efficiency, percent
π = pi
ρ = air density, kg/m^3
c = sound velocity, m/s
m = vibration-system mass, kg
a = effective radius of diaphragm, m
B = flux density, We/m^2
ℓ = coil length, m
R_c = coil resistance, Ω

In Eq. (7.55), the magnitude on the second term normally is approximately 50. The efficiency is only a few percentage points, which is very low. In contrast, the horn loudspeaker described in Sec. 7.6 has an excellent efficiency of a few 10 percents. Consequently, when a large sound pressure is required, it is advisable to use this type of speaker.

7.4.4 Nonlinear Distortion

The strain which takes place in a dynamic speaker includes the three types of distortion described below.

Driving-Force Distortion. Driving-force distortion occurs mainly because a drive coil flows out from the uniform magnetic field as amplitude varies, whereby the driving force ceases to be proportional to current. Figure 7.21a shows the magnetic-flux distribution and magnetic-flux-density distribution near the magnetic pole in a typical magnetic circuit. Figure 7.21b shows the relationship between the power coefficient generated by a coil located in such a magnetic circuit and the coil displacement. Consequently, the following nonlinear differential equation must be solved. Here a study may be made at an ultralow frequency with a large amplitude. Therefore, radiation impedance can be approximated with radiation mass and vibration-system impedance with stiffness. The basic Eqs. (7.5) and (7.6) are as follows, assuming the stiffness to be linear:

$$M_{MA}\frac{d^2\xi}{dt^2} = m\frac{d^2\xi}{dt^2} + r\frac{d\xi}{dt} + s_n - A(\xi)I(\xi) \qquad (7.56)$$

$$E_0 \sin \omega t = RI(\xi) + A(\xi)\frac{d\xi}{dt} \qquad (7.57)$$

where $A(\xi)$ = ξ function force factor, N/A
M_{MA} = radiation mass, kg
s_n = vibration-system stiffness, N/m
$E_0 \sin \omega t$ = applied voltage, V
R = coil resistance, Ω
$I(\xi)$ = current of ξ function, A
ξ = displacement, m

To reduce this distortion, it is preferable to adopt a method of decreasing the coil-winding width as shown in Fig. 7.22a so that it is not off the magnetic field or

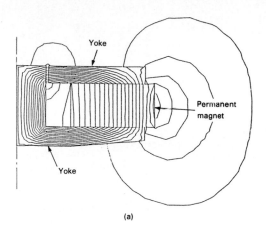

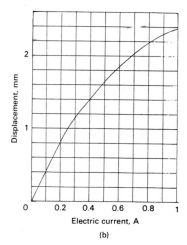

FIG. 7.21 Flux distribution of the half-magnetic circuit. (*a*) Typical flux lines in an air gap estimated by FEM. (*b*) Relation between the electric current and the displacement.

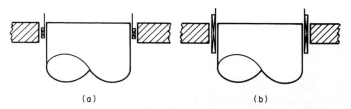

FIG. 7.22 Relation between the voice coil and the magnetic circuit for reducing distortion. (*a*) A voice coil shorter than the air gap. (*b*) A voice coil longer than the air gap.

sufficiently increasing the coil-winding width as shown in Fig. 7.22*b*. Since driving-force distortion develops as current distortion, this distortion can be reduced by detecting current flowing into a coil with a microresistance and feeding this current back into the input terminal of the amplifier. This is shown in Fig. 7.23. Other driving-force distortions include a strain generated by hysteresis of the

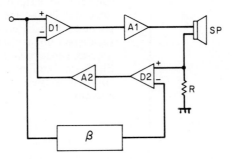

FIG. 7.23 System for reducing current distortion. *D*1, *D*2 = differential amplifiers; *A*1, *A*2 = amplifiers; β = feedback circuit; *SP* = loudspeaker; *R* = resistor for detecting current distortion.

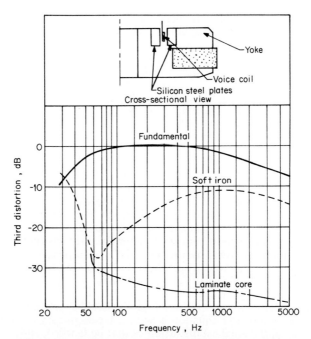

FIG. 7.24 Comparison of the third-harmonic distortion between soft iron and silicon plates. Solid-line curve = fundamental current level; dashed-line curve = soft-iron-type yoke; dash-dot-line curve = laminate-core-type yoke.

magnetic-circuit yoke. This can be substantially improved by using a silicon steel plate for a yoke and a magnetic material of small conductivity. This example is shown in Fig. 7.24.

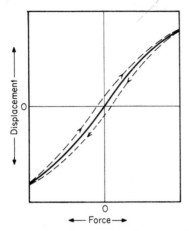

FIG. 7.25 Relation between force and displacement in a typical suspension.

Support-System Distortion. Support-system distortion is such that since elasticity of suspension is nonlinear, force and displacement cease to be proportional to each other. The force-versus-displacement characteristics of a general support system are shown in Fig. 7.25. The function showing such a curve is expressed by the following equation:

$$F(\xi) = \alpha\xi + \beta\xi^2 + \gamma\xi^3 \quad (7.58)$$

where $F(\xi)$ = force at displacement ξ, N

ξ = displacement, m

α, β, γ = constants

Consequently, stiffness ξ is found by

$$s(\xi) = \alpha + \beta\xi + \gamma\xi^2 \quad (7.59)$$

Assuming ω to be an ultralow frequency with this stiffness function substituted for the basic equation, Eqs. (7.56) and (7.57) are as follows:

$$M_{MA}\frac{d^2\xi}{dt^2} = m\frac{d^2\xi}{dt^2} + r\frac{d\xi}{dt} + s_n(\xi)\xi - A(\xi)I(\xi) \quad (7.60)$$

$$E_0 \sin \omega t = RI(\xi) + A(\xi)\frac{d\xi}{dt} \quad (7.61)$$

There are several methods of solving this equation. The calculation results on the assumption that the current is constant, using the indefinite-coefficient method and sample measurements, are shown in Fig. 7.26. The point to be considered in the support system in particular is that, for a large amplitude, suspension elasticity is suddenly lost, forming a cropped wave and leading to rupture. Since the support system is nonlinear, not only does distortion occur, but a so-called jumping phenomenon is found. As shown in Fig. 7.27, amplitude suddenly changes discontinuously for frequency and current. To prevent this, as large a suspension as possible is used, and such materials and construction are selected that the center-holding capacity is not lowered. Cone suspension uses a soft material wherever applicable, and corrugation and ribbing are provided to avoid edge resonance.

Air Distortion. Generally, on the assumption that changes in volume are very small when the sound-surge equation is solved, the secondary or more terms are ignored. However, the smallest distortion cannot be ignored, and the high-order term cannot be ignored when sound pressure is large. Equation (7.62) shows the degree of second-harmonic wave due to nonlinearity on this high-order term:

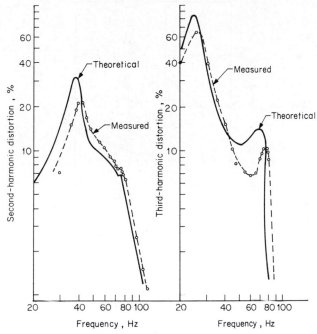

FIG. 7.26 Distortion characteristics of a driving force, calculated from Eqs. (7.60 and 7.61).

$$p_2 = \frac{(\gamma + 1)\omega}{2\sqrt{2}\gamma p_0 c} p_r^2 r \tag{7.62}$$

where p_2 = second-harmonic distorted sound pressure generated by plane waves at distance r, N/m^2

p_r = fundamental wave sound pressure of plane wave at distance r, N/m^2

p_0 = atmospheric pressure, N/m

γ = ratio between constant-pressure specific heat and constant-volume specific heat (air, 1:4)

ω = angular frequency, rad

c = sound velocity, m/s

r = distance, m

The calculation results of Eq. (7.62) are shown in Fig. 7.28.

Frequency-Modulation Distortion. Signals inputted to a speaker have various frequency spectra. When low- and high-frequency sounds are radiated from a diaphragm at the same time, high-frequency sound is subjected to modulation because the diaphragm is moving forward and backward significantly according to low-frequency signals. The frequency-modulated wave generated thereby is expressed by carrier and an unlimited number of sideband waves. The mean-

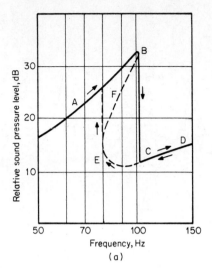

(a)

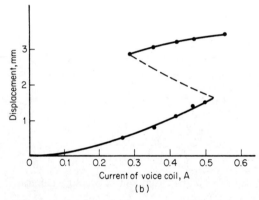

(b)

FIG. 7.27 Nonlinear suspension system. (*a*) The unstable portion of the response frequency characteristic is indicated by a dashed line. (*b*) The unstable portion of the response current characteristic is indicated by a dashed line.

square value of the ratio of sideband-wave energy to all energies of the sound wave is expressed in percentage as follows:

$$D = 2900 \frac{f_2 \sqrt{p_1}}{f_1^2 d^2} \tag{7.63}$$

where D = distortion, percent
f_2 = modulated wave (high-frequency), Hz
f_1 = modulated wave (low-frequency), Hz
p_1 = acoustic output of f_1, W
d = cone diameter, m

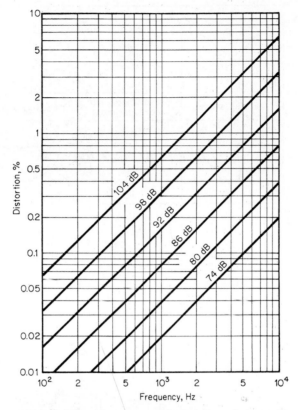

FIG. 7.28 Distortion generated in the air gap between the cone and the listening-point distance in a direct-radiator loudspeaker with a cone diameter of 20 cm, measured at a distance of 3 m.

One of the methods for reducing this distortion is to use a multiway speaker system.

7.4.5 Diaphragm and Support System

It is no exaggeration to say that the diaphragm and support system nearly determine speaker acoustic characteristics. A typical shape and features for the diaphragm and support system are described below.

Diaphragm. Diaphragms are classified by shape into cone, plane, and dome diaphragms. The cone diaphragm is one of the most frequently used types. Many researchers study this shape of diaphragm. Figure 7.29 shows typical shapes studied thus far. Any of these types is directed to widening the piston-motion area to enhance a high-range playback limit frequency and also to reduce distortion. For this purpose, it is important to know the vibrating conditions of the cone diaphragm, but it is very difficult to find them analytically. For example, six steps of

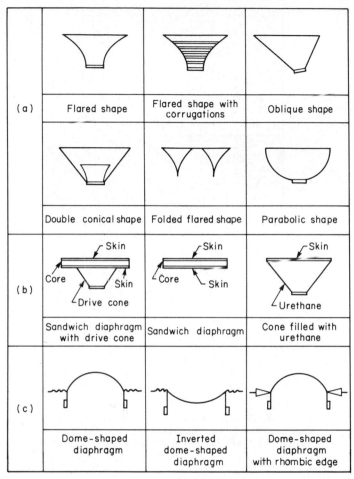

FIG. 7.29 Sectional views of various diaphragm shapes. (*a*) The diaphragm of the cone type extends the reproducing band by changing the shape of the curved surface. (*b*) The diaphragm of the plane type removes the cavity effect by using a flat radiation surface. (*c*) The diaphragm of the dome type improves bending elasticity by forming thin plates into a domelike shape.

ordinary differential equations must be solved even in checking symmetrical vibration around the axis. In recent years, however, FEM has been employed, and favorable results have been obtained. The results of eigenvalue analysis by using this method are shown in Fig. 7.30. The plane diaphragm was designed to eliminate the cavity effect which takes place with a cone diaphragm in order to realize a flat-frequency characteristic. This shape has made it possible to use highly rigid construction and materials such as honeycomb construction and plastic foam and adopt the optimum driving method. Figure 7.29 shows this summary. In the dome diaphragm a thin metallic foil, resin-impregnated cloth, or paper is formed into a sphere, and the periphery of the diagram is driven. A diaphragm with a smaller-aperture diameter is easy to realize because of circumferential drive, split vibration can be controlled up to a high frequency, and favorable directional char-

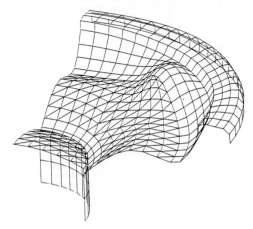

FIG. 7.30 Model shape of a 20-mm cone diaphragm is calculated by using FEM at 3408 Hz.

acteristics are also obtained. The sample shape of a dome diaphragm is shown in Fig. 7.29. Materials used in this diaphragm include sulfite cellulose, sulfate pulp, paper mixed with highly elastic fiber such as silicon carbide whiskers, carbon fiber, and alamido fiber, metal foil such as aluminum, titanium, and beryllium, high-polymer film such as polyethylene telephthalate or highly elastic materials reinforced by deposition such as carbon, boron, and beryllium, and composite materials using honeycomb and foamed urethane as a core.

Support System.   The support system is divided broadly into a cone suspension system and a center holder. The cone suspension system is required to absorb reflection from the frame as a termination of the diaphragm to control edge resonance and also to prevent an acoustic short circuit which would occur before and after the diaphragm along with a baffle board. This system must be constructed so that it is easy to move in the vibrating-axis direction of the diaphragm and difficult to move in the lateral direction along with the center holder. The principal construction features of the cone suspension system are shown in Fig. 7.31. Materials having proper mechanical resistance are preferable. For fixed suspension, a sample on which damping material is coated is provided. Requirements for centering suspension are to provide proper stiffness in order to maintain a restoration force, to hold a voice coil in the center of the gap formed by the magnetic circuit in order to smooth movement in the axial direction, to maintain favorable linearity of driving-force-to-displacement characteristics even when the diaphragm is given large amplitude, and to provide light weight. As shown in Fig. 7.32, most shapes of the support system are corrugated, but linearity is improved and the maximum allowable range is increased.

7.5   LOUDSPEAKER SYSTEMS

7.5.1   Open-Rear-Type Cabinet

Radiation efficiency lessens considerably at low frequencies with a simple plane baffle board. Therefore, a baffle of 1 m or more per side is necessary for repro-

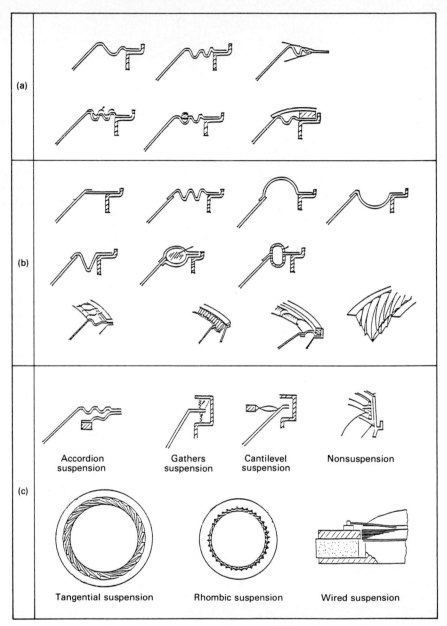

FIG. 7.31 Sectional views of cone suspension systems. (*a*) The thinned edge of a diaphragm fulfills the function of the cone suspension. (*b*) Material different from that of a diaphragm is used to fulfill the function of cone suspension. (*c*) Exceptional cone suspensions.

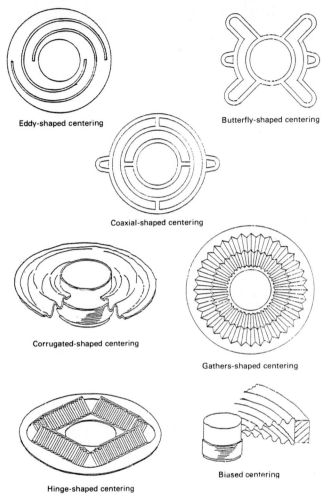

Eddy-shaped centering

Butterfly-shaped centering

Coaxial-shaped centering

Corrugated-shaped centering

Gathers-shaped centering

Hinge-shaped centering

Biased centering

FIG. 7.32   Various shapes of centering systems.

duction up to nearly 100 Hz. As a means of increasing the baffle effect without an increase in size, a cabinet with an open rear is used (see Fig. 7-33). Sound waves radiated from the rear of the speaker are of opposite phase from those radiated from the front and travel a longer distance around the sides of the cabinet to the reception point P.

Consequently, the sound-pressure-frequency-response characteristics at the reception point vary in amplitude with frequency because of the phase difference between the front and back waves resulting from the path difference, $\ell + \ell_0$. The amplitude is at a maximum at odd multiples of $\lambda/2$ and a minimum at even multiples when cancellation occurs.

Therefore, the practical low-frequency response limit f_L is lower (generally con-

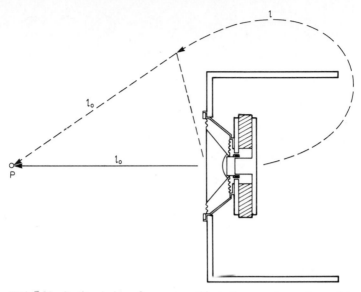

FIG. 7.33 Sectional view of open-rear cabinet. P = sound reception point; ℓ_o = distance between P and front surface of speaker; ℓ = differential difference.

sidered to be one-half) than that corresponding to the wavelength $\lambda/2$. This frequency is found by

$$f_L = \frac{C}{4\ell} \text{ Hz} \tag{7.64}$$

where C = velocity of sound in air.

With this type of cabinet a standing wave occurs at a frequency corresponding to $\lambda/2$ in interval length between the upper and lower surfaces of the interior cabinet and both surfaces. One end of the cabinet functions as an open pipe, and a standing wave occurs at a frequency whose length corresponds to $\lambda/4$. To prevent this standing wave, a sound-absorbing material layer must be provided at the internal side of the cabinet. This cabinet is used for television and radio sets but seldom for high-fidelity systems.

7.5.2 Enclosed Cabinet

With the enclosed type of open-rear cabinet the rear side is closed to eliminate the influence of sound from the rear of the speaker and to prevent lowering radiation efficiency in low ranges (Fig. 7.34a). However, since the rear is enclosed, the enclosed space comes to present air stiffness, and the minimum resonance frequency of the speaker system is determined according to the volume.

Figure 7.34b shows the equivalent circuit of this type of mechanical system. Stiffness S_{MB} in the space at the rear cabinet is

$$S_{MB} = \frac{\rho_0 C^2 S_d^2}{V_B} \tag{7.65}$$

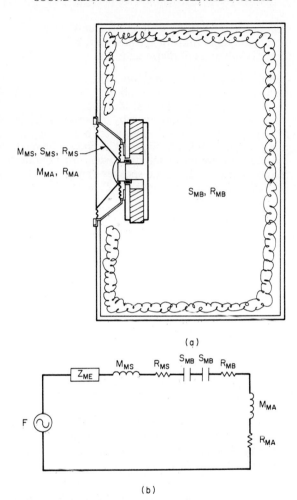

FIG. 7.34 (a) Sectional view of enclosed type of cabinet. (b) Equivalent circuit of the enclosed type of cabinet. $\dot{F}$ = driving force, N; Z_{ME} = motional impedance, mechanical ohms; M_{MS} = mass of vibrating system, kg; R_{MS} = mechanical resistance of vibrating system, mechanical ohms; S_{MS} = stiffness of vibrating system, N/m; S_{MB} = stiffness of cabinet, N/m; R_{MB} = mechanical resistance of cabinet, mechanical ohms; M_{MA} = radiation mass, kg; R_{MA} = radiation resistance, mechanical ohms.

where ρ_0 = air density, kg/m^3
C = sound propagation speed in air, m/s
S_d = speaker diaphragm area, m^2
V_B = cabinet volume, m^3

The lowest resonance frequency f_{0B} of the speaker system is determined by

$$f_{0B} = \frac{1}{2\pi} \sqrt{\frac{S_{MS} + S_{MB}}{M_{MS} + M_{MA}}} \tag{7.66}$$

where S_{MS} = vibrating-system stiffness of speaker unit, N/m
M_{MS} = vibrating-system mass of speaker unit, kg
M_{MA} = air-radiation mass of diaphragm, kg

As can be seen from Eqs. (7.65) and (7.66), when the cabinet volume is small and the diaphragm area is larger than the cabinet volume, the cabinet stiffness is larger than the vibrating-system stiffness of the speaker system ($S_{MB} \gg S_{MS}$). The low-range playback boundary is determined by the stiffness presented by the cabinet even when the minimum resonance frequency of the speaker unit is low, and low-range playback becomes difficult. Figure 7.35 shows the relationship of cabinet volume to sound pressure characteristics: when the volume becomes small, the lowest resonance frequency f_{OB} of the speaker system and the sharpness Q_0 of the resonance increase. When sound pressure P_r at a point $r(m)$ away from the

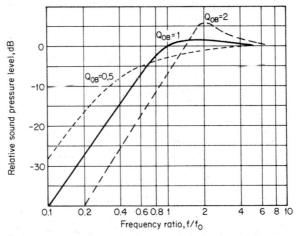

FIG. 7.35 Relation between cabinet volume and frequency response.

cabinet axis, sharpness Q_0, and cabinet volume V_B are determined, and the lowest resonance frequency of the speaker unit is very low, and $S_{MB} \gg S_{MS}$ conditions are satisfied, the lowest resonance frequency f_{OB} of the cabinet is

$$f_{OB} = \frac{1}{2\pi} \sqrt[3]{\frac{4C^2\pi^2 r^2 P_r^2 Q_0}{\rho_0 W_E V_B}} \qquad (7.67)$$

W_E is an electric input (power) supplied to the speaker unit from the outside, which is applied as a principle. For the enclosed cabinet, to eliminate the influence of the reflection of sound waves by diffraction and to prevent irregularities in sound-pressure-frequency characteristics, it is necessary to make the installation position of the speaker asymmetrical and the cabinet corner round (Fig. 7.36). A standing wave occurs at a frequency corresponding to $\lambda/2$ of the length between opposing surfaces within the cabinet, and it affects the vibration of the speaker-unit diaphragm. This is the same situation as with the open-rear cabinet. Consequently, to prevent this standing wave a sound-absorbing material must be provided at the internal side.

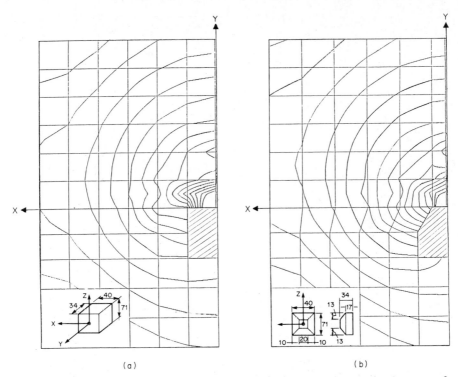

(a)   (b)

FIG. 7.36 Influence of diffraction from a 2-cm-diameter loudspeaker diaphragm at the corner of a cabinet shown as *x-y* contours of sound pressure levels. (*a*) Rectangular cabinet. (*b*) Tapered cabinet, estimated by FEM.

7.5.3 Phase-Inverting Cabinet

This type of cabinet inverts the phase of sound radiated from the rear of the speaker in order to widen a low-range playback boundary. Figure 7.37*a* and *b* shows the configuration and the equivalent circuit of the mechanical system. This cabinet is provided with a tube called a *port* that opens along with the speaker opening in front of the enclosed cabinet. The vibration of the diaphragm causes volume changes in the air within the cabinet, thereby radiating sound from the port. It produces a double sound source from which sound with the opposite phase is radiated at a very low frequency similarly to an open-rear type.

When the optimum constants of the speaker unit used and the cabinet including the port have been selected, a low-range playback band can be made nearly 30 percent wider than the minimum resonance frequency of an enclosed cabinet with the same volume. However, this resonance makes it impossible to invert the phase at a low frequency, and attenuation in sound pressure characteristics is noticeable (Fig. 7.38).

Since the amplitude of the diaphragm becomes very small near the counter-resonance frequency of the cabinet, harmonic distortion is lowered, while the amplitude becomes large at a lower frequency, thus increasing harmonic distortion. This is one of the drawbacks of this type of cabinet. When sound pressure P_r at a point $r(m)$ away from the cabinet axis, sharpness Q_0, and cabinet volume

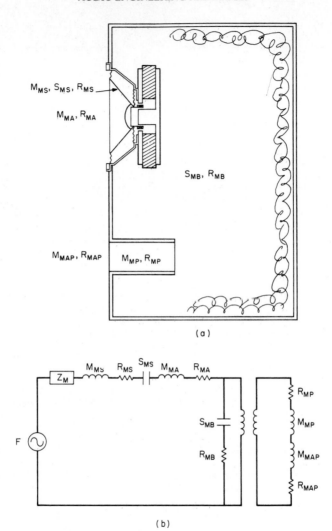

FIG. 7.37 Acoustical phase-inverting type of cabinet. (*a*) Sectional view of cabinet. (*b*) Equivalent circuit.

have been determined, sound pressure P_r and the lowest resonance frequency f_{0B} of the cabinet are found.

$$f_0'' = \frac{1}{2\pi} \sqrt{\frac{S_{MS}}{M_{MS}}} \qquad (7.68)$$

$$Q_0'' = \frac{2\pi f_0'' M_{MS}}{R_{ME} + R_{MS}} \qquad (7.69)$$

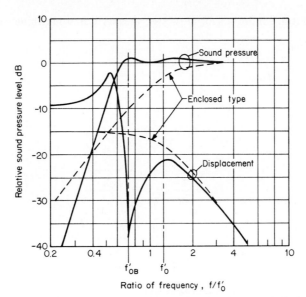

FIG. 7.38 Comparison of the sound pressure level and displacement versus frequency for the acoustical phase-inverter (solid lines) and enclosed (dashed lines) types of cabinets.

$$f'_{0B} = \frac{1}{2\pi} \sqrt{\frac{S_{MB}}{M_{MP}}} \tag{7.70}$$

$$\alpha = \frac{M_{MP}}{M_{MS}} \qquad \beta = \frac{S_{MB}}{S_{MS}} \tag{7.71}$$

$$A = \frac{1}{Q''_0}\left(1 - \frac{\beta}{\alpha}\right) \qquad B = \left(\frac{f}{f''_0} - \frac{f''_0}{f}\right)\left(1 - \frac{\beta}{\alpha}\right) - \beta\frac{f''_0}{f} \tag{7.72}$$

$$\frac{f_{0B}}{f''_0} = \sqrt{\frac{\beta}{\alpha}} \qquad \chi = \frac{f}{f''_0} \tag{7.73}$$

$$|p_r| = \frac{\rho_0 a^2 F}{2 r M_{MS}} \times \frac{x}{\sqrt{\frac{1}{Q''^2_0}\left\{1 - \left(\frac{\beta}{\alpha}\right)\frac{1}{x^2}\right\}^2 + \left[\left(x - \frac{1}{x}\right)\left\{1 - \left(\frac{\beta}{\alpha}\right)\frac{1}{x^2}\right\} - \frac{\beta}{x}\right]^2}} \tag{7.74}$$

$$f_{0B} = \frac{1}{2\pi} \sqrt[3]{\frac{4C^2\pi^2 r^2 Pr^2 Q_0}{\sqrt{2}\rho_0 W_E V_B}} \tag{7.75}$$

The optimum conditions for the above speaker unit and cabinet constants are

1. $S_{MB} = \frac{1}{2}S_{MS}$

2. $M_{MS} = \left(\dfrac{S_d}{S_p}\right)^2 M_{MP}$

3. $Q_0' = 1/\sqrt{3}$

4. $f_{0B}'/f_0' = 1/\sqrt{2}$

f_{0B}' and f_0' are defined by

$$f_{0B}' = \frac{1}{2\pi}\sqrt{\frac{S_{MB}}{\left(\dfrac{S_d}{S_p}\right)^2 M_{MP}}} \tag{7.76}$$

$$f_0' = \frac{1}{2\pi}\sqrt{\frac{S_{MS}}{M_{MS}}} \tag{7.77}$$

where S_{MB} = stiffness in cabinet rear space
$\quad\quad S_{MS}$ = vibrating-system stiffness of speaker unit
$\quad\quad M_{MS}$ = vibrating-system mass of speaker unit
$\quad\quad M_{MP}$ = air mass by port
$\quad\quad Q_0'$ = resonance sharpness of speaker unit
$\quad\quad S_d$ = speaker-unit diaphragm area
$\quad\quad S_p$ = port-opening area
$\quad\quad S_d/S_p$ = transformation ratio

In actual design, however, it is difficult to select these constants in optimum conditions, and it is common practice to use them slightly off the above conditions. Figure 7.39 shows changes in the characteristics under a variety of conditions. Consideration for the standing wave within the cabinet is the same as with the enclosed type. However, it is desirable to reduce sound-absorbing material to a minimum in order to prevent a standing wave and not increase resistance R_{MB} and port resistance P_{MP} within the cabinet (Fig. 7.39d and e).

7.5.4 Frequency Bands and Crossover Frequency

It is desirable to reproduce human audio frequency, that is, 20 to 20,000 Hz, uniformly for the playback frequency band of the speaker system, but it is difficult for one speaker unit to reproduce such a wide range of frequencies. Therefore, it is common practice to adopt a system of dividing the playback band and using special speakers for high, middle, and low ranges. The dividing network divides and applies electric input to each speaker. The frequency at the boundary for dividing the electric input is called the *crossover frequency*. The dividing network is normally configured by combination with high-pass and low-pass filters, divided into -6 dB per octave, -12 dB per octave, -18 dB per octave, etc., depending on attenuation (Figs. 7.40 and 7.41). To determine crossover frequency and attenuation, it is necessary to consider various characteristics including sound pressure characteristics, directional characteristics, and the harmonic dis-

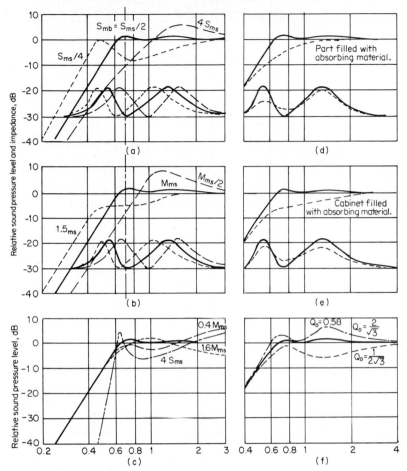

FIG. 7.39 Pressure-response-frequency characteristic of the acoustical phase-inverter loudspeaker. The changes in the pressure-response-frequency characteristics are shown with (*a*) cabinet volume, (*b*) length of port, (*c*) stiffness of loudspeaker mass, (*d*) absorbing material in the port, (*e*) absorbing material in the cabinet, and (*f*) *Q* of the loudspeaker.

tortion of the speaker used. Generally, the assigned lower frequency limit is less than the lowest resonance frequency of the speaker unit, and the amplitude of the vibrating system becomes large, thus increasing harmonic distortion, so that it should be more than 2 times this frequency. For the upper frequency limit priority is given to directional characteristics, and in 30° characteristics this frequency is selected at a lower level than −3-dB frequency below the axis. The speaker unit has available a wide variety of combinations such as a cone type for low frequencies and a horn type for middle and high frequencies. Therefore, efficiency is rarely constant. Consequently, the entire playback level must be adjusted to the speaker whose efficiency is the lowest of the system (in most cases, the speaker for lows). For this purpose, a volume-type attenuator and a constant-resistance-

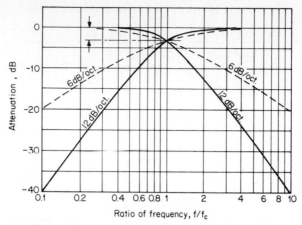

FIG. 7.40 Attentuation-frequency characteristic of the dividing network.

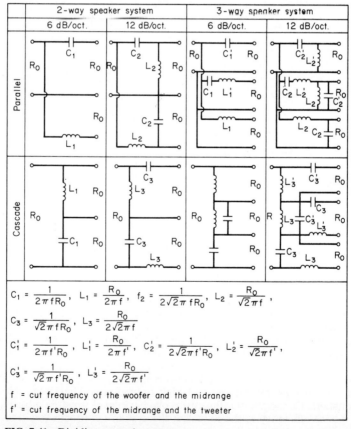

	2-way speaker system		3-way speaker system	
	6 dB/oct.	12 dB/oct.	6 dB/oct.	12 dB/oct.
Parallel				
Cascade				

$$C_1 = \frac{1}{2\pi f R_0}, \quad L_1 = \frac{R_0}{2\pi f}, \quad f_2 = \frac{1}{2\sqrt{2}\pi f R_0}, \quad L_2 = \frac{R_0}{\sqrt{2}\pi f},$$

$$C_3 = \frac{1}{\sqrt{2}\pi f R_0}, \quad L_3 = \frac{R_0}{2\sqrt{2}\pi f}$$

$$C_1' = \frac{1}{2\pi f' R_0}, \quad L_1' = \frac{R_0}{2\pi f'}, \quad C_2' = \frac{1}{2\sqrt{2}\pi f' R_0}, \quad L_2' = \frac{R_0}{\sqrt{2}\pi f'},$$

$$C_3' = \frac{1}{\sqrt{2}\pi f' R_0}, \quad L_3' = \frac{R_0}{2\sqrt{2}\pi f'}$$

f = cut frequency of the woofer and the midrange

f' = cut frequency of the midrange and the tweeter

FIG. 7.41 Dividing-network systems.

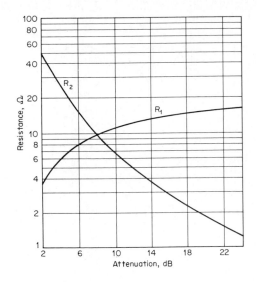

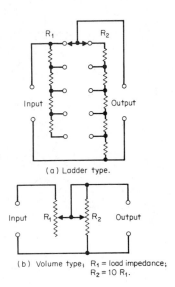

(a) Ladder type.

(b) Volume type; R_1 = load impedance; $R_2 = 10\ R_1$.

FIG. 7.42   Constant-impedance attenuators.

type attenuator are used (Fig. 7.42, also nomograph shown in Fig. 7.43). The previous network design was time-consuming because of adjustments necessary in using cut-and-try methods. The reasons are as follows:

1. In most cases there may be irregularities in the sound pressure characteristics of the speaker unit near the crossover frequency, and this part is emphasized by the opposite-crossing speakers.

2. There is a differential distance in sound source position between the sound-receiving point according to the shape (cone and horn types, for example) of each speaker unit and the installation position in the cabinet. The phase difference is produced by the time difference.

3. The band in which the impedance of the speaker unit can be considered as pure resistance is narrow, and in low ranges the dynamic impedance components caused by the resonance of the vibrating system exist, and in high ranges the reactance components of the voice coil exist. So the network constant with which the load is designed as constant resistance cannot produce the desired characteristics.

The network design will thus pose various complicated problems. Therefore, in recent years a computer simulation has been introduced to speaker-unit design in order to measure each speaker-unit characteristic in advance, perform a simulation to obtain the desired characteristics, and then determine the network constant.

7.5.5   Cabinet-System Variations

Drone-Cone Type.   This is a kind of phase-inverting type. It is structured so that only a unit of the diaphragm without the driving system is installed in the section

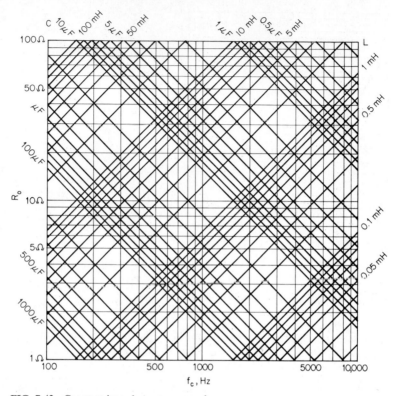

FIG. 7.43 Constant-impedance nomograph.

corresponding to the bass-reflex port (Fig. 7.44). In the schematic of the equivalent circuit of the mechanical system shown in Fig. 7.45, the mass of the diaphragm corresponds to the bass-reflex-port mass, and it forms another version to which the stiffness S_{Md} of the support system of the diaphragm is added. Therefore, this type has a disadvantage in that if bass characteristics are affected by the support-system stiffness S_{Md} and the support is too strong, thereby increasing stiffness, bass becomes harder to produce than in a bass-reflex type. The basic operation is almost the same as with a bass-reflex type.

Horn-Loaded Type. The horn-loaded type includes a front-loaded type with a horn loaded in front of the speaker, a back-loaded type with a horn loaded at the back of speaker, and a combination type with the first two types combined. Any of these types is directed to enhancing transformation efficiency in low ranges by means of the horn load. However, to produce a horn effect in bass, the horn becomes longer so that it is customary to adopt a return-horn type partitioned within the cabinet except for a large system for a theater and concert public address (PA) system (Fig. 7.46).

Acoustic-Labyrinth Type. In this type a partition panel is used within the cabinet to form an acoustic pipe, as with a return horn (Fig. 7.47). The principle is that when the pipe length is selected to produce a wavelength one-half of the bass fre-

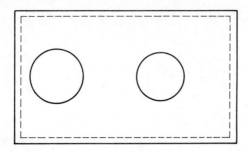

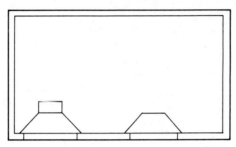

FIG. 7.44 Sectional view of the drone-cone type of cabinet.

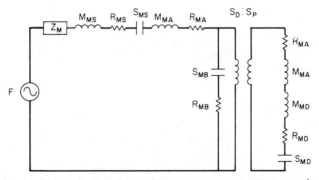

FIG. 7.45 Equivalent circuit of the drone-cone type of cabinet. $\dot{F}$ = driving force, N; Z_{ME} = motional impedance, mechanical ohms; M_{MS} = mass of vibrating system, kg; R_{HS} = mechanical resistance of vibrating system, mechanical ohms; S_{MS} = stiffness of vibrating system, N/m; S_{MB} = stiffness of cabinet, N/m; R_{HB} = mechanical resistance of cabinet, mechanical ohms; M_{MA} = radiation mass, kg; R_{MA} = radiation resistance, mechanical ohms; S_D = area of diaphragm, m²; S_D = area of drone, m²; R_{MD} = mechanical resistance of drone, mechanical ohms; M_{MD} = mass of drone with the mutual mass, kg; M_{MA} = mass of vibrating system with the mutual mass, kg; R_{MA} = mechanical resistance of vibrating system, mechanical ohms.

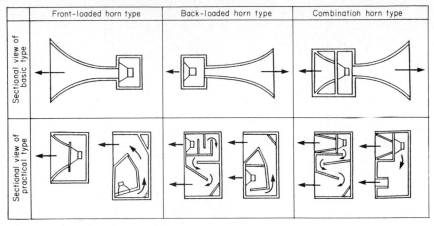

FIG. 7.46 Sectional view of horn-loaded type.

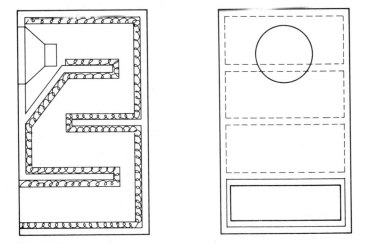

FIG. 7.47 Sectional view of acoustic-labyrinth type.

quency to be reproduced, the phase is the same as that of the sound wave of the front speaker unit at the opening, thereby increasing the level. To reproduce bass, as with a horn-loaded type a very long acoustic pipe is required, which is not suitable for a small-size system. Since sound waves radiated from the opening are opposite in phase at less than the resonance frequency of acoustic pipe, as is the case with a phase-inverting type, attenuation of radiation efficiency becomes large.

Double-Port Type.   In this type a vacant chamber of the bass-reflex type of cabinet is partitioned into two parts, and ports are provided (Fig. 7.48). This type aims at expanding low ranges with port resonance frequencies preset.

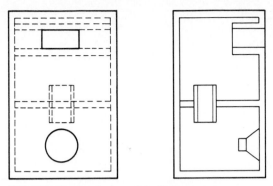

FIG. 7.48 Sectional view of double-port type.

Acoustic-Coupler Type. In a small-size system, the lowest resonance frequency is determined by cabinet stiffness. To avoid this limitation, the speaker aperture diameter may be made small while the diaphragm area is reduced, thus lowering radiation efficiency. To overcome this problem, an acoustic-coupler type is used. It employs a small speaker for drive, and a large-aperture-diameter diaphragm for radiation is provided in front of the speaker (Fig. 7.49).

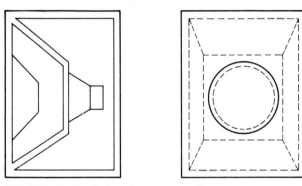

FIG. 7.49 Sectional view of acoustic-coupler type.

Double-Drive Type. The acoustic-coupler type has a radiation unit consisting only of a diaphragm without the drive system, but the double-drive type uses a large-aperture-diameter speaker in this part for drive with the same phase (Fig. 7.50).

Others. Other examples are shown in Fig. 7.51. They include the Karlson type, the R-J type of cabinet, and the acoustic-matrix type.

7.6 HORN LOUDSPEAKERS

Horn loudspeakers have been used for many years for reproducing sound efficiently within a specified sector. A horn speaker, as indicated by its name, is com-

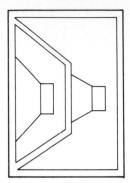
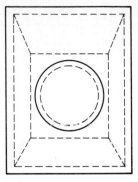

FIG. 7.50   Sectional view of double-drive type.

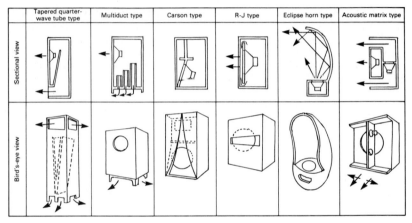

FIG. 7.51   Other loudspeaker systems.

posed of horn and speaker components. A *horn* is defined as a "sound pipe whose cross section changes gradually in the longitudinal direction."

7.6.1   Horn Form and Radiation Characteristics

A simple model of a horn with infinite length is shown in Fig. 7.52. Provided that sound is transmitted via plane waves within a horn, sound pressure P, medium vibration displacement ξ, and velocity potential ϕ at a given point x in the longitudinal direction can be expressed by the following equation:

$$\frac{d^2\phi}{dx^2} + \frac{1}{S} \times \frac{dS}{dx} \times \frac{d\phi}{dx} - \frac{\rho}{\kappa} \times \frac{d^2\phi}{dt^2} = 0 \qquad (7.65)$$

$$P = \rho \frac{d\phi}{dt} \qquad (7.66)$$

$$\frac{d\xi}{dt} = -\frac{d}{dx}\phi \qquad (7.67)$$

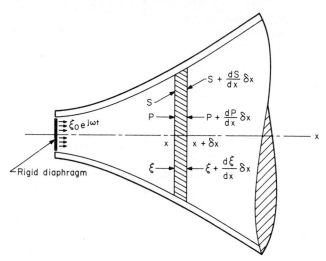

FIG. 7.52 One-dimensional sound-wave propagation in infinite horn length. $\xi_o e^{j\omega t}$ = displacement of diaphragm; P = pressure at arbitrary point; S = cross-sectional area; ζ = displacement of gas.

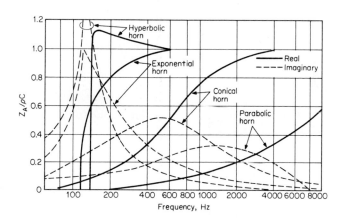

FIG. 7.53 Various shapes and impedance characteristics of loudspeaker horns.

	Shape	Equation		Shape	Equation
Parabolic horn	S_0 S	$S = S_0 X$	Exponential horn	S_0 S	$S = S_0 e^{mx}$
Conical horn	S_0 S	$S = S_0 X^2$	Hyperbolic horn	S_0 S	$S = S_0 (\cosh \frac{x}{x_0} + T \sinh \frac{x}{x_0})$ $T = 0.6 \,(T < 1)$

where S = cross sectional area at x, m^2

$\quad \rho$ = medium density, kg/m^3

$\quad \kappa$ = medium bulk modulus

In the case of a sound pipe without a cross-sectional change, dS/dx becomes 0 and 1 represents a wave equation for a sound pipe with a uniform cross section.

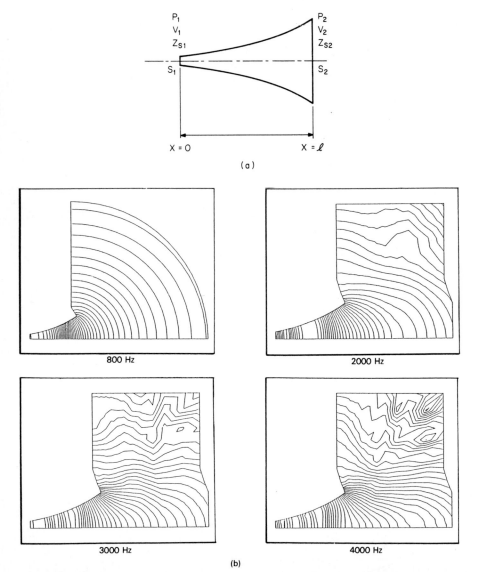

FIG. 7.54 Horn shape and normalized acoustic impedance at the throat of a horn. (*a*) Typical exponential horn shape. (*b*) Sound pressure distribution of an exponential horn estimated by FEM. (*c*) Normalized acoustic impedance at the throat of a horn.

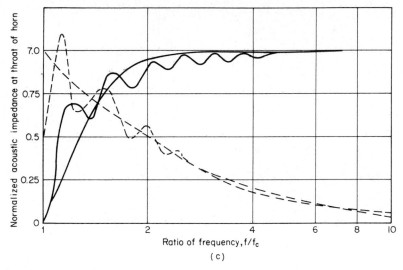

FIG. 7.54 (*Continued*)

Figure 7.53 shows the classification of various horn forms according to the rate of cross-sectional change, from a parabolic horn with the smallest change to a hyperbolic horn with the largest change.

The acoustic-impedance characteristic, as seen from the throat, varies according to the horn form. Figure 7.53 shows the acoustic-impedance characteristics of an infinitely long horn as seen from the throat, with horn forms. In the low-frequency range, the real part of the acoustic impedance is small whereas its imaginary part is large. This shows that the mass component of the sound pipe is dominant and that the acoustic impedance related to sound power is small. Accordingly, sound is reproduced efficiently in a frequency range in which the real part of the sound impedance characteristic is large. Especially for exponential horns the sound power is obtained only when the cutoff frequency f_c is smaller than f.

This cutoff frequency is determined by

$$f_c = \frac{mC}{4\pi} \text{ Hz} \tag{7.68}$$

where m = flare constant (showing rate of horn cross-sectional change)
$\quad\ C$ = speed of change

As the actual lengths of horns are finite, acoustic-impedance characteristics vary from those shown in Fig. 7.53. While only the effect of progressive waves must be considered for an infinitely long horn, the effect of reflection waves from the mouth cannot be ignored for a horn with a finite length.

Figure 7.54a shows a model of a horn with a finite length. Supposing that an exponential horn represents the typical flare function, the acoustic-impedance characteristics of a horn as seen from the throat can be calculated by

$$f > f_c \qquad Z_{A1} = \frac{\rho_0 C}{S_1} \left[\frac{S_2 Z_{A2} \times \sin(\theta - b\ell) + j\rho_0 C \times \sin(b\ell)}{jS_2 Z_{A2} \times \sin(b\ell) + \rho_0 C \times \sin(\theta + b\ell)} \right] \tag{7.69}$$

$$f = f_c \qquad Z_{A1} = \frac{\rho_0 C}{S_1} \left[\frac{S_2 Z_{A2}(1 - a\ell) + j\rho_0 Ca\ell}{jS_2 Z_{A2}a\ell + \rho_0(1 + a\ell)} \right] \tag{7.70}$$

$$f < f_c \qquad Z_{A1} = \frac{\rho_0 C}{S_1} \frac{S_2 Z_{A2} \times a/k\{b/a - \tanh(b\ell)\} + j\rho_0 C \times \tanh(b\ell)}{jS_2 Z_{A2} \times \tanh(b\ell) + \rho_0 C \times a/k\{b'/a + \tanh(b'\ell)\}} \tag{7.71}$$

The difference in acoustic impedance between exponential horns with infinite and finite lengths, as seen from the throat, is shown in Fig. 7.54c. For horns with

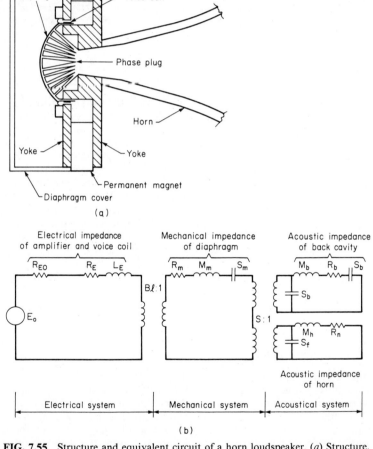

FIG. 7.55 Structure and equivalent circuit of a horn loudspeaker. (*a*) Structure. (*b*) Equivalent circuit. (*c*) Typical frequency characteristics. f_c = cut frequency of horn; f_0 = resonance frequency of vibration system; f_h = cut frequency caused by stiffness of air gap between diaphragm and horn.

finite lengths, resonance results from reflection waves from the mouth, causing irregularities in impedance characteristics. Sound-pressure-distribution characteristics within the horn and around the mouth of a horn speaker, calculated according to FEM, are shown in Fig. 7.54*b*.

7.6.2 Construction and Equivalent Network

The construction and equivalent network of a horn speaker are shown in Fig. 7.55*a* and *b*. A horn speaker consists of a driver and a horn. For diaphragms in drivers—for which lightness and a high resonance frequency of vibration of the normal mode are required—dome-formed shapes generally are used. The phase equalizer is installed at the junction between driver and horn. It enlarges the section of the route of the sound gradually by placing a rigid body closely in front of the diaphragm, for the cross section of the horn throat is smaller than the area of the diaphragm. The air room between the phase equalizer and the diaphragm front is designed to be as small as possible for the reproduction of a high compass,

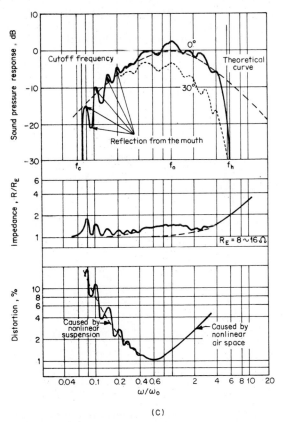

(C)

FIG. 7.55 (*Continued*)

and the distance between the phase equalizer and the route of sound is kept constant to prevent sound from being diminished by distance. Figure 7.55b shows the equivalent network, which can be divided into three portions: electrical, mechanical, and acoustic systems.

Direct-radiation speakers are designed to obtain a constant sound pressure characteristic within the mass-control range in which the acceleration-frequency characteristic is constant. On the other hand, horn speakers are used to obtain a constant sound pressure characteristic within the resistance control range by utilizing the acoustic load resistance of the horn. Accordingly, a light diaphragm is required to realize a constant sound pressure characteristic over a wide band. Typical frequency characteristics are shown in Fig. 7.55c.

7.6.3 Sound Radiation Power

In a direct-radiation speaker, the sound-pressure-frequency characteristic becomes constant in the mass-control range where acceleration is constant, and the sound radiation power becomes constant at frequencies ranging from the minimum resonance frequency to a frequency at which $ka = 3$ ($k = 2\pi f/C$; $a =$ diaphragm radius). On the other hand, horn speakers are of the speed control type, i.e., resistance control type, for the sound pressure characteristic becomes constant only within the range in which the speed of the diaphragm is constant.

The equivalent network is obtained by ignoring the capacity in front of the diaphragm and simplifying the equivalent network shown in Fig. 7.55c. That equivalent network of the horn speaker is a single-resonance system. Accordingly, the sound radiation power of the horn speaker can be calculated by

$$W_{\text{out}} = \left(\cfrac{E}{R_E + \cfrac{\dfrac{A^2}{R_s} \times \dfrac{A^2}{n\rho_0 CS_D}}{\dfrac{A^2}{R_s} + \dfrac{A^2}{n\rho_0 CS_D}}} \times \cfrac{\dfrac{A^2}{Rs}}{\dfrac{A^2}{R} + \dfrac{A^2}{nf_0 CS_D}} \right) 2 \times \frac{A^2}{n\rho_0 CS_D} \qquad (7.72)$$

The electrical input is determined by

$$W_{\text{in}} = \cfrac{E^2}{R_E + \cfrac{\dfrac{A^2}{R_s} \times \dfrac{A^2}{n\rho_0 CS_D}}{\dfrac{A^2}{R_s} + \dfrac{A^2}{n\rho_0 CS_D}}} \qquad (7.73)$$

Accordingly, the conversion efficiency η of the horn speaker can be calculated by

$$\eta = \frac{W_{\text{out}}}{W_{\text{in}}} \times 100 = \cfrac{100}{(n\rho_0 CS_D) \times \dfrac{\sigma}{G}\left(\dfrac{R_s}{n} + 1\right)^2 + \dfrac{R_s}{n} + 1} \% \qquad (7.74)$$

While the efficiency of direct-radiation speakers is 2 to 3 percent at best, horn speakers can realize an efficiency of 10 percent or more.

7.6.4 Nonlinearity Distortion

There are three main causes for the harmonic distortion of horn speakers:

1. Nonlinearity of the diaphragm supporting system
2. Nonuniformity of the magnetic-flux density in a magnetic void
3. Nonlinearity of air

Distortions caused by the nonlinearity of air (point 3) are peculiar to horn speakers. As the throat of a horn speaker is stopped by the phase equalizer, the sound pressure at this location sometimes exceeds 150 dB. Accordingly, a pressure change corresponding to approximately 1 percent of 1 atm results, leading to air distortions. These appear mainly in the form of secondary-harmonic distortions and are more frequent at high frequencies if the sound pressure is identical. The harmonic distortion D_h can be calculated by

$$D_h \fallingdotseq 7.5 \sqrt{W_a} \times \frac{f}{f_c} \times \frac{1}{S_{ho}} \%$$ (7.75)

where W_a = sound power
S_{ho} = cross sectional area of throat, $\wp m^2$

7.6.5 Directivity

The directivity of direct-radiation speakers is limited at higher frequencies. On the other hand, the directivity of horn speakers can be controlled by changing the wall or aperture form. Currently directivity control horns frequently are used to realize a constant sound pressure characteristic within a limited area over a wide frequency range. The form of a typical directivity control horn is shown in Fig. 7.56a, and an example of a directivity pattern in Fig. 7.56b.

7.7 OTHER TYPES OF LOUDSPEAKERS

7.7.1 Electrostatic Speaker

The fundamental principle and features were discussed in Sec. 7.1.3. In this section the structure and equation for sound pressure are described. The construction of an electrostatic speaker, as shown in Fig. 7.57, includes a single and a push-pull type. In the single type a fixed electrode consisting of a perforated metal plate, for example, is set against a diaphragm in which metal is deposited on a light, rugged polymeric film at intervals of approximately 0.3 to 0.5 mm. This type has the disadvantage that operation becomes unstable and distortion increases for a large amplitude; therefore, it is used mainly for a high-frequency-range speaker.

In the push-pull type the diaphragm is arranged between two fixed electrodes. Even when this type is vibrated at a large amplitude, operation is stable and distortion is significantly low; therefore, the push-pull type is also used as a midrange and low-range speaker. As compared with an electrodynamic speaker, however, these types are applied with only a limited amplitude, and the diaphragm area should be increased to obtain a large sound pressure.

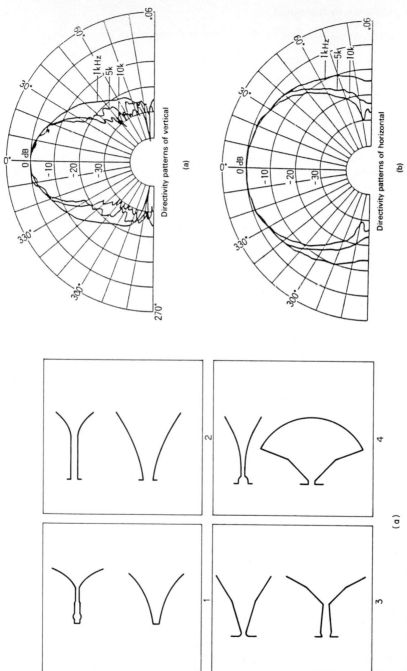

Directivity patterns of vertical

(a)

Directivity patterns of horizontal

(b)

(a)

FIG. 7.56 Shapes and directivity patterns of the constant-directivity horn. (*a*) Various shapes. (*b*) Typical polar directivity patterns.

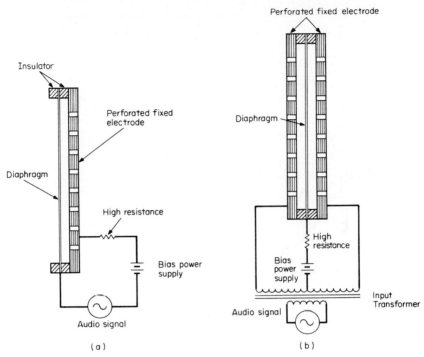

FIG. 7.57   Electrostatic-speaker configuration. (*a*) Single-ended drive. (*b*) Push-pull drive.

The sound pressure is shown in terms of the following equation:

$$P = \frac{2\pi f \rho_0 a^2}{2r} \cdot \frac{C_0^2 E_0 E}{\epsilon S(Z_M - A'^2 Z_0)} \tag{7.76}$$

where Z_M = mechanical-system impedance
   Z_0 = capacitive reactance when no electrode moves, $1/j\omega C_0$
   A' = force factor $G_0 C_0$ (G_0 = interpole field strength E_0/d_0)

In place of a high-voltage bias power supply some electrostatic speakers use electret electrified with a permanent charge on the surface of a polymeric film with a high insulation resistance. This type of speaker is used, for example, mainly for headphone and microphone applications which require a relatively low bias voltage even though a loss is introduced. Since signal voltage is divided by electret, the principle is the same as described in Sec. 7.1.3. The sample characteristics of an electrostatic speaker are shown in Fig. 7.58.

7.7.2   Piezoelectric Speaker

There are various methods for using PZT for a speaker, but since the material is hard and very stiff, it is difficult to secure a large amplitude if vertical oscillation is used; therefore, a bimorphic structure as shown in Fig. 7.59 is normally employed. This bimorph is designed so that when two piezoelectric plates are

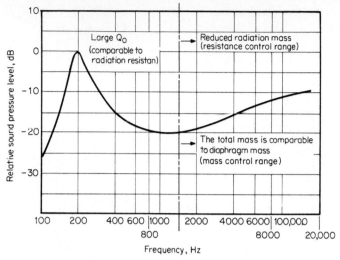

FIG. 7.58 Sound-pressure-frequency characteristic of a static loudspeaker.

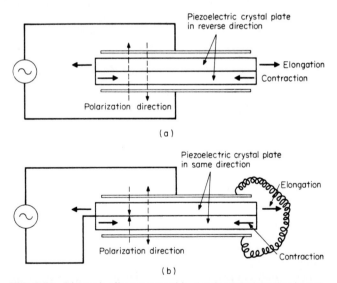

FIG. 7.59 Bimorph vibrator assembly. (*a*) Crystal plates laminated in reverse-polarity direction. (*b*) Crystal plates laminated in the same direction of polarity.

laminated and voltage is applied, one plate expands and the other contracts, causing bending oscillation as a whole. There are two methods to achieve this purpose. One is to laminate two plates to each other so that the polarization direction is the same (parallel type), and the other is to laminate both of them so that the polarization is in the opposite direction (series type). Voltage is applied between the upper and lower surfaces for the series and between the laminated surface of the two piezoelectric plates and the upper and lower surfaces for the parallel type. There are also other structures in which, for example, a metal plate is sandwiched between two piezoelectric plates or in which a piezoelectric plate and a metal plate are laminated.

As described above, since a piezoelectric plate is hard, its resonance point will unavoidably become high if the plate is small and resonance Q is also high, so that in most cases this type of speaker was frequently used as a compact sounding body rather than as a speaker. In recent years, however, a large-diameter slim type (50-mm diameter, 50-μm thickness) has become available, making it possible to reproduce a wide range of sound, including a low tone of approximately 300 Hz. Figure 7.60 shows the construction of a wideband piezoelectric speaker. In the

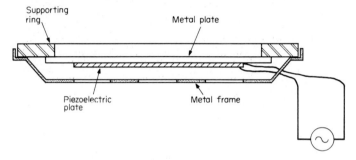

FIG. 7.60   Wideband piezo loudspeaker.

vibrator a piezoelectric plate is laminated on an aluminum disk. The peripheral section is secured to the metal frame by a supporting ring of foamed plastics.

In addition, a piezoelectric speaker provided with a cone in bimorph, as shown in Fig. 7.61, is often used to improve efficiency and flatten frequency characteristics. Polyvinylidene fluoride (PVF$_2$ or PVDF), a polymeric piezoelectric material, has the advantage of being soft and thin, molded to a filmy form. However, since the piezoelectric constant is smaller than PZT, efficiency is a little lower, so that this type is used as a high-range speaker and headphone.

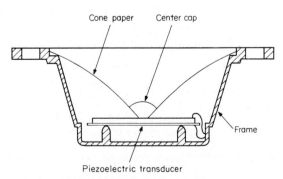

FIG. 7.61   Piezo loudspeaker with a paper cone.

7.7.3 Electromagnetic Speaker

This speaker is also called a *magnetic speaker*. It has the significant merit that it can be made compact and rugged. (The basic principle was discussed in Sec. 7.1.4.) At present, this speaker is used not for audio equipment but to a slight extent for telephone receivers.

The electromagnetic speaker, as shown in Fig. 7.62*a*, is constructed so that a diaphragm of magnetic substance is set against the magnetic pole of the electromagnet and the attractive force of the diaphragm is changed by current flowing into the coil. The equivalent circuit when an electromagnetic transducer is used as a receiver is shown in Fig. 7.62*b*.

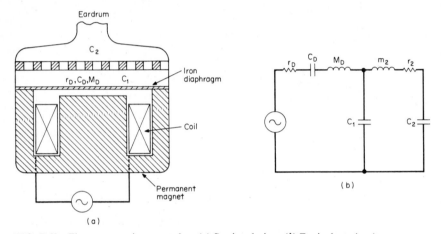

FIG. 7.62   Electromagnetic ear speaker. (*a*) Sectional view. (*b*) Equivalent circuit.

7.7.4 Ion Speaker (Discharging-Type Speaker)

As is apparent from a roll of thunder, it has been well known for many years that sound is produced by electrical discharges in air. However, this system cannot be put to practical use owing to the many noises caused by high-voltage arc discharges. In the 1950s, a system was developed wherein the arc is generated by an alternating current at a high frequency, for example, 20 MHz. Thus the arc is started and stopped continually at the high-frequency rate. The sound signal is generated by an amplitude modulation of the high-frequency carrier signal.

One electrode is a tube made of a dielectric such as silica to prevent corona arc discharge (see Fig. 7.63). This system was used in a commercial product called the Ionophone as a speaker with a wide frequency range. The Ionophone has no mechanical system such as a diaphragm, instead transmitting the molecular movement from the discharge action by means of a horn. Because of the lack of mechanical action, transient characteristics are excellent. However, this type has the disadvantages of electrode wear and the need for a high-frequency oscillator. For these reasons, this speaker device presently is only used rarely for very specialized applications.

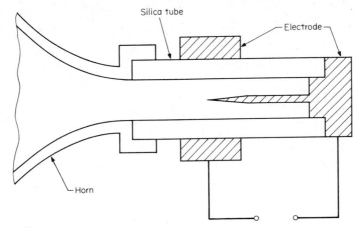

FIG. 7.63   Ion-speaker configuration

7.7.5   Airflow Speaker

In this type of speaker compressed air is sent out through a narrow flow line. Sound is generated by changing the cross-sectional area of the flow line, using a signal input. This construction is shown in Fig. 7.64. The speaker thus devised includes an electrodynamic type, an electromagnetic type, and a piezoelectric type. One example of each type is shown in Fig. 7.64a, b, and c. While a large acoustic output power can be obtained, noise caused by airflow poses a problem.

7.7.6   Parametric Speaker

When a sound wave with a large amplitude (finite-amplitude sound wave) propagates through a medium, a waveform is distorted progressively because of the nonlinearity of the medium, thus producing frequency components not present in the original waveform. When two finite-amplitude sound waves (primary wave) having different frequencies are subjected to nonlinear interaction in a medium, two sound waves (secondary wave) having a frequency of summation and difference of the two primary waves are generated. This secondary wave has no side lobe, showing very high directivity in the low-frequency range.

The sound velocity C of the finite-amplitude sound wave depends on particle speed u:

$$C = C_0 + \beta_u \tag{7.77}$$

where C_0 = sound velocity at infinite small amplitude
 β = nonlinear parameter in medium [$\beta = 1 + \frac{1}{2}(\gamma - 1)$ for gas; γ = specific-heat ratio]

When the primary wave is a plane wave and is satisfactorily collimated and the amplitude primary wave is relatively small so that quasi-linear theory is estab-

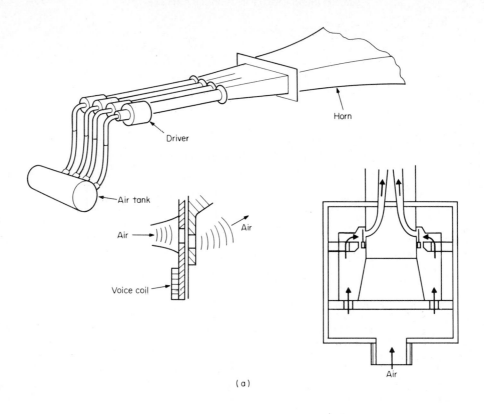

(a)

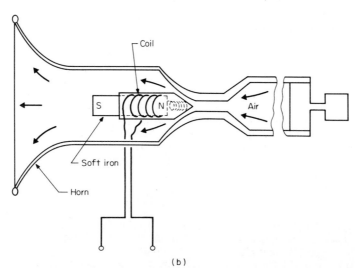

(b)

FIG. 7.64 Airflow loudspeakers. (*a*) Typical construction of an electrodynamic driver and speaker. (*b*) Electromagnetic type. (*c*) Piezoelectric type.

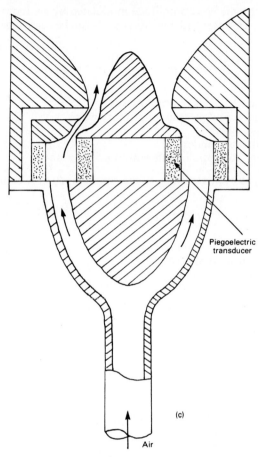

Piegoelectric
transducer

(c)

Air

FIG. 7.64 (*Continued*)

lished, the sound pressure P_s of the secondary wave satisfies the following wave equation:

$$
\begin{cases}
\nabla^2 P_s - \dfrac{1}{C_0{}^2} \dfrac{\partial^2 P_s}{\partial t^2} = -\rho_0 \dfrac{\partial q}{\partial t} \\[4mm]
q = -\dfrac{1}{\rho_0{}^2 C_0{}^4} \dfrac{\partial}{\partial t} P_1{}^2
\end{cases}
\tag{7.78}
$$

where ρ_0 = medium density
q = virtual sound source density of secondary wave
P_1 = sound pressure of primary wave

When an ultrasonic-wave amplitude modulated by an audio signal is used as a primary signal, a speaker with high directivity can be achieved. Assume primary wave P_1 to be

$$P_1 = P_0 \left[1 + m \times g\left(t - \frac{r}{C_0}\right) \right] e^{-\alpha r} \times \sin\left[\omega_0 \left(t - \frac{r}{C_0}\right) \right] \qquad (7.79)$$

where ω_0 = angle frequency of primary wave
   P_0 = initial sound pressure of primary wave
   $g(t)$ = audio signal
   m = modulation index
   α = linear absorption coefficient of primary wave

If Eq. (7.78) is solved according to the equation, $P_s(\omega)$ is obtained by

$$P_s(\omega) = -\frac{\beta P_0^2 a^2 m \omega^2}{8\rho_0 C_0^4 \alpha r} \times e^{-jrC_0\omega} \, G(\omega) \qquad (7.80)$$

where a = radius of sound source
   $G(\omega)$ = $g(t)$ Fourier transform

A −3-dB beam width $2\theta s$ of the secondary wave is found by

$$2\theta s = 4\sqrt{\alpha C_0 / \omega} \qquad (7.81)$$

Figure 7.65 shows one example of the system. The ultrasonic-wave source used is a 500 × 1500 focusing-convergence type of sound source consisting of approx-

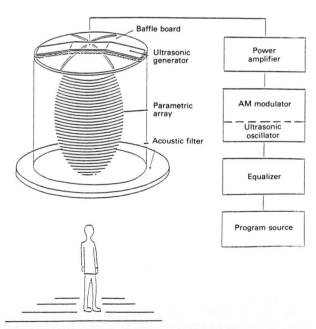

FIG. 7.65   Parametric-loudspeaker configuration.

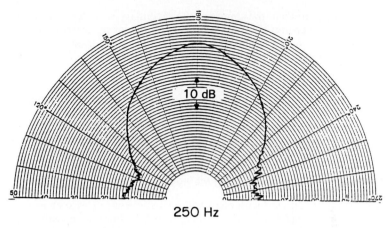

250 Hz

FIG. 7.66 Parametric-loudspeaker directivity pattern, 1 dB/gradation.

imately 6600 piezoelectric ceramic transducers of a bimorphic type. The acoustic filter consists of soft foamed urethane and polyethylene film alternately laminated in five layers. Furthermore, a pipe is installed to prevent an ultrasonic wave from scattering to the periphery. As a result, secondary-wave sound pressure produces 91 dB at 10 V, 1 kHz, at the sound-receiving point 2.5 m apart from the sound source. The primary-wave level at the sound-receiving point is attenuated from 140 to 80 dB through the acoustic filter.

Figure 7.66 shows the directional characteristics. A normal speaker is almost nondirectional at 500 Hz. Figure 7.67 shows the frequency characteristics of the sound pressure of the secondary wave. As can be seen from Eq. (7.78), a parametric speaker is indicative of 12-dB-per-octave characteristics since the sound

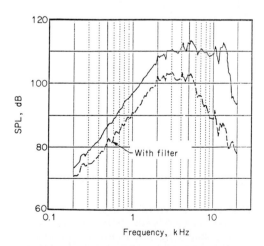

FIG. 7.67 Parametric-loudspeaker sound-pressure-frequency characteristic.

pressure is proportional to the square of the secondary-wave frequency. The characteristics do not become 12 dB per octave at 2 kHz or more since the ultrasonic transducer band is narrow. The primary-wave frequency used is 40 kHz. Problems in practical use for a parametric speaker include:

1. Low transform efficiency from primary to secondary wave
2. An acoustic filter required to protect a listener against a strong primary wave

7.8   PUBLIC-ADDRESS-SYSTEM LOUDSPEAKERS

7.8.1   Design by Sound-Ray-Tracing Methods

The problems encountered with electrical acoustic equipment such as the speakers, microphones, amplifiers, and mixers required for interior acoustic production under working conditions include the following:

1. Unequal sound pressure distribution in the service area
2. Echo generation
3. Spots of inferior articulation
4. Acoustical feedback

If these problems can be predicted in advance, speaker arrangement and component selection are simplified and performance is enhanced. To accomplish these objectives, a sound-field simulation program has been developed which employs a geometrical analysis technique that assumes that sound energy travels forward in a straight line like light. The mirror-image method is most suitable for examining initial sound reflections and echoes. The disadvantage of this method has been that calculation time increases exponentially with the number of reflections or the number of reflecting surfaces. For this reason, for practical calculations the number of reflections is limited to 2 to 3 times. However, calculation time can be shortened to a great extent by using the mirror-image technique. Calculation comprises the following three steps:

1. A mirror image is produced in relation to a wall.

2. Checks are made as to whether line segments connecting the sound-receiving point and the front of the wall and the sound ray and mirror image intersect at the front of the wall.

3. Checks are made as to whether the line segments mentioned in point 2 involve another wall.

7.8.2   Central-Cluster System and Distributor System

Central-Cluster System.   The central-cluster system, which uses high-efficiency midrange to high-range speakers with sharp vertical and horizontal directivity and high-power bass speakers, has the following advantages compared with the distributor system: (1) Echoes seldom occur. (2) The system can be used for various purposes such as improving sound-directional localization, producing special effects, etc. (3) Material, construction, and maintenance costs are low. On the other hand, there are drawbacks. Since speakers are concentrated in one or two locations in this system, volume is excessive near each speaker, thus increasing the level difference between the nearest and farthest positions.

Distributor System. This system functions satisfactorily for calling and announcing. However, since speakers are distributed over an area, an echo is liable to occur owing to the distance between speakers, and interference may be caused by reflected sound. In particular, when a full bass tone is required for music reproduction, a booming effect frequently will be encountered. When speakers are located around the rear seats, the sound is always localized behind the audience. Also, when speakers are installed around a field to cover seats, the volume becomes too low in the field, and large speakers cannot be used because they obstruct the view of spectators. Accordingly, there is a limit to the sound quality and sound pressure distribution realizable by this system.

Table 7.3 compares the distributor and central-cluster systems. These advantages and drawbacks do not apply to all cases. Rather, they vary depending on the complexity and cost of the facility, the kind of entertainments, methods of operation, and ambient environmental conditions, etc. Therefore, the speaker-system location, direction, and extent must be determined to meet field conditions.

TABLE 7.3   Comparison between Distributor and Central-Cluster Systems Employed in a Stadium

No.	Item	Central-cluster system	Distributor system
1	Speaker system	Multispeaker system employed relatively easily	Large speakers easily employed
2	Echo generation	Seldom	Often
3	Sound pressure level	Great level difference between near and distant positions	Relatively uniform
4	Workability	Labor for speaker house preparation, piping, and wiring saved	Speaker tower and pole installation, piping, and wiring executed separately
5	Speaker line transmission loss	Amplifier installed in or around speaker house, saving labor	Low-impedance drive impossible owing to long distance
6	Adjustment maintenance	Relatively easy owing to concentrated system	Sometimes difficult according to number of installation places and speaker structure
7	System price	Reasonable	More expensive

7.8.3 Theater and Auditorium Systems

Acoustically required items for a PA system vary according to application (type of entertainment). However, general requirements may be roughly outlined as follows:

1. Volume is satisfactory: *volume.*
2. Sound can be heard clearly: *clearness.*
3. Sound is pleasant: *reverberation.*

   These requirements cannot be fulfilled solely by adjusting the PA system; technical architectural conditions should also be met. A rough description is given below of the acoustic evaluation required for various applications and technical conditions in architecture and electronics as well as sound pickup systems, speaker systems, and voice-level adjustment systems. Furthermore, a system designed to facilitate setup and operation by employing computers, used in recently built multipurpose sports arenas, is described.
   Entertainment items and acoustic requirements are shown in Table 7.4. An electrical sound system for a hall is shown in Fig. 7.68, a sound pickup system is shown in Fig. 7.69, a sound control system is shown in Fig. 7.70, and a loudspeaker system is shown in Fig. 7.71.
   The size of the loudspeaker system is determined by the sound-pressure-level and frequency characteristics requested for the hall. The attenuation curve of the sound pressure level changes with interior conditions, which are quite different from free-field conditions. Therefore, the loudspeaker system is designed after the architectural and interior design has been completed. The average absorption α coefficient is given by the following equation:

$$\overline{\alpha} = \frac{\sum(\alpha_i - S_i)}{\sum S_i} \qquad (7.82)$$

where S_i = individual boundary surface area, m²
      α_i = absorption coefficient of area S_i

The room constant R is shown by the following equation:

$$R = \frac{\overline{\alpha}\, S}{1 - \overline{\alpha}} \qquad (7.83)$$

where S = total surface area, m².
   The attenuation equation is

$$\text{SPL} = \text{PWL} + 10 \log\left(\frac{Q}{4\pi r^2} + \frac{4}{R}\right) \qquad (7.84)$$

where SPL = sound pressure level at point from sound source, dB
     PWL = power level of sound source, dB
       Q = directivity index of sound source
       r = distance from sound source, m
       R = room constant

TABLE 7.4 Entertainment Items and Acoustic Requirements

Entertainment items	Acoustic requirements (overall evaluation standard)
Meetings, ceremonies, training courses, lectures, etc.	As speech is mainly transmitted, sound clearness is most important. As for electronics, howling margin should be increased to prevent howling. It is desirable that interiors be finished for sound absorption.
Popular music (broadcast via TV, etc.), popular songs, jazz	Ample reverberation and sufficient sound volume (sound pressure) are required. As for architecture, a finish to improve sound reflection is required. As for electronics, a large-capacity amplifier and a high-performance speaker system are required.
Traditional Japanese music, kabuki performances	As a rule, electrical acoustic equipment, if used, is employed only as an auxiliary to transmit speech and accompaniments. Since kotos and shamisens generate impact sound, an appropriate microphone is difficult to find. Interiors should be treated for sound absorption.
Opera, dance, plays	As a rule, electrical acoustic equipment is employed to produce special effects and not to transmit speech and songs. Accordingly, a comparatively large-capacity system is required. As for architecture, special precautions should be taken for ample reverberation.
Classical music	Electrical acoustic equipment is not used except for transmitting explanations and calling. As for architecture, special steps should be taken to secure a longer reverberation time.
Plays, folksongs	As in popular music, ample reverberation and sufficient volume (sound pressure) are required. Clearness is also required for plays.
Motion pictures	An electrical sound system for motion-picture acoustics is required. The power amplifier unit can be shared, and a special speaker system is required. Speakers for special effects may be installed on walls, ceilings, etc.

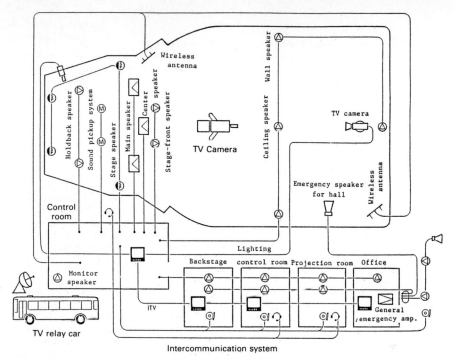

FIG. 7.68 Electrical sound system for an auditorium.

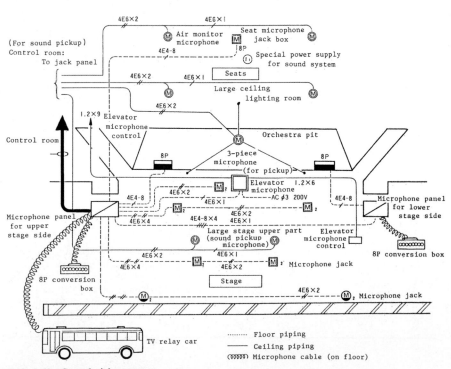

FIG. 7.69 Sound pickup system.

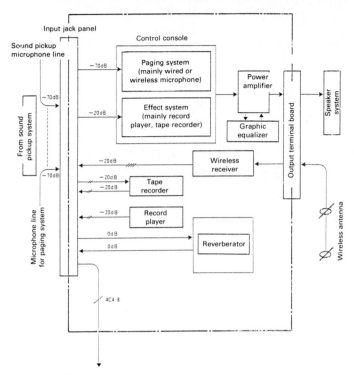

FIG. 7.70 Sound control system.

The first term, $10 \log (Q/4\pi r)$, of Eq. (7.84) shows inverse-square-law attenuation. The second term, $10 \log (4/r)$, shows the reverberant component. The relationship of attenuation and distance from the source is shown in Fig. 7.72. Examination of this figure makes the following clear. Sound pressure deviation is 5 dB between the front seats and the rear seats without a loudspeaker system. If a sound pressure level of 112 dB is generated at a point 1 m from the source, a sound pressure level of 90 dB can be obtained at the farthest seats. The power amplifier must apply 15.8 W to the loudspeaker, thus increasing the sound pressure level of 12 dB at the farthest seats.

The peaking factor of a speech source is 10 dB, and the peaking factor of a music source is 20 dB. Therefore, the power amplifier capacities are 158 W and 1580 W with the two sources, respectively.

PA System Using a Computer for a Multipurpose Sports Arena. Multipurpose sports arenas used for such events as popular music concerts, memorial ceremonies, lectures, exhibitions, and fashion shows require two or three types of stage setting according to use. When used for a sports contest or an exhibition, an arena will be utilized in a variety of ways. For example, an entire arena may be used as a stage. In this case, it may accommodate an audience of tens of thousands. Consequently, the speaker system will include center-cluster speakers (octahedron assembly directed downward) and distributed units installed at the upper part of the seats. When a temporary stage is required for concerts, gatherings, etc., speakers must be installed at both sides of the stage.

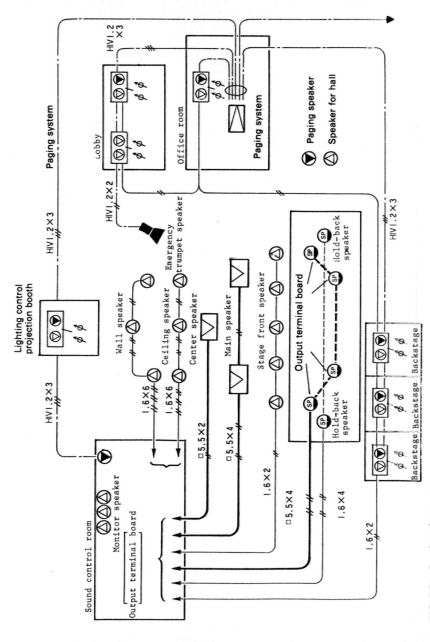

FIG. 7.71 Loudspeaker system.

7.72

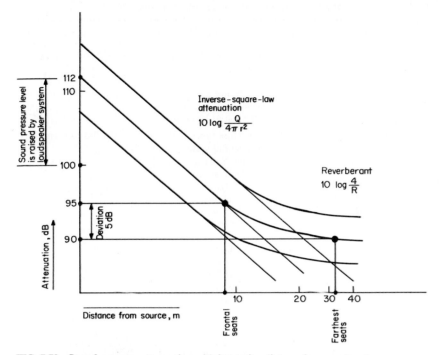

FIG. 7.72 Sound pressure attenuation with increasing distance in an enclosed space.

Adjustment of a PA system for such a multipurpose hall entails high labor costs. Speakers are selected according to the type of entertainment, delay time with distributed speakers must be adjusted, the sound field must be adjusted by using a graphic equalizer, the volume level among speakers should be balanced for two- or three-way speaker systems, etc. (see Table 7.5). Moreover, because a few hundred input-output lines are used, the patching operation associated with the audio control console is time-consuming. This problem is solved by computerized methods of connection and patching of input lines to the control console and of setting the speaker system according to the type of entertainment, as described and shown in Figs. 7.73 and 7.74.

7.8.4 Stadium PA Systems

Purpose of PA Systems in Stadiums. Stadiums are used for various purposes: baseball and football games, track meets, expositions, open-air shows, etc. (see Table 7.6). Possible applications of PA systems include:

1. Opening and closing ceremonies
2. Background music (when contestants enter or leave the stadium)
3. Musical accompaniment for vocal presentations
4. Musical accompaniment for action

TABLE 7.5 Electronics for Theater and Auditorium Systems

Technical conditions	Suggested measurement method	Suggested value
Maximum sound pressure level	1. Transmit pink noise with the electrical sound system and main speaker. 2. Measure sound pressure behind seats on the first floor, using the sound-level meter.	Continuously 95 dB or more.
Sound-pressure-distribution deviation within seats	1. Transmit pink noise with the electrical sound system, main speaker, etc. Measure sound pressure level at specified locations (10 or more) using a sound-level meter. 2. Determine deviation at each location against the center of seats on the first floor. 3. Measure sound pressure at the center at 80 to 85 dB. 4. For analysis at each frequency, measure at 125 and 500 Hz and 1 and 4 kHz.	± 3 dB maximum.
Transmission-frequency characteristics	1. Transmit pink noise with the electrical sound system and main speaker, and adjust the sound pressure level at the center of seats on the first floor to 80 to 85 dB. 2. Record the change in sound pressure level for each frequency via one-third-octave filter, using a level recorder. 3. Make measurements at 5 to 10 locations inside seats.	The transmission-frequency characteristics should be uniform and have no irregularities. The multiway speaker should have no extreme irregularities in characteristics near the crossover frequency.
Howling-frequency characteristics	1. Set a microphone to be used to the position of center microphone on the stage, and insert one-third-octave filter and attenuator (ATT) into the volume-intensifying loop. 2. Adjust the ATT so as to exceed the howling-limit point for every frequency; then enter ATT reading on graph paper.	The frequency characteristics should be uniform over the entire range. (In particular, no peak should be allowed.) When a peak is found, adjust so as to eliminate the peak by using a graphic equalizer. It is desirable that the level be low over the entire range.

TABLE 7.5 Electronics for Theater and Auditorium Systems (*Continued*)

Technical conditions	Suggested measurement method	Suggested value
Howling margin	1. Set a microphone to be used to the position of center microphone on the stage and install speaker 50 cm above the microphone axis as primary sound source. 2. Insert ATT into the volume-intensifying loop, and adjust frequency to 6 dB below the howling-limit point via ATT. 3. Transmit pink noise with the primary-source speaker, collect it with a microphone, and transmit with main speaker, increasing volume. 4. Measure the sound pressure level applied to the microphone by the primary-sound-source speaker, using a sound-level meter to obtain 80 dB. (*A*) 5. At that time, measure the sound pressure level at a representative seat location, using a sound-level meter. (*B*) 6. Determine the level difference (*B*) − (*A*) as the howling margin.	dB 0 — Very good −7 — Good −10 — Easily howling −15 — −20 — Bad

5. Guidance by announcer
6. Background music for exhibitions
7. Transmission for radio and TV broadcasting
8. Auxiliary use for concerts

Speaker-System Design Requirements

1. Speaker-unit performance and speaker-system scale, including the installation method, which secures the pressure required over the entire area between the main sound-source speaker and the farthest seat position
2. Weather resistance and durability of the speaker unit (for low ranges in particular), as stadium facilities are normally built for outdoor use
3. Directivity at midrange and high-range areas
4. Sustained feedback (howling) threshold and frequency characteristic

TABLE 7.6   System Classification

Electrical sound system
  Sound pickup system 1: sound pickup by wired microphone
  Sound pickup system 2: sound pickup by wireless microphone
  Speaker system
    Main speaker, center speaker
    Holdback speaker
    Stage-front speaker
    Wall speaker, ceiling speaker
    Stage speaker
    Monitor speaker
    Operation monitor speaker
  Voice-control system: voice-control console, power amplifier, record-player console,
                       tape-recorder console, wireless receiver, microphone mixer,
                       graphic equalizer, reverberator
Auxiliary system
  Communication unit
  Bell-and-buzzer unit
  TV equipment
  General and emergency broadcasting equipment
  ITV monitor unit

Computers have been actively utilized for these purposes, enabling sound pressure distribution and level to be calculated in advance.

Speaker-Unit Performance and Sound Pressure Level.   Assuming that the distance between the sound source and the farthest seat position is 300 m, that noise from the audience, etc., is 85 dB, and that the signal-to-noise ratio which can produce intelligible sound is 5 dB,

90 dB (sound pressure level required at farthest seat position)

$$+ \; 50 \text{ dB (attenuation is 300-m free space)} = 140 \text{ dB} \quad (7.85)$$

Accordingly, to cover the farthest seat position a sound pressure of 140 dB is required at a position 1 m from the speaker. This sound pressure must be generated by applying sufficient power and employing an appropriate number of speakers.

Assuming that sound pressure rises by 10 dB by applying a power of 100 W and by 8 dB by employing six additional speakers and that a system installed on both left and right sides can cover the farthest seat position,

$$140 \text{ dB} - 20 \text{ dB} - 8 \text{ dB} - 8 \text{ dB} = 104 \text{ dB} \quad (7.86)$$

Thus, it follows that to secure a 90-dB sound pressure at a position 300 m from the speaker 12 speaker units with 104 dB (1 W $\times$ 1 m) and a power of 600 W $\times$ 2 are required. Actually, considering the program peak factor, a 200-W power amplifier per unit is used with a 108 dB/(1 W $\times$ 1 m) driver unit, and a total of approximately 2400 W must be generated by the power amplifier units.

Installation Location.   The speaker system should be installed so as not to obstruct the audience's field of vision. It is desirable that the front side of the

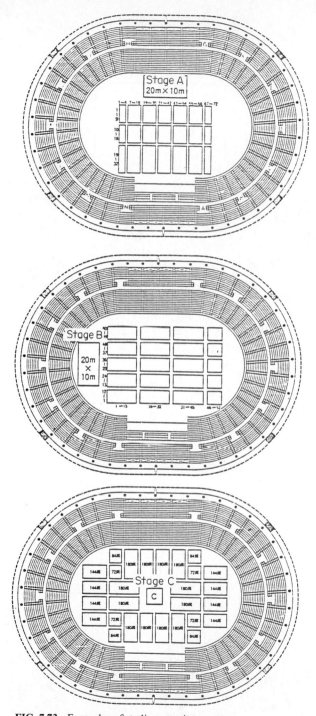

FIG. 7.73 Examples of stadium staging.

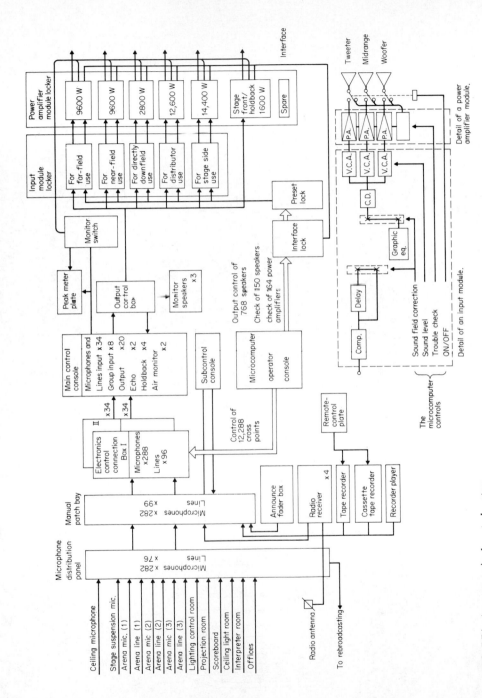

FIG. 7.74 A computerized control system.

7.78

system be acoustically transparent so as to emit sound as efficiently as possible. Also, proper measures should be taken against rain and wind. Moreover, in ballparks and other stadiums, the scoreboard, electric signboard, large-screen television display system, etc., are set up where they can be seen clearly by the audience, as they are important for the enjoyment of games. Accordingly, it is desirable that sound be transmitted from the scoreboard.

Weather Resistance of Speaker Unit.   As the horn loudspeaker's diaphragm for midrange and high range is metallic and the horn also is made of metal or reinforced plastic, weather resistance does not present a problem. However, for the low-frequency range the cone at the driver portion usually is made of paper and the housing of wood; therefore, proper measures should be taken to protect them from rain. It is necessary to apply sufficient preservative to the housing and assure proper surface treatment. The cone paper should be given a moistureproof treatment with silicone or have reinforced olefin applied to the surface.

Directivity at Midrange and High Range.   To transmit PA sound uniformly over an entire stadium, the frequency spectrum to be covered by midrange and high-range speakers should be determined after careful consideration. In many cases, sound reflected on buildings and grounds reaches seats, impairing clarity. Advances in speaker techniques have produced horn speakers with sharp horizontal and vertical directivity control, and computer-controlled simulation design technologies also have been developed. These developments have made it possible to calculate sound pressure distribution, the effect of long-distance echoes, etc., in advance of installation. In setting up a speaker system for a large outdoor facility, factors such as weather conditions, time, geography, etc., should be taken into consideration, as well as the noise level for residents near the facility.

Typical PA System: Memorial Colosseum, Los Angeles

Speaker system	Two-way system × 2 (configuration of one system shown in Fig. 7.75 and Fig. 7.76)
Low-range part	38-cm woofer × 12 Allowable input 300 W Output sound pressure 100 dB (1 W × 1 m)
Midrange and high-range part	*For long distance* Superdirectional horn × 6 Allowable input 100 W [108 dB/(1 W × 1 m)] Directivity, 40° horizontal and 30° vertical *For middistance* Superdirectional horn × 2 Allowable input 100 W [108 dB/(1 W × 1 m)] Directivity, 40° horizontal and 30° vertical

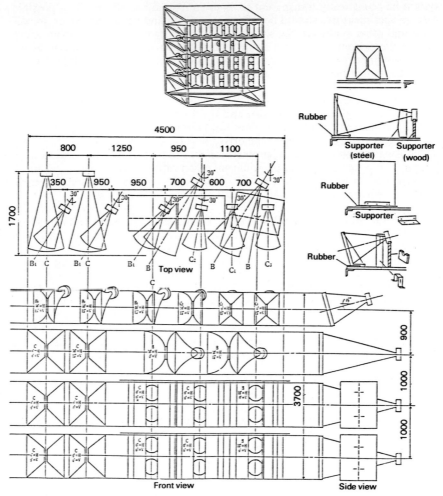

FIG. 7.75 Left-side speaker cluster assembly.

For short distance
Directional horn × 6
Allowable input 100 W [108 dB/(1 W
    × 1 m)]
Directivity, 60° horizontal and 40°
    vertical

A composite diagram for a loudspeaker system is shown in Fig. 7.77. The power amplifier is 200 W + 200 W × 13; the standby spare, × 1. The dimensions of a sample superdirectional horn are shown in Fig. 7.78, and its directivity in Fig. 7.79.

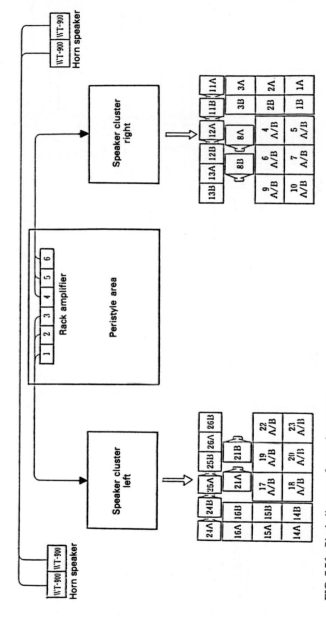

FIG. 7.76 Block diagram of a speaker system.

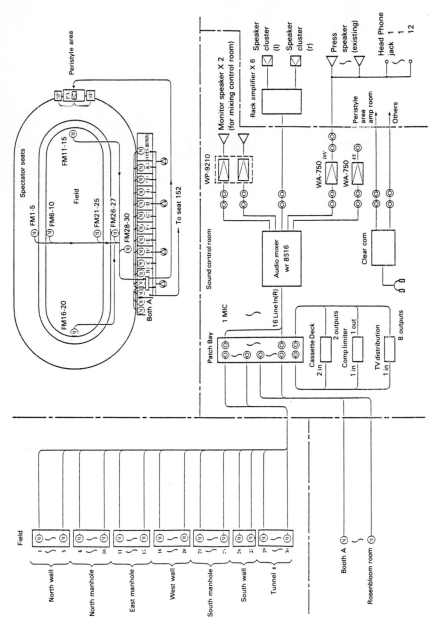

FIG. 7.77 Layout for a typical stadium system.

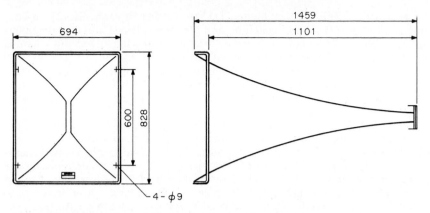

FIG. 7.78 Configuration and dimensions of a superdirectional horn.

7.9 HEADPHONES AND HEADPHONE SYSTEMS

7.9.1 Headphone Construction

A headphone consists of an electrical acoustic transducer, the ear cups containing it, ear cushions for forming a small space with the external ear, a headband connecting the right and left ear cups, and various adjusting mechanisms for attaching the headphone correctly.

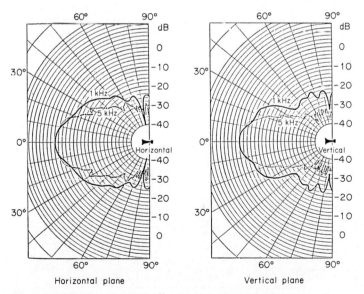

FIG. 7.79 Directivity patterns of a typical superdirectional horn.

Construction differs, depending on (1) the number of channels, (2) ear-coupling conditions, (3) sound insulation, and (4) the electricity and sound conversion principle. Headphones are classified into monaural, stereo, and four-channel headphones according to the number of channels, as shown in Fig. 7.80. The monaural headphone plays back the same sound at the right and left ears, while the four-channel headphone plays back the right and left front signal and rear signal from two transducers within the right and left ear cups. Most current headphones are stereo headphones.

Next, headphones are, as shown in Fig. 7.81, classified into pressure and velocity types according to ear-coupling conditions. A small space formed at the front side of the transducer that acts as the acoustic load is divided into a closed chamber or a leak space. In other words, for the pressure-type headphone the ear cushion is constructed so that a core material such as foamed urethane having excellent elasticity is wrapped with nonporous vinyl chloride sheet or synthetic leather, etc. Sometimes, liquid is sealed inside, improving sealing performance in the front chamber. In the velocity-type headphone the ear cushion may be formed of foamed urethane with acoustic permeability, or numerous through holes may be provided on the surface of the pressure-type headphone ear cushion. With ear-coupling conditions priority is given to the acoustic permeability of the ear cushion, while with sound insulation priority is given to both the ear cushion and the acoustic permeability of the ear cup. This depends on whether external sound is heard or not. If either the ear cushion or the ear cup is acoustically permeable, the headphone is an open-air type (velocity type). If both are nonporous, the headphone is a closed type (pressure type). (Refer to Fig. 7.81.) Since the closed-type headphone is interrupted acoustically from the outside, it suffers from a unique incompatibility, while the open-air type has no such drawback. Therefore, the open-air type has been most popular in recent years. The closed-type headphone is used for live recording and monitoring in broadcasting studios.

The type of electrical acoustic transducer used varies as described in Sec. 7.2, but a dynamic headphone is the principal type. Assuming voltage and current applied to the electric terminal of the transducer to be $\dot{E}$, $\dot{I}$, electric-system impedance to be Z_E, admittance to be Y_E, mechanical-system impedance to be Z_M, and load impedance converting the acoustic-system impedance to the mechanical-system impedance to be Z_{MA}, the vibrating speed V of the mechanical system is as

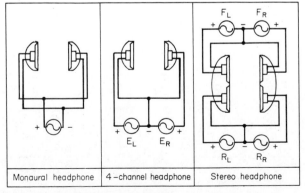

FIG. 7.80 Classification of headphones by channel.

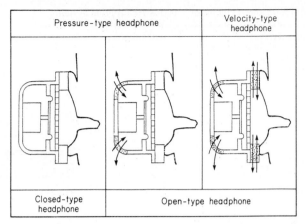

Pressure-type headphone	Velocity-type headphone

Closed-type headphone	Open-type headphone

FIG. 7.81 Classification of headphones by ear coupling and sound isolation.

shown in Table 7.7. However, A is the force factor, and for the dynamic type it corresponds to the product of magnetic-flux density of magnetic space B, in webers per square meter, and effective voice-coil wire length, in meters. For the static type, assuming the capacitance in stationary conditions to be C_0 in farads, and field strength to be G_0, in volts per meter, $A = C_0 G_0$; for an electret static type, assuming the induced charge to be q, in coulombs, and gap size to be d_0, in meters, $A = q/d_0$.

Normally, for the sound-pressure-frequency characteristics of the headphone, the sound pressure within a standard vessel (coupler) corresponding to the volume of space consisting of the ear and the headphone is measured, but since resonance occurs according to the shape, an objective comparative evaluation has been difficult.

Another tone evaluation method is a response-measuring method that uses actual ears to measure the sound pressure at the outer-ear entrance or eardrum surface with a probe tube microphone. However, since the results of this method differed among individuals and there was a danger of ear injury, the artificial ear shown in Fig. 7.82 was recommended by the International Electrotechnical Commission (IEC) in 1970. This is as near to the value of acoustic impedance of the human ear as possible: the space capacity is 2.5 cc at approximately 8 kHz or more, 11.8 cc at approximately 200 Hz, and 4.3 cc in between. At present, this artificial ear generally is used as a measuring instrument for headphone sound-pressure-frequency characteristics.

7.9.2 Equivalent Circuit and Operational Analysis

In the preceding section, the relationship between the electrical and mechanical systems was discussed. In this section the relationship of the mechanical system to the acoustic system is described; also shown is the equation for headphone sound pressure.

Figure 7.83 shows (*a*) a sketch of a headphone held at the ears and (*b*) mechanical and acoustic circuits. Assume that a system consists of a headphone, eardrum,

TABLE 7.7 Structure and Velocity of Various Headphone Systems

Velocity of diaphragm	Structure
Dynamic transducer type Concentrate drive $$V = \frac{A}{Z_E(Z_M + Z_{MA}) + A^2}\dot{E}$$ $A = B\ell$	
Distribution drive $$V = \frac{A}{Z_E(Z_M + Z_{MA}) + A^2}\dot{E}$$ $A = B\ell$	
Electrostatic transducer type Bias type $$V = \frac{A}{Y_B(Z_M + Z_{MA}) - A^2}\dot{I}$$ $A = \dfrac{2\varepsilon_0 S E_B}{d^2}$	
Electret type $$V = \frac{AI}{Y_E(Z_M + Z_{MA}) - A^2}$$ $A = \dfrac{2q}{g_0}$	

and ear cushion and that a small space of volume W_0, in cubic meters, including a volume equivalent to the ear acoustic impedance, is open to the outside by means of acoustic resistance r_A, in newton seconds per quintuple meter, caused by leaks and egress M_A, in kilograms per quadruple meter. The acoustic capacity C_A, in quintuple meters per newton, of this small space is determined by

$$C_A = \frac{W_0}{\rho_0 C^2} \qquad (7.87)$$

When pressure $\dot{P}$, in newtons per square meter, is applied to this small space by displacing the diaphragm of effective S_d, in square meters, to the inside by X, in meters, the volume velocity $\dot{U}$, in cubic meters per second, is relieved not only by the small space but by r, M, and ear acoustic impedance Z. Therefore, the following two equations are obtained:

$$\dot{U} = \left(j\omega C_A + \frac{1}{r_A + j\omega M_A}\right)\dot{P} \qquad (7.88)$$

$$\dot{U} = S_d \cdot \frac{d\dot{x}}{dt} = S_d \times \dot{V} \qquad (7.89)$$

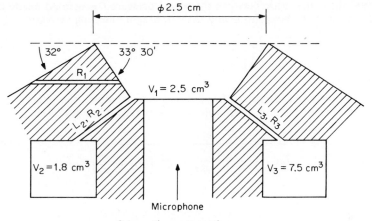

$\phi 2.5$ cm

$32°$

R_1

$33° 30'$

$V_1 = 2.5$ cm^3

L_2, R_2

L_3, R_3

$V_2 = 1.8$ cm^3

$V_3 = 7.5$ cm^3

Microphone

Schematic cross section

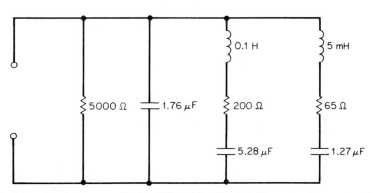

0.1 H

5 mH

5000 Ω

1.76 μF

200 Ω

65 Ω

5.28 μF

1.27 μF

FIG. 7.82 Standard ear specified in IEC Publication 318 *(Courtesy of International Electrotechnical Commission)*. In this analog 1 electrical ohm = 10^5 ns/m^{-5}.

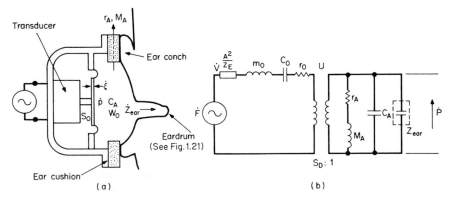

FIG. 7.83 (*a*) Placement of hearing aid in ear. (*b*) Equivalent circuit of acoustic and mechanical systems.

Next, find the relationship between the sound pressure $\dot{P}$ generated inside the small space through the headphone and the diaphragm vibrating velocity:

$$\dot{P} = \left(\frac{S_d}{j\omega C_A + \dfrac{1}{r_A + j\omega M_A}}\right) \dot{V} \qquad (7.90)$$

Consequently, taking a dynamic headphone, for example, the relationship between sound pressure $\dot{P}$ and input voltage E is as shown in Eq. (7.91).

$$\dot{P} = \frac{S_d}{j\omega C_A + \dfrac{1}{r_A + j\omega M_A}} \times \frac{A\dot{E}}{Z_E\left(Z_M + \dfrac{A^2}{Z_E}\right)} \qquad (7.91)$$

Pressure-Type Headphone. For a pressure-type headphone, normally $1/WC_A \ll r_A$, ωM_A in Fig. 7.81. Consequently, Eq. (7.91) is as follows:

$$\dot{P} = \left(\frac{S_d}{j\omega C_A}\right) \dot{V} = \frac{\rho_0 C^2 S d}{j\omega W_0} \frac{A\dot{E}}{Z_E} \frac{1}{Z_M + A^2/Z_E} \qquad (7.92)$$

If the value when acoustic capacity C_A is converted to the mechanical system is $C_{MA}\,(=\,C_A/S_d^2)$, the following equation is obtained:

$$Z_M + A^2/Z_E = A^2/Z_E + r_0 + j\left[\omega m_0 - \frac{(C_0 + C_{MA})}{\omega(C_0 \times C_{MA})}\right] \qquad (7.93)$$

Consequently, the sound pressure characteristics of a pressure-type headphone are found by

$$|\dot{P}| = \frac{\rho_0 C^2 S_d}{W_0} \frac{A|\dot{E}|}{Z_E} \frac{1}{\sqrt{\left(\dfrac{C_0 + C_{MA}}{C_0 \times C_{MA}} - \omega m_0\right)^2 + (A^2/Z_E + r_0)^2}} \qquad (7.94)$$

When $f \ll f_0$ and $f_0 \ll f$, check the operation in the equivalent circuit shown in Fig. 7.84.

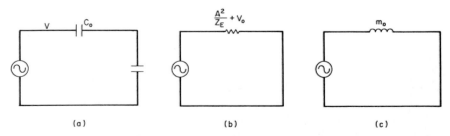

(a)   (b)   (c)

FIG. 7.84   Equivalent circuit of pressure-type headphone. (a) In the case of $f \ll f_0$, $\dot{V} = A\dot{E}/Z_E \times j\omega CC_0 + C_{MA}$. (b) In the case of $f = f_0$, $\dot{V} = A^2/Z_E + \gamma_0$. (c) In the case of $f \ll f$, $\dot{V} = A\dot{E}/Z_E \times 1/j\omega m$.

From Fig. 7.83 sound pressure $|\dot{P}|$ is determined by

$$|\dot{P}|_{f<f_0} = \frac{\rho_0 C^2 S_d}{W_0} \times \frac{A|\dot{E}|(C_0 \times C_{MA})}{Z_E(C_0 + C_{MA})}$$

$$= \frac{\rho_0 C^2 S_d}{W_0} \frac{A|\dot{E}|}{Z_E} \frac{1}{m_0 \omega_0^2} \tag{7.95}$$

$$|\dot{P}|_{f \gg f_0} = \frac{\rho_0 C^2 S_d}{W_0} \frac{A|\dot{E}|}{Z_E} \frac{1}{m_0 \omega^2} \tag{7.96}$$

$$|\dot{P}|_{f=f_0} = \frac{\rho_0 C^2 S_d}{W_0} \times \frac{A|\dot{E}|}{Z_E} \times \frac{Q_0}{m_0 \omega_0^2} \left(Q_0 = \frac{\omega_0 m_0}{r_0 + A^2/Z_E} \right) \tag{7.97}$$

To decrease sound pressure sensitivity from Eq. (7.97), increase the effective area of the diaphragm and the power coefficient and reduce W_0 and m_0. To make the sound-pressure-frequency characteristics flat, set the resonance frequency of the vibrating system to the high-frequency limit of the playback band for stiffness control. The solid line of Fig. 7.85 shows the sound-pressure-frequency characteristics of a general-pressure-type headphone. When Q_0 is high in the resonance zone, a peak is generated; therefore, satisfactory damping is required. Further, in the low range, if leak resistance r_A is present, sensitivity will be lowered at a low frequency: $1/WC_A > r_A$.

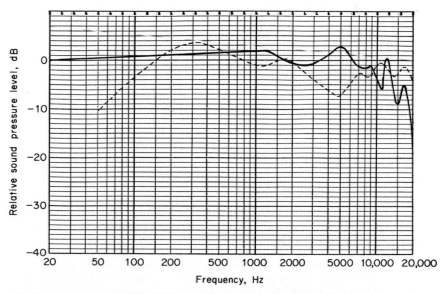

FIG. 7.85 Frequency characteristics of different types of headphones. Solid line: pressure type; dashed line: velocity type.

Velocity-Type Headphone. The velocity-type headphone should be set to the relation $WM_A \ll r_A \ll 1/WC_A$ in the acoustic circuit. Sound pressure $\dot{P}$ is as follows:

$$\dot{P} = r_A S_d \dot{V} = r_A S_d \frac{A\dot{E}}{Z_E} \times \frac{1}{Z_M + \dfrac{A^2}{Z_E}} \tag{7.98}$$

As with the pressure type, assume the value when C_A is converted to the mechanical system of acoustic resistance r_A to be $C_{MA} (= S_d^2 r_A)$. The following equation is obtained:

$$Z_M + \frac{A^2}{Z_E} = \frac{A^2}{Z_E} + r_0 + r_{MA} + j\left(\omega m_0 - \frac{1}{\omega C_0}\right) \tag{7.99}$$

The sound-pressure-frequency characteristics are determined by

$$|\dot{P}| = r_A S_d \times \frac{A|\dot{E}|}{Z_E} \sqrt{\left(\frac{A^2}{Z_E} + r_0 + r_{MA}\right)^2 + \left(\omega m_0 - \frac{1}{\omega C_0}\right)^2} \tag{7.100}$$

The equivalent circuit when $f \ll f_0$ and $f \gg f_0$ is shown in Fig. 7.86.

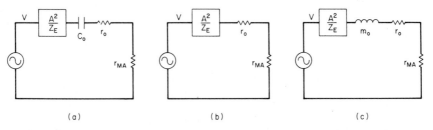

(a)   (b)   (c)

FIG. 7.86 Equivalent circuit of a velocity-type headphone. (*a*) In the case of $f \ll f_0$, $\dot{V} = (A \times \dot{E}/Z_E)/(A^2/Z_E + r_0 + r_{MA} + 1/j\omega C_0)$. (*b*) In the case of $f = f_0$, $\dot{V} = (A \times \dot{E}/Z_E)/(A^2/Z_E + r_0 + r_{MA})$. (*c*) In the case of $f_0 \ll f$, $\dot{V} = (A \times \dot{E}/Z_E)/(A^2/Z_E + r_0 + r_{MA} + j\omega M_0)$. $\dot{V}$ = velocity of diaphragm, m/s; A = force factor, N/A; $\dot{E}$ = signal voltage, V; Z_E electrical impedance, Ω; r_0 = mechanical resistance, mechanical ohms; r_{MA} = resistance of coupling space, mechanical ohms; C_0 = compliance of diaphragm, m/N; M_0 = mass of diaphragm, kg.

To increase sound pressure sensitivity from these equations, increase the effective area of the diaphragm and the power coefficient and reduce the mechanical impedance. To make the sound-pressure-frequency-characteristics flat, reduce the vibrating-system mass for high compliance to obtain the vibrating system of resistance control. Consequently, the vibrating velocity of the diaphragm inevitably becomes constant; this is called velocity type. The dashed line of Figure 7.85 shows the sound-pressure-frequency characteristics of a velocity-type headphone.

The preceding paragraphs presented the equations by which the sound-pressure-frequency characteristics of pressure- and velocity-type headphones are found for the simplest structures in which only the acoustic load at the front of the headphone is considered. Actually, optimum sound-pressure-frequency characteristics, including the acoustic load, are realized at the rear of the electrical acoustic transducer.

BIBLIOGRAPHY

Operational Analysis of Electroacoustic Transducers

Beranek, L. L.: *Acoustics,* McGraw-Hill, New York, 1954, p. 183.

Hayasaka, T., et al.: *Onkyo-Shindo Ron (Sound and Vibration),* Maruzen Kabushikigaishya, 1974, p. 201. (In Japanese.)

Kinsler, L. E., et al.: *Fundamentals of Acoustics,* Wiley, New York, 1982, p. 348.

Olson, H. F.: *Elements of Acoustical Engineering,* Van Nostrand, Princeton, N.J., 1957, p. 124.

Control System and Its Characteristics

Hayasaka, T., et al.: *Onkyo-Kogaku Gairon (An Introduction to Sound and Vibration),* Nikkan Kogyo Shinbunshya, 1973, p. 67. (In Japanese.)

Direct-Radiator-Loudspeaker Fundamentals

Beranek, L. L.: *Acoustics,* McGraw-Hill, New York, 1954, p. 185.

Hayasaka, T., and S. Yoshikawa: *Onkyo-Kogaku Gairon (An Introduction to Sound and Vibration),* 1983.

Morse, P. M.: *Vibration and Sound,* McGraw-Hill, New York, 1948, p. 326.

———— and K. U. Ingard: *Theoretical Acoustics,* McGraw-Hill, New York, 1968, p. 366.

Olson, H. F.: *Elements of Acoustical Engineering,* Van Nostrand, Princeton, N.J., 1957, p. 38.

Rayleigh, J. W. S.: *The Theory of Sound,* Dover, New York, 1945, p. 162.

Sakamoto, N.: *Loudspeaker and Loudspeaker Systems,* Nikkan Kogyo Shinbunshya, 1967, p. 18.

Dynamic-Type Direct-Radiation Speaker

Allison, R., et al.: "On the Magnitude and Audibility of FM Distortion in Loudspeakers," *J. Audio Eng. Soc.,* **30**(10), 694 (1982).

Beranek, L. L.: *Acoustics,* McGraw-Hill, New York, 1954, p. 183.

Hirata, Y.: "Study of Nonlinear Distortion in Audio Instruments," *J. Audio Eng. Soc.,* **29**(9), 607 (1981).

Kinsler, L. E., et al.: *Fundamentals of Acoustics,* Wiley, New York, 1982, p. 363.

Melillo, L., et al.: "Ferrofluids as a Means of Controlling Woofer Design Parameters," presented at the 63d Convention of the Audio Engineering Society, **1**, 177 (1979).

Niguchi, H., et al.: "Reinforced Olefin Polymer Diaphragm for Loudspeakers," *J. Audio Eng. Soc.,* **29**(11), 808 (1981).

Okahara, M., et al.: *Audio Handbook,* Ohm Sya, 1978, p. 285. (In Japanese.)

Olson, H. F.: *Elements of Acoustical Engineering,* Van Nostrand, Princeton, N.J., 1957, p. 123.

Sakamoto, N.: *Loudspeaker and Loudspeaker Systems,* Nikkan Kogyo Shinbunshya, 1967, p. 36. (In Japanese.)

———— et al.: "Loudspeaker with Honeycomb Disk Diaphragm," *J. Audio Eng. Soc.,* **29**(10), 711 (1981).

Shindo, T., et al.: "Effect of Voice-Coil and Surround on Vibration and Sound Pressure Response of Loudspeaker Cones," *J. Audio Eng. Soc.,* **28**(7–8), 490 (1980).

Suwa, H., et al.: "Heat Pipe Cooling Enables Loudspeakers to Handle Higher Power," presented at the 63d Convention of the Audio Engineering Society, **1**, 213 (1979).

Suzuki, H., et al.: "Radiation and Diffraction Effects by Convex and Concave Domes," *J. Audio Eng. Soc.,* **29**(12), 873 (1981).

Takahashi, S., et al.: "Glass-Fiber and Graphite-Flake Reinforced Polyimide Composite Diaphragm for Loudspeakers," *J. Audio Eng. Soc.,* **31**(10), 723 (1983).

Tsuchiya, H., et al.: "Reducing Harmonic Distortion in Loudspeakers," presented at the 63d Convention of the Audio Engineering Society, **2**, 1 (1979).

Yamamoto, T., et al.: "High-Fidelity Loudspeakers with Boronized Titanium Diaphragm," *J. Audio Eng. Soc.,* **28**(12), 868 (1980).

Yoshihisa, N., et al.: "Nonlinear Distortion in Cone Loudspeakers," *Chuyu-Ou Univ. Rep.,* **23**, 271 (1980).

Loudspeaker Systems

Adams, G. J., et al.: "Computer-Aided Design of Loudspeaker Crossover Networks," *J. Audio Eng. Soc.,* **30**(7–8), 496 (1982).

Ballagh, K. O.: "Optimum Loudspeaker Placement near Reflecting Planes," *J. Audio Eng. Soc*, **31**(12), 931 (1983).

Benson, J. E.: "Theory Design of Loudspeaker Enclosures," *Proc. IREE* (September 1969).

Beranek, L. L.: *Acoustics,* McGraw-Hill, New York, 1954, p. 208.

Bullock, R. M.: "Loudspeaker-Crossover Systems: An Optimal Crossover Choice," *J. Audio Eng. Soc.,* **37**(7–8), 486 (1982).

Cable, C. R.: "Acoustics and the Active Enclosure," *J. Audio Eng. Soc.,* **20**(10) (1972).

Engebretson, M. E.: "Low-Frequency Sound Reproduction," *J. Audio Eng. Soc.,* **32**(5), 340 (1984).

Mayr, H.: "Theory of Vented Loudspeaker Enclosures," *J. Audio Eng. Soc.,* **53**(2), 91 (1984).

Newman, R. J.: "A. N. Thiel, Sage of Vented Speakers," *Audio* (August 1975).

Normandin, R.: *J. Audio Eng. Soc.,* **32**(1–2), 18 (1984).

Okahara, M., et al.: *Audio Handbook,* Ohm Sya, 1978, p. 286. (In Japanese.)

Olson, H. F.: *Elements of Acoustical Engineering,* Van Nostrand, Princeton, N.J., 1957, p. 148.

————: "Direct Radiator Loudspeaker Enclosures," *J. Audio Eng. Soc.,* **17**(1), 22 (1969).

Penkov, G., et al.: "Closed-Box Loudspeaker Systems Equalization and Power Requirements," *J. Audio Eng. Soc.,* **33**(6), 447 (1985).

Sakamoto, N.: *Loudspeaker and Loudspeaker Systems,* Nikkan Kogyo Shinbunshya, 1967, p. 101. (In Japanese.)

Small, R. H.: "Closed-Box Loudspeaker Systems," part 1, *J. Audio Eng. Soc.,* **20**(10) (1972).

Horn Loudspeakers

Beranek, L. L.: *Acoustics,* McGraw-Hill, New York, 1954, p. 259.

Goldstein, S., et al.: "Sound Waves of Finite Amplitude in an Exponential Horn," *J. Acoust. Soc. Am.,* **6** (1935).

Hayasaka, T., and S. Yoshikawa: *Onkyo-Shindo Ron (Sound and Vibration),* Maruzen Kabushikigaishya, 1974, p. 661. (In Japanese.)

Kinsler, L. E., et al.: *Fundamentals of Acoustics,* Wiley, New York, 1982, p. 373.

Kyono, N., et al.: "Acoustic Radiation of a Horn Loudspeaker by the Finite Element Method," *J. Audio Eng. Soc.,* **30**(12), 896 (1982).

Merhault, J.: "Static Horn," presented at the 35th Convention of the Audio Engineering Society (1968).

Morita, S., et al.: "Acoustic Radiation of a Horn Loudspeaker by the Finite Element Method," *J. Audio Eng. Soc.,* **28**(7–8), 482 (1980).

Morse, P. M.: *Vibration and Sound,* McGraw-Hill, New York, 1948, p. 265.

Okahara, M., et al.: *Audio Handbook,* Ohm Sya, 1978, p. 281. (In Japanese.)

Olson, H. F.: *Elements of Acoustical Engineering,* Van Nostrand, Princeton, N.J., 1957, p. 184.

Rocard, Y.: "Distortion of Horn Loudspeakers," *Comptes rendus,* 196 (1933).

Sakamoto, N.: *Loudspeaker and Loudspeaker Systems,* Nikkan Kogyo Shinbunshya, 1967, p. 117. (In Japanese.)

Salmon, V.: "A New Family of Horns," *J. Acoust. Soc. Am.,* **17**(3) (1946).

Sinclair, R.: "Optimization of Two Section Exponential Horns," presented at the 63d Convention of the Audio Engineering Society, **2**, 231 (1979).

Thrus, A. L., et al.: "Extraneous Frequencies Generated in Air Carrying Intense Sound Waves," *J. Acoust. Soc. Am.,* **6** (1935).

Webster, A. G.: "Acoustic Impedance of a Horn," *Proc. Nat. Acad. Sci.,* **5** (1949).

Other Types of Loudspeakers

Huter, T. F., and R. H. Bolt: *Sonics,* Wiley, New York, 1955, p. 86.

Morse, P. M., and K. U. Ingard: *Theoretical Acoustics,* McGraw-Hill, New York, 1968, p. 781.

Oda, F.: *Ionophone,* Wright Air Dev. Center Tech Rep. 58, 1958, p. 368.

Olson, H. F.: *Elements of Acoustical Engineering,* Van Nostrand, Princeton, N.J., 1957, p. 333.

Rayleigh, J. W. S.: *The Theory of Sound,* vol. 2, Dover, New York, 1945, p. 228.

Sakamoto, N., et al.: "Frequency Response Considerations for an Electrostatic Horn Tweeter Using Electret Elements," *J. Audio Eng. Soc.,* **24**(5), 368 (1976).

———— and ————: "Wide-Range, High-Power Tweeter Using the Printed-Planar Voice Coil," presented at the 58th Convention of the Audio Engineering Society (1977).

Tamura, M., et al.: "Electroacoustic Transducers with Piezoelectric High Polymer Films," *J. Audio Eng. Soc.,* **23**(1), 21 (1975).

Westervelt, P. J.: "Parametric Acoustic Array," *J. Acoust. Soc. Am.,* **35**, 535 (1963).

Yoneyama, M., et al.: "The Audio Spotlight: An Application of Nonlinear Interaction of Sound Waves to a New Type of Loudspeaker Design," *J. Acoust. Soc. Am.,* **73**(5), 1532 (1983).

Public-Address-System Loudspeakers

Beranek, L. L.: *Acoustics,* McGraw-Hill, New York, 1948, p. 285.

Borish, J.: "Extension of the Image Model to Arbitrary Polyhedra," *J. Acoust. Soc. Am.,* **75**, 1827 (1984).

Davis, D. B.: *Sound System Engineering,* Howard W. Sams, Indianapolis, 1975.

Haas, H.: "Über den Einfluss eines Einfachecho auf die Horsamkeit von Sprache," *Acustica,* **1**(49) (1951).

Kinsler, L. E., et al.: *Fundamentals of Acoustics,* Wiley, New York, 1982, p. 313.

Knudsen, V. O., and C. M. Harris: *Acoustical Designing in Architecture,* Wiley, New York, 1949.

Krokstad, A., et al.: "Calculating the Acoustical Room Response by the Use of Ray Tracing Technique," *J. Sound Vib.,* **8**(1), 118 (1968).

Kuttruff, H.: *Room Acoustics,* Wiley, New York, 1973.

Morse, P. M., and R. H. Bolt: "Sound Wave in Rooms," *Rev. Mod. Phys.,* **16**(2) (1944).

———— and K. U. Ingard: *Theoretical Acoustics,* McGraw-Hill, New York, 1968, p. 576.

Olson, H. F.: *Elements of Acoustical Engineering,* Van Nostrand, Princeton, N.J., 1957, p. 397.

Satoh, K., et al.: "Application of Acoustic Simulation to the Olympic Main Coliseum," presented at the 76th Convention of the Audio Engineering Society. (1984).

Sabine, W. C.: *Collected Papers on Acoustics,* Harvard, Cambridge, Mass., 1922.

Schroeder, M. R.: "Digital Simulation of Sound Transmission in Reverberant Spaces," *J. Acoust. Soc. Am.,* **47**(2), 424 (1970).

———— et al.: "Digital Computers in Room Acoustics," 4th ICA (1962).

Taguch, G., et al: "An Efficient Algorithm for Tracing Reflected Rays in Acoustical Field Simulation by Geometrical Method," *J. Acoust. Soc. Am.,* **41**, 542 (1985).

Headphones and Headphone Systems

Bruel, P. V., et al.: *Bruel & Kjaer Tech. Rev.,* no. 4 (1961).

Kinsler, L. E.: *Fundamentals of Acoustics,* Wiley, New York, 1982, p. 375.

Olson, H. F.: *Elements of Acoustical Engineering,* Van Nostrand, Princeton, N.J., 1957, p. 295.

Sakamoto, N., et al.: "On 'Out of Head Localization' in Headphone Listening," *J. Audio. Eng. Soc.,* **24**(9), 710 (1976).

Zwislocki, J.: "Design and Testing of Earmuffs," *J. Accoust. Soc. Am.,* **27**, 1154 (1955).

CHAPTER 8
ANALOG DISK RECORDING AND REPRODUCTION

Gregory A. Bogantz
Manager, Quality Assurance, RCA Records

Joseph C. Ruda
Manager, Equipment and Process Development, RCA Records

8.1 EVOLUTION OF RECORDING TECHNOLOGY

8.1.1 Basic Elements

Acoustical or mechanical recording is the tree from which all recording technology grows. In the century since the filing of Thomas Edison's basic patents, which envisioned the cylinder, disk, and mechanically encoded tape, the state of the art of recording and reproduction has addressed the multitude of process limitations and has driven the end product toward true fidelity. Though F. Langford Smith's 1952 evaluation of sound reproduction,[1] that "it is manifestly impossible to reproduce at the two ears of the listener an exact equivalent of the sounds which he could hear in the concert hall," is technically true, analog disk recording and reproduction in the form of stereo and, in particular, discrete four-channel formats, have come very close indeed. While significant refinements have advanced the art to near perfection, the basic elements of recording technology, present at the turn of the twentieth century, are either with us today or are periodically being rediscovered. For example:

1. *Sound-powered diaphragm:* In 1877, Edison's work in multiplex telegraphy spun off the technology of a sound-powered diaphragm lashed to an embossing or cutting tool capable of generating a trace in a moving substrate which could later be reproduced. The use of a diaphragm in sound transducers such as microphones and loudspeakers is still basic to audio technology today.

2. *Vacuum metallizing:* The use of vacuum metallizing was introduced by Edison in 1887[2] to prepare wax masters for electroforming. This process was rediscovered in 1930 by Western Electric experimenters and, though not in general use for analog disks, is widely used today as a means of generating a reflecting surface in optical disks.

3. *Disk format:* The use of a disk format for recorded sound was promoted by Emile Berliner with his Gramophone (now gramophone) of 1887.[3] Today the disk format is basic to audio recording and other high-density information uses.

4. *Electroforming:* The use of electroforming to generate tools for replicating recorded disks and cylinders has been basic to the industry from the beginning.

5. *Thermoplastic molding:* The use of thermoplastic materials and the process of molding for the making of copies have also been basic to the industry from the beginning.

6. *Vertical and lateral recording:* Cylinder records utilized vertical recording, and lateral recording began with disks. Today's analog stereo disk is a balance of the two techniques with two transducers acting at opposing 45° angles to the surface of the record.

For an excellent summary of early practices, Refs. 2 and 3 are recommended.

8.1.2 Concepts of the Analog Process

Any analog process comprises the direct translation of an input to a means or medium such that reversing the process provides a replication of the original input. Inherent in this storage and recall process is the myriad of potential opportunities of having the original source modified in some undesirable way. In the early days of sound recording, the wonder of obtaining any near replication of the original sound was enough to bring revenues from exhibitions of the new art. But with technological advances the consumer of recorded sound has taken the means for granted and become increasingly intolerant of discernable defects in newly purchased records. What was commercially acceptable even a few short years ago no longer is. As the sources of general defects and distortions were eliminated, further improvements became exercises in precision.

To gain an understanding of the process's physical demands, consider the following general concepts:

1. *Groove surface speed (in/s):* $v = (\pi/30)rw$, where r = radius of groove and w = angular velocity, r/min.

2. *Recorded wavelength (in):* $\lambda = v/f$, where f = frequency, Hz.

3. *Groove length per record side (ft):* $1 = (\pi/12)(r_1^2 - r_2^2)d$, where r_1 = radius of first groove, in, r_2 = radius of last groove, in, and d = average recorded groove density, lines per radial inch.

4. *Peak writing velocity at industry-standard recording level (0 dB at 1 kHz):* v_p = 7 cm/s.

5. *Recorded-waveform peak amplitude:* $A_p = v_p/2\pi f$.

6. *Signal level (dB):* $dB = 20 \log (x_2/x_1)$, where x_1 and x_2 are similar characteristics such as velocity, amplitude, voltage, etc.

Applying the foregoing equations to the parameters of a 12-in long-playing (LP) record, we obtain the following values:

> Average surface speed at 33⅓ r/min = 14.2 in/s
> Average wavelength of 1-kHz signal = 0.014 in
> Groove length per side (d = 200) = 1436 ft
> Peak amplitude (1 kHz at 0 dB) = 0.00111 in

For an unrealizable perfect record, there would be no unwanted modulation of the stylus as it traced the groove wall. The ratio of signal (desired modulation) to noise (undesired modulation) would be infinite. Disregarding a number of variables, for a standard of reference assume that the typical present-day LP recording exhibits a signal-to-noise (S/N) ratio of roughly 50 dB. For an appreciation of the size of discernable defects, it may be calculated that an unwanted perturbation just 20 dB less than the standard recording level would have a dimension of 0.111 mil, which is 111 μin (2.8 μm). The average LP with an S/N ratio of 50 dB has deviations from smoothness amounting to only 0.00348 mil, which is about 3.5 μin (0.09 μm).

For another point of view, consider that over an average LP side, a total linear surface of about 2800 ft is in contact with the stylus (1400 ft times 2 groove walls). This, compared with the size of a defect, say, at a level 20 dB below that of average program modulation, is a ratio of over 300 million to 1. In a typical industrial process, a 0.1 percent error rate is considered very good. If record manufacturers abided by this standard, over 300,000 errors on an LP side would be acceptable.

7. As for the record material, the groove in a typical LP is not rigid. The stylus indents the groove because of its pressure and the elastic yielding of the record material in a manner given by the Hertz equation: $D = 0.825 \ (F^2/E^2R)^{1/3}$.

Assume that F (force on stylus) = 0.00208 lb (1 g), E = elastic modulus for the record material = 5×10^5 lb/in^2, and R (stylus-tip radius) = 0.00075 in. Then the indentation displacement D would be about 30 μin (0.77 μm). This calculation shows that the stylus can sense below the record surface itself. In fact, early record materials were inferior to present-day ones in that provision was not made in their formulation to reduce the incidence of discrete hard particles just below the surface of the molded disk. Such buried particles in the 2- to 3-μm range could generate a broadband background noise as high as 20 dB below the average program level.

As record materials become better (effectively homogeneous) in the stylus-penetration zone and as lower tracking forces and special stylus shapes decrease the penetration, more of the other manufacturing-process defects are evident. It is no accident that consistently well-engineered and well-controlled processes produce records with a high degree of satisfaction. In the following sections, details of the technology necessary to achieve this degree of excellence are described.

8.2   DISK RECORDING TECHNOLOGY

8.2.1   Vertical-Recording Development: The Phonograph

When Edison came upon his inspiration for the phonograph, he was working on a machine to repeat and transmit telegraph messages rapidly over the already-burgeoning telegraph cables of the day. It was to be a form of time compression of data. Toward this end, he had built a system which employed a stylus to puncture slots representing telegraphic dots and dashes in a nonconductive paper tape.[1] The tape was to be played back with another stylus, which would drop in and out of the punched slots and make electrical contact with the surface below as it retraced the original path of the recording stylus. The events leading up to details of Edison's dramatic revelation are not known in detail, but it is believed that as he observed the prototype machine in operation at high speed, he was reminded by the rhythmically chattering stylus of the sound of music or voice. A short time later, he had sketched the drawing of the first phonograph and handed it to his machinist to build. The registered date on the patent application is August 12, 1877.

The origin of vertical recording is clearly evident here. Having witnessed the noise from his repeating telegraph, Edison drew up a system employing a stylus connected to a flexible diaphragm. A horn was used to concentrate the air pressure of the speaker's voice onto the diaphragm, thereby increasing the intensity of its and the stylus's motion. The stylus rode just above a spiral slot cut into a metal cylinder around which was placed a sheet of metal foil. As the cylinder was turned, the stylus would emboss the foil (vertically, just as the paper tape was cut) with a mechanical analog of the vibrations occurring at the diaphragm. After the recording had been made, another stylus assembly was positioned over the foil at the start of the spiral. The embossed foil passing against this stylus caused its diaphragm to radiate the modulations in the foil back into the air to be heard as sound once again.

The phonograph was to be one of Edison's most inspired inventions, as it sprang nearly fully developed from concept to its first embodiment. It was one of Edison's favorite inventions, and the basic concept of analog disk recording remains unchanged today.

Edison's original patent on the phonograph covered the technique of vertical, or *hill-and-dale,* recording. It was Émile Berliner who patented the idea of lateral recording and called his machine a *gramophone* (see Sec. 8.1.2). It is only coincidental that the phonograph originally employed a cylinder and the gramophone used a disk. It should be noted, therefore, that up until the late 1950s, when stereophonic disks and vertical recording returned, Americans were listening to laterally cut gramophone 78s, 45s, and LPs and not to (vertically cut) phonograph records, as they were mistakenly called.

Edison had, in fact, contemplated the use of a disk for his phonograph but rejected the idea early in its development owing to the poorer sound quality that the metal-foil disk displayed at its inner diameter.[2] He had already discovered what was later to become one of the most troublesome problems with analog disk recording: inner-groove distortion (see Sec. 8.6.1).

Amid fierce competition, Edison stubbornly insisted on the superiority of his vertically cut cylinders. He introduced many improvements to his system which lengthened playing time, improved record wear, and kept the Edison phonographs sonically superior to all other "talking machines." The culmination of the Edison cylinder was the Blue Amberol unbreakable plastic cylinder, which played for 4 min, could be played "over 3000 times without wear," and exhibited remarkably low surface noise compared with the shellac-based gramophone disks of the day.

But the Berliner gramophone gained in popularity in later years, having now become known as the Victrola, manufactured by the Victor Talking Machine Company. Edison was forced to acquiesce to public demand and to the fact that flat disk records were much easier to mass-produce than were cylinders. In 1913 he introduced the Diamond Disc phonograph, which played vertically cut disks recorded on both sides.[3] As was the case with all the Edison machines, this one was sonically superior to all its competitors. It was also expensive, costing from $200 to over $1000. In its finer forms, the Diamond Disc machine employed such modern-day refinements as an individually ground diamond stylus, *floating-pickup construction,* whereby only the force of the stylus-and-diaphragm assembly weighed on the record, and a cuing lever to facilitate setting the stylus carefully into the groove. A motor-driven feed-screw mechanism was used to convey the rest of the massive acoustic reproducer's plumbing-and-horn assembly across the disk, thus preventing undue stress on the record groove. This latter feature was made possible by the fact that Edison disks were cut with a constant-groove pitch, as were his cylinders.

Edison maintained his aversion to lateral cutting as well as to electrical recording. In 1926, well into the electrical era, Edison even introduced an LP version of his disk which was an acoustical, vertically cut record capable of playing 20 min per side. But it proved to be too little, too late. The Edison company had become poorly managed by then, and the public was embracing the new, much louder electrical recordings, all of which were laterally cut. It is ironic that the acoustic phonograph, the favorite invention of the electrical Wizard of Menlo Park, should be put out to pasture by someone else's electrical (electronic, really) incarnation of it.

8.2.2 Lateral-Recording Development: The Gramophone

Lateral recording, generally acknowledged to have been developed by Emile Berliner in 1887,[4] followed a path parallel to that of Edison's vertical technique. Instead of positioning the recording and reproducing diaphragms parallel to the recording surface, thus resulting in vertical motion of the stylus, Berliner took his notion from an earlier machine called a *phonautograph.* This was a scientific curiosity which recorded a "picture" of acoustic waves by inscribing a laterally waving line on a revolving cylinder covered with lampblacked paper. The picture looked much like a present-day oscillograph. The phonautograph used a stylus attached to a diaphragm to pick up the sound waves, just as in Edison's phonograph. But in this case the diaphragm was oriented so as to cause the stylus to move laterally over the lampblacked recording medium. Berliner reasoned that if the resulting horizontally waving line could somehow be made to move a playback stylus, the device would re-create the original sound. He constructed his own version of the machine, using a zinc disk instead of a cylinder, coated the disk with a fatty material to serve as an acid *resist,* and devised an etching process to convert the scratched line into a groove. Thus was born what Berliner chose to call the gramophone, which was patentable by virtue of its lateral recording technique.

Another of the many ironies in the history of recording presents itself here, in that both Edison and Berliner first chose to record sound on a metal medium. Now, after many technological diversions through the use of wax and nitrocellulose (lacquer) materials, the industry finds itself once again back to recording on metal (copper) in the form of Direct Metal Mastering (DMM). With the rapidly growing popularity of digital compact disks, DMM could well be the final chapter in the book of analog disk recording (see Chap. 9).

With the invention of the gramophone, the first of the phonographic wars was on its way just 10 years after the birth of the invention. The world would yet experience the battle of vertical versus horizontal modulation, cylinder versus disk, the battle of the speeds, several versions of two-channel recording, and the battle of the quadraphonic systems, to name just the most prominent confrontations. It is a colorful story, and for more information about it the reader is encouraged to see Roland Gelatt's *The Fabulous Phonograph,* a delightful account of the history of recorded sound "from tin foil to high fidelity."

8.2.3   Comparison between Vertical and Lateral Recording

Vertical and lateral recording methods each had certain advantages and disadvantages which resulted in their close competition in the early days, but from now on this discussion will concentrate on the more modern technology of analog disk recording.

Today vertical recording really has no particular advantages, but it does exhibit several problems. Its chief disadvantage is that the playback stylus must resemble the recording stylus as closely as possible to reduce the geometrical phenomenon known as *tracing distortion*. Records now are cut with a relatively sharp recording stylus and played with a somewhat rounded playback stylus. The greater the difference between the two styli, the greater the tracing distortion, which can be quite annoying. (See Sec. 8.4.1 for more about recording and playback styli and Sec. 8.6.1 for a discussion of tracing distortion.)

Lateral recording has one very distinct advantage over vertical recording. It does not exhibit the nonlinear tracing distortion common with vertical modulation. Instead, it has a problem known as *diameter loss,* which is a loss of signal output with increasing frequency and decreasing groove diameter. This, too, is a result of the playback stylus's not exactly matching the recording stylus. There is also the phenomenon known as *pinch effect,* in which some of the desired recorded lateral motion is transformed into useless vertical motion. (See Sec. 8.6.1 for more details.)

Another advantage to lateral recording is that the groove can be a constant depth, which makes things easier for the disk-cutting engineer and for the manufacturing people. With vertical recording, the depth must be continuously varied, depending on the average loudness of the music, if the maximum recording time is to be realized. In both lateral and vertical recording, the groove pitch needs to be constantly varied to achieve maximum recording time. (See Sec. 8.3.1 for a discussion of the mechanisms used to accomplish this.)

8.2.4   Sterophonic (Two-Channel) Recording Development

Lest anyone believe that the battle between vertical and lateral recording was "won" during the 1930s through most of the 1950s, that period of lateral supremacy represented merely the victory of one battle. The acceptance of the present 45–45 system of stereophonic, or two-channel, analog recording has brought the war to a peaceful truce with a balanced compromise between the two modulation schemes. But a few skirmishes had to be endured along the way.

Cook Binaural Recording.   The first commercial system of recording two audio signals simultaneously on one disk was developed by Emory Cook and described in a paper published in 1953.[5] In these early days, two-channel recording was more apt to be called *binaural,* as the term *stereophonic* had not yet come into common use. In fact, there was some dissension over the use of stereophonic to describe specifically two-channel sound, since the root *stereo* implies *three-dimensional* and actually should be reserved as a more general descriptor, encompassing all forms of multichannel sound reproduction. Logical arguments aside, however, *stereo* is now the common parlance for *two-channel.* And, eventually, *binaural* came to be applied to recordings specifically recorded with two closely spaced microphones and intended to be reproduced through headphones.

Cook's two-channel system was really not much more than a laboratory curiosity, and not many of the old Cook two-channel records and even less of the playback equipment survive today. Cook used a brute-force technique which merely placed two laterally cut bands of signals on one disk, one at a smaller diameter than the other. The record required two separate pickup heads and styli to be started synchronously in their respective grooves. Cook's system was fairly easy to record because two cutter heads could be mounted on the same lathe and controlled with the same lead screw without much difficulty, even allowing for a variable recording pitch.

However, as proposed by Cook, the two-band record had an additional flaw: it was incompatible with existing monophonic (single-channel) playback systems. The Cook system recorded the sound of the left and right sides of the sound stage separately on the two bands of the disk. So if the record were played on a monophonic player, the listener would hear either the left of the sound stage or the right, depending on which band was played. It was impossible to get a proper reproduction of the sound of both the left and right sides of the sound stage at once.

Mullin Monogroove Recording.   This problem of incompatibility also plagued the next attempt at recording two-channel sound on a disk. This second system was simply the marriage of vertical and lateral recording together within a common groove as developed by J. T. Mullin for Bing Crosby Enterprises in 1954.[6] This *monogroove* two-channel recording system was the result of the clever observation that vertical and lateral modulations of a record groove are physically orthogonal, or at right angles to each other. It can be proved mathematically that orthogonal signals can exist independently; they do not interfere with one another. It was fairly easy to build a transducer capable of responding to purely lateral stimulation but not to vertical stimulation. Rotate another, similar transducer through 90°, and the opposite effect is produced. By mounting two such transducers oriented in this manner and connected to the same stylus, Mullin was able to demonstrate that the recording of two separate signals could be accomplished in a single groove.

But the incompatibility problem persisted because in the Crosby system one side of the sound field was recorded laterally and the other vertically. Playing this record on a monophonic player revealed only the lateral half of the desired sound field.

45-45 System.   Monophonic compatibility was achieved with the *45-45 system,* invented by engineers for Westrex in 1957.[7] Still the standard today, the system is so named because one side of the sound field is recorded with its axis of modulation rotated 45° to the left of vertical while the other side is recorded 45° to the right of vertical. (Refer to Fig. 8.1.) Notice that this places the two modulations at 90° to each other, and the system is orthogonal. Notice also that each side of the sound field has a component of its modulation lying laterally. There is also a vertical component of each. These components are smaller than the amplitude of the pure left or right modulations by a factor of the square root of 2, so there is some reduction in loudness. But when this record is played back on a monophonic player, equal parts of the left and right sides of the sound field are reproduced, and the listener hears all the music—a compatible system.

Since the 45-45 system is the present world standard for two-channel analog disk recording, it will now be discussed in more detail. Assume a cross-sectional view of the groove and that the disk is rotating toward the viewer. This corresponds to looking at the front of the pickup arm. Standard channel placement has

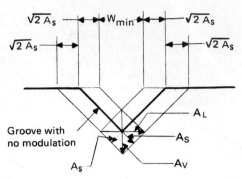

FIG. 8.1 Cross section of a stereo groove. [Disk Recording, *vol. 2,* J. Audio Eng. Soc., *379 (1981).*)

the left-channel modulation recorded on the inner (left) groove wall and the right on the outer (right) wall. These standards and more particulars are given in Secs. 8.3.1 and 8.3.2.

For the system to be compatible with lateral monophonic playback, attention must be paid to the relative phase of the signals from the two sides of the sound field. Suppose that positive sound pressure on the left-microphone diaphragm eventually results in left-groove-wall modulation which causes the playback stylus to move toward the left (and down). If the same sound source is also acting on the right microphone and results in right-wall modulation which causes the stylus to move to the left (and up), the system is said to be *in phase.* The lateral direction is called the *sum* of the left and right signals, and the vertical direction is called the *difference.* From this example, it is clear why this is so. If the two microphones are placed very close together, the system acoustically and physically degenerates to a purely lateral monophonic one. There will be no difference in the sound fields picked up by the two microphones. The lateral components of left and right modulation will add in the same direction and reinforce one another, and the vertical components will cancel each other completely, resulting in a net purely lateral stylus motion.

No discussion of two-channel disk recording schemes would be complete without a mention of other, ill-fated propositions. One was similar to the Cook system with two independent grooves interleaved, or bifilar-wound, on the same side of the disk. The obvious problem with this system was that it, like the Cook, reduced the playing time by half, and it required complex cutters and pickups. Another idea was to put one channel on each side of the disk. This would pose difficulties in manufacturing and in designing playback equipment. It would also halve the total playing time per disk. Another interesting scheme would prove to be providential: the carrier-disk system. This involved using the second audio channel to modulate a supersonic carrier frequency recorded in the same groove as the first channel. But at the time that this idea was conceived, technology was too primitive to permit successful recording or recovery of a signal of such a very high frequency from a disk. The system would later make a reappearance as the only discrete four-channel system put into commercial production with analog disks: CD-4.

The advantage of the 45-45 system over all two-groove systems is clear: it is the only system compatible with monophonic players, and that compatibility is reversible. If a monophonic (lateral) recording is played on a 45-45 stereo system, the same sound comes from both speakers in phase. The sound fields combine acoustically in the listening environment and create the effect of a single sound source located midway between the two reproducers. The other monogroove systems could have had this compatibility, too, if their designers had hit on the notion of electrically forming the sum-and-difference signals from the left and right sound sources and appropriately modulating their disks. This was done, in fact, with the later CD-4 system. However, the 45-45 system still has an advantage over a simple two-channel carrier-disk system in that it does not require expensive supersonic recording and reproducing equipment.

The chief disadvantage of the 45-45 system is the same one common to all systems that employ any form of vertical modulation: tracing distortion. It was a problem for Edison, and it continues to be a problem today. But technological advances have made possible reduced tracking forces, better transducers, and playback-stylus shapes that more closely approximate the recording stylus so that tracing distortion has become much less of a problem than it once was.

8.3 RECORDING CHARACTERISTICS

8.3.1 Electrical Parameters and Standards

The 78.26 r/min record has been obsolete since the 1950s. No detailed information will be given regarding these disks in this chapter. The interested reader is directed to the now-obsolete standard RS-211-C of the Electronic Industries Association (EIA) for more information regarding electrical and mechanical standards for 78 r/min records.

The three primary objectives of any sound recording are these:

1. To preserve the complete range of audible frequencies
2. To introduce no perturbations or distortions to the original signal waveforms
3. To maintain as high an S/N ratio in the recording as possible

It is possible to achieve these goals with a high degree of success in analog disk recording, and they will now be examined individually.

The generally accepted range of human hearing extends from about 20 Hz to 20 kHz, and it should be noted that this represents the limiting case rather than the average. It is the exceptional individual who can actually hear to either of these frequency extremes. A range of about 30 Hz to 15 kHz more closely approximates the average. Nevertheless, preserving even the extreme range is the easiest of the three goals to achieve. In fact, the high-frequency limitation of the 33⅓ r/min disk has been stretched upward to around 50 kHz in the case of the CD-4 system.

However, some care needs to be taken at both the highest and the lowest frequencies. For example, at the low end of the spectrum the compliance of the mechanical components of both the cutting (recording) and pickup (playback) systems can cause unevenness in the frequency response. The mechanical characteristics of the cutting and pickup systems are also responsible for most of the problems at the high end of the spectrum, but here the problems are due more to excessive mass than to too much compliance. (See Sec. 8.4.2 for more discussion on this.) High-frequency performance also depends greatly on the shape of the playback stylus (see Sec. 8.4.1).

The second objective of introducing no distortion in the process is a lot more elusive. There are several causes of distortion in the system, including diameter loss, tracing distortion, tracking distortion, vertical tracking-angle distortion, and horizontal tracking-angle distortion. (These will be discussed in detail in Sec. 8.6.)

The last objective of maintaining a high S/N ratio has been achieved fairly well by a combination of careful quality control in the manufacture of records and adoption of special filters which tailor the frequency response of the recorded waveform to help mask those defects which remain. As noted in Sec. 8.1.2, defects in the record groove of only 1 μm in size can be quite audible, so the need for extremely precise manufacturing techniques is clear.

The filters mentioned above perform what is known as *preemphasis* of the signal before recording and *deemphasis* of the signal upon playback. For an understanding of why this filtering is done, consider that most of the annoying defects heard in records are the result of deflections of the playback stylus from relatively small physical causes such as dirt in the groove and surface roughness in the molded disk. The small size of these defects is on the order of the smaller recorded wavelengths which correspond to the higher frequencies of sound.

The function of preemphasis in disk recording is not quite the same as in magnetic-tape recording (see Chap. 10). It happens that, from the standpoint of widest frequency range and lowest distortion, the best disk recording transducers (cutter heads) are of the magnetic type. In the early days of reproducing-transducer (pickup, or cartridge) development, magnetic types also were superior (see Sec. 8.4.3). But magnetic transducers have an electrodynamic characteristic, described as *constant velocity,* which exacerbates the problem of manufacturing defects in records.

To illustrate this, consider for a moment only sinusoidal signals. In the case of the cutter head, constant velocity means that if the head is driven with a *voltage* of constant peak amplitude at all frequencies, it will cut an analogous record groove which is not constant in amplitude but constant in the peak *velocity* of stylus motion. This results in a recorded waveform which exhibits a constant peak slope as traversed by the stylus. A consequence of this characteristic is that the amplitude of the waveform decreases by half with every doubling of frequency of the signal. This characteristic can be described as an amplitude response with a 6-dB-per-octave rolloff with increasing frequency. A magnetic pickup has the complementary characteristic that if it is used to play back a constant-velocity recording, it will produce a constant output voltage.

This is all very convenient, but the problem is that since the recorded signal becomes smaller with increasing frequency, defects in the record become more noticeable at higher frequencies than they would be if the recorded waveform were constant in amplitude. With constant-velocity recording, the ratio of signal (recorded waveform) to noise (record defects) becomes worse with increasing frequency.

So the purpose of preemphasis in disk recording and the complementary deemphasis in playback is to boost the amplitude of the recorded waveform at higher frequencies to improve the S/N ratio. A simple 6-dB-per-octave filter seems like a logical choice, since it would produce a constant-amplitude recording. But a glance at the response curve for the industry-standard emphasis filter reveals that it is not so simple (see Fig. 8.2). This emphasis, adopted as a standard by the Recording Industry Association of America and known as the *RIAA characteristic,* produces a shelved response which is essentially constant-amplitude

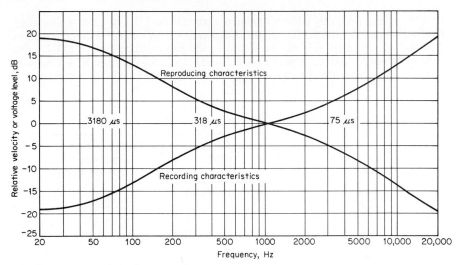

FIG. 8.2 Characteristics for fine-groove disk records. *(RIAA Dimensional Characteristics for 33⅓ r/min Records.)*

below 50 Hz and above about 2 kHz and constant-velocity between these frequencies.

The reason for this curious filter shape is one of practicality and compromise. Prior to the adoption of the present standard in 1954,[8] various "semistandards" were in use. Some were intended for 78 r/min and some for LP, some were in-house agreements used by certain record companies, and there was general confusion. By the early 1950s, the National Association of Broadcasters (NAB) and the EIA had jointly proposed a deemphasis standard for disk playback. Essentially the same characteristic has been in use ever since, and it was formally adopted by the RIAA in 1967.

The low-frequency portion of this standard curve is a compromise among the various characteristics in use in the early 1950s. The high-frequency portion constitutes a "shelf" of about 9 dB above what would otherwise be a constant-amplitude extension of the low-frequency characteristic. This results in a corresponding amplitude reduction in the recorded waveform at high frequencies, which was needed to lessen the distortion inherent in the phonograph pickups of the day with their fairly high-mass, conically tipped stylus assemblies.[9] Those early pickups could not cope with the stylus velocities and accelerations at the high frequencies required by a constant-amplitude recording. Although greatly reduced, these same problems of tracking and tracing distortion are still troublesome and will be discussed in Secs. 8.4 and 8.6.

8.3.2 Mechanical Dimensions and Speeds

As previously mentioned, 78.26 r/min records have been obsolete since the 1950s, so no additional reference will be made to them except to restate that the interested reader is referred to the obsolete EIA standard RS-211-C for more details.

Current standards[10] allow for 45 r/min records of only 7-in and 12-in diameters. Standards presently allow 33⅓ r/min records to be 7, 10, or 12 in in diameter. A detailed description of the physical dimensions and other characteristics of 33⅓ and 45 r/min records can be found in the EIA publication RS-211-D. The data in Tables 8.1 and 8.2 and in Figs. 8.2 and 8.3 are derived from RIAA Bulletin E-4 and summarize the dimensional standards for 33⅓ and 45 r/min records.

TABLE 8.1   Recording and Reproducing Characteristics

Recording relative level, dB	Frequency Hz,*	Reproducing relative level, dB	Play equalization for constant-amplitude pickup
−19.3	20	+19.3	−14.7
−18.6	30	+18.6	−11.9
−17.8	40	+17.8	−10.2
−17.0	50	+17.0	− 9.0
−16.1	60	+16.1	− 8.3
−15.3	70	+15.3	− 7.8
−14.5	80	+14.5	− 7.4
−13.1	100	+13.1	− 6.9
−12.4	110	+12.4	− 6.8
−11.6	125	+11.6	− 6.5
−10.2	150	+10.2	− 6.3
− 8.3	200	+ 8.3	− 5.7
− 6.7	250	+ 6.7	− 5.3
− 5.5	300	+ 5.5	− 5.0
− 3.8	400	+ 3.8	− 4.2
− 2.6	500	+ 2.6	− 3.4
− 1.9	600	+ 1.9	− 2.5
− 1.2	700	+ 1.2	− 1.9
− 0.7	800	+ 0.7	− 1.2
0	1,000	0	0
+ 1.4	1,500	− 1.4	+ 2.1
+ 2.6	2,000	− 2.6	+ 3.4
+ 4.7	3,000	− 4.7	+ 4.8
+ 6.6	4,000	− 6.6	+ 5.4
+ 8.2	5,000	− 8.2	+ 5.8
+ 9.6	6,000	− 9.6	+ 6.0
+10.7	7,000	−10.7	+ 6.2
+11.9	8,000	−11.9	+ 6.2
+12.9	9,000	−12.9	+ 6.2
+13.7	10,000	−13.7	+ 6.3
+15.3	12,000	−15.3	+ 6.3
+16.6	14,000	−16.6	+ 6.3
+17.2	15,000	−17.2	+ 6.3
+17.7	16,000	−17.7	+ 6.4
+18.7	18,000	−18.7	+ 6.4
+19.6	20,000	−19.6	+ 6.4

*The preferred frequencies shall be in accordance with ISO recommendation R266. (Courtesy of Recording Industry Association of America.)

TABLE 8.2 RIAA Dimensional Characteristics: 33 r/min Phonograph Records for Home Use*

Description	7-in records (Millimeters)	7-in records (Inches)	10-in records (Millimeters)	10-in records (Inches)	12-in records (Millimeters)	12-in records (Inches)
Outside diameter	(174.6 ± 0.8)	6.875 ± 0.031	(250.8 ± 0.8)	9.875 ± 0.031	(301.6 ± 0.8)	11.875 ± 0.031
Thickness Flush design	$\left(1.9 \begin{smallmatrix}+0.3\\-0.4\end{smallmatrix}\right)$	$0.075 \begin{smallmatrix}+0.010\\-0.015\end{smallmatrix}$	(1.9 ± 0.3)	0.075 ± 0.010	(1.9 ± 0.3)	0.075 ± 0.010
Contour design (see drawings)	Fig. 8.2; Fig. 8.3		Figure 8.1		Figure 8.1	
Center-hole diameter	Same as 10-in		$\left(7.26 \begin{smallmatrix}+0.025\\-0.05\end{smallmatrix}\right)$	$0.286 \begin{smallmatrix}+0.001,\\-0.002\end{smallmatrix}$	Same as 10-in	
Center of gravity maximum balance diameter concentric with hole	(11.1)	0.437	(11.1)	0.437	(11.1)	0.437
Lead-in spiral To start at record edge						
Grooves per inch Contour to be same as recording grooves (in addition, at least one complete unmodulated groove at recording pitch)	Same as 10-in		16±2		Same as 10-in	

TABLE 8.2 RIAA Dimensional Characteristics: 33 r/min Phonograph Records for Home Use* *(Continued)*

Description	7-in records (Millimeters)	Inches	10-in records (Millimeters)	Inches	12-in records (Millimeters)	Inches
Margin diameter (outer set-down limit of reproducing stylus)	(172.2)	6.781	(246.8)	9.719	(297.6)	11.719-in
Diameter of outermost groove at recording pitch	(168.3)	6.625 maximum	(241.3)	9.500 maximum	(292.1)	11.500 maximum
Recording-groove contour						
Included angle	Same as 10-in		90° ± 5°		Same as 10-in	
Bottom radius	Same as 10-in		(0.006)	0.00025 maximum	Same as 10-in	
Width—monophonic	Same as 10-in		(0.056)	(0.0022)	Same as 10-in	
Width—stereophonic—instantaneous	Same as 10-in		(0.025)	0.0010 minimum	Same as 10-in	
Minimum inside diameter of recording	(108)	4.250	(120.6)	4.570	Same as 10-in	
Runout of recording grooves related to center hole (this TIR measurement to be independent of recording pitch)	Same as 10-in		(0.41)	0.016 maximum	Same as 10-in	

Lead-out spiral (number of grooves per inch chosen so that the spiral contains at least one complete revolution)	Same as 10-in		2 to 6 grooves per inch		Same as 10-in
Stopping groove closed concentric circle					
Diameter	$\left(98.4 \begin{array}{c}+\,0 \\ -\,2\end{array}\right)$	$3.857 \begin{array}{c}+\,0.000 \\ -\,0.078\end{array}$	$(106.4 \pm .8)$	4.187 ± 0.031	Same as 10-in
Width	Same as 10-in		(0.08)	0.003	Same as 10-in
Direction of rotation (clockwise when observer faces side of record being played)					
Rotational speed (with 60-Hz line frequency, maximum speed error $\pm\,0.5\%$)	33⅓ r/min		33⅓ r/min		33⅓ or 45 r/min
Crossover spiral (number of grooves joining successive bands on a record not less than 16 per inch)					

* Courtesy of Recording Industry Association of America.

8.15

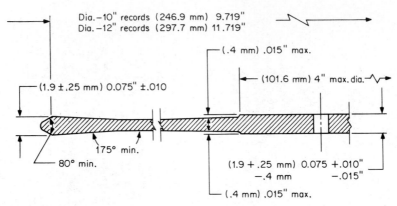

FIG. 8.3 Cross section of 10-in and 12-in contoured records. *(Recording Industry Association of America.)*

8.4 REPRODUCTION EQUIPMENT

Perhaps because the reproduction of phonograph records affects a much larger number of people than does the recording of them, much more has been written on the subject over the years as well. Whole books, magazines, and technical papers have been devoted to the science as well as the philosophy of the topics to be covered here in this one small section. However, over the course of the last century of recording technology, most of the misconceptions about analog disk recording and reproduction have been weeded out of the minds of audio engineers and designers. In spite of the facts, however, there remain a few who are still in search of the "holy grail" of LP playback. Those persons are advised to seek other literature in support of their theories of record playing, as this section will be devoted to the facts and physics of analog disk reproduction.

8.4.1 Playback Styli

Since the playback stylus is the first link in the chain of analog disk playback equipment, even a casual observer can well imagine that it is also an important one. But that is an understatement because the evolution of the playback stylus is arguably the most important development in the history of playback technology. As is pointed out several times in subsequent sections of this chapter, the primary sources of distortion in the analog disk are those having to do with the geometry and physical aspects of the recorded analog waveform. How well the playback stylus suits the groove in the record is of utmost importance.

Stylus Materials.   One of the earliest developments in the evolution of playback styli was the improvement in the materials used in their manufacture. The original Edison machines used ordinary metals, including steel, for both recording and reproducing styli. As phonograph and gramophone technology developed, refinements to stylus materials followed. It was a common sight to open the lid on a Victrola and observe several packets of *needles* in the needle tray bearing the descriptions "loud," "medium," or "soft." These names were meant to describe the nature of the sound produced by these styli, but they actually related to the hardness of the metal (usually steel) used in the needle. The reproducer assembly was so massive and stiff (low-compliance) that the stylus functioned very much like a spring in coupling the groove modulations to the sound diaphragm. Crude though it was by today's standards, the system functioned pretty much as advertised—never mind the vagaries of variable high-frequency loss caused by the mechanical filtering of the springy needle driving the recalcitrant *sound box*. The loud needle was the hardest and stiffest and, consequently, transferred the most energy to the diaphragm.

A further refinement to this scheme was less official but, born of necessity, was widely practiced. Because of the very heavy tracking force (nearly 1 lb), the relative softness of the steel needles, and the limestone which was included in the record compound to shape the needle, stylus life in a Victrola was poor. The typical needle was destroyed in one or two playings. Consequently, anything sharp and thin enough to be forced into the sound box was used to play records, including cactus needles and porcupine quills. A pocket knife and a good supply of rosebushes came in handy for an all-day listening session. The sound, however, would likely be soft.

The metal needle was still used into the electrical era, with ever-harder materials appearing periodically. This culminated in the osmium needle, which was available up into the 1950s. Metals gave way to gemstones when osmium was surpassed in durability and popularity by sapphire and ruby. Sapphire styli last about 2.5 times longer than those of osmium[11] and are still the most popular types in inexpensive record players.

The most durable of all stylus materials is diamond, which can be expected to last about 10 times longer than sapphire. Although the use of diamonds is not new (Edison employed them in his Diamond Disc phonograph), these styli have always been fairly expensive to manufacture and did not become widely used until the popularity of high-quality, high-fidelity *component* systems in the home.

Other aspects of stylus construction have evolved over the years as well. The original metal needles were simply made of one piece of material with a sharpened end. Beginning with osmium and up to the present day, styli have been tipped with a material different from that used in their shanks. Some means of bonding with an adhesive is usually employed to fasten the hard stylus tip to the shank.

From about the dawn of the stereo era, the typical *component-quality stylus assembly* has actually been composed of three parts. Increased concern for record and stylus wear was a natural consequence of the somewhat more delicate stereo groove. In addition to reducing the tracking force and increasing the compliance of the pickup, designers sought to reduce the effective tip mass of the assembly. The same objectives apply today, and the typical stylus shank is usually made of a strong lightweight material such as thin-walled aluminum tubing. A small piece of diamond or sapphire is bonded to a tip holder before it is ground to its desired shape. This holder allows much smaller and less expensive pieces of gemstone than would otherwise be necessary to be used. After the grinding, the tip holder is cut off from the finishing tooling, and the tip assembly is bonded to the stylus shank.

The most expensive styli employ what is called a *nude diamond,* which is to say that there is no tip holder in the assembly. A relatively large piece of diamond is bonded directly to the shank. These styli also tend to use rather exotic materials and shapes for the shank itself, such as a tapered solid beryllium rod with a machined tip-mounting surface. The purpose in doing all this is to produce the stiffest assembly with the lowest mass possible. Because of its relatively high mass, the diamond tip is kept as small as possible. This type of stylus assembly is vanishingly small: the tip can hardly be seen with the naked eye, and the short shank appears to have the diameter of only a few human hairs.

Conical Stylus Tips.   The conical tip shape, frequently described as spherical, was the first shape used for playback styli. The choice was made mostly because this shape was the easiest to grind, but in monophonic days there was very little reason to use any other shape. From the standpoint of producing the lowest tracing distortion, the optimum playback stylus shape is the same as that of the recording stylus. In the first Edison phonograph, for which recording was done by embossing the metal foil, both styli were and ideally should have been conical so that neither one would tear the foil. Later cylinder recordings were made with a sharpened recording stylus, and since the playback shape no longer matched the recording shape, the dawn of tracing distortion was upon the world of recorded sound.

Lateral recording is not subject to the distortion mechanisms inherent in vertical recording. Specifically, the large harmonic-distortion components associated with tracing distortion do not occur with lateral recording. Consequently, audiophiles were content to use conical playback styli up through the monophonic hi-fi era even though by this time recording styli had become sharp and chisel-shaped. The only real problem with using a conical stylus with lateral recordings is the phenomenon of *pinch effect,* or scanning loss. This causes a loss of output level with increasing frequency and decreasing record diameter.

Conical styli are still used today and are most commonly found in inexpensive record players. Many of these players are designed to handle 33⅓, 45, and 78 r/min records. The 78 r/min records used wider grooves than are now common with *microgroove* LPs, and the nominal radius for the appropriate playback stylus is about 3.0 mil. Monophonic LPs typically used a 1.0-mil stylus. Stereo LPs brought with them vertical modulation and the likelihood that groove width might become quite narrow on occasion. Consequently, the nominal radius for a conical stylus for stereo playback is generally agreed to be about 0.6 mil. The multispeed record player, then, should have at least two styli, one for 78s and one for stereo LPs. This is usually accomplished by using a *flipover* design for either the pickup itself or its stylus assembly. One side of the flipover unit is fitted with a 3.0-mil tip, and the other has a 0.6-mil tip.

The cost of the sapphire stylus tip has become so low that there is no longer any need to manufacture styli from any type of metal. Therefore, today's conical styli are available with only sapphire or diamond tips. With regard to the use of conical styli in high-quality applications, a few diehards still seem to prefer the "sound" of a conical. The very real advantages (audible and measurable) of elliptical and line-contact styli are evidently lost on them.

Elliptical Stylus Tips.   The elliptical, or biradial, stylus shape was developed specifically to address the disadvantages of the conical type. Tracing distortion is a direct result of the shape of the playback stylus not being the same as that of the recording stylus. The amount of this distortion is proportional to the difference between these two shapes. The elliptical shape attempts to reduce this difference by reducing the *scanning radius* of the stylus from about 0.7 mil to around 0.2 to 0.5 mil, which more closely approximates the sharp cutting edge of the recording tip (see Fig. 8.4).

This same effect could also be realized simply by using a smaller conical tip.

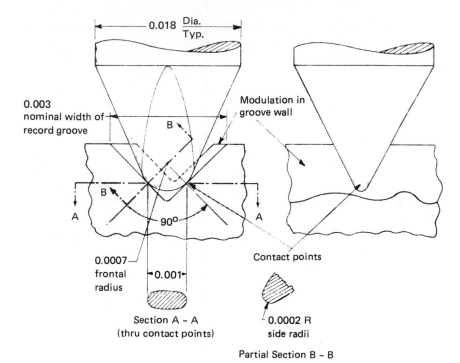

FIG. 8.4 Bilateral-elliptical-pickup-stylus dimensions and radii. *(Courtesy of Shure Brothers, Inc.)*

However, a small conical shape brings with it a smaller *bearing radius,* which allows the stylus to ride lower in the groove. This has the disadvantage of allowing the stylus to pick up more noise from debris or from stamper damage in the bottom of the groove. In the limiting case, the stylus would end up by being supported by the rounded bottom of the groove instead of by the sidewalls, thereby losing contact with the important lateral information in the groove. By having the same bearing radius as a conventional conical stylus (about 0.7 mil for stereo LPs), elliptical styli ride along the same part of the sidewalls and so do not pick up any additional noise.

There are a few disadvantages with the elliptical stylus. The most obvious is that it requires a different and more costly grinding procedure to arrive at its two different radii. From the above discussion, it can also be seen that the "footprint" left by the elliptical stylus as it indents the relatively soft sidewalls of the record will be smaller than that of a conical stylus with the same bearing radius and operating at the same tracking force (see Fig. 8.4). This results in a higher pressure being exerted on the record material, which will increase both record and stylus wear. Consequently, an elliptical stylus should be operated at approximately half of the tracking force of the comparable conical type to keep record wear constant. This requires that the pickup cartridge be of higher compliance and that the tip mass be sufficiently lower not to compromise the tracking ability of the system.

Elliptical styli offered a substantial improvement over conical ones with the advent of stereo recording. The improvement in tracing distortion was quite audible, particularly at the inner diameter of the record, where recorded wavelengths are on the order of the bearing radius. Even with lateral monophonic recordings, the elliptical stylus has a slight advantage because it reduces scanning loss, thereby improving high-frequency response.

The elliptical is probably the most popular of all stylus shapes today because it is an economical compromise between the inexpensive conical and the costly line-contact stylus. Elliptical styli are available with either sapphire or diamond tips, and some are made of nude diamonds as well.

Line-Contact Stylus Tips.   The line-contact type of stylus encompasses many variations and is usually known by the manufacturer's trade name. Names like Shibata, Pramanik, Quadrahedral, Stereohedron, and Micro-Ridge are used to describe this stylus shape. Regardless of the names and irrespective of a few minor variations, these styli share the same important parameters of a small scanning radius (0.1 to 0.2 mil) and a very large bearing radius (about 3.0 mil).

The first of these styli was the Shibata, which was named after its Japanese inventor. The introduction of this type of stylus was one of the long-lasting benefits to fall out of the development of the CD-4 four-channel analog disk system. The CD-4 required the reliable recovery of the very short wavelengths associated with its supersonic frequency-modulation (FM) carrier, which were so small that the typical conical stylus would not even fit into the undulations. The smaller scanning radius of the elliptical shape would scan the tiny carrier waveform well enough, but record wear proved to be excessive. Something better was needed.

The line-contact stylus was the next obvious step in the evolution of the playback stylus. The elliptical shape was a decided improvement over the conical in that its sharper scanning radius was a closer match to the sharp cutting edge of the recording stylus. If getting a little bit closer match was better, then getting a lot closer match should be better still, provided that record wear was not sacrificed. The line-contact stylus is so named because the ratio of the scanning to the bearing radii is so great (over 10:1) that the footprint left by the stylus on the groove wall resembles a line. This contrasts with the spotlike footprint of the conical stylus or the elongated spot of the elliptical stylus.

The line-contact stylus tip begins with a basically conical shape and then is ground with at least two flat sides symmetrically set at an obtuse angle with respect to the direction of groove motion. The Shibata stylus has only two of these flat facets, located at its front. The other line-contact variations include two more flat facets symmetrically placed at the back of the tip. Regardless of the variation, the stylus must be carefully and methodically polished to smooth and blend these flats into the otherwise conical shape of the tip and achieve the desired results of a large bearing radius and a much smaller scanning radius. It can easily be appreciated that this is a costly procedure, resulting in the most expensive of the three tip shapes.

The footprint of the line-contact stylus on the groove wall has about the same lateral dimension as that of the typical elliptical stylus operating at the same tracking force, but its vertical dimension is about 8 times greater. This results in about one-eighth of the pressure on the record surface, yielding correspondingly lower record wear. This benefit is usually traded off for increased tracking ability in the pickup by operating the system at a higher tracking force than would be used with an elliptical tip without sacrificing record wear.

Of the three stylus shapes considered here, the line-contact stylus most closely approximates the shape of the recording stylus. Consequently, it delivers the lowest tracing distortion. Properly matching this type of stylus to the dynamic requirements of the best pickup design results in a system that achieves the lowest tracing distortion and the highest tracking ability of any pickup-and-stylus combination.

The line-contact stylus is clearly the type of choice for the highest-fidelity reproduction in the playback of analog disk records. Because of their costly grinding requirements, line-contact styli are made only of diamond. Versions are available either with bonded tips or with nude diamonds.

8.4.2 Pickup Characteristics and Properties

Since the acoustical reproduction of analog disk records is now obsolete, this section is devoted to electrical means for the playback of records. The reproducing transducer used in disk playback is called a *pickup* or a *cartridge*. Over the years, pickups have been designed with several different voltage-generating technologies, some of which are now also obsolete. Because it is a transducer and is responsible for transforming one kind of energy to another, a pickup is a complex and critical link in the sound reproduction chain. It is characterized by several mechanical and electrical performance parameters, the interplay of which is also critical to the performance of the entire pickup-and-stylus system. This interconnection has only recently been understood well enough to be modeled accurately and to allow computer-aided designs to be practical.

As an introduction to a discussion of the different types of pickups is begun, it is useful to examine those characteristics that all pickups have in common. In the later discussion of transducer types, these characteristics can then be contrasted and compared.

Stylus Force.   A measure of the downward force exerted by the pickup on the record is the *stylus force*. It is also referred to as *tracking force* and is usually measured in grams. This is not to be confused with stylus pressure, which is the force per square unit of surface area indented by the stylus. Stylus pressure is, of course, a function of stylus shape.

The proper tracking force for a particular pickup is a function of several other factors in its design, notably its compliance and its effective stylus-tip mass. Manufacturers usually recommend a range of tracking forces through which they expect the pickup to operate with acceptably low tracking distortion and record wear.

Typical tracking forces for inexpensive conical-tipped pickups are in the 2- to 10-g range. Good-quality pickups of moderate cost using conical or elliptical tips usually operate in the 1- to 3-g range. The most expensive pickups, which usually employ elliptical or line-contact styli, operate from about 0.75 to 3 g but most often are grouped in the 1- to 1.5-g area.

Compliance.   The "stiffness" of the pickup's suspension system refers to the *compliance*. It is usually measured in centimeters of tip motion per dyne of applied force (cm/dyn). In early monophonic (lateral) pickups, which operated at relatively high tracking forces, the suspension system was often deliberately designed with more compliance in the lateral direction than in the vertical. For those pickups, separate compliance specifications were often given for the two directions. Since the advent of stereo recording, equal compliance in both the lateral and the vertical directions has been important. Most modern pickups are designed with mechanically symmetrical suspensions, so only one compliance specification is now given.

Generally speaking, the higher the compliance figure, the lower the tracking force necessary for a given pickup. This is particularly true of reproduction of low-frequency signals, for low frequency modulations tend to have higher amplitudes associated with them than do higher frequencies. This, in turn, is due partly to the natural distribution of amplitudes in the musical spectrum, particularly for pop and rock music. It is also due to the standardized recording preemphasis used in disk recording (see Sec. 8.3). However, high frequency modulation causes the effective tip mass of the pickup system to become the limiting factor in determining tracking ability, so this rule of thumb cannot be universally applied.

Typically, medium-priced pickups will exhibit compliances in the range of 10 to 20 μcm/dyn. Premium pickups are usually rated between about 20 and 30 μcm/dyn.

Amplitude-Frequency Response. One of the most useful measurements of the performance of any component of an audio system is the *amplitude-frequency response*. Pickups are transducers of energy, and transducers are notoriously prone to having uneven frequency responses unless care is taken in their design. A pickup is no exception. Considerable effort is required in balancing the mechanical factors of compliance, effective tip mass, and resonances with the electrical characteristics of inductance, capacitance, and field strength of the magnetic system to achieve a flat frequency response over the relatively wide range of human hearing, 20 Hz to 20 kHz.

It is beyond the scope of this chapter to discuss how the above-mentioned factors influence the frequency response of a pickup. Even more factors are involved, and whole treatises have been devoted to the subject. However, after many years of trial-and-error designs, the contributions of these factors can now be accurately modeled (see Ref. 12, for example), and most modern pickups are designed with the aid of computerized algorithms.

Inexpensive piezoelectric (PZT) pickups often have fairly uneven frequency responses, with as much as ± 10-dB variations from flat over the 20-Hz to 20-kHz range. Medium-priced pickups usually hold this variation to within ± 5 dB. Premium units often exhibit variations as low as ± 1 dB.

Output-Signal Level. A measure of the voltage generated by the pickup is the *output-signal level*. Pickups have never been designed to function as current sources. The FM type of cartridge, which was developed by Weathers in the 1950s, was nothing more than a variable capacitor and was one of the few pickups ever designed to be anything other than a voltage generator. The only other exceptions which come to mind were the semiconductor pickups developed by Euphonics in the 1960s and by Panasonic (Matsushita) for the CD-4 system. These units were essentially variable resistors.

The typical voltage levels developed by pickups fall into three major categories. Inexpensive PZT types, which are designed to be used at high tracking forces with simple amplifiers and in budget record players, usually generate voltages in the range of about 100 to 1000 mV/(cm·s) of groove velocity. (Standard average recording level is about 5 cm/s at 1 kHz.) Most medium- and high-quality pickups operate at a much lower voltage of about 1 to 5 mV/(cm·s). Some of the most expensive pickups are of the moving-coil design and generate voltages of only about 0.1 to 1 mV/(cm·s).

Effective Tip Mass.   A measure of the mass of the tip of the stylus is the *effective tip mass*. As the name implies, it is that lumped mass which, if located at the end of a perfectly rigid, zero-mass stylus assembly, would exactly represent the mass of the real stylus-tip-and-cantilever assembly as seen by the record groove. This concept is a useful mathematical aid in calculating and predicting the dynamic performance of a stylus assembly. Obviously, if a pickup has a tiny nude diamond mounted on the end of a thick and massive cantilever-and-generator assembly, it can be correctly advertised as having a small tip mass. But it will behave as if it had a much larger tip mounted on a much less massive cantilever: it has a relatively high effective tip mass.

The lower the effective tip mass, the better the potential performance of the pickup will be. This is true because less stress will be placed on the groove wall while it is accelerating the stylus tip. This will result in better tracking of the modulation waveform, less temporary strain of the groove wall, resulting in less distortion, and less permanent strain in the groove wall, resulting in less record wear.

All this assumes, of course, that the pickup has been properly designed to take advantage of the low effective tip mass. The cantilever-and-generator assembly must be rigid and of low mass to maintain a sufficiently high mechanical resonance with no *standing waves* on the cantilever. The suspension system must be compliant enough and sufficiently linear to assure good low-frequency tracking and low distortion. All these characteristics, together with several others not mentioned here, are difficult properties to balance in the design of a pickup and so usually are found in only the most expensive models.

Resonances.   In any vibrating system *resonances* are a natural occurrence. Unfortunately, they are usually unwelcome in a transducer because they bring with them irregularities in frequency response. The majority of pickups have two major sources of resonance. There are mechanical resonances of the moving system due to the presence of moving masses and the elasticity of the record material, the cantilever, and the suspension parts. In the case of magnetic pickups, a major electrical resonance exists in the generator system because of the inductance of its coil and the capacitance of the cable which connects the pickup to the amplifier. There are also secondary effects due to the intracoil capacitances in the pickup and the inductance of the connecting cable.

From the standpoint of reducing record wear, it is desirable to damp the mechanical resonances as much as possible and to make them fall above the normal range of music so that they are not likely to be excited by the signal content of a record. A poorly damped resonance which is easily excited will cause mechanical *ringing* of the stylus assembly and subsequent excessive stress on the groove walls, leading to permanent groove deformation. Of course, this same resonance would lead to a peak in the frequency response at that frequency as well, which is also undesirable.

Pickups are often designed to merge these unavoidable resonances in a constructive way. For example, a successful pickup design might be one in which the mechanical resonance is well damped and lies at about 20 kHz. This will ensure a minimal contribution to record wear. The electrical resonance can then be manipulated by selecting the proper capacitive and resistive loading on the pickup coil to smooth out some remaining response irregularity, which usually will occur just below the mechanical resonance.

Tracing Distortion.   Any of several different nonlinearities in the mechanical system of a pickup can result in distortion of the electrical signal. The most common one is *tracing distortion* (see Sec. 8.6.1). This effect is indigenous to all pickups because the playback stylus is not of the same shape as the recording stylus. Even though this source of distortion is actually a function of the stylus rather than of the pickup itself, it is mentioned here because it is by far the leading unavoidable cause of distortion in the pickup system. Even though it cannot be eliminated, it can be significantly reduced by the use of a line-contact stylus (see Sec. 8.4.1).

Tracking Distortion.   Also known as *mistracking, tracking distortion* is the next most significant type of distortion. It occurs when the stylus momentarily loses contact with the groove wall, resulting in a sound very much like *clipping* in an amplifier. Although it rates second place in this discussion, in a poorly designed pickup system mistracking can be far worse than tracing distortion. Nevertheless, theoretically it is possible to design a pickup with no tracking distortion, and in some premium models it has been virtually eliminated.

The essential mechanism of mistracking is that the stylus tip cannot be accelerated sufficiently by the groove wall. In such an instance, the tip has no other option but to slide upward along one wall, losing contact with the other. This is largely a function of pickup design, but the proper design of a pickup system in which tracking distortion has been minimized requires that the size and shape of the stylus be taken into account. This is true because mistracking is related to the effective tip mass, damping, compliance, resonance, and tracking force of the pickup.

In severe cases of mistracking, the stylus may jump out of the groove completely. This problem is most common with inexpensive pickups, which have very little compliance and are mounted in high-mass tone arms with substantial friction in their bearings. If the stylus tends to move inward on the record, the condition is called *skipping*. If it tends to move outward, which usually results in the repetition of a groove, the condition is called *sticking*.

The other sources of distortion in a pickup are probably one or two orders of magnitude less severe than tracing distortion or mistracking and so are nearly insignificant by comparison. These other sources are related to the nonlinearities which may exist in the generator system. Some magnetic-generator designs, for example, are more nearly linear over a wider angle of displacement of the stylus cantilever than are others. The suspension system can have resonant modes which may cause the effective fulcrum of the cantilever assembly to shift dynamically, resulting in a type of intermodulation distortion. Other distortion mechanisms are somewhat related to pickup design but are more a function of the interaction of the pickup and the tone arm. These are discussed in Sec. 8.5.

8.4.3 Types of Transducers

Piezoelectric Pickups.   Crystal or ceramic transducers are also known as *piezoelectric pickups*. Piezoelectrics (PZTs, for piezoelectric transducers) were one of the first types developed for consumer applications and are still widely used in inexpensive record players. A PZT pickup is built with a piece of PZT material (usually a flat, thin, and narrow rectangular sliver) mounted so that one of its small ends is fixed to the body of the pickup. The opposite end is connected to the cantilever assembly so that the PZT material is twisted or bent by the motions of the stylus.

Stressing a PZT element in this way causes the element to develop an electrical potential between its parallel broad faces. A PZT generator will produce a voltage proportional to its displacement from its mechanical equilibrium position. PZT pickups are therefore sensitive to the amplitude of the stylus motion and are known as *constant-amplitude transducers.* A PZT pickup is also a direct-current (dc) device. It will produce a constant unipolar (dc) voltage if its stylus is moved away from rest and held there. As with other types of constant-amplitude pickups, PZTs require a different deemphasis characteristic (playback equalization) in the preamplifier than do constant-velocity types (see Sec. 8.4.4).

The typical inexpensive PZT pickup has a rather large generator element which is also relatively stiff. This results in a pickup which produces high output voltages in the range of 0.1 to 1 V and with rather low compliance, which must then be used at fairly high tracking forces of about 3 to 10 g. This type of pickup, however, can then be used with a very simple, low-gain amplifier with a very simple equalization circuit. The inexpensive PZT pickup which requires only an inexpensive amplifier has led to the popularity of this combination in economy record players.

PZT pickups are not necessarily inexpensive or of poor quality. Several manufacturers, notably Sonotone and Micro-Acoustics, have marketed premium PZT designs which compare favorably with competitive magnetic types. With the use of very small and compliant generator elements, low-mass moving systems, and quality styli, these pickups can perform as well as any other type. Owing to the smaller and more compliant generator, these pickups produce considerably less voltage than do the economy versions. Since the magnetic pickup has become the preferred type for high-quality applications, high-fidelity preamplifiers are usually equipped with proper equalization for only constant-velocity pickups. Premium PZT units therefore are usually designed with an electrical compensation network built into them or are supplied with such a network which can be connected between the pickup and the preamplifier. This network tailors the pickup's frequency response to look like that of a constant-velocity pickup.

Magnetic Pickups.   The favored types for high-quality applications are *magnetic pickups.* There are three basic variations on the magnetic design, but they all result in producing the fundamental requirement of any magnetic generator: changing the magnetic lines of flux that pass through a coil of wire. Magnetic pickups are sensitive to the *change* of magnetic flux crossing the coil and not to the long-term intensity. Consequently, they respond to the velocity of stylus motion and are known as *constant-velocity generators.* They must be used with amplifiers employing a deemphasis characteristic (playback equalization) designed for this type of frequency response.

1. The most common type of magnetic pickup is the *moving-magnet pickup.* As the name implies, in this design the coil is held stationary and the magnet structure itself is moved, which causes the lines of flux to vary in the coil. The magnet is usually mounted directly to the cantilever assembly. Some of the most popular models are manufactured by Stanton/Pickering, Shure Brothers, and Audio-Technica. A whole range of models, from the inexpensive to premium state-of-the-art designs, is available.

For some years, moving-magnet pickups were thought to be a moving high-mass design compared with the other magnetic types. However, today's high-intensity magnets (samarium cobalt) and high-permeability magnetic materials have allowed the moving-magnet pickup to employ an effective tip mass as low as that of any other design. Moving-magnet pickups also have the advantages that they are fairly inexpensive to build, the stylus assembly can be easily interchanged, and the generator itself can be very efficient and linear while also being quite small and of low mass. This allows the entire pickup to be light in weight and suitable for use in the best low-mass tone arms.

2. The second most popular type of magnetic pickup is the *variable-reluctance pickup.* In this design, neither the coil nor the magnet moves. Instead, some other permeable member of the magnetic circuit is connected to be cantilever. This moving member functions like a variable magnetic valve and causes the magnetic-flux intensity to vary at the coil.

Variable-reluctance pickups have essentially the same characteristics as the moving-magnet types, with interchangeable styli, linear generator systems, low moving masses, and light weight being the important features. They are also comparable in price and output voltage. Models are available from the inexpensive to premium-price ranges.

Developed by William S. Bachmann of the General Electric Company, this type of pickup was marketed by GE under the trademark Variable Reluctance for a number of years. GE has since discontinued the manufacture of magnetic phonograph pickups, and many other manufacturers have moved in with a wide range of variations on this basic design. Some of the most popular units are now made by Bang & Olufsen, which terms its design the *moving micro-cross,* and ADC, which calls its design the *induced-magnet principle.*

3. The third type of magnetic pickup is the *moving-coil pickup.* Just as the name implies, the magnet structure is held fixed in the cartridge body, and the coil is attached to the cantilever.

Before the advent of high-intensity magnets, the moving-coil pickup was considered a premium design because the magnet assembly could be as large as necessary and the coil could be a small, low-mass assembly mounted to the cantilever. New materials and design techniques in moving-magnet pickups have erased this advantage.

The moving-coil design has certain disadvantages. To keep the effective tip mass low, the coil assembly has to be very small and contain relatively few turns of wire. Both of these requirements result in a generator which produces only a very small voltage, typically about one-tenth of that of a moving-magnet type (20 dB lower). This creates potential problems with maintaining an adequate immunity from hum and noise along the connecting cables between the pickup and the preamplifier. One manufacturer (Ortofon) attempted to alleviate this problem by building a step-up transformer directly into the pickup. This, of course, increases the size and weight of the cartridge, which can create other problems when trying to mate the pickup with low-mass tone arms. New high-intensity magnets and tiny coils made of very fine wire have allowed some moving-coil pickups to produce nearly as much voltage as moving-magnet types without the use of a transformer.

Another problem is that the stylus is difficult to replace. Since the coil must be attached firmly to the cantilever, when the stylus assembly is removed from the pickup, the coil wires must also be disconnected. Consequently, most moving-coil designs do not allow the stylus to be changed by the user: the pickup must be returned to a service center for stylus replacement. Some manufacturers have designed an electrical plug-and-socket arrangement to allow user replacement of the stylus and coil assembly.

Because of these disadvantages, moving-coil pickups are not nearly as popular as the other two types of magnetics. Some listeners seem to prefer the performance of moving-coil pickups, however, and are willing to pay the premium prices that most of them command. Moving-coil pickups are available from several manufacturers, including Denon (Nippon Columbia), Ortofon, and Audio-Technica.

Variable Resistance (VR). The technology of *variable resistance,* employed in cartridge design, is used for a unit known as a semiconductor pickup. Rather than employing an active voltage-generator system, this type of unit has a transducer which acts as a strain gauge. The transducer element usually is a type of semiconductor whose electrical resistance changes linearly with the displacement of one of its ends (similarly to a PZT type), or with the stress directed at one of its faces.

These pickups must be used with a bias-voltage source in order to place the operating range on the linear portion of the transfer-function characteristics. This usually is supplied by an adapter network connected between the pickup and the preamplifier. VR pickups respond to constant displacement and so are constant-amplitude transducers. The usual adapter network also transforms the output frequency response and signal level to match the input-signal requirements of typical phonograph preamplifiers which are designed for the output-signal characteristics of a constant-velocity pickup.

VR pickups have a very wide frequency response from dc to the ultrasonic range. This is true because the impedance of the transducer is usually very low and has little influence on the level of output voltage, which is easily controlled by the external bias source. The effective tip mass can be made quite low, and the total cartridge weight is also very small since the energy source is external to the pickup. The stylus assembly is easily interchangeable. The chief disadvantage of a VR pickup is that it is noisy compared with PZT or magnetic types. Probably because of their noisiness and the added complexity of their bias and equalization networks, VR pickups have never been popular. The leading manufacturer, Panasonic (Matsushita), promoted them for CD-4 use primarily because of their extended frequency range.

Variable Capacitance (VC). The fourth type of phonograph pickup is the VC, in which the stylus cantilever is connected to one plate of a capacitor while the other plate is held fixed to the pickup body. Two technologies have been used with VC pickups to transform variable capacitance into a voltage output.

The first method employs a local oscillator, usually operating in the radio-frequency (RF) range, which is detuned via the pickup's capacitance. The resulting signal is FM-modulated RF, which is then applied to a discriminator or demodulator circuit that recovers the desired audio signal. This method is sensitive to continuous deflection of the stylus and results in a constant-amplitude transducer. Weathers, the most notable manufacturer, built this type of pickup in the 1950s.

The second method is much the same as is used with most condenser microphones. A dc bias is applied through the pickup to the input of an amplifier having a very high input impedance. This can be accomplished by using a dc voltage source or by employing an *electret* type of dielectric in the transducer. The varying capacitance which occurs while the pickup is playing a record causes a varying bias to appear at the amplifier, whose primary function is to transform this very high transducer impedance to a much lower one. This method is not sensitive to continuous (dc) displacement of the stylus. Even though the transducer impedance is fairly high (usually a few picofarads), it is considerably smaller than that of the following amplifier. This causes the turnover frequency of this capacitively coupled network to be subsonic and results in a constant-amplitude characteristic over the audio-frequency range.

VC pickups have never been popular, probably because of their complexity. They also tend to be noisier than PZT or magnetic types. The dc bias type has no particular advantage over any other type of pickup. The FM type has an obvious problem with isolating the two RF fields, which would be necessary for stereo operation, and no stereo units have ever been commercially successful.

8.4.4 Playback-Signal Characteristics

The frequency responses of phonograph pickups can be grouped into two general categories. Pickups which are sensitive to the absolute displacement of the stylus regardless of frequency are said to have a *constant-amplitude* frequency response. Pickups which have an increasing output voltage with increasing frequency when the displacement is held constant are said to have a *constant-velocity* response. The details of these characteristics have been covered in Sec. 8.3.

Preamplifier Requirements.   Almost all phonograph pickups produce an output voltage which is too small to drive a loudspeaker or a headphone directly. The typical magnetic pickup produces about 5 mV at normal recording level at 1 kHz. This is also about 30 dB lower than the typical *line level* (about 220 mV) at which other consumer-type high-fidelity components such as tape decks or tuners operate. Therefore, it has become common practice to send the signal from the pickup through an additional amplifier, called a *preamplifier,* where it is boosted to a level comparable with that of other components. This line-level signal is the nominal voltage to properly drive most *power amplifiers,* which in turn drive headphones or loudspeakers.

The phonograph preamplifier also performs the important function of correcting the frequency response of the pickup to complement that used in cutting the record. As detailed in Sec. 8.3, the record is cut with a modified constant-amplitude characteristic. Since neither a constant-amplitude nor a constant-velocity pickup is properly suited to complement this characteristic, some response correction is necessary for either type. Table 8.1 shows the proper corrections necessary for both types of pickups. Figure 8.2 graphs the frequency responses of both the cutting and the reproducing equalizations necessary for use with constant-velocity cutters and pickups.

8.5   TRACKING THE RECORD WITH THE PICKUP

Until recently the only way to extract the recorded information from the groove of a record involved the physical tracing of that groove by a playback stylus. The optical technology which has been developed for tracking the spirals of information on the compact disk shows promise that it might be adapted for use in reading the information from a conventional analog disk record. However, as long as a playback stylus needs to be properly located in a record groove, some sort of support and guidance are required. *Tone arms* have traditionally performed this function, and this section will discuss some of the requirements of this important piece of playback equipment.

8.5.1 Pivoted Tone Arm

The pivoted tone arm is certainly the more common of the two basic types of arms, the other being the tangential, or radial, arm, which is discussed later. Today's pivoted arm is an example of the compromise necessary between the complex but theoretical ideal of radial tracking and the economy and simplicity of earlier pivoted designs.

The familiar pivoted tone arm should need little explanation. The pickup is mounted to one end of a movable arm having only two degrees of freedom, restricted by a two-axis pivot system at its other end. The pickup end of the arm can move in an arc vertically and laterally but cannot move along the axis of the arm itself, nor can it twist on the arm's axis.

Lateral Tracking-Angle Error. Given that the closest approximation to radial tracking is the ideal, consider the limiting case of a pivoted arm of infinite length. The motion of the pickup would then be perfectly radial from the record's center and perfectly vertical from the plane of the record. Since the practical limitations of this arrangement are obvious, consider a pivoted arm of some manageable length. A finite tone-arm length forces the pickup to traverse a noticeable arc, both laterally and vertically, which results in imperfect radial tracking. This deviation from perfect tangential alignment of the axis of the arm at the stylus tip is called *lateral tracking error,* or *tangent error.*

Several problems arise from this misalignment. As the error increases, the pickup is effectively twisted in the plane of the record. Since the playback stylus has a significant dimension between its right and left groove-wall contact points, this twisting of the pickup causes one groove-wall contact point to skew slightly fore and the other to skew slightly aft of their nominal positions. This will result in a time-delay error being introduced between the times when the right and left groove-wall modulations are being traced by the stylus.

A related problem is that as the axis of pickup sensitivity departs from that of the modulation in the groove, pickup output level decreases as the cosine of that angle of error.

The most significant ramification of tangent error is that it increases both harmonic (HD) and intermodulation (IM) distortion. Furthermore, IM distortion has been shown to consist of both amplitude- and frequency-modulated types. These distortions arise because the axis of recorded modulation differs from that of pickup sensitivity. The effect that this condition has when translated through the rounded scanning radius of the playback stylus is to make the reproduced waveform seem as though it were skewed or slanted to one side. The magnitudes of these distortions are also dependent on the shape of the playback stylus but are definitely audible and are on the order of a few percent even in well-designed tone arms. Further discussion on these phenomena is beyond the scope of this chapter. Many technical papers have been written on this subject, and the interested reader is referred to Refs. 13, 14, 15, and 16 for detailed information.

Skating Force. Another problem caused by tangent error in a straight pivoted tone arm is that it results in a *skating force* being applied at the stylus tip. Where there is no tangent error, the drag force on the stylus imparted by the groove lies perfectly along the axis of the tone arm and through the arm pivot. When tangent error exists, the drag force is applied along the tangent to the groove contact point, which is no longer in line with the arm pivot. This causes a *moment* to exist about the arm pivot, producing a torque on the arm which causes the stylus tracking force to become unbalanced, resulting in more force on one groove wall than on the other. This difference between groove-wall forces is called the skating force. In practice, this force is great enough to cause audible mistracking.

Offset Tone Arm.   The magnitude of the audible problems caused by the use of straight pivoted arms of practical length has led to the development of the *offset,* or curved, pivoted arm. By curving the tone arm or otherwise offsetting the axis of the pickup from that of the arm, the magnitude of tracking-angle error can be minimized. It can be shown mathematically that there is an optimum offset angle for any desired distance between the turntable pivot and the arm pivot. Again, a great deal of discussion exists in the literature on this topic, and Ref. 13 presents a good treatment.

Antiskate Compensation.   The chief disadvantage of the offset tone-arm design is that it trades off tangent error for considerably increased skating force. This is due, of course, to the fact that the lateral pickup axis is now greatly different from the stylus-tip-to-arm-pivot axis. This results in a rather large moment arm about the tone-arm pivot for the frictional force of stylus drag. Skating force is usually remedied by the inclusion of some mechanism which can apply an opposite torque to the arm; this is called *antiskate compensation.* The antiskate force must not be constant for all diameters of the record because the skating force is a function of stylus friction in the groove. If minor variations due to changes in the tangent error are disregarded, stylus friction decreases with decreasing diameter since the linear groove velocity also decreases. Therefore, most antiskate mechanisms allow for a decreasing antiskate force with decreasing diameter.

Several designs are employed in antiskate mechanisms. One popular technique involves hanging a weight on a thin string or wire whose other end is attached to the tone arm. By draping the string over a fixed post, the weight causes a lateral force to be applied to the arm. Varying the position of the string on the arm changes the moment arm of the antiskate assembly and, thus, the amount of antiskate force. Proper positioning of the fixed post allows the string to change angle as the record diameter changes, thereby changing the moment arm through which the weight acts, which accomplishes the necessary change in antiskate force.

Another design employs a spring which acts though a cam and bears laterally on the arm to provide the antiskate force. The design of the cam allows the force to change with changes in record diameter. Still other designs employ forces generated by weights, springs, and magnets.

8.5.2   Radial, or Tangential, Tracking Arm

In an attempt to solve the problem of lateral tracking-angle error, including the occurrence of skating force and the several distortions discussed above, the *radial,* or *tangential,* tracking arm was developed. Since the record is cut on a lathe employing a truly radially guided cutter head, it seems intuitively reasonable that radial guiding of the playback pickup would be the ideal method. However, a little thought will reveal the difficulty in trying to suspend a pickup so that its stylus rides in the record groove with very little force, having that force equally divided on both groove walls, and guiding the pickup accurately across the radius of the record as the groove spirals inward at an uneven speed. This uneven rate is, of course, due to the fact that the record was cut with a variable pitch to accommodate the varying loudness of its music. This last requirement rules out the use of a simple feed-screw arrangement, since some means would be necessary to vary the speed of the screw to track the variable pitch of the record. Furthermore, all of the above must be accomplished while tracking record warps and eccentricity.

Although this task is formidable, several designs have been developed to achieve this goal. The first ones employed somewhat ingenious mechanical methods to convey the pickup along a radial guide. Reference 17 describes an early arrangement for a broadcast type of player designed by the Radio Corporation of America (RCA) which involved having the pickup slide along a cylindrical rail that was made to have low friction by rotating it. This design was later modified for consumer use by Rabco with the addition of a roller bearing in the pickup arm which rode on the rotating guide rail to further reduce the lateral drag on the stylus.

The newest designs for radial arms employ some rather sophisticated electromechanical servo systems to sense in which direction the pickup needs to move and to get it there. Strain gauges or photooptical means are employed to sense the guiding force of the stylus in the groove. Some designs employ motorized chain- or belt-drive systems to move the pickup housing. Others use the magnetic drive of a linear motor to accomplish this.

8.5.3 Problems Common to Both Pivoted and Radial Arms

In addition to the problems of lateral tracking-angle-error distortion and skating force which are inherent in the pivoted arm and the complexity and costliness of the radial arm, both types share other common problems.

Arm Resonance. Since any tone arm has mass and since it is carrying an elastically suspended stylus vibrating in a record groove, this constitutes a dynamic system subject to one or more mechanical resonances. The most significant of these is a very-low-frequency resonance, typically in the 2- to 20-Hz range, which can be excited by the warpage of the record. Reference 18 describes a detailed investigation of the nature of record warpage. If this resonance is not well damped, record warp can cause severe mistracking, even to the point where the stylus jumps out of the groove.

Various techniques have been employed to damp this resonance. Early methods employed dashpots filled with viscous fluids and connected between the tone arm and the turntable base.[19] Newer methods employ electromechanical servo systems to damp the arm mostly at its resonant frequency.[20]

Additional resonances may exist at higher frequencies, depending on the mass of the arm and the compliance of the pickup-stylus assembly. This can become a significant problem in inexpensive record players with relatively stiff pickups and plastic arms, resulting in a resonance in the 20- to 200-Hz range. This range is easily excited by bass passages in music and can produce exaggerated bass response or can lead to groove jumping.

Warp Wow. Audible wow is a phenomenon usually associated with an eccentric record. As the groove is played at different diameters from that at which it was cut, the instantaneous linear velocity varies. This causes the music to play at a pitch higher or lower than it should be. This slowly wavering pitch is called *wow*.

This same kind of variation in pitch can occur with certain tone arms whose vertical bearing geometries are such that the axis for vertical motion is not in the plane of the record. Consider the usual case of the vertical axis above the record. When the arm is tracking up the warp of a record, the arm is rotated so that the stylus is given a slight resultant velocity in the direction of groove motion, thereby lessening the relative velocity between them and causing a lowering of the music pitch. As the arm tracks down the record warp, the reverse happens, and there is a slight additional relative velocity, resulting in a raising of the musical pitch. This effect is called *warp wow*.

Vertical Tracking-Angle (VTA) Error.   As the name implies, this is another form of tracking-angle error. It results in the same kinds of harmonic and IM distortions as does the lateral tracking-angle error explained above. VTA error occurs when the vertical axis of modulation in the cutter does not coincide with the vertical axis of stylus motion in the pickup.

It is nearly impossible to build a pickup with a stylus assembly and generator system whose vertical axis is really normal to the plane of the record. To do so would result in a cumbersome stylus suspension system. Accordingly, most pickups have their vertical axes skewed about 10 to 20° from the normal to the record to allow room for the generator system to ride a reasonable distance above the record without risk of being bumped by a warp in the disk. Cutter manufacturers have adopted 15° from true vertical as the nominal design angle for "vertical" modulation.

Much has been written on the effects of VTA error, its measurement, and efforts to reduce it. The mathematical treatment of this phenomenon is quite complicated and extensive and beyond the scope of this discussion. The interested reader is referred to the work of Cooper, White, and others in Refs. 14, 15, 16, 21, 22, 23, 24, and 25.

8.5.4   Automatic Record Players and Changers

Automatic record *changers* are, of course, devices which allow several records to be played in succession without the attention of the operator. Most consumer versions stack the unplayed records above the turntable and provide a means of moving the tone arm out of the way at the end of one record, dropping the next record onto the turntable, and resuming play at the beginning of the new disk. Automatic record *players* have much the same mechanism as changers, with the exception that they play only one record with automatic starting and stopping.

The tone arms typically used with these machines differ from those used in manual turntables in that they must somehow be linked to the automatic mechanism. Although this linkage is sometimes accomplished by optical or proximity sensors, mechanical linkages are most often used. This imposes additional frictions and encumbrances on the freedom of arm motion, which can lead to stylus force variations and tracking errors.

Most of today's premium automatic designs have reduced this problem to a nearly insignificant level even when the best pickups, which can be operated at tracking forces as low as 0.75 g, are used with them. However, many inexpensive players and changers which incorporate high-friction tone arms and uncompliant pickups are still on the market. These units exhibit considerable difficulty in tracking some highly modulated records and often show a tendency for the stylus to *skip* inward one or more grooves or to *stick* and repeatedly play the same groove.

Another problem with automatic changers is that the axis of vertical arm motion is fixed, usually at a level substantially higher than the plane of the turntable. This is needed to allow sufficient clearance when playing the last record in the stack. As discussed above, this situation promotes audible warp wow in addition to causing the VTA to be different for every record in the stack.

Inexpensive players and changers often have additional problems. They usually are equipped with poorly designed tone arms which exhibit considerable lateral tracking-angle error. This, in addition to the fact that they rarely incorporate any antiskate compensation, causes the skating force to be unusually high. This further increases the likelihood that these designs will exhibit groove skipping.

8.6   *DISTORTION AND OTHER DEGRADATIONS*

One of the problems associated with an analog process of any kind is that it is impossible to keep the analogy perfect at all times. Any minor modification or perturbation of the analogy makes it less accurate, although still similar and recognizable. Several kinds of perturbations can happen in the recording and reproduction of the analog disk which result in additions, deletions, or merely modifications to the analogy. In all cases, these changes are undesirable and are forms of *distortion.*

8.6.1   Tracing Distortion

Tracing distortion has been inherent with phonograph records since just after the tinfoil phonograph. Very simply, it is the result of the playback stylus's not having the same shape as the recording stylus. Edison's original tinfoil machine, oddly enough, was the only example of a phonograph or gramophone which did not have tracing distortion designed into it. This machine embossed the signal onto the foil, rather than cutting it, and so required a smoothed recording stylus. Both its recording and reproducing styli were of the same conical or spherical shape, and in some versions the same stylus was used for both functions. This was of small comfort, of course, because that first phonograph had a multitude of other distortions so great that there was little appreciation of its wonderfully low tracing distortion.

Since the days when disk masters were actually cut instead of being scratched or embossed, the recording stylus has had a sharp, chisel-like shape. If the playback stylus were to have exactly the same shape, the record would not so much be played as gouged. Some sort of rounded playback stylus is clearly necessary to avoid record wear. Tracing distortion is composed of several phenomena which are related by virtue of the fact that they are all caused by the dissimilar shapes of the recording and playback styli.

Scanning Loss.   This is the least consequential of the components of tracing distortion. It describes the problem of increasing loss of output level from the pickup with increasing signal frequency, decreasing record diameter, and increasing recorded level. The mechanism of scanning loss is that as the recorded wavelengths become smaller and smaller, they approach the curvature of the scanning radius of the playback stylus. Taken to extremes, the stylus will be unable to "fit" fully into a very sharp curve in the groove, so it cannot be fully deviated by the peaks in the groove. The result is that the playback stylus cannot faithfully reproduce the full amplitude of the original modulation, resulting in a loss of output signal from the pickup. This error increases with increasing signal frequency, decreasing record diameter, and increasing signal amplitude. The general effect is called *scanning loss,* and the particular aspect of it attributed to decreasing record diameter is called *diameter loss.* Extreme cases are called *curvature overload.*

Pinch Effect.   Consider the case of lateral modulation only. The cross section of the groove parallel with the cutting face of the recording stylus remains constant with modulation. When the groove is played by a conical stylus, the contact points between stylus and groove rotate around the stylus and describe a groove cross section taken normal to the instantaneous tangent to the groove. Notice that this cross section varies in size, becoming smaller with increasing signal amplitude. This narrowing has the effect of "pinching" the stylus upward and is called the *pinch effect.*

Consequently, the stylus is imparted with two axes of motion when playing a purely laterally cut groove. The lateral motion of the stylus faithfully traces the lateral cut with the exception of some scanning loss, but the stylus also has a vertical motion, which is a function of the instantaneous slope of the modulation. Furthermore, the stylus is pinched up and down twice for each single cycle of lateral motion. If this groove is played back through a monophonic pickup which responds only to lateral stimulation, the vertical motion of the stylus will be ignored and the desired modulation will be recovered. If this groove is played back through a 45-45 stereophonic pickup, this vertical motion will be reproduced and represents a second harmonic to the fundamental frequency of the lateral groove modulation. The net effect is that in addition to the desired modulation occurring in both of the stereo channels, in phase and of the proper amplitude, there will be an unwanted second harmonic in both channels but out of phase between them.

Harmonic Distortion.   As just discussed, pinch effect results in second-harmonic distortion. The same distortion mechanism is at work independently on each wall of the groove. Consider the case of single-channel sinusoidal modulation in a stereo groove. Just as with the laterally cut groove, the problem of the contact point rotating about the stylus exists in this groove. The result is that the actual motion of the stylus, and thereby the signal generated by the pickup, describes a cusp-shaped waveform rather than a sine wave. The degree of cusping increases as the wavelength of the signal approaches the dimension of the scanning radius of the stylus, just as in the case of pinch effect. This error represents a significant amount of even-ordered harmonic distortion, largely second.

Intermodulation Distortion.   As discussed above, the fact that the playback stylus has a rounded scanning radius where the recording stylus has a sharp edge causes the contact point of the stylus and the groove to rotate around the curvature of the playback stylus. In addition to the problems already mentioned, this situation causes a form of intermodulation distortion when the recorded signal is complex. Consider a case in which a signal is composed of a low-frequency (LF) and a high-frequency (HF) sine wave. As the stylus is tracing *down* the slope of the low frequency, the HF information is impinging on a spot slightly rotated toward the *trailing* side of the stylus. Then as the stylus traces *up* the slope of the low frequency, the HF undulations will impinge on a spot rotated slightly toward the *leading* side of the stylus. The net effect is that the presence of the LF signal causes the HF information to be retrieved, alternately, slightly earlier and then slightly later than when it was recorded. The LF signal is frequency-modulating the HF signal, which is a form of intermodulation distortion.

Additionally, the presence of the LF signal causes the amount of scanning loss to vary with the LF waveform. This causes the LF signal to modulate the peak-signal amplitude retrieved from the HF waveform. Thus, the LF signal also amplitude-modulates the HF signal, which is another form of intermodulation distortion.

These harmonic and intermodulation tracing distortions have been investigated exhaustively in the literature, and Refs. 14, 15, 16, 22, and 26 are recommended for further information. Suggestions have been made on how these distortions can be reduced if not completely remedied. As discussed in Sec. 8.4, the use of playback styli which more closely approximate the shape of the cutting stylus is one solution. Other solutions involve modeling and synthesizing the distorted waveform (usually electronically), inverting that waveform, and then recording it. When this inverted predistorted waveform is played back, the tracing distortion cancels out the predistortion, leaving the desired signal. Again, this subject has been thoroughly analyzed mathematically, and Refs. 27, 28, 29, 30, 31, and 32 are recommended to the interested reader.

8.6.2 Tracking Distortion

Tracking distortion, or *mistracking,* as it is often called, is a simple thing to describe. It is nothing more than the tendency of the stylus to lose contact with the groove wall. When this happens, of course, the stylus is no longer guided and is likely to continue moving in whatever direction it was last pushed. Minor cases of mistracking result in the stylus's continuing to move unguided until it suddenly slams into the groove wall again and is recaptured. This results in a recovered waveform which looks very much like clipping in electronic circuits. This type of distortion is quite aggravating to hear; it sounds like buzzing or rattling and is thoroughly unmusical.

Extreme cases of mistracking result in the stylus's jumping completely out of the groove. If it falls back into the same groove, there is a loud popping noise. If it falls into a groove at a smaller diameter, the condition is called *skipping.* If it falls into a groove at a larger diameter, it will usually jump back out again at the same place repeatedly; this condition is called *sticking.*

Extreme cases of mistracking are usually the result of a poorly functioning record player. The pickup may be of very low compliance, the stylus may be excessively worn, or the tone arm may have too much friction. Moderate cases of mistracking can also be caused by these same things or by incorrect antiskate compensation, use of a conical stylus, insufficient tracking force, or a lesser-quality pickup with a high effective tip mass.

Minor cases of mistracking are very difficult to eliminate because the recorded waveform usually contains at least a few instances in which the playback stylus will be accelerated beyond the pickup's ability to cope. This usually occurs when there is a very complex waveform consisting of high levels of midrange and high-frequency information. It can most often be noticed when sibilant sounds (*s, f,* and *t*) are recorded at high levels. The resulting mistracking sounds like an edgy, smashed, or sputtery version of the desired sibilant.

8.6.3 Wow and Flutter

Audible *wow* is a condition in which the pitch of the music is slowly varying up and down. It is a form of frequency modulation and is usually caused by the record's being eccentric or warped. It can also be caused if the record is periodically slipping on the turntable, which is sometimes the case with record changers employing heavy tracking forces. The modulating frequency is usually related to the rotational speed of the record, but in general it is a very low frequency in the range of about 0.1 to 4 Hz.

Flutter is a condition similar to wow, but with a higher unwanted modulating frequency, from about 4 to 30 Hz. Flutter in record players is usually the result of some defect in the turntable drive system. The motor shaft may be eccentric, or there may be a defect in the drive puck. In direct-drive players, the complicated motor itself may be exhibiting a problem with stability in its feedback speed-control circuit.

8.6.4 Acoustic Feedback

Acoustic feedback is fairly self-explanatory. It happens when sound from loudspeakers is allowed to impinge on the surface of a record and cause it to vibrate. The record has a rather large surface area, and if it is left poorly supported by the turntable, as when it is dish-warped, it can easily act as a sound-vibration-absorbing diaphragm. With the pickup stylus resting on the record, this mechanism acts very much like a microphone, and ambient acoustic vibrations can be picked up and fed into the amplifier. In this situation, the record and pickup are said to be *microphonic.*

The record-and-pickup combination will exhibit some natural mechanical resonances which will increase the sensitivity of the system at those frequencies. If the sound impinging on the record is delayed by the proper amount because of the distance between the speakers and the turntable, it will be in phase at certain frequencies with the signal being played back from the groove. If the microphonic gain of the system is sufficiently high at those frequencies where the desired and spurious signals are in phase, the system will experience positive feedback and will go into oscillation, which usually is heard as a howling sound. Lesser microphonic gain where the system is not oscillating will result in exaggerated loudness at the acoustic resonances. This causes frequency-response variations which are nonlinear with the loudness of the music in the room.

Acoustic feedback can be remedied by ensuring that the record is firmly held down on the turntable and that the turntable is fairly massive. This effectively damps out the acoustic vibrations that reach the record. Audio-accessory manufacturers market several products which can be useful in reducing this cause of acoustic feedback. One such product is a clamping mechanism which forces the record down and holds it securely by the turntable spindle. There are also turntable mats that are made of specially compounded foam materials which are very dense and which exhibit a hysteresis in their elastic compressibility. This characteristic makes the mats very good vibration dampers when they are used between the record and the turntable. Some of the more exotic and expensive turntables come equipped with a vacuum hold-down system which secures the record to the turntable platter in much the same way as the lacquer is held to the lathe platter in most cutting systems.

Sometimes, feedback can be the result of acoustic energy impinging on the deck or base of the turntable rather than on the record. The best remedy for this situation is to isolate the turntable-and-arm combination from the rest of the turntable assembly. Several turntable manufacturers have designed into their products effective suspension systems which perform this isolation. In these designs the turntable bearing and the tone-arm bearing are coupled rigidly together to prevent any motion between them. This subassembly "floats" on a fairly soft but well-damped suspension connected to the turntable base. It is very effective in isolating any external disturbances, including those occurring at the base itself such as drive-motor vibration. The natural resonance of this system is very low, usually about 1 to 5 Hz. Acoustic Research was one of the first manufacturers, around 1960, to recognize the effectiveness of this design.

Aftermarket remedies are also available for those turntables which do not have built-in isolation suspensions. Audio-Technica, EAR, and others offer sets of elastic damper feet which can be placed under the turntable base and help isolate building-borne vibrations from the record player. This fix is less effective than the isolation obtained with the Acoustic Research type of design because these isolators cannot reduce vibrations which occur at the turntable base.

REFERENCES

1. R. Gelatt, *The Fabulous Phonograph,* Lippincott, Philadelphia, 1955, p. 18.

2. Ibid., p. 28.

3. Ibid., p. 192.

4. Ibid., p. 60.

5. E. Cook, "Binaural Disc Recording," *Disk Recording,* vol. 1, *J. Audio Eng. Soc.,* 179 (1980).

6. J. T. Mullin, "Monogroove Stereophonic Disc Recording," *Disk Recording,* vol. 1, *J. Audio Eng. Soc.,* 182 (1980).

7. J. G. Frayne and R. R. Davis, "Recent Developments in Stereo Disc Recording," *Disk Recording,* vol. 1, *J. Audio Eng. Soc.,* 185 (1980).

8. H. E. Roys, "The RIAA Engineering Committee," *Disk Recording,* vol. 1, *J. Audio Eng. Soc.,* 466 (1980).

9. "AES Standard Playback Curve," *Disk Recording,* vol. 1, *J. Audio Eng. Soc.,* 451 (1980).

10. Recording Industry Association of America, Inc., *Standards for Analog Disc Records,* Bulletin E-1, 1977.

11. E. J. Marcus and M. V. Marcus, "The Diamond as an Industrial Material, with Special Reference to Phono Styli," *Disk Recording,* vol. 1., *J. Audio Eng. Soc.,* 315 (1980).

12. F. V. Hunt, "The Rational Design of Phonograph Pickups," *Disk Recording,* vol. 2, *J. Audio Eng. Soc.,* 186 (1981).

13. R. E. Carlson, "Resonance, Tracking, and Distortion: An Analysis of Phonograph Pickup Arms," *Disk Recording,* vol. 2, *J. Audio Eng. Soc.,* 259 (1981).

14. D. H. Cooper, "Compensation for Tracing and Tracking Error," *Disk Recording,* vol. 1, *J. Audio Eng. Soc.,* 39 (1980).

15. D. H. Cooper, "Integrated Treatment of Tracing and Tracking Error," *Disk Recording,* vol. 1, *J. Audio Eng. Soc.,* 44 (1980).

16. D. H. Cooper, "On Tracking and Tracing Error Measurements," *Disk Recording,* vol. 1, *J. Audio Eng. Soc.,* 61 (1980).

17. H. E. Roys and E. E. Masterson, "The Radial Tone Arm—An Unconventional Phonograph Pickup Suspension," *Disk Recording,* vol. 2, *J. Audio Eng. Soc.,* 271 (1981).

18. J. M. Kates, "Low-Frequency Tracking Behavior of Pickup Arm-Cartridge Systems," *Disk Recording,* vol. 2, *J. Audio Eng. Soc.,* 246 (1981).

19. C. A. Snow, Jr., "A New Viscous-Damped Tone Arm Development," *Disk Recording,* vol. 2, *J. Audio Eng. Soc.,* 275 (1981).

20. K. Clunis and M. J. Kelly, "Overcoming Record Warps and Low-Frequency Turntable Rumble in Phonographs," *Disk Recording,* vol. 2, *J. Audio Eng. Soc.,* 118 (1981).

21. J. B. Halter and J. G. Woodward, "Measurement of Distortions Due to Vertical Tracking Angle Errors in Stereodisk Systems," *Disk Recording,* vol. 1, *J. Audio Eng. Soc.,* 50 (1980).

22. D. H. Cooper, "Interaction of Tracing and Tracking Error," *Disk Recording,* vol. 1, *J. Audio Eng. Soc.,* 86 (1980).

23. D. H. Cooper, "Misinterpretation of Vertical Tracing Error," *Disk Recording,* vol. 1, *J. Audio Eng. Soc.,* 95 (1980).

24. C. R. Bastiaans, "Further Thoughts on Geometric Conditions in the Cutting and Playing of Stereo Disks," *Disk Recording,* vol. 1, *J. Audio Eng. Soc.,* 5 (1980).

25. J. V. White and A. J. Gust, "Measurement of FM Distortion in Phonographs," *Disk Recording,* vol. 2, *J. Audio Eng. Soc.,* 133 (1981).

26. E. C. Fox and J. G. Woodward, "Tracing Distortion—Its Cause and Correction in Stereodisk Recording Systems," *Disk Recording,* vol. 1, *J. Audio Eng. Soc.,* 31 (1980).

27. H. Redlich and H.-J. Klemp, "A New Method of Disc Recording for Reproduction with Reduced Distortion: The Tracing Simulator," *Disk Recording,* vol. 1, *J. Audio Eng. Soc.,* 78 (1980).

28. D. H. Cooper, "Construction of Tracing Correlator Waveforms," *Disk Recording,* vol. 1, *J. Audio Eng. Soc.,* 90 (1980).

29. D. H. Cooper, "Continuous Delay Regulator for Controlling Recording Errors," *Disk Recording,* vol. 1, *J. Audio Eng. Soc.,* 97 (1980).

30. D. Braschoss, "Development and Application of a New Tracing Simulator," *Disk Recording,* vol. 1, *J. Audio Eng. Soc.,* 131 (1980).

31. S. Washizawa, T. Nakatani, and T. Shiga, "Development of Skew-Sampling Compensator for Tracing Error," *Disk Recording,* vol. 1, *J. Audio Eng. Soc.,* 145 (1980).

32. E. G. Trendell, "Tracing Distortion Correction," *Disk Recording,* vol. 1, *J. Audio Eng. Soc.,* 159 (1980).

BIBLIOGRAPHY

Anderson, C. R., J. H. Kogen, and R. S. Samson: "Optimizing the Dynamic Characteristics of a Phonograph Pickup," *Disk Recording,* vol. 2, *J. Audio Eng. Soc.,* 213 (1981).

Bauer, B. B., R. G. Allen, G. A. Budelman, and D. W. Gravereaux: "Quadraphonic Matrix Perspective—Advances in SQ Encoding and Decoding Technology," *Quadraphony, J. Audio Eng. Soc.,* 102 (1975).

———, D. W. Gravereaux, and A. J. Gust: "A Compatible Stereo-Quadraphonic (SQ) Record System," *Quadraphony, J. Audio Eng. Soc.,* 145 (1975).

Bogantz, G. A., and S. K. Khanna: "Development of Compound for QuadraDiscs," *J. Audio Eng. Soc.,* **23,** 27 (January–February 1975).

——— and J. F. Wells: "The RCA Quadulator," *J. Audio Eng Soc.,* **25,** 99 (March 1977).

Burt, Leah S.: "Record Materials," *J. Audio Eng. Soc.,* 712–717 (October–November 1977).

Cooper D. H., and T. Shiga: "Discrete-Matrix. Multichannel Stereo," *Quadraphony, J. Audio Eng. Soc.,* 41 (1975).

————, ————, and T. Takagi: "QMX Carrier-Channel Disc," *Quadraphony, J. Audio Eng. Soc.,* 201 (1975).

Eargle, J. M.: "Multichannel Stereo Matrix Systems: An Overview," *Quadraphony, J. Audio Eng. Soc.,* 94 (1975).

————: "4-2-4 Matrix Systems: Standards, Practice, and Interchangeability," *Quadraphony, J. Audio Eng. Soc.,* 132 (1975).

Gerzon, M. A.: "Periphony: With-Height Sound Reproduction," *Quadraphony, J. Audio Eng. Soc.,* 56 (1975).

Groh, A. R.: "The Dynamic Vibration Absorber Principle Applied to a High-Quality Phonograph Pickup," *Disk Recording,* vol. 2, *J. Audio Eng. Soc.,* 251 (1981).

Hirsch F., and S. F. Temmer: "A Real-Time Digital Processor for Disk Mastering Lathe Control," *Disk Recording,* vol. 1, *J. Audio Eng. Soc.,* 282 (1980).

Hutto, Edgar, Jr.: "Emile Berliner, Eldridge Johnson, and the Victor Talking Machine Company," *J. Audio Eng. Soc.,* 666–673 (October–November 1977).

Inoue, T., N. Takahashi, and I. Owaki: "A Discrete Four-Channel Disc and Its Reproducing System (CD-4 System)," *Quadraphony, J. Audio Eng. Soc.,* 162 (1975).

Ishigaki, Y., K. Fukui, and G. A. Bogantz: "New Modulation Technique for CD-4 Recording," *J. Audio Eng. Soc.,* **24,** 112 (March 1976).

Isom, Warren Rex: "Record Materials," *J. Audio Eng. Soc.,* 718–723 (October–November 1977).

Itoh, R.: "Proposed Universal Encoding Standards for Compatible Four-Channel Matrixing," *Quadraphony, J. Audio Eng. Soc.,* 125 (1975).

Khanna, S. K.: "Role of Polymer Science in Developing Materials for Phonograph Discs," presented at the 52d Convention of the Audio Engineering Society (1975).

Kogen, J. H.: "Tracking Ability Specifications for Phonograph Cartridges," *Disk Recording,* vol. 2, *J. Audio Eng. Soc.,* 221 (1981).

Owaki, I., T. Muraoka, and T. Inoue: "Further Improvements in the Discrete Four-Channel Disc System CD-4," *Quadraphony, J. Audio Eng. Soc.,* 170 (1975).

Ruda, Joseph C.: "Record Manufacturing: Making the Sound for Everyone," *J. Audio Eng. Soc.,* 702–711 (October–November 1977).

Scheiber, P.: "Analyzing Phase-Amplitude Matrices," *Quadraphony, J. Audio Eng. Soc.,* 111 (1975).

————: "Four Channels and Compatibility," *Quadraphony, J. Audio Eng. Soc.,* 79 (1975).

Smith, F. Langford, *The Radiotron Designer's Handbook,* 4th ed., Radio Corporation of America, Harrison, N.J., 1953, p. 603.

Takahashi, N., T. Muraoka, and T. Inoue: "Noise Reduction in the CD-4 Disc System," *Quadraphony, J. Audio Eng. Soc.,* 191 (1975).

Tremaine, H. M.: *Audio Cyclopedia,* Howard W. Sams, Indianapolis, 1969, pp. 693–710.

White, J. V.: "Mechanical Playback Losses and the Design of Wideband Phonograph Pickups," *Disk Recording,* vol. 2, *J. Audio Eng. Soc.,* 233 (1981).

————: "A Theory of Scanning Loss in Phonographs," *Disk Recording,* vol. 1, *J. Audio Eng. Soc.,* 150 (1980).

Woodward, J. G.: "NQRC Measurement of Subjective Aspects of Quadraphonic Sound Reproduction—Part I," *Quadraphony, J. Audio Eng. Soc.,* 19 (1975).

————: "NQRC Measurement of Subjective Aspects of Quadraphonic Sound Reproduction—Part II," *Quadraphony, J. Audio Eng. Soc.,* 31 (1975).

CHAPTER 9
DIGITAL DISK RECORDING AND REPRODUCTION*

Hiroshi Ogawa
Optical Disk Drive Division, Sony Corporation, Tokyo, Japan

Kentaro Odaka
Audio Technology Center, Sony Corporation, Tokyo, Japan

Masanobu Yamamoto
Disk Development Division, Sony Corporation, Tokyo, Japan

9.1 COMPACT-DISK DIGITAL FORMAT

This section describes the digital format of the compact-disk (CD) digital audio system: its basic specifications and the process by which audio signals are converted into digital signals and recorded on the disk. In addition, subcodes which can be put to a variety of uses are described.

9.1.1 Basic Specifications

Audio specifications, signal format, and disk specifications are summarized in Table 9.1.

Sampling Frequency. *Pulse-code modulation* (PCM) is used to convert audio signals into digital signals. Stereo audio signals are sampled simultaneously at a rate of 44.1 kHz. This sampling frequency was chosen for the following reasons:

1. From the standpoint of filter design, a 10 percent margin with respect to the Nyquist frequency is needed. The frequency of 44 kHz is the minimum sam-

---

* Technical Consultant: Dr. Toshi T. Doi, Sony Corporation, Tokyo, Japan.

pling frequency required to cover audible frequencies up to 20 kHz. (20 kHz × 2 × 1.1 = 44 kHz.)

2. The frequency of 44.1 kHz* is used in digital audio tape recorders based on videotape recorders (VTRs). Note that when a continuous signal in a limited bandwidth is sampled, it can be converted to a discrete signal with no degradation in sound quality.

TABLE 9.1 Basic Specifications of the CD System

Recording method	
Signal detection	Optical
Linear recording density	43 kbit/in (1.2 m/s)
Area recording density	683 Mbit/in^2
Audio specifications	
Number of channels	2-channel stereo
Playing time	Approximately 60 min
Frequency response	20 ~ 20,000 Hz
Dynamic range	> 90 dB
Total harmonic distortion	< 0.01%
Channel separation	> 90 dB
Wow and flutter	Equal to crystal oscillator
Signal format	
Sampling frequency	44.1 kHz
Quantization	16-bit linear/channel
	2′ complement
Preemphasis	No or $^5\!/_{15}$ μs
Modulation	EFM
Channel-bit rate	4.3218 Mbit/s
Error correction	CIRC
Transmission rate	2.034 Mbit/s
Redundancy	≃ 30%
Disk specifications	
Diameter of disk	120 mm
Thickness of disk	1.2 mm
Diameter of center hole	15 mm
Program area	50 ~ 116 mm
Scanning velocity	1.2–1.4 m/s, CLV
Revolution speed	500 ~ 200 r/min
Track pitch	1.6 μm
Pit size	0.11 × 0.5 × 0.9 ~ 3.2 (μm)

Quantization. Quantization is the key factor in determining the sound quality of a digital system. A 16-bit linear quantization has been chosen to maintain the same quality as that of master tapes. Coding of 16 bits is also preferable from the point of view of digital data application. The theoretical dynamic range of

---

* There are 525 and 625 lines per frame in the NTSC and CCIR TV systems, respectively. Each line can record three words per channel including redundant data, and 490 and 588 lines per frame are available for data recording. Thus, 44.1 kHz comes from the following calculation:

$$3 \times 490 \times 30 \text{ Hz (NTSC bandwidth)} = 3 \times 588 \times 25 \text{ Hz (CCIR)} = 44.1 \text{ kHz}$$

the system at maximum-amplitude input is about 97.8 dB, or substantially greater than that of conventional analog systems. This results from a lower noise level. To reduce quantization noise, preemphasis of a $^{15}\!/_{50}$-μs time constant can be used. Coding is $2'$ complement, so the positive peak level is 0111 1111 1111 1111, and the negative peak level is 1000 0000 0000 0000.

Signal Format.   The error correction system used in the CD system is the *cross-interleave Reed-Solomon code* (CIRC). CIRC employs two Reed-Solomon codes which are cross-interleaved. The total data rate, which includes CIRC, sync word, and subcode, is 2.034 Mbit/s.

The modulation method used is 8-to-14 modulation (EFM), and 8-bit data are converted to $14 + 3 = 17$ channel bits after modulation. Thus the channel-bit rate is $2.034 \times {}^{17}\!/_8 = 4.3218$ Mbit/s.

Playing Time.   Playing time depends on disk diameter, track pitch, and linear velocity. The CD system was designed for 60 min of playing time, but maximum possible playing time at the lowest linear velocity is 74.7 min.

Disk Specifications.   The diameter of the disk is 120 mm, and the thickness is 1.2 mm. The track pitch is 1.6 μ, which is about one-sixtieth of that of the conventional long-playing (LP) record. The disk rotates counterclockwise, as seen from the readout side, and the signal is recorded from inside to outside. Because the CD system adopts the *constant-linear-velocity* (CLV) recording method, which maximizes recording density, the speed of revolution of the disk is not constant. The standard linear velocity is 1.25 m/s. Thus, as the pickup moves from the starting area outward, the rate of rotation gradually decreases from 500 to 200 r/min. (See Fig. 9.1.)

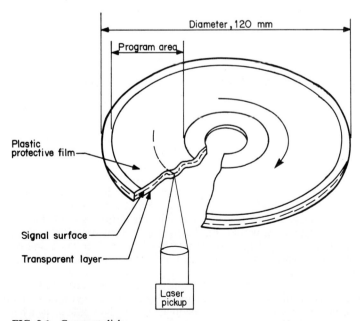

FIG. 9.1 Compact disk.

9.1.2   Error Correction and Control Technique

This section describes the error control technique and the CIRC error correction code: its construction and performance.

Necessity of Error Control.   The CD system employs the optical noncontact readout method. Because the signal surface is protected by a plastic layer and the laser beam is focused on the signal surface, the disk surface itself is kept free from defects such as scratches. As a result, most of the errors which occur at and in the vicinity of the signal surface through the mastering and manufacturing process are random errors of several bits. Even though the CD system is resistant to fingerprints and scratches, defects exceeding the limit will naturally cause large burst errors. A typical bit error rate of a CD system is 10^{-5}, which means that a data error occurs 2×10^6 bits/s $\times 10^{-5} = 20$ times per second. Such data errors, even though they may be 1-bit errors, cause unpleasant pulsive noise; so an error correction technique must be employed.

Unlike an error in computer data, an error in digital audio data (if the error can be detected) can be concealed. Indeed, simple linear interpolation is sufficient in most cases. The error correction code used in a CD system must satisfy the following criteria:

1. Powerful error correction capability for random and burst errors

2. Reliable error detection in case of an uncorrectable error

3. Low redundancy

CIRC satisfies these criteria and can control errors on the disk properly.

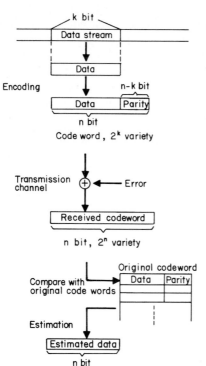

FIG. 9.2   Basic error correction technique.

Basic Error Correction Code.   The basic error correction procedure is shown in Fig. 9.2. A group of data is translated into a code word by adding check data and transmitted through the recording channel. At the receiver side, received data are compared with all the code words, and the nearest are selected. If a group of k symbols (the data) is encoded to a longer word of n symbols (the code word) and the code words satisfy special check equations, then this code is called an (n, k) linear block code. The encoding process is, in other words, a process of assigning as much nonparity check data to the original data. For example, suppose $X = (X_1, X_2, \ldots X_n)$ and $Y = (Y_1, Y_2, \ldots Y_n)$ are code words, as in Fig. 9.3, then the Hamming distance between the two code words is defined as the number of different pairs of symbols. If t symbol errors induced in the channel are not to lead to confusion at the receiver side as to whether X or Y was transmitted, X and Y should differ from each other (as in Fig. 9.4) by at least

$(2t + 1)$ symbols. Therefore, a figure of merit of the code called minimum distance d is defined as the minimum distance among all pairs of different code words X and Y. A code is t-error-correcting if and only if $d \geqq (2t + 1)$; and if the locations of the errors (erasure location) are known, $d - 1$ erasure correction is possible. If the number of errors exceeds these bounds, error correction and detection capability are no longer guaranteed and the decoder may make an erroneous decoding.

Cross-Interleave Reed-Solomon Code (CIRC).   The encoder of CIRC is shown in Fig. 9.5. To handle errors generated on the disk effectively, CIRC uses two

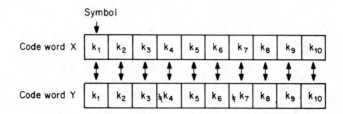

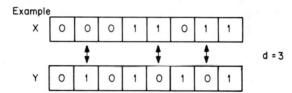

FIG. 9.3 Hamming distance.

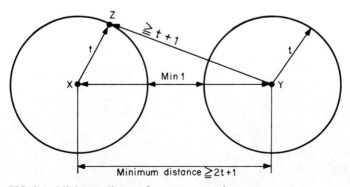

FIG. 9.4 Minimum distance for t error correction.

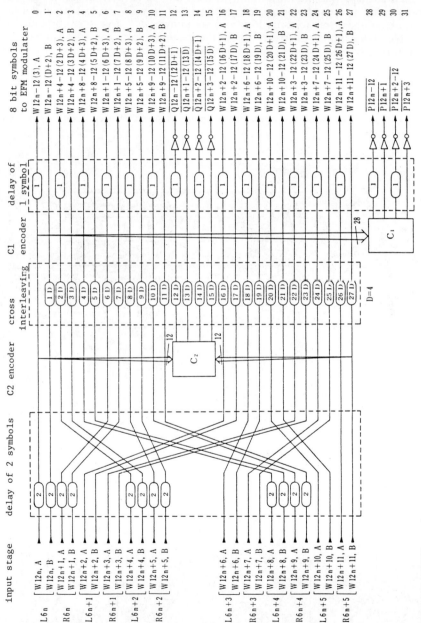

FIG. 9.5 CIRC encoder.

Reed-Solomon codes and a sophisticated interleaving technique. The CIRC encoder is composed of the following five stages.

1. *Input stage:* Sixteen-bit data of 12 words (6 words per channel) are input per frame [F frame = F sampling (44.1 kHz)/6 = 7.35 kHz]. Twelve words are divided into 24 symbols of 8 bits, which comprise the error correction code. After that, a delay of 2 symbols and scrambling are given to maximize concealment capacity.

2. *C_2 Reed-Solomon code:* Twenty-four symbols of data are encoded into a (28, 24) Reed-Solomon code over GF(2^8).* Four parity symbols are used for error correction, and the code words satisfy the following equation:

$$H_q \cdot V_q = 0 \qquad (9.1)$$

H_q and V_q are shown in Fig. 9.6a and b. This C_2 code is effective for burst-error correction.

3. *Cross interleaving:* Cross interleaving is applied to the C_2 code to make a product code with the C_1 code and also to increase burst-error controllability.

4. *C_1 Reed-Solomon code:* Cross-interleaved 28 symbols of the C_2 code are encoded again into a (32, 28) Reed-Solomon code over GF(2^8). Four parity symbols are used for error correction, and code words satisfy the following equation:

$$H_p \cdot V_p = 0 \qquad (9.2)$$

H_p and V_p are shown in Fig. 9.7a and b. This code is effective for random-error correction and burst-error detection.

5. *Output stage:* At the output stage, half of the C_1-encoded 32-symbol code word is given a 1-symbol delay to avoid a 2-symbol error at the boundary of the symbols. The total code rate of CIRC becomes

$$R = {}^{24}\!/_{32} = \tfrac{3}{4} \qquad (9.3)$$

CIRC is a code over GF(2^8), which means that the decoding process is made in 8-bit symbol units. Thus, the modulation method to be used in this system should generate errors also in symbol units without error propagation.

Performance of CIRC. Performance of CIRC depends on the decoding strategy. As shown in Fig. 9.8, the CIRC decoder is composed of two Reed-Solomon code decoders, C_1 and C_2. Both codes have four parities, and their minimum distance is 5. If the error location is known, distance-5 code can correct up to four symbols; if the location is not known, up to two symbols. At the C_1 decoder, error location information can be derived from the eight-to-fourteen modulation (EFM) demodulator and the radio-frequency (RF) signal detector, and at the C_2 decoder more reliable information can be derived from the C_1 decoder. Thus, in practice both decoders work adoptively with error location information to maximize error correction and detection capability. If the errors exceed the correction limit, they are concealed by interpolation. Since even-numbered sampled data and odd-numbered sampled data are interleaved as much as possible, CIRC can conceal long-burst errors by simple linear interpolation. Burst-error controllability is shown in Table 9.2. The maximum correction length and concealment length are, respec-

---

* Galois field.

$$
H_q = \begin{bmatrix}
1 & 1 & 1 & 1 & 1 & 1 & 1 & 1 & 1 & 1 & 1 & 1 & 1 & 1 & 1 & 1 & 1 & 1 & 1 & 1 & 1 & 1 & 1 & 1 & 1 & 1 & 1 \\
\alpha^{1} & \alpha^{2} & \alpha^{3} & \alpha^{4} & \alpha^{5} & \alpha^{6} & \alpha^{7} & \alpha^{8} & \alpha^{9} & \alpha^{10} & \alpha^{11} & \alpha^{12} & \alpha^{13} & \alpha^{14} & \alpha^{15} & \alpha^{16} & \alpha^{17} & \alpha^{18} & \alpha^{19} & \alpha^{20} & \alpha^{21} & \alpha^{22} & \alpha^{23} & \alpha^{24} & \alpha^{25} & \alpha^{26} & \alpha^{27} \\
\alpha^{2} & \alpha^{4} & \alpha^{6} & \alpha^{8} & \alpha^{10} & \alpha^{12} & \alpha^{14} & \alpha^{16} & \alpha^{18} & \alpha^{20} & \alpha^{22} & \alpha^{24} & \alpha^{26} & \alpha^{28} & \alpha^{30} & \alpha^{32} & \alpha^{34} & \alpha^{36} & \alpha^{38} & \alpha^{40} & \alpha^{42} & \alpha^{44} & \alpha^{46} & \alpha^{48} & \alpha^{50} & \alpha^{52} & \alpha^{54} \\
\alpha^{3} & \alpha^{6} & \alpha^{9} & \alpha^{12} & \alpha^{15} & \alpha^{18} & \alpha^{21} & \alpha^{24} & \alpha^{27} & \alpha^{30} & \alpha^{33} & \alpha^{36} & \alpha^{39} & \alpha^{42} & \alpha^{45} & \alpha^{48} & \alpha^{51} & \alpha^{54} & \alpha^{57} & \alpha^{60} & \alpha^{63} & \alpha^{66} & \alpha^{69} & \alpha^{72} & \alpha^{75} & \alpha^{78} & \alpha^{81}
\end{bmatrix}
$$

$$
V_q = \begin{bmatrix}
W12n-24,A \\
W12n-24,B \\
W12n+4-24,A \\
W12n+4-24,B \\
W12n+8-24,A \\
W12n+8-24,B \\
W12n+1-24,A \\
W12n+1-24,B \\
W12n+5-24,A \\
W12n+5-24,B \\
W12n+9-24,A \\
W12n\div9-24,B \\
Q12n \\
Q12n+1 \\
Q12n+2 \\
Q12n\div3 \\
W12n+2,A \\
W12n+2,B \\
W12n\div6,A \\
W12n+6,B \\
W12n+10,A \\
W12n+10,B \\
W12n+3,A \\
W12n+3,B \\
W12n+7,A \\
W12n+7,B \\
W12n+11,A \\
W12n+11,B
\end{bmatrix}
$$

FIG. 9.6 (a) H_q. (b) V_q.

$$
H_p =
\begin{bmatrix}
1 & 1 & 1 & 1 \\
1 & \alpha & \alpha^{2} & \alpha^{3} \\
1 & \alpha^{2} & \alpha^{4} & \alpha^{6} \\
1 & \alpha^{3} & \alpha^{6} & \alpha^{9} \\
1 & \alpha^{4} & \alpha^{8} & \alpha^{12} \\
1 & \alpha^{5} & \alpha^{10} & \alpha^{15} \\
1 & \alpha^{6} & \alpha^{12} & \alpha^{18} \\
1 & \alpha^{7} & \alpha^{14} & \alpha^{21} \\
1 & \alpha^{8} & \alpha^{16} & \alpha^{24} \\
1 & \alpha^{9} & \alpha^{18} & \alpha^{27} \\
1 & \alpha^{10} & \alpha^{20} & \alpha^{30} \\
1 & \alpha^{11} & \alpha^{22} & \alpha^{33} \\
1 & \alpha^{12} & \alpha^{24} & \alpha^{36} \\
1 & \alpha^{13} & \alpha^{26} & \alpha^{39} \\
1 & \alpha^{14} & \alpha^{28} & \alpha^{42} \\
1 & \alpha^{15} & \alpha^{30} & \alpha^{45} \\
1 & \alpha^{16} & \alpha^{32} & \alpha^{48} \\
1 & \alpha^{17} & \alpha^{34} & \alpha^{51} \\
1 & \alpha^{18} & \alpha^{36} & \alpha^{54} \\
1 & \alpha^{19} & \alpha^{38} & \alpha^{57} \\
1 & \alpha^{20} & \alpha^{40} & \alpha^{60} \\
1 & \alpha^{21} & \alpha^{42} & \alpha^{63} \\
1 & \alpha^{22} & \alpha^{44} & \alpha^{66} \\
1 & \alpha^{23} & \alpha^{46} & \alpha^{69} \\
1 & \alpha^{24} & \alpha^{48} & \alpha^{72} \\
1 & \alpha^{25} & \alpha^{50} & \alpha^{75} \\
1 & \alpha^{26} & \alpha^{52} & \alpha^{78} \\
1 & \alpha^{27} & \alpha^{54} & \alpha^{81} \\
1 & \alpha^{28} & \alpha^{56} & \alpha^{84} \\
1 & \alpha^{29} & \alpha^{58} & \alpha^{87} \\
1 & \alpha^{30} & \alpha^{60} & \alpha^{90} \\
1 & \alpha^{31} & \alpha^{62} & \alpha^{93}
\end{bmatrix}
$$

$$
V_p =
\begin{pmatrix}
\text{W12n}-12(2)\,,\text{A} \\
\text{W12n}-12(1\text{D}+2)\,,\text{B} \\
\text{W12n}+4-12(2\text{D}+2)\,,\text{A} \\
\text{W12n}+4-12(3\text{D}+2)\,,\text{B} \\
\text{W12n}+8-12(4\text{D}+2)\,,\text{A} \\
\text{W12n}+8-12(5\text{D}+2)\,,\text{B} \\
\text{W12n}+1-12(6\text{D}+2)\,,\text{A} \\
\text{W12n}+1-12(7\text{D}+2)\,,\text{B} \\
\text{W12n}+5-12(8\text{D}+2)\,,\text{A} \\
\text{W12n}+5-12(9\text{D}+2)\,,\text{B} \\
\text{W12n}+9-12(10\text{D}+2)\,,\text{A} \\
\text{W12n}+9-12(11\text{D}+2)\,,\text{B} \\
\text{Q12n}-12(12\text{D}) \\
\text{Q12n}+1-12(13\text{D}) \\
\text{Q12n}+2-12(14\text{D}) \\
\text{Q12n}+3-12(15\text{D}) \\
\text{W12n}+2-12(16\text{D})\,,\text{A} \\
\text{W12n}+2-12(17\text{D})\,,\text{B} \\
\text{W12n}+6-12(18\text{D})\,,\text{A} \\
\text{W12n}+6-12(19\text{D})\,,\text{B} \\
\text{W12n}+10-12(20\text{D})\,,\text{A} \\
\text{W12n}+10-12(21\text{D})\,,\text{B} \\
\text{W12n}+3-12(22\text{D})\,,\text{A} \\
\text{W12n}+3-12(23\text{D})\,,\text{B} \\
\text{W12n}+7-12(24\text{D})\,,\text{A} \\
\text{W12n}+7-12(25\text{D})\,,\text{B} \\
\text{W12n}+11-12(26\text{D})\,,\text{A} \\
\text{W12n}+11-12(27\text{D})\,,\text{B} \\
\text{P12n} \\
\text{P12n}+1 \\
\text{P12n}+2 \\
\text{P12n}+3
\end{pmatrix}
$$

$$D = 4$$
$$n = 0,\ 1,\ 2,\ \ldots$$

FIG. 9.7 (a) H_p. (b) V_p.

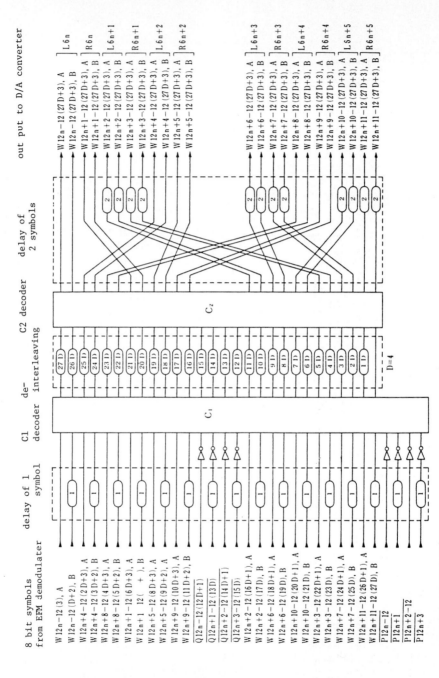

FIG. 9.8 CIRC decoder.

TABLE 9.2 CIRC Burst-Error Controllability

C_2 decoder	Dimensions	Correction length	Concealment length
2-symbol correction	No. of frames (data bit)	8 ($\approx$2000 bits)	48 ($\approx$12,300 bits)
	Actual length on disk (1.25 m/s)	1.36 mm	8.16 mm
2-symbol correction + 1 erasure correction	No. of frames (data bit)	12 ($\approx$3000 bits)	48 ($\approx$12,300 bits)
	Actual length on disk (1.25 m/s)	2.04 mm	8.16 mm
4-symbol erasure correction	No. of frames (data bit)	14 ($\approx$3600 bits)	48 ($\approx$12,300 bits)
	Actual length on disk (1.25 m/s)	2.38 mm	8.16 mm

tively, 2.38 and 8.16 mm on the disk surface. Random-error controllability also depends on the decoding strategy, and the most popular configuration is a two-symbol error decoder for each stage. Calculated performance results of this decoder configuration are shown in Fig. 9.9. The performance of CIRC is sufficient for the CD system, and this code has still more capacity for error control.

9.1.3 Modulation Method

This section describes how CIRC-encoded data are modulated and recorded on the disk.

Basic Requirements for a Modulation Method. CIRC-encoded data cannot be directly recorded on the disk because they do not satisfy the following requirements for optical recording; thus, EFM modulation is employed. The basic requirements are:

1. *Correct readout of high-density recording:* The frequency characteristics of the CD system are basically the same as those of a low-pass filter, and the cutoff frequency is $\dfrac{2NA}{\lambda}$ *V*, where λ is the wavelength of the beam, NA is the numerical aperture of the lens, and *V* is the linear velocity. (See Fig. 9.10.) Therefore, to avoid intersymbol interference caused by a limited bandwidth, T_{min} (minimum run length of the channel data) must be as large as possible. On the other hand, if the detection window T_w is too small, the deterioration of the signal caused by such factors as lens aberration, defocus, and skew may cause random errors. As a result, a large T_{min} and a proper T_w are preferable.

2. *Clock content:* A bit clock which must be regenerated from the readout signal edge is used for demodulating the data and for CLV control. To maintain clock stability the modulated signal must have a sufficient number of transitions, and T_{max} (the maximum run length) must be small.

3. *Low-frequency components:* If the modulated signal contains no low-frequency components, low-frequency disturbances caused by dirt and scratches on the disk surface or asymmetry of the readout signal can be removed easily. Also, low-frequency components leak to the servoloop, making the servo unstable.

4. *Error propagation:* The error correction system employed in the CD system treats 8-bit symbols as a unit; thus, 8-bit unit modulation without error propagation is preferable.

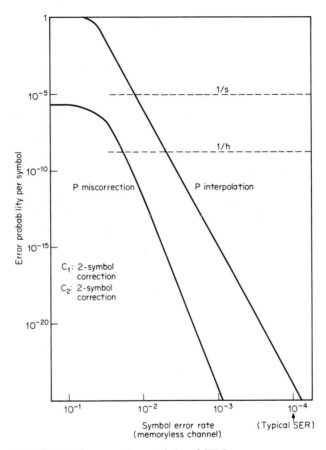

FIG. 9.9 Performance characteristics of CIRC.

EFM (Eight-to-Fourteen Modulation). EFM is a run-length-limited (RLL) code developed for the CD system. First, 8-bit data are mapped on a 14-channel-bit pattern. (See Fig. 9.11.) To satisfy the aforementioned requirements, $(2^8 = 256)$ patterns are selected from the 267 possible different 14-bit patterns that satisfy $T_{min} = 3$ channel bits and $T_{max} = 11$ channel bits. Part of this mapping table is shown in Fig. 9.12, where 1 means "transition" and 0 means "no transition." It is clear that to connect these patterns by maintaining the run-length constraint, at least two channel bits must be inserted between all the patterns. But in the case of EFM, 3 channel bits are inserted so as to control not only run length but also the low-frequency components of the modulated signal. An example of this con-

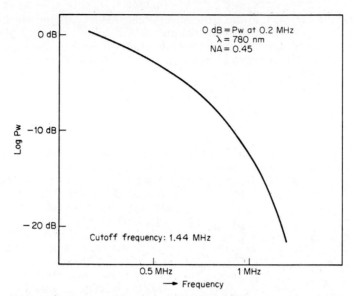

FIG. 9.10 Frequency response of the compact-disk system at a scanning velocity of 1.25 m/s. 0 dB = P_w at 0.2 MHz; wavelength = 780 nm; NA = 0.45.

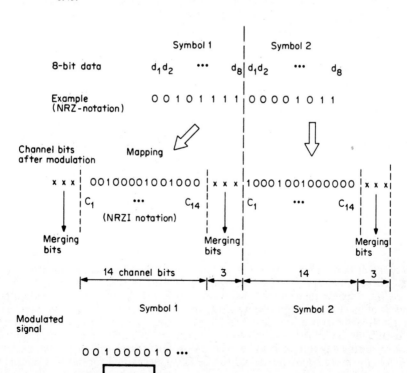

FIG. 9.11 EFM modulation.

trol is given in Fig. 9.13. In this case, possible channel-bit patterns which satisfy the T_{min} and T_{max} constraint are 000, 010, and 001. To control low-frequency components, the digital sum variation (DSV) is calculated for these three cases, and the best pattern (000) is selected. In such a way, the 8-data bit is converted to a $(14 + 3 = 17)$ channel-bit pattern.

The basic parameters of EFM are shown in Table 9.3, and the Table 9.3 frequency spectrum is shown in Fig. 9.14. Demodulation in Fig. 9.14 is effected by detecting the 14-channel-bit pattern. Thus, error propagation is limited to 8 bits, which suits CIRC.

Frame Format.   For demodulation and deinterleaving of the data, channel-bit stream synchronization and frame synchronization must be effected by using the synchronization pattern. A 24-channel-bit synchronization pattern which incorporates a double T_{max} pattern is inserted in a frame, as shown in Fig. 9.15. (A double T_{max} pattern is not permitted in ordinary EFM modulation.) One frame consists of a synchronization pattern (24 channel bits), 32 symbols of CIRC code word $(14 \times 32 = 448$ channel bits), 1 symbol of subcode (14 channel bits), and marging bits (3×34), for a total of 588 channel bits. F frame is 7.35 kHz, and the channel-bit rate is 7.35 kHz $\times$ 588 = 4.3218 Mbit/ s. The total data rate is 4.3218 Mbit/s $\times$ %₁₇ ≃ 2.034 Mbit/s.

```
100  01100100    01000100100010
101  01100101    00000000100010
102  01100110    01000000100100
103  01100111    00100100100010
104  01101000    01001001000010
105  01101001    10000001000010
106  01101010    10010001000010
107  01101011    10001001000010
108  01101100    01000001000010
109  01101101    00000001000010
110  01101110    00010001000010
111  01101111    00001001000010
112  01110000    10000000100010
113  01110001    10000010000010
114  01110010    10010010000010
115  01110011    00100010000010
116  01110100    01000010000010
117  01110101    00000010000010
118  01110110    00010010000010
119  01110111    00100010000010
120  01111000    01001000000010
121  01111001    00001001001000
122  01111010    10010000000010
123  01111011    10001000000010
124  01111100    01000000000010
125  01111101    00001000000010
126  01111110    00010000000010
127  01111111    00100000000010
```

FIG. 9.12   Part of the EFM conversion table.

9.1.4   Subcodes

Many features of the CD player are based on various subcodes recorded on the disk. This section describes the subcodes of the CD system.

Basic Concept.   One of the advantages of digital recording is that the digital format can handle not only the main audio signal but also subcoded nonaudio digital data. In the CD system 3 percent of total recordable data is reserved for subcodes whose main purpose is control and display.

Subcode Format.   Eight bits per frame are used for subcoding, as shown in Fig. 9.16. These 8 bits are used as eight different subcoding channels (P, Q, R, S, T, U, V, W), thus giving each channel a bit rate of 7.35 kbit/s. One subcode block consists of 98 subcode symbols, resulting in a block rate of 7.35 kHz/98 = 75 Hz. For block synchronization, two special 14-channel-bit synchronization patterns are used; thus, 96 bits are available for each channel. Channel P is a simple music-track separator flag intended to be used in low-cost search systems. Channel Q is available for more sophisticated controls. The general data format of Channel Q is shown in Fig. 9.17.

First, 4 control bits indicate essential information such as the number of channels, whether or not there is preemphasis, and so on. The 4-bit address (ADR) and the succeeding 72-bit DATA-Q section have several data modes. The basic mode indicates the track number, the elapsed time of current selection, and the total elapsed time. In the lead-in track, which is located inside the music tracks, Channel Q indicates the table of contents, information which is very helpful for high-speed accessing. The other modes can be used for such information as the disk manufacturer wishes to make available. The last 16 bits are the cyclic-redun-

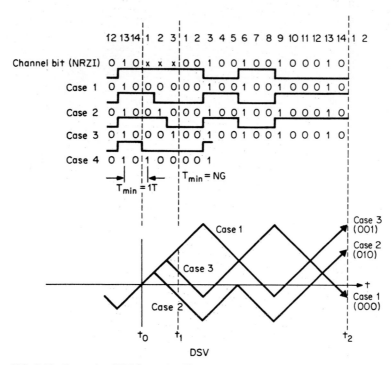

FIG. 9.13 Example of EFM marging bits control.

TABLE 9.3 Basic Parameters of EFM

Conversion ratio	$8 \rightarrow 14 + 3$
T_w	$0.47T^*$
T_{min}	$1.41T$ (3 channel bits)
T_{max}	$5.18T$ (11 channel bits)
Constraint length	$8T$ (no error propagation)
Channel-bit rate	$17/8T$ bit/s
Sync pattern	Double T_{max}
DC component	$\simeq$ free
Density ratio (T_{min}/T)	1.41
$T_w \times T_{min}$	0.66

*T = data bit interval.

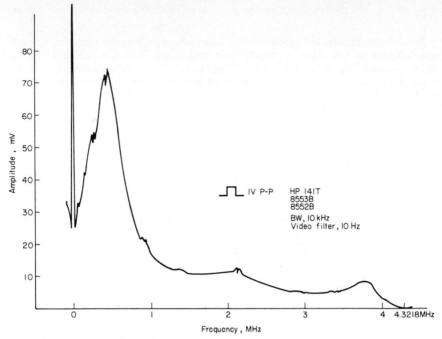

FIG. 9.14 Power spectrum of EFM.

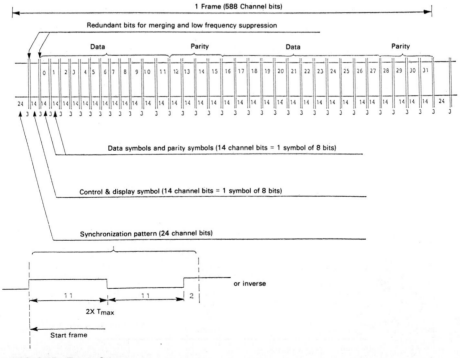

FIG. 9.15 Frame format.

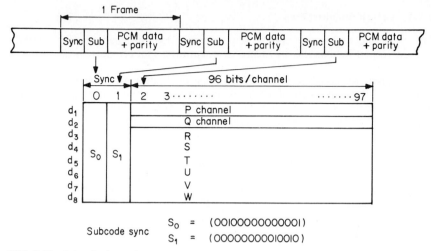

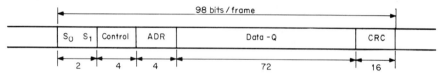

FIG. 9.16 Subcode channels.

FIG. 9.17 General data format of Channel Q.

dancy-check (CRC) code for error detection. Channels R through W can be used for display purposes. The maximum available data rate is $6 \times 96 \times 75 = 43.2$ kbit/s. Examples of possible graphic applications are shown in Table 9.4. Other applications (still picture, voice channel, etc.) are planned for introduction in the future.

9.2 COMPACT-DISK PLAYER SYSTEM

This section describes the CD player system: its principle, its structure, and the process by which the signals recorded on the disk are converted to digital sound. In addition, two extended applications of the CD system are described.

TABLE 9.4 Examples of Compact-Disk Graphic Applications

Mode	Pixels (horizontal × vertical)	Color	Memory size	Maximum display speed	Features
Line graphics	288 × 24	8	16 kbit	0.32 s	Scroll
TV graphics	288 × 192	16 out of 4096	64 kbit	2.56 ~ 10.24 s	Scroll
					Channel-select

9.2.1   Optical Requirements

The principle and some optical requirements for the readout of a digitally encoded signal from a disk by means of a scanning spot are described.

Basic Optics for Reading.   The basic optics for reading are shown in Fig. 9.18. This simple figure consists of a light source, a microscope objective lens to concentrate a spot onto the information layer of a disk, a beam splitter, and a pin diode as a photodetector which converts to electric current.

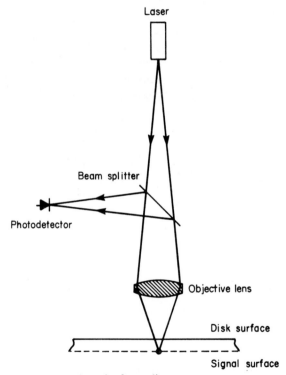

FIG. 9.18   Basic optics for reading.

The optical principle of noncontact readout is based on diffraction theory. Though this phenomenon by means of a narrow slot is well known, an analogous situation occurs if a light beam impinges on a reflective signal surface with pitlike depressions. In the case of a flat surface (between pits), nearly all the light is reflected, whereas if a pit is present, the major part of the light is scattered and substantially less light is detected by the photodetector (see Fig. 9.19).

Laser Diode (LD).   The light source used in the CD system must satisfy the following conditions:

1. It must be small enough to be built into the optical pickup.
2. It uses coherent light in order to focus on an exceedingly small spot.
3. Enough light intensity for readout must be provided.

GaAlAs semiconductor laser diodes satisfy the above requirements. The specifications of such an LD are the following.

Wavelength = 0.78 to 0.83 μm
Light power = about 3 mW
Lateral mode = fundamental
Transverse mode = fundamental
Longitudinal mode = multiple

When the light from the LD is returned from the reflective surface of the disk, it has an effect on the light-generating characteristics of the LD and generates large

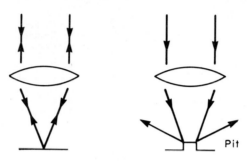

Scattering of light by phase object (pit)

FIG. 9.19   Principle of noncontact readout.

optical noise fluctuations. Thus, a *multiple longitudinal mode* is necessary to prevent the phenomenon. A typical structure and optical and electrical characteristics are shown in Figs. 9.20 and 9.21.

Lens.   The lens requirement can be described by means of numerical aperture (NA). By using the angle from Fig. 9.22, it is shown by NA $= n \sin \theta$, where n is the refractive index.

Owing to diffraction at the lens aperture, the light beam has a limited value. It is well known that when a beam with a uniform distribution of flux is incident to a lens, the beam projects a pattern known as the Airy disk. The diameter of the first ring, in which about 84 percent of the energy is concentrated, is given roughly by

$$1.22 \times \lambda/\text{NA} \qquad (9.4)$$

where λ = wavelength. If the strength is defined as $1/e^2$ (e is the base of the natural logarithm), the effective beam diameter is

$$0.82 \times \lambda/\text{NA} \qquad (9.5)$$

From these equations, it can be concluded that to focus on a small spot it is better to have a smaller rather than a larger NA. But NA also defines the following important factors:

Depth of focus is proportional to $\lambda/(\text{NA})^2$

Allowance for skew (tilt) is proportional to $\lambda/(\text{NA})^3$

Allowance for variations in disk thickness is proportional to $\lambda/(\text{NA})^4$

For these reasons, an NA which satisfies the following equation is recommended:

$$\lambda/\text{NA} \leq 1.75 \tag{9.6}$$

Accordingly, NA must be within the range of 0.45 to 0.50 in combination with the wavelength of the LD.

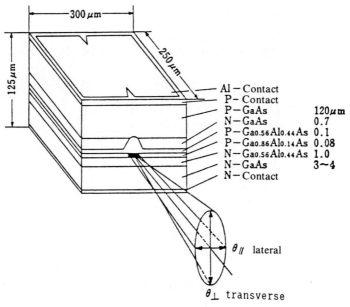

FIG. 9.20 Structure of the laser diode.

Modulation Transfer Function (MTF).   MTF is the frequency characteristics of the optical channel. In other words, it is the parameter which determines the smallest size of pits that can be detected. To make this determination, the *optical transfer function* (OTF) is defined and expressed by a complex number. MTF is the absolute expression of OTF. The phase term of OTF is called the *phase transfer function* (PTF). Generally, OTF is expressed by the cross-correlation function for the input and output apertures. In the case of a CD, a form of reflective optical disk, this becomes the autocorrelation function in the following equation:

$$F(x) = \frac{2}{\pi} \cos^{-1} \frac{x}{x_o} - \frac{x}{x_o} \sqrt{1 - \left(\frac{x}{x_o}\right)^2} \tag{9.7a}$$

where $x = x_o$.

$$F(x) \leq 0 \tag{9.7b}$$

where $x > x_o$. Here x shows the spatial frequency, and x_o shows the optical cutoff; x_o is expressed with a given NA and λ as follows:

$$x_o = 2\text{NA}/\lambda \tag{9.8}$$

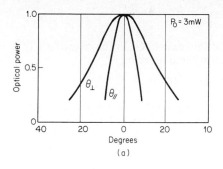

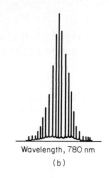

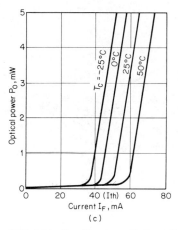

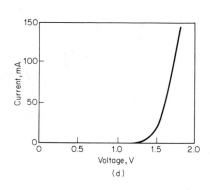

FIG. 9.21 Specifications of a laser diode. (*a*) Far-field pattern. (*b*) Longitudinal multimode spectrum. (*c*) *I-L* characteristics. (*d*) *V-I* characteristics.

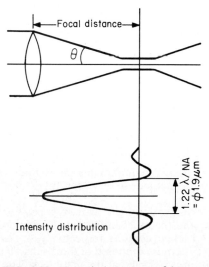

FIG. 9.22 Numerical aperture of lens and Airy disk.

As shown in Fig. 9.23, it is a form of low-pass filter. In the case of a CD, λ = 0.78 μm, NA = 0.45, and the optical cutoff frequency is

$$x_o = 1.154 \times 10^6 \tag{9.9}$$

In other words, this optical system can detect pits as dense as 1154 per millimeter. As shown in Sec. 9.3, the smallest pit of a CD is about 0.87 μm at a linear

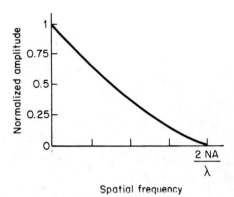

Spatial frequency

FIG. 9.23   Modulation transfer function (MTF).

velocity of 1.25 m/s. If the track were occupied by these pits, the spatial frequency would be

$$1/(0.87 \ \mu\text{m} \times 2) = 0.581 \times 10^6 \tag{9.10a}$$

This wideband characteristic facilitates accurate reading of the pit modulation over a wide range.

In terms of temporal frequency, the cutoff frequency is

$$\frac{2\text{NA}}{\lambda} \times V = 1.44 \ \text{MHz} \tag{9.10b}$$

where the linear velocity V = 1.25 m/s.

All the equations are for theoretically ideal optics and ideal conditions. For design and analysis purposes, they must be modified for actual operational conditions and available hardware.

9.2.2   Servo Method

In the preceding section, optical requirements for accurate readouts were given. This section describes some methods of servo control to meet these requirements.

Servo System.   For tracking with a light beam, two position controls are necessary, one in the vertical and the other in the radial direction. These controls are called *focus-* and *radial-tracking controls,* respectively.

Generally, the servo system is composed of three subsystems, as shown in Fig. 9.24. The error of position is detected at the first block. The second block is the

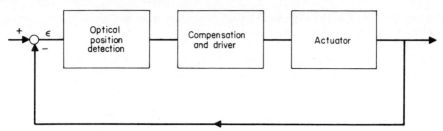

FIG. 9.24 Block diagram of the servo system.

electronic compensation network, which is necessary for the stability of a closed-loop system. In the last stage, the electronic signal is converted into actual spot displacement by means of the electromechanical system.

Focus Servo System

1. *Focus servo:* This system is used to keep the laser beam focused on the reflective layer of the disk within the focus depth of the optical system. The focus depth is

$$\pm \frac{\lambda}{(\mathrm{NA})^2} = \pm 2 \ \mu\mathrm{m} \tag{9.11}$$

where $\lambda = 0.78$
$\mathrm{NA} = 0.45$

On the other hand, the specified deviation in the vertical direction is

Maximum deviation $= 0.5$ mm
Maximum acceleration $= 10$ m/s

This translates into a requirement of more than 48 dB for low-frequency response.

2. *Astigmatic method:* One method to detect the light-beam position in the vertical direction is the astigmatic method (see Fig. 9.25). By using this method, it is necessary to modify the basic optics shown in Fig. 9.18. That is accomplished by placing a cylindrical lens between the beam splitter and the photodetector. The photodetector is divided into four segments. When the beam is focused on the disk surface within the focus depth, a circular spot is created on the four-segment detector surface. When the beam is focused before or after that point, elliptic spots are imaged on the detector. If an $(A + C) - (B + D)$ operation is performed, the result is the focus-error signal.

3. *Foucault method:* There are differing forms of this method, one example of which is shown in Fig. 9.26. In this case a wedge is used instead of a cylindrical lens, and two two-segment detectors are employed. If the beam is in focus, the operation $(A + D) - (B + D)$ is zero. If the disk and lens move closer, the image of the reflected light moves further away. On the other hand, if this distance increases, the resultant polarity of the signal becomes the opposite sign.

4. *Actuator:* The mechanism used in the vertical direction is the same as that employed in loudspeakers. For example, as in Fig. 9.27, an objective lens (or the complete pickup, if possible) can be attached to a voice coil, which moves up and down according to the electronic signal command from the focus-error detector through the phase-lead circuit.

Radial-Tracking Servo Requirements.   The laser spot should follow the center of the track to within about 0.1 mm, with no interference from adjacent tracks merely 1.6 μm away.

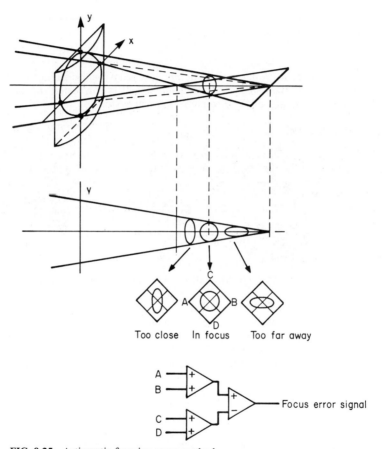

FIG. 9.25   Astigmatic-focusing servo method.

The permissible radial variation is specified as:

$$\text{Maximum eccentricity} = 70 \ \mu m$$
$$\text{Maximum acceleration in radial direction} = 0.4 \ \text{m/s}$$

Accordingly, a reduction in low-frequency area of more than 57 dB is needed.

1. *Twin-spot method:* When using this method for detection of the beam position in the radial direction, the basic optics must be modified. This is accomplished by placing a grating between the LD and the objective lens and two detectors in the detector plane. As shown in Fig. 9.28, two extra beams are projected, one on each side of the main beam. When the main beam is directly over the track, the edges of the secondary beams (E and F) barely encroach upon the track, and the remainder of each beam is on the so-called mirror surface. In this case,

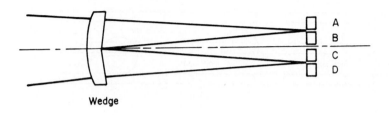

Wedge

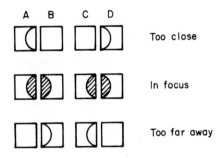

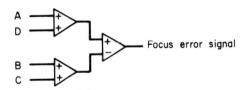

FIG. 9.26   Foucault method for the focusing servo system.

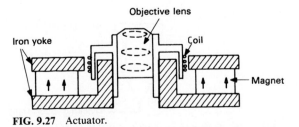

FIG. 9.27   Actuator.

the light output $(E - F)$ is essentially zero. If all three beams should be misaligned slightly, the diffractions from E and F become different. Accordingly, the resultant output $(E - F)$ becomes the radial-tracking-error signal.

2. *Push-pull method:*   In contrast to the twin-spot method, in this method the radial error signal is obtained from one spot, as shown in Fig. 9.29. When the

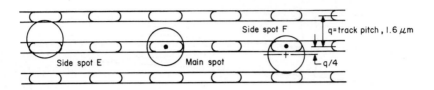

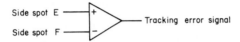

FIG. 9.28   Twin-spot radial-tracking method.

position of the beam is exactly on the track (pit), there is an equal distribution in signal strength on the left and right sides of the detector. If this relationship of position should be changed slightly, however, the distribution of signal strength on the left and right sides becomes asymmetrical. Accordingly, the resultant left half–right half becomes the radial-tracking-error signal.

Although this method is extremely simple, there are some drawbacks; that is, (*a*) it is sensitive to variations in pit depth and pit shape; and (*b*) when the lens

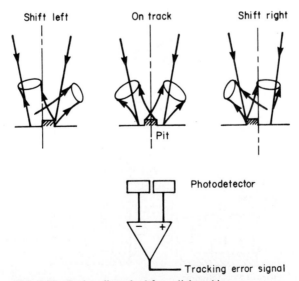

FIG. 9.29   Push-pull method for radial tracking.

is moved only to follow the track, a dc offset is produced in the radial-tracking-error signal.

3. *Actuator in radial direction:*   There are two methods for moving the light beam in the radial direction. One uses the so-called two-axis device and slide movement. The two-axis device is constructed by attaching additional coil assemblies to the voice coil of Fig. 9.27. This method is a two-stage radial movement. A two-axis device mainly takes care of fine radial tracking and the slide drive of coarse tracking in the radial direction. This type of twin-spot actuator with astigmatic correction is a popular combination.

The other method is the so-called swing-arm pickup or segment meter. This pickup is mounted in a swing arm which describes an arc across the disk during playback. This type of actuator, a single-beam push-pull with Foucault focusing, is another popular combination.

Spindle Servo (Constant Linear Velocity).   The specified CD linear speed typically is 1.25 m/s, but a speed of 1.2 to 1.4 m/s is permissible. On the other hand, a CD player must rotate the disk at exactly the same speed as when the signal was recorded in mastering. Spindle servo control is accomplished in two sequential stages as follows (Fig. 9.30):

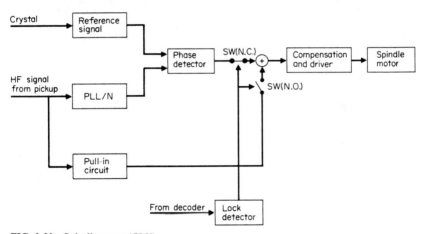

FIG. 9.30   Spindle servo (CLV).

1. *Pull-in stage:*   The disk spindle motor is controlled by some means so that it rotates within the capture range of the phase-lock loop (PLL) used for clock recovery. In most cases this is done by detecting the T_{max} (the longest signal length) or T_{min} (the shortest signal length).

2. *Lock stage:*   After confirming that the PLL is in *lock* condition, the spindle motor is locked to the reference signal from the crystal in the digital signal processor.

9.2.3   Compact-Disk Player

This section describes the configuration of the CD player and signal processing from light modulated by pits on the disk to the output audio signal.

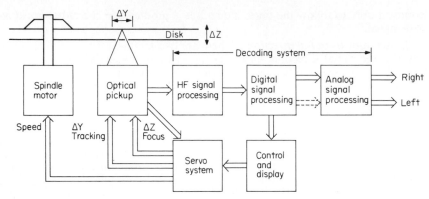

FIG. 9.31   Configuration of the compact-disk player.

Functional Components.   A block diagram of the CD player is shown in Fig. 9.31. The concentrated spot onto the information layer reads the signal, which has been recorded on the disk in digitally encoded form. The readout signals are processed (added and/or subtracted) and separated into (1) servo status signals and (2) the audio program signal. The audio signal is processed in the decoding block into the conventional but highly precise audio signal waveforms for the right and left channels. Concurrently, the servo status signals drive the servo system, which maintains precise control of spindle speed and laser-beam tracking and focus. The control and display system, using a microprocessor, is a control center; it not only simplifies user operation but also provides a display of visual data (using subcoding Channel Q information derived from the decoding block), which consists of brief notes about the musical selections as they are played.

High-Frequency Signal Processing.   After the compensation of frequency response, if necessary, we can obtain the so-called eye diagram, shown in Fig. 9.32. This is the result of processing by optical low-pass filter, expressed by MTF.

   To convert into a two-level bit stream, it is necessary to take care of the "pit" distortion. By looking at Fig. 9.32 carefully, it can be understood that the center

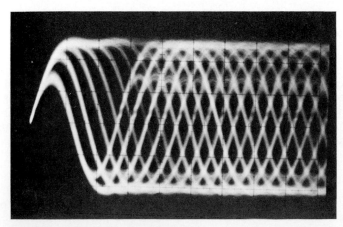

FIG. 9.32   Eye diagram of the EFM signal.

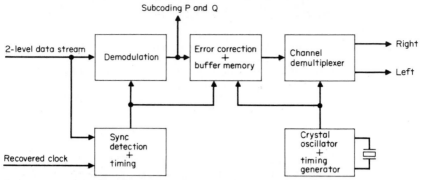

FIG. 9.33 Block diagram of digital signal processing.

of the eye is not in the center of the amplitude. This is called *asymmetry*, a kind of pit distortion. It cannot be avoided when disks are produced in large quantities because of changes resulting from variations in mastering and stamping parameters as well as differences in the players used for playback. Accordingly, a form of feedback digitizer, using the fact that the dc component of the EFM signal is zero, is recommended. In addition, the clock for timing signals is regenerated with a PLL circuit locked to the channel-bit frequency (4.3218 MHz).

Digital Signal Processing. Figure 9.33 is a block diagram of digital signal processing. The demodulation of EFM can be accomplished by using the conversion process shown in Figs. 9.8 and 9.12. This provides the digital audio data and parities for error correction (CIRC). At the same time, the subcoding that directly follows the synchronization signal is demodulated and sent to the control and display block. The data and parities are then temporarily stored in a buffer memory (2K bytes) for the CIRC decoder circuit. The parity bits can be used here to correct errors or merely to detect them if they cannot be corrected. Although CIRC is one of the most powerful error-correcting codes, if more errors than a permissible maximum occur, they can only be detected and used to provide estimated data by linear interpolation between preceding and new data.

At the same time the CIRC buffer memory operates as the deinterleaver of the CIRC and is used for time-base correction (TBC). If the data are written into the memory by means of the recovered clock signal with the PLL and then read out by means of the crystal clock after a certain amount of data has been stored, data can be arranged in accordance with a stable timing rate. In this way *wow* and *flutter* of the digital audio signal are reduced to a level equal to the stability of the crystal oscillator.

Analog Signal Processing. The error-corrected and time-base-corrected digital data must be converted into the analog values that they represent. This is the role of the digital-to-analog converter (DAC), and the necessary conditions for the CD system are:

1. 16-bit resolution
2. Conversion speed of at least 15 μs
3. Low cost (monolithic integrated circuit)

For these requirements, several types of conversion methods have been developed. They are:

1. R-2R ladder network

2. Dynamic element matching (DEM)

3. Integration method using a high-frequency clock

The popular R-2R ladder-type schematic diagram is shown in Fig. 9.34.

At the last stage of analog signal processing is the low-pass filter to reduce the energy outside the band of the audible frequency range (20 Hz to 20 kHz). Instead

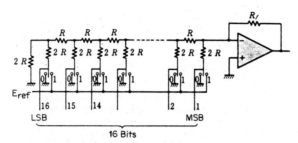

FIG. 9.34   Type R-2R digital-to-analog converter.

of using only the analog filter, a combination of a digital oversampling filter with a simple analog filter has recently become popular. A block diagram is shown in Fig. 9.35.

9.2.4   Applications of Compact-Disk System

Two extended applications of the CD system are described in this section. One is the so-called CD-ROM (read-only memory). The other is the optical video disk with digital sound.

Read-Only Memory (ROM).   The CD-ROM system, based on the CD system, has been designed for use as data storage for computers. Its data format is shown in Fig. 9.36. In a data track the data are divided into addressable blocks of 2352 sequential bytes. Block size is based on a subcode frame equal to 98 frames of the CD format. One block contains:

$$\text{Sync field} \ = \ 12 \text{ bytes}$$
$$\text{Header field} \ = \ 4 \text{ bytes}$$

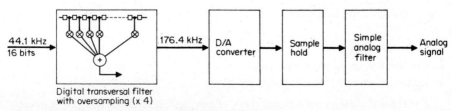

FIG. 9.35   Digital-to-analog conversion using digital filtering.

User-data field = 2048 bytes

Auxiliary-data field = 288 bytes

A new error correction code (ECC) is added by using the auxiliary-data field because the interpolation after CIRC cannot be used for digital data. The format is shown in Fig. 9.37.

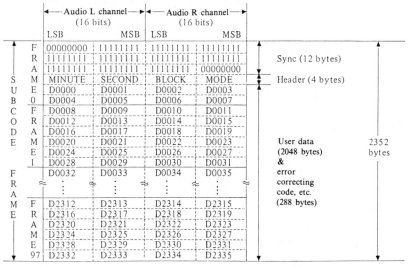

FIG. 9.36 Block diagram of the compact-disk ROM.

	0	1	2	•	•	•	40	41	42	
0	0000*	0001	0002	••••	••••	••••	0040	0041	0042	Header
1	0043	0044	0045	••••	••••	••••	0083	0084	0085	4 bytes
2	0086	0087	0088	••••	••••	••••		0127	0128	+
3	0129	0130	0131	••••	••••			0170	0171	User Data
4	0172	0173	••••	••••					0214	2048 bytes
•									•	+
•										EDC (CRCC)
•	P sequence				Q sequence				•	4 bytes
•										+
•									•	Space
•										8 bytes
21	0903	0904	••••	••••					0945	
22	0946	0947	0948	••••	••••	••••	••••	0987	0988	/2†
23	0989	0990	0991	••••	••••	••••	••••	1030	1031	
24	1032	1033	1034	••••	••••	••••	1072	1073	1074	Parity P
25	1075	1076	1077	••••	••••	••••	1115	1116	1117	172 bytes /2
26	1118	1119	1120	••••	1143					Parity Q
27	1144	1145	1146	••••	1169					104 bytes/2
	0	1	2	•	25					

* Consecutive 16-bit words in a block without sync.

† There are two planes for this ECC; the first plane contains the MSB of words, and the second plane contains the LSB. On each plane, the same ECC is defined.

FIG. 9.37 Configuration of the layered ECC.

The system specification is as follows:

Memory capacity = 60 min × 60 s × 75 subcodes

$$× 2048 \text{ bytes} = 540 \text{ Mbytes/side}$$

Video Disk with Digital Sound. Since in the optical video disk format analog stereo signals are recorded, the digital system was developed to improve audio

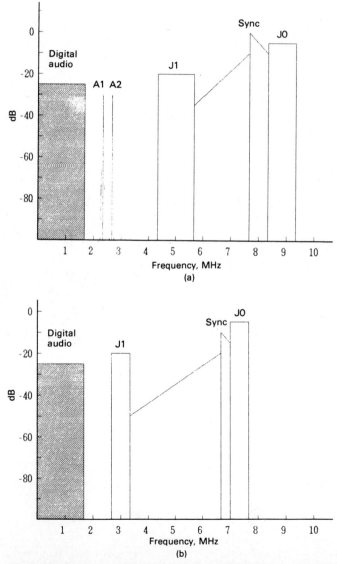

FIG. 9.38 Spectrum of the combined compact-disk format for NTSC and PAL video format standards. (*a*) NTSC format. (*b*) PAL format.

quality. The spectrum of the combined digital audio and National Television System Committee (NTSC) and PAL video formats is shown in Fig. 9.38. The principle is to record the CD format channel signals in the gaps of the frequency spectrum of the video disk format. First, the two-level output of the CD modulator is low-pass-filtered with a cutoff frequency of approximately 1.75 MHz. After low-frequency preemphasis, the signal is applied to the pulse-width input of the video disk modulator (Fig. 9.39).

In the player, the EFM signal is reconstructed by deemphasis and low-pass filtering. Then the signal is passed to a normal CD decoder, which eventually supplies the high-quality audio signal. To use simple filter playback, the nonuniform group delay of the playback filter is precompensated in the encoding stage.

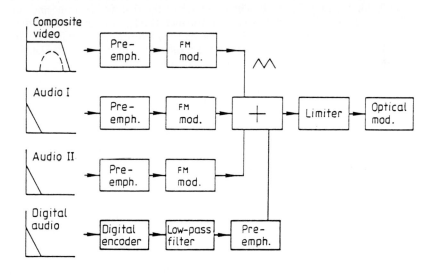

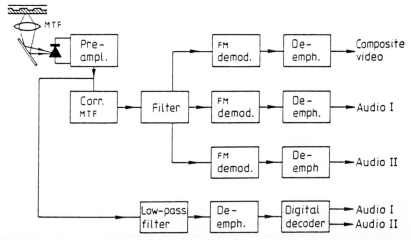

FIG. 9.39 Block diagram of the signal processing of an optical video disk player (NTSC format).

9.3 CONFIGURATION AND MANUFACTURING PROCESS OF COMPACT DISKS

This section describes the configuration and manufacturing process of compact disks: the basic specifications, the signal characteristics produced by the pit, and the mastering and replication sequence to produce disks.

9.3.1 Disk Specification and Pit Geometry

Disk Specification. The specifications and dimensions of the compact disk are shown in Table 9.5 and Fig. 9.40. The diameter of the disk is 120 mm, and the center hole is 15 mm. The signal is read out through the 1.2-mm transparent disk substrate. The disk rotates counterclockwise as seen from the reading side. The spiral track pitch is 1.6 μm and is read out from the inside to the outside. Density is about 16,000 tracks per inch. The track length is given by

$$l = \frac{1}{p} \int_{r_i}^{r_o} 2\pi r \; dr = \frac{\pi}{p} (r_o^2 - r_i^2) = \frac{S}{p} \qquad (9.12)$$

where p = track pitch
S = area of program zone
r_o = outside diameter of program area
r_i = inside diameter of program area

TABLE 9.5 Specifications of Compact Disk

Readout mode	In reflections through transparent disk
Track shape	One spiral
Outer diameter of disk	120 ± 0.3 mm
Disk weight	14 to 33 g
Diameter of center hole	15 + 0.1/0 mm
Thickness of disk	1.2 + 0.3, −0.1 mm
Clamping area	26 to 33 mm
Maximum deflection	±0.4 mm
Maximum angular deviation (skew)	±0.6°
Refractive index of substrate	1.55 ± 0.1
Maximum birefringence	100 nm
Reflectivity	70% minimum
Starting diameter of program area	50 mm
Maximum diameter of program area	116 mm
Track pitch	1.6 ± 0.1 μm
Sense of disk rotation	Counterclockwise as seen from readout side
Scanning velocity	1.2 to 1.4 m/s
Maximum vertical acceleration	10 m/s^2 at scanning velocity
Maximum eccentricity	±70 μm
Maximum radial acceleration	0.4 m/s^2
High-frequency modulation amplitude	
I_3/I_{top}	0.3 to 0.7
I_{11}/I_{top}	≧0.6
Track-following signal magnitude	0.04 to 0.07 at 0.1-μm radial offset
Average block error rate	Less than 3%

The program area starts at a 50-mm diameter and ends at a maximum of 116 mm. The total track length derived from Eq. (9.12) is about 5 km. The lead-in and lead-out zones are used for controls of the player system such as track access and automatic playback. To maximize playing time, the CD is recorded by the CLV method. The scanning linear velocity of the disk (v) is specified as 1.2 to 1.4 m/s. The revolution speed decreases from 500 to 200 r/min. However, the frequency response of the readout signal is the same at any disk radius.

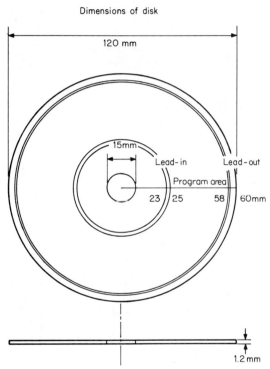

FIG. 9.40   Dimensions of the program area of the compact disk.

The playing time of a music program (T) is given by

$$T = l/v \qquad (9.13)$$

From this equation, the maximum recording time of a CD is about 74 min at 1.2 m/s.

Cross Section of the Compact Disk.   Figure 9.41 shows a cross section of the compact disk. The signal is picked up by a focused laser beam through a transparent substrate. Its 1.2-mm thickness prevents signal disturbance by dust or fingerprints. The material of the substrate must satisfy various optical and mechanical requirements such as birefringence, absence of defects, and reliability. Polycarbonates, polymethyl methacrylates, and glass are suitable for disk-production requirements.

The replicated pits on the signal surface are about 0.1 μm deep, 0.5 μm wide, and several micrometers long. The signal surface is covered with an aluminum layer to reflect a laser beam. This reflective layer is coated with ultraviolet-light-cured resin to protect it from scratches, moisture, and other harmful effects. The label is printed on the protective layer by a silk-screen method.

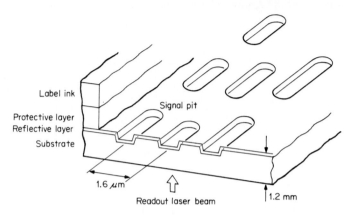

FIG. 9.41 Cross section of a compact disk.

Pit Profile and Signal Characteristics.   The principle of CD signal detection is based on the diffraction phenomenon of a laser spot caused by the *phase pit*. A reading laser beam and pit geometry determine signal performance from an optical pickup. The relation between pit shape and signal amplitude when the phase pit is illuminated by a readout laser beam is reviewed in the following paragraphs.

Pit Depth.   There is a $2\pi d/\lambda$ phase difference between the reflected light rays from a pit and those from a land (see Fig. 9.42). When the phase difference is π

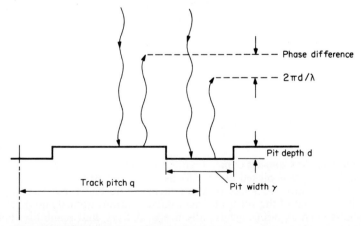

FIG. 9.42 Phase difference of a reflected beam.

$= \lambda/2$, the modulation index of the reflected beam is at a maximum value by the resultant diffraction. Since a laser beam is reflected from a pit and the pit exists inside the transparent substrate of which the refractive index is $n = 1.5$, the $\lambda/4n$ pit depth gives the maximum high-frequency signal amplitude:

$$\lambda/4n = 0.78 \ \mu\text{m}/4 \times 1.5 = 0.13 \ \mu\text{m} \tag{9.14}$$

On the other hand, the push-pull signal for tracking is at a maximum value when the pit depth is $\lambda/8n$. In view of the performance of high-frequency and push-pull signals the pit depth of the replica has been chosen at about 0.1 μm.

Pit Width. This parameter also affects signal quality, viz., the amplitude, distortion, and frequency response of high-frequency and track-following signals. The pit width is equal to a recording spot size of 0.5 $\sim$ 0.7 μm in mastering.

Figure 9.43 shows the relation between the signal amplitude and the square cross-section pit profile.

Pit Length. Pit length is related to the pulse width of the CD signal format. With a scanning velocity of 1.25 m/s, there are nine different pits on the signal surface: 0.87, 1.16, 1.45, 1.74, 2.02, 2.31, 2.60, 2.89, and 3.18 μm. Each pit length is effected by the disk-production processing operation and the readout charac-

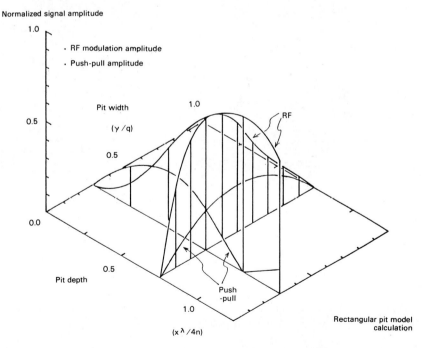

Pit period ≫ spot size on disk surface.

FIG. 9.43 Normalized signal amplitude versus pit shape. Example of RF and push-pull signal amplitude: a curved surface that is determined by RF or push-pull amplitude intersects a pit depth = 0.75 constant plane and a pit width = 0.30 constant plane. $I_{pp} \propto (\beta/p) \cdot \sin (\gamma/q) \cdot \sin (2\phi)$. Rectangular-pit model calculation. Pit period ≫ spot size on disk surface.

teristics of the optical pickup. This phenomenon is called asymmetry. Within a certain range asymmetry is not a problem because the correction circuit corrects it automatically.

Pit Edges.   The replicated pit does not have an ideal square cross section but does have a slope of pit edges (see Fig. 9.44). This pit shape is called the "soccer

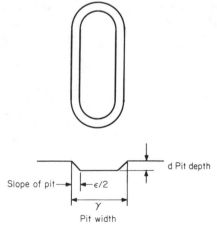

FIG. 9.44 "Soccer stadium" model.

stadium" model. The signal characteristics can be simulated by using a computer. An example of a simulated signal is shown in Fig. 9.45.

9.3.2 Premastering and Mastering Process

Figure 9.46 shows the compact-disk manufacturing process. *Premastering* means the preparation of an edited master tape to be used in the recording process. *Mastering* is the process of making a glass master and nickel stamper.

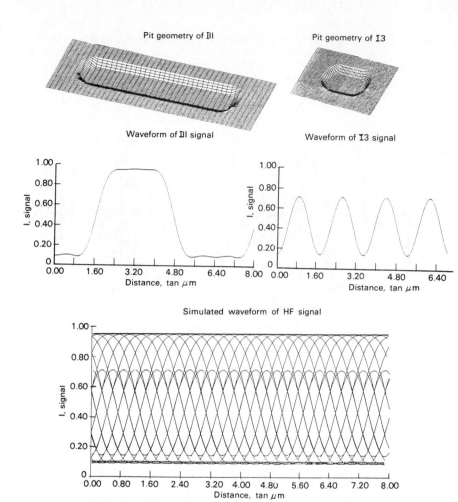

Pit geometry of I11

Pit geometry of I3

Waveform of I11 signal

Waveform of I3 signal

Simulated waveform of HF signal

FIG. 9.45 Simulated waveform of a high-frequency signal.

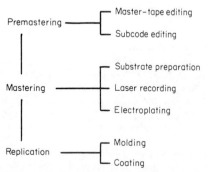

Premastering ——— Master-tape editing
                      — Subcode editing

Mastering ——— Substrate preparation
                — Laser recording
                — Electroplating

Replication ——— Molding
                — Coating

FIG. 9.46 Manufacturing process of the compact disk.

Editing the Master Tape. The editing system for the master tape is shown in Fig. 9.47. Music programs are edited in the ¾-in videotape cassette. After editing a music program, the table-of-contents (TOC) information is inserted in the beginning of the cassette. The completed master tape is then used in the laser recording process of mastering.

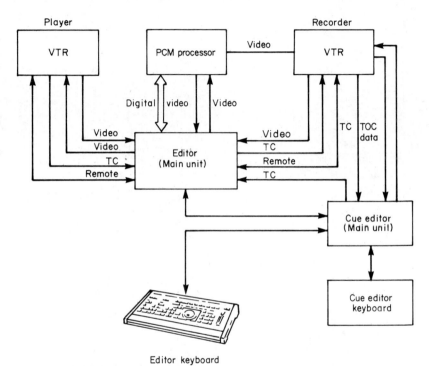

FIG. 9.47 Editing system for the master tape.

Mastering-Process Flow Sequence. Figure 9.48 shows the mastering-process flow sequence. During mastering 10 billion pits are made on the thin photosensitive layer. Mastering operations are carried out in a clean-air room to prevent deleterious contamination.

Preparation of Glass Master. A highly polished and cleaned glass substrate is prepared in the mastering process. Flatness, smoothness, and lack of defects in the glass are important to produce good-quality disks. A positive photoresist about 0.1 μm thick is coated on the glass surface by a spinning method. The positive photoresist is suitable for the production of optical disks because of its high resolution, smooth surface, and polarity of matrix. An ellipsometer is used to measure the resist thickness in order to determine the pit depth.

Laser Recording. A photoresist on the glass is exposed by a laser spot that is intensely modulated by a CD signal. The recording laser should satisfy the following requirements:

1. Capability of producing a small spot (about 0.5 μm)
2. Sensitivity to photosensitive material
3. Continuous-wave emission and light-source stability

HeCd laser (441.6 μm) and Ar ion laser (457.9 μm) are suitable for recording.

A high-speed light modulator is also an important part of a laser recording system. An acoustooptic modulator (AOM) which uses ultrasonic waves and an

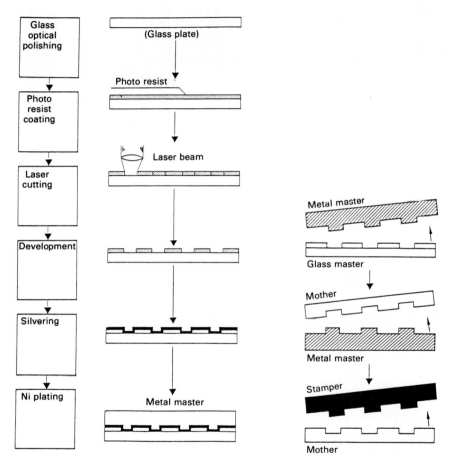

FIG. 9.48 Mastering-process flow sequence.

electrooptic modulator (EOM) which makes use of the Pockels effect are employed to modulate laser light. Recording quality primarily depends on the performance of the *master code cutter,* the accuracy of track pitch, scanning velocity, and stability of exposure. Figure 9.49 is a block diagram of the master code cutter.

After the subsequent development process the exposed photoresist is washed away, leaving the signal pits.

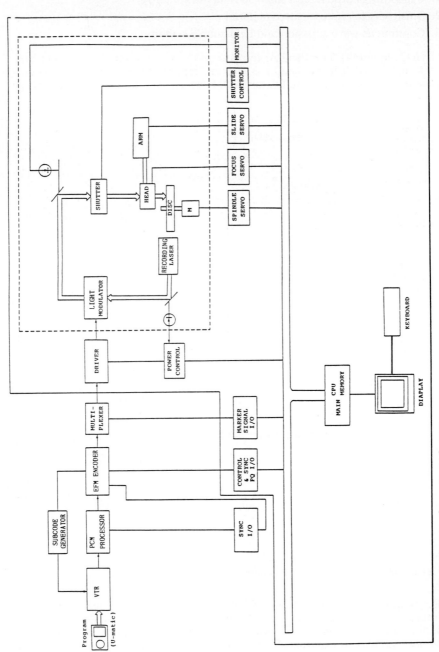

FIG. 9.49 Block diagram of a master code cutter.

Stamper Production. Since the molding process needs a high temperature and high pressure, a glass master cannot be used. The information pits must be transferred to a nickel stamper.

As shown in Fig. 9.48, silvering metallizes on the signal surface. After silvering, nickel is electroplated to make a metal master about 300 μm thick. The process from a metal master to a stamper is similar to that of an analog long-playing (LP) disk. Several mothers and stampers can be obtained from one metal master by use of the matrix.

9.3.3 Replication Process

Replication-Process Flow Sequence. Replication is the process whereby many CD replicas are produced from the stamper. The flow sequence is shown in Fig. 9.50.

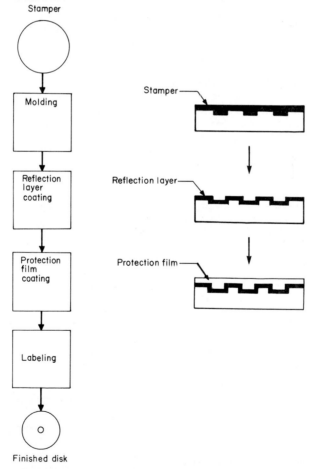

FIG. 9.50 Replication-process flow sequence.

Molding Method. There are about 9 Gbits of information on the signal surface of a CD stamper. The molding process is designed to make many good replicas with high productivity. Typical molding methods are outlined below.

Injection Molding. In this method melted resin is injected at high pressure into a mold and solidified (see Fig. 9.51). Injection molding is widely used in CD production because of its high productivity.

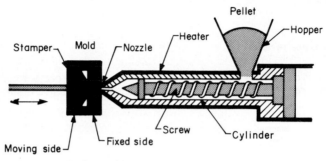

FIG. 9.51   Injection mold.

Compression Molding. The stamper is attached to one side of the molding die, and both sides are heated by steam. Plastic cake is then inserted and molded by a hydraulic press (Fig. 9.52). LP disks are made by this method.

Photopolymerization Method. Figure 9.53 shows the photopolymerization process. A transparent plate is prepared, and ultraviolet-light-curing resin is inserted between plate and stamper. From the transparent-plate side, an exposure to ultraviolet light is made, after which the resin is cured.

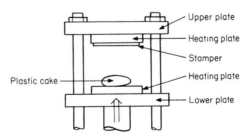

FIG. 9.52   Compression mold.

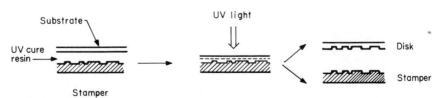

FIG. 9.53   Photopolymerization process.

1. Mastering

Digital 2-channel recording is done on a 3/4 ″ U-matic tape, while subcode editing is performed to make the tape complete with all the data necessary for cutting.

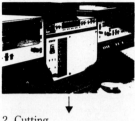

2. Cutting

A glass master is made by laser-cutting data in real time on the photoresist layer of a glass plate.

3. Stamper Production

A metal master is produced from the glass master, a metal mother from the metal master, and production stampers from the metal mother.

4. Disk Injection Molding

Injection molding of polycarbonate resin results in volume production of disks from the same stamper.

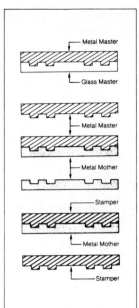

Metal Master

Glass Master

Metal Master

Metal Mother

Stamper

Metal Mother

Stamper

5. Reflective-Layer Coating

Aluminum is evaporated and deposited on the signal surface of each disk to enable data detection with a laser beam.

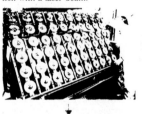

6. Protective-Layer Coating

Ultraviolet curing resin is applied over the aluminum coating and exposed to ultraviolet rays to form a transparent protective layer.

Transparent Poly-Carbonate Disk

Reflective-Layer Coating

Protective Layer Coating

7. Inspection

The disks are quality-tested invidually, using a computerized automatic inspection system.

8. Label Printing/Packaging

Each disk is labeled and wrapped for shipment as the final product.

FIG. 9.54 Production process of the compact disk.

The most appropriate molding method is selected, for example, by conducting a study of the materials to be used, producibility, and facilities.

Coating. After molding, a layer of metal aluminum is evaporated onto the pit surface. Subsequently, a protective layer is spun onto the reflective layer. This protective layer consists of ultraviolet-light-curing resin about 10 μm thick.

The label is printed on the protective layer. The compact disk is now finished and ready for shipment after final inspection. Figure 9.54 shows the complete production process of the compact disk.

BIBLIOGRAPHY

Bouwhuis, G., and J. J. M. Braat: "Recording and Reading of Information on Optical Disks," in *Applied Optics and Optical Engineering,* vol. IX, Academic, New York, 1983, chap. 3.

———, ———, A. Pasman, G. van Rosmalen, and K. A. Schouhamer Immink: *Principles of Optical Disc Systems,* Adam Hilger Ltd., Bristol, England, 1985.

Driessen, L. M. H. E., and L. B. Vries: "Performance Calculations of the Compact Disc Error Correcting Code on a Memoryless Channel," International Conference on Video and Data Recording, University of Southampton (April 1982).

Immink, K. A. Schouhamer, A. H. Hoogendijk, and J. A. Kahlman: "Digital Audio Modulation in the PAL and NTSC Laser Vision Video Disc Coding Formats," presented at the 74th Convention of the Audio Engineering Society, New York (1983), preprint 1997.

Isailovic, J.: *Videodisc and Optical Memory Systems,* Prentice-Hall, Englewood Cliffs, N.J., 1985.

Miyaoka, S.: "Digital Audio Is Compact and Rugged," *IEEE Spectrum* (March 1984).

Nakajima, H., and H. Ogawa: *Compact Audio Disc,* TAB Books, Blue Ridge Summit, Pa. (to be published).

Odaka, K., T. Furuya, and A. Taki: "LSI's for Digital Signal Processing to Be Used in Compact Disc Digital Audio Players," presented at the 71st Convention of the Audio Engineering Society (March 1982), preprint 1860 (G-5).

——— and L. B. Vries: "CIRC: The Error Correcting Code for the Compact Disc Digital Audio System," presented at the Premier Audio Engineering Society Conference (June 1982).

Ogawa, H., and K. A. Schouhamer Immink: "EFM—The Modulation Method for the Compact Disc Digital Audio System," presented at the Premier Audio Engineering Society Conference (June 1982).

Philips Tech. Rev., **40**(6) (1982). This issue contains four articles about the CD system.

Sako, Y., and T. Suzuki: "CD-ROM System," Topical Meeting on Optical Data Storage, WCCI (October 1985).

Vries, L. B., et al.: "The Compact Disc Digital Audio System: Modulation and Error Correction," presented at the 67th Convention of the Audio Engineering Society (October 1980), preprint 1674 (H-8).

CHAPTER 10

ANALOG MAGNETIC-TAPE RECORDING AND REPRODUCTION

E. Stanley Busby, Jr.

Senior Staff Engineer, Ampex Corporation, Redwood City, California

10.1 PRINCIPLES OF MAGNETIC RECORDING

10.1.1 History

The Danish inventor Valdemar Poulsen made the first magnetic sound recorder. In 1898 he passed the current from a telephone through a recording head held against a spiral of steel wire wound on a brass drum. Upon playback, the magnetic variations in the wire induced enough voltage in the head to power a telephone receiver. Amplification was not available at the time.

The hit of the Paris Exposition of 1900, Poulsen's recorder won the grand prize. In this magnetic analog of Edison's acoustic recorder (which impressed a groove on a rotating tinfoil-covered drum), one whole cylinder held only 30 s of sound. In a few years, the weak and highly distorted output of Poulsen's device was vastly improved by adding a fixed magnetizing current, called *bias,* to the output of the telephone. This centered the signal current variations on the steepest part of the curve of remanent magnetism, greatly improving the gain and linearity of the system.

In 1923, two researchers working for the U.S. Navy first applied high-frequency ac bias. This eliminated even-order distortion, greatly reduced the noise induced by the surface roughness of the medium, and improved the amplitude of the recovered signal. Except in some toys, ac bias is used in all audio recorders.

Wire recording, further developed in the United States, found wide use during World War II and entered the home recording market by the late 1940s. Wire recorders had no capstan and pinch roller to establish uniform speed. Instead, a relatively large takeup spool, having a small difference between empty and full diameters, rotated at a constant angular speed. The wire speed therefore varied slightly between start and finish. As long as the change in diameter during playback equals the change during record, tonal changes do not occur.

A recorder using solid steel tape on large reels was developed in Europe.

Licensed for manufacture by Marconi and others, it was used by European broadcasters before 1940. In some installations, a wire cage around the recorder protected operators from the consequences of breakage of the spring-steel tape.

Development of coated magnetic tape began in Germany in 1928. The first tapes consisted of black carbonyl iron particles coated on paper, using a technique developed by Fritz Pfleumer to bronze-plate cigarette tips. By 1935 Badische Anilin und Soda Fabrik (BASF), a division of I. G. Farben, had produced cellulose acetate base film coated with gamma ferric oxide. During the war years, the tapes used for broadcasting were a suspension of oxide particles throughout the thickness of the acetate. Beginning in 1939, polyester substrates, which have superior strength and tear resistance, replaced acetate.

During World War II, German broadcasters used Magnetophons made by the Allgemeine Elektrizität Gesellschaft (AEG). At the end of the war, a U.S. Signal Corps major, John T. Mullin, obtained two machines. Too large for a mail sack, they were dismantled and gradually shipped home to California in pieces along with 50 rolls of tape. Unlike the military field dictation recorders, which used dc bias, the machines used for broadcasting were equipped with high-frequency ac bias.

In 1946, using modified electronics, Mullin demonstrated a Magnetophon at a San Francisco meeting of the Institute of Radio Engineers. Among the engineers attending the meeting were Harold Lindsay and Charles Ginsburg. Both men were to influence greatly the future of magnetic recording.

Mullin and his partner William Palmer, a San Francisco filmmaker, took a machine to Hollywood to demonstrate it at the Metro-Goldwyn-Mayer film studios. Alexander M. Poniatoff, founder of the Ampex Corporation, then a maker of electric motors, heard a demonstration. In search of a postwar product, he determined then to develop a tape recorder. He hired Lindsay to lead the design team.

Mullin demonstrated his recorder to the renowned singer Bing Crosby. Recorded on disk, Crosby's Sunday-evening radio show had such poor sound quality that the sponsor began pressing him for live broadcast. Crosby disliked live broadcast intensely and hired Mullin to record the 26 shows of the 1947–1948 season. These were recorded on the captured Magnetophons by using the captured tape. Lacking confidence in the new technology, the American Broadcasting Company (ABC) network transferred each show to disk for broadcast.

Contractual arrangements with others prevented Mullin from providing any circuit details to Lindsay. Nevertheless, Lindsay completed a prototype and demonstrated it to Crosby. Twenty recorders were ordered by the ABC network, saving the faltering company.

In the absence of wartime restrictions, applications of the new technology spread quickly. In 1949 performers Les Paul and Mary Ford pioneered the technique of recording multiple parts performed by one person. Recorders were used to overcome the 3-h time displacement between the east and west coasts of the United States and Canada. Used as data recorders, they aided vibration analysis, medical research, and other endeavors involving signals occupying the audio spectrum.

About 1950 the recording of a frequency-modulation (FM) carrier, or of a pulse-code-modulated signal, extended the low-frequency response to zero. Recording of strain gauges, pressure sensors, depth sensors, seismic events, and other slowly varying signals became possible. Called *instrumentation recorders,* these machines recorded in automotive test vehicles, flights of experimental airframes, submarines, and space vehicles.

In the 1950s developments in magnetic recording diverged into five paths, each growing within its own domain, and a sixth path which used the technical advances made by the others.

1. The professional audio recording industry developed multitrack recorders, portable audio recorders, electronic editing techniques, and machine synchronizers which can speed-lock an audio reproducer to other audio recorders, television recorders, or film cameras.

2. Several researchers extended the high-frequency response of magnetic recorders to include the wide bandwidth of a (then monochromatic) television video signal. At the time, kinescope recordings were made by photographing a TV picture tube on 16-mm movie film. Sprocketed film is less stable positionally than television. *Picture weave* made recordings obvious. The input-output curve of film did not complement that of monochrome television. Processing dirt and chemical stains were the rule. These flaws seriously impacted the enjoyment of television.

Mullin, by then employed by Crosby Laboratories, developed an 11-track recorder which divided the video bandwidth into 10 equal portions. The first to be demonstrated, the recorder failed to achieve acceptance by broadcasters. The recorder was modified to serve as an instrumentation recorder and, along with the laboratories, sold to the Minnesota Mining and Manufacturing Company to seed a line of wideband data recorders.

The Radio Corporation of America (RCA) showed an experimental machine having four tracks, one for each of the three primary colors and one for sound and synchronization. Its effort and a similar one by the British Broadcasting Corporation (BBC) failed for lack of market support.

Ginsburg, then employed by Poniatoff, developed the first practical videotape recorder. It used 2-in-wide tape and a rotating drum with four heads spaced 90° apart around its periphery. One television picture required 32 traverses across the width of the tape. Further developed over 25 years, the technology was expanded to adapt to color television, stereo audio, longer playing time, and automated editing methods. Given the name *quadruplex,* the technology was extended to the recording of digitized video. A quadruplex digital TV recorder was demonstrated in 1976 but was not commercialized.

Helical-scan recording replaced the quadruplex method. Long diagonal tracks are recorded at a shallow angle across 1-in-wide tape. Each track contains one television field. Less expensive to operate and maintain than quadruplex recorders, helical-scan recorders were capable of visual "tricks," for example, stopping and slow motion.

A television recorder must accommodate the associated sound. In both technologies, sound is recorded longitudinally, as in audio recorders. The audio tracks are located at or near the edges of the tape, the area most difficult for the rotating video heads to contact reliably.

The use of audio FM carriers, written by the video heads, was borrowed from home video technology for use in ½-in professional recording formats. This method offers excellent performance but is not amenable to editing audio separately from video, nor can it easily offer more than two channels.

3. As early as 1950 multichannel data recorders became available. They offered a wide range of speeds to provide time-base expansion and contraction and bandwidths to 4 MHz per track, with tape speeds to 240 in/s. Adapted for data recording, rotary-head recorders achieved data rates of 500 Mbit/s. All rotary-head machines record at least one track along the length of the tape.

4. Audio recorders for the home, introduced in the early 1950s, and the pre-recorded tapes provided for them were offered as long-life replacements for disks. These fell victim to the development of small lightweight recorders in which a narrow tape and its reels were housed in a small cassette. The ease of handling brought commercial success.

Very small battery-powered playback machines, having counterrotating fly-wheels to cancel the angular acceleration induced by walking or running, are part of the street scene. They have become so popular that laws have been enacted in many jurisdictions prohibiting their use by motor-vehicle drivers lest the drivers not hear sirens and other alarms.

The insulation of the public from the mechanical niceties of preparing a reel of tape for use was an essential element in the introduction of *video* recorders into the home, all of which now use cassette tape. At first, television audio recording used the conventional longitudinal method, with limited performance. By 1983 two audio channels were impressed on frequency-modulated carriers and recorded along with the video by using the video record head. The audio perfor-mance of these home systems rivals or exceeds the best of the extant professional analog recorders.

5. Magnetic *disk* recorders, on which the record is either a spiral track on a flat platter of magnetic medium or takes the form of concentric circles on it, are used as computer peripherals to record digital data. A flat circular magnetic medium for audio recording was briefly offered as a literal replacement for the grooved phonograph disk, to be used by radio disk jockeys.

6. Recording for dictation at first infrequently employed disk recorders, then increasingly wire recorders, then reel-to-reel tape recorders, and finally, in great numbers, cassette tape recorders. A microcassette recorder was developed, with its tape usage tailored to the limited frequency response needed for intelligible speech. The entire device, with batteries, is smaller than a packet of cigarettes.

10.1.2 General Recording and Reproduction Theory

The essential elements of a magnetic recorder are shown in Fig. 10.1. A *supply reel* holds unused tape. A *takeup reel* collects used tape. A *capstan* establishes a constant linear tape speed. These mechanical elements combine to move the tape past the following:

1. *An erase head (optional):* This is not a necessary element but is conve-nient. If it is not used, the tape must be erased elsewhere, usually on the reel in a device designed for bulk erasure. More information about erase heads can be found in Sec. 10.4.

2. *A recording head (mandatory):* The magnetic particles on the tape are influenced by the signal current in the record head as they pass by its gap. A bias signal is added which is either subsonic (dc) or supersonic (ac). It is important to remember that the addition of bias is a simple linear mix, and no modulation takes place. Additional details about record heads and recording are in Secs. 10.4 and 10.6.

3. *A reproducing head (the record head can be used after rewinding):* The magnetized particles on the tape have fields which can link with the metal struc-ture of the head and thereby induce a voltage in its winding. For more details about reproducing heads and reproduction see Secs. 10.4 and 10.5.

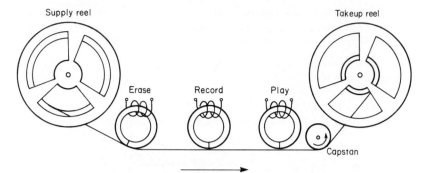

FIG. 10.1   Essential elements of a tape recorder.

Recording Methods.   If the signal current in the record head is directly proportional to the input signal, the recording is a *direct* recording. Almost all analog audio recorders use direct recording.

If the record current is a frequency-modulated carrier on which the input signal is impressed, the recorder uses the *FM method.* Seldom employed for audio recording, FM recording is useful when the low-frequency response must be extended to zero or when the tape speed is too slow to support adequate frequency response, as in home video recorders. In this last case, two FM carriers are recorded by the rotating video heads.

If the record current is a series of *binary* pulses whose repetition *time* varies according to the input signal, the recording method is called *pulse-position modulation.* This is not a digital recording in the arithmetic sense but is a form of phase modulation analytically similar to FM.

If the record current is a series of binary bits or a carrier modulated by binary bits, the method is called *pulse-code modulation* (PCM). In PCM, the input signal is sampled at a uniform rate that is greater than twice the input frequency range. Each sample is converted to a binary number, typically using 16 bits. The binary numbers are recorded, then later reproduced and converted to voltages. PCM optical disk recording is discussed in Chap. 9, and PCM tape recording is found in Chap. 11.

In direct recording, the magnitude of the remanent magnetism left on the tape is a function of the input signal. In all other methods, it is constant, and the data are stored in the form of time variations or numeric values. Also, all other methods record at or near the maximum magnetic field that the tape can sustain. A large constant recording field causes considerable erasure of previous recordings. Some systems therefore need no erase head. All audio direct recorders, aside from toys, have an erase head.

Physical and Magnetic Relations.   The *maximum* signal which can be recovered by a reproduce head is a function of many physical, electrical, and magnetic parameters. Some of these are defined in the following short glossary:

1. *Wavelength:*   The distance along the tape, in the direction of tape motion, which is occupied by one cycle of a recorded signal. It is given by

$$\lambda = \frac{v}{f} \qquad (10.1)$$

where λ = wavelength, any unit of length
　　　v = tape speed, same unit per second
　　　f = frequency of recorded signal, Hz

2. *Magnetomotive force (F):*　The magnetic analog of electrical voltage, often expressed in ampere-turns, the product of a current and the number of turns in a coil of wire through which the current flows.

3. *Magnetic field (H):*　The magnetomotive force per unit length. It is usually expressed in oersteds. The relation between oersteds and ampere-turns is

$$H = \frac{1000 \times \text{ampere-turns}}{4\pi \times \text{length (meters)}} \tag{10.2}$$

4. *Flux density (B):*　The intensity of a magnetic field per unit of cross-sectional area. A magnetic analog of electrical current, flux density is usually expressed in gauss.

5. *Permeability:*　The magnetic analog of electrical conductance. The permeability of air is taken as unity. The permeability of metals and alloys used in recording range from the low thousands to the tens of thousands. For a given magnetomotive force, the resulting flux density is proportional to permeability. Initial permeability (at low flux densities) is given by

$$\mu = 1 + \frac{B}{H} \tag{10.3}$$

where μ = permeability, a ratio
　　　H = magnetizing field
　　　B = resulting flux density

6. *Saturation:*　The maximum flux density that a material can sustain. As an applied magnetomotive force is increased, the permeability diminishes, until, at saturation, the permeability is unity and the flux density fails to increase further. In general, materials with high permeability have low saturation. It is important to select record-head materials, for example, which do not saturate at a lower level than the tape material. The efficiency of reproduce heads is maximized by choosing materials of the highest permeability.

7. *Remanence:*　The ability of a magnetic material to retain magnetism after a magnetomotive force has been removed. Permanent magnets and recording media are selected for high remanence. Record and reproduce heads, shields, and transformer cores are chosen for high permeability and low remanence.

8. *Coercivity:*　The measure of the magnetomotive force required to demagnetize a previously saturated remanent material.

9. *Squareness ratio:*　The ratio of the saturation flux density to the remanent flux. High squareness ratio is a desirable property of recording media.

10. *Weber:*　A unit of flux. An ac magnetic field of 1 Wb at a frequency of 1 Hz, if linked with one turn of wire, will induce 1 V. Recording levels are typically expressed in terms of nanowebers per meter of track width.

Basic Direct Recording.　With the addition of ac bias, the remanent magnetism remaining on the tape is a reasonably linear function of the signal current in the record head. The linearity and frequency response are a function of the magnitude of the ac bias current, treated in greater detail in Sec. 10.6.1.

Basic Direct Reproduction.   The maximum voltage available at the reproduce-head terminals is directly proportional to the track width, the remanent magnetism of the tape material, the rate of change of magnetism (and therefore, frequency), and the number of turns of wire on the head assembly. The basic expression is

$$e = KN \frac{d\phi}{dt} \qquad (10.4)$$

where e = instantaneous peak induced voltage
  $d\phi$ = rate of change of induced flux
  N = number of turns
  dt = rate of change of time
  K = scale factor, representing all other effects

K is influenced mostly by losses related to short wavelengths. These are discussed in greater detail in Sec. 10.5.1.

10.1.3   Magnetization

Almost all the magnetic properties of materials used in recording stem from the axial spins of the third shell of orbiting electrons of the atom. The electrical charge of the electron rotates, generating a current, which in turn generates a magnetic field. In nonmagnetic materials, electrons occur in pairs having opposing spin, canceling the magnetic effect. Iron, in particular, is heavily unbalanced, and nickel and chromium also exhibit magnetism. Compounds and alloys of these are useful in tape recorders. Applications include motors, transformers, loudspeakers, heads, tape, and shields.

The crystalline structure of magnetic materials includes groupings of millions of atoms whose spin axes are aligned. Each group is called a *domain* and in effect is a tiny saturated magnet. The direction of magnetization can be reversed by the application of a strong opposing field. In demagnetized materials, the direction of magnetization of the domains is randomly distributed, resulting in a net sum of zero.

Hard and Soft Materials.   Figure 10.2*a* illustrates a hysteresis curve of a remanent or hard magnetic material, i.e., one which is difficult to demagnetize and

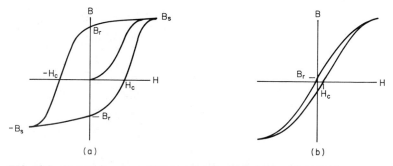

FIG. 10.2   Hysteresis curves of (*a*) a hard material and (*b*) a soft material.

therefore is useful for permanent magnets and recording media. Figure 10.2*b* is a curve representative of a *soft,* easy-to-demagnetize material useful for transformers, heads, and shields.

In Fig. 10.2*b* the curve of initial magnetization shows the result of increasing an applied field on a demagnetized material. Around the origin, the effect is reversible; i.e., upon removal, the material will return to its random state. As the field is increased, the flux density increases as more domains switch direction in response to the applied field.

At point B_s, not only have all domains switched, but those whose spin axes are aiding but are not perfectly aligned have their axes deflected to line up with the applied field. This is known as *saturation.* If the magnetizing field H is removed, the flux density decreases somewhat as the domains that were not perfectly aligned revert to their undeflected axis angle, i.e., not 100 percent aiding but not opposing either. This is shown in Fig. 10.2*a* as point B_r.

The ideal tape particle is a single domain with its spin axis aligned with the lengthwise dimension of the tape. If these alignments were perfect, B_r would equal B_s and the hysteresis loop approach a square. The ratio B_r/B_s, called the *squareness ratio,* is therefore a measure of the success in aligning tape particles during manufacture.

If the applied field is increased in the opposite direction, more and more domains reswitch until point $-H_c$ is reached. Here, half of the domains have switched and half have not, resulting in a net flux density of 0. The force required to reach this point in a previously saturated material is the measure of the coercivity of the material. Figure 10.2 cannot adequately illustrate the magnitude of the difference between soft and hard materials. Reference 1 gives the magnetic and physical characteristics of some useful magnetic materials.

Bias. Figure 10.3*a* is a plot of remanent flux versus an applied field, showing the effect of dc bias. The curve is not symmetric about the bias point; therefore, the spectrum of distortion components of a recorded sine wave will contain even as well as odd multiples of the fundamental frequency. A tape recorded without audio still will generate a signal as the tape moves over the reproduce head. Sur-

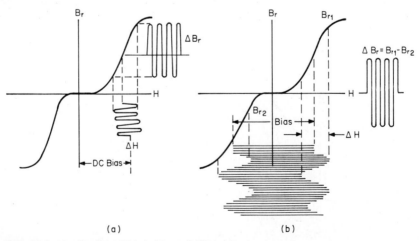

(a)   (b)

FIG. 10.3 Application of (*a*) dc bias and (*b*) ac bias.

face roughness and a coating thickness that varies at audio rates will directly modulate the field in the reproduce head, generating noise.

Figure 10.3*b* illustrates ac bias. The peak-to-peak amplitude of the supersonic signal is constant and is about twice the dc value. The bias signal can be thought of as a high-frequency switching signal, magnetizing for half of the time in one direction and half in the other. The noise performance is vastly improved because the net average magnetization is 0. The sum of the shapes of the upper and lower portions of the curve is such that even-order-harmonic-distortion components of the audio signal cancel. The design measures needed to maintain the advantages of ac bias are discussed in Sec. 10.6.1.

Erasure. Figure 10.4 shows the hysteresis loops traced as a remanent material is exposed to a large, slowly decreasing magnetic field. The net result as the ac field approaches 0 is to randomize the domains, leaving the material demagnetized.

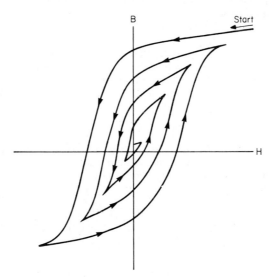

FIG. 10.4   Erasure by a diminishing ac field.

The high-frequency excitation of an erase head is constant, and the diminishing-field effect is obtained as a given spot on the tape moves away from the gap of the head. The choice of frequency and tape speed must cause the tape to experience several field reversals.

10.2   MAGNETIC RECORDING MATERIALS

The active component of magnetic tape is the first of four components:

1. The magnetic material itself.

2. A binder, or glue, which surrounds the magnetic material and holds it to a plastic support.

3. A plastic support, usually polyethylene terephthalate, also known as *polyester*. After coating, if slit into strips, it becomes tape. If punched into circles, it becomes floppy disks.

4. A conductive back coating is applied if the application includes severe winding-speed requirements. Floppy disks are coated on both sides; tape, on one side.

The last three of the components are discussed in Sec. 10.3. There are four magnetic materials in popular use for making tape and a fifth in development.

10.2.1   Iron Oxide

Having a coercivity of 300 to 360 Oe, gamma ferric oxide is by far the most widely used recording material. The first step in its preparation is the precipitation of seeds of geothite [alpha FeO (OH)], from scrap iron dissolved in sulfuric acid, or of lepidocrocite [gamma FeO (OH)], produced from ferrous chloride.

After further growth the seeds are dehydrated to hematite (alpha Fe_2O_3), then reduced to magnetite (Fe_3O_4). It is then oxidized to maghemite (gamma Fe_2O_3), which not only is magnetic but has the desired acicular (rod-shaped) form with an aspect ratio of 5 or 10:1. The length of the particles is 0.2 to 1.0 μm.

10.2.2   Cobalt-Doped Iron Oxide

Having a coercivity of 500 to 1200 Oe, the preferred preparation causes cobalt ions to be adsorbed upon the surface of gamma ferric oxide particles as an epitaxial layer. This is one form of *high-bias tape*.

10.2.3   Chromium Dioxide

Offering coercivities of 450 to 650 Oe, this material provides a slightly higher saturation magnetization, 80 to 85 emu/g, compared with 70 to 75 emu/g for gamma ferric oxide. It has high acicularity and lacks voids and dendrites. It has a low curie temperature, making it a likely candidate for contact duplication of video tapes or other short-wavelength recordings.

Chromium dioxide is abrasive, tending to reduce head life. It is less stable chemically than iron oxide. At extremes of temperature and humidity, it can degrade to nonmagnetic compounds of chromium. Tapes made with cobalt or chromium oxides yield output levels of 5 to 7 dB greater than gamma ferric oxide of the same coating thickness. Chromium dioxide does have a problem in respect to disposal. In many countries, chromium and its compounds are subject to special treatment when discarded.

10.2.4   Iron Particle

Tapes made from dispersions of finely powdered metallic iron particles are capable of 10- to 12-dB greater signal output than gamma ferric oxide tapes. These tapes have high saturation magnetization (150 to 200 emu/g), a retentivity of 2000 to 3000 G, and a coercivity of 1000 to 1500 Oe.

Several processes generate metal particles. One is the reduction of iron oxide in hydrogen. Another is the reduction of ferrous salt solutions with borohydrides. Metal particles, being very small, take longer to disperse, a disadvantage in manufacture. When dry, iron particles are highly reactive in air and present a processing hazard. Corrosion at elevated temperatures and humidity is also a problem.

10.2.5   Plated Metal

The use of a flexible substrate which has been plated with a magnetic material in a vacuum is under investigation. This substance will probably find application in systems which require (and allow) a narrow range of recorded wavelengths. While its thinness (100 to 150 nm) tends to limit the absolute output level, this is partially offset by a very high retentivity (12,000 G). Good noise performance is expected because a plated layer is less granular than a coated one. Plated tapes will probably first be used in digital audio and digital video recorders.

10.3   MAGNETIC TAPE

In this section, keep in mind that the processes employed in the manufacture of tape are, for the most part, trade secrets closely guarded by the several competing manufacturers and are not likely to be published.

10.3.1   The Substrate

Virtually all flexible magnetic recording media are made by coating a plastic substrate, or base film, with a slurry of magnetic particles suspended in a volatile solvent. The plastic of choice is polyethylene terephthalate, also called *polyester* or PET.

PET has good tensile strength, excellent tear resistance, and good chemical stability, and its cost is reasonable. Its strength is improved by stretching in two dimensions after extrusion from the melt. In the case of very thin base films, less than 0.5 mil, additional strength is needed in the direction of motion. This is provided by additional stretching in that direction. Films receiving the extra stretch are said to be *tensilized.*

Organic particles of very small size are added to PET to give the surface optimum roughness. If the surface is too smooth, the film is difficult to handle and there are adhesion problems. If it is too rough, the smoothness of the finished coating can be compromised. In audio direct recording, excessive surface roughness will decrease short wavelength response and contribute to *modulation noise,* noise produced only in the presence of a recorded signal. If the recording surface is too smooth, the tape can "wring," or suffer molecule adhesion to smooth nonrotating tape-path elements. These include guides and heads.

Spools of base film range to 15,000 ft long, from 0.2 to 1.5 mils thick, and 12 to 60 in wide. Thin films and thin coatings are used for video and digital recording. Audio tapes tend to have thicker coatings and a moderately thick base.

10.3.2 Manufacture

Mixing.   The first step in manufacture is the dispersion of the dry magnetic material in a liquid mixture consisting of the following components:

1. Binders, to enhance adhesion of the coating to the base film.

2. Stabilizers, to prevent aging of the binders.

3. Dyes and conductive agents, to color the coating and provide protection from the accumulation of static electricity during winding.

4. Plasticizers, to make the coating as flexible as the base film. The complete evaporation of plasticizers marks the end of the lifetime of a magnetic recording.

5. Lubricants, to reduce wear.

6. Dispersants, having high surface tension, tend to aid the dispersion of the magnetic particles and inhibit their tendency to cohere.

Dispersion takes place in a mill containing either steel balls or pebbles. Since the magnetic particles are equivalent to single-domain magnets, they tend to agglomerate. Milling defeats this tendency, especially if the viscosity of the mix is properly chosen. A uniform dispersion leads to minimum modulation noise.

Dry oxide is abrasive. One function of milling is to assure that each magnetic particle is individually coated with the relatively soft binder and separated from other particles. Abrasiveness is also influenced by surface treatment applied later.

Coating.   All known coating processes are continuous; i.e., if the process is stopped, the results are ruined. Figure 10.5 illustrates three coating methods. Discussed below are five methods:

1. *Reverse-roll coating:*   The total wet thickness is the distance between the surfaces of the rollers.

2. *Gravure coating:*   The depth of the indentations in the roller control the coating thickness, and the viscosity of the mix controls the evenness of the coating.

3. *Knife-blade coating:*   The coating material is applied by gravity, and a blade is used to scrape off the excess. Thickness is determined by the spacing between the blade and the base-film surface. This method is falling into disuse.

4. *Extrusion coating:*   A carefully controlled amount of coating mixture is extruded onto a highly polished large-diameter roller. Later, the resulting film is transferred to the base film by the roller.

5. *Spray coating:*   Pneumatic or electrostatic forces are used to propel the mix onto the base film.

Particle Orientation.   Before the coating hardens, while it is still viscous, it is passed through a strong magnetic field oriented in the direction of tape motion. Magnetic particles which are not oriented in the direction of tape motion tend to rotate in order to become so oriented. The extent to which they succeed deter-

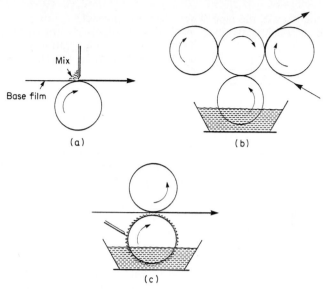

FIG. 10.5 Coating methods. (*a*) Knife coating. (*b*) Reverse-roll coating. (*c*) Gravure coating.

mines the *squareness ratio,* the ratio of saturation flux to remanent flux. If all magnetic particles were perfectly formed rods of one magnetic domain each and all became physically aligned while passing through the aligning field, the squareness ratio would be 1.

Surfacing.   The surface of the coating that contacts the recording and reproducing heads must be smoothed to an optimum roughness. The best roughness is just rougher than that at which molecular adhesion occurs at the heads, fixed guideposts, or other smooth surfaces which the tape contacts.

The methods which have been used are these:

1. *Brushing* with a horsehair or nylon brush to dislodge protruding oxide particles from the surface.

2. *Scraping* with a sharp edge, either lifting out protruding crystals or fracturing them at the surface.

3. *Abrasion* by rubbing the coating over itself. In this case, protruding particles are used to break off other protruding particles.

4. *Ironing* particles, or pushing them into the surface by using a highly polished roller, results in a smooth surface with few broken oxide particles at the surface.

Back Coating.   The maximum rewind or fast-forward speed is limited by the maximum tension which can be used without stretching the tape or collapsing the hub of the reel. The greater the tension, the more rapidly the air between the outside layer and the tape pack can be forced out.

Professional and some consumer tapes have a conductive, fairly rough coating applied to the back of the tape. The roughness provides an air path even when the top layer is touching the inner pack. The conductive component is a further deterrent to the accumulation of static electricity. Figure 10.6 shows the relative positions of the coatings.

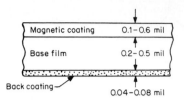

FIG. 10.6   Tape coatings.

Slitting.   The coated base film is slit into multiple strands of the desired width between 0.15 and 2.0 in. The strips along each edge of the wide coated base film are discarded because the thickness of coating at the edges of the base film cannot be adequately controlled.

Rotary shears are usually employed, and the precision of the tape-width dimension is dependent on proper maintenance of the shears. It is typical to slit tape so that the advertised width is the maximum dimension, never to be exceeded. The guiding of tape usually involves upper and lower edge guides. If the tape width exceeds the distance between the guides, the tape can buckle and, in extreme circumstances, curl under itself with catastrophic results.

The sharpness of the shears is critical. If the force necessary to cut the tape is great enough, the tape can be stretched beyond the elastic limit at the cut edge, producing the visual effect of a lettuce leaf. Since iron oxide is abrasive, it can easily be understood that sharpening is an ongoing process.

Testing.   Anything that goes wrong anywhere in the process can ruin a batch of tape. Physical and magnetic tests are applied all along the process line to trap failures as early as possible. It is pointless to continue applying labor and material to a product which is already doomed.

Packaging.   Audio tape is packaged and sold in many forms and thicknesses:

1. Wound on plastic or metal flanged reels, a properly wound tape pack does *not* touch the flanges.

2. Wound on a hub without flanges, the assembly is called a *pancake.*

3. Enclosed in a cassette, the tape is wound onto two small reels.

4. Wound on one hub and enclosed in a cartridge, the tape is pulled from the layer next to the hub, used, then wound on outside the same tape pack. Since the layers must constantly slide over each other, tape for cartridge use is heavily lubricated.

10.3.3   Physical Properties

Generally, wide (1- to 2-in) audio tapes employ the thickest substrate and the thickest coating. Guiding forces applied to the edge of the tape are proportional to tape width, and the increased column stiffness offered by the increased thickness allows guiding without increased risk of buckling.

Winding.   Figure 10.7 shows the effect of poor tape packs caused by transport misalignment (usually a nonvertical tape guide) and by excessive winding speed.

If the air film between the top layer of the tape pack and the next layer down is not squeezed out in the time of one revolution, the pack will be loose and will occasionally slide down and contact the lower flange. Even on a vertically mounted transport, high speeds enhance the lubrication of the tape by air, and the tape can weave about. It will be contained by the flanges but will touch them, inviting edge damage if the reel is picked up by the flanges. Many professional recorders are equipped with a special spooling speed (about 80 to 160 in/s). Lacking that feature, tapes should be wound at play speed and stored with the end of the program on the outside.

Storage. Tapes in archival storage should be put on a transport every few years and spooled back and forth to relieve stresses which might accumulate with age. Any tendency of a tape to shrink with age, humidity, or temperature results in longitudinal stress. This stress, multiplied thousands of times, is applied to the hub as compression. In extreme cases, plastic hubs have been crushed during storage.

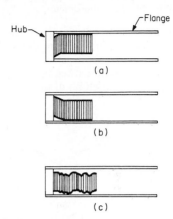

FIG. 10.7 Poor tape packs. (*a*), (*b*) Tape pack resulting from mechanical misalignment. (*c*) Tape pack resulting from excessive winding speed.

10.3.4 Magnetic Properties

The available long-wavelength output from a recorded tape is proportional to the remanence of the magnetic material, the ratio of magnetic material to the binder which holds it in place, and the thickness of the coating as long as the thickness is equal to or less than the gap of the reproduce head.

The short-wavelength response is proportional to the same parameters except that coating thickness is not a factor. Thin coatings are typical of video and digital tapes, which employ mostly short wavelengths. Professional audio recording uses a wide range of wavelengths and profits from tapes with thick coatings.

The contribution of any given magnetic particle to the total signal induced in the playback head is determined by its distance from the reproduce gap and the wavelength of the recorded signal. Compared with the contribution of a particle at the surface of the tape, the *separation loss* of a buried particle is

$$\text{Loss (dB)} = 54.6 \frac{d}{\lambda} \tag{10.5}$$

where d = distance of particle from head gap
   λ = wavelength in same units as d

Coating thickness also affects the ability to minimize harmonic distortion, discussed in Sec. 10.6.

10.4   HEAD DESIGN

10.4.1   Physical Dimensions

Figure 10.8 shows the major dimensions of a magnetic head. The number and thickness of the laminations determine the recorded track width. The gap length determines the depth of recording of record heads and the upper frequency response of reproduce heads. The gap depth will influence the head efficiency and determines the lifetime of the head.

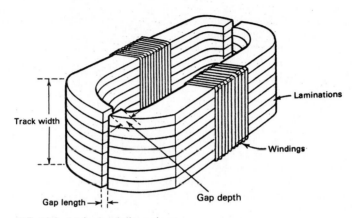

FIG. 10.8   Major head dimensions.

10.4.2   Magnetic Relationships

Figure 10.9 is an electrical analog of a record head. When a current I is passed through a coil having N turns, a magnetomotive force (mmf) is produced:

$$\text{mmf} = 0.4\pi NI \tag{10.6}$$

As a result of the mmf, a magnetic flux flows in the head core. The flux is analogous to electrical current, the mmf is analogous to electrical voltage, and the magnetic reluctance of the core and the gaps is analogous to electrical resistance. Just

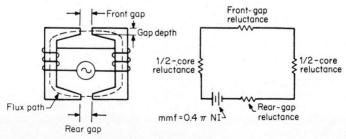

FIG. 10.9   Electrical analog of a record head.

as the resistance of wire is determined by the conductance of the material and the physical dimensions of the wire, so is the reluctance of a head core:

Wire: $$R = \frac{1}{\gamma}\frac{l}{A}$$ (10.7)

where R = resistance
$\quad A$ = wire cross-sectional area
$\quad l$ = length
$\quad \gamma$ = conductance of wire

Head core: $$R = \frac{1}{u}\frac{l}{A}$$ (10.8)

where R = reluctance
$\quad A$ = mean cross-sectional area of core
$\quad l$ = mean length of core
$\quad u$ = permeability of core material

Formula (10.8) may be used to determine the reluctance of a head gap by setting l equal to the gap length and the permeability u to 1. High efficiency exists when most of the mmf appears across the gap and a small percentage across the core.

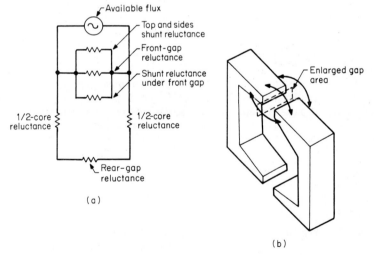

FIG. 10.10   (*a*) Electrical analog of a reproduce head. (*b*) Illustration of stray flux.

Figure 10.10*a* is the electrical analog of a reproduce head. The available flux is shunted by the gap reluctance. As shown in Fig. 10.10*b*, the stray flux that fringes the sides of the front gap tends to enlarge the gap cross-sectional area, hence lower the reluctance of the gap, and therefore decrease head efficiency. The effect of stray flux is proportional to the ratio of gap length to track width and is pronounced in video heads because of their very narrow tracks. It is a minor factor in most audio playback heads.

The permeability of the core material is a function of frequency. In low-resistivity materials such as metals, the reduction in permeability with rising frequency is due to eddy currents in the material, which force the flux to flow on the surface of the material in a manner analogous to the skin effect experienced in electrical conductors at radio frequencies.

In high-resistivity materials such as ferrite, high-frequency losses are mostly spin-relaxation effects,[2] while eddy-current losses are minimized by the material's high resistivity.

Metal heads are often formed from stacks of thin laminations of magnetic material, interleaved with even thinner laminations of nonconductive cement. In this way, eddy currents are confined to one dimension, and high-frequency losses are minimized. Lamination thickness ranges from 0.001 to 0.0001 in.

The gap may be filled with any suitable nonmagnetic material. Ideally, the gap material should wear at about the same rate as the rest of the structure. Early heads used paper. Later, malleable metals such as copper were used, as well as mica and silicon dioxide.

Ferrite heads often use sputtered glass as the gap separator. After being lapped to a smooth plane surface, the opposing surfaces are exposed in a low-pressure atmosphere of inert gas, to glass atoms which have been dislodged from a target by accelerated gas ions. Controlled by the accelerating voltage and the gas pressure, deposition is continued until each face has been coated to half of the desired gap length. The faces are later brought into contact and heated to the fusing temperature of the glass. Some ferrites lose their magnetic properties if heated in the presence of oxygen and require a controlled atmosphere.

10.4.3 Head Structures

Figure 11.8 illustrates the salient dimensions of a typical symmetrical ring head. The presence of the *back gap* is the practical outcome of maintaining the opposing faces of the gap as parallel planes. This is necessary to keep the gap length constant with wear. Figure 10.11 shows how the added reluctance of the back gap can be reduced by increasing its cross-sectional area.

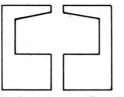

FIG. 10.11   Reducing the effect of the back gap.

To the extent that the back gap equals the front gap, there is a tendency for interfering magnetic fields to induce voltages which cancel, making the structure more immune to the influence of hum fields originating in the recorder's power supply.

Figure 10.12 describes an asymmetric structure. This structure has the advantage of having only one gap and needing only one coil. It is often used with ferrite heads.

A composite design is shown in Fig. 10.13. It presents to the tape a material magnetically and physically best suited for tape contact, yet it retains for the bulk of the structure a material (such as ferrite) which has less loss at high frequencies than does metal.

Compromises must be made when a head is used for both recording and play-

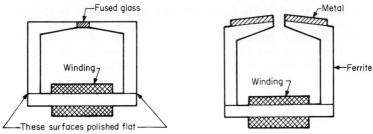

FIG. 10.12 One-coil asymmetric structure.   **FIG. 10.13** Composite head structure.

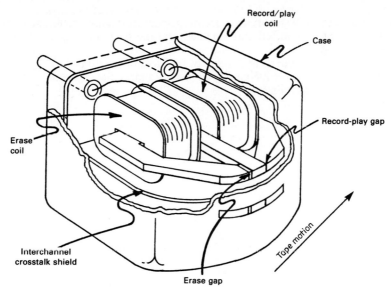

FIG. 10.14 Combination head structure.

back. The ideal gap length for playback is seldom the ideal choice for recording. The core material must be able to sustain recording fields, whereas a playback-only head is free to use the highest-permeability material available.

Figure 10.14 shows a *combination head,* which combines the functions of erasure and record-playback into a single structure. Since the central magnetic path is shared by the record and erase functions, the erase current and the record bias must be derived from the same source.

A head used for both record and playback is typically connected to the appropriate amplifier by a relay. One novel design, called the *flux-gate head,* is described in Fig. 10.15. In playback the record winding is shorted, and in the record mode the playback winding is shorted. If magnetic flux

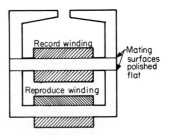

FIG. 10.15 Flux-gate head.

were to attempt to enter the leg having the shorted winding, it would induce a voltage across that winding. Since the winding is shorted, this produces a current, which produces an mmf opposing that which created the voltage. The result is a magnetic path which has been switched to a high-reluctance state by virtue of the shorted winding. The short circuit can be a metallic contact or a saturated semiconductor junction.

10.4.4 Head Manufacture

The steps in the manufacture of a typical head are illustrated in Fig. 10.16. Figure 10.16*a* shows the preparation of the back core which supports the winding. The back core will be joined with the front piece after high-temperature processing has been completed. Figure 10.16*b* shows the preparation of the nosepiece and the installation of ferrite shields and ceramic separators. Figure 10.16*c* shows how the back pieces are supported and shielded and the back and front halves assembled.

All magnetic-core parts and many of the faces of the supporting structure that fit together are lapped to a high degree of smoothness, flatness, and parallelism so that air gaps are minimized.

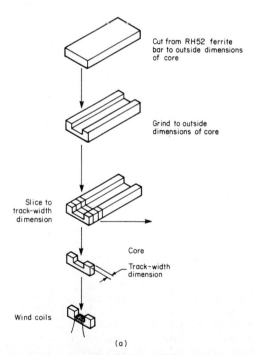

(a)

FIG. 10.16 Stages in the construction of a ferrite head. (*a*) Making the back core. (*b*) The steps in making the front assembly. (*c*) Bringing the front and rear halves together.

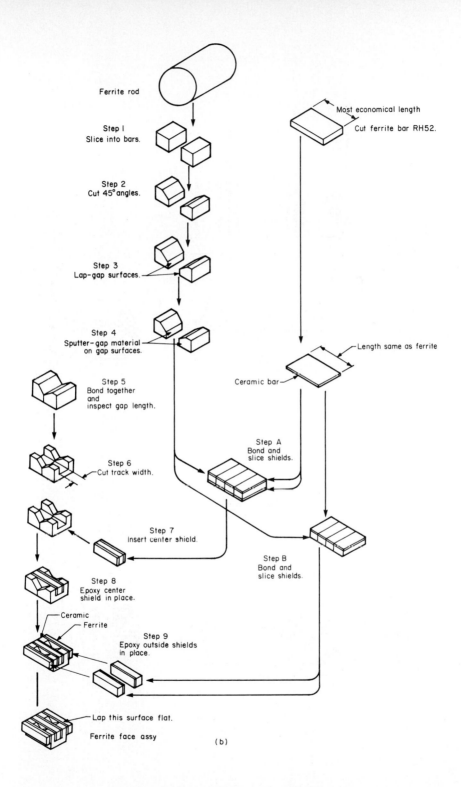

Ferrite rod

Step 1
Slice into bars.

Step 2
Cut 45° angles.

Step 3
Lap-gap surfaces.

Step 4
Sputter-gap material
on gap surfaces.

Step 5
Bond together
and
inspect gap length.

Step 6
Cut track width.

Step 7
Insert center shield.

Step 8
Epoxy center
shield in place.

Ceramic
Ferrite
Step 9
Epoxy outside shields
in place.

Lap this surface flat.

Ferrite face assy

Most economical length
Cut ferrite bar RH52.

Length same as ferrite

Ceramic bar

Step A
Bond and
slice shields.

Step B
Bond and
slice shields.

(b)

10.21

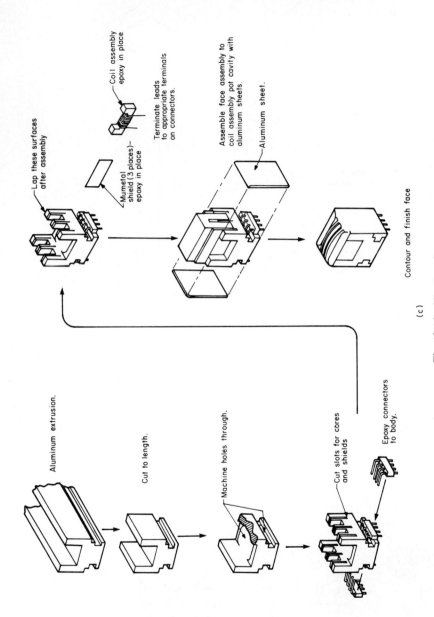

Lap these surfaces after assembly

Mumetal shield (3 places)— epoxy in place

Coil assembly epoxy in place

Terminate leads to appropriate terminals on connectors.

Assemble face assembly to coil assembly pot cavity with aluminum sheets.

Aluminum sheet.

Contour and finish face

Aluminum extrusion.

Cut to length.

Machine holes through.

Cut slots for cores and shields

Epoxy connectors to body.

(c)

Fig. 10.16 (Continued)

The preparation of metal heads is similar except in the following respects:

1. The head cores are not sliced but are formed by stacking thin laminations of core material interleaved with very thin layers of adhesive to achieve the desired track width.

2. Ferrite shields and ceramic spacers are not used. Shields are Mumetal.

3. The sides forming the gap are not sputtered to apply the gap material. After lapping, the gap separator is simply applied to one half of the core structure and the other half laid on top. The two halves are adjusted under magnification until the two core halves are precisely opposite each other, clamped, and then epoxied together in an external shield with the pole pieces protruding through slots in the front face of the shield.

10.4.5 Finishing

The nosepiece of the head assembly (the part that touches the tape) is *contoured* (polished) by rotating it in the vertical axis while the front surface is in contact with a flat turntable charged with an abrasive. If the rotation is around a fixed center, the result is a cylindrical surface. Sometimes the center of rotation is modified so as to produce a parabolic cross section, deemed by some to be advantageous for reproduction at long wavelengths.

In the mounting which holds the head to the tape transport, certain adjustments may be supplied, listed here in the order of likelihood:

1. The head gap must be perpendicular to the direction of tape travel. Deviation from perpendicularity, called *azimuth-angle error,* has a strong effect on high-frequency response and stereo phasing. This effect is discussed in more detail in Sec. 10.5.1.

2. The head may be rotated on its vertical axis until the points of tangency of the tape on the nosepiece are equidistant from the gap. This is called *centering the footprint.* Errors affect high frequencies and, in the extreme, cause complete loss of signal.

3. The head may be tilted until the face of the head is perpendicular to the plane of the tape transport. Failure to do so can cause poor tape guiding and, in the extreme, damage the tape, especially the edges.

10.5 AUDIO REPRODUCTION PROCESS

10.5.1 Frequency Response

Within the audio passband, frequency-dependent recording losses are generally negligible, consisting mainly of changes in the permeability of reproduce-head cores versus frequency. Most reproduce losses are directly related to the recorded *wavelength,* which, at a given tape speed, can be expressed in terms of frequency.

In an imaginary perfect reproduce system, the output from the reproduce head would double with each doubling of frequency. Various effects cause the output at high frequencies to be less than ideal. These are named and summarized below.

Thickness Loss. The particles at the surface of the tape which have reversals of magnetic direction link with the reproduce-head pole pieces and generate a signal. Their neighboring particles within the depth of the coating have their fields partly canceled by other nearby particles of opposite magnetization which are also distant from the pole pieces. The influence of a given particle on the output diminishes at 55 dB per wavelength of separation from the head. The thickness loss in decibels is

$$20 \log \frac{1 - \exp{(-2\pi d/\lambda)}}{2\pi d/\lambda} \qquad (10.9)$$

where d = depth of recording
λ = wavelength, in same units

Spacing Loss. The surface of the tape is not perfectly flat. If it was, it would adhere to points of sliding contact with disastrous results. Surface particles, therefore, vary in their distance from the pole pieces. The loss due to this average separation in decibels is

$$20 \log \exp{(-2\pi a/\lambda)} \qquad (10.10)$$

where a = average spacing of surface particles
λ = wavelength, in same units

Azimuth Loss. If the *angle* of the reproduce gap in respect to the direction of tape motion is different from the angle of the recording gap, there is an additional loss (see Fig. 10.17). The loss in decibels is

$$20 \log \frac{\sin{[(W \tan \theta)/\lambda]}}{(W \tan \theta)/\lambda} \qquad (10.11)$$

where θ = differential angle
W = track width
λ = wavelength, in same units as width

This loss can be very severe, especially with wide tracks. Head assemblies are usually provided with means to adjust the verticality of the gap. Typically, a reference tape made by a certified supplier is reproduced and the azimuth angle of the reproduce head adjusted for maximum output while reproducing a high frequency.

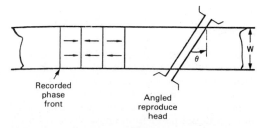

Recorded
phase
front

Angled
reproduce
head

FIG. 10.17 Dimensions affecting azimuth loss.

Gap Loss. When the recorded wavelength is equal to the gap length, the summation of the influence of the magnetic particles within the gap is zero, and there is a null in response. For wavelengths longer than the gap, the loss can be expressed as

$$20 \log \frac{\sin (1.11\pi g/\lambda)}{1.11\pi g/\lambda} \qquad (10.12)$$

where g = optically determined gap length
λ = wavelength, in same units

Gap loss is typically less than 6 dB. Compensation for this loss is often provided by resonating the head inductance with cable capacitance at a frequency well above the system's upper band limit. Alternatively, a dedicated circuit may be used to provide a rising response to cancel the gap loss. Reference 3 will give a very close fit.

Long-Wavelength Effects. Except for the particular case of a circular head structure,[4] at those low frequencies that produce wavelengths which approach the width of the head structure undulations in response occur, including reinforcement. These are known as *head bumps*. Making pole pieces of the head structure very wide tends to move the undulations below the audio spectrum. This, however, makes the head a more efficient transformer, therefore increasing crosstalk with adjacent heads. There is no easy electronic compensation for head bumps, so there is a range of tradeoffs between crosstalk and low-frequency response.

Equalization. Equalization, the process of correcting deviations from uniform frequency response, is distributed between the record and reproduce circuits. In general, losses attributable to the reproduce process are corrected in the reproduce circuits, and vice versa.

The major loss during reproducing is inversely proportional to wavelength for wavelengths which are short compared with the tape coating thickness. If we assume a recording having uniform record current with frequency and no other losses, the system response is dominated by the thickness loss. Thickness loss has been found to approximate the response of a simple resistance-capacitance (RC) low-pass circuit. The reproduce system must therefore have an inverse response, rising with frequency.

On the basis of measurements made on typical tape samples, a standard reproduce curve is selected and promulgated by various standards organizations to effect tape interchange among similar machines. The response at high frequencies is expressed in terms of an RC product, or time constant. The reproduce-system response is given by Eq. (10.13). Values range from 15 to 120 μs. Thicker tape coatings and slower tape speeds require the larger values.

$$\text{Gain (dB)} = 10 \log [1 + (2\pi f R_1 c_1)^2] \qquad (10.13)$$

In some systems, the low frequencies are boosted during recording and attenuated during playback to reduce ac hum. The associated inverse reproduce response is given by

$$\text{Gain (dB)} = 10 \log \left[1 + \frac{1}{(2\pi f R_2 C_2)^2} \right]^{-1} \qquad (10.14)$$

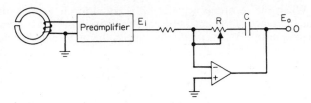

FIG. 10.18   Elements of a reproduce equalizer.

A typical RC value is 3180 μs. Where RC is nonzero, there is a frequency, usually between 400 and 1000 Hz, at which the influences of the two equalizations are equal and their sum is minimum. The frequency, given by Eq. (10.15), is useful as a test frequency and is obtained by equating Eqs. (10.13) and (10.14) and solving for B.

$$f = \frac{1}{2\pi} \sqrt{\frac{1}{R_1 C_1 R_2 C_2}} \qquad (10.15)$$

Figure 10.18 highlights the essential elements of a reproduce equalizer. At low frequencies the impedance of the feedback path is predominantly capacitive, and the response of the amplifier falls at 6 dB per octave, compensating for the rising frequency response of the head. At high frequencies, the response of the amplifier is determined by the value of R and becomes flat. Figure 10.19 illustrates how the response of the head-tape interface and the reproduce equalizer complement each other.

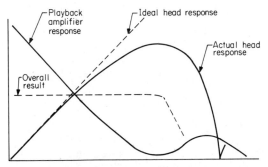

FIG. 10.19   Complementary responses of the reproduce system and equalization.

Adjustment of reproduce equalization circuits may be accomplished in two ways:

1. A reference tape prepared under laboratory conditions and containing several frequencies is reproduced and circuits adjusted for the most uniform response. Some reference, or *alignment,* tapes are recorded full-width to avoid errors due to imperfect vertical positioning of heads relative to the recorded tracks. Formula (10.16) in conjunction with Fig. 10.20a will calculate the rise in response due to fringing fields from the parts of the tape that are not ordinarily

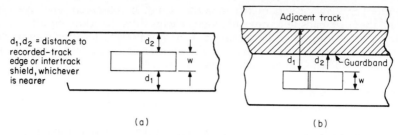

(a)   (b)

FIG. 10.20 Dimensions for (a) fringing-gain calculation and (b) crosstalk calculation.

recorded upon. Equation (10.16) is sufficiently accurate to correct for the rise in output at frequencies usually employed to set the playback-system gain. At longer wavelengths, the rise is more pronounced and accuracy suffers. Reference 5 can provide greater accuracy.

$$\text{Fringing gain (db)} = 20 \log \left[1 + \frac{2 - \exp(-kd_1) - \exp(-kd_2)}{2kW} \right] \quad (10.16)$$

where $k = \pi$ frequency/velocity
W = head width

2. The desired reproduce response is calculated from Eq. (10.13) and the inverse of Eq. (10.12). The head is excited by a small coil of wire driven by a test oscillator. The reproduce circuits are adjusted until the obtained response is most nearly equal to the calculated response. Alternatively, a circuit having a response which is the inverse of the calculated response can be interposed between the test oscillator and the coupling loop. The reproduce circuitry is then adjusted for flat response.

10.5.2 Noise

Noise is anything that appears at the output that was not present at the input and is not a function of any of the input signals. Crosstalk and distortion products are not noise.

Coherent interference may be injected into the reproduce path either magnetically (coupled into the reproduce head) or electrically (introduced into the reproduce circuitry). The usual source of coherent interference is the ac power supply. Radiation from the power transformer into the reproduce head and coupling of the third harmonic of the power line frequency into high-gain circuitry are typical sources.

Encasement of the power transformer in a surrounding enclosure of magnetic material is highly recommended. AC motors may be shielded and/or rotationally oriented for minimum field radiation in the direction of the reproduce head. The circuit path for ac motors should never share any wiring or even any part of the transport structure with any signal circuit.

Audio recorders in a television environment frequently experience interference from the magnetic fields originating in the scanning yokes of television monitors. The vertical scanning waveform is rich in harmonics which lie within the audio passband and is therefore difficult to cancel. Only the fundamental of the horizontal scanning frequency is of interest. Shielding of television monitors is difficult. The viewing end of the monitor cannot be obscured, and shielding around the yoke tends to remove too much energy from the scanning yoke. Keep audio recorders away from TV monitors. The worst possible location is inside the same metal frame (rack) that contains a monitor. The monitor injects energy into the frame, which couples the energy into the recorder.

Random Noise.   Unrelated to the recorded signal, random noise stems from two sources. The random distribution of magnetic particles in the tape is, ideally, the major source.

Electronic noise includes the thermal noise of the resistive component of the head windings and the semiconductor junction noise in the preamplifier. If electronic noise is kept at least 10 dB below tape noise, its contribution to the overall signal-to-noise (S/R) ratio will be limited to 1 dB or less.

Electronic noise in the preamplifier can be minimized by the following design steps:

1. Locate the preamplifier as closely as possible to the reproduce head to minimize the capacitance of the wiring to the head.

2. Choose a head inductance as high as possible without having the inductance and associated capacitance resonate too close to the upper band edge. Resonance at 2 or 3 times the upper band edge is reasonable. This move maximizes the number of turns of wire on the head winding and therefore the induced voltage.

3. Carefully choose a small-signal transistor. It should have low *shot* ($1/F$) noise at low frequencies. Calculate the source impedance of the head at 6.3 kHz, approximately the frequency of maximum sensitivity of the human ear. Choose the current through the transistor to produce the minimum noise figure at the calculated source impedance. Avoid the use of balanced (push-pull) designs which involve the use of two active junctions. Two junctions make more noise than one.

The playback noise from a tape subjected to ac bias current, but no signal current, is usually greater than that from a tape subjected to nothing. This effect can be minimized but not eliminated. Means to minimize it are given in Sec. 10.6.1.

10.5.3   Reproduced Crosstalk

The coupling of a magnetic track into a neighboring reproduce head is given by Eq. (10.16) in conjunction with Fig. 10.20*b*.

$$\text{Crosstalk (dB)} = 20 \log \left[\frac{\exp(-kd_1) - \exp(-kd_2)}{2kW} \right] \qquad (10.17)$$

where $k = \pi$ frequency/velocity
     W = head width

Equation (10.16) assumes no intertrack shield. Another source of intertrack crosstalk is the magnetic coupling between the two head structures, similar to the relation between the primary and the secondary of a transformer. The combination of these two effects is a wildly gyrating function at low frequencies.

A degree of cancellation of intertrack crosstalk can be effected by injecting a small fraction of the reproduced voltage of a channel into its neighboring ones in antiphase. The cancellation is most effective in the middle range of frequencies.

10.5.4 Circuit Design Considerations

The establishment of a point in an electrical system that may be considered as reference zero is not trivial and is the subject of many books and learned papers. Audio-recorder designs tend to establish a reference ground at the reproduce preamplifier. Another approach is to declare reference ground as the point of attachment of the power supply filter capacitors.

In all cases, the interference between circuits caused by currents developing voltages across *ground* wires can be minimized by reducing the impedance of those wires. Ground pins on plug-in circuit boards should be numerous. Ground interconnections should be massive, consisting of either large-cross-sectional-area conductors or multiple wires of equivalent conductance.

With larger systems having longer interconnections, the use of balanced transmission on two wires for each signal path is highly recommended, as it can bring great reductions in conductive crosstalk.

High-impedance circuits can suffer interference from nearby signals by capacitive coupling. This form of interference can be diminished by the use of an electrostatic shield, one that is conductive but not magnetic. Examples include aluminum shield cans, braided or wrapped shields around wires, and metal enclosures.

Low-impedance circuits, especially the reproduce head and its wiring, can suffer from interfering ac magnetic fields. Notable sources of interference include power supply transformers and reel-and-capstan motors.

Sometimes it is necessary to attenuate the interference at the source, i.e., to enclose a motor in a can made of magnetic material. The greatest source attenuation is had by encasing the offending item in an inner shield of material which has moderate permeability but is capable of sustaining fairly strong fields without saturating. An example is the material known as *netic*. The outer shield is formed of a material with very high permeability. Such materials tend to saturate even in moderate fields, but the inner shield attenuates the field to a tolerable level. An example is the material known as *conetic*.

Shielding of the reproduce head is difficult. It is obviously not possible to fully enclose the head. The maximum practical shielding is obtained by mounting the head in a cup made of a sandwich of Mumetal separated by copper. (See Fig. 10.21.) A cap made of the same material is formed to cover the cup. Small slots are cut in the cup to allow passage of the tape. The cap is retracted to thread the tape but pressed against the cup in normal operation.

Some magnetic materials (Mumetal is one) lose their magnetic properties when worked. After bending or other major stress, their magnetic property can be restored by annealing in a hydrogen atmosphere.

The wiring between the reproduce heads and the associated preamplifiers is especially critical. If the distance is more than a few inches, it would be wise to encase the wires in a tubular magnetic (and electrostatic) shield. In any event the head wires should be tightly twisted.

10.6 AUDIO RECORDING PROCESS

10.6.1 Bias

As explained in Sec. 10.1.3, for all applications other than toys the audio signal to be recorded is mixed with a supersonic single-frequency ac signal prior to being

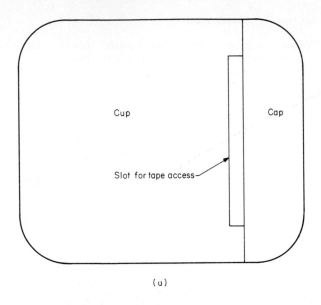

(u)

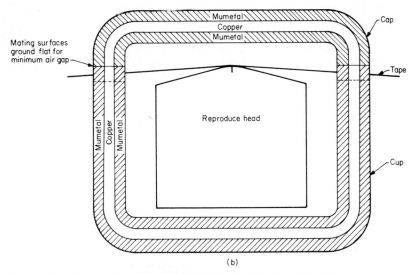

(b)

FIG. 10.21   High-quality head shield. (*a*) Side view. (*b*) Top cross section.

coupled to the record head. It is important to understand that the addition of bias is strictly linear. No modulation is intended, and no multiplicative products of modulation are needed or desired.

Figure 10.22 shows how the spectrum of noise due to the granularity of the magnetic particles in the surface of the tape is distributed around the bias frequency. The lower skirt of the spectrum invades the audio spectrum. This explains the commonly observed difference between noise measured from virgin

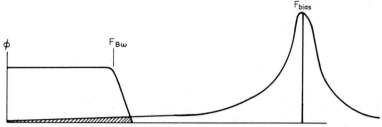

FIG. 10.22 Intrusion of the bias noise spectrum.

bulk-erased tape and noise measured from tape which has been biased (and recorded) with zero signal. Increasing the bias frequency will reduce the magnitude of *biased noise* slightly. Obtaining adequate bias and erase currents at reasonably low voltages is a problem at high bias frequencies.

The erase frequency is usually equal to the bias frequency. Sometimes it is less. If so, it should be an odd submultiple of the bias frequency.

If too low a bias frequency is chosen, then the recording of high-amplitude, high-frequency signals will, in a process akin to phase modulation, generate a family of sidebands spaced at N times the signal frequency above and below the bias frequency, where N is an integer. Figure 10.23 illustrates how these artifacts can intrude into the audio passband. The effect is easily heard by recording a high-amplitude sine wave of rising frequency and listening for descending tones upon playback. A bias frequency at least 7 times but not more than about 20 times the highest frequency to be recorded is reasonable.

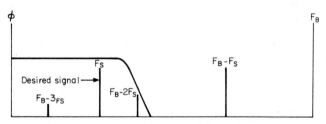

FIG. 10.23 Alias interference due to large distortion products.

Figure 10.24 shows the relation between bias amplitude and the remanent audio signal. Note that the high-frequency, short-wavelength signal reaches a maximum at a lower bias current than the long-wavelength signal. The bias field is strongest at the surface of the tape and diminishes as it penetrates the thickness of the tape coating. The particles contributing to low-frequency output include some near the surface, which are overbiased, and some within the depth of the recording, which are underbiased. The particles responsible for high frequency response are confined to the surface and are all overbiased.

Operationally, bias current is adjusted by recording a moderately high-frequency signal, producing a wavelength which is short compared with the thickness of the tape coating. The bias amplitude is slowly increased until the audio output reaches a maximum, then decreases by an amount prescribed by the manufacturer. The method is adequately sensitive and is designed to result in a min-

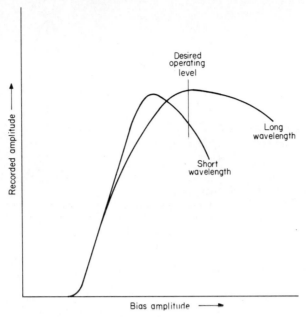

FIG. 10.24 Influence of bias amplitude.

imization of distortion at low and medium frequencies. In the particular case of thick tape coatings and record heads having a gap length approaching the coating thickness, a sharp reduction in distortion can be obtained by careful adjustment of bias amplitude.

Some recorders which have separate record and playback heads offer automatic bias adjustment. Two built-in test oscillators, one at a low frequency and the other near the upper band edge, are mixed in a known ratio and injected into the record path. A playback circuit examines the ratio between the reproduced tones and adjusts the bias amplitude until the correct ratio is achieved. The adjustment value is stored as a binary number in nonvolatile memory.

10.6.2 Measurement of Record Amplitude

The choice of a "normal" recording level is a careful tradeoff between noise and distortion. A tape recorded consistently at too high a level of magnetization will exhibit excessive and perhaps noticeable odd-order harmonic distortion. If recorded at too low a level, the S/N ratio will be degraded and the complaint will be *tape hiss*. A typical normal record level is 8 or 9 dB below the level resulting in 3 percent third-harmonic distortion.

Two methods of signal-level measurement are used, sometimes together. The volume-unit (VU) meter, standardized in the United States, indicates decibels above 1 mW across a 600-Ω line. The ballistics of the meter are closely specified and controlled to obtain repeatable results. The meter is limited in its ability to respond mechanically to very short signal peaks. Use of this meter to adjust loudness dynamically results in occasional bursts of high distortion depending on the program content but in a relatively constant S/R ratio.

In Europe and on many consumer products, metering of the record level is done with a peak-reading instrument consisting of a fast-charge–slow-discharge circuit driving either a conventional meter movement or a linear array of light-emitting diodes. This display method indicates instantaneous peaks of amplitude long enough for one to see and react to them. Use of peak-reading instruments tends to produce a constant maximum distortion level and an S/R ratio which varies according to the program content.

10.6.3 Dynamic Noise Reduction

The concept of compressing the dynamic range occupied by an audio signal before passing it through a noisy transmission channel was employed in the days of the vacuum tube.[6] During the compression phase, soft sounds were made louder. After exposure to the noisy channel, the dynamic range was restored by reducing the system gain during soft passages, thereby reducing noise as well. One popular expander of its time consisted only of a tungsten-filament lamp in parallel with the loudspeaker voice coil. During soft passages, the loudspeaker was shunted by the cold resistance of the lamp's filament. During loud passages, the filament heated, raising the shunt resistance and thereby stealing a smaller proportion of the output power.

Compression, recording, and then expansion are particularly applicable to audio recording as the process takes advantage of the *masking* effect.[7] When the ear is exposed to loud sound, its ability to discern noise is impaired. In the presence of very soft sounds there is little impairment, and noise, if present, is more readily noticed.

Dolby Systems.   Dolby Laboratories developed a series of dynamic noise reducers suitable for recording and sometimes used in radio transmission as well. The first, Dolby A,[8] divides the audio spectrum into four bands. The lowest band is really a low-pass filter, extending to 80 Hz and including hum and $1/F$ noise. The second band extends from 80 Hz to 3 kHz and includes most of the spectral content of music and voice. The third and fourth bands are really high-pass filters. The third begins at 3 kHz, and the fourth at 9 kHz. These last two include much of the noise associated with tape recording. Beyond 9 kHz two bands are involved, and noise reduction above 9 kHz is thereby increased.

Within each band of frequencies the spectral energy is measured and the gain in that path adjusted to reduce the dynamic range. Figure 10.25 shows how the variation in gain versus absolute amplitude is confined to input amplitudes which are well above the anticipated tape noise and well below the maximum input amplitude. The rate of gain reduction is confined to less than 2:1; i.e., a 6-dB variation in input level results in an output change of less than 6 but more than 3 dB. The fact that above 9 kHz there are two active bands results in some additional noise reduction above 9 kHz. Overall noise reduction is on the order of 10 dB.

Dolby B,[9] widely used on early cassette tape recorders, can be thought of as Dolby A with only one of the high-pass filters but one which moves up and down the spectrum according to the amplitude and spectral content of the record signal. The intent is to boost only those frequencies higher than those containing the bulk of the energy at any moment. This avoids boosting a signal which is already large, thereby avoiding tape saturation.

Dolby C[10] has been described as two Dolby B's in series. While not untrue, this description is inadequate. Two high-pass filters of the ilk of Dolby B are used, but

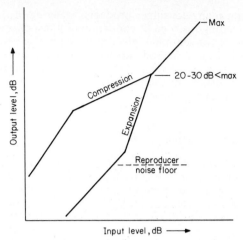

FIG. 10.25 Input-output relation in a Dolby system.

the levels at which each begins to compress are staggered. The result is a modest increase in compression ratio and an increase in noise reduction to a maximum of 20 dB.

For the Dolby SR system, see Chap. 15.

Telcon.   Telefunken, of West Germany, developed a noise reduction circuit called Telcon C4.[11] One of its two versions can be used in Dolby A systems. As in Dolby A, the audio spectrum is broken up into four bands. The compression ratio, shown in Fig. 10.26, is constant through the entire dynamic range.

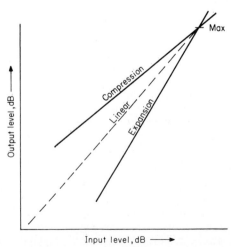

FIG. 10.26 Input-output relation in the Telcom C4 system.

dbx. The dbx noise reduction system, developed by dbx, Inc., does not divide the spectrum. Treating all frequencies alike, it offers a 2:1 compression ratio over the entire input-amplitude range.

All noise reduction schemes act upon the record signal and restore the playback signal on the basis of the absolute amplitude of the audio signal itself. Therefore, maintenance of signal-level calibration in both record and playback modes is crucial. Also, variations from uniform frequency response are magnified by noise reduction processing. The degree of magnification is proportional to the compression ratio.

10.6.4 Distortion Reduction

The only distortion products which should be detectable at the output of a properly designed and maintained tape recorder are the odd-order harmonics of the signal frequency. The predominant harmonic is the third. The absolute amplitude of the harmonic is closely proportional to the cube of the amplitude of the recorded signal. The sign of the harmonic is such that the peak amplitude of the signal is reduced. The limiting case is that of a totally overdriven system with a sine-wave input and a square-wave output.

One technique to make the system more linear is to create, in the recording process, odd-order distortion of the opposite sign and add it to the signal to be recorded, thus canceling in advance the effects of the inherent distortion produced by the magnetic medium. Called *predistortion,* this technique is presented in Fig. 10.27, which shows ways to approximate the desired function. There is no inherent reason why distortion correction must be applied as a part of the record process. A generalized approach, given in Ref. 12, may be applied as part of the

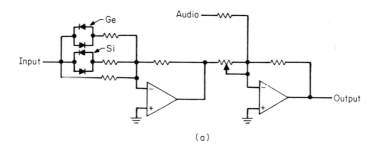

(a)

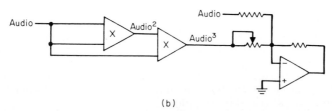

(b)

FIG. 10.27   Two circuits for amplitude predistortion. X = four-quadrant multiplier.

record *or* the playback process. The record path is usually chosen because so few reproducers are equipped for postdistortion correction.

The recording process also introduces delay distortion, the nonuniform time response to the various frequencies in the input spectrum, brought about by the interaction of the longitudinal and vertical components of the recording field. This effect may be compensated for by introducing delay distortion of the opposite sense. Figure 10.28 shows a second-order all-pass circuit which will partially compensate for the delay distortion. An extensive treatment of the subject with an excellent bibliography is given in Ref. 13. In at least one recorder[14] the delay predistortion is produced in the record equalizer. As in the case of amplitude predistortion, there is no reason other than economics that predistortion must be accomplished in the record process. The easiest but not necessarily best way to establish circuit values in a phase predistorter is to determine experimentally the values which result in the best square-wave response at midrange frequencies, i.e., 500 to 2000 Hz.

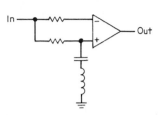

FIG. 10.28 Second-order delay correction circuit.

In the process of copying audio recordings, the accumulation of phase distortion can be minimized by making alternate generations of copy in the reverse direction.

If both amplitude and phase predistortion are used in the record path, phase predistortion should be applied first. Phase predistortion can affect peak amplitude, but amplitude predistortion does not affect phase.

10.6.5 Record Equalization

Most recorders have at least one adjustment in the record path to set the frequency response at the upper end of the spectrum. In simple consumer recorders, a single RC variable boost usually suffices. Professional mastering recorders have as many as four, including adjustment of low-frequency response. Record equalization is always set after setting reproduce response and after setting bias amplitude in order to achieve the flattest overall system response.

10.6.6 Record Crosstalk

The degree to which a record signal is also recorded, in part, on an adjacent track depends on whether the adjacent track was also being recorded upon at the time. If a bias field is present on the adjacent track, that track is most sensitive to the presence of leakage flux from its neighbor. Two paths exist for introducing one signal path into another. The first magnetic path extends from the face of the record head into the face of the neighbor. The other path is the *transformer coupling* between the two heads within the structure of the head assembly. Transformer coupling can be greatly reduced by the introduction of interchannel magnetic shields, as described in Sec. 10.4.

Record crosstalk may be partially canceled by injecting into each neighboring channel's record path a fraction of the record signal in antiphase. The cancellation signal is frequently passed through a circuit which varies its amplitude and phase as a function of frequency. Generally the adjustments are critical, and generally the cancellation is effective only over the midrange frequencies, roughly 500 to 5000 Hz.

10.6.7 Circuit Design

Consumer recorders have simple input circuits. The input cable is typically a single shielded conductor with the shield connected to ground. While this is adequate when the signal source is a meter or two away, professional recorders are often operated with sources which are tens of meters removed. To avoid introducing interfering signals due to currents in the ground paths, professional recorders usually have a balanced input with bipolar signals symmetrical about ground. The input circuit is sometimes a transformer, but better rejection of common-mode interference can be gained with an operational amplifier with one or two adjustments to maximize common-mode rejection (CMR). Figure 10.29 shows a typical circuit. The potentiometer adjusts CMR at low frequencies, and the variable capacitor minimizes CMR at high frequencies.

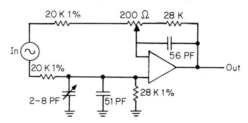

FIG. 10.29 Input differential-amplifier circuit.

Two methods of adding the bias signal to the audio are in use. Figure 10.30 shows both. In one, the bias-generator output is added to the audio record-amplifier output by using passive components. In the other, the bias is added at the input to the record amplifier, which must be designed to have the bandwidth and output-amplitude capability to amplify the mixture without distortion.

The design of the bias source is critical. The bias current must be free of any even-order distortion and must be spectrally pure. Even-order distortion will result in even-order distortion of the audio signal and in increased tape noise. Spectral impurity will result in increased modulation noise, i.e., noise which occurs only in the presence of a signal.

Additionally, in recorders used for editing, the bias and erase signals are turned on and off slowly to prevent clicks, pops, and thumps at the edit point. It is important that the bias and erase waveforms remain free of even-order distortion during the turn-on–turn-off period.

The following record controls may be found in record electronics, usually repeated for each channel:

1. If the recorder is equipped with one or more noise reduction circuits, there is usually a record calibration control which is set to produce a standard level at the input to the noise reduction circuit. Another record calibration control is used to establish the desired tape flux at the standard input level.

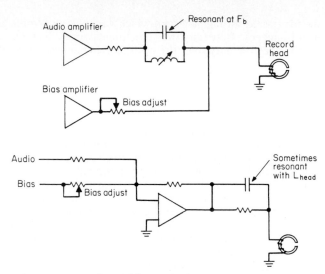

FIG. 10.30   Two bias-addition methods.

2. There is a user front-panel record level control which compensates for the variation in level at the input terminals.

3. There is usually a calibration control to adjust the sensitivity of the record level display device.

4. There is often a record equalization control to set the overall frequency response to maximum flatness.

5. There is almost always an adjustment to set bias amplitude. Cassette recorders and the less expensive reel-to-reel machines often provide a single bias adjustment, with the different amplitudes required by different tape formulations being set by a resistive voltage divider using fixed components. Top-quality professional machines usually provide separate adjustments for each tape type and an adjustment for erase amplitude as well.

10.6.8   Editing

Where the tape is accessible, the end of one passage may be mechanically joined to the beginning of the next by cutting the two tapes at the appropriate points, abutting the two ends, and securing them with adhesive tape on the nonoxide side of the tape. The cutting is done in a jig with a groove equal to the width of the tape. The two tapes are put in the groove and overlapped. The cut is always made through both layers at once, assuring a precision fit. Usually, a diagonal cut is made to spread the effect of the splice over a period of time, producing a cross-fade between the two signals.

When the finality of a mechanical splice is too risky or when there is a multi-track recorder on which some tracks need editing and others must be retained, electronic editing is used. When the record command is issued, the erase current is ramped up over a period of 5 to 100 ms. Later, when the beginning of the erased tape reaches the record head, the bias current and audio signal are ramped up

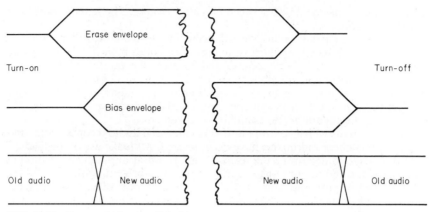

FIG. 10.31   Erase and bias on-off timing.

over a similar time. When recording is terminated, the procedure is reversed, with the erase being ramped down first. Figure !0.31 shows the timing and resulting effect. The on and off delays are different for bias and erase, different for ramping up and ramping down, and different for each tape speed. To avoid holes in the recording at either the start or the end of the edit, each of the delays is, in some machines, made adjustable.

In some applications, as when the sound in a movie being filmed is magnetically recorded, it is necessary to assure that the tape recorder plays back at precisely the same speed used during recording even when the tape has shrunk or stretched. An early method of doing this was to record a narrow track of a single reference frequency in the guard band between two tracks. The frequency was derived either from the ac power line, if the camera was equipped with a synchronous motor, or from an ac generator attached to the camera drive shaft. During playback, the reproduced reference signal was compared with the reference and the speed of the recorder controlled to cause their frequencies to be the same.

Early recorders used synchronous ac motors, and speed was controlled by driving the motor with a power amplifier driven with a variable-frequency oscillator. In later machines, the capstan is driven by a dc motor having a tachometer disk on one end of its shaft. Speed is controlled by comparing the tachometer frequency with a suitable variable-frequency generator. A typical nominal tachometer frequency is 9600 Hz.

In both of the above schemes, initial synchronism is achieved manually and maintained by the servo system thereafter.

A digitally encoded time and control code suitable for recording was developed under the auspices of the Society of Motion Picture and Television Engineers (SMPTE).[15] The code is also supported by the European Broadcasting Union (EBU).[16] Time is expressed, using two binary-coded decimal digits per 8-bit byte, as hours, minutes, seconds, and television or film frames and is iterated once each frame. A total of 80 binary bits are recorded per frame; 16 bits provide synchronism and direction sense, 32 are used to express time, and another 32 are available to the user for any purpose. The signal is very useful in a television environment and is employed in situations in which audio is recorded separately from video or the audio of a television program is to be separately manipulated before broadcast. The time code is recorded either on one track of a multichannel recorder or on a narrow track between two audio tracks. The latter is called *centerline time code.*

A synchronizer is either an external electronic device or a plug-in accessory circuit board to a recorder which compares time codes replayed from a master recorder and from a slave reproducer and controls the capstan of the slave to maintain the difference between the two time codes at zero or some desired fixed offset. In this way, the slave, usually an audio reproducer, and the master, usually a video recorder, are kept in synchronism. Unlike earlier rate-only servos, synchronizers can both attain and maintain synchronism.

Editing systems which control numerous video and audio recorders and video and audio switchers and mixers have been devised. All make use of the SMPTE-EBU time code to determine the relative time position of video and audio program materials and to control the various machines presenting those materials. The rehearsal of proposed edits, the accumulation of a list of edits within a program, and the generation of a master tape conforming to the edit decision list are typical features of these systems.

10.7 MECHANICAL CONSIDERATIONS

10.7.1 The Supporting Frame

The essential elements which may be mounted on the frame are shown in Fig. 10.32. If the elements are intended to be mounted vertically, as in an equipment rack, the mounting method must isolate planar irregularity of the rack from the

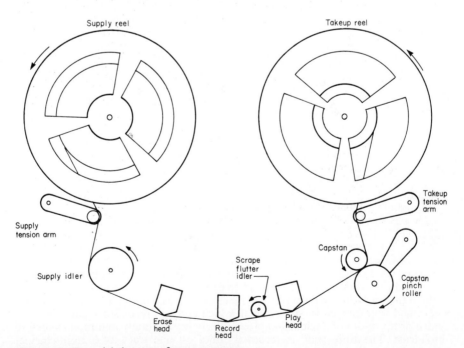

FIG. 10.32 Essential elements of a tape transport.

frame. If vertical *or* horizontal mounting is intended, the bending of the frame due to the weight of the components mounted upon it must be calculated and determined to keep the plane of the mounting surfaces adequately flat. The frame, in its simplest form, is a sheet of rolled metal. In its most complex form, it is a casting with deep webs to increase stiffness.

In larger recorders, some of the electronic elements are often mounted directly on the frame. These are mostly circuits which benefit from short wiring or which are electronic sensors of mechanical elements. Included are playback preamplifiers, motor-drive amplifiers, optical tachometer sensors, tension arm-deflection sensors, and solenoids which move some of the mechanical elements.

10.7.2 The Tape Path

The purpose of the elements shown in Fig. 10.32 is to keep the tape under tension while moving it across the head assemblies. The supply reel, whether driven by a separate motor or by a friction clutch, supplies torque in the direction opposite to normal tape travel. In the play mode and the fast-forward mode, this maintains tape tension. In the rewind mode, it serves to accelerate the tape and the takeup reel and return the tape to the supply reel. The takeup reel, in a like manner, supplies torque in the forward direction.

In friction-drive systems and those with ac motors, the torque applied to the reels is relatively constant, causing the tape tension to vary with the diameter of the tape pack. For this reason, the ratio between full and empty reel diameter is usually restricted to 2.5 or 3:1.

In friction-driven reel systems and in separate-motor systems with unipolar motor-drive amplifiers, the torque is always in the direction shown. In larger recorders, especially those which handle large reels of wide tape, the motor-drive amplifiers are often bipolar. This allows the motor to aid in the acceleration of a reel rather than depend on the increased tension on the tape to do it alone. Quick response to rewind and fast-forward commands can thus be obtained while restricting tension transients in the tape to approximately 2:1. Tension transients are often the cause of tape *cinching,* shown in Fig. 10.33. It occurs when the outside of the tape pack rotates in respect to the inner part.

The supply and takeup reels are usually supplied with frictional brakes even if

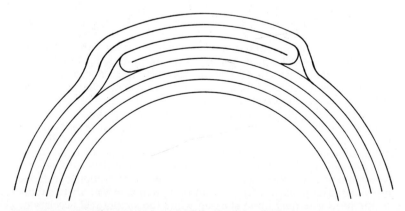

FIG. 10.33 Cinching, or interlayer folding of tape in winding.

these are used only in the event of power failure. Figure 10.34 shows how an active element, a solenoid, is used to hold the brakes *off* so that power failure will result in brakes *on*. The springs at each end of the brake band are unequal, resulting in the greater braking force being applied to the *unwinding* reel. This maintains tension even when the system stops in the absence of power.

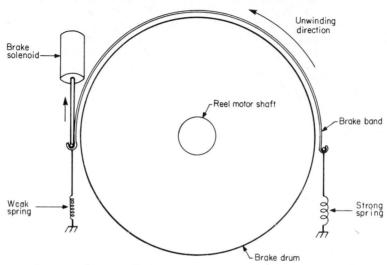

FIG. 10.34 Brake operation.

The braking force is the product of the spring force and the *capstan effect,* a multiplicative parameter which reflects the tendency of things wrapped around a spindle to tighten further. The effect is a function of the coefficient of friction and the wrap angle (in radians) and is given by

$$\frac{\text{Output tension}}{\text{Input tension}} = e^{\mu\theta} \qquad (10.18)$$

where e = 2.71828
μ = coefficient of friction
θ = angle of wrap, rad

The effect is a strong function of the angle of wrap. It is overwhelming in nautical applications, in which a few turns of rope can multiply the holdback force of a sailor by millions. The angle of wrap of tape around the nosepiece of a head is so small as to seem negligible but, when multiplied by (not summed with) the effect of *each* wrap around *each* frictional element that the tape encounters, can result in a ratio of output tension to input tension approaching 2:1. The coefficient of friction of typical tape against typical polished metal surfaces ranges between 0.2 and 0.3 when the tape is in motion and about twice that when it is stationary. Depending on tension and the surface roughness of the tape, there is a tape speed, about 5 in/s, above which friction is reduced somewhat. It results when the air film between tape and guide exceeds the roughness of the rubbing surfaces.

Supply and takeup tension arms, in simple systems, serve only to supply some tape to the head assembly upon start-up while the supply reel accelerates. This diminishes the tension transients associated with starting and stopping tape motion. In more complex systems, the position of the tension arms is sensed and used to regulate the torque applied to the associated reels (discussed later).

Variations in holdback torque due to motor cogging or to an off-center tape pack on the reel will tend to vary the tension (and therefore the elongation) of the tape and thus result in variations in tape velocity at the playback head. The supply idler suppresses this tendency by coupling the tape to a rotating member having high inertia, thus tending to isolate the tape motion at the head from disturbances at the supply reel.

The inertia of the idler is a compromise. Too much, and the time from the beginning of play to stable speed is excessive, as the tape slips over the idler until the idler is fully accelerated. If there is too little inertia, the isolation is insufficient. In some film transports, the idler is given a jump start (by independent means) at the beginning of the play cycle instead of depending on the film to accelerate the idler. This minimizes the time between the start of the play mode and stable motion.

The difference between stationary friction and moving friction gives rise to the *stick-slip,* or *violin-string,* phenomenon, also called *scrape flutter.* The effect is most pronounced when the span of tape between stationary frictional elements is relatively large, as in professional transports. In the case of tapes improperly stored so that the plasticizers and lubricants have evaporated, the effect can be so pronounced as to render the tapes unusable.

The *flutter idler* helps to diminish the high-frequency flutter component associated with scrape flutter by lightly coupling the tape to an inertial element. The roundness of the idler and the quality of its bearings (usually jeweled) are important, as any deviations from uniformity will directly perturb the tape motion. The angle of contact is usually small, on the order of 1 or 2°.

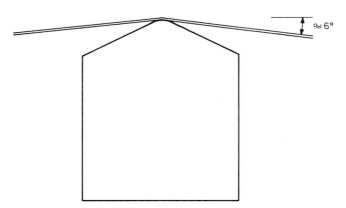

FIG. 10.35   Head-to-tape contact by wrap.

Contact of the tape and the erase, record, and playback heads is assured by having the tape subtend a total angle over the nose of the head on the order of 10 to 16°. This is shown in Fig. 10.35. In consumer-grade cassette recorders, contact is assured by a felt pad which presses the tape against the head.

The tape-path element which determines the absolute speed of the tape is the capstan. In some designs, the capstan is coated with a plastic having a high coefficient of friction, and the wrap angle is high, 90 to 270°. Reel servos are used to maintain relatively constant tape tension so as to restrict the work done by the capstan. This limits the possibility of slippage of the tape over the capstan.

In typical designs, a manual or solenoid-operated rubber roller presses the tape against a steel shaft. Figure 10.36 shows two circumstances. In the first, the roller is narrower than the tape. In this case, the tape speed must be calculated by using the radius of the capstan shaft plus one-third of the thickness of the tape. In the second case, it must be assumed that the coefficient of friction of rubber and tape is greater than that of steel and tape; thus the capstan drives the roller, and the roller drives the back side of the tape, while the front side of the tape slips over the shaft. The *rolling radius* of the roller depends upon its elasticity and the pressure against the shaft. It is a complex relationship best resolved by measurement.

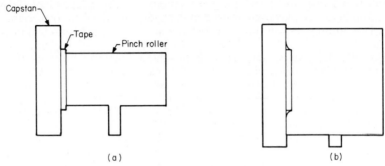

FIG. 10.36 Capstan pinch-roller relationships. (*a*) Capstan moves tape; tape moves roller. (*b*) Capstan moves roller; roller moves tape.

Measurement of absolute tape speed can be approximated by reproducing a flutter-measurement tape and measuring the reproduced frequency, typically 3000 Hz, nominal. The percentage by which the frequency deviates from 3000 Hz is the percentage by which the tape deviates from the design value. The most accurate measure is as follows:

1. Measure the tape tension in the vicinity of the capstan in the play mode.

2. Remove a length of tape, the longer the better. Place it under the same tension as measured in Par. 1, using a spring scale. Make two marks, one near each end of the tape, and measure their separation with a tape measure. (Note that many accurate tape measures must themselves be tensilized.)

3. Return the tape to a reel and measure the time required to play the span between the marks. A photoelectric timer is best, but a stopwatch might serve if the tape is long enough.

The takeup arm serves much the same purpose as the supply arm, isolating the capstan from transients produced at the takeup reel.

10.7.3 Capstan and Reel Servos

Figure 10.37 shows, in schematic form, the operation of a reel servo. The tension arm is fitted with a spring, which determines the tape tension. The position of the arm is sensed by a potentiometer (or other means). Any deviation from the

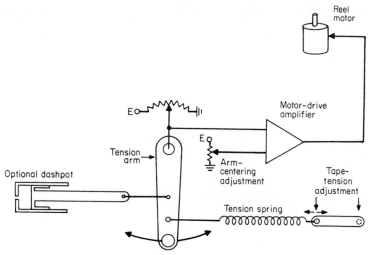

FIG. 10.37   Reel-servo arrangement.

desired deflection of the arm causes the motor torque to be adjusted so as to reduce the deviation toward zero. In some designs, any tendency to oscillate is damped by a dashpot, a piston in a cylinder with a leak. The leak is often adjustable. Usually, servomechanisms are applied to both supply and takeup reels.

The frequency response of the reel-servo system must take into account the resonant systems formed by the inertia of the reel and motor, the spring constant of the tension arm, the mass of the arm, the modulus of elasticity of the tape, the length of tape between the reel and the supply idler (or capstan), and the moment of inertia of the idler (or capstan). Considerable insight into the performance of a proposed design can be had by modeling the mechanical components as electrical elements and using one of the many computer programs designed to analyze the response of electrical circuits.

A capstan servo is a rate servo, in which the rotational rate of the capstan is compared with a reference frequency and any deviation from the reference rate causes an increase or decrease in capstan speed, so as to tend to reduce differences in rate to zero. The capstan shaft is fitted with a tachometer disk, usually optical, which generates a frequency, typically 9600 Hz, at normal play speed. The capstan tachometer frequency is compared with a reference derived from the power line frequency, a crystal-derived frequency, or the scanning frequency of a television system. The result of the comparison varies the current to the capstan motor so as to maintain phase coherency of the tachometer and the reference. While this guarantees a constant rotational rate of the capstan, it does not cause a precisely repeatable tape speed, since the dimensions of the tape can change with time.

To maintain time coherency with another device, typically a film or television camera, it is necessary to record, on the audio transport, a signal derived from the motion of the film camera or the scanning rate of a television camera. During replay, the film or TV rate is compared with the replay of the record, and any tendency to depart from phase coherency is caused to vary the capstan speed so as to diminish that tendency toward zero. In this way, audio recorded separately from video can be reproduced in lip synchronism. The earliest reference frequency recording was a narrow stripe between the two tracks of a two-channel recorder, recording the output of a selsyn motor coupled to the drive shaft of a movie camera. A modern analog is the recording of SMPTE time code[15] on a narrow track in the center of the tape or on one track of a multitrack recorder.

10.7.4 Sources of Flutter and Wow

1. Variations in the supply-reel torque, caused by motor cogging, poor ball bearings, out-of-round mounting of the turntable, dragging brakes, out-of-round tape pack, or the scraping of bent reel flanges against the edges of the tape. The effect of these variations is reduced by the inertia of the supply idler and by the effect of the reel servo, if present.

2. Out-of-round tension arm idlers or bad ball bearings on them. These effects tend to be diminished by the inertia of the supply idler and possibly by the reel servo, depending on frequency.

3. Out-of-round supply idler or bad bearings thereon. These will not be much diminished by the reel servo.

4. Scrape flutter in the absence of a scrape-flutter idler or out-of-round condition in the presence of one. This is not diminished by servos.

5. Out-of-round capstan. This is undiminished by servos.

6. Off-center mounting of a tachometer disk to the capstan shaft will cause the servo to generate perturbations at the once-around rate.

7. Bad bearings in the capstan or pinch roller. These will be diminished by a capstan servo depending on ball size (frequency) and the response of the servo.

8. The effects of irregularities in the takeup reel and the takeup idler are the same as those discussed in Pars. 1 and 2.

9. Vibration of portable recorders, especially angular vibration in the plane of the reels. This effect is diminished by all servos, but since all rotating elements are involved, it is very easy to overload some servo systems by exposing them to the vibration experienced in a helicopter, for instance. Some cassette designs are equipped with counterrotating inertial elements which are designed to cancel the angular acceleration induced by a running person.

10. Slippage of the tape over the capstan due to insufficient pressure of the pinch roller or, in a pinch-roller-less design, due to the detritus which has attached itself to the somewhat tacky plastic capstan surface, thus giving it a reduced coefficient of friction.

10.8   RECORDING FORMATS

Track-width dimensions shown are for the *recorded* tracks. Where erase heads are separate, it is usual for the head width of the erase gap to be 0.010 to 0.020 in wider than the track width to assure full erasure on an interchange basis. Similarly, where reproduce heads are separate, it is typical for their gaps to be 0.005 to 0.010 in smaller than the track width to assure constant output with variations of tracking accuracy.

10.8.1 Two-Track Cassette System

In terms of the number of manufactured recorders, the 0.150-in-width two-reel cassette is undoubtedly the most popular format ever designed. These cassettes are to be found in automobile dashboards and broadcasting studios and are worn by joggers in the park.

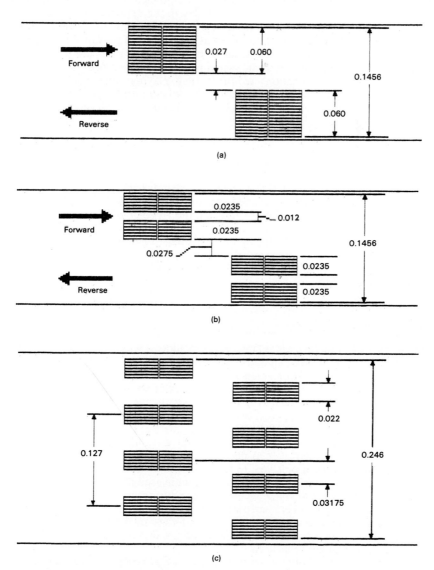

FIG. 10.38   Cassette formats. (*a*) Monophonic recording tracks. (*b*) Stereophonic recording tracks. (*c*) Eight-track recording tracks.

In the simplest form, there are two monophonic tracks, one to each side of the centerline of the tape. When one side is completed, the user removes the cassette, flips it over, and plays the second side over the same head used for the first side. The same method is used on simple stereophonic recorders. Figure 10.38*a* illustrates the monophonic case, and Fig. 10.38*b* the stereo case.

Many recorders, especially automotive installations, offer an autoreverse feature. When the first side of the tape has been completed, the physical end of the tape is sensed, the capstan is reversed, and play in the opposite direction begins.

In some machines, the single head or single stereo pair of heads is moved downward until it is in the position shown at the bottom of the tape in Fig. 10.38*a* and *b*. In other implementations, separate heads or head pairs are provided for the reverse direction, with electronic switching choosing the proper head or heads.

In monophonic applications requiring long playing time, such as talking books, it is typical to use the stereo format to squeeze four separate tracks onto one tape. The reproducer must have a left-right balance control capable of reducing the output of each channel to zero.

10.8.2   Eight-Track Cartridge System

Figure 10.38*c* describes the physical track dimensions of this once-popular stereo format. The stereo pairs are identified as the tracks separated by 0.127 in. A *cartridge* is a single-reel tape assembly in which the tape is pulled up and out of the innermost turn of the tape pack, passed over the heads, and returned to the outside of the same tape pack. It has the advantage of being unidirectional and requiring only one reel. The layers of tape in the pack constantly slip in relation to their neighbors, requiring tape with special lubricants. Performance at high winding speeds is dubious.

10.8.3   Reel-to-Reel Formats

The number of these formats is large, for it includes a wide range of tape widths, each tape width supporting a number of tracks.

The simplest of the ¼-in formats is called *full track.* A monaural format, it is shown in Fig. 10.39. Capable of superlative performance, it is used mostly in monaural amplitude-modulation (AM) and shortwave broadcasting. An early stereo format which also supports two independent channels (as in the case of two languages) is shown in Fig. 10.40. The spacing between the two tracks provides adequate isolation. This format also allows for a monaural implementation in which the tape is flipped over to play the second side, similarly to the way in which simple cassettes are played. In this case, the lower of the two heads shown in Fig. 10.40 may be omitted. When this format is used for recording stereo associated with a film or videotape recording, it is customary to record a *neo-pilot-tone* or time code on two very narrow (about 0.016-in) tracks which are very close together and located so as to straddle the centerline of the tape width. The two heads are located in a separate head stack and are driven in antiphase to reduce crosstalk to negligible proportions.

A European stereo-only format is depicted in Fig. 10.41. This format makes a tradeoff between increased channel crosstalk, which is allowable in a stereo system, and a better S/N ratio resulting from the wider track width.

A bidirectional stereo format is shown in Fig. 10.42. As in the case of the cas-

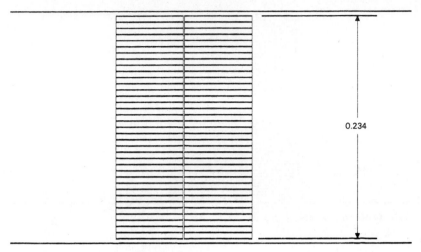

FIG. 10.39   ¼-in full-track recording format.

sette format, a particular implementation may furnish only the heads identified by the right-pointing arrows, requiring the user to flip the tape reel midway, or it may furnish all four heads for use on machines equipped with autoreverse mechanisms. Prerecorded music using this format has a sliding low-frequency tone ranging from 15 to 20 Hz recorded at the end of the first side. A few quadraphonic tapes were published toward the end of the popularity of this format. The appropriate format drawing is Fig. 10.44.

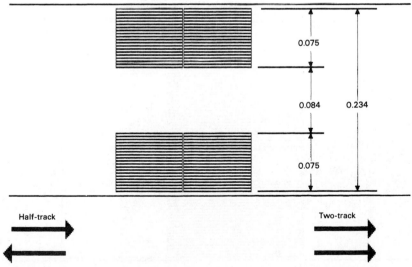

FIG. 10.40   ¼-in two-track–half-track format.

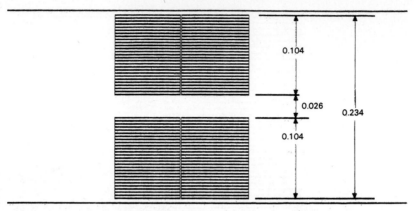

FIG. 10.41   ¼-in stereo-only format.

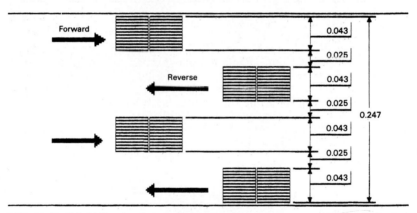

FIG. 10.42   ¼-in bidirectional stereo format.

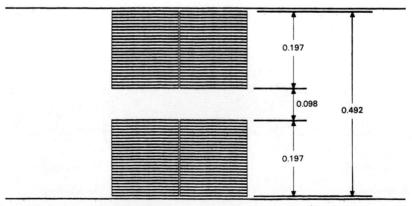

FIG. 10.43   ½-in stereo-master format.

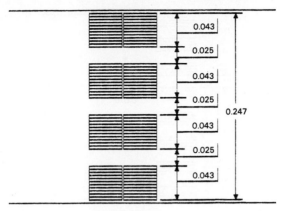

FIG. 10.44 Quadraphonic format.

A stereo format for ½-in-wide tape is detailed in Fig. 10.43. The wide tracks provide very low noise. This format, usually operated at 15 or 30 in/s, is often used to convey the final two-channel mix-down to the cutting lathe for making disks. The format is also used to provide the one-turn delay needed with record lathes having variable groove pitch, using a tape loop transport. Sometimes both the tape playback and the lathe are operated at half speed, reducing by 2 the maximum acceleration required by the cutting head. Figure 10.45 shows a four-channel implementation. Aside from general multitrack recording, this format is often used as the master tape to be copied onto the cassette stereo format. In this case two stereo pairs are copied at once, one in reverse. Both the ½-in reproducer and the cassette recorder are operated at a high speed, usually an integer multiple of normal play speed. By these two means copying time is minimized.

The ½-in four-track format was simply repeated, as shown in Fig. 10.46, to provide an eight-track 1-in format. The first use of a multitrack recorder to allow a single performer to perform several different parts was on an eight-track 1-in

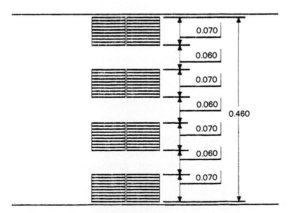

FIG. 10.45 ½-in four-channel or four-track stereo-master format.

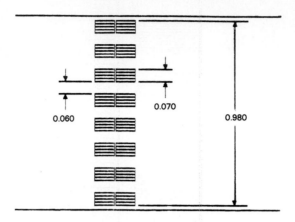

FIG. 10.46   1-in eight-track format.

recorder used by the performers Les Paul and Mary Ford. Using the record head as a reproduce head, the performer, listening with headphones, was able to maintain tempo while recording another part onto another track.

The number of tracks was increased by the use of 2-in-wide tape, already a popular tape width for early video recorders. The two format drawings are Fig. 10.47a and b. While the typical tape speeds of multitrack recorders are 7.5, 15, and 30 in/s, all offer variable-speed reproducing, and some allow small deviations in record speed. This allows music already recorded to be tuned to synchrony with another live instrument in the studio as it is being recorded onto another track. This is a particular advantage when recording a piano or organ track, as those instruments are expensive to retune.

10.8.4   Audio Recording on Video Recorders

Video recording formats provide for two to four associated audio tracks. Recording, for the most part, uses the same methods as with audio recorders, with the tracks located at or near the edges of the tape. One audio track is usually dedicated to the recording of the time code. Similar technology is used to record the *control track,* which is essentially a record of the phase position of the rotating video head assembly. Recorded on another longitudinal track, the playback control-track signal is compared with the phase position of the video head, and any difference is used to control the capstan so as to reduce the difference. This causes the video head to land on a recorded track, a necessary but not sufficient aspect of video recording.

Video recorders use very short wavelengths for the video channel, so there is nothing to be gained by using thick tape coatings. Video tapes therefore have thin coatings. This causes the 3-dB frequency of the reproduce equalization curve to be higher than in an equivalent audio-only application. It also reduces the output available at the reproduce head, which, coupled with the many sources of magnetic pollution on a video recorder, makes the control of induced noise difficult.

Digital video recorders use even shorter wavelengths than analog recorders. Tape coatings are about half the thickness of analog video tapes (about 100 μin). Digital recording formats provide for three longitudinal tracks: a low-quality

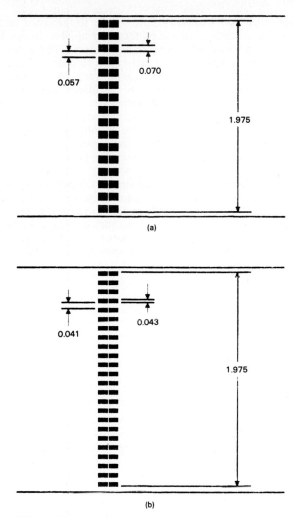

FIG. 10.47 Typical 2-in multitrack formats. (*a*) Eight-track.
(*b*) 24-track.

audio channel not intended for on-air use, a control track, and a time-code track.
All longitudinal tracks use bias recording to minimize crosstalk.

10.8.5 Overview of Format Developments

Many more tape formats exist or have existed than are described here. Early
stereo research and demonstrations used a three-track format on 1-in tape or
coated 35-mm film. There are a few machines offering eight tracks on ¼-in tape
and 12 or 16 channels on 1-in tape. One long-duration recorder uses a rotary disk
having four heads around its periphery. It records narrow tracks transversely

across 3-in-wide tape. The method is quite similar to that used on the first 2-in video recorders. The recording time is on the order of 24 h. Before the advent of the cassette recorder, a magnetic-disk recording system called a *mat recorder* was devised to differentiate it legally from a reel-to-reel recorder. Music was recorded in a fashion similar to the vinyl disk, in a spiral track, on a round, about 0.005-in-thick, flat magnetically coated substrate. Developed in response to certain union rules, this system suffered a quick demise.

In addition, a large number of recording formats have evolved for magnetically coated film. Film widths range from 8 to 70 mm and include 16-, 17.5-, and 35-mm film widths. Track usage is twofold: magnetically striped film, which also contains an optical image; and magnetically coated film totally devoted to audio recording.

Many of the formats are maintained only by manufacturers who supply replacements for worn-out heads. These manufacturers are the best source of data relating to supported formats. Among them are Nortronics, in the United States, and Bogen, of West Germany. Their catalogs include heads for tape, magnetic-disk, and coated film. Makers of video recorders which also record audio include Ampex Corporation of the United States, Robert Bosch of West Germany, and Sony and Hitachi of Japan.

REFERENCES

1. K. Blair Benson (ed.), *Television Engineering Handbook,* McGraw-Hill, New York, 1986, chap. 15, p. 15.16, Table 15-2.

2. B. R. Gooch, in Benson, op. cit, p. 15.34.

3. Benson, op. cit., secs. 15-59 through 15-63, p. 15.127.

4. S. Dinker and J. Guest, "Long Wavelength Response of Magnetic Reproducing Heads with Rounded Outer Edges," *Philips Res. Rep.*, **19**(1) (1964).

5. A. Van Herk, "Side Fringing Response of Magnetic Reproducing Heads," *J. Audio Eng. Soc.*, **26**(4) (April 1978).

6. V. C. Henriquez, "Compression and Expansion in Transmission Sound," *Philips Tech. Rev.*, **3.7**, 284 (July 1938).

7. I. M. Young and C. H. Wenner, "Masking of White Noise by Pure Tone, Frequency-Modulated Tone, and Narrow-Band Noise," *J. Acoust. Soc. Am.*, **41**, 700 (1967).

8. R. M. Dolby, "An Audio Noise Reduction System," *J. Audio Eng. Soc.*, **15**, 383–388 (October 1967).

9. Ibid., "A Noise Reduction System for Consumer Tape Applications," presented at the 39th Convention of the Audio Engineering Society, *J. Audio Eng. Soc. (Abstracts),* **18**, 784 (December 1970).

10. Ibid., "A 20 dB Audio Noise Reduction System for Consumer Applications," *J. Audio Eng. Soc.*, **31**, 98–113 (March 1983).

11. Jurgen Wermuth, "Kompandersystem 'Telcom 04,'" *Fernseh-Kino-Tech.*, no. 3, 91–94 (1980; in German).

12. D. Preis and H. Polchlopek, "Restoration of Nonlinearly Distorted Magnetic Recordings," *J. Audio Eng. Soc.*, **32** (February 1984).

13. D. Preis, "Phase Equalization for Magnetic Recording," *IEEE Conf. Proc.*, 1981 ICASSP (Mar. 30–Apr. 1, 1981).

14. A. M. Heaslett, "Phase Distortion in Audio Magnetic Recording," presented at the 55th Convention of the Audio Engineering Society (October 1976), preprint 1178 (P-3).

15. *Time and Control Code for Video and Audio Tape Recordings for 525-Line/60 Field Television Systems,* ANSI V98.12M, American National Standards Institute, New York, 1981.

16. *Time-and-Control Codes for Television Tape Recordings (625 Line Systems),* EBU TECH 3097-E, Technical Centre of the EBU, Brussels, April 1972.

BIBLIOGRAPHY

Principles of Magnetic Recording

Busby, E. Stanley: in K. Blair Benson (ed.), *Television Engineering Handbook,* McGraw-Hill, New York, 1986, chap. 15, sec. 8.

"An Evening with Jack Mullin," oral history, distributed on cassette tape by the Audio Engineering Society, Los Angeles Chapter.

Fantel, Hans: "Sound," *The New York Times* (Feb. 12, 1984).

Ginsberg, Charles P., and Beverley R. Gooch: in K. Blair Benson (ed.), *Television Engineering Handbook,* McGraw-Hill, New York, 1986, chap. 15, sec. 1.0.

Gooch, Beverley R.: in K. Blair Benson (ed.)., *Television Engineering Handbook,* McGraw-Hill, New York, 1986, chap. 15, sec. 1.4.

Lowman, Charles E.: *Magnetic Recording,* McGraw-Hill, New York, 1972, chap. 2.

Magnetic Recording Materials

Lowman, Charles E.: *Magnetic Recording,* McGraw-Hill, New York, 1972, chap. 6.

Perry, Robert, H.: in K. Blair Benson (ed.), *Television Engineering Handbook,* McGraw-Hill, New York, 1986, chap. 15, sec. 2.2.

────── and A. A. Nishimura: in Kirk Othmer (ed.), *Encyclopedia of Chemical Technology,* 3d ed., vol. 14, Wiley, New York, 1982, pp. 732–753.

Magnetic Tape

Hawthorne, J. M., and C. J. Hefielinger: "Polyester Films," in N. M. Bikales (ed.), *Encyclopedia of Polymer Science and Technology,* vol. 11, Wiley, New York, 1969.

Lueck, L. B. (ed.): *Symposium Proceedings Textbook,* Symposium on Magnetic Media Manufacturing Methods, Honolulu, May 25–27, 1983.

Perry, Robert H.: "Magnetic Tape," in K. Blair Benson (ed.), *Television Engineering Handbook,* McGraw-Hill, New York, 1984, chap. 15, sec. 2.

────── and A. A. Nishimura: "Magnetic Tape," in Kirk Othmer (ed.), *Encyclopedia of Chemical Technology,* 3d ed., vol. 14, Wiley, New York, 1981, pp. 732–753.

CHAPTER 11
DIGITAL MAGNETIC-TAPE RECORDING AND REPRODUCTION

W. J. van Gestel
Philips Research Laboratories, Eindhoven, Netherlands

H. G. de Haan
Philips Consumer Electronics, Eindhoven, Netherlands

T. G. J. A. Martens
Philips Consumer Electronics, Eindhoven, Netherlands

11.1 DIFFERENCES BETWEEN ANALOG AND DIGITAL AUDIO RECORDING

Except for live music, all the music we listen to comes to us via some form of recording. This means that the quality of the music we hear largely depends on the quality of the original tape recording and copies of it. Even the best conventional tape recording system still suffers from a number of limitations in the form of noise and dynamic-range restrictions. These limitations are inherent in tape, heads, and other mechanical factors, and although they can be minimized by conventional means, it is virtually impossible to eliminate them completely. Instead of further refining and perfecting presently known recording technology, a new method of recording, *digital magnetic recording,* is now being applied. This method overcomes the limitations of present recording techniques and makes it possible to achieve a great advance in the quality of reproduced music. Digital techniques were first introduced in the studios, but they are finding increasing application in consumer equipment. Apart from the well-known advantages of digital techniques, such as reproducibility and insensitivity to temperature changes, further advantages are found in magnetic recording.

Signal-to-Noise Ratio. By definition the *signal-to-noise (S/N) ratio* is the difference between the maximum signal level and noise in the absence of the signal. Using linear pulse-code-modulation (PCM) coding when quantizing the samples, the S/N ratio is given by[1]

$$S/N = 6m + 1.8 \text{ dB} \qquad (11.1)$$

where m is the number of bits per sample. In most situations the 1.8 dB is simply ignored. In many current systems 16 bits per sample are used; then the S/N ratio is almost 100 dB. In an analog recorder 60 dB can hardly be met even when preemphasis and deemphasis of the analog signal, weighting curves for the measurement of noise, and harmonic distortion of several percent in maximum signal level are accepted.

Nonlinear Distortion.   Only the input and output filters and the analog-to-digital and digital-to-analog converters (ADC and DAC) contribute to nonlinear distortion. Harmonic distortion can be kept small (<0.1 percent), much smaller than is usual in analog recording (1 to 3 percent).

Frequency Response.   Only the ripple in the input and output filters is important. This ripple does not depend on bias setting, tape parameters, or heads. Frequency response is independent of the recording level.

Effects of *print-through* and *crosstalk* from other tracks can be removed completely. A properly designed error correction system permits exact reconstruction of the original signal. *Repeated copying* will not degrade the signal quality. The uniqueness of each bit in the bit stream enables time-base correction. In this way all effects of *wow and flutter* are removed. The system also makes *time-base compression* possible, which is very useful in system design. *Time multiplexing* of several audio channels in one track can easily be realized.

Of course, there are drawbacks in the digital system. There is a need for an effective *error correction system.* After passing the DAC, misdetected bits result in annoying clicks in the audio signal. Error correction should be able to handle large burst errors (several thousands of bits) caused by dropouts. The *hard clipping* of the ADC makes it necessary to avoid even small overloads. Some bits should be reserved for the peaks in the audio signal.[1] (This stricture is relevant only in the first recording. In copies the maximum signal is known exactly.)

A 20-kHz bandwidth is generally accepted for high-quality audio signals. Typical sample frequencies for this bandwidth are in the range 44 to 48 kHz. With two audio channels, 16 bits per sample, extra bits for channel coding, error correction, and word synchronization, a bit rate of about 2 Mbit/s is the result. If we assume 2 bits per wavelength, we need a minimum bandwidth of 1 MHz. This clearly demonstrates the *bandwidth problem* in digital recording. Two systems have been adopted to solve bandwidth problems.

   1. *Use of helical-scan recorders:*   In these systems the scan speed and so the bandwidth are increased with a rotating drum. Examples of these systems are found in videotape-recorder (VTR) adapters (Sec. 11.7.1), 8-mm video systems (Sec. 11.7.3), and R-DAT (Sec. 11.7.5).

   2. *Application of many tracks:*   The bit rate of 2 Mbit/s is multiplexed over several tracks in such a way that the bit rate in each track is sufficiently low. Examples of these systems are the DASH recorder (Sec. 11.7.2) and the S-DAT system (Sec. 11.7.4).

Different manipulations of the signals are shown in greater detail in the block diagram of Fig. 11.1. At the input a low-pass filter is required to prevent aliasing frequencies higher than half of the sampling frequency. A distinction is made between channel coding (often called channel modulation), error correction coding, and source coding.

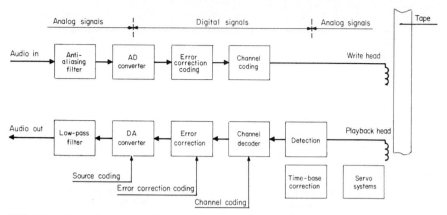

FIG. 11.1   Block diagram of a digital audio recorder.

This chapter begins with an analysis of the recording channel. The blocks shown in Fig. 11.1 are then explained. At the end of the chapter several standardized systems are treated.

11.2   RECORDING AND PLAYBACK CHANNELS

In digital magnetic recording systems there is continuous development toward more efficient use of available storage space. The ultimately achievable density is determined by the tolerable *bit error rate* (BER). On the playback side performance can be considerably improved by linear pulse-shaping networks, error correction techniques, and detection methods adapted to the type of interference encountered in the recording system.

11.2.1   Playback Process

Although the recording process precedes reproduction, it is more convenient to start with the playback side. The treatment of the replay process is usually based on the reciprocity theorem.[2] From the law of mutual induction the following formula is derived:

$$\phi = \frac{\mu_0}{J} \int \mathbf{M} \cdot \mathbf{H} \, dv \qquad (11.2)$$

The flux ϕ through a coil due to the magnetization distribution $\mathbf{M}$ in the tape is related to the magnetic field $\mathbf{H}$ of the head caused by the current J through the coil. Both distributions $\mathbf{H}$ and $\mathbf{M}$ must be known to predict the flux and the output signal $e(t) = -d\phi/dt$.

Edge effects on the sides of the track are neglected. This restricts the distribution of head field and magnetization to two dimensions. (See Fig. 11.2.) The coordinates of the head field are denoted by x and y and those of magnetization by x_1

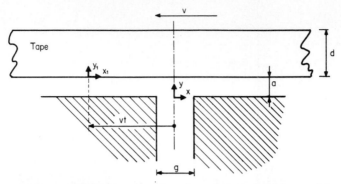

FIG. 11.2 Head-tape configuration; d = magnetized thickness of the tape; a = head-to-tape distance; g = gap length of the head; w = track width; v = tape speed.

and y_1. The coordinates are related to each other by the tape speed and the head-to-tape distance: $x = x_1 - vt$, and $y = y_1 + a$.

The head-field distribution with 1-A magnetomotive force across the gap is $\mathbf{H}_0(x, y)$, and the number of turns is n. The efficiency coefficient η is by definition the ratio between $\mathbf{H}_0(x, y)$ and the actual head field $\mathbf{H}(x, y)$ when the applied magnetomotive force nJ is taken into account. So,

$$\mathbf{H}(x, y) = \eta n J \mathbf{H}_0(x, y) \tag{11.3}$$

and

$$\phi(t) = \mu_0 n \eta w \int_a^{a+d} dy \int_{-\infty}^{\infty} \mathbf{M}(x + vt, y - a)\mathbf{H}_0(x, y)\, dx \tag{11.4}$$

Since $\mathbf{M}$ is the only component that depends on time t (via $x = x_1 - vt$), we can write

$$\frac{d\mathbf{M}}{dt} = v\left(\frac{\partial \mathbf{M}}{\partial x}\right) \tag{11.5a}$$

and

$$e(t) = -\mu_0 n \eta w v \int_a^{a+d} dy \int_{-\infty}^{\infty} \frac{\partial \mathbf{M}(x + vt, y - a)}{\partial x} \mathbf{H}_0(x, y)\, dx \tag{11.5b}$$

Expressions for $\mathbf{H}_0(x, y)$ from various head configurations can be found in the literature.[2,3,4,5] We have used the well-known Karlqvist approximation:

$$H_{0x}(x, y) = \frac{1}{\pi g}\left(\arctan \frac{x + \dfrac{g}{2}}{y} - \arctan \frac{x - \dfrac{g}{2}}{y}\right) \tag{11.6a}$$

$$H_{0y}(x, y) = -\frac{1}{2\pi g}\left[\ln \frac{\left(x + \dfrac{g}{2}\right)^2 + y^2}{\left(x - \dfrac{g}{2}\right)^2 + y^2}\right] \tag{11.6b}$$

At a sufficient distance from the gap ($y < g/3$) the field can be approximated by that of a head with zero gap. (See Fig. 11.3.) Then the field has a circular shape:[3]

$$H_{0x}(x, y) = \frac{1}{\pi} \cdot \frac{y}{x^2 + y^2} \tag{11.7a}$$

$$H_{0y}(x, y) = -\frac{1}{\pi} \cdot \frac{x}{x^2 + y^2} \tag{11.7b}$$

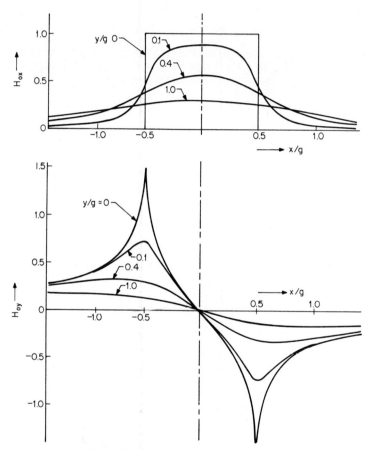

FIG. 11.3 Head field from the Karlqvist approximation. The head field is normalized on the field in the gap.

Step Response. Most investigations of magnetic recording have been based on an analysis with the transmission of sine waves. This is rather obvious because this method is well matched to sound recording, which was the first application of magnetic recording. In digital magnetic recording the write current is a two-level signal consisting of a series of step functions at multiples of the bit cell. For the analysis of digital recording it is therefore useful to introduce the step response.[6] Suppose that a longitudinal magnetized tape ($M_y = 0$) is used.

$$M_x(x_1, y_1) = + M \quad x_1 > 0$$

$$0 \quad x_1 = 0 \qquad (11.8)$$

$$- M \quad x_1 < 0$$

The differentiation of $\partial M(x)/\partial x$ results in a δ function at $t = -x/v$. For a thin layer with thickness Δy at distance y_0 we find

$$e(t) = -\mu_0 n\eta wv \, \Delta y \cdot 2M \, H_{0x}(-vt, y_0) \qquad (11.9)$$

The shape in the time domain of the output pulse is similar to the shape of the head field $H_x(x)$, $y = y_0$. For a thick tape we should integrate the head field over the thickness. With a perpendicular magnetization ($M_x = 0$)

$$M_y(x_1, y_1) = + M \quad x_1 > 0$$

$$0 \quad x_1 = 0 \qquad (11.10)$$

$$- M \quad x_1 < 0$$

the asymmetrical output pulse given by the H_y field in Fig. 11.3 is found. Measured pulse shapes show much more correspondence with H_x (the symmetrical curve) than with H_y. The longitudinal magnetization component is in fact far more important than the perpendicular component.

Sine-Wave Response. The playback process is essentially linear. In general, complicated magnetization distributions in the tape will not result in a closed expression of the output signal. The influence of the playback function on the output can be analyzed by taking the transfer function in the frequency domain, as is done with electrical networks. For a sinusoidal magnetization distribution we have

$$M_x(x_1, y_1) = M \cos\left(2\pi \frac{x_1}{\lambda}\right) \qquad (11.11)$$

where λ = wavelength on the tape. The frequency of the playback signal is

$$f = v/\lambda \qquad (11.12)$$

By combining Eqs. (11.11) and (11.6a and b), the flux through the head is given by[2,7]

$$\phi(\lambda) = \phi_0 \underbrace{\left(\frac{1 - e^{-2\pi d/\lambda}}{2\pi d/\lambda}\right)}_{} \underbrace{e^{-2\pi a/\lambda}}_{} \underbrace{\left(\frac{\sin(\pi g/\lambda)}{\pi g/\lambda}\right)}_{\text{gap-length losses}} \qquad (11.13)$$

distance losses

thickness losses

flux without losses

$$\phi_0(t) = n\eta w d\mu_0 M \left[\cos\left(2\pi \frac{vt}{\lambda}\right)\right] \qquad (11.14)$$

and the output signal without losses is given by

$$e(t) = n\eta w d\mu_0 \underbrace{M} \cdot \underbrace{2\pi f[\sin(2\pi f t)]}$$

flux from tape   differentiator   (11.15)

To find the output signal of a complicated magnetization pattern we can calculate the transfer function of each frequency component. The output signal in the time domain can then be calculated with the inverse Fourier transform.

11.2.2 Recording Process

In digital recording no dc or high-frequency bias current is used to linearize the recording channel. The write current is a two-level signal with amplitudes $+I$ and $-I$ and with transitions at multiples of the channel-bit length. Each transition in the write current results in a transition in the magnetization on the tape.

Two methods of digital recording are distinguished: *saturation recording* and *partial-penetration recording.* In saturation recording the whole thickness of the magnetic layer is magnetized. This method is applied in low-density recording and in disk systems with very thin layers. With partial-penetration recording the amplitude of the record current is optimized for maximum output at short wavelengths. Only part of the (thick) layer is magnetized. This method is used in digital audio recording.

In Fig. 11.3 the x and y components of the head field are given. Lines of constant field strength H_x, H_y, and $|H|$ are shown in Fig. 11.4 for the situation in which H_x at ($x = 0$, $y = g$) is equal to the coercivity of the tape (H_c).

The area where the write field is higher than the coercivity of the tape is magnetized in the direction of the write field, while the area where $H < H_c$ remains unchanged. For a perfectly oriented tape in the x direction magnetization is caused by the x component of the head field. In nonoriented tapes it is the ampli-

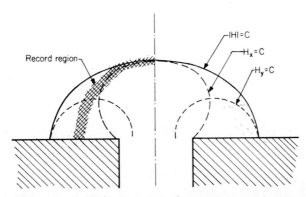

FIG. 11.4 Lines of constant field strength. The recording depth is one gap length deep ($c = H_c$). The shaded area is the estimated transition region.

tude $|H|$ of the head field that determines the magnetized area. The practical situation will be somewhere in between. This is shown schematically in Fig. 11.4. The shaded area, which is more rectangular than the curves $H_x = H_c$ and $|H| = H_c$, represents the transition region. With a moving tape only transitions at the trailing edge of the head are left. The magnetized thickness of the tape is estimated at 0.2 to 0.3 μm (less for thinner tapes).

This is checked in the following way. A very short record pulse magnetizes an erased tape. During playback two peaks in the output signal are found at the transition regions. From the distance between these pulses the magnetized area can be calculated. More accurate measurements are possible with broader record pulses. Then no interference from both transitions occurs during playback.

Magnetization distribution in the tape can be clearly illustrated by simulations with a large-scale model.[8] An example is shown in Fig. 11.5.

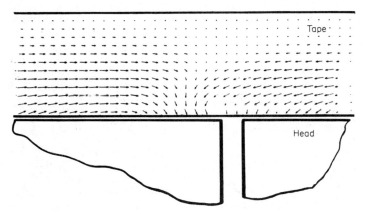

FIG. 11.5   Magnetization pattern from a single transition.

Transition Width.   The width of the transition zone is determined not only by the switching-field distribution of the particles in the tape (the switching field is determined by the coercivity of the particles, the orientation of the particles, and the interacting demagnetizing fields) but also by the demagnetizing field of the written transition. A sharp transition will result in very high demagnetizing fields, which might even be higher than the coercivity of the tape. The tape will then be demagnetized until everywhere in the tape the demagnetizing field is lower than the coercive force. This demagnetizing takes place as soon as the tape leaves the surface of the record head. Many assumptions have been made for the distribution of magnetization in the transition region. We will restrict ourselves to the one most frequently used, the *arctan transition*. Experimental results do agree very well with this kind of transition, which also leads to simple expressions. For a longitudinally magnetized tape we have

$$M_x(x_1) = \frac{2}{\pi} M \arctan\left(\frac{x_1}{c}\right) \tag{11.16}$$

The parameter c determines the transition width. The output pulse from a single transition is found by combining Eqs. (11.16) and (11.6) in Eq. (11.4). Many slightly different expressions for the playback pulse are given in the literature[9-12].

Gap length, tape thickness, head-to-tape distance, and transition width are taken as parameters.

We will follow a somewhat different approach which turns out to be very practical in combination with equalization and detection. If there are no playback losses, then the flux through the head will be given by

$$\phi(t) = n\eta w d\mu_0 M \cdot \frac{2}{\pi} \cdot \arctan\left(\frac{vt}{c}\right) \tag{11.17}$$

So

$$e(t) = \frac{E_p}{1 + \left(\dfrac{t}{t_0}\right)^2} \tag{11.18}$$

with

$$\text{with } E_p = n\eta w d\mu_0 M \cdot \frac{2}{\pi} \cdot \frac{v}{c} \tag{11.19}$$

$$t_0 = \frac{c}{v} \tag{11.20}$$

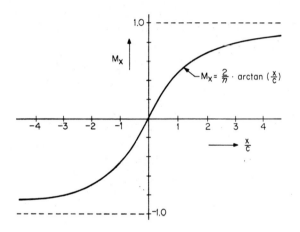

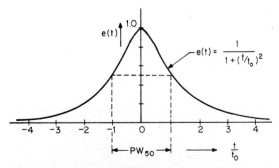

FIG. 11.6 Arctan transition of magnetization and the corresponding playback pulse; c = transition constant; PW_{50} = pulse width at 50 percent of peak amplitude.

E_p is the peak amplitude. The pulse width (PW) is often defined as the width at 50 percent of the peak amplitude (PW_{50}); so

$$PW_{50} = 2c \ \mu m \qquad \text{or} \qquad PW_{50} = 2t_0 \ s \tag{11.21}$$

The frequency spectrum found with Fourier transformation of the pulse shape is

$$E(f) = \pi E_p t_0 \cdot e^{-2\pi f t_0} \tag{11.22}$$

The surface area of the pulse (in the time domain), which is $\pi E_p t_0$, corresponds to the difference in flux through the head on both sides of the transition.

In practice there will be wavelength-dependent playback losses [see Eq. (11.13)].

Distance Losses.   By comparing distance losses and the losses given by the transition width, it is easy to see that the result is the same. The parameters for head-to-tape distance and transition width can be taken together: both result in a widening of the pulse width.

Thickness Losses.   The magnetized thickness d of the tape is less than 0.3 μm. Thickness losses as a function of the wavelength are shown in Fig. 11.7. The dashed lines represent an exponential decrease in the output spectrum. In the most interesting frequency range thickness losses can be approximated by the following transfer function:

$$H_d(\lambda) = e^{-2\pi d^*/\lambda} \qquad \text{with} \qquad d^* \approx \frac{d}{3} \tag{11.23}$$

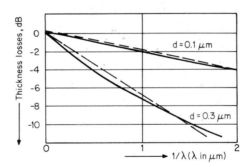

FIG. 11.7   Thickness losses as a function of $1/\lambda$. The dashed lines represent an exponential-loss function.

The thickness losses are thus treated in the same way as the transition-width losses and the distance losses; so we can write

$$t_0 = \frac{c + a + \dfrac{d}{3}}{v} \tag{11.24}$$

Gap-Length Losses. The effect of gap-length losses in the time domain is simply an averaging of the pulse shape over the gap length (in the time domain g/v). If we define $t_g = g/2v$, then we find for the output signal

$$e^*(t) = E_p \cdot \frac{t_0}{t_g} \cdot \frac{1}{2}\left(\arctan\frac{t + t_g}{t_0} - \arctan\frac{t - t_g}{t_0} \right) \tag{11.25}$$

The measured peak amplitude and the pulse width are

$$E_p^* = E_p \cdot \frac{t_0}{t_g} \cdot \arctan\left(\frac{t_g}{t_0}\right) \tag{11.26}$$

$$\mathrm{PW}_{50}^* = 2(t_0^2 + t_g^2)^{1/2} \tag{11.27}$$

In Fig. 11.8 both values are shown as a function of the gap length.

The measured playback pulses look very much like the differentiated arctan transition. Frequency spectra of playback pulses (corrected for gap-length losses) indeed show an exponential decrease at high frequencies. Pulse widths of some head-tape combinations are shown in Table 11.1. Chromium dioxide tape and ME tape have been measured with a ferrite head, and MP tape with a ribbon Sendust head. No correction for the gap-length ($g = 0.25\ \mu m$) losses has been made. (See also Fig. 11.9.)

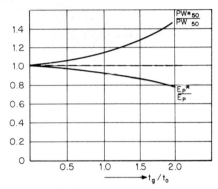

FIG. 11.8 Influence of gap length on E_p and PW. E_p, PW_{50} = values without gap-length losses; E_p^*, PW_{50}^* = measured values.

Pulse Asymmetry. The read-back pulse from an isolated transition shows a characteristic asymmetry. This asymmetry is attributed to the perpendicular component in magnetization, the asymmetry in the transition zone, and phase errors in playback electronics. A proper electronic design eliminates this last-mentioned effect.

The y component of magnetization, which need not be in phase with the x component, adds an uneven function to the output pulse shape, as we have seen in Eqs. (11.8), (11.9), and (11.21).

The asymmetry of the transition region is easily recognized in Fig. 11.5. Low-frequency signals from the middle of the magnetized thickness are delayed when compared with high-frequency signals from the tape surface.

Effects from perpendicular magnetization and the asymmetrical transition region accumulate in the output signal. The result is shown in Fig. 11.9.

TABLE 11.1

Tape	PW_{50}, μm
CrO_2	0.7
MP (metal powder)	0.5
ME (metal evaporated)	0.45

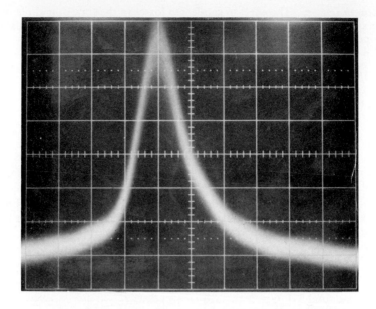

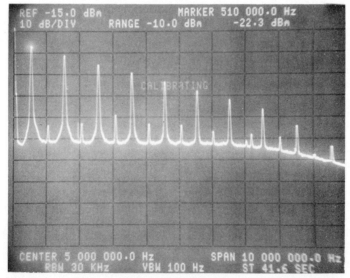

FIG. 11.9 Playback pulse of a chromium dioxide tape. The tape speed is 5 m/s. The tape is recorded with a square-wave record current. The harmonics in the spectrum show the exponential decreasing function. (*a*) Playback pulse (100 ns/div.). (*b*) Frequency spectrum of playback signal.

Peak Shift and Pulse Crowding.   Isolated transitions were used to analyze the reproduction process. Any data signal may be considered as a series of step functions with closely spaced transitions in high-density recording. Interactions between transitions should be taken into account.

The external fields from tapes are low, low enough to avoid nonlinear effects in the heads. On the playback side, therefore, superposition may be applied. The write process is basically nonlinear. However, with two-level write currents it behaves like a linear process up to very high densities. Superposition is shown in Fig. 11.10. Transitions close to each other result in a lower peak amplitude (pulse crowding) and in a displacement of the peaks (peak shift). As pulse crowding and peak shift are results of linear operations, they can be removed. These techniques are used in equalization and detection as we will see later on.

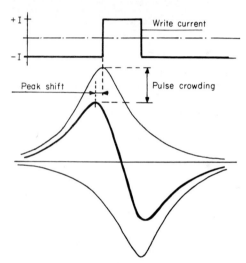

FIG. 11.10   Peak shift and pulse crowding caused by superposition of two transitions.

11.2.3   Thin-Film Heads

Fabrication of multitrack ferrite heads with narrow track widths and small guard bands is difficult. In the S-DAT system (see Sec. 11.7) there are 22 tracks on a 1.9-mm tape width. Thin-film technologies—techniques similar to those which have become established in the production of silicon integrated circuits—make it possible to manufacture multitrack heads for this application.[13] The different geometric structures of the process steps are obtained with photolithographic techniques. Permalloy is used for the magnetic flux guides, gold for the conductors, and quartz as an insulator. These materials are deposited on a magnetic substrate by a series of sputtering, plasma-deposition, and etching steps. The end product is a wafer comprising a large number of magnetic heads. From this wafer individual multitrack heads are obtained by adding protective blocks, cutting and lapping the head surface. Finally, each head is mounted in a special housing and attached to a connecting foil with an appropriate connector. Separate record and

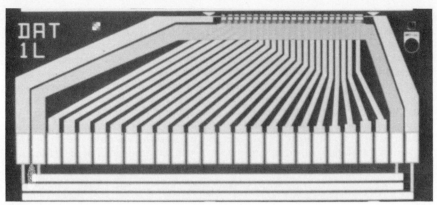

FIG. 11.11   Layout of the S-DAT thin-film head.

playback heads are used. Owing to the limited number of turns (only a few turns can be made in these heads), the playback signal of this inductive record head (IRH) is rather low. That is why the IRH is used only as a write head. During playback magnetoresistive heads (MRH) are used. In an MRH the electrical resistance of the sensor, which is a very thin and narrow stripe of permalloy, depends on the externally applied magnetic field (the field from the tape).[14] The effect is nonlinear. Biasing, e.g., with a current through a bias line in the vicinity of the sensor, is needed to linearize the element. The change in electrical resistance is determined with a measuring current (typical value, 10 mA). Such different configurations as unshielded, shielded, and yoke heads are possible in an MRH.[15] Yoke-type magnetoresistive heads have proved to be suitable for multitrack digital audio. A schematic view and layout of these heads are shown in Fig. 11.11.

11.3   EQUALIZATION AND DETECTION

In the preceding section we have seen the effects of intersymbol interference which resulted in peak shift and pulse crowding. These effects can be removed by linear filtering insofar as this intersymbol interference is caused by superposition. This reduction of interference is realized with equalizer and shaping filters. The nonlinear behavior of the write process is often compensated by write current equalization. Write current equalization should not be used to reduce linear symbol interference (e.g., peak shift). The write process is essentially nonlinear and depends on heads and tapes. It should be possible to interchange prerecorded tapes. With write current equalization too many parameters must be standardized.

Equalization and shaping methods can be divided into *linear equalization,* with only frequency-response correction (amplitude and phase), and *decision feedback and feed-forward techniques.* These methods can be made adaptive to cope with changing transfer functions.[16,17] Equalization and shaping characteristics should be treated together with detection methods.

11.3.1 Detection Methods

Several detection methods are applied. They include:

1. Pulse-position detection (peak detection)
2. Pulse-amplitude detection (pulse slimming)
3. Level detection (restoring the write current)
4. Viterbi-like detection

The most frequently employed equalization and detection methods will be explained here.

Pulse-Position Detection. Differentiation of the playback pulse results in a zero crossing at the transition (see Fig. 11.12). Far from the transition the differentiated signal decays to zero; so noise will cause numerous zero crossings. That is why amplitude detection is needed to gate out the correct transition (see Fig. 11.13). Peak shift results in displacement of the zero crossings, and severe peak shift shifts the zero crossing out of the window in the bit cell. A certain equalization is needed to keep the transitions at the right place.[18] Owing to the differentiator high-frequency noise is boosted, which results in a poor detection S/N ratio. For that reason this direction method is not used in digital audio recording with its narrow tracks and high linear densities.

Pulse-Amplitude Detection. By using Nyquist criteria the shape of the playback pulse may be changed so that no intersymbol interference occurs at the detection (clocking) moment. In pulse-amplitude

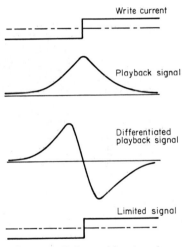

FIG. 11.12 Pulse-position detection.

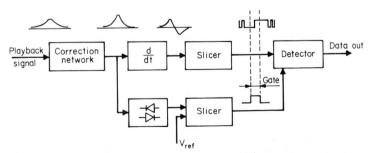

FIG. 11.13 Block diagram of pulse-position detection. V_{ref} is proportional to peak amplitude. In the detector it is checked if there is a transition in the gate interval.

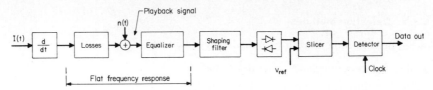

FIG. 11.14 Block diagram of pulse-amplitude detection. V_{ref} is proportional to peak amplitude. ($V_{ref} \approx 0.5\ V_p$.) The detector consists of a flip-flop which is clocked in the middle of the eye opening.

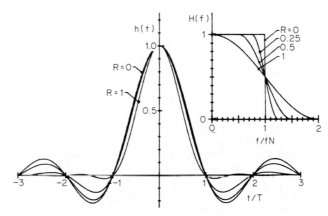

FIG. 11.15 Nyquist 1 shaping filter (transfer function and impulse response).

detection transitions in the write current are detected. A block diagram is shown in Fig. 11.14.

The equalizer compensates for the losses in the recording channel with the inverse (amplitude as a function of frequency) transfer function. At the output of the equalizer δ pulses are found again together with a lot of noise due to the high-frequency boost. To reduce this noise and widen the pulse, shaping filters which satisfy the Nyquist 1 criterion are used, e.g., sine rolloff filters with transfer function.

$$
H_1(f) = \begin{cases} 1 & f < (1 - R)f_N \\[2mm] \dfrac{1}{2}\left[1 - \sin\left(\dfrac{\pi}{2} \cdot \dfrac{f - f_N}{R \cdot f_N}\right)\right] & (1 - R)f_N \le f \le (1 + R)f_N \\[2mm] 0 & f > (1 + R)f_N \end{cases} \quad (11.28)
$$

where f_N = Nyquist frequency
R = rolloff factor

With $R = 0$ the ideal low-pass filter is obtained, and with $R = 1$ the raised cosine filter.

The impulse response of the sine rolloff filter is given by

$$h_1(t) = \frac{1}{T} \cdot \frac{\cos\left[\pi R\left(\dfrac{t}{T}\right)\right]}{1 - \left[2R\left(\dfrac{t}{T}\right)\right]^2} \cdot \frac{\sin\left[\pi\left(\dfrac{t}{T}\right)\right]}{\pi\left(\dfrac{t}{T}\right)} \tag{11.29}$$

The Nyquist pulses extend from $t = -\infty$ to $t = \infty$, but at the clocking moments ($t = nT$) they do not disturb one another. The eye pattern is shown for two values of the rolloff factor in Fig. 11.16. Only in the eye opening is a faultless data recognition possible. With small rolloff factors the eye opening is narrow. If the sampling moment is unstable (clock jitter), a high bit error rate will be the result. On the other hand, a large rolloff factor results in a large bandwidth and so in an increasing noise level. Practical values for the rolloff factor are $R = 0.3$ to 0.5.

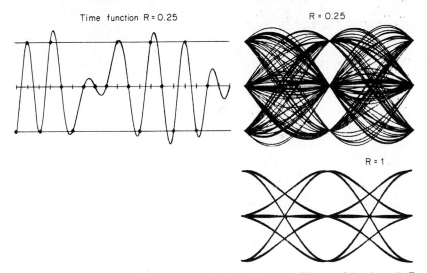

FIG. 11.16 Eye pattern of Nyquist 1 shaping filter; R = rolloff factor of the sine rolloff filter.

Pulse-Amplitude Detection with Partial-Response Shaping. The wide bandwidth in Nyquist 1 pulse shaping may lead to high noise levels. In partial-response systems the bandwidth is reduced below the Nyquist frequency, which results in intersymbol interference. With certain shaping filters this interference is restricted to a few bits. The most frequently used partial-response system (Class 4) will be described.[19] The transfer function of the partial-response shaping filter is

$$H_2(f) = \cos\left(\frac{\pi}{2} \cdot \frac{f}{f_N}\right) \qquad f \leq f_N$$
$$= 0 \qquad f > f_N \tag{11.30a}$$

and the impulse response

$$h_2(t) = \frac{1}{2\pi} \cdot \frac{T}{\left(\dfrac{T}{2} + t\right)\left(\dfrac{T}{2} - t\right)} \cdot \cos\left(\pi \times \frac{t}{T}\right) \qquad (11.31)$$

This given transfer characteristic may be modified with an even function around f_N as follows from the Nyquist 2 criterion.[20] A practical transfer characteristic using sine rolloff filters is

$$H_2(f) = \cos\left(\frac{\pi}{2} \cdot \frac{f}{f_N}\right) H_1(f) \qquad (11.30b)$$

Clocking is done in the middle of the bit cell (see Fig. 11.17). Only at two instants is a nonzero value found; the value at the clocking moments is half of the value of the Nyquist 1–shaped signal. This reduced signal level should be compensated by a much lower noise level (because of the smaller bandwidth). The eye pattern looks very much the same as the one from the Nyquist 1–shaped signal (see Fig. 11.18).

The signal value at the clocking moments is determined by two bits, the preceding bit and the next bit. Signal levels can be $+v$ and $-v$ (one transition either left or right from the clocking moment) and 0 (no transitions or a transition at

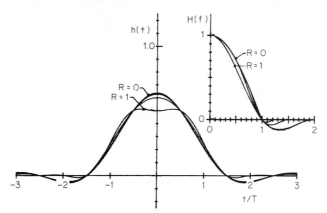

FIG. 11.17 Partial-response Class 4 shaping filter (transfer function and impulse response).

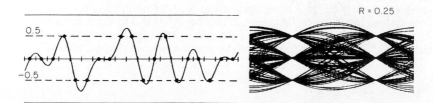

FIG. 11.18 Eye pattern of a partial-response Class 4 shaping filter.

the left and one at the right of the clocking moment). If we know the preceding bit, we can determine the next bit from the measured signal level. Error propagation might occur when one bit is misdetected. Methods used to prevent error propagation are described in Sec. 11.4.2.

Level Detection (Restoring the Write Current).   The two-level write current is restored by means of an equalizer and an integrator, which compensate for the differentiating action of the playback head. (See Fig. 11.19.) At the input of the shaping filter, the original write current appears, but with a lot of noise (low-frequency noise due to the integrator and high-frequency noise from the high-frequency boost in the equalizer). The high-frequency noise is removed with the shaping filter, which is just a Nyquist 1 filter with compensation for the length of the bit cell.

$$H_3(f) = H_1(f) \left[\frac{\dfrac{\pi f}{f_N}}{\sin\left(\dfrac{\pi_F}{f_N}\right)} \right] \tag{11.32}$$

At the clocking moments a positive or a negative signal is found. The reference level for the limiter is 0 V. The fact that it is not amplitude-dependent is a great advantage because of the amplitude fluctuations found in magnetic recording.

Level detection can handle some intersymbol interference caused by deviations at high frequencies from the ideal transfer characteristic, but it is more sensitive to deviations at low frequencies. (See Figs. 11.20 and 11.21.) In a practical situation integration cannot be carried out at very low frequencies, for the influence of low-frequency noise and disturbances would be too severe. That is why dc-free channel codes are advantageous when level detection is applied. To overcome problems at low frequencies, dc-restoring circuits might be used[21] (see Fig. 11.22).

The high-pass circuit in the signal path removes low-frequency noise but also low-frequency signal components. If a rather low bit error rate is expected at the output, the missing low-frequency components could be added to the signal at the input of the limiter. A further decreasing bit error rate will be the result. Careful matching of amplitude levels is required.

Level detection can be used also with *partial-response* shaping. Then a trace-level signal occurs. Reference levels at half of the peak amplitude are used.

Viterbi Decoding.   In Viterbi detection one detected bit is not determined by the signal at just one clocking moment.[22,23] Several successive signal values are stored

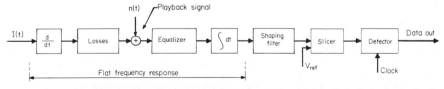

FIG. 11.19   Block diagram of a level detector.

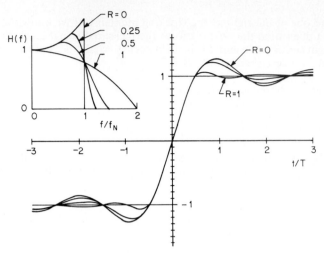

FIG. 11.20   Step response of a level-detector shaping filter; R = roll-off factor of the sine rolloff filter.

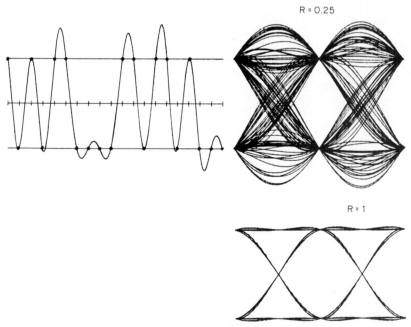

FIG. 11.21   Eye pattern of a level-detector shaping filter.

in a memory, and the probable sequence is taken. A gain of several decibels in S/N ratio is expected. This method is more complicated and more sensitive to changes in the transfer characteristic than those mentioned earlier. Perhaps that is the reason why it is not yet widely used in magnetic recording.

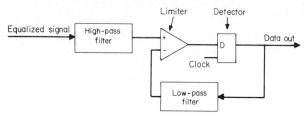

FIG. 11.22 DC-restoring circuit.

11.3.2 Transversal Filters

Equalizing and shaping filters are often implemented with transversal filters[24] (see Fig. 11.23). Signals from a tapped delay line are multiplied by adjustable coefficients and then added together. In this way the desired impulse response can be made. Some simple transversal filters are shown in Fig. 11.24.

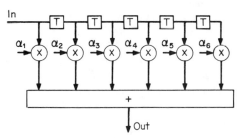

FIG. 11.23 Transversal filter; T = delay time; α_i = multiplier constant.

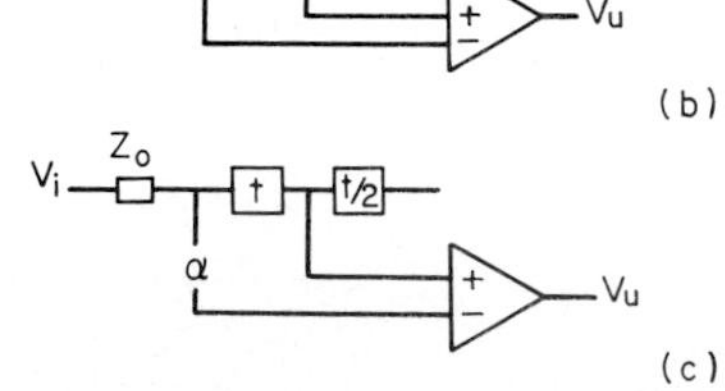

$$\frac{V_u}{V_i} = e^{-j\omega t} \cdot \cos(\omega t)$$

(a)   delay

$$\frac{V_u}{V_i} = e^{-j\omega t} \cdot \frac{1}{2}\left[1 - 2\alpha \cdot \cos(\omega t)\right]$$

(b)

$$\frac{V_u}{V_i} = e^{-\frac{3}{2}j\omega t} \cdot \left[\cos(\omega \, t/2) - \alpha \cdot \cos(\omega^3 t/2)\right]$$

(c)

FIG. 11.24 Special cases of transversal filters. (a) Shaping filter for the partial-response Class 4 detector. (b, c) Equalizer circuits.

11.3.3   Bit Errors

Noise from tape, head, and electronics may result in erroneously detected bits. For additive noise with a gaussian amplitude distribution a relation between the BER and the S/N ratio can be derived. (see Figs. 11.25 and 11.26.) Suppose the amplitude density function $\rho(E)$ is given by

$$\rho(E) = \frac{1}{\sigma\sqrt{2\pi}} \cdot e^{-E^2/2\sigma^2} \tag{11.33}$$

where σ = rms value of the noise voltage.

For a two-level signal (level detection) the probability that, for instance, the $-V_0$ level is misdetected is given by

$$p(E > V_0) = \int_{V_0}^{\infty} \rho(E) \times dE \tag{11.34}$$

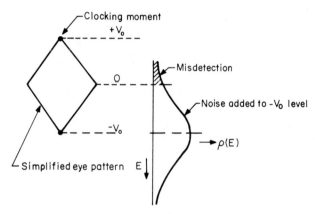

FIG. 11.25   Two-level detection with additive noise.

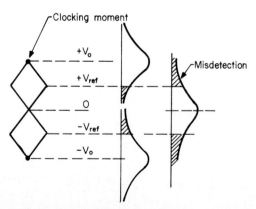

FIG. 11.26   Three-level detection with additive noise.

If we expect that there are equal probabilities for the signal levels $+V_0$ and $-V_0$ and that the reference level is midway between $+V_0$ and $-V_0$, then the error probability is

$$p(E > V_0) = \frac{1}{2}\left[1 - \text{erf}\,\frac{V_0}{\sigma\sqrt{2}}\right] \qquad (11.35)$$

The error function erf (x) is tabulated in many books. The S/N ratio at the moment of the detection is V_0/σ. Figure 11.27 shows that the BER $= f(S/N)$. Here we can see that S/N $=$ 16 dB is high enough to have a BER $< 10^{-10}$.

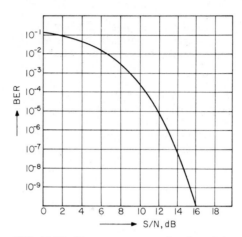

FIG. 11.27 Bit error rate as a function of the S/N ratio.

Similar calculations can be made for three-level detection. The probability of misdetection of the zero level is twice the expression given in Eq. (11.35). Owing to the deep slope in the curve, Fig. 11.27 gives a very good approximation for the BER in three-level detection. The signal level in the expression of the S/N ratio is always the distance between the signal level at the clocking moment and the closest reference level. Additive noise is only one reason for bit errors. Others are:

1. *Amplitude modulation:* This results in a high noise level around the carrier frequency. In amplitude detection the reference level should be adjusted to the instantaneous signal level.

2. *Dropouts:* Dropouts are characteristic of magnetic recording. Some may extend over several thousands of bits.

3. *Crosstalk.* No guard band is used in rotary-head systems. Sometimes the playback head is wider than the written tracks on the tape, resulting in crosstalk. Even with the track width of the playback head the same as the track width on the tape, mistracking during playback and side-reading effects result in crosstalk. The crosstalk signal should not be treated as additive noise. The amplitude distribution is not gaussian, and the maximum amplitude is well defined. In a worst-case situation this maximum crosstalk level may be subtracted from the signal level when calculating that the BER $= f(S/N)$.

4. *Nonlinearities:* Especially when tapes are overwritten (without erasing), residual signal may be left and nonlinearities may occur in the write process. Some detection methods (amplitude detection) are more sensitive to nonlinearities than others (level detection).

5. *Clock jitter:* Residual intersymbol interference, noise, and scan-speed variations result in clock jitter. The signal is not clocked in the middle of the eye opening, resulting in a loss of S/N ratio.

11.4 CHANNEL CODING

Channel coding (often called *channel modulation* or *line modulation*) is used to match data to the particular characteristics of the transmission channel. The magnetic recording channel is band-limited and nonlinear, and it suffers from crosstalk, timing errors, noise, amplitude modulation, and dropouts. Each of these factors poses constraints on the selection of channel codes and detection methods.

The recorder will not reproduce very low frequencies (because of the differentiating action of the playback head) or high frequencies.

With a two-level write current most nonlinearities in the recording process are eliminated, but some distortion occurs, especially in the overwriting of data (without erasing the tape). The playback process is expected to be linear. This holds for the ring head; the MRH exhibits nonlinear behavior.

The use of narrow tracks, without a guard band and in some cases with a wider playback head than the written tracks on the tape, results in crosstalk. Detection methods and channel codes should be optimized with respect to this kind of crosstalk.

Timing jitter of clocking signals is caused by residual symbol interference, noise, crosstalk, and scan-speed variations. This necessitates run-length-controlled codes which are self-clocking. A wide eye opening reduces the effect of clock jitter on the BER.

Narrow tracks and small wavelengths on the tape result in a low S/N ratio.

A typical shortcoming of the recording channel is amplitude modulation of the playback signal. In worst-case situations severe dropouts occur.

11.4.1 Code Parameters

In channel coding the data bit stream is converted into a bit stream suitable for the recording channel (see Fig. 11.28). (The function of the precoder will be explained in Sec. 11.4.2.) In the channel coder n input bits are converted into m output bits. As $m > n$, some m-bit symbols can be left out. Only those code words which have favorable properties with respect to bandwidth, dc content, etc., are used. Converting n bits into m bits can be accomplished either by using logical rules which take into account the previous bits (examples are the Miller square, HDM-1) or by using tables to convert n bits into m bits (examples are the 4–5

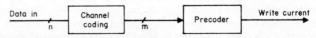

FIG. 11.28 The channel coder.

group code and the 8–10 dc-free code). The suitability of the codes is determined by such code parameters as:

1. *Rate of the code:* $R = n/m$ is called the rate of the code.

2. *Clock window:* $\Delta T = (n/m)T$. A large clock window can tolerate more clock jitter. T is the data-bit length, and ΔT is the channel-bit length.

3. *Run-length distribution (distances between transitions):* It is assumed that a 1 in the coded bit stream results in a transition in the write current; with a 0 there is no change. (This is achieved in the precoder.) The following definitions are used to characterize the run lengths: d = the minimum number of 0's between successive 1's; k = the maximum number of 0's between succeeding 1's; r = the number of 0's at the beginning of a code word; and ℓ = the number of 0's at the end of the code word. The minimum distance T_{min} between two transitions is the lower value of $(d + 1) \Delta T$ and $(r + \ell + 1) \Delta T$, and the maximum distance T_{max} is the higher value of $(k + 1) \Delta T$ and $(r + \ell + 1) \Delta T$. In block codes sometimes *merging* rules are used to limit T_{min} and T_{max} at the boundaries of the code words. A high value of T_{min} results in fewer problems if deviations from the ideal transfer function occur at high frequencies, and with a low value of T_{max} fewer problems are expected at low frequencies and with clocking. The guaranteed number of transitions makes the code self-clocking.

4. *Density ratio:* DR = $(d + 1)n/m$. The normalized value of T_{min} is often called the density ratio. It gives the minimum distance between transitions compared with the data-bit length T.

5. *Constraint length:* This is the number of channel bits required to decode the present bit. In block codes the constraint length is limited to 1 block (to 2 blocks when merging rules are used). The constraint length is important with respect to error propagation.

6. *DC content and digital sum variation (DSV):* The DSV is the running integral of the bits. Here 1 is taken as +1 and 0 as −1, just as with the record current. A limited value of the DSV results in a dc-free channel code. The DSV can be shown in a plot of the trellis diagram (see Fig. 11.29).

Parameters of some codes are shown in the Table 11.2. Code conversion tables on these codes can be found in Refs. 19 and 25 to 30.

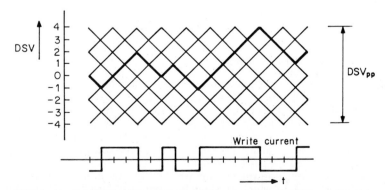

FIG. 11.29 Trellis diagram showing digital sum variation (DSV) as a function of the time.

TABLE 11.2   Some Properties of Channel Codes

Code	Rate	d	k	T_{min}/T	T_{max}/T	DC-free
NRZ-M	1	0	∞	1	∞	No
Biphase	1–2	0	1	0.5	1	Yes
Miller	1–2	1	3	1	2	No
Miller square	1–2	1	5	1	3	Yes
Group 4–5	4–5	0	2	0.8	2.4	No
HDM-1	1–2	2	8	1.5	4.5	No
3PM	1–2	2	11	1.5	6	No
EFM	8–17	2	10	1.4	5.2	Yes
Block code 2–3	2–3	1	7	1.3	2.7	No
Block code 8–10	8–10	0	3	0.8	3.2	Yes

Nonreturn to zero (NRZ) is not suitable for recording unless some boundaries on T_{max} are already present in the data. Undefined maximum run lengths can cause problems in clock recovery. Frequency-modulation (FM) recording (biphase) requires a large bandwidth, but it has good properties with regard to clocking, dc content, and immunity to crosstalk, nonlinearities, etc.

It is hard to decide which code is the best in high-density recording. All codes are optimized for a certain application and with the limitations of the recording channel for that particular application. The choice is often determined by the experience one has had with a certain kind of channel code and by the patent rights of others.

Codes are often described by their power spectral-density function (well known from communication theory). The aim is to match the power spectral-density function to the transfer function of the channel. However, spectral-density functions are found by averaging over a long bit sequence. Separate bits are detected by clocking at a certain moment. In general, BERs are less than 10^{-4}. Worst-case patterns and temporary fluctuations in the transfer characteristic of the recording channel may be largely responsible for these errors. It is the aim of channel coding to improve the worst-case patterns and to make detection more reliable in case of fluctuations in the transfer characteristic. The gain in the performance of the worst-case situations compensates for the loss under normal circumstances. Considerations in the time domain (step and impulse response, T_{min}, T_{max}, clock window, etc.) are more important than the power spectral-density function (which is found for long sequences and under normal circumstances).

11.4.2   Precoders and Scramblers

It was noted that a 1 in the channel-bit stream resulted in a transition in the write current. The reason for this result will be given here.

The playback head differentiates the flux from the head (which is similar to the record current). In pulse-amplitude detection only transitions in the write current are detected. If we know the starting point, we can reconstruct the data pattern. Misdetection of a transition results in error propagation. This error propagation can be avoided by using precoders.

In the time-discrete and digital domain the differentiator can be replaced by the function $(1 + D)$, in which D is a delay operator[19] (see Fig. 11.30). With the precoder this transfer function is divided by $(1 + D)$. Now a 1:1 transfer function

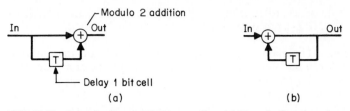

FIG. 11.30 Precoder for an NRZ-1 recording. (*a*) Transfer-function play-back side (differentiator). (*b*) Precoder which compensates for the transfer function.

between channel code and detected bits is found (see Fig. 11.30). In this way every 1 in the channel-bit stream results in a transition of the record current. No error propagation occurs, as can be seen in the following example.

Bit pattern	0	0	1	0	1	1	1	0	0	1	1	1	1	0
Write current	−	−	+	+	−	+	−	−	−	+	−	+	−	−
Playback signal	.	.	↑	.	↓	↑	↓	.	.	↑	↓	↑	↓	.
Detected bits	0	0	1	0	1	1	1	0	0	1	1	1	1	0

Furthermore, detection is independent of the polarity of the signal. The polarity of the connections of the write and the playback head is no longer important. Therefore, this method is also used for level detection. Here the output signal of the precoder is detected. This signal should be differentiated to find the output from the channel coder.

This kind of precoding results in NRZ-M (mark) recording of the channel bits [also called NRZ-1 (inverse) recording]. It must be noted that the desired channel characteristics (T_{min}, T_{max}, DSV) should be met after the channel bits have passed through the precoder.

The transfer characteristic of the partial-response Class 4 amplitude detector is ($1 + D^2$) (see Fig. 11.31). To avoid error propagation for this kind of detection the corresponding precoder with the transfer function $1/(1 + D^2)$ is used. The precoder is explained with the following example.

Bit pattern		0	0	1	0	1	1	1	0	0	1	1	1	1	0
Current	−	−	−	−	+	−	−	+	+	+	+	−	−	+	+	+
Playback signal	.	.	.	↑	.	↓	↑	↑	.	.	↓	↓	↑	↑	.
Detected bits		0	0	1	0	1	1	1	0	0	1	1	1	1	0

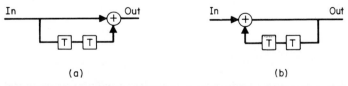

FIG. 11.31 Precoder for an I-NRZ-1 recording. (*a*) Transfer-function play-back side. (*b*) Precoder which compensates for the transfer function.

This kind of recording is often called I-NRZ-1 (interleaved NRZ-1 recording) because the NRZ-1 precoder with interleave factor 2 is used.

Scramblers. The main disadvantage of NRZ recording is that no transitions are guaranteed. On the other hand, NRZ has the advantage of a wide clock window. If some statistics are present in the data stream (long run lengths), it is possible to convert these data bits without increasing the number of bits into another bit stream which has many more transitions or no correlation between succeeding bits. Changing the sequence by interleaving might be a solution, but often scramblers are used.[24] An example of a scrambler is given in Fig. 11.32. Scramblers are used in the same way as precoders. On the recording side the bit stream is divided by a transfer function, while on the playback side it is multiplied by the same function. The transfer functions are known from Galois-field arithmetic and pseudo-random noise generators.[31]

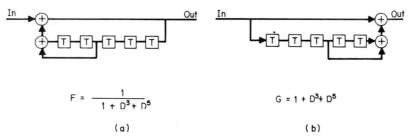

$$F = \frac{1}{1 + D^3 + D^5}$$

$$G = 1 + D^3 + D^5$$

(a)   (b)

FIG. 11.32   Scrambler-descrambler circuit. (*a*) Scrambler on the record side. (*b*) Descrambler (playback side).

Scramblers should be used carefully. Some data patterns will result in long run lengths, and single bit errors may be converted into multiple errors.

11.4.3 Multilevel Coding

Advantages and disadvantages of multilevel coding are explained with the following example. The four combinations of 2 data bits are converted into 1 channel bit with four discrete amplitude levels (equally spaced). So bit rate and bandwidth are halved. The maximum amplitude level in the channel remains the same. In the detector the difference between a certain level and the closest reference level is one-third of the signal level found in two-level detection. This loss in signal should be compensated by a much lower noise level (because of the lower bandwidth). This is not yet true.

The nonlinear write process and the amplitude modulation act against the use of multilevel codes.[32]

11.5 *ERROR CONTROL CODES*

Digital characterization of information provides us with an accurate and yet simple way to manipulate signal content. It allows detection of transmission errors and makes it possible to correct these errors. Although the design and evaluation of codes seem to be a highly specialized area in engineering, we will show that the concept is very simple.

You will have noticed the word *control* in the heading of this section. More than *correction,* it indicates the goal of the code designer to offer reliable transmission over a relevant area of error probabilities. Operation outside this area generally shows less reliable transmission than using no error control at all.

We may distinguish between random and burst errors. In the case of random errors, the probability of a transmission error in a succeeding bit is independent of the present bit position. In a burst error, this dependency is clearly present. To illustrate this, we state that in magnetic recording random errors are caused by additive noise whereas burst errors are generated by signal interruptions (dropouts).

In simulations one often refers to error generators of a structure known as *Markov sources* (Fig. 11.33). It shows two states, one good and one bad. During each unit of time the source emits one symbol of the message and assumes a new state. The transitions from the old and new states are given in terms of conditional probabilities P(new-old). Error conditions are also denoted along the branches.

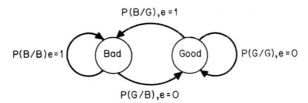

FIG. 11.33 Markov source; $e = 1$ is error; $e = 0$ is correct.

When a message which has been transmitted over a noisy channel is received, it is checked for an error event before it is used. To do so, we may employ known properties of the information itself. For instance, when we read a text produced by handwriting, we automatically use this kind of detection in checking bad characters by using our knowledge of words and context. Obviously the text contains excess information. In coding theory, this kind of information is called *redundancy.* If we delete the redundant information from the message, the transmission will be very efficient. Also, the message will be vulnerable. In a text one deformed character could alter the entire context of a letter. Therefore, if we want to transmit a message which has no redundancy, we should provide for excess information ourselves. For example, we could send the same message twice instead of once. By comparing the two messages, reliability may be checked. If differences are found, we do not know which message is wrong; therefore, to make corrections we must add even more redundancy. One method would be send the information three times. With a majority vote all single errors can be corrected.

This system is a simple and yet illustrative example of coding for error control. It shows a number of general principles:

1. To be able to detect transmission errors, we must add redundant information.

2. To be able to correct transmission errors, we must add even more redundant information.

3. If a protected signal is corrupted by more than a certain amount of errors, the protection fails.

11.5.1 Construction of a Code

In the first example a maximum BER of 1 error in 3 consecutive bits of information is expected. All possible combinations of 3 bits which differ in only 1 bit therefore should represent the same information. From the 8 available words only 2 can be used, 1 from Table *a* and its inverse from Table *b*.

a. 000; 001; 010; 011

b. 111; 110; 101; 100

In our second example we will show how to construct a code with 10-bit-wide code words. It should be possible to correct all error fractions of 3 bits or less. First, we assign the code word A, which is a random selection from all 10-bit possibilities. Then, we delete all code words which differ in 3-bit positions or less from the first code word. We could visualize this by saying that we have constructed a sphere with radius 3 around the code word A. The center of the sphere is the code word A. All other elements in the sphere are nonvalid code words. If a message with 3 or less bit errors is sent, we know therefore that message A has been sent.

To find the second code word, we locate a second sphere which does not touch the first sphere. The center of the sphere is code word B. The procedure is repeated until the entire space is filled with spheres. Then the number of available code words is given by the largest integer which is smaller than

$$m \leq \frac{\text{total number of 10-bit code words}}{\text{number of code words in one sphere}} = \frac{1024}{176} \qquad (11.36)$$

Here only five codes words are found. One can show that the codes perform better if the length of the code words increases. With such long codewords A, B . . . cannot be chosen arbitrarily. During decoding it would take too much time to check step by step to which sphere the received code word belongs. A systematic approach to construct these code words concentrates on mathematical procedures found in group theory and Galois-field computation.[31] In this section we will not detail these methods but conclude with a few statements:

1. Most practical codes encode k information bits into n-bit code words by adding $(n - k)$ bits. These codes are called *systematic*. The $(n - k)$ redundant bits are known as *parity bits*. All the computations may be performed on $(n - k)$-bit-wide words (using the information of n bits). This results in an acceptable hardware.

2. Many codes are not optimal in the sense that words are "lost in the space between spheres." Moreover, words need not be equally spaced. That is why the minimum distance d between any two code words (called the Hamming distance) is given in the code descriptor (n, k, d).

3. Most practical decoders operate by digital computation of the remainder of a division. This remainder contains the information on the location of the erroneous bits.

11.5.2 Detection of Transmission Errors

The cyclic-redundancy-check (CRC) method, which is often used to detect error-free transmission, is explained with a numerical example.

Suppose that symbols (decimal numbers) in a message can have values 0, 1, ..., 9. The message contains 5 symbols ($k = 5$) numbered $s1, ..., s5$. One symbol $s0$ is added to these 5 symbols. The number $s5.10^5 + s4.10^4 + s3.10^3 + s2.10^2 + s1.10 + s0$ divided by 11 (prime number) should result in a remainder which is zero. So $s0$ is just 11 minus the remainder which is found when $s5, ..., 0$ is divided. [The situation that the remainder is 10 (2 digits) is excluded for the moment.] The message which is sent is $s5, s4, ..., s0$.

At the receiving point we know that the message $s5, ..., s0$ should be a multiple of 11. So all errors will be detected except those which are multiples of 11. Apparently the coding is straightforward and yet powerful for decimal numbers.

We can also divide binary data by some divisor and produce encoded data by the same procedure. To do so we define a binary polynomial in terms of a delay operator. This polynomial behaves like the prime number in the foregoing example. Because all encoded sequences of bits are multiples of this divisor we call it a *generating polynomial*. Generating polynomials are known from Galois-field arithmetic. Often a 16-bit CRC code is used. The generating polynomial for this code, given in the usual notation, is

$$g(x) = x^{16} + x^{12} + x^5 + 1 \qquad (11.37)$$

x is equivalent to the delay operator. The circuit diagram is given in Fig. 11.34.

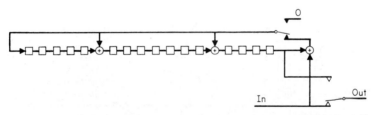

FIG. 11.34 CRC encoder and decoder. The generating polynomial is $g(x) = x^{16} + x^{12} + x^5 + 1$. Encoder: switch is closed during transfer of k information bits and opened during transfer of 16 parity bits. Decoder: switch is closed during $n = k + 16$ data bits. Then the shift register is checked to see whether all registers are 0.

In the numerical example we have seen the detecting properties. The choice of the generator polynomial determines the power of the code.

11.5.3 Correction of Random Errors

By group theory rules are formulated to find generators which produce BCH (Bose-Chaudhuri-Hocqueghem), RS (Reed-Solomon), and other famous codes. The procedure to correct errors will be demonstrated by using the polynomial $g(x) = x^3 + x^2 + 1$ (in binary terms, 1 0 1 1). Suppose that the information to be sent is 1 1 0 1 ($k = 4$ bits). The remainder after division of $x^3(x^3 + x^2 + 1) = x^6 + x^5 + x^3$ by $g(x)$ results in 1. The message that is sent is 1 1 0 1 0 0 1; it is called a code word $C(x)$. During transmission the word $C(x)$ may have been corrupted by an error pattern $E(x)$. The received message is $R(x) = C(x) + E(x)$. During detection this message is divided by $g(x)$. A transmission error is detected when the remainder is not zero. If we are able to derive one or more position pointers from the remainder, we can correct these errors. Therefore, we introduce a check matrix H, which is defined so that for every encoded message $H \cdot C = 0$. In our case

$$H = \begin{bmatrix} 0 & 0 & 1 & 1 & 1 & 0 & 1 \\ 0 & 1 & 1 & 1 & 0 & 1 & 0 \\ 1 & 1 & 1 & 0 & 1 & 0 & 0 \end{bmatrix} \tag{11.38}$$

The received message $R(x)$ is a code word only when $(H \cdot R) = 0$; if not, the result is $(H \cdot E)$. This result is called a *syndrome* (sign of disease). Every syndrome is related to one correctable-error pattern, which can be found, for example, by a read-only-memory (ROM) lookup table.

Reed-Solomon codes are very efficient in the sense of parity bits to be added. Here the minimum distance $d = 2t + 1$ (t = radius of the sphere). If we want to correct t error symbols, we only need to add $2t$ parity symbols. If the positions of the error symbols (by pointers found, for instance, with the CRC method) are known, we can even correct $2t$ error symbols.

This is illustrated in Fig. 11.35. Here a (12, 10, 3) RS code is combined with a CRC code. The CRC code detects errors in each column. These columns are marked with an erasure pointer. Then the RS code corrects the rows with up to two pointers.

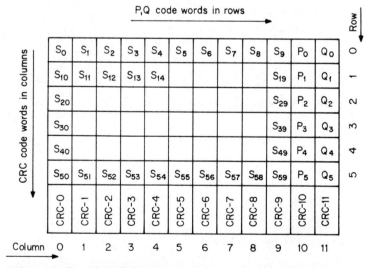

FIG. 11.35 Two-dimensional structure. Data symbols and P, Q error correction symbols are 8 bits long, and the CRC word is 16 bits long.

In the RS decoder multipliers are needed. To avoid these multipliers, simpler codes with only a parity check (see Sec. 11.7.3) can be used. This results in simpler hardware.

11.5.4 Correction of Burst Errors with Interleaving

It is obvious that correction runs short if burst errors occur. Then many symbols within one code word are wrong. If we could separate the burst error into many single errors which are distributed over different code words, even a burst error could be corrected. This separation of errors is obtained with interleaving (see Fig. 11.36). After deinterleaving, the burst error is changed into many single errors, which can be corrected.

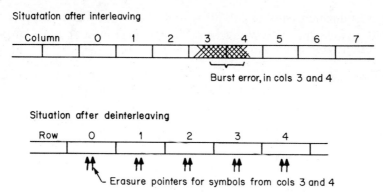

FIG. 11.36 Effects of interleaving. A burst error in the serial bit stream of rows 3 and 4 is expected.

In magnetic recording interleaving techniques improve correction possibilities significantly. The interleave factors used depend on the maximum dropout length and on the way in which concealment is applied if error correction fails.

11.6 SOURCE CODING

In the source coder the analog audio signal is converted into a digital signal. Since analog-to-digital conversion is treated in Chap. 4, only the methods used in digital recording are mentioned here.

Linear Pulse-Code Modulation (PCM). Each analog sample is quantized and converted into an m-bit code word. Quantization steps are equal for all signal levels. The S/N level is given by[1]

$$S/N = 6m + 1.8 \text{ dB} \qquad (11.39)$$

Important parameters are linearity, monotonicity, and jitter in the sampling point.

Companded PCM. To reduce the number of bits a nonlinear quantizer is used. At low input levels quantizing steps are small and S/N is high, while at large input levels steps are large. Companding techniques result in nonlinear distortion. An example of companded PCM is given in digital audio for the 8-mm video system

(Sec. 11.7.3). Here the bit rate is 256 kb/s per channel. (Sampling frequency is 32 kHz, 8 bits per sample.)

DPCM (Delta PCM).   In an oversampled signal differences between successive samples will be small.[33] These differences are coded in only a few bits and then recorded.

One-Bit Coding.   The sampling rate in this situation is high (much higher than 40 kHz). Two methods of coding are distinguished:

   1. Δ modulation, equal to DPCM, but differences are coded in 1 bit.[33]

   2. Σ Δ modulation.[1,33,34] With feedback in the coder most of the quantization noise is shifted out of the audio bandwidth.

Transform Coding.   The audio signal is sampled and quantized in linear PCM. Blocks of a number of samples are formed, and redundancy of the audio signal is removed.

Concealment Techniques (Interpolation).   These techniques are used when error correction fails. With delta modulation and in situations where all redundancy in the audio signal has been removed, concealment with interpolation is no longer possible.

11.7 STANDARDIZED SYSTEMS

A complete survey of all articles and investigations on digital audio would take up too much space. Most of the papers can be found in the preprints of Audio Engineering Society conventions, the *AES Journal,* and notes from working groups on standardization of the systems. An attempt is made here to show schematically the progress that has been made and the connections between the systems (see Fig. 11.37).

Preliminary investigations at the British Broadcasting Corporation (BBC) and elsewhere resulted in fixed-head multitrack systems for professional use. These recorders were meant to replace the multichannel analog recorders (24 to 48 audio channels) in the studios. Systems were announced by the 3M Company,[35] Matsushita,[36] Mitsubishi,[37] and others. They all have different formats. In 1980 Sony and Studer (later followed by Matsushita) started standardization activities. This resulted in the DASH system (digital audio with stationary heads). Together with the Mitsubishi solution, DASH is now the most important system in this area. The first announcements of fixed-head multitrack systems for consumer applications (two audio channels) were made by Sharp. At the beginning investigations were related to reel-to-reel recorders; later efforts were concentrated on cassette recorders. This led to standardization of the S-DAT system (stationary-head digital audio on tape) with multitrack thin-film heads and a compact cassette.

With the introduction of the VTR in 1975–1976 new systems became available to handle the high bit rates of digital audio systems. Adapters which convert the digitized audio signal into a video signal were developed. These PCM adapters were standardized by the Electronic Industries Association of Japan (EIAJ) for National Television System Committee (NTSC) video systems and for PAL-SECAM systems. PCM adapters are now on the market.

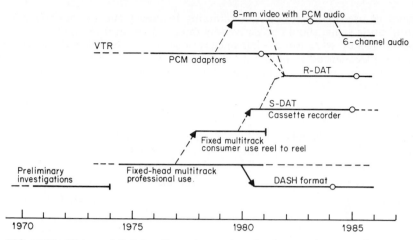

FIG. 11.37 History of digital audio on tape. —| = development has stopped; -o- = standardization has taken place; --- = reduced effort.

The 8-mm video system has an option for digital audio. This system was standardized in 1984. In 1985 an 8-mm tape recorder in which the video information is replaced by six stereo channels was announced.[38]

Perhaps initiated by 8-mm video and PCM adapter activities, Sony announced in 1982–1983 a rotary-head digital audio cassette recorder with very small dimensions. This type of recorder is standardized in the working group on R-DAT (rotary-head digital audio on tape).

The standardized systems are treated in the rest of this chapter.

11.7.1 PCM Encoder-Decoder for Use with Video Recorders

Video recorders offer the large bandwidth required by digital audio systems. So it is obvious that after the introduction of the VTR attempts were made to record digital audio signals on these recorders. Here only the result of the standardization is given. The standard is supported by the EIAJ and can be found in the technical files of the Stereo Technical Committee and the Video Technical Committee.[39]

The adapter containing the PCM encoder-decoder (see Fig. 11.38) delivers a black-and-white video signal. Of course, this adapter may be incorporated in the

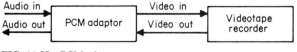

FIG. 11.38 PCM adapter.

VCR, but unfortunately there are different TV systems: the NTSC with 60 Hz, 515 lines; and the PAL-SECAM with 50 Hz, 625 lines. In synchronizing signals some restrictions had to be imposed on the sampling frequency and bit format of the audio signal. Each line in the TV signal had to contain a complete number of samples, but not all lines should contain information. Vertical synchronization cannot be used. Furthermore, the sampling frequency and the horizontal synchronization signal should be derived by integer division from the same crystal clock frequency, while this clock frequency must be sufficiently low (MHz region). Sampling frequencies in both TV systems should be almost the same. This has led to the rather peculiar sampling frequency of 44.056 kHz for NTSC and 44.100 kHz for PAL-SECAM.

Signal Specification

Number of audio channels	Two channels $A + B$ ($L + R$ for stereo)
Audio bandwidth	0 to 20 kHz
Preemphasis and deemphasis	Optional; $T_1 = 50 \ \mu s$, $T_2 = 15 \ \mu s$
Sampling frequency	44.056 kHz (NTSC); 44.10 kHz (PAL-SECAM)
Quantization	14-bit linear PCM; two's complement binary code; most significant bit (MSB) first
Transmission rate	2.625 Mbit/s
Error correction	CRC detection, P, Q correction

PCM Signal Format.   Horizontal lines contain one data or control block. The data block consists of six samples, P and Q error-correcting words, and one error-detecting CRC word (see Fig. 11.39). Video input and output signals are 1 V peak to peak. The data signal is only 0.3 V peak to peak. It cannot be larger because the VTR uses preemphasis of the video signal together with a clipper, and larger data signals would result in nonlinear behavior.

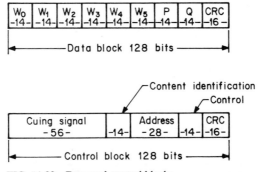

FIG. 11.39   Data and control blocks.

The NTSC format will be explained with reference to Figs. 11.40 and 11.41. Data for the PAL-SECAM system are given in parentheses. A total of 16 lines in the odd field and 17 lines in the even field of vertical synchronization are not used for data signals. One control-signal block is added in each field. The control-signal block includes a cuing signal word (56 bits), a content identification (ID) signal (14 bits), an address-signal word (28 bits), a control-signal block (14 bits), and an error-detecting (CRC) word (16 bits).

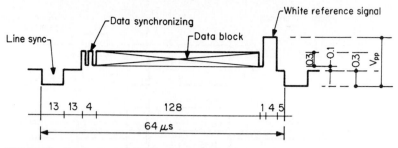

FIG. 11.40   One horizontal TV line; units are in bits.

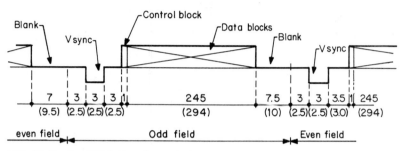

FIG. 11.41   One TV field; units are in horizontal TV lines. The situation is given for NTSC with PAL figures in parentheses. In NTSC 245 lines per frame are used, and in PAL 294 lines per frame.

Error Correction.   The CRC error-detecting word is a 16-bit word. This word is the remainder that results when the sum of the six samples and the P and Q words (112 bits) is divided by the following generating function:

$$g(x) = x^{16} + x^{12} + x^5 + 1 \qquad (11.40)$$

The CRC code delivers after deinterleaving the erasure pointer for the separate symbols. The error-correcting words P and Q are 14-bit words:

$$P = A_n + B_n + A_{n+1} + B_{n+1} + A_{n+2}B_{n+2} \qquad (11.41)$$

$$Q = T^6A_n + T^5B_n + T^4A_{n+1} + T^3B_{n+1} + T^2A_{n+2} + TB_{n+2} \qquad (11.42)$$

where n is an address of consecutive samples. As three samples of each audio channel are used in one data block, n is a multiple of 3; $+$ is a modulo 2 summation of the bits in each column, and T is the generating matrix. With this error-correcting system two of the eight words can be corrected.

To handle burst errors, interleaving is used (Fig. 11.42). For the signal symbols and the P and Q error-correcting symbols within each block an interleaving of D = 16 blocks is used (Fig. 11.43). As a result of this interleaving the eight words from one data block are recorded far from each other (maximum distance, 112 video lines). Owing to the incline of the written track on the tape, scratches on the tape do not disturb samples from one coded data block. Successive samples from one audio channel are spaced 32 TV lines from each other.

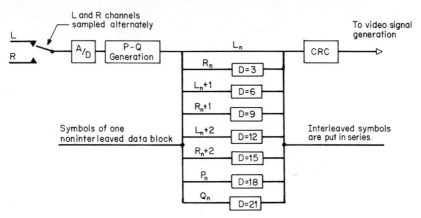

FIG. 11.42   Interleaving of data words; D = delay in blocks (horizontal TV lines).

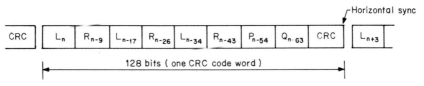

FIG. 11.43   Interleaved data words in one block.

Some PCM adapters can code in 16-bit linear PCM. The Q correction is not used and is replaced by the 2 extra bits from each sample. However, this system is not standardized, and it should not be used when many errors occur.

11.7.2   Digital Audio on Stationary-Head Recorders (DASH)

As already mentioned, initial experiments were carried out on recorders with stationary heads. In professional audio recording there is still a need for these recorders. More than two audio channels can be recorded simultaneously by increasing the tape speed and/or the number of tracks. Linear tape speeds may be high; tape consumption and playing time are not as important as they are in consumer systems.

The standard should define not only track geometry, tape speed, and tape width but also the position and meaning of every bit (data, control, error corrections). The DASH format accepts several sampling frequencies, tape speeds, and tape widths. In each format four auxiliary tracks are used for addressing, control data, cuing, etc. An option is provided with thin-film heads with 3 times as many tracks on the tape. The principal parameters are given below and in Table 11.3.

Sampling frequencies   48 kHz, 44.1 kHz, and 32 kHz
Linear tape speed   Proportional to sampling frequency
With f_s = 48 kHz   DASH-S (slow): v = 19.05 cm/s
                             DASH-M (medium): v = 38.1 cm/s
                             DASH-F (fast): v = 76.2 cm/s

TABLE 11.3

Tape width, in	Number of tracks		Number of channels		
	Data	Auxiliary	DASH-S	DASH-M	DASH-F
Normal					
¼	8	4	2	4	8
½	24	4	6	12	24
Thin-film heads*					
¼	16	4	4	8	16
½	48	4	12	24	48

*Optional.

Channel code	HDM-1 ($T_{min} = 1.5T$; $T_{max} = 4.5T^{25}$)
Quantization	In 16-bit linear PCM
Error correction	CRC detection; P, Q error correction

Additional Details. The track geometry for the ¼-in normal system is shown in Fig. 11.44. The track width of the recording head is 300 μm, and the track width of the playback head is 150 μm. Toler-
ances in recording head and playback head and in tape width (tape guidance) should not exceed certain values. The realization of the DASH-F format for ¼-in tape is shown in Fig. 11.45. Even- and odd-numbered samples are written on the tape far from each other. Inter- polation will still be possible if error correction fails because of large dropouts.

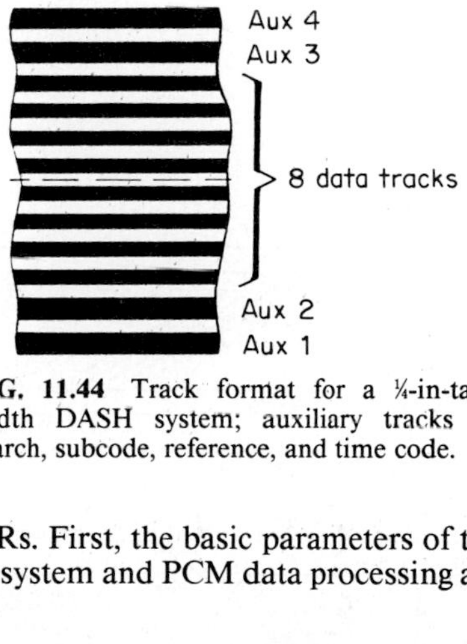

FIG. 11.44 Track format for a ¼-in-tape- width DASH system; auxiliary tracks for search, subcode, reference, and time code.

11.7.3 PCM Sound in the 8-mm Video Format

This section deals with the PCM sound concept of the 8-mm video standard for VCRs. First, the basic parameters of the tape deck are summarized; then the tracking system and PCM data processing are described.

Concept of 8-mm Video. The 8-mm video format employs state-of-the-art tape and head technology. The sound section of the recorder incorporates a mandatory FM sound system and an optional digital recording mode.[40] Figure 11.46 shows the tape format on 8-mm-wide magnetic tape and the tape wrap on the rotating drum with video heads.

In a period of time equal to one-half rotation of the drum, the information of one video field is read from the tape by one head as in standard VTRs. When this head leaves the tape, the second head starts reading the next video field. The video heads will also reproduce the pilot signals needed in the tracking system (Fig. 11.47).

The four pilots are recorded track-sequentially: Track 1 records f_1; Track 2, f_2, etc. The playback head also reads crosstalk information from adjacent tracks. By

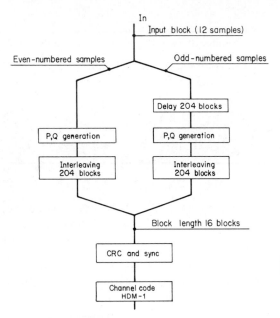

FIG. 11.45 Generating the channel-bit stream for the DASH-F ¼-in system.

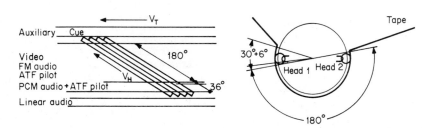

FIG. 11.46 Tape format and tape wrap.

	60-field system		50-field system	
	Short play	Long play	Short play	Long play
Tape width	8.000 ± 0.010 mm		8.000 ± 0.010 mm	
Drum diameter	40 mm		40 mm	
Wrap angle	221°		221°	
Track pitch	0.0205 mm	0.0102 mm	0.0344 mm	0.0172 mm
Track angle (tape stop)	4°53′06″		4°53′06″	
Tape speed (V_T)	14.3 mm/s	7.1 mm/s	20.05 mm/s	10.02 mm/s
Head speed (V_H)	3.8 m/s		3.1 m/s	

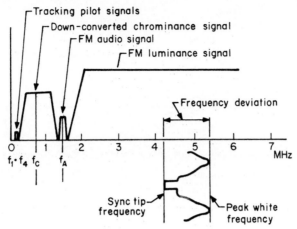

FIG. 11.47 Frequency-spectrum allocation of recording signals.

controlling tape speed it is possible to give the crosstalk signals from both adjacent tracks the same average amplitude and therefore guarantee proper tracking of the head.

The 180° part of the wrap angle is used to get continuous video information while playing back a tape. Figure 11.46 shows that the remaining tape wrap is used to create an interval where two heads contact the tape. In this interval, one head plays the video signal while the other reproduces PCM signals. By this method continuous analog video signals are combined with time-compressed digital audio data.

In the International Radio Consultative Committee (CCIR) recorder the drum rotates with 25 r/s (50-Hz video field frequency), and in the NTSC recorder the drum rotates with 30 r/s (60-Hz video field frequency). Both recorders are available in a short-play version and a long-play version (reduced tape speed and track width).

PCM Sound and the Magnetic-Tape Format. Specifications for 8-mm video PCM sound recording are as follows:

Number of audio channels	2
Sampling frequency	$2 \times F_h$ (F_h = horizontal-line frequency)
Bits per sample	8 bits, nonlinear
Noise reduction	2:1 (analog compandor)
ID code per video field	6 bytes
Redundancy (total bits − data bits)/ (total bits)	40.5 percent
Linear recording density, bit/mm	1800 (50 Hz), 1500 (60 Hz)
Transmission rate, Mbit/s	5.75 (50 Hz), 5.79 (60 Hz)

Digital Signal Processing. One PCM area contains the information required to reproduce the sound accompanying one recorded field (Fig. 11.48). This infor-

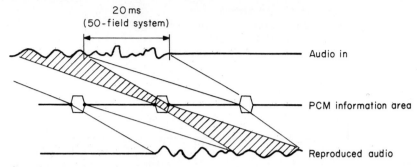

FIG. 11.48   Time-compression audio.

mation is built up with blocks of identical structure. Each block consists of (Fig. 11.49):

A synchronization pattern
An 8-bit address code

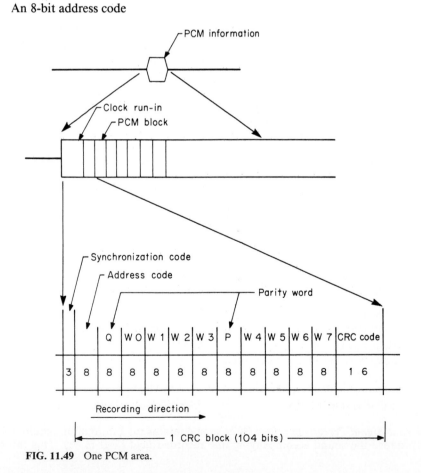

FIG. 11.49   One PCM area.

8 data bytes

2 parity bytes (P, Q)

A 16-bit CRC code

To retrieve the recorded information, a voltage-controlled oscillator (VCO) in the playback circuit is phase-locked to the tape data. Once phase lock has been achieved, the oscillator provides the sampling moments of the tape data. When the rotating head reads the PCM burst, the VCO should quickly obtain phase lock. To achieve this, the VCO loop bandwidth should be large. On the other hand, the sample timing of the tape information should be as stable as possible (and not be influenced by noise). This calls for a small loop bandwidth. A biphase mark code contains a phase reference for the clock at least every 2 channel bits. Therefore, a bandwidth that is a good compromise can easily be chosen. Figure 11.50 shows a data pattern and its possible phase and frequency lock moments. It is obvious that when the VCO frequency equals twice the data clock, unambiguous synchronization can be obtained.

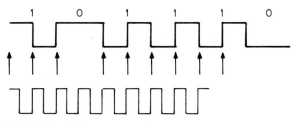

FIG. 11.50 Biphase mark code and clock recovery.

In fact, the tape-transfer characteristics do not produce a square-wave output at the playback heads. A typical frequency response of a tape-head assembly is plotted in Fig. 11.51. Ideally, the phase response should be linear. In practice, however, frequency and phase equalization are needed.

Figure 11.52 shows an eye pattern of a noiseless equalized PCM signal. By proper equalization all zero crossings are discrete.

Figure 11.53 shows the block diagram. Once the data and clock have been retrieved, the data are checked for the occurrence of a synchronization pattern. This pattern (0 0 0 1 1 1 or 1 1 1 0 0 0) is not consistent with the coding rules of the biphase mark data and therefore cannot occur from the information itself. The 88 bits following the synchronization pattern are divided by a polynomial which is given by the CRC code:

$$g(x) = x^{16} + x^{12} + x^5 + 1 \qquad (11.43)$$

When the remainder equals zero, we know that a reliable transfer of information has taken place.

Eighty data bits are stored in a random-access memory (RAM), starting with a RAM address equal to the first 8 bits (Fig. 11.54). This procedure assures rapid frame synchronization if a synchronization failure has occurred (for example, after a large dropout). During a RAM address cycle, the data byte will also be marked "reliable" by a *flag bit*. After 157 blocks (50 Hz) have been received, one frame has been completed.

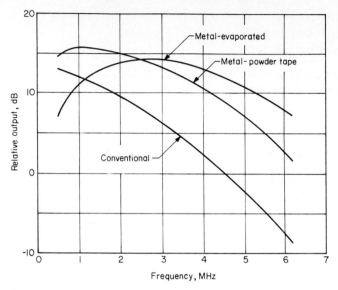

FIG. 11.51 Frequency response of different tapes.

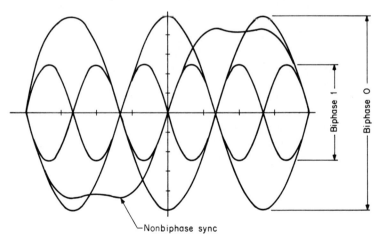

FIG. 11.52 Eye pattern of the biphase mark code.

Figure 11.55 shows the exact arrangements of the data as standardized for 50-Hz and 60-Hz systems.

Control of Transmission Errors.   To understand the error correction system used for 8-mm video, we should recall that the CRC code provided a reliability indicator for every column in the table. So if a transmission error has occurred in column 0, all bytes of column 0 are marked "unreliable" by a flag bit. Additionally, at the time of tape recording the P and Q parity symbols are generated. These *even parities* are computed by using the interleave structure of Fig. 11.56.

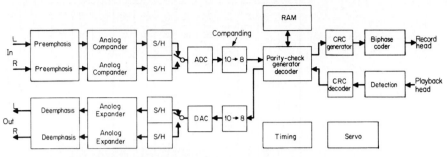

FIG. 11.53 Block diagram of a PCM system.

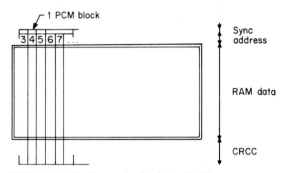

FIG. 11.54 Block organization in the RAM.

For example, the even-parity byte $Q1, 1$ at column 1 and row 1 will be generated by

$$Q1, 1 = W15, 2 + W29, 3 + W33, 4 + W47, 5$$

$$+ P61, 6 + W75, 7 + \cdots \quad (11.44)$$

If an interleave line exceeds column 156 (50-Hz recorder), the valid column will be X-156. By defining this arithmetic, all parity bytes P and Q depend only upon the data of one RAM content. Note that every element except the Q bytes is an element of two interleave lines. This so-called cross-interleave principle is of fundamental importance for error correction capability. The correction process starts by reading one interleave line from the RAM into the correction circuit while checking for the flag bit. Three situations are possible:

1. Every deinterleaved byte proves to be reliable.

2. 1 deinterleaved byte is not reliable.

3. More than 1 byte is not reliable.

Situation 1 obviously does not call for action. If situation 2 occurs, the error correction procedure is started. As an example, suppose $W15, 2$ to be corrupted by an error pattern *(syndrome)* E. Then,

$$Q1.1 + (W15.2 + E) + W29.3 + \cdots = E \quad (11.45)$$

Data Arrangement in 525-Line, 60-Field System

Sychronization code

RAM

A 0	A 43	A 44	A 87	A 88	A 131
Q 0	Q 43	Q 44	Q 87	Q 88	Q 131
ID 0 ID 1 L 0 R 0	R 60	ID 2 ID 3 L 1 R 1	R 61	ID 4 ID 5 L 2 R 2	R 62
L 63	R 126	L 64	R 127	L 65	R 128
L 129	R 192	L 130	R 193	L 131	R 194
L 195	R 258	L 196	R 259	L 197	R 260
P 0	P 43	P 44	P 87	P 88	P 131
L 261	R 324	L 262	R 325	L 263	R 326
L 327	R 390	L 328	R 391	L 329	R 392
L 393	R 456	L 394	R 457	L 395	R 458
L 459	R 522	L 460	R 523	L 461	R 524

CRC code

—— 44 ——   —— 44 ——   —— 44 ——   —— 44 ——

——————— 132 blocks ———————

11.46

Data Arrangement in 625-Line, 50-Field System

Synchronization code

RAM ← →

A 0	A51	A 52	A 53	A 104	A 105	A 156
Q 0	Q 51	Q 52	Q 53	Q 104	Q 105	Q 156
ID 0 ID 1 L 0 R 0	R72	L75	ID 2 ID 3 L 1 R 1 R 73		ID 4 ID 5 L 2 R 2 R 74	
L 75	L 151	R 153	R 74	L 152	R 77	L 153
L 130	R 229	L 232	L 155	R 230	L 156	R 231
R232	L308	R 310	R 233	L 309	R 234	L 310
P 0	P 51	P 52	P 53	P 104	P 105	P 156
L 311	R 386	L 389	L 312	R 387	L 313	R 388
L 389	L 465	R 467	R 390	L 466	R 391	L 467
L 468	R 543	L 546	L 469	R 544	L 470	R 545
L 546	L 622	R 624	R 547	L 623	R 548	L 624

CRC code

——— 53 ——— ——— 52 ——— ——— 52 ———

——— 157 blocks ———

FIG. 11.55 Data arrangements for two systems. A— = address byte, no. —; L— = audio sample, L channel no. —; R— = audio sample, R channel no. —; P— = parity check, byte no. —; Q— = parity check, byte no. —; ID— = identification code no. —.

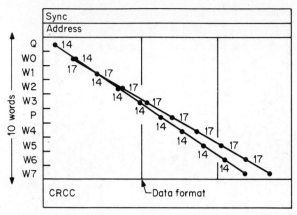

FIG. 11.56 Interleaving (50-Hz system); P parity $= 17$ blocks; Q parity $= 14$ blocks.

The erroneous byte (marked by the flag) is corrected with the error pattern. Also the flag pointer of $W15, 2$ will be set to the reliable condition.

If situation 3 occurs, error correction is not necessarily possible, as the algorithm used produces the sum $E_t = E_1 + E_2$ and not the respective components E_1 and E_2. However, because of the cross-interleave principle, every word is an element of two interleave lines (Fig. 11.57).

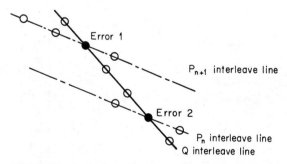

FIG. 11.57 Correction of two errors in one code word.

It is therefore possible that the other interleave line contains only that unreliable byte. If so, that error can be corrected (situation 2) and would eliminate one error from the first interleave line. Therefore, by repeating the error correction process several times, the possibility of correction is improved, as can be seen in Fig. 11.58.

For the correction of random errors, it may be calculated that a BER of 10^{-5} results in a probability of an uncorrectable error of less than 1 byte per day. This uncorrectable byte is marked as such and recognized by an interpolation circuit. The audio bytes are read from the RAM to the concealment circuit (interpolation) in the right sequential order. From the tables of Fig. 11.55 it is apparent that two successive audio samples are many data blocks (columns) apart. Therefore, when a large dropout on tape causes a number of columns in error which exceeds correction capacity, an unreliable byte is still surrounded by reliable neighbors and successful interpolation is possible (Fig. 11.59).

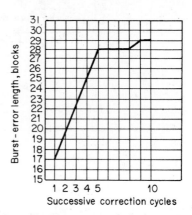

FIG. 11.58 Improvement in burst-error correction by successive correction cycles.

Analog Processing for 8-mm Video PCM Sound. The digital audio information in the 8-mm video system is restricted in resolution to 8 bits per sample. Therefore, the ratio between signal power and quantization noise is about 48 dB.

Two measures have been taken to maintain an optimal S/N ratio over a wide range of audio levels:

1. Use of a digital compandor
2. Use of an analog compandor

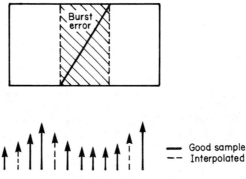

FIG. 11.59 Interpolation with very long burst errors.

As the digital compandor operates instantaneously, a sine wave will be nonlinearly compressed in the recording mode. In the playback mode an inverse expansion is performed to reconstruct the original signal. As all the relevant signal parameters are quantized digitally, full inverse processing is guaranteed. The improvement due to the nonlinear compandor is shown in Fig. 11.60. Small signals will be quantized with 10-bit accuracy.

The analog compandor (see Fig. 11.61) operates on an average signal level. By using well-chosen attack and release times, a high compression factor of 2 may be achieved (Fig. 11.62). Since the analog compandor doubles the dynamic range by a factor of 2, it is a simple matter to align the analog signals to the converter at the time of recording. Strong preemphasis and deemphasis ($t_1 = 120$ μs, $t_2 = 15$ ns) are used at high frequencies.

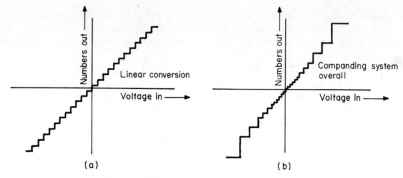

FIG. 11.60 Digital companding. (*a*) Linear PCM. (*b*) Nonlinear PCM.

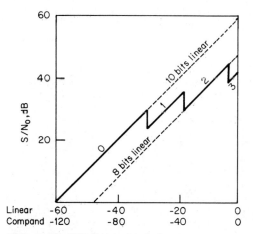

FIG. 11.61 S/N (input signal) for the 10–8 companded PCM signal.

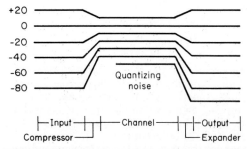

FIG. 11.62 Analog compandor (ratio 1:2). The resulting performance with preemphasis and deemphasis of $t_1 = 120\ \mu s$, $t_2 = 15$ ns: frequency range = 20 Hz to 13,500 Hz (-3-dB point); dynamic range = 100 dB (*A*-weighted); S/N ratio > 43 dB (-20 dB to 0 dB); distortion = 0.35 percent (-12 dBr).

11.50

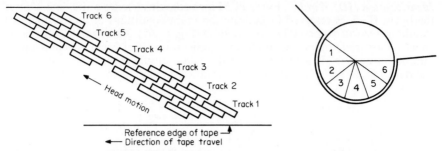

FIG. 11.63 Track format, multichannel system.

PCM Multichannel Format.   Recall that only 30° of the tape wrap angle of 210° is used to record the audio information of one stereo channel. Once we decide to use the recorder for audio only, the tape area for video can be used for audio signals as well. Therefore, the servomechanism provides the possibility of shifting the PCM recording and playback windows to six different positions along one scan of the video head. Figure 11.63 shows the resulting multichannel tape format and tape wrap. The resulting playing time is increased by a factor of 6.

Like the video mode, tracking is controlled by the four pilot signals. A fifth pilot frequency may be used to indicate that PCM signals are available for the specific track. By means of this pilot and a suitable display, one can easily allocate recorded and nonrecorded tracks on the tape even in search modes. Another feature of multichannel PCM is the autoreverse recording and playback condition. With a suitable mechanism, the tape-transport direction is reversed at the end of the tape. In this way nearly continuous recording times of 24 h (50 Hz) or 18 h (60 Hz) are available (Fig. 11.64).

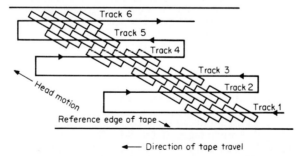

FIG. 11.64 Multichannel system with an autoreverse possibility.

In a practical condition, music recordings on different channels will show unequal lengths. Therefore, it is necessary to indicate that a piece of music has ended, where the next sound information is to be found, and whether this should be played in the forward or the reverse mode. To provide this kind of information, the 8-mm video PCM is equipped with identification words.

Identification (ID) Words. Every PCM area contains 6 bytes of ID data. One of the bytes, ID 5, is reserved to indicate the main conditions of a recording and should be recorded when ID codes are used (Fig. 11.65). To be able to use the ID codes for a variety of known and future applications, ID 1 is employed as a page number to decode ID 2 to ID 4. For the video mode, pages 0 to 6 have been standardized. Page 7 is reserved for the multichannel mode.

	Utility word [9] (optional)					Control word	
	ID 0	ID 1	ID 2	ID 3	ID 4	ID5	
B7	Mode code	Data code				1	Dubbing protect
B6 B5						B5, B6 1 0 0 1 1 1 0 0	 Recorded start point [5] Recorded end point [6] Recorded period [7] Ignore the bits [8]
B4						Ch. 2 1 0	Audio Others
B3						Ch. 1 1 0	Audio Others
B2 B1						B1, B2 0 0 0 1 1 0 1 1	 Mono [1] Stereo [2] Bilingual [3] Others
B0						1 0	Valid Invalid (all 0) [4]

FIG. 11.65 Identification words. (1) For monaural sound both channels are recorded. (2) Ch. 1 is for *L* and Ch. 2 for *R;* (3) Ch. 1 is for main sound and Ch. 2 for subsound. (4) B 0 of ID 5 is a valid-invalid bit for the following B 1 to B 7. Valid 1 should be written at least once per second. (5) The record length at the recorded start point is at least 30 fields but up to 60; (6) the record length at the recorded end point is at least 1 field. (7) These bits are recorded between recorded start and recorded end points. (8) In case that these bits are not used, (9) ID 0 and ID 1 and ID 4 are for the mode code symbolizing the sort of data and for the data code, respectively. It is possible to assign application modes up to 2°.

11.7.4 Stationary-Head Digital Audio on Tape (S-DAT)

In the stationary-head digital audio recorder information is recorded on tape in 22 parallel tracks. The advantages of the S-DAT system are relatively simple mechanics and easy head adjustments. A disadvantage is lower areal density compared with the R-DAT system (see Sec. 11.7.5). Thin-film heads are used during recording and playback. Duty-cycle writing is applied to reduce power consumption and crosstalk.[41]

For playback a yoke-type magnetoresistive head (Y-MRH) is used. A combined IRH (inductive-record head) and MRH assembly can be utilized with switching electronics and appropriate amplifiers to provide both recording and playback functions (see Fig. 11.66 and Ref. 13).

Specifications. S-DAT specifications are presented in Table 11.4.

Modes 3, 4, and 5 are optional and will not be considered here. An 8–10 dc-

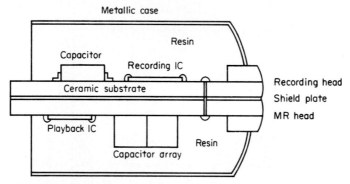

FIG. 11.66   Schematic layout of a combined IRH-MRH.

free channel code is used, with a minimum distance between transitions of $0.8T$ and a maximum distance of $3.2T$.[26] For all modes the minimum distance between transitions on tape is 0.32 μm, which corresponds to a linear density of 3000 channel bits per millimeter.

Cassette and Tape.   The cassette is a flangeless type. Its tape is protected against fingerprints by a lid that is easily opened inside the tape deck. The dimensions of the cassette are 86 $\times$ 55.5 $\times$ 9.5 mm (see Fig. 11.67). The tape width is 3.81 mm, and the tape thickness is 13 μm.

A metal-powder tape with a coercivity of $H_c = 1400$ Oe is used as a reference tape. The recording current is optimized for maximum output at a 75-kHz signal.

Data Format on Tape.   The PCM-coded audio signals are recorded in the longitudinal direction on the tape; 20 parallel tracks are used. Track pitch is 80 μm, and track width is 65 μm. Two extra tracks (auxiliary and cuing) are available for subcode or search information (Fig. 11.68).

The data on the tape are shown in Fig. 11.69. Multiples of 8 data bits are used as data symbols (ID and frame address are taken together). In the channel coder the 8-bit symbols are coded in 10 channel bits. Frames on the tape are 240 data bits (300 channel bits) wide. The C_2 parity symbols protect the subcode and the PCM data. These parity bits are written in four tracks (see Fig. 11.70).

TABLE 11.4

Mode	1	2	3	4	5
Number of audio channels	2	2	2	2	2 $\times$ 2
Sampling frequency, kHz	48	44.1	32	32	32
Quantization, bits					
Linear	16	16	16		
Nonlinear	. . .	. . .		12	12
Tape speed, cm/s	4.76	4.37	3.17	2.38	4.76
Transmission rate, Mbit/s	2.4	2.2	1.6	1.2	2.4
Redundancy, percent	36	36	36	36	36
ID code, kb/s	10	9.2	6.7	5	10
Subcode, kb/s	128	117	85	64	64

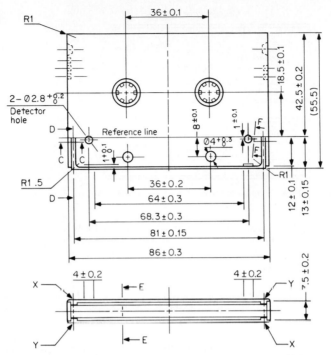

FIG. 11.67 S-DAT cassette; tape width, 3.81 mm; tape thickness, 13 μm.

In the C_1 parity generator the bits in each frame (sychronization excluded) are protected by two symbols. The error correction codes are product codes of two Reed-Solomon codes. The calculation is performed in the Galois field (GF (2^8)). The primitive polynomial $g(x) = x^8 + x^4 + x^3 + x + 1$ is used. The generating polynomials

$$C_1 = G_p(x) = \prod_{i=0}^{1} (x - \alpha^i) \qquad (11.46)$$

$$C_2 = G_Q(x) = \prod_{i=0}^{7} (x - \alpha^i) \qquad (11.47)$$

Here α is the primitive element in GF(2^8) = 0 0 0 0 0 0 1 0. In this way codes C_1 (29, 27, 3) and C_2 (40, 32, 9) are made.

Error Correction Strategy. C_1 is used to check whether there are errors in the frame of each track. Erroneous tracks are marked with a flag. With the C_2 parity bits any four erroneous tracks can then be corrected. Strong interleaving in each track is used to handle burst errors. Multiplexing and interleaving of the data symbols over the tracks are optimized for the best possible concealment (interpolating) if error correction fails (Fig. 11.71). Even with a typical symbol error rate of 5.10^{-2} caused by random bit errors only, one interpolation is found in 10

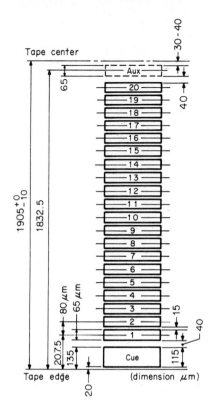

FIG. 11.68 Track pattern.

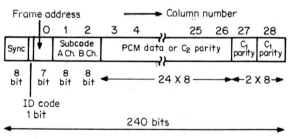

FIG. 11.69 Frame configuration.

min and one misdetected error in a year. Burst-error performance is plotted in Fig. 11.71.

Subcode. Subcode information can be allocated as:

1. *Identification code (ID):* One bit per frame is reserved for the ID (Fig. 11.70). Tape speed, track configuration, subcode, etc., can be encoded.

2. *Cue code:* This optional code is written in the cue track (see Fig. 11.68). Such basic parameters as quantization, number of data tracks, sample frequency,

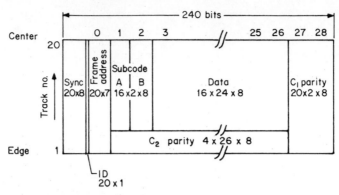

FIG. 11.70 Block configuration.

program time, and time code are encoded. The data are protected by a CRC code with polynomial $g(x) = x^{16} + x^{12} + x^5 + 1$. FM is used as a channel code. The basic configuration of the data is shown in Fig. 11.72.

3. *Subcode in the main tracks:* This optional code (Fig. 11.70) consists of a 2-byte channel (A and B). Subcode information of the compact disk can be recorded in this area.

4. *Auxiliary code:* This code has not yet been specified.

11.7.5 Rotary-Head Digital Audio on Tape (R-DAT)

Recording digital signals offers the freedom of easy compression and expansion in the time domain, which is almost impossible in analog recording. Thus the well-known helical-scan recording method with its advantage of high area density can be combined with a small wrapping angle (90°) and a small drum (diameter, 30 mm). This results in a compact apparatus with an easy-loading mechanism, reduced tape load, and larger tolerances (Fig. 11.73). A small recorder with reduced tape consumption and audio quality equal to that of a compact disk can be produced for consumer use.

Two audio channels pass through an antialiasing filter and are converted by a sample-and-hold device (quantization in time) into a quantized amplitude (ADC; see Fig. 11.74). Coding these successive samples results in a typical bit stream of

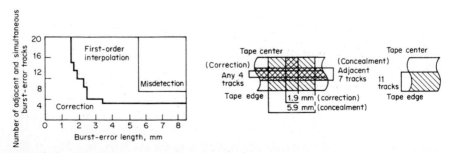

FIG. 11.71 Burst-error and concealment performance.

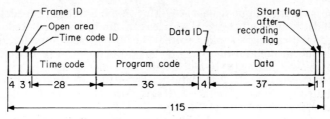

FIG. 11.72   Basic configuration of data.

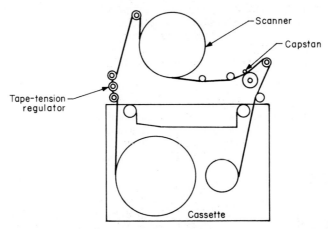

FIG. 11.73   Schematic layout of an R-DAT.

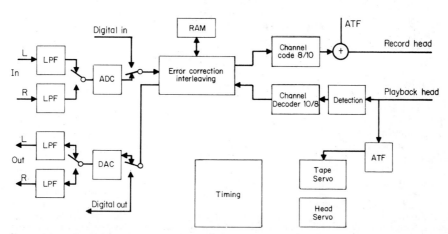

FIG. 11.74   Block diagram of an R-DAT system.

11.57

1.536 Mbit/s. Digital input signals according to the European Broadcast Union (EBU) standard[42] from other digital sources can also be accepted. Redundancy is added, and interleaving is applied so that during playback imperfections of the tape that result in random bit errors or large dropouts can be detected and/or corrected. Channel coding (8–10 block code) then takes place. The resulting continuous bit stream equals 2.46 Mbit/s. The data are time-compressed and recorded burstwise on tape together with servo signals, subcode information, etc., resulting in a channel-bit rate of 9.4 Mbit/s.

In the playback mode the analog signals from the tape are amplified and equalized. The clock is regenerated, and bit detection is applied. Time-base correction is performed to eliminate jitter from the tape-transport mechanism. Servo information is extracted from the playback signal to control tracking of the heads. The digital signal is demodulated, decoded, deinterleaved, interpolated when needed, and fed to a DAC which, together with a low-pass filter, exactly reconstructs the analog audio signal. A digital output is also possible. Subcode information can be used for control and/or display purposes.

Specifications.   Five modes are specified (see Table 11.5). The first two are mandatory; the last three, optional.

Cassette and Tape.   The cassette is a flangeless type. The tape inside the cassette is protected from external influences by a slider and a lid. Inside the tape deck the cassette can easily be opened. The basic dimensions are $73 \times 54 \times 10.5$ mm, the hub span is 30 mmm, and the hub diameter 15 mm (Fig. 11.75). The tape width is 3.81 mm, and the tape thickness is 13 μm. Maximum length of the tape is about 70 m.

A metal-powder tape ($H_c \approx 1400$ Oe) is used as a reference tape. The recording current is adjusted for maximum output at 4.7 MHz. (See Fig. 11.76.) Because no separate erase head is used in this R-DAT standard, special attention should be paid to overwrite characteristics. Overwriting depends on the maximum and minimum distances between the transitions and on the recording current. Erasing becomes more difficult with lower currents and longer wavelengths. In the 8–10

TABLE 11.5

Mode	I	II*	III	IV	V
Number of audio channels	2	2	2	2	4
Sampling frequency, kHz	48	44.1	32	32	32
Quantization, bits					
Linear	16	16	16	. . .	. . .
Nonlinear	. . .	. . .	. . .	12	12
Redundancy, percent	37.5	42.6	58.3	37.5	37.5
Subcode capacity, kb/s	273.1	273.1	273.1	136.5	273.1
ID code capacity, kb/s	68.3	68.3	68.3	34.1	68.3
Transmission rate, Mbit/s	2.46	2.46	2.46	1.23	2.46

* For software standard IIa, b, see tape format (Fig. 11.79). Redundancy is calculated according to the formula (bits of the data area – data bits)/(bits of the data area). The bits of the data area consist of synchronization, ID code, block address, parity, PCM data, parities for PCM data, and blanks (see also Fig. 11.86). The data bits consist of PCM data only.

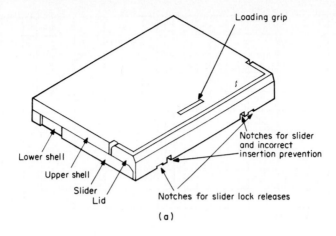

(a)

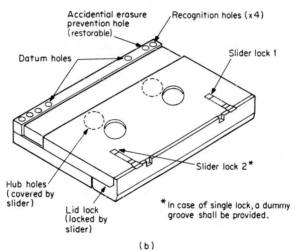

(b)

FIG. 11.75 R-DAT cassette.

channel code the minimum distance corresponds to 4.7 MHz and the maximum distance to 1.2 MHz. The residual signal after overwriting should be less than - 20 dB of the original signal. The influence of the recording current on overwrite performance (BER) is shown in Fig. 11.77.

Tape-Format R-DAT.   Optimum areal density can be achieved when guard-band-free recording is used. The crosstalk levels which occur when the reading head is not properly aligned to the recorded track can be reduced by using azimuth recording.

The amount of crosstalk is a function of overlap with neighboring tracks, wavelength, and the azimuth angle of the head (Fig. 11.78). The crosstalk should be low (< -20 dB) for the PCM data, and attenuation of low-frequency automatic-track-finding (ATF) pilot signals from neighboring tracks is much less.

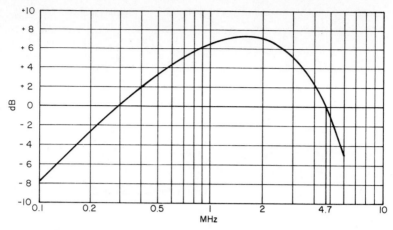

FIG. 11.76 Output frequency response of typical head; constant recording current and metal-powder tape.

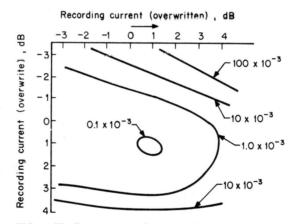

FIG. 11.77 Error-rate map for overwrite.

The tape format is depicted in Fig. 11.79. Each track is divided into 16 parts, or 196 blocks (90°, or 7.5 ms), of which 128 blocks are allocated for PCM audio (58°, or 4.9 ms). The PCM data, the ATF signals, phase-locked-loop (PLL) run-in, subcode data, interblock-gap (IBG) signals, and postamble and margin signals are recorded in a time-multiplex way (Fig. 11.80).

Tracking. To realize high-areal-density recording good tracking in the helical-scan recorder is of prime importance. There are two widely known methods of achieving optimum alignment between the recording tracks and the heads during playback:

1. *Control track (CTL):* In the VHS (video home system) system approach control pulses are written on the tape in a separate longitudinal track. During

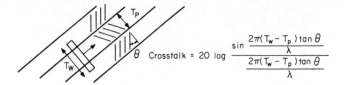

$$\text{Crosstalk} = 20 \log \frac{\sin \dfrac{2\pi(T_w - T_p)\tan\theta}{\lambda}}{\dfrac{2\pi(T_w - T_p)\tan\theta}{\lambda}}$$

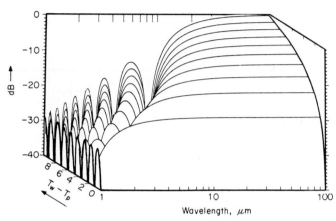

FIG. 11.78   Azimuth recording; $T_p = 10 \ \mu$m; $\theta = 20°$.

playback the system is locked to these pulses. The disadvantages are that (*a*) mistracking is measured some distance from the scanning heads, is therefore influenced by temperature changes and tape tension variations, and involves problems of compatibility; (*b*) an extra CTL head plus electronics is needed; and (*c*) in practical situations an erase head and a tracking knob also are needed.

2. *Pilot signals in the track itself:*   During playback the difference in crosstalk signals between the pilots of neighboring tracks is measured. The head is positioned on the track by means of the capstan control (ATF). In dynamic track following (DTF) the fast changes in track position are controlled with a piezoelectric actuator on which the heads are positioned. The pilot signals can be used in a frequency-division-multiplex (FDM) mode and in a time-division-multiplex (TDM) mode. DTF is not possible in the TDM mode. Owing to the relatively short R-DAT track length (23.5 mm) it suffices to measure tracking error at two discrete positions along the track.

Because the PCM audio spectrum covers a broad frequency range a TDM implementation of tracking signals has been chosen to minimize crosstalk between PCM audio and ATF signals. Of the 196 blocks, 10 (0.3836 ms) are allocated for ATF information. The ATF track pattern is depicted in Fig. 11.81.

Scanner rotation and longitudinal tape speed are fixed in the recording mode. During playback scanner rotation speed is kept constant. Tracking is controlled by longitudinal tape-speed variation.

The recorded signal consists of a pilot signal f_1 (130.67 kHz $= f_{ch}/72$) for detecting the track deviation of the scanning head, two synchronization frequencies f_2

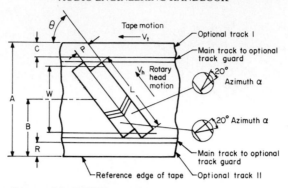

FIG. 11.79 Tape format of the R-DAT system.

Items	Mode	DAT Mandatory	Option 1	Option 2	Option 3	Prerecorded tape Normal track	Wide track
1. (A) Tape width	(mm)	3.81 ($+0$, -0.02)				3.81 ($+0$, -0.02)	
2. (W) Effective recording width	(mm)	2.613				2.613	
3. (L) Track length	(mm)	23.501				23.501	23.171
4. (P) Track pitch	(μm)	13.591				13.591	20.41
5. (θ_0) Track angle (still)	(°)	6° 22″				6° 22″	
6. (θ) Track angle (tape runs)	(°)	6° 22′ 59.5″				6° 22′ 59.5″	6° 23′ 29.4″
7. (α) Head gap azimuth angle	(°)	±20				±20	
8. (B) PCM center	(mm)	1.905				1.905	
9. (C) Optional track I (including optional edge guard (0.1)	(mm)	0.5				0.5	
10. (R) Optional II track (including optional edge guard (0.1)	(mm)	0.5				0.5	

Recommended cylinder specifications	Mode	DAT Mandatory	Option 1	Option 2	Option 3	Prerecorded tape Normal track	Wide track
1. (ϕ) Drum diameter	(mm)	30.0				30.0	
2. (N) Drum revolution speed	(r/min)	2000		1000	2000	2000	
3. (V_h) Writing speed	(m/s)	3.133		1.567	3.133	3.133	3.129
4. (ϕ) Wrap angle	(°)	90.0				90.0	

(522.67 kHz) and f_3 (784.0 kHz) to generate timing signals for crosstalk measurement, and an erasing signal f_4 (1.560 MHz). The length of the pilot signal f_1 equals 2 blocks; f_2 and f_3 equal 1 or 0.5 block. The remainder is allocated to the f_4 erasing signal. The pilot signal f_1 (130.67 kHz) is measured by the head with the other

Track format

1	2	3	4	5	6	7	8	9	10	11	12	13	14	15	16

Allocation	Signal	Normal track (for DAT and prerecorded tape)			Wide track (for prerecorded tape)		
		Angle, °	Number of blocks	Period, μs	Angle, °	Number of blocks	Period, μs
1. Margin	1/2 f channel	5.051	11	420.9	5.051	11	420.9
2. PLL (sub)	1/2 f channel	0.918	2	76.5	0.918	2	76.5
3. Sub 1		3.673	8	306.1	3.673	8	306.1
4. Postamble	1/2 f channel	0.459	1	38.3	0.459	1	38.3
5. IBG	1/6 f channel	1.378	3	114.8	0.918	2	76.5
6. ATF		2.296	5	191.3	3.444	7.5	287.0
7. IBG	1/6 f channel	1.378	3	114.8	0.689	1.5	57.4
8. PLL (PCM)	1/2 f channel	0.918	2	76.5	0.918	2	76.5
9. PCM		58.776	128	4898.0	58.776	128	4898.0
10. IBG	1/6 f channel	1.378	3	114.8	0.918	2	76.5
11. ATF		2.296	5	191.3	3.444	7.5	287.0
12. IBG	1/6 f channel	1.378	3	114.8	0.689	1.5	57.4
13. PLL (sub)	1/2 f channel	0.918	2	76.5	0.918	2	75.5
14. Sub 2		3.673	8	306.1	3.673	8	306.1
15. Postamble	1/2 f channel	0.459	1	38.3	0.459	1	38.3
16. Margin	1/2 f channel	5.051	11	420.9	5.051	11	420.9
Total		90	196	7500	90	196	7503

FIG. 11.80 Track format of the R-DAT system.

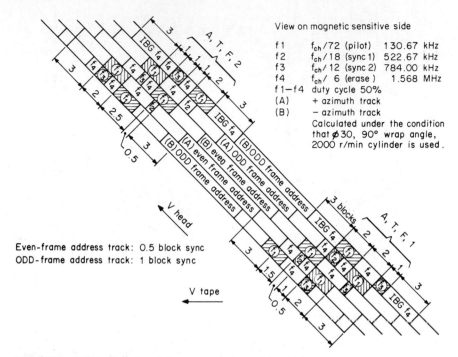

View on magnetic sensitive side

f1	$f_{ch}/72$ (pilot)	130.67 kHz
f2	$f_{ch}/18$ (sync 1)	522.67 kHz
f3	$f_{ch}/12$ (sync 2)	784.00 kHz
f4	$f_{ch}/6$ (erase)	1.568 MHz
f1—f4	duty cycle 50%	
(A)	+ azimuth track	
(B)	− azimuth track	

Calculated under the condition
that ϕ 30, 90° wrap angle,
2000 r/min cylinder is used .

Even-frame address track: 0.5 block sync
ODD-frame address track: 1 block sync

V tape

FIG. 11.81   ATF track pattern (view on magnetic-sensitive side).

azimuth angle, but because of the relatively long wavelength azimuth loss is small. This ATF signal is embedded in two IBG areas of 3 blocks each. Since the ATF pattern is recorded twice in one track, tracking is guaranteed even if one ATF part is completely lost owing to tape damage. The ATF track pattern is periodic over four tracks. The synchronization frequency f_2 is recorded by the positive-azimuth head; the synchronization frequency f_3, by the negative-azimuth head. For tracks with an even-frame address the synchronization frequency has a length of 0.5 block; for those with an odd-frame address it has a length of 1.0 block. This extension of periodicity supports the possibility of ensuring proper tracking for curved tracks and in cases when cue and review modes are used with different tape speeds.

A block diagram of the servo system for R-DAT is depicted in Fig. 11.82.

Scanner Servo.   During recording as well as during playback the output of the frequency generator [FG (s): tachometer signal, typically 800 Hz] is compared with a reference frequency. Normally this is done by converting the frequencies into voltages and comparing these voltages (speed loop).

The phase loop is implemented by comparing the output of the phase generator with a reference phase generated by the signal-processing unit, which is controlled by a crystal. The error signal controls the scanner motor so that it rotates in phase at 2000 r/min.

Capstan Servo.   During recording the tape speed should be constant at 8.15 mm/s to record with desired track width. This can be achieved by comparing the tachometer signals with a reference frequency (speed loop) and a reference phase

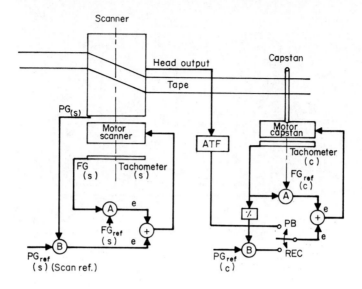

A: frequency comparison
B: phase comparison

FIG. 11.82 Block diagram of a servo system; A = frequency comparison; B = phase comparison.

(phase loop). The error signal controls the capstan motor. During playback the average tape-speed loop is the same, but the phase error is replaced by the tracking error detected by the ATF circuit. The track width of the head equals 1.5 times the track pitch on the tape. So the head overlaps the adjacent tracks. This overlap and the side-reading effect of the head enable the pilots of the neighboring tracks to be measured (reversed azimuth but low frequency), which is an indication of mistracking at any moment. Figure 11.83 explains detection timing, and Fig. 11.84 depicts the ATF circuit. Two different paths can be observed:

1. *Synchronization path:* The playback signal is high-pass-filtered, integrated, and clipped. This signal is used for synchronization detection and provides for the generation of SP_1 and SP_2 pulses.

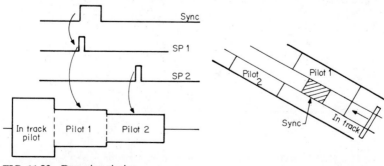

FIG. 11.83 Detection timing.

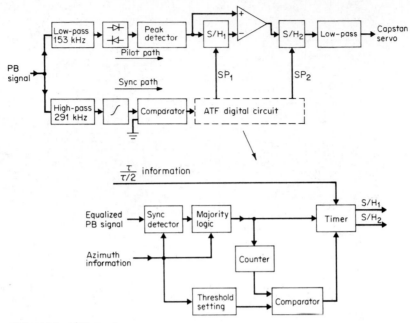

FIG. 11.84   ATF circuit.

2. *Pilot path:*   The playback signal is low-pass-filtered, rectified, and sampled by SP_1 and SP_2 pulses generated by the digital part of the ATF circuit. The two pilot amplitude samples are subtracted, filtered, and fed to the capstan motor control to obtain optimal alignment between the recorded tracks and the scanning heads. A synchronization detection circuit together with a majority logic determines the start of a timer which generates an SP_1 pulse and later an SP_2 pulse for sampling the two pilot amplitudes. Different strategies can be implemented for high-speed lock-in, high-speed search, etc.

Capstan Wow and Flutter.   Track linearity is affected by the wow and flutter of the capstan motor. This wow and flutter causes extra tracking errors and timing problems for the pulses SP_1 and SP_2 (Fig. 11.85). If the tape speed is given by $v_t(t) = v_0 + \hat{v}_x \sin(2\pi ft)$, then the maximum track-pitch error equals $\Delta T_p = \hat{v}/2\pi f \times \sin \theta$.

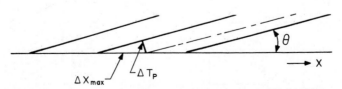

FIG. 11.85   Track-pitch error due to tape-speed variation.

Scanner Wow and Flutter.   The limiting factor in allowable scanner jitter is the ATF pattern generation on tape. The amplitude of the pilot frequencies (f_1) of the adjacent tracks is measured on the basis of the timing information of the synchronization frequencies f_2 and f_3. Track shifts should be limited in order to detect the amplitude of the pilot frequencies effectively in all circumstances.

Channel Coding.   For R-DAT a dc-balanced 8–10 conversion code with good overwrite characteristics is used. The minimum distance between transitions is $0.8T$, and the maximum distance is $3.2T$.[26]

Error Correction.   A PCM block consists of a synchronization pattern of 8 bits, an ID code of 8 bits, a block address of 8 bits, parity $P = W_1 + W_2$ (+ means modulo 2 addition) on the ID code and block address, and 32 symbols of 8 bits each of PCM data plus parity (C_1) or parity only (C_2). (See Fig. 11.86.) The MSB of the block address identifies a subcode (1) or a PCM (0) block; so 7 bits are left for addressing. A total of 128 blocks are allocated per track.

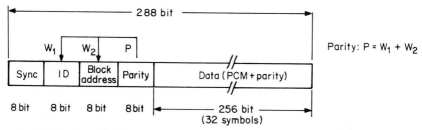

FIG. 11.86   4-Block format. Parity $P = w_1 + w_2$ (modulo 2 addition). Block address: MSB identifies subcode block or PCM data block (address = 7 bits).

For error correction or detection a product code of two Reed-Solomon codes is used because of their high performance for random as well as burst errors. Vertically, at the C_1 level, two RS (32, 28, 5) code words are interleaved to increase the capability of correcting random bit errors or small burst errors (few symbols). Horizontally, at the C_2 level, 4 RS (32, 26, 7) code words are interleaved (Fig. 11.87).

This calculation is performed in the Galois field GF(2^8). The primitive polynomial is $g(x) = x^8 + x^4 + x^3 + x + 1$. The generator polynomials are

$$C_1 : G_p(x) = \prod_{i=0}^{3} (x - \alpha^i) \tag{11.48}$$

$$C_2 : G_Q(x) = \prod_{i=0}^{5} (x - \alpha^i) \tag{11.49}$$

Here α = a primitive element in GF(2^8) = 0 0 0 0 0 0 1 0.

Interleaving.   Interleaving of audio PCM data is accomplished in such a way that:

1. The most and the least significant symbols of a 16-bit audio PCM sample

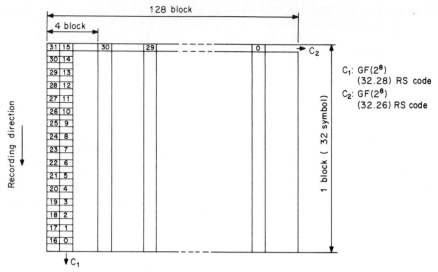

FIG. 11.87 Error-correcting format.

are always in one C_1 code word; so even if some data of a C_1 code word are uncorrectable at the C_2 level, a minimum number of samples are in error.

2. Two-field interleaving is applied to make it possible to interpolate the audio PCM data when single-head clogging occurs. (In mode I the odd samples of the right channel and the even samples of the left channel are always in the positive azimuth track.) Audio interleaving is illustrated in Fig. 11.88. In case of random bit errors the number of misdetections and interpolations is negligible up to a symbol error rate of 10^{-2}.

The situation for burst errors is somewhat different. The maximum correctable burst length is 2.8 mm.

Subcode. A distinction between different types of subcode information must be made:

1. *PCM area subcode (Fig. 11.89); mode I with 68.3 kb/s:* This subcode information is coded in relation to the PCM audio data in the PCM headers and is called PCM-ID (1 to 8). This code can only be changed together with the PCM audio. ID 1 to 7 are used for audio information such as sample frequency and emphasis. ID 8 can be used for data (e.g., graphics in pack format). The optional code is used for time information, search code, etc.

2. *Subcode area; mode I with 273.1 kb/s:* This subcode information can be changed independently of the audio information. It contains information on program time, program number, etc. The information is coded in the subcode area (see Fig. 11.81): Sub 1 and Sub 2 (8 blocks each) and subcode headers (Fig. 11.90).

3. *Subcode for compact-disk format (software only); 44.1 kHz, sample frequency:* This subcode (prerecorded tapes) is composed of the P, Q, and R-W channels (see also CD standard). The P and Q channels of the CD subcode are converted to the DAT subcode format and are recorded in the subdata area of DAT. The R-W channels of the CD subcode can be recorded in the main data of the DAT.

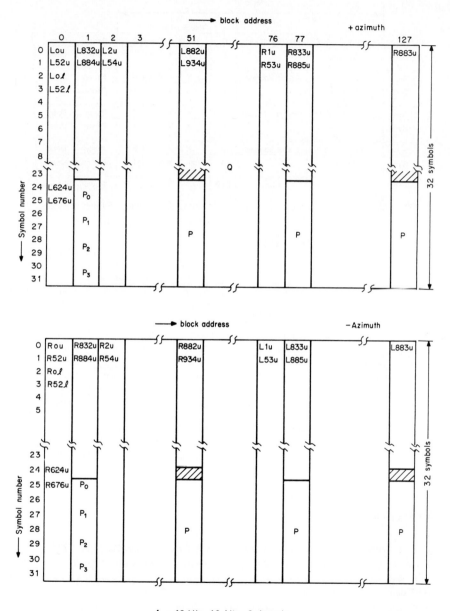

FIG. 11.88 1 Interleave format.

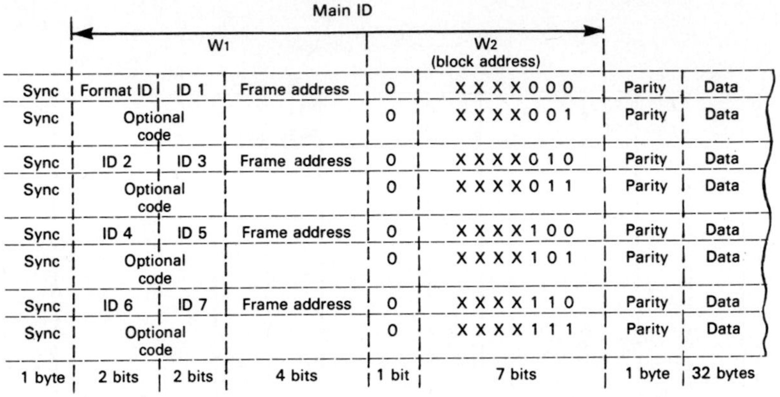

Main ID

		W1			W2 (block address)			
Sync	Format ID	ID 1	Frame address	0	X X X X 0 0 0	Parity	Data
Sync	Optional code			0	X X X X 0 0 1	Parity	Data
Sync	ID 2	ID 3	Frame address	0	X X X X 0 1 0	Parity	Data
Sync	Optional code			0	X X X X 0 1 1	Parity	Data
Sync	ID 4	ID 5	Frame address	0	X X X X 1 0 0	Parity	Data
Sync	Optional code			0	X X X X 1 0 1	Parity	Data
Sync	ID 6	ID 7	Frame address	0	X X X X 1 1 0	Parity	Data
Sync	Optional code			0	X X X X 1 1 1	Parity	Data
1 byte	2 bits	2 bits	4 bits	1 bit	7 bits	1 byte	32 bytes

FIG. 11.89 PCM header area. The eight blocks shown are repeated 16 times per track.

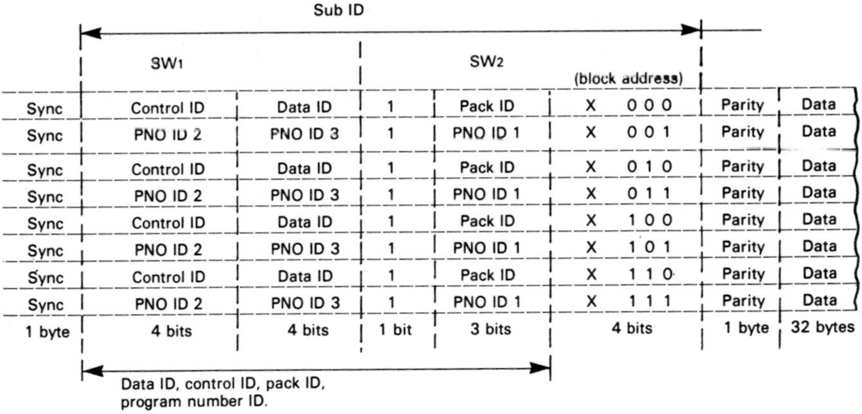

Sub ID

	SW1			SW2 (block address)			
Sync	Control ID	Data ID	1	Pack ID	X 0 0 0	Parity	Data
Sync	PNO ID 2	PNO ID 3	1	PNO ID 1	X 0 0 1	Parity	Data
Sync	Control ID	Data ID	1	Pack ID	X 0 1 0	Parity	Data
Sync	PNO ID 2	PNO ID 3	1	PNO ID 1	X 0 1 1	Parity	Data
Sync	Control ID	Data ID	1	Pack ID	X 1 0 0	Parity	Data
Sync	PNO ID 2	PNO ID 3	1	PNO ID 1	X 1 0 1	Parity	Data
Sync	Control ID	Data ID	1	Pack ID	X 1 1 0	Parity	Data
Sync	PNO ID 2	PNO ID 3	1	PNO ID 1	X 1 1 1	Parity	Data
1 byte	4 bits	4 bits	1 bit	3 bits	4 bits	1 byte	32 bytes

Data ID, control ID, pack ID, program number ID.

FIG. 11.90 Subcode header area. The eight blocks shown are repeated 1 time per Sub 1 and Sub 2 areas.

REFERENCES

1. B. A. Blesser, "Digitization of Audio," *J. Audio Eng. Soc.,* no. 10, 739 (1978).

2. W. K. Westmijze, "Studies on Magnetic Recording," *Philips Res. Rep.,* **8** (1953).

3. F. Jorgensen, *The Complete Handbook of Magnetic Recording,* 3d ed., TAB Books, Blue Ridge Summit, Pa., 1986.

4. O. Karlqvist, "Calculation of the Magnetic Field in the Ferromagnetic Layer of a Magnetic Drum," *Trans. Royal Inst. Tech. Stockholm,* **86,** 3 (1954).

5. L. G. Sebestyen, *Digital Magnetic Tape Recording for Computer Applications,* Chapman and Hall, London, 1973.

6. K. Teer, "Investigations of the Magnetic Recording Process with Step Functions," *Philips Res. Rep.,* **16,** 469 (1961).

7. R. L. Wallace, "The Reproduction of Magnetically Recorded Signals," *B.S.T.J.,* **30,** 1145 (1951).

8. D. L. A. Tjaden and L. Leyten, "A 5000-1 Scale Model of the Magnetic Recording Process," *Philips Tech. Rev.,* **25**(11), 319 (1963).

9. M. K. Loze et al., "A Model for a Digital Magnetic Recording Channel," *IERE Conf. Proc.,* no. 59, 1 (1984).

10. B. K. Middleton, "Performance of a Recording Channel," *IERE Conf. Proc.,* no. 54, 137 (1982).

11. B. K. Middleton and P. L. Wisely, "Pulse Superposition and High Density Recording," *IEEE Trans. Magn.,* **MAG-14,** 1043 (1978).

12. B. K. Middleton and P. L. Wisely, "The Development and Application of a Simple Model of Digital Magnetic Recording to Thick Oxide Media," *IERE Conf. Proc.,* no. 35, 33 (1976).

13. S. Imakoshi et al., "Thin Film Heads for Multi-Track Tape Recorders," presented at the 79th Convention of the Audio Engineering Society (1985), preprint 2287.

14. W. J. van Gestel et al., "Read-Out of a Magnetic Tape by the Magnetoresistance Effect," *Philips Tech. Rev.,* **37,** 42 (1977).

15. W. F. Druyvesteyn et al., "Magnetoresistive Heads," *IEEE Trans. Magn.,* **MAG-17,** 2884 (1981).

16. R. W. Lucky, "Automatic Equalization for Digital Communication," *B.S.T.J.,* **44,** 547 (1965).

17. R. W. Lucky, "An Automatic Equaliser for General Purpose Communication Channels," *B.S.T.J.,* **46,** 2179 (1967).

18. M. Tachibana et al., "Equalization in Digital Recording," *NEC Res. Dev.,* no. 35, 37 (1974).

19. M. Kobayashi and D. T. Tang, "Application of Partial Response Channel Coding to Magnetic Recording Systems," *IBM J. Res. Dev.,* 368 (1970).

20. W. R. Bennett and J. Q. Davey, *Data Transmission,* McGraw-Hill, New York, 1965.

21. R. W. Wood and R. W. Donaldson, "Decision Feedback Equalization of the DC Null in High Density Digital Magnetic Recording," *IEEE Trans. Magn.,* **MAG-14,** 218 (1978).

22. G. D. Forney, "The Viterbi Algorithm," *Proc. IEEE,* **61,** 268 (1973).

23. R. W. Wood, "Viterbi Reception of Miller Squared Code on a Tape Channel," *IERE Conf. Proc.,* no. 54, 333 (1982).

24. K. Sam Shanmugam, *Digital and Analog Communication Systems,* Wiley, New York, 1979.

25. T. T. Doi, "Channel Codings for Digital Audio Recording," presented at the 70th Convention of the Audio Engineering Society (1981), preprint 1856.

26. S. Fukuda et al., "8/10 Modulation Codes for Digital Magnetic Recording," *IEEE Trans. Magn.,* **MAG-22,** 1194 (1986).

27. G. V. Jacoby, "A New Look-Ahead Code for Increased Data Density," *IEEE Trans. Magn.,* **MAG-13,** 1202 (1977).

28. J. C. Mallinson and J. W. Miller, "Optimal Codes for Digital Magnetic Recording," *Radio Electron. Eng.,* **47,** 172 (1977).

29. T. Moriyama et al., "New Modulation Technique for High Density Recording on Digital Audio Discs," presented at the 70th Convention of the Audio Engineering Society (1981), preprint 1827.

30. H. Ogawa and K. Schouhamer Immink, "EFM, the Modulation Method for the Compact Disc Digital Audio System," *AES Conf.,* Rye, N.Y. (1982).

31. Shu Lin, *An Introduction to Error-Correcting Codes,* Prentice-Hall, Englewood Cliffs, N.J., 1970.

32. N. D. Mackintosh and F. Jorgensen, "An Analysis of Multi-Level Encoding," *IEEE Trans. Magn.,* **MAG-17,** 3329 (1981).

33. R. W. Adams, "Companded Predictive Delta Modulation: A Low Cost Conversion Technique for Digital Recording," presented at the 73d Convention of the Audio Engineering Society (1983), preprint 1978.

34. K. J. Gundry, "Recent Developments in Digital Audio Techniques," presented at the 73d Convention of the Audio Engineering Society (1983), preprint 1956.

35. J. A. McCracken, "A High Performance Digital Audio Recorder," presented at the 58th Convention of the Audio Engineering Society (1977), preprint 1268.

36. H. Matsushima et al., "A New Digital Audio Recorder for Professional Applications," presented at the 62d Convention of the Audio Engineering Society (1979), preprint 1447.

37. Y. Ishida et al., "On the Signal Format for the Improved Professional Use 2 Channel Digital Audio Recorder," presented at the 79th Convention of the Audio Engineering Society (1985), preprint 2270.

38. S. Itoh et al., "Multi-Track PCM Audio Utilizing 8 mm Video System," *IEEE Trans. Cons. Electron.*, **CE-31**(3) (1985).

39. EIAJ Technical Committee, file STC007, 1979; file STC008, 1981.

40. Recommended standard for the 8-mm video system.

41. W. J. van Gestel et al., "A Multi-Track Digital Audio Recorder for Consumer Applications," presented at the 70th Convention of the Audio Engineering Society (1981), preprint 1832.

42. Recommended EBU standard on I/O interface.

BIBLIOGRAPHY

Magnetic Recording

Chi, C. S., and D. E. Speliotis: "The Isolated Pulse and Two Pulse Interactions in Digital Magnetic Recording," *IEEE Trans. Magn.*, **MAG-11**, 1179 (1975).

Potter, R. I.: "Digital Magnetic Recording Theory," *IEEE Trans. Magn.*, **MAG-10**, 502 (1974).

Digital Audio in General

Zander, H.: "Grundlagen und Verfahren der digitalen Tontechnik," *Fernseh Kino Tech.* (1984–1985).

Coding, Equalization, and Detection

Doi, T. T.: "Error Correction for Digital Audio Recorders," presented at the 73d Convention of the Audio Engineering Society (1983), preprint 1991.

Franaszek, P. A.: "Sequence State Methods for Run-Length-Limited Coding," *IBM J. Res. Dev.*, 376 (1970).

Jacoby, G. V.: "Signal Equalization in Digital Magnetic Recording," *IEEE Trans. Magn.*, **MAG-4**, 302 (1968).

Lindholm, D. A.: "Fourier Synthesis of Digital Recording Waveforms," *IEEE Trans. Magn.*, **MAG-9**, 689 (1973).

Nakagawa, S., et al.: "A Study in Detection Methods on NRZ Recording," *IEEE Trans. Magn.,* **MAG-16,** 104 (1980).

Steele, R.: *Delta Modulation Systems,* Pentech Press, London, 1975.

Digital Audio Systems

Kogure, T., et al.: "The DASH Format: an Overview," presented at the 74th Convention of the Audio Engineering Society (1983), preprint 2038.

Legadec, R., and M. Schneider: "A Professional 2-Channel 15 ips DASH Recorder," presented at the 78th Convention of the Audio Engineering Society (1985), preprint 2259.

Owaki, I., et al.: "The Development of the Digital Compact Cassette System," presented at the 71st Convention of the Audio Engineering Society (1982), preprint 1861.

Recommended standard on S-DAT recorders, August 1985.

Sekiya, T., et al.: "Digital Audio Compact Cassette Deck with Thin Film Heads," presented at the 71st Convention of the Audio Engineering Society (1982), preprint 1859.

PCM in the 8-mm Video System

Martens, T. G. J. A., and J. P. Schuddemat: "A Versatile PCM IC Set for 8 mm Video," *IEEE Trans. Cons. Electron.,* **CE-30,** 575 (1984).

Rotary-Head Systems

Arai, T., et al.: "Digital Signal Processing Technology for R-DAT," *IEEE Trans. Cons. Electron.,* **CE-32,** 416 (1986).

de Haan, H. G.: "R-DAT: A Rotary Head Digital Audio Tape Recorder for Consumer Use," SAE Conf., Detroit (February 1986).

Itoh, S., et al.: "Magnetic Tape and Cartridge of R-DAT," *IEEE Trans. Cons. Electron.,* **CE-32,** 442 (1986).

Hitomi, A., et al.: "Servo Technology of R-DAT," *IEEE Trans. Cons. Electron.,* **CE-32,** 425 (1986).

Nakajima, N., et al.: "The DAT Conference: Its Activities and Results," *IEEE Trans. Cons. Electron.,* **CE-32,** 404 (1986).

Odaka, K. et al.: "A Rotary Head High Density Digital Audio Tape Recorder," *IEEE Trans. Cons. Electron.,* **CE-29**(3) (1983).

————: "Format of Pre-Recorded R-DAT Tape and Results of High Speed Duplication," *IEEE Trans. Cons. Electron.,* **CE-32,** 433 (1986).

Othaka, N., et al.: "Magnetic Recording Characteristics of R-DAT," *IEEE Trans. Cons. Electron,* **CE-32,** 372 (1986).

Recommended standard on R-DAT recorders, August 1986.

Vries, L., "Digital Audio Tape Recording," *ICCE* (June 1987).

CHAPTER 12
FILM RECORDING AND REPRODUCTION*

Ronald E. Uhlig
Senior Photographic Engineer, Motion Picture and Audio Visual Product Department, Eastman Kodak Company, Rochester, New York

12.1   INTRODUCTION

In the presentation of motion-picture films, sound is equal in importance to the visual images. Consequently, preparation and reproduction of the sound tracks warrant a comparable degree of attention and care. The various aspects of motion-picture sound can be divided into three sequential operations:

1. Original production recording
2. Postproduction editing and sweetening
3. Duplication

In the original production recording and postproduction editing phases, there are two fundamentally different techniques for handling the sound. These are single-system and double-system.

Single-system sound indicates that picture and sound information are contained on the same piece of film. *Double-system sound* denotes that the picture is on one piece of film and the sound on a separate film or magnetic tape. Depending on production and distribution requirements, each method has advantages and disadvantages. The obvious advantage of single-system sound is that equipment operators have only one piece of film to handle. Any operation performed on the pictures, such as cutting out an undesired segment, performs the same operation on the sound track. This can be an advantage where operational simplicity and editing speed are important factors. Conversely, serious difficulties may be encountered when it is necessary to replace a section of either the picture or the sound without affecting the other. In that case, double-system sound clearly is preferable so that independent operations can be performed. However, even this advantage is offset by the need to deal with two strips of film and to maintain

---

* With contributions by Joseph J. Charles, Eastman Kodak Company, Rochester, New York.

synchronism between them. Either single- or double-system techniques may be used in each of the phases of sound production, and the techniques for each are described in Secs. 12.2.1 and 12.2.2.

In the original production recording and reproduction phases, two major technologies are utilized for recording sound on motion-picture film. These are magnetic sound tracks and optical sound tracks.

Magnetic sound tracks involve recording with conventional magnetic recording heads on a strip of magnetic oxide in a binder, usually coated near the edge of the film. *Optical sound tracks* (also known as *photographic sound tracks*) use the imaging layers of the film to record the sound information, which is read back with a beam of light. Advantages of magnetic sound tracks are that (1) better sound quality is obtained with single-system recording on camera original films and (2) the sound track subsequently can be re-recorded or changed. Advantages of optical or photographic sound tracks are (1) lower costs for producing a number of prints, (2) capability of virtually all projectors to reproduce optical sound, whereas relatively few are equipped with magnetic sound, and (3) excellent quality on prints made on negative-positive-print films. In the sections on original recording and on reproduction, both magnetic and optical sound tracks will be discussed and further advantages and disadvantages of each will be given.

12.2 ORIGINAL RECORDING

Original recording is the process of capturing the sound that occurred when the pictures were being filmed. The stage of original photography and original sound recording for a motion picture is sometimes referred to as the *production stage.* Some of the sound recorded at this time may be used in the final presentation, and some of it may not, being replaced or modified during the *postproduction stage.*

Single-system original sound recording, in television production, is used most often when filming news stories or documentaries. Since only one piece of film and equipment is involved, there is no problem in maintaining synchronism between sound and pictures. The use of a clapstick or more sophisticated control-track recording in the shooting process is not necessary.

It should be noted that although the basic editing functions are simple with single-system sound, any sophisticated editing can be difficult. This is true because of the separation of sound and pictures along the film and the difficulty of replacing either the sound or the pictures, but not both, as is necessary in a cutaway shot. Consequently, it is often necessary to transfer the sound to a separate piece of film so that editing may be done double-system. These techniques and limitations are discussed in Chap. 14.

12.2.1 Single-System Recording

Magnetic Sound. The most common type of single-system sound recording on film is magnetic sound recording on prestriped 16-mm film. Several film manufacturers produce films with a narrow strip of magnetic oxide coated along one edge of the film. Super-8 (type S) film is also produced in a prestriped format, but this is used primarily for consumer applications. Prestriped 35-mm-camera films are not available.

Since a single-system camera is recording picture material at a frame-by-frame intermittent rate and sound at a uniform rate, it is essential that there be adequate isolation between the sound recording head and the picture gate to ensure that there is no modulation of the sound signal by the film pull-down action. Therefore, sound is recorded 28 frames ahead of the picture at a point in the camera where the film is moving smoothly. A rotating drum in the sound recording head has a flywheel attached to it to ensure uniform film motion. If the intermittent motion at the picture gate is not sufficiently isolated from the sound head, the velocity of the film at the sound head will be varying, normally with a 24-Hz pull-down rate. These speed variations are known as *flutter,* and when they are excessive, they cause the reproduced sound track to be garbled.

In most modern cameras, the amplifier circuitry necessary to record sound is included inside the camera body itself. Often, the camera operator is provided with an indication of excessive signal level by means of a flashing or blinking light in the viewfinder. Generally, little in the way of adjustments or maintenance is necessary, other than perhaps setting the level during recording and keeping the recording heads clean. Many cameras include switch-selectable automatic volume control circuitry to relieve the operator of that concern also. For additional information on magnetic recording, see Chap. 10.

Optical Recording. Single-system optical sound recording is accomplished by exposing a photographic sound track. While optical sound is the most common method for creating a sound track on prints of films, it is no longer used to any extent for single-system original sound recording, principally because of the poor sound quality obtained. This is due primarily to two factors: (1) The photographic characteristics of the film are adjusted to give optimum picture quality. Specifically, the contrast of camera films is too low, the granularity is too high, and the image spread is too great for good-quality variable-area sound recording. (2) A high-quality optical recording system cannot be packaged in a camera at a reasonable price.

12.2.2 Double-System Recording

Double-system original sound recording involves recording the sound and pictures on two separate media. Specifically, the pictures are recorded on photographic film, either negative or reversal, and the sound generally is recorded on ¼-in- (6.35-mm-) wide audio tape. An alternative has been to record the sound on perforated magnetic film, but this is no longer common practice.

Special tape recorders designed specifically to be used for recording double-system sound have been developed. These recorders, besides being highly portable and capable of recording high-quality audio, have special features to satisfy some of the requirements of recording double-system sound. The main requirement discussed in this chapter is the synchronism of sound and pictures. The system must permit the maintenance of synchronism even in situations where several minutes of sound and pictures are recorded without interruption, and, furthermore, synchronism must be maintained within approximately ¼₄ s (one film frame). This requirement is dictated by tests which have shown that if the sound either precedes or follows the corresponding picture by more than one frame, the loss of synchronism is noticeable and even objectionable to many viewers.

There are two aspects to maintaining synchronism: (1) alignment of the sound and pictures at the beginning of a sequence of film and (2) maintenance of the alignment throughout the length of a sequence. Generally, it is not necessary to synchronize the original tape recording with the picture film. As discussed in Sec. 12.3, the sound is almost always transferred from ¼-in (6.35-mm) tape to perforated magnetic film for editing. It is this magnetic film that is synchronized with the pictures. Therefore, it is necessary to transfer the sound to magnetic film so that there is a one-to-one correspondence between the frames of picture and the frames of sound.

The usual method of maintaining equal speed on both the picture and sound rolls is to record a special signal on the ¼-in tape known as the pilot-tone track. The pilot-tone track is a recording of a nominally 60-Hz sine wave. The frequency of the tone is proportional to the frame rate of the camera and is 60 Hz when the camera frame rate is exactly 24 frames per second. This pilot-tone track is then used when the audio is transferred from the ¼-in tape to perforated magnetic film to ensure that 24 frames of film are recorded for each 60 cycles of pilot-tone track, thus maintaining a one-to-one relationship between frames of sound and frames of picture.

There are several systems for generating the pilot-tone signal. One common method is to have a tachometer-generator attached to the drive shaft of the camera. This device generates a signal whose frequency is proportional to the frame rate of the camera and is the required 60 Hz when the camera frame rate is exactly 24 frames per second. The signal may be transmitted from the camera to the tape recorder by cable or by radio-frequency (RF) transmission.

Another common method involves the use of a quartz-crystal-oscillator speed control circuit in the camera, ensuring that the frame rate of the camera will be exactly 24 frames per second. A similar quartz crystal oscillator in the tape recorder generates a precise 60-Hz tone that is recorded on the tape. The quartz oscillators used in the cameras and tape recorders are accurate enough to permit the filming of sequences lasting many minutes without loss of synchronism. Advantages of this system are that several cameras can be used at the same time without cables connecting the camera or cameras to the tape recorder.

In the commonly used Nagra neopilot system, the pilot-tone signal is recorded on the ¼-in tape in two special out-of-phase tracks. (See Fig. 12.1.) By recording

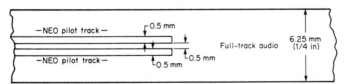

FIG. 12.1 Nagra neopilot pilot-tone track location and dimensions. [*From R. R. Epstein, Leo O'Donnell, and L. Green, "Lightweight Synchronous Stereo Recording System," J. Soc. Motion Pict. Telev. Eng., 75, 29–31 (January 1966).*]

the signal out of phase on the two tracks, the audio signal can be played back on a conventional full-track head without picking up the pilot-tone signal. This permits the pilot-tone signal itself to be reproduced by using a special head consisting of two tracks with their windings connected out of phase. This configuration is insensitive to pickup of sound-track audio signals even when there is a moderate degree of misalignment of the track position.

While the pilot-tone track provides a means of keeping the speeds of picture and sound rolls equal, there still is a need to establish the initial synchronization of a film sequence. The most common method used is the venerable clapstick or slate, the latter providing production identification information.

Automatic slating systems also may be used. These generally involve the use of a camera with a small light source near the film gate. After both the camera motor and sound recorder have been started, the camera operator presses a button to flash the light, which light exposes one or more frames of film and, at the same time, causes a tone to be recorded on the sound track. These two signals can then be used later for synchronization purposes.

12.3 POSTPRODUCTION

Much of the artistic character of a film production results from the manipulations conducted during the editing and related operations of the postproduction phase. For the sound track, this might be just a simple editing operation of removing undesired material and rearranging the remaining material in the desired order, with the same editing operations being performed on both the sound and the pictures. On the other hand, much more complex operations are possible. For example, undesirable or unusable location dialogue can be replaced by dialogue recorded in the studio. Music and sound effects are recorded and added. A whole new sound track, bearing little if any resemblance to the original recording, can be created. Some of the fundamentals are discussed in this chapter. Chapter 14 describes in more detail complex postproduction editing of both sound and picture.

It is to be emphasized that the type of original recording is not a constraint on the type of editing, nor is the method of release. For greater flexibility, it is feasible to record the original sound single-system, edit in a double-system mode, and then convert to single-system recording for the final print.

12.3.1 Single-System Editing

Single-system postproduction techniques normally are used only with film shot single-system. The editing operation is fast, the equipment simple and inexpensive, and, furthermore, the picture and sound can be monitored directly, in sync, on a viewer and loudspeaker.

However, a major shortcoming arises from the displacement between corresponding pictures and sound on the film. Because the sound is recorded 28 frames ahead of the picture, slightly more than 1 s of running time, it is not possible to make precise cuts. As a result, a common fault is to have the sound from one scene continuing while the picture has already cut to the next scene.

Displacement Recorder. To overcome this effect with a magnetic sound track, a device called a *displacement recorder* is often used. This device plays back the sound from a strip of film and re-records it displaced 28 frames. The sound is now said to be in line with the pictures or in editorial sync. That is, a given sound is immediately adjacent to the corresponding picture frame, thus permitting frame-accurate editing. When editing is complete, the film is run through the displacement recorder again to restore the sound to the 28-frame displacement so that it is now in projection sync.

12.3.2 Double-System Editing

Because of its simplicity, single-system editing has some other very serious limitations. Single-system editing is limited to little more than cutting out undesired sections and rearranging scenes. Not only is it very difficult to do cutaway shots, but also the addition of narration or dialogue, sound effects, or music cannot be easily accomplished. The solution is double-system editing. As the name implies, two pieces of film are involved—one for sound and the other for pictures. In practice, the sound may involve the use of many reels of film, each running in synchronism with the picture. Individual rolls are required to provide, for example, music, effects, and dialogue. In some instances, music and effects may be combined on a single M&E track.

It is worth restating that while most original recording done double-system uses ¼-in tape as the recording medium, the audio is invariably transferred from the tape to perforated magnetic film for editing. This procedure serves two purposes: (1) The editor is provided with sound on a perforated medium, which results in less complex equipment and editing operations than with ¼-in tape. (2) The transfer provides a backup and protection of the original recording. Editing the original directly provides no room for errors.

While the use of perforated magnetic film as the sound-track medium is traditional, the use of multitrack nonperforated magnetic tape is becoming more popular. Thus, two subsections will follow, one devoted to double-system editing using perforated magnetic film and the other to double-system editing using magnetic tape.

Editing with Perforated Film. The flexibility of double-system editing necessitates maintaining synchronism between the pictures and sound. When transferring from ¼-in tape to magnetic film, the pilot-tone signal must be used to control the tape velocity during transfer. Two different systems are in use. In the first, the 60-Hz pilot-tone signal is amplified and filtered by a sync pulse amplifier to approximately 115 V and used to power a synchronous-drive motor on the magnetic-film transport. In the other system, the film recorder is driven by a synchronous motor fed from the ac power line. The tape recorder used to play back the ¼-in tape recording has a variable-speed motor and circuitry that phase-locks the pilot-tone signal being played from the tape with the line frequency.

For a simple film consisting of only pictures and the associated dialogue, such as news film, a simple double-system editor may be all that is required. The editor has great flexibility in splicing in cutaway shots into the picture roll or narration into the sound roll. In more complex situations, it is often necessary to combine different sounds from M&E and dialogue tracks. Multisprocket synchronizers are useful in this effort, as may be flat-bed editing tables.

At the end of the editing process, it is necessary to add all these sounds together in a operation known as *mixing*. Each roll of sound is placed on an individual reproducer, all of which can be interlocked electrically to run and stop together. Using a multichannel sound-mixing console, one or more operators watch a projection of the picture and, at the same time, adjust the levels of the dialogue, music, and sound-effects rolls to produce the desired balance. This is then recorded on a single roll of magnetic film, which becomes the *master mix*. Of course, the scale and complexity of these operations can vary drastically, depending on whether the production is a large-budget movie or a small documentary for a local television station.

Generally, the format of the sound film matches the format of the picture film.

For example, if 35-mm pictures are being shot, 35-mm magnetic film will be used for the sound. However, in special situations formats may be mixed. A studio equipped primarily with 16-mm sound equipment may choose to do all sound work in 16-mm film even though the pictures are shot in 35-mm film. Special synchronizers that allow the mixing of formats are available and would be necessary in such a situation.

Editing with Nonperforated Magnetic Tape. Recently, there has been a trend toward the use of multitrack nonperforated magnetic tape for sound editing and sweetening.[1]

Sweetening is a term used to describe the addition of music and sound effects to a sound track. Instead of using multiple rolls of film for the various dialogue, music, and effects tracks, multiple tracks on a single roll of 16- or 24-track magnetic tape are used. The key to such an operation is the use of a time and control code such as the Society of Motion Picture and Television Engineers (SMPTE) time code. The time code occupies one of the tracks and is used by a computer to control the operation of the multitrack recorder and also other recorders that are used to play back the sounds to be added to the sound track. The process then is one of electronic editing as opposed to the *cut-and-splice editing* used with perforated magnetic film.

The equipment permits the operator to specify the time address of the beginning and end of the desired sequence to be added to the sound track and the time address of the spot in the sound track where this sequence is to be inserted. The computer then controls the equipment to make the desired transfer.

12.4 OPTICAL (PHOTOGRAPHIC) SOUND TRACKS

12.4.1 General Characteristics

There are two types of photographic sound tracks: variable-area and variable-density tracks. While *variable-density* tracks were used through the early 1950s, virtually all current photographic sound tracks are of the *variable-area* type.

Most release-print sound tracks are printed from a sound negative film. However, when only a very few prints are needed, often the additional cost of a separate sound negative cannot be justified. In that case, the photographic sound track is *recorded* directly on the print. This method of reproducing the sound track is called *electrical printing,* and the print itself is called an *electrical print.*

Variable-area photographic sound tracks are generally bilateral or dual-bilateral. A few multilateral tracks are produced. Stereophonic photographic tracks consisting of two bilateral[2,3,4] or four unilateral[5] tracks side by side have been produced.

Bilateral stereophonic tracks should not be confused with dual-bilateral monaural tracks that look similar. Outline drawings of a stereo track and a dual-bilateral track are shown in Fig. 12.2.

The predominant formats are 35-mm and 16-mm films. Type-S (8-mm) films having photographic sound tracks are also used to a limited extent.

Track Width and Position. The standardized width and position of the photographic sound track ensure interchangeability of product. If the sound track is not in the proper position or is of greater than normal width, reproduction of the

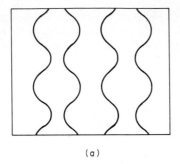

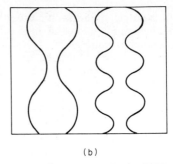

(a)   (b)

FIG. 12.2 Outline drawings of monophonic dual-bilateral (*a*) and stereophonic (*b*) 35-mm photographic sound tracks.

sound track may be severely distorted, or the sound track may encroach on the picture area of the film. Figures 12.3, 12.4, and 12.5 show the location and dimensions for sound tracks on 35-mm, 16-mm, and Super-8 films, respectively, taken from the appropriate American National Standards. Figure 12.6 shows the location and dimensions of 35-mm stereophonic sound tracks.

Prior to performing any other tests on the quality of a sound track, the position of the track should be checked. The tolerances given in the above figures are realistic and should be observed. If the track on a photographic sound-track negative is found to be out of position, the instruction or service manual supplied with the recorder should be consulted. If the sound track is out of position in the print but the negative position is satisfactory, then the threading and operation of the printer should be checked.

Velocity.   The velocity or speed of a motion-picture film, with or without a sound track, is specified in terms of the number of perforations or frames per second. However, since the nominal perforation pitch is known, the speed in units of distance per unit time can be calculated. Table 12.1 gives the track velocities for 35-mm, 16-mm, and Super-8 sound tracks.

Short-term variations in the velocity of a sound track are known as *wow* and *flutter* and are discussed in Sec. 12.5.5.

Sound-to-Picture Separation.   When a motion picture is viewed on a screen, the motion of the film at the picture aperture is intermittent, while at the sound head it must be continuous. Thus, to isolate the different types of motion the sound and picture on the film must be separated by several frames. Table 12.2 indicates the standard separation for 35-mm, 16-mm, and Super-8 motion pictures.

Output Level.   The output level of a variable-area photographic sound track depends on three parameters: (1) the modulation level or the amplitude of the modulation of the width of the clear area of the sound track, (2) the transmittances of the light portions of the track, and (3) the transmittances of the dark portions of the track. To maximize signal-to-noise ratios (SNRs), the output level of a sound track should be as high as possible. If the output level is lower than necessary, the gain of the projector must be increased, which in turn increases sound-track noise and electrical system noise. The level of the sound track as affected by the transmittance of the light and dark portions of the track is referred

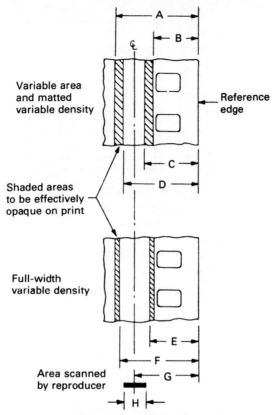

FIG. 12.3 Dimensions of photographic sound records on 35-mm motion-picture prints. *(American National Standard PH22.40-1984.)*

Dimensions	Inches		Millimeters	
A	0.308	nominal	7.82	nominal
B	0.192	nominal	4.88	nominal
C	0.205 ± 0.001		5.21 ± 0.03	
D	0.281 ± 0.001		7.14 ± 0.03	
E	$0.193 \begin{array}{l}+\,0.004 \\ -\,0.000\end{array}$		$4.90 \begin{array}{l}+\,0.10 \\ -\,0.00\end{array}$	
F	$0.293 \begin{array}{l}+\,0.000 \\ -\,0.004\end{array}$		$7.44 \begin{array}{l}+\,0.00 \\ -\,0.10\end{array}$	
G	0.243 ± 0.001		6.17 ± 0.03	
H	0.084 ± 0.001		2.13 ± 0.03	

to as *relative-output level*. Modulation level and relative-output level are independent of each other and will be discussed separately.

Modulation Level. Modulation has two distinct meanings in photographic sound-track discussions: (1) the amplitude of the modulation of the width of the

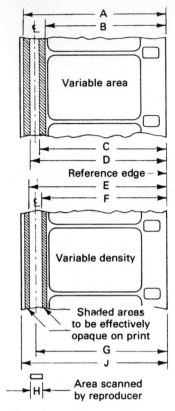

FIG. 12.4 Dimensions of photographic sound records on 16-mm motion-picture prints. *(American National Standard PH22.41-1983.)*

Dimensions	Inches		Millimeters	
A	0.611	maximum	15.52	maximum
B	0.513	reference	13.03	reference
C	0.540 ± 0.002		13.72 ± 0.05	
D	0.600 ± 0.002		15.24 ± 0.05	
E	0.610 ± 0.002		15.49 ± 0.05	
F	0.530 ± 0.002		13.46 ± 0.05	
G	0.570	reference	14.48	reference
H	0.071	reference	1.80	reference
J	0.628	reference	15.95	reference

clear area of the sound track and (2) the amplitude modulation of a carrier signal as in the cross-modulation test signal. In this section we are concerned only with the first; the second will be discussed under distortion tests in Sec. 12.5.4.

The modulation of a constant-amplitude signal is defined as the sum of the peak-to-valley displacements d_i of the signal divided by the total width W available for the signal (see Fig. 12.7):

$$m = \frac{d_1 + d_2}{W} \qquad \text{(for a bilateral track)} \qquad (12.1)$$

$$m = \frac{d_1 + d_2 + d_3 + d_4}{W} \qquad \text{(for a dual-bilateral track)} \qquad (12.2)$$

where W = 0.076 in (1.93 mm) for 35-mm sound tracks
0.060 in (1.53 mm) for 16-mm sound tracks
0.020 in (0.51 mm) for Super-8 sound tracks

Very often the modulation level is multiplied by 100 percent to obtain the level in percentage.

The modulation level of a sound track may be measured by using a microscope and appropriate scales. To increase accuracy, both modulations of a bilateral track or all four modulations of a dual-bilateral track should be measured separately, rather than measuring merely one modulation and multiplying by the number of modulations. For even greater accuracy, the entire measurement may

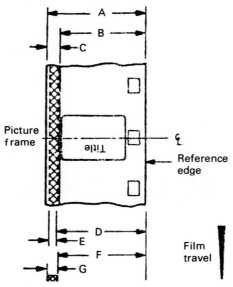

FIG. 12.5 Dimensions of photographic sound records on Super-8 motion-picture prints. *(American National Standard PH22.182-1978.)*

Dimensions		Inches		Millimeters	
A	Film width	0.314	reference	7.98	reference
B		0.283 ± 0.001		7.19 ± 0.03	
C	Printed width	0.028	minimum	0.71	minimum
D		0.288 ± 0.001		7.32 ± 0.03	
E	Modulated width (100%)	0.020	maximum	0.51	maximum
F		0.285 ± 0.001		7.24 ± 0.03	
G	Scanned width	0.025 ± 0.001		0.64 ± 0.03	
H	Sound record centerline	0.298	nominal	7.57	nominal

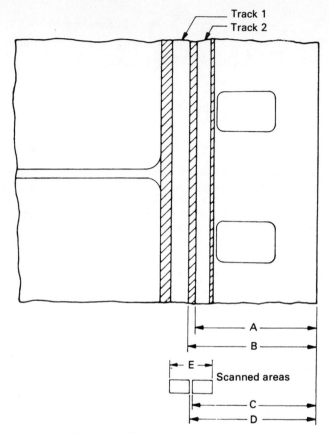

FIG. 12.6 Dimensions of two-track photographic sound records on 35-mm motion-picture prints. *(American National Standard PH22.203-1981.)*

Dimensions	Inches	Millimeters
A	0.238 ± 0.002	6.05 ± 0.05
B	0.248 ± 0.002	6.30 ± 0.05
C	0.242 ± 0.001	6.15 ± 0.03
D	0.244 ± 0.001	6.20 ± 0.03
E	0.084 reference	2.13 reference

be repeated and the results averaged. Since the output level of a photographic sound track depends on the transmittances of the light and dark portions of the track in addition to the modulation level, the modulation level cannot be determined accurately by measuring the output of a projector. Visual examination is the only reliable method of determining the modulation level.

Relative-Output Level.   The relative output of a photographic sound track is dependent upon the transmittances of the light and dark portions of the track.

TABLE 12.1   Film Velocities

			Velocity	
Format	Frames/s	Perforations/s	cm/s	in/s
35-mm	24	96	45.72	18.0
16-mm	24	24	18.288	7.2
Super-8	24	24	10.16	4.0

TABLE 12.2   Sound-to-Picture Separations

Format	Sound-to-picture relationship
35-mm	21 ± ½ frame advance
16-mm	26 ± ½ frame advance
Super-8	22 ± ½ frame advance

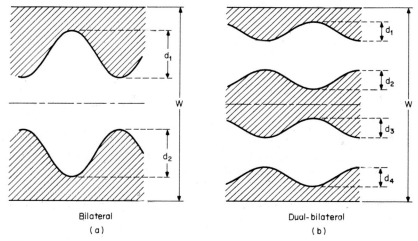

Bilateral   Dual-bilateral
(a)   (b)

FIG. 12.7   Measurements to determine modulation of a photographic sound track. (See text for formula.) (*a*) Bilateral. (*b*) Dual-bilateral.

Clifford and Charles[6] provide a graph and a nomograph which relate the relative output (RO) to the high and low densities of the sound track. (See Fig. 12.8.) Alternatively, relative output can be calculated from the following equation:

$$RO = 20 \log (T_{hi} - T_{lo}) \text{ dB} \qquad (12.3)$$

where T_{hi} and T_{lo} are the transmittances of the clear and opaque portions of the track, respectively. The transmittances are related to the sound-track densities by Eqs. (12.4) and (12.5).

$$T_{hi} = 10^{-D_{lo}} \qquad (12.4)$$

$$T_{lo} = 10^{-D_{hi}} \qquad (12.5)$$

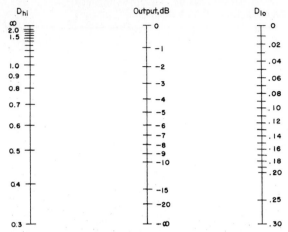

FIG. 12.8 Nomograph to determine the relative output of a photographic sound track. Connect D_{hi} and D_{lo} with a straight line. The intersection with center scale yields relative output. [*From Joseph J. Charles and Dexter Clifford, "The Relative Output of Photographic Sound Tracks,"* J. Soc. Motion Pict. Telev. Eng., *84, 730–731 (September 1975).*]

Either of the figures or the equation for relative output can be used to determine the relative output of a sound track given its high and low densities. An important point to be realized from these graphs is the importance of the density value for the dark portions of the track. It can be seen that the relative output is more strongly dependent on D_{lo} than on D_{hi}. For a sound track having densities of 0.06, 1.30, an increase of 1.0 in D_{hi} results in about 0.5-dB output increase, while a decrease of only 0.02 in D_{lo} results in that same increase.

Measuring the Relative-Output Level.   The RO of a sound track can be measured by reproducing a 400-Hz 80 percent-modulated signal on a projector and comparing the result to either a reference-level test film or a 400-Hz 80 percent-modulated track on another piece of film. When comparing sound track with the reference-level test film (see Chap. 16 for a listing of test films), care should be taken that the signal on the sound track to be tested is exactly 80 percent-modulated. In the following section on frequency-response tests, a procedure for recording 80 percent-modulated test signals is presented. It should be followed carefully.

12.4.2 Film Characteristics That Affect Quality

The Characteristic Curve.   The characteristic curve shows the relationship of film density to log exposure. Figure 12.9 shows typical sound-track-negative characteristic curves. Figure 12.10 shows typical print-stock sound-track characteristic curves.

Film Speed.   The photographic sensitivity, or speed, of a sound negative is a quality factor that is important to the sound laboratory which makes the rerecording on the sound negative. The sound negative must have sufficient speed to be exposed at reasonable recorder-lamp intensities. It should be possible to obtain the proper exposure without using the lamp at its maximum voltage or

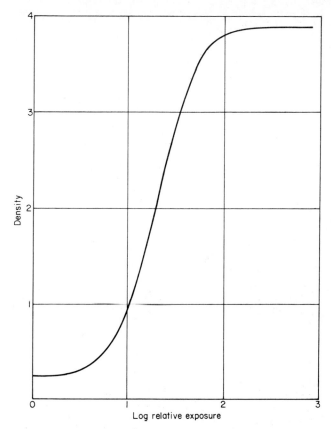

FIG. 12.9 Characteristic curve of Eastman sound-recording II film 5373/7373.

current rating. Using the lamp at less than the maximum rating greatly extends its life and avoids frequent replacement with the necessary recorder recalibration.

Negative-speed determination must be based upon conditions similar to those under which the film is used. Since the exposure times in a photographic sound recorder are on the order of 25-μs duration, reciprocity-law failure may be an important consideration. In the final analysis, the recorder-lamp voltage or current that is required to produce the proper exposure is the only important measure of negative speed.

The speed of the print emulsion layers used for the sound track is also important. These layers must be fast enough to be exposed by using printer sound-head lamps and optical systems which are practical. It must also be possible to obtain sufficient exposure when the printer is operated at production rates. Print-film speed should be sufficient to allow slight-undervoltage operation of the sound-head lamp for the reasons described above for the negative.

Minimum Density. The minimum density D_{min} of a sound negative is usually of little importance unless it becomes abnormally high. Most sound-negative emulsions are coated on a gray or bluish-gray base to reduce halation. These products

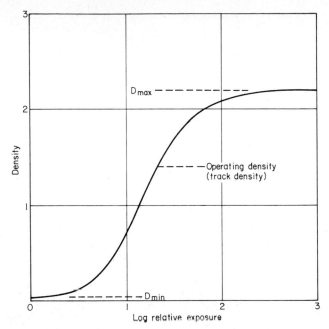

FIG. 12.10 Characteristic curve of sound-track exposure on Eastman color-print film 5384/7384.

usually have a D_{min} of 0.20 to 0.30 due to base, fog, and stain densities. Since the print sound track must be exposed through the negative D_{min}, the D_{min} can be thought of as equivalent to a gray or bluish-gray filter in the printer acting essentially like a neutral-density filter. However, while the sound-negative base density contributes to the attenuation of the light reaching the print film during printing, sound-head lamps are able to provide sufficient light for exposure by a comfortable margin.

An abnormally high negative D_{min} is a sign of trouble, e.g., a processing problem or a fogged negative. A high D_{min}, whatever the cause, is a serious problem because it alters the shape of the toe of the characteristic curve.

The toe characteristic is quite important since it represents the densities that will be produced by the lower levels of scattered light within the emulsion. From an analysis of sound-track image formation such as that given by Ferrier and Desprez[7] one can intuitively gather that toe shape may have an important effect on the sound-track image and hence on quality. However, no studies on this subject have been published recently. Staes and associates[8] mention that studies made using a mathematical model of photographic sound indicated that the negative toe shape has a great influence on sound-track characteristics, particularly on the exposure tolerance.

The D_{min} of the print sound track is extremely important because it profoundly affects the relative-output level as well as the noise level of the track. Thus, it has a doubly important effect on the SNR of the track. Negative-positive print sound tracks typically have a D_{min} of about 0.035 to 0.05. A D_{min} of 0.035 is about as low as possible because of Fresnel reflection losses at the film base. Reversal films having negative-positive sound tracks have a D_{min} of about 0.07. Inadequate quality control in the processing of these products can result in an excessively high D_{min} with the resulting losses in sound-track quality mentioned above. A D_{min} greater than 0.10 should be considered a cause for concern. Reversal films having reversal silver sulfide sound tracks are capable of producing a D_{min} only as low as about 0.20. The resulting SNR is several decibels lower than that of a silver sound track on the same product. However, these tracks are produced in a process having only one stage of sound-track application rather than two, and some feel that the lower SNR is an acceptable price to pay for a single application stage.

Maximum Density.   *Maximum density* means the highest density that can be produced by a product in a given process, i.e., the maximum density on the shoulder of the characteristic curve. The maximum density, or D_{max} as it is commonly called, should not be confused with the *track operating density,* which is described in the next section.

If the D_{max} obtained when a characteristic curve is processed is lower than that which should be obtained in a normal process, the process is abnormal. In such a case, the rest of the characteristic curve should then be compared with a normal curve. If the two curves agree for densities up to and including the operating density, normal performance can be expected. However, the low D_{max} should be considered an abnormal condition and possibly an indication that further process problems may be encountered.

Track Operating Density.   The *track density* is the density of the dark portion of a variable-area track. It is the density which is actually obtained on a given track under a given set of exposure and processing conditions. The track density can be thought of as being the point on the characteristic curve at which one is operating; thus the term *operating density* may be used synonymously with track density. In practice, both of these terms are usually shortened simply to *density,* as in the *print density* or the *negative density.*

Negative track densities range in value from 2 to 4 or higher, while print track densities typically range from 1.0 to 1.6. The significance of the negative track density will be discussed after that of the print.

The print density which is recommended as the operating point by the manufacturer of the product is determined on the basis of two print behavior considerations: (1) SNR versus density behavior and (2) frequency response versus density behavior.

Generally, as the print density increases the SNR increases until it reaches some maximum value while the frequency response continuously decreases. A family of frequency-response curves, each obtained for a different print density, generally do not cross each other; thus the response at a single high frequency can be used to convey some idea of the density dependence of frequency response. Figure 12.11a shows the decrease in response at 7 kHz relative to that at 1 kHz versus density for Eastman color-print film 7384. The response at 7 kHz relative to that at 1 kHz is seen to decrease as track density increases. Figure 12.11b shows the SNR versus track density. The SNR is seen to increase rapidly until a density of about 1.0 is reached and to become approximately constant beyond a density of 1.3. On the basis of data such as these, the manufacturer recommends that this product be used at a density of 1.30 ± 0.20.

Once the operating density of the print is decided upon, the operating density of the negative must be determined. The operating density of the negative is not arbitrary; the negative must be used at a density which cancels cross-modulation distortion in the print. Cross-modulation distortion is discussed in Sec. 12.5.4.

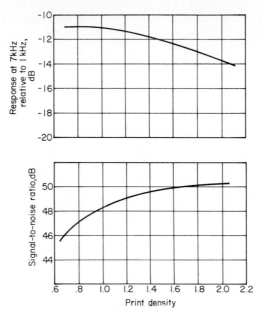

FIG. 12.11 Effect of sound-track density on (*a*) frequency response (upper curve) and (*b*) SNR (lower curve).

Aside from cross-modulation considerations, the negative density must be sufficiently high so that the exposure E to the print through the high-density portions of the negative is insufficient to produce a density above the print D_{min}. Thus, the difference between negative operating density and D_{min} must exceed the difference between the log E at the print's operating point and the log E at the point at which the characteristic curve just begins to rise above the D_{min}. Using Eastman color-print film 7384 and Eastman sound-recording II film 7373 as examples, we conclude from Fig. 12.10 that the negative density must be at least 1.20 above its minimum. Thus for a D_{min} equal to 0.23, the negative operating density must be at least 1.43. Other than for the two considerations mentioned here, there is no particular requirement on negative track density.

Gamma. *Gamma* is the slope of the straight-line portion of the characteristic curve, also known as *contrast.* Sound-negative-film gammas lie between 3 and 6. Together with the modulation transfer function (MTF), the gamma largely determines the cross-modulation distortion-density relationship for the product. Figure 12.12 shows the amount of cross-modulation distortion in a print-versus-negative density for two negatives which differ only in gamma but have identical MTFs. (See Sec. 12.5.4 for a complete discussion of cross-modulation distortion.)

All other factors being equal, a low-gamma negative will contain more cross-modulation distortion than a high-gamma negative. Since to cancel the cross-modulation distortion in a print a negative must contain a certain required amount of distortion, a low-gamma negative will require less density than a high-gamma negative.

Sound tracks made on a high-gamma negative will appear sharper, with the

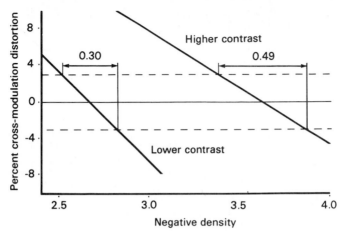

FIG. 12.12 Effect of negative gamma on cross-modulation distortion in the print. [*From Ronald E. Uhlig, "The Relationship of Film Parameters to Photographic Soundtrack Quality," J. Soc. Motion Pict. Telev. Eng., 89, 229–234 (April 1980).*]

area between modulation peaks appearing *cleaner,* i.e., D_{min} extending deeper between the peaks. However, sound-negative quality is judged by performance rather than appearance, although appearance can provide a clue to poor performance. The images on high-gamma and low-gamma sound negatives must be photographically equivalent to cancel the cross-modulation distortion in a print regardless of how they look.

A high-gamma sound negative film is likely to be more tolerant of recorder flare and thus may perform better than a lower-gamma film in recorders with higher amounts of flare. The reason for this can be seen by considering Fig. 12.13, which shows characteristic curves of a high-gamma and a low-gamma negative. The curves have been shifted horizontally to align at the operating point. By assuming that the exposure caused by flare in the recorder is 1.0 log E below the aim exposure, we see that the flare will produce a density of 0.43 in the low-gamma negative but a density of only 0.30 in the high-gamma negative.

Print sound-track gamma affects the amount of image spread produced by the print. All other factors being equal, the lower the gamma, the more image spread produced. This is true because scattered light will result in more density if the gamma is lower. Hence, low-gamma prints will require sound negatives having higher densities and thus more cross-modulation (XM) distortion for cancellation.

Since print gamma affects image spread, it is reasonable to expect that the lower-gamma print stocks might have a lower frequency response than the higher-gamma stocks.

Spectral Sensitivity. The spectral sensitivity of commercially available sound negative films varies with the brand and type. Among the various types are ultraviolet and blue-sensitive, orthochromatic, and panchromatic.

Extension of the spectral sensitivity of the negative beyond the blue region effectively increases its speed since the recorder lamp can be used at less intensity to produce the required exposure. Muramatsu[9] reports that by extending the spec-

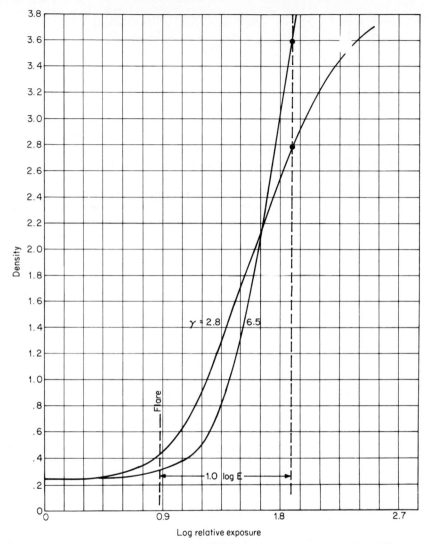

FIG. 12.13 High- and low-contrast characteristic curves used to show the effect of flare.

tral sensitivity to a wavelength of 630 nm Fuji fine-grain sound-recording film (variable-area) type II could be made with a finer grain than usual with the extended spectral sensitivity compensating for the lower speed of the smaller grains.

Ordinarily, the film manufacturer considers the spectral sensitivity of the print film and the spectral energy distributions of printer light sources when making exposure recommendations. Optical filters are sometimes recommended when sound tracks are printed to restrict or modify the quality of the exposing light. Thus, while the user generally need not consider the spectral sensitivity of the print film when printing sound tracks, it should be considered if other than conventional printing is being done. Such considerations, for example, might indicate a choice for spectrally neutral rather than dichroic beam splitters if any are to be used.

Modulation Transfer Function.   Modulation transfer function is a measure of the light-scattering properties of a raw-stock emulsion. The closer an MTF remains to unity (100 percent) as a function of spatial frequency, the less the emulsion scatters the exposing light. The MTF data should pertain to the layers in which the sound track is formed.

While an emulsion may scatter the exposing light, whether or not the scattered exposure produces any density depends on the exposure level and the film's characteristic curve. Any image density produced by the scattered light will affect the cross-modulation and frequency-response characteristics of the sound track. All other factors being equal, a product with a low MTF will produce more cross-modulation distortion than a high-MTF product. This is true for both negative and print tracks.

In general, one would expect the frequency response of a sound track on a low-MTF print stock to be less than that of a high-MTF print stock. However, because the frequency response of the print track depends on its density as well as on the density of the negative, the actual differences, if any, should be determined by testing prints optimized for cross-modulation. It is not easy to verify this in practice because differences other than MTF usually also occur.

Granularity.   The granularity of the print-film sound track ultimately determines the maximum SNR which a clean, new print film is capable of producing. To the extent that the granularity of the sound negative is printed through to the print sound track, it too is important, although the effect of negative granularity is less significant than print-film granularity.

The precise relationship between granularity and sound-track noise is not well understood. Measurements of the audio noise produced when uniformly flashed samples of film are reproduced shows that noise is lowest for both high and low print densities and is higher for intermediate densities (see Fig. 12.15).

The noise which is audible in a sound track containing a single-frequency constant-amplitude signal increases as the frequency of the signal increases. This is due to the increased presence of intermediate densities caused by image spread between the signal peaks.

Granularity-caused noise also depends on the total width of the low-density portion of the track relative to the width of the high-density portion at the same longitudinal point in the track. This is shown in Fig. 12.14. This phenomenon is also evidenced by the *breathing* of biasing noise reduction systems which can sometimes be heard in noisy tracks.

From a quality standpoint, it can be said that the finer the grain in the sound track, the quieter it will be for a clean, new print. After the print has been used extensively, the noise is more likely to depend on its physical condition than on its intrinsic granularity.

Latent-Image Keeping.   *Latent-image keeping* (LIK) refers to the stability of the latent image during the time between when a film is exposed and when it is processed. In films having good LIK, relatively little exposure loss will be noted when the time between exposure and processing is long. The opposite is true for a film product having poor LIK. Either the negative film or the print film may have poor

FIG. 12.14 Effect of the width of the sound-track clear area on noise.

LIK. In a film having poor LIK, the loss in exposure usually occurs most rapidly immediately after a film is exposed.

LIK loss can be an important source of variability which would be noticed especially in the cross-modulation test. Suppose, for example, that a cross-modulation family was obtained by using a negative which was exposed on a Friday but processed on the following Monday after having been kept at room temperature over the weekend. If the negative has poor LIK, then the results of the test would not apply to negatives which are recorded and processed the same day. Several other variations of this example are also possible.

Measurement of Densities. The type of density measurement which is used, whether visual or infrared, specular or diffuse, depends upon the intended use of the product. A print film which is being contact-printed is exposed to all the light transmitted through the sound negative. Since the geometry closely corresponds to that specified for diffuse transmission densitometry, diffuse negative density should be measured. In principle, the spectral quality of the density measurement should agree with the spectral sensitivity of the print-film layers being used for the sound track, but this is always modified by practical considerations. Since conventional sound negatives are composed of silver images and since silver is a relatively nonselective absorber, visual diffuse densities are usually measured.

Print sound tracks are usually reproduced in projectors or reproducers having a specular optical system. However, diffuse print densities are used for quality control purposes.

Projectors for 16-mm and 35-mm film contain photodetectors whose response is typically characteristic of either a silicon or an S-1 photosurface (see Sec. 12.4.5). These photodetectors are sensitive primarily in the infrared, having peak sensitivity at a wavelength of about 800 nm. Thus, infrared transmission density should be used for 16- and 35-mm prints.

Super-8 photographic sound-track images are commonly composed of the normal picture dyes, and the spectral responses of Super-8 photographic sound-projector photodetectors typically peak in the visible region of the spectrum. Thus Super-8 print film sound-track densities should be read with a color filter so that the response of the densitometer approximates that of the projector. Unfortunately, there are no standards that specify the responses of projectors or densitometers which are to be used for Super-8 photographic sound tracks.

12.4.3 Recorder Characteristics Affecting Quality

Galvanometer Recorders. Moving-mirror galvanometers are commonly used together with a triangular-shaped aperture to modulate variable-area sound-track exposures. Figure 12.16 illustrates the elements of a galvanometer modulator.[10]

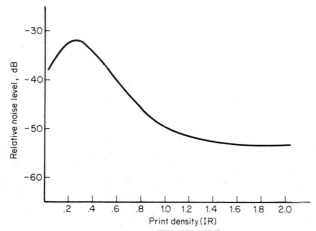

FIG. 12.15 Noise of a uniformly flashed track versus density.

The lamp uniformly illustrates the aperture A through the condenser C; the image of the aperture, reflected off the galvanometer mirror G, is formed on the recording slit S by the converging lens E; the objective lens images the recording slit onto the film. The audio-signal input to the galvanometer causes the mirror to deflect, thereby varying the width of the illuminated portion of the slit according to the amplitude of the audio signal.

The dynamics of galvanometer deflection depend upon the mechanical and electrical properties of the galvanometer movement. The frequency response of a galvanometer also depends upon the electrical properties of the driving circuit.

Light-Valve Recorders. Light-valve modulators are used in many photographic sound recorders, particularly those manufactured by Westrex. The basic elements of a light-valve recorder are shown in Fig. 12.17. The light-valve ribbons are located in a magnetic field that is oriented so that the ribbons will be deflected alternately toward and away from each other when electrical current is passed through them.

The dynamics of ribbon deflection depend on the electrical, magnetic, and mechanical properties of the light valve as well as the input signal. Frayne[11] has derived an expression for the ribbon deflection and shows a family of theoretical response curves.

Recorder Aperture. The sound-negative film is exposed by an image of an aperture which is brought to focus at the emulsion plane. This "optical" aperture is

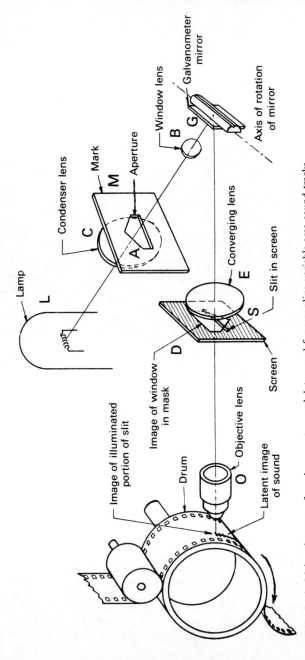

FIG. 12.16 Major elements of a galvanometer modulator used for recording variable-area sound tracks. [*Reprinted with permission of E. W. Kellogg, "The ABC of Photographic Sound Recording," J. Soc. Motion Pict. Telev. Eng., **44**, 151–194 (March 1945).*]

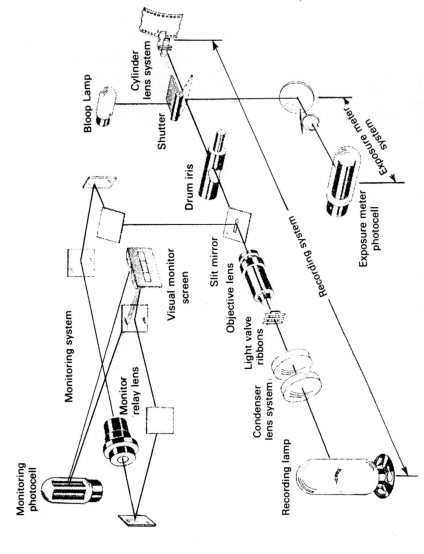

FIG. 12.17 Major elements of a light-valve modulator used for recording variable-area sound tracks. [*From Lewis B. Browder, "Variable-Area Light-Valve Modulator," J. Soc. Motion Pict. Telev. Eng., 51, 521–533 (November 1948).*]

the image of a physical slit which is illuminated through a modulator whose function is to vary the length of the illuminated portion in proportion to the amplitude of the audio signal. There are two common types of modulators: the light-valve type and the galvanometer type. The light-valve type divides the slit into one or more rectangles, while the galvanometer type divides it into one or more trapezoids. If the slit is broken up into one, two, or more rectangles or trapezoids, the recorder will produce bilateral, dual-bilateral, or multilateral tracks, respectively. It makes little difference whether the aperture is rectangular or trapezoidal. In this section we are concerned only with the optical aperture which is brought to focus at the film plane. We shall refer to this image as the *aperture,* and for convenience we will discuss an aperture having only one section, i.e., one which will produce a bilateral track. The extension to dual-bilateral or multilateral recorders will be obvious.

We consider the dimension of the aperture in the direction of film travel (longitudinal) to be the width a of the aperture and in the perpendicular direction (transverse) to be the length l. The length of the aperture is modulated in accordance with the amplitude of the audio signal. The maximum length L is made to equal the standard width of the track for the given format. Thus, L should equal 0.029 in (0.50 mm), 0.060 in (1.52 mm), or 0.076 in (1.93 mm) for 8-, 16-, and 35-mm formats, respectively. The width of the aperture affects the frequency response of the recorder and is primarily responsible for the *aperture effect* discussed in the literature. Stryker,[12] Foster,[13] and Cook[14] have studied the effects of the recording aperture. The effects of the aperture cannot be fully described without considering the properties of the emulsion in which the image is produced as well as those of the sound-negative process. Unfortunately, such an analysis including the light-scattering properties of the film does not exist. Modern computer simulations of photographic sound have included models of recorder apertures.[15,16,17] These simulations can be used to determine the effects of aperture size and shape.

The most important effect of the aperture is the frequency-response loss caused by its finite width. Cook[14] showed that the frequency-response loss for an aperture of width a is given by

$$R(f) = \sqrt{a^2 + b^2} \tag{12.6}$$

where $a = (1 + \cos \theta) \cdot (\frac{1}{2} - \theta/4\pi) + (\sin \theta/2\pi)$
$\quad\quad b = (\cos \theta - 1)/2\pi - (\frac{1}{2} - \theta/4\pi) \cdot \sin \theta$
$\quad\quad \theta = 2\pi af/v$
$\quad\quad f =$ audio frequency
$\quad\quad a =$ aperture width
$\quad\quad v =$ velocity with which the film travels
$\quad\quad R =$ relative output on the film

Recorder aperture-effect losses in commercially available recorders are small for the audio frequencies of interest in each format. At 10 kHz the falloff for a 35-mm recorder ($a = 3$ μm) is about 0.2 dB, for a 16-mm recorder ($a = 3$ μm) about 1.1 dB, and for a Super-8 recorder ($a = 2$ μm) about 1.6 dB.

Spectral Filtering. In the past it has been customary to use a blue optical filter when recording on blue-sensitive sound-negative films. Although there still may be a case for using an optical filter under certain circumstances (such as to eliminate the effects of chromatic aberration), it is usually unnecessary. In case of doubt, the recommendations of the film and recorder manufacturers should be followed.

Ultraviolet recording, developed during the 1930s to produce sharper sound negatives, is not necessary with modern negative films; so an ultraviolet optical filter is not required.

When recording electrical prints, the recommendations of the film manufacturer should be followed. As a rule, if the color temperature of the recorder lamp is assumed to be close to that of a printer sound-head lamp, one should use the filters recommended for conventional printing in the recorder.

The filters should be placed in the position designated by the recorder manufacturer or, if none is specified, preferably in a non-image-forming part of the optics.

Exposure Control. Negative exposure is usually controlled by adjusting the recorder-lamp current or voltage to provide different lamp intensities. Since negative exposure is a critical factor in obtaining cancellation of cross-modulation distortion in the print, one must be able to adjust the lamp intensity accurately to provide any desired negative exposure with a high degree of repeatability.

Density Patching. By *density patching* we mean the recording of distinct areas so as to obtain each of two densities: the operating density and the negative D_{min}. These areas can be recorded by recording a slightly overmodulated signal of very low frequency (about 40 Hz), by manually deflecting the galvanometer by hand as for Radio Corporation of America (RCA) recorders, or by applying dc input signals to the galvanometer or light valve to give areas that are alternately clear and opaque.

The clear patch on the negative is used to measure negative D_{min} and, after printing and processing the print, the print density in the corresponding area. The opaque patch of the negative provides an area that can be used to measure the negative operating density and the print sound-track D_{min}. Recording these areas without bias lines makes it easy and convenient to read the densities.

Aperture Focusing. To obtain optimum sound quality, the recorder aperture must be sharply focused on the negative by the objective lens. It is necessary to check the recorder focus for each type of film used in the recorder. It is not sufficient to assume that two different films of the same thickness will have the same focus, since other factors such as the combined effects of film spectral sensitivity and recorder chromatic aberration can affect focus. Since a focus test is so easy to conduct, one should not even assume that a recorder newly received from the manufacturer will be optimally focused for any particular film stock.

A focus test is conducted by recording an 80 percent-modulated high-frequency signal (10 kHz for 35-mm, 7 kHz for 16-mm, and 5 kHz for 8-mm film) at several focus positions. Best focus is achieved at the position that provides the highest signal level.

Compression and Limiting. It is often necessary to make a 16-mm or Super-8 print of a 35-mm motion picture that was originally intended for theatrical release. Since the noise level in areas where 16-mm or Super-8 prints are projected is normally higher than the noise level in a theater, it is possible that lower-level dialogue and sounds, which were audible in the theater, may become inaudible because of masking. It may therefore be desirable to use a compression amplifier in the photographic recorder to reduce the dynamic range of the original recording to a smaller dynamic range that might be more appropriate to the 16-mm or Super-8 formats.

Many photographic sound-track recorders have compression amplifiers built

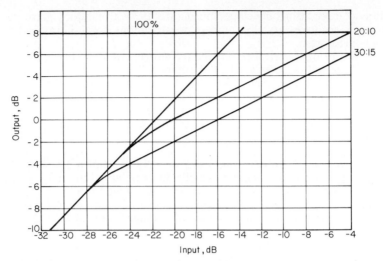

FIG. 12.18 Typical compression characteristics for a photographic sound-track recorder. *(Courtesy of Mitsubishi Pro Audio Group.)*

in. Figure 12.18 shows the input-output characteristic for a typical compression amplifier. Curves are shown for two compression characteristics. In both cases, the compression ratio is 2:1. That is, each 2 dB of input dynamic range is compressed to 1 dB of output range. For curve *A,* compression is applied to approximately the upper 20 dB of input range, compressing it to 10 dB of output range. Curve *B* shows compression being applied to the upper 30 dB of input range. In each case, there is a threshold below which no compression is applied and the input-output relationship is linear. Since many compressors have a tendency to increase the relative amplitude of the sibilant sounds in dialogue recordings, they often have a "de-essing" function, switchable in or out, which increases the amount of compression at high frequencies to reduce the level of the sibilant sounds.

If the modulation level of a variable-area sound track is allowed to go above the 100 percent modulation point, the level of distortion is very high. On the other hand, if the modulation level is lowered so that no peaks are over 100 percent-modulated, the average level of modulation may now be quite low. To keep the average modulation level high but yet not have excessive distortion on those occasional high-level program-material peaks, a limiter may be used with the photographic sound-track recorder. A limiter is basically a compressor with a very high compression ratio, usually 10:1. It is adjusted so that its threshold of operation is just below 100 percent modulation. It will then reduce the level of any signals that would have been over 100 percent modulation and prevent them from being clipped.

Frequency-Response Equalization. Equalization is used in photographic sound-track recording to modify the frequency response of the recorder to compensate for high-frequency losses in the negative and print films. The equalization is important, as it plays a large role in determining the final frequency response of the photographic sound-track system. It is desirable to use an amount of equalization that exactly compensates for the film losses. For this reason, some recorder manufacturers make the amount of equalization adjustable so that the user can more accurately match the losses of the films used. At 10 kHz, equalization available on one type of recorder ranges from about 8 to 14 dB.

When high-frequency equalization is used, there is always the risk of overmodulating high-frequency material whose level has been boosted by the equalization. Therefore, it is not always possible to use as much equalization as is necessary to compensate for film losses. The maximum amount of equalization that can be used depends on the level of the high-frequency material in the program being recorded and therefore varies from one recording to the next. Various studies have been made of the average spectral content of various types of program material.[18,19,20] For average program material good practice[19] dictates that not over 15 dB of equalization be used, for example, at 10 kHz. It should be noted that certain types of program material, especially some types of modern electronic music, have significantly greater high-frequency output and may lead to distortion if this amount of equalization is used.

12.4.4 Printer Characteristics

Contact and Slippage.   Virtually all sound tracks are contact-printed. Most modern contact printers contain both a picture head and a sound head for simultaneous printing of picture and sound in one pass. On a printer containing only one head, two passes are required to print both picture and sound because each must be contained on a separate negative and because they require different exposures. Figure 12.19 illustrates schematically the sound head on a modern contact printer.

Slippage of the print over the negative no longer seems to be a problem on modern well-adjusted printers. Contact has been improved by the use of a backup roller instead of a shoe. The quality of contact and amount of slippage can be determined by examination under 10-times magnification. Excessive slippage, if it occurs, should be seen in a high-frequency sinusoidal signal of constant amplitude as a degradation of the image occurring every two to four perforations. Poor contact can be measured objectively by measuring the amplitude modulation which results.

Commercial sound-negative stocks are perforated with a shorter pitch (distance from one perforation to the next) than print stocks to reduce slippage. The print stock requires a longer arc length between perforations because it is wrapped around the sprocketed printing drum on the outside of the sound negative. In any applications where other than a commercially available sound-negative film is to be used as a sound negative, the product used should be perforated with the appropriate short pitch. Table 12.3 lists the pitches for the various formats.

Filtration.   The manufacturers of color-print films usually recommend the use of one or more color filters. It is usually desirable to reduce the exposure to the bottom layer on the film because the exposure distribution is degraded significantly by scattering in passing through the upper layers. A blue-light-absorbing filter such as the Kodak Wratten filter no. 12 is generally used with negative-positive color-print films to restrict the exposure to the top two (green- and red-light-sensitive) layers. On reversal color-print films, a cyan filter is sometimes recommended because the red-sensitive layer is on the bottom. Since all light-sensitive film layers retain their intrinsic sensitivity to ultraviolet (UV) light, the UV light must be

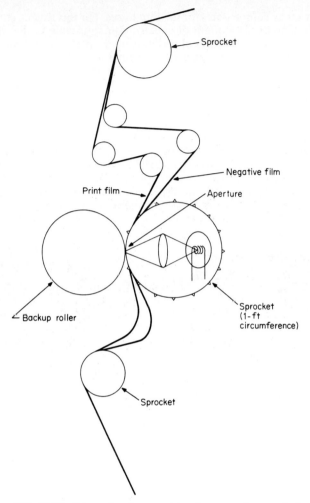

FIG. 12.19 Schematic of a sound head on a modern contact printer.

removed to allow control of the exposure in the individual layers. Film manufacturers recommend that a filter such as the Kodak Wratten filter no. 2B be used to remove the UV component from the printer source.

12.4.5 Reproducer Characteristics

To reproduce a photographic sound track, the film is transported past an optical system such as that shown in Fig. 12.20. Light from the exciter lamp is restricted by the narrow slit. The slit is imaged on the film by the objective lens. The condenser lens produces an image of the lamp filament within the objective lens.

TABLE 12.3 Perforation Pitches

Format	Negative films	Print films
35-mm	4.740 ±0.010 mm 0.1888 ±0.0004 in	4.750 ±0.010 mm 0.1870 ±0.0004 in
16-mm	7.605 ±0.010 mm 0.2994 ±0.0004 in	7.620 ±0.010 mm 0.3000 ±0.0004 in
Super-8	4.227 ±0.010 mm 0.1664 ±0.0004 in	4.234 ±0.010 mm 0.1667 ±0.0004 in

Ideally, the image of the slit on the film would be a line of light of infinitesimal width. In practice, however, the slit must have a finite width to allow enough light to fall onto the photodetector. For the reproduction of 35-mm tracks a slit width of 0.001 in is typical, and for 16-mm tracks slit widths are most often in the range of 0.0003 to 0.0005 in. The output current of the photodetector is proportional to the total amount of light falling upon it. In an ideal variable-area sound track, the amount of light transmitted by the film and consequently the photodetector current are proportional to the width of the clear area of the sound track.

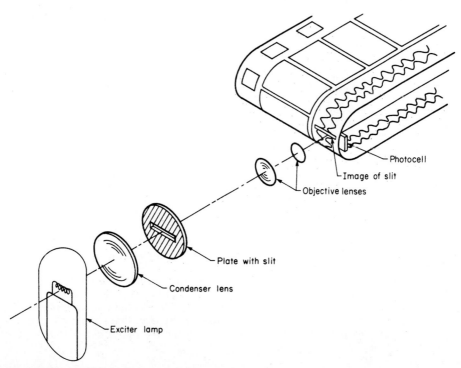

FIG. 12.20 Photographic sound-reproducing optical system.

Photodetector Types. It is virtually universal practice in 16- and 35-mm projectors to use a photodetector that is sensitive primarily to infrared light. The two most common types of photodetectors used are the gas phototube with S-1 response and the silicon solar cell. Typical spectral responses are shown in Fig. 12.21. The germanium phototransistor is less common but is used in some 16-

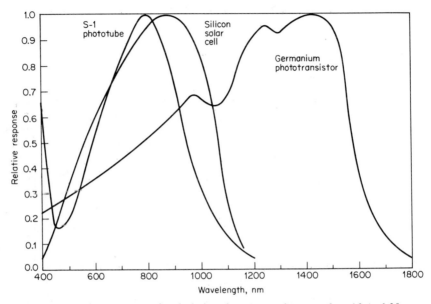

FIG. 12.21 Spectral response of typical photodetectors used to reproduce 16- and 35-mm photographic sound tracks.

mm projectors. The peak response of the germanium phototransistor is at a considerably longer wavelength than either the S-1 gas phototube or the silicon solar cell.

Less standardization exists among projectors designed for reproducing Super-8 photographic sound tracks. Most common is either the silicon solar cell or the silicon blue cell. The silicon blue cell is similar to the solar cell except that the response to visible light has been enhanced by either or both of the following methods: careful control of the "doping" of the semiconductor material during manufacture of the crystal or placing an appropriate filter over the cell. Silicon blue cells have a peak response at a lower wavelength than solar cells and are less sensitive. Some Super-8 projectors incorporate an optical filter to reduce their sensitivity to infrared light (see Fig. 12.22).

In many projectors that use the gas phototube, the S-1 response phototube can be removed and replaced with an S-4 response phototube. The S-4 response phototube is sensitive primarily to visible light and therefore is suitable for reproducing sound tracks that contain only the normal picture dyes that are largely transparent to infrared light. The spectral response of the S-4 phototube is shown in Fig. 12.22.

Focus of Scanning Beam. It is important that the image of the slit on the film be focused as well as possible to obtain the best high-frequency response. Improper

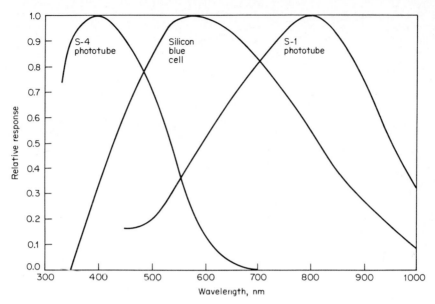

FIG. 12.22 Spectral response of typical photodetectors used to reproduce Super-8 photographic sound tracks.

focus can cause a falloff of almost 14 dB at 9 kHz. Some projectors are focused during manufacture and have no provision for focus adjustment by the user. Others are equipped with levers or knobs so the user may accurately focus the slit image on the film. Since the emulsion position on 16-mm films may be either toward or away from the projection lens, frequent changing of the focus may be necessary to accommodate films with different emulsion positions. Test films (see Chap. 16) that are suitable for projector focusing are available. These films contain a high-frequency signal (usually either 7000 or 10,000 Hz), and the projector output is adjusted to obtain maximum output from the signal.

Azimuth.   The azimuth of a projector scanning beam refers to the angle that the slit image on the film makes with the edge of the film. Ideally, that angle should be 90°. If the angle is not 90°, attenuation of high-frequency signals will result. The loss may be calculated with the following formula:[12]

$$\text{Scanning loss (dB)} = 20 \log \frac{\sin (\pi f)/f_0}{(\pi f)/f_0} \tag{12.7}$$

where $f_0 = V/W \tan (\theta)$
  V = film velocity
  W = track width
  θ = azimuth error = 90° − azimuth
  f = frequency of interest

Figure 12.23 shows the effect of an azimuth error of 40 min of arc (0.012 rad) on the frequency response of a 16-mm photographic sound track (film velocity = 7.2 in/s; track width = 0.060 in).

Test films (usually the same films used for focusing) that can be used to adjust

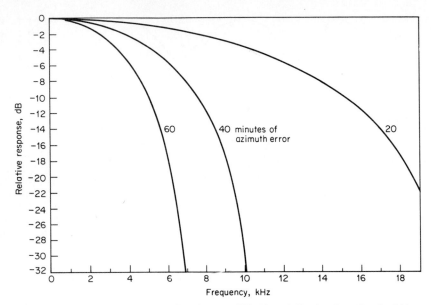

FIG. 12.23 Response due to an azimuth error of 20, 40, and 60 min of arc. Track width = 0.060 in; film velocity = 7.2 in/s.

the azimuth of a projector are available. These test films consist of a high-frequency signal whose azimuth is certified to be within a few min of 90°. The azimuth is adjusted for maximum output of the test-film signal.

Width and Position of Scanning Beam. When the scanning beam is correctly positioned on the film, the area scanned is slightly wider than the width of a variable-area sound track. If the scanned area is too narrow or is improperly positioned, the sound-track peaks will be clipped and distortion, including sibilant or cross-modulation distortion, will result. If the scanned area is too wide, excessive noise will result.

Figure 12.24 shows a test film designed to check for proper scanned area and position. If the scanning beam is correctly positioned, neither square wave will be reproduced. If the scanned area is too wide or out of position, either or both of the square waves will be heard. The scanning-beam position should be adjusted so that neither square wave is heard.

Uniformity of Scanning Beam. A lack of uniformity of the intensity of the scanning beam along its length can cause distortion when variable-area sound tracks are being reproduced. This lack of uniformity may be caused by dirt on the lenses, dirt in the slit, a nonuniform slit, an improperly positioned exciter lamp, or nonuniform photodetector response. Scanning-beam-illumination test films are available for checking uniformity. These test films are often called *snake tracks* because they consist of a narrow variable-area track (usually about 0.005 in wide) which begins near one edge of the sound-track area and gradually traverses or *snakes* across the track area. The scanning-beam uniformity is considered to be satisfactory if the output of the test film is ±1.5 dB across the entire width of the scanned area.

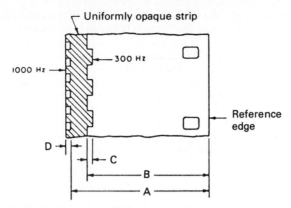

FIG. 12.24 16-mm scanning-beam-position test film. (*From SMPTE Recommended Practice 67-1983,* Specifications for Buzz-Track Test Film for 16-mm Motion Picture Reproducers, Photographic Type.)

Dimensions	Inches		Millimeters	
A	0.6060	+0.0 −0.0005	15.392	+ 0.0 − 0.013
B	0.5340	+0.0005 −0.0	13.561	+ 0.013 − 0.0
C	0.022	minimum	0.56	minimum
D	0.022	minimum	0.56	minimum

Measuring the Frequency Response of Photographic Reproducers and Projectors. After the adjustments of focus, azimuth, and scanning-beam width, position, and uniformity have been made as described in the preceding sections, it is often desirable to measure the overall frequency response of the projector. Test films that consist of a series of sinusoidal signals of various frequencies are available for this purpose. Each test film is calibrated and supplied with a list of correction factors to be added to the measured results. Frequency-response test films are designed to reproduce with uniform response at all frequencies on a reproducer or projector with a scanning beam of negligible width. The response measured with the test film includes the effects of not only the optical system but also the photodetector and amplifiers used.

Flutter. The reduction of flutter in motion-picture projectors is somewhat more difficult than in other types of sound-recording equipment owing to the proximity of the sound reproduction head to the picture aperture, where the motion of the film is intermittent and therefore very nonuniform. In a typical 16-mm projector a free loop of film is allowed to form between the picture gate and the sound drum. This loop takes up most of the variation in speed at the picture aperture and allows the film speed to be relatively uniform at the sound drum. The sound drum is driven only by the film and is coupled to a large flywheel to ensure uniform motion. The film is pulled past the sound drum by the sprocket. A damped compliance roller between the sound drum and the sprocket serves to isolate the sound drum from speed variations of the sprocket. The sound-drum pressure roller guides the film onto the sound drum to ensure correct scanning-beam position and also serves to increase the friction between the film and the sound drum to reduce slippage.

Test films that can be used to measure the flutter of a projector are available. The film consists of a 3000- or 3150-Hz signal, which has been recorded on equipment with very uniform motion. To use it, the test film is reproduced and the flutter is measured with an appropriate flutter meter. An abnormally high flutter level would indicate possible malfunction or misadjustment of the projector. The projector manufacturer's instructions should be followed closely when attempting to correct such problems or when otherwise disassembling or assembling a projector, as some of the adjustments of roller tension and dampening are rather critical.

12.5 OPTICAL SYSTEM QUALITY FACTORS

12.5.1 Frequency Response

Frequency response is a measure of the ability of the recording-reproducing system to reproduce signals of different frequencies. It is generally desired that a photographic sound-track system reproduce all frequencies as uniformly as possible in order to re-create the original recording accurately. In other words, the frequency response should be flat over as broad a frequency range as possible. There are several cases, however, where the frequency response of the entire system or part of it intentionally departs from a flat response. An intentional modification of the frequency response is generally known as *equalization.* Unintentional and usually unavoidable modifications of the frequency response by various elements in the system are referred to as *losses.* As the term is used here, losses will include increases as well as decreases in frequency response. In some cases, equalization is used to compensate for specific losses. In other cases, equalization is used for aesthetic reasons. That is, it is used to make the recording sound more pleasing. A good example of aesthetic equalization is the equalization that is commonly done to dialogue recording. The high- and low-frequency response is rolled off to increase naturalness and intelligibility.

High-frequency losses can arise from a variety of causes in photographic sound systems. These include recorder galvanometer and aperture losses, negative- and print-film sharpness losses, printer contact losses, and reproducer losses. Each of these factors was discussed in Sec. 12.4.

Recording and reproducing low frequencies (below 200 Hz) are not inherently difficult for the photographic sound-track system. If desired, it would be relatively easy to have a frequency response which extended to dc. However, it has been found that if the high-frequency response of the system does not extend to the limits of hearing, then the low-frequency response should also be rolled off. Doing this helps maintain a balanced sound; that is, a predominance of neither high- nor low-frequency information exists.

Measurement.   In general, frequency response is measured by recording a series of sinusoidal signals the amplitude of which, at the input of the recorder or at the modulator, is constant. Care must be taken so that none of the frequencies overmodulate the recording system. Any compressors or limiters normally used in the system should be switched out or off.

Frequency response can be measured either with or without the film-loss equalization. The frequency response with the film-loss equalization represents the system as actually used for recording program material. An unequalized, or constant-percent-modulated, frequency response indicates the intrinsic response of the system. It is most useful for comparing the response of different systems, since the amount of film-loss equalization can vary from recorder to recorder. Unequalized frequency-response tests are generally recorded so that each frequency is 80 percent modulated. Even with the film equalizer switched out, the frequency response of most recorders is not perfectly flat. Thus, it is usually necessary to make small adjustments in the amplifier gain to ensure that each frequency is recorded at exactly 80 percent modulation.

Equalization.   As mentioned previously, equalization is sometimes used to compensate for frequency-response losses elsewhere in the recording system. Such is the case in the photographic sound system. Photographic sound recorders contain an electronic circuit element known as a *film-loss equalizer* or, simply, *film equalizer.* This equalizer compensates for the frequency-response losses in the negative and print films. The amount of film equalization used varies from recorder to recorder.

12.5.2   Noise

Noise is any undesired signal present in a motion-picture sound track. Several types of noise may be present. The two most important are the noise due to film granularity and the noise due to dirt and scratches on the film. In addition, there may be noise originating in the various amplifiers used in the recording and reproducing system.

The noise due to film granularity, or grain noise, is broadband and fairly uniform in nature. It sounds much like the sound of air rushing through a small orifice and is often described as *hiss.*

The noise due to dirt and scratches on the film is impulsive and very nonuniform. It sounds somewhat similar to radio static. On a freshly processed print little of this type of noise should be present, and with careful handling it can be kept to a minimum throughout the life of a print. However, the noise in a badly dirtied or scratched print can be much louder than other types of noise present and can seriously affect the usefulness of the motion-picture print.

Several types of noise originate in the amplifiers used in the recording and reproducing system. One is amplifier hiss, which sounds similar to grain noise. Another is *hum,* which is a combination of low-frequency tones related to the power line frequency. Also, various static-type sounds can originate within the amplifiers.

Signal-to-Noise Measurements.   The ratio of the amplitude of the maximum signal the sound track is capable of to the amplitude of the noise present in the sound track is a quantitative expression of noise characteristics. The SNR is measured by recording a section of a standard reference signal and a section of unmodulated sound track. A print made from this recording is then played back on a reproducer or projector, the outputs from both the reference-signal section and the noise section are measured, and the ratio is calculated. The SNR is almost always expressed in decibels, which can be calculated with the following formula.

$$\text{SNR (dB)} = 20 \log \frac{V_{\text{sig}}}{V_{\text{noise}}} \qquad (12.8)$$

where V_{sig} = reference-signal voltage
V_{noise} = noise voltage

Measuring Circuits.   When the frequency response of the measuring system is flat and no frequencies have received any more *weight* than any others, the SNR measured is considered to be *unweighted*. However, such a measurement may not always yield numbers which accurately reflect the subjective noise quality of the noise in a system. This is true because the listener's auditory system does not respond equally to sounds of different frequencies, especially when the sounds are of fairly low level, as is the background noise in a sound track. Specifically, sounds of low frequency are less objectionable than higher-frequency sounds. In addition, the human hearing system does not respond to impulsive sounds in the same manner as most meters. Impulsive sounds sound more objectionable than indicated on a standard rms or average-responding type of meter. Thus, special metering circuits have been developed that yield SNR measurements which correspond more accurately with subjective impressions of noise than unweighted measurements. Wilms[21] provides an excellent review of the various measurement techniques used to measure audio noise. Figure 12.25 shows some of the standard weighting curves used for noise measurements.[21] The *A* curve has been used in the United States for noise measurements for many years. It is basically the inverse of the 30-phon equal-loudness curve of Fletcher and Munson.[22] It has been found more recently, however, that frequencies between 1 and 9 kHz are more annoying than indicated by the *A*-weighting curve. This is recognized by the *P* curve, which has been frequently used in Europe but rarely in the United States. The most recent work by the International Radio Consultative Committee (CCIR) has resulted in adoption of the *Q* curve by that organization.[23] In addition, the CCIR has adopted a quasi-peak-reading-meter characteristic. Thus, the use of a special weighting and metering circuit is recommended for noise measurements which compare dissimilar types of noise. CCIR Recommendation 468-2 is particularly recommended since it represents the most recent work. A broadband measuring system should be used only when comparing systems for which the noise is similar and nonimpulsive.

In Table 12.4, typical SNRs for motion-picture sound tracks are given. These measurements are intended to be measurements of the sound-track grain noise. Since this type of noise is similar from one film system to another and since meters complying with weighted standards are not readily available, measurements given were made of the broadband signal, expressed in rms values, and measured with a vacuum-tube voltmeter (VTVM). The readings were made on clean prints with relatively little dirt and scratch noise, and where it existed, meter fluctuations due to dirt and scratches were ignored.

As there are several different sound-track conditions under which the noise may be measured, it is important, when reporting SNR data, to note which type of noise measurements have been made.

1. *Unbiased, unmodulated (UBUM) noise measurements:* These measurements are made on a section of track which contains no signal and on which noise reduction biasing, also known as ground-noise reduction (GNR), has not been used. This is the most common type of SNR measurement made on photographic sound tracks and is the type reported in Table 12.4.

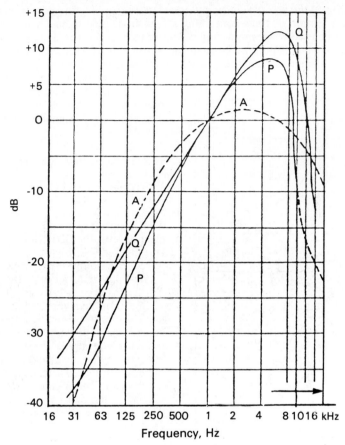

FIG. 12.25 Weighting curves used for noise measurements. (See text for description of curves.) [*From Herman A. O. Wilms, "Subjective or Psophometric Audio Noise Measurement: A Review of Standards,"* J. Audio Eng. Soc., *18, 651 (December 1970).*]

2. *Biased, unmodulated (BUM) noise measurements:* These measurements are made on a section of track which has no signal but does have noise reduction biasing. BUM measurements indicate the amount of noise present during a quiet passage in the program.

TABLE 12.4 Typical Signal-to-Noise Ratios

Print-film type	Signal-to-noise ratio, dB
Monochrome-print film, 16-mm	42–45
Color-print film, 16-mm	46–49
Reversal color-print film, 16-mm	40–43
Color-print film, Super-8 (dye)	37–40

3. *Noise-in-the-presence-of-signal measurements:* These measurements are made on a section of track containing a high-frequency signal. A narrow-notch filter must be used when measuring the noise to filter out the signal and measure only the noise that is present. Noise is measured in the presence of signal because the noise in a photographic sound track increases when a high-frequency signal is recorded owing to the greater edge length of such a signal. The SNR in the presence of signal is usually smaller than the UBUM signal-to-noise ratio.

12.5.3 Noise Reduction Techniques

When all other factors have been eliminated, it is frequently found that a low SNR is due to a high sound-track D_{min}. The importance of the density of the clear area to the SNR cannot be overemphasized. A high D_{min} works to lower the sound-track SNR in two ways. First, it lowers the signal level. This can be easily seen from Fig. 12.26b. The high D_{min} reduces the signal level by absorbing light that should be falling on the photodetector, thus reducing the signal level. The other effect of high D_{min} is to cause a dramatic increase in the noise level. The importance of this effect can be seen in Fig. 12.26a. If the density is very low, say, 0.05, the noise level is also low. If the D_{min} increases to 0.15, the noise level increases by approximately 2 dB. At the same time, this same increase in D_{min} has caused a loss of 2.2 dB in the level of the reference signal, resulting in an overall loss in the SNR of over 4 dB. Figure 12.26c shows this overall effect graphically. The bottom curve shows how the noise level is affected by D_{min}, the middle curve shows how the signal is affected, and the top curve shows the overall effect.

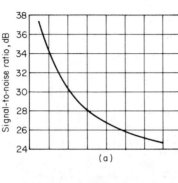

(a)

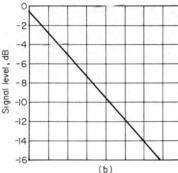

(b)

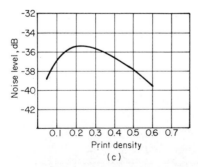

Print density

(c)

FIG. 12.26 Effect of sound track D_{min} on (a) noise, (b) signal level, and (c) signal-to-noise ratio.]

Ground-Noise-Reduction (GNR) Biasing. Ground-noise-reduction biasing refers to the technique of reducing the clear area of the sound track during quiet passages in the program material. Figure 12.27 shows photographic sound tracks with and without noise reduction biasing. The biasing is accomplished electrically in the photographic sound recorder; see Sec. 12.4.3 for a description of the electronic techniques used. GNR is effective because most of the noise in a photographic sound track, whether due to granularity, dirt, scratches, or other physical defects in the sound track, comes from the D_{min} area of the sound track. If the clear area that is not carrying modulations can be reduced, the noise level can also be reduced. The width of the clear area is reduced to about 0.05 to 0.10 mm (0.002 to 0.004 in). The use of GNR is common practice when recording all types of photographic sound tracks.

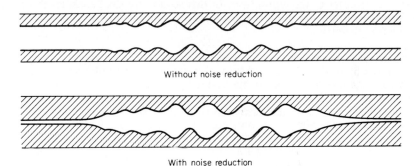

Without noise reduction

With noise reduction

FIG. 12.27   Sound tracks with and without noise reduction biasing.

Preequalization and Postequalization.   Both of these procedures can also be used for noise reduction. During recording, preequalization is added in the form of high-frequency boost. During playback, a complementary high-frequency rolloff is added. The net result is zero for the program material which encounters both boost and rolloff. However, noise which encounters only the playback rolloff has its high-frequency content reduced, resulting in a subjectively lower noise level. At first it might seem that boosting the high frequencies during recording might cause overmodulation and distortion of high-frequency sounds. However, it has been found that most program material has considerably less energy at high frequencies than at low frequencies.[18,19,20] Thus, the high-frequency level may be boosted without excessive overmodulation. For 16-mm and Super-8 sound tracks, a large amount of high-frequency equalization is required just to overcome recording losses. If any more preequalization were added for the purpose of noise reduction, excessive high-frequency overmodulation would result. Thus, preequalization and postequalization for noise reduction purposes are not used for 16-mm or Super-8 sound tracks but are used for 35-mm photographic sound tracks.

Compression-Expansion Systems.   These systems have been experimented with for many years as a means of noise reduction.[24] By means of an electronic volume control circuit, the dynamic range of the program material is compressed during recording. A complementary expansion circuit is used during playback to restore the program material to its original dynamics. Noise which was added after recording (such as film-grain noise and dirt and scratch noise) is expanded downward, resulting in a subjectively greater SNR. The Dolby noise reduction system is currently in widespread use with stereo photographic sound tracks. (See Chap. 6 and Refs. 2, 3, and 4.)

12.5.4 Distortion

Distortion occurs in a photographic sound track when there is a nonlinear relationship between input and output. Sources of distortion in the photographic sound-track system are (1) nonlinearities in amplifiers used in the recorders or reproducers, (2) the galvanometer or light valve that produces the variable-area sound track, (3) image spread in the negative and print films, (4) too large a signal (overmodulation distortion), (5) a mispositioned sound track or reproducer scanning beam (clipping distortion), and (6) a misadjusted lamp or optical system in either the recorder or the reproducer. In this section we shall consider three categories of distortion: harmonic distortion, cross-modulation distortion, and intermodulation distortion.

Harmonic Distortion. Harmonic distortion occurs when a sinusoidal signal is applied to a nonlinear system. Additional frequencies, multiples or harmonics of the original frequency present in the input signal, are generated. Harmonic distortion is measured by applying a sinusoidal signal to the input of the system. The output signal from the system is passed through a filter which removes the fundamental frequency and leaves only the harmonics. These harmonics are measured and expressed as a percentage of the amplitude of the fundamental. If all the harmonics are measured together, the result is total harmonic distortion. If a narrow-bandpass filter is used, the harmonics can be measured individually. Specific meters suitable for measuring harmonic distortion are available.

To measure the harmonic distortion of a photographic sound track, record a section of tone of the desired frequency at normal negative density and have it printed at the normal print density. The cross-modulation test should be used to determine the proper densities. The recorded signal should be longer than usually recorded for other tests, since making a distortion measurement requires more time than just measuring the level as in a frequency-response test. The frequency most commonly used for distortion measurements of photographic sound tracks is 400 Hz, although any frequency within the range of the recording system may be used. Because of image-spread effects, the distortion will not be the same at all frequencies. Harmonic-distortion measurements at frequencies above 3000 or 4000 Hz may not yield an accurate measure of the distortion present. Distortion components may fall outside the passband of the system, resulting in low distortion readings. However, distortion may still occur, especially on listening material containing more than one tone at a time (known as intermodulation distortion; see Sec. 12.4.6).

Figure 12.28 shows a plot of second-harmonic distortion, third-harmonic distortion, and total harmonic distortion versus frequency for a typical 16-mm sound track. Notice that the decrease in harmonic distortion in the region above 3000 Hz is due primarily to the fact that the harmonics fall outside the passband of the reproducer and are attenuated.

Cross-Modulation Distortion. The single most important quality test for photographic sound tracks is the cross-modulation test. Even if the best recording equipment and the best film stocks are used, cross-modulation distortion can still be present in the final print. This is true because cross-modulation distortion is a function of exposure of both the negative and the print. The cross-modulation test should be a routine part of a laboratory's quality control procedure to ensure that the proper exposure levels are maintained and distortion is minimized.

A high level of cross-modulation distortion is most noticeable in its effect on the sibilant speech sounds. Many of the sibilant speech sounds (*s, sh, ch, z,* etc.)

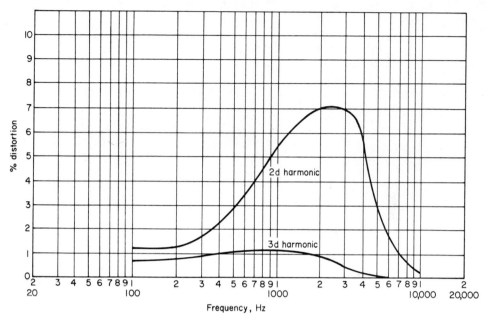

FIG. 12.28 Harmonic distortion in a 16-mm photographic sound track.

and some of the voiced and voiceless stop sounds (*b, p,* and *t*) become distorted. The *s* sound, however, is the sound most affected by cross-modulation distortion. These sibilant speech sounds contain high-frequency content of rapidly varying amplitude (Fig. 12.29). Image spread causes the valleys of the variable-area sound track to fill in, resulting in a variable dc shift, which is heard as the distortion that accompanies the sibilant sound (see Fig. 12.30). Image-spread distortion that occurs when a negative is recorded can be essentially eliminated when that neg-

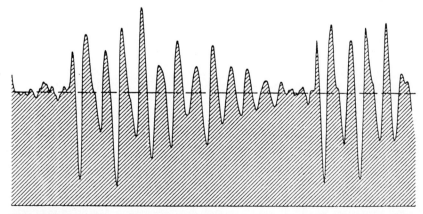

FIG. 12.29 Variable-area sound track of a spoken *s* sound. [*From Ronald E. Uhlig, "The Optimum Carrier Frequency for Cross-Modulation Tests,"* J. Soc. Motion Pict. Telev. Eng. *(August 1976).*]

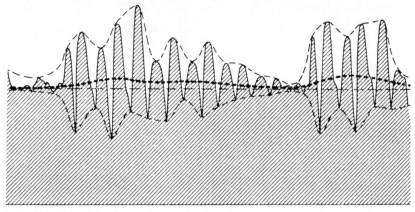

FIG. 12.30   Variable-area sound track with image spread.   [*From Ronald E. Uhlig, "The Optimum Carrier Frequency for Cross-Modulation Tests," J. Soc. Motion Pict. Telev. Eng. (August 1976).*]

ative is printed by an equal but opposite shift in the print film. The cross-modulation test is used to ensure that the amount of shift in the print exactly cancels the shift present in the negative.

The cross-modulation test signal, shown in Fig. 12.31, consists of a high-frequency carrier which is amplitude-modulated at 400 Hz. Figure 12.32 is an illustration of a variable-area recording of the cross-modulation test signal. Image-spread distortion causes a shift that repeats for each cycle of the envelope, thus generating a 400-Hz signal which is proportional to the amount of image-spread distortion. The 400-Hz signal is measured with a bandpass filter and voltmeter. The aim is to get minimum voltage, signifying maximum cancellation. Those interested in more detail can consult the literature.[25,26]

The carrier frequency of the cross-modulation signal plays an important part in determining the effectiveness of the cross-modulation test. For sound tracks on 35-mm film, it has been common practice to use 9000 Hz for the carrier frequency, as originally suggested by Baker and Robinson.[26] American National Standard PH22.52-1960 states that a 4000-Hz carrier frequency shall be used for cross-modulation tests on 16-mm sound tracks.[27] However, both 4-kHz and 6-

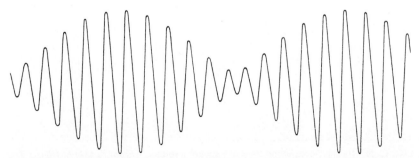

FIG. 12.31   Cross-modulation test signal.   [*From Ronald E. Uhlig, "The Optimum Carrier Frequency for Cross-Modulation Tests," J. Soc. Motion Pict. Telev. Eng. (August 1976).*]

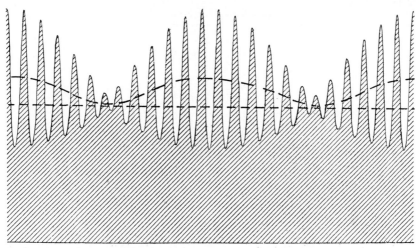

FIG. 12.32 Variable-area recording of the cross-modulation test signal. [*From Ronald E. Uhlig, "The Optimum Carrier Frequency for Cross-Modulation Tests," J. Soc. Motion Pict. Telev. Eng. (August 1976).*]

kHz carrier frequencies are commonly used. In addition, Uhlig[28] has described tests which showed that, for a wide-bandwidth 16-mm photographic sound-track system, the cross-modulation carrier frequency should be 8000 to 9000 Hz. If the recording system has a more restricted bandwidth, the carrier frequency should be approximately at the cutoff frequency of the system.

Generally, when the cross-modulation signal is recorded, a 400-Hz sine wave of the same amplitude is also recorded. When the cross-modulation signal is analyzed, the voltage due to the 400-Hz signal present in the cross-modulation signal is divided by the voltage of the 400-Hz reference. This figure is then multiplied by 100 to give percent distortion. Often, the amount of distortion is expressed in decibels rather than percent and is called the cross-modulation product.

$$\text{Cross-modulation product} = 20 \log \frac{V_{XM}}{V_R} \qquad (12.9)$$

where V_{XM} = cross-modulation signal, V
$ V_R$ = reference signal, V

The cross-modulation signal may be formed either by amplitude-modulating a high-frequency carrier or by mixing together two high-frequency signals separated by 400 Hz. The two signals appear very similar (Fig. 12.33), and either may be used. If accurate distortion measurements are to be made, it is necessary that the 400-Hz reference signal and the cross-modulation signal be recorded at the correct level. Both signals should be recorded at 80 percent of the maximum modulation level. In addition, the cross-modulation signal should have an amplitude-modulation factor of 0.80. Referring to Fig. 12.33, the amplitude-modulation factor is given by

$$m = \frac{E_{max} - E_{min}}{E_{max} + E_{min}} \qquad (12.10)$$

If $m = 0.8$, then $E_{min} = \frac{1}{9} E_{max}$.

Amplitude-modulated cross-modulation signal

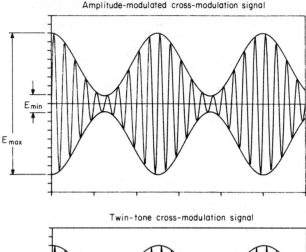

Twin-tone cross-modulation signal

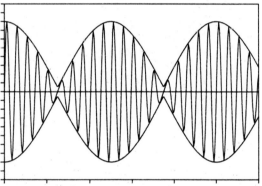

FIG. 12.33   (*a*) Amplitude-modulated and (*b*) twin-tone cross-modulation signals. For 80 percent amplitude modulation, $E_{min} = \frac{1}{9}$ E_{max}.

An oscilloscope can be used to measure the modulation factor. If the cross-modulation signal is obtained by mixing two high-frequency signals, the amplitudes of the two signals should be in a ratio of 1:1.25 in order to obtain a modulation factor of 0.80. The peak amplitude of the cross-modulation signal should be at 80 percent of maximum modulation. If a meter is available in the recording system on which the voltage required for 100 percent modulation is recorded, then the two tones should be set to the following levels:

$$V_1 = 0.444 \, V_{100} \tag{12.11}$$

$$V_2 = 0.356 \, V_{100} \tag{12.12}$$

If an amplitude-modulated high-frequency signal is used for a cross-modulation signal, the amplitude of the cross-modulation signal, as measured on an average-responding meter, should be 5.1 dB less than a sinusoidal signal of the same peak amplitude. When measured on a true rms-responding voltmeter, the cross-modulation signal will measure 5.8 dB less than a sinusoidal signal of the same peak amplitude.

It is occasionally necessary to make measurements of cross-modulation distortion from a negative or print on which the reference and/or cross-modulation signals are not at the correct level. Under these circumstances, the amount of distortion measured will not be the same as it would have been had the signals been recorded at the correct amplitude. If the cross-modulation signal is over 100 percent modulation, the clipping that has occurred will cause additional distortion which invalidates the test. However, if the cross-modulation signal has not been recorded at over 100 percent modulation, the measurements may still be used. Reference 1 contains a procedure for correcting the measurements, based on measurements of the signal amplitudes on the film. It should be noted that, in addition to requiring a fairly accurate means of measuring distances on the film, the method is somewhat tedious, and every effort should be made to record the signals at the correct amplitude initially.

The maximum amount of cross-modulation distortion that can be tolerated in a photographic sound track depends on several factors, including the bandwidth of the recording system and the sibilance of the speaker. It is generally accepted that distortion should be less than about 2.5 to 3 percent for optimum quality. (This corresponds to a cross-modulation product that is less than -30 to -32 dB.) In order to keep distortion under this level, there must be a conscientiously applied program of quality control using the cross-modulation test. Reference 25 contains a step-by-step procedure for sound-track quality control. This procedure includes the method for performing the original cross-modulation test in which the cross-modulation family is obtained, as well as using these data in day-to-day operation to obtain prints with acceptably low levels of cross-modulation distortion.

Intermodulation Distortion.   Intermodulation distortion occurs when the various components of a complex signal interact to produce frequency components not found in the original signal. The intermodulation test is of particular interest with respect to variable-density sound tracks, where nonlinearities in the film's exposure-transmittance characteristic cause amplitude modulation of the higher-frequency components by the lower-frequency components. For producers of variable-density sound tracks, the intermodulation test is the basic quality control test, much as the cross-modulation test is for the variable-area sound track.

There are actually two types of intermodulation-distortion tests. One type, known as the SMPTE intermodulation test,[29] uses a test signal which is a combination of a low frequency, nominally 60 Hz, and a high frequency, nominally 2000 Hz. The other type, known as the CCITT intermodulation test,[30] uses two high-frequency tones of equal amplitude with a frequency difference in the order of 10 percent. This test is also called a twin-tone distortion test. The cross-modulation test, described in the preceding section, is a slight variation of the CCITT intermodulation test. This type of intermodulation test will not be further discussed.

In the SMPTE intermodulation test, the amplitude of the high frequency is one-fourth of the amplitude of the low frequency. The intermodulation-distortion analyzer consists basically of a means for measuring the amount of amplitude modulation in the high-frequency signal. (Figure 16.36 in Chap. 16 shows the basic block diagram of an intermodulation analyzer.)

The intermodulation test signal is recorded onto the negative film at a series of exposure levels. This series of negatives is then printed to obtain a series of print densities, resulting in a family of prints. The intermodulation distortion is then measured in each of the prints, and a plot of the distortion in the print versus

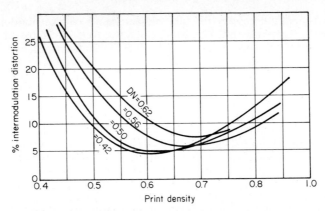

FIG. 12.34 Intermodulation distortion as a function of print density for various negative densities of a variable-density sound track. *(From John G. Frayne and Halley Wolfe,* Elements of Sound Recording, *Wiley, New York, 1949.)*

print density is made for each of the negative exposure levels. Figure 12.34 is an example of such a plot.[31] From such a plot the negative and print densities which yield the lowest distortion can be determined.

Reference 31 contains valuable additional information on the use of the inter-modulation-distortion test in the production of variable-density sound tracks.

Amplitude Modulation. Amplitude modulation occurs in photographic sound tracks when the amplitude of high-frequency signals is nonuniform. It can be heard as a wavering of the signal level or, in extreme cases, as a gurgling of low-frequency sounds.

Amplitude modulation is measured by using the same analyzer that is employed for measuring intermodulation distortion. It can be measured at any frequency from about 1000 Hz or greater. The most commonly used frequencies are 2000 and 3000 Hz. A section of a continuous sinusoidal signal of the desired frequency is recorded. The negative produced is then printed, and the amount of amplitude modulation in the print is measured. The amount of amplitude modulation in the negative may also be measured. An abnormally high amount of amplitude modulation in the negative might indicate poor or varying focus of the negative recorder. A high amount of amplitude modulation in the print usually indicates poor contact in the printer. It is normal for the amount of amplitude modulation in the print to be somewhat higher than the amount of amplitude modulation in the negative. Also, the amount of amplitude modulation in both the negative and the print increases as the frequency of the test signal used increases. Amplitude modulation of 3 percent or less of a 3000-Hz signal usually indicates satisfactory printer contact.

12.5.5 Flutter

Flutter is frequency modulation of recorded audio listening material. It is most often caused by variations in recorder and reproducer transport speed, but in the case of photographic sound tracks it can also be caused by slippage in the motion-picture printer. Flutter is objectively measured by measuring the amount of variation in frequency of a constant-frequency recording.

Definition.   In its most general sense, the term flutter includes all variations in speed of a recording. In a more limited sense, however, the terms *drift, wow, flutter,* and *modulation noise* have been used to describe frequency modulation of various rates. Frequency modulation which occurs at rates below 1 Hz is heard as a drift of pitch. If the frequency modulation is in the region of 1 to 8 Hz, it is heard as a wow. In the region between 8 to 50 Hz, a pitch change itself is not audible, but a roughening of the tone quality is heard. If the frequency modulation is above 50 Hz, the sidebands themselves are heard as an added noise which is called modulation noise.

Measurement Procedures.   Flutter must be measured with some care if the resulting measurement is to compare well with the subjective impression of flutter. Generally, flutter measurements include all flutter frequencies from 0.2 to 200 Hz. Since the ear is more sensitive to some frequencies of flutter than to others, a weighting circuit is sometimes used in the flutter-measuring device to suppress the measurement of those frequencies to which the ear is less sensitive and to emphasize those to which the ear is more sensitive. (Figure 16.10 in Chap. 16 shows common weighting filters.)

The response characteristics of the meter circuit are also important in determining how subjectively accurate the measurements will be. The National Association of Broadcasters (NAB) standard[33] specifies that a volume-unit (VU) indicating meter which has the same dynamic characteristics as the standard VU meter be used. The standard VU meter characteristic follows an average rectified full-wave measurement law. On the other hand, the more recent Deutsche Industrie Normenanschus (DIN) and CCIR standards specify a quasi-peak-reading meter.[34,35]

Frequencies of either 3000 or 3150 Hz are most generally used for measuring flutter. When measuring the flutter of a reproducer, an essentially flutter-free test film is reproduced and the flutter is measured. To measure the flutter of a recorder, a recording of a 3000- or 3150-Hz constant-frequency tone is made. After the sound track has been processed (and printed, if desired), the flutter in the recording should be read on a reproducer which has a negligible amount of flutter compared with that of the recorder. Since few reproducers which have less flutter than many high-quality recorders are available, it is important to measure the flutter of the reproducer alone, using a test film, before attempting to measure the flutter in the recording. If the flutter in the recording is not significantly higher than the flutter of the reproducer alone, it should be recognized that the measured flutter is due primarily to the reproducer rather than the recorder. In the photographic sound-track system, flutter can also be introduced by the motion-picture printer. This source of flutter can be measured by comparing the flutter in the negative with the flutter in a print made from the negative. The flutter in the print will generally be somewhat higher, but a large difference could be an indication of slippage in the printer.

When reporting a flutter measurement, it should be noted whether the measurement is a peak or an rms value and is weighted or unweighted. Most flutter meters are accompanied by manuals which give fairly complete instructions on their use. These instructions should be followed closely since accurate measurements depend on the proper interpretation of a fluctuating meter reading.

12.6 MAGNETIC SOUND TRACKS

12.6.1 Introduction

Magnetic sound tracks are used extensively in the production, postproduction, and distribution of motion pictures. The basic principles of the magnetic recording process as used in the motion-picture industry are the same as other analog magnetic recording applications and are discussed in Chap. 10.

One-fourth-inch magnetic tape is used almost universally for production recording of motion-picture sound tracks. *Production recording* is the recording that takes place during the original photography stage of shooting motion pictures. The formats used, the recording characteristics, and the methods of synchronization with the pictures are discussed in Sec. 14.2 in Chap. 14.

The first step in *postproduction,* which comprises the steps following production, is to transfer the production audio from the ¼-in tape to striped or full-coat film. This is the film that is used in the editing process and provides the input to the mixing process. The formats used and the processes involved are discussed in detail in Secs. 14.2 and 14.3.

12.6.2 Release-Print Formats

Roughly one-fourth of motion-picture release prints, that is, the prints of motion pictures that are sent to theaters, contain a magnetic sound track. A number of formats have been used in the past, but the only magnetic format currently in widespread use for theatrical films is the 70-mm six-track format. This format consists of four magnetic stripes, two wide and two narrow, on which are recorded six audio tracks. The film format and stripe location are shown in Fig. 12.35. Four-track 35-mm formats have been employed in the past for release prints, but the use of these formats has been discontinued. The magnetic stripes are applied to the prints after the pictures have been printed and the film has been processed.

Some 16-mm films are made with magnetic sound tracks in the format shown in Fig. 12.36. This format is primarily used when the quantity of prints required does not justify the expense of having a photographic sound-track negative made. Many 16-mm projectors can reproduce either magnetic or photographic sound tracks.

Magnetic sound tracks are also found on Super-8 films used for single-system sound recording and also on print films used for mass duplication (see Fig. 12.37). Both 16-mm and Super-8 format film are supplied by film manufacturers *prestriped,* that is, with the magnetic stripes already in place.

12.7 MAGNETIC SYSTEM QUALITY FACTORS

The following paragraphs discuss several factors that can affect the reproduced quality of motion-picture sound tracks.

12.7.1 Equalization

Equalization refers to the amplitude-versus-frequency characteristic of the circuitry used to record and reproduce magnetic sound tracks. Several different standards exist for this characteristic. Therefore, it is important that the record and

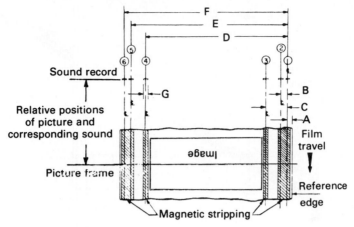

FIG. 12.35 Stripe location for 70-mm film. *(From American National Standard PH22.185-1980.)*

Dimensions	Inches	Millimeters
A	0.052 ± 0.002	1.32 ± 0.05
B	0.110 ± 0.002	2.79 ± 0.05
C	0.316 ± 0.002	8.03 ± 0.05
D	2.328 ± 0.002	59.13 ± 0.05
E	2.534 ± 0.002	64.36 ± 0.05
F	2.644 ± 0.002	67.16 ± 0.05
G	$0.060 \, {+ 0.004 \atop - 0.000}$	$1.52 \, {+ 0.10 \atop - 0.00}$

reproduce circuitry be correctly aligned to complement the recording characteristic and to ensure uniform frequency response of the sound track. Multifrequency test films that have been recorded according to the applicable standards are available for use in aligning and maintaining equipment. (See Chap. 16 on test materials.)

12.7.2 Azimuth

Azimuth refers to the orientation of the magnetic head around an axis normal to the plane of the magnetic coating. The ideal position is to have the gap of the magnetic head positioned at exactly 90° to the direction of film motion. Departure from the ideal position in either recording or reproduction will result in a reduction of high frequencies. Test films are available to assist in setting up the proper azimuth. (See Chapter 16.)

12.8 THEATER SYSTEMS

This section on reproduction or playback of sound on film provides a brief list of the different formats that may be encountered and a description of some of the factors that affect the quality of the reproduced sound.

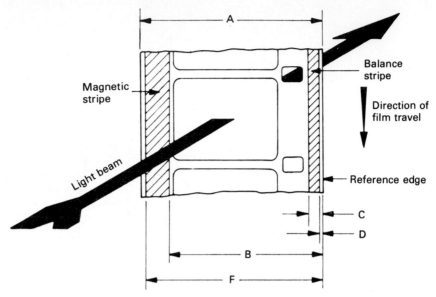

FIG. 12.36 Stripe location for 16-mm film. *(From American National Standard PH22.112-1983.)*

Dimensions	Millimeters		Inches	
A	15.95	reference	0.628	reference
B	13.25	$+0.00$ -0.15	0.522	$+0.000$ -0.006
C	0.80	$+0.00$ -0.15	0.031	$+0.000$ -0.006
D	0.15	maximum	0.006	maximum
F	15.80	minimum	0.622	minimum

12.8.1 Single-System Sound Tracks

The basic mechanism for the reproduction of single-system sound tracks is in many ways similar to that required in the camera for recording single-system. Since the film must be moving in a smooth and continuous manner at the point where the sound is reproduced, a free loop is required to isolate that point from the intermittent motion at the film gate. Many 16-mm projectors are capable of playing either optical or magnetic sound tracks. The displacement between picture and sound is slightly different for the two formats, being 26 frames for optical and 28 frames for magnetic sound tracks. To switch from one format to the other merely requires a mechanism for lifting or lowering the magnetic head onto the film and switching the preamplifier to input from either the magnetic head or the photoreceptor.

Spectral Response of Photocell Receptors. One important consideration is the spectral sensitivity of the photoreceptors used in motion-picture projectors. The standard photoreceptor for 16- and 35-mm motion-picture projectors is sensitive

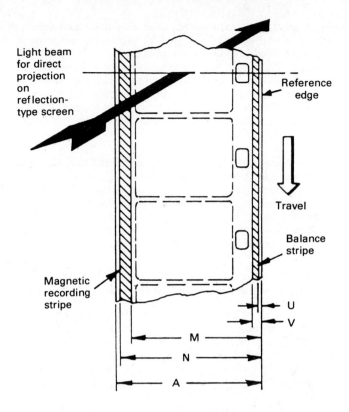

Film as seen looking toward lens

FIG. 12.37 Stripe location for Super-8 film. *(From American National Standard PH22.164-1982.)*

Dimensions	Inches	Millimeters
A	0.314 nominal	7.98 nominal
M	0.285 ± 0.002	7.24 ± 0.05
N	0.312 ± 0.002	7.92 ± 0.05
U	0.003 ± 0.003	0.08 ± 0.08
V	0.015 ± 0.003	0.38 ± 0.08

primarily to infrared light. The reason for this spectral response rather than a response to visible light is one of history. When optical sound tracks were first becoming used in the 1920s, there was only one type of photocell available that had the required high-frequency response and high sensitivity. That was the infrared-sensitive gas phototube, now known as the S-1 phototube response. At that time there was no problem, since the incandescent-light bulbs used as light sources for sound reproduction output produced large amounts of infrared light, and the black-and-white films, which used silver to form the images, were excellent modulators of infrared light as well as visible light. However, with the advent of color films, it was found that the dyes used were poor modulators of infrared light. Techniques were therefore developed for processing the color-print film so that the sound track would retain a silver image.

Later, photocells that were sensitive to visible light were developed, but while these gave good results in reproducing dye sound tracks, they gave less-than-ideal results when playing back the specially processed color films, for they had, in addition to the silver image, a dye image of the sound track. Suffice it to say that infrared-sensitive photocells continue to be used, and it remains necessary to process print film to obtain a silver sound track.

Color-Print Film Processing. The extra step necessary to obtain a silver sound track on color-print film involves the application of a viscous developer to the sound-track area only following the bleach step in the color-print film process. This step is called sound-track *redeveloper application* or often just *application*. When reversal color-print film is used, two sound-track application steps are required. The first is a sound-track fix application, and the second, somewhat later in the process, is a sound-track redeveloper application.

12.8.2 Reproduction of Double-System Sound Tracks

There are two major reasons why it may be necessary to project a film double-system. The first is that origination and/or editing was done double-system and it is more convenient to project or broadcast double-system than to make a single-system print. This is especially true of certain news-gathering operations in which there is essentially only a single showing. The second reason for using double-system is that a higher quality of audio reproduction can be obtained. A separate sound track offers a wider track width and the use of a transport with better film motion. The use of double-system sound for this reason is more common in European broadcast operations.

For double-system reproduction, a magnetic-film transport that can be interlocked to the telecine projector is required. Given this, the only other concern of the operator is that the sound and picture rolls be properly synchronized at the beginning of projection.

REFERENCES

1. K. Blair Benson (ed.), *Handbook of Television Engineering,* McGraw-Hill, New York, 1986, p. 14.109.

2. Ronald E. Uhlig, "Stereophonic Photographic Sound Tracks," *J. Soc. Motion Pict. Telev. Eng.,* **82,** 292–295 (1973).

3. Ronald E. Uhlig, "Two- and Three-Channel Stereophonic Photographic Sound Tracks for Theaters and Television," *J. Soc. Motion Pict. Telev. Eng.,* **83,** 729–733 (1974).

4. Ioan Allen, "The Production of Wide-Range, Low-Distortion Optical Soundtracks Utilizing the Dolby Noise Reduction System," *J. Soc. Motion Pict. Telev. Eng.,* **84,** 720–729 (September 1975).

5. J. Mosely, D. E. Blackmer, and K. O. Johnson, "The Colortek Optical Stereophonic Sound Film Systems," *J. Soc. Motion Pict. Telev. Eng.,* **87,** 222–232 (1978).

6. Joseph J. Charles and J. Dexter Clifford, "The Relative Output of Optical Soundtracks," *J. Soc. Motion Pict. Telev. Eng.,* 730–731 (September 1975).

7. V. Ferrier and R. Desprez, "Image Structure in the Problems of Sound Recording by Photographic Means," *Proc. 9th Cong. Int. Union Tech. Cinematog. Assoc., Modern Techniques for the Recording, Transmission, and Reproduction of Audio and Visual Information*, 253–264 (1970; in French).

8. K. Staes, L. A. Hayen, and R. G. L. Verbrugghe, "ST 8: A New Agfa-Gavaert Sound Negative Film Especially Suitable for Super-8," *J. Soc. Motion Pict. Telev. Eng.*, **84**, 593–596 (1975).

9. K. Muramatsu, "Improving 8 mm Type S (Super-8) Optical Sound by Design of Film and Recording System," *J. Soc. Motion Pict. Telev. Eng.*, **83**, 117–124 (1974).

10. E. W. Kellogg, "The ABC of Photographic Sound Recording," *J. Soc. Motion Pict. Telev. Eng.*, **44**, 151–194 (1945).

11. J. G. Frayne, "Variable-Area Recording with the Light Valve," *J. Soc. Motion Pict. Telev. Eng.*, **51** (1948).

12. N. R. Stryker, "Scanning Losses in Reproduction," *J. Soc. Motion Pict. Eng.* (November 1930).

13. Donald J. Foster, "The Effect of Exposure and Development on the Quality of Variable Width Photographic Sound Recording," *J. Soc. Motion Pict. Eng.*, **XVII**, 749–764 (November 1931).

14. E. D. Cook, "The Aperture Effect," *J. Soc. Motion Pict. Eng.*, **XVI**, 650–662 (June 1930).

15. J. Jespers, "The Influence of Photographic Imaging Properties on Sound Reproduction," *BKSTS J.*, **52**, 6–11 (January 1970).

16. V. V. Rakovsky, "A Mathematical Model of Variable Width Sound Tracks Recorded on Film," *Tekh. Kino Telev.*, no. 4 (1974), translated by F. H. Holland, Jr.

17. Joseph J. Charles and C. F. Mitasik, "Computer Simulation of Photographic Sound Recording," *J. Soc. Motion Pict. Telev. Eng.*, **87**, 429–435 (July 1978).

18. John G. McKnight, "The Distribution of Peak Energy," *J. Audio Eng. Soc.*, 65 (April 1969).

19. Banjamin Bauer, "Octave Band Spectral Distribution," *J. Audio Eng. Soc.*, 165 (April 1970).

20. Josef W. Dorner, "Why Use 15-IPS Tape Speed?" *db*, 40 (June 1975).

21. Herman A. O. Wilms, "Subjective or Psophometric Audio Noise Measurement: A Review of Standards," *J. Audio Eng. Soc.*, **18**, 651 (December 1970).

22. H. Fletcher and W. A. Munson, *J. Acoust. Soc. Am.*, **5**, 82 (1933).

23. *Measurement of Audio-Frequency Noise in Broadcasting, in Sound-Recording Systems, and on Sound Programme Circuits*, CCIR Recommendation 468-2.

24. Ray N. Dolby, "An Audio Noise Reduction System," *J. Audio Eng. Soc.* (October 1967). The article contains a number of references to earlier work in compression-expansion noise reduction systems.

25. *Cross-Modulation Distortion Testing for the Small Motion-Picture Laboratory*, Kodak Publication H-44.

26. J. O. Baker and D. H. Robinson, "Modulated High-Frequency Recording as a Means of Determining Conditions for Optimal Processing," *J. Soc. Motion Pict. Eng.*, **30**, 3–17 (January 1938).

27. *Cross-Modulation Tests for 16 mm Variable-Area Photographic Sound Prints*, SMPTE Recommended Practice 104-1981.

28. Ronald E. Uhlig, "The Optimum Carrier Frequency for Cross-Modulation Tests," *J. Soc. Motion Pict. Telev. Eng.* (August 1976).

29. *Intermodulation Tests for 16 mm Variable-Density Photographic Sound Prints*, SMPTE Recommended Practice 120-1983.

30. CCITT intermodulation test.

31. John G. Frayne and Halley Wolfe, *Elements of Sound Recording,* Wiley, New York, 1949.

32. C. E. K. Mees, "The Theory of the Photographic Process," *Photographic Aspects of Sound Recording,* 1st ed., Macmillan, New York, 1942, chap. XXII.

33. *NAB Standard—Magnetic Tape Recording and Reproducing* (reel-to-reel), National Association of Broadcasters, Washington, April 1965.

34. "DIN Standard—Measurement Equipment for Frequency Variations" (flutter and drift), *Sound Recording Equipment,* DIN 45-507 (October 1976).

35. *Measurement of Wow and Flutter in Recording Equipment and in Sound Reproduction,* CCIR Recommendation 409-2, Geneva, 1974.

BIBLIOGRAPHY

BKSTS Training Committee: *Photographic Sound Recording and Reproduction,* 1968.

————: *Sound for Film and Television,* 1968.

Frater, Charles B.: *Sound Recording for Motion Pictures,* Tantivy Press, London, 1979.

Frayne, J. G., A. C. Blaney, G. R. Groves, and H. F. Olson: "A Short History of Motion Picture Sound Recording in the United States," *J. Soc. Motion Pict. Telev. Eng.,* **85,** 515–528 (1976).

———— and H. Wolfe: *Elements of Sound Recording,* Wiley, New York, and Chapman & Hall, London, 1949.

Kellogg, E. W.: "The ABC of Photographic Sound Recording," *J. Soc. Motion Pict. Telev. Eng.,* **44,** 151–194 (March 1945).

————: "History of Sound Motion Pictures," *J. Soc. Motion Pict. Telev. Eng.,* **64,** 291–302, 356–374, 422–437 (1955).

Mees, C. E. K.: "The Theory of the Photographic Process," *Photographic Aspects of Sound Recording,* 1st ed., Macmillan, New York, 1942, chap. XXII.

Schuller, Edgar A.: "Trouble Chart for Variable-Area Sound," *J. Soc. Motion Pict. Telev. Eng.,* **73,** 4–8 (October 1964).

Sponable, E. I.: "Historical Development of Sound Films," *J. Soc. Motion Pict. Telev. Eng.,* **48,** 275–303, 407–422 (1974).

Theisen, W. E.: "Pioneering in the Talking Picture," *J. Soc. Motion Pict. Telev. Eng.,* **36,** 415–444 (1941).

Uhlig, Ronald E.: "The Relationship of Film Parameters to Photographic Soundtrack Quality," *J. Soc. Motion Pict. Telev. Eng.,* **89,** 229–234 (April 1980).

CHAPTER 13
STUDIO PRODUCTION SYSTEMS

Ernst-Joachim Voelker
Institut für Akustik und Bauphysik, Oberursel, West Germany

13.1 INTRODUCTION

Sound recording in a studio and its balancing in the control room have always been of special importance in the development of audio systems and components. The technology not only has influenced the design of microphones and loudspeakers but has led to new standards for the quality of sound reproduction. For example, it is inconceivable that the revolution of sound motion pictures and stereophonic recording could have taken place without the development of increasingly more sophisticated studio techniques.

Nevertheless, the application of audio technology in other fields, such as communication and public address systems, has been a relatively independent technological advance. From telegraphic wire transmission, in 1861 Philip Reiss devised the contact microphone, from which later evolved the carbon microphone. However, it was not until 1876 that Alexander Graham Bell invented the complementary device, the telephone receiver, which used the principle of electromagnetism and which remained in use until the recent decade.

The main goals of electroacoustic transmission for speech and music were (1) sufficient loudness and (2) quality of reproduction. As early as 1921 very large systems with horn loudspeakers and power amplifiers were in use in the United States to project the inauguration of President Harding to an audience of over 125,000 persons.[1] These techniques soon were adopted by the film industry for the first talking pictures.

The first electrodynamic moving-coil loudspeakers were described by H. Riegger in 1924[2] as a so-called *Blatthaller*; with these units distances of several kilometers could be covered. The first stereophonic transmissions using microphones were made much earlier from the stage of the Paris Opera to Bell Telephone receivers in the telephone receiving room at the International Exhibition of Electricity in Paris in 1881.[3] The stereo pickup was accomplished with carbon microphones installed to the left and right of the prompt box. Electromagnetic telephones were used for reception. The event was reported in 1881 in the *Scientific American* by M. Hospitaller as follows:

Everyone who has been fortunate enough to hear the telephones at the Palais de l'Industrie has remarked that, in listening with both ears to the two telephones, the sound takes a special character of relief and localization which a single receiver cannot produce. It is a common experience that, in listening on a single telephone receiver, it is practically impossible to have even a vague idea of the distance at which a person at the other end of the line appears to be. To some listeners this distance seems to be only a few yards; to others the voice apparently proceeds out of a great depth of the earth. In this case there is nothing of the kind. As soon as the experiment commences, the singers place themselves, in the mind of the listener, at a fixed distance, some to the right and others to the left. It is easy to follow their movements, and to indicate exactly, each time that they change their position, the imaginary distance at which they appear to be.

The stage of the opera house can be called the first studio, the microphones the first studio microphones, and the receiving room the first control room. Arrangement of the microphones in the footlights of the stage and listening with high-quality headphones are still usable today, although the intervening 100 years have seen many developments, for example, in amplifier technology, microphones, loudspeakers, quality of cables, improved signal-to-noise (S/N) ratio, and magnetic-recording techniques. The studio technique gave a significant impetus to the improvement of quality in recording, transmission, and reproduction. In 1954 H. Scherchen acknowledged the importance of these developments. He undertook very important investigations in his experimental studio in Gravesano in Tessin, Switzerland.[4] Figure 13.1 is a block diagram of the recording equipment for his Studio 1. By that time an artificial head was in use. Recorded signals were artificially reverberated and delayed. The reproduction used broadband loudspeakers built in a stone enclosure in addition to 20 ceiling-mounted loudspeakers.

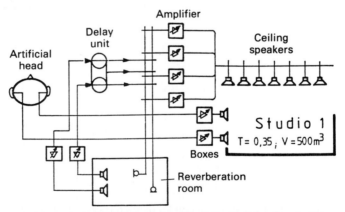

FIG. 13.1 Experimental Studio 1 of Prof. Dr. H. Scherchen in Gravesano, Switzerland, with recording facilities and loudspeaker system, 1954.

R. Vermeulen developed an ambiophony from these ideas.[5] The combination of direct sound, delayed signals, and reverberation was studied. Vermeulen said: "The human ear has the impression of spaciousness when delayed repetitions of a sound arrive from several different directions."[6] Alkin used this principle at the British Broadcasting Corporation (BBC) in Studio G in Lime Grove with 65 loudspeakers. Microphones picked up the sound close to the musical instruments of the orchestra in the studio. Reproduction took place over the 65 loudspeakers. As amplification is increased, there is a greater sense of spaciousness. Ambiophony therefore is a first method for producing a variable acoustic characteristic by electroacoustic means.

A new field of study was opened by the question of the importance of short-term delayed signals. Joseph Henry opened the door to acoustics as a natural science in 1854 when he demonstrated in the Lecture Theater of the Smithsonian Institution the advantage of reflected sounds when their delay times were less than or equal to 53 ms. If this delay time is increased, the signal is heard as an echo which reduces the intelligibility of speech.[7] Recently, some notebooks belonging to Wallace Clement Sabine were found which confirm the importance of these early studies. In 1895, Sabine had found the fundamental relationship between reverberation time and total absorption, which is shown by Eq. (13.1).

$$T = \frac{0.163V}{\sum\limits_{i=1}^{n} \alpha_i S_i} \tag{13.1}$$

where T is the reverberation time, s; V, the volume, m^3; α_i, the absorption coefficient; and S_i, the corresponding area, the individual surfaces being identified by $i = 1$ to n.[8]

Sabine's acoustic consulting work in the first two decades of this century is described in his notebooks. His work was concerned with echoes, and he made recommendations for churches and other auditoria. His discoveries and proposals are described briefly here:

1. Carpet should be thin, to deaden the noise of footsteps without unduly damping resonance (*resonance* is used here in the sense of reverberation).

2. Carpet should be used in the aisles between the seating areas in a church which is designed for good understanding of speech. The carpet should be thick to absorb the sound which arrives at the audience. If this is not done, late reflections will disturb the speaker.

3. Wood paneling on the rear wall should be thin and spaced at a distance from the wall to obtain a resonance effect.

4. Many reflections are required from the room surfaces, for example, from the balcony fronts.

5. There should be a reflector above the speaker at an optimum distance to prevent echoes.

6. There should be a reflector behind the speaker with a folded surface to produce many diffuse reflections.

7. Plaster spaced at a distance from the wall is better than plaster applied directly to the wall. The latter gives a hard surface which degrades the acoustics.

8. Measurements of the sound isolation in the laboratory were recorded as a received level on a logarithmic scale. This was the forerunner of decibel measurements.

These fundamental findings were the basis for research on the quantitative influence of reflections in concert halls and studios. They form the acoustics at the listener's position or the acoustical conditions around the microphone. Dr. Richard Thiele defined *Deutlichkeit* as the relationship of the energy which

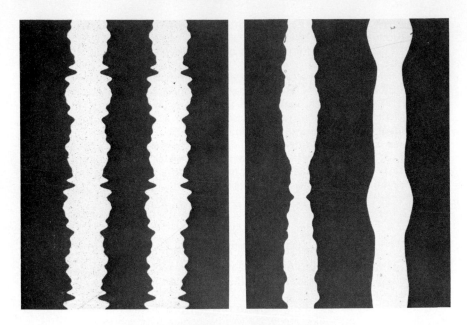

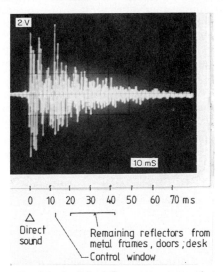

2 V

10 mS

0   10   20   30   40   50   60   70 ms

△
Direct
sound

Remaining reflectors from
metal frames, doors ; desk
—Control window

FIG. 13.2 Impulse reflectogram measured at
the listening position. The impulse is produced
in front of the control-room monitoring
speaker.

arrives in the first 50 ms compared with total energy. The measurement was possible only with an oscilloscope on which the direct sound and the later-arriving reflections could be shown.[10] As an example, Fig. 13.2 is an impulse response *(reflectogram)* of a control room. The greater part of the energy arrives within the first 50 ms, and therefore Deutlichkeit lies close to 93 percent.

With the development of broadcasting in the 1920s, very highly damped studios were built. Draperies were hung on the walls and the ceiling, and the announcer's position was divided from the studios by draperies. The floors were covered with a carpet. A single carbon microphone was followed by an amplifier and telephone lines to the transmitter. The control room was called an amplifier room.

For 30 years, radio transmissions were monophonic. A long time had elapsed since the first two-channel transmission in Paris in 1881. In the 1960s stereophony was introduced along with very-high-frequency (VHF) transmission. Concurrently a new generation of studios was built. More light was thrown upon the mysteries of sound recording, for example, in the use of sound effects. In the following years there was a marked improvement in the quality of recording. The expectations of listeners were carefully taken into consideration and influenced studio production. A close relationship now existed between the market and studio production.

13.2 STUDIOS: THEIR LAYOUT AND SOME FUNDAMENTAL PROPERTIES

13.2.1 Introduction

Studios are constructed to record a variety of sound pictures with microphones. Their acoustic properties are very important and cause specific room impressions. The use of close microphones can eliminate such room impressions. Artificial sound effects are possible. Fine tuning is carried out in the control room. Monitoring is usually effected with high-quality loudspeakers in an appropriate acoustic environment. Studios permit the use of production techniques suited for recordings, in which interruptions and repetitions are common. While an audience may be present, it will accept the production type of studio operation. A studio production thus differs from a live transmission from a concert hall or an opera house, where the audience or the listener at home expects an uninterrupted high-quality performance.

Studios should provide stimulus for the performer. For that, good acoustics are necessary. In addition, the color, the daylighting, the effect lighting, and modern furniture are important. Television and film studios have special requirements for lighting and air conditioning. Sets may cover the acoustical wall treatment. Microphones must be used at greater distances to be out of the picture. The view through the control-room window is often obscured, and the picture monitor provides a direct view.

13.2.2 Survey of Studios

Studios can be divided into three groups as in Table 13.1:

1. Broadcasting studios for radio and television
2. Recording studios for music, speech, and television and film and dubbing studios
3. Studios in theaters, multipurpose halls, and concert halls

Studios are combined with control rooms except for self-operated and disk jockey studios. The control rooms may be used in different ways: for recording

TABLE 13.1 Survey of Speech and Music Studios

Broadcasting stations		Recording studios			Concert hall Multipurpose hall Theater sound systems
Radio	Television	Music	Speech	Motion pictures	
Large studio for music, shows, and theater with and without audience					Announcement studio
Announcement studio; on-air studio		Announcement studio			
Rock, pop studio	Large studio Multipurpose hall	Pop, rock studio	Drama studio Reverberation room Living room Reflection-free room	Large studio halls	
Chamber music	Disco-effect studio	Chamber music Choir, soloists		Disco-effect studio	
Drama studio		Control room also as studio			
News studio	Film-dubbing studio for speech and music with film and video equipment				Control room at center of theater or hall Video monitoring
Disk jockey Interview studio	Reverberant or partly reverberant room				
Studio for weather, elections, traffic, special news	Electronic and live music			Cinema	Control room
Control rooms for multipurpose use, connected with switching room					
Rehearsal studio; also for recording					

13.6

the output of the studio, for high-quality monitoring, or for monitoring and recording musical instruments. In all three cases a high-quality monitoring loudspeaker system is used. Figures 13.8 through 13.15 show studios in simplified forms with their associated control rooms. The layouts are based primarily on well-known studios. Acoustical details will be described later. Tables 13.2 through 13.24 show the following data relating to the studios:

T_m, s   Reverberation time as an arithmetic mean for the frequency range of Δf.

T, s   Simple indication of the preferred reverberation time as a function of frequency at low, middle, and high frequencies.

Δf, Hz   Frequency range with low- and high-frequency limits.

NR, dBA   Noise-rating curve according to ISO R1996 (1971)[11] with A-weighted sound-level equivalent. Recommended values after Voelker, considering international recommendations (see below).

$L_{p,max}$, dB   Maximum sound pressure level in the studio at the recording-microphone position, in the vicinity of the sound source, or near the room surface.

D, dB   Average sound-level difference between the studio and the recording room for wall, door, and window.

R Sound reflections which arrive at the microphone. Depending on the studio and recording technique, they can be either an advantage or a disadvantage.

13.2.3 Large Music Studios without an Audience or Television Recording Use (Fig. 13.3)

These studios are used for large orchestras, small orchestras, or choirs. Volume is normally 2000 m³ or more. Reverberation time may be adjusted between 1.5 and 1.2 s, depending on the distribution of draperies and other sound-absorbing materials. Changes of reverberation time are limited to the middle and high frequencies. The maximum sound level of 96 dBA within the studio must be taken into account when designing a studio adjacent to another studio.

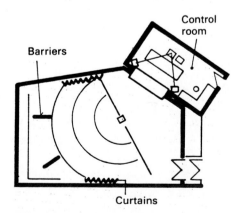

FIG. 13.3 Large music studio.

13.2.4 Large Music Studios with and without an Audience (Fig. 13.4)

Such studios may have a volume of about 5000 m³ and are used for large orchestras, small orchestras, and soloists. When the orchestras are rehearsing in the studio, available volume may amount to 50 m³ per person, but when an audience is present, this figure falls to about 15 m³ per person. If audience seating is removed from the studio, reverberation time may rise as high as 2.4 s. With draperies that

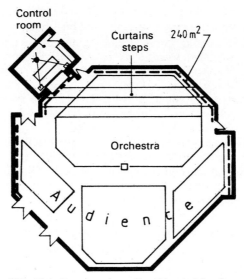

FIG. 13.4 Large music studio with provision for an audience.

TABLE 13.2 Requirements for a Large Music Studio

T_m, s	T for f, kHz	Δf, Hz	NR, dBA	$L_{p,max}$, dB	Sound reduction, studio/control room D, dB	
1.5		50	15		Wall	68
1.2		↓	25	96	Door	..
	0.1 1 10	12.500			Window	62
					Σ	64

Sound reflections R at the recording microphone

First strong R desired	No R permitted	Many R's, even first R, desired	Higher-ordered R's permitted	Strong first R's not permitted	Less R's desired
		x		x	

TABLE 13.3 Requirements for a Large Music Studio with Audience

T_m, s	T for f, kHz	Δf, Hz	NR, dBA	$L_{p,max}$, dB	Sound reduction studio/control room D, dB	
2.4		50	25		Wall	68
1.7	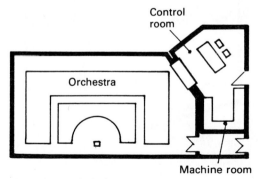	↓		96	Door	..
1.2**		12,500	30*		Window	62
					Σ	64

Sound reflections R at the recording microphone					
First strong R desired	No R permitted	Many R's, even first R, desired	Higher-ordered R's permitted	Strong first R's not permitted	Less R's desired
x		x	x		

may be 10 to 12 m high and have an area as great as 240 m², reverberation time declines to about 1.2 s with audience and orchestra present. The permitted noise level can vary between NR_{15} in studio use and NR_{20} with an audience present.

13.2.5 Chamber Music Studio: Multipurpose Studio for Small Symphony Orchestra, Choir, and Local and Instrumental Soloists (Fig. 13.5)

The volume of this type of studio is about 1000 m³. The short reverberation time of about 0.9 s when the chamber orchestra is playing will be lengthened to about

FIG. 13.5 Chamber music studio.

1.2 s when only soloists are present. Additional variation of reverberation time by movable sound-absorbing elements on the wall may be an advantage. Strong first reflections can be prevented by mounting sound-absorbing material in the most effective positions on the walls or ceiling.

TABLE 13.4 Requirements for a Chamber Music Studio

T_m, s	T for f, kHz	Δf, Hz	NR, dBA	$L_{p,\max}$, dB	Sound reduction, studio/control room D, dB	
1.2		50			Wall	68
0.9		↓	25	90	Door	..
	0.1 1 10	12,500			Window	62
					Σ	64

Sound reflections R at the recording microphone					
First strong R desired	No R permitted	Many R's, even first R, desired	Higher-ordered R's permitted	Strong first R's not permitted	Less R's desired
		x	x		

13.2.6 Dance Music Studio for Orchestra with String Instruments or Big-Band, Jazz, Folk, or Country Music (Fig. 13.6)

A lot of acoustic absorption is necessary to separate individual instruments or groups from each other. Draperies and freestanding screens are used for this purpose. Movable wall elements may be employed instead of draperies. In many

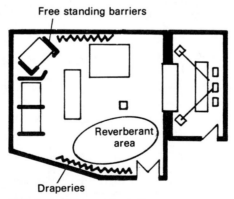

Free standing barriers

Reverberant area

Draperies

FIG. 13.6 Dance music studio.

cases, a reverberant area which suits strings, flutes, or acoustic guitars is provided. The volume of such a studio may be about 800 m³. Carpet may be used in some parts of the studio. The drummer plays in a drum booth to prevent interference with other microphones, as when an acoustic guitar is being recorded. Some studios have movable ceilings which can be lowered or raised to vary reverberation time. The frequency range of interest extends to low frequencies which must be strongly damped by resonators.

Table 13.5 Requirements for a Dance Music Studio

T_m, s	T for f, kHz	Δf, Hz	NR, dBA	$L_{p,max}$, dB	Sound reduction studio/control room D, dB	
0.9 0.5	(0.1 1 10)	40 ↓ 12.500	25	100	Wall Door Window Σ	68 .. 62 64

Sound reflections R at the recording microphone					
First strong R desired	No R permitted	Many R's, even first R, desired	Higher-ordered R's permitted	Strong first R's not permitted	Less R's desired
		x (selected areas)	x	x	

13.2.7 Rock and Pop (Fig. 13.7)

The use of closely spaced microphones is normal in this type of studio, with clusters of microphones for drums, piano, or other instruments. In order to discriminate against the sounds of other instruments, reflections must be avoided. In many cases the studio is small and lacks natural acoustics. A separate drum booth or enclosure is normally provided. The windows of such a booth should be continually adjustable to achieve the desired isolation between studio and booth. Sometimes individual reflecting surfaces are used to raise the sound level of the instruments (for example, the piano or sometimes the drum) at the ear of the players. Using these reflecting surfaces gives a local impression of liveliness.

The control-room window often is a fully glazed door. The following aspects must be considered:

1. It is common to monitor at high sound levels in the control room. Sensitive instruments near the glass door can be affected, and feedback may even occur.

2. The door facilitates the direct injection of electronic instruments, which can be arranged around the open door.

3. The control room is visually enlarged when the big door to the studio is opened. The high-quality loudspeaker system in the control room can be used both for mixing and for monitoring individual instruments which may be playing behind the control engineer.

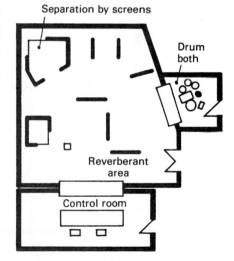

FIG. 13.7 Rock and pop music studio.

TABLE 13.6　Requirements for a Rock and Pop Studio

T_m, s	T for f, kHz	Δf, Hz	NR, dBA	$L_{p,max}$, dB	Sound reduction studio/control room D, dB	
0.3	 0.1 1 10	25 ↓ 12,500	25	100	Wall Door Window Σ	68 · · · · 64

Sound reflections R at the recording microphone					
First strong R desired	No R permitted	Many R's, even first R, desired	Higher-ordered R's permitted	Strong first R's not permitted	Less R's desired
x				x	x

13.2.8　Concert Hall with Announcer Booth and Control Room and Adjacent Equipment Room (Fig. 13.8)

The concert hall provides the necessary acoustic environment for both audience and orchestra. Sound recordings or live transmissions must take these priorities into account. Audience and orchestra require a volume of about 12 m³ per person.

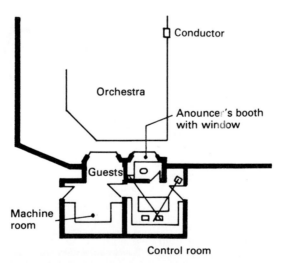

FIG. 13.8　Concert studio with announcer booth and control room.

The walls and ceiling are sound-reflecting to achieve the necessary reverberation time while avoiding echoes. The equipment room can be separated from the control room to avoid interference when operating recording equipment. The announcer booth, which has a view into the auditorium, is controlled by the

TABLE 13.7 Requirements for the Concert Hall

T_m, s	T for f, kHz	Δf, Hz	NR, dBA	$L_{p,max}$, dB	Sound reduction, studio/control room D, dB	
2.0		80 ↓ 12,500	25	90	Wall Door Window Σ	68 · · · · 64

Sound reflections R at the recording microphone

First strong R desired	No R permitted	Many R's, even first R, desired	Higher-ordered R's permitted	Strong first R's not permitted	Less R's desired

TABLE 13.8 Requirements for the Announcer Booth

T_m, s	T for f, kHz	Δf, Hz	NR, dBA	$L_{p,max}$, dB	Sound reduction studio/control room D, dB	
0.3		125 ↓ 12,500	25	70	Wall Door Window Σ	62 · · · · 64

Sound reflection R at the recording microphone

First strong R desired	No R permitted	Many R's, even first R, desired	Higher-ordered R's permitted	Strong first R's not permitted	Less R's desired
			x	x	x

sound engineer. Activities in the concert hall, such as applause or the sound of the instruments, to some extent may be allowed to reach the announcer's microphone. In the example shown in Fig. 13.8 it is a disadvantage that the sound engineer has no direct view into the concert hall; in this case, closed-circuit TV is used.

13.2.9 Studio Complex with On-Air and Production Studio (Fig. 13.9)

Such a complex may consist of a control room which works with a talk studio or a multipurpose studio. The adjacent equipment room serves as a control room for separate operation of the multipurpose studio. Nonreverberant recordings can be made in the very dead room. Reverberation times and other properties are described in Tables 13.9, 13.10, and 13.11. For the differing requirements of speech, choir, orchestra, or even a drummer in the multipurpose studio, acoustics

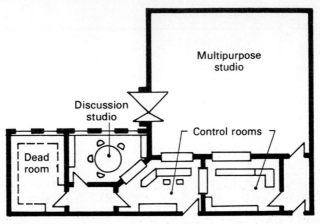

FIG. 13.9   On-air and production studio complex.

TABLE 13.9   Requirements for a Multipurpose Studio

T_m, s	T for f, kHz	Δf, Hz	NR, dBA	$L_{p,\mathrm{max}}$, dB	Sound reduction studio/control room D, dB	
1.2 0.6		80 ↓ 12,500	25	100	Wall Door Window Σ	68 ·· 62 64

Sound reflections R at the recording microphone

First strong R desired	No R permitted	Many R's, even first R, desired	Higher-ordered R's permitted	Strong first R's not permitted	Less R's desired
			x	x	x

TABLE 13.10   Requirements for the Announcer Booth

T_m, s	T for f, kHz	Δf, Hz	NR, dBA	$L_{p,\mathrm{max}}$, dB	Sound reduction, studio/control room D, dB	
0.35		125 ↓ 12,500	25	70	Wall Door Window Σ	68 ·· 62 64

Sound reflections R at the recording microphone

First strong R desired	No R permitted	Many R's, even first R, desired	Higher-ordered R's permitted	Strong first R's not permitted	Less R's desired
			x	x	

TABLE 13.11 Requirements for the Nonreverberant Interview Studio

T_m, s	T for f, kHz	Δf, Hz	NR, dBA	$L_{p,max}$, dB	Sound reduction studio/control room D, dB	
0.15	(curve) 0.1 1 10	100 ↓ 10,000	10 20	100	Wall Door Window Σ	68 65 · · 64

| | | Sound reflections R at the recording microphone | | | | |

First strong R desired	No R permitted	Many R's, even first R, desired	Higher-ordered R's permitted	Strong first R's not permitted	Less R's desired
	x				

are varied with movable wall elements or adjustable absorbent roller blinds.[12,13] The talk studio is suitable for announcements or for discussion. Possible operation of either control room with either studio requires a high level of sound isolation from the windows, doors, and walls.

13.2.10 Drama Complex Including a Larger Studio; Occasional Music Use

Such a complex is normally used for speech recordings. Each room has an individual acoustic condition. The large studio provides a reverberant area and, in the corner, a nonreflecting area for intimate speech. Many specific facilities are provided for sound effects, among them staircases of steel or wood, carpeted or wooden floors, and sand or gravel trays in the nonreflecting room. The impression of a receding voice can be provided by the wall arrangement shown in the nonreflecting room. In some organizations the large studio is divided into three parts

TABLE 13.12 Requirements for a Large Studio in a Drama Complex

T_m, s	T for f, kHz	Δf, Hz	NR, dBA	$L_{p,max}$, dB	Sound reduction, studio/control room D, dB	
0.80	(curve) 0.1 1 10	80 ↓ 12,500	10	100	Wall Door Window Σ	68 57 62 64

| | | Sound reflections R at the recording microphone | | | | |

First strong R desired	No R permitted	Many R's, even first R, desired	Higher-ordered R's permitted	Strong first R's not permitted	Less R's desired
		x	x		

TABLE 13.13   Requirements for a Nonreverberant Recording Studio in a Drama Complex

T_m, s	T for f, kHz	Δf, Hz	NR, dBA	$L_{p,max}$, dB	Sound reduction studio/control room D, dB	
0.15	(graph: 0.1 1 10)	80 ↓ 12,500	10 20	100	Wall Door Window Σ	68 57 62 64

Sound reflections R at the recording microphone

First strong R desired	No R permitted	Many R's, even first R, desired	Higher-ordered R's permitted	Strong first R's not permitted	Less R's desired
	x				

TABLE 13.14   Requirements for a Reverberant Recording Studio in a Drama Complex

T_m, s	T for f, kHz	Δf, Hz	NR, dBA	$L_{p,max}$, dB	Sound reduction, studio/control room D, dB	
1.5	(graph: 0.1 1 10)	80 ↓ 12,500	10 20	100	Wall Door Window Σ	68 57 62 64

Sound reflections R at the recording microphone

First strong R desired	No R permitted	Many R's, even first R, desired	Higher-ordered R's permitted	Strong first R's not permitted	Less R's desired
x		x	x		

by hanging draperies; one end will be reverberant and the other end dead, while the center area simulates a normal living-room condition. This type of studio has the disadvantage that while a recording is being made in one section the other parts cannot be used even for rehearsals. The large studio shown in Fig. 13.10 is usable for the following activities:

1. Large speech recordings with up to 30 persons, for example, simulating congressional hearings or auditorium presentations. Figure 13.11 is a view into the large studio of the drama complex at Hessen Broadcasting in Frankfurt.

2. Many small recordings to create individual sound images, such as a corridor in a house, a table in a kitchen, or a telephone conversation in an office.

The control room normally occupies a central position and has a view into the individual areas of the complex (see Fig. 13.12). The many sources of sound effects from tape recorders and electronic effects for coloration, delays, and reverberation need much space either in a control room or in a separate room. Recordings in drama studios are normally made with distant microphones; the speech

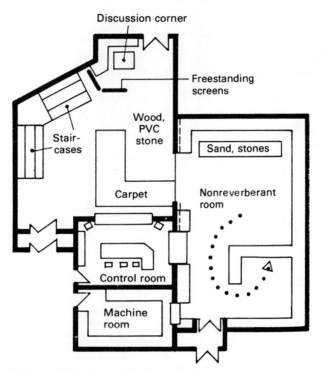

FIG. 13.10   Studio complex for dramatic productions.

level at the microphone is therefore lower, and any interfering background noise will be amplified in the same way as the speech. Therefore, the requirements for background music are more stringent in drama studios.[14]

13.2.11   Television Studio for Live Broadcasting (Fig. 13.13)

A cyclorama and sets together with extensive lighting and air-conditioning equipment are the important features of television studios. In many cases a catwalk is constructed above the cyclorama. Normally it is not necessary for the control rooms to have a direct view into the studio. In any case, the production control room normally will have a bank of monitors that would obscure any studio window. The acoustic characteristics of such studios often are poor because of unavoidable reflections from the studio sets, the necessary equipment at ceiling level, and the hard reflective floor needed for stable camera movement (see Table

FIG. 13.11 Large studio in the dramatic production complex of Hessen Broadcasting in Frankfurt. Recording of Kurt Weill's *The Threepenny Opera* is in progress.

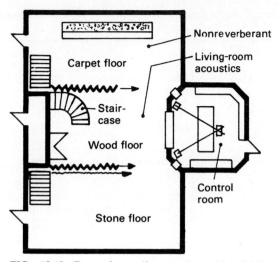

FIG. 13.12 Dramatic studio complex with dividing draperies.

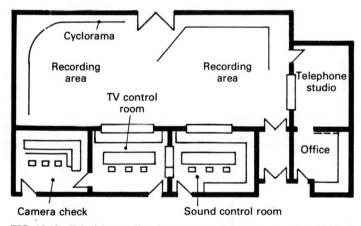

FIG. 13.13 Television studio with separate video and audio control rooms.

13.15). The adjacent telephone studio is included in studio production, showing the activities involved with incoming phone calls. The acoustic conditions of this telephone studio are those of a normal talk studio.

13.2.12 Television Complex with Two Studios (Fig. 13.14)

Two studios, each having its own control room but sharing a common equipment room, are combined here. Each studio includes an announcer booth which opens directly from the control room (see Fig. 13.15). Double doors and sound locks

TABLE 13.15 Requirements for a Television Studio with Video and Audio Control Rooms

T_m, s	T for f, kHz	Δf, Hz	NR, dBA	$L_{p,max}$, dB	Sound reduction studio/control room D, dB	
0.6	(graph: 0.1 1 10)	80 ↓ 12,500	20 30	100	Wall Door Window Σ	62 52 52 54

Sound reflections R at the recording microphone					
First strong R desired	No R permitted	Many R's, even first R, desired	Higher-ordered R's permitted	Strong first R's not permitted	Less R's desired
			x	.	x

provide the necessary isolation of the studios from the hectic activities in the control area. Acoustic requirements are similar to those shown in Table 13.15. The larger studio has a design reverberation time of about 0.9 s. Table 13.16 also provides technical information for the announcer room. In many cases, a single control room serves for both sound and production control. During production close communication between sound engineer and producer is normally more important than the quality of the sound. The side area is open to give a direct view to the announcer booth but is acoustically dead to act as a sound lock. The sound engineer can improve listening conditions and separate himself or herself from

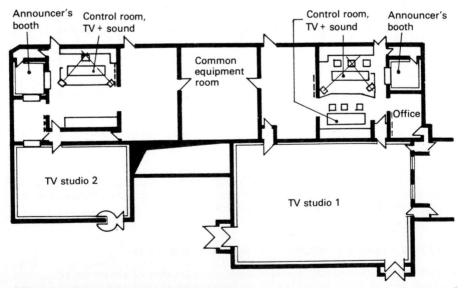

FIG. 13.14 Television complex with two studios.

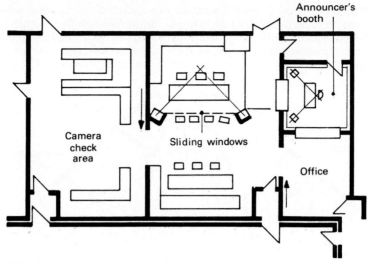

FIG. 13.15 Announcer booth with a combined television and audio control room.

activities in the control room by closing the movable window between the two areas. The engineer can then listen at a higher level without interfering with other activities.

13.2.13 News Studio Complex for Broadcasting (Fig. 13.16)

Two control rooms are combined with three studios in this complex. The disk jockey studio is self-operated with its own tape recorders, cassette recorders, and

TABLE 13.16 Requirements for a Television Complex with Two Studios

T_m, s	T for f, kHz	Δf, Hz	NR, dBA	$L_{p,max}$, dB	Sound reduction, studio/control room D, dB	
0.30		125	15		Wall	68
		↓		80	Door	· ·
		12,500	25		Window	62
					Σ	64

Sound reflections R at the recording microphone

First strong R desired	No R permitted	Many R's, even first R, desired	Higher-ordered R's permitted	Strong first R's not permitted	Less R's desired
			x	x	

record players. It can also work with the other studios, in this case acting as a control room. There are many ways to use the studios, the larger studio having the possibility of including an invited audience to take part in discussions. Actual news transmissions require an atmosphere in the studios, and a certain amount of sound transfer from one area to another is therefore permitted. The same aim

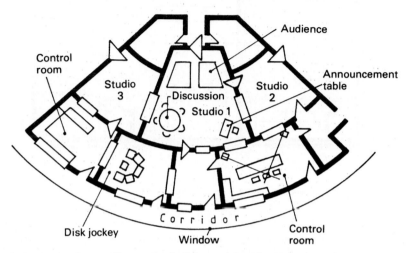

FIG. 13.16 News studio complex for live, on-air broadcasting.

is achieved by windows that link all the areas together. On the other hand, the windows result in undesirable acoustic characteristics with strong reflections, and they also limit the wall area available for acoustic treatment. In discussions in which microphone distance may be greater because of inexperienced participants, these strong reflections produce a small-room impression and lead to a colored sound. The disk jockey (DJ) must use a close-speaking microphone to exclude the noise of equipment and its operation.

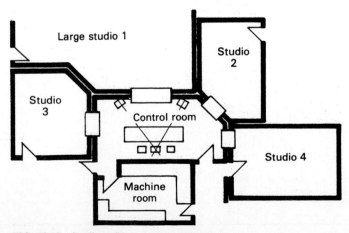

FIG. 13.17 Studios with a central control room.

TABLE 13.17 Requirements for Studios 1, 2, and 3

T_m, s	T for f, kHz	Δf, Hz	NR, dBA	$L_{p,max}$, dB	Sound reduction, studio/control room D, dB	
0.40		125 ↓ 12,500	15 25	80	Wall Door Window Σ	68 · · 62 64

Sound reflections R at the recording microphone					
First strong R desired	No R permitted	Many R's, even first R, desired	Higher-ordered R's permitted	Strong first R's not permitted	Less R's desired
			x	x	x

13.2.14 Studios with a Central Control Room (Fig. 3.17)

Studio 1 could be a multipurpose studio for music and speech, while Studios 2, 3, and 4 would be designed primarily for speech with the following acoustic conditions:

1. Highly damped or nonreverberant condition

2. Reverberant condition as in a normal living room

3. Very reverberant condition as in an empty room or a stairwell

There could be other uses, such as discussions.

The control and equipment rooms together form a technical center. It is a disadvantage that the control room can work with only one studio at a time. Rehearsals or preparations for later recordings take place in the other studios at that time. In radio stations the control room can go on the air by taking from each studio a different program such as interviews, weather, or music. (See Fig. 13.18.)

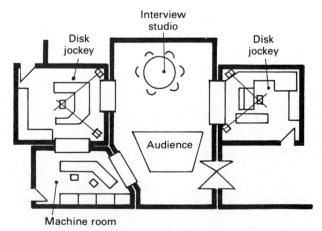

FIG. 13.18 Single-studio local radio station.

13.2.15   Radio Station

A small radio station may have two disk jockey studios, each of which can act as a control room operating with the common interview studio, with or without an audience (see Table 13.18). It is usual also to have a small studio for news inserts, weather, and other announcements. Small music groups may be recorded in the larger studio. Most recordings are speech-orientated and include discussions, news, weather, and telephone calls. A certain level of background noise may be permissible and even desirable, but there are certain types of transmission for which noise is disturbing, for instance, comments on serious events or poetry readings. To reduce the necessity to construct expensive, highly insulated studios, close-microphone techniques are normally employed. Figure 13.19 shows another arrangement of studios, control room, and disk jockey studio. For full utilization, one studio may be used for tape editing and preparation of computer-controlled

TABLE 13.18   Requirements for the Disk Jockey Studio

T_m, s	T for f, kHz	Δf, Hz	NR, dBA	$L_{p,\max}$, dB	Sound reduction studio/control room D, dB	
0.30		125 ↓ 12,500	15 25	80	Wall Door Window Σ	52 ·· ·· 45

Sound reflections R at the recording microphone					
First strong R desired	No R permitted	Many R's, even first R, desired	Higher-ordered R's permitted	Strong first R's not permitted	Less R's desired
			x	x	x

TABLE 13.19   Requirements for Studios 2, 3, and 4

T_m, s	T for f, kHz	Δf, Hz	NR, dBA	$L_{p,\max}$, dB	Sound reduction studio/control room D, dB	
0.30		125 ↓ 12,500	15 25		Wall Door Window Σ	68 ·· 62 64

Sound reflections R at the recording microphone					
First strong R desired	No R permitted	Many R's, even first R, desired	Higher-ordered R's permitted	Strong first R's not permitted	Less R's desired
			x	x	

TABLE 13.20 Requirements for Large Studio 1 (Volume, 1000 m³) as a Music-Recording Studio

T_m, s	T for f, kHz	Δf, Hz	NR, dBA	$L_{p,max}$, dB	Sound reduction, studio/control room D, dB	
1.5		50	15		Wall	68
		↓		100	Door	..
1.2	0.1 1 10	12,500	25		Window	62
					Σ	64

Sound reflection R at the recording microphone

First strong R desired	No R permitted	Many R's, even first R, desired	Higher-ordered R's permitted	Strong first R's not permitted	Less R's desired
		x		x	x

TABLE 13.21 Requirements for an Interview and Multipurpose Studio

T_m, s	T for f, kHz	Δf, Hz	NR, dBA	$L_{p,max}$, dB	Sound reduction studio/control room D, dB	
		100	20		Wall	68
0.50		↓		90	Door	..
	0.1 1 10	12,500	30		Window	..
					Σ	64

Sound reflections R at the recording microphone

First strong R desired	No R permitted	Many R's, even first R, desired	Higher-ordered R's permitted	Strong first R's not permitted	Less R's desired
		x		x	x

TABLE 13.22 Requirements for a Disk Jockey Studio

T_m, s	T for f, kHz	Δf, Hz	NR, dBA	$L_{p,max}$, dB	Sound reduction, studio/control room D, dB	
		125	20		Wall	52
0.30		↓		80	Door	..
	0.1 1 10	12,500	30		Window	..
					Σ	45

Sound reflections R at the recording microphone

First strong R desired	No R permitted	Many R's, even first R, desired	Higher-ordered R's permitted	Strong first R's not permitted	Less R's desired
			x	x	

TABLE 13.23   Requirements for a Weather and Traffic Studio with Telephones and Telex

T_m, s	T for f, kHz	Δf, Hz	NR, dBA	$L_{p,max}$, dB	Sound reduction studio/control room D, dB	
0.25		125 ↓ 10,000	25 35	80	Wall Door Window Σ	62 ·· ·· 58

Sound reflections R at the recording microphone					

First strong R desired	No R permitted	Many R's, even first R, desired	Higher-ordered R's permitted	Strong first R's not permitted	Less R's desired
			x	x	

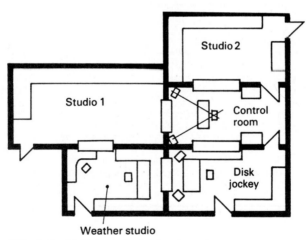

Weather studio

FIG. 13.19   Multiple-studio local radio station.

transmissions. During transmission the control room, disk jockey studio, and weather studio work together.

13.2.16   Film-Dubbing Studio (Fig. 13.20)

Here the sound from the studio is synchronized with the picture projected on the screen. There are areas of different sound absorption, for example, a highly damped commentator's booth and an area enclosed by draperies and screens. The film is projected from the projection room; certain sound tracks containing music or background noise may already exist, while others are recorded from the studio.

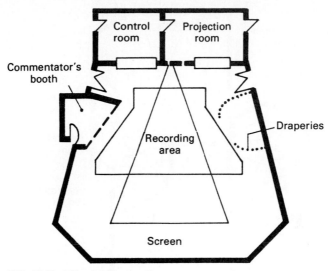

FIG. 13.20 Film-dubbing studio.

Nonreverberant studio conditions satisfy the many different scenes to be reproduced. A wide range of electronic techniques is available to brighten dead acoustic conditions, for example, by artificial reverberation, filtering, or delay.

13.2.17 Combined Production and Film-Dubbing Studio (Fig. 13.21)

The complex shown in Fig. 13.21 combines the functions of two dubbing studios and one sound-recording studio. Both dubbing studios need highly damped commentator's booths. The larger of the two studios accommodates an entire orches-

TABLE 13.24 Requirements for a Film-Dubbing Studio

T_m, s	T for f, kHz	Δf, Hz	NR, dBA	$L_{p,max}$, dB	Sound reduction, studio/control room D, dB	
0.40		50 ↓ 12,500	15 25	100	Wall Door Window Σ	68 ·· 62 64

Sound reflections R at the recording microphone					
First strong R desired	No R permitted	Many R's, even first R, desired	Higher-ordered R's permitted	Strong first R's not permitted	Less R's desired
	x			x	x

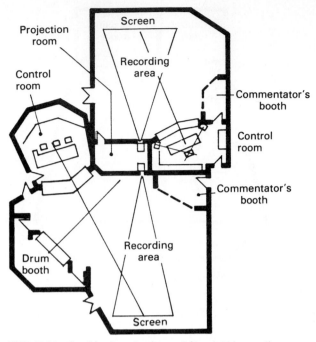

FIG. 13.21 Combined production and film-dubbing studio.

tra in front of the screen. Acoustic requirements differ with the type of music and the instruments that are playing, and variable acoustics therefore are desirable.

13.3   MICROPHONE RECORDING IN A STUDIO

13.3.1   Listener's Expectations

Reproduced sound must be natural. The listener in front of a loudspeaker expects the quality experienced in a concert hall, in a theater, or, insofar as speech is concerned, in conversation with a neighbor. Placing a microphone, for example, in the twentieth row of the concert hall does not produce the same sensation. This is true also when special recording systems are used. To replace what has been lost, the microphone must be moved closer to the sound source. At some position the correct relationship between direct sound and room effect is apparent. In extreme cases the microphone is drawn so close to the source that the effect of the room is completely excluded. Then electronic manipulation is possible. The missing effect of the room can be reproduced artificially, sometimes more satisfactorily than the effect of the actual room.

The listener is usually satisfied by these manipulations. A good example is the transmission of a concert to millions of listeners who hear a better sound than the audience in the concert hall does. In one hall, an artificial head recording was made in the twentieth row.[15] The full 1200-person audience, together with orchestra and choir, reduced reverberation time to about 1.3 s. In the hall the sound was dead with a very abrupt cutoff and with a lack of loudness in the rear seats. The microphones which were positioned close to the orchestra allowed the above-mentioned manipulation in two ways:

1. Addition of delayed signals as strong reflections
2. Addition of reverberation from a reverberation room

The stereo microphone in the reverberation room picked up two-channel sound, which was mixed into the stereo sound picture from the hall. The broadcast sound showed a reverberation time of 2.3 s, or 1 s more than in the real auditorium. The room seemed bigger. The singer and the choir were understandable. The orchestra, choir, and soloists were clearly located along the line between the stereo loudspeakers, and, as an additional benefit, there was no disturbance from coughs, paper rustling, or movement.

Since 1954 many concerts had taken place in this hall. As a consequence of the improved sound picture from the hall during broadcasts, the acoustics of the building were to be changed in 1987.

In addition, the influence of home listening has affected live performances on the stage for other types of music. Therefore, a complete sound system must be installed between the stage and the audience. Microphones are used extremely close to the sound source or to the mouths of the singers in order to exclude completely the sound of the hall and to prevent feedback. It is then possible to create the desired sound image for the audience, which can be achieved for each individual instrument. Only with these techniques is a multichannel reproduction (for example, left, middle, and right) possible.

13.3.2 Direct Sound, Reflections, and Reverberation

Without the room effect or in the open air there is only the direct sound, for which the sound pressure level (SPL) is normally measured at a distance of, say, 1 m. In a room the measuring microphone also picks up many sound reflections. The direct sound D and reflections R are added together. Near the sound source D predominates; at a greater distance, R. Figure 13.22 illustrates these conditions for several rooms. In a small room, the reduction of sound level with distance is restricted to 1 or 2 dB. In a concert hall, there is a distance of up to 4 or 6 m in which the sound level from D is bigger than that from R. For example, following curve 4 in Fig. 13.22, a microphone at a 2-m distance would measure $L_{pD} = 70$ dB; $L_{pR} = 60$ dB. The addition of the two sound pressures yields

$$L_{pD+R} = 10 \log \left(10^{0.1 L_{pD}} + 10^{0.1 L_{pR}} \right)$$ (13.2)
$$= 70.4 \sim 70 \text{ dB}$$

The influence of R can be ignored. The curves in Fig. 13.22 follow Eq. (13.3):

$$L_{pr} = L_{p,1m} + 10 \log \left(\frac{1}{r^2} + \frac{16\pi}{QA} \right)$$ (13.3)

where L_{pr} = SPL at r, dB
$L_{p,1m}$ = SPL at $r = 1$ m
r = distance from source, m
Q = directivity factor
A = total absorption area, m^2 [A after Eq. (13.1)]

The directivity characteristics of the sound source are well known for musical instruments and speech (that is, for a human head).[16] The curves in Fig. 13.22 are calculated for $Q = 1$, that is, for omnidirectional sound sources. They are first-order radiators.

For a first approximation, speech and musical instruments can be calculated also with $Q = 1$. This does not hold true for highly directional instruments, such

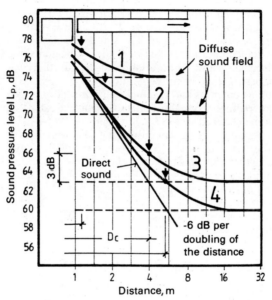

FIG. 13.22 Falloff of sound pressure level with increasing distance. The critical distances are indicated by arrows. (1) Living room, 70 m³, 0.5 s. (2) Small studio, 100 m³, 0.4 s. (3) Church, 500 m³, 1.8 s. (4) Concert hall, 5000 m³, 1.8 s.

as trumpets and tubas, nor for most instruments at high frequencies. For $Q = 2$, the diffuse-sound level will be reduced by 3 dB. This can be seen from Eq. (13.3) for two special cases:

1. Increased r means $1/r^2 \rightarrow 0$.

$$L_{p,\text{diff}} = L_{p,1m} + 10 \log \left(\frac{16\pi}{QA} \right)$$

$$\text{(13.4)}$$

$L_{p,\text{diff}}$ dB SPL in the diffuse sound field

2. Increased A means $1/A \rightarrow 0$.

$$L_{p,\text{dir}} = L_{p,1m} + 10 \log \left(\frac{1}{r^2} \right)$$

$$\text{(13.5)}$$

$L_{p,\text{dir}}$ dB SPL in the direct sound field

The arrows in Fig. 13.22 show the point at which direct and reflected sound pressures are equal, that is, $D = R$, or from Eqs. (13.4) and (13.5),

$$r_H = \sqrt{\frac{QA}{16\pi}} = 0.14 \sqrt{QA} = 0.057 \sqrt{\frac{QV}{T}} \qquad (13.6)$$

where r_H = critical distance, m. The total sound level at this point is 3 dB greater than either individual sound level.

The influence of individual strong reflections can be calculated as follows. The SPL is derived as shown in Fig. 13.23 from an image source at the greater distance

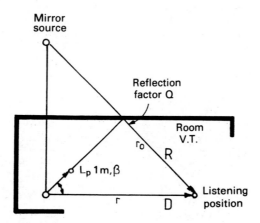

FIG. 13.23 Direct sound D and reflected sound R in a room.

(see Fig. 13.24). Only the direct sound is important, so that Eq. (13.5) can be modified as shown in Eq. (13.7).

$$L_{pR} = L_{p,1m,\beta} + 10 \log \frac{1 - \alpha}{r_0^2} \qquad (13.7)$$

where L_{pR} = SPL of single reflections in a distance of $r = r_0$, dB
$L_{p,1m,\beta}$ = SPL at $r = r_0 = 1$ m at angle β, dB
$1 - \alpha = Q$, reflection factor
r_0 = distance from mirror source, m

With $r_0 = 4$ m and $\alpha = 1$, that is, total reflection, and with $L_{p,1m} = 75$ dB, an SPL of 63 dB is calculated as in Eq. (13.8).

$$L_{pR} = L_{p,1m} + 10 \log \frac{1}{r_0^2} = 75 + 10 \log \frac{1}{16} = 63 \text{ dB} \qquad (13.8)$$

For the example of curve 4 in Fig. 13.22, this means that at a distance of $r = 2$ m, the sound level is not 70.4 dB as in Eq. (13.2), but after the addition of one strong reflection the resulting sound level is raised to 71.1 dB as shown in Eq. (13.9).

$$L_p = 10 \log (10^{0.1 \times 70.4} + 10^{0.1 \times 63}) = 71.1 \text{ dB} \qquad (13.9)$$

For two equally strong reflections, this gives a level of 71.7 dB; for four reflections, 72.8 dB.

When a source radiates sound, the received signal is formed from several different parts: direct sound, single strong reflections, and many other individual reflections which form the diffuse sound field. When this sound source is switched

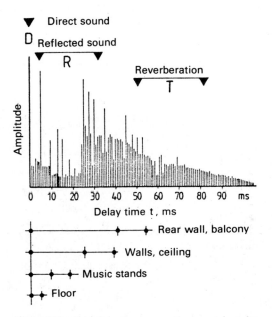

FIG. 13.24   Sound pressure versus time as an impulse response.

off, a decay process starts which can be described in general terms by the Sabine equation [Eq. (13.1)]:

1. The path length of sound is related to the volume of the room.

2. The absorption coefficient of the room surfaces describes the amount of sound which is converted into heat.

3. The additional absorption arises from dissipation in the air.

13.3.3   Time-Related Structure of Sound

At the recording-microphone position each individual acoustic path gives rise to a sound signal. These signals together convey the impression of the studio as well as the sound source.

1. D, the direct sound, contains information relating to the sound source, its SPL, and its spectrum.

2. *R*, the first individual strong sound reflections arriving, for example, from the floor with a delay of 5 ms or from music stands, from the rostra, and from neighboring instruments.

3. There exists an initial time-delay gap of between 5 and 20 ms. After that gap, stronger later reflections up to about 40 ms arrive from the ceiling and the walls.

4. *T*, reverberation, is formed from the total amount of later and multiple reflections which form a decay characteristic with increase of time.

An example of a reflectogram illustrating the arrival of individual signals is shown in Fig. 13.25. The microphone was placed near the string section of an

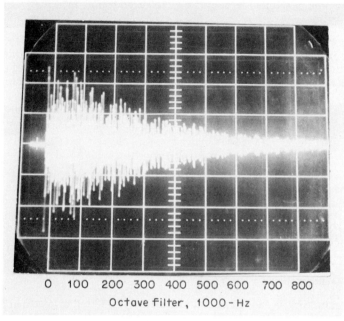

0   100   200   300   400   500   600   700   800

Octave filter, 1000 - Hz

FIG. 13.25 Impulse response reflectogram recorded near the strings excited at the midsection of the orchestra.

orchestra. A spark in the middle of the rear section of the orchestra (percussion) formed the excitation signal. The direct signal *D* is the strongest, followed by many single reflections which form a recognizable tree pattern. By comparing Figs. 13.24 and 13.25 it is apparent that there is practically no initial time-delay gap. It is filled in this case with reflections from nearby surfaces such as the floor, the music stand, and adjacent walls. The filling of the initial time-delay gap is considered good for the quality of the sound field (after Beranek, Ref. 17). The measurement method used gives no information on the direction of the arriving reflections. A stereo microphone or an artificial head[18] is preferable because reflectograms can be obtained from each channel.

The individual reflections carry sound energy which, according to Eq. (13.10), is to a first approximation proportional to the square of the sound pressure shown in the reflectogram. For the single reflection, no integration has taken place over the duration, but this may be neglected because each individual impulse has approximately the same form.

$$E = \left(\frac{p^2}{\rho c}\right) St \qquad E \sim p^2 \tag{13.10}$$

where E = energy, W
$\quad p$ = sound pressure, Pa
$\quad \rho$ = density of medium, kg/m^3
$\quad c$ = velocity of sound, m/s
$\quad S$ = area penetrated by sound, e.g., reflected sound, m^2
$\quad t$ = time, s

For the reflectogram of Fig. 13.25 the first 50 ms contains most of the energy in direct sound and reflections. According to Thiele's definition,[10] Deutlichkeit is given by Eq. (13.11), which, after squaring the pressure and integrating over the appropriate times, leads to a value of $D = 92$ percent for the reflectogram in Fig. 13.25.

$$D = \frac{\int_0^{50} p^2(t)\, dt}{\int_0^{\infty} p^2(t)\, dt} \qquad \% \tag{13.11}$$

This relationship between arriving energies is important for effective evaluation of sound fields.[19] High values of Deutlichkeit are found for small studios and for large studios with many local reflecting surfaces. For more distant listening positions (for example, the twentieth row of a concert hall), Deutlichkeit decreases because of the arrival of later reflections.

13.3.4 Reverberation

Reverberation time is defined as the time for an SPL to fall by 60 dB after cutoff of the sound source. The decay curve of a typical studio is plotted by a level recorder on a paper traveling at 30 mm/s (Fig. 13.26). In the control room the sound engineer has the opportunity to mix in reverberation from a reverberation device with 3-s reverberation. This gives rise to the double-sloped curve in which the level of the second decay can be adjusted. With electronic reverberation devices, reverberation time can be reduced from 3 s to, for instance, 1 s and reverberation level increased. In such a case decay can be smoother and more linear.

Reverberation time differs to a large extent in different rooms, as seen in the examples given above. However, there is general agreement on the correct reverberation time for a given type of studio. Figure 13.27 contains these recommendations. The work of Kuhl in this field since 1954 should be acknowledged; he found optimum reverberation times for recording studios in which romantic or classical music is produced.[20]

Given the volumes and reverberation times, critical distances can be calculated according to Eq. (13.6). Within the critical distance the early decay time is

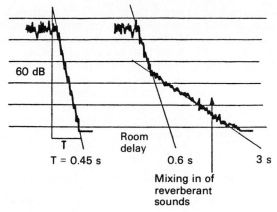

FIG. 13.26 Decay curves in a room with mixing of reverberant sounds.

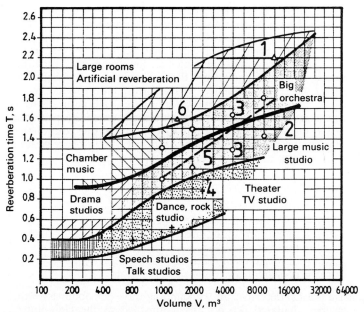

FIG. 13.27 Survey of reverberant times for studios as a function of volume. (1) After W. Kuhl [*"Optimale akustische Gestaltung von Räumen für Aufführende, Zuhörer und Schallaufnahmen,"* Schalltechnik, *no. 20 (1956)*] for romantic music. (2) As in (1) for classical music. (3) o indicates average values for several recommendations. (4) + indicates measurements in dance music studios. (5) Multipurpose halls with changeable acoustics. (6) Artificial reverberation often used for musical recordings.

very short, down to the level at which the first strong reflections arrive. After this point the real decay process starts with the reverberation time of the studio. The entire decay process indicates the relative importance of direct sound and the first strong reflections compared with the total amount of later-arriving reflections in diffuse sound. To determine reverberation time, the early part of the decay characteristic should be ignored.[21] For curves 1 and 2 in Fig. 13.22, the measurement distance must be greater than 2 to 4 m. Even at this distance the effect of strong first reflections is important.[22] Nevertheless, the short reverberation times[23,24,25] are not incorrect. They can still be called reverberation times even though only a small number of reflections are measured.

13.3.5 Frequency Response of Reverberation Times; Eigentones

At high and middle frequencies reverberation times are clearly understood as follows:

1. At midfrequencies, from 400 to 4000 Hz, values are as given in Fig. 13.27.

2. For high frequencies, above 4000 Hz, absorption of the air and of all the acoustic treatment in the studio increases with a consequent reduction in reverberation time.

At low frequencies, below 400 Hz, there are certain important requirements. For music an increase in the low-frequency response usually is desirable and obtainable from a longer reverberation time. On the other hand, reverberation depends only on the existence of eigentones, standing waves or modes. The smaller the studios, the fewer the modes at low frequencies and therefore the greater the frequency spacing between them. These single modes must be damped to reduce their disturbing influence, with a corresponding reduction in reverberation time. The long-wave length at low frequencies leads naturally to the buildup of standing waves. A superimposition takes place between the direct and reflected sounds, where the wave repeats itself in the same form continuously. It was described by Cremer as a *gleichphasiger Anschluss*,[26] an in-phase summation. The wave is a cosine form as in Eq. (13.12):

$$p(x,y,z) = P_{max} \cos \frac{n_x x}{l_x} \cos \frac{n_y y}{l_y} \cos \frac{n_z z}{l_z} \qquad (13.12)$$

where $p(x,y,z)$ = sound pressure at the spot x,y,z, Pa
P_{max} = maximum sound pressure, Pa
n_x, n_y, n_z = numbers 0, 1, 2, 3, ...
l_x, l_y, l_z = dimensions of room, m
x, y, z = coordinates

Equation (13.12) describes all the standing waves or nodes for which the frequency can be calculated. To do this it must satisfy the Helmholtz equation, shown in Eq. (13.13):

$$\frac{d^2p}{dx^2} + \frac{d^2p}{dy^2} + \frac{d^2p}{dz^2} + k^2p = 0 \qquad (13.13)$$

The solution is possible, leading to the eigenfrequencies given in Eq. (13.14):

$$f_n \frac{c}{2} \sqrt{\left(\frac{n_x}{l_x}\right)^2 + \left(\frac{n_y}{l_y}\right)^2 + \left(\frac{n_z}{l_z}\right)^2} \text{ Hz} \qquad (13.14)$$

where f_n = frequency of modes, Hz
n_x, n_y, n_z = numbers 0, 1, 2, 3, . . .

For the simplified case in which the standing wave in the x direction exists between two parallel walls, the eigenfrequency can be calculated according to Eq. (13.15), with $n_1 = 1$ and both n_2 and $n_3 = 0$:

$$f = \frac{c}{2} \frac{n_1}{l_x} = \frac{340 \times 1}{2 \times l_x} \qquad (13.15)$$

For a distance $l_x = 10$ m, the eigenfrequency is 17 Hz. This normal mode is described by 1, 0, 0, and all the modes between two parallel surfaces are known as axial modes. 1, 1, 0 describes a mode which exists between two pairs of parallel surfaces called tangential modes. Calculation for $l_x = 10$ m, $l_y = 5$ m, leads to a mode frequency for this tangential mode of 38 Hz according to Eq. (13.16):

$$f_2 = \frac{c}{2} \sqrt{\left(\frac{n_1}{l_x}\right)^2 + \left(\frac{n_2}{l_y}\right)^2} = \frac{340}{2} \sqrt{\frac{1}{10^2} + \frac{1}{5^2}} = 38 \text{ Hz} \qquad (13.16)$$

Taking into account all the reflection possibilities from the corners and edges of a rectangular room and including the oblique series of modes from three pairs of parallel surfaces, the mode frequencies for a small rock studio measuring 12 by 8 by 3 m can be calculated. Rounded to the nearest hertz, these mode frequencies are 14, 22, 26, 29, 36, 43, 46, 52, 58, 61, 63, 64, 65, 72, 73, etc.

It becomes obvious that at low frequencies only a few modes can exist. By following Cremer and others,[26] the numbers can be calculated from the volume and surface area of the room. The numbers do not depend on the individual room dimensions indicated by l_x or l_y or on the reverberation time.

$$N = \frac{4}{3} \pi V \left(\frac{f}{c}\right)^3 + \frac{4}{\pi} S \left(\frac{f}{c}\right)^2 \qquad (13.17)$$

where N = number of modes up to f
V = volume $v = l_x l_y l_z$, m³
S = surface of room, m² [surface = $2 (l_x l_y + l_x l_z + l_y l_z)$]
c = velocity of sound, m/s
f = frequency, Hz

For the dimensions of the small rock studio mentioned above, the approximate number of modes up to 50 Hz is 9, up to 80 Hz 28, and up to 125 Hz 40. The number of modes is identical to the number of sound reflections in the time up to t, as given in Eq. (13.18):

$$N_R \sim \frac{4}{3} \pi \frac{c^3}{v} t^3 \qquad (13.18)$$

where N_R = number of reflections
t = time of decay after source is switched off, s

With the same volume of 288 m^3 and a time interval of 50 ms, the number of reflections is 71.

The eigentones form a landscape of modes with distinct hills and deep valleys, as seen in Fig. 13.28. In this case the valley is about 1 m long and is located close to the ear of the sound engineer. The measurements were carried out by moving

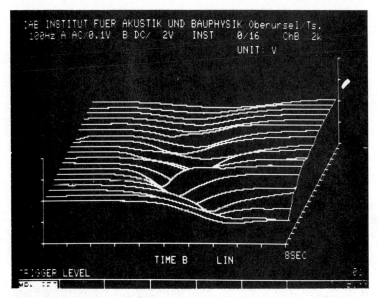

FIG. 13.28   Landscape of modes at the listening position produced by the sinosoidal signal of 60 Hz.

a measurement microphone along parallel lines, each 2 m long and spaced 5 cm apart. The information was stored in a computer and plotted on the oscilloscope as a waterfall display. A listening position or a microphone in this deep valley would register no sound.

It is difficult to damp out single low-frequency modes because the efficiency of sound-absorbing materials at low frequencies is poor. When exciting a small room with a pure tone at a frequency which corresponds to a natural mode of the room, a long decay time will be measured when the tone is cut off. If the driving frequency is between two mode frequencies, normally a short decay time would result. In many cases where the bandwidth of the modes is sufficiently wide, however, the decaying energy will be transferred into the normal mode, which decays at its usual rate.

A mode layout exists in both the studio and the control room. Either the right position for a microphone must be found in this landscape of modes in the studio, or a flat landscape without hills and valleys must be designed in the region of the control desk. To flatten this mode landscape, low-frequency sound absorbers or even Helmholtz resonator absorbers must be installed.[27,28]

The number of modes falling in each one-third-octave or octave bandwidth is often important. In Table 13.25 the center frequencies and cutoff frequencies f_i

TABLE 13.25 Octave and One-Third-Octave Filters with Center and Cutoff Frequencies

Center frequency, f_m, Hz	Filter passband, f_1 to f_2, Hz	Center frequency, f_m, Hz	Filter passband, f_1 to f_2, Hz
	Octave filter		
63	45–90	2,000	1,400–2,800
125	90–180	4,000	2,800–5,600
250	180–355	8,000	5,600–11,200
1,000	710–1,400	16,000	11,200–22,400
	One-third-octave filter		
40	35.5–45	1,000	900–1,120
50	45–56	1,250	1,120–1,400
63	56–71	1,600	1,400–1,800
80	71–90	2,000	1,800–2,240
100	90–112	2,500	2,240–2,800
125	112–140	3,150	2,800–3,550
160	140–180	4,000	3,550–4,500
200	180–224	5,000	4,500–5,600
250	224–280	6,300	5,600–7,100
315	280–355	8,000	7,100–9,000
400	355–450	10,000	9,000–11,200
500	450–560	12,500	11,200–14,000
630	560–710	16,000	14,000–18,000
800	710–900	20,000	18,000–22,400

and f_2 are shown for each one-third-octave and octave band. The relationship of f_1 and f_2 to the mean frequency for each bandwidth is shown in Eq. (13.19):

$$f_1 = 0.71\,f_m \quad f_2 = 1.40\,f_m \quad \text{for octaves}$$
$$f_1 = 0.90\,f_m \quad f_2 = 1.12\,f_m \quad \text{for one-third octaves} \tag{13.19}$$

The number of modes in the one-third-octave band centered on 125 Hz is found according to Eq. (13.17) by calculating the number of modes up to each frequency f_1 and f_2. The number within the band then is the difference between these two numbers and is seen in Eq. (13.20) to be 74 modes:

$$\text{For } f = f_1 = 112 \text{ Hz} \quad N_1 = 96$$
$$\text{For } f = f_2 = 140 \text{ Hz} \quad N_2 = 170 \tag{13.20}$$
$$\text{For } f_1 \text{ to } f_2 \quad N = N_2 - N_1 = 74 \text{ modes}$$

The number of modes within the one-third-octave band can indicate the validity of measurements of reverberation time [according to Eq. (13.1)] within this frequency band. A significant limit to the measurement of reverberation time in small rooms is contained in the measurement standards for dwellings.[29,30] These standards require measurement in the 100-Hz one-third-octave band. For a typical room of 5 by 6 by 2.7 m, the number of modes may be shown to be 19. For comparison, a very small control room of 4 by 3 by 2.4 m would have only 5 modes in the same one-third-octave band.

13.3.6 Microphones in Direct and Diffuse Sound Fields

It is apparent that some microphones will be better suited to close-microphone records and some to diffuse-field recordings. They can be designed for specific applications as follows:

1. Microphones having a free-field calibration for recording in the direct sound field virtually without diffuse sound
2. Microphones having a diffuse-field calibration for recording at great distances in almost completely diffuse sound fields

The term *calibration* is used here in the sense that construction of the microphone leads to a smooth frequency response in the appropriate sound field. Measurements are made in a dead reflection-free room for the direct sound field or in a reverberation room for the diffuse sound field. Manufacturers strive for a microphone with a flat characteristic in both sorts of sound field as in Fig. 13.29, curve 6. This implies that moving the microphone from the diffuse sound field into the near sound field of the source will result in no change of coloration. As an example, two universally renowned old microphones were used for many decades by sound engineers for good recordings in either sound field.

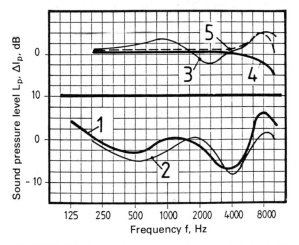

FIG. 13.29 The human ear and microphones in direct and diffuse sound fields. *Curve 1:* Equal-loudness curve for 60 dB in a direct sound field. *Curve 2:* Equal-loudness curve for 60 dB in a diffuse sound field. *Curve 3:* Same as curves 1 and 2. *Curve 4:* Microphone with a rolloff at high frequencies in the diffuse sound field (Neumann Co. M49 or Schoeps Co. MK2). *Curve 5:* Microphone with an increase at high frequencies in the diffuse sound field (Neumann Co. KM54a). *Curve 6:* Microphone with a flat frequency-response curve.

Example: M49 microphone: Used as a close-speaking microphone at distances from 50 cm to 1 m, this microphone has a flat response following curve 6. Moving this microphone into the diffuse sound field results in a fall in the high-frequency response, as in curve 4. Subjectively, the M49 microphone sounded smooth and had a well-rounded response. This effect varied with the distance from the source.

The acoustical image of the room changes in the same way; for instance, the sense of reverberation in the room is changed. This microphone has regained popularity.

Example: KM54a microphone: This is also a free-field calibrated microphone. It has a linear characteristic as shown in curve 6 when it is used at a distance of about 1 m. When moved into the diffuse field, it exhibits a rise at high frequencies. As a consequence, strings sound edgy and sharp; speech is sibilant. The sound becomes clear and direct, which is an advantage for quiet instruments. This microphone leads to a very different room impression when compared with the M49.

Measurement microphones can also be constructed to have a linear response in a direct or a diffuse sound field. Figure 13.30 presents two microphones from

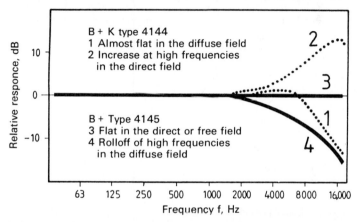

FIG. 13.30 Measurement microphones in diffuse and direct sound fields. [*H. Moller, "Relevant Hi-Fi Tests at Home," presented at the 47th Convention of the Audio Engineering Society, Copenhagen (1974).*]

Bruel and Kjaer. Type 4145 is suitable for free-field measurements (curve 3), while Type 4144 is correct for diffuse-field use. Using these microphones in the wrong environment would lead to incorrect results.[31] The change in frequency response of these microphones is similar to that of the M49 and KM54a (see Fig. 13.30). The use of a measurement microphone and a level recorder in a studio must take account of the calibration of the microphone if, for instance, the studio monitoring chain is being equalized.

Figure 13.29 also shows the sensitivity of the human hearing system in free field and diffuse field. At 8000 Hz, for instance, a lower SPL in a diffuse field will give the same impression of loudness. This implies that the ear is more sensitive in the diffuse sound field. It "records" more in the same way as the KM54a microphone.

The directivity index of a microphone is derived from its sensitivity in free field and diffuse field [Eq. (13.21)].

$$10 \log Q_M = 10 \log \frac{B_{\text{free}}^2}{B_{0,\text{free}}^2} - 10 \log \frac{B_{\text{diff}}^2}{B_{0,\text{diff}}^2} \qquad (13.21)$$

where $10 \log Q_M$ = directivity, dB
Q_M = directivity factor
B_{free} = sensitivity factor in free or direct sound field, V/Pa
$B_{0,\text{free}}$ = sensitivity factor in free or direct sound field for 1000 Hz, V/Pa
B_{diff} = sensitivity factor in diffuse sound field, V/Pa
$B_{0,\text{diff}}$ = sensitivity factor in diffuse sound field for 1000 Hz, V/Pa

The directivity index ($10 \log Q_M$) and the directivity factor (Q_M) are listed in Fig. 13.31 for some common microphone types. Signal voltage from the micro-

Directivity Pattern	Directivity factor Q_M $10 \log O_M$		Distance factor	Equation for directivity $F(\varphi)$
		dB		
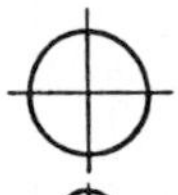 Omnidirectional	1	0	1	1
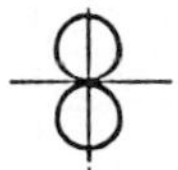 Bidirectional	3	4,8	1,73	$\cos \varphi$
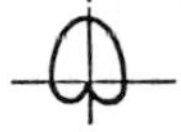 Cardioid	3	4,8	1,73	$\frac{1}{2}(1+3\cos\varphi)$
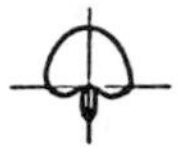 Hypercardioid	4	6,0	2,00	$\frac{1}{4}(1+3\cos\varphi)$
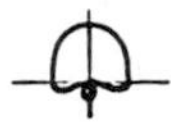 Supercardioid	3,75	5,7	1,93	$37 + 36\cos\varphi$
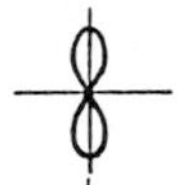 2d-order bidirectional	5	7,0	2,24	$\cos^2\varphi$
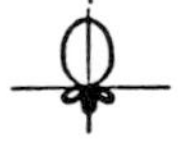 2d-order cardioid	7,5	8,8	2,74	$(1+\cos\varphi)\cos\varphi$
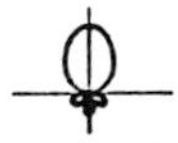 2d-order hypercardioid	8	9,0	2,83	$(6+\cos\varphi)\cos\varphi$

FIG. 13.31 Directivity factors of different microphones and their gain with distance.

phone depends on the Q_M factor as in Eq. (13.22). In a diffuse sound field when operating close to feedback, a microphone with a greater Q_M is advantageous. The signal level is lower, and the stability margin before feedback is increased. Alternatively, the greater stability margin could be exchanged for a greater distance between microphone and source.

$$L_{U,\text{diff}} = L_{p,\text{diff}} + 10 \log \frac{B_{\text{diff}}^2 \, p_0^2}{Q_M \, U_0^2} \qquad (13.22)$$

where $L_{U,\text{diff}}$ = voltage level of microphone in diffuse sound field, dB
 $\quad L_{p,\text{diff}}$ = SPL in diffuse sound field, dB
 $\quad p_0$ = reference pressure, 2×10^{-5} Pa
 $\quad U_0$ = reference voltage, $U_0 = 1$ V

As an example, what feedback margin is obtainable when a microphone with an omnidirectional characteristic $Q_M = 1$ is compared with a hypercardioid $Q_M = 8$?

1. The diffuse sound level around the microphone according to Eq. (13.5) may have a value of 80 dB.

2. The sensitivity of the microphone in the direct sound field is 20 mV/Pa.

3. For the hypercardioid, the signal level is -57 dB, which corresponds to a voltage of 1.4 mV.

4. For the omnidirectional characteristic, the signal level is -48 dB, or 4 mV.

5. The feedback margin is increased by 9 dB for the hypercardioid microphone compared with an omnidirectional one. This is equal to 10 log Q_M.

The possible increase in distance is given by $\sqrt{Q_M}$, as may be seen in Fig. 13.31. The maximum distance factor is 2.83 for a hypercardioid microphone. Some microphones show greater rear-facing sensitivity than others. For example, the hypercardioid with $Q_M = 4$, although its directivity may be lower than that of the cardioid microphone, has a greater front-to-back ratio.

13.4 SOUND-LEVEL CONDITIONS IN STUDIO AND HOME

13.4.1 Music, Speech, and Noise

The sound level and spectra of music, speech, and noise, such as traffic, aircraft, or air-conditioning noise, are known and must be taken into account in designing studios or dwellings. Figure 13.32 shows typical values for music and speech. The sound levels can be higher or lower with almost the same frequency response. The maximum values have been given in the studio descriptions in Sec. 13.2. The minimum usable sound level, which is about 5 dBA above background noise, occurs for solo instruments or quiet passages of speech including whispering [Eq. (13.23)].

$$S - N \geq 5 \text{ dB} \qquad (13.23)$$

where S = signal, dB
 $\quad N$ = noise, dB

Both signal and noise levels must take into account the statistical variation of level and the averaging carried out during measurements. A typical variation in level for music and speech and the corresponding levels which are exceeded for various percentages of time are shown in Fig. 13.33. An approximate relationship between the levels is shown in Table 13.26.

The level variations can be seen in the control room or in the domestic environment with certain volume indicators. To follow the very fast variation in

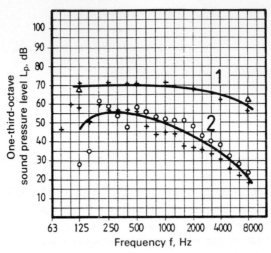

FIG. 13.32 Sound pressure levels for speech and music. *Curve 1:* Spectrum of radio and TV programs after H. Jakubowski [*"Das Problem der Programmlautstärke,"* Rundfunktech. Mitt. *(1968)*], 80 dBA, "+" music of Mozart after H. Kuhl [*"Optimale akustische Gestaltung von Räumen für Aufführende, Zuhörer und Schallaufnahmen,"* Schalltechnik, no. 20 *(1956)*], 80 dBA, and "triangle" music of Brahms *(Kuhl, op. cit.),* 80 dBA. *Curve 2:* Average spectrum of quiet speech after T. Tarnóscy [*"Das durchschnittliche Energie-Spektrum der Sprache (für sechs Sprachen),* Acustica *(1971)*] for female speech "o," 60 dBA, and male speech "+," 60 dBA.

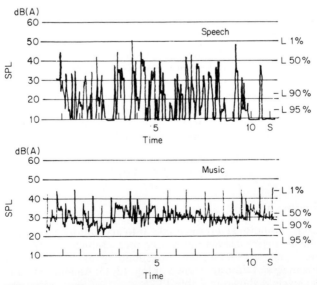

FIG 13.33 Different sound pressure levels of speech and music recorded with paper speed of 10 mm/s and writing speed of 1000 mm/s.

sound level, we may use a light beam whose response time is about 10 ms, compared with a normal impulse-measuring sound-level meter whose response time is defined as 70 ms.[32] In Fig. 13.33 level variations are plotted by a level recorder using a writing speed of 1000 ms. The volume-unit (VU) meter has a comparable response time and is also comparatively slow.[33] This slow indication is an advan-

TABLE 13.26 Sound Pressure

Level	Decibels
Peaks, L, 1%	0
Medium peaks, L, 5%	-3
Medium peaks, L, 10%	-7
Average level, L, 50%	-12
Background level, L, 90%	

tage because impulse signals would otherwise be overestimated. Such impulse signals are very short, their energy is small, and normally they present little danger to transmission equipment. Sometimes light indicators and VU meters are used in parallel to check both aspects.

During pauses in speech or music, background noise may be heard. It arises from the air-conditioning system and from other activities inside or outside the studio. The question of permissible background noise is extremely important because of its relationship to building costs. As described previously, using microphones close to the sound source excludes the effects of room influence and also reduces the impact of background noise. Here that means that using only close-microphone techniques simplifies many aspects of building construction.[34,35] It must be remembered that once the decision has been made, microphone techniques cannot be changed during the lifetime of a studio. There are certain cases in which weak studios have been used with distant-field-microphone techniques, such as artificial head recordings or the PZM microphone on the studio surface.[18,19] Here, noise together with the total room information which characterizes studio acoustics is evident, particularly because of the comparatively low level of direct sound. Permissible background noise levels in studios from several different sources are shown in Fig. 13.34. The stringent requirements for German recording studios are obvious. They are based on the work of Kuhl[36] for quiet sound sources, such as quiet speech with the necessary amplification added in the control room. It is apparent that amplification in the control room or at home to raise volume will also increase the background noise level. An increase of 10 dB in volume means that during a pause in speech studio background noise of, for example, NR_{20}, corresponding to 30 dBA, will be raised to 40 dBA. As the lowest achievable level, Kuhl took the noise of a good-quality microphone. Following Eq. (13.22), the signal level of a dynamic microphone consists of two parts:

1. Noise from a 200-Ω resistor as a limit, calculated according to Eq. (13.24).

2. Electrical signal level produced when sound pressure falls on the microphone membrane. The sensitivity factor may be taken as $B_{dir} = 2$ mV/Pa.

$$L_u = 10 \log \frac{4\, kTnR_i\, \Delta f}{U_0^2} \tag{13.24}$$

where L_u = voltage level, dBm
     k = Boltzmann factor, $k = 1.38 \times 10^{-23}$
     T = absolute temperature, K
     n = number of microphones
    Δf = frequency range, Hz
    U_0 = reference voltage, 0.775 V

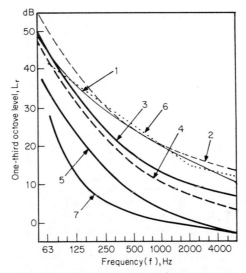

FIG. 13.34 Permissible sound pressure levels in studios for radio and television. 1. BBC studios for light entertainment and shows, 35 dBA [*S. Brown, "Acoustic Design of Broadcasting Studios," J. Sound Vib., I(3), 238–257 (1964)*]. 2. Noise-rating curve (Noise Rating Curves, *ISO R1996, 1971*). 3. German recommendation for TV studios after W. Kuhl [*"Zulässige Geräuschpegel in Studios, Konzertsälen und Theatern," Acustica (1964)*], 29 dBA; also BBC standard for announcers, music, and television, 30 dBA *(Brown, op. cit.)*. 4. NR_{15} = 25 dBA. 5. BBC drama studios, 25 dBA. 6. German recommendation for music studios with cloth-covered microphone pickup technique, 33 dBA [*after L. L. Beranek, "Preferred Noise Criterion Curves and Their Application to Rooms," J. Acoust. Soc. Am., 50(5), 1223–1228 (1971)*]. 7. German recommendation for music studios, announcer booth, and drama studios, 13 dBA *(Kuhl, op. cit.)*.

Figure 13.35 shows these significant levels. When loud or quiet speech is produced, the corresponding signal levels exist at the output of the microphone or at the input to the following amplifier.

Background noise having a spectrum of an NR_{25} curve is shown as curve 4 in Fig. 13.35. Quiet speech, shown as curve 5, is not greatly above curve 4, and the

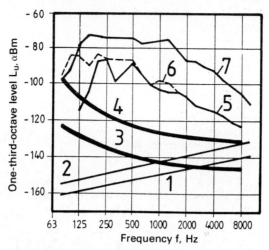

FIG. 13.35 Voltage level at the output of a dynamic microphone with an impedance of 200 Ω. *Curve 1:* Noise of a 200-Ω resistor, −127 dB lin, or −131 dBA. *Curve 2:* As in curve 1 for four microphones. *Curve 3:* Permissible sound pressure levels in studios [*after H. Kuhl, "Zulässige Geräuschpegel in Studios, Konzertsälen und Theatern,"* Acustica *(1964)*], 13 dBA. *Curve 4:* Noise-rating curve NR$_{25}$, approximately 35 dBA. *Curve 5:* Female announcer, quiet speech, after T. Tarnóscy [*"Das durchschnittliche Energie-Spektrum der Sprache (für sechs Sprachen),"* Acustica *(1971)*]; microphone distance, 60 cm, 57 dBA. *Curve 6:* As in curve 5, male announcer, 61 dBA. *Curve 7:* As in curve 6, loud speech, microphone distance 35 cm, spectrum after Tarnóscy *(op. cit.)*, 76 dBA.

noise is audible during pauses in speech. Loud speech and, in addition, a small microphone distance increase the S/N ratio enormously, by about 20 dB, as curve 7. The same effect is obtainable by reducing the studio noise level from curve 4 to curve 3.

13.4.2 Sound Isolation

In studios the sound-level difference [Eq. (13.25)] is the main factor of interest. Sound transmitted through a dividing partition constitutes a direct sound field near the wall or door or window and a diffuse sound field at greater distances.

$$D = L_1 - L_2 \qquad (13.25)$$

where L_1 = SPL at sending end, dB
L_2 = SPL at receiving end, dB

D, the sound-level difference, depends on the sound reduction index of the walls, the presence of flanking paths, and the acoustical conditions of the room. When interest is focused upon the partition, the sound reduction index may be calculated according to Eq. (13.26).

$$R = D + 10 \log \frac{S}{A} = D + 10 \log \frac{ST}{0.163 \, v} \qquad (13.26)$$

where R = sound reduction index, dB
    S = wall area, m^2
    A = total absorption, m^2
    T = reverberation time, s
    v = volume of receiving room, m^3
  0.163 = factor in metric system, s/m^2

Curve 1 in Fig. 13.36 is a combination of the mean program level for speech and music (see Fig. 13.32) with traffic noise after De Lange and Kosten,[37] which

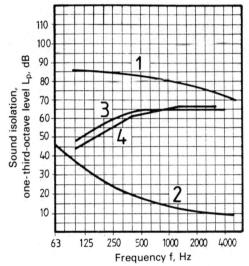

FIG. 13.36 Sound pressure levels and sound reduction. *Curve 1:* Average spectrum of speech, music, and automobile and traffic noise, 90 dBA. *Curve 2:* Permissible noise levels according to NR$_{20}$ with approximately 28 dBA between 100 and 3200 Hz. *Curve 3:* Difference of curve 1 − curve 2, 62 dB. *Curve 4:* Reference curve (Schallschutz im Hochbau, *DIN 4109, Beuth-Verlag, Berlin; E. J. Voelker,* Ein kleiner Hörfunk-Studiokomplex—Schalltechnische Mindestanforderungen und ihre Realisierung, *VDE-Verlag, Berlin, 1981) R$_w$* = 63 dB.

may exist in a source room such as a studio. In the adjacent studio the background noise may correspond to the NR curve shown as curve 2. The difference between these two curves, as given in Eq. (13.25), is curve 3, which is almost equal to the reference curve for the sound reduction index shown as curve 4. For this reason, it is permissible to derive the required sound isolation by subtracting the required background noise level from an assumed source level. For example, a studio may have a source level of 100 dBA. The adjacent announcer's room has a requirement for a background noise level of NR_{15} equivalent to 25 dBA. To a first approximation $D = R = 75$ dB. This represents a very stringent requirement for sound reduction between two studios with difficult and expensive considerations for the construction of studios.

13.4.3 Sound Level and Isolation in Dwellings

Normal standards of house construction are just sufficient to achieve an acceptable sound isolation around 52 dB between adjacent dwellings. Permissible noise levels in apartments are about 25 dBA during the night.[38] Sanitary installations may be allowed to reach 30 dBA. By starting with this 30 dBA in a bedroom and adding the sound insulation of 52 dB, an allowable level of 82 dBA will be permitted on the other side of the wall:

$$L_1 = D + L_2 = 52 + 30 = 82 \text{ dBA} \tag{13.27}$$

This level will frequently be exceeded by parties, playing musical instruments, or a loud TV set. The resulting complaints are well known. For comparison with the 30-dBA background noise, the noises of normal activities in a house will frequently exceed 40 dBA. A normal listening level for radio or TV is 75 dBA. So the remaining S/N ratio is around 35 dB. Speech or music must therefore be recorded so that the dynamic range does not exceed 35 dB. Rémonit has examined more than 30 samples of serious music and found a dynamic range (difference between peak signal levels and quiet signal levels) of 36 to 45 dB, having a mean value of 40 dB.[39] Other authors found a similar result of 30 dB when they asked many thousands of people at home to describe their listening levels.[40,41] This result, of course, does not apply for persons who listen with headphones or who live in detached houses. Nor does it hold true for dwellers in privately owned apartments for whom much higher building costs would result from requirements to achieve higher sound insulation. For many sound engineers, their own home listening serves as a reference standard. They may even make a cassette copy of a sound recording to check in their houses or their cars that the correct result has been achieved. The living room has its own acoustic characteristics and normally some acoustical disadvantages. It adds to the direct signal from the loudspeaker a number of strong first reflections from the ceiling and the walls. The reverberation time in living rooms is around 0.3 to 0.4 s. It has almost no influence on the reverberation of the recording. It seems to be important that the listener get used to his or her own listening conditions which are thus unconsciously taken into account. As a consequence, there is no necessity for a standard listening room or a standard living room with a standard loudspeaker system. The same compensation occurs with music producers who are able to sit beside the sound engineer and outside the stereophonic listening area and yet make valid judgments about balance.

13.4.4 Survey of Sound Insulation

Table 13.27 shows the usual sound insulation values between studios and adjacent rooms as described above. Control rooms and domestic rooms are included.

TABLE 13.27 Survey of Sound Insulation between Studios, Control Rooms, and Dwellings, dB

	Studio	Control-room sound	Control-room TV	Announcer's booth	Camera check	Editing room	Corridor	Office	Plant, workshop	Equipment room	Projection room	Disk jockey	Weather studio	Telephone studio	Concert hall
Studio	72/72	68/64	62/58	62/58	57/52	68/64	68/64	68/64	72/72	68/64	68/64	52/45	68/64	57/52	72/72
Control-room sound	68/64	68/64	62/58	62/58	57/45	68/64	52/45	68/64	68/64	62/58	62/58	52/45	62/58	57/52	68/64
Control-room TV	62/58	62/58	57/45	62/58	57/45	57/45	52/45	68/64	62/58	52/45	58/52	52/45	52/45	57/52	68/64
Announcer's booth	62/58	62/58	62/58	62/58	62/58	62/58	68/64	68/64	72/72	68/64	68/64	52/45	68/64	62/57	68/64
Camera check	57/52	57/45	57/45	62/58	52/45	52/45	45/37	45/37	62/58	52/45	52/45	52/45	52/45	52/45	62/58
Editing room	68/64	68/64	57/45	62/58	52/45	52/45	45/37	45/37	58/58	52/45	52/45	52/45	52/45	52/45	62/58
Corridor	68/64	52/45	52/45	68/64	45/37	45/37	:	45/37	45/37	45/37	45/37	52/45	45/37	45/37	68/64
Office	68/64	68/64	68/64	68/64	45/37	45/37	45/37	:	45/37	52/37	52/45	52/45	52/52	52/52	68/68
Plant, workshop	72/72	68/64	62/58	72/72	62/58	58/58	45/37	45/37	62/62	62/58	62/62	62/62	62/62	57/52	72/72
Equipment room	68/64	62/58	52/45	68/64	52/45	52/45	45/37	52/37	62/58	58/58	58/52	62/57	62/57	52/45	68/64
Projection room	68/64	62/58	58/52	68/64	52/45	52/45	45/37	52/45	62/62	58/52	52/45	52/45	62/57	52/45	68/64
Disk jockey	52/45	52/45	52/45	52/45	52/45	52/45	52/45	52/45	62/62	62/57	52/45	62/58	58/52	45/45	62/58
Weather studio	68/64	62/58	52/45	68/64	52/45	52/45	45/37	52/52	62/62	62/57	62/57	58/52	58/52	45/45	62/58
Telephone studio	57/52	57/52	57/52	62/57	52/45	52/45	45/37	52/52	57/52	52/45	52/45	45/45	45/45	62/58	62/58
Concert hall	72/72	68/64	68/64	68/64	62/58	62/58	68/64	68/68	72/72	68/64	68/64	62/58	62/58	62/58	72/72

It should be noted that the sound insulation curve is similar to curve 4 or curve 3 in Fig. 13.36. The sound-level difference follows Eq. (13.26) and is the most important figure.

13.5 CONTROL ROOMS

13.5.1 Definition; History

Ever since studios have existed and recordings have been made, control rooms have been necessary. The listening room at the International Exhibition of Electricity in Paris in 1881 was treated with draperies to reduce noise and reverberation.[3] In the 1920s the control room was known as an amplifier room. Like studios, it was treated with draperies on walls and ceiling. Then there came a period in which control rooms were constructed to have acoustics similar to those of living rooms.[42] At this time an omnidirectional loudspeaker radiated sound to all the reflecting surfaces of the room to achieve a diffuse sound field in the same way as in a home.[43] The same thinking held true for speech studios. Why, it would be asked, should the speaker not be heard as if from a normal room? Subjectively, this was not found pleasing, and further developments led to a highly damped speech studio and control room. In recent years, the control room with a certain reverberance has reappeared, and a reverberation time of about 0.5 s has been proposed.[44] This type of control room had its forerunner in many control rooms with their inevitable sound-reflecting surfaces from desks, windows and doors, and technical equipment. In 1972 Voelker found[45] that sound engineers created better recordings in a control room which they knew than in one with which they were not so well acquainted. There was a surprise in 1974 when four control rooms containing high-quality monitoring systems were studied and showed a very uneven frequency response at the listener's position.[46] In these cases, unpleasant sound reflections could not be avoided, and in the following years the sound field in control rooms had to be investigated more carefully.[47]

The basic requirement for a control room is that the reproduced sound picture not be influenced by the control room to an extent that affects the sound engineer's judgment concerning the quality of the recorded sound.

13.5.2 Standard Control Room: Necessary or Desirable?

It is significant that no standard control room has even been felt to be necessary or been built. In the past the control room was always the technical center and contained the mixing desk, amplifiers, equalizers, and racks. Despite the resulting limitations, the sound engineers, program producers, and sound mixers did not refuse to work in this environment. These limitations still exist. It seems that a standard control room is not necessary, and this implies that in the future there can be a wide variety of control rooms. These will include designs suitable for speech or music or specific types of music, such as pop, folk, and rock, for multipurpose use, or for mix-downs.

In 1981 the European Broadcasting Union (EBU)[23] made certain recommendations, which should be discussed:

1. The volume of the control room should be about 40 m^3 but always greater than 30 m^3. This volume is too small. With a volume of 40 m^3 and a reverberation time of 0.25 s, according to Eq. (13.18) there are only seven modes up to a frequency of 80 Hz. This number is too small.

2. Below 100 Hz, there are no recommendations for reverberation time, which would be allowed to rise or fall. There are, of course, control rooms whose frequency response extends to 25 Hz with the necessary sound absorption and damping of mode amplitudes as discussed by Duncan.[27]

3. Reverberation time is allowed to be 0.3 ± 0.1 s. In this range, from 0.2 to 0.4 s is large and includes both highly damped and reverberant control rooms.

4. The maximum loudness for listening should not exceed 85 dBA. When background noise does not exceed 30 dBA, this level will provide an adequate S/N ratio of around 55 dBA. In practice, many control rooms have higher noise levels from equipment, sometimes amounting to 45 to 50 dBA, and in these cases it will be necessary to listen at a higher level, which may exceed 100 dBA.[48,49]

5. The stereo listening area is defined by an included angle of 60 ± 10°. This angle is generally achieved in most control rooms. However, in some recent control rooms, there has been a tendency to bring the main monitoring loudspeakers closer to the mixing desk, and in these cases the included angle can be as great as 90°.

13.5.3 Aimed Acoustics for Control Rooms

By *aimed acoustics* is meant the acoustic design which takes into consideration direct sound, reflections, and reverberation, the short reverberation times, modes, and the placing of sound-absorbing material. Voelker defined this term in 1964.[50] It is also described in published work relating to control rooms for music use[51] and for speech use.[52] The features can be summarized as follows:

1. The sound of the loudspeakers travels directly to the ears of the sound engineer.

2. Sound reflections that arrive shortly after the direct sound at the engineer's listening position, for example, from the ceiling, walls, or other items, must be avoided.

3. The strength of the reflections is reduced with sound-absorbing material placed in appropriate locations on the ceiling and the walls between the loudspeaker and the listener.

4. The rear wall is totally absorbing and forms what might be called an *acoustic sink.*

5. The reverberation time is about 0.25 s.

6. The frequency response of the reverberation time is linear down, perhaps, to 50 Hz. This standard can be achieved only by using very effective low-frequency sound absorbers, including resonator absorbers.[27,28]

7. Higher-order reflections are allowed to obtain a certain reverberance and prevent an overdamped room.

13.5.4 Control Room with Loudspeakers Producing Artificial Reflections

The control room described above can be brightened by artificially introduced reflections from up to 40 loudspeakers. These are mounted in the rear half of the control room, and their signals are delayed so that they arrive 30 to 50 ms after the direct signal. Their frequency response can be equalized with one-third-octave filters, as shown in principle in Fig. 13.37. Comparing acoustic conditions with and without loudspeakers shows that the loudspeakers have advantages for certain types of music.[51] It is possible to switch the system on and off.

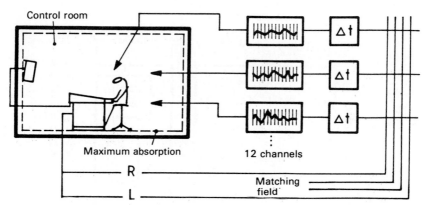

FIG. 13.37 Artificial sound reflections produced by loudspeakers mounted in the ceiling and on sidewalls and back walls.

13.5.5 Half-Reverberant Control Room with Permitted Late Reflections

The sidewalls and the rear wall have sound-reflecting surfaces that are orientated to reflect the sound away from the listener's ears (Fig. 13.38). The sound paths attain delays of more than 20 ms before reaching the ears. This design ensures an initial time-delay gap of 5 to 20 ms after the direct sound; during this period the control room adds no information to that contained in the recorded sound. The dotted line in Fig. 13.38 indicates the area in which highly sound-absorbing finishes are included. The reverberation time in this control room is higher than in the room described previously. This design is preferred for disco, pop, country, and jazz music;[51] "with a reverberation time of 0.4 s this control room is quite reverberant and is rejected for drum sounds. The control room is clearly heard with these sounds." This half-reverberant control room is not satisfactory for listening to speech.[52]

13.5.6 Four Types of Control Room and Their Acoustic Properties

Voelker in the Institut für Akustik und Bauphysik (IAB) had the opportunity of constructing within the same enclosure four different control rooms, one after the other. Their properties are summarized in Fig. 13.39, where the different rooms are identified by numbers 1 through 4 as follows:[51]

Type 1: A very reverberant control room. It is generally not liked for speech and music, but some subjects liked this type for organ music.

Type 2: Half-reverberant room, as described in Sec. 13.5.5.

Type 3: Aimed acoustics, as described in Sec. 13.5.3. This is a well-damped control room.

Type 4: Same as Type 3 with loudspeakers, as described in Sec. 13.5.4.

The reflectograms for Type 1, 2, and 3 rooms are shown in Fig. 13.40. In all three cases the source was a spark approximately 5 cm in front of the surface of

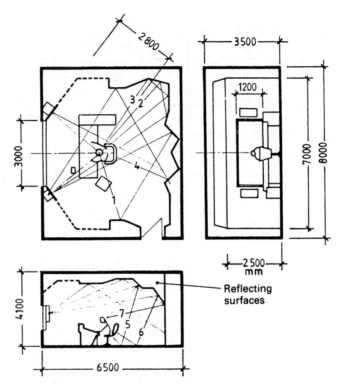

FIG. 13.38 Half-reverberant room with favorable late reflections: *Path 1,* 1 ms. *Path 2,* 27 ms. *Path 3,* 30 ms. *Path 4,* 36 ms. *Path 5,* 18 ms. *Path 6,* 21 ms. *Path 7,* 19 ms. The volume of the control room is 160 m³.

the left monitoring loudspeaker. An omnidirectional microphone picked up the signal, which was was displayed on an oscilloscope and photographed.

Room Type 1: Very reverberant with many reflections, this type produces a broad, full tree characteristic. The reverberation time is 0.8 s.

Room Type 2: This type is half-reverberant. There is an initial time-delay gap that is almost free of sound reflections. Even the later part of the tree shows far fewer reflections. The reverberation time is equal to 0.4 s.

Room Type 3: A highly damped control room, it follows the design of aimed acoustics. The elimination of first-order and many higher-order reflections means that the tree is very small. The reverberation is 0.2 s.

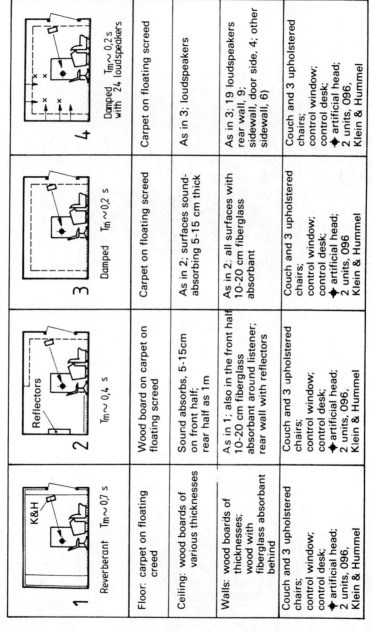

	1 — Reverberant $T_m \sim 0{,}7$ s	2 — Reflectors $T_m \sim 0{,}4$ s	3 — Damped $T_m \sim 0{,}2$ s	4 — Damped $T_m \sim 0{,}2$ s with 24 loudspeakers
Floor:	carpet on floating creed	Wood board on carpet on floating screed	Carpet on floating screed	Carpet on floating screed
Ceiling:	wood boards of various thicknesses	Sound absorbs, 5-15cm on front half; rear half as 1m	As in 2; surfaces sound-absorbing 5-15 cm thick	As in 3; loudspeakers
Walls:	wood boards of thicknesses; wood with fiberglass absorbant behind	As in 1; also in the front half 10-20 cm fiberglass absorbant around listener; rear wall with reflectors	As in 2; all surfaces with 10-20 cm fiberglass absorbant	As in 3; 19 loudspeakers rear wall, 9; sidewall, door side, 4; other sidewall, 6)
	Couch and 3 upholstered chairs; control window; control desk; ◆ artificial head; 2 units, 096, Klein & Hummel	Couch and 3 upholstered chairs; control window; control desk; ◆ artificial head; 2 units, 096, Klein & Hummel	Couch and 3 upholstered chairs; control window; control desk; ◆ artificial head; 2 units, 096 Klein & Hummel	Couch and 3 upholstered chairs; control window; control desk; ◆ artificial head; 2 units, 096, Klein & Hummel

FIG. 13.39 Properties of four different control rooms, all of identical size with different surface treatment and furnishings. MF = mineral fiber.

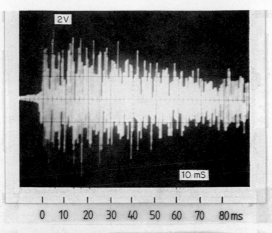

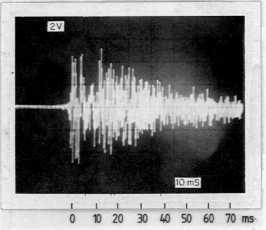

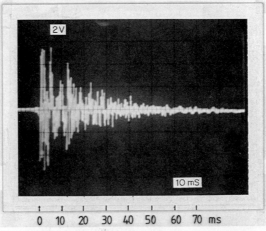

FIG. 13.40 Impulse reflectograms of three different control rooms pictured in Fig. 13.35. Reverberation times are (1) 0.8 s, (2) 0.4 s, and (3) 0.2 s.

13.5.7 Noise in Control Rooms

Control rooms are very often affected by high, disturbing noise levels of 35 to 45 dBA. The sound arises from technical equipment that sometimes must be ventilated: air conditioning, tape recorders, and so on. The corresponding noise-rating curves have been shown in Figs. 13.34, 13.35, and 13.36.[11] These high noise levels are less important when listening at high volume, as noted by Kuhl[48] and Burd.[49] To exclude many of these noise sources from the control room, a separate equipment room may be designed, as seen in many of the examples in Sec. 13.2. It may often be necessary to monitor at high sound levels in order to assess the importance of noise in the studio or during the recording process. Further improvement in reducing the noise level can be achieved by using noise reduction systems.

13.5.8 Modes and Equalization

The monitoring system is usually equalized by narrowband filters.[51] There are some difficulties in low-frequency regions where single modes may exist. Any mode forms a mode pattern with hills and valleys, as seen in Fig. 13.28. An example of improving acoustical conditions at a very low frequency is shown in Fig. 13.41. The left loudspeaker did not produce a sufficient sound level at the listening position (see curve 1). While trying to equalize this channel, the studio engineer increased the gain of the channel until the loudspeaker burned out. The reason for this was that the listening position or the measurement position for equalization, which was the same position, was in a deep valley in the mode pattern. By introducing reflecting surfaces at several positions in the room, the mode pattern was moved so that the listening position was no longer in the valley. Curve 3 shows the increased SPL from the left loudspeaker, which now was comparable with that from the right loudspeaker. The same effect could not be produced by introducing

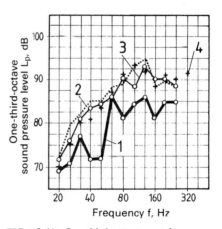

FIG. 13.41   One-third-octave sound pressure levels at the listening position in a small control room. *Curve 1:* Left loudspeaker. *Curve 2:* Right loudspeaker. *Curve 3:* Same as curve 1 after constructional changes. *Curve 4:* Same as curve 3 for right loudspeaker.

standard sound-absorbing materials, even 40-cm-thick mineral wool. Equalization of the monitoring chain in the control room must be approached cautiously if a situation such as that described above exists.

Another important aspect of equalization at low frequencies is found in small rooms in which there are only a few modes with a wide frequency spacing. To attenuate a single mode a narrowband filter should be used.

The aim of acoustic design should be to create a monitoring room with sufficient sound-absorbing material covering the whole frequency range so that equalization is not (or almost is not) necessary.

REFERENCES

1. W. Green and J. P. Maxfield, "Public Address Systems," presented at the Midwinter Convention of the American Institute of Electrical and Electronics Engineers, New York (1923).

2. F. Trendelenburg, *Einführung in die Akustik,* Springer-Verlag, Berlin, 1939, p. 123.

3. B. F. Hertz, "100 Years with Stereo: The Beginning," presented at the 68th Convention of the Audio Engineering Society, Hamburg (1981).

4. A. Moles and F. Trautwein, "Das elecktroakustische Institut Hermann Scherchen," *Gravesaner Blätter,* no. 5, 51–64 (1956).

5. R. Vermeulen, "Akustik und Elektroakustik," *Gravesaner Blätter,* no. 7 (1960).

6. R. Vermeulen, "Stereo Reverberation," *Philips Tech. Rev.,* **17** (1956).

7. R. S. Shankland, "Architectural Acoustics in America to 1930," *J. Acoust. Soc. Am.,* **61** (1977).

8. W. C. Sabine, *The Collected Papers on Acoustics,* Dover, New York, 1964.

9. L. L. Beranek and J. W. Kopec, "Wallace C. Sabine, Acoustical Consultant," *J. Acoust. Soc. Am.,* **69** (1981).

10. R. Thiele, "Richtungsverteilung und Zeitfolge der Schallrückwürfe in Räumen," *Acustica,* **3** (1953).

11. *Noise Rating Curves,* ISO R1996, 1971.

12. U. Kath, "Ein Hörspielstudio mit variabler Nachhallzeit," *Rundfunktech. Mitt.,* no. 1 (1972).

13. E. J. Voelker and M. Brückmann, "Raum- und Bauakustik des neuen Funkhauses des Hessischen Rundfunks in Kassel," *Fortschr. Akustik,* 439–442, VDI-Verlag, Düsseldorf (1973).

14. E. J. Voelker, "Akustik und Aufnahmetechnik im modernen Hörfunk- und Fernsehstudio—Anforderungen im Wandel," *NTG Fachber.,* **56,** VDE-Verlag, Berlin (1976).

15. E. J. Voelker, "The Alteration of the Reverberation Times in a Small Theater and a Concert Hall Using Loudspeaker Equipment," presented at the 40th Convention of the Audio Engineering Society, Los Angeles (1971), preprint 785 (F-3).

16. J. Meyer, *Akustik und musikalische Aufführungspraxis,* Buch Verlag des Musikinstrument, Frankfurt.

17. L. L. Beranek, *Music, Acoustics and Architecture,* Wiley, New York, 1962.

18. H. Wilkens, "Kopfbezüglich Stereophonie—Ein Hilfsmittel für Vergleich und Beurteilung verschiedener Raumeindrücke," *Acustica,* **26,** 213–221 (1972).

19. D. Gottlob, "Vergleich objektiver akustischer Parameter mit Ergebnissen subjektiver Untersuchungen an Konzertsälen" (1973).

20. W. Kuhl, "Optimale akustische Gestaltung von Räumen für Aufführende, Zuhörer und Schallaufnahmen," *Schalltechnik,* no. 20 (1956).

21. H. Kuttruff, *Room Acoustics,* Applied Science Publishers, London, 1973.

22. T. J. Schultz, "Problems in the Measurement of Reverberation Time," *J. Audio Eng. Soc.,* **11,** 4 (1963).

23. "EBU: Determination of the Acoustical Properties of Control Rooms and Listening Rooms for Broadcasting Programmes," *Tech. Rec.,* R-22, Brussels (1980).

24. H. Larsen, "Reverberation Process at Low Frequencies," *Tech. Rev.,* no. 4 (1978).

25. G. M. Jackson and M. G. Leventhal, "The Acoustics of Domestic Rooms," *Appl. Acoust.,* no. 5 (1972).

26. L. Cremer and H. A. Müller, *Die wissenschaftlichen Grundlagen der Raumakustik,* S. Hirzel-Verlag, Stuttgart, 1976, p. 227.

27. K. Duncan, *Studio Design Requirements for the Next Decade,* Sierra Audio, Burbank, Calif., 1979.

28. U. Kath, "Abstimmbare Helmholtzresonatoren und die Messung ihrer Absorptionsfläche," presented at the Fifth International Congress on Acoustics, Liège (1965).

29. *Luft- und Trittschalldämmung,* DIN 52210 (ISO R717), Beuth-Verlag, Berlin.

30. *Schallschutz im Hochbau,* DIN 4109, Beuth-Verlag, Berlin.

31. H. Moller, "Relevant Hi-Fi Tests at Home," presented at the 47th Convention of the Audio Engineering Society, Copenhagen (1974).

32. *Impulsschallpegelmessgerät,* DIN 45633 (IEC 651), Beuth-Verlag, Berlin.

33. *Peak Programme Meter,* DIN 45406 (IEC 268-10).

34. E. J. Voelker, "Zur Akustik im Büro—Neue Wege beim Bau des Verlagshauses Bertelsmann," *Technik am Bau,* no. 2, 120–123 (1976).

35. E. J. Voelker, "Das akustische optimale Grossraumbüro," *VDI Ber.,* **291,** 121–128 (1977).

36. W. Kuhl, "Zulässige Geräuschpegel in Studios, Konzertsälen und Theatern," *Acustica* (1964).

37. C. W. Kosten, *Acustica,* 10 (1960).

38. "Beurteilung von Arbeits- und Freizeitlärm hinsichtlich Gehörschäden," *VDI-Richtlinie,* 2058, VDI-Verlag, Düsseldorf.

39. J. Rémonit, "Dynamics of Discs," presented at the 44th Convention of the Audio Engineering Society (1973).

40. K. Müller, "Welche Konzertdynamik wünscht der Rundfunkhörer," *Rundfunketech. Mitt.,* **14**(6), 268–274 (1970).

41. H. Schiesser, "Optimale Lautstärke von Rundfunkprogrammen beim Hörer und im Studio," *Fernseh Kino Tech.,* no. 11, 391–397 (1971).

42. W. K. E. Geddes, "The Influence of Listening Conditions on the Quality of Reproduced Speech" (1954).

43. H. Haas and H. Kösters, "Ein neuer Gesichtspunkt für die Entwicklung von Lautsprechern?" *Tech. Hausmitt. Nordwestdeutschen Rundfunks,* annual 3 (1951).

44. D. Davis, "Engineering an LEDE™ Control Room for a Broadcasting Facility," presented at the 67th Convention of the Audio Engineering Society, New York (1980), preprint 1688.

45. W. Reinicke, "Eine dünne, leichte Wand mit hoher Schalldämmung," dissertation, Berlin (December 1983).

46. E. J. Voelker, "Bauakustische Massnahmen bei den neuen Sprecher- und Tonträgerräumen des Hessischen Rundfunks," *Rundfunktech. Mitt.,* **10,** H-6 (1966).

47. F. Mechel and J. Royar, "Hohlraumdämpfung in zweischaligen Trennwänden," *WKSB,* H-5 (1977).

48. W. Kuhl, "Keine Gehörschädigung durch Tanzmusik, sinfonische Musik und Maschinengeräusche beim Rundfunk," *Rundfunktech. Mitt.* (1976).

49. A. Burd, *Sound Recording Practice,* Oxford University Press, London, 1977, pp. 17–33.

50. E. J. Voelker, "Gezielte raumakustische Ausgestaltung der Nachrichtensprecherräume des Hessischen Rundfunks und der Studios der Werbung im Rundfunk GmbH in Frankfurt," *Schalltechnik,* **26**(67/68), 1–9 (1966).

51. E. J. Voelker, "Control Rooms for Music Monitoring," *J. Audio Eng. Soc.,* **33**(6), 452–462 (1985).

52. E. J. Voelker, Acoustical Design of Control Rooms for Speech and Music Monitoring," presented at the 74th Convention of the Audio Engineering Society, New York (1983), preprint 2002 (C-3).

CHAPTER 14

POSTPRODUCTION SYSTEMS AND EDITING*

Tomlinson Holman
Assistant Professor, School of Cinema-Television, University of Southern California; Corporate Technical Director, Lucasfilm Limited, San Rafael, California

14.1 DEFINITION OF POSTPRODUCTION

14.1.1 Relationship to Production

The term *postproduction* loosely applies to all the processes needed to prepare finished picture and sound masters from the original-production materials ready for duplication and distribution. The term can be more explicitly defined by discipline:

Motion Pictures. The course of a motion-picture production is broken down in various stages as *preproduction,* consisting of scripting, production planning, and the like; *production,* consisting of principal and second-unit photography with their attendant production sound recording; and *postproduction,* consisting of picture editing and the making of special visual effects, as well as our primary interest, sound postproduction. It consists of finishing the sound tracks available from production while adding new ones as needed to make a coherent final sound mix.

Television. The terminology follows a similar course, but the term *production* is more likely to embrace the total sum of the project, and the term *principal photography* generally gives way to *taping.* Postproduction (often abbreviated in slang to the one word *post*) still encompasses the activity needed to produce finished-looking and -sounding masters.

---

* Registered trademarks and trademark names used in this chapter: Dolby® is a registered trademark of Dolby Laboratories, Inc.; Spectral Recording™ is a trademark of Dolby Laboratories, Inc.; Dolby® Surround™ is a trademark of Dolby Laboratories, Inc.; THX® is a registered trademark of Lucasfilm, Ltd.; Nuoptix™ is a trademark of Nuoptix Inc.; Nagra™ is a trademark of Nagra Magnetic Recorders, Inc.; Compact Cassette™ is a trademark of Philips; Q-Lock™ is a trademark; and Editron™ is a trademark of Editron.

14.1.2   Similarities and Differences between Picture Sources

Whether a motion picture or television is being shot, it is the job of the production sound recordist to record sound tracks which capture the actors' performances as accurately as possible. In order to do this, a medium different from the one carrying the picture is generally used, since it is difficult to optimize analog media for best picture and sound quality simultaneously. Since the picture and sound occupy different media, some method of providing for absolute synchronization between them is necessary, as a speed drift measured in only very small fractions of a percent becomes obvious in a synchronous sound take within seconds. So the material delivered to the transfer room for the start of the postproduction process usually includes recordings of the actors' performances, perhaps some usable sound effects from the set or possibly audience reaction, and a means of synchronizing the sound to the picture.

It is the task of the sound postproduction crew, consisting of sound designers, editors, mixers, transfer-room operators, and others, to take the production sound track and manipulate it as necessary, including even substituting dialogue where necessary, and combine it with sound effects and music to produce the final experience sought by the director and producer of the production. In television usage, the addition of tracks other than production ones is termed *sweetening.*

Note.   There are situations in which the distinction between production and postproduction activity as described above becomes more vague. For example, music may be prerecorded in a multitrack studio, played back on the set for a dance number while being shot, then used in postproduction as a component of the sound of the scene. Since the same personnel and equipment are often involved in prerecording and postproduction, the distinctions become blurred. We will describe conventional, linear production first, then have a word to say about such complex production later.

14.1.3   Production Planning

As we shall see through the course of this chapter, the relationship between shooting and postproduction must be close, since there are many interdependencies if operations are to run smoothly. There are legions of stories about problems which could have been solved through production planning. A disproportionate share of these stories involves synchronization of sound to picture, so a thorough understanding of the issues involved is one of the tasks of this chapter. But audio recording can also cause problems: there is the story of the picture recorded all in stereo that sounded great at the dailies but produced perspective jumps when cut together, requiring expensive looping of the entire picture. By understanding the underlying processes, personnel in both production and postproduction can cooperate to produce film and television smoothly.

14.2   TRANSFER ROOM: INPUT TO THE POSTPRODUCTION PROCESS

14.2.1   Audio Standards for Playback of Source Materials

Original-production materials may be supplied to postproduction in many forms; so the transfer room must be prepared to play them back aligned to a variety of audio and synchronization standards.

The most common form of field recording for film remains the ¼-in analog tape, which is difficult to beat for its utility, employing as it does high-quality and very portable recorders that also have low power consumption, such as the Nagra. Although some inroads into the universal popularity of ¼-in analog recording have occurred in the form of pulse-code-modulation (PCM) digital audio converted to video and recorded on portable videotape recorders, such recording currently requires larger equipment of greater power consumption than the analog method and thus has not won a major market position. At this writing, consumer rotary digital audio tape (R-DAT) recorders are to be introduced soon. Whether this format is robust enough for professional use and whether machines having other features needed by professionals (such as a time-code channel) will be introduced remain to be seen.

Of the various methods of production sound recording, ¼-in-wide full-track magnetic analog monaural recordings, at 7½ in/s, with National Association of Broadcasters (NAB) equalization[1] in United States usage, on 5-in reels of low-print-through tape, are easily the most popular. Many recordings are also made with ¼-in-wide two-track magnetic analog stereo recording, at 7½ or 15 in/s, with NAB equalization in the United States, although many of these "stereo" recordings are better described as twin-channel mono, since the channels are often used to record uncorrelated information. In television, the sound tracks of the original videotape are sometimes used for production sound recording, or some channels of a multitrack recorder can be used to record the original directly. For low-budget filmmaking, a method has been commercialized to record audio on one of the stereo pair of conventional Compact Cassette channels, with 60-Hz synchronization on the other.

The task of the transfer room is to convert the original materials into another medium, usually magnetic film for motion pictures or selected tracks of a multitrack recorder for television. It is extremely important that this task be done with strict adherence to standards since transfers made months apart must intercut without any audible change. To ensure this goal, at least standardization of azimuth, equalization, and level must be practiced.

Azimuth. Full-track 7½ in/s recordings are highly susceptible to azimuth error since the track is very wide and the tape speed is relatively slow. Also, many field recorders are infrequently aligned. So it is essential to match the playback machine's azimuth to the original. The tone oscillator on Nagra recorders facilitates matching since the tone is not pure but has a deliberately added *spike* in an otherwise sinusoidal waveform. By using either a spectrum analyzer or the ear, it is relatively easy to set azimuth from the tone by adjusting for maximum high-frequency content; the tone is usually recorded at the head of each reel. (The setup from *one* field recorder is usually stable: changes come as the transfer room constantly interchanges among tapes made on a variety of recorders.)

Azimuth in other media must also be adhered to, at least by adjustment to relevant test tapes. Audio on videotape is often hampered from attaining the highest-quality interchangeability by azimuth differences between machines on which the original is recorded and played.

Equalization. Relatively small frequency-response differences are known to be easily audible on A/B tests, and this accounts for the need to maintain frequency response accurately. (After all, the editing process produces a nearly constant stream of A/B's, that is, one for each cut.)

In the Nagra machines, the spiky sinusoid is factory-adjusted so that the ninth harmonic is at precisely -28 dB re the fundamental (the frequencies are 1.1 and

10 kHz). So playback equalization can be checked with an audio-spectrum analyzer, such as a Hewlett-Packard 3580A or a one-third-octave bandpass filter centered at 10 kHz, which can resolve the harmonics separately.

For other machines, a direct recording from a *pink-noise generator,* displayed on a one-third-octave real-time analyzer, can prove flatness of equalization.

CCIR Equalization. In United States usage, NAB equalization of 3180 and 50 μs (corresponding to 50- and 3150-Hz break frequencies) is used. Most European recorders are set to IEC-DIN-CCIR* equalization of ∞ and 35 μs. A correction factor is given in Table 14.1, which specifies the amount of equalization needed

TABLE 14.1 Equalization for CCIR-Recorded Tapes Played on NAB-Equalized Player

Frequency, Hz	Level, dB
25	+6.6
50	+2.6
125	+0.3
250	−0.2
500	−0.2
1,000	0
2,000	−0.7
4,000	−1.6
8,000	−3.0
10,000	−3.1
16,000	−3.1

to correct a tape recorded to CCIR standards played on a machine having NAB equalization. This is a problem commonly encountered by transfer facilities handling original materials shot in Europe. For a discussion of the time constants and the relevant equations which specify the frequency response of the flux on the tape, see Chap. 10.

For other media, adherence to the standards relevant for the particular medium is equally important.

Level Setting. Most monaural recordings are made with a quasi-peak-responding modulometer for program-material setting where 0 dB equals 320 nWb/m. The level-setting tone is at −8 dB re 320 nWb/m DIN in mono Nagra machines, which makes the tone level 118 nWb/m ANSI (American National Standards Institute), equaling −4 dB re the reference fluxivity 185 nWb/m. For a discussion of ANSI versus DIN flux levels, see Chap. 10. SMPTE EG-15, *Recording Level for Dialog in Motion-Picture Production,* gives information about recording with such a meter.

In Nagra stereo machines, the modulometer is set for 510 nWb/m DIN; the original impetus for a higher level in stereo was that it improved interchange-

---

* IEC = International Electrotechnical Commission; DIN = Deutsche Industrie Normenanschus; CCIR = International Radio Consultative Committee.

ability with mono on a full-track machine and tape-distortion-reduction circuitry kept distortion low. Of course, the added center synchronization channel prevents using tapes from stereo machines on mono machines, but the gain in signal-to-noise (S/N) ratio for equal-distortion performance nevertheless is valuable. The level-setting tone is again at -8 dB, which converts to 188 nWb/m ANSI, sufficiently close to 185 nWb/m to be interchangeable.

To see how the level is set for recording to another medium, consult Sec. 14.2.4, "Transfer Processes."

Print-Through.   Analog magnetic-tape recording is subject to *print-through,* a layer-to-layer transfer of information in storage. Print-through is often the worst noise problem on production sound recordings that have been made in quiet, dead studio environments since the "holes" of near silence between syllables of speech promote the audibility of printed-through information. Various actions have been taken against print-through, including using tape optimized for print-through characteristics on production sound recordings, storing tape tails out and at moderate temperature, using companding noise reduction such as Dolby A on such recordings, selectively reducing the level of print-through by running the tape past a head excited with small amounts of bias current (which has the property of reducing print more than the principal recording; see Chap. 10 for an explanation), and, as a last resort, selectively scraping the magnetic oxide off the sprocketed sound track in editing.

Videotape Sources.   For many television applications, the original sound source is recorded directly on one or more of the original-production videotape audio channels. Such recording serves well for many nondemanding services, but the longitudinal track of 1-in type C videotape and ¾-in type E U-matic video cassettes have less low-frequency headroom and more noise than audio tape or film, thus limiting quality at the source. (The differences are 8 dB less headroom for equal distortion at 200 Hz, but with equal high-frequency performance, and 10dB greater weighted noise, measured with representative samples of contemporary video and audio media.[2] The differences arise out of the need to optimize the videotape for very-short-wavelength recording rather than audio properties.)

14.2.2   Synchronization Methods

There are two levels of synchronization: simple absolute-speed control, called *resolving,* which was the first available method; and synchronization via the SMPTE (Society of Motion Picture and Television Engineers) time code, which provides absolute position as well as speed. These are tabulated for the various media in Table 14.2. The 60-Hz-based methods of synchronization provide correct absolute speed, but they do not provide an absolute time reference; i.e., they give no start point. For this, conventional production makes use of the time-honored clapboard slate. (Note that throughout the following discussion 60 Hz is used generically; in Europe, 50 Hz is used for the same purpose.)

The synchronization signal for making the nominal 60 Hz, for both mono and stereo ¼-in recordings, must be derived from the same source as the camera. Most often today, the camera uses a speed servo controlled from a crystal oscillator, making its speed performance very precise, and the tape recorder has its own crystal oscillator, divided down to 60 Hz. This is the simplest system in practice because it is wireless, permitting great distance between the camera and the

TABLE 14.2 Synchronization Methods for Various Media

Source	Relative speed	Absolute position
¼-in monaural	60-Hz neopilot-tone*	Clapboard slate
¼-in stereo	13.5-kHz carrier, frequency-modulated at 60 Hz*	Clapboard slate
¼-in stereo time code†	Center-track time code†	Time code†
Compact Cassette	60 Hz on one channel*	Clapboard slate
All videotape	SMPTE time code† recorded on cue or audio channel or vertical-interval time code† in picture	SMPTE time code†
Multitrack audio tape	60 Hz on one channel,* or SMPTE time code† on one channel, or both on two channels	Clapboard slate SMPTE time code†
Digital audio encoded as video on video tape in various formats: Sony F1, 1610; dbx 700; etc.	Video record-play cycle maintains crystal accuracy; alternatively, SMPTE time code†	Clapboard slate SMPTE time code†

* Source for 60 Hz on sound recorder *must* match camera source.
† Source for SMPTE time code must match same code standard recorded by camera (see Sec. 14.3.9).

recorder. However, if the camera uses a synchronous motor operated off the power lines, then the pilot-tone synchronization source must be a sample of the same power line, or if the camera operates on a non-crystal-controlled dc motor, then it will include a pilot-tone generator on the shaft of the motor intended for connection to the pilot-tone input of the tape recorder. *Unless these conventions have been observed on the set, playing the tape in the transfer room to produce a copy on sprocketed magnetic film having the identical frame-for-frame length of the picture will be impossible.*

Common Mono Recordings. For mono ¼-in recordings, the synchronization method most common is called neo-pilot-tone. It uses two narrow out-of-polarity tracks of 60 Hz (for 24 frames per second, in United States usage), which together cancel at the full-track play head but which can be recovered by the same two-narrow-track head that recorded them by wiring the two head windings out of polarity. The neo-pilot-tone tracks are each 0.4 mm wide, separated by 0.45 mm, and are centered on the tape width.

Resolvers. To play the tape in frame-for-frame synchronization with a sprocketed recorder, a device called a *resolver* is used. Several different methods are employed for resolving. In the most common method, the resolver compares the 60 Hz on the tape to the 60-Hz reference for the sprocketed recorder and produces a correction voltage for the ¼-in machine's speed-control servo, ensuring synchronization. *The resolver must have available both the 60 Hz from the original tape and the 60-Hz reference used for the sprocket drive.* The sprocket-drive reference might be the power line, or it could be an internal crystal oscillator; the source controlling the speed of the film must be applied to the reference input of the resolver. An older method simply drives the sprocketed recorder from an amplified version of the 60 Hz from the tape.

One particular problem for resolvers is receiving tapes from Europe with 50-Hz nominal sync while generally having available only 60-Hz-based equipment. For this, a reference generator capable of conversion to accommodate the correct combination of frame rate and pilot-tone frequency must be employed. Alternatively, a phase-locked–loop-based device may be used to produce 60 Hz locked to the source 50 Hz. Then the derived 60 Hz can be applied to the input of the resolver.

Some resolvers can also use a time-code input by simply stripping all the time-code information except the frame rate and comparing it with the reference frequency. For example, a time code of 30 frames per second is an even submultiple of the 60-Hz reference. In such cases, a slate is still required for absolute synchronization.

More commonly with time-code recordings a *synchronizer* rather than a resolver is used. Synchronizers are discussed in Sec. 14.3.9.

Other Mono Methods.   An older method still in some use is called Picsync, developed by Fairchild. It uses a 14-kHz carrier amplitude modulated at 60 Hz mixed in with the audio. In this case the playback equipment contains complementary notch and peak filters which separate the audio and the sync signal and further demodulates the 60 Hz from the 14-kHz carrier for application to the resolver.

In addition, there are a number of other methods of recording a 60-Hz synchronization signal which are of historical interest. They are documented in the *Audio Cyclopedia.*[3]

Stereo Methods.   For stereo ¼-in recordings, one of two synchronization methods is now used. The older but still more common synchronization method uses a narrow center channel, between the audio tracks, on which a 13.5-kHz carrier frequency is frequency-modulated at 60 Hz (the channel also has capacity for an intercom-quality voice channel, useful for slating). The center track is 0.014 in wide, and the audio tracks use the NAB two-track recording format, in which the tracks are 0.080 in wide, rather than the 0.102-in stereophonic format used in *butterfly* heads in Europe. Once the frequency has been demodulated, resolving proceeds along the same lines as for mono recordings.

New Nagra machines record SMPTE time code on the center track from a multistandard time-code generator built into the recorder. *It is essential that the multistandard generator be set to the correct type of time code, which is the same one as the corresponding image recorder.* The switch-settable standards are 24 frames per second for film applications, 25 frames per second for European film or television (European Broadcasting Union, or EBU), 29.97 frames per second for United States color television ("color time" with optional internal crystal), and 30 frames per second for United States black-and-white television ("real time"). In addition, the 29.27-frames-per-second mode requires a choice of "drop frame" (eliminating the error of 29.97 ÷ 30 by dropping frames to restore real time) or "non-drop frame." The names in quotation marks are from ANSI-SMPTE 12M-1986.

There are four methods to record time code on motion-picture cameras. The simplest one uses a slate with a running code matching the sound code, although this method only provides synchronization while the slate can be seen in the picture. There are two optical methods of recording time code: one for serial code with dimensions documented in SMPTE Recommended Practice 116-1983, *Dimensions of Photographic Control and Data Record on 35-mm Motion-Picture Camera Negatives;* and another being developed for a parallel code. At the time of writing, debate is being heard both nationally and internationally on the inter-action among the so-called superformats, utilizing a greater picture area on the negative than normal, and various time-code proposals. The fourth method uses magnetic recording on a low-dispersion magnetic coating, documented in SMPTE Recommended Practice 137-1986, *Data Tracks on Low-Disperison Magnetic Coatings on 35-mm Motion-Picture Film.*

For audio-cassette recordings, one channel of the normally inseparable stereo pair is assigned to be a 60-Hz pilot track from either a crystal-oscillator source or from camera-derived pilot tone. A resolver is used in transfer to control the speed of the modified cassette recorder.

One simple further method has not been mentioned, although it is often used in some applications, particularly music recording: one track of a stereo recorder can be devoted to recording picture-synchronous 60 Hz.

For videotape and multitrack audio-tape formats, SMPTE time code is often used as a reference. Once again, the note regarding multiple standards for time code applies, as on the stereo ¼-in recorders which employ time code. Alternatively, or additionally on multitrack recorders, a channel can be devoted to recording picture-synchronous 60 Hz.

14.2.3   Transfer Recorder Standards

For motion-picture production, 35-mm film can contain from one to six tracks. See Table 14.3 for the track dimensions and numbering.

Monaural recording generally is made on stripe-coat magnetic film, which carries two "stripes": one wide enough to record a 0.200-in track and a *balance stripe* to ensure even winding. Recently, SMPTE has standardized the balance stripe so that secondary recordings, such as time code, can be recorded on it.

All other track configurations are usually recorded on *full-coat* magnetic film, with coating extending across the width of the film, although a limited amount of three-stripe-coated film is in use for the three-track format. The tracks are normally used by following these rules:

1. Track assignments virtually always use and start on Track 1, so that it always contains identifying information such as head slates and the like.

2. Tracks are assigned so that pairs representing stereophonic information are as close together as possible; e.g., a two-channel tape is copied to Tracks 1 and 2 of a three-track format if a stereo copy is desired. An example, using the same rule, is a stereo source pair copied to Tracks 2 and 3 of a three-track format with a monaural sum recorded on Track 1. This permits playback in monaural on a simple stripe dubber or editing machine but in full stereo with a three-track head.

3. If the tracks are intended to represent positional information, then the typical use is left, center, and right, corresponding to Tracks 1, 2, and 3 in the three-track format; left, center, right, and surround in the four-track format; and left, left extra, center, right extra, right, and surround in the six-track format.

4. If the tracks are for television submasters, the track assignments are given in SMPTE Recommended Practice 147, *Audio Channel Assignments of Multi-Channel Sub-Masters Used in Preparation for Two-Track Masters for Transfer to Video.* (See Fig. 14.1.)

TABLE 14.3 Magnetic-Film Track Dimensions, Numbers, and Locations for Two, Three, Four, and Six Tracks

A. Dimensions for Two Magnetic Sound Records

Dimensions	Inches	Millimeters
A	0.200 + 0.004 − 0	5.0 + 0.1 − 0
A_1	0.150 + 0.004 − 0	3.8 + 0.1 − 0
B	0.339 ± 0.002	5.6 ± 0.06
C	0.725 ± 0.002	18.4 ± 0.06
H ref.	1.337	34.97

B. Dimensions for Three Magnetic Sound Records

Dimensions	Inches	Millimeters
A	0.200 + 0.004 − 0	5.0 + 00.1 − 0
B	0.119 ± 0.002	8.6 ± 0.05
C	0.350 ± 0.002	8.9 ± 0.05
D	0.700 ± 0.002	17.8 ± 0.05
H ref.	1.377	34.97

C. Dimensions for Four Magnetic Sound Records

Dimensions	Inches	Millimeters
A	0.150 + 0.004 − 0	3.8 + 0.1 − 0
B	0.314 ± 0.002	7.9 ± 0.05
C	0.250 ± 0.002	6.4 ± 0.05
D	0.500 ± 0.002	12.8 ± 0.05
E	0.750 ± 0.002	19.2 ± 0.05
H ref.	1.377	34.87

D. Dimensions for Six Magnetic Sound Records

Dimensions	Inches	Millimeters
A	0.100 ± 0.002	2.40 ± 0.10
B	0.289 ± 0.002	7.34 ± 0.05
C	0.150 ± 0.002	4.06 ± 0.05
D	0.320 ± 0.002	8.12 ± 0.05
E	0.480 ± 0.002	12.18 ± 0.05
F	0.540 ± 0.002	15.24 ± 0.05
G	0.500 ± 0.002	20.30 ± 0.05
H ref.	1.377	34.97

Note: The metric values listed in the tables are not exact conversions and deviate from accepted conversion practices. They are based upon the practice of those countries using the metric system. Head assemblies made to either system of dimensions will, for all practical purposes, be interchangeable.

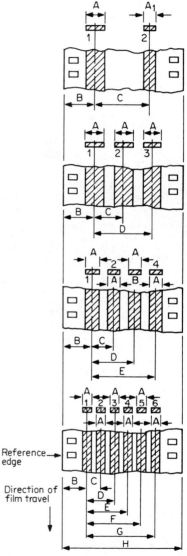

Reference edge

Direction of film travel

Viewed base down (magnetic surface facing upward)

**Audio Channel Assignments of Multi-Channel Sub-Masters used in
Preparation for Two-Track Masters for Transfer to Video**

1. Scope

This Recommended Practice specifies the audio channel assignments of multi-channel sub-master recordings for transfer to two-channel stereo audio tracks on video tape and video cassettes.

2. Format

2.1 Non-sprocketed tape. The recording may be 16 or 24 channel on 1 or $2''$ audio tape.

2.2 35-mm magnetic film. The recording format may be on 3-track, 4-track, two 4-tracks interlocked, or 6-track.

3. Channel assignments

3.1 Using non-sprocketed tape or two 35-mm magnetic films interlocked, in the 4 track format (producing 8 channels):

Track	Program
1	Left Dialog
2	Right Dialog
3	Left Music
4	Right Music
5	Left Effects
6	Right Effects
7	Left Laugh or Sweetener
8	Right Laugh or Sweetener

3.2 Using 35-mm magnetic recording film, in the 3-track format, or the single 4-track format:

Track	Program
1	Left Music & Effects
2	Center Dialog
3	Right Music & Effects

3.3 Using 35-mm magnetic film, in the 6-track format:

Track	Program
1	Left Dialog
2	Right Dialog
3	Left Music
4	Right Music
5	Left Effects
6	Right Effects

3.4 For non-sprocketed formats the second to last track should be reserved for sync pulse and the last track should be reserved for SMPTE time code, using line-referenced non-drop frame. (However, if the video system is locked to a crystal or drop-frame code, then the same time base must be used for the audio reference.) The hour digits may be assigned to reel numbers and the minutes, seconds, and frames should be set to zero on the START frame of the SMPTE frame leader. (See SMPTE/RP136 Time and control codes for 24, 25 or 30 frame-per-second Motion Picture systems.)

FIG. 14.1   SMPTE Recommended Practice for Track Formats.

TABLE 14.4   ANSI-SMPTE Standards for 16-mm Magnetic Film

0.100-in track for release prints	ANSI PH22.112-1977
0.200-in edge track	ANSI PH22.97-1982
0.200-in center track	ANSI/SMPTE 218M-1985
Two 0.150-in audio records + control track	ANSI PH22.210M (proposed)
Equalization ("recorded characteristic")	ANSI/SMPTE 213M-1984

Formats on 17.5-mm film usually result from slitting 35-mm film into two equal strips; in this case, the record adjacent to the perforation marked *Track A* is the only relevant one (see Table 14.3*A*).

In the United States 16-mm magnetic film is used in documentary production, while in Europe it is widely used for television, including stereo formats. The applicable SMPTE-ANSI standards are listed in Table 14.4.

Track formats and standards for ¼-in, ½-in, 1-in, and 2-in analog audio tape are identical when used synchronized to picture as for general music recording (see Chap. 10 for track formats and equalization standards). Usually the highest-numbered track available will be used for SMPTE time code, and the second-highest-numbered track may be used, in addition, for 60-Hz reference. If only an absolute-speed reference is needed, such as for music recording which will be edited to picture without start-mark references, 60 Hz can be used alone. Crosstalk both from and to time-code channels can cause problems. Crosstalk from code to audio channels can prove highly audible, since the predominant energy in time code lies in the most sensitive frequency region for hearing. But crosstalk *into* code, from adjacent sound, can also cause problems. For example, it is not uncommon to put strong bass tracks on channels adjacent to code, since for crosstalk into the audio channel a filter can be applied to reduce the effect. But crosstalk of strong bass signals into time code can confuse synchronizers to the point of their not operating. It is advisable to test before vital synchronization is necessary.

If the tracks are used for television submasters, reference is again made to SMPTE RP-147.

Equalization.   SMPTE and international standards agree on ∞ and 35-μs time constants to describe the frequency response of the flux recorded on 35-mm film containing no picture. Sixteen-millimeter film uses ∞ and 70-μs equalization. Test films are available from commercial sources and SMPTE for setup to the relevant standard (see Chap. 17).

In using these test films, be certain to compensate for low-frequency side fringing, since the films are recorded full-width and the head responds to flux outside the area swept by the head tracks at low frequencies, as explained in Chap. 10. Table 14.5 details fringing for one widely used type of head assemblies. Although these amounts are typical of many heads, variations among designs mean that the exact values for each assembly should be determined by individual measurements. Head *bump* patterns of undulating low-frequency response also change with head wear, so a value measured on unworn heads will differ from that for fairly worn ones.

Caution.   Do not extrapolate the values in the table to other heads even from the same manufacturer, as the values of fringing are unique to a given model head, depending on shielding, other internal factors, and even wear.

TABLE 14.5 Amount to Be Subtracted from Reading to Account for Fringing Effects for MagnaTech Electronics 35-mm Recorders and Dubbers Using Branch & Appleby Hi-μ 80 Heads*

Format	Track or tracks	Frequency, Hz	Amount, dB
1-track ("stripe")	All	50	0.8
		100	0.5
3-track	All	50	0.6
		100	0.6
4-track	All	50	3.2
		100	1.5
6-track	1, 6	50	3.5
		100	1.6
6-track	2–5	50	1.5
		100	0.8

* Data from measurements made with full-track test film.

Level Setting. As discussed below in Sec. 14.2.4 under "Reference Fluxivities," the reference level for flux on magnetic film is 185 nWb/m (SMPTE EG-9, *Audio Recording Reference Level for Post-Production of Motion-Picture Related Materials*). For a discussion of transfer level, see Sec. 14.2.4.

Head-Height Setting. Many head-mounting arrangements require the user to set the *head height,* defined as the alignment of the head core or cores to the width of the records on the film, when changing heads. Simplifying this task are commercially available *buzz-track* test films[4] which have pairs of narrow tracks recorded just outside the area to be swept by the conventional core. Each pair of tracks is recorded with one higher- and one lower-frequency tone, which are the same for each pair. So a simple sum of all the channels displayed on a spectrum analyzer (or even just listened to) can be used to set the head height unambiguously.

14.2.4 Transfer Processes

This section will outline the *processing* possible in making a transfer from simple level setting to pitch-compensated speed changes to make dialogue fit.

Level Setting. Since it has been found by experiment that the headroom and S/N ratio of ¼-in tapes are similar to those of the magnetic film to which it will be copied (despite their equalization, track-width, and speed differences), the best day-to-day level-setting practice is to make the flux level in the recorded medium equal to the flux level in the source medium. Another important factor in choosing this *equal-flux method* is that we find in practice that the distortion buildup over the number of generations through which the signal will go is perceptually acceptable on even difficult program material.

Thus a 185 nWb/m test tape can be used to bring the output of the playback machine to the transfer room's standardized bus level, such as 0 dBu, and the 35-mm magnetic-film recorder can be aligned so that such an input level yields a flux level on the film of 185 nWb/m (see Table 14.6). This procedure will usually yield the best results since it is very repeatable and since the dynamic ranges of the source and recorded media are so close.

Alternatively, the Nagra tone from mono field tapes can be set to -4 dB re the studio bus level, and with the film recorder set so that the studio bus level produces 185 nWb/m the same result will be accomplished. (The stereo Nagra level tone should be equal to a 185 nWb/m test tape; thus the tapes would be set to the bus level directly.)

If the source medium should be very underrecorded or overrecorded, some correction may have to be applied to avoid pileup of noise or distortion. Level correction from conventional 1:1 copying should be noted so that identical copies can later be made for reprints.

TABLE 14.6 Comparison of Some Commonly Used Test-Tape Fluxivities to 185 nWb/m ANSI Reference Fluxivity

Test-tape fluxivity	dB re reference
185 nWb/m ANSI	0
250 nWb/m ANSI	+2.6
320 nWb/m DIN	+4.1

Summing Multiple Channels.   When two or more channels are combined, the resulting signal will usually have a higher peak level than in any of the source channels. However, the amount by which the peak level will be greater is unpredictable. For example, if a narrator is recorded identically on two channels of a source tape which are to be combined in transfer to make a single monaural channel, the addition will be by 6 dB. If, however, uncorrelated noise is recorded in two source channels, the level will increase by only 3 dB. Since cancellations between the source channels are possible (although unlikely), the level might even go down.

Therefore, the best rule of thumb on combining source channels is to make the copy with a peak flux level equal to the highest peak flux level in the highest single source channel. That is, with peak meters on each of the source and summed channels, adjust the gain so that the highest peak in the summed channels equals the highest peak in any one of the source channels. One advantage of this method is that it applies to any arbitrary number of source and summed channels. Most real-world stereo recordings will contain spatial information causing the need to lower the gain by *between* 3 dB (if the channels are equal in level but uncorrelated) and 6 dB (if the channels are completely correlated). This means that the gain must be lowered from that which would produce a 1:1 copy by 6 dB for the narrator example, by 3 dB for the uncorrelated noise, and by somewhere between 3 and 6 dB for average stereo material.

Reference Fluxivities.   The test-tape level used to align multitrack recorders has drifted upward as tape has improved, so that 250 nWb/m is a common reference fluxivity in music-recording studios today (see Table 14.6). In film sound, however, we are more greatly interested in interchangeability and intercuttability over the long run; so maintaining a constant-level reference over time is more important. For this reason, SMPTE[5] has standardized 185 nWb/m as the reference level for interchange (SMPTE EG-9, 1985). (When multitrack tapes from music studios are employed in postproduction, the reference fluxivity used is more commonly that of the music studio, such as 250 nWb/m.)

Digital Audio Sources. For PCM original recordings which must be copied to analog media for postproduction, the issue is: "What is the correct relationship between digital peak level (11111 . . .) and the peak flux on film?" Experts disagree by more than 12 dB on how this relationship should be set (if it were to be fixed), so for the present it is best to say that monitoring the peaks of modulation on a quasi-peak-responding meter from a digital source and setting the level so that the recorded film's dynamic range is used effectively are what is important. Also important again is the ability to do precisely the same dubbing months later for intercutting; therefore, all settings must be recorded.

Metering PCM digital audio recordings is made difficult by the abrupt overload characteristic of the medium. Near-instantaneous peak meters are required since digital overload even under 1 ms is audible on critical program material. For this reason, attack time constants of 0.1 to 0.5 ms are used to ensure that the meter captures the peak. Since there is no fixed relationship between peaks occurring in such short time intervals and those occurring in the longer time intervals captured by a quasi-peak meter or a volume-unit (VU) meter, no fixed level offset can be given as a rule of thumb. This factor is what leads to the "12-dB disagreement" mentioned above.

Companding Noise Reduction or Other Complementary Record-Play Processing. The use of companding noise reduction, explained in Chap. 12, is currently nearly universal for 35-mm magnetic-film recordings. Since the typical minimum number of generations that the sound encounters before reaching us in a 70-mm screening is six, noise reduction is essential. However, almost no field recordings are made with noise reduction since for the most part background noise on the set usually masks tape hiss (but note that noise reduction is useful in the reduction of print-through; see Sec. 14.2.1). [Note that the residual noise reduction action of Dolby-A at 1 kHz and reference level is enough ($\sim\frac{1}{2}$ dB) so that the noise reduction should be switched off for accurate level setting.] The newly introduced Dolby Spectral Recording™ process is likely to displace Dolby-A noise reduction as time goes by, since it offers both greater noise reduction and headroom extension, thus providing a larger dynamic range than heretofore available on analog media.

Polarity of Multiple Channels. Until recently most practitioners standardized only the relative polarity of multiple channels on a given machine, since if a pair of channels containing stereo material were to be added to make monaural, a polarity reversal *(relative polarity)* would cause a null in the important center information. Published evidence for the audibility of *absolute polarity* of audio signals has led SMPTE to publish Recommended Practice 134-1986, *Polarity for Analog Audio Magnetic Recording and Reproduction,* setting recommended practice for absolute polarity.

Off-Speed and Reverse-Direction Transfers. Frequently, editors and sound designers will ask for deliberately off-speed transfers. This technique is used especially with sound effects in order to make ordinary, day-to-day sounds unfamiliar to the listener, so that the sound indicates something other than what it is. Backward transfers are made as well, although this technique is limited by obviousness when reverberation is heard before the event causing it.

A special case of off-speed transfers is requested by dialogue editors: lengthening or shortening a *take* or *line* from an automated-dialogue replacement (also called *looping*) session so that it fits into the original performance. The speed change brings with it a corresponding pitch change that can be corrected by a digital electronic pitch shifter. For this reason, it is important that the speed-changing device on the playback machine have accurate percentage speed indication so the pitch shifter can be set for an equal and opposite correction. For the principles employed in pitch shifters, see Chap. 4.

Cleanup Devices. A continual dichotomy faces operators of a transfer room: should each transfer be made to sound as good as possible, employing all available cleanup techniques, or should all transfers be made identically, emphasizing the ability to intercut material? The first approach calls for many judgments on the part of the operator, such judgments being made over an often inadequate monitor system and out of context with the program material which will surround the transfer. Taking these arguments to heart leads to an assembly-line approach to the problem: make all transfers on the standards, and let the mixers do their job in cleaning up the sound when they can hear it in context over an appropriate monitor.

On the other hand, the program material is sometimes so badly distorted, hissy, or noisy from factors out of the control of the production sound recordist that perpetuating the problems will accumulate trouble. For example, if there is a great deal of very-low-frequency noise on a dialogue recording, it will intermodulate with the voice and "roughen" the recording. Thus it is best to get such noise out as early in the postproduction process as possible (although it is better to get it out before it gets on tape in the first place).

An added factor in the decision as to whether to employ cleanup devices in transfer is: "How is it going to sound at dailies?" Production sound recordists rise and fall on the strength of how the transfer sounds immediately after it is shot, before postproduction processing is applied. This problem is in the realm of politics and thus outside the scope of a handbook on audio technology.

Cleanup devices which could be used in transfer are the same ones used in cleanup in mixing and so are covered in Sec. 14.4.2.

Matching Other Transfers. It is hoped that the foregoing discussion has convinced the reader of the need to produce, above all else, *consistent* high-quality results from the transfer room. It is more important, however, that the results be *consistent* than that they be of the *highest quality* obtainable at any given time. While at first glance this may seem to be a heretical notion, there is a very good reason for the stance: intercuttability is all-important. That is, an editor must be able to take a new transfer and intercut it with transfers made months earlier. It is simply too big a job to keep track of the time when various transfers were made and to keep transfers made at the same time together in different reels for different treatment by the mixer. An editor must be able to cut in a single syllable of speech newly transferred with old material, and this need causes consistency to outweigh ultimate quality.

As an example, when dubbing backup digital recordings to magnetic film to match original magnetic-film recordings made on an ADR stage, it is more important to match the equalization of the original recorder than it is to make a perfectly flat recording. For this reason, all recording sessions ought to have recorded as frequently as possible (at least daily) 1-kHz tone at reference level and pink noise on the recorder in use. These two signals form a "Rosetta stone" for the particular recording session: level, azimuth, and equalization can all be derived *and subsequently matched in the transfer room.* In this way, transfers which are indistinguishable when interspersed with the original recording can be made.

14.2.5 Monitoring in the Transfer Environment

Most transfer rooms have limited audible monitoring capability. Some of the problems which arise are due to acoustical factors, and others to psychoacoustical ones. They include:

1. The small-volume rooms employed for transfer have low modal density at low frequencies, leading to unsmooth and uneven bass response.

2. The monitor loudspeakers are commonly not equalized for even a small-room extrapolation of the standardized theater electroacoustic response ISO (International Organization for Standardization) 2969 curve X and thus give the wrong high-frequency timbre. (To do this accurately, a dummy head must be employed.[6])

3. Despite acoustical treatment used to deaden both the transfer room and the theater environment so that the rooms add only a minimum of their own *room sound,* the ratio of direct to early-reflection to reverberant sound fields cannot be made the same in a small and a large room.

4. Transfer rooms usually operate without picture, thus giving a different psychological impression of the sound than if synchronized picture were shown (but showing the picture tends to mask problems with the sound).

The first and third of these problems are due purely to the physical size required by economic dictates of the transfer room, and they are not amenable to correction. The second problem can be solved by using the method outlined in Ref. 6. The fourth "problem" actually works in our favor, since it tends to exacerbate sound problems.

For these reasons, some transfer operators prefer to operate with headphones, duplicating the impression that the production sound recordist had of the original recording. With training, operators become good at making a mental picture of how different a recording sounds between headphones and the dubbing stage and learn to concentrate on problems which will be audible at subsequent stages. Unfortunately, headphones have the psychoacoustical effect of "compressing" sound, thus making low-level sounds, including reverberation, more audible than they are in normal loudspeaker playback.

14.3   EDITING

14.3.1 Tape Editing

Most motion-picture and television postproduction uses either sprocketed-film-based editing or one or more of various electronic systems usually based on SMPTE time code. But an additional editing mode should not be overlooked: simply cutting unsprocketed tape. This method is very useful to save expensive magnetic film, for example, when editing a voice-over narration. There simply is no reason to transfer material which later will be cut out by an editor.

Conventional tape-based editing is also useful for material which bears only a rough relationship to the picture and for which internal edits are more important than picture synchronization. An example is the cutting of temporary music tracks, that is, library music which bears no fixed relationship to picture (specifically composed music does usually have at least points of synchronization to picture). An editor might know that a specific length of time is needed for a particular cue and often can work more efficiently in cutting tape than in cutting film. Then the finished cue can be dubbed to film for editing into synchronism with the picture.

There are a few tricks of the trade to know about editing audio tape by physically splicing it:

1. Obviously, a higher tape speed makes editing easier than a lower speed, and a sharp cutting instrument works better than a dull one. Also, the tape machine must be equipped with a mode whereby the tape can be moved past the playback head slowly, back and forth, to find the precise point for an edit (this technique is called *rock-and-roll editing*).

2. Most editors work with three tape reels, or pancakes, at a time: one source reel and two output reels (one for *in-takes* or *kept-takes* and one for *out-takes*). With this method, tape from the source reel is progressively wound onto either the in-take or the out-take reel. This procedure leaves both the in-take reel and the out-take reel in the same order and thus facilitates changes which may arise. Another source reel may be needed if *room tone* is being cut for spacing between takes (see Par. 4), and more reels are necessary if the original recording is not in the order required for the finished product.

3. Splicing blocks offer a choice of 90° cuts or angled ones. The angled cut is used more often, as smoothing the transition in time from one piece of tape to another reduces the likelihood of hearing a click at the cut. On the other hand, certain kinds of edits, such as ones on plosives in speech, may benefit from an abrupt transition and so would use the 90° cut. For wide tapes, a splicing machine has been developed to give a "pinking shears" effect, producing a zigzag of diagonal cuts across the width of the tape while still maintaining close synchronism of the cut across the width along with the advantages of a smoothed transition.

4. Cutting a recording of room tone (also called *presence* or *atmosphere*) into the gaps between edited segments helps smooth transitions. The room tone must match the rest of the original recording and thus must be recorded at the time of the original at the same gain setting employed for the principal program material.

5. Leadering between takes is often done with plastic leader tape. Under low-humidity conditions, this tape can build up a static charge, exacerbated by winding back and forth on a tape transport. The static charge may discharge at the (grounded) heads and thus become crackling noise. Paper-based leader, although more fragile, is not a good enough insulator to build up charge and so is preferred. Note that leader tape without a magnetic layer is not useful for use with tapes recorded with time code, since many synchronizers need continuous code to "know where they are."

6. Splicing tape varies in quality. Some tapes ooze sticky material shortly after application and cause subsequent tape-handling problems. A test for the quality of splicing tape before use is suggested.

7. When tapes with splices are stored, they should be put through a wind cycle (rewound, then wound on at a speed that produces a smooth pack) at least once a year. Storage with tails out is recommended in Chap. 10.

8. If the reels being cut already have time code recorded on them, some means must be provided to resolve the frame rate of the original tape while re-recording continuous code on the finished reel; otherwise, synchronization will be lost. While this may not generally be important, since the reel is being edited in any case, one might still want long segments to stay in sync with the picture. Therefore, the synchronization means must be carried across to the edited tape. Since most of the electronic synchronizers to be used subsequently will generally not deal well with discontinuities in time code, continuous code is required. So two time-code tracks become necessary, one of original code and one of continuous code, and the continuous code must be locked to the frame rate of the original code as it is recorded.

9. Some formats of digital audio-tape recordings use error codes robust enough so that physical editing nearly identical to analog tape cutting is possible. Some differences may remain: one common one is a need for greater general cleanliness such as keeping the oxide side of the tape untouched.

10. For each editing specialization—dialogue, music, and sound effects—many of the techniques used to edit sprocketed film apply to cutting similar program material on unsprocketed tape. These are explained in Secs. 14.3.8 through 14.3.10.

14.3.2 Magnetic-Film Splicing

Splicing is an underlying requirement of all nonelectronic editing functions. Splicing of sprocketed film obeys many of the rules listed in Sec. 14.3.1 but in addition has the following requirements:

1. The diagonal angle for a sound splice is chosen so that the line of the splice does not go through sprocket holes, thus providing the best strength in the splice (documented in SMPTE Recommended Practice 129-1985, *Requirements for 35-mm, 16-mm and 8-mm Type S Tape Splices on Magnetic Audio Recording Motion-Picture Film*).

2. Perforated splicing tape, with the same width as the film to be spliced and having the same perforation pattern as the base film, is used.

3. Splicing blocks are used to provide precise angles and placement of cuts. These blocks have pins which register to the film perforations as well as integral cutting blades.

4. The condition of the splicing block, especially alignment of the cutting blade, is far more important in perforated-film cutting than in tape splicing because the backing is much thicker and correspondingly stronger for film than for tape.

14.3.3 Sync-Block Editing

The simplest form of synchronous editing for sprocketed magnetic film employs a *sync block*. This device uses multiple drive-sprocketed wheels on a common shaft to provide sprocket-locked synchronization; it also includes separate foot and frame counters. A frame-counter disk mounted on the front of the frontmost sprocketed wheel indicates frame lines as well as count (70-, 35-, and 17.5-mm film use more than one perforation per frame, so a frame line indicator is necessary; 16- and 8-mm film use only one perforation per frame, so a frame line indicator is not used). Both the foot and the frame counters can be reset to zero at any time.

Sync-block editing generally follows the principle that while film to the left of the block may or may not be *in sync,* film to the right of the block is always in sync. Typically the task of an editor using a sync block is to synchronize *dailies* or *rushes.* A work print consisting of *circled takes* (those chosen by the director at the time of shooting: "Cut—print it") is obtained from the laboratory or picture editor. Next, sound transfers corresponding to the circled takes must be obtained. Then, take by take, the clapboard slate beginning each take is found, and the frame in which the "sticks" come together is marked. Then the corresponding frame in the sound track is found, and the sound track is spliced so that picture and sound will be in sync. The sync block is used to provide:

1. Absolute synchronization
2. A method of hearing the sound track by means of magnetic heads mounted on the frame, together with an amplifier-speaker combination called a *squawk box*
3. A running foot and frame count, which can be converted into time as required

Sync-block editing generally depends on the film supplied on reels mounted on at least a pair of *rewinds.* Since differences in the thickness of picture and sound films would lead to differing diameters of the film packs for equal footages of film, the film-stock thickness favored by editors for sound is usually kept the same as for picture: about 0.005 in. (There are, however, mechanical slip clutches for use between film reels that will take up a difference in the speed of rotation of two adjacent reels and thus permit different thicknesses of film stock to be wound from a common shaft.)

14.3.4 Moviola Upright Editor

The Moviola upright editor is used to synchronize sound to picture by mounting a picture work print on the picture head, mounting sound film on the sound head, and locking and unlocking the mechanical connection between the heads as required. Typical practice is to maintain a roll of sound synchronous to picture by making up *dummy reels* of leader for the sound in the same length as the picture. Then sound film is substituted for the leader as needed. Cut reels are called *units;* the leader is usually old picture film *with the picture emulsion kept opposite the sound oxide* so that it does not rub off on sound heads and cause *spacing loss* (see Chap. 10). While using a Moviola, it is common practice to employ *film bins* for temporary storage, since feeding from reels may be inconvenient.

14.3.5 Flat-Bed Editors

There are a number of *flat-bed editors* on the market, including ones from KEM, Steenbeck (Fig. 14.2), and Moviola. These machines have electronic or mechanical means to synchronize *picture heads* with *sound heads.* The typical practice is the same as described in Sec. 14.3.4, with one difference: film is more likely to be kept on reels or in pancakes wound on cores than in film bins. Some editors prefer flat-bed editing machines to upright machines since flat-bed machines can be interlocked from one machine to the next, thus expanding the capacity to run

FIG. 14.2 Steenbeck flat-bed editor.

multiple tracks simultaneously. The ability to hear a number of units in combination, with at least separate volume controls, helps the editor preview the work
under way in context with other sound tracks.

14.3.6   Track Editing on Multitrack Recorders

Various systems have been developed to use multitrack tape recorders ranging
from 4 through 32 tracks. Some larger-scale systems even include multiple audio
machines. Such systems depend on SMPTE time and control code to produce
synchronization of the audio medium with the picture medium (see Sec. 14.3.11).
   Multitrack editing also depends on the ability of the recorder electronics to
punch in and *punch out* on each channel separately or on any combination of
channels. The *punch* terms refer to the ramping up and down of bias, audio, and

erase currents in the correct time relationship to the erase and record heads so that minimum disturbance is heard at the edit points in the final product.

In television usage, the original videotape sound recording of dialogue is transferred to one or more tracks of the multitrack recorder; then sound effects, music, and audience-reaction tracks are added sequentially (in the parlance, the original tracks are *sweetened*). Generally, all the various tracks needed for final mixing are applied to one tape, with the number of channels adjusted to the scale of the production, although multiple recorders can be interlocked. The disposition of the tracks depends greatly on the production, the only quasi standard being that time code usually occupies the highest-numbered channel and that the penultimate channel is used for 60-Hz reference if one is needed.

In motion-picture usage, multitrack recording is more likely to carry only a part of the elements needed for a final mix. Most commonly, the multitrack will carry music. The reason that multitrack recording has not replaced separate dubbers is the need for flexibility in changes: it is impossible to "slip" tracks (resynchronize them separately) without time-consuming copying of the tracks to other media and back in a new placement. Separate strips of film on different machines allow for resynchronization, sound by sound, when picture changes occur. In television production, with its greater time pressure, changes do not occur to the picture nearly as often as they do in the production of theatrical motion pictures. So the multitrack editing technique has been used more widely in television production than in motion-picture production.

Another motion-picture application of multitrack recording is in the building of sound effects. Many sound effects are more effective when layered with others to make up new sounds which never occurred in reality. The multitrack recorder, under the control of a synchronizer, provides a means for efficiently producing these layered tracks, which, if they were cut on film, would be more time- and material-consuming. A typical method is to provide specialized software for the synchronizer, by means of either manufacturer programming or *soft-key* programming, that will do the sound-editing job. A typical sequence is:

1. Move the picture, first quickly and then frame by frame, until a point is found where a sound is needed. The picture-moving mechanism must be able to rock backward and forward one accurate frame at a time.

2. Mount an appropriate sound-effects tape on a playback machine. This might be a ¼-in machine synchronized with time code or an NAB cartridge machine synchronized with a start signal. Find the moment of sound which is to be synchronized with the picture, and mark it.

3. Determine record start and stop points, or use default values built into the system.

4. Audition the punch-in and punch-out. The synchronizer can operate switches so that what is on the multitrack recorder can be heard up to the record start point, then change to the source tape, and change back to the multitrack recorder at the record stop point.

5. If the synchronization looks good and the record edit points sound good, record the effect. Otherwise, trim the sync, in, or out points as required.

Good systems are those that permit quick location of synchronization and edit points, complete computer control of all motion control and record functions, and rapid lockup of synchronization on different media and have the best control utility.

14.3.7 Random-Access Editing Systems

Using hardware developed originally for random-access computer files, computer-based editing systems are becoming a practical reality. By digitizing sound, usually with 16-bit linear PCM coding and a 48-kHz clock, the storage medium may become whatever digital hardware is most cost-effective, given access time and throughput requirements. Since a great deal of effort goes into increasing storage capacity and minimizing access time for computer applications, the audio field can greatly benefit from a scale of production and research which it could never support alone.

Available and forthcoming systems differ in their details, but the principles remain the same: paramount is the ability to pull sounds rapidly from a library and synchronize them to picture, then play back the results, adding together a number of tracks. Those systems which are intended to be used by personnel trained in the film industry may have one set of human interfaces mimicking conventional film editing, while systems which are to be used by television-trained personnel are more likely to have an interface reminiscent of a video editing system, with time-code displays and the like.

14.3.8 Dialogue-Editing Specialization

Production sound recording was originally used to capture all the sound on the set, including dialogue and sound effects. The sound track became just what had been recorded at the time of shooting. Before long and for a variety of reasons, the role of the production sound recordist changed to concentration on dialogue, with sound effects left to postproduction. While a good production sound mixer still records sound effects on the set, the recordist usually concentrates on getting the best-quality dialogue tracks possible under the circumstances. If unique sound effects can be recorded in isolation on the set, so much the better.

In theatrical motion-picture production, the tasks of the dialogue editor are complex and artful. The editor must construct a performance out of available materials at hand, even though those materials may show technical defects where the best performance is to be had and poor performances where the recording is perfect. Smoothly blending dialogue from many sources depends on the cooperation of the editor and the re-recording mixer, but the editor has first crack at the material and can make the mixing job easy or impossible, depending on skill and understanding of the whole editing and mixing process.

A number of techniques are used to overcome technical faults in the original-source recordings. These faults arise out of the necessity of operating special-effects equipment, poor control of set background noise and reverberation, and, perhaps greater than any other factor, the fact that sound *can* be reconstructed off line during postproduction, thus downgrading its importance on the set. Methods to overcome faulty production recording include:

1. Looping the performance, also called automated dialogue replacement (ADR). The original actor comes to a specialized ADR stage, where he or she hears the original performance in headphones and reproduces it in synchronization with the picture. The recording thus made is free of significant background noise and reverberation. Then appropriate background noise and reverberation can be added in mixing to produce a reasonably close match to the conditions of the original recording, thus enhancing the illusion of a continuous recording. Multiple takes of the performance are usually necessary and form a good deal of the material for the dialogue editor. (An enhancement available to the ADR stage is Wordfit, a specialized digital audio processor which improves synchronization by taking the spectrum of the original recording and comparing it, every 10 ms, with the ADR stage performance. Through a *time-warping algorithm,* the newly recorded performance is made to synchronize with the original recording. The algorithm splices out silent periods for shortening. It finds the base pitch period of vowels and splices in a synthetic extension of them for lengthening.)

2. Scanning all recorded performances, even those of unprinted takes, for useful material which can solve technical or artistic problems. Often a good word or phrase from an out-take can be substituted into a longer good take without difficulty.

3. Using a variety of splicing techniques to overcome discontinuities associated with edits. A very long diagonal cut can be used to fade in on a background sound a moment before a line starts, thus smoothing a transition; or a 90° cut might be the most appropriate for cutting in the middle of a word from a vowel to a plosive consonant. The psychoacoustic basis for the utility of an abrupt cut is that premasking and postmasking are being invoked by the editor; that is, a loud sound will mask a soft one for even a little time before it and for a longer time after it. (To produce the same effect as a long diagonal cut *mag wipe* was formerly used. A chemical dissolver of the magnetic material, it was rubbed on the film selectively to remove oxide, but health concerns over the use of its main ingredient led to its demise.)

4. Splitting characters and method of recording across various tracks or strips of film. That is, one might want a two-character scene to be available to the mixer on four tracks: one for the original production recording of each character and one for the ADR of each character. This procedure gives the mixer the greatest flexibility in trying to match the recorded level, equalization, and reverberation of the separate recordings.

5. Filling tracks between words with background presence which matches that of the original recording or, if no such presence is available, cutting out as much of the original presence as possible and putting a similar continuous presence on a separate track, which the mixer can add in the right amount to mask discontinuities in the dialogue track.

6. Doing the best job possible with the difficult situation arising from dialogue overlaps between characters. It is far easier to overlap in editing characters who are supposed to talk simultaneously than it is to edit a sequence of master shot, one actor's close-up, and another actor's close-up, in which both actors are allowed to talk over one another in all takes, since it is virtually impossible for actors to overlap each other at precisely the same time in each of many takes. Simple edits then lead to either doubled-up or missing dialogue from one of the actors. This is a problem best solved in production planning.

14.3.9 Music-Editing Specialization

Most motion-picture and television postproduction completes picture editing before elaborate work on the sound track begins. Starting with a *locked picture cut,* the composer can write the score with frame accuracy, that is, with musical events, "stings" and the like, synchronized to absolute points in time. For the scoring session, a work print marked with *streamers* and punched holes provides the start point, internal sync point or points, and endpoint cuing for the conductor. (The streamer is simply grease-pencil marking diagonally along the length of the film for a number of frames in a sync block. When projected, it becomes a line moving across the screen from left to right by convention. It hits the right-hand border to mark the cue.) The typical original music recording is done on multitrack analog or digital recorders. The *scoring mixer* subsequently produces a mix to three-track left, center, and right (LCR) or four-track left, center, right, and surround (LCRS) magnetic film or to tape to be run as music units. Music editing for such a situation consists of *syncing up* the tracks resulting from the *marked takes* from the scoring stage. Typical usage is to cut two or, at most, three units, thus allowing dissolves. The checkerboard pattern promotes the mixer's ability to compensate for small changes across edits that were unanticipated during the music mix by spreading the tracks across console channels.

Power-line-frequency synchronization is often used on a separate track of the mix if an unsprocketed medium is employed. The 60 Hz on the mix-down copy must be related to the 60 Hz recorded on the original tape: it may be copied, or if the multitrack machine is run with a resolver, it may be a recording of the power line at the time of playback of the source.

On large-scale productions without the extreme time pressure of television and smaller-scale productions, the *picture lock* is more tenuous, with likely changes between the time that the picture is scored and the final mix. Under such circumstances, the music editor's task becomes much more difficult. Since the length of the music may no longer fit the scene and synchronization points are missed, much creative music editing is required. Although no specific methods can be given since characteristics vary greatly from case to case, some principles are:

1. Repetitive bars can be cut out, or they can be extended by having a second identical mix available and intercutting between them.

2. If a cut results in a bad key change without an available bridge, one section can be copied through a digital *pitch changer* to avoid the change or at least to make the edit a tolerable transition.

3. A quick dissolve can be designed to go "behind" a sound effect, making the sound effect mask the edit.

14.3.10   Effects-Editing Specialization

The coming of sound to film brought added complication for foreign releases: the pictures had to be dubbed into the language of the target country rather than simply substituting title cards in a new language, as had been the practice in the silent-movie era. Since looped dialogue in a foreign language lacked any sound effects, it became immediately clear that sound effects were necessary to preserve the illusion of the film. As the field grew and became more sophisticated, sound-effects editing became its own discipline, separate from what had been shot on the set. Where originally the production track had captured sound effects such as gunshots, "cleaner," more closely miked recordings or recordings with an interesting echo pattern came to be *cut in* in place of the production sound recording.

Today, sound effects are found in many sources. First, the production track serves as a useful record and at least a *guide track* to the original. Some theatrical films have been made with a documentary style using all original sound, but such films are a rarity. More often, the production track is combined with effects from a stock library of sound effects. If the desired effect cannot be found there, it can be traded from another library or purpose-recorded by the sound editor or someone hired to make specific sound-effect recordings.

Over the years, sound effects have been broken into discrete disciplines according to the type of effect. Predubs are usually divided by these disciplines, since the internal balance of one unit with another can be determined during the premixing of one type of effect and it would be more difficult to control balance while mixing two wholly different types of effects at once. The usual breakdown is:

1. *Ambience:*   This is the general underlying background of a scene. Although it may change from cut to cut to simulate shifts of perspective, there is little correspondence with screen action. (The term can be confusing, as the word ambience is also used interchangeably with *presence* or *atmosphere* to describe the background intercut with dialogue tracks to prevent them from going dead between pieces of material which are used. The ambience sound-effects track is not usually the same as that used to fill out dialogue tracks.)

2. *Foley:*   Foley sound effects are those made in a studio while watching a picture. A performer, called a *Foley walker,* named for the most common Foley effect, watches the screen and makes appropriate noise in synchronization with the screen image. The classic Foley effect is footsteps, and Foley stages are equipped with pits having a variety of surfaces to simulate walking on metal, sand, stone, etc. But many other kinds of sound effects are made on such a stage, using the same technical facilities as an ADR stage: film motion is under computer control to rock and roll over a given scene until synchronization is achieved and the required effects have been recorded.

3. *A, B, C FX:*   These sets of effects are those which generally do synchronize with screen action. The assignment of any given effect to A, B, or C premixes is determined by the chief editor, mixer, or sound designer so that sounds which the director may want to emphasize or remove are uniquely recorded, that is, not mixed together with other sounds.

This list is typical of many theatrical production features, but the type of film controls usage of the available tracks and console channels. For example, a music film might use virtually all the available resources for music, leaving little for sound effects and dialogue.

Although books can be written about the emotional content of film sound tracks, a few underlying principles of using sound on film have an impact on the technique used:

1. Film sound is a sparse symbolic representation of reality or fantasy. Some sound editors say that the ear cannot hear more than five sounds at one time. This rule of experience dictates that there is a practical upper limit on the number of sounds to be presented for recognition at one time.

2. The perspective of a useful sound effect very often is not a perspective which matches the picture. A great deal of film sound is a caricature which involves more close miking than a *reality recording* would have.

3. The speed of sound often is not factored in. Sound effects of cannon fire which are delayed to put them in authentic synchronization for the camera's point of view do not usually work for audiences unless the time delay has been set up by the preceding script.

4. Most sound effects are cut in *dead sync* with the frame of picture that they represent, but sound effects which are too early often seem better synchronized than ones which are equally late.

5. Many sound effects which work well to help set the mood of a scene are drawn from an *emotional dictionary* that each person carries around in his or her head; that is, the sound effect relates to learned experience from the world. One is reminded of the Bergman film of a house in the country, little occupied, where the only sound for minutes is of a ticking clock. This tells us that we are alone, for the sound of the clock is not being masked as it is in ordinary rooms at most times when activity is occurring.

14.3.11   SMPTE Time Code

The widespread application of the SMPTE time and control code, American National Standards Institute standard number SMPTE 12M, has greatly enhanced the utility of unsprocketed media, since it permits synchronizing a wide variety of picture film, audio film, videotape, and audio-tape machines in ever more complex patterns to meet production and postproduction needs. Although time code is a great boon to the industry, its intricacies unfortunately are often misunderstood, causing innumerable problems[7].

There are several decisions to be made regarding the type of time code to use on a production, and it is best if these decisions are made during preproduction so that the entire production can be recorded, edited, and mixed while using one set of code standards. The first decision is to choose the basic frame rate: 24, 25, 29.97, or 30 frames per second. Table 14.7 details which kinds of production use the various frame rates. The second decision applies only to 29.97-frame-rate recordings: whether the time code is to use the *drop-frame format,* thus maintaining synchronization with clock time, or not. The drop-frame mode is most commonly applied to recordings for video transmission in the United States, since its use means that the time code corresponds closely to real time. If the rule to employ a common time code for all parts of a production has been violated, a few commercial products can be of help, including the Gear Box from Q-Lock and the synchronizers made by Editron.

The third important decision involves the placement of the time code relative to the picture. For productions in which the camera and audio recorder are disconnected but are running on synchronized crystals, time of day is often used. (This works well unless the schedule calls for working through midnight, when an offset starting time might be useful.) One common postproduction usage is to make time code 00:00:00:00 coincident with the picture-start frame of an SMPTE universal leader and make all preceding frames, for example, 23:59:59:29 for a system of 30 frames per second. After the picture-start frame, the time-code numbers ascend through the end of the roll. Another postproduction method for a multireel film or tape is to start each reel with a new number in the hours digit; thus the picture-start frame for the first reel is 01:00:00:00, for the second, 02:00:00:00, etc.

Tips for time-code-based editing systems follow.

1. Mixing code types prevents synchronization with most equipment. The Q-Lock Gear Box can change the code type before injection into a synchronizer, and the synchronizers made by Editron can use a mixed code.

2. Time code can be recorded at the record head and played at the play head or the record head of a multitrack recorder. The correct head must be used for

TABLE 14.7 SMPTE Time and Control Code

Frame rate, frames per second	Special frame sequence	Countries of widest application	Prime use
24	No	All, for "pure" film production	Most film production and specialized video generally for release on film
25	No	Those using PAL and SECAM television systems, including Europe	Both film and video for television production
29.97	No	Those using NTSC television system, including United States	Video production with continuously ascending code numbers but without correction for consequent 3.6 s/h error from real time
29.97 (drop)	Yes	Those using NTSC television system, including United States	Video production corrected to real (clock) time; frames "dropped" to accommodate
30	No	All	Most used in audio postproduction of film

each purpose; otherwise, an unintentional offset will be added. For an example of use, see Sec. 14.4.5.

14.3.12 Editing Material for Lip-Sync Playback

Many types of music recordings must be prerecorded for playback on the set. Several methods are used to assure both relative and absolute synchronization:

1. Two tape machines are used. One contains the material to be played back, and the other is used to make a voice slate at the beginning of the take and then re-record the prerecorded music so that an editor can find synchronization. The difficulty with this method lies in long takes. Starting the playback tape in the middle to save film which would be wasted if it were rolled from the head of the take to the middle means that an editor must wind through considerable material to find a sync point, and repetitive music tracks can lead to synchronization errors.

2. Only one machine, the playback machine, is used. It must be equipped with time code. The time code played from the playback machine is read on an electronic slate, which the camera can pan to at any time for synchronization. This method has the advantage that every point of the sound track is uniquely identified. Separate playback cuts could be numbered in the hours columns and thus prevent further confusion.

3. In both cases, the playback recorders must be used with a resolver to a crystal reference source, thus ensuring synchronization with the camera. The time code employed should match the camera frame rate so that no translation is needed in postproduction. In the first case, the recording machine must record a crystal-synchronized signal, either 60-Hz or time-code.

14.4 MIXING

14.4.1 The Hourglass

An outline of the process of mixing sound tracks for motion pictures can be likened to an hourglass (see Fig. 14.3). At the top of the process are the *units,* or *elements,* cut by the editors on magnetic film or laid down in synchronization to picture on a multitrack recorder in checkerboard fashion. A group of elements belonging to one discipline, such as ambience sound effects, are mixed together for form *premixes.* The premixes are subsequently combined into the *final mix.* The foregoing processes tend to limit the number of tracks which must be dealt with at one time. A corresponding tendency is to have fewer total tracks at each progressive stage so that the final mix becomes the waist of the hourglass. From the final mix, many materials must be prepared to produce the various outputs which are required. These include *print masters* for 70- and 35-mm motion-picture releases, *D, M, and E masters* for monaural use, and, by substituting tracks of the final mix for others, dubbed foreign-language releases.

14.4.2 Premix Audio Technique

Dialogue Premixing. Often thought of as not requiring the highest quality because of its inherent fairly low bandwidth and loudness ranges, dialogue mixing

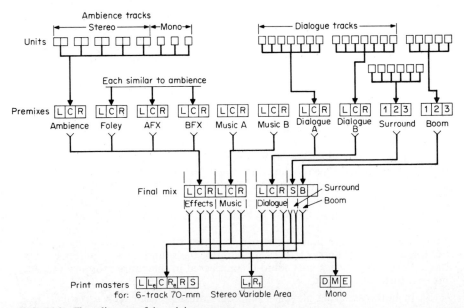

FIG. 14.3 Flow diagram of the mixing process.

is actually a large fraction of the overall task. Partly this is due to the fact that the dialogue carries the story line forward, often more than any other single factor, and partly because the human hearing mechanism is very sensitive to changes in the quality of speech. Since achieving intelligibility is essential to the story line, a large amount of time and a great deal of equipment are often applied to make the best-sounding dialogue premixes.

Among the techniques employed to promote intelligible, well-balanced recordings are equalization, filtering, compression, limiting, de-essing, noise gating, multiband noise reduction, and reverberation. Techniques used for special effects include *worldizing,* which is a special case of reverberation, and various processing tricks, including pitch shift and the addition of short-time-delayed versions of the signal to itself. Another common trick is to put well-recorded sound through bad transducers and acoustic environments to simulate telephone calls or public address systems.

1. Equalization is used to make speech intelligible and pleasant, to match the spectral balance of one recording with another, and to overcome film-system losses (especially in monaural film mixing). It is also used to overcome the losses associated with varying microphone techniques, such as equalizing a lavaliere microphone which is buried under clothing, equalizing for proximity effect a directional microphone used close up, and improving the spectral balance of recordings made in rooms with longer reverberation time in the bass than in the midrange and treble. Equalization is surely the most widely used technique for improving the quality of recordings.

Concern in earlier years over the *phase behavior* of equalizers led some designers to work within a limited range of circuit topologies for equalizers; such equalizers were sometimes called *combining* in the mistaken notion that equalizers with other topologies could not combine well from band to band. More recent work[8] has shown that all topologies in widespread use in audio are *minimum-phase.* Thus the amplitude response with respect to frequency (conventionally called the *frequency response*) and its adjustability are the principal concerns in choosing an equalizer. Various equalizers provide differing ability to adjust parameters: the range from simple virtual tone controls to multiband parametric graphic equalizers is vast, with many tradeoffs available among size, complexity, and ease of use. One caution should be applied to looking at conventional specifications and reviews: the usual frequency-response curves show only the action of the equalizer at full boost-and-cut conditions. But there is more than one way for an equalization curve to get from here to there. For example, a new class of one-third-octave-band equalizers called constant-Q offers greater selectivity for small amounts of boost and cut than do conventional equalizers.

Another primary concern in the postproduction use of equalizers must be the ergonomics of the unit. Since postproduction usually involves working with a picture, the attention of the mixer should not be diverted to the equipment any more often than is necessary. This factor explains the continuing popularity of octave-band graphic equalizers, with their immediately understood graphical display, despite the fact that other forms of equalizers offer greater packing density.

2. Filtering is used to reduce the background noise of recordings by attenuating undesired signals while minimizing the impact on speech. Commonly available filters include steep high- and low-pass filters as well as notch filters for discrete tonal noise. Commonly found filters can be quite steep, up to 24 dB per octave, which is useful in discriminating between speech and noise that are close together spectrally. The *telephone filter* has been commonly used to limit speech to the approximate bandwidth of a telephone line to simulate phone calls, although more severe processing than bandwidth restriction is now considered useful in simulating telephones.

3. Compression and limiting of dialogue tracks are both used, especially if the target output medium has limited dynamic-range capacity. The degree to which they are applied is generally less for media having the widest output dynamic-range capacity, such as 70-mm film release, and relatively more for media having less range, say, monaural optical sound tracks. Another factor that strongly influences the amount of compression or limiting is the amount of "interference" to intelligibility created by sound effects and music. Compressing the lowest-level sounds from a voice may prove useful in keeping it above the "noise" of the other tracks. Finally, the individual actor's performance greatly influences the amount of compression or limiting which is useful.

The upper limit on the useful range for compression or limiting is the occurrence of audible artifacts. These can include distortion due to tradeoffs between time constant and program-material content and audible *pumping* or *breathing* effects as the channel contains both signal and noise and the noise level is modulated by the presence or absence of signal. To ameliorate these effects compressors or limiters can be made available for each track. This helps prevent modulation of one channel by another one, which is another telltale artifact of compression processes. Thus one may conclude that overall compression of a completed program is less effective than compression of individual tracks.

4. *De-essing* is related to compression and limiting. It is a special form of dynamic signal processsor, having a frequency-discriminatory side chain. That is, high frequencies are emphasized in importance to the gain reduction action. The application of proper de-essing reduces the levels of *s*'s without disturbing the rest of speech. De-essing is particularly useful for mixes intended for release on optical sound tracks, since the optical track produces sibilant distortion as the first audible artifact of any misexposure or processing.

5. Wideband noise gates turn down the channel gain when the level is below a settable threshold. This technique may be useful on some tracks of a mix where the available signal from other tracks blocks audible artifacts, but a noise gate by itself, especially on a composite signal, often exhibits *noise breathing,* a quality that the background noise is swishing, which can be more annoying than the noise itself.

6. More widely used than wideband noise gates are multiband noise reducers. The most commonly employed of these is Dolby® Catalog No. 43, which uses the four bands of Dolby A (see Chap. 15). It is a complementary noise reduction system used in a unique single-ended and adjustable mode (this type of compander is always intended for complementary use; here is an example of a design made to be used in a complementary fashion that is also useful in a noncomplementary mode). This system provides noise attenuation of signals falling below adjustable thresholds in the four bands.

7. Reverberation is commonly added to overly dry voice tracks to put them in perspective in space, since otherwise they might sound like narration or voice-over recordings. The primary characteristic needed in a reverberator for dialogue mixing is the availability of adjustment of the reverberator to simulate small rooms. Many reverberators built for music simply do not have short enough reverberation programming to be useful for dialogue. A second requirement is ease of matching the reverberant characteristics of recorded spaces, since a great deal of dialogue premixing involves matching sound from ADR recordings with sound from the set.

8. *Worldizing* is a special case of reverberation, using a loudspeaker system and a microphone in an acoustical space setting to add the sound of the space to dry recordings. It may be used as a wideband, high-quality reverberator, but more often than not worldizing is used to duplicate the *bad* reverberation characteristics of a space, leaving the synthesis of good-quality spaces to reverberation devices.

Since many of these processes are dynamic, their order is important. While some general principles can be given, this is a field in which informed experimentation on a case-by-case basis is recommended.

1. Usually it is useful to filter out any tonal noise or large amount of low-frequency noise before employing other processes so that the tone or noise does not dominate the gain control function of dynamic processes.

2. The next process after filtering is often use of a multiband noise reduction device. It should generally precede compression or limiting, which would tend to undo its effect, and in practice it is found better to noise-reduce before equalization.

3. The primary choice is whether to equalize before or after compression or limiting. Little help can be offered here, as both arrangements have proved useful. The mixer should be aware that the characteristics differ with the order.

4. De-essing usually occurs late in the chain, since the level of *s*'s which will cause a problem is related to the high-level properties of the optical track, and a time late in the chain is closer to the track than an earlier time. The line may thus be more easily calibrated through experience than if de-essing were earlier in the chain. Also, placing de-essing after equalization prevents overly aggressive high-frequency boost equalization from causing high distortion. The equalization is made completely effective only at low levels, and the de-esser tends to remove the boost at high levels. The audible effect of a de-esser can be made quite benign compared with the benefits which it offers.

Mapping frequency response versus level of the combination of the foregoing processes shows variations from flat to 20 dB in one direction, with ± 15-dB variations not uncommon. Although conventionally thought of as radical, such processing is not uncommon, and it is useful for tracks recorded under less than ideal conditions.

Panning. With the advent of stereo in the 1950s, characters were routinely pan-potted into position across the width of the screen. For several reasons, such extensive dialogue panning is no longer used or even considered desirable, and it is the rare line which is panned away from the center in today's mixes. One reason not to pan is that panned voice often suffers from audible frequency-response changes as the pan is undertaken, as the voice moves from one channel to another and the lack of completely uniform coverage of the loudspeakers is revealed. Another psychoacoustic problem with panned dialogue is that the ear is not prepared for discontinuous cuts in perspective in the same way that the eye has been trained through the experience of seeing thousands of perspective changes with picture cuts.

Track Usage. There are several ways to use the available number of tracks in a dialogue premix. One way is a spatial representation, left, center, and right (LCR); another is to maintain the characters on separate tracks so that individual characters can be adjusted in level at the final mix. The LCR method has the advantage that three uncorrelated return signals from the reverberation device are recorded and the reverberator is thus free for other jobs at the final mix. (It is not particularly useful to record reverberation on tracks split by character: if the level of one character must be reduced at the final mix, the ratio of direct to reverberant sound would change, and the one character would sound more distant than another.) A combination of these two techniques for a two-character-dialogue split premix is to record LCR for one character and LCR for another character, both on a six-track recorder.

Sound-Effects Premixing.   Premixing of sound effects uses many of the same techniques as dialogue premixing, but the relative importance of the various techniques is substantially different. For example, it would be rare to see a de-esser or a compressor in use on sound-effects tracks. Also, single-ended noise reduction devices are rarely used since the tracks are often inherently cleaner than dialogue tracks, having been specifically recorded in isolation and thus being unpolluted with interfering noise.

But equalization, filtering, reverberation, worldizing, and, especially, panning are all extremely useful with sound effects. The amount of such manipulation can often be greater than on voice tracks, since the listener has little experience in comparing film sound effects with sounds from everyday life, whereas dialogue is relatively more familiar. [It's like color television, in which one need get only skin, grass, and sky (the dialogue) the right color because the viewer doesn't know the color of anything else.] The meaning of this to the audio design engineer is that a different tradeoff between range and resolution of controls is desirable between dialogue and sound-effects sections of large consoles. Anything greater than ± 12 dB of equalization for a dialogue track is probably a gross rescue job, whereas greater equalization might routinely prove useful for sound-effects premixing.

A factor more important in sound-effects than in dialogue premixing is that premixes are generally made complete with fades and the relative level differences that are to occur in the final mix. This means that, moment by moment, the usage of the dynamic range of the storage medium is not optimized (we aren't recording with peaks hitting the top of the available range). Since from a practical standpoint it is essential to reduce the amount of level manipulation during the final mix to reasonable proportions, a number of premixes will be underrecorded relative to good-practice criteria. The solution to this dilemma is having enough dynamic range available on the premix medium to permit free artistic expression without concern for the fact that the medium is not "correctly" loaded. Occasionally whole premixes will be made so that the mix is recorded "hot" by some number of decibels, which will subsequently be pulled back into the correct relationship with the other premixes at the final mix. A useful amount of such an offset is 10 dB, and a typical premix might be for Foley sound effects, which are generally not too loud in the final mix. By putting the premix at a higher level which still does not exceed tolerable distortion limits, the effect of noise in the premix is reduced by 10 dB when the premix is put back in context.

The foregoing notion depends on a factor which is better controlled in the film industry than elsewhere in audio recording: the fact that the flux or other reference level on the final mix is designed to produce a specified sound pressure level (SPL) at the time of listening. In almost every other application of sound systems, someone is in charge of setting the volume control for the "correct loudness" at the time of listening. In contrast, the film industry, in order to give control of loudness to the director and producer of a film, has set standards which promote uniformity of presentation, including loudness, across many theaters.

Panning is one of the most important elements of sound-effects premixing, since sound effects, unlike music and dialogue tracks, routinely must be set into a space and many of them moved to accommodate the picture. For this the panning law, the relationship between angle of rotation and relative attenuation of the signal feeding various output channels, is important. Since virtually all stereo mixes are currently made for the Dolby Surround format, a panning law which works best through this matrix is best. Such a law has experimentally been found to have crossover levels of -4.2 dB rather than the -3 dB of a sine-cosine panner.

Music Premixing.   This term is a misnomer, since normally one avoids premixing music if possible. The problem here is the number of generations which a sound track must go through and the consequent pileup of noise and distortion from generation to generation. If a music track is originally recorded with a multitrack technique, then mixed down to film, that film becomes the music units as it is synchronized to the picture. Then there would be a premix stage, if one were employed, a final mix, the print master, and the prints themselves. Thus the signal encounters six generations by the time that it is heard in the theater, and deletion of the premix stage saves at least one of the six.

So music units are most often cut in checkerboard fashion between two dubbers, giving overlap and butting capability between cues, so that the cut music units themselves in effect become the premix. Another reason that premixing music is largely unnecessary is that no large amount of signal processing is usually applied to music. Commonly only a little high-frequency boost equalization (about $+2$ dB at 10 kHz) and reverberation are applied to music tracks, although compression might be useful for tracks which are meant to underscore dialogue.

Mix-in-Context.   This procedure involves having available multiple mix buses in the console for the following purpose. If units can be brought into the console, mixed together, and then sent to a recorder and if formerly made premixes can be brought in through another set of channels assigned to new outputs and mixed with the returns from the recorder, the console operator can, in effect, mix both a premix and a scratch version of the final mix simultaneously (see Fig. 14.4).

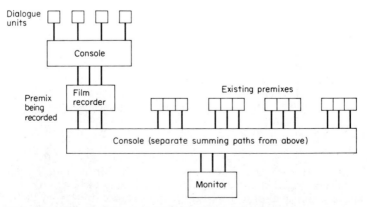

FIG. 14.4   Flow diagram of mix-in-context for a dialogue premix.

This permits hearing the effect that sound effects, say, are going to have on the dialogue premix and allows the mixer to shape the results for best performance, given the other elements that will be present in the final mix. Another common usage for mix-in-context is to choose and manipulate music and sound effects so that each can be heard simultaneously without serious masking of the other element by the opposing one. Thus a scene that calls for a large rumble sound effect would be better scored with high brasses than with tympani, and mix-in-context reveals such problems before the final mix.

Premix Use of Stereo Matrix.   The process of premixing yields fewer surprises if monitoring of the resulting mixes is made through a 4:2:4 matrix encoder-decoder. Early use reveals sound effects and music which, having decorrelated phase relationships, will produce undesirable levels of sound from the surround channel. Use also reveals out-of-polarity conditions immediately, since such information will come from the surround channels instead of the intended one.

14.4.3   Final-Mix Audio Technique

The final-mix stage can be relatively straightforward if the sound design, that is, the disposition of the tracks and the premixing, has been handled with forethought. The purpose of the final mix is to blend the premixes together seamlessly, with dialogue, music, and sound effects having a mutually beneficial relationship. Massive amounts of mixing per se are not needed if the fades and level relationships have been handled during premixing. Instead, changes among the premix tracks no greater than ± 5 dB are usual.

The final mix is also the point at which to make the overall film reel-to-reel loudness consistent. Until this time it is typical to work on films in 10-min reels, with concentration on what goes into each reel. Final mixing is often done in sequence so that transitions between the reels are given due consideration.

The same audio processes are available to be used in final mixing as in premixing, although most of the processing has already been done at the premix stage. This leaves the final mix to touch up such factors as equalization. In addition, if the dialogue tracks have been left dry (so the maximum number of tracks is available for character splitting), reverberation must be added at this stage. Since dialogue and music usually require different reverberation programs (dialogue typically uses shorter reverberation times than music), at least two and sometimes more reverberators are necessary.

Several interrelated factors have to be considered at the time of the final mix. Since there is a reasonably well-accepted standard for setting volume control in theaters, the flux on the film or the equivalent intensity measure in other media lies in a 1:1 relationship with loudness in the theater. The final mix thus solely determines the volume range of the film, with special importance on the relationship between the level of average dialogue and the loudest sounds. Another factor is the available dynamic range of the various output media. Seventy-millimeter film has greater range than stereo optical, and stereo optical has more range than mono optical.

There is an important choice to be made which is best considered at the final mix: Shall the film be released with single inventory for the 35-mm optical track prints, with reasonable mono compatibility, or should there be no concession to compatibility and dual-print inventory? The question hinges on the difference between average dialogue level and the loudest sounds on the optical track and on the fact that stereo tracks have more dynamic-range capacity than mono ones. If the average dialogue level is kept low so that there is a great deal of headroom for louder sounds, then the tendency is for the theaters to turn the volume down from the standardized level, which tends to make the dialogue unintelligible. Prints having such a large difference are less mono-compatible than are ones with relatively higher dialogue level. Most films released in optical stereo today are made for single-print inventory, offering the producer maximum economy, with the compromise that the dialogue must be mixed at a relatively high level.

14.4.4 Print Mastering

Once the final mix has been finished, it is necessary to make a wide range of *print masters* for a variety of purposes. Print masters of motion pictures are virtually always on sprocketed media, and the track format and levels correspond 1:1 with what is recorded magnetically or optically on the prints, with one exception, for mono tracks, as explained below.

There are three basic differences among the print masters:

1. The track format varies. Print masters for 70-mm release contain six discrete audio tracks; for 35-mm stereo releases they contain two tracks, left total (L_t) and right total (R_t), matrix-encoded with four-channel information; for 35-mm mono they contain one or three tracks (D, M, and E intended for 1:1:1 summed mono); and for video-only release one or two tracks. For common release of stereo format in both film and video, the motion-picture stereo matrix master is commonly employed for both tasks.

2. The volume-range requirements vary since the dynamic range of the releasing medium varies, and the setting where the end product is to be used also has an inpact (a 70-mm print master would probably have too much volume range for living-room listening). The 70-mm release prints have the greatest dynamic range, 35-mm stereo less, and 35-mm mono far less. Requirements for video release seem to equal those for 35-mm stereo. Beyond the actual dynamic range available on the medium is consideration of how the medium behaves close to and in overload: optical tracks and digital media are *hard-clipping* media, whereas magnetic film has a *soft-overload* characteristic.

3. The language of the primary dialogue varies according to the country of release.

These various considerations could result in a very wide range of output mixes since the possible matrix of the factors is large. Fortunately, in practice some simplification is possible, and the number of mixes on a single-print-inventory film (no mono) is not so large. Simplifying the requirements is the fact that the Dolby Stereo Matrix is downward-compatible, with acceptable results in listening over the hierarchical range of four-channel decoded, two-channel (direct listening to L_t, R_t), and mono (listening to the sum $L_t + R_t$). Typical print masters on a theatrical large-scale film might be:

1. Seventy-millimeter six-track Dolby noise reduction encoded, English, used only for 1:1 copying to the 70-mm release prints. The six tracks on the print master correspond 1:1 to the six tracks on the prints: one left, two left extra, three center, four right extra, five right, and six surround.

2. Thirty-five-millimeter Dolby Stereo Matrix, English, used for striking 35-

mm stereo optical sound negatives and for video release. L_t and R_t are recorded respectively on the first two tracks of a three-track film.

3. Additional 70-mm six-track-format print masters in any other languages for which 70-mm dubbed prints are appropriate (some markets use English-language 70-mm release prints with burned-in subtitles in the vernacular).

4. Additional 35-mm stereo print masters in other primary languages.

The original six-track format called for five evenly spaced speakers across the width of the screen and a *surround* or *effects* channel covering the auditorium. Because of the decreasing screen size in most of today's theaters, increasing use of "room" equalization for loudspeaker systems to promote uniformity across various speakers, and better psychoacoustic understanding of panning, three speaker channels are now commonly employed for full-frequency-range signals. (The use of the other two channels caused problems from lack of five-channel pan pots to *phasing* as sound was smoothly panned across the screen.) Since this left two unused speakers in many auditoria and since the tracks were available on the 70-mm film, the two extra loudspeaker channels, called left extra and right extra, have been pressed into service to improve the bass power-handling capacity of the other three front channels. Called the *baby-boom format,* this is now the most popular format for 70-mm release.

Use of the proprietary Dolby Stereo Matrix starts by recording left, center, right, and surround channels as L_t and R_t signals on the magnetic print master and then copying 1:1 to the film negative. This is a 4:2:4 matrix, using two mono-compatible, dual-bilateral, variable-area tracks on 35-mm prints. Subsequently, a matrix decoder in the theater equipment or in the home environment for video releases decodes the two channels on the medium into four (three for some home-style decoders). Since the matrix must, by application of information theory, lose something (after all, not all the information in four channels can be piped through two channels having the same bandwidth as the four), it has been well designed to lose the least perceived information on practical program material. Program bandwidth and S/N ratio are not compromised, but proper localization decoding depends on perceptual mechanisms of time-intensity tradeoffs. Problems which remain include the fact that very "phasy" recordings, such as orchestra recordings with widely spaced microphones, will appear at higher levels in the surrounds than they would in a fully discrete system. Such *magic surrounds* can be ameliorated by recording with M-S style recording technique on both music and stereo sound effects. A second problem consists of Toddisms, named for the developer of the matrix system at Dolby. These are short-term events (in the range of 50 to 100 ms) localized in the wrong place before the playback decoder circuitry can properly place the signal. The most obvious Toddisms are usually the initiation of a centered dialogue phrase, which may appear at left or right and then quickly center. This problem arises when a sound effect just prior to the line is more intense in one side channel and has caused preferential matrix steering to that channel. It can be solved by ducking the offending sound just before the dialogue line or by adding a sound in the opposite channel to center the matrix before the entrance of the line. The possibility of these problems arising at the final mix is minimized if the encode-decode hardware is employed throughout both premixing and final mixing.

Monaural format masters are commonly recorded as D, M, and E tracks, kept separate and designed for summing at the time of optical transfer. This permits last-minute balance changes among the elements or substitution of another language for the dialogue track, which would not be possible if the tracks were mixed.

Monaural monitoring uses a high-frequency rolloff to reduce noise. Sometimes called the *Academy filter,* this filter was not a fixed element but depended on additional losses from slit-scanning loss, loudspeaker high-frequency rolloff, and screen high-frequency attenuation. Such electrical rolloff as is necessary is described in Sec. 14.4.8.

14.4.5   Television Lay-Down–Lay-Back

Television's usual compressed production schedule does not generally permit extensive premixing. Instead, original-production sound is copied from the production tapes to one or more tracks of a multitrack recorder. Then sound-effects and music sweetening tracks are added, as described in Sec. 14.3.6. Mixing consists of balancing among the available tracks. Then, in the *lay-back* stage, the composite audio is re-recorded back to the video master. Although multiple recorders are occasionally used on complex productions and digital recorders have been used, by far the largest amount of work is done currently with a 24-track recorder, saving space for the time code and the final mix on tracks of the recorder.

Time-code synchronization can be complicated by the *sel-sync mode* of the recorder. That is, the time code can be played from either the record or the play head of the recorder, and the correct head to use varies with what is being done. The time code should be placed in *dead sync* with the production track, either by *prestriping* a reel of multitrack tape with the time code and synchronizing to playback from the record head *(sel-rep)* at the time of the lay-down or by laying time-code and production audio at the same time by synchronizing to a common source.

Then, as tracks are added, it is best to use all channels at the record head by recording there or by using the sel-rep mode for playback. Finally, when all tracks have been recorded, they can be played, including the time code from the playback head, for best audio quality. The mix can then be recorded on another machine, or the mix-down can be made by using all the channels, including the time code, on sel-rep and recorded to an unused channel. Figure 14.5 shows the various operating modes.

14.4.6   Mix-Studio (In-Plant) Synchronization Techniques

The first synchronization method used in studios employed *selsyns,* specialized electric motors that are designed, when interconnected, to run together. By changing the voltage on the main drive distributor, equipment could be brought up to speed together and reversed by changing phases on the drive-distributor motor. Today electronic synchronization of sprocketed machines employs a pair of *biphase synchronization signals* to maintain sync from machine to machine. These are usually TTL-level (0 to $+5$ V) square waves at a nominal rate related precisely to the frame rate, although there may be from 2 to 100 pulses per frame, depending on the make of the equipment. Two quadrature signals present the machine with speed and direction information over the range from zero to many times (such as 10 times) speed.

Several levels of more sophisticated control are possible in a system containing many dubbers. The first level interposes a control box which permits the operator to offset a single dubber and to restore the machine to absolute sync when required. A higher-level microprocessor-based device can store offset for each of

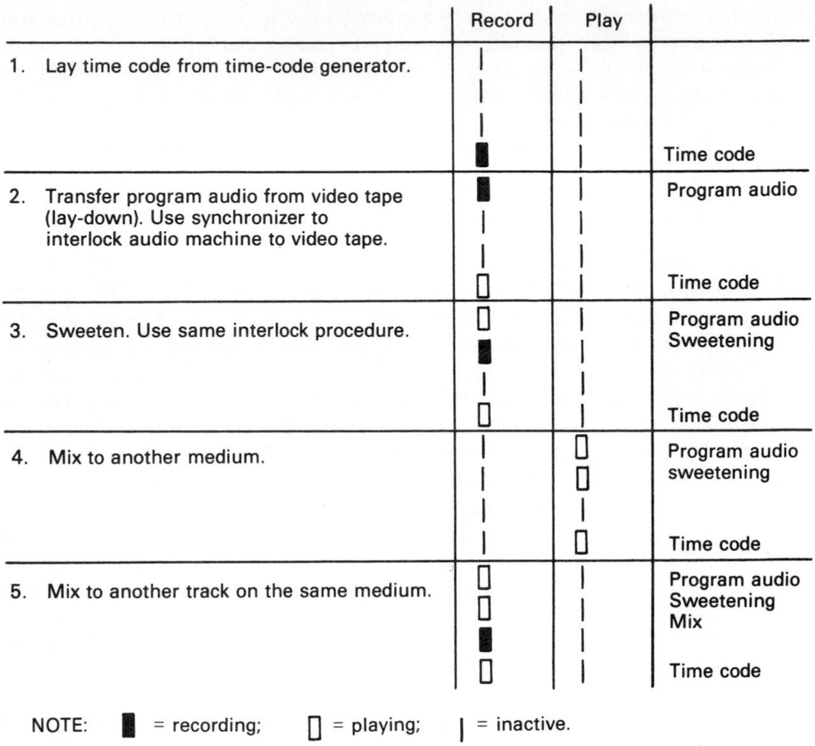

	Record	Play	
1. Lay time code from time-code generator.	∣ ∣ ∣ ■	∣	Time code
2. Transfer program audio from video tape (lay-down). Use synchronizer to interlock audio machine to video tape.	■ ∣ ∣ ▯	∣	Program audio Time code
3. Sweeten. Use same interlock procedure.	▯ ■ ∣ ▯	∣	Program audio Sweetening Time code
4. Mix to another medium.	∣ ∣ ∣ ∣	▯ ▯ ∣ ▯	Program audio sweetening Time code
5. Mix to another track on the same medium.	▯ ▯ ■ ▯	∣	Program audio Sweetening Mix Time code

NOTE: ■ = recording;   ▯ = playing;   ∣ = inactive.

FIG. 14.5 Television lay-down–lay-back program and time-code-synchronization block diagram.

the machines in a system and "memorize" where the machine should be, permitting it to be taken off line (for track repairs, say) and then restored to absolute sync without having to return all tracks to zero.

Film dubbers have had such a long life and generally have not been replaced by multitrack recorders owing to the flexibility of being able to shift one or more machines relative to the others. To do the same job on a multitrack recorder requires copying the track to be moved to another medium and then putting it back in the new sync.

Film dubbers and recorders maintain synchronization to the biphase signals either by using a low-inertia moving system which can keep step with the speed changes sent out by a control unit that contains speed-shape-changing circuitry or by storing the difference between the position demanded by the biphase signal and the actual position and driving the film to minimize the difference through a servomechanism. In order to do this the latter machines employ a large digital buffer.

Unsprocketed media generally use time-code-based synchronization systems, described in Sec. 14.3.11. Some synchronizers are equipped with purpose-built programs useful for mixing. Such programs automate machine control of motion and punch-in–punch-out capability, allowing the mixer greater freedom for concentrating on the audio details of a mix. Some synchronizers also have available *soft-key facilities* or a connection to a higher-level computer, both of which can more fully automate the mix studio.

14.4.7 Role of Automation in Postproduction

Console automation systems, including fader automation, grouping of faders, mutes, snapshots of console pots, and reset of switch functions to stored configurations, can contribute to the productivity of a studio. Early users of automation in postproduction found, however, that the level of sophistication available in automation systems that were useful to music studios was inadequate for postproduction. Compounding factors include the very high number of faders, which may be in nearly continuous use during a film mix and which stressed the data capacity and carrying rates of early systems. Today automation is becoming better accepted in some circles, especially for the more routine functions, and more advanced forms of automation, including full-console control, are regarded as becoming available and useful in the near-term future.

Fully automated mixing offers one large advantage in the production of multiple copies of a final mix or a print master, in that personnel need make only one pass, making the original mix, and automation can then be used to produce multiple identical copies. This is a great advantage when time is short and, for example, multiple copies of 70-mm print masters are needed so that more than one *sounding house* can be employed.

14.4.8 Postproduction Audio Monitoring

In the 1930s, the concept of a dubbing stage was that it ought to represent an average theater and that, as the state of the art progressed, theaters would tend to become more and more average, thus promoting interchangeability of product from dubbing stage to theater to theater. Thus such factors as background noise of the stage, power output capability of the sound system, available dynamic range on the sound tracks, intelligibility of voices, and many others were given due consideration, *since the mixers were monitoring in the same environment that the final user heard.*

Fifty years later our notion is more universal. That is, we now have a better grasp of the wide range of conditions under which the product will be seen and heard. That range is larger than it was in the 1930s, since it involves the home as well as the theater, and variance from theater to theater is better understood. So the conception we have today is to build dubbing stages as practical laboratories of how good we can make all factors (since at least some listeners will hear the product under conditions which are virtually this good) and *to provide appropriate degrading systems so that the mixers can be certain that the film will still play as best as it can even under degraded conditions.* Actually, we are supporting the notion of the past that the mixer should hear the sound under the same conditions as the final user in order to render the best judgment about the sound. What has changed is that the variety of conditions which require different monitoring schemes is greater and that today it is possible to achieve a closer approximation to the sound of the variety of systems to be simulated than it was 50 years ago.

Dubbing-stage monitoring systems are quite complicated compared with their cousins in the music studio because the tasks of the dubbing stage are more varied. Premixing requires one kind of monitor system, final mixing another, and print mastering a third, and there are endless variations within each of these frameworks. An example of the functions of a dubbing-stage monitor system is shown in Table 14.8. Here can be seen two fundamental elements: many processes done to the audio both before and after recording it and a method of configuring the processes for the job at hand. A list of the processes available and what they do follows:

TABLE 14.8   Functions of a Dubbing-Stage Monitoring-Mastering System

1. Cross-point routing for interconnect
    a. Used, for example, so that one can monitor the effect of a 4:2:4 matrix recording while recording discretely or, alternatively, record the matrixed output of the 4:2 encoder
    b. Multiple "levels" needed to bring switch size into practical range

2. Electronics for playback of source media
    a. Magnetic playback preamplifiers
    b. Optical playback preamplifiers
    c. Magnetic-optical playback A-chain filters

3. Stereo 4:2:4 matrix recording
    a. 4:2 encoder with surround on-off and bass sum on-off
    b. Delay line limiter for optical tracks
    c. Optical track simulator for overload, noise, laboratory processing simulation
    d. Noise-reduction-as-required encoders and decoders

4. Monitor frequency-response equalizer-filter set
    a. Wide range (flat)
    b. Equalized average theater loudspeaker
    c. Unequalized average theater loudspeaker
    d. Television (to simulate flat near-field monitor with dubbing-stage system)
    e. Diffuse-sound-field to frontal-field equalizer for surround channel

5. Monitor dynamic-range controls
    a. Volume control with calibrated detent at standardized SPL
    b. Dim −15 dB
    c. Cut
    d. Average theater clip headroom versus frequency in-out
    e. Average theater background noise in-out

6. Enhancements
    a. Optical bass enhancement
    b. Stereo surround encoder-decoder (70-mm only)
    c. Subwoofer summer and crossover

7. Self-test
    a. Pink-noise sequencer into each channel in turn
    b. Fixed-boundary-layer microphone on ceiling to measure transfer function
    c. Computer controller

8. Monitor system
    a. Electronic crossover
    b. Constant-Q one-third-octave-band equalizers
    c. Power amplifiers
    d. Loudspeakers, local acoustical environment, global acoustical environment
    e. Flat near-field monitors

1. *Dolby Stereo matrix encoder:*   From left, center, right, and surround channel information it produces two-track L_t, R_t format signals.

2. *Dolby Stereo matrix decoder:*   From L_t, R_t signals it produces left, center, right, and surround output channels.

3. *Delay line limiter:*   Based on a BBC delay line limiter, this Dolby design prevents a program from exceeding the 100 percent limit of the optical track and also provides a gain-reduction-meter drive.

4. *Nuoptix optical track simulator:* It synthesizes the processes which occur in optical recording, including light-valve or galvanometer simulation, film-loss simulation, laboratory negative processing, film printing, and laboratory positive processing, including simulating overload of the optical variable-area track, noise modulation effects, grain noise injection, dirt noise injection, image-spread and cancellation effects, and the like. It prevents making magnetic masters with too wide a dynamic range that cannot be subsequently recorded optically, and it greatly reduces the need for multiple negatives to determine the correct levels.

5. *Magnetic and optical filters:* These roll off high-frequency response in a prescribed way, considering alignment of the monitoring system to ISO 2969 curve *X*. Optical filter is used for the presentation of mono films; magnetic filter, for four-track magnetic release prints from the era before noise reduction was employed. Both filters also are used if old films are to be employed as elements in contemporary films.

6. *High-pass–low-pass filters or equalizers:* These simulate various conditions encountered in the field. The filters or equalizers are named *wide-range* (flat), *equalized A4* (simulating the most commonly found loudspeaker system when used with one-third-octave equalization to meet, insofar as possible, ISO 2969 curve *X*), *unequalized A4* (simulating the same loudspeaker system but without benefit of equalization), *unequalized A4* with Academy filter (matching the response specified in SMPTE 221 for mono theaters), and *television* (matching the characteristic frequency response of a near-field flat monitor from a far-field design, +2 dB at 10 kHz). All these filters simulate the entire system response from the electrical input to the power amplifier through loudspeaker response, screen attenuation, and room acoustics and are made as differences from the response delivered by the wide-range monitor system.

7. *Frontal-to-diffuse equalizer:* It equalizes surround loudspeakers to account for the fact that the sound field from the screen speakers is largely frontal and, from the surrounds, largely a diffuse field. Thus a wideband sound such as pink noise panned from the screen to the surrounds will undergo a timbre shift unless such an equalizer is employed. The amount of the correction lies within +3 to −4 dB over the range from 20 Hz to 16 kHz.

8. *Dolby Stereo Surround encoder-decoder:* It is used for putting left-right information into the surround channel on 70-mm prints by employing the unused high-frequency range of the baby-boom Channels 2 and 4 to carry the information. In the few equipped theaters, the high-frequency split-surround information is extracted from the *extra left* and *right* tracks (2 and 4) and combined with a low-frequency signal on the mono surround track (6) to form left and right surround speaker feeds (see Sec. 14.4.4).

9. *Dolby optical bass enhancement:* It provides a means for extracting bass information from an optical track without interference from dialogue or noise. This is accomplished by a low-frequency, low-pass filter set and a downward expander to prevent low-level, low-frequency noise from being accentuated. In this case, it forms an optional feed for the subwoofer when playing an optical track.

10. *Volume-dim:* It provides a calibrated volume control and a facility to dim the monitor system (attenuate all speaker signals by 15 dB). The volume control in a motion-picture facility is calibrated to the same standard as that of the theater, so the volume control is used only for special cases (such as wanting to record a soft premix at higher levels to reduce noise; in such a case the monitor level can be lowered so that the mixer will put more level on the medium).

11. *Average theater clip:* Dubbing stages generally have more power available than do many theaters, so a clipping simulator, including the effect of differences in speaker sensitivity with frequency, is useful. The necessary curve has been compiled empirically from field measurements since a number of factors influence the octave-by-octave overload level.

12. *Noise adder:* Dubbing stages are generally quieter than theaters, leading mixers to mix too wide a volume range. Soft information simply gets lost under the masking noise of the theater. Artificial air-conditioning noise, formed from multiple uncorrelated electronic noise generators, equalized to a spectral shape as measured in the average of many theaters, and injectable at a variety of levels into left, center, right, left surround, and right surround separately, is useful. The average theater level is NC 30, and provision is made for this and a lower level simulating conditions in the best theaters.

13. *Pink-noise tester:* Part of a building-wide system to prevent mixing to a bad monitor, this system sends pink noise out of each channel in turn in the middle of the night and picks up the sound with a ceiling-mounted microphone. The microphone is connected to an analyzer which can compare the measurements with previous records and flag unusual responses for an engineer to investigate.

14. *Source-tape switching:* This is used to make comparisons between the source for a recording and the recording itself to ensure the quality of the recording.

15. *Monitor speaker select:* This permits using near-field monitors for television mixes and for checking film mixes on near-field speakers, as opposed to conventional monitoring over screen speakers.

16. *Graphic equalizers:* These are used for equalizing for the frequency-response difference observed in a particular room compared with the average room for which the crossover is designed to produce a standardized response. There are two primary factors to be considered which cause response changes that must be equalized. One occurs in the low-frequency (20- to 315-Hz) region and is the result of modal density pattern and the presence of acoustical factors such as the knee cavity beneath the console. The other is at high frequencies (2 to 20 kHz) where a correction is needed for room volume (smaller rooms require a brighter response to have the same perceived timbre as larger rooms).

17. *THX crossover:* A set of electronic crossover cards contains electrical filters which, when combined with specific loudspeaker elements, produce a fourth-order Linkwitz-Riley response characteristic measured acoustically, with time delay for driver offset, and compensation for driver responses, screen loss, and correction to ISO 2969 curve X.

Cross-point switches under computer control provide the necessary means for quickly reconfiguring the monitor system and for storing studio setups. Relays controlled by the same computer as the cross point are used to switch the various logic lines associated with the processes listed above to change their operating modes.

Theater Sound Systems. To understand postproduction monitoring requirements, one needs to know how theaters are equipped and how they perform, ranging from the best to the worst. By making many field measurements, the knowledge gained can serve as input to the variety of simulation processes described above. But what sets the upper limit on quality; i.e., how good should the dubbing-stage monitor be made? For that, one must understand the theater sound system itself and a little of its history.

The prints manufactured from the postproduction materials are played over theater sound systems, consisting of an A chain and a B chain. The division between these chains occurs at the top of the volume control. The A chain consists of:

1. *Playback pickup:*   It provides optical or magnetic sound heads.

2. *Playback preamplifier:*   It provides correction for the *recorded characteristic* (frequency response) of the optical or magnetic recording and any losses in the playback head as well as standardization of level.

3. *A-chain filters:*   These are flat filters for magnetic or optical recordings which employ noise reduction encoding, per SMPTE 221 for mono optical recordings or for magnetic recordings not employing noise reduction encoding.

4. *Stereo matrix decoder:*   It is used for stereo variable-area recordings.

The B chain consists of:

1. Volume control
2. Room equalization (one-third-octave-band equalizer per channel)
3. Electronic crossover (if used)
4. Power amplifiers
5. Loudspeaker systems
6. Local acoustical environment of loudspeakers
7. Global acoustical environment of room

In the 1950s, the best recorded sound one could hear was in the road-show film house. By the mid-1960s, home high-fidelity systems were available with greater frequency range and better octave-to-octave musical balance over the range than were being offered to theaters. The systems which were designed for theaters had become "standard." While this promoted uniformity of reproduction across many theaters, both nationally and internationally, development came to a halt. There seemed to be no reason to change the loudspeaker since the Academy mono standard track could hardly benefit from speaker improvements. Even stereo of the 1950s brought limited advancement, since the noise of the magnetic tracks was necessarily curtailed by the high-frequency rolloff associated with the loudspeaker-screen-room system.

The early 1970s saw the application of new technologies to the old systems present in theaters. By extending the frequency range and using noise reduction companding to improve the S/N ratio, acceptable wide-range performance became available from an optical track. The addition of stereo, in a form compatible with mono, greatly improved acceptance of the better-quality track. Widespread use of "room" equalization became practical because of advancing technology. The word *room* is used in quotation marks, since the equalizer was actually equalizing more for speaker deficiencies than it was for acoustical variation among rooms. Along with the use of equalization came the accumulated knowledge among theater installers that loudspeaker systems in widespread use had very notable deficiencies which are only ameliorated but not cured through equalization. Through the 1970s, development concentrated on increasing sophistication of the A chain and part of the B chain through the point of one-third-octave-band equalization, but the limitations of the loudspeakers and rooms in which they were used increasingly became the weak link in the chain.

The most noticeable problems of older loudspeaker designs which are now solvable are that (1) low-bass and high-treble response is deficient; (2) distortion at high SPLs is evident on bass program material; (3) the combination of cross-over network and midrange dispersion characteristics gives rise to the all-too-familiar camelback-shaped power response evident in one-third-octave pink-noise measurements made in hundreds of theaters; and (4) the audience is not uniformly covered.

By combining appropriate developments which have been made since the standardization of the theater environment in the 1940s, on both theoretical and practical grounds, new system designs have emerged as being the best available today. The incorporated developments cover a wide range of fields, including loudspeaker design, acoustics, psychoacoustics, and electronics. The *THX Sound System,* developed by the author at Lucasfilm, employs direct-radiator low-frequency woofers flush-mounted in a large, flat baffle; constant-directivity high-frequency horns with improved compression drivers; and an electronic crossover network offering flat axial and power response, with excellent lobing behavior. These features have been demonstrated to result in greater frequency range and smoother frequency response, greater low-frequency acoustic output, and more uniform coverage of the audience. Furthermore, the complete B chain, following the equalizers, is made a comprehensive part of the system by setting specifications for the local acoustical environment of the loudspeakers and the global acoustical environment of the room, including reverberation time, control of echoes, background noise level, and intrusive noise control. Acceptance of the system has been high both in professional usage and in theaters.

REFERENCES

1. National Association of Broadcasters, 1771 N Street N.W., Washington, D.C. 20036, *Magnetic Tape Recording and Reproducing Standards,* Table 4 and Fig. 5.

2. Minnesota Mining and Manufacturing Company, *Measurements on 3M 350 Magnetic Film and 3M 480 1-Inch Video Tape.*

3. Howard M. Tremaine, *Audio Cyclopedia,* Howard W. Sams & Co., Indianapolis, 1959.

4. Norton Associates, 10 Di Thomas Court, Copiague, N.Y. 11726, *Buzz Track Test Film.*

5. Society of Motion Picture and Television Engineers, 595 West Hartsdale Avenue, White Plains, N.Y. 10607, Recommended Practice, *Recording Level for Dialog in Motion-Picture Film.*

6. Henrik Staffeldt, "Measurement and Prediction of the Timbre of Sound Reproduction," *J. Audio Eng. Soc.,* **32**(6) (June 1984), 410–414.

7. Gert-Jan Vogelaar, "CD Video and Audio Engineering," presented at the 83d Convention of the Audio Engineering Society (October 16–19,1987), preprint 2541.

8. R. A. Greiner and M. Schoessow, "Design Aspects of Graphic Equalizers," presented at the convention of the Audio Engineering Society (May 12–15, 1981), preprint 1767.

CHAPTER 15
NOISE REDUCTION SYSTEMS

Ray Dolby
Chairman, Dolby Laboratories Inc., San Francisco, California

David P. Robinson
Senior Vice President, Dolby Laboratories Inc., San Francisco, California

Leslie B. Tyler
Vice President, Engineering, dbx Inc., Newton, Massachusetts

15.1 INTRODUCTION

All forms of electric or electronic transmission or storage have noise limitations. Sometimes these limitations are inevitable (as when they are determined by the physical properties of the medium), while in other cases the limitations are by choice (such as a determination of quality required compared with decisions about how many radio channels can be fitted into an available bandwidth). Often a choice made at one time becomes unacceptable in later years as standards and expectations rise with the introduction of new technology.

The usual limitations on a system are at the extremes. There is a maximum signal level which cannot be exceeded without introducing unacceptable distortion and a minimum level where the system noise becomes predominant. The difference between these levels is usually called the dynamic range of the system; for example, the compact cassette has a dynamic range of about 55 dB (without noise reduction), and the compact disk about 90 dB.

There are many available techniques to increase this dynamic range. Clearly noise is not so audible in the presence of a loud program, so that an obvious ploy used widely in recording and broadcast studios is to raise the level of low-level signals. This is relatively easy to do when the program is known, for example, after several rehearsals of a piece or during the broadcast of a published work when the score will alert the recording engineer to changing dynamics. However, this approach is applicable only when the modification to the dynamic range is neither large nor sudden, so that the listener is not aware of the changes introduced. The greater the difference between the dynamic range of the program and that of the transmission or recording process, the more compression must be applied and the more obvious it becomes.

As well as noise reduction by modification of program transmission, there is noise reduction by modification of reception. Clearly, a simple technique is to introduce filters to remove the offending noise, such as low-pass filters to remove hiss and high-pass filters to remove hum. (Tone controls are a crude example of such filters.) Static filters have their uses, but unfortunately they usually remove wanted program as well as the noise; so they are not usually employed for high-quality use.

Dynamic filters, usually controlled by the program itself, have certain uses especially when the content of the program is of more interest than its quality. There are available a variety of professional devices[1,2] and a few consumer versions, the most notable of which is a system known as DNR (dynamic noise reduction), marketed by National Semiconductor,[3] with some 25 million products on the market at the end of 1986. These devices are active when there is no program to cover the offending noise and are switched off or modified automatically when the program contains levels and frequencies which mask the noise.

For high-quality use, any signal processing performed on the signal before it reaches the noisy recording or transmission medium must be capable of being undone at the playback or receiving stage. Thus, in broad terms, if the signal was compressed in recording, it must be expanded in playback, restoring the original signal dynamics. The noise introduced in the recording process is subject only to the expanding or decoding process and so is reduced relative to the wanted signal. Such a system is easy to conceptualize but extremely difficult to make so that its operation is inaudible. Most simple systems introduce artifacts such as breathing (the background noise varies audibly in sympathy with the program), modulation effects (the average program level changes in response to a particular sound), and distortion on abrupt changes in level (transient or overshoot distortion).

A system of compressing and later expanding is known generically as a *compandor*. The history of the noise reduction or compandor techniques is long, with the first applications in the 1920s in the telecommunication industry. These early systems were for voice circuits and had no place in high-quality audio engineering, but interest turned to such use in the 1950s. Even so, the demands of high quality meant that these conventional approaches were not commercially successful. An initial period of acceptance by the industry of a particular commercial product was followed by realization that other problems, often more objectional than a uniform layer of hiss, were created. One of the few ideas introduced at that time that are still in use today is ground-noise reduction in optical film recording (see Chap. 12).

In 1965 the Dolby A-type noise reduction system was developed, with the first sales in 1966. This system revolutionized analog audio recording. Once the initial disbelief based on past experience was overcome, the system became a success in all forms of recording and communications; by the end of 1986, more than 100,000 channels were in use. This success was due to the novel approach of the system's signal processing, which allowed noise reduction without any of the fundamental artifacts of conventional techniques.

Audio noise reduction is now legitimized and has applications wherever there is not an engineering solution to a problem; that is, it should not be used to cover up bad engineering such as leakage of hum into circuits from poorly designed power transformers. Some of these applications are described in Chap. 10, "Analog Magnetic-Tape Recording and Reproduction," Chap. 12, "Film Recording and Reproduction," Chap. 14, "Postproduction Systems and Editing," and others.

The following section by R. M. Dolby on the Dolby A-type system serves as a good introduction to all forms of noise reduction and compandor systems as well as describing the totally different approach of Dolby systems. In particular, Refs. 4 to 15 form a useful background to conventional approaches to noise reduction.

15.2 DOLBY A-TYPE NOISE REDUCTION*

15.2.1 Introduction*

In an audio recording or transmission channel, noises of varying degrees of avoidability arise in the channel itself. Apart from correction at the source, any scheme to reduce the audibility of such noises, which may include hum, crosstalk, printthrough, hiss, and other undesired signals, can be classified broadly into one of two types (Fig. 15.1):

1. Noncomplementary, in which the signal is postprocessed only, thereby producing an overall alteration of the signal while reducing noise
2. Complementary, in which both preprocessing and postprocessing are used, the attempt being to produce no overall alteration while reducing noise

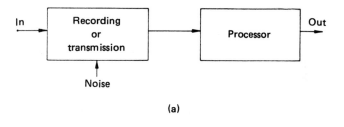

(a)

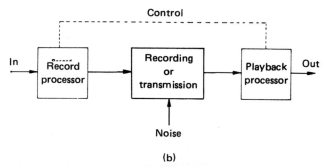

(b)

FIG. 15.1   Noise reduction systems, illustrating two basic types with reference to effects on signal. The control path shown in *b* is optional. (*a*) Noncomplementary system. (*b*) Complementary system.

* Section 15.2 is adapted from a paper by R. M. Dolby, "An Audio Noise Reduction System," *J. Audio Eng. Soc.*, **15**(4), 383–388 (1967). It is published here by courtesy of the AES.

Examples of noncomplementary noise reduction systems include simple tone controls and filters. In more sophisticated forms, the filtering action may be made dynamic, as in the Dynaural system of Scott[4] or the multiple-band diode expander system of Olson.[5] Automatic signal-controlled attenuators, which function similarly on a wideband basis, have also been described.[6,7]

The noise problem has also been attacked in complementary ways, the simplest method being the use of optimized equalization characteristics.[8] Various types of compressors and expanders have been devised, both of the instantaneous variety, employing nonlinear networks, and of the syllabic type, in which linear variable-gain devices are controlled in accordance with the signal envelope[9-12]; in some systems pilot tones are used in the expansion process.[13,14] An electronically switched two-channel (low-level–high-level) noise reduction system has also been developed by Mullin.[15]

15.2.2 Requirements

It is possible to draw up a set of requirements which any noise reduction system must meet if it is to be used without reservation in high-quality recording or transmission channels. The system will necessarily be of the complementary type.

Overall Signal Quality Requirements

1. The output signal should not be perceptibly different from the input in frequency response, transient response, and dynamics; stereo signals thus should be perceptibly free of image wandering or shifting.

2. The system should not introduce perceptible nonlinear distortion of transient or steady-state signals at any level or at any frequency or combination of frequencies; the overload point should be substantially above the normal peak-signal level.

3. The system should have a low internal noise level and should not generate any additional perceptible noises in the presence of signals.

4. All the above requirements should be met in tandem operation of the system (i.e., with multiple processing and deprocessing of the signal).

Requirements Relating to Recording or Transmission Channel

1. The output from the recording-sending processor should be suitable for transmission through one channel of normal audio bandwidth.

2. Correct operation should not be dependent upon linear phase-frequency response in the channel.

3. Normally encountered errors or fluctuations in gain and frequency response of the channel should not cause audibly significant changes in the system output.

4. The system should not modify significantly the overall steady-state or transient overload characteristics of the channel.

Interchangeability Requirements

1. The operating characteristics of the system should be fixed and reproducible.

2. The processing units should be sufficiently stable with time, temperature, and other factors to permit interchange of recordings or channels.

Noise Reduction Requirements

1. The amount of noise reduction should be perceptibly similar for all types of noises encountered.

2. The noise reduction action should be perceptibly free of signal-modulated noise effects with any normally encountered combination of program material and noise.

15.2.3 Compandors

Of the possible noise reduction methods which have been investigated, the syllabic compressor and expander (compandor) technique (Fig. 15.2) has been the subject of the most development effort. Since the noise reduction system to be described here may be roughly classified as a compandor, it is worth noting some of the limitations of previous approaches to compression and expansion.

Well-known compandor difficulties—which by now are regarded as classical—include poor tracking between recording-sending and reproducing-receiving, both statically and dynamically; high sensitivity to gain errors in recording or transmission; inadequate dynamic range (high noise level versus high distortion); overshooting with transient inputs; audible modulation-product generation under dynamic conditions; distortion of low frequencies by control-signal ripple modulation; and production of noticeable signal-modulated noise effects.

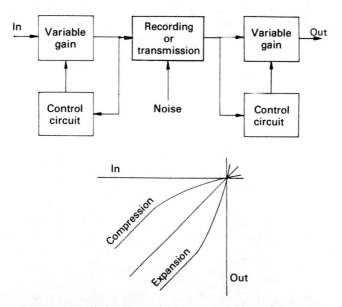

FIG. 15.2 Layout and input-output transfer characteristics of a compandor noise reduction system.

Comparison of compandor performance with the previously listed requirements for high-quality applications shows that the normal compression and expansion approach is inadequate. Compandors have thus been found to be usable without qualification only in relatively low-grade narrowband applications such as telephone circuits.

15.2.4 Noise Reduction System: Differential Method

A noise reduction system which is capable of meeting the listed requirements has been developed and is described below.

In normal compression or limiting, a primary object is to modify high-level-signal dynamics; it is thus unfortunately necessary to subject the signal as a whole to the hazards of passage through a variable-gain system. In applying compression techniques to the noise reduction problem, in which the objective does not include modification of signal dynamics, it is unnecessary and undesirable to operate upon high-level signal components; noise amplitude in a high-quality channel is only of the order of 0.1 percent of maximum signal amplitude. It would clearly be preferable to generate a small correction or differential component which could be appropriately subtracted from the signal, thereby canceling or reducing noise while leaving the larger aspects of the signal untouched.

The differential treatment of the signal in the present noise reduction system is illustrated in Fig. 15.3. The networks (operators) G_1 and G_2 are signal multipliers controlled by the amplitudes, frequencies, and dynamic properties of the signals fed into them. During reproduction, network G_2 passes low-level components (noise) back to the subtractor, which partially cancels these components in the signal from the channel. In the process of reducing noise, G_2 and the subtractor also partially cancel low-level signal components. To compensate for this cancellation, the network G_1, which has the same characteristics as G_2, adds an identical component prior to recording or sending.

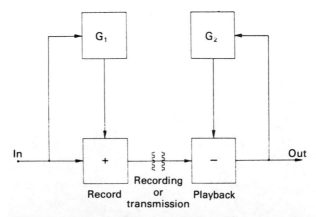

FIG. 15.3 Basic layout of the noise reduction system. In practice, the operators G_1 and G_2 comprise identical sets of four filters and low-level compressors.

These operations may be expressed in the following way. If the input to the recording processor is x (some function of time), the signal in the channel is y, and the output signal from the reproducing processor is z, we have

$$y = [1 + G_1(x)]x \tag{15.1}$$

and $\qquad z = y - zG_2(z) \qquad \text{or} \qquad z = \{1/[1 + G_2(z)]\}y \tag{15.2}$

Combining Eqs. (15.1) and (15.2),

$$z = \{[1 + G_1(x)]/[1 + G_2(z)]\}x \tag{15.3}$$

The solution of interest is $G_1 = G_2$; $z = x$. Thus, the output signal will be equal to the input signal if the recording and reproducing differential networks (i.e., the operators G_1 and G_2) are identical, on condition that $G(z)$ is not allowed to become -1 (no oscillation) and that the functions in Eqs. (15.1) and (15.2) are continuous and single-valued (no tracking ambiguity).

The prime requirement of any high-quality noise reduction system—that the signal should be unchanged overall—is thereby satisfied, and it is necessary only to choose an operator that yields a recording-sending signal which is compatible with the channel and that produces satisfactory noise reduction properties.

Steady-State Properties. Referring to the steady-state transfer characteristics shown in Fig. 15.4, the noise reduction requirement, together with the desirability of interfering as little as possible with high-level-signal components, dictates a reproducing (expansion) curve of the type shown in Fig. 15.4*b*; that is, the gain at low levels must be reduced, while a unity-gain condition should prevail at high levels. The required differential-component transfer characteristic, shown in Fig. 15.4*c*, is then determined, being linear up to the compression threshold, rising slightly with increasing input, and finally decreasing with larger inputs. In practice, such a characteristic is formed by deriving the compressor control voltage from a combination of feed-forward and feedback signals.

The recording (compression) transfer characteristic shown in Fig. 15.4*a* is complementary to the reproducing characteristic, amplifying low-level-signal components in order to compensate for the corresponding deficiencies produced by the noise reduction action during reproduction.

Comparison of the differential method of forming the compression and expansion laws with the conventional approach depicted in Fig. 15.2 shows that the scheme has several advantages. Nonlinear and modulation distortion are both reduced since the compressor (limiter) contribution is negligible at high levels. System noise problems are alleviated, and the variable-gain device can be operated at higher levels than would be possible if it were called upon to pass the whole dynamic range.

Tracking-accuracy problems between units are also reduced, since the transfer characteristic is largely determined by two readily controlled factors: the compression threshold and the addition or subtraction coefficient of the differential component. At low and high levels the possibility of mistracking is minimal, and in the transition region it is not a difficult design matter to hold the error to a small fraction of a decibel.

A further tracking characteristic concerns the compatibility of the system with the audio channel. To a first order, gain variation in the channel manifests itself only at a level change at the output, not as an alteration of signal dynamics. For the parameters used in the present system the maximum tracking error, having a

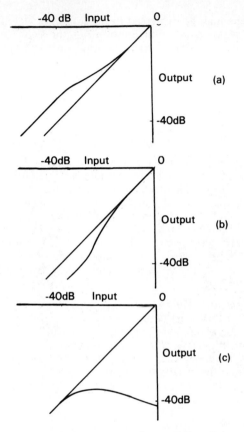

FIG. 15.4 Input-output characteristics of the noise reduction system. The compression characteristic is formed by adding the differential component to the input signal; the expansion characteristic is formed by subtracting the differential component from the recorded-transmitted signal in accordance with the negative-feedback configuration shown in Fig. 15.3. (*a*) Compression. (*b*) Expansion. (*c*) Differential component.

decibel value approximately equal to that of the decibel error in gain, occurs at about 30 dB below peak operating level, where its effect is unobtrusive. The method is thus, in practice, tolerant of moderate errors in gain. This tolerance is especially significant in stereo, as it enables the noise reduction system to operate without control-signal interconnections.

A related matter is the tracking behavior of the system with channels having nonlinear phase-frequency response. For a given rms value, the peak and average values of a complex wave depend on the phase relationships of the various frequency components. With a channel of uncertain phase response it is in principle necessary to control the compression and expansion operations by using the rms value of the signal, a procedure which at best is inconvenient. However, in practice a combination of peak and average values is a sufficiently accurate indicator of the rms value to permit the use of relatively simple rectification and smoothing circuits; in the present system such circuits are used. Good tracking is thereby obtained even when the signal has suffered considerable phase distortion.

A further channel-compatibility aspect concerns the possibility of overloading channels with frequency-dependent overload characteristics. The overload properties may be further complicated if preemphasis is used. Since preemphasis is usually based on the energy probability distribution with frequency for normally encountered sounds, it is evident that any practical noise reduction system should not interfere unduly with this distribution. The compression of comparatively high-level signal components thus must be avoided; the transfer characteristic of the present system satisfies this condition (see Fig. 15.4a).

Dynamic Properties. Overshoots, arising because of control-circuit time lag, normally have maximum amplitudes equal in value to the degree of compression. Such overshoots waste some of the dynamic range of the audio channel if they are passed linearly. Furthermore, if they are clipped by the channel, various undesirable side effects can be created: for example, blocking of amplifiers, breakthrough from groove to groove with disks, and interference with other channels if modulated carriers are used. Controlled clipping of the output signal in the compressor itself is a method of avoiding these difficulties, but it has the disadvantage of reducing the overload margin.

The usual solution is to make the attack time as short as possible and either to clip within the device or to depend upon the shortness of the overshoot to minimize side effects with clipping in the channel. Unfortunately, the use of short attack times results in side effects in the signal. Rapid changes in gain cause significant modulation products to be generated, which may or may not be canceled by reciprocal treatment following transmission.

With the method under discussion it is possible not only to confine overshoots to small values but to use relatively long attack times, thereby reducing modulation distortion. Referring to the differential-network portion of Fig. 15.5, the method used is to follow the compressor circuit (linear limiter) with a conventional symmetrical clipper (nonlinear limiter). A suddenly applied signal is thus momentarily passed without attenuation to the clipper; the differential component is confined to an amplitude which results in negligible overshoot when added to the main signal. In the present system the clipping level has been chosen to limit the overshoot to 2 dB with peak-amplitude step inputs.

The addition of the low-amplitude clipped signal to the large-amplitude pure main signal results in momentary distortion of a few percent, but the degradation is so small and of such short duration (1 ms or less, depending on the frequency) that it is masked by transient components present in the input signal, as well as subjectively attenuated by the relatively slow loudness-growth characteristics of the ear.[16] In practice, the clipper circuit is rarely called upon to perform its function, the compressor operating linearly except with the most percussive types of program material.

Regarding modulation distortion, it is evident that at high levels such effects are negligible because of the diminished influence of the differential component. By the use of nonlinear control-signal smoothing circuits, distortion is minimized at low levels as well. A relatively long attack time (of the order of 0.1 s) is used for small variations in signal amplitude, the gain changes produced being slow

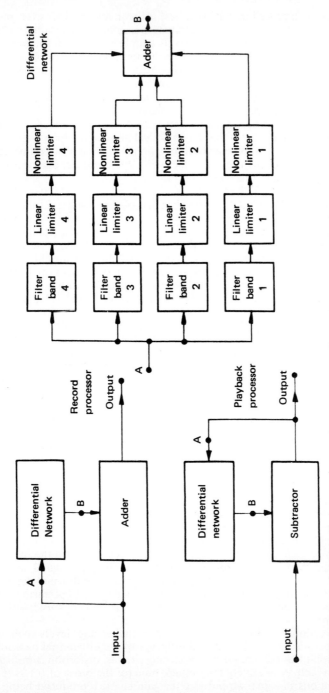

FIG. 15.5 Basic block diagram of the noise reduction system. The differential network, shown at the right, is the same for both recording and playback; the filters and compressors work under identical conditions, both statically and dynamically, in the two modes.

enough that they do not generate audible modulation products. The time constant is decreased in accordance with the size of the amplitude transition, and for steps large enough to cause the compressor output to exceed the clipper threshold the attack time is reduced to such an extent that the modulation-clipping distortion produced is masked by the transient components present in the input signal.

The use of long attack times as described not only reduces modulation distortion but tends to improve the noise reduction of the system. Since the amount of noise reduction depends upon the amplitude of the differential component in relation to that of the signal in the main path, it is an advantage if short transients of moderate amplitude are prevented from causing unnecessary compression of the differential component. Overshoots of several decibels may be produced under these conditions, but they are of such low amplitude compared with the peak level that they are handled linearly in all respects.

While the attack behavior is undoubtedly the most important dynamic aspect of the system, particularly in relation to ensuring compatibility of the recording-sending-processor output with the audio channel, the decay or recovery time is of equal significance when the noise reduction properties are considered. The problem in this regard is to reduce the recovery time to such a value that noise reduction following cessation of high-amplitude signals is provided adequately by the residual masking phenomenon,[17] by which the sensitivity of the ear is momentarily reduced. The noise reduction action of the system must thus be restored in an interval of the order of 0.1 s, during which residual masking prevails.

The use of short recovery times in normal compressors results in high distortion at low frequencies. Furthermore, modulation distortion, which was discussed previously from the point of view of attack time, is a product of short recovery time as well as short attack time.

As with the attack aspects of the matter, the recovery problem in the present system is solved jointly by the differential method itself and by suitable choice of characteristics of the nonlinear control-signal integration circuitry; the smoothing time constant is made long under equilibrium conditions but is decreased appropriately for large, abrupt reductions in signal amplitude. In this way, low-frequency distortion in the recording-sending-processor output is readily held to negligible values at high and low levels and to moderate values (a fraction of a percent) at intermediate levels, while the recovery time is made sufficiently fast that perceptible noise modulation effects are avoided following cessation of the signal.

Because of the undistorted character of the recording-sending-processor-output signal, the system does not depend upon subsequent distortion cancellation during reproduction for correct operation. Phase errors in the audio channel thus are not troublesome; the signal may be re-recorded a number of times or be sent through transmission lines, both being important applications in which nonlinear phase-frequency characteristics prevail. Also, the signal may be processed and deprocessed repeatedly with negligible cumulative distortion effects.

It may be remarked that some of the operating characteristics discussed, which have generally been attributed to the differential method, are in fact properties of the overall compression law produced (see Fig. 15.4a). Good tracking, high tolerance of gain errors in the audio channel, avoidance of steady-state overloading of highly equalized channels, and negligible formation of modulation products at high amplitudes are features of the overall transfer characteristic, not of the method of forming it. However, the weaknesses of a direct approach to such a transfer characteristic would appear in the usual forms: overshoots, high noise level, high nonlinear distortion, difficult reproducibility, and poor stability.

15.2.5   Noise Reduction System: Band Splitting

The advantages of the differential method of deriving the compression law are dependent upon the existence of a large ratio between the maximum amplitude of the signal in the main path and the maximum amplitude of the differential component; it follows that the compression threshold must be set at a low value. Unfortunately, a low compression threshold is detrimental to good noise reduction properties. With moderate and high-level signals the noise reduction action technically disappears, so that if only one full frequency-compression band were used, an unacceptably high degree of program-modulated noise would be evident. This difficulty has been overcome in the present system by splitting the differential component into four frequency bands (Fig. 15.5). Dependence is placed on the masking effect for subjective noise reduction in portions of the spectrum occupied by signals having amplitudes appreciably higher than the compression thresholds.

Beginning with the early studies of Wegel and Lane,[18] investigations of the masking effect have been concerned almost exclusively with the masking of pure tones by tones or noise.[19] The considerable body of results available unfortunately is not very relevant in the noise reduction application, in which the masking of a band of noise by one or more tones is of interest. A closer approach to the conditions required is the masking of one band of noise by another band of noise.[20] But systematic research into the use of wideband noise as the maskee has only recently been undertaken,[21] and it would appear that it will be some time before sufficient work has been done to permit the choice of noise-reduction-system design parameters simply by reference to published psychoacoustic data.

In applying the masking phenomenon to the noise-reduction-system design problem, the number of bands used (circuit complexity) must be balanced against other parameters and the overall system performance requirements. It was found that for normal high-quality audio channels the use of four bands yields satisfactory noise reduction properties while permitting the compression thresholds to be set at a value low enough to obtain the advantages of the differential method.

In the system under discussion, using four bands with compression thresholds of 40 dB below the peak operating level, the frequency divisions are Band 1, 80 Hz low-pass; Band 2, 80 Hz to 3 kHz bandpass; Band 3, 3 kHz high-pass; Band 4, 9 kHz high-pass. Bands 1, 3, and 4 are conventional 12-dB-per-octave filters, while Band 2 has a frequency response which is complementary to that of Bands 1 and 3. The outputs of all the bands are combined with the main signal in such a way as to produce a low-level output from the recording-sending processor which is uniformly 10 dB higher than the input signal up to about 5 kHz, above which the increase in level rises smoothly to 15 dB at 15 kHz.

The figure of 10 dB represents a compromise among a number of design factors, not the least of which is the desirability of minimizing sensitivity to gain errors in the audio channel. At the high end of the spectrum an extra 5 dB of noise reduction is obtained without appreciable disadvantage in this regard. Bands 3 and 4 contribute approximately equally in this region, so that with normally encountered sounds the output of Band 3 is usually compressed substantially before the threshold is reached in Band 4. The maximum compression ratio is thereby reduced, and the possibility of program-modulated frequency response under gain-error conditions is decreased.

Because of the use of four bands, with consequent interactions between these bands, the noise reduction properties of the system under signal conditions are not altogether simple. These properties are, however, amenable to investigation and measurement by the use of low-level probe tones.

The overall noise reduction action of the system may be summarized as follows: Band 1 provides noise reduction in the hum-and-rumble frequency range; Band 2, in the midaudio range (broadband noise, crosstalk, print-through); and Bands 3 and 4, in the hiss range. With average orchestral music, Band 1 is compressed fairly often; Band 2, almost all the time; Band 3, fairly often; and Band 4, rarely. The noise reduction action thus arises most of the time from low- and high-frequency preemphasis and complementary deemphasis. The high-frequency deemphasis not only attenuates hiss but in magnetic-tape recording reduces high-frequency modulation noise. High-frequency sidebands of lower-frequency signals suffering frequency modulation due to scrape flutter are treated similarly.

15.3 OTHER SYSTEMS

Since the introduction of the Dolby A-type system in 1966, almost all the commercial systems then on the market have disappeared. Some of these earlier systems are discussed in Refs. 10 to 15. Interest in other methods of achieving noise reduction grew with the commercial success of the A-type system, and two other professional noise reduction systems for tape recording have since been introduced and remain on the market.

dbx Type I Noise Reduction System. This first design, introduced in 1971, was a modern version of the conventional approach using sophisticated control circuits. In 1982 dbx proposed a system for multichannel TV sound. This is described in the introduction to Sec. 15.7 and in Sec. 15.7.3.

ANT-Telefunken C4 Noise Reduction System. The second system is the ANT C4 compandor system (1976), which is a mixture of the linear compansion approach of dbx, but using in most of its implementations a 1:1.5 compression ratio, and the band-splitting technique used in the Dolby A-type system.[22] (ANT Nachrichtentechnik GmbH is a company formed from a divested division of the German Telefunken company, the original inventors of the C4 system.) The system is in fairly widespread use by broadcasters in Germany and Austria, but there is only limited broadcast use outside central Europe or in professional recording studios.

dbx 321 Noise Reduction System. While the dbx Type I and Type II systems have 2:1:2 companding ratios, it is, of course, possible to design systems with other ratios for other purposes. The ratio 2:1:2 was chosen because it provides sufficiently aggressive companding to eliminate the perception of background noise in tape-based recorders. Wideband compandors have also been applied to transmission-reception systems in which the transmission channel has limited dynamic range. One example is dbx's 321 noise reduction system, designed for National Public Radio's analog satellite network. This compandor must cope with a channel with only about 45-dB dynamic range and so required a higher companding ratio than 1:2.

The 321 system incorporates the basic block diagram of the Type I and Type II systems but has an extra gain of 2 between each rms detector and the voltage-controlled-amplifier (VCA) gain-control port. This produces a companding ratio of 1:3:1. The other frequency-selective networks are quite different from those of Type I and Type II, to match the signal and noise conditions of the channel and to suit the companding ratio. However, the basic principles of operation are the same. The 321 system provides better than a 85-dB dynamic range from the 45-dB channel on which it is used.

15.4 CONSUMER NOISE REDUCTION SYSTEMS: DOLBY B

Many of the concepts of Dolby A-type noise reduction are equally applicable to consumer equipment; however, the complexity and therefore the cost of the circuit preclude a direct application. Fortunately, slow-speed tape recordings are highly emphasized (for good frequency response), so that the resulting perceived noise is high-frequency in character (hiss); therefore, a system which removes hiss gives a subjective reduction in all noise. Such a system can be made economically and repeatably.

In sound-recording systems the high frequencies are often preemphasized during recording and deemphasized during reproduction to improve the signal-to-noise (S/N) ratio. However, the equalization characteristics must be chosen so that even with high-level, high-frequency signals there are no detrimental effects. Therefore, the allowable boost with fixed equalization is not as great as it might be for optimum equalization of the recording medium. For example, recording an instrument such as a violin or a piano does not usefully load the tape over the whole audio spectrum, and thus high-frequency noises are noticeable during reproduction.

It is clear that the situation could be improved with a more flexible equalization method. The B-type noise reduction system provides a characteristic, controlled by the incoming signal, which achieves a much more efficient utilization of the tape-recording medium under all signal conditions. During playback a complementary characteristic is applied which restores all signal components to their correct amplitudes and phases and, in the process, attenuates any noise introduced during recording.

In the professional Dolby A-type system (described in Sec. 15.2) the signal and noise frequency spectrum is split into four bands. In consumer tape systems, however, the main noise problem is tape hiss, and it can be handled inexpensively but adequately by the use of a single high-frequency noise reduction band. The B-type system uses such a method and is effective from approximately 1 kHz upward; the noise reduction provided is 3 dB at 500 Hz, 6 dB at 1 kHz, and 10 dB at 5 kHz and above.

In the B-type system the width of the noise reduction band is variable, being responsive to the amplitude and frequency distribution of the signal. In this way it is possible with relatively simple circuitry to obtain significant amounts of noise reduction down to quite low frequencies without causing audible modulation of the noise by the signal.

The B-type signal utilizes the same differential method of signal processing as in the A-type system. Since the high-level signals are treated separately from the low-level signals, there are no high-level signal-handling problems, the low-level signals being the only ones which undergo any kind of variable action.

A block diagram of the B-type noise reduction system is shown in Fig. 15.6. The symmetrical nature of the system can be seen at the bottom of the figure. On the playback side a network is provided which passes only low-level, high-frequency signals. These signals are allowed to return to the subtractor and partially

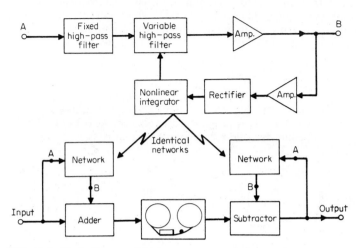

FIG. 15.6   Block diagram of the Dolby B-type noise reduction system.

cancel low-level noise components coming from the tape. High-level signals are blocked and not allowed to pass through the network and thus do not cancel; the high-level signals therefore pass through essentially unchanged.

In partially canceling the low-level noise components from the tape, the playback half of the system also partially cancels legitimate low-level components of the signal itself. Therefore, the reason for the existence of the record half of the system is to precompensate for the low-level-signal cancellation which takes place in the playback portion of the system. If, in the configuration shown, a network having characteristics identical to those used in playback is used on the record side, the system signal output will be identical to the signal at the system input. There will be no alterations of frequency response, phase response, or transient response. In other words, the system will be a truly complementary one which preserves the integrity of the signal.

From the point of view of maintaining signal integrity it is almost immaterial what type of network is used, provided only that the two networks are identical. But from a noise reduction point of view, the characteristics of the network are crucial. If the frequency response or the signal-limiting characteristics of the network are incorrect, then there may be either insufficient noise reduction or, even worse, an apparently changing amount of noise reduction, depending on the signal.

To maximize the amount of noise reduction obtained under signal conditions the high-level blocking circuit mentioned previously is a variable high-pass filter. Under given signal conditions the cutoff frequency is caused to shift upward sufficiently to attenuate any high-level signal components but not so far that low-level signals at higher frequencies cannot pass through. It is important that all low-level, high-frequency components be able to pass through, since in the playback mode these return to the subtractor and produce the noise reduction. Thus, the desired action of attenuating high-level signal components, so that there is no danger of tape overload, is achieved without impairing the noise reduction action at frequencies higher than that of the high-level signal. The cutoff frequency of the filter automatically conforms to the amplitude and frequency of the incoming signal. This technique yields sufficient noise reduction even under high-level signal conditions to avoid noise modulation effects (breathing).

The variable filter follows a 1.5-kHz fixed high-pass filter, which defines the lower effective limit of the noise reduction action and further reduces noise modulation effects. The variable high-pass filter is controlled by an amplified, rectified, and smoothed signal taken from the output of the filter.

The frequency response of the record unit under single-signal conditions at various levels is shown in Fig. 15.7. When the signal level increases, the amount of high-frequency boosting is progressively reduced. At 0 VU (volume unit) the boosting is negligible, and the record output signal is substantially equal to the input signal.

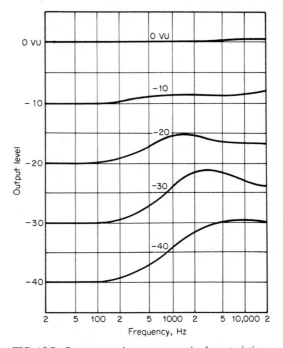

FIG. 15.7   B-type record-processor static characteristics.

The characteristics of the playback unit are opposite to those of the record unit; the inverse of the low-level encoding curve also indicates the amount of noise reduction given by the circuit. This measures just less than 10 dB when using a weighting filter such as the CCIR (International Radio Consultative Committee) or CCIR ARM (average-responding meter) network.

The Dolby B-type noise reduction system was introduced in 1969 and has become an essential part of all high-quality cassette recorders; indeed, by the end of 1986 more than 150 million products using B-type noise reduction had been manufactured. The system shares the Dolby A-type system's attributes of gentle signal processing with extremely low audible artifacts. While the early versions used discrete circuits, for many years realizations have made use of about 30 different integrated circuits from several worldwide manufacturers. The noise reduction characteristics of all these devices are identical; differences are in the number of channels in one package, the types of mode switching, voltage supplies required, etc.

15.5 RECENT CONSUMER DEVELOPMENTS

As the consumer became used to this level of quality and as new forms of home storage of music and of transmission became available [such as the compact disk and pulse-code-modulation (PCM) recordings on tape], so did expectations of even more noise reduction. A consumer version of the dbx noise reduction circuit called dbx Type II was launched; then, in 1980, Dolby C-type noise reduction was introduced. This followed the same general concept of the sliding-band technique used in the B-type circuit, but it staggered two such circuits operating at different signal amplitudes and also covered a wider bandwidth. The amount of noise reduction in the C type approaches 20 dB when measured with a filter which approximates the ear's sensitivity. In addition, the circuit uses techniques to overcome the fundamental high-frequency, high-amplitude saturation effect of magnetic tape. A fuller description of the circuit is given in Sec. 15.6, taken from a paper by R. M. Dolby. The system found acceptance in higher-quality cassette recorders and, helped by many integrated circuits designed for a variety of applications, had been used in over 20 million products by the end of 1986.

15.6 DOLBY C NOISE REDUCTION*

15.6.1 Comparison of Tape and Disk Noise Characteristics

The B-type noise reduction system[23,24] was developed in 1967–1968 and first applied to open-reel recording (KLH models 40 and 41). However, by this time there was a general feeling that a more convenient tape format was required for widespread use. In late 1968 we therefore began experimenting with eight-track cartridges and the B-type system. The results were encouraging if suitable tape formulations and oxide thicknesses were used, but ergonomic and aesthetic considerations persuaded us that the eight-track cartridge would not be a success as a quality recording medium; anyone willing to tolerate an endless-loop format would be unlikely to be very much interested in sound quality.

In early 1969 we turned to the Philips compact cassette, which was another of several tape formats competing for the popular market at that time. The compact cassette offered the advantage of rapid access, which appeared to be a requirement for acceptance by critical listeners. The disadvantage of very low tape speed (1⅞ in/s, or 4.75 cm/s) was to some extent offset by the special tape formulations and oxide thicknesses that had to be created, since there was no practical possibility for the industry to use standard thick oxide ¼-in (6.3-mm) tape in cassettes (as there had been in eight-track cartridges).

---

* Section 15.6 is adapted from a paper by R. M. Dolby, "A 20 dB Audio Noise Reduction System for Consumer Applications," *J. Audio Eng. Soc.*, **31**(3), 98–113 (1983). It is published here by courtesy of the AES.

Throughout 1969 the properties of available cassette recorders and cassette tapes were researched by Dolby, and by the end of that year we had adapted and improved several cassette decks to provide wide-frequency-response, low-distortion performance with high stability. Using the B-type noise reduction system, we demonstrated our results to cassette-deck manufacturers and cassette-duplication firms. There was general agreement that this was a promising development; under good conditions it was possible to produce overall results that were comparable with the best disks. The technology has since been adopted and widely used, and by this time it is possible to draw up a comparative list of the main technical defects of disks and B-type encoded cassettes when produced and reproduced under the best conditions (see Table 15.1).

TABLE 15.1   Comparison of Tape and Disk Noise Characteristics

Disks	Cassettes
Mold-grain noise	Hiss
Hiss	High-frequency-overload distortion
Ticks and pops	

The low-frequency mold-grain noises (rumbling and rushing sounds) produced by disks are evidently unnoticed by most listeners; perhaps these noises are masked by the ambient noises of typical listening environments. Disk-processing hiss is variable but usually not too obtrusive. The main audible defect of most disks is low-level ticks and pops. In contrast, cassette tapes have no audible rumble or other low-frequency noises, and, of course, there are no ticks and pops. However, the hiss level is audibly greater than that of disks; the continuing presence of this hiss has evidently been the main factor in causing the cassette to fall just short of disks in the estimation of quality-conscious listeners. A further element is that cassette tapes, especially the ordinary formulations used in mass duplication, do not have the high-level, high-frequency recording capability of disks. For economic reasons, most duplicators are reluctant to use tapes that might overcome this problem.

In 1978 we developed a system, HX (headroom extension), to improve the high-level, high-frequency performance of normal cassette tapes.[25] This system was introduced in consumer cassette recorders in 1979–1980. (Later, a new approach, HX Pro, was introduced.[26]) While these developments were welcomed by the technical community, there was still a feeling that the basic noise performance of the cassette, using the B-type noise reduction system, was inadequate. Several different noise reduction systems offering more than 10 dB of noise reduction became available, and many cassette-deck manufacturers requested a response from us to this activity.

Until early 1980 the author remained unconvinced that the underlying demand for an improved (and more costly) system would be sufficient to justify the industry infrastructure required to support a new high-performance standard. However, performance expectations do not appear to diminish. Thus a new noise reduction system called C type has been developed. It is hoped that it will meet a reasonable proportion of these expectations. The author, as well as many others, will be waiting with interest to see whether the long-term demand is broadly based enough to result in a significant change in usage patterns.

This section describes the new system, which utilizes two series-connected sliding-band compressor and expander stages, operating at different levels, to solve the problem of increasing overall compression, expansion, and noise reduction without introducing side effects. Further developments reduce high-frequency tape saturation and improve the tolerance of the system to irregular response of the recorder at very high frequencies. Good frequency response and level reliability are nonetheless required at lower frequencies.

15.6.2   Staggered-Action Dual-Level Format

In the development of the A-type noise reduction system in 1965–1966 (see Sec. 15.2), the author found that a two-path configuration and a maximum dynamic action of the order of 10 dB, placed some 30 dB below the nominal maximum level, provided a good margin of safety in solving the problem of suppressing compressor overshoots without introducing audible distortions caused by rapid modulation of the signal. In the development of the B-type system in 1967–1969 these facts, coupled with tests to determine the maximum dynamic action likely to be allowable for reasonable compatibility when encoded recordings were reproduced without decoding, established the maximum noise reduction at 10 dB.

In the development of the C-type system in 1980, the compressor overshoot and modulation-distortion consideration pointed strongly toward the retention of the dual-path 10-dB low-level format which had proved to be successful in the A-type and B-type systems. While it was tempting to contemplate stretching the capability of the basic 10-dB circuit to performance levels in the 15- to 20-dB region, only a few experiments were enough to reconfirm that such an approach would be hazardous at best; it would be better to accept the cost penalty of a more complex method and to be safe. A two-band configuration would not be of much help, since each band would still be required to operate with the full dynamic effect. However, if two stages could be cascaded, then the stage gains and resultant compression and expansion would be multiplied (or added on a decibel basis) to yield an overall noise reduction of, say, 20 dB. While early tests indicated that this was an attractive method under ideal conditions, the resulting high compression ratios (up to 4:1) would clearly be a problem with the production and operating tolerances of practical cassette recorders. A method was therefore devised whereby the dynamic actions of the two stages could be spread out or staggered into different level regions. Such dynamic-action staggering, in which one stage operates at levels comparable with those of the B-type circuit and the second stage treats signals some 20 dB lower in level, is possible with compressor and expander stages having a certain type of transfer characteristic which will be discussed. This staggering technique proved to be a key element in the development of the C-type system.

Referring to Fig. 15.8, the A-type and B-type noise reduction systems employ a level transfer characteristic which at any particular frequency comprises the following elements:

1. A low-level linear portion up to a threshold (where *linear* in this context denotes constant gain with changing input level)

2. An intermediate-level nonlinear portion (changing gain with changing input level) above the threshold and up to a finishing point, providing a certain maximum compression or expansion ratio

3. A high-level linear portion having a gain different from the gain of the low-level portion

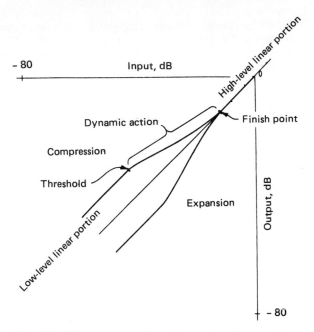

FIG. 15.8   Bilinear compression and expansion characteristics.

This type of characteristic can be designated a bilinear characteristic because there are two portions of substantially constant gain. Such characteristics may be distinguished from other types of characteristics, namely:

1. A logarithmic or nonlinear characteristic with either a fixed or a changing slope and with no linear portion (the gain changes over the whole dynamic range)
2. A characteristic having two or more portions of which only one portion is linear

An advantage of a bilinear characteristic is that the threshold can be set above the input noise level or transmission-channel noise level to exclude the possibility of control of the circuit by noise; the low-level region is a reliable *gain floor,* which contributes to overall stability of the signal. The high-level portion of substantially constant gain avoids the nonlinear treatment of high-level signals which would otherwise introduce distortion, either by rapid modulation of the signal or by overshoots and subsequent clipping. In the region of dynamic action, at intermediate levels, relatively long attack and recovery times are used to reduce modulation distortion. The attack and recovery times are progressively reduced with increasing amplitude steps, the high-level portion providing a region within which to deal with the overshoots, which in a dual-path system are suppressed by clipping diodes acting upon the noise reduction signal only.

Thus with 10 dB of dynamic action spread over an input-signal-level range of about 20 to 25 dB, so that the maximum compression ratio does not substantially exceed 2:1, it is possible to set the threshold at a level high enough to be well clear of input-signal noise and recorder noise, that is, in the region of 40 dB below the nominal peak level. This leaves a high-level linear region of some 20 dB for the suppression of overshoots.

Note that bilinear compressors and expanders determine the two end regions of constant gain by means of fixed, preset circuit elements, such as resistors and capacitors, which are inherently stable and cannot cause dynamic errors, waveform distortions, and the like. Only in the transitional area can any dynamically active portions of the circuits introduce signal errors.

In contemplating the possibility of a multistage circuit, it should be noted that prior attempts have resulted in a multiplication of the maximum compression ratios of the individual stages with the consequence of an overall high compression ratio, which is not very useful in a practical noise reduction system (for example, one circuit with a compression ratio of 2:1 and the other with a compression ratio of 3:1 will yield an overall ratio of 6:1). Other cascaded approaches have utilized compressor stages operating in mutually exclusive frequency stages. While such an arrangement may not necessarily result in any increase in the maximum compression ratio over that of a single stage, it cannot provide an overall increase of noise reduction at a particular frequency.

Experience has shown that with a compression ratio of much more than 2:1 it becomes increasingly difficult to ensure complementarity between the compressor and the expander; in particular, level errors or errors in the frequency response of the recorder lead to correspondingly multiplied errors at the output of the expander.

An examination of bilinear circuits used in a series connection shows that they not only have the previously discussed advantages but further ones as well, namely, a way of solving the high-compression-ratio problem and a way of dealing with the larger overshoots which accompany greater overall compression.

Note that the superposition of the high- and low-level linear regions does not increase the compression ratio in these regions (since by definition the compression ratio is 1). The compression ratio is increased only in the limited region in which dynamic action takes place. Therefore, it becomes possible to separate the areas of dynamic action of the two stages in such a way as to obtain the required overall increase in compression without altering the overall maximum compression or expansion ratio significantly. A further feature is that the overall result is bilinear, with all the attendant advantages. Thus the action-staggering possibility of bilinear compressors and expanders represents a further advantage of this type of device.

At any given frequency, the thresholds and dynamic regions of the compressor or expander stages are set to different values so as to stagger the intermediate-level portions of the characteristics of the stages. This results in a change of gain over a wider range of intermediate input levels than for each of the stages individually, an increased difference between the gains at low and high input levels, and a maximum compression or expansion ratio which is substantially no greater than the maximum compression ratio of any single stage.

The thresholds of the overshoot suppressors are also staggered along with the stagger of the syllabic thresholds. The overshoots of the low-level stage are correspondingly reduced.

Figure 15.9 shows the basic block diagram of the staggered-action method. A high-level bilinear compressor feeds the low-level bilinear compressor connected in series. During playback a pair of series-connected bilinear expanders receives the input from the signal channel and provides an overall noise-reduction-system output at the output of the high-level expander.

For overall complementarity of the system, the order of the stages in the com-

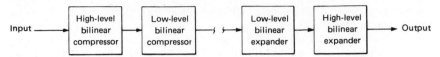

FIG. 15.9   Basic block diagram of a staggered-action bilinear noise reduction system.

pressor is reversed in the expander. Thus the last stage of the expander is complementary to the first stage of the compressor (and likewise the first stage of the expander to the last stage of the compressor) in all respects, both steady-state and time-dependent.

The separation or staggering of the high- and low-level stages is depicted in Fig. 15.10, which plots compression ratio versus input amplitude (horizontal axis) for the compressor or expander stages operating at a particular frequency. The top curves are those of compressors; the bottom curves, those of expanders. In this example the areas of action as a function of input level are separated so that the product of the two curves results in an overall characteristic having a compression ratio or expansion ratio which does not exceed 2:1 (1:2) between the two maximum compression points 1a and 2a (1b and 2b) of the two devices. For

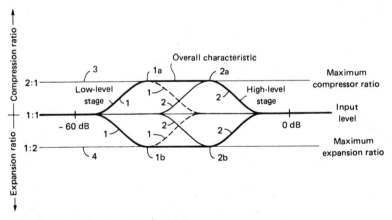

FIG. 15.10   Action-staggering principle.

clarity, the curves are shown in idealized form; as a practical matter the curves may be somewhat asymmetrical. The compressor portion of curve 2 represents the variations of the compression ratio of the high-level stage as a function of the input level to the high-level stage, while the compressor portion of curve 1 is the variation of the compression ratio of the low-level stage as a function of the input level to the high-level stage, as if the high-level stage had a constant gain. In practice, the high-level stage modifies the input signal to the low-level stage as a function of signal level. The overall characteristic produced is the left-hand portion of curve 1, the section from 1a to 2a, and the right-hand portion of curve 2. Analogous considerations apply in the case of the expanders depicted on the lower half of the figure.

Thus even with two compressors or expanders in series, the end regions of operation still remain fixed, the maximum compression and the maximum expansion ratios are not increased beyond those of single devices, and the advantages of single bilinear devices are retained. Consequently, the maximum error in level occurring within the range of dynamic action caused by the devices in series should not substantially exceed the maximum error of a single device. With the continually changing levels of real signals, however, the time probability of a level error is increased because of the greater range of dynamic action of the cascaded devices over that of a single device.

Note that in the representation of Fig. 15.10 the dynamic action of a logarithmic compressor or expander becomes a horizontal line; line 3, for example, is the characteristic of a 2:1 compressor, and line 4 is that of a 1:2 expander. It is clear that there is no opportunity for separating or staggering the actions of such devices.

To obtain a first-order approximation of the parameter relationships in action staggering, it is useful to idealize Fig. 15.10 even further. Assume that each compressor (and expander) immediately reaches its maximum compression ratio at a threshold level and holds that ratio until it reaches a finishing point at a higher level where its dynamic action abruptly stops.

Based on observations of the resulting transfer characteristics (Fig. 15.11), Eq. (15.4) sets forth the relationship between threshold level T, finishing point F, compression ratio C, and gain G of the stages:

$$T = F - \frac{CG}{C-1}.$$

(15.4)

Using this equation is straightforward for the first stage. For the second stage, the first-stage threshold becomes the second-stage finishing point. However, the calculated threshold is the overall threshold, referred to the first-stage input. To

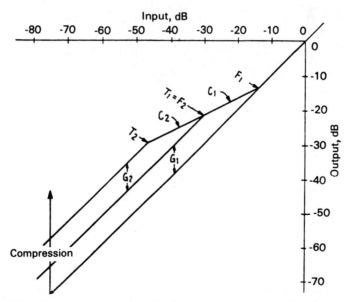

FIG. 15.11 Idealized construction to show parameter relationships [Eq. (16.4)]. C = compression ratio; T = threshold; F = finishing point; G = stage gain.

obtain the threshold of the second stage referred to its own input, the low-level signal gain of the first stage is taken into account. The equation can also be arranged to give the finishing point F, the compression ratio C, or the gain G.

Consideration of Eq. (15.4) and Fig. 15.11 shows that for the case of a 2:1 compression ratio, half of the threshold staggering is provided by the signal gain of the first stage and the other half must be provided by the control circuitry of the second stage.

As previously mentioned, a 2:1 compression ratio appears to be about the maximum that can be used in cassette recording systems because of error amplification effects during decoding. A lower compression ratio (such as 1.5:1) would permit an expander to track the compressor more easily, but, on the other hand, the dynamic action would have to extend down to lower levels, resulting in greater susceptibility to noise modulation for a given maximum amount of noise reduction. Hence there is a tradeoff between undesirable effects caused by both high and low compression ratios.

Similar considerations apply in arranging the staggering of a dual-stage system. Once the maximum allowable compression ratio has been decided, it is best to employ the minimum amount of staggering consistent with keeping the overall ratio within the design goal. Squeezing the area of dynamic action of the low-level stage up close to that of the high-level stage results in improved noise modulation performance of the low-level stage; there is little virtue in keeping the two areas well separated.

The two stages of the C-type system are each of the sliding-band type, similar to that of the B-type circuit.[23,24] The first stage of the compressor is set for operation at levels similar to that of the B-type circuit, and the second stage is set for operation at lower levels. In this order there is a useful interaction between the stage gains and the areas of dynamic action; the area of action of the downstream stage is partly determined by the signal gain of the preceding stage. Thus with 10 dB of low-level gain per stage, the control-amplifier gain requirement of the second stage is reduced by 10 dB. When a high-level signal appears, the 10-dB gain of the first stage is eliminated from the overall effective amplification used to derive the control signal of the second stage. This improves the noise modulation performance of the second-stage sliding band.

If the arrangement were reversed, with the low-level stage first, there would be reduced interaction. The control amplifier of the first stage would need a high gain to achieve the required low threshold. This high gain and low threshold would then apply even in the presence of high-level signals, which in the case of a sliding-band system would result in poorer noise modulation performance. Thus the arrangement actually used takes best advantage of the prevailing signal gains of the individual stages, namely:

1. Under very-low-level (subthreshold) signal conditions the control-amplifier gain requirement of the second stage is reduced by 10 dB over what would otherwise be required to achieve the desired staggering.

2. A signal-dependent variable-threshold effect is achieved, which with sliding-band stages reduces noise modulation effects.

15.6.3 Noise Reduction Characteristic

The maximum amount of compression and expansion to be used in the C-type system was more or less arbitrarily set at 20 dB. This seemed a natural goal, neither too little nor too ambitious, moreover offering the possibility of adapting existing B-type integrated circuits before dedicated C-type integrated circuits would become available. Nevertheless, it was necessary to determine an optimal spectral distribution of the noise reduction. If the frequencies to be treated were restricted to as narrow a range as possible, compatibility would be improved and noise modulation performance enhanced, and there would be fewer troubles caused by recorder response irregularities at the frequency extremes.

In connection with the development of the B-type system, beginning in 1967, listening tests were made to determine what range of frequencies had to be treated to bring the noise of 3¾ in/s (9.5 cm/s) open-reel recording into subjective spectral balance by using moderate to high listening levels, so that the tape hiss, with noise reduction, was discernible but not excessive. Thus the high-pass filter cutoff frequency used in the B-type circuit was set at 1.5 kHz. This cutoff frequency was retained in adapting the circuit for use with cassettes in 1969, although the filter configuration was changed to provide more noise reduction in the 300-Hz to 1.5-kHz range, as well as improved noise modulation performance.

The same kinds of listening tests were made in the development of the C-type system, using high-quality Type II cassette tape, 70-μs equalization, a quiet residential listening environment, and volume settings corresponding to rather loud listening conditions. That is, as in the B-type tests, the volume was set so that tape noise with noise reduction was perceptible but not annoying. Many filter configurations and combinations were tried. In the early stages of the development it had been hoped that one of the two stages could be left as a standard B-type circuit for easy switchable compatibility between B-type and C-type operation. However, the spectral distribution tests eventually proved that this placed too heavy a burden on the second stage; it was required to produce substantially more than 10 dB of noise reduction in the region of several hundred hertz to 2 kHz. The solution to this problem was to abandon the attempt to retain one stage as a standard B-type circuit; both circuits had to be nonstandard. Unfortunately, this approach increased the switching and component complexity, but it yielded a system in which the dynamic-action burdens are more evenly shared between the two stages. The listening tests ultimately set the filter cutoff frequencies of the two circuits equal, at two octaves below that of the B-type circuit, namely, at 375 Hz.

The use of equal cutoff frequencies yields a full compounding of the frequency discriminations of the two circuits, giving a steeply rising overall characteristic. This results in leaving the low-frequency region, in which little treatment is necessary, essentially untouched while providing substantially the full amount of noise reduction above about 500 Hz. The resulting noise reduction begins at about 100 Hz (3 dB), is about 8 dB at 200 Hz and 16dB at 500 Hz, and is essentially 20 dB above about 1 kHz. This characteristic was determined by using several types and qualities of loudspeakers and headphones, with both daytime listening and late-night listening, when the ambient noise level (in San Francisco) is significantly reduced.

The cassette recorders used in the tests were standard production models selected for low hum levels. The selection process revealed such wide variations in hum level and character that only the best recorders were used in the final tests so that hum reduction would not be a factor in determining the noise reduction characteristic. It was abundantly clear that it is possible to design recorders which are free of audible hum; a specification simply had to be established for allowable levels for the power line fundamental and each of its harmonics. Thus the shape of the low-level noise reduction characteristic was set only on tape-noise considerations; with good head preamplifiers, tape noise predominates down to about 200 Hz. Below this frequency the audible noise, relative to noise at higher frequencies, is negligible with C-type noise reduction switched in from either the amplifier or the tape.

15.6.4   Spectral Characteristic: High Frequencies

During the tests to determine the low-frequency characteristics of the system, attention was also directed to the high-frequency end of the spectrum. Consideration of the shape of the CCIR noise-weighting characteristic (Fig. 15.12), which was established for wideband, relatively low-noise audio systems, shows that there is a significantly reduced need for noise reduction at extremely high frequencies (above about 10 kHz). Cassette tape recording has problems with record-playback frequency-response reliability and tape saturation in this frequency region. Moreover, with certain kinds of signals, compressor-expander tracking accuracy is affected. It seemed that the introduction of a new noise reduction system could be used as an opportunity to optimize the overall performance of the cassette medium, including the noise reduction system, by using the above facts.

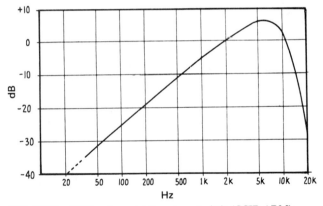

FIG. 15.12   CCIR noise-weighting characteristic (CCIR ARM).

Midband Modulation Effect.   Compressor-expander complementarity requires not only that the expander have the inverse characteristics of the compressor but also that the transmission channel between the compressor and the expander preserve relative signal amplitudes, and preferably also phases, at all frequencies within the bandwidth of the signals compressed. As received by the expander, changes in level caused by the transmission channel are indistinguishable from signal processing by the compressor. The resulting errors in the expanded signals can be significant and audible, depending on the spectral content of the signals. With the sliding-band B-type system, the most audible error is not the direct effect on very-high-frequency signals themselves but rather the modulation effect on midfrequency signals, such as in the region of several hundred hertz. For discussion purposes, this effect will be referred to as the *midband modulation effect.*

In widespread companders an amplitude error at the controlling frequency will manifest itself to the same degree in all other portions of the spectrum; this may or may not be acceptable. In sliding-band companders (B-type and C-type) an error at a dominant high frequency is substantially multiplied at midfrequencies. (Conversely, if the controlling frequencies are at midfrequencies, as they usually are, then any errors at the high-frequency extreme are reduced; this is an advantage of sliding-band companders.) The midband modulation effect is rare with normal music sources; it may, for example, be audible with intermittent high-level, high-frequency signals such as brushed cymbals in combination with a more or less continuous low-level midfrequency sound, such as background violins. In such a case, the violins may be modulated in amplitude, even after decoding, because the cymbals cause the encoder band to slide without a complementary sliding of the decoder band. This effect is basically a frequency-response error effect, as opposed to a tape-saturation effect; it might be caused by inaccurate biasing and equalization or by gap loss, poor azimuth, and the like. However, the effect will be worse if there is also saturation in the controlling-frequency region.

Reduction of the midband modulation effect is one reason for the incorporation of sharp low-pass filters, popularly known as multiplex (MPX) filters, in audio products using the B-type noise reduction system. Such band-limitation filters have corner frequencies at the edge of the useful bandpass of the system (about 16 kHz) in order to avoid limiting the system bandwidth unduly. Such filters have several functions:

1. Attenuation of subcarrier components and the 19-kHz pilot tone used in FM broadcasting in order to avoid bias *birdie* beats (whistles), impairment of the noise reduction action, and encoder-decoder mistracking

2. Attenuation of tape-recorder bias which may leak into the signal circuits in order to avoid encoder-decoder mistracking

3. Attenuation of supersonic signal components or of spurious radio-frequency components in the encoder input signal which may otherwise result in audible intermodulation products and/or bias birdies

4. Attenuation of supersonic tape noise or other transmission-channel noise at the decoder input in order to avoid encoder-decoder mistracking

5. A signal bandwidth definition to promote complementarity of the encoder-decoder; that is, to reduce the midband modulation effect

Strictly speaking, if an ideal channel exists between the encoder and the decoder, then the input filter to the decoder should be disconnected, as its inclusion theoretically results in a slight noncomplementarity (the encoder signal is subjected to one stage of filtering, the decoder to two). However, removal of the decoder input filter must be done with caution because of the considerations listed above.

Spectral Skewing.   The solution to the midband modulation problem is rather surprising in its simplicity and is termed *spectral skewing*. Advantage is taken of the fact that the high-frequency signals which cause the problem are usually complex in nature; that is, they occupy a relatively broad band of frequencies and are not at single discrete frequencies. The method used is to subject the signals to be processed by the compressor to an abrupt high-frequency drop-off which is within the useful bandpass of the system but somewhat below the frequency at which the record-playback response becomes highly unreliable. A corner frequency of 10 to 12 kHz fulfills these conditions. In this way the distributions of the signals processed by the compressor are altered or skewed so that the compressor action is significantly less susceptible to the influence of signals beyond the abrupt rolloff

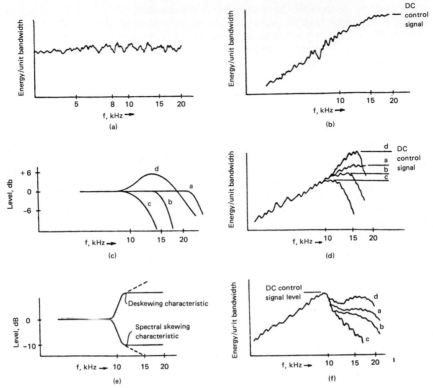

FIG. 15.13 Example showing how spectral skewing tends to desensitize the noise reduction system to recorder errors at very high frequencies. (*a*) Representation of spectral distribution of a signal having a significant wideband component. (*b*) The signal of *a* after control-amplifier preemphasis in the compressor. (*c*) Four different tape-recorder responses (a, b, c, and d). (*d*) The signal of *a* is compressed and then sent through recorder channels a, b, c, and d, resulting in the signal distributions shown at the point of rectification in the expander; different dc control signals a, b, c, and d are thereby produced. (*e*) Idealized spectral-skewing characteristic. (*f*) Same as *d*, but with spectral-skewing treatment at the input of the compressor; the same dc control signal is produced in the expander with the four different recorder responses a, b, c, and d.

frequency. Signals processed by the expander are subjected to a complementary boost so that an overall flat frequency response is maintained. The spectral-skewing network is situated at the compressor input; the deskewing network, with complementary characteristics, is located at the expander output.

The spectral-skewing principle as applied to sliding-band companders can best be understood by reference to Fig. 15.13. Figure 15.13*a* shows the spectrum of a signal that might provoke the midband modulation effect (such a signal might be generated by a wideband percussive sound). The compressor-control-circuit preemphasis results in an energy spectrum as shown in Fig. 15.13*b*. After rectification, the peak in the preemphasized ac control-signal spectrum provides the dc signal that controls the sliding-band action of the compressor.

Figure 15.13*c* illustrates the different frequency responses of four tape recorder channels, a, b, c, and d. The effect on the spectrum of Fig. 15.13*a* is to cause four different spectra (Fig. 15.13*d*) to be present in the control circuit of the expander, resulting in the four dc control signals shown; clearly, errors in decoding will result.

An idealized spectral-skewing characteristic (Fig. 15.13*e*) causes the compressor and expander to generate the same dc control signal in each case, as shown in Fig. 15.13*f*), which results in accurate decoding not only of the high-frequency signals but also of any other signals at lower frequencies. Note that the network does not eliminate the sliding of the frequency band. Indeed, sliding may be only slightly reduced. However, the sliding now becomes recoverable during playback.

The spectral-skewing characteristic used in the C-type system has a simpler and more economical form than the idealized curve of Fig. 15.13*e*. A 12-dB notch characteristic is formed by combining the input and output signals of a resonant notch filter with a center frequency of 20 kHz and a *Q* of 1. The resultant characteristic within the audio band can be seen in Fig. 15.14. Compare this with Fig. 15.15, which shows representative measured high-frequency response curves for several typical cassette recorders. These curves show that, for levels below saturation, the typical recorder in good adjustment has little deficiency in response below 10 to 20 kHz. Hence, at most levels the spectral-skewing network will ensure that there will be a significantly reduced discrepancy in the decoder control signal caused by uncertainties in response at extremely high frequencies.

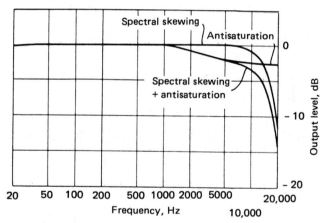

FIG. 15.14 Spectral-skewing and antisaturation characteristics used in the C-type system. The overall antisaturation effect is produced by a combination of the two characteristics.

The spectral-deskewing network used during decoding results in about a 12-dB loss of noise reduction in the 20-kHz region, leaving only about 8 dB of noise reduction. However, reference to the CCIR weighting curve (Fig. 15.12) shows that the frequencies above 10 kHz are on the steeply declining portion of the curve. In the 20-kHz region the ear is some 30 dB less sensitive to noise than in the 5-kHz region; this fact makes the spectral-skewing technique possible.

The reduced psychoacoustic need for maintaining substantial noise reduction at frequencies above 10 kHz is the high-frequency counterpart of the ordinarily observed ability of the B-type noise reduction system to provide a subjectively

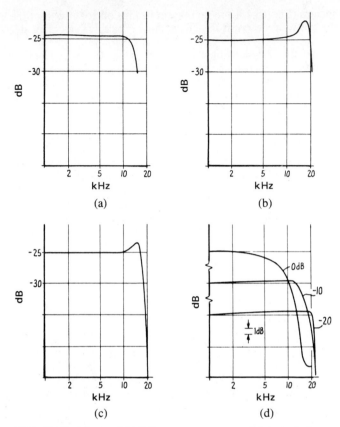

FIG. 15.15 Measured high-frequency responses of four typical cassette recorders.

useful amount of noise reduction even though the low frequencies are not treated at all. Good engineering can eliminate hum, which, as mentioned previously, is the only low-frequency noise which is subjectively troublesome in cassette tape recording.

Note should be taken that the use of a spectral-skewing network does not obviate or replace an overall band-limitation filter (MPX). As discussed, band-limitation filters used in both recording and playback have several functions in addition to reducing the midband modulation effect. Therefore, even in the case of the highest-quality recorders, it is essential to have band-limitation filters and to use them. Cleaner, more accurate recordings will be the result. It may be noted, however, that when spectral skewing and deskewing are employed, as in the C-type system, then the band-limitation filters may have comparatively high cutoff frequencies (such as 20 kHz) without provoking the midband modulation phenomenon (but a switchable 19-kHz notch should be provided for recording FM broadcasts).

15.6.5 Saturation Reduction

Inspection of Fig. 15.15*d* shows that high-frequency saturation is a serious problem in cassette recording. Usable peak levels at lower frequencies are some 8 to 10 dB higher than shown in this particular graph, with an even further deterioration of performance at high frequencies.

A useful by-product of the use of the spectral-skewing network is the reduction of very-high-frequency saturation. Thus not only does the network desensitize the compressor to the frequency components likely to cause trouble during decoding, but it also reduces the chance for recording deficiencies at those frequencies, compounding the advantage. The significant improvement observable in single-tone frequency-response curves is likely to be interpreted as the advantage of the technique; the improvement is easy to demonstrate graphically. The spectral-skewing network by itself improves the high-frequency saturation performance of cassette tapes by several decibels in the 10- to 20-kHz region. However, cassette tapes suffer from saturation problems down to frequencies as low as 2 kHz. To accommodate this it is not possible to increase the bandwidth of the spectral-skewing notch or to extend the effective cutoff frequency downward significantly for two reasons: (1) the noise reduction effect would be audibly impaired, and (2) the effectiveness of the spectral-skewing network in treating the midband modulation effect would be reduced. The CCIR weighting curve (Fig. 15.12) shows that full noise reduction action must be maintained up to about 10 kHz. Moreover, the efficiency of the spectral-skewing action is dependent upon a relatively abrupt characteristic (Fig. 15.13*e*). On the other hand, at least in approximately the 2- to 8-kHz frequency range, the saturation characteristics for typical cassette tapes are comparatively gradual, as can be seen in Fig. 15.15*d* (0-dB curve).

The above considerations point to the need for a different method of solving the saturation problem in the mid-high-frequency area. A changed tape-equalization characteristic could be used, but this would have a direct bearing on the overall noise level. An equalized high-frequency limiter could be employed, but this would be costly and in addition require complementary treatment during decoding. Headroom extension[25] is relevant but has the drawback of cost.

The following antisaturation method, which is both simple and effective, is incorporated into the C-type noise reduction system. Note that in a dual-path compressor or expander circuit the output at very low signal levels is provided mostly by the noise reduction path. For 10 dB of dynamic action, the contributions of the main and the noise reduction paths are in the ratios of 1 and 2.16, respectively. At high signal levels the roles of the two paths are reversed: the main path provides the predominant signal component, and the further path contribution is negligible.

The saturation reduction method is based on the above observations; that is, an equalizer providing the required attenuation of high-frequency drive is placed in the main path of the compressor, as shown in Fig. 15.16. At high signal levels essentially the full effect of the equalization is obtained, with a consequent reduction in high-frequency saturation. However, at low levels the equalization effect is reduced, since the contribution of the noise reduction path becomes significant. If, for example, the antisaturation network provides for a 3-dB attenuation at a particular frequency, then, with phase considerations ignored, the low-level effect will be

$$0.71 \times 1 + 2.16 = 2.87 \quad (9.2 \text{ dB}) \quad (15.5)$$

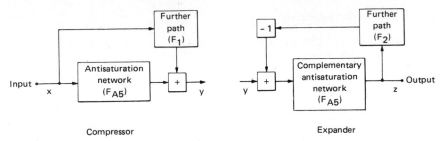

Compressor   Expander

FIG. 15.16 Placement of antisaturation networks in the main signal paths of a compressor and an expander.

That is, a 3 dB reduction in high-level recording drive is obtained for a 0.8-dB loss in noise reduction effect.

It is necessary that a complementary correction be provided on the playback side so that the signal is restored. The type of correction required can be deduced from Fig. 15.16, which shows a symmetrical compressor and expander configuration, including the placement of networks in the main signal path. Let the input signal to the compressor be x, the signal in the recorder channel be y, and the output signal of the expander be z. Let F_1 and F_2 be the transfer characteristics of the noise reduction path of the compressor and expander, respectively, and F_{AS} the transfer characteristic of the antisaturation network. Let F'_{AS} be the required compensating characteristic in the decoder.

$$y = (F_{AS} + F_1)x \tag{15.6}$$

and

$$z = yF'_{AS} - zF_2F'_{AS} \tag{15.7}$$

Thus,

$$z = \frac{F'_{AS}F_{AS} + F_1F'_{AS}}{1 + F_2F'_{AS}} x \tag{15.8}$$

Inspection shows that $z = x$ if $F_1 = F_2$ and if $F'_{AS} = 1/F_{AS}$.

The above shows not only that the two noise reduction networks should be identical, as is known in the A-type and B-type systems, but also that the antisaturation compensation network in the decoder should have an inverse characteristic to that of the network employed in the encoder.

The antisaturation network used in the C-type system is a simple shelf network (two resistances and one reactance) with time constants of 70 and 50 μs, corresponding to turnover frequencies of about 2.3 and 3.2 kHz, respectively. High-frequency attenuation is provided in the encoder, with a corresponding boost in the decoder. Referring to Fig. 15.14, this results in a saturation reduction of about 1 dB at 2 kHz, 2.3 dB at 5 kHz, and 2.8 dB at 15 kHz.* At frequencies above 10 kHz, the spectral-skewing network augments the overall antisaturation effect, as shown in Fig. 15.14.

_____

*Thanks are due to K. J. Gundry for reviewing the saturation properties of contemporary high-performance cassette tapes and for recommending this 50-μs–70-μs characteristic for use in the C-type noise reduction system.

15.6.6 Block Diagram: C Type

Based on the principles discussed, Fig. 15.17 shows the basic block diagram of the C-type compressor and expander. The networks N_1 and N_2 are the noise reduction side chains. The spectral-skewing network is placed at the input of the high-level stage of the compressor, thereby affecting the operation of both the high- and low-level compressor stages. Note that the deskewing network, being situated at the output of the whole system, has no effect on the operation of either of the expander stages; its only function is to restore an overall flat frequency response. For simplicity and economy the antisaturation network is placed only in the low-level stage.

Figure 15.18 includes more complete diagrams of the individual stages and also shows the distinctions between the B-type and C-type systems. The figure shows the function changes necessary to provide a switchable record-play circuit with either B-type or C-type capability. If desired, further switching can be provided so that one spectral-skewing network and one antisaturation network can serve in both the record and the play modes with the required complementary characteristics.

For B-type operation the low-level stage and spectral-skewing and deskewing networks are switched out of the circuit; the filter frequencies, overshoot suppression level, and control-circuit smoothing time constants are set to the B-type values.

For C-type operation, the spectral-skewing and deskewing networks are switched in. The low-level stage is connected in series, with its preset low-level area of action, including overshoot suppression; the variable-filter quiescent cutoff frequency is preset to 375 Hz; and the antisaturation network is connected in the main signal path. In the high-level stage the fixed- and variable-filter frequencies are both lowered to 375 Hz. The latter changes, together with the retention of control circuitry with B-type characteristics, result in a modified spectral distrib-

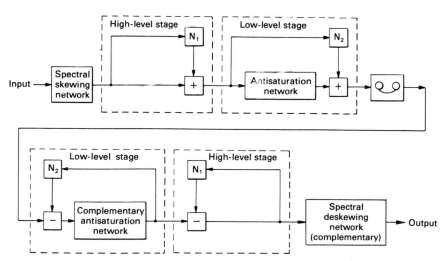

FIG. 15.17 Basic block diagram of a C-type compressor and expander. N_1 and N_2 are the noise reduction networks.

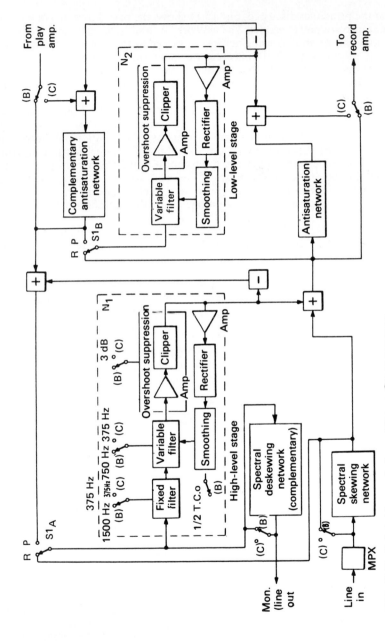

FIG. 15.18 Switchable record-play and B-type–C-type processor.

ution and slightly higher level at the side-chain output. Overshoot suppression for these conditions is optimized by setting the suppression threshold 3 dB higher than in B-type operation. The potential maximum overshoot is therefore somewhat greater than in the B-type system.

In the development of the C-type circuit, the opportunity was taken to incorporate full-wave rectification in the control circuitry of both stages (for economy, half-wave rectification is normally used in the B-type circuit). This significantly reduces distortion caused by control-signal ripple modulation and makes it possible to decrease the smoothing time constants used. Halving the time constants eliminates the last vestiges of noise tails upon abrupt cessation of high-amplitude, high-frequency signals (which generate the largest control signals). The attack time constants are also reduced, which tends to offset the higher overshoot suppression level of the high-level stage as well as the (somewhat lower) overshoot contribution of the low-level stage. As shown in Fig. 15.18, the smoothing time constants of the high-level stage are made switchable in order to retain compatibility with the B-type characteristics.

A minimum amount of staggering is used in separating the areas of action of the two circuits, consistent with maintaining the overall compression ratio at a maximum of about 2. Figure 15.19 shows the single-tone compression characteristics of the high-level stage; spectral skewing is omitted for clarity. Note that the frequencies from about 1 Hz to 8 kHz include areas which have compression ratios in the region of 2. Thus the low-level stage must have an action area arranged to be well clear of these. Above and below this frequency range the compression ratios are generally lower, so that some overlapping of the characteristics is possible in these ranges.

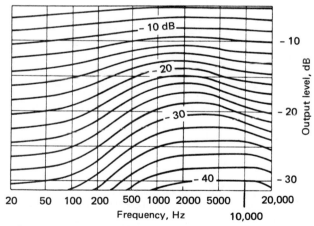

FIG. 15.19 Input-output characteristics of the high-level stage only, without spectral skewing.

Staggering is achieved by increasing the effective amplification employed in generating the control signal of the low-level stage. As previously discussed, this increased gain is provided partly in a fixed way and partly in a variable way, by virtue of the low-level signal boosting of the high-level stage.

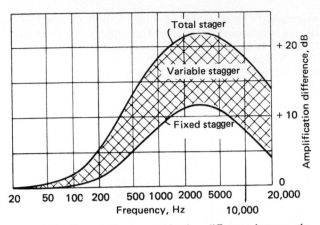

FIG. 15.20 Control-circuit amplification difference between the high-level stage and the low-level stage. The low-level stage has a fixed gain increase which is augmented by a variable increase caused by the signal-processing action of the high-level stage.

Figure 15.20 shows the fixed and variable elements of the amplification differ-ence used in the low-level stage of the C-type system. In the development of the system, the variable-gain component was taken as given, and the fixed-gain com-ponent was experimentally determined to provide the best overall fitting together of the characteristics.

For convenience and flexibility, the development of the C-type system was done with discrete components and field-effect transistors (FETs).

In adapting the design to integrated-circuit technology, it was necessary to match the external impedances used in the variable filter to the variable-resistance characteristics of the integrated circuits. Therefore, it was essential to specify C-type filter impedances which would be as compatible as possible with such inte-grated-circuit resistance characteristics, especially bearing in mind the increased requirements of the C-type circuit.

Referring to Fig. 15.18 and Refs. 23 and 24, the fixed filter is simply a series capacitor and shunt resistor; there is no problem with this stage. The variable filter is a series-connected parallel combination of a resistor R and a capacitor C (with a turnover frequency of $\frac{1}{2}\pi\ RC$) which is shunted by the variable-resistance R_v: this combination provides a variable shelf characteristic. In the B-type circuit there is a one-octave difference between the turnover frequencies of the two sec-tions (1500 and 750 Hz), which yields a quasi two-pole filter with a more steeply rising noise reduction characteristic in the presence of signals than a simple single-pole filter might provide.

In lowering the fixed-filter cutoff frequency in the C-type circuit by two octaves, the available integrated-circuit characteristics made it seem unlikely that the variable-filter turnover frequency could be lowered by a similar amount. For this reason and a further reason to be discussed, the variable-filter turnover fre-quency was lowered by only one octave (to 375 Hz).

The component values used in the variable filter are a compromise which stretches the capability of R_v at both ends of the range, regarding limiting values and their repeatability, as well as repeatability within the range (especially at high resistances). Attention in dedicated C-type integrated-circuit designs has been directed to these matters.

Using the same turnover frequency (375 Hz) for the fixed and variable sections causes this particular filter configuration to perform in the same manner as a single-pole variable filter.* Replacement of the combination with a single-pole filter saves a resistor and a capacitor; this saving can be realized in the low-level stage, which need not be switchable to B-type operation.

The performance limitations of available integrated-circuit variable resistances thus were one consideration in selecting a C-type filter arrangement which, by itself, is not as efficient as the filter of the B-type circuit with respect to noise modulation. However, the steepness-compounding effect of the two-stage arrangement used in the C-type system more than compensates for the deficiency. The resulting noise modulation margin of safety, while not quite that of the B-type system, is adequate, if not good, on nearly all program material, especially taking into account the lower real noise level achieved in the presence of signals.

Even if available integrated-circuit characteristics had made it possible to lower the variable-filter turnover frequency by a full two octaves to retain quasi two-pole performance in each stage, it is unlikely that such a choice would have been made. Throughout the development, the midband modulation effect, transposed two octaves lower than in the B-type system, was a hazard borne in mind at least as much as noise modulation (thereby stimulating the development of the spectral-skewing technique). It is inevitable that a steeply rising noise reduction characteristic (in each stage) results in a greater susceptibility to the midband modulation effect. Even with the advantages afforded by spectral skewing, it would be difficult to predict all the possibilities for error in the mass production of C-type machines and prerecorded tapes. Thus it is to be hoped that the modest filter characteristics used in the C-type system will in due course prove to have been a good design compromise.

15.6.7 Performance

Characteristic Curves. Figure 15.21 shows the overall input-output transfer characteristic of the C-type compressor at 1 kHz. The high-level stage by itself is also shown in order to demonstrate how the actions of the two stages blend together without increasing the maximum compression ratio.

In Fig. 15.22 the overall single-tone compression characteristics can be seen. The reduced drive to the tape at very high frequencies and high levels significantly extends the frequency response which can be obtained routinely. High-frequency distortion under test and real signal conditions is also notably reduced.

The corresponding expansion curves are given in Fig. 15.23. While the curves of Figs. 15.22 and 15.23 do not appear to be symmetrical, or complementary, it should be noted that the expander is normally not fed by an unprocessed signal; rather, it is always supplied with a signal from the output of a compressor. Consideration of these curves will show that the expander characteristic restores the compressed signal to its original state. Reference to Eq. (15.8) shows that the restoration is theoretically exact in all respects: frequency-response, phase, and dynamic properties. This ideal can be achieved in practice to any extent desired in the tolerancing and matching of components and operating conditions. How-

---

* Thanks are due to the audio group at Sony Corporation for pointing this out.

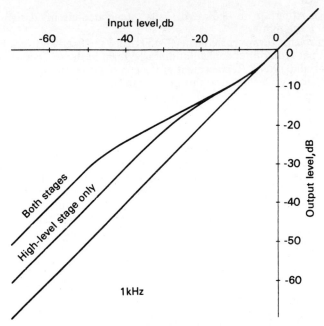

FIG. 15.21 Input-output transfer characteristic of a C-type compressor at 1 kHz. The high-level stage also is shown.

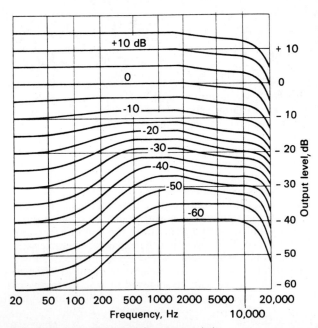

FIG. 15.22 C-type compression characteristics.

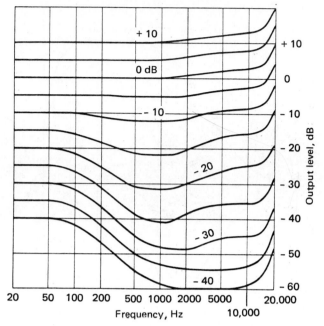

FIG. 15.23 C-type expansion characteristics.

ever, from Figs. 15.21 and 15.22 it should be noted that the maximum compression ratio of the C-type system prevails over a significantly greater range of amplitudes and frequencies than in the B-type system. For optimal reproduction it is thus essential to maintain high standards of tape-recorder gain setting and frequency response.

In Fig. 15.24 the subthreshold frequency responses of the compressor and expander are shown. The expander curve determines the maximum noise reduction effect of the system, which is obtained with no signal input.

The presence of signals reduces the noise reduction effect attributable to compression and expansion. However, this real noise reduction merges into the subjective noise reduction provided by the masking effect, on which all compressor-expander noise reduction systems depend. Figure 15.25 shows the effect on the noise reduction frequency band of several different frequencies applied at a high signal level, in this case at the nominal maximum level of the system, 0 dB (reference level). It is, of course, impermissible to boost a signal at such a high level, so the band slides upward to eliminate the boosting action. Low-level signal components at higher frequencies continue to be boosted. The complementary attenuation provided by the expander then produces whatever real noise reduction action is possible under those signal conditions.

The curves of Fig. 15.25 were obtained by mixing a sweeping probe tone at a level of −65 dB into the compressor input signal and detecting the tone at the output with a tracking wave analyzer.

Figure 15.26 shows the operation of the compressor in response to a 500-Hz signal over a range of levels; the corresponding expander characteristic is given in Fig. 15.27. The compressor and expander progressively slide the frequency band

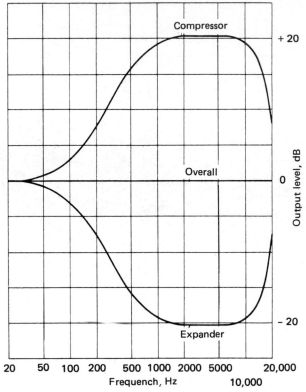

FIG. 15.24 Low-level (subthreshold) frequency response of a C-type compressor and expander.

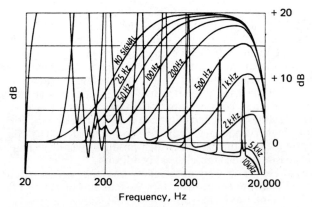

FIG. 15.25 Sliding-band action of a compressor in response to high-level (0-dB) signals at the frequencies shown (−65-dB probe tone).

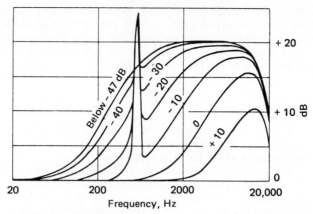

FIG. 15.26 Sliding-band operation of a C-type compressor with 500-Hz signals at the levels indicated (−65-dB probe tone).

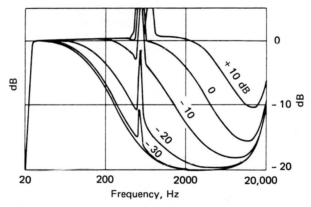

FIG. 15.27 Sliding-band operation of an expander with a 500-Hz signal at the levels indicated (−45-dB probe tone).

upward with increasing signal levels; the masking effect, working in cooperation with the expander, creates the overall illusion of a low, virtually unchanging noise level.

Figures 15.19 through 15.27 have shown the response to a single tone or to the simulation of a dominant signal together with other signals at much lower levels. Often, however, the signal will comprise a complex combination of frequencies and levels. The action of the spectral-skewing network in tilting or altering the spectrum of very-high-frequency signals has been discussed. A similar but variable type of skewing action affecting the operation of the system also takes place at lower frequencies, by virtue of the two-stage sliding-band layout. With complex input signals the high-level stage alters the spectral content of the signal. Thus the low-level stage is actuated by a signal which is not only different in level but different in spectral balance. This has the tendency of spectrally spreading out the chance for error in the decoding function. If the high-level stage is controlled by signal components in a certain frequency range, then the low-level stage will tend to be controlled by signal components somewhat higher in frequency. Thus the spectral shifting effect reduces the overall dynamic and frequency-response errors of the decoded result when the tape recorder has an uneven frequency response.

Compatibility.   In the design of the B-type system, the subjective acceptability of encoded recordings when used with conventional players was a matter of some concern; the dual-inventory production of cassettes was not judged to be commercially feasible. Thus the B-type system represents a three-way balance of (1) operating characteristics which are practical, economical, and technically safe in implementation, (2) a noise reduction effect which is sufficient to be acknowledged as useful, and (3) an amount and type of dynamic action which could be judged as "compatible" on simple players.

The conditions relating to the development of the C-type system were somewhat different. For one thing, the majority of listeners were already adequately catered to with the B-type system, which gave greater latitude in the design of the new system. At least in the beginning, the C-type system would be an audiophile or critical-listener system. Therefore the main consideration had to be the provision of a usefully increased amount of noise reduction without provoking undesirable side effects under full encode-decode conditions, taking into account the strengths and deficiencies of practical production-model tape recorders and tapes. Thus no specific design concessions were made to the issue of compatibility (except to the further consideration of providing a circuit which would be B–C-switchable). However, a certain compatibility happens to be a useful by-product of the design philosophy used in producing these noise reduction systems, namely, that the best treatment of the signal is the least treatment. If the action of the system is constrained to the bare minimum with respect to the signal levels handled and the frequency ranges covered, then an inevitable consequence is that the bulk of the encoded signal is simply the original input signal. The compatibility of this or that kind of C-type encoded program material (with B-type reproduction, or with a tone control, or with nothing) is a matter of opinion. It may well be possible that the single-inventory production of certain types of C-type recordings or signal sources is workable. However, in relation to the various potential applications and markets, this matter must be judged on a case-by-case basis.

15.6.8 Conclusion

A new high-performance noise reduction system, designated C-type, has been developed for consumer applications. Primarily designed for use with cassette tapes, the system is switchable between the B-type and C-type modes.

The new system avoids many of the problems associated with large amounts of dynamic action through the use of a dual-level staggered-action arrangement of series-connected compressors and expanders. Specific problems relating to cassette recording are addressed: an antisaturation method extends useful high-level, high-frequency response and reduces distortion, and a technique called spectral skewing further reduces saturation and desensitizes the system to recorder errors at very high frequencies.

15.7 COMPANDING FOR MULTICHANNEL TELEVISION SOUND

In 1982, dbx proposed a new noise reduction system (called dbx-TV) for use with multichannel television sound. Late in 1983, dbx-TV, along with a transmission-system proposal from Zenith, was selected by the television industry for stereo and multichannel television broadcasting for the United States. (In Chap. 5, Fig. 5.17 is a block diagram of the TV stereo generator showing the inclusion of dbx encoding.) The dbx-TV system has a common heritage with the previously described wideband compandors but differs in its use of a spectral compandor as part of the system.

15.7.1 Zenith Transmission System

The Zenith transmission system transmits stereo information via a subcarrier located at 31.468 kHz, amplitude-modulated with a signal representing the difference between the two stereo channels $(L - R)$. Except for the subcarrier frequency, the system is essentially the same as that used for transmitting stereo FM in the United States. The $L - R$ channel is limited in its dynamic range with respect to the $L + R$ (main) channel, owing to its location higher in frequency (the $L + R$ signal contains only frequencies up to 15 kHz, while the modulated subcarrier bandwidth extends from about 17 kHz to 46 kHz). This results in a peak S/N ratio of less than 43 dB for the $L - R$ channel without preemphasis and under Grade B reception conditions (a somewhat snowy but viewable picture).

The Zenith system also includes a Second Audio Program (SAP) channel which consists of a frequency-modulated subcarrier located at 78.67 kHz. The dynamic range of this channel without preemphasis and under Grade B reception conditions is a very poor 26 dB.

15.7.2 Where to Use Noise Reduction

dbx-TV was applied directly to the noisy channels: the $L - R$ channel and the SAP channel. By leaving the $L + R$ channel unmodified, complete compatibility with monaural TV sets was assured. The same compandor was used in both companded channels, so that receivers could be designed with one expander which could be switched between SAP and $L - R$ service.

15.7.3 dbx-TV Noise Reduction

Because of the poor dynamic range of the channels to be compressed, a traditional wideband compandor was considered inadequate to provide high-quality noise reduction. A wideband compandor would have betrayed its presence through excessive modulation noise, especially on the SAP channel under poor reception conditions. Therefore, dbx chose to combine elements from its wideband compandors (preemphasis and 1:2:1 companding) with a new concept: spectral companding.

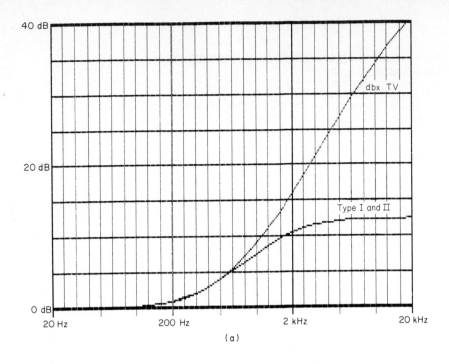

(a)

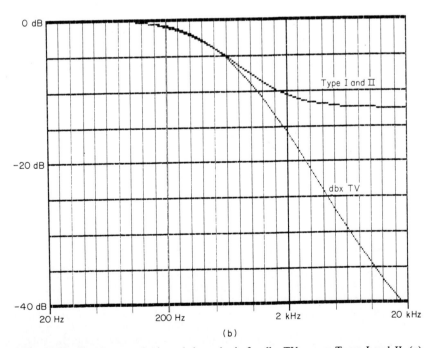

(b)

FIG. 15.28 Signal preemphasis and deemphasis for dbx-TV versus Types I and II. (*a*) Preemphasis. (*b*) Deemphasis.

15.44

dbx-TV Preemphasis. Both the $L - R$ and, especially, the SAP channel have poor dynamic range at high frequencies. To overcome these limitations, strong preemphasis was provided in the compressor, followed by strong deemphasis in the expander. The frequency responses of these networks are plotted in Fig. 15.28 along with the response of Type I and Type II preemphasis for comparison.

This strong preemphasis carries with it a liability: the channel can be more easily overloaded by high frequencies in the program material. Of course, overload can occur only when the program contains high levels of high frequencies. In dbx-TV, the spectral compressor is designed to aid the signal preemphasis by providing consistently even spectral balance in the signal to be transmitted. In the process, it will sense conditions which would cause overload and correct them.

Spectral Compression. The spectral compressor monitors the spectral balance of the input signal (How much high-frequency energy is there?) and varies the high-frequency preemphasis accordingly. When very little high-frequency information is present (and masking is least likely), the spectral compressor provides large high-frequency preemphasis. When strong high frequencies are present (and overload is most likely), the spectral compressor actually provides deemphasis, thereby reducing the potential for high-frequency overload. The resulting encoded signal is therefore dynamically adjusted to contain consistently a substantial proportion of high frequencies before transmission, which masks the channel noise.

The spectral compressor consists of a variable preemphasis-deemphasis stage and a band-limited rms-level detector (see Fig. 15.29*a*). The filtering that precedes the detector restricts its sensing range to high audio frequencies (the passband centers at about 8 kHz). The detector output is therefore proportional to the high-

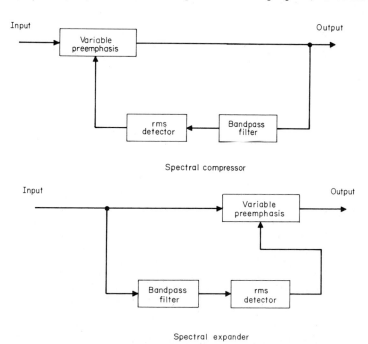

Spectral compressor

Spectral expander

FIG. 15.29 Block diagram of a spectral expander for companding.

frequency energy in the program. Figure 15.29*b* shows the spectral-expander configuration. The control sense of the variable-response network in the expander is reversed from that in the compressor, thereby inverting its frequency-response-versus-energy characteristic (hence preemphasis-deemphasis in the compressor and deemphasis-preemphasis in the expander).

The variable preemphasis-deemphasis stage works by varying the gain of a VCA embedded in a frequency-selective network, producing a continuum of frequency responses depending on the rms-detector output signal. Some of the available responses are shown in Fig. 15.30. A range from +27 dB to −27 dB at 15 kHz is available.

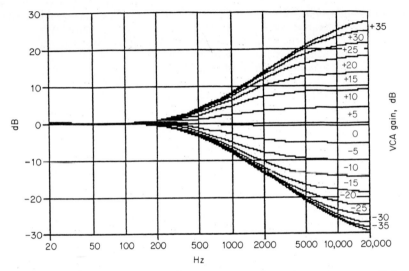

FIG. 15.30 Spectral-compressor frequency responses for various voltage-controlled-amplifier (VCA) gains.

The combination of the variable preemphasis-deemphasis stage and the signal preemphasis provides a range of overall preemphasis responses from nearly flat (with maximum deemphasis from the compressor) to +55 dB at 15 kHz (see Fig. 15.31). This large range allows the compander to provide good masking with an extremely wide range of program material.

Wideband Companding. To provide good masking with low-frequency program material, a 1:2:1 wideband compandor is also incorporated into the dbx-TV system. As in the tape systems, the *unaffected-level point* of the wideband-compandor section is set below the maximum signal level in the transmission channel, in this case, 21 dB below 100 percent modulation (Fig. 15.32). This keeps the signal consistently above the noise floor but consistently below 100 percent modulation (therefore providing room for transient overshoots in both the wideband and the spectral compandors). In conjunction with the fixed-signal preemphasis and variable preemphasis, this forces the system to unity gain at 17 dB below 100 percent modulation at 300 Hz.

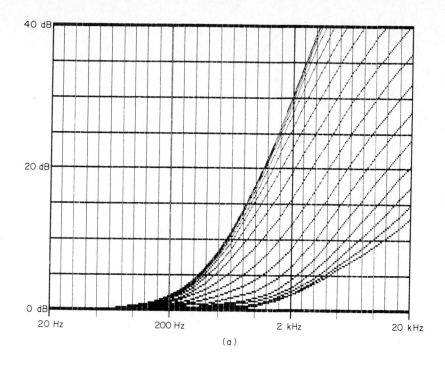

(a)

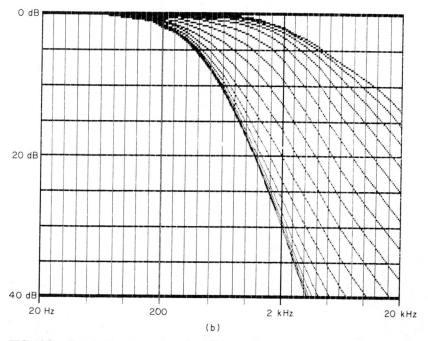

(b)

FIG. 15.31 Frequency response for a fixed-plus-variable preemphasis and deemphasis. (*a*) Preemphasis. (*b*) Deemphasis.

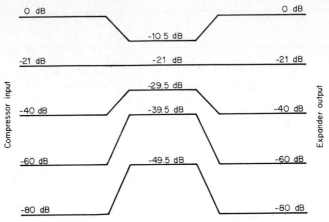

FIG. 15.32 dbx-TV wideband-compandor action.

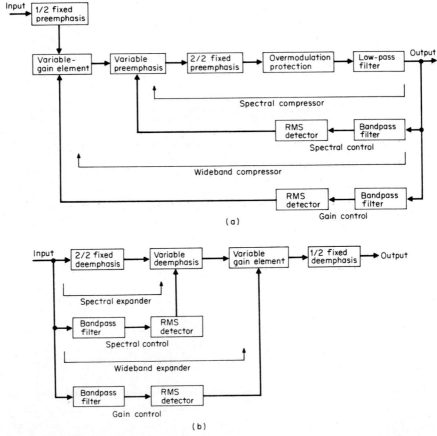

(a)

(b)

FIG. 15.33 dbx-TV compandor block diagram. (*a*) Compressor (encoder). (*b*) Expander (decoder).

The detectors in the wideband compandor are band-limited to the lower portions of the audio band (below approximately 2 kHz). This prevents the wideband compandor from acting on high frequencies in the program material where high frequencies dominate the spectrum (leaving this area to be controlled by the spectral compandor). Figure 15.33 shows a block diagram of the entire compandor, including the elements discussed below.

Transient Protection. In television broadcasting, it is important not to overmodulate the audio channel to prevent splatter into the picture and adjacent channels. Even brief overmodulation must be avoided. Therefore, dbx-TV includes a transient protection stage designed to prevent even very-short-duration overloads. This stage usually takes the form of a simple clipper, which is active only during transient overshoots caused by the application of suddenly increasing signals at the input to the compressor. Because the compressor response time is relatively short, the clipper is usually active for less than 1 ms at a time. This is of very little audible consequence.

So that the energy lost during clipping does not cause mistracking between the expander and the compressor, the clipper is incorporated within the compressor feedback loop (see Fig. 15.33). This forces the compressor detector to sense the same signal (after clipping) that the expander detector will see. Any energy lost is lost to both detectors, so no mistracking can result from it.

Out-of-Band Filtering. Because the $L - R$ subcarrier is transmitted via an suppressed carrier channel, a pilot is provided at 15.734 kHz to allow the receiver to reconstruct the 31.468-kHz carrier for demodulation. The spectrum around the pilot must be kept free of interfering signals so that the pilot may be clearly recovered. Since dbx-TV produces substantial gain at high frequencies, filtering is necessary following the gain to prevent noise around the frequency of the pilot from interfering with its successful demodulation. As with the transient protection, the filter used to keep the pilot clear is placed within the feedback loop of the compressor, again to prevent its effect on signal energy from causing mistracking in the expander.

Results. The combination of dbx-TV and the Zenith MTS transmission system [referred to as the BTSC (Broadcast Television Systems Committee) system] provides true high-fidelity stereo performance for all viewers within the range of monaural TV signals. When switching into stereo, there will be none of the noise added which accompanies the switch into stereo with FM radio. Neither the fidelity nor the coverage area need be compromised.

For the SAP channel, the combination allows adequate performance to be achieved out to the Grade B contour. City-grade (Grade A) performance is quite good, consistent with the SAP channel's 10-kHz bandwidth. The uncompanded channel S/N ratio is so low that some compandor artifacts are inevitable in Grade B reception. However, this still provides acceptable-quality service.

15.8 DOLBY SPECTRAL RECORDING

A recent development from Dolby Laboratories is called Dolby SR (spectral recording).* This new approach to analog recording was introduced in 1986 and,

---

* Section 15.8 is adapted from Paper 2413, presented by R. M. Dolby at the Audio Engineering Society's 81st Convention in Los Angeles in November 1986. It is published here by courtesy of the AES.

when used with a professional analog recorder, provides a dynamic range somewhat greater than 16-bit PCM recording, as well as being more forgiving to overloading the tape (and to underrecording as well). It is called a recording system rather than a noise reduction system since it utilizes processing techniques to improve all the analog recording or transmission functions as well as a reduction of noise.

15.8.1   Introduction

In 1980, some 14 years after the introduction of A-type noise reduction (see Sec. 15.2), the author began work on the development of the next-generation system for general-purpose professional recording and transmission. A configuration that would employ the A-type characteristics as part of the new system, with switchable compatibility, was considered initially. However, this would not take full advantage of the new technology embodied in the C-type system (see Sec. 15.6), nor would it readily allow the incorporation of some further new concepts. Therefore, the particular parameters of the A-type system were abandoned as a starting point for the new development. However, the basic principles, which appear to be as valid as when they were first introduced, were retained: the use of a main signal path without any dynamic processing to pass high-level signals, coupled with a low-level side-chain compressor to provide dynamic action.

The design goals of the new system were set high. The new technology, called spectral recording, should provide master recordings of the very highest quality, especially with regard to audible-signal purity. Yet the system should be practical and economical for routine applications, being suitable for easy and trouble-free use in a wide variety of professional recording and transmission environments. Certain new techniques, to be described, provide the required signal quality and practicality but result in circuit complexity. Reliance has been placed on improved circuit implementation and manufacturing techniques to overcome the problems of complexity and to ensure economical production of the new system.

15.8.2   Brief Outline

The goal of the SR process is to modify the various components of the incoming signal so as to load an imperfect recording or transmission medium in the most rational way. Generally, high-level signal components at both ends of the spectrum are attenuated, whereby a better match with the overload characteristic of the medium is provided. At the same time, low-level components of the signal are amplified substantially, in a highly frequency-selective way. These effects are reversed during reproduction, restoring the original signal. The result is a significant reduction of distortion and noise, in both the absence and the presence of signals.

The process has a number of layout and operating characteristics in common with the A-type (Sec. 15.2), B-type,[23,24] and C-type (Sec. 15.6) noise reduction systems. The SR process takes these developments considerably further in the same general direction. With regard to general principles, reference should be made to the technical papers on these systems, the C-type paper (Sec. 15.6) being particularly relevant.

Referring to Fig. 15.34, which is described later in detail, a main signal path is responsible primarily for conveying high-level signals. A side-chain signal with

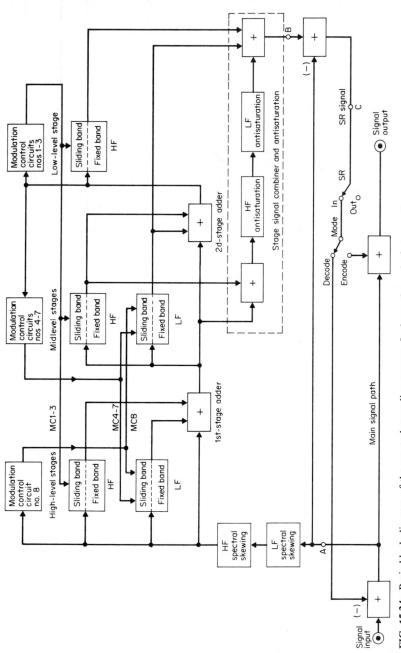

FIG. 15.34 Basic block diagram of the spectral recording process. It shows the main features of process: multistage high-frequency and low-frequency dynamic-action staggering, action substitution (fixed bands and sliding bands), modulation control, high-frequency and low-frequency spectral skewing, and high-frequency and low-frequency antisaturation.

the SR process characteristic is combined additively with the main signal in the encoding mode and subtractively in the decoding mode, whereby an overall complementary action is obtained.

The SR stage layout resembles that of the C-type system, except that three levels or stages of action staggering are used: high-level, midlevel, and low-level (HLS, MLS, and LLS). Various advantages arise from the use of multilevel stages, including accuracy and reproducibility, low distortion, low overshoot, and action compounding for good spectral discrimination. For the high-level and midlevel stages both high-frequency and low-frequency circuits are used, with a crossover frequency of 800 Hz. The low-level stage is high-frequency only, with an 800-Hz high-pass characteristic.

Each of these stages has a low-level gain of somewhat over 8 dB, whereby a total dynamic effect of about 16 dB is obtained at low frequencies and of about 24 dB at high frequencies. A further dynamic action of about 1 dB takes place above the reference level.

The spectral-skewing network has the same purpose and function as in the C-type system, except that a spectral-skewing action is provided at low frequencies as well. The spectral-skewing networks desensitize the SR process to the influence of signal components at the extreme ends of the audio-frequency band. This effect is particularly helpful if the recording or transmission system has an uncertain frequency response in these regions. The networks are also important in attenuating subsonic and supersonic interferences of all kinds. The spectral-skewing action is compensated in the decoder, resulting in an overall flat frequency response.

Both high-frequency and low-frequency antisaturation networks are provided in the main signal path, again operating in substantially the same way as in the C-type system. There is an effective compounding of the antisaturation effects produced by the antisaturation networks and the spectral-skewing networks. In this way the SR process achieves a significant increase in high- and low-frequency headroom.

15.8.3 Design Principles

Least-Treatment Principles. A design philosophy used in the development of the new system is that the best treatment of the signal is the least treatment. The operating goal of the encoder is to provide fixed, predetermined gains for all frequency components of the signal, with corresponding attenuations in the decoder. If a large-signal component appears at a particular frequency or frequencies, then the gains should be reduced at those frequencies only, in accordance with predetermined compression laws for restoration of the signal during decoding. In other words, the compressor should try to keep all signal components fully boosted at all times. When the boosting must be cut back at a particular frequency, the effect should not be extended to low-level signal components at other frequencies.

The audible effect of this type of compression is that the signal appears to be enhanced and brighter but without any apparent dynamic compression effects (the ear detects dynamic action primarily by the effect of a gain change due to a signal component at one frequency on a signal component at some other frequency, somewhat removed). If the ear cannot detect dynamic effects in the compressed signal, then (1) it is unlikely that noise modulation effects will be evident in the decoded signal, and (2) it is unlikely that signal modulation effects will be evident in the decoded signal if there should be a gain or frequency-response error in the recording or transmission channel.

In the SR process two new methods greatly reduce the circuitry required to achieve the design goal of a full spectrally responsive system. In particular, both fixed and sliding bands are used in a unique combination, called *action substitution,* that draws on the best features of both types of circuits. A further technique, called *modulation control,* greatly improves the performance of both the fixed and the sliding bands in resisting any modulation of signal components unless necessary.

The use of the new methods reduces the basic encoder to two frequency bands only (high-frequency and low-frequency), each with a fixed-band circuit and a sliding-band circuit (this combination being referred to as a *stage*). When the three-level action-staggering layout is taken into account, five fixed bands and five sliding bands are employed in the spectral recording process.

Action Substitution.　A new type of compression and expansion action that is highly responsive to spectral changes can be achieved by superposing or overlaying the individual characteristics of different types of dynamic-action circuits. One circuit may provide a quiescent characteristic or defining umbrella; a further characteristic is hidden until signal components appear that cause the hidden characteristic to be revealed and become active.

For discussion purposes let the gains in a compressor system be arranged so that subthreshold signals pass without attenuation. That is, the maximum possible action is that of providing a certain gain, unity, for instance. Somehow to achieve this gain over as broad a range of frequencies as possible, in the presence of higher-level (dominant) signals, is the task of the system.

Thus, in a superposed action compressor circuit, represented in Fig. 15.35, a signal is fed into a first compressor circuit. The output from this circuit represents the completed part of the total potential action. The uncompleted part is therefore the input signal minus the completed part; this is so derived and fed into the next compressor circuit, which has some different characteristic. The output of the second circuit is then added to that of the first, augmenting the action of the first. In an extreme condition, in which the output of the first circuit may be negligible at

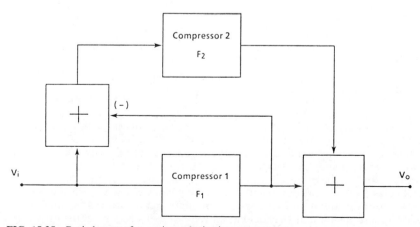

FIG. 15.35　Basic layout of an action-substitution compressor.

a particular frequency, the action of the second circuit is effectively substituted for that of the first.

The operation of the action-substitution compressor can be characterized directly from the above description. With an input signal V_i and an output signal V_o, a first-compressor transfer function F_1, and a second-compressor transfer function F_2, we have

$$V_o = V_i[F_1(V_1) + F_2(V_1) - F_1(V_1) \times F_2(V_1)] \qquad (15.9)$$

This equation shows that the overall transfer function is the sum of the individual transfer functions minus their product. In other words, to the extent that the transfer functions may overlap, a factor is subtracted from the sum of the transfer functions.

The above type of action can be achieved with various circuit topologies, the one used in the present implementation of the SR system being shown in Fig. 15.36. In this arrangement, the compressor circuits are arranged in a stack. Both

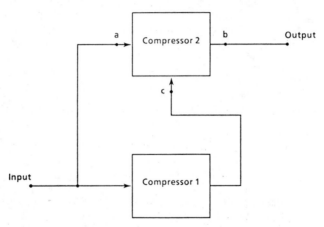

FIG. 15.36   Another action-substitution-compressor configuration.

circuits are fed in parallel, and the output is taken from the top circuit, which is configured as a three-terminal network with terminals a, b, and c. The output of the first circuit is fed to the reference terminal c of the top circuit. It can be shown that the signal components at the output terminal b are those specified by Eq. (15.9).

The usefulness of the superposition technique can be appreciated by consideration of Fig. 15.37a and b. The advantages of fixed-band-compressor circuits (Fig. 15.37a) arise from the fact that all signal frequencies within the band are treated equally, in contrast with sliding-band action (Fig. 15.37b). Thus the appearance of a dominant signal component actuating the compressor results in a loss of noise reduction effect that manifests itself in a uniform manner throughout the band (2 dB in the example shown). The loss is not concentrated in any particular frequency region as it is in sliding-band circuits; note the 5-dB loss shown in the example of Fig. 15.37b. The main significance of this is that if the recorder or transmission channel has an error in gain and/or frequency response, there is no amplification of the error at other, nondominant signal frequencies; in sliding-band circuits the amplification may be significant (the midband modulation effect, discussed in Sec. 15.6.4).

In contrast, the advantages of sliding-band compression and expansion circuits derive from the fact that all signal frequencies are not treated equally. In particular, compression, expansion, and noise reduction action are well maintained above the frequency of the dominant signal component in high-frequency circuits and below the frequency of the dominant signal component in low-frequency circuits. This action-maintenance effect, except on a one-to-one basis, is absent in fixed-band circuits.

Clearly, it would be desirable to have the benefit of fixed-band operation on the stop-band side of the dominant signal frequency and sliding-band operation on the passband side. The action-substitution technique provides this useful combination. In Fig. 16.37c the response of an action-substitution compressor to the signal conditions of Fig. 16.37a and b is shown. As is seen, the output is primarily from the fixed band for frequencies up to the dominant signal component and

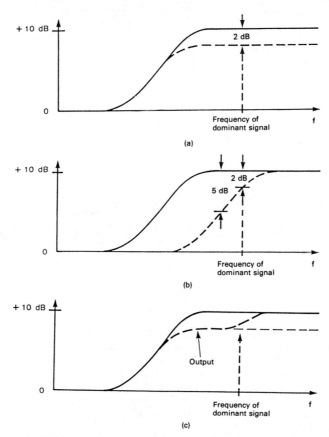

FIG. 15.37 Types of compressor characteristics. (a) Fixed-band-compressor characteristic. (b) Sliding-band-compressor characteristic. (c) Action-substitution-compressor characteristic.

from the sliding band above that frequency. Conversely, for a low-frequency stage the output is from the fixed band for frequencies down to a low-frequency dominant component and from the sliding band below that frequency. This cooperative effect is particularly useful in the level region from the circuit threshold up to some 20 dB above it.

In the SR process, action-substitution operation is used in both the high- and the low-frequency circuits. Thus both fixed-band and sliding-band dynamic actions are used in each of the five stages, or in a total of 10 compressor circuits. While there is an effective interaction of the fixed and sliding bands in any particular stage, all the stages operate independently. Depending on the levels and spectral conditions in each stage, fixed-band operation is used whenever it provides best performance; sliding-band operation is substituted whenever it has an advantage. The substitution is effective on a continuous and frequency-by-frequency basis.

Even though the frequency division of the stages is nominally 800 Hz, the use of what are effectively single-pole band-defining filters results in a significant overlap region between the high- and low-frequency stages. The high-frequency stages extend their effects down to about 200 Hz, and the low-frequency stages extend their effects up to about 3 kHz. This overlap, together with the use of action substitution, contributes to the achievement of a very good spectral tracking effect under all frequency and level conditions. The practical significance is that an excellent noise reduction effect is obtained in the presence of signals and that the system has a remarkable tolerance to gain and frequency-response errors in the signal channel.

A further aspect of action substitution relates to the transient recovery characteristics of the system. A fixed-band-compressor circuit has a recovery time that is essentially independent of frequency, at least in the passband. A sliding-band circuit has a fast recovery time for nondominant signals at the passband end of the spectrum and a slow recovery time for nondominant signals at the stop-band end of the spectrum. The choice of integrator recovery times is therefore a matter of compromise between this recovery-time situation and the amount of steady-state and modulation distortion obtained. The compromise is made much easier by the use of the action-substitution technique. In particular, the fixed band provides a definite and rapid recovery time for the overall system, so that the sliding band can employ longer time constants than would otherwise be desirable. This results in both low modulation distortion and a fast recovery time.

Thus the action-substitution technique provides the advantages of fixed- and sliding-band circuits while avoiding their disadvantages. In other words, there is a significantly improved adherence to the ideal of least signal treatment; in the level region somewhat above the circuit threshold the signal more closely approaches fully boosted conditions in the encoding mode, with a consequently improved noise reduction effect in the decoding mode. For signals at higher levels the technique of modulation control, described below, is employed.

Modulation Control. In the A-type, B-type, and C-type systems the signal from the side chain is highly limited under high-level signal conditions. This high degree of limiting, beginning at a low-level threshold, is responsible for the low distortion, low overshoot, and low modulation distortion which characterize these systems.

A closer examination shows that it is unnecessary to utilize such a low threshold and such a strong limiting characteristic under certain signal conditions. In particular, whenever the side-chain signal departs from an in-phase condition with respect to the main-path signal, the threshold can be raised. Moreover, after an appropriate degree of limiting has taken place at a given frequency (in order to create the desired overall compression law), it is unnecessary to continue the limiting when the signal level rises even further. Rather, the level of the side-chain signal can be allowed to rise as a function of a further increase in signal level, whereby it stabilizes at some significant fraction of the main-path signal level.

In the fixed-band portions of the spectral recording process the above arrangement results in conventional performance in the passband (in-phase) frequency region. However, in the stop-band region the modulation control scheme causes the limiting threshold to rise and the degree of limiting to be reduced. The possibility of doing this can be appreciated by consideration of the phasor diagrams of the two conditions shown in Fig. 15.38*a* and *b*. In the passband (in-phase) condition the side-chain signal and the main-path signal add directly; therefore, a relatively low threshold must be maintained at all passband frequencies (Fig. 15.38*a*). However, in the stop band the effective amplitude contribution of the side-chain signal may be minimal owing to the phase difference between it and the main-path signal; because of this it is possible to raise the threshold significantly and to reduce the limiting strength once the desired amount of attenuation has been obtained at a given frequency (Fig. 16.38*b*). The result is that large signals in the stop band do not cause signal modulation in the passband and consequently create an impairment of the noise reduction effect achieved during decoding.

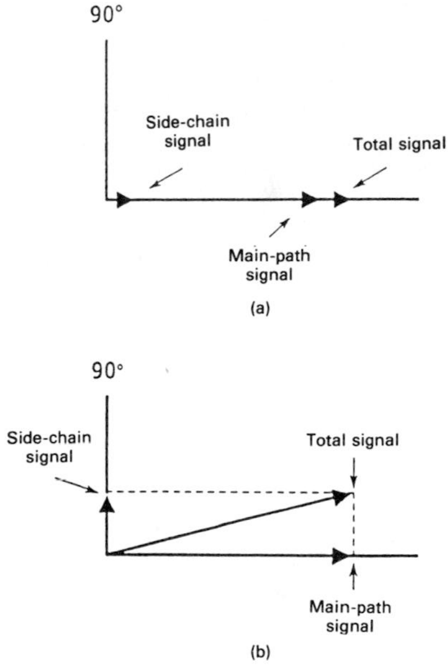

Similar considerations apply in the SR sliding-band circuits. By way of introduction, in the B-type and C-type

FIG. 15.38 Phasor diagrams of a dual-path compressor. (*a*) In the passband, a low threshold and a strong limiting characteristic are required. (*b*) In the stop band, phase shift results in the side-chain signal having negligible influence on the total signal amplitude; therefore, a higher threshold and weaker limiting can be used.

sliding-band circuits a variable filter follows a fixed filter, which has proved to be an efficient and reproducible arrangement. At frequencies outside the passband a pure two-pole filter would result in overall amplitude subtraction from the main-path signal because of the large phase angles created. Therefore, the type of filter which has been employed is only quasi-two-pole (a single-pole fixed filter plus a variable shelf characteristic).

The same type of arrangement is used in the spectral recording process, with a one-octave difference (in the stop-band direction) between the variable-filter turnover frequency (under quiescent conditions) and the fixed-filter cutoff frequency. Above the threshold at a particular frequency the variable filter slides to the turnover frequency needed to create the overall (main-path plus side-chain signal) compression law. As the input level rises and once an overall gain of about unity is obtained (when the variable-filter cutoff frequency is about two to three octaves above the dominant signal frequency), there is no reason for further sliding of the variable filter. At this point the modulation control arrangement counteracts further sliding of the filter; as with the fixed-band circuits, this arrangement prevents unnecessary modulation of the signal.

The above effects in both the fixed and the sliding bands are created by circuits called *modulation control circuits.* Suitably filtered or frequency-weighted signals from the main signal path are rectified, and in some cases smoothed, and are fed in opposition to the control signals generated by the control circuits of the various stages. The result at higher signal levels, relatively (beginning at about 20 dB above the threshold of the relevant compressor circuit), is to tend to create a balance, or equilibrium, between the compressor-circuit control signals and the modulation control signals. Under these conditions there is a significantly reduced gain reduction or sliding of the variable filters as a function of increasing input-signal levels.

Figure 15.39a and b illustrates the action of modulation control with a high-frequency fixed-band-compressor circuit. The circuit has a low-level gain of about 8 dB and an 800-Hz high-pass characteristic. Figure 15.39a shows the response of the circuit in the absence of modulation control. Ideally there should be no attenuation in response to a 100-Hz signal because the overall shape of the envelope is such that there is negligible signal boosting at 100 Hz. Nevertheless, with a conventional compressor circuit as shown here, when the 100-Hz signal increases in level, there is a reduction of low-level signal boosting over the whole frequency band. The unnecessary attenuation has two effects: (1) substantial noise reduction action is lost during expansion; and (2) when the amplitude of the 100-Hz signal varies, it can modulate low-level signal components at higher frequencies, resulting in possible incorrect restoration of the signal by the expander if the recording channel has an irregular frequency response in the vicinity of 100 Hz.

Figure 15.39b shows the operation of the same circuit with modulation control. A greatly reduced attenuation occurs when the 100-Hz signal is varied over the same range of levels as in Fig. 15.39a. Thus a significant immunity to strong signals in the stop-band frequency region is achieved, the effect decreasing as the dominant signal frequency approaches the passband frequency region of the circuit.

Referring to Fig. 15.40a, the operation of a sliding-band circuit under comparable conditions is shown. As with the fixed-band circuit, ideally there should be no sliding in response to a strong 100-Hz signal. Nonetheless, as the 100-Hz signal increases in level, the band slides upward. As with the fixed-band circuit, the unnecessary sliding results in a loss of noise reduction action and the modulation of signals at higher frequencies when the sliding band varies under the control of the 100-Hz signal.

Figure 15.40b shows the operation of the same circuit with modulation control. Minimal sliding occurs when the 100-Hz signal is varied over the same range of levels as in Fig. 15.40a. Thus the sliding-band compressor is also made essentially immune to strong signals outside its passband.

The effect of modulation control is further illustrated by Fig. 15.40c and d, except that the frequency of the dominant signal is changed to 800 Hz, a frequency within the passband of the circuit. Ideally, sliding is required to go only so far as not to boost the 800-Hz signal above the 0-dB reference level. Thus, in the Fig. 15.40c response, without modulation control, the sliding produced by the 800-Hz signal at levels above −10 dB is excessive. Figure 15.40d shows the response of the circuit with modulation control: sliding at and above the 0-dB

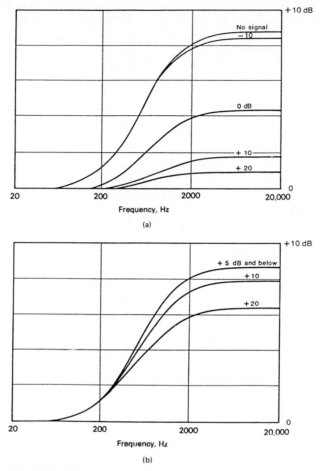

FIG. 15.39 Effect of modulation control on a fixed-band-compressor circuit. (*a*) Probe-tone curves with a 100-Hz signal at the levels indicated: no modulation control. (*b*) Same as *a*, with modulation control.

level is greatly reduced. The effect is progressively reduced for low signal levels but is observable to some extent at the −10-dB level.

The use of modulation control techniques also has advantages under transient conditions, both from their use in the steady-state circuits and also because of their use in the overshoot suppression circuits. Modulation control generally prevents any further fixed-band attenuation or sliding of the variable filter than is required to respond to a given signal situation. Therefore, (1) signal modulation is reduced, (2) the SR process is rendered very tolerant of channel errors, (3) subsequent noise modulation during decoding is reduced, and (4) recovery from transient signal conditions is faster. The electronic reality in both the steady-state cir-

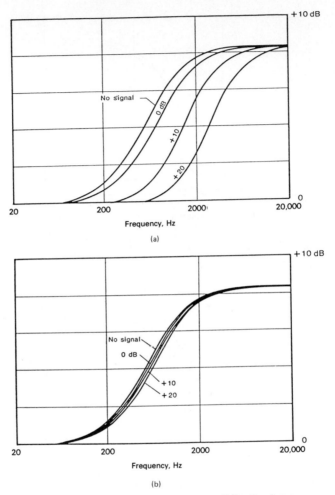

FIG. 15.40 Effect of modulation control on a sliding-band-compressor circuit, with a signal in the stop band and a signal in the passband. (*a*) Probe-tone curves with a 100-Hz signal at the levels indicated: no modulation control. (*b*) Same as *a*, with modulation control. (*c*) Probe-tone curves with an 800-Hz signal at the levels indicated: no modulation control. (*d*) Same as *c*, with modulation control.

cuits and transient-control circuits is that the integrator capacitors are prevented from charging to voltages as high as they normally would in the absence of modulation control; with lower fully charged voltages, recovery is faster.

The modulation control aspects of the SR process result in an encoding action which is remarkably free of noticeable signal-related modulation effects. Working together with action substitution, modulation control contributes to the goal of least treatment, in providing a highly boosted, audibly stable encoded signal.

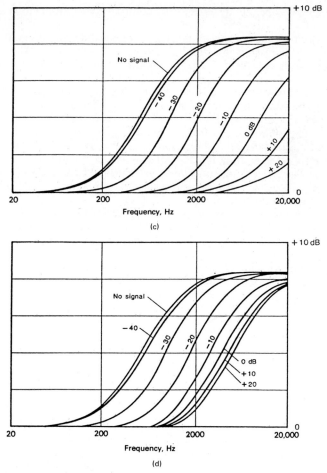

FIG. 15.40 (*Continued*)

Overshoot Suppression.   A side effect of the modulation control scheme is that at high signal levels the amplitudes of the signals from the several stages are relatively high in comparison with the situation in the A-type, B-type, and C-type systems. Because of this it is not possible to employ simple overshoot suppression diodes as in these previous systems. A more flexible but necessarily more complex scheme that operates directly upon the control signals is used.

In common with the A-type, B-type, and C-type systems, the SR process features overshoot suppression thresholds that are significantly higher than the steady-state thresholds; this results in low modulation distortion. The overshoot suppression thresholds are set about 10 dB above the relevant steady-state thresholds. The net result is that for most musical signals the overshoot suppressors rarely operate; the compressors are controlled by well-smoothed signals. When the suppressors do operate, the effect is so controlled that modulation distortion is minimal.

Under extreme transient conditions, e.g., from a subthreshold signal situation, the overshoot suppression threshold is set at its lowest point. The overshoot suppression effects are then phased in gradually as a function of increasing impulse level.

Under relatively steady-state but nonetheless changing signal conditions the overshoot suppression effects are gradually phased out as a function of increasing signal levels; this action further ensures low overall modulation distortion from the system. The phasing-out effect is achieved by increasing the overshoot suppression thresholds; the thresholds are controlled by signals that are the same as or derived from the modulation control signals used to control the steady-state characteristics, whereby a tracking action between the transient and steady-state behavior is obtained. This arrangement results in both well-controlled overshoots and low modulation distortion.

Both primary and secondary overshoot suppression circuits are employed, the latter acting as fallback or long-stop suppressors. In the high-frequency circuits the secondary overshoot suppressors improve the performance just inside the stop band, that is, in the 400-Hz to 800-Hz region. In the low-frequency circuits these additional suppressors improve the performance under extreme complex signal conditions (e.g., high-level, low-frequency and midfrequency transient signals in combination with high-level, high-frequency signals). In the low-frequency circuits a further overshoot suppressor (LF O/S) is used for very-low-frequency signals; this is a very gentle, slow-acting circuit which reduces low-frequency transient distortion.

Staggered-Action Multilevel Format.   The principles discussed above are incorporated into each stage of the multilevel staggered-action encoder and decoder. (See Sec. 15.6.2 for a detailed discussion of staggered-action circuits.) In the SR system two stages are employed at low frequencies; three, at high frequencies. The thresholds used are approximately -30 dB, -48 dB, and -62 dB below reference level (20 dB below SR peak signal level). In the series-connected staggered-action format there is a compounding of the actions of the individual stages; the transfer functions of the several stages are multiplied, whereby the dB characteristics add. In this way a large total dynamic action can be achieved with very low modulation distortion, low overshoot, and good manufacturing reproducibility. An important additional result is that there is an overall steepness enhancement of the frequency-discrimination abilities of the circuit, further inhibiting signal modulation and noise modulation effects.

Spectral Skewing.   The spectral-skewing networks employed in the SR process comprise both high-frequency and low-frequency sections, with the same rationale and mode of operation as discussed in Sec. 15.6.4. The spectral distributions of the signals processed by the encoder are altered or skewed, well within the passband, so that the encoder, or compressor, action is significantly less susceptible to the influence of signals beyond the abrupt rolloff frequencies of the spectral-skewing networks.

The high-frequency network is a low-pass filter with an attenuation characteristic similar to that of a 12-kHz two-pole Butterworth filter but with a limiting attenuation of about 35 dB (i.e., a shelf). The low-frequency network is a 40-Hz high-pass filter, connected in series with the high-frequency network, also with a two-pole Butterworth-like characteristic but with about a 25-dB limiting attenuation. These shelves do not interfere with the attenuation within the audio band but provide phase characteristics that are essential in the decoding mode.

Antisaturation.   The general principle of antisaturation was described in Sec. 15.6.5. Briefly, by placing a fixed-attenuation network, usually a shelf, in the main path of a dual-path compressor, it is possible to create a very effective antisaturation characteristic at the extremes of the audio band without any undue adverse effect on the noise reduction effect achieved during decoding. In the SR process high- and low-frequency networks are operative above about 5 kHz and below about 100 Hz, respectively. In addition, the spectral-skewing networks have a secondary but very useful antisaturation effect, especially at very low and very high frequencies.

15.8.4   Block Diagrams

Basic Block Diagram.   As mentioned previously, Fig. 15.34 shows the basic layout of an SR processor. While the whole system comprises an encoder and a complementary decoder, the figure as drawn shows a switchable configuration, which generally is the most useful one. The main signal path transmits high-level signal components. To this is added in the encoding mode, and subtracted in the decoding mode, the output of the side-chain circuitry, designated the SR signal, point *C*. The stage circuits, as well as the spectral-skewing networks and antisaturation networks above, are driven from point *A*. (See Sec. 15.2.3 for a mathematical explanation of these arrangements.)

A secondary main path which does not include any antisaturation is employed as the basis of the side chain, to which the outputs of the high-level stages and midlevel stages are added in the first-stage adder and second-stage adder, respectively. The low-level stage and modulation control circuits 1 to 7 are driven directly from the output of the second-stage adder. Modulation control circuit 8 is driven from the output of the spectral-skewing network, as will be discussed.

The antisaturation effects are created in the dashed block labeled "Stage signal combiner and antisaturation." The arrangement shown provides a high-frequency deemphasis effect on the secondary main-path signal, which includes the output of the high-level stages, and on the high-frequency midlevel-stage signal. This deemphasis is effective not only on the steady-state aspects of these signals but on all transient effects as well. The output of the low-level stage is then added directly. For low-frequency antisaturation the low-frequency deemphasis is effective on the secondary main-path signal, including the high-level-stage outputs. The low-frequency midlevel signal is then added directly. (Section 15.6.5 describes the mathematical basis for these arrangements.)

With the final combination of signals in the last adder, an SR encoded signal appears at point *B*. The encoded signal can be considered to comprise an unmodified component from the input plus an SR signal which carries all of the SR characteristics. Thus the SR component can be derived by subtracting the unmodified input signal at point *A* from the SR encoder output at point *B*. This provides an SR signal at point *C* that can be handled and switched in the same way as in the A-type system. This simplifies practical use of the system.

Modulation Control Circuits.   Figure 15.34 shows how the inputs of the various modulation control circuits are connected and how the resultant signals are distributed. Modulation control signals MC1 to MC7 are derived from the output of the second-stage adder. In this way the modulation control signals begin to have a significant influence at relatively low levels, such as at -30 dB (because of the contributions of the HLS and MLS stages). The phase relationships between the modulation control signals and the signals in the control circuits of the several stages are also optimized. In the generation of MC8, which is used for low-frequency-stage overshoot suppression inhibition under high-frequency transient-signal conditions, the influences of the HLS and MLS stages are undesirable. MC8 is therefore derived from the first feed point of the stages, just following the spectral-skewing networks.

Figure 15.34 also shows the distribution scheme of the modulation control signals. MC1 to MC3 are used for the high-frequency stages; MC5 to MC8, for the low-frequency stages.

In Fig. 15.41, the basic layout of the modulation control circuits is shown. MC1 controls the high-frequency sliding-band circuits. The signal from the take-off point is fed through a 3-kHz single-pole high-pass filter, full-wave-rectified (all rectifiers in the system are full-wave), and fed in opposition to the control signals generated by the high-frequency stages. An all-pass phase-shift network is used to optimize the phase of the MC signal in relation to the stage control signal at low frequencies; this reduces control-signal ripple. MC1 is also smoothed by a two-stage 1-ms integrator and is employed, as MC2, to oppose the operation of the high-frequency sliding-band overshoot suppression circuits; the overshoot suppression thresholds thereby track the steady-state thresholds. MC2 must be smoothed because the phase relationships of MC1 and the signals in the stages vary (because of the sliding-band action) throughout the audio band, being a function of frequency and level.

MC3 controls the high-frequency fixed-band circuits. The signal from the take-off point is weighted by cascaded 400-Hz and 800-Hz single-pole low-pass filters, rectified, and fed in opposition to both the steady-state and transient control circuits of the high-frequency fixed-band circuits. There is no need to provide a smoothed MC signal for the overshoot suppressors of the high-frequency fixed-band stages because a fixed phase relationship exists between the stage signals and the control signals throughout the audio band.

MC4 controls the sliding-band circuits of the low-frequency stages. The signal from the takeoff point is fed through a 200-Hz single-pole low-pass filter, rectified, and fed in opposition to the sliding-band control signals generated in the stages. The phase relationship of the modulation control signal is optimized by the use of an all-pass phase shifter, as with MC1; low-frequency control-signal ripple is thereby reduced. MC4 is smoothed by a two-stage 2-ms integrator to form MC5; this signal is used to control the low-frequency sliding-band overshoot suppressors.

MC6 controls the low-frequency fixed-band circuits. The signal from the take-off point is weighted by cascaded 800-Hz and 1.6-kHz single-pole high-pass filters, rectified, and used to oppose the steady-state fixed-band control signals. MC6 is also smoothed in a two-stage 2-ms integrator, forming MC7, which is used to control the low-frequency fixed-band overshoot suppressors. This smoothing is necessary in the low-frequency fixed-band stages because, unlike the situation in the high-frequency fixed-band stages, there is no fixed phase relationship between the stage signals and the overshoot suppression signals. MC7 is also used in a supplemental way to control the low-frequency sliding-band overshoot suppressors.

MC8 is used to control the overshoot suppression circuits of both the fixed- and the sliding-band low-frequency circuits. MC8 compensates for the fact that

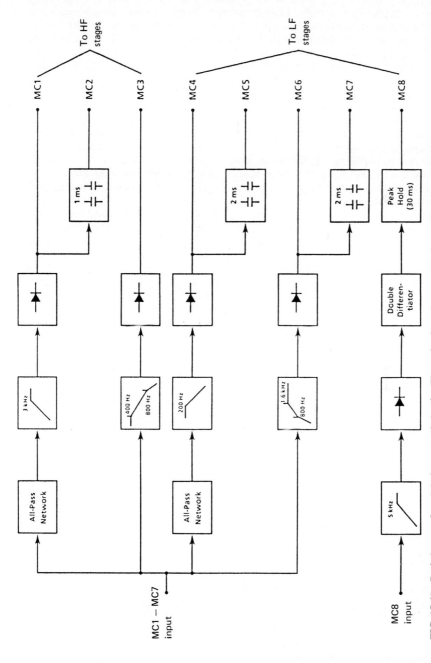

FIG. 15.41 Basic layout of modulation control circuits. These circuits reduce modulations of the gains and frequency-response characteristics used in the system, especially at signal levels significantly above the compressor thresholds.

no frequency weighting is used in the generation of the low-frequency primary overshoot suppression signals. High-frequency transient-signal components are detected and used to oppose the operation of the low-frequency primary overshoot suppression circuits. The signal from the MC8 takeoff point is fed through a 5-kHz high-pass filter, rectified, double-differentiated with 15-μs time constants, and peak-held with about a 30-ms time constant. The resultant high-frequency transient modulation control signal MC8 is then employed to oppose the low-frequency overshoot suppression action.

High-Frequency Stage.   Figure 15.42 shows both steady-state and transient-control aspects of the high-frequency stages. The diagram shows only the basic parameter-determining elements; the practical circuits of course contain other details such as buffering, amplification, and attenuation. The high-level, midlevel, and low-level stages have the same basic block diagrams and schematics. The main distinctions are that the ac and dc circuit gains are increased for the midlevel and low-level stages.

Referring to the block diagram, each stage comprises a fixed-band section on the bottom and a sliding-band section on the top, each with its own control circuits. The fixed- and sliding-band circuits are fed in parallel, and the output signal is taken from the sliding-band circuit. The sliding-band variable filter is referenced to the output of the fixed band; that is, the fixed-band output is fed directly to the bottom end of the sliding-band variable-resistance RV_s. This connection results in the action-substitution operation as discussed previously. At any given frequency the overall output will be the larger of, or some combination of, the fixed- and sliding-band contributions. If there is a signal situation in which the fixed-band output is negligible, then the sliding band predominates. Conversely, if there is little or no sliding-band contribution, the output from the fixed band will still feed through to the output through RV_s. In this way the action of one circuit augments that of the other and, as the occasion requires, may be substituted for that of the other.

The incoming signal is fed through an 800-Hz single-pole band-defining filter. This is followed by a 400-Hz single-pole filter which attenuates the low-frequency signal levels fed to both the fixed- and the sliding-band circuits; this reduces waveform distortion and complex-signal transient distortion at high signal levels. The filter also forms part of the fixed-band control-signal weighting network. The output signal is taken from the sliding-band stage and is fed through a 400-Hz network having a reciprocal characteristic to that of the 400-Hz high-pass filter at the input. Thus the overall quiescent (subthreshold) frequency response of the circuit is that of a single-pole 800-Hz high-pass network. The low-frequency stages have a complementary 800-Hz single-pole low-pass characteristic, which overall results in optimal combination of the signals from the high- and low-frequency stages.

The fixed-band output from RV_f (i.e., the variable-gain circuit) is fed to two control circuits, the main control-signal circuit (top) and the passband control circuit (bottom). In the main control circuit the signal is rectified and opposed by the modulation control signal MC3. The resulting dc signal is smoothed by an integrator circuit with a 15-ms time constant (the overall steady-state control-signal characteristic in this and all other stages is average-responding). The control signal is then fed to one input of a maximum selector circuit, which passes to its output the larger of two signals applied to the input.

The fixed-band output is also fed to the passband control circuit, which comprises a 1.6-kHz single-pole high-pass filter, a rectifier, and a smoothing circuit (15 ms). The passband control signal is applied to the other input of the maxi-

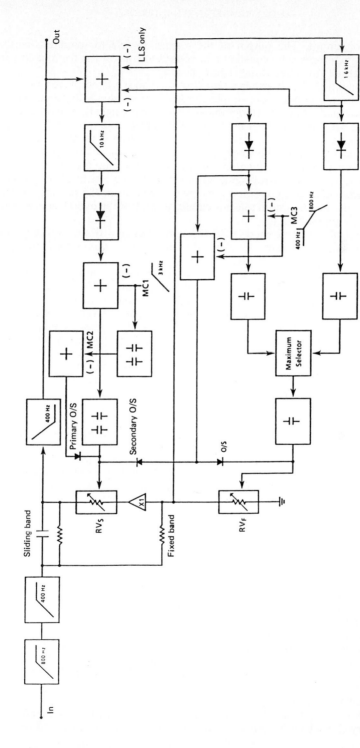

FIG. 15.42 High-frequency-stage block diagram.

mum selector circuit. The output of the maximum selector circuit is further smoothed by a 160-ms time constant and is used to control the fixed-band variable resistance RV_f or other variable-gain means.

The dual-control circuit arrangement described above is employed to obtain optimal performance under both simple-signal situations (single dominant signal) and complex-signal situations (more than one dominant signal). The modulation control signal MC3 is optimized in frequency weighting and amount for simple-signal conditions, in which the modulation control action is most useful. Under complex-signal conditions, however, the modulation control signal developed becomes larger, and the subsequent modulation control action is then greater than necessary; that is, the dc control-signal output from the main control circuit is less than required. Under this condition the control signal from the passband circuit is phased in, via the maximum selector circuit, to control the overall action of the fixed-band-compressor circuit.

The output of the fixed band is fed through a buffer with an overall gain of unity to provide the reference for the sliding-band filter; this is the only signal output of the fixed-band-compressor circuit.

The sliding-band control signal is derived from the stage output. The signal is fed through a single-pole high-pass weighting network (about 10 kHz, different for each stage) and is rectified. The rectified signal is opposed by modulation control signal MC1; since MC1 also has a single-pole high-pass characteristic, the ratio between the rectified control signal and MC1 monitors the signal attenuation (this ratio creates an end-stop effect on the sliding-band action). The result is smoothed first by a time constant of about 5 ms (different for each stage) and finally by a time constant of 80 ms. The smoothed control signal is then used to control the sliding-band variable-resistance RV_s. A single control circuit suffices in the sliding-band circuit because the 10-kHz high-pass control weighting network tends to offset the effect of complex signals on the modulation control voltage developed (MC1).

A modification is made in the sliding-band control characteristic at low levels. Signals from the fixed-band circuit are combined in opposition with the sliding-band output signal (see combining circuit at the right of Fig. 15.42). The effect is in the direction of simulating the derivation of the sliding-band control voltage from the voltage across the sliding-band variable filter only (i.e., from the voltage across RV_s). This tends to raise the sliding-band threshold at high frequencies, which reduces unnecessary sliding of the band. (The 10-kHz control weighting network provides the correct amount of control signal for the variable filter at medium and high levels, but it produces the undesirable side effect of lowering the threshold at high frequencies. The differential-control-signal-derivation method counteracts this threshold-lowering effect.)

The overshoot suppression (O/S) arrangements are also shown in Fig. 15.42. In the high-frequency circuits a general feature is that unsmoothed rectified signals from the control-circuit rectifiers are opposed by appropriate modulation control signals and are fed via diodes to the final integrator circuits. The low-frequency arrangements follow the same pattern, with some modifications.

Referring to the diagram, in the high-frequency fixed-band circuit the O/S signal is derived from the rectifier of the main control circuit. As with the steady-state control signal, the rectified signal is opposed by MC3, so that the O/S threshold is appropriate for conditions in the steady-state regime. The resultant O/S signal is coupled by a diode to the final integrator circuit.

In the sliding-band circuit two O/S signals, primary and secondary, are used. The primary O/S signal is derived from the control-circuit rectifier and opposed by MC2, a smoothed version of MC1 (MC1 controls the steady-state characteristics). The smoothing is necessary because, unlike the situation in the fixed-band circuit, there is no constant and favorable phase relationship between the signal in the control circuit and MC1 (because of the sliding band); the smoothing enables reliable bucking action to take place.

The secondary overshoot suppressor supplements the action of the primary overshoot suppressor under certain conditions. The primary O/S signal is derived from the same rectifier used in the steady-state control circuit, with the consequence not only of economy but of a favorable phase relationship between the O/S impulse and the signal to be controlled; this results in low transient distortion. However, the control-circuit frequency weighting responsible for this situation also causes a reduction of control-signal amplitude with falling frequency. A dc bias is used in the O/S circuit to create the required suppression threshold; when the signal amplitude in the O/S circuit decreases, the bias results in the O/S effect falling away faster than the signal amplitude. For frequencies below about 400 Hz, a reduced O/S effect is appropriate because of the attenuation and phase shift of the stage input filter (see Fig. 15.38). However, in the 400-Hz to 800-Hz region there is a slight O/S deficiency; this can be compensated or trimmed very simply by feeding a small amount of O/S signal from the fixed-band circuit into the sliding-band circuit. This supplemental signal is called the secondary O/S signal.

Regarding recovery times, the use of action substitution and modulation control contributes to rapid action, as already mentioned. Nonetheless, reverse-biased recovery speedup diodes are used in a fairly gentle way (series resistors) to provide a further increase in speed.

Low-Frequency Stage: Steady-State Aspects.   Figure 15.43 shows only the steady-state layout of the low-frequency stages. As with the high-frequency stages, only the basic parameter-determining elements are shown. The high-level and mid-level low-frequency stages have the same block diagrams and circuits, but the ac and dc gains are increased for the midlevel stage; there are also some other minor differences.

Referring to the block diagram, certain similarities and differences may be noted with respect to the high-frequency diagrams. The dual-layer arrangement of the fixed band on the bottom and the sliding band on the top is similar. However, the sliding band acts downwardly, using a simulated inductance (gyrator circuit). As with the high-frequency stages, the fixed- and sliding-band circuits are fed in parallel, and the output signal is taken from the sliding-band circuit. The fixed-band output is coupled to the bottom of the sliding band to provide the action-substitution operation described previously.

A notable difference from the high-frequency circuit is that the fixed 800-Hz band-determining filter follows rather than precedes the variable filter. This arrangement has several advantages: (1) O/S signals can be generated without the delay inherent in a low-pass filter, resulting in lower transient distortion; (2) any transient distortion produced by the circuit is attenuated by the 800-Hz low-pass filter; and (3) noise generated by the gyrator circuit is attenuated by the filter. The price to be paid for these advantages is the resulting high signal levels that the variable resistances RV_f and RV_s must be capable of handling at high frequencies (there is no active attenuation at all at very high frequencies, since sufficient passive attenuation and phase shift are provided by the 800-Hz low-pass filter). Special control arrangements, called high-mode, comprising complementary bootstrapping and control-circuit gain boosting, enable the fixed- and sliding-

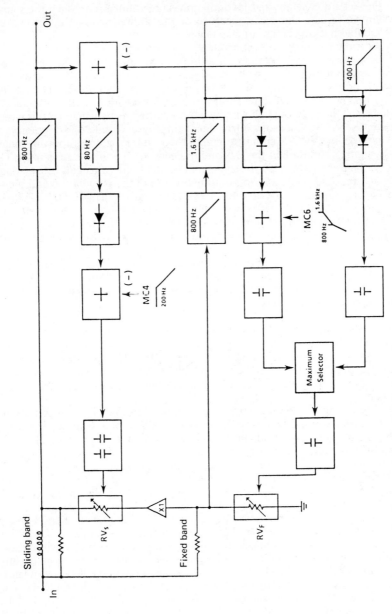

FIG. 15.43 Low-frequency-stage block diagram: steady-state aspects.

band-signal circuits to handle the required levels with low distortion and low noise.

Referring to the fixed-band section, the incoming signal is applied directly to the variable-gain circuit. Control-circuit frequency weighting is provided by cascaded single-pole 800-Hz and 1.6-Hz low-pass filters (the corresponding filters in the high-frequency stages are the 800-Hz and 400-Hz filters at the inputs of the circuits). The main control circuit rectifies the filtered signal; the resulting dc signal is bucked by modulation control signal MC6, smoothed by a 15-ms integrator, and fed to one input of the maximum selector circuit. The maximum selector circuit has the same purpose and mode of operation as in the high-frequency circuits.

The 800-Hz and 1.6-kHz frequency-weighted output of the fixed-band circuit is also fed to the passband control circuit. Here the control signal is further weighted by a 400-Hz single-pole low-pass filter, rectified, smoothed by a 15-ms integrator, and fed to the other input of the maximum selector. The larger of the two signals is passed to the final integrator (300 ms) to become the fixed-band control signal applied to RV_f; in this way, both simple and complex signals are accommodated, as in the high-frequency stages.

As in the high-frequency circuits, the sliding-band control signal is derived from the stage output, that is, from a point following both the fixed 800-Hz band-determining filter and the variable filter. The signal is frequency-weighted by an 80-Hz single-pole low-pass filter, rectified, and bucked by modulation control signal MC4 (which also has a single-pole low-pass characteristic, with the same type of sliding-band end-stop effect as in the high-frequency circuits). The result is smoothed by a 7.5-ms integrator and finally smoothed by a 150-ms integrator to become the sliding-band control signal applied to RV_s. As in the high-frequency stages, a single control circuit suffices for the sliding band.

The same type of low-level control characteristic modification is made in the low-frequency circuits as in the high-frequency circuits. Namely, a signal from the fixed band is combined in opposition with the sliding-band output signal (see combining circuit at the right of Fig. 15.43). This differential control modification raises the sliding-band threshold at low frequencies.

Low-Frequency Stage: Transient-Control Aspects.   The transient-control (including steady-state) aspects of the low-frequency stages are shown in Fig. 15.44. In a manner generally similar to that of the high-frequency circuits, unsmoothed rectified signals from the outputs of the variable elements are opposed by appropriate modulation control signals and are fed via diodes to the final integrator circuits.

The fixed and the sliding bands each have primary and secondary overshoot suppressors, which operate at frequencies above about 100 Hz. Additionally, each has a gentle and slow-acting low-frequency overshoot suppressor, operating at frequencies below about 200 Hz; there is a crossover effect between the two types of overshoot suppression in the 100- to 200-Hz region. The primary overshoot suppressors provide the earliest and strongest suppression effect in simple transient situations. With more complex signals the primary overshoot suppression thresholds rise, and eventually the secondary overshoot suppression circuitry takes control.

In contrast with the high-frequency situation, the low-frequency general strategy is to derive the primary overshoot suppression signals from signal points that do not include any control-circuit frequency weighting. This is true because the required control-circuit weighting networks of the low-frequency stages are low-pass in character, resulting in delays (the high-pass networks used for control-

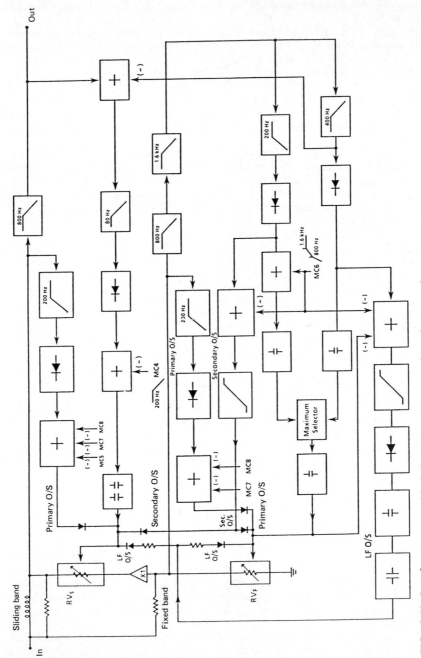

FIG. 15.44 Low-frequency-stage block diagram: steady-state and transient-control aspects.

circuit weighting in the high-frequency stages do not introduce delays). However, because of the lack of a weighting factor in the primary overshoot suppression signal, there is no inherent tracking between the steady-state and overshoot suppression thresholds of the circuits involved, particularly in the stop bands. Therefore, further modulation control techniques are employed to obtain the required tracking; secondary overshoot suppression signals are derived from a point in the fixed-band circuitry that provides adequate tracking in both the fixed and the sliding bands.

Referring to Fig. 15.44, the fixed-band primary overshoot suppression signal is generated by passing the variable-attenuator output through a 200-Hz single-pole high-pass filter. This filter reduces the influence of the primary overshoot suppressor at low frequencies, allowing the gentler low-frequency overshoot suppressor to take over the transient-control function. The signal is rectified and then opposed by modulation control signal MC7, a 2-ms smoothed version of MC6 (the fixed-band steady-state modulation control signal); the effect is in the direction of improving the steady-state and overshoot suppression threshold tracking on a steady-state basis. However, the thresholds must also track on a transient basis. This is the function of the high-frequency transient modulation control signal MC8, which is a high-frequency weighted, peak-detected signal that opposes the primary overshoot suppression signal in the time interval before MC7 becomes effective. The overshoot suppression signal is then diode-coupled to the final integrator circuit of the fixed-band circuit.

In the generation of the sliding-band primary overshoot suppression signal, the output of the variable filter is fed through a 200-Hz single-pole filter to reduce the effect of the circuit at low frequencies (as in the fixed-band circuit). The signal is rectified and then opposed by modulation control signals MC5 and MC7 to provide an adequate degree of tracking between the steady-state threshold and the overshoot suppression threshold on a steady-state basis. As in the fixed-band circuit, MC8 provides the required degree of tracking on a transient basis. The resultant overshoot suppression signal is diode-coupled to the sliding-band final integration circuit.

In both the fixed- and the sliding-band circuits, the effects of the primary overshoot suppression circuits are maximized for the most significant transient-signal situation, that is, a single impulse or tone burst starting from a subthreshold signal level. A side effect of the use of smoothed MC5 and MC7 signals is that the overshoot suppression levels for low- and medium-frequency transient signals are raised under certain complex signal conditions, especially those in which relatively steady-state high-frequency signals at high levels are also present. To compensate for this effect, secondary overshoot suppression signals are derived from the fixed-band overshoot suppression signal and are diode-coupled to the fixed-band and sliding-band final integrator circuits. The secondary overshoot suppressors have higher thresholds than the primary suppressors and operate only rarely because of the unusual circumstances for which they are designed.

The secondary overshoot suppression signals are generated from the frequency-weighted point (800-Hz low-pass and 1.6-kHz low-pass) in the fixed-band steady-state control circuit. To prevent interference with the low-frequency overshoot suppression circuit at low frequencies, the signal is further filtered by a 200-Hz single-pole high-pass network, as in the primary overshoot suppression circuits; the filtered signal is then rectified. (Note that for clarity this filter is not shown in Fig. 15.43. On a steady-state basis the passband control circuit controls the circuit at very low frequencies, via the maximum selector circuit; this arrangement allows the main control-circuit rectifier to serve a double function.) The dc signal is opposed by MC6 in order to phase out the secondary overshoot suppression effect at high frequencies; an optimal phase relationship is obtained between the rectified signal and MC6, apart from the effect of the 200-Hz filter (which is negligible). An ideal tracking effect is achieved between the steady-state and secondary overshoot suppression thresholds.

The effect of the 800-Hz and 1.6-kHz frequency-weighting networks is to introduce a time delay into the secondary overshoot suppression signal. The effective delay is significantly reduced by increasing the gain used in the secondary overshoot suppressor circuit and applying limiting. The resultant overshoot suppression signal is more in the nature of a nearly fixed amplitude impulse, applied in the rare circumstances when necessary, than it is a proportional response. The signal is coupled through a diode to the fixed-band final integrator circuit and is also used, suitably biased, for secondary overshoot suppression in the sliding-band circuit, also coupled through a diode.

The low-frequency overshoot suppression signal is developed by tapping the rectified but unsmoothed output of the passband control circuit of the fixed-band circuit. The signal is opposed by MC6 to desensitize the circuit to high-level, high-frequency components. The signal is further opposed by the resulting fixed-band smoothed control signal, in a negative-feedback fashion (when the fixed-band control signal has risen to a sufficient level, there is no further need for low-frequency overshoot suppressor action). The signal is then highly amplified and limited, peak-rectified, and smoothed by an integrator with about a 20-ms decay time constant. The resulting high-amplitude pulses are fed through a differentiating network, with a time constant of the same order as the integration time constant, to provide low-frequency overshoot suppression impulses of defined strength for distribution to the fixed-band and sliding-band final integrators, via high-value resistors and series diodes. The result is a decaying *constant-current charging* of the capacitors of the final integrator circuits. This is in contrast with the higher-peak currents and correspondingly more abrupt control-voltage changes produced by the relatively low-impedance primary and secondary overshoot suppressors. The use of the low-frequency overshoot suppression method results in low waveform distortion of relatively slowly changing low-frequency signal impulses applied to the system.

The control-signal recovery characteristics are similar to those of the high-frequency circuits, although they are about half as fast because of the longer time constants employed. As in the high-frequency stages, the recovery time is favorably affected by the use of action-substitution and -modulation control but is further augmented by the use of speedup diodes.

15.8.5 Operating Characteristics

The objective of the SR process is to provide a very clean and accurate-sounding replica of the input signal. This result is achieved by suitable actions on both the encoding and the decoding sides of the process. By means of the antisaturation technique, the incoming signal is first encoded in such a way as to reduce harmonic and intermodulation distortion generated in the recording or transmission channel. Then the decoding process reduces any noise and/or distortion introduced by the channel.

Dynamic (Compression) Action for Steady-State Dominant Signals.   Referring to the single-tone compression curves shown in Fig. 15.45, several features are noted in the following subsections.

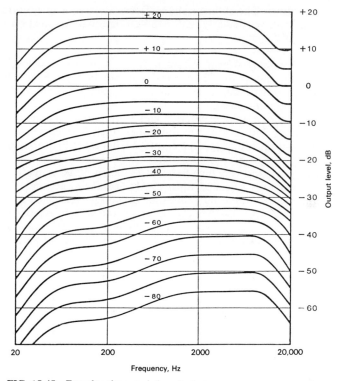

FIG. 15.45 Encoder characteristics: single-tone.

Low Frequencies. Dynamic action occurs in the range from about −48 dB to −5 dB (with respect to reference level). That is, there is no action (but full boosting) in the lower 35 to 40 dB of the dynamic range. Similarly, there is no action in the top 25 dB of the total dynamic range. A linear dynamic characteristic (a bilinear characteristic) prevails in these two regions.

High Frequencies. Dynamic action occurs in the range from about −62 dB to −5 dB. That is, there is no action in the lower 20 to 25 dB (but full boosting) or the top 25 dB of the dynamic range (a linear dynamic characteristic in these regions).

In the intermediate-level regions of dynamic action the effects of the multilevel stages are joined together to create a compression ratio of about 2:1.

Referring to the high-level low- and high-frequency portions of the curves, the effective antisaturation of the system can be seen, with the combined effects of the spectral-skewing and antisaturation networks, the SR stages, and about 1 dB of wideband-level compensation built into the coefficients of the stage signal combiner (Fig. 15.34). The overall result is an antisaturation effect of about 2 dB at 5 kHz, 6 dB at 10 kHz, and 10 dB at 25 Hz and 15 kHz. At high frequencies this amount of antisaturation significantly reduces distortion, reduces signal compression effects, and, with tape recording, improves the long-term stability of the recording. The high-frequency improvements are especially significant with

35-μs CCIR recordings. The antisaturation effect at low frequencies usefully counteracts tape overload, particularly with 3180-μs National Association of Broadcasters (NAB) recordings.

Quiescent (Subthreshold) Signal Characteristic. The very-low-level, or subthreshold, characteristic of the SR process is shown in Fig. 15.46. The general shape of this characteristic was determined in a way that takes good advantage of the properties of human hearing.

First, there is less of a noise generation and perception problem at moderately low frequencies (e.g., 200 Hz) than at moderately high frequencies (e.g., 3 kHz); therefore, two low-frequency stages are employed, but three high-frequency stages are used.

Second, at very low and very high frequencies (below 50 Hz and above 10 kHz) even less noise reduction is needed. Strong spectral-skewing actions can therefore be used in these regions, resulting in accurate decoding even when the recording medium has response irregularities. Additionally, the spectral-skewing networks provide for good immunity to high- and low-frequency interference (supersonic audio components, tape-recorder bias, subsonic noise components arising from wind, traffic, or other rumble sources).

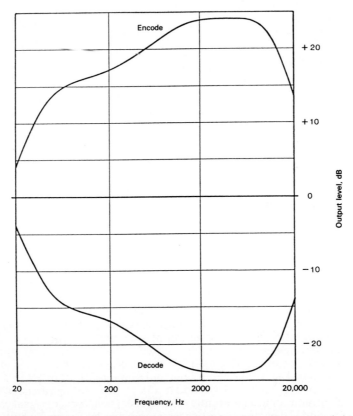

FIG. 15.46 Low-level (subthreshold) encoding and decoding characteristics.

Note that the overall shape of the low-level SR decoding characteristic resembles the low-level Fletcher-Munson and Robinson-Dadson curves; the encoding characteristic resembles the subsequently derived CCIR noise-weighting curve.

Thus the SR system is designed to reduce only those noises that can be heard. The prevention of action in inaudible-signal regions promotes accuracy in the audible region.

Treatment of Nondominant-Signal Components. The behavior of the system with low-level nondominant-signal components in the presence of higher-level dominant-signal components can be simulated by the use of probe tones. This representation is significant because it is an indicator of the noise reduction effect achieved with signals. Refer to the curves shown in Figs. 15.47, 15.48, and 15.49, which were obtained by adding a swept frequency probe tone at levels between -60 dB and -80 dB into the encoder input signal and detecting the tone at the output with a tracking wave analyzer.

Nondominant signals are boosted over and above the dominant signal toward the two spectrum ends by high- and low-frequency sliding-band actions. If there are two dominant signals, a fixed-band-compression effect prevails for the nondominant-signal components between the frequencies of the dominant-signal components.

Thus, nondominant-signal components are boosted by an amount at least equal to the amount of the boost of the dominant signal. The boosting of the nondominant signals is maintained toward the spectrum ends even though the level of the dominant signal is relatively high (e.g., in the range -30 dB to 0 dB). This boosting action spectrally tracks the dominant-signal frequency or frequencies.

It is advantageous to have a steeply rising boosting effect away from the frequency of the dominant-signal component. In this connection the SR circuit profits from the steepness-enhancing effect of cascaded stages. The low frequencies

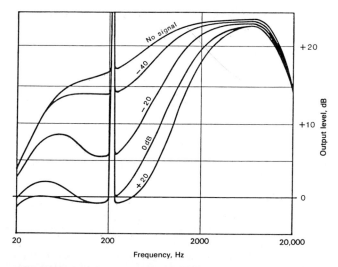

FIG. 15.47 Low-level encoding characteristic in the presence of a 200-Hz signal at the levels indicated.

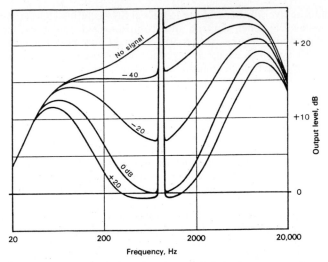

FIG. 15.48 Low-level encoding characteristic in the presence of an 800-Hz signal at the levels indicated.

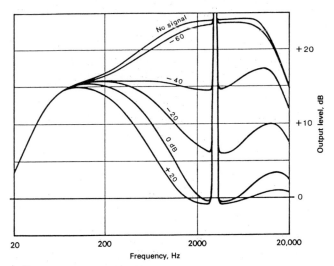

FIG. 15.49 Low-level encoding characteristic in the presence of a 3-kHz signal at the levels indicated.

have two stages of steepness compounding; the use of three stages at high frequencies further improves the effect. These effects are particularly evident in the high-level areas of the probe-tone curves.

The curves show that the compressor circuit tends toward keeping all low-level signal components boosted at all times. Only those components above the threshold are subject to a reduction of boosting. With regard to the overall system the advantages of this type of characteristic are (1) a powerful noise reduction effect in the presence of signals and (2) a relative tolerance level and frequency-response errors in the channel between the encoder and the decoder.

The audible encoding effect of the system is to create a dense, bright-sounding signal with little or no apparent dynamic action. Harmonics, overtones, and small-scale components of the sound, including noise, are all enhanced. The anti-saturation characteristics tend to compensate for this brightness at very high signal levels.

The decoding effect of the system is to create a very clean-sounding signal; the decoder significantly reduces tape bias noise and modulation noise. An audible reduction of intermodulation distortion is achieved by the low-frequency noise reduction capabilities of the process.

The decoder can also reduce audible and measurable harmonic distortion produced by the recording medium. Steady-state third-harmonic distortion is typically reduced to less than one-half; fifth-harmonic distortion is reduced to less than one-quarter. Higher-order harmonics are even further reduced. Thus, especially if the medium has a hard-clipping characteristic, the subjective cleanliness of the signal at high recording levels is significantly improved.

15.8.6 Calibration

The spectral recording calibration procedures are conceptually similar to those of the Dolby A-type, B-type, and C-type systems. That is, signal levels in the decoder circuit ideally should match those in the encoder circuit even though the SR process has been designed to be more tolerant of gain and frequency-response errors than these previous systems. For tape-interchange standardization it is also preferable if, at least within a given organization, the reference level of the encoder and decoder corresponds to a known and fixed flux level. Whether or not a standardized flux is used for this, the matching of the decoder to the encoder is accomplished by a calibration signal generated in the encoder and recorded on the tape; this allows the tape replay gain to be set correctly, using the meter in the decoder unit.

Most problems in the studio use of noise reduction and, indeed, analog recording in general can be traced to incorrect level settings and/or frequency-response errors in the recorder. This may be true because checking these factors is a time-consuming and boring process. A faster and more interesting method of accomplishing these checks would be more likely to produce reliable and consistent results. For this reason, practical embodiments of the SR process include pink-noise generators which are used for both level and frequency-response calibration instead of single-tone sine-wave oscillators. For identification, the pink noise is interrupted with 20-ms "nicks" every 2 s. During recording this signal is fed to the tape at a level of 15 dB below reference level, which is low enough not to cause saturation problems with low-speed tape recording or highly equalized transmission channels.

During playback the tape signal is automatically alternated with internally generated reference pink noise (uninterrupted) in 4-s segments (8-s total cycle time) and passed to the monitor output. An audible comparison can thus be made between the reference pink noise and the calibration noise coming from the tape. Any discrepancies in level and/or spectral balance are immediately noticeable and can be corrected or at least taken note of. If desired, the signal can also be fed to a spectrum analyzer.

In using the new calibration method it is important to be able to tell when the 4-s tape segments are being passed to the monitor and when the signal heard is from the reference pink-noise generator. Differentiation of the tape segments from the reference segments is accomplished in two ways. First, the reference segments are 4 s of continuous pink noise, and the tape segments begin with a nick, have a nick in the middle, and end with a nick; this time sequence is easily identified with a little practice. Second, colored lights identify the two different signals.

The new calibration facility gives recording and production personnel a useful control of the recording process. At any time the recorder can be checked; the result can be heard immediately and conclusions drawn about whether adjustments might be necessary.

With tape and signal interchanges it is possible to tell quickly whether there is any error or misunderstanding about levels, equalization, azimuth, and the like. If the original recording of calibration noise stays with the tape, the quality of the ultimate playback, even after copying, can be retained. Thus the comparison function serves to ensure that the recorder and spectral recording process provide on a routine basis the signal quality and reliability of which they are capable.

15.8.7 Conclusion

A new professional recording format, designated spectral recording, has been described. The objective of the new encoding and decoding process is to record and reproduce audio signals with a high degree of audible-signal purity.

The system employs a dual-path, multilevel staggered-action arrangement of two low-frequency compressor stages and three high-frequency compressor stages, each with a fixed band and a sliding band. The outputs of the bands are combined in a unique way, called action substitution, which results in an unusually responsive treatment of the signal with respect to both frequency and level. A technique referred to as modulation control augments the spectral tracking abilities of the system. Spectral skewing contributes to a tolerance of channel errors, and the employment of both high- and low-frequency antisaturation techniques results in a significantly improved channel-overload characteristic.

15.9 PRACTICAL USAGE OF NOISE REDUCTION SYSTEMS

Noise reduction systems have applications in all forms of signal transmission and storage. These include magnetic-tape recording, radio and television transmissions, land lines, and film dubbing, mixing, and release formats, both optical and magnetic. They also have applications in digital signal processing, where the combination of an analog noise reduction system and a low bit number may often be a more cost-effective solution to a transmission problem than a greater number of bits.

Most of these applications are covered in other chapters in this book; however, some specialized operational procedures are discussed here.

Calibration.   All noise reduction systems need calibration except in very specialized circumstances. To this end, many systems use special tones of a characteristic nature intended for recording at the head of a tape or for sending through a communications system. These tones are originated in the encoder and inform the listener (1) that a noise reduction system is in use, (2) what type of system is being employed, and (3), by using meters or the equivalent on the noise reduction unit, whether the levels are correctly set for correct decoding.

If these tones have been removed from tapes, it is good practice to mark the tape box and the reel with details. Preprinted labels are available from manufacturers of noise reduction equipment.

Miscalibration. Since noise reduction systems use variable-gain amplifiers in the decode mode, in order to expand the compressed recorded signals and thereby reduce the noise of the transmission path there is the potential for errors if the signal received by the decoder is not identical with that leaving the encoder. The nature of the errors produced depends on the particular noise reduction system in use.

Dolby noise reduction systems operate only on low-level signals. (Other systems usually operate on all signal levels.) Referring to Fig. 15.4, low-level signals are boosted in the encode mode by a fixed amount, and high-level signals are unaltered. There is only a small area, typically around −20 dB, where the gain is changing; at this point the compression is about 2:1, and it is less at levels above and below.

Amplitude errors between encoder and decoder are thus reproduced over most levels with no change; that is, the error is not altered. This is of especial value for high-level signals, where the ear is most sensitive. Only at intermediate levels are level errors accentuated, by a maximum of 2:1. Thus the systems are tolerant of the errors likely to occur in the day-to-day operation of a studio or broadcasting organization.

Similarly, frequency-response errors are confined not only to these medium levels but also the the frequency area in which the errors occur, since the various systems split the frequency range into separate independent domains.

Constant-slope compandors have an advantage in that, since the slope of the decoder action is constant, the actual level into a decoder from a single source is relatively unimportant because the decoding will always be correct. However, in practical recording terms, the compandors also require accurate calibration, since they are sensitive to frequency errors (and may be also to level errors) in the transmission or recording link.

Level matching is important if tapes are to be spliced or if different tapes are to be played back through a single decoder. Any difference in the recorded flux level across a splice or between tapes will be amplified by the expansion slope whatever its level. For example, a difference of 2 dB in a compandor system using a 2:1 compression ratio will be amplified to one of 4 dB after decoding.

Similarly, a 2-dB frequency-response error will produce errors at all frequencies and not just at the actual frequency in question. Out-of-band interfering frequencies (such as low-frequency hum) can cause modulation effects through a similar mechanism.

Bandwidth limitations can be another source of error. Systems using fast time constants in their gain-control amplifiers will perform well when connected directly together, that is, with the encoder output taken directly to the decoder input. In practical situations, where the transmission or recording link does not have the bandwidth to pass the high-frequency signals generated by fast attack or decay times, signal dispersion will occur and correct decoding cannot happen. Transients may thus become smeared.

Copying. Encoded tapes may be copied without decoding if the overall playback response of the master recorder and the record response of the copying slave recorder are such that a 1:1 copy is made in both amplitude and frequency. In theory, the least treatment of a signal will cause the least modification of its integrity, so that in these circumstances tapes can be copied with the master-decode and slave-encode noise reduction units switched off.

However, the signal is often routed via a mixing console which can introduce unwanted and unsuspected changes. Additionally, in many cases some signal conditioning is required (for example, there may be reasons to introduce deliberate changes in equalization or levels or to mix in other signals). In these situations the noise reduction units must be switched on so that this conditioning is performed with decoded signals and the changed signal is reencoded onto the slave recorder. Thus, in practical terms it is usually best always to leave the noise reduction units switched on even for 1:1 copying.

REFERENCES

1. R. Orban, "A Program-Controlled Noise Filter," *J. Audio. Eng. Soc.,* **22,** 2–9 (January 1974).

2. R. S. Burwen, "A Dynamic Filter," *J. Audio Eng. Soc.,* **19,** 115–120 (February 1987).

3. M. Giles, *A Non-Complementary Audio Noise Reduction System,* Application Note AN 386, National Semiconductor Corp., Santa Clara, Calif., 1985.

4. H. H. Scott, "Dynamic Noise Suppressor," *Electronics,* **20,** 96 (1947).

5. H. F. Olson, "Audio Noise Reduction Circuits," *Electronics,* **20,** 118 (1947).

6. N. J. Hudak, "Transistorized Audio AGC Amplifier," *IEEE Trans. Broadcast.,* **BC-9**(1), 26 (1963).

7. A. Kaiser and B. B. Bauer, "A New Automatic Level Control for Monophonic and Stereo Broadcasting," *IRE Trans. Audio,* **AU-10**(6), 171 (1962).

8. J. G. McKnight, "Signal-to-Noise Problems and a New Equalization for Magnetic Recording of Music," *J. Audio Eng. Soc.,* **7,** 5–12 (1959).

9. A. C. Norwine, "Devices for Controlling Amplitude Characteristics of Telephone Signals," *Bell Syst. Tech. J.,* **17**(4), 539 (1938).

10. R. O. Carter, "Theory of Syllabic Compandors," *Proc. Inst. Elec. Eng.,* **111**(3), 503 (1964).

11. Several papers on compandor techniques appear in the *IEEE Conf. Proc.: Transmission Aspects of Communications Networks,* Institution of Electrical Engineers, London (1964).

12. D. Aldous, "NoisEx Recording System," *Int. Broadcast. Eng.,* no. 10, 510 (1965).

13. L. H. Bedford, "Improving the Dynamic Range of Tape Recording," *Wireless World,* **66,** 104 (1960).

14. H. Fletcher, "The Stereophonic Sound-Film System," *J. Soc. Motion Pict. Eng.,* **37,** 331–352 (1941).

15. J. T. Mullin, "Advanced Tape Mastering System: Electronic Features," *IEEE Trans. Audio,* **AU-13**(2), 31 (1965).

16. W. A. Munson, "The Growth of Auditory Sensation," *J. Acoust. Soc. Am.,* **19,** 584 (1947).

17. E. Luescher and J. Zwislocki, "Adaptation of the Ear to Sound Stimuli," *J. Acoust. Soc. Am.,* **21,** 135–139 (1949).

18. R. L. Wegel and C. E. Lane, "The Auditory Masking of One Pure Tone by Another and Its Probable Relation to the Dynamics of the Inner Ear," *Phys. Rev.,* **23,** 266 (1924).

19. J. P. Egan and H. W. Hake, "On the Masking Pattern of a Simple Auditory Stimulus," *J. Acoust. Soc. Am.,* **22,** 622–630 (1950).

20. C. E. Bos and E. de Boer, "Masking and Discrimination," *J. Acoust. Soc. Am.,* **39,** 708–715 (1966).

21. I. M. Young and C. H. Wenner, "Masking of White Noise by Pure Tone, Frequency-Modulated Tone, and Narrow-Band Noise," *J. Acoust. Soc. Am.,* **41,** 700–706 (1967).

22. J. Wermuth, "Compander Increases Dynamic Range," *db,* **10**(6), 25–30 (1976).

23. R. M. Dolby, "A Noise Reduction System for Consumer Tape Applications," *J. Audio Eng. Soc. (Abstracts),* **18,** 704 (1970).

24. R. Berkovitz and K. J. Gundry, "Dolby B-Type Noise Reduction," *Audio,* **57**(9), 15–16; 33–36 (1973).

25. K. J. Gundry, "Headroom Extension for Slow-Speed Magnetic Recording of Audio," *J. Audio Eng. Soc. (Abstracts),* **27,** 1026 (1979), preprint 1534.

26. J. S. Jensen, "Recording with Feedback-Controlled Effective Bias," *J. Audio Eng. Soc. (Abstracts),* **29,** 938 (1981), preprint 1852.

CHAPTER 16

AUDIO TESTS AND MEASUREMENTS*

Dr. Richard C. Cabot, P.E.

Prinicpal Engineer, Audio Precission, Inc. Beaverton, Oregon

16.1 PURPOSE OF AUDIO MEASUREMENTS

Measurements are made on audio equipment to check performance under specified conditions and assess suitability for use in a particular application. They may be used to verify specified system performance or as a way of comparing several pieces of equipment for use in a system. Measurements may also be used to identify components in need of adjustment or repair. Whatever the application, audio measurements are an important part of audio engineering.

Many parameters are important in audio devices and merit attention in the measurement process. Some common audio measurements are frequency response, gain or loss, harmonic distortion, intermodulation distortion, noise level, phase response, and transient response. There are other, equally important tests too numerous to list here. This chapter will explain the basics of these measurements, describe how they are made, and give some examples of their application.

Most *measurements* in audio (and other fields) are composed of measurements of fundamental parameters. These parameters include signal level, phase, and frequency. Most other measurements consist of measuring these fundamental parameters and displaying the results in combination by using some convenient format. For example, signal-to-noise ratio (SNR) is a pair of level measurements made under different conditions expressed as a logarithmic, or *decibel* dB, ratio.

When characterizing an audio device, it is common to view it as a box with input terminals and output terminals. In normal use an audio signal is applied to the input, and the audio signal, modified in some way, appears at the output. In

---

* The author is indebted to Bruce Hofer of Audio Precision for many of the ideas presented here and for sharing his knowledge about audio measurements. Bob Metzler of Audio Precision provided most of the material in the section on wow-and-flutter measurements. The editor, Blair Benson, deserves special thanks for encouraging the writing of this chapter and for extreme patience with the inevitable delays caused by my busy schedule. The cooperation of Audio Precision, Tektronix, *Sound and Video Contractor* magazine, and the other copyright holders who allowed their material to be used is greatly appreciated.

the case of an equalizer the modification to the signal is an intentional change in the gain with frequency *(frequency response)*. Often it is desired to know or verify the details of this gain change. This is accomplished by measurement. Real-world behavior being what it is, audio devices will also modify other parameters of the audio signal which should have been left alone. To quantify these unintentional changes to the signal we again turn to measurements. Using the earlier example of an equalizer, changes to the amplitude-versus-frequency response of the signal inevitably bring changes in phase versus frequency. Some measurements are what are known as *one-port measurements,* such as impedance or noise level. These are not concerned with both input and output signals, only with one or the other.

As mentioned above, measurement of level is fundamental to most audio specifications. Level can be measured either in absolute terms or in relative terms. Power output is an example of an absolute level measurement; it does not require any reference. SNR and gain or loss are examples of relative, or ratio, measurements; the result is expressed as a ratio of two measurements. Though it may not appear so at first, frequency response is also a relative measurement. It expresses the gain of the device under test as a function of frequency, with the midband gain as a reference.

Distortion measurements are a way of quantifying the amount of unwanted components added to a signal by a piece of equipment. The most common technique is *total harmonic distortion* (THD), but others are often used. Distortion measurements express the amount of unwanted signal components relative to the desired signal, usually as a percentage or decibel value. This is also an example of multiple level measurements which are combined to give a new measurement figure.

16.2   LEVEL MEASUREMENTS

The simplest definition of a level measurement is the alternating-current (ac) amplitude at a particular place in a system. However, in contrast to direct-current (dc) measurements, there are many ways of specifying ac voltage. The most common methods are average response, root-mean-square (rms) response, and peak response. Strictly speaking, the term *level* refers to a logarithmic, or decibel, measurement. However, common parlance employs the term for any ac amplitude measurement, and that convention will be followed here.

16.2.1   Root-Mean-Square Technique

The rms technique measures the effective power of the ac signal. It specifies the value of the dc equivalent which would dissipate the same power if either were applied to a load resistor. This process is illustrated in Fig. 16.1 for voltage measurements. The input signal is squared, and the average value is found. This is equivalent to finding the average power. The square root of this value is taken to get the signal from a power value back to a voltage. For the case of a sine wave the rms value is 0.707 of its maximum value.

Suppose that the signal is no longer a sine wave but rather a sine wave and several of its harmonics. If the rms amplitude of each harmonic is measured individually and added, the resulting value will be the same as an rms measurement

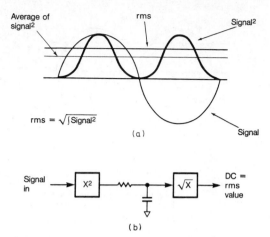

FIG. 16.1 Root-mean-square (rms) measurements. (*a*) Relationship of rms and average values. (*b*) The rms measurement circuit.

on the signals together. Because rms voltages cannot be added directly, it is necessary to perform an rms addition. This is illustrated in Eq. (16.1). Each voltage is squared, and the squared values are added.

$$V_{\text{rms total}} = \sqrt{V_{\text{rms 1}}^2 + V_{\text{rms 2}}^2 \cdots + V_{\text{rms } n}^2} \qquad (16.1)$$

The square root of the resulting value is taken, yielding the rms voltage of their combination. Note that the result is not dependent on the phase relationship of the signal and its harmonics. The rms value is determined completely by the amplitude of the components. This mathematical predictability is very powerful in practical applications of level measurement, enabling measurements made at different places in a system to be correlated. It is also extremely important in correlating measurements with theoretical calculations.

An interesting result for gaussian random noise is that the rms value equals the standard deviation of the amplitude distribution. In fact, if the amplitude distribution of any signal is plotted, the standard deviation of the distribution is, by definition, the rms value.

16.2.2 Average-Response Measurements

Average-responding voltmeters were the most common in audio work until a few years ago, mainly because of their low cost. They measure ac voltage by rectifying it and filtering the resulting waveform to its average value as shown in Fig. 16.2. This results in a dc voltage which can be read on a standard dc voltmeter. As shown in the figure, the average value of a sine wave is 0.637 of its maximum amplitude. Average-responding meters are usually calibrated to read the same as an rms meter for the case of a single-sine-wave signal. This results in the measurement being scaled by a constant K of 0.707/0.637, or 1.11. Meters of this type are called *average-responding, rms calibrated*. For signals other than sine waves

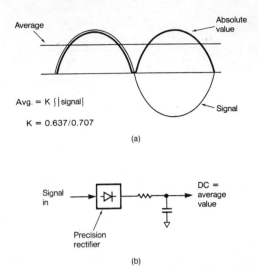

FIG. 16.2   Average measurements. (*a*) Illustration of average detection. (*b*) Average-measurement circuit.

the response will be different and hard to predict. If multiple sine waves are applied, the reading will depend on the phase shift between the components and will no longer match the rms measurement. A comparison of rms and average-response measurements is made in Fig. 16.3 for various waveforms. If the average readings are adjusted as described above to make the average and rms values equal for a sine wave, all the numbers in the average column should be increased by 11.1 percent, while the rms-average numbers should be reduced by 11.1 percent.

16.2.3   Peak-Response Measurements

Peak-responding meters measure the maximum value that the ac signal reaches as a function of time. This is illustrated in Fig. 16.4. The signal is full-wave-rectified to find its absolute value. This is passed through a diode to a storage capacitor. When the absolute value of the voltage rises above the value stored on the capacitor, the diode will conduct and increase the stored voltage. When the voltage decreases, the capacitor will maintain the old value. Some means for discharging the capacitor is required to allow measuring a new peak value. In a true peak detector this is a switch. Practical peak detectors usually use a large resistor to discharge the capacitor gradually after the user has had a chance to read the meter.

The ratio of the true peak value to the rms value is called the *crest factor*. As can be seen from Fig. 16.5, this is a measure of the peakedness of the signal. For any signal but an ideal square wave the crest factor will be greater than 1. A comparison of crest-factor values for various waveforms is shown in Fig. 16.5. As the signals become more peaked, the crest factor will increase. The q parameter in the gaussian-noise example is a measure of the percent of time during which the sig-

Waveform		rms	Avg.	rms avg.	Crest factor
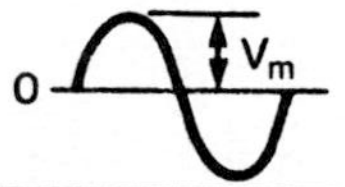	Sine wave	$\dfrac{V_m}{\sqrt{2}}$ = 0.707 V_m	$\dfrac{2V_m}{\pi}$ 0.637V_m	$\dfrac{\pi}{2\sqrt{2}}$ = 1.111	$\sqrt{2}$ = 1.414
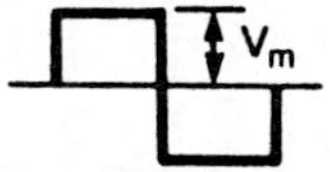	Symmetrical square wave or DC	V_m	V_m	1	1
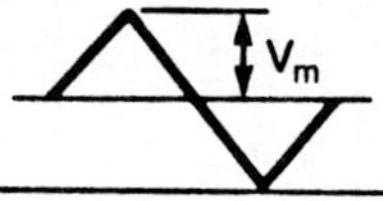	Triangular wave or sawtooth	$\dfrac{V_m}{\sqrt{3}}$	$\dfrac{V_m}{2}$	$\dfrac{2}{\sqrt{3}}$ = 1.155	$\sqrt{3}$ = 1.732
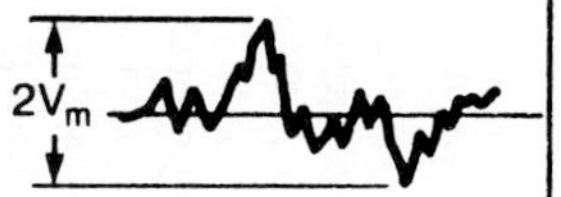	Gaussian noise 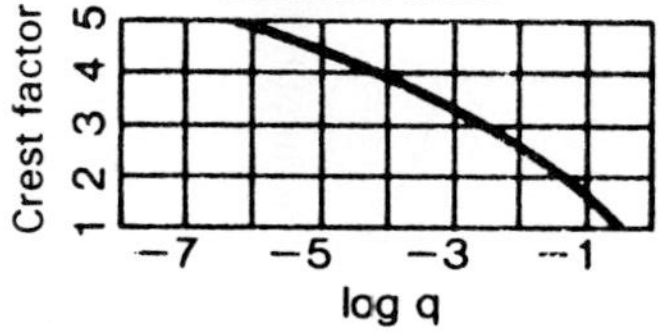	rms	$\dfrac{\sqrt{2}}{\pi}$ rms = 0.798 rms	$\sqrt{\dfrac{\pi}{2}}$ = 1.253	C.F. / q: 1 → 32%, 2 → 4.6%, 3 → 0.37%
	Pulse train	$V_m\sqrt{\eta}$	$V_m\eta$	$\dfrac{1}{\sqrt{\eta}}$	$\dfrac{1}{\sqrt{\eta}}$

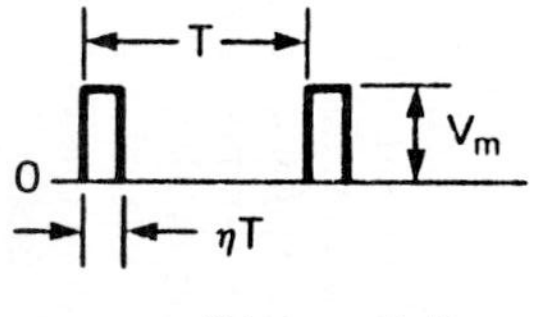

Gaussian noise graph: Crest factor vs log q (axis markings 1 2 3 4 5 and −7 −5 −3 −1)

Pulse train sub-table:

η	Mark/space	rms	Avg.	rms avg.	Crest factor
1	∞	V_m	V_m	1	1
0.25	0.3333	0.5V_m	0.25V_m	2	2
0.0625	0.0667	0.25V_m	0.625V_m	4	4
0.01	0.0101	0.1V_m	0.01V_m	10	8
					10

η = "duty cycle"

FIG. 16.3 Comparison of rms and average characteristics. *(Courtesy of EDN, Jan. 20, 1982.)*

16.5

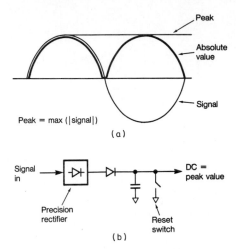

Peak

Absolute value

Signal

Peak = max (|signal|)

(a)

Signal in

DC = peak value

Precision rectifier

Reset switch

(b)

FIG. 16.4   Peak measurements. (*a*) Illustration of peak detection. (*b*) Peak-measurement circuit.

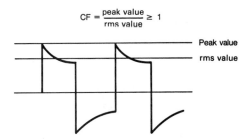

$$CF = \frac{\text{peak value}}{\text{rms value}} \geq 1$$

Peak value

rms value

FIG. 16.5   Definition of the crest factor.

nal is greater than the rms value. True gaussian noise has infinitely large peaks and therefore an infinite crest factor.

By introducing a controlled charge and discharge time with resistors a quasi-peak detector is achieved. These charge and discharge times are picked to simulate the ear's sensitivity to impulsive peaks. International standards define these response times and set requirements for reading accuracy on pulses and sine-wave bursts of various durations. Quasi-peak detectors normally have their gain adjusted so that they read the same as an rms detector for sine waves. For details on the quasi-peak standard see International Radio Consultative Committee (CCIR) Recommendation 468.

Another method of specifying signal amplitude is called *peak-equivalent sine.* It is the rms level of a sine wave having the same peak-to-peak amplitude as the signal under consideration. This is the peak value of the waveform scaled by the correction factor 1.414, corresponding to the peak-to-rms ratio of a sine wave. This is useful when specifying test levels of waveforms in distortion measurements. If the distortion of a device is measured as a function of amplitude, a point will be reached where the output level cannot increase any further. At this point the peaks of the waveform will be clipped, and the distortion will rise rapidly with further increases in level. If another signal is used for distortion testing on the same device, it is desirable that the levels at which clipping is reached correspond. Signal generators are normally calibrated in this way to allow changing between waveforms without clipping or readjusting levels.

16.2.4 Types of Meters

Most meters of a few years ago were of the average-responding, rms-calibrated type. Newer meters measure the true rms value of the waveform by using special integrated circuits. This allows accurate measurements of voltage for all signals, not just sine waves. As mentioned earlier, rms measurements accurately reflect the heating power of the waveform in a resistor or a loudspeaker. This is critical to many measurements such as specification of power in amplifiers. However, many noise specifications were developed in the days of average-responding meters, and verifying these requires an average-responding unit. Therefore, good-quality audio test equipment allows selection between these two responses, giving compatibility with old and new techniques.

One obvious difference between various audio voltmeters is the type of display, analog or digital. Each type has its advantages. Analog meters are not easy to use for exact measurements because of their multiple scales and the need to interpolate numbers from the printed scale. In contrast, a digital meter gives a direct readout of the value to more digits of precision than could ever be obtained from an analog-meter scale. This enables very precise measurement of gain and output power with little chance for error.

However, nothing is perfect. The digital meter is suited only for measuring relatively stable signals. When trying to monitor program level to determine system operating levels under actual use, it becomes very difficult to extract a single number from the mass of flashing digits. The analog meter can handle this job with ease. Another application for analog meters is monitoring the results of an adjustment for a peak or a null. Some manufacturers have put both analog and digital displays on the same instrument to enable the best of both worlds. The analog scale on such meters typically does not have very fine graduations on it and is intended only for approximate measurements of rapidly changing signals.

The bandwidth of a voltmeter can have a significant effect on the accuracy of the reading. For a meter with what is called a *single-pole rolloff,* i.e., one bandwidth-limiting component in the signal path, significant errors can occur in measurements. For such a meter with a specified bandwidth of 100 kHz, there will be a 10 percent error in measurements of signal at 50 kHz. To obtain 1 percent accurate measurements (with other error sources in the meter ignored), the signal frequency must be less than 10 kHz.

Another problem with limited-bandwith measuring devices is shown in Fig. 16.6. It is a distorted sine wave being measured by two meters with different bandwidths. The meter with the narrower bandwidth does not respond to all the harmonics and gives a lower reading. The severity of this effect varies with the frequency being measured and the bandwidth of the meter; it can be especially severe when measuring wideband noise. Most audio requirements are adequately served by a meter with a 500-kHz bandwidth. This allows reasonably accurate measurement of signals to about 100 kHz. Peak measurements are even more sensitive to bandwidth effects. Systems with restricted low-frequency bandwidth

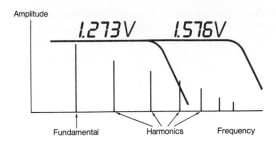

FIG. 16.6   Effect of bandwidth on measurements.

will produce tilt in a square wave, and bumps in the high-frequency response will produce an overshoot. The effect of either situation will be an increase in the peak reading.

Accuracy is a measure of how well a meter measures a signal at a midband frequency, usually 1 kHz. This sets a basic limit on the performance of the meter in establishing the absolute amplitude of a signal. It is also important to look at the flatness specification to see how well this performance is maintained with changes in frequency. The flatness specification describes how well the measurements at any other frequency will track those at 1 kHz. If a meter has an accuracy of 2 percent at 1 kHz and a flatness of 1 dB (10 percent) from 20 Hz to 20 kHz, the inaccuracy can be as wide as 12 percent at 20 kHz.

Meters often have a specification on accuracy which changes with voltage range, being most accurate only in the range in which they were calibrated. A meter with 1 percent accuracy on the 2-V range and 1 percent accuracy per step would be 3 percent accurate on the 200-V scale. By using the flatness specification given earlier, the overall accuracy for a 100-V 20-kHz sine wave is 14 percent. In many meters an additional accuracy deration is given for readings as a percentage of full scale, making readings at less than full scale less accurate.

However, the accuracy specification is not normally as important as the flatness. When performing frequency response or gain measurements, the results are relative and are not affected by the absolute voltage used. When measuring gain, however, the attenuator accuracy of the instrument is a direct error source. Similar comments apply to the accuracy and flatness specifications for signal generators. Most are specified in the same manner as voltmeters, with the inaccuracies adding in much the same way.

16.2.5   Decibel (dB) Measurements

Measurements in audio work are often expressed in decibels. The following paragraphs review the concepts and rationale behind decibel measurements. Audio signals span a wide range of level. The sound pressure of a rock-and-roll band is about 1 million times that of rustling leaves. This range is too wide to be accommodated on a linear scale. The decibel is a logarithmic unit which compresses this wide range down to a more easily handled range. Order-of-magnitude (factor-of-10) changes result in equal increments on a decibel scale. Furthermore, the human ear perceives changes in amplitude on a logarithmic basis, making measurements with the decibel scale reflect audibility more accurately.

A decibel may be defined as the logarithmic ratio of two power measurements or as the logarithmic ratio of two voltages. Equations (16.2) and (16.3) define the decibel for both power and voltage measurements.

$$dB = 20 \log (E_1/E_2) \tag{16.2}$$
$$dB = 10 \log (P_1/P_2) \tag{16.3}$$

There is no difference between decibel values from power measurements and decibel values from voltage measurements if the impedances are equal. In both equations the denominator variable is usually a stated reference. This is illustrated with an example in Fig. 16.7. Whether the decibel value is computed from the power-based equation or from the voltage-based equation, the same result is obtained.

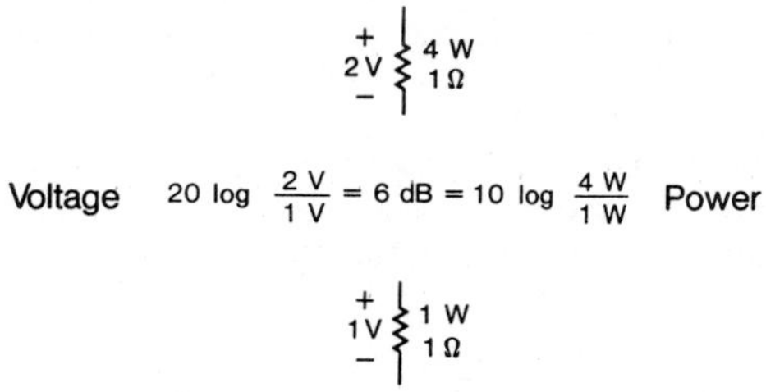

$$\text{Voltage} \quad 20 \log \frac{2\text{ V}}{1\text{ V}} = 6 \text{ dB} = 10 \log \frac{4\text{ W}}{1\text{ W}} \quad \text{Power}$$

FIG. 16.7 Equivalence of voltage and power decibels.

A doubling of voltage will yield a value of 6.02 dB, while a doubling of power will yield 3.01 dB. This is true because doubling voltage results in a factor-of-4 increase in power. Table 16.1 shows the decibel values for some common voltage and power ratios. These are handy to commit to memory, and they make quick comparisons of readings especially easy.

TABLE 16.1 Some Common dB Values

dB value	Voltage ratio	Power ratio
0	1	1
+1	1.122	1.259
+2	1.259	1.586
+3	1.412	1.995
+6	1.995	3.981
+10	3.162	10
+20	10	100
+40	100	10,000
−1	0.891	0.794
−2	0.794	0.631
−3	0.707	0.501
−6	0.501	0.251
−10	0.3163	0.1
−20	0.1	0.01
−40	0.01	0.0001

The above example showed the decibel value obtained from two measured quantities. Often audio engineers express the decibel value of a signal relative to some standard reference instead of another signal. The reference for decibel measurements may be predefined as a power level, as in dBm (decibels above 1 mW), or it may be a voltage reference. When measuring dBm or any power-based decibel value, the reference impedance must be specified or understood. For example, 0 dBm (600 Ω) would be the correct way to specify level. Both 600 and 150 Ω are common reference impedances in audio work.

The equations assume that the circuit being measured is terminated in the reference impedance used in the decibel calculation. However, most voltmeters are high-impedance devices and are calibrated in decibels relative to the voltage required to reach 1 mW in the reference impedance. This voltage is 0.775 V in the 600-Ω case. Termination of the line in 600 Ω is left up to the user. If the line is not terminated, it is not correct to speak of a dBm measurement. The case of decibels in an unloaded line is referred to as dBu (or sometimes dBv) to denote that it is referenced to a 0.775-V level without regard to impedance.

Another common decibel reference in voltage measurements is 1 V. When using this reference, measurements are presented as dBV. Often it is desirable to specify levels in terms of a reference transmission level somewhere in the system under test. These measurements are designated dBr where the reference point or level must be separately conveyed.

16.2.6 Crosstalk and Separation Measurements

One application of decibel measurements using two measured quantities is *crosstalk*. Crosstalk is the leakage of signal from one audio channel into another. In the general case of crosstalk the channels are not necessarily related. For the special case of crosstalk between the two channels of a stereo system (or the four channels in a quadraphonic system) the term *separation* is used. As a general rule, if the two channels under consideration carry two channels of the same audio program, the term separation is used. If the two channels are unrelated, the term crosstalk is used.

Crosstalk or separation is defined as the difference in decibels between the interfering-signal level in the source channel and the receiving channel. Crosstalk and separation specifications are usually expressed as a positive decibel value. Measuring crosstalk or separation consists of applying a sine wave to one channel of the device under test and measuring the level of the signal in the other channel. The amount of leakage is likely to depend on the frequency used, so these measurements are normally made as a function of frequency and expressed in graphical form as with an amplitude-frequency-response curve.

Take the case of a 10-V, 1-kHz sine wave in the left channel of a stereo system. If the right channel is not driven with signal, there should be no 1 kHz present at its output. However, if a level measurement on the right channel yields 10 mV of signal, the separation is defined to be 60 dB.

One possible problem with this procedure is that the 10 mV may not be 1 kHz leaking from the other channel but may represent the noise floor of the system under test. If this is true, the separation measurement is inaccurate. The solution is to use a bandpass filter tuned to the frequency of the test tone, thereby rejecting system noise and other interfering components. If the measurements are to be made as a function of frequency, the bandpass-filter frequency should be enslaved to the generator frequency. This is illustrated in Fig. 16.8. One channel is driven

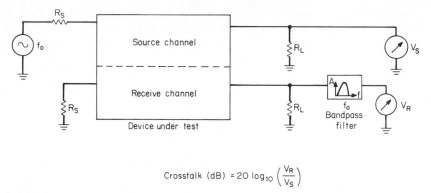

$$\text{Crosstalk (dB)} = 20 \log_{10}\left(\frac{V_R}{V_S}\right)$$

FIG. 16.8 Crosstalk measurement with a bandpass filter.

from a sine-wave generator at its nominal operating level and terminated in its normal load impedance. The other channel input is terminated by the normal source impedance, and the output is terminated by the normal load impedance. The level at the output of the driven channel is measured with a voltmeter, and the output of the undriven channel is measured by a voltmeter with a bandpass filter centered on the test-signal frequency. The level difference between these measurements, expressed in decibels, is the separation. When the two channels have different gains, it is common to correct the measurements for the gain difference so as to present the crosstalk referred to the channel inputs.

Crosstalk between two audio channels is sometimes nonlinear. The presence of a signal in one channel will sometimes yield tones of other frequencies in the receiving channel. This is especially true in transmission systems where cross-modulation can occur between carriers. These tones disappear when the source signal is removed, clearly indicating that they are due to the suspected source. Measuring them can be tedious if sine waves are used because the frequency of the received interference may not be easily predictable. There may also be some test frequencies which cause the interference products to appear outside the channel bandwidth, hiding the effect being tested. Therefore, this test is often performed with a random noise source so that all possible interference frequencies are tested.

16.2.7 Noise Measurements

Noise measurements are simply specialized level measurements. It has long been recognized that the ear's sensitivity varies with frequency, especially at low levels. This effect was studied in detail by Fletcher and Munson and later by Robinson and Dadson. The Flecher-Munson hearing-sensitivity curve for the threshold of hearing is given in Fig. 16.9. The ear is most sensitive in the region of 2 to 4 kHz, with rolloffs above and below these frequencies. This effect is responsible for the apparent loss of bass when the volume is reduced on a hi-fi system. To predict how loud something will sound it is necessary to use a filter which duplicates this nonflat behavior electrically. The filter weights the signal level on the basis of its frequency, thus earning the name *weighting filter*.

Various attempts have been made to do this, resulting in several standards for noise measurement. Some of these weighting filters are shown overlaid on the hearing-threshold curve in Fig. 16.10. The most common filter in use in the United States is the *A*-weighting curve. This filter is placed in front of a high-sensitivity voltmeter, and the amplitude of the noise is measured (see Fig. 16.11). An average-responding meter is often used for *A*-weighted noise measurements, though rms meters are gaining acceptance for this application.

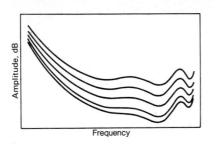

FIG. 16.9   Fletcher-Munson curves of hearing sensitivity versus frequency.

CCIR Noise Measurements. European equipment is usually specified with a CCIR filter and a quasi-peak detector. The CCIR-filter response is shown with the *A*-weighting curve in Fig. 16.10. It is significantly more peaked than the *A* curve and has a sharper rolloff at high frequencies. The CCIR quasi-peak standard was developed to quantify the noise in telephone systems. The quasi-peak detector more accurately represented the ear's sensitivity to impulsive sounds which occur when telephone switching systems operate. When used with the CCIR-filter curve, it is supposed to correlate better with the subjective level of the noise than *A*-weighted average-response measurements do.

Owing to the cost of true quasi-peak meters, Dolby Laboratories have proposed the use of the CCIR curve with an average-response meter. To make the readings correlate with noise measurements made by using other techniques, they have further proposed modifying the unit-gain frequency of the filter to 2 kHz from the 1-kHz standard. This modification will shift the CCIR weighting curve down by 6 dB, introducing a simple gain difference. This measurement technique

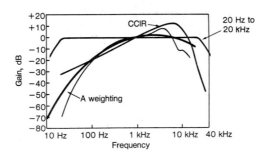

FIG. 16.10   Common weighting filters for audio measurements.

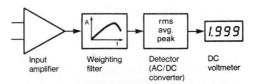

FIG. 16.11   Weighted-voltmeter architecture.

is referred to as CCIR ARM, the ARM denoting an average-responding meter. For more information on the background of this technique, see Dolby.[1]

Other Noise Measurements. Some manufacturers specify noise with a 20-Hz to 20-kHz bandwidth filter and an rms-responding meter. This is done to specify the noise over the audio band without regard to the ear's differing sensitivity with frequency. The International Electrotechnical Commission (IEC) defines the audio band as all frequencies between 22.4 Hz and 22.4 kHz. Measurements over such a bandwidth are referred to under IEC standards as *unweighted*. About a dozen different weighting-filter–voltmeter combinations have been proposed for measuring noise. Each technique has its group of supporters. The important thing is that the measurement technique used be specified and be consistent from test to test. Meters designed for measuring noise and containing appropriate weighting filters are sometimes called *psophometers*. This term is more common in Europe than in the United States. In the United States such a device would more often be referred to simply as a voltmeter.

European telephone noise levels are often specified as dBmp, meaning that a dBm value has been measured in the system impedance by using a weighting filter corresponding to the International Telegraph and Telephone Consultative Committee (CCITT) psophometric curve. In the United States telephone noise measurements are normally made with a *C*-message weighting filter and an average-responding meter. The *C*-message curve is a combination of the ear's response and the response of the typical telephone handset. These are denoted dBrnc. Measurements made with an *A*-weighting filter are termed dBA. The term dBq refers to noise voltages measured with a quasi-peak detector and one of the filters specified in CCIR Recommendation 468-1. These may be either the CCIR weighting curve or the 22.4-Hz to 22.4-kHz audio band filter.

Noise Analysis. Power line (mains) hum is low-frequency interference at the power line frequency or its multiples. This interference is generally grouped with noise when making measurements. For North American lines the components occur at 60 Hz, 120 Hz, 180 Hz, 240 Hz, etc. For 50-Hz power lines the corresponding frequencies are 50 Hz, 100 Hz, 150 Hz, 200 Hz, etc. The dominant components are usually fundamental, second, and third harmonic which can be removed with a high-pass filter at approximately 400 Hz. With a three-pole or sharper filter, 1-dB-accurate measurements may be made down to 1 kHz. By making unweighted noise measurements both with and without the high-pass filter the effects of hum may be estimated. Subtracting the two decibel measurements results in a level ratio measurement called the *hum-to-hiss ratio*. Good-quality equipment will have hum-to-hiss ratios of less than 1 dB.

Even more information about the underlying sources of noise may be obtained with a spectral analysis of the noise. This may be accomplished with any of the spectrum-analysis techniques described later in the chapter: fast-Fourier-transform (FFT) analyzers, heterodyne analyzers, real-time analyzers (RTAs), etc. Each offers advantages for particular applications, but all provide considerable insight to the measurement being made. Figure 16.12 shows a spectrum analysis of the output noise from a professional equalizer. The measuring equipment uses a sweeping one-third-octave filter and an rms detector. Note the presence of power-line-related signals, both 120-Hz and 180-Hz components. The 120-Hz product is due to asymmetrical charging currents in the power supply, while the 180-Hz product is from transformer field leakage.

Another approach which is often useful in noise analysis is to view the noise

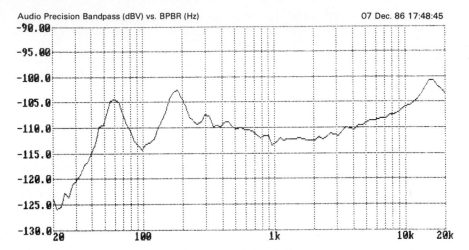

Audio Precision Bandpass (dBV) vs. BPBR (Hz)   07 Dec. 86 17:48:45

FIG. 16.12 Typical spectrum of noise and hum measured with a sweeping one-third-octave filter.

on an oscilloscope and trigger the oscilloscope with an appropriate synchronization signal. The components of the noise related to the synchronization signal will remain stationary on the screen, and the unrelated energy will produce fuzz on the trace. For example, to investigate line-related components the oscilloscope should be triggered on the power line. If interference is suspected from a nearby television signal, the oscilloscope can be triggered on the television vertical and/ or horizontal sync signals. The photograph in Fig. 16.13 is an example of the display when measuring power line noise obtained with this technique.

Noise may be expressed as an absolute level (usually in dBm or dBu) by simply measuring the weighted voltage (proper termination being assumed in the case of dBm) at the desired point in the system. However, this is often not very meaningful. A 1-mV noise voltage at the output of a power amplifier may be quite good, while 1 mV of noise at the output of a microphone would render it useless for anything but measuring jet planes. A better way to express noise performance is the signal-to-noise ratio (SNR). SNR is a decibel measure of the noise level

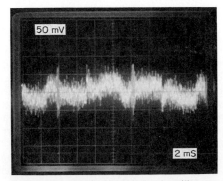

FIG. 16.13 Power-line-triggered-oscilloscope display of noise and hum.

using the signal level measured at the same point as a reference. This makes measurements at different points in a system or in different systems directly comparable. A signal with a given SNR can be amplified with a perfect amplifier or attenuated with no change in the SNR. Any degradation in SNR at later points in the system is due to limitations of the equipment that follows.

An extension of this technique to the spectral analysis of noise has been proposed by Moller.[2] The noise spectrum is analyzed by an appropriate method, in this case by using an RTA. The clipping point as a function of frequency is measured and plotted on the same graph. The resulting display, shown in Fig. 16.14, is a graphical illustration of the dynamic range of the device under test as a function of frequency. This is in effect the SNR as a function of frequency.

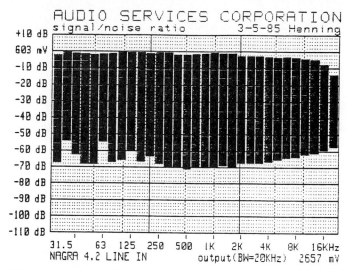

FIG. 16.14 Graphical display of dynamic range versus frequency. [*From H. Moller, "Computerized Audio Testing," Audio Engineering Society preprint 2251 (1985).*]

16.3 PHASE MEASUREMENT

16.3.1 Time Relationships

When a signal is applied to the input of a device, the output will appear later. For a sine-wave excitation this delay between input and output may be expressed as a proportion of the sine-wave cycle, usually in degrees. One cycle is 360°, one half-cycle is 180°, etc. This measurement is illustrated in Fig. 16.15. The phasemeter input signal no. 2 is delayed from, or is said to be lagging, input no. 1 by 45°.

Most audio measuring gear measures phase directly by measuring the proportion of one signal cycle between zero crossings of the signals. This can be done with an edge-triggered set-reset flip-flop as shown in Fig. 16.15. The output of this flip-flop will be a signal which goes high during the time between zero crossings of the signals. By averaging the amplitude of this pulse over one cycle (i.e., measuring its duty cycle) a measurement of phase results.

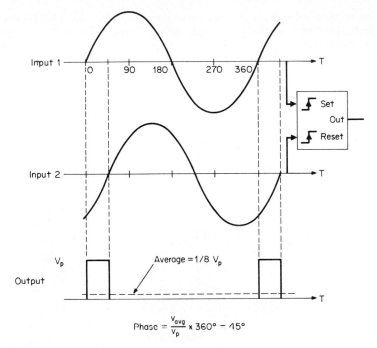

$$\text{Phase} = \frac{V_{avg}}{V_p} \times 360° - 45°$$

FIG. 16.15   Basic measurement of a phase shift between two signals.

Phase is typically measured and recorded as a function of frequency over the audio range. For most audio devices phase and amplitude responses are closely coupled. Any change in amplitude which varies with frequency will produce a corresponding phase shift. A device which has no more phase shift than what is required by the amplitude-response variation with frequency is called *minimum-phase*. A typical phase-and-amplitude-versus-frequency plot of a graphic equalizer is shown in Fig. 16.16.

A fixed time delay will introduce a phase shift which is a linear function of frequency. This time delay can introduce large values of phase shift at high frequencies which are of no significance in practical applications. The time delay will not distort the waveshape of complex signals and will not be audible in any way. There can be problems with time delay when the delayed signal will be used in conjunction with an undelayed signal. This would be the case if one channel of a stereo signal was delayed and the other was not. If we subtract out the absolute time delay from a phase plot, the remainder will truly represent the audible portions of the phase response. In instances where absolute delay is a concern, the original phase curve is more relevant. For a discussion of measuring high-frequency phase shifts and their importance to audio, see Jensen.[3]

Relation to Frequency.   When dealing with complex signals, the meaning of phase becomes unclear. Viewing the signal as the sum of its components according to Fourier theory, we find a different value of phase shift at each frequency. With a different phase value on each component, which one is to be used? If the signal is periodic and the waveshape is unchanged passing through the device

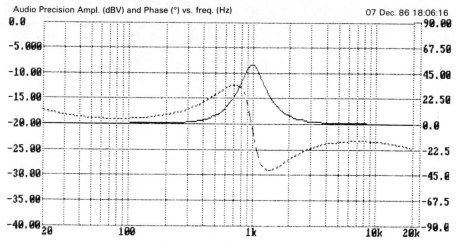

FIG. 16.16 Typical phase-and-amplitude-versus-frequency plot of a graphic equalizer.

under test, a phase value may still be defined. This may be done by using the shift of the zero crossings as a fraction of the waveform period. Indeed, most commercial phasemeters will display this value. However, if there is differential phase shift with frequency, the waveshape will be changed. It is then not possible to define any phase-shift value, and phase must be expressed as a function of frequency.

Another useful expression of the phase characteristics of an audio device is *group delay*. Group delay is the slope of the phase response. It expresses the relative delay of the spectral components of a complex waveform. This describes the delay in the harmonics of a musical tone relative to the fundamental. If the group delay is flat, all components will arrive together. A peak or rise in the group delay indicates that those components will arrive later by the amount of the peak or rise. It is computed by taking the derivative of the phase response versus frequency. Mathematically,

$$\text{Group delay} = -(\text{phase at } f_2 - \text{phase at } f_1)/(f_2 - f_1) \qquad (16.4)$$

This requires that phase be measured over a range of frequencies to give a curve which can be differentiated. It also requires that the phase measurements be performed at frequencies which are close enough together to provide a smooth and accurate derivative. For a discussion of group-delay measurements, see Jensen.[3]

The most common application of phase measurement in a studio is aligning heads in tape recorders. If a multitrack tape head is tilted relative to the direction of tape travel (an azimuth error), the signals in each channel will be slightly delayed. This delay results in a phase shift on sine waves. Since azimuth error results in a fixed time delay, the phase error will increase with increasing frequency. At a sufficiently high frequency the phase error may exceed 360°. Since sine waves repeat every 360°, the phasemeter will not be able to tell that this has occurred and the readings will be in error. To avoid this, first measure the phase at a midfrequency where it will be less than 360°, such as 1 kHz. Increase the frequency to about 3 kHz and remeasure, then increase it again to 10 kHz. The head azimuth is adjusted for a minimum-phase reading at 1 kHz; then this is fine-tuned at 3 kHz and again at 10 kHz. By measuring the phase shift at several frequencies the head misalignment becomes easy to see and correct. If an automatic measurement set is being used, this procedure becomes very simple. The equipment is set to scan these three frequencies and measure phase. The test equipment repeats this sweep several times per second, allowing essentially real-time display of the head alignment.

16.4 FREQUENCY MEASUREMENTS

16.4.1 Frequency Characteristics

Frequency is a fundamental characteristic of periodic signals. It is simply the number of times per second that the signal being measured repeats its pattern. An alternative way to specify this parameter is the period of the signal, i.e., the time taken for one cycle of the pattern to occur. Care should be taken not to confuse *pitch* and *frequency*. Pitch is essentially the perceived frequency. Indeed, for complex waveforms such as narrowband noise of frequency-modulated sine waves frequency is difficult to define. For example, what is the "frequency" of a signal consisting of 2-kHz, 3-kHz, 4-kHz, and 5-kHz sine waves? When this signal is heard, the brain will "insert" the missing 1-kHz fundamental and perceive a 1-kHz pitch. Pitch, though not always obvious from electrical measurements, is readily apparent to a listener.

16.4.2 Frequency Measurement

Early methods of frequency measurement employed vibrating reeds or frequency-to-voltage conversion circuits. These were hardly precision measurement techniques, but the frequency-to-voltage-converter approach was easy to use and became popular. Frequency measurement has advanced greatly since the development of digital logic. Early designs used digital counters to count the number of zero crossings during a fixed time window. For ease of design these time windows (called *gates*) were decimal fractions or multiples of 1 s. For example, if the gate is open for 1 s while measuring a 1-kHz tone, the counter will accumulate 1000 counts. This value is then displayed on a suitable readout such as light-emitting diodes (LEDs). The resolution of this technique is very limited for most audio purposes. To obtain a 4-digit-accurate readout of the frequency of a 10-Hz tone would require a 1000-s (15-min) gate.

Newer designs take advantage of the computing power of microprocessors and measure period, reciprocating the result to obtain the frequency. To perform this measurement both a high-frequency reference clock and the input signal are counted during the gate interval as illustrated in Fig. 16.17. The frequency of the input signal may then be computed by the formula

$$F = \text{clock frequency} \times \text{no. of signal cycles/count} \qquad (16.5)$$

Note that the gate interval does not enter into the calculation and may be chosen on the basis of the speed of measurements desired. Longer gate intervals and higher-frequency clocks will result in higher-resolution measurements. However, the gate interval must be an integer multiple of the input-signal period. This is

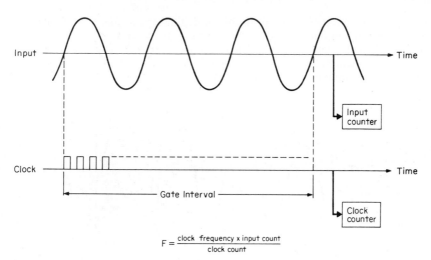

$$F = \frac{\text{clock frequency} \times \text{input count}}{\text{clock count}}$$

FIG. 16.17 High-resolution frequency measurement.

easy to ensure with appropriate logic circuitry. For the fairly typical case of a 10-Hz signal, a 0.1-s gate, and a 10-MHz clock, we would have a 1-cycle gate and a count of

$$10 \text{ MHz} \times 1 \text{ cycle}/10 \text{ Hz} = 1 \text{ million} \qquad (16.6)$$

giving a resolution of 6 digits. A 1-s gate would allow 10 cycles of input signal, giving a count of 10 million.

Another scheme is sometimes used for measuring low frequencies quickly and to high resolution. This involves locking a voltage-controlled oscillator (VCO) to a multiple of the input frequency, usually 100, with a phase-locked loop (PLL). The counter then counts the VCO output and obtains a factor-of-100 improvement in resolution for the same gate time. This scheme requires several cycles of input signal for the PLL to acquire and lock to the input. This time must be included in the measurement time, reducing the improvement. Increasing the multiplication factor much above 100 is difficult because of problems of oscillator instability and tuning range. Although the factor-of-100 improvement is substantial, period-based measurement schemes achieve even better resolution, yet are quite inexpensive.

All these measurement techniques are limited as to achievable accuracy by the accuracy of the reference. Typical quality crystal oscillators provide an accuracy of several parts per million at room temperature at a cost of a few dollars. By temperature-compensating the crystal oscillator the ambient-temperature effects may be removed. Adding an oven around the circuitry to maintain a constant environment further reduces drift. Order-of-magnitude improvements in accuracy tend to require order-of-magnitude increases in cost. Fortunately, for most audio applications the basic crystal accuracy is adequate.

16.4.3 Spectrum Analysis

A *spectrum analyzer,* generally speaking, is a device that displays a signal in the frequency domain. The most common approach is the sweeping-filter technique.

It may be visualized as a bandpass filter which sweeps in frequency as shown in Fig. 16.18. The output level from the filter drives the vertical axis of a display, while the signal frequency is the horizontal-axis variable. This gives a graph of the frequency content of the signal. A single sine wave will give a display of one peak at a horizontal point corresponding to the frequency of the input.

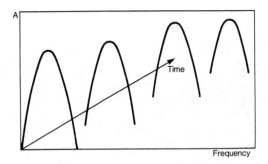

FIG. 16.18 Sweeping spectrum-analyzer response.

Because of the problems in tuning a bandpass filter electronically most spectrum analyzers are implemented according to the block diagram in Fig. 16.19. A sweeping oscillator (called the LO, for *local oscillator*) is mixed with the input signal in a multiplier, shifting the frequency of the signal to that of the fixed-frequency bandpass filter. This process is called *heterodyning* and is used in most radio receivers. This has also prompted some manufacturers of these units to call them *heterodyne analyzers.* Two important characteristics identify this type of analyzer. First, the bandwidth of the analysis filter is fixed by the characteristics of the fixed-frequency filter. The bandwidth of the analysis will not depend on the analysis frequency. Second, the analyzer must sweep through the frequency range of interest. If something happens at one frequency when the analyzer is tuned to another frequency, it will be missed.

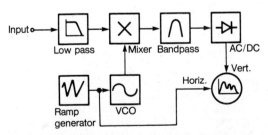

FIG. 16.19 Block diagram of a heterodyne spectrum analyzer.

The fixed-frequency-filter stage, called the *intermediate-frequency (IF) amplifier,* is typically a multiple-stage filter with amplifiers between each stage. This allows a very sharp rolloff characteristic and very small bandwidths. Means are normally provided for setting the IF bandwidth, allowing the resolution of the spectrum analyzer to be adjusted. The frequency-analysis range, or *span,* of the analyzer is set by the tuning of the LO. A minimum bandwidth is required for any value of span and sweep speed. This requirement allows the IF filter to settle to its steady-state response on the input signal. If the sweep is too fast or the bandwidth too small, the filter output will give an incorrect reading. The shape of the response seen on the analyzer screen for different sweep rates is shown in Fig. 16.20. As the sweep rate is increased above the optimum value, the peak will start to drop and its frequency will shift in the direction of the sweep. The optimum bandwidth B for a particular sweep time T and dispersion or total frequency sweep range D is given in Fig. 16.21.

Another approach to spectrum analysis is using real-time analyzers (RTAs). A parallel bank of bandpass filters is driven with the signal to be analyzed. The outputs of the filters are rectified and displayed in bar-graph form on a cathode-ray tube (CRT) or other suitable display as shown in Fig. 16.22. The resulting display is shown in Fig. 16.23. The filters are at fixed frequencies, usually spaced every one-third octave or full octave from 20 Hz to 20 kHz. This results in 30 filters for the one-third-octave case and 10 filters for octave-band units. These frequencies have been standardized by the IEC and are given in Table 16.2. Some units have been built with 12 filters per octave, or a total of 120 filters, for even higher resolution, but these are rarely used because of cost. Because RTAs are normally made with these fractional-octave filters, they are constant-percentage-bandwidth devices. This means that the bandwidth of the filters is always a fixed percentage of the center frequency. The advantage of parallel-filter analyzers is their instantaneous display and their ability to see transient events. Since all filters are constantly monitoring the signal, all transients will be seen. Severe disadvantages are the low-resolution display and the inability to trade resolution for frequency range after the unit is manufactured.

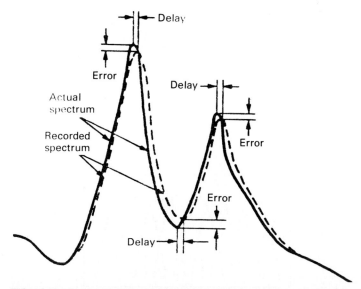

FIG. 16.20 Error and delay (bias errors) in writing out peaks and valleys in a spectrum. *(R. B. Randall,* Application of B & K Equipment to Frequency Analysis, *2d ed., B & K Instruments, Naerum, Denmark, 1977.)*

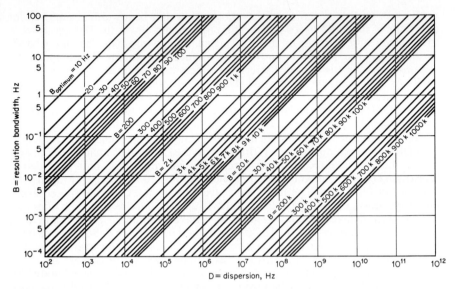

FIG. 16.21 Optimum resolution setting for spectrum analyzers. Read values of $B_{optimum}$ for a given dispersion and sweep time. *(M. Engelson and F. Telewski,* Spectrum Analyzer Theory and Applications, *Artech House, Norwood, Mass., 1974.)*

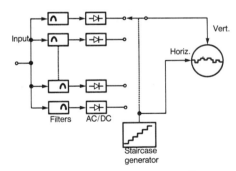

FIG. 16.22 Real-time-analyzer block diagram.

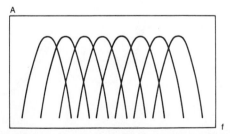

FIG. 16.23 Real-time (parallel-filter) analyzer response.

TABLE 16.2   ANSI-ISO Preferred
Frequencies

25 Hz	250 Hz	2.5 kHz
31.5 Hz	315 Hz	3.15 kHz
40 Hz	400 Hz	4.0 kHz
50 Hz	500 Hz	5.0 kHz
63 Hz	630 Hz	6.3 kHz
80 Hz	800 Hz	8 kHz
100 Hz	1 kHz	10 kHz
125 Hz	1.25 kHz	12.5 kHz
160 Hz	1.6 kHz	16 kHz
200 Hz	2	20 kHz

RTAs are commonly used with a random-noise or multitone test signal to measure a device or system response quickly. A random-noise signal is a signal whose instantaneous amplitude is a random, usually gaussian variable. Random noise has a spectrum (amplitude versus frequency) made up of all frequencies over the bandwidth of the noise. Various terms are used to describe the spectral distribution of noise; the most common are *pink noise* and *white noise.* White noise has an equal energy per hertz of bandwidth. If it is measured by using a filter whose bandwidth is constant with frequency (such as a heterodyne analyzer), the spectrum will be flat. If it is measured with a fractional-octave filter, as are all RTAs, the spectrum will rise at 3 dB per octave. Pink noise is random noise which has an equal energy per octave. If it is displayed on an RTA, the response will be flat. A heterodyne analyzer will show a rolloff of 3 dB per octave.

For most audio testing work with RTAs the system or device under test is excited by the pink-noise test signal. The output of the system is measured with the RTA, and the frequency response is displayed without waiting for a sweep. Because of the random nature of the noise signal there is significant fluctuation in the amplitude of each filter output. The average level will be correct, but the instantaneous value will change considerably with time. This puts significant uncertainty in the response being measured. This uncertainty may be reduced, but not eliminated, by increasing the averaging time in the ac-to-dc converters after the filters. A study of the fluctuations in narrowband noise signals and the resulting measurement error may be found in Hassall and Zaveri.[4]

Multitone test signals which consist of a sine wave at the center frequency of each filter used in the analysis may be constructed. This is most easily done digitally, but units have been built with discrete analog oscillators. When this signal is displayed on an RTA, the response will be shown without the random fluctuations common to pink noise. However, since the signal consists of a small number of sine waves, the response shown on the RTA is the steady-state response at each filter's center frequency. Because multitone signals measure at a single frequency in each filter, they will be greatly affected by sharp peaks and dips in the response being measured. When pink noise is used to make this same measurement, the RTA's response will be the average over the frequency range of each filter. This becomes a distinct advantage of random noise as a source for some acoustic measurements. It will average the response over the range of the analyzing filter, resulting in a measurement less affected by room modes and resonances in transducers.

16.5 FAST-FOURIER-TRANSFORM (FFT) MEASUREMENTS

Time and frequency domains are alternate ways of looking at a signal. The French mathematician Fourier proved that any signal may be represented as a series of sine waves summed together. Indeed, this is the justification for analyzing signals with a narrowband-tunable-filter spectrum analyzer to examine these components. Advances in technology have made it possible to implement directly Fourier's theory with digital computing circuits. Instruments which perform Fourier analysis digitize the signal, sampling the waveform at a rate faster than the highest-frequency input signal, and convert these samples into a numerical representation of the signal's instantaneous value. Fourier series provides a way to convert these signal samples into samples of the signal spectrum. This transforms the data from the time domain to the frequency domain. The FFT is merely a technique for efficiently computing the Fourier series by eliminating redundant mathematical operations.

The FFT operates on a piece of the signal which has been acquired and stored in memory for the calculation. Take, for example, the section of a sine wave shown in Fig. 16.24. This is a piece of a sine wave which continues in time on both sides of the selected segment. The FFT algorithm does not know anything about the waveform outside this piece that it is using for calculations. It therefore assumes that the signal repeats itself outside the "window" it has of the signal. This is important because an incorrectly selected piece of the signal may lead to very strange results. Consider the sine wave of Fig. 16.24 and the possible pieces of it which have been selected for analysis. In the first example the beginning and end of the window have been chosen to coincide with zero crossings of the signal. If the selected segment is repeated, an accurate representation of the signal is obtained. The FFT of this will give the correct spectrum, a single-frequency component. If the window is chosen incorrectly, as in the second example, there is a noninteger number of cycles in the waveform. When this segment is repeated, the resulting waveform will not look like the original sine wave. The computed spectrum will also be in error; it will be the spectrum of the discontinuous waveform. Transients which start at zero and decay to zero before the end of the sample segment will not suffer from any discontinuities. Continuous random or periodic signals will, however, be affected in a manner analogous to the effects on sine waves.

Clearly, then, the choice of windows for a signal which is to be transformed is critical to obtaining correct results. It is often difficult to select the correct endpoints of the window, and even more difficult without operator involvement. The window function may be thought of as a rectangular-shaped function which multiplies the signal. Intuitively it seems that the sharp discontinuities introduced by the endpoints of the window are at fault for the spurious components in the FFT. This may be proved theoretically but is beyond the scope of this discussion. A simple solution to the windowing problem is to use nonrectangular windows. Multiplying the signal by a window which decreases to zero gradually at its endpoints eliminates the discontinuities. Using these windows modifies the data and results in a widening of the spectral peaks in the frequency domain. This is illustrated in Fig. 16.25. This tradeoff is unavoidable and has results in the development of many different windowing functions which emphasize the spectral widening or the rejection of spurious components. The most common window function in use today is the Hamming window, illustrated in Fig. 16.26, which is

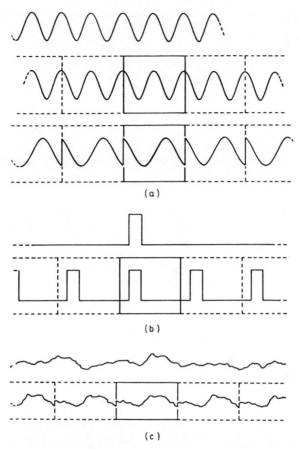

FIG. 16.24 The FFT assumes that all signals are periodic and that they duplicate what is captured inside the FFT window. (*a*) Periodic signal: integer number of cycles in the measurement window. (*b*) Nonperiodic signal: transient. (*c*) Nonperiodic signal: random. *(R. Ramirez, The FFT: Fundamentals and Concepts, Tektronix Inc., Beaverton, Oreg., 1975.)*

a cosine function raised above zero. It rejects spurious signals by at least 42 dB but spreads the spectral peaks by only 40 percent.

The FFT algorithm always assumes that the signal being analyzed is continuous. If transient signals are being analyzed, the algorithm assumes that they repeat at the end of each window. If a transient may be guaranteed to have decayed to zero before the end of the window time, a rectangular window may be used. If not, a shaped window must still be used. However, if there is significant transient energy at the end of the window, the computed spectrum will not include the frequency contribution of that data.

Fourier-transform algorithms may be written for any number of data points. However, it is easiest if the number of points may be expressed as the product of two smaller numbers. In this case the transform may be broken into the product

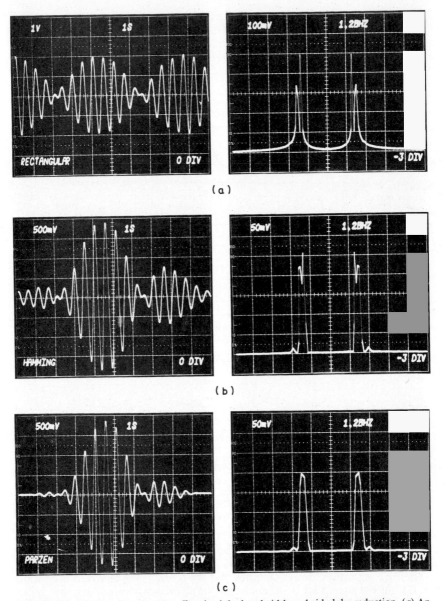

FIG. 16.25 Window shapes trade off major-lobe bandwidth and side-lobe reduction. (*a*) An almost periodic waveform in the rectangular acquisition window. The FFT magnitude (expanded 4 times for detail) shows closely adjacent, nearly equal components; one has substantial leakage. Also a small wrinkle at two divisions from center hints at a possible third component. (*b*) Multiplying the waveform by a Hamming window reduces side-lobe leakage and reveals a third low-level component in the FFT magnitude (expanded 4 times for detail). (*c*) A Parzen window offers more side-lobe reduction, but the increased bandwidth of the major lobe causes the two nearly equal components to merge completely into each other. (R. Ramirez, The FFT: Fundamentals and Concepts, *Tektronix Inc., Beaverton, Oreg.,* 1975.)

Unity-amplitude Window	Shape equation	Frequency-domain magnitude	Major-height	Highest side lobe dB	Bandwidth 3 dB	Theoretical roll-off, dB octave
Rectangle 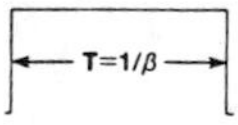	A = 1 for t = 0 to T	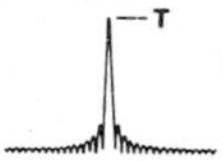	T	−13.2	0.86β	6
Hamming 	A = 0.08 + 0.46 (1 — cos 2πt/T) for t = 0 to T	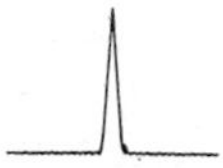	0.54 T	−41.9	1.26β	6 (beyond 5β)

FIG. 16.26 Some common FFT data windows and their frequency-domain parameters. *(R. Ramirez,* The FFT: Fundamentals and Concepts, *Tektronix Inc., Beaverton, Oreg., 1975.)*

of two smaller transforms, each of a length equal to the smaller numbers. The most convenient lengths for transforms, based on this scheme, are powers of 2. The most commont transform lengths are 512 points and 1024 points. These would ordinarily provide a spectrum with 256 and 512 components, respectively. However, because of errors at high frequencies due to aliasing and the rolloff introduced by windowing only 200 or 400 lines are displayed.

The transformation from the time domain to the frequency domain by using the FFT may be reversed to go from the frequency domain to the time domain. This allows signal spectra to be analyzed and filtered and the resulting effect on the time-domain response to be assessed. Other transformations may be applied to the data, yielding greater ability to separate the signal into its components. The cepstrum is probably the best known of these techniques.[5]

16.6 NONLINEAR DISTORTION

Distortion is a measure of signal impurity. It is usually expressed as a percentage or decibel ratio of the undesired components to the desired components of a signal. Distortion of a device is measured by feeding it one or more sine waves of various amplitudes and frequencies. In simplistic terms, any frequencies at the output which were not present at the input are distortion. However, strictly speaking, components due to power line interference or other spurious signals are not distortion. There are many methods of measuring distortion in common use: harmonic distortion and at least three different types of intermodulation distortion. These are different test procedures rather than different forms of distortion in the device under test.

16.6.1 Harmonic Distortion

Take the case of harmonic-distortion measurement first. The transfer characteristic of a typical device is shown in Fig. 16.27. This represents the output voltage at any point in the signal waveform for a given input voltage; ideally this is a straight line. The output waveform is the projection of the input sine wave on the device transfer characteristic. A change in the input produces a proportional

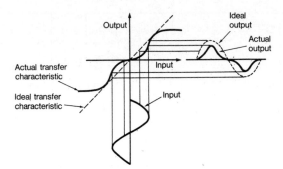

FIG. 16.27 Total-harmonic-distortion (THD) test of transfer characteristics.

change in the output. Since the actual transfer characteristic is nonlinear, a distorted version of the input waveshape appears at the output.

Harmonic-distortion measurements excite the device under test with a sine wave and measure the spectrum of the output. Because of the nonlinearity of the transfer characteristic, the output is not sinusoidal. By using Fourier series, it can be shown that the output waveform consists of the original input sine wave plus sine waves at integer multiples (harmonics) of the input frequency. The spectrum of the distorted signal is shown in Fig. 16.28. For a 1-kHz input the output consists of 1 kHz, 2 kHz, 3 kHz, etc. The harmonic amplitudes are proportional to the amount of distortion in the device under test. The percentage harmonic distortion is the rms sum of the harmonic amplitudes divided by the rms amplitude of the fundamental.

To measure harmonic distortion with a spectrum analyzer the procedure illustrated in Fig. 16.28 is used. The fundamental amplitude is adjusted to the 0-dB mark on the display. The amplitudes of the harmonics are then read and converted to linear scale. The rms sum of these values is taken and represents the THD. This procedure is time-consuming and difficult for an unskilled operator. Even skilled operators have trouble in obtaining accuracies better than 2 dB in the final result because of equipment limitations and the problems inherent in reading numbers off a trace on the screen of an analyzer.

A simpler approach to the measurement of harmonic distortion is the *notch-filter distortion analyzer*. This device, commonly referred to as simply a distortion

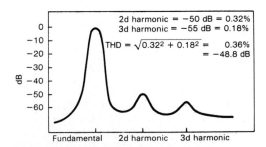

FIG. 16.28 Reading THD from a spectrum analyzer.

analyzer, removes the fundamental of the signal to be investigated and measures the remainder. A block diagram of such a unit is shown in Fig. 16.29. The fundamental is removed with a notch filter, and its output is then measured with an ac voltmeter. Since distortion is normally presented as a percentage of the fundamental level, this level must be measured or set equal to a predetermined reference value. Additional circuitry (not shown) is required to set the level to the reference value for calibrated measurements. Some analyzers use a series of step attenuators and a variable control for setting the input level to the reference value.

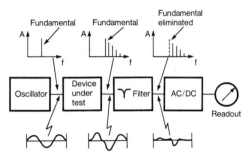

FIG. 16.29   Basic block diagram of a harmonic-distortion analyzer.

More sophisticated units eliminate the variable control by using an electronic gain control. Others employ a second ac-to-dc converter to measure the input level and compute the percentage by using an analog divider or a microprocessor. Completely automatic units also provide autoranging logic to set the attenuators and ranges. This provision significantly reduces the effort and skill required to make a measurement.

The correct method of representing percentage distortion is to express the level of the harmonics as a fraction of the fundamental level. However, commercial distortion analyzers use the total signal level as the reference voltage. For small amounts of distortion these two quantities are equivalent. At large values of distortion the total signal level will be greater than the fundamental level. This makes distortion measurements on these units lower than the actual value. The relationship between the measured distortion and the true distortion is given in Fig. 16.30. The errors are negligible below 10 percent measured distortion and are not significant until 20 percent measured distortion.

The need to tune the notch filter to the correct frequency can also make this a very tedious measurement. Some manufacturers have circumvented this problem by including the measurement oscillator and analyzer in one package, placing the analyzer and oscillator frequency controls on the same knob or button. This eliminates the problem only when the signal source used for the test is the internal oscillator. If a tape recorder with a prerecorded test tape is being used, the generator frequency will not be the frequency coming from the tape and the user will be back to manual tuning. Similar problems occur when testing broadcast links or communications lines because the generator may be hundreds or thousands of miles away. A better approach, used by a few manufacturers, is to measure the input frequency and tune the filter to the measured frequency. This eliminates any need to adjust the analyzer frequency.

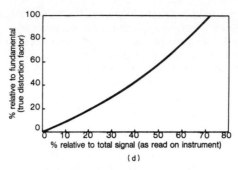

FIG. 16.30 Conversion graph for indicated distortion and true distortion. *(From H. W. Tremaine,* Audio Cyclopedia, *Howard W. Sams, Indianapolis, 1975.)*

Because of the notch-filter response, any signal other than the fundamental will influence the results, not just harmonics. Some of these interfering signals are illustrated in Fig. 16.31. Any practical signal contains some hum and noise, and the distortion analyzer will include these in the reading. Because of these added components, the correct term for this measurement is *total harmonic distortion and noise* (THD + N). Although this does limit the readings of equipment for very low distortion, this is not necessarily bad. Indeed it can be argued that the ear hears all components present in the signal, not just the harmonics. Some interfering signals, such as the 19-kHz pilot tone used in frequency-modulation (FM) stereo, may be outside the range of audibility and therefore totally undesirable.

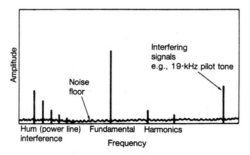

FIG. 16.31 Interference in distortion and noise measurements.

Additional filters are included on most distortion analyzers to reduce unwanted hum and noise as illustrated in Fig. 16.32. These usually consist of one or more high-pass filters (400 Hz is almost universal) and several low-pass filters. Common low-pass-filter frequencies are 22.4 kHz, 30 kHz, and 80 kHz. Better equipment will include filters at all these frequencies to ease the tradeoff between limiting bandwidth to reduce noise and the reduction in reading accuracy from removing desired components of the signal. When used in conjunction with a good differential input on the analyzer, these filters can solve most practical measurement noise problems.

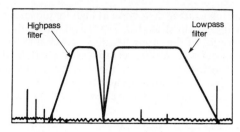

FIG. 16.32   Use of filters to reduce interference.

The use of a sine-wave test signal and a notch-type distortion analyzer has the distinct advantage of simplicity in both instrumentation and use. This simplicity has an additional benefit in ease of interpretation. The shape of the output waveform from a notch-type analyzer indicates the slope of the nonlinearity. Displaying the residual components on the vertical axis of an oscilloscope and the input signal on the horizontal gives a plot of the transfer characteristics' deviation from a best-fit straight line. This technique is diagramed in Fig. 16.33. The trace will be a horizontal line for a perfectly linear device. If the transfer characteristic curves upward on positive input voltages, the trace will bend upward at the right-hand side. Examination of the distortion components in real time on an oscilloscope will show such things as oscillation on the peaks of the signal, crossover distortion, and clipping. This is an extremely valuable tool in the design and development of audio circuits and one which no other distortion measurement method can fully match. Viewing the residual components in the frequency domain by using a spectrum analyzer also gives much information about the distortion mechanism inside the device under test.

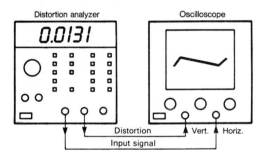

FIG. 16.33   Transfer-function monitoring.

Both the frequency and the amplitude of the sine-wave stimulus are adjustable parameters in harmonic-distortion testing. This often proves to be of great value in investigating the nature of a distortion mechanism. By measuring at low frequencies, thermal distortion and effects may be examined in detail. Using frequencies near the power line frequency and looking for beats in the distortion products can reveal power supply limitations and line-related interference. Measurements at high frequencies can reveal the presence of nonlinear capacitances or slew-rate limiting. By examining the slope of the distortion change with frequency, several mechanisms which are active in the same frequency range may be isolated. This is covered in detail by Cabot.[6]

Limitations when measuring distortion at high frequencies are the major problem with THD testing, as illustrated in Fig. 16.34. Since the components being measured are harmonics of the input frequency, they may fall outside the passband of the device under test. A tape recorder with a cutoff frequency of 22 kHz (typical for a good machine) will allow measurement only up to the third harmonic of a 7-kHz input. THD measurements on a 20-kHz input are impossible because all the distortion components are filtered out by the recorder.

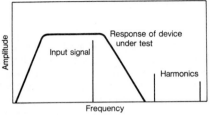
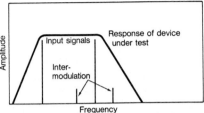

FIG. 16.34 Problems in measuring harmonic distortion in band-limited systems.

FIG. 16.35 Measuring intermodulation in band-limited systems.

16.6.2 Intermodulation Distortion

The commonly accepted solution to this problem is to measure distortion by the interaction or intermodulation (IM) of two or more signals passing through a device simultaneously. Many methods have been devised to measure this interaction. The most common of these is SMPTE IM, named after the Society of Motion Picture and Television Engineers, which first standardized its use. IM measurements according to the SMPTE method have been in use since the 1930s. The test signal is a low-frequency tone (usually 60 Hz) and a high-frequency tone (usually 7 kHz) mixed in a 4:1 amplitude ratio. Other amplitude ratios and frequencies are used occasionally. The signal is applied to the device under test, and the output signal is examined for modulation of the upper frequency by the low-frequency tone. The amount by which the low-frequency tone modulates the high-frequency tone indicates the degree of nonlinearity. As with harmonic-distortion measurement, this may be done with a spectrum analyzer or with a dedicated distortion-analysis instrument. The modulation components of the upper signal appear as sidebands spaced at multiples of the lower-frequency tone as illustrated in Fig. 16.35. The amplitudes of the sidebands are rms-summed and expressed as a percentage of the upper-frequency level.

The most direct way to measure SMPTE IM distortion is to measure each component with a spectrum analyzer and rms-sum them together. The spectrum-analyzer approach has a drawback in that it is sensitive to frequency modulation of the carrier as well as amplitude modulation. Since Doppler effects cause frequency modulation, this approach cannot be used on loudspeakers. Similar problems result from the wow and flutter in tape recorders and disk recording equipment.

A distortion analyzer for SMPTE testing is quite straightforward. The signal to be analyzed is passed through a high-pass filter to remove the low-frequency tone as shown in Fig. 16.36. The high-frequency tone is then demodulated as if it were an amplitude-modulation (AM) radio signal to obtain the sidebands. These are low-pass-filtered to remove any remaining high-frequency energy. The resul-

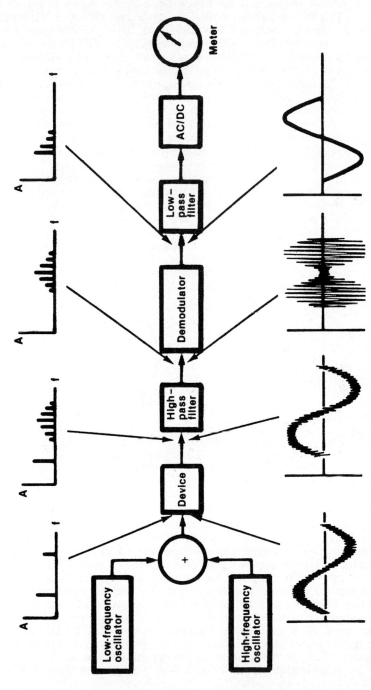

FIG. 16.36 Basic block diagram of an SMPTE intermodulation analyzer.

tant demodulated low-frequency signal will follow the envelope of the high-frequency tone. This low-frequency fluctuation is the distortion and is displayed as a percentage of the high-frequency tone's amplitude. Since this low-pass filtering sets the measurement bandwidth, noise has little effect on SMPTE measurements. The analyzer is very tolerant of harmonics of the two input signals, allowing fairly simple oscillators to be used to generate the test signal. Indeed, early analyzers used a filtered version of the power line for the low-frequency tone: hence the 60-Hz low tone frequency in the SMPTE standard. It is important, however, that no harmonics of the low-frequency signal generator extend into the measurement range of the high-frequency tone. The analyzer will be unable to distinguish these from sidebands. After the first stage of filtering in the analyzer, there is little low-frequency energy left to create IM in the analyzer. This considerably simplifies the remaining circuitry.

As shown in Fig. 16.37, when this composite signal is applied to the test device, the output waveform is distorted. As the high-frequency tone is moved along the transfer characteristic by the low-frequency tone, its amplitude changes. The high-frequency tone is being used to measure the gain at each point of the transfer characteristic. This results in low-frequency amplitude modulation of the high-frequency tone. This modulation results in sidebands around the high-frequency tone as described earlier. This test is therefore quite sensitive to such things as crossover distortion and clipping. High-order nonlinearities create bumps in the transfer characteristic which produce large amounts of SMPTE IM.

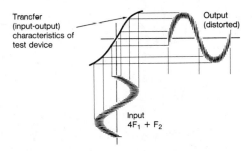

FIG. 16.37   SMPTE intermodulation test of transfer characteristics.

SMPTE testing is also good for exciting low-frequency thermal distortion. As the low-frequency signal moves around, exciting the thermal effects, the gain of the device changes, creating modulation distortion. Another excellent application is the testing of output inductance-capacitance (LC) stabilization networks in power amplifiers. Low-frequency signals may saturate the output inductor, causing it to become nonlinear. Since the frequency is low, very little voltage is dropped across the inductor, and there is little low-frequency harmonic distortion. The high-frequency tone will develop a signal across the inductor because of the rising impedance with frequency. When the low-frequency tone creates a nonlinear inductance, the high-frequency tone becomes distorted. This illustrates an important advantage of SMPTE IM testing. The sensitivity may be quite high to low-frequency distortion mechanisms in that the components occur at high frequencies. In most electronic audio circuits there is feedback which decreases at high frequencies. This lower feedback allows the distortion components to escape much of the reduction otherwise achieved at low frequencies by the feedback.

The inherent insensitivity of SMPTE IM to wow and flutter has fostered widespread use of the SMPTE test in applications which involve recording the audio signal. Much use is made of SMPTE in the disk recording and film industries. When applied to disks, the frequencies used are usually 400 Hz and 4 kHz. This form of IM testing is especially sensitive to excessive polishing of the disk surface even though harmonic distortion is not.

It is often claimed that because the distortion components in an SMPTE test are not harmonically related to either input they will be more objectionable to the ear. Musical instruments are rich in harmonics but contain few if any components which are inharmonic. With the typical 60-Hz low-frequency tone used in SMPTE measurements, it is doubtful that the sidebands could be outside the masking range of the ear. However, it is quite possible for the test to be indicative of audible performance even if the test-signal distortion is not audible. For a thorough discussion of these problems, see Cabot.[7a]

Several papers compare SMPTE IM readings with harmonic-distortion readings. For most classic transfer-function nonlinearities the SMPTE test is approximately 12 dB more sensitive than THD. However, when heavy feedback is employed or when dynamic distortion effects are present, the difference becomes considerably less predictable. These limitations are discussed in Cabot[6] and the references cited therein.

Twin-tone intermodulation or International Telephone Consultative Committee (CCIT) difference-frequency distortion is another method of measuring distortion by using two sine waves. The test signal consists of two closely spaced high-frequency tones as shown in Fig. 16.38. When these are passed through a nonlinear device, IM products are generated at frequencies related to the difference in frequency between the original tones. For the typical case of signals at 14 kHz and 15 kHz the IM components will be at 1 kHz, 2 kHz, 3 kHz, etc., and 13 kHz, 16 kHz, 12 kHz, 17 kHz, etc. Even-order, or asymmetrical, distortions produce low-frequency difference-frequency components. Odd-order, or symmetrical, nonlinearities produce components near the input-signal frequencies. The most common application of this test measures only the even-order components since they may be measured with only a multipole low-pass filter. Measurement of the odd-order components requires a spectrum analyzer or a selective voltmeter. The measurement residuals in the two cases are approximately 110 dB and 85 dB below the input signals, respectively. The CCIT test has several advantages over either harmonic or SMPTE IM testing. The signals and distortion components may almost always be arranged to be in the passband of the device under test. This method ceases to be useful below a few hundred hertz when the required selectivity in the spectrum analyzer or selective voltmeter becomes excessive. However FFT-based devices can extend the practical lower limit substantially below this.

The distortion products in this test are usually very far removed from the input signal. This positions them outside the range of the auditory system's masking

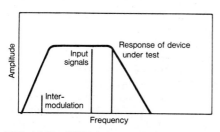

FIG. 16.38 CCIT intermodulation in band-limited systems.

effects. If a test which measures what the ear might hear is desired, the CCIT test is the most likely candidate. The question of correlation with audibility for this test is covered by Stanley and McLaughlin[8] and Cabot.[7]

Ladegaard[9] discusses the use of swept-frequency two-tone IM tests to study transient intermodulation (TIM), or slope-induced distortion. This approach has numerous advantages over the specialized tests which have been developed for the same purpose. The ability to adjust the test frequency enables qualitative study of the underlying distortion mechanism. Factors such as the steepness of the change in distortion with frequency and the frequency at which the change begins are useful in separating static from dynamic distortion mechanisms. The dominant order of the nonlinearity also gives useful information about its origins.

The totally in-band character of the test is one of its most attractive attributes. The difference product at $f_1 - f_2$ is widely separated in frequency and is easy to measure with a low-pass filter. This provides a simple implementation of the measurement and is the one most commonly used. However, the difference-frequency product is responsive only to even-order, or asymmetrical, nonlinearities in the device under test. It is possible to measure the odd-order products without a spectrum analyzer by using a precision squarer and bandpass filters. This approach has limitations in dynamic range because of the multiplier or squarer and its attendant inaccuracies.

Another approach, suggested by Thiele[10] and Small,[11] involves a clever choice of test frequencies to place both even- and odd-order components near each other. The idea is to choose the two test frequencies in almost a 3:2 frequency ratio. If they were exactly a 3:2 ratio, the second-order and third-order products would both fall at the 1 position in frequency; i.e., for tones of 10 kHz and 15 kHz both distortion components would fall at 5 kHz. Both components may then be measured with a single multipole bandpass filter tuned to this frequency. To prevent possible cancellation of the two distortion products if they should happen to be of opposite phase, the frequencies are offset slightly. The distortion components will then be at slightly different frequencies, yielding an unambiguous measurement. This test has been proposed as a measurement standard within the IEC.

The sine-wave–square-wave IM test was originally proposed by Leinonen, Otala, and Curl.[12] It consists of summing a square wave at 3.18 kHz and a sine wave at 15 kHz (of one-fourth of the square-wave amplitude) and applying them to the device under test. The signal is low-pass-filtered at either 30 kHz or 100 kHz and is nomenclated the DIM (for dynamic intermodulation) 30 or DIM 100, respectively. As the amplifier slews on the corners of the square wave, it becomes nonlinear and distorts the sine wave. The resulting IM components are measured with a spectrum analyzer, rms-summed, and expressed as a percent of the 15-kHz sine-wave amplitude. The IEC has since proposed that the frequency of the square wave be shifted to 3.15 kHz.

The test-signal spectrum is shown in Fig. 16.39. Leinonen and associates[12] define nine IM components in the audio band to be summed when making the measurement. If the square wave is not exactly 50 percent duty cycle, there will be even-order harmonics of the 3.18 kHz in the test signal. These even-order-harmonic components of the square wave when introduced by the device under test are not included in the measurement. However, these components may be as large as the IM components with some test devices and do provide valuable insight into the device nonlinearities. Making this measurement as originally defined requires a sine-wave generator, a square-wave generator, a single-pole low-pass filter, a spectrum analyzer, a calculator, and a considerable amount of

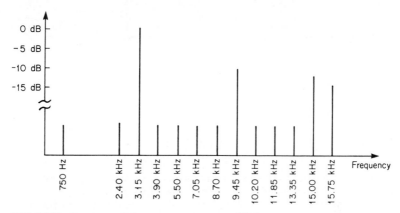

FIG. 16.39 Spectrum of sine-wave–square-wave TIM test.

time. The procedure is a fixed-frequency test, for there is no practical way to adjust the test frequencies to examine intricacies of the device under test.

Owing to its extreme complexity in measurement, the test was slow to be adopted by the audio industry despite widespread interest in *transient* forms of distortion. Skritek[13] and later Hofer[14] developed a procedure which simplifies this measurement considerably. The basic approach is illustrated in Fig. 16.40. Both an even-order and an odd-order IM product fold down to the 2-kHz region from interaction of the square wave and sine wave. By using a square wave of 3.15 kHz and a sine wave at 15 kHz, these appear at 750 Hz and 2.4 kHz. The 3.18-kHz square wave will produce components at 900 Hz and 2.28 kHz. The amplitude of these two components may be measured with a high-order elliptic low-pass filter at approximately 2.5 kHz. Their amplitude is expressed as a percentage of the 15-kHz tone amplitude. Owing to the practical difficulties of measuring the 15-kHz signal directly, the rms amplitude of the total signal is measured and a correction factor is applied. Additional high-pass filtering at approximately 400 Hz may be used to eliminate the effects of hum on the measurement. A block diagram of a DIM distortion analyzer using this measurement approach is shown in Fig. 16.41. Extensive testing by Hofer has shown that these two products correlate adequately with the results obtained by adding all nine IM components.

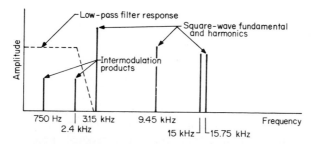

FIG. 16.40 Simplified TIM test-measurement system.

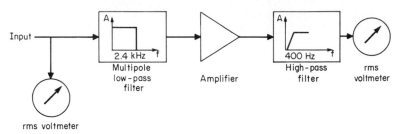

FIG. 16.41   Block diagram of a simplified DIM distortion meter.

The IEC has adopted the square-wave–sine-wave test as a proposed standard but has altered the frequencies somewhat. The square-wave frequency has been shifted to 3.15 kHz to make it conform to the standard one-third-octave filter frequency. Otala has also proposed a change in the test frequencies for broadcast use. Broadcast systems which are limited to a firm 15-kHz bandwidth will not pass the third harmonic of the square wave and thus will lose much of the sensitivity of the test. By shifting the square wave to 2.96 kHz and the sine-wave frequency to 14 kHz all appropriate components will now be passed by the system under test. The IM components change frequency slightly. However, the two low-frequency components used in the simplified version of the test shown in Fig. 16.40 remain within the bandwidth of the proposed filters.

16.6.3   Distortion-Measurement Hardware

Distortion measurements should be performed with an rms-responding meter in the distortion analyzer. This is necessary to make the reading represent the true power in the distortion. Older instruments used average-responding meters, but these are rapidly becoming outdated. With most practical distortion measurements the rms response will read about 2 dB higher than the average response. Some arguments can be made for measuring distortion with peak or quasi-peak detectors. The averaging time of the ear is between 50 and 250 ms, depending on test conditions and procedure. This has led to the definition of the quasi-peak meter for measuring telephone noise as described earlier. Petri-Larmi and associates[15] have proposed that the ear can hear the narrow spikes of distortion which occur on transients from slew-rate limiting. These would be very much like the noise pulses in telephone switchgear that the quasi-peak standard was developed to measure.

Accuracy of most distortion analyzers is specified at 1 dB, but this can be misleading. Separate specifications are often put on the bandwidth and ranges, as explained above for voltmeters. A more important specification for distortion measurements is the residual distortion of the measurement system. Manufacturers of distortion analyzers often specify the oscillator and the distortion analyzer separately. A system in which the oscillator and the analyzer are each specified at 0.002 percent THD can have a system residual distortion of 0.004 percent. If the noise of the analyzer and/or the oscillator is specified separately, this must be added to the residual specification to find the residual THD + N of the system. It is not uncommon to find this limiting system residual at most input voltages. For example, an analyzer specified at 0.002 percent distortion and 20-μV input noise will have a 0.003 percent residual at 1-V input and 0.02 percent at 0.1-V input. These voltages are common when measuring mixing consoles and pream-plifiers, resulting in a serious practical limitation with some distortion analyzers.

Many commercial units specify the residual distortion at only one input volt-age or at the full scale of one range. The performance usually degrades by as much as 10 dB when the signal is at the bottom of an input range. This is true because THD + N measurements are a ratio of the distortion components and noise to the signal level. At the full-scale input voltage the voltage in the notch filter is a maximum and the filter's noise contribution will be minimized. As the level drops, the residual noise in the notch filter becomes a larger percentage of the reading. When the next input range occurs, the residuals will improve again. This limitation is in addition to the input-noise problem discussed earlier because it results from noise in a later portion of the instrument.

16.6.4 Addition and Cancellation of Distortion

Another often-overlooked problem is that of distortion addition and cancellation in the test equipment or the device under test. Consider the examples in Figs. 16.42 and 16.43. Suppose one device under test has a transfer characteristic sim-ilar to that diagramed at the top of Fig. 16.42a and another has the characteristic diagramed at the bottom. If they are cascaded, the resulting transfer-characteristic nonlinearity will be magnified as shown. The effect on sine waves in the time domain is illustrated in Fig. 16.42b. The distortion component generated by each nonlinearity can be seen to be in phase and will sum to a component of twice the magnitude. However, if the second device under test has a complementary trans-fer characteristic as shown in Fig. 16.43, we obtain quite a different result. When

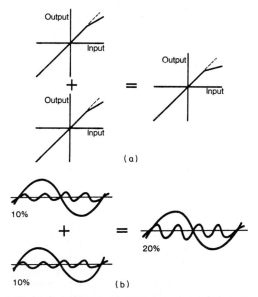

FIG. 16.42 Addition of distortion. (a) Addition of transfer-function nonlinearities. (b) Addition of dis-tortion components.

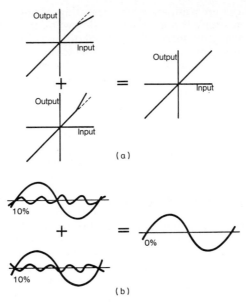

FIG. 16.43   Cancellation of distortion. (*a*) Cancellation of distortion waveform. (*b*) Cancellation of transfer-characteristic nonlinearity.

the devices are cascaded, the effects of the two curves will cancel, yielding a straight line for the transfer characteristic. The corresponding distortion products are out of phase with each other, resulting in no distortion components in the final output.

It is quite common for this to occur at low levels of distortion, especially between the test equipment and the device under test. For example, if the test equipment has a residual of 0.002 percent when connected to itself and readings of 0.001 percent are obtained from the circuit under test, cancellations are occurring. It is also possible for cancellations to occur in the test equipment itself, with the combined analyzer and signal generator system giving readings lower than the sum of their individual residuals. If the distortion is from an even-order (asymmetrical) nonlinearity, reversing the phase of the signal between the offending devices will change a cancellation to an addition. If the distortion is from an odd-order (symmetrical) nonlinearity, phase inversions will not affect the cancellation.

16.7 SIGNAL-SOURCE EFFECTS IN MEASUREMENTS

The signal source is an often-overlooked factor in the accuracy of level measurements. Let us consider the measurement of a low-pass filter's gain above its −3-dB frequency. This is shown in Fig. 16.44 for a three-pole low-pass filter. If the frequency of the generator is off by 3 percent, the gain measurement will be off by 1 dB. A higher-order filter or a less accurate generator will give more error.

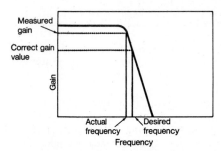

FIG. 16.44 Frequency-accuracy effects in measuring filters.

Figure 16.45 shows the effect of generator distortion on the gain measurement of a multipole high-pass filter. The harmonics of the generator are not attenuated as much by the filter as is the fundamental. If the signal-source distortion is high, as with function generators, the gain measurement will be in error. This effect is most important when measuring notch filters in an equalizer, where the distortion will appear as inadequate notch depth.

Figure 16.45 suggests that the effect of these errors on distortion measurements is more severe. The gain introduced by a filter on the harmonics of the generator can make them exceed the distortion of the filter itself. A three-pole high-pass filter will introduce 18 dB of gain at the second harmonic and 29 dB of gain at the third. Under these conditions an oscillator which has 0.001 percent second- and 0.001 percent third-harmonic distortion will read 0.03 percent when measuring a distortion-free filter. These errors necessitate the use of an oscillator with very low distortion.

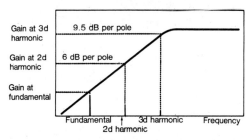

FIG. 16.45 Source-distortion effects in high-pass filters.

Another source of error in measurements is the output impedance of the generator. The amplitude and phase response of a device under test will often be affected by its input impedance interacting with the source impedance of the generator. They form a resistive divider in which the shunt leg is the nonconstant impedance of the device under test. This causes a variation of the voltage at the input to the test device, thus corrupting the measurements. Low-output-impedance generators will suffer less variation with load than high-impedance generators. However, if the system response is being measured, the generator impedance should be equal to the source impedance of the device normally driving that input. Transformer input stages often require a specific source impedance to provide correct damping for optimum high-frequency response. Too large a source impedance will cause excessive rolloff, while too low a source impedance will produce an underdamped or peaked response. For example, most microphone inputs are designed to be driven from a 150-Ω source, a value close to the typical microphone source impedance.

16.8   TIME-DOMAIN MEASUREMENTS

So far only the frequency-domain behavior of devices has been considered. It is also informative to examine the time-domain behavior of audio components. The most common signals for this purpose are sine waves, triangle waves, square waves, and tone bursts.

Sine waves are used in the time domain to measure clipping behavior. The top of a sine wave normally has a rounded appearance as shown at the top of Fig. 16.46. When a device is driven into saturation or clipping with a sine wave, the top, bottom, or both will flatten as in the lower trace. If the device is well behaved, the end of the flat region should change smoothly to a sine wave. There should be no glitches or ringing on the signal as the device comes out of saturation. Triangle waves are sometimes used instead of sine waves for this application because their peaks are sharper, making the flattening easier to see.

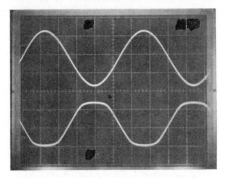

FIG. 16.46   Sine wave showing the effect of clipping: top undistorted; bottom clipped.

Square waves are used to determine the time-domain equivalents of amplitude and phase versus frequency measurements. The appearance of the output waveform from the device under test gives much qualitative information about its behavior. A table of square-wave responses from the *Audio Cyclopedia*[16] is given in Fig. 16.47. Quantitative measurements may also be obtained from the square-wave response. The most common of these are rise time, overshoot, ringing, tilt, and slew rate. The first four are measurements of the linear behavior of the device and may be related to the frequency-domain behavior. These are illustrated in Fig. 16.48.

The *rise time* is the time required for the signal amplitude to change from 10 to 90 percent of the total square-wave amplitude. For a single-pole low-pass device the rise time (RT) and the bandwidth (BW) are related by Eq. (16.7):

$$RT = 0.35/BW \qquad (16.7)$$

For multipole systems this equation will be only approximate.

The *overshoot* of a device is the amount by which the peak of the square wave exceeds steady-state positive or negative amplitude as shown. Large overshoots are indicative of peaking or excess phase shifts in the high-frequency response of the device under test. The maximum overshoot is normally the parameter spec-

Waveform	LF gain	LF delay	HF gain	HF delay	Damping
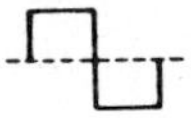	Ideal	Ideal	Ideal	Ideal	Ideal
	Insufficient	Good	Excessive	Good	High
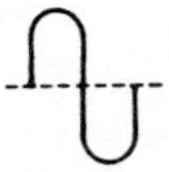	Excessive	Good	Insufficient	Good	High
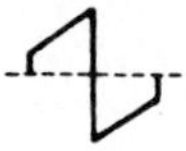	Good	Excessive	Good	Insufficient	High
	Good	Insufficient	Good	Excessive	High
	Excessive	Excessive	Insufficient	Insufficient	High
	Excessive	Insufficient	Insufficient	Excessive	High
	Insufficient	Excessive	Excessive	Insufficient	High
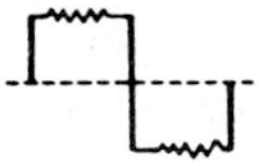	Good	Good	Excessive	Good	Medium
	Good	Good	Excessive	Good	Low
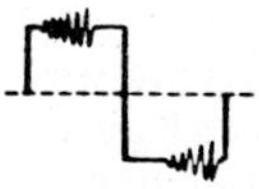	Good	Good	Excessive	Good	Negligent
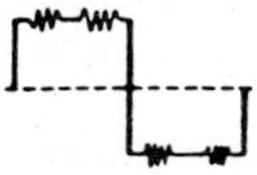	Good	Good	Sharp cutoff or peaked	Good	Low

FIG. 16.47 Effects of amplitude and phase response on square-wave characteristics. *(From H. M. Tremaine,* Audio Cyclopedia, *Howard W. Sams, Indianapolis, 1975.)*

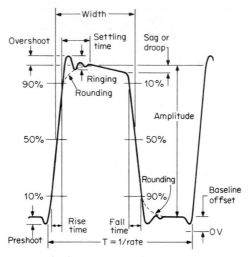

FIG. 16.48 Definition of rise time, overshoot, ringing, and droop. *(From H. M. Tremaine,* Audio Cyclopedia, *Howard W. Sams, Indianapolis, 1975.)*

ified, but the subjective appearance of the overshoot is also of interest. Well-behaved devices will have smooth overshoot, symmetrical on both positive and negative peaks. Overshoot normally occurs only on the leading edges of a square wave. However, if the device is linear-phase, as are many digital filters, there will be symmetrical overshoot on both leading and trailing edges.

Ringing is the tendency of band-limited square waves to oscillate on the peaks. This is largely a subjective measurement with the results stated as the severity of ringing. The greater the high-frequency peaking, the greater will be the ringing.

Tilt is a measure of low-frequency behavior. As low frequencies are filtered, phase shifts are introduced which cause the leading edge of the square wave to rise and the trailing edge to fall. This produces a tilt to the top and bottom of the square wave. The tilt is usually expressed as a percentage of the peak amplitude of the square wave.

Slew rate is a measure of how fast a signal changes from one instantaneous value to another. The ideal square wave changes from one amplitude extreme to the other instantly. Practical devices cannot keep up with this transition and will often have a maximum speed with which they can change. This speed limitation will result in a tilted straight-line portion of the square-wave edge as shown in Fig. 16.49. This should not be confused with the exponential rounding of square-wave edges which results from a high-frequency rolloff (the effect measured by rise time). The effects of bandwidth limiting are linear; the effects of slew-rate limiting are not. A simple way to determine whether a signal is slew-limited is to increase the signal amplitude. A bandwidth-limited signal will make the transition in the same time; a slew-limited signal will take longer.

Tone bursts are another technique for evaluating the response of audio devices to transients. They are created by gating a sine wave on and off at its zero crossings. A tone burst concentrates the energy of the waveform closer to a particular frequency, enabling evaluation of individual sections of the audio-frequency range. However, they still contain substantial high-frequency energy as shown in

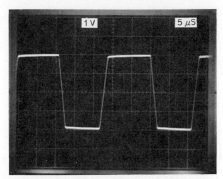

FIG. 16.49 Effect of slew-rate limiting on a square wave.

Fig. 16.50, taken from Linkwitz.[17] The number of cycles on and off significantly affects the frequency spread of the energy. This frequency spreading can yield anomalous results, requiring extreme care in interpretation. Linkwitz proposed the use of shaped bursts, employing a windowing function much the same as the Hamming window employed in FFT analysis. The shaping of the burst rise and fall reduces the spread in frequency, concentrating the energy near the frequency of the sine wave.

Tone-burst testing is common with loudspeakers, yielding qualitative information on the damping characteristics of the drivers at a glance. As with square waves, the common parameters specified in tone-burst measurements are overshoot and ringing. The overshoot or undershoot on a tone burst is usually taken to be the amount by which the burst envelope goes above or below the steady-state on level. Ringing on a tone burst refers to the tendency to continue oscillating after the burst has stopped. This gives the appearance of a tail which continues after the body of the burst.

The bursts considered so far have been sine waves gated completely off. It is often useful to gate a sine wave between two different levels. The most common applications of this procedure are testing amplifiers and compressors. When an amplifier is driven into clipping, its circuitry loses feedback and portions of the circuitry become saturated. As the amplifier comes out of this overload condition, it may do unpredictable things. These are often easier to see when a signal is present. A waveform such as a dual-level tone burst can overload the amplifier periodically while maintaining signal between overloads, enabling examination of this behavior. The Institute of High Fidelity (IHF) specifies a 20-dB ratio between on and off levels for this application. Compressors, expanders, limiters, etc., are designed to change the dynamic range of audio signals. To evaluate the dynamic, or time, behavior of these devices it is necessary to have a signal which has significant changes in level with time. The two-level tone burst is ideal for this application, enabling observation of the transition of the compressor from one gain to another. An example of typical compressor behavior is shown in Fig. 16.51.

Tone bursts may be used to make response measurements in the presence of interfering reflections such as occur in rooms. The basic principle is to stimulate the device under test with a burst and perform measurements on the resulting signal with a gate (electronic switch) which eliminates later-arriving reflections. The amplitude of the impulse is sampled during the body of the burst after any ringing on the leading edge has died away. The sample gate is turned off before

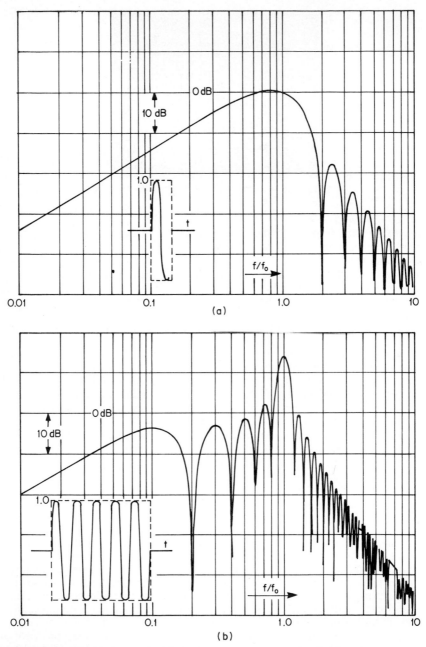

FIG. 16.50 Tone-burst spectra. (*a*) Single-cycle sine-wave burst. (*b*) Five-cycle sine-wave burst. [*From S. Linkwitz, "Narrow Band Testing of Acoustical Systems," Audio Engineering Society preprint 1342 (May 1978).*]

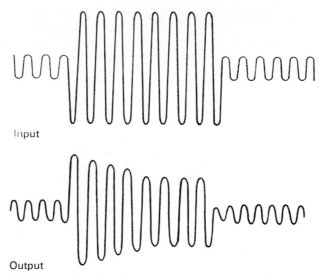

Input

Output

FIG. 16.51 Typical tone-burst response of a compressor, illustrating the time response of the compressor. Input (*top*). Output (*bottom*). [*From R. C. Cabot, "Limiters, Compressors, and Expanders,"* Sound and Video Contractor, *26 (November 1985).*]

any reflections have arrived, yielding the free-field response. Linkwitz[17] modified this procedure to use a shaped tone burst which concentrates the energy much more within the frequency band of interest. This allows the maximum amplitude of the burst to be measured, eliminating the need to gate the measurement during the center portion of the burst. The reflections may usually be ignored because they are lower in level than the direct signal.

Another method for checking the time-domain behavior of devices is the *impulse response.* The device under test is excited by a very narrow pulse whose amplitude is set to the maximum allowed for linear operation. The response may be viewed on an oscilloscope for qualitative judgments. However, the power of the technique lies in capturing the response with a digital storage oscilloscope or FFT analyzer. Performing an FFT will yield the frequency-domain behavior of the device, both amplitude and phase. Under most conditions this information is identical to what would be obtained by a sine-wave-based sweep of frequency. If linear operation is maintained by proper choice of levels, the only differences will be in terms of heating effects (as occur in loudspeaker voice coils) and dynamic level effects (as occur in compressors).

16.9 INPUT AND OUTPUT INTERFACING

Balanced inputs and outputs are common in audio to eliminate ground loops and reduce interference. It is even more important to maintain balanced operation when connecting to audio test equipment. Use of a balanced differential input on a voltmeter or distortion analyzer is essential to accurate readings and to verification of today's low distortion and noise levels.

Let us first examine what a balanced line is and what problems it solves. Figure 16.52a shows a basic source-load connection. No grounds are indicated; both source and load float. Either the source or the load may be tied to ground with no problems, but not both. Unbalanced systems occur when each piece of equipment has one of its connections tied to ground as shown in Fig. 16.52b. This occurs, for example, because the source is an amplifier output whose power supply is tied to the chassis. The difference in ground potential causes current to flow in the ground wire and develops a voltage across the wire resistance. The ground-noise voltage directly adds to the signal itself. Since this ground current is usually derived from leakage in power transformers and line filters, the current is 60 Hz ac and gives rise to hum. If the wire resistance is reduced by using heavier ground wire, the hum will be reduced, but it is difficult to get an adequately low resistance.

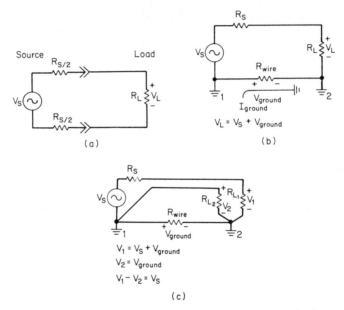

FIG. 16.52   Interfacing of inputs and outputs. (*a*) Ideal source-load connection: both source and load float. (*b*) An unbalanced system in which each piece of equipment has one of its connections connected to ground. (*c*) Cancellation of ground-loop noise by use of a differential input. [*From R. C. Cabot, "Active Balanced Inputs and Outputs," Sound and Video Contractor, 30 (March 1986).*]

By amplifying both the high side and the ground side of the source and subtracting the two, it is possible to cancel the ground-loop noise as shown in Fig. 16.52c. This is the basis of a differential-input circuit. The differential input also aids in the rejection of magnetic and electrostatic noise picked up in the cabling. Figure 16.53a shows what happens when an unbalanced line is exposed to an interfering signal. The resulting signal cannot be separated into the desired and undesired components. If a balanced connection is used (Fig. 16.53b) between source and load, the interference will couple into both sides of the line equally. The differential input subtracts the two sides of the line and cancels the interference from the signal.

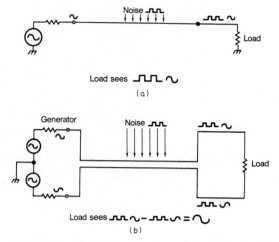

FIG. 16.53 (*a*) Noise pickup in unbalanced lines. (*b*) Rejection of noise in balanced lines.

The measure of how well an input rejects signals present on both inputs is called the common-mode rejection ratio (CMRR). This is illustrated in Fig. 16.54. The desired signal is applied between the plus and minus inputs of the amplifier. The amplifier will have a certain gain, called the *differential gain,* for this signal condition. The ground-noise voltage appears on both plus and minus inputs simultaneously; i.e., it is *common* to the two inputs. Since the amplifier subtracts the two inputs, giving only the difference between the voltage at the two terminals, the output voltage (and therefore the gain under this condition) should be zero. In practice it is not. The CMRR is the ratio of these two gains in decibels. The bigger the number, the better. For example, a 60-dB CMRR means that a ground signal common to the two inputs will have 60 dB less gain than the differential signal. If the ground noise is 40 dB below the desired signal level, the differential input will make it 100 dB below. However, if the noise is already part of the differential signal, the CMRR will do nothing to improve things.

Common-mode range is a specification of the largest common-mode signal which can be handled at the input without clipping or other malfunction. The common-mode range is usually a function of the input range of the test equip-

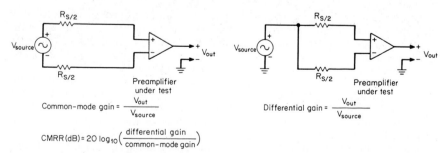

FIG. 16.54 Definition of common-mode rejection ratio. [*From R. C. Cabot, "Active Balanced Inputs and Outputs,"* Sound and Video Contractor, *30 (March 1986).*]

ment. Ranges which employ gain at the input will normally have a common-mode range of about 5 to 10 V. For ranges which are attenuated at the input, the common-mode range will increase with the maximum input rating of the input. However, these ranges will also have a degraded CMRR because of mismatch in the two attenuators used on the two sides of the input.

Some manufacturers are now offering an electronically balanced and floating output on their equipment. The basis of these designs is shown in Fig. 16.55. The circuit consists of two operational amplifiers which are cross-coupled with positive and negative feedback. The output of each amplifier is dependent on the input signal and the signal present at the output of the other amplifier.

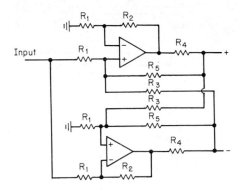

FIG. 16.55 An electronically balanced and floating output. (R_5 may be omitted.) [*From R. C. Cabot, "Active Balanced Inputs and Outputs,"* Sound and Video Contractor, *30 (March 1986).*]

Output floatability is often unspecified in the actively balanced and floating outputs. When driving a test device, there is often a large potential difference between chassis. This may be due to the equipment being on different phases of the power line. A transformer floating output will have a small capacitance from the center tap of the balanced line to ground and will induce very little 60-Hz common mode onto the line. An active balanced and floating output has an impedance from each output to ground, typically several tens of thousands of ohms. This induces a common-mode potential between the chassis which must then be rejected by the CMRR of the device input.

Balanced and unbalanced outputs and inputs can be mixed if care is taken in the connections. Simply remember that the ground of one device is not quite the same as the ground of another. There may be an ac voltage difference between any two points called ground. The resulting current flow should be predicted, and the connection scheme which minimizes this effect should be used.

A differential input is also valuable to avoid inducing noise when measuring circuits. If an additional ground is introduced by the connection of an unbalanced meter to the system, it may introduce hum which was not previously there. A differential input allows monitoring unbalanced lines without introducing any additional ground paths.

Similar concerns about balanced operation apply to the signal source. When a balanced system is unbalanced by connection to a grounded generator, there may be hum introduced if the CMRR of the system under test is not adequate. With an unbalanced generator driving an unbalanced line it will not be possible to separate the hum introduced by connection to the generator from that inherent in the system.

If measurements are made in a high-radio-frequency-interference (RFI) field, it is essential to maintain balanced operation. Most inexpensive pieces of test equipment will not operate properly in such environments. Using these devices will certainly result in many hours of wasted time fighting with shields and filters or recording incorrect data.

Susceptibility to RFI is a common problem with test equipment. Strong radio signals can often be rectified by nonlinearities in the input operational amplifiers or transistors. Although wideband low-distortion circuits will be less prone to this problem, they are not immune. Therefore, any signals which are outside the range of the active circuits must be filtered out before they can be inadvertently demodulated. Most manufacturers add small series resistors and capacitors to ground at the input terminals. Inductors may also be added, but if package shielding is inadequate, they may pick up as much interference as they are supposed to filter out. They are, after all, coils of wire waiting for a passing magnetic field.

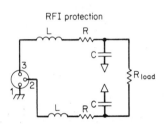

FIG. 16.56 A typical input RFI rejection filter. [*From R. C. Cabot, "Active Balanced Inputs and Outputs,"* Sound and Video Contractor, *30 (March 1986).*]

The use of toroidal inductors will usually reduce pickup of external signals substantially. A schematic of a typical input RFI rejection filter is shown in Fig. 16.56. For the reasons cited above and because of cost the inductors are often omitted.

16.10 IMPEDANCE

Impedance is the ac equivalent of resistance. It also follows Ohm's law relating the voltage across an impedance to the current flowing through it. The input impedance and output impedance of audio devices are generally a function of frequency. To measure these parameters a known current is forced through the device under test, and the voltage developed across the terminals is measured. This voltage is proportional to the unknown impedance. By choosing the value of current correctly, the scale factor becomes a convenient multiple of 10. For most measurement requirements a large resistance in series with a voltage source makes an adequate current source.

This technique is diagramed in Fig. 16.57. The known voltage is applied through the resistor to the device under test. The voltage developed across the test device is measured by a voltmeter. The phase shift between this voltage and the source voltage is measured with a phasemeter. If the resistor is adequately large, the current through the unknown impedance will be approximately constant and proportional to the voltage of the source. In addition, the phase of the current is the same as the phase of the source voltage. Therefore, the voltmeter will read the magnitude of the impedance, and the phasemeter will read the phase of the impedance.

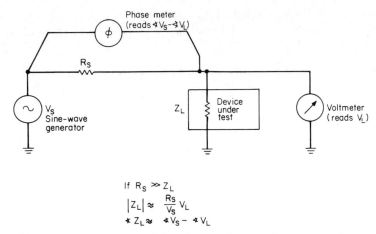

$$\text{If } R_S \gg Z_L$$

$$|Z_L| \approx \frac{R_S}{V_S} V_L$$

$$\angle Z_L \approx \angle V_S - \angle V_L$$

FIG. 16.57 Measurement of impedance using a voltage-source-resistance approximation to a current source.

Applying this technique to measure the impedance of a loudspeaker yields the curve shown in Fig. 16.58. This same procedure may be used to measure the input or output impedance of electronic devices. However, when measuring high impedances such as amplifier inputs, care must be taken to make the source resistor adequately large. Very low test impedances such as amplifier outputs may

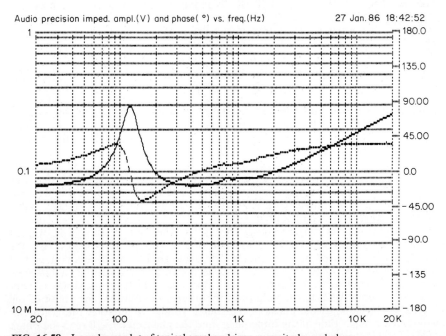

FIG. 16.58 Impedance plot of typical speaker driver, magnitude, and phase.

require small source resistors and large currents from the generator to obtain adequately large voltages across the test impedance.

16.11 WOW AND FLUTTER

Wow and flutter are the undesirable frequency modulation of an audio signal due to rapid speed variations in an audio storage medium such as a tape recorder or a disk player. These speed variations may be caused by mechanical imperfections in the device, noise in the servomechanisms, external influences such as floor vibration, etc. Wow-and-flutter measurements are made by playing back a tape having a prerecorded tone, usually at 3.15 kHz. The reproduced tone is fed to the wow-and-flutter meter. It contains an FM discriminator whose output is proportional to the instantaneous frequency deviation of the test tone. For most applications the flutter components are weighted, based on their frequency, according to the ear's sensitivity to them. The block diagram of a wow-and-flutter meter is shown in Fig. 16.59.

The bandwidth of wow-and-flutter meters with the weighting filter turned off usually extends from about 0.5 Hz to 200 Hz. This is the range where problems occur in rotating components such as idler wheels, capstans, pulleys, motors, etc. However, variations in tape speed can also be caused by frictional effects of the tape sliding over guides or the tape heads themselves. These effects are called *scrape flutter* and produce FM components as much as 5 kHz away from the signal. Modern servo motor transports can also exhibit FM products substantially above the 200-Hz top end of conventional wow-and-flutter meters. These high-frequency FM products are perceived more as added noise, "grit," or "harshness" than as the wavering sound usually associated with wow and flutter.

To measure this form of flutter it is necessary to use a test-tone frequency higher than the usual 3.15 kHz. A test-tone frequency of 12.5 kHz allows a 5-kHz bandwidth in the measurement if the tape-machine bandwidth is at least 17.5 kHz. Because of the wideband nature of the test a weighting filter is not used. For typical professional tape recorders with a scrape-flutter idler the scrape-flutter measurement of components above 200 Hz will read approximately as high as the conventional wow-and-flutter measurement. For lesser-quality machines the scrape-flutter reading will be much higher, indicating the presence of excessive instability in the tape motion. If the tape machine under test has a more limited bandwidth, it may be necessary to shift the test frequency down or compromise the bandwidth of the scrape-flutter measurement.

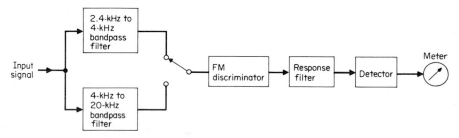

FIG. 16.59 Wow-and-flutter-meter block diagram. (*Courtesy of Audio Precision.*)

16.11.1   Standards for Measurement

Four major standards exist for the measurement of wow and flutter: IEC, Deutsche Industrie Normenausschus (DIN), National Association of Broadcasters (NAB), and Japanese Industrial Standard (JIS). All recommend the measurement of weighted frequency modulation of a test tone, but they differ in specific test-tone frequency, detector type, and/or meter ballistics (dynamic response). All the standards specify the same weighting curve for weighted measurements. This curve is shown in Fig. 16.60. The IEC and DIN standards are identical and recommend a 3.15-kHz test tone with a quasi-peak detection characteristic. Both

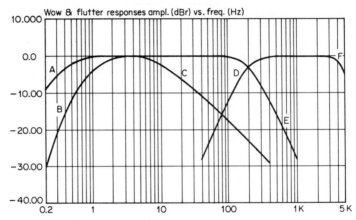

FIG. 16.60 Wow-and-flutter-analyzer response: *B-C* weighted, *A-E* unweighted, *A-F* wideband. (*Courtesy of Audio Precision.*)

NAB and JIS recommend a 3.0-kHz test tone but differ in detector type. NAB specifies an average-responding meter (rms-calibrated) with volume-unit (VU) meter ballistic characteristics. The JIS standard specifies an effective response which is similar to NAB detection but with a much longer integration time constant. Scrape flutter is normally measured with average detection rms-calibrated (NAB) characteristics.

Some engineers adhere to the NAB flutter standard, which specifies measuring with a flutter-free test tape on playback. This standard test tape is, by its nature, a very difficult thing to produce. Several laboratories specialize in making such test tapes to the required precision. However, professional machines which push the state of the art for performance will leave doubts as to the accuracy of the test tape.

For this reason the IEC flutter standard specifies that testing shall use a tape which has been recorded on the machine undergoing test. This cannot be done during the simultaneous record-playback mode. The time delay caused by the physical spacing of the record and playback heads will cancel flutter components at frequencies given by the following expression:

$$\text{Flutter frequency} = N \times \text{speed/gap-to-gap distance} \qquad (16.8)$$

$$= N/\text{time delay between heads} \qquad (16.9)$$

$$N = 1, 2, 3, \ldots$$

Components at frequencies near these will be reduced in amplitude as well. To avoid this the tape must be recorded, rewound, and played back.

Tape tension varies with the amount of tape on the supply and takeup reels. This requires that readings be taken at random intervals throughout the length of the test reel. It may be necessary to splice segments of the test tape into a full reel to test beginning, midreel, and end of reel performance. To randomize the phase of the various flutter components, the tape should be stopped between readings, and each roller and idler should be turned slightly by hand. This will tend to catch combinations of effects which, when occurring together, create large peak-speed deviations.

16.11.2 Related Measurements

To identify the source of the wow and flutter in the machine under test the ac output from the wow-and-flutter meter may be analyzed with a low-frequency spectrum analyzer. Because typical wow and flutter have components down to 0.5 Hz, it is extremely slow and tedious to do this with a sweeping-filter type of analyzer. The speed of an FFT approach is essential in obtaining accurate information in a reasonable measurement time. The high frequency resolution provided by an FFT analyzer also helps in separating components which may be relatively close in frequency such as a 5-Hz capstan imbalance and a 5.5-Hz servo resonance. The sweeping filters available in some wow-and-flutter meters are too wide a bandwidth to distinguish these components. An interesting example of the use of spectrum analysis of wow and flutter was in the Watergate tape-recording investigation. By analyzing the spectrum of the wow and flutter on the hum products during the famous 18-min gap, it was possible to identify the machine used to make the erasure.

Magnetic recording tape often has flaws in its surface coating which introduce fluctuations in the recorded level. These are called dropouts and represent one of the major performance factors between various brands of tape. Standards have been developed which concern the measurement of dropouts and their annoyance factor. They depend upon characterizing the width and depth of the dropout as shown in Fig. 16.61. The tape is recorded with a 3150-Hz tone, and the level is

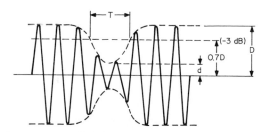

FIG. 16.61 Measurement of dropouts.

monitored on playback. The width of the dropout is measured in milliseconds from the time when the signal decreases by 3 dB from the nominal level to the time when it returns to within 3 dB of nominal. The ultimate depth of the dropout is also measured and used to grade the dropout. The resulting score, ranging from 2 to 12, for each dropout is based on both depth and duration. By adding them to measures of how often in a given time interval the dropouts occur a total score is reached.

Surface irregularities in tape will also result in high-frequency variations in amplitude. These are discussed by Manquen in his paper on scrape flutter.[18] They result in amplitude modulation which appears as modulation-noise sidebands on signals recorded on the tape. Recall that SMPTE IM measures the amplitude modulation of a high-frequency tone by a low-frequency tone. By recording a high-frequency tone with no low-frequency tone present, a conventional SMPTE analyzer may be used to measure this effect. The modulation noise will be demodulated by the analyzer and will appear as noise in the SMPTE IM measurement. This makes an excellent test of tape quality and is used by some recording studios to test incoming batches of tape before use. However, no standards exist to date for these measurements, and the absolute readings obtained will depend greatly on the model of wow-and-flutter meter used.

Another important measurement on recording devices is speed accuracy and drift. This is measured with a standard test tape or disk which has a stable frequency recorded on it. Changes in speed will produce a change in frequency which can be measured with a frequency counter. The frequency is monitored on playback as a function of time. The percentage difference between the measured value and the recorded value represents the percentage speed error. Changes in this value over the length of the tape are the speed drift. A plot of the speed drift and wow and flutter for a typical cassette recorder is shown in Fig. 16.62.

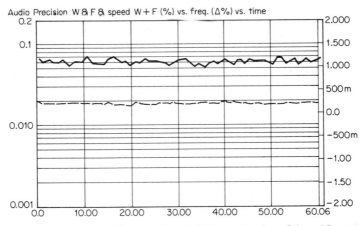

FIG. 16.62 Wow and flutter and speed drift as a function of time. (*Courtesy of Audio Precision.*)

16.12 AUDIOMETRIC MEASUREMENTS

Audiometric measurements are measurements of hearing acuity and related characteristics of the ear. Audiometers are unique in the field of audio measurements in that the device under test is a person. This invokes many measurement problems that are well known to psychologists but are quite foreign to audio engineers. These stem from the subjective aspects of people's response to stimuli and the difficulty in obtaining a quantifiable response from the subject.

The fundamental measurement in audiology is that of the ear's threshold sensitivity. This is commonly performed with a sine-wave (*pure-tone* in audiological parlance) stimulus presented over headphones. A tone is presented to the subject, who responds as to whether it is audible or not. If it is, the amplitude is lowered by 15 dB and the signal is presented again. If it is not, the amplitude is raised by 15 dB and the signal is presented again. This process is repeated until the threshold is found. After it is found, several more stimulus-response cycles are performed with a 5-dB-step size to bracket the threshold. A flowchart from Martin[19] illustrating this process is shown in Fig. 16.63. The levels are specified in decibels HTL, which refers to decibels above the standardized "average" hearing thresholds for humans in this test. A level of 0 dB HTL at any frequency will be just audible to an average listener.

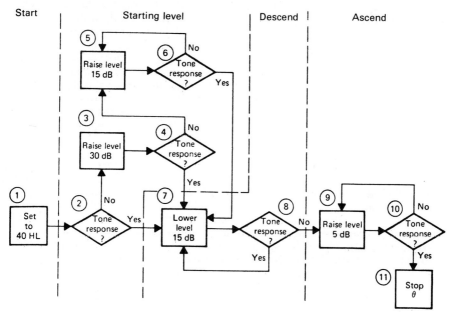

FIG. 16.63 Flowchart showing the procedure for pure-tone audiometry with masking. (*From F. N. Martin*, Introduction to Audiology, *Prentice-Hall, Englewood Cliffs, N.J., 1975.*)

Instructions for Flow Chart

1. Start with tone at 40 dB HTL.
2. Is there response to the tone?
   Yes. Proceed to 7.
   No. Proceed to 3.
3. Raise level 30 dB.
4. Is there response to the tone?
   Yes. Proceed to 7.
   No. Proceed to 5.
5. Raise level 15 dB.
6. Is there response to the tone?
   Yes. Proceed to 7.
   No. Return to 5.
7. Lower level 15 dB.
8. Is there response to the tone?
   Yes. Return to 7.
   No. Proceed to 9.
9. Raise level 5 dB.
10. Is there response to the tone?
    Yes. Proceed to 11.
    No. Return to 9.
11. Stop! Threshold.

HTL translates to a sound pressure level (SPL) which will depend on the stimulus frequency in roughly the same way as the Fletcher-Munson hearing-threshold curve described earlier. Audiometric testing is generally performed at a few fixed frequencies: 250 Hz, 500 Hz, 1 kHz, 2 kHz, 4 kHz, 8 kHz. These are graphed with O's and X's for the right and left ears respectively and connected by lines. A typical audiometric recording form is shown in Fig. 16.64.

Though pure-tone audiometry may seem straightforward, it rapidly becomes complicated when the person being tested has elevated thresholds (is hard of hearing) in one or both ears. When sufficient level is applied to the ear being tested to approach the subject's hearing threshold, the sound may leak to the opposite ear. This will result in the subject hearing the sound in the ear not being tested, invalidating the results. This leakage may be airborne around the head or be via bone conduction through the skull.

The solution to this problem is to apply to the untested ear a masking signal of a sufficient level to mask the test tone. The level of the masker chosen must be high enough to guarantee masking but low enough not to leak to the ear under test and interfere with the threshold determination. Usually the masking signal is wideband white or pink noise, but narrowband maskers may be used. The flowchart for this procedure is shown in Fig. 16.65. The thresholds obtained with masking are displayed on the audiogram by using triangles and squares for the right and left ears, respectively. Selecting the proper masker level is often a difficult task, requiring experience and some thought about hearing loss in the particular subject being tested. Indeed, for highly unequal hearing loss in the two ears it may not be possible to mask the better ear correctly. For a complete discussion of the masking problem see Martin.[20]

Pure-tone audiometry is also performed by using a vibrator placed on the subject's skull bone. This allows bypassing occlusions of and damage to the middle ear, testing only the inner ear and the neural portion of the auditory system. By placing the vibrator on the bone mass directly behind the outer ear some degree of selectivity between the two ears may be obtained. It is usually necessary to augment this procedure with a masking signal presented via earphones if any significant asymmetrical loss is encountered. Bone-conduction thresholds are graphed by using $>$ and $<$ symbols for the right and left ears, respectively. Masked bone-conduction thresholds are graphed with closed arrows.

An alternative to conventional pure-tone audiometry is Békésy audiometry. A tone is applied to the ear under test, and the subject is given a control button which raises the level when pressed and decreases the level when released. The subject is instructed to maintain the level of the tone at threshold. The level is then plotted on a graph versus time. The stimulus starts at low frequency, incrementing every inch or so of pen travel, tracing out the audiogram on the chart paper as shown in Fig. 16.66. Békésy audiometers are commonly used for simple audiometric screening when large numbers of people must be tested and time or skill availability is important. They are not as reliable as conventional audiometry because a skilled operator is not involved to assess the validity of each measurement. Masking is difficult to design into a Békésy machine, and there is no provision for detailed diagnostic tests to determine the source of the hearing loss (conductive, sensory neural, etc.).

Problems are sometimes encountered with patients attempting to fool the audiologist. This may be done for a number of reasons: insurance claims, fear of the social stigma of wearing a hearing aid, etc. These situations require the involvement of a skilled professional audiologist to identify that deception is taking place and to obtain accurate data anyway. Often there will be clues to the fraud because of inconsistencies in the test results.

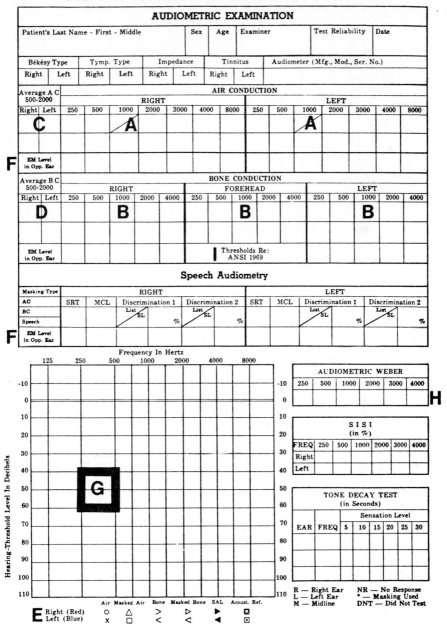

FIG. 16.64 An audiometric worksheet. Identifying information is listed regarding the patient, examiner, and audiometer used. Data include the following: (*a*) Air-conduction thresholds (numerical); (*b*) bone-conduction thresholds (numerical); (*c*) pure-tone air-conduction average; (*d*) pure-tone bone-conduction average; (*e*) plotting symbols; (*f*) effective masking level in the nearest ear used, where applicable, during air-conduction and bone-conduction tests; (*g*) squares formed 1 octave (across) by 20 (down); (*h*) audiometric results in webers; and (*i*) indication that the hearing-threshold levels are with reference to ANSI-1969 values. (*From F. N. Martin,* Introduction to Audiology, *Prentice-Hall, Englewood Cliffs, N.J., 1975.*)

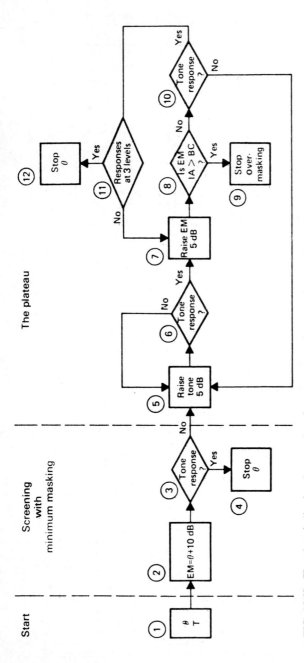

FIG. 16.65 Flowchart indicating the procedure for pure-tone audiometry with masking. (*From F. N. Martin*, Clinical Audiometry and Masking, *Bobbs-Merrill, Indianapolis, 1972.*)

Instructions for Flow Chart
1. Start with tone at threshold in test ear.
2. Put EM into nontest ear at threshold level of nontest ear. The additional 10 dB shown in block 2 may be eliminated if that safety factor is included in the original calibration of effective masking.
3. Is there response to the tone?
   Yes. Proceed to 4.
   No. Proceed to 5.
4. Stop! Unmasked threshold is correct.
5. Raise tone 5 dB.
6. Is there response to the tone?
   Yes. Proceed to 7.
   No. Return to 5.
7. Raise EM level 5 dB.
8. Is EM-IA greater than *BC* of test ear?
   Yes. Proceed to 9.
   No. Proceed to 10.
9. Stop! Overmasking has taken place.
10. Is there response to the tone?
    Yes. Proceed to 11.
    No. Return to 5.
11. Are there responses to the tone at three consecutive EM levels?
    Yes. Proceed to 12.
    No. Return to 7.
12. Stop! This is masked threshold.

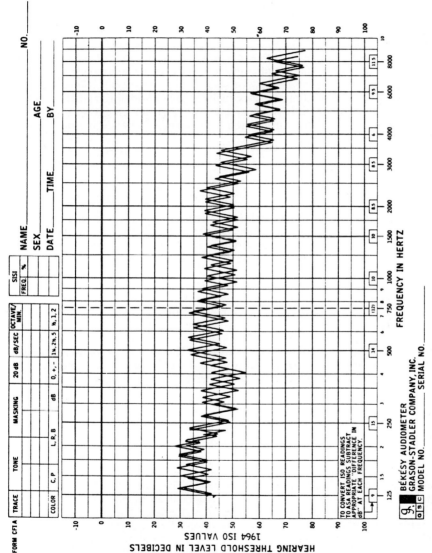

FIG. 16.66 Typical Békésy audiogram results. The downward peaks of the graph show where the patient pressed the hand switch, indicating that the tone was heard, automatically causing it to decrease in intensity. The upward peaks of the graph show where the patient released the hand switch, indicating that the tone could no longer be heard, causing it automatically to increase in intensity. *(From F. N. Martin, Introduction to Audiology, Prentice-Hall, Englewood Cliffs, N.J., 1975.)*

16.61

One example of a technique used to identify this behavior is the swing test. Speech is presented to the subject in one ear at a level near threshold. Questions are asked of the subject to test how much of the text has been understood. Key words which would radically alter the meaning of the sentence presented are presented in the other ear. Most subjects will not notice that the other ear received one word of the sentence but will still hear it if it is above threshold. If the ear which receives the swing word really has the hearing loss determined by the audiogram, the subject will not have heard the word and will misinterpret the sentence. Similar techniques involve changing the level of one word in a sentence to verify that the threshold in a given ear is accurate. Again, the change in level will not be noticed, and the person attempting to deceive the audiologist will be tripped up.

There are many more audiometric tests, including speech-intelligibility testing, eardrum-impedance testing, tone-in-noise tests, and short-increment-sensitivity-index (SISI) testing. For a good introduction to these and other audiometric tests, see Martin.[20]

16.13 SOUND-LEVEL METERS

Measurement of SPL is a simple extension of amplitude measurements to the acoustical domain. A sound-level meter consists of a microphone, amplifiers, weighting filters, and a voltmeter. The circuitry of a sound-level meter is essentially the same as that of a weighted voltmeter, with the addition of a microphone. (The typical block diagram was shown in Fig. 16.11.) The signal is picked up by the microphone and amplified to a convenient level. The ac signal is converted to a dc value and displayed on a meter or digital readout. The conversion is normally performed by an rms detector with a high-crest-factor capability. Acoustic signals often have large crest factors which require care if the signals are to be measured accurately. If required, an appropriate weighting filter is inserted after the amplification and before the ac-to-dc converter. The most common weighting filter in use for sound-level measurements is the *A*-weighting curve. It provides an approximation to the level which would be perceived by a human listening to the sound.

16.14 TIME-DELAY SPECTROMETRY (TDS)

When measuring loudspeakers in rooms, it becomes difficult to separate the response of the loudspeaker from that of the room. The sound emitted from the loudspeaker is picked up by the measuring microphone as intended. Also picked up by the microphone is the sound reflected from the boundaries of the room. This problem was the impetus for the invention of time-delay spectrometry (TDS) by Heyser.[21] The original TDS system was a modified sweeping spectrum analyzer with a tracking-signal generator. A fixed-frequency offset was inserted between the analyzer-filter frequency and the tracking-generator frequency. Figure 16.67 diagrams the operation of a TDS analyzer. The tracking-generator output is fed to the loudspeaker under test. The time delay between the loudspeaker and the microphone results in the delayed sweep shown in the diagram. At any instant the direct-sound wave received by the microphone will be lower in frequency than

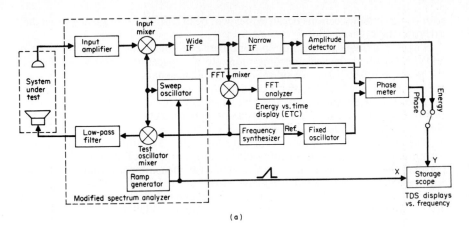

(a)

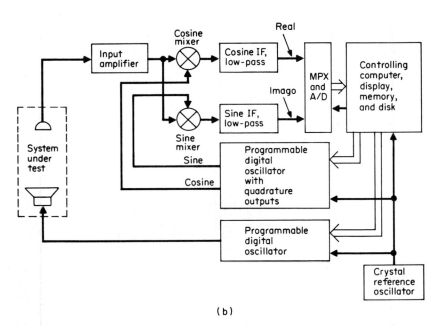

(b)

FIG. 16.67 Block diagram of two TDS measurement approaches. (*a*) TDS implementation by traditional means. (*b*) Block diagram of the TEF 10. [*From G. Stanley, "TDS Computing," Audio, 38–42 (November 1983).*]

the signal emitted from the speaker. Reflections from the walls of the room result in a signal delayed further in time and therefore still lower in frequency. By delaying the frequency sweep of the spectrum analyzer-filter frequency relative to the tracking-generator frequency the direct-sound wave may be measured. The bandpass-filter response will reject the reflections since they lag behind in frequency. By offsetting the filter frequency further, any of the reflections may be measured instead of the direct sound. The bandpass-filter response will reject both the direct sound and other reflections because they will be of a different frequency when they arrive at the microphone.

There is a frequency-resolution–time-between-reflections tradeoff inherent in TDS. When the reflections become more closely spaced than one wavelength at the lowest frequency of analysis, it is impossible to separate their effects. This sets a lower frequency limit on the TDS analysis equal to the path length difference between the direct sound and the reflection from the closest surface. However, this limitation also exists in other forms of signal selective measurement such as FFT analysis and gated tone-burst analysis.

The basic TDS measurement displays the amplitude-versus-frequency response of a system. The resulting plot of amplitude as a function of frequency is called the energy-frequency curve (EFC). TDS measurements may also be performed with the phase-versus-frequency information included. This gives a more complete description of the frequency-domain behavior of the system under test. By a simple Fourier transform of the output of the TDS analyzer a display of

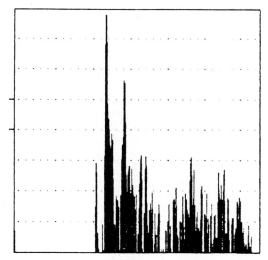

FIG. 16.68 Typical energy-time curve (ETC). [*From G. Stanley, "TDS Computing,"* Audio, *38–42 (November 1983).*]

Vertical	6 dB per division with base of display at 39.8 dB; 0 dB located at 0.00002 Pa
Horizontal	0 μs or O m to 20,154 μs or 6.91274 m
Scale	1.8900E+00 m/in or 6.4410E m/cm, 5510 μs/in or 2169 μs/cm
Line spacing	50.5106 μs or 1.73251E-2 m
Line width	68.6944 μs or 2.25622E-2 m
Sweep rate	1001.91 Hz/s
Sweep range	200.24 Hz to 19,998.10 Hz
Window file name	A: Hamming. WBT
Input configuration	Inverting with 18 dB of input gain and 9 dB of IF gain

signal energy versus time may be displayed. This is referred to as the energy-time curve (ETC). An example of this display is shown in Fig. 16.68. Indeed, the EFC and ETC are views of the same data from different domains.

For an excellent treatment of time-delay spectrometry, the reader is referred to the papers by Heyser[21,22] and Stanley[23] as well as the newsletter and *Tech-Topics* published by Syn-Aud-Con.

16.15   AUTOMATED MEASUREMENTS

Audio testing has become more complex and time-consuming as the performance levels of the devices under test have steadily improved. This has required more skill on the part of the equipment operator and has naturally raised the cost of such testing. Increasing production volumes and decreasing product prices have increased the need for economical testing alternatives. This challenge has been met by automating many tests which previously required laborious operations.

This has been accomplished with programmable (computer-controlled) audio test equipment. This equipment permits making multiple measurements and recording the results automatically, with data presented to the user in whatever form is desired. The user may use this flexibility in a number of different ways, depending on the requirements of the application. In a manufacturing environment the extra power of a programmable measurement system may be used to reduce the skill level of the operator and thus reduce labor costs and improve reliability of the results. Alternatively, the programmable system may be used to increase the thoroughness of testing, resulting in a more reliable product for the customer. In an engineering environment the programmable system can deliver data in a fraction of the time previously spent, freeing the engineer for more creative tasks. The computational capability of the system may also be used to provide data reduction and display in formats never before available.

The typical programmable audio measurement system consists of an oscillator, a voltmeter, a distortion analyzer, a frequency counter, a phasemeter, a wow-and-flutter meter, and some means for switching and routing signals. All these devices are connected to a computer via an appropriate interface bus. Figure 16.69 shows a block diagram of a typical computer-based audio test system. The computer may have peripherals such as a printer, a plotter, a mass storage system, etc. The computer commands the generator to output a signal appropriate for the test to be performed. It then selects the measuring device and measuring mode. The computer may input readings from the equipment, check for settled data, and process the data for display, storage, and decision making as needed.

By making a series of measurements under various test conditions the system can completely characterize the device under test. The resultant data may be displayed in graphic or tabular form, may be compared with predefined pass-fail limits, or may be stored in a file for use in establishing statistical information. For a more thorough discussion of the advantages and tradeoffs in a programmable audio test system, see Metzler.[24]

The most common method for connecting test equipment to a computer is via the IEEE (Institute of Electrical and Electronics Engineers)-488 interface bus, commonly called GPIB for general-purpose interface bus. This bus has the distinct advantage of being standardized, at least in terms of the hardware interconnection. Equipment available from many manufacturers connects via this bus. However, the number of audio-specific test devices available is significantly

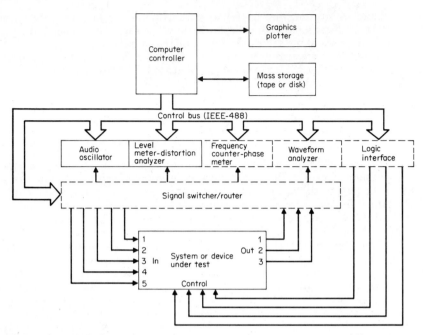

FIG. 16.69 Block diagram of a typical automated audio test system. Items shown dashed are optional, depending on the particular application. *(Journal of the Audio Engineering Society.)*

smaller. This is due partly to the smaller market for such equipment and partly to the difficulty of combining computer-control capability and high-performance analog circuitry. The noise problems and performance tradeoffs in combining high-performance analog circuits and digital computer circuits in the same package are considerable. Cabot[7] discusses some of these problems in the design of a GPIB programmable distortion analyzer and oscillator.

The latest developments in automated measurements are personal-computer-based measurement instruments. These use commonly available personal computers for the human interface and computational functions of the test equipment. The idea is to remove as much of the processing circuitry from the test equipment as is practical and place it in the computer. This allows the test equipment to concentrate on the collection of data or measurements and not on the human interaction requirements.

The manufacturing volumes of personal computers are orders of magnitude greater than those of instrumentation controllers or of instruments themselves. This gives a tremendous cost advantage to the personal-instrumentation approach because it leverages off the high computational power per dollar of the computer. Most such instruments omit the front-panel displays and controls found on conventional equipment. These components typically account for 20 percent of the cost of electronic instrumentation. Another advantage of the personal-instrument approach is the flexibility provided by the software-based features. By providing a new disk with an appropriate code, entire instrument functions may be changed or added.

The close coupling of computer processing with instrument operation also allows optimization of measurement speed and settling. Characteristics of instrument operation such as settling after range changes and filter response times may be directly accounted for in program operation. In most personal instruments the hardware is mapped into the computer memory or input-output (I/O) space. The protocol overhead associated with the GPIB bus may therefore be eliminated, speeding computer operation. By including appropriate software hooks the computer may also be interfaced to conventional GPIB equipment if a necessary measurement function is not otherwise available.

The block diagram of a typical personal-computer-based test system is shown in Fig. 16.70. This system provides all the common measurement functions in audio. It consists of a signal generator which provides various combinations of sine-wave, square-wave, and random-noise test signals. These are mixed to produce the desired waveform and passed to a variable-gain stage for setting output level. This signal is amplified and passed through an amplifier to the output transformer, which provides a balanced and floating output. The resulting signal is the stimulus for most system measurements.

The output from the device under test is connected to the voltmeter input. This is a balanced differential input which allows rejection of ground loops and common-mode interference. The signal is amplified as necessary to obtain adequate amplitude for the subsequent measurement stages. These include the frequency counter, phasemeter, wow-and-flutter meter, input voltmeter, and distortion-analysis circuits. A second input channel allows testing stereo systems and provides the second input signal required for the phasemeter. The level, frequency, and distortion measurement circuits switch between the two inputs. The phasemeter is always connected to both.

The frequency counter is a period-based measurement circuit, enabling quick measurements at low frequencies. The phasemeter employs two sets of edge-triggered set-reset flip-flops to cancel the effects of signal asymmetry and even-order distortion on the phase measurement. Both the phasemeter and the frequency counter include special comparators to convert the input waveform to a square wave. These comparators find the average voltage of the signal and set the comparison thresholds and hysteresis appropriately. This improves rejection of noise and other interfering signals.

The notch-bandpass filter can either remove components for harmonic-distortion testing or selectively filter components for spectrum analysis. The intermodulation-distortion-measurement circuits access the signal at this point to perform the filtering or demodulation functions necessary for their particular measurement. A voltmeter constantly monitors the input to the distortion measurement circuits. This provides the reference-level information for percentage or decibel distortion readings. It also allows simultaneous measurement of input voltage when distortion measurements are made.

The output of the distortion-measurement circuits is amplified by an autoranging gain stage. Various weighting and bandwidth-limiting filters are applied to the signal at this point. Any one of three low-pass filters and any one of three high-pass filters may be switched in. Additionally, a weighting filter such as an *A*-weighting or a CCIR-weighting filter may be selected. The filtered signal is converted to direct current by one of three detectors: rms-, average-, or peak-responding converters. This current is then measured and sent to the computer as reading information.

One aspect which becomes critical when automation is introduced to the measurement process is data settling. When a stimulus is applied to a device under test, the device takes a finite time to reach steady-state operation. This effect is

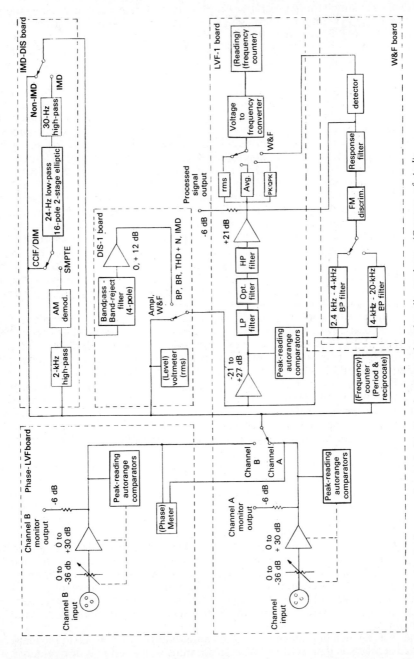

FIG. 16.70 Block diagram of a typical personal-computer-based audio analyzer. (*Courtesy of Audio Precision.*)

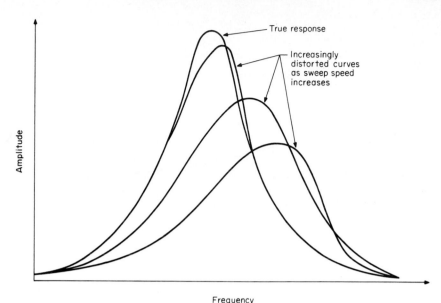

FIG. 16.71 Effect of sweep speed on response measurement.

especially pronounced with high-Q bandpass filters or devices such as compressors or limiters. The settling time is usually a function of frequency, being longer at low frequencies and in devices which are designed to operate at low frequencies. Equipment which performs a sweep at a fixed rate regardless of the measured data will introduce errors in response if the speed is set too fast. An example of this is shown in Fig. 16.71 for the case of a high-Q bandpass filter. At an infinitely slow sweep rate the true response of the filter will be measured. As the speed is increased, the peak amplitude of the curve will be reduced and the peak frequency will shift in the direction of the sweep. If the sweep is of increasing frequency with time, the peak in the response curve will be shifted upward. There is also a distortion of the curve shape. As the sweep rate increases, these effects become more pronounced.

There may also be time delays between the application of the stimulus and the resulting output. This is common with satellite links or tape recorders in a simultaneous record-play mode, both of which produce delays of several hundred milliseconds. Audio time-delay units and reverberators can produce delays as long as several seconds.

All these times are substantially longer than the reading rate of quality audio test equipment. A trained audio engineer or test technician using manually operated equipment will compensate mentally for these delays, waiting the required time for the measurements to settle. With automated test equipment this function must be performed by the computer. The computer software must compare successive readings and, using information supplied by the user about the device under test, make decisions on when the data are adequately settled. This will ensure data integrity and repeatability.

One approach to implementing a settling algorithm, illustrated in Fig. 16.72, is employed in Audio Precision System 1. The most recent reading from the hardware is compared with previous readings. When it falls within a predetermined

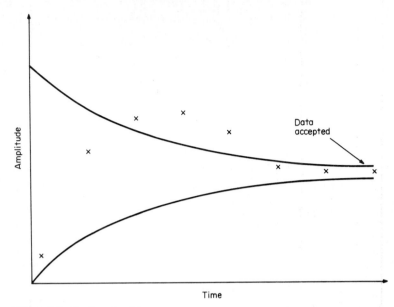

FIG. 16.72   Settling algorithm.

window, the reading is accepted as valid data. This window is usually tapered so that progressively older data are weighted less heavily. This is designed to follow the exponential settling characteristics of the measurement hardware and typical test devices. For more stringent testing requirements the window may be made flat instead of tapered. This requires all points used in the algorithm to be within a fixed percentage of each other.

For the example data shown in Fig. 16.72, seven comparison points are used. The current data point is compared with the previous data point to within the specified tolerance percentage. The point before it is compared with the current data point at 2 times the programmed tolerance. The third point back is compared at 4 times and the fourth point back at 8 times the programmed tolerance, etc. If any of these comparisons fail, the data will not be accepted. Whether accepted or not, this point replaces the previous reading in the algorithm. The older readings are all pushed back by 1, and the oldest reading is discarded. Measurements of very small quantities are often disturbed by interfering noise. This noise will often produce a fixed amplitude of reading jitter. As the signal amplitude decreases, this will represent a greater percentage of the reading. It is therefore helpful to include a *floor* value in the settling algorithm which passes data points closer to one another than the floor amount.

REFERENCES

1. R. Dolby, D. Robinson, and K. Gundry, "A Practical Noise Measurement Method," *J. Audio Eng. Soc.,* **27**(3), 149 (1979).

2. H. Moller, "Computerized Audio Testing," Audio Engineering Society preprint 2251 (1985).

3. D. Jensen, "High Frequency Phase Response Specifications—Useful or Misleading? Audio Engineering Society preprint 2398 (November 1986).

4. J. R. Hassall and K. Zaveri, *Acoustic Noise Measurements,* 4th ed., Bruel and Kjaer, Copenhagen, 1979.

5. P. Bauman, S. Lipshitz, and J. Vanderkooy, "Cepstral Techniques for Transducer Measurement," Audio Engineering Society preprint 2172 (October 1984).

6. R. C. Cabot, "A Comparison of Nonlinear Distortion Measurement Methods," Audio Engineering Society preprint 1638 (May 1980).

7. Ibid., "Design Factors in a Programmable Distortion Measurement System," *J. Audio Eng. Soc., 32*(12) (December 1984).

7a. Ibid., "Perception of Nonlinear Distortion," Audio Engineering Society preprint C1004 (May 1984).

8. G. Stanley and D. McLaughlin, "Transient Intermodulation Distortion and Measurement," Audio Engineering Society preprint 1308 (November 1977).

9. P. Ladegaard, *Swept Distortion Measurements—An Effective Tool for Revealing TIM in Amplifiers with Good Subjective Correlation to Subjective Evaluation,* B&K Application Note 17-234, 1977.

10. A. N. Theile, "Measurement of Nonlinear Distortion in a Bandlimited System," *J. Audio Eng. Soc., 31,* 443–445 (June 1983).

11. R. Small, "Total Difference Frequency Distortion: Practical Measurements, *J. Audio Eng. Soc., 34*(6), 427 (June 1986).

12. E. Leinonen, M. Otala, and J. Curl, "Method for Measuring Transient Intermodulation Distortion," Audio Engineering Society preprint 1185 (October 1976).

13. P. Skritek, "Simplified Measurement of Squarewave/Sinewave and Related Distortion Test Methods," Audio Engineering Society preprint 2195 (1985).

14. B. Hofer, "Practical Extended Range DIM Measurements," Audio Engineering preprint 2334 (March 1986).

15. M. Petri-Larmi et al., "Threshold of Audibility of Transient Distortion," Audio Engineering Society preprint 1392 (1978).

16. H. M. Tremaine, *Audio Cyclopedia,* Howard W. Sams, Indianapolis, 1975.

17. S. Linkwitz, "Narrow Band Testing of Acoustical Systems," Audio Engineering Society preprint 1342 (May 1978).

18. D. Manquen, "Measurement of High Frequency Scrape Flutter," Audio Engineering Society preprint 1637 (May 1980).

19. F. N. Martin, *Clinical Audiometry and Masking,* Bobbs-Merrill, Indianapolis, 1972.

20. Ibid., *Introduction to Audiology,* Prentice-Hall, Englewood Cliffs, N.J., 1975.

21. R. C. Heyser, "Acoustical Measurements by Time Delay Spectrometry," *J. Audio Eng. Soc., 15* (October 1967).

22. Ibid., "Some New Audio Measurements," Audio Engineering Society preprint 1008 (May 1975).

23. G. Stanley, "TDS Computing," *Audio,* 38–42 (November 1983).

24. R. E. Metzler, "Automated Audio Test Systems for Professional Audio Test Requirements," *dB, 17*(3) (March 1983).

BIBLIOGRAPHY

Bauman, P., S. Lipshitz, and J. Vanderkooy: "Cepstral Techniques for Transducer Measurement: Part II," Audio Engineering Society preprint 2302 (October 1985).

Berman, J. M., and L. R. Fincham: "The Application of Digital Techniques to the Measurement of Loudspeakers," *J. Audio Eng. Soc.,* **25** (June 1977).

Cabot, R. C.: "Measurement of Audio Signal Slew Rate," Audio Engineering Society preprint 1414 (November 1978).

Lipshitz, S., T. Scott, and J. Vanderkooy: "Increasing the Audio Measurement Capability of FFT Analyzers by Microcomputer Post-Processing," Audio Engineering Society preprint 2050 (October 1983).

Metzler, R. E.: "Automated Audio Testing," *Studio Sound* (August 1985).

———— and B. Hofer: "Wow and Flutter Measurements," *Audio Precision 1 Users' Manual,* July 1986, chap. 15.

Moller, H.: *Electroacoustic Measurements,* B&K Application Note 16-035.

———— and C. Thompsen: *Swept Electroacoustic Measurements of Harmonic, Difference Frequency and Intermodulation Distortion,* B&K Application Note 15-098.

Otala, M., and E. Leinonen: "The Theory of Transient Intermodulation Distortion," *IEEE Trans. Acoust. Speech Signal Process.,* **ASSP-25**(1) (February 1977).

Preis, D.: "A Catalog of Frequency and Transient Responses," *J. Audio Eng. Soc.,* **24** (June 1976).

Schrock, C.: *The Tektronix Cookbook of Standard Audio Measurements,* Tektronix Inc., Beaverton, Oreg., 1975.

Vanderkooy, J.: "Another Approach to Time Delay Spectrometry," Audio Engineering Society preprint 2285 (October 1985).

CHAPTER 17
STANDARDS AND RECOMMENDED PRACTICES

Daniel Queen

Daniel Queen Associates, New York

17.1 STANDARDIZATION REQUIREMENTS

17.1.1 Industrial Dependency on Standards

Broadly stated, industrial development is dependent to a large degree upon the adoption of system and component standards to permit the exchange of products and services. Thus, operational interchangeability is a prime consideration in the formulation of standards.

System Performance. In a narrower view, a group of standards may be dedicated to a specific system to ensure that the system is designed, tested, and operated to meet, first, the user's requirements; second, the interface requirements of other interconnected systems; and, third, the performance requirements of the overall system.

17.1.2 Scope of Standards Activities

Government Regulation. In order to permit the end user, both professional and consumer, to acquire products that meet the performance requirements dictated by the intended application, test procedures and performance standards are necessary. These may be by government edict in the case of operations, such as broadcasting, or products for which either quality or safety for consumer protection may be a criterion.

Industry Regulation. In addition to government regulation, there exists a large body of technical information consisting of recommended standards and practices that represent the consensus among those involved in a particular industry. These recommendations and industry-sponsored standards represent good engineering practice that ensures practical manufacturability within the current state of the art and, by consent of those skilled in the art, may serve as the basis for the generation of regulatory action by appropriate government agencies.

International Relationships. Because of the increase in foreign markets and the interchange of recorded information and entertainment products, the need extends beyond national borders and consequently has resulted in international standards activities involving industry representatives, professional and trade organizations, and government regulatory bodies. In fact, at present over 200 international committees and a comparable number of domestic groups are involved in the development of electrotechnical standards necessary to facilitate international exchange of goods and services as well as to coordinate intellectual, scientific, technological, and economic activities.

Development of International Standards Organizations. The demand for a common language and for mutual agreement on technical items prompted the beginning of international work, which dates back to the establishment in 1875 of the International Bureau of Weights and Measures and in 1904 of the International Electrotechnical Commission (IEC). Much later, in 1926, the International Federation of National Standardizing Associations (ISA) was organized to cope with the growing international exchange of goods and services. Replaced in 1942 with the United Nations Standards Coordinating Committee (UNSCC), after 6 years it was reorganized as the International Standards Organization (ISO).

The ISO technical committees cover the fields of audio equipment and systems, cinematography, recording, and consumer questions in addition to maintaining liaison with the standardizing committees of national professional organizations, for example, in the United States the American National Standards Institute (ANSI).

17.1.3 Process of Standards Development

Standards proposals are derived from industry-sponsored committees and working groups composed of voluntary individuals from industry, government, and academic areas. In the United States the government representative's status generally is that of a nonvoting observer. The inputs he or she receives may be used by the related government agency in formulating any regulations deemed necessary.

The industry committees, sponsored by engineering societies such as the Audio Engineering Society (AES) or trade associations such as the Recording Industry Association of America (RIAA), are formed and assigned areas of expertise by agreement among the sponsoring parent organizations.

Usually, a standards committee will not immediately develop recommendations for a new technology. A careful balance is maintained so that publication of specifications, tests, or performance limits does not stifle creative development. As new technology (for example, digital recording) comes into existence, many valid systems and methods will be suggested. A period of test and experience must determine which ones are widely accepted.

Typical Examples. In the past such a process generally proceeded in an orderly manner; thus the evolution of the long-playing (LP) record was able to include a variation on its configuration: the 45 r/min 7-in disk. In this case the economic consequences to both producer and consumer were minimal. Compatible hardware was quickly and inexpensively developed.

Similarly, in the case of stereo recording the process proceeded without complications, although the time span between initial development and final configuration was longer. In the course of it many recordings were made and issued which, while playable, suffered seriously in quality when used on noncompatible equipment.

With the coming of the quadraphonic record, systems came into the market having no compatibility and requiring expensive playback equipment which could not easily be adapted from one format to the other. The standardization process did not work well in this case, perhaps contributing to the demise of the development.

The compact cassette, on the other hand, was developed and licensed by a single company, which published its own closely controlled standard. Thus, by the time that national and international standards committees began work, the configuration was well established by testing and modifications in practice.

Sources.   Hundreds of published standards on audio and acoustics are now available from dozens of sources. The majority in the United States are published by various industry associations. Fewer are available as American National Standards and still fewer as international standards. Besides American National Standards, standards are available in English from other national standards committees, including those of Canada, Australia, and Great Britain. In addition, standards are sometimes available in English from Japan, Germany, the Netherlands, the Soviet Union, Italy, and other industrialized countries.

17.2   TYPES OF STANDARDS

Standards used in audio fall into several principal categories: standards setting limits of performance, configuration standards, methods of measurement, procedures for operating equipment, and terminology. (See Sec. 17.8.)

Existing standards in the audio field fall into several categories. The most commonly recognized category is the *configuration standard,* which provides dimensional and operating limits for a device or a process. Such standards have provided us with interchangeable analog tape recordings, for example. Another category is the *method for measurement,* which is sometimes combined with a configuration standard and provides repeatable and reproduceable tests for a device or a process. Other categories include *standard definitions, procedures,* and *performance levels.* Such standards usually arise out of a need in the industry and are put into writing by several organizations not always in concert with one another.

17.2.1   Configuration

A much more common category of standards contains configurations. Configurations include dimensions of media for recording such as compact cassettes, disks, and audio tape. Such configuration standards may also designate the position of tracks on recording media or the protocols for digital audio.

Configuration standards may exist also for some types of marking, particularly for audiovisual equipment. Others provide uniform designations for controls, inputs, and outputs.

Configuration standards for digital audio are being developed through similar processes initiated by individual companies and consortia. Typical is the configuration of the compact disk. However, new configurations for professional audio equipment continue to appear, partially in response to rapid development of processor technologies. Thus, the activity of professional audio configuration standards is concerned mainly with facilitating the interfacing of such equipment.

17.2.2 Measurement

Much more common are standards which can be generally categorized as methods for measurement. Such standards usually do not mandate the characteristics to be measured but provide methods for measuring when those characteristics are specified. However, some are published for the purpose of listing the characteristics which must be specified for a product to be certified under the standards, together with methods for measuring the required characteristics. Others may only reference other standards for methods of measurement.

Thus, the AES publishes a recommended practice for specifying loudspeaker components used in sound reinforcement systems or in professional audio. The standard, also issued by the American National Standards Institute (ANSI), is a listing of the characteristics which are needed by system designers in order to develop adequately either components or their systems.

17.2.3 Procedures

Procedural standards are usually issued as recommendations from professional organizations. For example, the AES has published a procedure for plane-wave-tube measurement which includes a review of construction methods for the tube, long a task more craftlike than conceptual. More often, procedural standards provide means for establishing a particular type of audio environment. Such procedures are sometimes published as appendixes of standards for measurement. An example is the ISO standard method for measuring the response of cinemas, which includes in its appendix recommendations for the placement of loudspeakers so that the measurements will be valid.

17.2.4 Performance

Performance standards set specifications which equipment must meet in order to be certified according to the standard. For example, the IEC has a series of standards under the category 581 for the performance of high-fidelity equipment. In the United States there are no national standards of such scope, but there are industry standards for the performance of certain specialized types of audio equipment. For example, there are standards set by the National Association of Broadcasters (NAB) for tape recorders used in broadcasting. Similarly, performance limits on consumer audio tapes are published by the International Tape Association (ITA). The largest industry group influencing audio practice, particularly consumer audio equipment, the Electronic Industries Association (EIA), does not promulgate performance limits standards for such equipment.

17.2.5 Terminology

The final category is that of definitions. Nearly every standard contains a section on definitions of the terms used in it. Usually these are terms unique to the standard. In addition, by reference or implication, standards refer to various standard glossaries such as IEC Publication 50.

17.3 STANDARDS-MAKING ORGANIZATIONS

17.3.1 Government Regulatory Standardization

In most countries national governments sanction or organize standards-making organizations, usually for the purpose of issuing safety standards. Some countries, such as Germany and Japan, place most standards-making organizations in the governmental structure. Thus, Deutsche Industrie Normenausschus (DIN) and Japanese Standards Association (JSA) standards have some mandatory aspects for nationals. Most governments also sponsor the voluntary standards organizations associated with the IEC.

All countries issue regulatory standards published by government agencies, although such regulations are often references to existing voluntary standards.

The United States is unique in that voluntary standards, including those for safety, are usually written by nongovernmental organizations.

Metrological. Metrological standards in the United States are written by the National Bureau of Standards (NBS), which maintains the physical materials on which the standards are based. Thus basic reference quantities for mass, length, time, charge, and some of their derivatives are maintained by the NBS. The NBS also has published derivative research reports in the field of acoustics, such as reports on the measurement of sound power, but has left the publication of standards based on the research to the voluntary standards organizations.

Audio and Sound. In the audio field, United States government regulations relate to audio associated with broadcasting and to certain safety aspects of sound. Internationally, most nations are official sponsors of United Nations–controlled regulatory agencies such as the International Radio Consultative Committee (CCIR) and the International Telegraph and Telephone Consultative Committee (CCITT) and do not publish separate standards relating to audio. While in the past the Federal Communications Commission (FCC) has issued such standards in the United States, it, too, is beginning to follow the international regulations. FCC regulations relating to audio include performance limits for broadcasting and for communications.

Other agencies, such as the Environmental Protection Agency (EPA) and the Occupational Safety and Health Administration (OSHA), issue standards that can affect the amount of sound energy which may lawfully be produced by audio equipment.

17.3.2 Quasi-Governmental Standardization

Regional bodies producing audio-related standards are found mainly in Europe. Typical are the European Broadcast Union (EBU) and the International Radio and Television Organization (OIRT). They are sponsored by trading groups such as the European Economic Community (Common Market) and COMECON (the eastern European economic bloc).

The principal international regulatory bodies affecting audio are the CCIR, the Study Group on Television and Sound Transmission (CMTT), and the CCITT.

17.3.3 Voluntary Standardization

Commonly, when technologists refer to standards, they are thinking of voluntary consensus standards. Such standards carry the weight of regulation and of law only when adopted by regulatory agencies.

Voluntary consensus standards come about as a need is expressed by producers and users of products or processes. Such needs are usually expressed by trade organizations, producers, or users. In response, a standards-making organization will set up committees to discuss the need for the standard. If such a need can be shown, it will set up a writing or working group to attempt to develop the standard. The working group would consist of representatives of various producers and users. An effort is always made to get as wide a representation as possible so that no single interests are able to dominate the activities of the group. In the United States, in fact, such domination of the activities of the group can bring about serious legal problems.

The concept of consensus means that all parties involved in such working groups should agree substantially before a document is issued. This concept is carried through to the official standards-making bodies of the particular organizations. Such bodies are governed by careful rules and procedures which assure representative voting on the standards.

17.3.4 International and National Coordinators

Most industrialized countries have a national consensus standards organization which is generally associated with either or both the IEC and the ISO. In the United States the generally recognized standards organization and the one to which audio standards ultimately go is ANSI. Promulgation of a standard by ANSI carries the weight of a consensus of all interested groups, producers, and users rather than a consensus only of industry or of users. Nevertheless, even its standards are only voluntary in scope: they carry no regulatory weight.

International Standards Organization (ISO). The ISO, based in Geneva, is a nongovernmental membership organization currently made up of 74 standards coordination organizations "most representative of standardization" in their respective countries. The organizations represent 89 countries. The ISO's work is carried out through technical committees (TCs). Its scope covers all fields except electrical and electronics engineering.

The TCs of main concern for audio are TC-12, Quantities, Units, Symbols, Conversion Factors, and Conversion Tables; TC-36, Cinematography; TC-37, Terminology; TC-43, Acoustics; and TC-97, Information-Processing Systems.

International Electrotechnical Commission (IEC). In the audio field, most international standards are issued under the coordination of the IEC, a not-for-profit nongovernmental body based in Geneva that was founded in 1906 and is loosely associated with the ISO. Like the ISO, it is a membership organization, composed of 42 national bodies, but its scope is limited to electrical and electronic engineering.

The Commission's parent technical committees concerned with sound and audio include TC-84, Audio, and TC-60, Recording.

Since the mid-1970s this organization has tried to bring the more important audio standards together in single multivolume sets. Thus, sound-system measurement standards have been grouped in Publication 268, which includes volumes on amplifiers, microphones, loudspeakers, automatic gain controls, connectors, etc. While mainly covering measurements, the set includes some configuration standardization. Audio performance standards have been grouped in Publication 581, which is now in the process of issue. Definitions are in Publication 50, which includes all electrotechnical definitions. Volume 50(801) covers electroacoustics, and Volume 50(806) covers recording and reproduction.

Magnetic-recording standardization is treated in the form of methods for measurement and configuration in IEC Publication 94. Disk recording is covered in Publication 98. IEC Publication 574 contains additional standards on audiovisual equipment.

American National Standards Institute (ANSI). In the United States professional audio standards are published by ANSI under the direction of Accredited Standards Committee S4 on audio engineering, which is administered by the AES. S4 reviews existing literature to fill the gaps in the American National Standards catalog, that is, to subject existing industry standards to the consensus process to see if they can be accepted by the representatives of producers, consumers, and general-interest groups that must vote on American National Standards. In addition, some existing American National Standards, as they come up for review, are reviewed in the light of current international standards.

17.3.5 Professional-Organization Standards

Audio Engineering Society (AES). A unique situation exists internationally in the field of professional audio. The main international organization of users and producers of professional audio is the AES. The AES maintains a standards committee (AESSC) which supervises the work of several subcommittees and working groups covering the various fields of sound reinforcement, digital processing, etc. In general, subcommittees and working groups are set up as a need is expressed within the society and by others to the society.

If a working group completes a draft of a standard, it is submitted to the AESSC for review for its procedure, for the thoroughness of the consensus, and for the advisability of contacting others before the standard is processed further. If the committee decides that the standard has been discussed sufficiently, it will be prepared for publication in a document distributed with the *Journal of the Audio Engineering Society (JAES)*. Thus, it will go to the entire membership for discussion.

Following such publication, comments will be collected. If they are editorial in nature, that is, not such that they will cause a major change in the substance of the standard, the standard will be modified and redistributed for a vote to the AESSC. If it is then approved, it will be published in the *JAES* as an audio engineering standard. At the same time, the standard may be submitted to various other standardization organizations, such as the S4 Committee coordinated by ANSI. ANSI may then submit it to the IEC.

The functioning of the AES in the standardization process is not a rubber-stamp process. Many areas do not yet have standards, some because of new technology and some because of refined methods of measurement. For example, a working group on the measurement of absolute polarity is now functioning in the AES. Such groups have the task of gathering together standard methods, codifying industry practice, and utilizing the scientific literature to produce the type of standard useful to the particular needs of the professional audio community.

Society of Motion Picture and Television Engineers (SMPTE).   The first standards relating to audio recording were published by the SMPTE for the photographic sound-track medium. SMTPE promulgates both standards which it publishes as an accredited standards organization coordinated by ANSI and what it calls recommended practices, published as SMPTE documents. Because of the increasing interrelation of sound, film, and video, SMPTE and the AES maintain a close working relationship.

Acoustical Society of America (ASA).   The ASA, through its Committee on Standards (ASACOS) and its technical committees, administers four accredited standards committees coordinated by ANSI. S1 concerns itself with basic acoustics, electroacoustics, and measurement. The applications of these basic standards are handled by S2 on shock and vibration, S3 on bioacoustics, and S12 on noise.

Institute of Electrical and Electronic Engineers (IEEE).   The IEEE issues standards both as an organization and as an accredited standards organization administered by ANSI. Audio-related standards are developed principally by its broadcast and speech-processing groups, although many electronics-related standards are of interest, particularly those related to electrical noise and interference.

17.3.6   Industry Standards

Often it is desirable to publish a standard to help develop new technology or to cover subjects too detailed for general interest. Such standards are promulgated by trade associations. They are voluntary, developed by consensus, but the consensus is usually only that of the members of the organization.

Some trade associations are also accredited standards organizations coordinated by ANSI. Standards issued by them through ANSI must receive full consensus approval according to ANSI procedures.

Electronic Industries Association (EIA).   The largest trade organization which includes producers in the audio field is the EIA. It publishes a large catalog of standards, the most important to audio being those developed by its Parts Division (standards on components) and those by its Consumer Electronics Group (standards on consumer audio equipment).

The EIA is an accredited standards organization; so some of its standards are listed in a catalog published by ANSI.

Recording Industry Association of America (RIAA).   The RIAA publishes configuration standards for phonograph records (see Chap. 9).

National Association of Broadcasters (NAB). The NAB publishes performance limits and configuration standards for audio equipment such as tape recorders used in broadcasting.

Underwriters Laboratories (UL). The particular case of voluntary consensus standards which take on the characteristics of regulation is found in the field of safety standards. In most countries a single government agency promulgates safety standards and also conducts investigations of the safety of products. In the United States this function is carried out by private organizations, in particular by the Underwriters Laboratories of the National Board of Fire Underwriters.

Underwriters Laboratories promulgates safety standards which are developed by committees consisting principally of manufacturers of the devices to be measured together with representatives of insurers. When a standard is of such general use that it may be desirable to obtain a wider consensus, UL will seek broader consensus by submitting it for approval through an ANSI procedure. In such cases other organizations, such as the S4 Committee, will become involved if the safety standard affects equipment or processes under their jurisdiction.

UL safety standards gain the force of law when they are adopted by government agencies such as cities promulgating fire codes, etc.

The principal UL standard of interest to professional audio is UL813.

17.4 AUDIO-STANDARDIZATION ACTIVITY IN THE UNITED STATES

17.4.1 History

Of all the possible areas of standardization activity of interest to the Audio Engineering Society, the one that perhaps has created the most discussion and controversy has been the usage of audio connectors. In the late 1940s, the generally accepted microphone connector both nationally and internationally was the European UA connector. However, it was not long before the XL type of connector came on the scene, quickly replacing the UA connector. Unfortunately, no effort was made at that time to standardize usage of the XL connector, with the exception that, because of its mechanical configuration, the no. 1 pin was always used as the shield connection. However, the absolute polarity of the no. 2 and no. 3 pins was left to industry practice. The problem arose because at that time each major company in the audio industry had its own approach. Thus today most, but not all, users of XL connectors for microphones use no. 2 as the high terminal and no. 3 as the low terminal. On the other hand, many users of XL connectors for line level use the opposite polarity. In an effort to resolve this problem, the IEC has been able to achieve a compromise in which the no. 2 connection is suggested for use as the high terminal. Many other connectors are vying for use in professional audio applications.

17.4.2 Participating Organizations

Only recently have standards makers in the United States taken an active interest in international activity. As a result, a large number of existing American standards do not correspond to their international counterparts and are less organized and accessible. American National Standards on audio have been written by several organizations, principally the EIA, the IEEE, and the ASA. In some cases all these organizations have issued their own standards covering the same subject, each covering it differently. Which of the standards becomes an American National Standard has been as much a question of jurisdictional maneuvering as of technical relevance. For example, all three organizations have methods for the measurement of loudspeakers. Draft methods of measurement have been written by working groups in the ASA. Included are measurements of frequency response, directivity, and distortion. However, none has ever been accepted as an American National Standard, possibly because of jurisdictional conflicts. These measurements were to have replaced the IEEE measurement standard written in 1961 and withdrawn in 1978.

The EIA document was written in 1949. It provides similar measurements and, in addition, standard methods for reporting loudspeaker characteristics. The most commonly used characteristic based on this standard is *EIA sensitivity,* which provides a measurement of the pressure produced axially by a loudspeaker with the given input. In the 1970s, with the greater recognition of the need to coordinate American standards with international standards, the IEEE rewrote its old loudspeaker standard, basing its document on IEC document 268-5. The standard is largely a paraphrase of the IEC document with the addition of some methods drawn from IEC 268-4 on microphones and from the Australian loudspeaker standard, which was being drafted at the same time.

The only American National Standards for microphones are for precision laboratory devices (configuration standards) and a short document on phasing. An EIA standard written in 1949 does cover microphones. It provides measurements of axial pressure, frequency response, and directivity.

Amplifiers are covered by various older standards, most of them drafted on the basis of power matching; so concepts of insertion gain and power gain are important to them. This emphasis is in contrast to the IEC 268-3 standard, which does provide measurements more in keeping with current practice.

There are several standards for headphones, most of which involve headphones used for audiometric purposes. One standard deals with headphones used for audiovisual applications. However, there is no American National Standard or IEC publication for the measurement of high-fidelity headphones.

In the recording field, a substantial number of standards were developed by the former S4 Committee, which is now the S4-1 Subcommittee. Some of the more fundamental standards were developed by the IEEE and adopted as S4 American National Standards. Others were developed by the EIA and mainly cover components used in recording as well as configuration standards for disks and tape. The EIA has also contributed several American National Standards listed in the electrical group (C83). These include standards for loudspeaker driver configurations, standard magnets, methods for measuring flux, and methods for measuring the characteristics of driver components. Other American National Standards developed by the EIA cover connectors, many of which are used in audio. Unfortunately, the most common audio connectors are not clearly defined in American National Standards. This omission is partially due to controversy over the usage of some of the more common connectors.

Another body of standards generated by the EIA provides configuration and measurement methods for amplifier components. Some are American National Standards. These include standards for capacitors, resistors, transformers, and active devices, among others. In the professional recording field, no American

National Standards are in existence. The standards generally used have been generated by the NAB.

17.5 PROCEDURES FOR DEVELOPING STANDARDS

17.5.1 International and National Standards Relationships

When no similar international work exists, a working group examines the work of national committees in other nations. By this process, a standard developed nationally can be brought before the international organizations and adopted internationally. In many cases, such a process results in an international standard which differs in some way from the national standard. During the 5-year review such differences are taken into account and revisions made if they are acceptable to the national consensus. An example occurred in the related field of audiovisual equipment. When Philips developed its original industry standard for the compact cassette, it included a provision for synchronization of visual material for educational audiovisual purposes. Because of the great interest in education spawned by the various federal education acts of the late 1960s in the United States, this application of the cassette was strongly developed there. A standard was adopted in 1974 for the use of the cassette in the synchronized mode. The standard was brought before the IEC, which shortly afterward adopted it with modifications to suit practice as it had been developing internationally. The differences between the standards were resolved at the time of the 5-year review of the American National Standard. Thus, the conflict with the international standard existed for only 2 years, a relatively short time in the standardization process.

17.5.2 Differences in Procedures among Organizations

Agreement and Disagreement Appeals Procedures. A procedure exists for appeals at all points in the development of standards. The consensus process provides that substantial agreement must be obtained among the participants in a standardization process. There will be times when a particular participant cannot agree with the majority and the majority must go ahead, so that the standard can be promulgated. In such cases the individual who feels strongly enough has a right to appeal through procedures in the organization. The appeal must be reviewed thoroughly and should be settled to the satisfaction of the individual.

Initiation of Standards Work. All standards-making organizations have procedures for initiating activities on new standards. Proposals for standards in the United States should be sent to ANSI, 1430 Broadway, New York, N.Y. 10018, or to the AES, 60 East 42d St, New York, N.Y. 10017, or to both.

Termination of Standards Work. An individual or an organization that feels that a working group is carrying on an inappropriate activity may contact the appeals board of the particular standards organization.

Legal Considerations and Restrictions. In the United States, antitrust laws are sometimes interpreted to preclude different producers for a single market from meeting privately to discuss product configurations. Standards committees therefore maintain openness in both membership and proceedings.

17.6 USE OF STANDARDS

17.6.1 Product and Design Specifications

The most common use of standards in the audio field is in the specification of products and product designs. Methods of measurement may be alluded to in specifications either from users or from manufacturers of products. For example, the purchase of a loudspeaker to be used in a system may refer to standard-size configurations for the mounting of loudspeakers and to standard methods for measuring the characteristics of drivers. The specification is more easily understood and is less ambiguous because of the presence of a voluntary consensus standard.

17.6.2 Development of Government Regulations

Voluntary consensus standards are also used in the development of government regulations. Such regulations as may be promulgated, for example, by the EPA or the FCC become legal documents only as applied to the specific field over which such agencies have jurisdiction.

An important application of voluntary standards occurs in the implementation of General Agreement on Tariffs and Trade (GATT) tariffs. Noncompliance with specified voluntary standards may prevent a product from being traded with GATT nations.

17.7 VALIDITY OF STANDARDS

An essential characteristic of voluntary consensus standards is that they are constantly changing.

17.7.1 Review, Reaffirmation, and Revision

Most voluntary standards organizations require that a standard be reviewed periodically to decide whether it should be reaffirmed, revised, or withdrawn. For ANSI, ISO, and IEC, the period is 5 years. Users of standards should always check the currency of a document with its publisher.

17.7.2 Legal Questions

Any claim that a product adheres to a voluntary standard is open to civil court review. However, claims on a standard with regulatory status may come under criminal review. Note that a standard need not be approved by a national consensus organization to have regulatory status.

17.8   CURRENT AUDIO STANDARDS

17.8.1   Overview

Standards undergo constant revision and replacement with the development of new technologies and changes in operational requirements. Consequently, published lists of applicable documents must be continually updated and expanded. Nevertheless, the following tabulation, compiled from literature available in 1987, provides an overview of the work of various standards-making committees and organizations in the field of audio.

Because of the ongoing activities in standards development, it is suggested that, in the utilization of any standards, the cognizant organization be contacted to determine the currency of specific documents and to obtain the latest releases.

In the United States, ISO, IEC, and some ITU documents are available from ANSI. Information on other standards may be obtained from the sponsoring body or from the Audio Engineering Society Standards Committee.

17.8.2   Configuration Standards

ANSI PH7.404-1984   issued

Abbreviated title: *Audio-Visual and Educational Use of Coplanar Magnetic Cartridge Type CPII (Compact Cassette)*

Coding for synchronization of single-frame visual material

ANSI C18.1-1986   issued

Abbreviated title: *Specifications for Dry Cells and Batteries*

Sizes, voltages, and electrolyte types

EIA RS-297b-1956   issued

Abbreviated title: *Cable Connectors for Audio Facilities for Radio Broadcasting*

Sizes and performance minima

EIA RS-299a-1968   issued

Abbreviated title: *Loudspeakers, Dynamic, Magnetic Structures and Impedance*

Preferred dimensions and impedances

EIA RS-355-1968   issued

Abbreviated title: *Dimensions for Unrecorded Magnetic Sound Recording Tape*

EIA RS-399a-1975   issued

Abbreviated title: *Dimensional Standard Coplanar Magnetic Tape Cartridge Type CPII (Compact Cassette)*

EIA RS-332a-1978   issued

Abbreviated title: *Dimensional Standards—Endless Loop Magnetic Tape Cartridges, Types I, II, III*

EIA RS-433-1976   issued

Abbreviated title: *Magnetic Tape Records: Compact Cassette with Four Track Mono-Stereo Compatible Records*

Dimensions and tracks

EIA RS-432-1976   issued

Abbreviated title: *Magnetic Tape Records: Endless Loop Cartridges for 8-track Stereophonic Records at 3.75 in/s (9.53 cm/s)*

Dimensions and tracks

EIA RS-387-1971   issued

Abbreviated title: *Magnetic Tape Records, Four Channel Sound*

ANSI S4.28–1984 AES 5-1984   issued

Abbreviated title: *Preferred Sampling Frequencies: Sampling Frequencies for Digital Recordings*

ANSI S4.40–1985 AES3-1985   issued

Abbreviated title: *Serial Transmission Format: Standard Interface for Professional Digital Audio Processors*

EIA RS-434-1976   issued

Abbreviated title: *Magnetic Tape Records, 4-track Open Reel Stereophonic Records at 3.75 and 7.5 in/s (9.5 and 19 cm/s)*

ANSI PH22.112-1983   issued

Abbreviated title: *Position, Dimensions, and Reproducing Speed of 100-Mil Magnetic Sound Record on 16 mm Film*

ANSI-SMPTE 87M-1985   issued

Abbreviated title: *100-Mil Magnetic Striping on 16 mm Motion-Picture Film, Perforated One Edge*

Dimensions

EIA RS-243-1961   issued

Abbreviated title: *Color-coding of Stereo Pickup Leads*

IEC 94   issued

Abbreviated title: *Magnetic Tape Recording and Reproducing Systems: Dimensions and Characteristics* (plus four amendments through 1978)

All Audio-tape recording configurations

IEC 98 (1964)   issued
Abbreviated title: *Processed Disk Records and Reproducing Equipment* (plus four amendments)
Dimensions and recording characteristics

IEC 574-10 (1977)   issued
Abbreviated title: *A-V video and Television Equipment and Systems: Audio Cassette Systems*
Equivalent to ANSI PH7.4-1975

ANSI C83.117 EIA RS-278b (1976)   issued
Abbreviated title: *Mounting Dimensions for Loudspeakers*
Preferred mounting holes and basket-rim dimensions with designations

NAB (1965)   issued
Abbreviated title: *Magnetic Tape Recording and Reproducing* (reel-to-reel)
Open-reel configuration and performance

NAB (1964)   issued
Abbreviated title: *Cartridge Tape Recording and Reproducing*
Configuration and performance of endless-loop cartridge with cue track

NAB (1964)   issued
Abbreviated title: *Disk Recording and Reproduction*
Configuration of disks for broadcast

ANSI/IEEE 152-1953   issued
Abbreviated title: *Volume Measurements of Electrical Speech and Program Waves*
Standard VU meter

ISO 2969-1977   issued
Abbreviated title: *Electro-Acoustic Response of Motion-Picture Control Rooms and Indoor Theatres*
Minimum performance and measurement techniques for listening rooms

EIA RS-215 (1958)   issued
Abbreviated title: *Broadcast Microphone Cables*

ANSI/EIA RS-221a (1979)   issued
Abbreviated title: *Polarity of Broadcast Microphones*
Marking and testing of microphone phase

EIA RS-224 (1959)   issued
Abbreviated title: *Magnetic Recording Tapes*
Track locations and playback characteristics for 6.35-mm tape

EIA RS-233a (1965)   issued
Abbreviated title: *Phasing of Loudspeakers*
Loudspeaker polarity and marking

ANSI/EIA RS-310c-1977 (r1983)   issued
Abbreviated title: *Racks, Panels, and Associated Equipment*
Dimension and compatibility of 19-in relay racks and panels

17.8.3   Definitions, Symbols, and Preferred-Usage Standards

ANSI S3.17-1975 ASA 4-1975   issued
Abbreviated title: *Rating the Sound Power Spectra of Small Stationary Sound Sources*
Single-number rating for noise emitted by small machines and appliances

ANSI S1.23-1976 ASA 5-1976   issued
Abbreviated title: *Designation of Sound Power Emitted by Machinery and Equipment*
Descriptor in bels for sound power emission

ANSI S2.9-1976 ASA 6-1976   issued
Abbreviated title: *Specifying Damping Properties of Materials*
Preferred nomenclature (parameters, symbols, definitions)

ANSI S3.14-1977 ASA 21-1977   issued
Abbreviated title: *Rating Noise with Respect to Speech Interference*
Calculation of single-valued index called speech-interference level

ANSI S1.1-1960 (r1976)   issued
Abbreviated title: *Acoustical Terminology*
Dictionary of acoustical terms

ANSI S1.6-1984   issued
Abbreviated title: *Preferred Frequencies and Band Numbers for Acoustical Measurements*
Cyclical series of numbers to use as test frequencies and band centers

ANSI S1.8-1969 (r1974)   issued
Abbreviated title: *Preferred Reference Quantities for Acoustical Levels*

Quantities to which levels such as sound pressure level and sound power level are referred

ANSI S3.20-1973 (r1978)   issued
Abbreviated title: *Psychoacoustical Terminology*
Definitions of terms

ANSI Y10.11-1953 (r1959)   withdrawn
Abbreviated title: *Letter Symbols for Acoustics*
Preferred symbols for equations

EIA RS-356-1968   issued
Abbreviated title: *Record Changers and Manual Phonographs, Definitions and Terminology*

IEC 574-1 (1977)   issued
Abbreviated title: *Audio-Visual, Video and Television Equipment and Systems; Part 1: General; Part 2: Explanation of General Terms; Part 3; Tape/Visual Sync; Part 8: Symbols and Identification*
List of parts of 574 as planned, general conditions, terms

ASTM C634-84a   issued
Abbreviated title: *Definition of Terms Relating to Environmental Acoustics*
Terms used in noise control, etc.; applicable to appliance noise

ISO 16-1975   issued
Abbreviated title: *Standard Tuning Frequency*
Set musical A to 440 Hz

IEEE Std-151   issued
Abbreviated title: *Standard Definitions for Terms for Audio and Electroacoustics* (1965)
Terms used in audio

IEC Publication 50   issued as draft
Abbreviated title: *International Electrotechnical Vocabulary*
Chapters for each field

17.8.4   Standards for Instrumentation and Test Materials

ANSI S1.4-1983   issued
Abbreviated title: *Specification for Sound Level Meters*
Requirements, types, grades, and features of sound-level meters including weighting networks; revision of S4.1-1971 (r1976)

ANSI S1.11-1966 (r1986)   issued
Abbreviated title: *Octave, Half Octave, and Third-Octave Filter Sets*
Filter shapes (width, skirts, etc.) for three classes of filters

ANSI S1.12–1967 (r1977)   issued
Abbreviated title: *Laboratory Standard Microphones*
Acoustical measurement microphones for free-field, pressure, and random incidence

ANSI S3.6-1969 (r1973)   issued
Abbreviated title: *Specifications for Audiometers*
Requirements for audiometric instrumentation, including earphones

ANSI PH22.61-1969   withdrawn
Abbreviated title: *9 kHz Sound Focusing Test Film for 35 mm Motion Picture Sound Reproducers*
Replaced by SMPTE RP 64-1976

ANSI PH22.113-1966 (r1971)   withdrawn
Abbreviated title: *16 mm 3 kHz Flutter Test Film, Magnetic Type*
Replaced by SMPTE RP

ANSI PH22.43-1970   withdrawn
Abbreviated title: *16 mm 3 kHz Flutter Test Film, Photographic Type*
Replaced by SMPTE RP 70-1977

IEC 94-2 (1975)   issued
Abbreviated title: *Part 2: Calibration Tapes*

ANSI S3.29-1983   issed
Abbreviated title: *Occluded Ear Simulator*
Describes dimensions and characteristics of Zwislocki-type coupler

17.8.5   Standards for Methods of Measurement

ANSI S3.19-1974 ASA 1-1975   issued
Abbreviated title: *Measurement of Real Ear Protection of Hearing Protectors and Physical Attenuation of Earmuffs*
Psychophysical procedures and physical requirements for determining effectiveness of hearing protector

ASA Std-3-1975 issued
Abbreviated title: *Test-Site Measurement of Maximum Noise Emitted By Engine Powered Equipment*
Measurement of vehicle noise

ANSI 3.1-1977 ASA 9-1977 issued
Abbreviated title: *Permissible Ambient Noise during Audiometric Testing*
Maximum noise in room during hearing tests

ANSI S1.2-1962 (r1976) withdrawn
Abbreviated title: *Physical Measurement of Sound*
Largely superseded by S1.13 and S1.21

ANSI S1.10-1966 (r1976) issued
Abbreviated title: *Calibration of Microphones*
Procedures for calibration of laboratory precision microphones meeting the requirements of S1.12

ANSI S1.13-1971 (r1976) issued
Abbreviated title: *Measurement of Sound Pressure Levels*
Guide to use of precision microphones and sound-level meters for measuring sound pressure both in laboratory and in the field

ANSI S1.21-1972 withdrawn
Abbreviated title: *Determination of the Sound Power Levels of Small Sources in Reverberation Rooms*
Procedures for measurement and for qualification of instruments and measuring rooms (replaced by S1.30 series)

ANSI S3.2 1960 (r1982) issued
Abbreviated title: *Measurement of Monosyllabic Word Intelligibility*
Procedures and lists of words for testing intelligibility by using human subjects

ANSI S3.4-1980 issued
Abbreviated title: *Computation of Loudness of Noise*
Procedures for computing perceived loudness of noise from multiple-frequency measurements; expressed in sones or phons

ANSI S3.5-1969 (r1978) issued
Abbreviated title: *Calculation of the Articulation Index*
Procedures for computing articulation index, a measure of intelligibility, from multiple-band measurements of signal and noise

ANSI S3.7-1973 (r1986)   issued

Abbreviated title: *Coupler Calibration of Earphones*

Compilation of various methods and couplers for earphones; no one method favored

ANSI PH7.2-1974 (r1981)   issued

Abbreviated title: *Audio Amplifier Single Frequency Output for Institutional Audio-Visual Equipment Used Primarily for Speech*

Method for measuring output power including provision for dynamic headroom

ANSI S1.5-1961 IEEE 219-1961   withdrawn

Abbreviated title: *Loudspeaker Measurements*

Largely obsolete standard but contains valuable tutorial material; IEEE has issued revision based on IEC 268

ANSI C16.29 IEEE Std 150-1956   withdrawn

Abbreviated title: *Gain Amplification Loss Attenuation and Amplitude-Frequency Response*

Largely superseded by IEC 268-3

ANSI/ASTM C423-77   issued

Abbreviated title: *Sound Absorption of Acoustical Materials in Reverberation Rooms*

Test of materials in which sample covers partial surface of reverberation room

ANSI/SAE J986 Nov 81

Abbreviated title: *Sound Level for Passenger Cars and Light Trucks*

Passerby noise measured on specially prepared site

ANSI S4.6-1982 AES 7-1982

Abbreviated title: *Measuring Recorded Flux of Magnetic Sound Records at Medium Wavelengths*

Short-circuit flux measurement requires calibrated head

ANSI S4.1 IEEE Std 192-1958   withdrawn

Abbreviated title: *Calibration of Mechanically Recorded Lateral Frequency Records*

ANSI C83.69 EIA RS-386-1971   issued

Abbreviated title: *Measurement of Phonograph Rumble*

ANSI S4.12-1982 EIA RS-238b-1975   issued

Abbreviated title: *Stylus Tips Used for Disk Phonograph Reproducing*

ANSI 4.3-1982 AES S6-1982   issued

Abbreviated title: *Weighted Peak Flutter of Sound Recording and Reproducing Equipment*

Compatible with IEC

IEC 268   issued

Abbreviated title: *Sound System Equipment, Parts 1–15: General, Amplifiers, Mics, Speakers, Passive Elements, AGC, Reverberation-Delay, etc.*

Encyclopedia of test methods and configurations

IEC 98a (1972)   issued

Abbreviated title: *Measuring the Characteristics of Disk Record Playing Units*

IEC 386 (1972)   issued

Abbreviated title: *Measurement of Speed Fluctuations in Sound Recording and Reproducing Equipment*

Equivalent to ANSI S4.3

ASTM C384-77 (1981)   issued

Abbreviated title: *Impedance and Absorption of Acoustical Materials by the Impedance Tube Method*

Method usable in incoming quality control for measuring materials, e.g., fiberglass

ANSI/ASTM E596-78   issued

Abbreviated title: *Noise Reduction of Sound Isolating Enclosures*

Precision method for measuring small enclosures used for acoustical testing

ANSI/ASTM C423-84a   issued

Abbreviated title: *Sound Absorption and Sound Absorption Coefficients by the Reverberation Room Method*

Primary method for rating acoustical absorption materials; contains method for measuring reverberation time

ISO 3382-1975   issued

Abbreviated title: *Measurement of Reverberation Time in Auditoria*

ANSI S1.30-1979ASA-10   issued

Abbreviated title: *Guidelines for Use of Sound Power Standards to Prepare Test Codes*

Introduction to series

ISO 3741-1975   issued   (ANSI S1.31-1980)

Abbreviated title: *Determination of Sound Power of Noise Sources—Precision Methods for Broad-Band Sources in Reverberation Rooms*

Use of reverberation rooms for measuring sources having no discrete tones; useful for noise measurement of speaker response

ISO 3742-1975   issued   (ANSI S1.32-1980)

Abbreviated title: *Determination of Sound Power of Noise Sources—Precision Methods for Discrete Frequency and Narrow Band Sources in Reverberation Rooms*

Requires costly equipment and measuring room

ISO 3743-1976   issued   (ANSI S1.33)

Abbreviated title: *Determination of Sound Power Levels of Noise Sources— Engineering Methods for Special Reverberation Test Rooms*

Simplified methods requiring fewer measurements than precision methods

ISO 3744-1981   issued   (ANSI S1.34-1980)

Abbreviated title: *Determination of Sound Power Levels of Noise Sources— Engineering Methods for Free-Field over a Reflecting Plane*

Pressure measurements in large room or outdoors

ISO 3745-1977   issued   (ANSI S1.35-1979)

Abbreviated title: *Determination of Sound Power Levels of Noise Sources— Precision Methods for Anechoic and Semi-Anechoic Rooms*

Uses multiple pressure measurements in laboratory free-field to integrate to power levels

ISO 3746-1979   issued   (ANSI S1.36-1979)

Abbreviated title: *Determination of Sound Power Levels of Noise Sources— Survey Method*

Calculates power from several pressure measurements made near-field in situ

IEEE Std-258   issued

Abbreviated title: *Test Procedure for Close-Talking Pressure Type Microphones (1965)*

Measurement of near versus far field for noise cancellation, etc.

ASHRAE 36-72   issued

Abbreviated title: *Testing for Sound Rating*

Contains useful reverberation-room construction data and techniques for power measurement

EIA Se105 (1949)   issued

Abbreviated title: *Microphones for Sound Equipment*

Basis for many ratings now in use but not always directly applicable; being made obsolete by IEC 268-4

IEEE Std-219-1975   issued

Abbreviated title: *Recommended Practice for Loudspeaker Measurement*

Based on IEC 268-5 and 268-4 with enhancements from Australian standards

EIA RS-157   review

Abbreviated title: *Measurement of Loudspeaker Magnetic Air Gap Energy*

Search coil flux density method

ANSI PH7.305-1981   issued

Abbreviated title: *Test Method for Headphones for Audio-Visual Equipment Used Primarily for Speech*

Sensitivity and impedance

ANSI PH7.3-1977   issued

Abbreviated title: *Measuring Effective Output Power Bandwidth for Institutional Audiovisual Equipment Used Primarily for Speech*

Technician methods including headroom test

ANSI/EIA RS-426-A-1980   issued

Abbreviated title: *Loudspeakers, Power Rating, Full Range*

Noise signal for testing damage-related power handling of single drivers (differs from IEC and IEEE)

IEC 94-3 (1979)   issued

Abbreviated title: *Part 3: Methods of Measuring the Characteristics of Recording and Reproducing Equipment for Sound on Magnetic Tape* (plus one amendment)

17.8.6 Standard Procedures

ANSI S1.26-1978 ASA 23-1978   issued

Abbreviated title: *Calculation of the Absorption of Sound by the Atmosphere*

Provides tables and formulas for calculation of propagation absorption which is particularly dependent on temperature and humidity

ANSI S3.21-1978 ASA 19-1978   issued

Abbreviated title: *Manual Pure-Tone Threshold Audiometry*

Procedure for measuring hearing using pure-tone method with operator-patient interaction

IEC 543 (1976)   report

Abbreviated title: *Informative Guide for Subjective Listening Tests*

Procedures, conditions, statistical methods, etc., for listening tests on audio equipment

IEEE Std-297 (1969)   issued

Abbreviated title: *Recommended Practice for Speech Quality Measurements*

Methods for jury-preference testing

EIA RS-160 (1951)   issued

Abbreviated title: *Sound Systems*

Formulas for electrical calculation for sound systems; acoustical calculations largely obsolete

17.8.7 Quality-Level Requirements and Recommendations

ANSI S2.19-1975 ASA 2-1975   issued

Abbreviated title: *Balance Quality of Rotating Rigid Bodies*

Permissible unbalances re speed; balance-quality grades

ANSI/UL 464-1981 C33.43

Abbreviated title: *Safety Standard for Audible Signaling Devices*

Includes free-field method for evaluating output; diffuse-field method under consideration

IEC 581   issued

Abbreviated title: *High Fidelity Audio Equipment and Systems: Minimum Performance Requirements; Part 1: General; Part 3: Record Players; Part 4: Tape Recorders; Part 6: Amplifiers*

ITA ITA-a-101   issued

Abbreviated title: *Audio Cassette Specifications—Up to 90 Minutes Total Playing Time*

September 1978; minimum quality requirements; based on IEC, ANSI, and EIA, but compatibility to be checked; commercial test materials required

ITA-a-102 issued

Abbreviated title: *Audio Cassette and Associated Hardware*

September 78; cassette-player interface minimum quality requirements; based on IEC but compatibility and errors to be checked

ITA ITA-a-103 issued

Abbreviated title: *Audio-Eight-Track Cartridge*

September 78; Minimum mechanical and recorded-reproduced quality requirement

ITA ITA-a-104 issued

Abbreviated title: *Duplication Guidelines for Eight Track Cartridges and Four Track Cartridges*

Minimum quality requirements for pancake duplication of commercial tape records for CPII cassette and eight-track cartridge

17.8.8   Specification-Writing Standards

ANSI S3.22-1982 ASA 7-1982 issued

Abbreviated title: *Specification of Hearing Aid Characteristics*

Electroacoustical characteristics and tolerances useful for specifying selecting and fitting hearing aids

ANSI S2.4-1976 ASA 8-1976 issued

Abbreviated title: *Specifying the Characteristics of Auxiliary Analog Equipment for Shock and Vibration Measurements*

Uniform terminology and format for specification

ANSI S4.26-1984 AES 2-1984 issued

Abbreviated title: *Specification of Loudspeaker Components Used in Professional Audio and Sound Reinforcement*

Describes units and characteristics of speakers and horn drivers

EIA RS-174 (1956, r1975) issued

Abbreviated title: *Audio Transformers for Electronic Equipment*

General guide to transformer specification

EIA RS-183 (1957, r1975) issued

Abbreviated title: *Output Transformers for Radio Receivers*

INDEX

ABOUT THE EDITOR

K. Blair Benson, currently a consultant, has been in the forefront of many important advances in the recording and television industry. He began his career during World War II as an electrical engineer with General Electric, where time spent on radar design was shared with the design of wire recorders and radio receivers for postwar manufacture. In 1948 he joined the Columbia Broadcasting System Television Network Engineering Department, where he led in the development of many new technologies, the most noteworthy of which was the commercial introduction and implementation of videotape in broadcasting in 1956. From 1961 through 1966 he was responsible for the engineering design and installation of the CBS Television Network Broadcast Center facilities in New York, a project that introduced many new techniques and designs to broadcasting. This was followed by an assignment as vice president, technical development, of the newly formed CBS Electronic Recording Division. From 1972 to 1976, as engineering vice president of Goldmark Communications Corporation, in addition designing and operating one of the first videocassette duplication plants, he implemented Dr. Goldmark's visionary ideas for stereophonic audio conferencing systems. In 1976 he joined Video Corp. of America as vice president of technical operations and engineering. Since 1980 he has been active in both audio and television systems and facilities designs. A senior life member of the IEEE, a life fellow of the SMPTE, and a member of the AES, he has served on numerous engineering committees and for various terms with the SMPTE as editorial vice president, television affairs vice president, and governor. He is the author of over 40 technical papers and editor in chief of the McGraw-Hill *Television Engineering Handbook.*